S0-BFC-672

Copyright © 1996, 2004 Dianne Onstad. All rights reserved.

Unless otherwise noted, all illustrations are copyright © Robin Wimbiscus. All rights reserved. No part of this book may be transmitted in any form by any means without permission in writing from the publisher.

Managing Editor: Collette Leonard
Copy Editor: Sarah Baldwin
Proofreader: Laura Jorstad
Indexer: Peggy Holloway
Designed by Peter Holm, Sterling Hill Productions

Printed in the United States of America.
08 07 06 05   1 2 3 4 5

This book has been written and published solely for informational and educational purposes. Please be advised that it is not our intention to provide medical advice or to substitute for the role of a physician in treating illness. While every care has been taken to ensure the accuracy of the contents herein, the author and publisher cannot accept legal responsibility for any problem arising out of experimentation with the substances described.

Library of Congress Cataloging-in-Publication Data

Onstad, Dianne, 1962-
Whole foods companion : a guide for adventurous cooks, curious shoppers &
lovers of natural foods / Dianne Onstad.-- Rev. and expanded ed.
     p. cm.
Includes bibliographical references and index.
ISBN 1-931498-62-8 (pbk. : alk. paper) -- ISBN 1-931498-68-7 (hardcover : alk.
paper)
1. Natural foods. 2. Cookery (Natural foods) I. Title.
TX369.O54 2004
641.5'63--dc22

                        2004017697

Chelsea Green Publishing Company
Post Office Box 428
White River Junction, VT 05001

WHOLE FOODS
COMPANION

a guide for adventurous cooks, curious
shoppers, and lovers of natural foods

REVISED AND EXPANDED EDITION

DIANNE ONSTAD

CHELSEA GREEN PUBLISHING COMPANY
White River Junction, Vermont

This book is dedicated with love to Kevin,
my companion in life's many adventures.

ACKNOWLEDGMENTS

I would like to acknowledge all the friends, family, and business associates who have helped in their innumerable ways with this book. And to all those who pick this book up and take it home, thank you, and may you have many happy hours of reading!

CONTENTS

No man can be wise on an empty stomach.

—GEORGE ELIOT

Food is necessary for life to exist. Much of our time on this planet is devoted to either thinking about food, hunting and gathering it (now called shopping), or preparing and consuming it. Trade routes, agriculture, and spices have occasioned war and conquest, and many fortunes have been made and lost because of food. The time is ripe to celebrate food for the central role it plays in our lives. It is a magical, precious gift from nature, one not to be taken lightly. This book provides a starting point for an exploration into the fascinating world of food and offers a wealth of information both historical and practical: where our foods originated, how they received their botanical and common names, the stories associated with them throughout their travels, how they are used for culinary purposes, and their many nutritional benefits.

There is a growing demand for wholesome and flavorful foods, a demand that will influence the way food is grown, packaged, and shipped in the future. Sales of organic produce are rapidly increasing as the public becomes aware of the dangers of food additives, chemical fertilizers, and insecticides. The term *organically grown* refers to a method of growing fruits and vegetables the way they were raised before the advent of industrial farming—without synthetic fertilizers, pesticides, or herbicides. Researchers at Rutgers University recently tested produce to find out just how much more nutritious organic produce really is. Their conclusion: organic produce has as much as a 75 percent higher mineral content than non-organic produce. Freshly picked and unprocessed food can supply over two thousand different enzymes; these enzymes are destroyed by heat greater than 105 degrees Fahrenheit and by pasteurization, and their beneficial effects are greatly inhibited by chemical substances added either to the soil or during processing.

The foods profiled in this book are organized by category, for instance "Fruits" and "Vegetables," and then organized alphabetically within each category. Some foods are placed by botanists in one category while popular use places them in another. For example, tomatoes and eggplants are botanically fruits but are used as vegetables. For the purposes of this book, popular use prevails. Products made from whole foods (such as apple juice or peanut butter) do not have separate entries but are covered along with their parent whole food. If you are unsure where to find a particular food, please check the index. Dairy products and eggs were omitted in order to concentrate solely on plant-based foods. Like the animals from which they come, these foods may carry large amounts of toxic chemicals, including antibiotics, hormones, and pesticides, which are dangerous to health. Margarine, though not derived from animal sources, was also excluded because it is neither a whole nor a healthful food. However, a brief discussion of butter and margarine can be found in the introduction to the **Nuts, Seeds, and Oils** section.

This book is intended to be used as a reference, but I hope it will also be entertaining. Each entry contains information on the plant's botanical name and the food's history, folklore, culinary uses, and nutritional data. Although entries vary according to how much information was available, there should be enough information in each case to identify an unfamiliar item at the market and then prepare and serve it successfully. The nutritional composition tables, which present all available information from a number of sources, provide only an estimate of each food's fat, carbohydrate, protein, vitamin, and mineral content; nutrient value may vary up to 100 percent depending upon the quality of the soil in which the plants grew, the stage at which they were picked for shipment, and even weather conditions; methods and duration of storage and preparation also cause wide variations. Measurements are given in the standard gram (g), milligram (mg), microgram (mcg), and IU (International Unit) increments.

A note on botanical names: The botanical name of a plant consists of two parts. Of these, the first word indicates the genus or family, while the second identifies the species within the genus. These botanical names change from time to time, sometimes at a speed that must be disconcerting even for botanists. Some of the names given here may already be scheduled for replacement, but fortunately obsolete names have a sort of afterlife and continue to enjoy some currency for a decade or more after they have been replaced.

The idea for this book grew out of my combined interests in organic gardening, cooking, and holistic health. After an initial study of food and its relation to health, I decided to research and compile the information I had found on natural foods into one comprehensive volume.

This book is the culmination of my effort to discover the relationship between the foods we eat, the health of our bodies, and the clarity of our minds. It was not my intention to promote one manner of eating over another, and thus there is no recommendation for any particular "diet." There are many excellent books already written on that subject, quite a few of which are mentioned in the bibliography. Bon appétit!

It is an obvious truth, all too often forgotten, that food is not only inseparable from the history of the human race, but basic to it. Without food there would be no human race, and no history.
—REAY TANNAHILL, *FOOD IN HISTORY*

FRUITS

Every fruit has its secret.
—D. H. Lawrence

FRUITS

FRUITS

The English word *fruit* derives from the Latin verb *frui*, meaning "to enjoy or take pleasure in." Most people do enjoy these utterly irresistible delicacies of nature, and fruits generally have the edge over vegetables (for young and old alike) because they appeal to the voracious sweet tooth in us all. Fruit forms an increasingly significant proportion of the American diet: total consumption in the mid-1980s was over two hundred pounds per person annually, compared to around 140 pounds at the turn of the century. However, most of this growth has been in the form of processed fruit, especially orange juice. Starting in the late 1950s, Americans began consuming more processed fruit than fresh, an unhealthful trend that continues even today. Rather than having your fruit sliced, diced, canned, juiced, jarred, jellied, frozen, sweetened, or concentrated, eat it fresh to enjoy its full flavor and nutritional properties.

When most people think of fruit, they think of such sweet, soft, succulent, refreshing, and delicious fruits as apples, oranges, berries, and melons. However, by strict definition, a fruit is the ripened ovary of a female flower. This scientific definition covers what we commonly call fruit as well as nuts and some vegetables, including squash, pumpkins, and tomatoes. In 1893 the U.S. Supreme Court dealt with this confusion and ruled that a vegetable refers to a plant grown for an edible part that is generally eaten as part of the main course, while a fruit refers to a plant part generally eaten as an appetizer, dessert, or out of hand.

The following section on fruit deals only with those natural foods commonly used as fruits; the "vegetable fruits," as well as nuts, will be found in their respective sections. Botanically, fruits fall into four categories: aggregate fruits, such as bananas and dates, which grow in clusters; berries, such as strawberries and raspberries, which have many seeds throughout; drupes, such as peaches and plums, which contain a single stone or pit; and pomes, such as apples and pears, which contain cores and small seeds. All fresh fruits contain the natural acids (malic, citric, and tartaric, among others) necessary for the proper and prompt elimination of toxins, poisonous acids, and other impurities produced partly as natural byproducts of digestion and metabolism, and partly from external sources (air, water, pesticides, etc.). These natural fruit acids are highly alkaline after they have been reduced in the body, and

3

besides being strong cleansers, they provide excellent protection against germs and disease. The human digestive tract is believed to have evolved around a diet of fruits and their close relatives, nuts and seeds. Fresh raw fruits and nuts contain all the vitamins, minerals, natural sugars, and amino acids required for human nutrition, and a diet consisting solely of fruit will quite rapidly disinfect the stomach and alimentary canal, with fresh fruits being far more effective for this purpose than stewed or canned fruits. Regular fruit consumption, like regular vegetable consumption, has been shown to offer significant protection against many chronic degenerative diseases, including cancer, heart disease, cataracts, and strokes.

Most fruit tastes best softened at room temperature and eaten within a few days of purchase. Once ripened, it can be stored in a cool place such as the refrigerator, where some varieties may keep for several weeks. If you are in a hurry for a fruit to be ripe, that old tip about putting it in a brown paper bag really works. The bag traps ethylene gas, naturally released during ripening, that helps soften the fruit. Most fruit should not be kept in plastic bags because the plastic holds moisture, which will cause mold to grow. Also, keep vegetables away from fruit, since the ethylene gas from the fruit can cause premature brown spotting on the vegetables.

CANNED AND FROZEN FRUIT

Canning is the most common way to preserve fruit to make it available out of season. In 1920 only 3 percent of the fruits and vegetables sold were canned; the vast majority were fresh from home gardens or nearby farms. Today canned goods are almost as popular as fresh produce: 40 percent of the fruits and vegetables sold in 1990 were fresh, while 27 percent were canned. Canned fruits lose varying amounts of vitamin C and beta carotene during processing (along with smaller quantities of other vitamins and minerals), and the processing turns their alkaline properties acidic and therefore detrimental to the body. Additionally, fruit packed in heavy syrup can be highly caloric. Freezing fresh fruit, however, has the effect of prolonging its life; the majority of frozen fruits are flash-frozen without having been heated, so there is very little nutrient loss, and most have no added sugar.

DRIED FRUIT

Another way to preserve fruit is by drying, either in the sun or with heated air, to reduce the water content to between 15 to 25 percent. Only a few nutrients are lost in the drying process, the main one being vitamin C. Dried fruits provide quick energy and are a compact source of dietary fiber. Though there is no more fruit sugar in dried fruit than in raw, dried fruit has been concentrated and thus tastes sweeter. Also, most people tend to eat more dried fruit than they would whole, undried fruit at one sitting, thereby consuming more sugar. Fruits dried early in the season may undergo certain natural changes over subsequent months, the most obvious one being "sugaring," in which tiny white crystals appear on the skin. This is just the crystallization of the natural sugars in the fruit collecting on the surface and not a mold growth of some kind, as some people mistakenly think. To reconstitute dried fruit, cover with warm to hot water and let stand for several hours. The reconstituted fruit can be refrigerated in its soaking water for several weeks. Apricots, peaches, figs, and prunes in particular all taste much better when soaked, and the resulting liquid makes a delicious drink.

SULFURED FRUIT

Dried fruits are frequently dipped in a sulfur solution or subjected to the fumes of burning sulfur. This is done for two reasons: (1) bleaching the fruit gives it a more appealing color and appearance; (2) sulfuring dried fruits enables the producers to put them on the market with a much higher water content—as high as 30 percent—so that proportionally less fruit is sold for the same price.

The main proponents for sulfuring claim that the process kills insects and prevents them from getting into the stored fruit. True, no self-respecting insect will eat sulfured fruit, but this is also an excellent reason for you to avoid it. Sulfur dioxide is a poison and the body treats it as such, combining the sulfurous acids with alkalies before eliminating them. This process robs the body of necessary alkalies bases. Also, sulfur compounds destroy B vitamins and can cause allergic reactions in sensitive individuals. Experiments conducted by Dr. H. W. Wiley, former chief chemist of the U.S. Department of Agriculture, demonstrated that the use of sulfurous acid in food is always harmful, degenerating the kidneys, retarding the formation of red corpuscles, and destroying vitamins.

Akee
(Blighia sapida)

Blighia was given in honor of the notorious Captain Bligh, who brought the plant to the West Indies. *Sapida* means "savory" or "pleasant-tasting." *Sapida* may also mean "belonging to the soapberry family," the Sapindaceae.

General Information

This tropical tree is native to the Ivory and Gold Coasts of West Africa and was brought by Captain Bligh to the West Indies along with the breadfruit tree in the late eighteenth century. It was readily adopted there, and the akee became a familiar sight in dooryards and along roadsides. The fruit is leathery, pear-shaped, and yellow, flushed with a scarlet, three-lobed capsule. When fully mature, the three-inch-long fruits split open, exposing their large black seeds, which are encased in a fluffy yellow or cream-colored pulp resembling scrambled eggs. The akee must be allowed to open (preferably fully) before being detached from the tree. This allows the toxic properties of the arils to be largely dispelled by light as the fruit splits.

Buying Tips

Select only firm, unbruised, fully open fruit. Timing is everything, as both immature and overripe fruit are poisonous. Fruit that has fallen from the tree should never be eaten.

Culinary Uses

The yellow pulp (arils) is the only edible part. Although it can be eaten raw, the pulp is usually parboiled in salted water or milk and then lightly fried in butter, at which time it is said to be delicious. The pink tissue and seeds are extremely poisonous, as are underripe fruits that have not yet opened. The fruit is popular in Jamaica, and the canned arils are exported to the United Kingdom, where they are welcomed by Jamaican immigrants. Although technically a fruit, akee is usually served with meat or fish like a vegetable. Importation to the United States has been banned by the Food and Drug Administration because of the health hazards associated with the fruit.

Ambarella
(Spondias dulcis, S. cytherea)
Also Known As: Otaheite Apple, Tahitian Quince, Polynesian Plum

Spondias was the name used by Theophrastus for this family of plants. *Dulcis* means "sweet to the taste" or "mild." The common name *ambarella* is a Sinhalese name for the fruit.

General Information

The ambarella is native from Melanesia through Polynesia but has spread into tropical areas of both the Old and the New World. It was introduced into Jamaica both in 1782 and in 1792, the second time by Captain Bligh. The grayish-orange fruits are produced in pendant clusters of twelve or more, each hanging from a long stalk. Oval and somewhat irregular or knobby, the fruits have a thin but tough skin that is often russeted. While still green and hard, the fruits fall to the ground over a period of several weeks; as they ripen, the skin and flesh turn a beautiful golden-yellow. Each fruit is about the size of an egg and contains several seeds surrounded by a yellowish pulp. The ambarella has suffered for decades by comparison with the mango. At the proper stage, however, the fruit is relished by many and yields a delicious juice for beverages.

Culinary Uses

Still-firm fruits have flesh that is crisp, juicy, and subacid, and a flavor and fragrance somewhat like pineapple. If allowed to soften, the aroma and flavor become musky and the flesh difficult to slice because of conspicuous and tough fibers. The unripe fruits are usually made into relishes, pickles, or sauce. Stewed with a little water and sugar

Akee / Nutritional Value Per 100 g Edible Portion			
	Raw Arils		Raw Arils
Protein	5.75 g	Phosphorus	98 mg
Fat	18.78 g	Thiamine (B₁)	0.10 mg
Fiber	3.45 g	Riboflavin (B₂)	0.18 mg
Calcium	83 mg	Niacin (B₃)	3.74 mg
Iron	5.52 mg	Ascorbic Acid (C)	65 mg

Ambarella / Nutritional Value Per 100 g Edible Portion			
	Raw		Raw
Calories	157.3	Fiber	0.85-3.60%
Protein	0.50-0.80%	Ascorbic Acid (C)	42 mg
Fat	0.28-1.79%		

and then strained through a sieve, the ambarella makes a product comparable to applesauce, but with a richer flavor; it can be cooked down to make a preserve similar to apple butter. Young ambarella leaves are appealingly acid and are consumed raw in southeast Asia. In Indonesia they are steamed and eaten as a vegetable with salted fish and rice, and also used as seasoning for various dishes.

Apple
(Malus sylvestris, M. pumila)

> September fruits are on the bough
> And the bright apple is king of all,
> Red, golden, russet—brimming now,
> Ripe for picking before they fall.

> —DAVID SQUIRE

> If you wish to make an apple pie truly from scratch, you must first invent the universe.

> —CARL SAGAN

Malus is the classical Greek name for a round fruit, from the Greek *malon* or *melon*; *sylvestris* means "of woods and forests," and *pumila* means "dwarf." The English word *apple* comes from the province of Italy called Abela, where the modern apple is thought to have first appeared.

General Information
Apple trees are members of the large rose family. They are probably native to the Caucasus Mountains of western Asia, and perhaps to Anatolia, the Asian part of Turkey, where carbonized apples dating to 6500 B.C. have been found. Apples came to Britain with the Roman conquest, quite possibly with Julius Caesar himself, who took a keen interest in botany. Apple orchards were planted by Roman officers within their walled gardens, but they also sprang up about the native villages, evidence of a plundered orchard here and there. The apple was introduced into Massachusetts as early as 1623 by William Blackstone, minister to the settlers at Plymouth. So important were these trees to the early colonists that by 1646 Massachusetts had passed its first law stipulating "proper punishment" for anyone robbing an apple orchard. Almost every farm had an orchard of apples, grown for fermenting into hard cider. Visitors were offered

not coffee, tea, or water, but cider: it was the common drink. The spread of apple cultivation in America was encouraged by a notably eccentric personality known as Johnny Appleseed. This itinerant preacher and accomplished nurseryman was christened John Chapman in the town of Leominster, Massachusetts, in 1775. The barefoot Chapman wore an inverted mush pan hat, an old burlap bag shirt, and ragged trousers. The apple tree stock that he sold, gave away, and planted throughout the Midwest helped future generations of pioneers. At the time of his death in March 1845, he had pushed as far west as Indiana, where he died at Fort Wayne.

The most popular temperate-zone fruit, apples are grown in almost every state. Washington State, however, produces more than one-quarter of the whole U.S. apple crop. That state's orchards supposedly began from seeds of an apple given to Captain Aemilius Simpson of the Hudson's Bay Company by a young woman from London at a farewell party. To please her, he had kept the seeds and planted them at Fort Vancouver, Washington, in 1824. Only one of the seeds sprouted, and the tree in its first producing year bore only one apple but in following years bore many more. Just eight varieties account for 80 percent of domestic apple production: Golden Delicious, Granny Smith, Jonathan, McIntosh, Red Delicious, Rome Beauty, Stayman, and York. American consumption of apples (and their processed products) is about 120 apples, or roughly forty pounds, annually per capita. Of fresh apples, Americans eat an average of just eighteen pounds a year— less than an apple a week. Belgians and Italians put away three times that amount, while the average person in France consumes five times as many apples, mostly in the form of fermented cider. And they fall short of the Dutch, who approach the health maxim's idea of an apple a day.

The British have a head start on the apple revival. There the old varieties have become a symbol of resisting the uniformity imposed by three mighty forces: supermarkets, the European Union, and American-style fast food. The Agriculture Ministry is encouraging stores to stock more domestic apple varieties, and some now offer as many as forty. This initiative comes none too early. Roughly two-thirds of Britain's orchards have been lost, and three out of five apples are imported. In North America government pomologists haven't been deaf to the fuss. They are testing varieties with more concern for taste and developing impressive new disease-resistant varieties that will change the way apples are grown. But the folk heroes of the apple's rebirth are the orchardists rescuing old favorites from extinction, while celebrating the best of the new imports.

Buying Tips

To Henry David Thoreau, ever the grouchy purist, an apple had no spirit if not eaten under the tree from which it was picked. Nevertheless, most of us will continue to shop for apples. Purchase firm, well-colored fruit with intact stems and few or no blemishes. However, be aware that looks can be deceiving. Organic apples are more prone to have blemishes than non-organic, but the taste is far superior. Elspeth Huxley, in her 1965 book *Brave New Victuals*, writes, "You cannot sell a blemished apple in the supermarket, but you can sell a tasteless one provided it is shiny, smooth, even, uniform and bright." Apples will keep for two to three weeks in the refrigerator. However, if you store a number of apples in the refrigerator, you may notice undesirable changes in their neighbors because of the ethylene gas emitted. Carrots become bitter, potatoes tend to sprout and shrivel, asparagus toughens, brown spots may appear on lettuce, and cucumbers turn yellow. Most of us buy our fruit by the pound at the supermarket. You'll pay considerably less if you shop in quantity from growers, and that will introduce you to the arcana of bushels and pecks. One bushel equals four pecks equals approximately forty-two pounds. One pound equals two big apples, or three medium apples, or four small apples. Most apples look and feel waxy because the skin secretes a protective covering of wax; this layer serves to hold water in and keep disease out. Shoppers may confuse the dusty wax coating on an unbuffed apple with chemical residue, and supermarket apples are routinely machine-rubbed to a high gloss. Plus, not all wax jobs are natural. In the 1950s it occurred to a Yakima, Washington, shipper that apples could be waxed just like cars. His mirror-finish apples brought a dollar a box more than untreated fruit, and the practice caught on.

Culinary Uses

Apples are one of the most versatile of all fruits. They make an appearance in every manner of dish, from main courses to salads and desserts, but are especially popular for apple pie. When you cook apples, do so over low heat so that the delicate pectin, vitamins, and minerals will be preserved as much as possible. Sliced apples can be kept from turning brown by dipping them into an acidic solution such as lemon juice and water. Apple seeds are best discarded, as they contain moderate levels of cyanide. Seventy-five per-

cent of the insecticide spray that is used on apples ends up in the core and seeds. That said, the small number of seeds in the typical core poses little risk of serious poisoning; it takes an estimated half cup of seeds to kill the average adult. It is best, however, to remove the seeds before giving apples to children.

Health Benefits

pH 3.30–4.0. Astringent, carminative, digestive, diuretic, emollient, laxative, tonic. In medicine the disinfectant and therapeutic qualities of the apple are highly valued. Naturally antitoxic, apples can modify the intestinal environment by reactivating the beneficial bacteria that normally flourish there. A highly digestible alkaline food, they have a high water content (around 85 percent), which quenches both immediate and cellular-level thirst. Fibrous, juicy, and nonsticky, they help clean the teeth and exercise the gums when eaten raw. Apples contain both malic and tartaric acids, which help to remove impurities in the liver and inhibit the growth of ferments and disease-producing bacteria in the digestive tract. They also contain pectin, a gel-forming fiber that supplies galacturonic acid to prevent the putrefaction of protein. Pectin content helps make apples an excellent intestinal broom, working as a bulking agent to gently push through the digestive tract and cleanse it along the way. This effect is particularly noticeable when impactions are present. Pectins are also powerful in protecting against the toxic effects of certain chemicals in the diet, such as cyclamates. Studies indicate that eating apples daily will help reduce skin diseases, arthritis, and various lung and asthma problems; European research shows that apple pectin binds with radioactive residues and removes them from the body, along with lead, mercury, and other toxic heavy metals. Pectin is an ingredient in the well-known antidiarrhetic medicine Kaopectate, and apples also relieve diarrhea; after diarrhea symptoms subside, applesauce or apples grated with the skin are a good first step back to solid foods. Another benefit of pectin is that it limits the amount of fat our adipose (or fatty) cells can absorb by building a "barrier" that naturally controls the buildup of fat in the body. Although the apple itself is not particularly high in iron, it contains an element that improves the assimilation of iron in companion foods. All apples, although especially green apples, cleanse the liver and gallbladder and help soften gallstones. Apple leaves contain an antibiotic that, when crushed, can temporarily substitute for a bandage. To reduce fever in children, serve them grated raw apples. To ease a dry cough, steam apples with honey. To eliminate mucus from the lungs, prepare apples with agar.

VARIETIES

There are over seventy-five hundred varieties of cooking and dessert apples, all descended from the very tart and scarcely edible wild crab apple (*Pyrus baccata*) and the ancient apple of the Near East (*P. malus*). Dessert apples, as the name implies, are delicious out of hand, and most are also delicious cooked. Cooking or culinary apples may or may not be delicious raw since they tend to be tart, but when cooked they become succulent and sweet as the heat reduces acidity.

Ambrosia apples were developed naturally from a chance seedling in 1990 in Cawston, British Columbia. They have a distinct honeyed and slightly perfumed flavor. A smooth-skinned apple with an iridescent pink/red blush over a sweet yellow flesh, they are crunchy, tender, and juicy with a crisp texture. Ambrosias retain their shape when cooked so are excellent for use in open pies and tarts.

Api apples were named for Appius, the Etruscan horticulturist who developed them, and they remained in high esteem through many centuries. Grown in the royal French gardens, it was one of only seven varieties of apples deemed worthy to be served to Louis XIV. In France it can still be purchased under its original name, the *pomme d'Api*; in the United States it is generally known as the **Lady Apple**. It is a winter apple, small, somewhat flattened, and ranging in color from creamy yellow to deep crimson according to its exposure to the sun. The flesh is delicately perfumed and juicy, and because the skin is particularly flavorful it should not be peeled.

Baldwin apples were first called Pecker or Woodpecker and later named Baldwin in honor of the colonel who propagated them in Massachusetts in 1740. Readily available

Apple / Nutritional Value Per 100 g Edible Portion					
	Raw w/ Skin	Raw w/o Skin	Processed Juice	Sweetened Applesauce	Dried Sulfured
Calories	59	57	47	76	275
Protein	0.19 g	0.15 g	0.06 g	0.18 g	1.00 g
Fat	0.36 g	0.31 g	0.11 g	0.18 g	1.60 g
Fiber	0.77 g	0.54 g	0.21 g	0.46 g	3.10 g
Calcium	7 mg	4 mg	7 mg	4 mg	31 mg
Iron	0.18 mg	0.07 mg	0.37 mg	0.35 mg	1.60 mg
Magnesium	5 mg	3 mg	3 mg	3 mg	n/a
Phosphorus	7 mg	7 mg	7 mg	7 mg	52 mg
Potassium	115 mg	113 mg	119 mg	61 mg	569 mg
Sodium	0 mg	0 mg	3 mg	3 mg	5 mg
Zinc	0.040 mg	0.040 mg	0.030 mg	0.040 mg	n/a
Copper	0.031 mg	0.041 mg	0.022 mg	0.043 mg	n/a
Manganese	0.023 mg	0.045 mg	0.113 mg	0.075 mg	n/a
Beta Carotene (A)	53 IU	44 IU	1 IU	11 IU	n/a
Thiamine (B$_1$)	0.017 mg	0.017 mg	0.021 mg	0.013 mg	0.060 mg
Riboflavin (B$_2$)	0.014 mg	0.010 mg	0.017 mg	0.028 mg	0.120 mg
Niacin (B$_3$)	0.077 mg	0.091 mg	0.100 mg	0.188 mg	0.500 mg
Pantothenic Acid (B$_5$)	0.061 mg	0.057 mg	n/a	0.052 mg	n/a
Pyridoxine (B$_6$)	0.048 mg	0.046 mg	0.030 mg	0.026 mg	n/a
Folic Acid (B$_9$)	2.8 mcg	0.400 mg	0.10 mcg	0.60 mcg	n/a
Ascorbic Acid (C)	5.70 mg	4.00 mg	0.90 mg	1.70 mg	10.00 mg
Tocopherol (E)	0.590 mg	0.270 mg	0.010 mg	n/a	n/a

in the Northeast, Baldwins are a medium-red apple, dull crimson on the side that faced the sun, with some yellow flecks and streaks underneath. An excellent eating and all-purpose apple, they have a sweet and slightly tangy flavor with a unique aftertaste that is pleasing and inviting. They sweeten during cooking but still retain their unique Baldwin flavor. Picked late in the season after the first frost, they retain their crispness and whiteness well into late November or early December.

Blenheim Orange apples are among the best of the pippin family. The variety was popular in England for a century after its introduction around 1818 but it is not often found in today's marketplace. This large, dull yellow and red apple has crisp flesh and a flavor of unusual acidity. It is the classic Christmas apple, ripening in midwinter.

Braeburn was introduced in 1952, a chance seedling from New Zealand's South Island. That country, with its reverse seasons, ships the apples to reach our supermarkets in May and June. The variety is now being planted here but has met some resistance because it isn't as red as a fire engine. Nevertheless, Braeburn's tall shape and bright color are attractive in their own right. Uncut, Braeburn may have a faintly cidery perfume. The skin is thin and seems to disappear in the mouth. The flesh is yellow-green to creamy yellow, breaking and crisp in texture. If the apples are harvested at the right time, they offer a complex, sweet-tart flavor, with a noticeably aromatic aftertaste—a match and then some for another popular newcomer, Fuji. When cooked, Braeburn turns simpler but doesn't go flat. As sauce it needs little or nothing in the way of added sweetening, and in Australia the variety has been used to make applesauce for diabetics.

Bramley's Seedling, or simply **Bramley,** is the most widely sold cooking apple in Britain, in part because it has a very long keeping season, from early autumn right through to the following summer. Usually very large and irregular in shape, it is harvested commercially as a green apple, or green with faint red stripes, but will turn yellow if left on the tree. There are also crimson varieties.

Citerion is a tart, crisp apple, very good for all uses: eating fresh, baking, juicing, or as sauce. However, it is not widely available.

Cortland apples are a modern American variety, bred in 1898 from the Ben Davis and the McIntosh in New York. Grown in New England, Cortlands are medium-sized, dark red or purplish-red all-purpose apples with lots of flavor. They have very white meat, good juice, and a semi-sweet flavor. Cortlands are exceptional as cooking or eating apples because they do not darken quickly when cut and exposed to oxygen. Cooking sweetens the flavor considerably, making for a rich, thick applesauce, as well as great traditional high-crust pies, because the pieces do not melt and cause the crust to collapse. Cortlands are crisper earlier in the season but store well. They are available in late autumn.

Cox's Orange Pippin was developed in 1830 by a retired brewer named Richard Cox, and the British boast that this is the finest dessert apple in the world. One of the best of the large family of pippins, since its introduction in the first half of the nineteenth century it has become the most popular British apple. It is a medium-sized, round apple, dull brownish green with faint red stripes and a red flush on one side. It usually has a matte brown russeted area around the stem. The texture is crisp, the flavor solidly acid but balanced by sweetness. The seeds are loose, and you can hear them when you shake the fruit. This apple is not widely available in North America; it is much more common in Britain and New Zealand.

Crab apples (also known as **American Sweet, Garland,** and **Prairie Crab**) are a wild species of small, acidic fruits that can be either deeply red or yellow; they have a high pectin content, and thus their main use is in making jellies and preserves. They are briefly available in autumn.

Crispin (or **Mutsu**) are a large green apple developed from crossing a Golden Delicious with a Japanese apple variety called Indo. Grown extensively in New York State, it is an all-purpose variety, with a firm texture and sweet flavor. The Crispin looks like a large Granny Smith and has that apple's crispness but possesses the flavor and sweetness of a Golden Delicious. It is available year-round.

Discovery, so named because it was a chance discovery by an amateur grower, is one of the first British apples to appear each season. It was first marketed on a large scale in the 1970s. The apple is bright green and crimson like a brighter version of a Worcester Pearmain, and the flesh often has a pink tinge on the sunny side. At first light and crisp, it softens quickly and must be eaten at once. The flavor is unique, with a hint of raspberries.

Empire is a relatively new variety from New York State, the result of crossing the McIntosh with the Red Delicious. The deep red skin is rather thick, but the crisp texture and sweet-tart taste make it ideal for eating fresh. The juicy yet crisp combination contributes to its growing popularity. Good but not great for pies and sauce. The Empire is available September through spring.

Fuji is a Ralls Janet and Red Delicious cross that originated in Japan. Pale green and pink striped or blushed, it has a sweet-tart juicy taste and is ultracrisp like an Asian pear. An excellent eating apple, it works widely in all uses and will keep for months if refrigerated.

Gala is a striking new apple that has a peachlike appearance, with its pinkish yellow skin striped or blushed with red. Sweet, flavorful, and wonderfully crisp, it is excellent for fresh consumption and also makes a delicious pie.

Golden Yellow Delicious (or simply **Golden Delicious**) is an American apple that appeared as a chance seedling on Anderson H. Mullin's West Virginia farm in 1890. Now the most widely grown apple in many countries, it is second in popularity in the United States only to the Red Delicious. Golden Delicious apples are somewhat smaller than their red cousins and are actually a hybrid development from a totally different source. They appear earlier than the red variety and keep longer, have a smooth shiny skin with a slight green tinge in early season, and become a deep, dark yellow by March. Firm and crisp when the skin is greenish, or less crisp but sweeter when completely golden. A versatile apple good for eating as well as cooking and juice. They are always sweet and make perfect dried apple slices, delicious unsweetened applesauce, and excellent cheese and wine companions. When the apple is grown in a cool climate, so that a reasonable amount of acid is formed, it can be very good; in warmer regions it can be insipid. The variety is popular with growers because the tree produces heavily.

Granny Smith are the leading apples in Australia. The original tree, from the seed of an apple thrown out into the yard of Mrs. Thomas Smith of Eastwood, near Sydney, was bearing by 1868. The Granny Smith is a medium-to-large apple, oval to round in shape, with a very green, very bright white-dotted skin. The fruit is superhard, with white and juicy flesh. It has a delightfully tart taste in early season and a somewhat sweeter flavor later on. The most popular of all the green apples, they are a worldwide choice both for cooking and eating (although they take longer than many to soften during cooking). Today Granny Smiths are grown primarily in Australia, New Zealand, and South Africa. The commercial imported fruit is often sprayed with an oil formula that, combined with the variety's naturally tough skin, makes the peel difficult to digest. Yellow Grannies are overaged or under-refrigerated or both and are unacceptable.

Gravenstein apples originated in northern Germany or Denmark before 1800, and the variety was imported to the United States in 1824, when scions (cuttings for grafting) were taken to California; the Gravenstein soon became a popular American variety, especially for cooking. It is also eaten by those who like rather acidic apples. It is large, roundish, and slightly lopsided, yellow with bright red and orange stripes. Its main use is for applesauce, but it is also good eaten on its own or in desserts.

Idared is an American apple, bred in Idaho in the 1930s and 1940s from the better-known Jonathan and Wagener. A medium-sized red and yellow apple with a sweet, moderately acid flavor, it keeps and cooks well.

Jonathan apples (originally called Rick, after their discoverer) were first found on the farm of Philip Rick in Woodstock, New York, in 1880. This old favorite is a deep yellow apple with both bright and dull red stripes. It is very round, with creamy-white meat that is semisweet in early season and sweeter later on. Considered one of the best eating apples, it has a highly aromatic, spicy taste that makes it very good for pies or applesauce. An excellent keeper, the Jonathan is not a very hard apple when fresh-picked, but it doesn't soften much during storage.

Jonagold, a thin-skinned Jonathan/Golden cross, is a wonderfully sweet and crisp apple, but it does not store well. Buy only a few of these apples at a time, for quick and enjoyable consumption. It is an excellent eating apple.

Laxtons are a large and important group that owe their name to Thomas Laxton (1830–1890), who worked mainly on peas and strawberries but whose sons began in 1893 to experiment systematically in crossing apples. They produced thousands of crossbred apples, from which many of the best British dessert apples are derived. A high proportion of them retain the name

Laxton. They bear a general resemblance to Coxes, although they can usually be distinguished by their brighter color. The texture is crisp and the flavor light. The best known are **Laxton's Pearmain**, **Laxton's Superb**, **Laxton's Advance**, **Laxton's Leader**, and **Laxton's Fortune**.

Macouns first appeared in 1926, when a McIntosh was crossed with a Jersey Black. Today's Macouns have a light gray-maroon to deep vermilion shading with some striping and both white and very dark flecks. The meat is very white, crisp, juicy, and sweet, with no bitter taste to the peel. Macoun apples are considered the finest of all dessert apples. They are a small-to-large apple, but the medium size eats best. Fresh-picked Macouns are as good as any apple anywhere and are considered the premium eating apple of the northeastern United States, where they are mostly grown. However, they keep poorly.

McIntosh is a popular North American variety, named in 1811 for John McIntosh of Ontario, Canada, who discovered the chance seedling. A pioneer, John McIntosh settled at what is now Dundela, Ontario. In 1796, while clearing a forest along the St. Lawrence River, he came across some small wild seedling apple trees. These he planted near his house. One of the trees bore especially delicious apples, and it was given the name *McIntosh Red.* This tree lived and bore fruit for 112 years, dying in 1908 after being injured by a fire. Paid for by popular subscription, a monument was later erected to mark the site of the original tree of one of the finest American apples. This all-purpose apple has also been excellent for crossbreeding; it has in turn given us such varieties as the **Cortland**, **Spartan**, **Melba**, **Macoun**, **Niagara**, and **Puritan**, among others. In New York State, the world's largest producer of McIntosh apples, they are first picked on September 15 and show mostly green with a red blush. These early apples are excellent for an apple pie mix, because they tend to be slightly tart and very crisp. By October the McIntosh is three-quarters red and has sweetened considerably. By November the color is almost all red, the taste is very sweet, and the crispness and crunch seem to soften more than just a little. The late McIntosh makes a thick applesauce that requires little sweetener. This round, squat, shiny red-green apple has a fine high flavor, a spicy-sweet taste with an ever-so-slight tartness. Texture is tender but crisp. Does bruise easily and can get mushy if not kept consistently cold.

Newton is a tart, crisp apple that is very good to eat and excellent for cooking; it also has an excellent keeping quality.

Newtown Pippin (or **Yellow Newtown**) was originally found growing in Newtown, New York, site of present-day Flushing, soon after 1700. The tree produced a heavy crop of yellowish-green apples that were crisp but juicy, acid but sweet, and had exceptional keeping qualities. The variety, spread by cuttings taken from this tree (which perished in 1805 as a result of excessive cutting), was soon grown over most of the settled parts of North America. The tree is awkwardly sensitive to soil and climate, and as a result it lost popularity among growers toward the end of the nineteenth century. This green-to-yellow apple (sometimes with an attractive blush, but often simply with a green-yellow skin) has a moderately tart or even winelike taste, similar to Granny Smith. With its sweet, semi-juicy flavor and fairly crisp texture, it is excellent to eat and is also used in pies and for drying but most often for juice.

Northern Spy apples have a somewhat obscure origin; some say that the name may derive from the fact that Bloomfield, New York, where it originated in about 1800, was a site of activity for the Underground Railroad, a secret escape route by which Southern slaves were brought to freedom in the North. This apple was long considered the perfect specimen and became something of a legend. Brightly striped with red-green skin, firm yellow flesh, and a tart, slightly acid flavor, it is suitable for pies or snacking.

Pink Lady is fast becoming one of the most popular varieties. The bi-colored apple originated in Australia as a cross between Golden Delicious and Lady Williams. The fruit is medium in size and conical in shape, with a distinctive pink blush over a yellow background. The fine-grained flesh is crisp and crunchy and does not brown easily after being cut.

Pippin, originally referring to any apple grown from a pip (seed), is derived from the French *pepin,* meaning both "pip" and "apple." By the sixteenth century the term had come to denote a hard, late-ripening, long-keeping apple of acid flavor. **Golden Pippin**, **Ribston Pippin**, **Cox's Orange Pippin**, and **Sturmer Pippin** are common varieties.

Red Astrachan is a Russian apple introduced into the United States in 1835. Grown in California, this green-red to entirely green apple has uses in cooking and is also enjoyed fresh. An early apple with a fruity, acid taste and plenty of character, it is apt to fall off the tree before it is fully ripe.

Red Delicious (or simply **Delicious**) began as a chance seedling on the farm of Hesse Hiatt of Peru, Iowa, in the late 1860s. Because it was self-planted, the tree was cut down in 1870, when it had grown big enough to become an obstacle. However, new shoots appeared from the stump the following year, and the tree was allowed to grow back. When the first apples appeared on the regrown tree, Hiatt found them so superior in taste that he entered them in a contest held by a canning company. The judges agreed to award the apple a prize but discovered that the basket had lost its identifying label. Fortunately, Hiatt resubmitted the fruit the following year, and its career began. First marketed as Hiatt's Hawkeye, it was bought out by the Stark Brothers, a large fruit-growing concern, which renamed the variety Delicious. Since the 1940s it has been the leading American apple; however, it has been developed to a high state of color and uniformity, and thus its taste is greatly diminished. For most of the selling season it remains crisp and juicy, but by March it starts to soften and becomes mealy. The Red Delicious is triangular or heart-shaped, with the tapered bottom closing with the recognizable five points, or sheep nose, at the blossom end. It is sweet but insipid, lacking in acid, very juicy in its early stage, and wrapped in a thick peel. The size varies, but most are medium to very large, with the largest available around Christmas. Not necessarily the most flavorful or juicy of apples, they are good for eating but only fair in cooking or juice making.

Rhode Island Greening is a variety developed in Rhode Island in approximately 1740 by a tavern keeper named Green, at Green's End, Rhode Island. Rarely seen in commercial markets, this pale yellow-green apple is often larger on one side. The skin is very tough and thick, often slightly bronzed, and with a touch of roughness. Picked after the frost, they are hard and crunchy with a crisp, sharp, refreshing, brisk acid taste, and they make an excellent companion for wine and cheese. An excellent pie apple because of its juice, which thickens well in baking, this variety is used commercially for applesauce and frozen pies.

Rome Beauty is an American apple named for Rome, Ohio, near where it was discovered in 1832 by the farmer Joel Gillett. One of his grafted trees had shot from below the graft. The stray branch began to produce large, red-striped apples of handsome appearance and rocklike solidity. The variety became popular, especially among growers, for it was easy to manage and the attractive fruit sold well. Hybrids like the **Gallia Beauty**, **Monroe**, and **Ruby** come from this variety. The Rome Beauty is a medium-to-large, deep red, shiny apple with crisply firm, very juicy, and full-flavored flesh. This is America's most popular cooking apple, but it is also good for eating out of hand. Early Rome apples (picked in September or October) are very hard, with a tart winey taste. They are excellent as part of an apple pie mix, since the pieces hold their shape and become sweeter in the baking. Later Rome apples, either picked ripe or allowed to ripen off the tree, are the true baking apples. They soften evenly without saucing up. The skin holds the fruit together, and the large size makes them a generous and attractive serving.

Shamrock, a new variety, is a green apple much like a McIntosh: tart and tender.

Spartan is a McIntosh/Pippin cross grown primarily in Canada. The Danes developed this firm apple with a custardlike taste that is popular for eating and cooking. Fairly tart, tender yet very flavorful and crisp, this variety cooks well and holds its firmness. Excellent allpurpose apple and a good keeper.

Starking, also called **Starking Delicious,** is a French variety and a crisp dessert apple with red-streaked skin and very white, sweet flesh. It is, indeed, delicious with cheese or made into fritters.

Wealthy is a variety that arose in approximately 1860 from an unusually intent search by Peter Gideon of Minnesota for the perfect apple. Of all the seeds that he planted, the best fruit came from the cold-tolerant tree we know today; *Wealthy* was the given Christian name of his wife. This variety reached the height of its commercial success in the 1910s and 1920s but is commercially unimportant today. The medium red apple has a mildly acid taste and is good for desserts or eating. The pinkish flesh softens quickly, so it lasts poorly and should be eaten soon after purchased. It is available in midautumn.

White Astrachan was introduced to the United States in approximately 1820 from Russia. Now grown primarily in California, this greenish-white apple is good for cooking.

White Pearmains are part of the pearmain family, the

LORE AND LEGEND

The apple seems to have had the widest and most mystical history in the popular tales of all countries. Aphrodite bears it in her hand, as does Eve. The serpent guards it, and the dragon watches it. It is the healing fruit of the Arabian tribes, and it bestows immortality on the Turks. Greek mythology relates that the origin of the Trojan War was attributed to the Apple of Discord, a golden apple thrown down in front of an assembly of the gods by the goddess of hate, Eris. Inscribed "For the Fairest," the apple was claimed by the three most eminent goddesses—Hera, Athena, and Aphrodite. Appointed to choose the most beautiful of the three, Paris was offered power and riches by Hera, wisdom and fame by Athena, or the most beautiful woman in the world by Aphrodite. Yielding to passion, Paris chose Aphrodite. He got what he desired, but in the process started the lengthy Trojan War, since the beautiful Helen just happened to be somebody else's wife. Another myth involves Hercules's obtaining the golden apples from the Gardens of the Hesperides, faithfully guarded by a sleepless dragon. One of the Norse myths tells of the goddess Idun, who supplied magic apples to all the gods so that they could stay eternally young. The fairy tales of the Brothers Grimm, which are all taken from old folktales and myths, have at least four stories involving apples, including the famous story of Snow White.

oldest English apple name, first recorded in a Norfolk document of 1204. Although the place and date of its origin are unknown, the name is derived from the old French apple name *parmain* or *permain*, referring perhaps to a group of apples rather than a single variety. Today this yellow apple is grown primarily in California and is good for baking.

White Transparent is an early-ripening apple of Scandinavian or Russian origin. It was introduced to Britain and the United States in the mid–nineteenth century. As its name suggests, it is very pale with a transparent skin. The taste is mild but agreeable. The fruit should be used quickly, while still crisp, for cooking rather than dessert. It is available in late summer.

Winesap is one of the oldest American varieties, dating back to the colonial period. It was so named because it was often used as a cider apple. The Winesap is a rugged country apple of dull rusty-red color with a touch of yellow in its ripe stage. Picked after the first frost, this apple has a hard, juicy texture, white meat, and a definite wine flavor. For the wine, cheese, and apple lover the Winesap is the first choice. Winesap apples make excellent apple pies either as part of an apple mix or by themselves since they cook up into a light-textured sauce with that distinctive Winesap flavor. They are also excellent cider apples, producing sweeter and sweeter juice as the apple season lengthens.

The variety has a good keeping time and was very popular for this reason until controlled-atmosphere storage made other varieties more available.

York Imperial was developed in Pennsylvania, in approximately 1830. The apple has pinkish-red skin that is often dotted with pale spots, which don't affect the quality of the fruit, and a lopsided shape. The flesh is yellow and moderately juicy, neither too tart nor too sweet. Yorks are good baking apples, holding their shape and flavor when cooked, and are now mostly a processing apple.

BYPRODUCTS

Apple cider is freshly pressed juice that has not been pasteurized or sweetened. This is the best-tasting form of apple juice, full of vitamins and free of all processed interference. Compared to store-bought apple juice, it is more flavorful but less sweet. Unlike clear, pasteurized apple juice, cider looks cloudy, and sediment often collects at the bottom of the bottle. Because it is highly perishable, it must be kept under constant refrigeration and even then may only last from ten to fourteen days. Freshly squeezed apple cider is excellent for the body and is especially helpful in cleansing or reducing diets. Beneficial for the liver and gallbladder, it tends to speed up bowel action but will produce flatulence if the bowels are not moving well. The English brought the cider habit with them to America. Since medieval times they had looked upon apples as a source of beverage rather than as something to eat, and for good reason. If you grind up a few apples and express their juice, a minor miracle of alchemy takes place: that clear, sugary liquid starts to change immediately to a cloudy brew that, left to its own devices, will pitch itself into a fizzing tempest. The end product is a complex and stable beverage, mildly alcoholic, with an agreeable bitterness. It was once the most popular beverage in America, serving in the place of water, milk, wine, and hard liquor in households and taverns. Fully fermented cider was distilled to make apple brandy, a concentrated drink that could be stored and shipped more easily. New Jersey sent more than its share through the coils, and in 1810 a local orchardist reported that Essex County alone had distilled 307,310 gallons of apple brandy. But the cider and brandy boom would not continue much longer. Temperance movements not only did away with the drink but also bowdlerized the name.

Apple cider vinegar—see the entry under **Herbs, Spices, and Other Foods.**

Apple juice is fresh cider that has been pasteurized to guarantee that it will not turn into hard cider or vinegar. During this process most of the cider's vitality is lost and the sugar content is dramatically increased by the heat process or by additional sweetening. All canned and bottled fruit juices are pasteurized but need refrigeration after opening to prevent them from souring. Like most other processed foods, it is best avoided.

Hard cider has been left to ferment naturally. It can be dry or sweet, depending on the apple varieties used and whether fresh cider was added back after fermentation. The alcohol content ranges from 3 to 7 percent. European cider is usually sparkling, either bottled before fermentation is complete or perhaps with carbonation added afterward.

Apricot
(Prunus armeniaca)

> The flavors of the peach and the apricot are not lost from generation to generation. Neither are they transmitted by book learning.
>
> —EZRA POUND

Botanists have characterized this fruit as part of the large plum family, thus the *Prunus* genus. *Armeniaca* signifies that the ancients believed that this tree originated in Armenia, a region in southwest Asia. The English word *apricot* came from the Latin *praecoquum*, which means "precocious," because the fruit is early ripening.

General Information
The apricot is believed to be native to China and to have been introduced by Alexander the Great to the Greco-Roman world around the fourth century B.C. A member of the large rose family, the apricot is a drupe, like its cousins the peach, plum, cherry, and almond. The oval orange-colored fruit resembles the related peach in shape, and the plum in flavor. Its cleft pit protects a kernel that tastes remarkably like the almond and is often used in brandies, preserves, marzipan, amaretti, and other confections. In bitter varieties, however, this kernel contains a strong compound that can be poisonous if eaten raw in large quantities over an extended period—an unlikely possibility. The Franciscan friars brought apricots to California in the late 1700s, and this state now produces almost all our fresh apricots. Apricots have been sun-dried in the Far and Middle East since ancient times. It requires six pounds of fresh fruit to result in one pound of dried, but the fruit loses nothing but water, and the nutrients are concentrated. Try to find apricots that have been dried naturally, without sulfur dioxide, which is harmful to the body and imparts a bitter taste.

Buying Tips
Most apricots come from the West Coast, are available during the summer season, and cannot be shipped when fully ripe. A truly ripe apricot is golden-orange all over with no traces of green. They are best when deep orange with a red blush, plump, and slightly soft to the touch. Avoid those that are overly soft, have bruises, or are wilted and shriveled. Most dried apricots contain sulfur dioxide, a noxious gas used to prevent discoloration. Look for the darker, nonsulfured variety instead.

Culinary Uses
There are many apricot varieties, all of which are delectable. Tree-ripened apricots have the best flavor, but the fruit is so delicate that tree-ripened fruit is rarely available in stores. Immature apricots are greenish yellow and never attain the right sweetness or flavor; their flesh is firm and their taste sour. Once fully ripened, refrigerate promptly, as these delicate gems spoil rapidly. They are a natural partner to almonds in baked goods since they are closely related, as their almond-shaped pits attest. Their sharp sweetness complements meats, quick breads, and desserts; they are also excellent and convenient snacks for children, picnickers, and hikers.

Health Benefits
pH 3.3–4.8. Laxative. Like other bright orange fruits or vegetables, apricots contain highly concentrated amounts of beta carotene, or provitamin A, which has been shown to be successful in thwarting certain cancers, especially those of the lung and skin. In a landmark study of one thousand men,

Apricot / Nutritional Value Per 100 g Edible Portion		
	Fresh	Dried
Calories	48	260
Protein	1.40 g	5.00 g
Fat	0.39 g	0.50 g
Fiber	0.60 g	3.00 g
Calcium	14 mg	67 mg
Iron	0.54 mg	5.50 mg
Magnesium	8 mg	n/a
Phosphorus	19 mg	108 mg
Potassium	296 mg	979 mg
Sodium	1 mg	26 mg
Zinc	0.260 mg	n/a
Copper	0.089 mg	n/a
Manganese	0.079 mg	n/a
Beta Carotene (A)	2,612 IU	10,900 IU
Thiamine (B_1)	0.030 mg	0.010 mg
Riboflavin (B_2)	0.040 mg	0.160 mg
Niacin (B_3)	0.600 mg	3.300 mg
Pantothenic Acid (B_5)	0.240 mg	n/a
Pyridoxine (B_6)	0.054 mg	n/a
Folic Acid (B_9)	8.60 mcg	n/a
Ascorbic Acid (C)	10 mg	12 mg

LORE AND LEGEND

For those familiar with the rich sensuous smell of ripe apricots, it is perfectly clear why nectar (a beverage of fruit juice and pulp generally made from apricots) was the preferred drink of the Greek and Roman gods. In Eastern countries the apricot is known by the beautiful name of "Moon of the Faithful."

researcher Dr. Richard Shekelle found a definite connection between the rate of lung cancer and the amount of beta carotene in a person's diet. Several other studies have shown the protective effect of beta carotene against cigarette-smoking cancers such as cancer of the lung and pancreas and possibly the larynx, esophagus, bladder, and stomach. Dried apricots have an even higher concentration of beta carotene than the raw fruit. Tree-ripened apricots are one of the finest sources of copper, cobalt, and the organic iron, necessary for building red corpuscles in the blood. This mineral richness makes them beneficial in cases of blood-related disorders such as anemia, acne, toxemia, and tuberculosis. Apricots offer a special bonus for healthy hearts—plenty of potassium, which scientists say is valuable in helping to control high blood pressure. Apricot juice is also a powerful fat fighter. As an added bonus, crack open the apricot kernel, grind the nut inside, and add it to the juice. The nut is a little-known source of nitrilosides, substances that help promote a marvelous fat-flushing response.

Atemoya
(Annona squamosa x A. cherimola)

Annona means "year's harvest" and is suggested by the Haitian name *anon*, which is applied to one of the species. *Squamosa* means "full of scales" or "having scalelike leaves"; *cherimola* derives from *chirimuyu*, the native name (see **Cherimoya**, below). The English name *atemoya* is a combination of *ate* (an old Mexican name for the sugar apple) and *moya* (from cherimoya).

General Information
Native to tropical America and the West Indies, the atemoya is one of a family of puddinglike creamy fruits whose arrival is fairly recent. As its name implies, it is a cross between a cherimoya and a sugar apple. The flesh is prized for its custardlike texture and delicate taste, frequently described as reminiscent of vanilla, mango, milk, or sherbet. Others have described it as having a piña colada flavor without the alcohol. This tough-skinned, grayish-green fruit resembles in size and shape a distorted, slightly melted, Stone Age artichoke. The rind has more prominent and angular areoles than those of the sugar apple, with tips that are rounded or slightly upturned. Although the atemoya was supposedly "invented" in 1908 by P. J. Wester, an employee of the U.S. Department of Agriculture, it turned out nature had already come up with the same cross in 1850 in Australia, and did so again in Israel in 1930. The first man-made hybrids were produced in an attempt to combine the cold tolerance of the cherimoya with the more tropical qualities of the sugar apple; subsequently, some of the most successful cultivars were developed in Israel. The atemoya is now grown commercially in that country as well as in Australia, India, South Africa, and the United States, particularly in Florida, California, and Hawaii.

Buying Tips
Choose pale green atemoyas that are unblemished and have not cracked open. Those that are relatively thin-skinned and somewhat tender have the best flavor.

Culinary Uses
This delicacy has a creamy, ivory-colored, virtually acid-free flesh studded with dark, slippery, watermelon-like seeds. At its best, the rich flesh tastes astonishingly like cooked vanilla custard with a hint of mango. When less than perfect, it can be rather starchy, like winter squash blended with pear. Atemoyas tend to be rather messy to

Atemoya / Nutritional Value Per 100 g Edible Portion			
	Raw		Raw
Calories	94	Sodium	4-5 mg
Protein	1.07-1.40 g	Zinc	0.2 mg
Fat	0.4-0.6 g	Beta Carotene (A)	10 mcg
Fiber	0.05-2.50 g	Thiamine (B₁)	0.05 mg
Calcium	17 mg	Riboflavin (B₂)	0.07 mg
Iron	0.3 mg	Niacin (B₃)	0.80 mg
Magnesium	32 mg	Ascorbic Acid (C)	50 mg
Potassium	250 mg		

eat; the best way is to cut them in half and eat the flesh a spoonful at a time, daintily spitting out the inedible seeds. The fruit can also be used in fruit salads or puréed and served as a fruit sauce. Blended with orange juice, lime juice, and cream, it makes a delicious ice cream.

Bael
(Aegle marmelos)
Also Known As: Bengal Quince, Indian Quince, Stone Apple

Aegle comes from the Latin *Aegle*, one of the Hesperides (mythical guardians of a golden apple orchard). *Marmelos* is a Portuguese name for the fruit.

General Information
Belonging to the citrus family, this tree grows wild in much of central and southern India and Southeast Asia. It is cultivated throughout India, mainly in temple gardens, because of its status as a sacred tree. The fruits look something like grayish-yellow oranges and may have a thin hard shell or a less hard but thick skin.

Culinary Uses
The segmented pulp inside is yellow, gummy, and full of seeds but has an aromatic, refreshing flavor. It can be eaten plain, served with jaggery (palm sugar), or made into a marmalade, jelly, or drink. One popular Indian drink is made by beating the seeded pulp together with milk and sugar. Both the central core and seeds are inedible. Mature but still unripe fruits are made into jam with the addition of citric acid.

Health Benefits
The fresh ripe pulp of the higher-quality cultivars, and the sherbet made from it, are taken for their mild laxative, tonic, and digestive effects. It has been surmised that the psoralen in the pulp increases tolerance of sunlight and aids in maintaining normal skin color. Marmelosin, derived from the pulp, is given as a laxative and diuretic; in

> ### LORE AND LEGEND
> Hindus hold the tree sacred to Shiva and use its leaves in his worship. It is sacrilegious to cut down a bael tree, but to die under one assures immediate salvation.

larger doses it lowers the rate of respiration, depresses heart action, and causes sleepiness.

Bakuri
(Platonia insignis)

Platonia derives from a personal name. *Insignis* means "remarkable" or "distinguished."

General Information
The bakuri tree was first reported in European literature in 1614. The tree commonly grows wild in the Amazon region of northern Brazil and is especially abundant in the state of Para. Its native territory extends across the border into Colombia and northeast to the humid forests of Guyana. Seldom cultivated, the tree is always left standing for the sake of its fruits when land is cleared for planting or pastures. The roundish fruits, three to five inches wide, are yellow when ripe. Each has a hard rind and may weigh up to thirty-two ounces.

Culinary Uses
Bakuri pulp is white and pithy, with a pleasant odor and subacid flavor. It contains up to four inedible seeds. Infertile seed compartments filled with pulp (called "filho") are the parts preferred by the natives. Although the fruit is eaten raw, it is more commonly used to make sherbet, ice cream, marmalade, or jelly.

Bael / Nutritional Value Per 100 g Edible Portion			
	Raw		Raw
Protein	1.80–2.62 g	Riboflavin (B$_2$)	1.19 mg
Fat	0.20–0.39 g	Niacin (B$_3$)	1.10 mg
Beta Carotene (A)	55 mg	Ascorbic Acid (C)	8–60 mg
Thiamine (B$_1$)	0.13 mg		

Bakuri / Nutritional Value Per 100 g Edible Portion			
	Raw		Raw
Calories	105	Phosphorus	36.0 mg
Protein	1.9 g	Thiamine (B$_1$)	0.04 mg
Fiber	7.4 g	Riboflavin (B$_2$)	0.04 mg
Calcium	20.0 mg	Niacin (B$_3$)	0.50 mg
Iron	2.2 mg	Ascorbic Acid (C)	33.0 mg

Health Benefits

The seeds contain 6 to 11 percent of an oil that is mixed with sweet almond oil and used to treat eczema and herpes.

Banana
(Musa acuminata)

Time flies like an arrow; fruit flies like a banana.

—GROUCHO MARX

Little by little grow the bananas.

—CONGO PROVERB

The banana plant was named *Musa* in honor of Antonius Musa, the personal physician to Octavius Augustus, first emperor of Rome (63–14 B.C.). Euphorbus Musa, the brother of Antonius, discovered the banana while in Africa as physician to the king of Numidia, an ally of Rome. He sent samples to Antonius, urging the banana's cultivation and use, and Antonius promoted it so successfully that it has carried the family name ever since. *Acuminata* means "long-pointed" or "tapering" and usually refers to the flower petals. The classical writer Theophrastus recounted from Alexander the Great's reports of India that wise men were said to sit in the shade of the banana tree and eat its fruit—hence the earlier term *sapientum*, meaning "of the wise men." The first European contact with the fruit came not long after 1402, when Portuguese sailors encountered it in West Africa; this is why the English name *banana* comes from a West African word, the Guinean *banema* or *banana*.

General Information

The origin of the banana is thought to be in East Asia and Oceania, but the tree and its long slender fruit (the red and green cooking varieties) have been known and used since ancient times, even before the cultivation of rice. During the first millennium A.D. the banana reached Africa, probably taken directly from the Malay region to Madagascar. In 1482 the seafaring Portuguese found the banana on the Guinean coast and carried it with them to the Canary Islands. The Spanish missionary Friar Tomas de Berlanga took banana roots from the Canaries to Santo Domingo in the West Indies in 1516; later, when he was made bishop of Panama, the fruit reached the American mainland with him. The new plant spread so quickly and became so well established that some early travelers thought it an indigenous American plant. Only in 1836 did the yellow banana appear, a mutant from the original red and green cooking banana. A Jamaican named Jean François Poujot observed one morning that the bananas on one of his plantation trees were uniquely yellow. Tasting the strange new fruit uncooked, he found it edible—ripe, sweet, and delicious—and, recognizing their potential, soon planted acres of sweet yellow bananas. The international banana trade was started by two American entrepreneurs, Captain Lorenzo D. Baker in 1870 and Minor C. Keith in 1872, who independently of each other began to ship bananas from the Caribbean to New Orleans, Boston, and New York. They were offered as an exotic imported delicacy, to be eaten with a knife and fork. At the 1876 Philadelphia Centennial Exposition, yellow bananas were sold as a "curiosity of the Indies" for ten cents each and proved highly popular. By 1899 these two men had merged their interests to form the United Fruit Company, which still has great influence in Central America and the Islands. The flourishing banana industry is now one of the most profitable agricultural resources of many tropical countries.

The banana plant, contrary to popular notion, is not actually a tree but a giant perennial herb. Probably the largest plant without a woody stem, the trunk consists of a cylinder of tightly wrapped leaf-petiole sheaths. Pushing up through the center is the true stem, which emerges at the top as a flower spike or bud. Blossoms held in spirals on the tip grow into upturned "fingers," as many as twenty in a "hand," as many as fifteen hands in a bunch. After each harvest the pseudo-stem is either manually removed or allowed to die down naturally, but side shoots or suckers from the same underground corm continue to grow, and these stems will produce bunches of bananas in the following season. Some plants have been known to remain in production for up to one hundred years. In a sense the plant is immortal, although in practice most banana plantations are started anew every five to twenty years. The long slender banana fruit is sterile; the tiny partial seeds will not regenerate, but serve only to release the hormone (ethylene gas and carbon dioxide) that turns green bananas ripe and yellow. Most bananas are cut while still quite green, even for local use in the tropics, where they are allowed to ripen in a shady place near the house. Fruit intended for export is shipped green and ripened using ethylene gas under carefully controlled conditions. Bananas are one of the most popular fresh fruits in the United States, with an average twenty-five pounds consumed per capita annually.

Buying Tips

Bananas are harvested and shipped while still green. Thus you'll see bananas in various degrees of ripeness at the store. Those that are full and plump generally have more flavor and delicacy. Slightly green bananas will quickly ripen at room temperature. They are perfectly ripe when they have a few brown spots on them or even when there is still just a touch of green at the tips. The riper they are, the sweeter they are.

Culinary Uses

Unripe bananas are mostly starch and are hard to digest, while fully ripe fruits have converted most of their starch content into sugar, and the tannin element (which makes fresh fruit taste bitter and puckery) is greatly reduced.

Banana / Nutritional Value Per 100 g Edible Portion	Raw	Dried
Calories	65.5-111.0	298
Protein	1.10-1.87 g	2.80-3.50 g
Fat	0.16-0.40 g	0.80-1.10 g
Fiber	0.33-1.07 g	2.10-3.00 g
Calcium	3.2-13.8 mg	n/a
Iron	0.4-1.5 mg	n/a
Magnesium	29 mg	n/a
Phosphorus	16.3-50.4 mg	n/a
Potassium	396 mg	n/a
Sodium	1 mg	n/a
Zinc	0.160 mg	n/a
Copper	0.104 mg	n/a
Manganese	0.152 mg	n/a
Beta Carotene (A)	81 mg	n/a
Thiamine (B$_1$)	0.040-0.540 mg	n/a
Riboflavin (B$_2$)	0.050-0.067 mg	n/a
Niacin (B$_3$)	0.600-1.050 mg	n/a
Pantothenic Acid (B$_5$)	0.260 mg	n/a
Pyridoxine (B$_6$)	0.578 mg	n/a
Folic Acid (B$_9$)	19.1 mcg	n/a
Ascorbic Acid (C)	5.60-36.40 mg	n/a
Tocopherol (E)	0.270 mg	n/a

Bananas can be eaten raw straight out of their jackets, peeled and used in fruit salads, baked, fried, flambéed with liqueurs, and added to pies, ice creams, cakes, and bread. Where appearance is important they should be used immediately, or sprinkled with lemon juice to prevent discoloration. Refrigeration will stop the ripening process but turns the banana skins brown; the fruit itself is not harmed.

Although more than 90 percent of the bananas grown are used directly for food, several products are made from the remainder. A banana flour or powder is sometimes produced (but rarely exported) by spray-drying or drum-drying the mashed fruits. Candies and various confections are made by splitting and drying the bananas. Banana chips of commercial origin are made from bananas that are picked green, before the starch base turns to sugars, then sugar-sweetened and deep-fried like potato chips. Unsweetened chips are a dull product—with an oily texture (from frying) and no banana flavor—that few people would purchase twice. Make your own banana chips in a dehydrator; they will be more chewy than crunchy, with a rich, dense banana flavor, and are quite definitely healthier. Dehydrated banana flakes are also available in some markets in vacuum-sealed cans; these are used on cereals, in baked goods, desserts, sauces, and other products.

Health Benefits

pH 4.50–5.29. The banana is not only one of the neatest and most conveniently packaged food items but also a powerhouse of nutritional energy. Fully ripe bananas are composed of 76 percent water, 20 percent sugar, 12 percent starch, a large contingent of vitamins and minerals, and a great deal of fiber. Green bananas contain antinutrients, proteins that inhibit the actions of amylase, an enzyme that permits digestion of starch and other complex carbohydrates; thus wait until they are fully ripe before eating. Antifungal and antibiotic principles are found in both the peel and pulp of fully ripened bananas. Bananas feed the natural acidophilus bacteria of the bowel; their high vitamin and mineral content (especially potassium) benefits the muscular and nervous systems; their sugars are readily assimilated for use as fuel; and their pectin content helps heal ulcers and lower blood cholesterol. Bananas strengthen the surface cells of the stomach lining, thus creating a thicker barrier against digestive acid and pepsin—the two main causes of ulcers. Because high blood pressure medication may lower potassium levels dangerously, some

LORE AND LEGEND

There is an old Islamic myth, probably of Indian origin, that the banana was the forbidden fruit of the Tree of Knowledge of Good and Evil, which grew in the Garden of Eden. Furthermore, after the Fall, Adam and Eve covered their nakedness with banana leaves rather than those of the fig. This may account for the common West Indian practice of calling the banana fruit a fig.

patients are told to eat bananas because they are full of potassium. Potassium itself plays a direct role in controlling blood pressure, according to a classic Japanese study. Bananas are also rich in the amino acid tryptophan, which is known to promote sleep, and contain enzymes that assist in the manufacture of sexual hormones. For those striving to gain weight or build muscle bulk, bananas are a wonderful food (along with appropriate exercise). They are especially good for young children and infants, as they are easily digested and can be puréed with water to form a milky beverage. Make sure to use only ripe bananas. Unripe bananas tend to be constipating, while ripe ones are more laxative.

VARIETIES

Lady Fingers, also called **Chicaditas,** are small dull-yellow bananas that are incredibly sweet. Their small size makes them perfect finger food for children (or adults).

Red bananas, or **Clarets,** are shorter and fatter than yellow bananas and have thick red skins, dark creamy flesh, and a higher oil content. The taste of a red banana compared to a yellow banana is analogous to that of cream to milk; the red bananas are richer, more aromatic, smoother, and sweeter. To be fully ripe, a red banana must be swollen, slightly soft with perhaps a split skin, and the color turned from red to orange.

Apple bananas have a more acid flavor than a regular yellow banana and taste something like a mellow apple. These also must be very ripe before eating, or their consistency will be starchy.

Yellow bananas were introduced to North America by the United Fruit Company, now called United Brands.

It is largely because of the efforts of this unusual and controversial company that we enjoy a constant supply of this tropical fruit. By far the most common variety of yellow banana in the past was **Manque** or **Gros Michel** (Big Mike). The varieties known as **Valery** and **Cavendish,** which are more resistant to disease, are now the major varieties. These produce large, straight, compact bunches, which makes them easy to ship.

Barberry
(Berberis vulgaris, Mahonia aquifolium)

Berberis derives from the Arabic for "Barbary" (North Africa). *Mahonia* was named in honor of Bernard M'Mahon, a prominent American horticulturist (1775–1816). *Vulgaris* means "common," while *aquifolium* means "having pointed leaves" or "spiny-leaved." The English name *barberry* is a corruption of the Arabic name.

General Information
The barberry (*B. vulgaris*), a native of Europe and Asia, has been thoroughly naturalized in the eastern and middle United States, especially in New England. Formerly planted for its edible fruits as well as for ornamentation, today it has to compete with many other species and hybrids. *Berberis* berries are generally red, varying from coral to deep crimson, and tart. American barberries (*Mahonia* spp.) are usually blue, either pale or dark-colored. *M. aquifolium*, the mountain grape or Oregon grape, which is the floral emblem of the state of Oregon, has blue-gray berries.

Culinary Uses
Barberries are pleasantly acid and make a fine jelly or jam, as well as excellent juices and wines. In India some species are sun-dried to make "raisins," which are eaten as a dessert. The fruits ripen in September.

Health Benefits
The root and stem bark of the plant contain tannin and a substance known as berberine, which may account for the plant's effectiveness in treating diarrhea. Berberine salts, derived from barberry and other plants, are used in eyedrops and eyewashes. In ancient Egypt a syrup made of common barberry mixed with fennel seed was used against plagues; this concoction was probably effective because, as modern research indicates, the plant has antibacterial

properties that would help ward off infectious diseases. Barberry jelly provides relief for catarrhal infections, and the plain juice with a little sugar is a healing throat gargle.

Bignay
(*Antidesma bunius*)
Also Known As: Chinese Laurel, Currant Tree, Salamander Tree

Antidesma derives from a Greek term for "banding," signifying that the bark was used for cordage. The English name *bignay* derives from the Philippine name *bignai*.

General Information
The bignay tree is native to India, Ceylon, and southeast Asia. It is grown in every village in Indonesia, where the clusters of fruit are common in the marketplaces. Quite a few trees were planted in southern Florida and the fruits utilized for jelly, but they are rarely used today. The round or ovoid fruits are borne in grapelike, pendant clusters that are extremely showy. Since the berries ripen unevenly, there are pale yellowish-green, white, bright red, and nearly black stages all present at the same time. The thick skin is tough and leaves a bright purple stain on fabrics.

Culinary Uses
Whole bignay fruits are very acid when unripe, much like cranberries; ripe fruits are subacid and slightly sweet. For some there is an unpleasant aftertaste; others don't experience this. Each fruit contains a single inedible stone. The fruits are popular with Malayan children. Elsewhere the fruits are made into high-quality wine or preserves, and the richly colored jelly was actually produced on a small commercial scale in southern Florida for a number of years. Juice from the fruit makes an excellent syrup and has been fermented into wine and brandy.

Bilimbi
(*Averrhoa bilimbi*)

The *Averrhoa* genus was named in honor of *Averrhoes*, a twelfth century Arabic physician and philosopher. *Bilimbi* is the common name in India.

General Information
Probably a native of the Moluccas, the bilimbing asam is cultivated throughout much of Indonesia, the Philippines, Ceylon, and Burma. Introduced into Queensland, Australia, in about 1896, the tree was readily adopted and is now quite common. The fruit is ellipsoid or nearly cylindrical and 1½ to 4 inches long. Crisp when unripe, it turns from bright green to yellowish green or nearly white when ripe.

Culinary Uses
The outer skin is glossy, very thin, soft, and tender, and the flesh green, jellylike, juicy, and extremely acid. There may be perhaps six or seven flattened, disklike brown seeds about a quarter of an inch wide. Generally regarded as too acidic to eat raw, the fruit is frequently used for making pickles, flavoring curries, and stewing as a vegetable.

Health Benefits
In Java the fruits are combined with pepper and eaten to cause sweating when people are feeling under the weather. A paste of pickled bilimbis is smeared all over the body to hasten recovery after a fever. A conserve made from the fruit is administered as a treatment for coughs, beriberi, and biliousness. Syrup prepared from the fruit is taken as a cure for fever and inflammation and to stop rectal bleeding and alleviate internal hemorrhoids. Very acid bilimbis are employed to clean the blade of a kris (dagger), and they serve as mordants in the preparation of an orange dye for silk fabrics. The juice, because of its oxalic acid content, is useful for bleaching stains from the hands, rust marks from white cloth, and tarnish from brass.

Bignay / Nutritional Value Per 100 g Edible Portion			
	Raw		Raw
Protein	0.75 g	Thiamine (B₁)	0.031 mg
Calcium	0.12 mg	Riboflavin (B₂)	0.072 mg
Iron	0.001 mg	Niacin (B₃)	0.530 mg
Phosphorus	0.040 mg		

Bilimbi / Nutritional Value Per 100 g Edible Portion			
	Raw		Raw
Protein	0.61 g	Beta Carotene (A)	0.035 mg
Fiber	0.6 g	Thiamine (B₁)	0.010 mg
Calcium	3.4 mg	Riboflavin (B₂)	0.026 mg
Iron	1.01 mg	Niacin (B₃)	0.302 mg
Phosphorus	11.1 mg	Ascorbic Acid (C)	15.5 mg

Biriba

(Rollinia mucosa)
Also Known As: Wild Sugar Apple

The *Rollinia* genus was named in honor of the French historian Charles Rollin. *Mucosa* means "slimy." *Biriba* is the popular Brazilian name.

General Information

Many people find the biriba fruit the best of the large Annonaceae family (which includes cherimoyas, atemoyas, and others). Native to Brazil, it is the favorite fruit in western Amazonia. In Rio de Janeiro the biriba is so esteemed as to be called "the countess's fruit." Seeds were first introduced into the United States by O. W. Barrett in 1908, and seedlings later distributed to pioneers in southern Florida, but only a few trees exist there today. Biriba fruits are three to four inches long and conical to heart-shaped, with a creamy yellow skin when fully ripe. Handling causes the wartlike protuberances on the ripe fruit to turn brown or near black.

Culinary Uses

The white or cream-colored flesh is sweet, juicy, and flavorful. It has a slender, opaque-white core and numerous dark brown seeds, which are inedible. The fruit is eaten fresh or is fermented to make wine.

Health Benefits

In its native lands, the biriba is regarded as a refrigerant and antiscorbutic.

Biriba / Nutritional Value Per 100 g Edible Portion	
	Raw
Calories	80
Protein	2.8 g
Fiber	1.3 g
Calcium	24 mg
Iron	1.2 mg
Phosphorus	26 mg
Thiamine (B₁)	0.04 mg
Riboflavin (B₂)	0.04 mg
Niacin (B₃)	0.50 mg
Ascorbic Acid (C)	33.0 mg

Blackberry

(Rubus laciniatus, R. procerus, R. villosus)

One of the most astonishing of recent trends in science is that many top physicists and cosmologists now defend the wild notion that not only are universes as common as blackberries, but even more common.

—Martin Gardner

O, blackberry tart, with berries as big as your thumb, purple and black, and thick with juice, and a crust to endear them that will go to cream in your mouth, and both passing down with such a taste that will make you close your eyes and wish you might live forever in the wideness of that rich moment.

—Richard Llewellyn,
Welsh novelist (1907–1983)

Rubus comes from the Latin *ruber*, meaning "red." *Laciniatus* means "torn"; *procerus* means "tall"; *villosus* means "villous" or "soft-hairy." The English name *blackberry* is a very good description, since the berries are a deep rich black color when fully ripe.

General Information

Blackberries are a relative of the rose and like roses grow on thorny brambles or canes. The bushes are so vigorous and invasive that they quickly become a thick, scratchy, impenetrable mass that is hard to eradicate. Since they grow wild in such abundance throughout the country, cultivation has been slow. Just the mere mention of blackberries will bring to mind for many people annual excursions to gather this delicious fruit. They are well worth the cuts, scratches, and stains of picking. The berry itself has a distinct shape: a single berry is actually a group of "drupelets," tiny fruits, each containing one seed, clustered together around a core. This core does not separate from the fruit like the raspberry's does.

Dewberries (*Rubus procumbens, R. canadensis*) are a more delicately flavored type of blackberry; grown on trailing rather than upright plants, they are regarded as one of the tastiest varieties. Boysenberries, loganberries, ollalieberries, tayberries, and youngberries are hybrids of blackberries and either dewberries or red raspberries.

Buying Tips
Look for bright, clean berries with uniform dark coloring. Check the bottom of the container to make sure it has not been stained from crushed or moldy fruit. Blackberries should be refrigerated as soon as you get them home. Before storing, throw away those that are already damaged and put the rest in a flat container to avoid any further damage. Use care when washing them.

Culinary Uses
Plump, sweet blackberries are larger, juicier, and grainier than raspberries, with a more assertive flavor. They deteriorate faster than most fruits and should be used the day they are gathered or purchased. When fully ripe, each drupelet turns a shiny purple-black, and the whole berry is soft and lush. Blackberries can be used in a multitude of ways. Straight off the bush is best, but they are also good mixed with cream, or cooked into cobblers, jams, pies, and other baked goods.

Health Benefits
pH 3.85–4.50. Astringent, tonic. Blackberries are valuable as a general tonic and blood cleanser. They are highly esteemed in relieving diarrhea because of their astringent and tonic effects, as well as for contracting tissues and reducing secretions. Overindulgence may cause constipation.

Blueberry
(*Vaccinium corymbosum, V. ashei, V. angustifolium, V. myrtillus*)
Also Known As: Whortleberry, Bilberry, Hurtleberry

> Blueberries as big as the end of your thumb,
> Real sky-blue, and heavy, and ready to drum
> In the cavernous pail of the first one to come!
> And all ripe together, not some of them green
> And some of them ripe! You ought to have seen!
>
> —Robert Frost

Vaccinium is the ancient Latin name for the blueberry bush, derived from *vacca*, meaning "cow," because cows like the plants. *Corymbosum* means "corymbose," or having a flat-topped inflorescence; *angustifolium* means "narrow-leaved"; *myrtillus* refers to the bush's myrtlelike leaves. The English name *blueberry* is a good description of this blue-fruited plant; *bilberry* derives from the Danish *bolle*, meaning "ball," referring to the berry's round, smooth appearance.

General Information
It's no wonder that the delectable blueberry, not too juicy and not too sweet, is the second most popular berry after the strawberry. A relative of azaleas and rhododendrons, blueberries grow in the same climates. Low-bush blueberries (*V. angustifolium*), which flourish at ankle height, grow wild in the rocky uplands and sandy pine barrens of the upper northeastern United States and Canada, and locally provide berries that are very small but superbly fla-

Blackberry / Nutritional Value Per 100 g Edible Portion			
	Raw		Raw
Calories	52	Copper	0.140 mg
Protein	0.72 g	Manganese	1.291 mg
Fat	0.39 g	Beta Carotene (A)	165 IU
Fiber	4.10 g	Thiamine (B$_1$)	0.030 mg
Calcium	32 mg	Riboflavin (B$_2$)	0.040 mg
Iron	0.57 mg	Niacin (B$_3$)	0.400 mg
Magnesium	20 mg	Pantothenic Acid (B$_5$)	0.240 mg
Phosphorus	21 mg	Pyridoxine (B$_6$)	0.058 mg
Potassium	196 mg	Folic Acid (B$_9$)	n/a
Sodium	0 mg	Ascorbic Acid (C)	21 mg
Zinc	0.270 mg	Tocopherol (E)	0.600 mg

Blueberry / Nutritional Value Per 100 g Edible Portion			
	Raw		Raw
Calories	56	Copper	0.061 mg
Protein	0.67 g	Manganese	0.282 mg
Fat	0.38 g	Beta Carotene (A)	100 IU
Fiber	1.30 g	Thiamine (B$_1$)	0.048 mg
Calcium	6 mg	Riboflavin (B$_2$)	0.050 mg
Iron	0.17 mg	Niacin (B$_3$)	0.359 mg
Magnesium	5 mg	Pantothenic Acid (B$_5$)	0.093 mg
Phosphorus	10 mg	Pyridoxine (B$_6$)	0.036 mg
Potassium	89 mg	Folic Acid (B$_9$)	6.4 mcg
Sodium	6 mg	Ascorbic Acid (C)	13 mg
Zinc	0.110 mg		

vorful. Rabbit-eye blueberry bushes (*V. ashei*), which are more abundant in the southern United States, grow to towering heights of thirty feet and produce medium-sized berries that are generally processed rather than marketed fresh. The variety of blueberry found in most grocery stores comes from the high-bush blueberry plant (*V. corymbosum*), which produces large, firm, light blueberries. In the early 1900s Elizabeth White of New Jersey encouraged the cultivation of blueberries by offering prizes for outstanding bush specimens, and today nearly all commercially cultivated blueberry varieties sold in the United States are the result of her work. Some varieties of blueberry are mistakenly called huckleberries: the red huckleberry (*V. parvifolium*) of the Northwest United States, the squaw huckleberry (*V. stamineum*) of the North, and the California huckleberry (*V. ovatum*). Because of its superior shipping properties, the blueberry is a sizable business in the northeastern states, especially Maine. The United States produces 95 percent of the world's blueberry crop.

Buying Tips

Ripe blueberries should be plump, clean, dry, and full of color, with a powdery "bloom" on the skins. This bloom is a natural, protective, waxy coat. Overripe berries are dull in appearance, soft and watery, or moldy. Watch out for stained or leaking containers, which indicate crushed or moldy berries within. Blueberries should be refrigerated as soon as you get them home. Before storing, throw away those that are already damaged and put the rest in a flat container to avoid any further damage. Use care when washing them. Blueberries are easily frozen in sealed containers for later use.

Culinary Uses

Highly perishable, the berries will last only about seven days after picking. The use of blueberries as a fresh or stewed fruit, and in such dishes as blueberry pie and blueberry muffins, is well known. Fresh or frozen, blueberries are a colorful and tasty addition to cakes, shortcakes, pies, cobblers, preserves, and syrup. Combined with other fruits that provide additional tartness and pectin, they make an excellent jelly. They dry well and are used in numerous prepared foods. Blueberries darken if stored in a metal container, and if combined with excessive alkaline ingredients (like baking soda), the berries turn a greenish blue.

Health Benefits

pH 3.11–3.33. Laxative. Blueberries are well known for their laxative effect, but they also make excellent blood and liver cleansers, improve sluggish circulation, and benefit the eyesight (particularly nocturnal vision). During World War II, British Royal Air Force pilots consumed bilberry (a variety of blueberry) preserves before their night missions to improve their ability to see at night. After the war, numerous studies demonstrated that blueberry extracts do in fact improve nighttime visual acuity and lead to quicker adjustment to darkness and faster restoration of visual acuity after exposure to glare. Bilberry's active ingredients, anthocyanosides, are antioxidant flavonoids that help prevent free-radical damage to the eyes. Anthocyanosides support and protect collagen structures in the blood vessels of the eyes, assuring strong, healthy capillaries that successfully carry vital nutrients to eye muscles and nerves. Additional research suggests that blueberries may protect against the development of cataracts and glaucoma; they may also be quite therapeutic in the treatment of varicose veins, hemorrhoids, and peptic ulcers. Their bacteria-fighting capabilities are particularly useful in countering urinary tract infections. Fresh berries have a healing effect on any infection of the mouth and rejuvenate the pancreas, and their antiseptic value helps in relieving dysentery. Of the fresh, temperate-region fruits, the blueberry is one of the highest in iron. Blueberry leaves effectively lower high blood sugar in adult-onset diabetes.

Boysenberry
(Rubus ursinus, var. loganobaccus, cv. "Boysen")

Rubus is from the Latin *ruber*, meaning "red." The English name *boysenberry* was given in honor of its creator, Rudolf Boysen, who experimentally crossed the black raspberry and loganberry in 1923.

General Information
The boysenberry is a slightly larger and more acidic blackberry that looks exactly like the black parent it came from. California plant breeders had said it was genetically impossible to cross black, logan, and raspberry varieties, but Rudolph Boysen managed to do it. Mr. Boysen never cashed in on his discovery, and the plants were largely forgotten for many years. In 1933 boysenberries were rediscovered, and a southern California grower named Walter Knott started planting them extensively on his family's farm in Anaheim, California (Knott's Berry Farm), where they soon became the keystone of his family's fortune. Grown primarily for canning, the large, long, dark reddish-black berries are fully ripe only when each drupelet turns deep purple; just one light-colored drupelet will make the whole berry bitter.

Culinary Uses and Health Benefits
pH 3.11–3.33. Same as blackberries.

Boysenberry / Nutritional Value Per 100 g Edible Portion			
	Raw		Raw
Calories	50	Copper	0.080 mg
Protein	1.10 g	Manganese	0.547 mg
Fat	0.26 g	Beta Carotene (A)	67 IU
Fiber	2.70 g	Thiamine (B₁)	0.053 mg
Calcium	27 mg	Riboflavin (B₂)	0.037 mg
Iron	0.85 mg	Niacin (B₃)	0.767 mg
Magnesium	16 mg	Pantothenic Acid (B₅)	0.250 mg
Phosphorus	27 mg	Pyridoxine (B₆)	0.056 mg
Potassium	139 mg	Folic Acid (B₉)	63.3 mcg
Sodium	1 mg	Ascorbic Acid (C)	3.10 mg
Zinc	0.220 mg		

Breadfruit
(Artocarpus altilis)

Gather the breadfruit from the farthest branches first.

—Samoan proverb

Artocarpus comes from the Greek words *artos*, meaning "bread," and *carpos*, meaning "fruit." The term *altilis* refers to the tallness of the tree. Its English name *breadfruit* comes from the fact that when the fruit is roasted whole between hot stones, the pulp achieves the consistency and taste of freshly baked bread.

General Information
The handsome breadfruit tree is believed to be native to a vast area extending from New Guinea through the Indo-Malayan Archipelago to western Micronesia. A member of the mulberry family, the breadfruit is a valuable crop from southern Florida to Brazil, and during its eight-month season it provides the natives around the Gulf of Mexico and the Caribbean Sea with an important fruit, often the mainstay of their diet. The greenish-yellow fruit, with its

Breadfruit / Nutritional Value Per 100 g Edible Portion	Underripe, Raw	Ripe, Cooked
Calories	105-109	n/a
Protein	1.30-2.24 g	1.34 g
Fat	0.10-0.86 g	0.31 g
Fiber	1.08-2.10 g	1.50 g
Calcium	0.05-17.00 mg	0.022 mg
Iron	0.61-2.40 mg	n/a
Magnesium	25 mg	n/a
Phosphorus	0.04-30.00 mg	0.062 mg
Potassium	490 mg	n/a
Sodium	2 mg	n/a
Zinc	0.120 mg	n/a
Copper	0.084 mg	n/a
Manganese	0.060 mg	n/a
Beta Carotene (A)	35-40 IU	n/a
Thiamine (B₁)	0.080-0.085 mg	n/a
Riboflavin (B₂)	0.033-0.070 mg	n/a
Niacin (B₃)	0.506-0.920 mg	n/a
Pantothenic Acid (B₅)	0.457 mg	n/a
Ascorbic Acid (C)	15-33 mg	n/a

LORE AND LEGEND

The breadfruit was regarded as a romantic symbol of abundance and easy living by early inhabitants of the Pacific Islands. Captain James Cook, the English navigator who explored the Pacific in 1770-1780, saw the tree during his voyages and reported in such glowing terms about the value of the breadfruit that the British government decided to transplant young breadfruit trees for use in its thriving slave colonies in the Jamaican West Indies. Captain William Bligh, who had sailed with Cook, was duly commissioned; thus began the infamous voyage of the HMS *Bounty* in 1786. The ship left Tahiti with more than a thousand young trees, but as a result of the mutiny led by Fletcher Christian, neither trees nor crew ever reached their destination. Bligh remade the journey in 1792, and in January 1793 successfully landed a quantity of plants at the island of St. Vincent. The unfortunate breadfruit never became an important food plant in the West Indies, however, as the natives much preferred the already familiar bananas, plantains, and other native foods. Captain Bligh has been honored by having another fruit tree named after him, *Blighia sapida*, the akee; its fruit is edible, but only barely—eaten either unripe or overly ripe, the fruit is highly poisonous and can cause death.

reticulated pattern of small protrusions, sometimes reaches a foot in diameter and weighs up to ten pounds. It is similar to a pineapple in that the fruit is actually multiple fruits that have developed from the ovaries of a tight cluster of flowers rather than from a single flower. Both seedless and seeded forms of breadfruit are known. All seedless varieties must be cooked. The seeded type is grown primarily for its seeds, called breadnuts, which when cooked and eaten are said to taste like chestnuts.

Buying Tips

If you don't plan to use breadfruit for a few days, select a specimen that is all green, evenly colored, hard, and with large scales. It should feel dense and heavy for its size, not spongy. If you want to use it immediately, choose one as your recipe calls for (immature through mature). All breadfruit store poorly, ripening very quickly.

Culinary Uses

No one tasting breadfruit for the first time is likely to dispute that it is an acquired taste (and texture). When green and immature, raw breadfruit is hard and starchy like a raw potato, and equally unappealing. At this stage, the pulp is generally sliced and roasted, or baked whole in its thick skin between hot stones so that it nearly achieves the consistency and taste of freshly baked whole-wheat bread. As it gradually ripens and turns yellowish green, the pulp when cooked acquires the flavor of a yam and a texture that might be likened to that of an extremely starchy potato mixed with plantain, but much stickier than either. At this stage it is also frequently cored, stuffed with a rich filling of meat or cheese, and baked. Fully ripened, it becomes a dessert fruit, since its flesh becomes rather sweet and tacky with a slightly musky, fruity flavor, which at the same time is very bland. In countries that cultivate them, the breadfruit is cooked in all the ways that Europeans and North Americans prepare both white and sweet potatoes: boiled, baked, roasted, fried, steamed, mashed, creamed, and puréed; it is also made into smooth soups, puddings, cakes, and pies. The pulp from ripe breadfruits is combined with coconut milk, salt, and sugar, and baked to make a pudding. Dried fruit is ground into flour, and when added to wheat flour the combination is more nutritious than wheat flour alone. The seeds from seeded breadfruit are edible. Usually boiled, roasted, or fried before being eaten, they are said to be so close to chestnuts in flavor and texture that they may be freely substituted in any chestnut recipe.

Calamondin
(Citrofortunella mitis)
Also Known As: Calamansi, Calamondin Orange, Panama Orange, Golden or Scarlet Lime

Citrofortunella is a hybrid of *citrus* and *Fortunella* (see **Kumquat**). *Mitis* means "mild, gentle, ripe, without thorns." The English name *calamondin* derives from the Tagalog name *kalamunding*.

General Information
It is believed that this small citrus fruit is native to China and was taken early to the Philippines. Widely grown in India and throughout southern Asia and Malaysia, it is a common ornamental dooryard tree in Hawaii, the Bahamas, and parts of Central America. Dr. David Fairchild introduced the tree into Florida from Panama in 1899, and it quickly became popular in that state and Texas. The round, orange-red, very aromatic and showy fruits are 1¾ inches wide and contain no or only a few seeds.

Culinary Uses
Looking like a small mandarin orange, the peeled fruit contains pulp that is orange, very juicy, highly acidic, and usually seedless. Halves or quarters may be served like orange slices or pressed for the juice, like lime or lemon juice in salads, desserts, and custard pies. An excellent marmalade is made by using equal quantities calamondins and kumquats or papaya.

Health Benefits
Rubbing calamondin juice on insect bites eliminates itching. Slightly diluted and drunk warm, it serves as a laxative. Combined with pepper, the juice is prescribed in Malaya to expel phlegm.

Canistel
(Pouteria campechiana)
Also Known As: Yellow Sapote, Egg Fruit

Pouteria is a native name for the plant, as is *canistel* for the fruit.

General Information
Sometimes called egg fruit, or yellow sapote because of its orange flesh, the canistel occurs wild in parts of southern Mexico, Belize, Guatemala, and El Salvador. The tree was introduced at low and medium elevations in the Philippines before 1924; it reached Hawaii about the same time. During World War II, RAF pilots and crewmen training in the Bahamas showed great fondness for the canistel and bought all they could find in the Nassau market. The fruit, widely variable in form and size, may be nearly round or somewhat oval, and is often bulged on one side. When unripe the fruit is green-skinned, hard, and gummy internally. Upon ripening, the skin turns lemon yellow or pale orange-yellow and is very smooth and glossy.

Culinary Uses
The yellow flesh is relatively firm and mealy, with a few fine fibers; toward the center the fruit is softer and more pasty, often likened in texture to the yolk of a hard-boiled egg. Fruits should not be allowed to become too soft and mushy before eating. The flavor is sweet, more or less musky, and somewhat like that of a baked sweet potato. There may be up to four hard, inedible freestone seeds. Some people enjoy the fruit with salt, pepper, and lime or lemon juice, either fresh or lightly baked. The puréed flesh may be used in custards or added to ice cream mix just before freezing. A rich milk shake, or "egg-fruit nog," is made by combining ripe canistel pulp, milk, sugar, vanilla, and nutmeg or other seasonings in an electric blender.

Calamondin / Nutritional Value Per 100 g Edible Portion			
	Raw		Raw
Calories	173/lb	Iron	0.003%
Protein	0.86%	Phosphorus	0.07%
Fat	2.41%	Ascorbic Acid (C)	88.4–111.3 mg
Calcium	0.14%		

Canistel / Nutritional Value Per 100 g Edible Portion			
	Raw		Raw
Calories	138.8	Phosphorus	37.3 mg
Protein	1.68 g	Beta Carotene (A)	0.32 mg
Fat	0.13 g	Thiamine (B₁)	0.170 mg
Fiber	0.10 g	Riboflavin (B₂)	0.010 mg
Calcium	26.5 mg	Niacin (B₃)	3.720 mg
Iron	0.92 mg	Ascorbic Acid (C)	58.1 mg

Cape Gooseberry
(Physalis peruviana)
Also Known As: Poha

Physalis is Greek for "bladder," a name given to this plant because its thin calyx enlarges and encloses the fruit; *peruviana* means "of Peruvian origin." The *cape* in *cape gooseberry* refers to the Cape of Good Hope, where the plant was grown by early settlers before 1807. It is called gooseberry because its taste reminded the settlers of that fruit.

General Information
Although the fruit is thought to be native to Peru and Chile, it has been introduced into many other countries and is now widely cultivated. The plant seems to be successful wherever tomatoes can be grown. The small yellow-green or orange fruit, about the size of a cherry, enjoyed an early popularity in the Cape province of South Africa, and when it traveled from there to New South Wales in Australia, where it was one of the few fresh fruits of the early settlers, it became widely known as the cape gooseberry. Throughout Australia and New Zealand the plant has become abundantly naturalized. It is surprising that this useful little fruit has received so little attention in the United States.

Buying Tips
Avoid greenish ones; choose those that are yellow or orangey. A bit of dinginess on the balloony husks will not hurt the fruit. The fresh fruits can be stored in a sealed container and kept in a dry atmosphere for several months.

Culinary Uses
Within the thin waxy skin is a juicy pulp and many small seeds, all with a distinctive flavor and grapelike tang. Cape gooseberries can be eaten raw, used like strawberries in desserts, canned whole, or used to make a good jam, when combined with a high-pectin fruit. They add an intriguing flavor, texture, and color to apple pies. The husk is bitter and inedible. Unripe fruits are poisonous.

Capulin
(Prunus salicifolia)
Also Known As: Wild Cherry, Black Cherry

The large plum family was given the genus *Prunus*, a name derived from the ancient Greek name *proumne*. *Salicifolia* means "having leaves like the willow or *Salix* tree." *Capulin* is a colloquial name for the fruit.

General Information
The capulin is a true cherry and is native throughout the Valley of Mexico from Sonora to Chiapas and Veracruz. Cultivated since early times, it is an important food in those areas. The aromatic fruit is round and three-eighths to three-quarters of an inch wide, with red or nearly black smooth, tender skin.

Culinary Uses
The pale green juicy pulp has an agreeably acid but slightly astringent flavor. Ripe fruits are eaten raw (minus the single stone), stewed, or made into jam. With skin and seeds removed, they are mixed with milk and served with vanilla and cinnamon as a dessert. They may also be fermented to make an alcoholic beverage.

Cape Gooseberry / Nutritional Value Per 100 g Edible Portion			
	Raw		Raw
Protein	0.054 g	Beta Carotene (A)	1.613 mg
Fat	0.16 g	Thiamine (B1)	0.101 mg
Fiber	4.9 g	Riboflavin (B2)	0.032 mg
Calcium	8 mg	Niacin (B3)	1.73 mg
Iron	1.23 mg	Ascorbic Acid (C)	43 mg
Phosphorus	55.3 mg		

Capulin / Nutritional Value Per 100 g Edible Portion			
	Raw		Raw
Protein	0.105–0.185 g	Beta Carotene (A)	0.005–0.162 mg
Fat	0.26–0.37 g	Thiamine (B$_1$)	0.016–0.031 mg
Fiber	0.1–0.7 g	Riboflavin (B$_2$)	0.018–0.028 mg
Calcium	17.2–25.1 mg	Niacin (B$_3$)	0.640–1.140 mg
Iron	0.65–0.84 mg	Ascorbic Acid (C)	22.2–32.8 mg
Phosphorus	16.9–24.4 mg		

Carambola

(Averrhoa carambola)
Also Known As: Star Fruit, Chinese Star Fruit, Belimbi

The carambola tree was given its Latin name in honor of Averrhoes, a twelfth-century Arabic physician and philosopher; *carambola* is an Indian name for the fruit, from the Sanskrit *karmara*, meaning "food appetizer."

General Information

A tree melon that originated in Ceylon and the Moluccas, the carambola is now grown throughout Asia and Florida. The fruit is 2½ to 6 inches long, with a waxy skin that ranges in color from orange-yellow to pale yellow, and has crisp, yellow, juicy flesh when ripe. Hanging on the tree, the fruit resembles yellow Chinese lanterns. There may be up to twelve flat, thin brown seeds, or none at all. With its five or six prominent ridges, similar to an acorn squash, the fruit when sliced provides perfectly shaped stars that delight the eye and lighten the spirit. Of the two principal sorts of carambola, one is small and acidly sour, while the other is larger with a mild, almost bland, but sweeter flavor. Most tart varieties have very narrow ribs, while the sweet yellow varieties have thick, fleshy ones. The two white varieties marketed commercially are sweet.

Buying Tips

Look for full, firm fruits from two to five inches long, with juicy-looking ribs. If green-ribbed fruit is purchased, be sure to let it ripen until it has a full floral-fruity aroma and the skin has turned yellow. Avoid those with brown, shriveled ribs.

Culinary Uses

The carambola when green is very astringent, like green gooseberries or sorrel, but when ripe is pleasantly acid-sweet and refreshing. The Chinese and Hindus eat the carambola when green as a vegetable, and when ripe as a fruit. Fully ripened sweet carambolas have a flavor that combines the flowery best of plums, McIntosh apples, pineapples, and Concord grapes with a citric edge. When sour, the flesh is brightly sharp, as clean as a lemon, but less harsh and more fruity. Use fresh carambola as you would melons. Eat it plain, mix it with salads, add it as a garnish on avocado or seafood, or float it in punch bowls. For the winter solstice, Christmas, Hanukkah, or New Year's Eve, a golden star on anything makes a festive and glamorous garnish. The fruits are also cooked into puddings, tarts, stews, and curries. Dried star fruit is available in some natural food stores.

Health Benefits

In India ripe fruits are administered to halt hemorrhages and to relieve bleeding hemorrhoids. A conserve of the fruit is said to allay biliousness and diarrhea, and to relieve hangovers from excessive alcohol consumption.

Carambola / Nutritional Value Per 100 g Edible Portion			
	Raw		Raw
Calories	35.7	Sodium	2 mg
Protein	0.38 g	Zinc	0.110 mg
Fat	0.08 g	Copper	0.120 mg
Fiber	0.80-0.90 g	Manganese	0.082 mg
Calcium	4.4-6.0 mg	Beta Carotene (A)	0.003-0.552 mg
Iron	0.32-1.65 mg	Thiamine (B$_1$)	0.030-0.038 mg
Magnesium	9 mg	Riboflavin (B$_2$)	0.019-0.030 mg
Phosphorus	15.5-21.0 mg	Niacin (B$_3$)	0.294-0.380 mg
Potassium	163 mg	Ascorbic Acid (C)	26-53 mg

Carissa and Karanda

(Carissa macrocarpa, C. grandiflora, C. congesta)
Also Known As: Natal Plum

Carissa is an Aboriginal name for the fruit. *Macrocarpa* means "bearing large fruits or seedpods"; *congesta* means "congested or brought together." The fruit received its alternate name *Natal plum* because it was from the Natal province of South Africa.

General Information

Two closely related fruits, the carissa is indigenous to the coastal region of Natal, South Africa, and the karanda to India, Burma, and Malacca. First introduced into the United States in 1886 by the horticulturist Theodore L. Meade, the carissa was then introduced into Hawaii in 1905 and extensively distributed throughout the islands over the next few years. The fruit looks like a small scarlet plum with dark red seams. About 2½ inches long and up to 1½ inches wide, the fruit is green and rich in latex when unripe. As it ripens, the tender, smooth skin turns to a bright magenta red coated with a thin, whitish bloom, and finally dark crimson. The flesh is soft and juicy, strawberry red flecked with white, and contains about a dozen thin brown seeds. The karanda was widely cultivated in India, where the fruit was popular with British residents because it reminded them of the gooseberry. Planted in the Philippines, the tree first fruited in 1915 and was described by P. J. Wester as "one of the best small fruits introduced into the Philippines within recent years." It has been cultivated in a limited manner in Florida and California. The small, half-inch to one-inch fruits turn dark purple or nearly black when ripe.

Culinary Uses

The carissa must be fully ripe, dark red, and slightly soft to the touch to be eaten raw. It can be eaten out of hand, without peeling or removing the seeds; the texture is slightly granular, the flavor mildly sharp and strawberry-like. Halved or quartered and seeded it is suitable for fruit salads, adding to gelatins, and as a topping for cakes, puddings, and ice cream. Ripe fruits make a filling for pies. In the semi-ripe stage the fruits are used for making jellies and jams. Ripe karandas have very acid to fairly sweet, juicy, red or pink pulp, which exudes flecks of latex. There may be two to eight small brown seeds. The sweeter types of karanda may be eaten raw out of hand, but the more acid ones are best stewed with plenty of sugar. Even so, the skin may be found to be tough and slightly bitter. The cooked syrup has been successfully utilized on a small scale by at least one soda-fountain operator in Florida. In Asia the ripe fruits are employed in curries, tarts, puddings, and chutneys. Green, sour fruits are turned into pickles.

Health Benefits

Unripe fruits are used medicinally as an astringent, while ripe fruits are taken as an antiscorbutic and remedy for biliousness. The fruits have also been employed as agents in tanning and dyeing.

Cashew Apple
(Anacardium occidentale)

The genus name *Anacardium* means "heart-shaped"; *occidentale* means "western." The English word *cashew* is derived from the Brazilian Tupi-Indian word *acaju*.

General Information

The tropical evergreen cashew shrub, whose relatives include the mango and pistachio, is native to northeast Brazil. In the sixteenth century, Portuguese traders introduced the tree into Mozambique and coastal India, but only as a soil retainer to stop coastal erosion. The cashew flourished, and soon extensive forests were formed in these locations and on nearby

Carissa and Karanda / Nutritional Value Per 100 g Edible Portion		
	Raw Carissa	Raw Karanda
Calories	62	338-342/lb
Protein	0.50 g	0.39-0.66%
Fat	1.30 g	2.57-4.63%
Fiber	0.90 g	0.62-1.81%
Calcium	11 mg	n/a
Iron	1.31 mg	n/a
Magnesium	16 mg	n/a
Phosphorus	7 mg	n/a
Potassium	260 mg	n/a
Sodium	3 mg	n/a
Copper	0.210 mg	n/a
Beta Carotene (A)	40 IU	n/a
Thiamine (B₁)	0.040 mg	n/a
Riboflavin (B₂)	0.060 mg	n/a
Niacin (B₃)	0.200 mg	n/a
Ascorbic Acid (C)	38 mg	9-11 mg

Cashew Apple / Nutritional Value Per 100 g Edible Portion			
	Raw		Raw
Protein	0.101-0.162 g	Beta Carotene (A)	0.030-0.742 mg
Fat	0.05-0.50 g	Thiamine (B₁)	0.023-0.030 mg
Fiber	0.4-1.0 g	Riboflavin (B₂)	0.130-0.400 mg
Calcium	0.9-5.4 mg	Niacin (B₃)	0.130-0.539 mg
Iron	0.19-0.71 mg	Ascorbic Acid (C)	146.6-372.0 mg
Phosphorus	6.1-21.4 mg		

islands. The true fruit of the tree is the cashew nut, which resembles a miniature boxing glove. The nut hangs like an appendage from the base of the pseudo-fruit, the peduncle (stalk), which fills out, becoming fleshy and pear-shaped with yellow or red skin. An interesting feature is that the nut develops before the cashew "apple" or peduncle. In some countries the apple has been highly utilized and the nut simply thrown away. Since the cashew apple spoils within twenty-four hours of harvest, it is almost never exported, and the fortunate few who have tried this fruit, either ripe or in preserves, say it is even tastier than the cashew nut.

Culinary Uses

The fruit has pulp that is spongy, fibrous, very juicy, astringent, and acid to subacid. Locally, the fruits are chewed for their refreshing juice, the fibrous residue is discarded. The apples are also preserved in syrup on a small commercial scale.

Health Benefits

Fresh cashew apple juice, without removal of tannin, is prescribed as a remedy for sore throat and chronic dysentery in Cuba and Brazil; fresh or distilled, the juice is a potent diuretic and said to possess sudorific properties.

Cassabanana

(Sicana odorifera)

Also Known As: Sikana, Musk Cucumber

Sicana is a Peruvian name for the plant. *Odorifera* means "fragrant" or "scented."

General Information

This fruit is probably native to Brazil, where the plant is grown as an ornamental vine. It was first mentioned by European writers in 1658 as cultivated and popular in Peru. People like to keep the fruit around the house, and especially in linen and clothes closets, because of its long-lasting fragrance and the belief that it repels moths. It is also placed on church altars during Holy Week. Trial plantings in the United States have generally failed. Renowned for its strong, sweet, agreeable, melonlike odor, the striking fruit is ellipsoid or nearly cylindrical, twelve to twenty-four inches long, and three to five inches wide, with an orange-red to dark purple or jet-black hard shell.

Culinary Uses

The juicy orange or yellow flesh is firm, cantaloupe-like in texture, and highly aromatic. In the central cavity there is softer pulp, a soft, fleshy core, and numerous rows of flat, oval seeds. Unripe fruits can be used in soups and stews as a vegetable. Ripe ones are refreshing if eaten raw but more often end up as jam.

Health Benefits

In Puerto Rico the flesh is cut up and steeped in water with added sugar, then usually left overnight at room temperature so that it will slightly ferment. The resultant liquor is sipped frequently. Strips of the flesh are eaten to relieve sore throat.

Cherimoya

(Annona cherimola)

Also Known As: Sherbet Fruit, Custard Fruit

Annona means "year's harvest" and is suggested by the Haitian name *anon*, which is applied to one of the species. The English name *cherimoya* comes from *chirimuya*, a Quichuan word (from Incan Peru) meaning "cold seeds," presumably an allusion to the wet freshness of the fruit and the large seeds.

Cassabanana / Nutritional Value Per 100 g Edible Portion			
	Raw	(without peel, seeds, central pulp)	Raw
Protein	0.145 g	Beta Carotene (A)	0.11 mg
Fat	0.02 g	Thiamine (B₁)	0.058 mg
Fiber	1.1 g	Riboflavin (B₂)	0.035 mg
Calcium	21.1 mg	Niacin (B₃)	0.767 mg
Iron	0.33 mg	Ascorbic Acid (C)	13.9 mg
Phosphorus	24.5 mg		

Cherimoya / Nutritional Value Per 100 g Edible Portion			
	Raw		Raw
Calories	94	Phosphorus	30-40 mg
Protein	1.3-1.9 g	Beta Carotene (A)	10 IU
Fat	0.1-0.4 g	Thiamine (B₁)	0.100-0.117 mg
Fiber	2.0-2.2 g	Riboflavin (B₂)	0.110-0.140 mg
Calcium	21.7-32.0 mg	Niacin (B₃)	0.900-1.300 mg
Iron	0.5-0.8 mg	Ascorbic Acid (C)	5-16 mg

General Information

Cherimoya trees began their history in the uplands of Colombia, Bolivia, and Ecuador as a wild tree taken into cultivation by the Incas. The nineteenth-century German naturalist and traveler Friedrich W. K. Humboldt, who left his scientific imprint throughout South America and Mexico, declared that this delicious fruit was well worth the hazardous trip across the Atlantic. Generally heart-shaped and ranging in size from a large apple to a small cantaloupe, cherimoyas look rather like leathery fat green pinecones or light green armadillos, as their skins are patterned with shingles or scales.

Buying Tips

Select cherimoyas of any size with smooth, slightly yellow-green skin and that are firm or with a little give if you want to eat them within a day or so. Avoid fruits that are dark or splotched with many dark areas, as they may have been subjected to cold in transit and will not ripen properly. Handle them gently, as the skins are not as tough as they appear to be.

Culinary Uses

When ripe, the fruit will give to pressure all around like a papaya or plum; do not cut until it is uniformly quite soft. The sweet, low-acid flesh is silky smooth and juicy, white or cream-colored, with a slight granular finish like a custard of fine pears. The ambrosial flavor is very sweet and fruity, touching on mango, pineapple, strawberry, papaya, or vanilla custard in varying proportions. Scattered at random throughout are quite a few watermelon-like black seeds, which are inedible. The easiest way to eat a cherimoya is to cut it in half lengthwise and take a spoon to it, daintily spitting out the seeds as you go; it can also be peeled and either diced or puréed with other fruits to make drinks and sherbets.

Cherry, Acerola

(*Malpighia punicifolia, M. emarginata*)
Also Known As: Barbados Cherry, West Indian Cherry

The botanical name *Malpighia* was given in honor of Marcello Malpighi, an Italian anatomist. *Punicifolia* means "having leaves of reddish purple." The English word *cherry* can be traced back to the Assyrian *karsu* and Greek *kerasos*. The term *acerola* was adopted by the six-teenth-century colonizers of Puerto Rico, who thought the fruit resembled the fruit of a well-known but not closely related tree, the acerolo.

General Information

Acerola cherries are native to the Lesser Antilles and South America. Although they resemble the common American cherry, they are not botanically related. The fruits are borne singly or in twos or threes and are oblate to round in shape but more or less obviously three-lobed. Each one-half- to one-inch bright red fruit contains orange-colored, very juicy but rather acidic pulp and three small seeds. In 1945 there was enormous interest in the acerola cherry because of its high ascorbic acid (vitamin C) content, and numerous groves were planted. It was soon realized that synthetic sources of ascorbic acid were much cheaper to produce, and the acerola cherry could not compete economically.

Culinary Uses

Unless fully ripe, the acerola cherry is very acidic, but when mature it has a pleasant flavor. The flesh is juicy and moderately acid, more like a raspberry than a cherry in flavor. When cooked, it tastes like a tart apple. In its native West Indies, the fruit is eaten fresh or made into pies and preserves. The seeds are inedible.

Cherry, Acerola / Nutritional Value Per 100 g Edible Portion		
	Raw Fruit	Raw Juice
Calories	32	21
Protein	0.40 g	0.40 g
Fat	0.30 g	0.30 g
Fiber	0.40 g	0.30 g
Calcium	12 mg	10 mg
Iron	0.20 mg	0.50 mg
Magnesium	18 mg	12 mg
Phosphorus	11 mg	9 mg
Potassium	146 mg	97 mg
Sodium	7 mg	3 mg
Beta Carotene (A)	767 IU	509 IU
Thiamine (B$_1$)	0.020 mg	0.020 mg
Riboflavin (B$_2$)	0.060 mg	0.060 mg
Niacin (B$_3$)	0.400 mg	0.400 mg
Pantothenic Acid (B$_5$)	0.309 mg	0.205 mg
Pyridoxine (B$_6$)	0.009 mg	0.004 mg
Ascorbic Acid (C)	1,677.60 mg	1,600.00 mg

Health Benefits
This cherry is higher than any other known food source in natural vitamin C (twenty to fifty times that of an orange) and is frequently combined with other high-ascorbic-acid foods, such as rose hips, in vitamin C pills and liquid drops.

Cherry, Common
(Prunus avium, P. cerasus)

In the cherry blossom's shade
There's no such thing as a stranger.

—Issa

Prunus derives from the ancient Greek name *proumne*, their name for the plum tree family, of which the cherry is a member. *Avium* means "of or for the birds," because of the birds' delight in this fruit; the term *cerasus* is from a region in Pontus (Northeast Asia Minor). The English word *cherry* can be traced back to the Assyrian *karsu* and the Greek *kerasos*.

General Information
The cherry tree is native to the temperate climates of eastern Europe and western Asia, where it has been cultivated since at least 600 B.C. Although cherries were being grown in Italy already by this time, the Roman general and gourmet Lucullus probably introduced a more popular variety around 69 B.C. and thus his name has become synonymous with the arrival of the fruit into Italy from Cerasus. The Egyptians, Greeks, and Romans all cherished and cultivated this tree, both for its beautiful blossoms and for its fruit. In America cherries were present early enough to have developed distinct species by the time the first colonists arrived; the colonists, however, brought the European variety with them. The European cherry was one of the plants that crossed the ocean to America soon after Columbus's discovery, increasing the already large number of Euro-Asiatic plants that arrived here during that period. The fruits, soft and small with thin skins surrounding juicy flesh and a large seed (pit), are borne on long, thin stems.

Buying Tips
Select firm cherries that are bright, glossy, and plump, with fresh green stems, as dry brittle stems are a sign of over-ripeness and age. Avoid those that are soft, leaking, or too dark in color. When buying dark cherries, look them over very carefully as the color can hide signs of decay or mold. Of all fresh fruits, commercial cherries and grapes often contain the most toxic chemical residues; favor organic cherries whenever possible, and wash the commercial ones well. Cherries should be refrigerated immediately, stored in a plastic bag, and used within a couple of days.

Culinary Uses
Cherries when tree-ripened are sweet, lush, juicy, and incomparably superb. There are two basic varieties of cherries: sweet and sour. Sweet cherries (both red and yellow) should be plump and hard rather than soft to the touch, with the deepest-colored ones being the sweetest. Highly perishable, they must be stored in the refrigerator until eaten (which usually does not take very long!). Sweet cherries can be eaten fresh or cooked. They also freeze and can well. As for pitting fresh cherries, find the method that suits you and watch out for the juice, which stains. Europeans

Cherry, Common / Nutritional Value Per 100 g Edible Portion	Raw Sweet	Raw Sour	Maraschino w/ Liquid
Calories	72	50	116
Protein	1.20 g	1.00 g	0.20 g
Fat	0.96 g	0.30 g	0.20 g
Fiber	0.40 g	0.20 g	0.30 g
Calcium	15 mg	16 mg	n/a
Iron	0.39 mg	0.32 mg	n/a
Magnesium	11 mg	9 mg	n/a
Phosphorus	19 mg	15 mg	n/a
Potassium	224 mg	173 mg	n/a
Sodium	0 mg	3 mg	n/a
Zinc	0.060 mg	0.100 mg	n/a
Copper	0.095 mg	0.104 mg	n/a
Manganese	0.092 mg	0.112 mg	n/a
Beta Carotene (A)	214 IU	1,283 IU	n/a
Thiamine (B$_1$)	0.050 mg	0.030 mg	n/a
Riboflavin (B$_2$)	0.060 mg	0.040 mg	n/a
Niacin (B$_3$)	0.400 mg	0.400 mg	n/a
Pantothenic Acid (B$_5$)	0.127 mg	0.143 mg	n/a
Pyridoxine (B$_6$)	0.036 mg	0.044 mg	n/a
Folic Acid (B$_9$)	4.2 mcg	7.5 mcg	n/a
Ascorbic Acid (C)	7 mg	10 mg	n/a
Tocopherol (E)	n/a	0.130 mg	n/a

LORE AND LEGEND

There is a Japanese story about a warrior who had for many of his youthful years played at Iyo beneath the branches of a cherry tree. Upon attaining a great age, and outliving all his family and friends, the only object that linked him to his past was his beloved cherry tree. One summer the tree died; this the old warrior took for a sign and was not consoled when a young sapling was planted nearby. During that winter, he spoke to the dead tree and pleaded with it to bear blossoms just once more. If it did, he promised, he would give up his life. Having given his promise, he spread a white sheet upon the ground and committed hara-kiri. As his blood soaked into the roots of the tree and his spirit into its sap, the dead tree burst into bloom; every year on his death day, though the ground is hard and all other trees lie dormant for the winter, this tree at Iyo blossoms.

often leave the pits in pastries as part of the sport (and to add more flavor), a practice Americans are unaccustomed to and generally dislike. Dried sweet cherries are becoming widely available but are still comparatively expensive. Sour cherries can be made into excellent jams and jellies, canned, frozen, dried, or used to make wine and liqueurs, which brings out their rich flavor. Black cherry juice is wonderful for flavoring teas as a sugar substitute.

Health Benefits

pH 3.32–4.52. Detoxifying, laxative, stimulant. Cherries are a good "spring cleaner" to stimulate and cleanse the digestive system, the darker ones being all the more valuable to the system as they contain a greater quantity of magnesium, iron, and silicon. They are a well-known remedy for gout, arthritis, and rheumatism; part of their action in rheumatic disorders occurs from their ability to eliminate excess body acids. Their potent antiphlogistic and antiputrid properties make them an excellent adjunct in combating the harmful effects of animal protein, and their high iron content makes them beneficial for the liver, blood, and gallbladder. One teaspoonful of concentrated cherry juice in a glass of water taken several times a day brings miraculous results in stopping constant urination and can also help relieve painful urinary infections. Cherries are a potent antibacterial agent against tooth decay. In fact, studies have shown that black cherry juice blocked 89 percent of the enzyme activity that leads to plaque formation and ultimately tooth decay.

VARIETIES

Sweet cherries are generally dark and heart-shaped, with a sweet, rich flavor. The more popular varieties are **Bing**, **Lambert**, **Chapman**, **Tartarian**, and **Royal Ann** (Napoleon). The heaviest demand is for the Bing (named after Ah Bing, a Chinese gardener who lived in the United States): it is an extra-large, deep maroon to black fruit that is firm, highly flavored, and stands up well for shipping. The Royal Ann is the leading light-colored cherry, being light amber to yellow with a red blush and having a delightful fresh flavor. The majority of each season's Royal Ann crop are dyed and bottled as maraschino cherries. The original maraschino was fermented in a liqueur made from the juice and crushed pits of marasca, a wild sour Italian cherry. Today's maraschino cherry that tops a banana split is tough, sugary (75 percent sugar), and beggarly.

Sour or **pie cherries** are smaller and lighter-colored than sweet cherries. Since only a few types are actually sweet enough to eat from the tree, most sour cherries are marketed frozen or canned for sauce and pie filling. If and when you find them fresh in the market, they will be as soft and juicy as dead-ripe plums. It is impossible to find them unbruised, so don't bother to try. Almost every familiar dessert that calls for cherries would do better with sour ones; many of these recipes were invented for the sour cherry. Their soft skins and pulp become creamy tender when subjected to heat, and the flavor blooms, delightfully fresh and acid. The only change in the recipe might be the need for additional sugar. Less common types of sour cherries are **chokecherries**, small, red, very tart cherries often eaten by birds before any fruit can be harvested for human consumption; **sand** cherries, small, dark red fruits growing wild in the Rocky Mountains; **ground** cherries, related to tomatoes, that grow on short, sprawling plants; and the **black** cherry, a wild native American tree that yields small, edible cherries that can be used in pies.

Cherry, Cornelian
(Cornus mas)

Cornus is derived from the Latin word for "horn," alluding to the hardness of the wood; *mas* means "masculine" or "bold," referring to young trees, which produce only male flowers (they produce both male and female flowers plus fruit as they mature). The English name *cornelian* refers to the similarity of the fruit's coloring to that of the cornelian (or carnelian) quartz, which has a waxy luster and a deep reddish color.

General Information
The cornelian cherry is native to regions of eastern Europe and western Asia. Botanically, the tree is a species of dogwood, unrelated to the common cherry. It was well known to the ancient Greeks and Romans, and references to the plant abound in their literature. The plant was grown in monastery gardens of Europe through the Middle Ages and introduced to Britain in about the sixteenth century. By the eighteenth century the plant was common in English gardens, where it was grown for its fruits, which were sometimes called cornel plums; the fruit was even familiar enough to be found in European markets up to the end of the nineteenth century. Over most of Europe and North America today, the cornelian cherry is admired solely as an ornamental plant, but the bright fruits do not go completely unnoticed. Generally oval in shape and sometimes as large as a small plum, they are fire-engine red, with a single, elongated stone and a flavor, akin to a tart cherry, that develops sweetness and aroma with full ripeness.

Culinary Uses
This cherry has a tart flavor, and some varieties can be slightly bitter. Western Europeans rarely ate this fruit out of hand (it was more bitter than current varieties) but rather made it into a thickened, sweet syrup and highly esteemed tarts. The juice also added a bright flavor to cider and perry (pear cider). Unripe fruits were pickled as a substitute for olives. In the Ukraine cornelian cherries are a frequent ingredient in bottled soft drinks, conserves, wines, and liqueurs.

Health Benefits
In folk medicine the fruit is used to combat gout, anemia, skin diseases, painful joints, and disrupted metabolism. Fruit, leaves, or bark have been employed for gastrointestinal

---

LORE AND LEGEND

The famous and unsolvable Gordian knot was believed to have been formed from a thong of the cornelian cherry's leathery bark. (Alexander the Great, acquainted with the problem, drew his sword and severed the knot, then went on to fulfill the prophecy that whoever could unfasten it would conquer the world.) In an old Turkish legend, it seems that when the Devil first saw the cornelian cherry tree (called *kizilcik* in Turkish) covered with blossoms when no other fruit showed even a bud, he smiled to himself and said: "Aha! This tree will produce fruit first of all. I must be first there to secure it." So he made preparations, gathered up his basket, and took up his position under the tree. He waited and waited patiently, yet all the other fruit trees came into bloom and formed fruit, but still the *kizilcik* was not ready and ripe for eating. To his great surprise and chagrin he discovered that this was one of the very last fruits to ripen at the end of summer. Ever since then the Turks have called the tree *Seytan alditan agaci—*"the tree that deceived Satan."

---

disorders and tuberculosis. Russian scientists have reported that the fruit contains components that leach radioactivity from the body. Sugar content ranges from 4 to 12 percent, and the acidity ranges from 1 to 4 percent. The vitamin C concentration commonly averages twice that of oranges.

Cherry, Jamaican
(Muntingia calabura)
Also Known As: Jam Tree, Strawberry Tree, Panama Cherry, Calabura

The Jamaican cherry tree is named for its small, red, sweet fruits.

General Information
Indigenous to southern Mexico, Central America, tropical South America, the Greater Antilles, St. Vincent, and

Cherry, Jamaican / Nutritional Value Per 100 g Edible Portion			
	Raw		Raw
Protein	0.324 g	Beta Carotene (A)	0.019 mg
Fat	1.56 g	Thiamine (B₁)	0.065 mg
Fiber	4.6 g	Riboflavin (B₂)	0.037 mg
Calcium	124.6 mg	Niacin (B₃)	0.554 mg
Iron	1.18 mg	Ascorbic Acid (C)	80.5 mg
Phosphorus	84.0 mg		

Trinidad, the Jamaican cherry tree is an abundant producer. The trees have a reputation for thriving with no care in poor soils; they grow wild on denuded mountainsides and on cliffs. They are presently being evaluated for reforestation in the Philippines where other trees have failed to grow and also for wildlife sanctuaries since birds and bats are partial to the fruits. The fruits are round, with red or sometimes yellow smooth, thin, tender skins and light brown, soft, juicy pulp.

Culinary Uses

The flesh has a very sweet, musky, somewhat figlike flavor and is filled with exceedingly minute yellowish seeds, too fine to be noticed in eating. Usually eaten out of hand, the fruit is also often cooked into tarts or made into jam.

Health Benefits

The flowers are said to possess antiseptic properties. An infusion of the flowers is valued as an antispasmodic; it is taken to relieve headaches and the first symptoms of a cold.

Cherry, Nanking
(Prunus tomentosa)
Also Known As: Downy Cherry, Mongolian Cherry, Manchu Cherry

Prunus derives from the ancient Greek name *proumne*, their name for the plum tree family, of which the cherry is a member. *Tomentosa* means "thickly matted with hairs." The alternate name *downy cherry* derives from the downy hair that covers the plant in summer—the leaves, the new shoots, and even the fruits.

General Information

The Nanking cherry is native to central Asia but has become naturalized from Japan and Korea west across China and Russia to Turkistan and the Himalayas. Generally grown in cold, semi-arid regions, the plant is the most common garden fruit plant in the Russian Far East. A beautifully colored spreading shrub or small tree, it is usually wider than its nine- to fifteen-foot height. Late spring brings the fruits, borne in profusion and ornamental in their own right. The plant was introduced into North America in 1882 and met with great enthusiasm. By the late twentieth century, however, enthusiasm had died down, and today the plant is relatively anonymous. The cherries ripen in early summer. Ripe fruits are generally brilliant red, although there are also pink and white varieties, and are about a half inch in diameter.

Culinary Uses

These cherries have a sprightly, true cherry flavor (including the single pit) and a meaty texture. Because of their softness, they are rarely seen in commercial quantities. The best way to enjoy these gems is to stroll out into the garden and pop the ripe fruits straight into your mouth. Or perhaps pick a few to use for a dessert. These cherries make a refreshing summer drink and, for those who wish to preserve them, a beautiful, clear jelly.

Cherry, Surinam
(Eugenia uniflora)
Also Known As: Brazilian Cherry, Cayenne Cherry, Pitanga

The *Eugenia* genus was named in honor of Prince Eugene of Savoy. *Uniflora* means "one-flowered." The English name *Surinam cherry* results from the fact that the fruit is native to Surinam and is the size of a cherry.

General Information

The Surinam cherry is native to the region from Surinam and French Guiana to southern Brazil and Uruguay. It was

Cherry, Surinam / Nutritional Value Per 100 g Edible Portion			
	Raw		Raw
Calories	43-51	Phosphorus	11 mg
Protein	0.84-1.01 g	Beta Carotene (A)	1,200-2,000 IU
Fat	0.40-0.88 g	Thiamine (B₁)	0.030 mg
Fiber	0.34-0.60 g	Riboflavin (B₂)	0.040 mg
Calcium	9 mg	Niacin (B₃)	0.030 mg
Iron	0.2 mg	Ascorbic Acid (C)	20-30 mg

first described botanically from a plant growing in a garden in Pisa, Italy; it was believed to have been introduced from Goa, India. Portuguese voyagers are said to have carried the seed from Brazil to India, as they did the cashew. It was long ago planted on the Mediterranean coast of Africa and the European Riviera. The first Surinam cherry was introduced into coastal Israel in 1922 and aroused considerable interest because it produced fruit in May, when other fruits are scarce. In Florida the tree is one of the most common hedge plants throughout the central and southern parts of the state and the Florida Keys, where the fruits are eaten mostly by children. There are two distinct types: one bears the common bright red fruit, while the other bears the rarer dark crimson to nearly black fruit, which tends to be sweeter and less resinous. Each fruit is from ¾ to 1½ inches wide, oblate with seven or eight ribs. When mature, the fruits are bright red to deep scarlet or dark, purplish maroon.

Culinary Uses

Surinam cherries have thin skins and orange-red flesh that is melting and very juicy, acid to sweet, with a touch of resin and slight bitterness. There may be one fairly large, round seed or perhaps two or three smaller seeds, which are extremely resinous and inedible. Children enjoy the ripe fruit out of hand. For table use, they are best slit vertically along one side, spread open to release the seeds, and kept chilled for two or three hours to dispel most of their resinous character. If seeded and sprinkled with sugar before being refrigerated, they will become very mild and sweet, exuding a quantity of juice. These then can be served instead of strawberries on shortcake and topped with whipped cream. Surinam cherries are an excellent addition to fruit cups, salads, and custard puddings; they also add a delicious flavor to ice cream and sauces.

Chupa-Chupa
(Quararibea cordata)

Cordata means "cordate," or "heart-shaped." *Chupa-chupa* is the colloquial name in Colombia and Peru, where it is descriptive of the manner in which the flesh is chewed from the large seeds.

General Information

The chupa-chupa tree grows wild in lowland rainforests of Peru, Ecuador, and adjacent areas of Brazil, especially

Chupa-Chupa / Nutritional Value Per 100 g Edible Portion			
	Raw		Raw
Protein	0.129 g	Beta Carotene (A)	1.056 mg
Fat	0.10 g	Thiamine (B₁)	0.031 mg
Fiber	0.5 g	Riboflavin (B₂)	0.023 mg
Calcium	18.4 mg	Niacin (B₃)	0.330 mg
Iron	0.44 mg	Ascorbic Acid (C)	9.7 mg
Phosphorus	28.5 mg		

around the mouth of the Javari River. The fruit is round, ovoid, or elliptic, with a prominent, rounded knob at the apex, and is capped with a leathery calyx at the base. About five inches long and weighing up to twenty-eight ounces, the fruit has a rind that is thick, leathery, greenish brown, and downy.

Culinary Uses

The flesh is orange-yellow, soft, juicy, sweet, and of agreeable flavor, tasting something like a cross between an apricot and mango. There are usually two to five seeds, and long fibers extend throughout the flesh, making it difficult to eat. It is most commonly eaten out of hand; only those with the least fibrous flesh may be suitably utilized for juice or other processing.

Citron
(Citrus medica)

Moses had specified the cedar cone, *kadar* (*kedron* in Greek), to be used during the Feast of Tabernacles. When it fell into disfavor, the cedar cone was replaced by the citron, the Palestine Greeks calling the latter *kedromelon* (cedar apple). *Kedros* was Latinized as *cedrus*, and this evolved into *citrus* and subsequently into *citron*. The Latin term *medica* means "coming from Media" (a name for Persia); it also means "healing."

General Information

The citron's place of origin is unknown, but seeds have been found in Mesopotamian excavations dating back to 4000 B.C. The fruit was long used in India as a medicine and fragrance, and the armies of Alexander the Great, upon their return from India to Macedonia in 325 B.C., brought stories and seeds of the citron back to Europe. Soon afterward the Greek writer Theophrastus com-

Citron / Nutritional Value Per 100 g Edible Portion		
	Raw	Candied
Calories	n/a	314
Protein	0.081 g	0.200 g
Fat	0.04 g	0.30 g
Fiber	1.1 g	1.4 g
Calcium	36.5 mg	83.0 mg
Iron	0.55 mg	0.80 mg
Phosphorus	16.0 mg	24.0 mg
Potassium	n/a	120 mg
Sodium	n/a	290 mg
Beta Carotene (A)	0.009 mg	n/a
Thiamine (B$_1$)	0.052 mg	n/a
Riboflavin (B$_2$)	0.029 mg	n/a
Niacin (B$_3$)	0.125 mg	n/a
Ascorbic Acid (C)	368 mg	n/a

mented that "the Median or Persian apple is not eaten, but is very fragrant," adding that it would protect clothes against moths. The Jews cultivated the citron intensely, with only the best fruits used during the Feast of Tabernacles. A Jewish coin struck in 136 B.C. bore a representation of the citron on one side. In A.D. 300, a Chinese writer documented the gift of "40 Chinese bushels of citrons from Ta-ch'in" in A.D. 284, *Ta-ch'in* being understood to mean the Roman Empire, where the citron was a staple commercial food item.

Culinary Uses

The citron looks like a huge, rough lemon, with most of its bulk being its thick dense skin. The flesh inside is dryish, either sour or sweet, with a weak lemon flavor. The peel, which has a unique resinous fragrance, is the most useful part. It is cut into small pieces, preserved in brine or seawater, then cooked, and finally candied. It may be crystallized to be eaten for its own sake, like other candied fruits, or the firm pulp may be used to make jellies or preserves. Candied fruit is used in fruitcakes and plum pudding. The peel may also be pressed to obtain an oil that is quite fragrant and is used in the manufacture of medicines, liqueurs, and perfumes.

Health Benefits

In ancient times and during the Middle Ages, the citron was employed as a remedy for seasickness, pulmonary troubles, intestinal ailments, and other disorders. Citron

LORE AND LEGEND

In modern Orthodox Jewish ritual, a special type of citron (in Hebrew, *etrog*) is used during the Feast of Tabernacles as a symbol of God's bounty. It is ungrafted, inedible, and must have its calyx intact. The original command for the Jewish practice is given in the Bible in the book of Leviticus, composed at a time when the Jews could not yet have known the citron. Scholars believe that the cedar cone was meant, and that the Jews substituted the citron later because they were unhappy about the use of the cedar cone in rituals of other religions. The citron came to represent wealth in India, perhaps because of its splendid size. Thus the god of wealth, Kuvera, is always represented as holding a citron in one hand and a mongoose spewing jewels in the other. After the plant reached China in the fourth century A.D., a freak form (variant *sarcodactyla*) developed in which the fruit separated into five lobes like the fingers of a hand. This type, called Buddha's hand, was considered a symbol of happiness. For this reason and because of its especially fine scent, it was placed on household altars.

juice with wine was considered an effective purgative to rid the system of poison. The candied peel is sold in China as a stomachic, stimulant, expectorant, and tonic.

Cocona
(Solanum sessiliflorum)

> *Solanum* comes from the Latin *solamen*, meaning "solace" or "quieting." *Sessiliflorum* means "with stalkless flowers."

General Information

The spineless cocona is apparently unknown in the wild, having been observed by botanists only in cultivation from Peru and Colombia to Venezuela and Brazil. In 1760 a Spanish surveyor, Apolinar Diez de la Fuente, found the

Cocona / Nutritional Value Per 100 g Edible Portion

	Raw		Raw
Protein	0.6 g	Phosphorus	14 mg
Fiber	0.4 g	Beta Carotene (A)	140 mcg
Calcium	12 mg	Thiamine (B₁)	25 mcg
Iron	0.6 mg	Niacin (B₃)	500 mcg

cocona with maize and beans in an Indian garden between Guaharibos Falls and the juncture of the Casiquiare and Orinoco rivers. Borne singly or in compact clusters, the fruit may be round, oblong, or conical. The thin, tough skin is coated with a slightly prickly, peachlike fuzz until the fruit is fully ripe, at which point in becomes smooth, golden- to orange-yellow, red, or deep purple. Within is a quarter-inch to three-quarter-inch layer of cream-colored firm flesh enclosing the yellow, jellylike central pulp.

Culinary Uses

The cut-open fruit has a faint tomato-like aroma. The flesh has a mild flavor also faintly suggestive of tomato, while the pulp has a pleasant, limelike acidity. Abundant throughout the central pulp are thin cream-colored seeds, which are edible. The ripe fruit is peeled and eaten out of hand, used in salads, or cooked with fish and meat stews. Sweetened, it is used to make sauce and pie filling. It is often processed as a nectar or juice, which when sweetened with sugar is a popular cold beverage.

Cranberry
(Vaccinium oxycoccos, V. macrocarpon)

> Whatever the regional differences, one thing is constant all over the nation—the cranberry. The red berry is jellied and cut in quivering slices, stewed and served with whole berries, squeezed and poured into glasses as a cocktail; nationwide it is spiked with spirits, baked in bread, chopped into a relish, embalmed in gelatin or cubed in a salad.
>
> —HORACE SUTTON

Vaccinium is the ancient Latin name for plants of the blueberry family, derived from *vacca*, meaning "cow," given because cows like the plant. *Oxycoccos* refers to its sharp leaves; *macrocarpon* means that it bears large fruits or seed pods. The English name *cranberry* is a shortened form of the earlier *craneberry*, given because the plant's blossoms grow downward and look like the head and neck of a crane; cranes also like to eat cranberries, which often grow in sandy peat bogs, one of their favorite habitats.

General Information

The cranberry is a small evergreen shrub related to the blueberry. The plants, with their slender creeping vines, are native to open bogs and swampy marshes from Alaska to Tennessee, preferring poor acidic soil. The oblong or nearly round berries are green at first but turn red in September or October. When well protected by snow, they often will remain on the vine all winter. The American Indians, who paid homage to the cranberry in their legends, taught the settlers to make pemmican, a dried buffalo, venison, or bear meat preserve pounded with animal fat and berries, that they took on hunting trips as a high-energy convenience food. The benzoic acid

Cranberry / Nutritional Value Per 100 g Edible Portion

	Raw	Canned Sweetened Sauce	Bottled Sweetened Juice
Calories	49	146	65
Protein	0.39 g	0.10 g	0.10 g
Fat	0.20 g	0.20 g	0.10 g
Fiber	1.20 g	0.20 g	trace
Calcium	7 mg	6 mg	5 mg
Iron	0.20 mg	0.20 mg	0.30 mg
Magnesium	5 mg	n/a	3 mg
Phosphorus	9 mg	4 mg	3 mg
Potassium	71 mg	30 mg	10 mg
Sodium	1 mg	1 mg	1 mg
Zinc	0.130 mg	n/a	0.020 mg
Copper	0.058 mg	n/a	0.013 mg
Manganese	0.157 mg	n/a	0.157 mg
Beta Carotene (A)	46 IU	20 IU	4 IU
Thiamine (B₁)	0.030 mg	0.010 mg	0.010 mg
Riboflavin (B₂)	0.020 mg	0.010 mg	0.010 mg
Niacin (B₃)	0.100 mg	trace	0.039 mg
Pantothenic Acid (B₅)	0.219 mg	n/a	0.067 mg
Pyridoxine (B₆)	0.065 mg	n/a	n/a
Folic Acid (B₉)	1.7 mcg	n/a	0.4 mcg
Ascorbic Acid (C)	13.5 mg	2.0 mg	2.0-40.0 mg

LORE AND LEGEND

It is believed that the Pilgrims learned how to prepare cranberries from the Indians. The berries kept so long without decay and were prized so highly by the colonists that ten barrels of them were shipped across the ocean as a gift to King Charles II, a long journey in slow-moving sailing vessels. The Pilgrims supposedly dined on cranberry dishes at the first Thanksgiving celebration in 1621, but cranberry sauce did not become a national tradition until after the Civil War, when General Ulysses S. Grant considered cranberry sauce such an essential part of Thanksgiving that he ordered it served to Union troops during the siege of Petersburg in 1864.

in the berry acted as a preservative that kept the mixture from turning rancid.

Buying Tips

Look for firm, bright-colored, plump cranberries. Avoid those that are soft, crushed, shriveled, or soft and sticky. In early days berries were selected by being rolled down a short flight of stairs. Good ones bounced like little rubber balls; soft ones stayed on the steps. Today's grading machines work on the same principle, with each berry being given seven chances to bounce over four-inch-high barriers as it passes along a conveyor belt. If the fruit does not pass the high-jump test, it is discarded.

Culinary Uses

Because of their very tart taste, few people eat cranberries in their fresh, raw state. Cranberries are excellent used in cranberry nut bread and pair well with nuts, wild rice, and whole grains. The fruit is compatible with other fall fruits such as apples and pears, and its red color can magically enhance an otherwise mundane dish. Cranberries are generally made into sauces and jellies with a great deal of sugar syrup, rendering them highly acidic and distinctly harmful to the body; these sauces and jellies are best used either sparingly or avoided altogether. Dried cranberries can be used like raisins. Cranberry juice is always sweetened and diluted with water to make it palatable.

Health Benefits

pH 2.30–2.52. Cranberries are excellent curative and preventive therapy for the entire breathing apparatus as they contain one of nature's most potent vasodilators, which opens up congested bronchial tubes. They also contain large amounts of benzoic acid, a natural preservative, which accounts for the Native American practice of adding the dried fruits to pemmican (a dried, preserved meat product). Long touted for their powers against bacterial infections and viruses of the bladder, kidneys, and urinary tract, cranberries are very high in tannic and oxalic acids, which create a distinctly acidic reaction within the body. A recent study in the *New England Journal of Medicine* confirms that there are tannins in the juice called proanthocyanidins, which wrap up bacteria in a kind of Teflon coating and prevent the germs from sticking to the walls of the urinary tract. If the bacteria can't attach themselves to anything, they're flushed away and can't cause infection. There's also reason to believe that cranberries can help treat diaper rash. When urine and feces mix in the diaper, the result is a high pH (alkalinity) level that irritates skin and leads to diaper rash. Giving older infants two to three ounces of cranberry juice leaves an acid residue in the diapers, helps lower pH, and reduces irritation.

Currant

(Ribes rubrum, R. nigrum, R. americanum, R. odoratum)

Ribes is believed to be derived from *ribas*, the Arabic name for *Rheum ribes*; it is thought by some to be the latinized form of *riebs*, which is an old German word for the fruit. The term *rubrum* signifies the red berries, while *nigrum* specifies the black variety; *americanum* means "native to America," while *odoratum* means "fragrantly scented." The English word *currant* is said to be derived from the resemblance of the fruit to the Corinth grapes or raisins.

General Information

Currants are a type of berry that should not be confused with the dried Zante currant, a small raisin made from dried Corinth grapes. Popular in northern European countries such as Great Britain, Germany, Scandinavia, and Russia, the currant has never caught on in southerly regions. The European black currant (*R. nigrum*) is a cold-climate plant native to northern Europe and north and central Asia. It is closer to the gooseberry than to the red currant, with fruit that is neither as sweet nor as flavorful as the red currant. Although red, white, yellow, and black currants grow wild throughout the northern temperate regions of the world, the black currant has the greatest commercial availability. It grows on shrubs and emits a peculiar, heavy aroma. Fruits are borne in strings, or chains, each fruit averaging three-eighths of an inch in diameter. Red currants (*R. rubrum*) are native to northeastern Europe as far as the Arctic Sea, and the steppes of northern Asia as far as Siberia and eastern Manchuria. The plant produces small, red, semi-transparent berries with a pleasantly sour taste. The white currant is botanically a red currant that has lost its pigmentation and some of its acidity. The American black currant (*R. americanum*) is native from New Mexico to Virginia, and north into Canada. Fruits, leaves, and shoots have the same pungent aroma as the European currant. The clove currant (*R. odoratum*) is native to the American Midwest as far north as Minnesota and as far south as Texas. Every spring, when the plant flowers, the profusion of red-tinged yellow trumpets puts on quite a show, and the whole plant has a heavy fragrance of clove and vanilla. The fruits are borne singly or in small clusters, and range in size from one-quarter to three-quarters of an inch in diameter. Usually the fruits are smooth, shiny, and blue-black, though some plants bear yellow or orange fruits.

Buying Tips

Currants should be quite firm and translucent, with a deep rich color for the most flavor and a good acid balance. No matter their color, they are hard to find in domestic markets. This smooth, small berry is thin-skinned and has a matchless flavor—not exceptionally sweet, juicy, or tart but decidedly enjoyable. The white currant is the sweetest; the black is the most tart and is favored for preserves. Look for shiny skins and plump berries. Refrigerate and use within three days.

Culinary Uses

Red currants, when sufficiently dosed with sugar, can be eaten fresh, but their principal use has been in jellies, preserves, sauces, Scandinavian fruit soups, and desserts. Try substituting them in recipes for raspberries or cranberries and adjusting the sweetener as necessary. White currants show up well when they are combined with more colorful fruits and are usually less acidic than the red. The black currant lacks the brilliant flavor of the red currant, especially when the fruit is raw. A few of them make a welcome addition to mixed-fruit salads. The flavor of clove currants is intense, somewhat resinous, but fruity. In Finland peasants make a currant-strawberry drink to carry them through the long dark winter. In England the berry is essential to summer pudding, usually made with raspberries, which also ripen in midsummer.

Health Benefits

Fresh currant berries or their juice promote the appetite and can also be taken for an upset stomach. Long recommended for colds and as a laxative, when the berries are eaten whole the indigestible seeds provide bulk to help regulate activity of the bowels. Currant juice has a cleansing, antiseptic effect on the system, helping to purify the blood

Currant / Nutritional Value Per 100 g Edible Portion		
	Raw Black	Raw Red/White
Calories	63	56
Protein	1.40 g	1.40 g
Fat	0.41 g	0.20 g
Fiber	2.40 g	3.40 g
Calcium	55 mg	33 mg
Iron	1.54 mg	1.00 mg
Magnesium	24 mg	13 mg
Phosphorus	59 mg	44 mg
Potassium	322 mg	275 mg
Sodium	2 mg	1 mg
Zinc	0.270 mg	0.230 mg
Copper	0.086 mg	0.107 mg
Manganese	0.256 mg	0.186 mg
Beta Carotene (A)	230 IU	120 IU
Thiamine (B$_1$)	0.050 mg	0.040 mg
Riboflavin (B$_2$)	0.050 mg	0.050 mg
Niacin (B$_3$)	0.300 mg	0.100 mg
Pantothenic Acid (B$_5$)	0.398 mg	0.064 mg
Pyridoxine (B$_6$)	0.066 mg	0.070 mg
Ascorbic Acid (C)	181 mg	41 mg
Tocopherol (E)	1.00 mg	0.10 mg

and counteract anemia, and is beneficial for kidney and nervous system problems. When cooked with sugar, the berries tend to lose much of their beneficial medicinal value and become acid-forming. Oil from black currant seeds complements omega-3 fatty acids and is a quality source of gamma-linoleic acid (GLA), a substance that contributes to prostaglandin synthesis and has a profound positive effect on health, especially in ameliorating premenstrual symptoms.

Custard Apple
(Annona reticulata)
Also Known As: Bullock's Heart

Annona means "year's harvest" and is suggested by the Haitian name *anon*, which is applied to one of the species. *Reticulata* means "reticulated" or "netted." The English name *custard apple* results from the fruit's custardlike texture and apple shape. The coloration of the fruit (reddish or brownish on the sunny side, dull yellow on the other) and its shape show enough resemblance to the heart of a bullock or other large mammal to justify the West Indian name *bullock's heart*.

General Information
This tree is believed native to the West Indies and thrives in coastal and lowland regions. Generally rated as the mediocre variety or "ugly duckling" of the genus, the tree is not especially attractive and has ill-smelling leaves and flowers that never fully open. The heart-shaped or lopsided fruit varies from three to six inches in diameter and may weigh over two pounds. The skin, which when ripe is yellow or brownish with a blush, may be either faintly or distinctly netted.

Custard Apple / Nutritional Value Per 100 g Edible Portion			
	Raw		Raw
Calories	80–101	Sodium	4 mg
Protein	1.17–2.47 g	Beta Carotene (A)	0.007–0.018 mg
Fat	0.5–0.6 g	Thiamine (B$_1$)	0.075–0.119 mg
Fiber	0.9–6.6 g	Riboflavin (B$_2$)	0.086–0.175 mg
Calcium	17.6–27.0 mg	Niacin (B$_3$)	0.528–1.190 mg
Iron	0.42–1.14 mg	Pantothenic Acid (B$_5$)	0.135 mg
Magnesium	18 mg	Pyridoxine (B$_6$)	0.221 mg
Phosphorus	14.7–32.1 mg	Ascorbic Acid (C)	15.0–44.4 mg
Potassium	382 mg		

Culinary Uses
The flesh of the custard apple is yellowish white and has the typical custardlike granular texture of the *Annona* genus, along with its many inedible seeds and a fibrous, central, pointed core that extends more than halfway through the fruit. Although the flavor is sweet and agreeable, it lacks the distinct character of the cherimoya, sugar apple, or atemoya. Most often it is used as a dessert fruit, or puréed, strained, and added to confections such as ice cream and milk shakes. The yellow-skinned varieties usually are superior to the brownish ones, with thicker and juicier flesh.

Health Benefits
The unripe fruit is rich in tannin; dried and pulverized, it is employed against diarrhea and dysentery. The seeds, leaves, and young fruits are insecticidal. The leaves have been employed in tanning and yield a blue or black dye. Crushed leaves or a paste of the flesh may be poulticed on boils, abscesses, and ulcers. The seeds are so hard that they may be swallowed whole with no ill effects, but the kernels if chewed are very toxic.

Date
(Phoenix dactylifera)

Theophrastus gave the name *Phoenix* to the date palm, perhaps thinking of Phoenicia, where it was first encountered by the Greeks, or else of the fabled phoenix of Egypt; for like the mythological phoenix that rises from the ashes, the date tree has its feet in water and its head in the fires of heaven (oases or irrigation providing the former, desert sun the latter). The term *dactylifera* means "finger bearing," in reference to the fruits, which hang fingerlike from the trees. The English word *date* derives (with a few convolutions) from the Greek *dactylos*, meaning "finger."

General Information
Date palms are believed to have originated in the Persian Gulf region and in ancient times were especially abundant between the Nile and Euphrates rivers. Nomads carried dates as sustenance on their travels and planted great quantities of pits at desert oases. In the Sahara Desert every oasis is a beautiful garden of date palms. As far back as 50,000 B.C. the date palm flourished on favorable lands, and developing humans must have always found it valuable; even now it is said to have a different use for every day of the

year, and many more besides. The stems and leaves are used for building huts, while the fibers of the leaves are used to manufacture baskets, ropes, hats, mats, and many other everyday objects. The wood of the tree is fairly combustible and in some areas is the only wood product available to make fires. The palm itself made other contributions to the diet, the crown being tapped for its sugary sap, which could be fermented to make palm toddy. During the useful life of the tree the tapping was done with moderation, but when it had passed its peak a good deal more was drawn off, and ultimately, the tree was drained completely. Extremely long-lived, the palm produces a new section of leaves each and every year, often growing to a hundred feet in height; after a century or so it is usually so tall that it falls over. Date palms start bearing in their fourth year and have their greatest production when they are about eighty years of age, producing on average a hundred pounds of fruit annually. The large bunches of fruit weigh over twenty pounds and contain as many as a thousand dates. So productive are these trees that dates are among the cheapest of staple foods (and often the only abundantly available food) for many African and Middle Eastern populations. During the eigh-

teenth century Franciscan and Jesuit missionaries introduced the date palm into California, where it now thrives. The California date industry began only in the twentieth century—in 1902 according to some authorities—but now California produces over 99 percent of all dates sold in the United States.

Buying Tips

Fresh, undried dates should be plump with shiny skins. Most varieties have smooth skins, but the large Medjools are usually wrinkled, sometimes with a thin white film of invert sugar on the surface that is quite normal. Excessive shriveling, a dry flaky appearance, or a fermented aroma indicates dates that are old or have been improperly stored. Soft, fresh dates should be refrigerated or frozen; they can be stored in an airtight container for up to one year in the refrigerator and for up to five years in the freezer. They will become drier in the refrigerator over time. Frozen dates have almost no loss in quality. Dried dates store indefinitely at room temperature.

Culinary Uses

Referred to as "candy that grows on trees," dates are sweet and chewy fruits that are delicious when eaten fresh. Most packaged dates, especially domestic ones, are dried and pasteurized to prevent molding, and corn syrup is often added to keep them from further drying out. Fresh dates keep extremely well under refrigeration for long periods of time, so there is no need to buy the poorer-quality, commercial dried fruits. Before using, slit them open and remove the stone. Dates also freeze well and so may be kept for an extended period. Dry or fresh dates can be eaten out of hand, seeded and stuffed, or added to many dishes such as fruit salads, cereals, puddings, and baked goods, often substituting for raisins or currants. Pitted dates, stuffed with either nuts or nut butters and rolled in coconut, are a delight to adult and child alike. Chopped dates on cereal make a wonderfully healthy sweetener, while crystallized dates (date sugar) can be used to replace other sweeteners in baked goods with excellent results. Date sugar, made solely from pitted, dehydrated, and pulverized dates, is technically considered not a sugar but a food, since the whole fruit is used. This sweetener contains about 65 percent fructose and sucrose. The taste is mildly date-flavored, with the same sweetening power as white sugar. Its only drawback for baking is that the granules do not dissolve when added to liquids.

Date / Nutritional Value Per 100 g Edible Portion		
	Fresh	Dried
Calories	142	274-293
Protein	0.9-2.6 g	1.7-3.9 g
Fat	0.6-1.5 g	0.1-1.2 g
Fiber	2.6-4.5 g	2.0-8.5 g
Calcium	34 mg	59-103 mg
Iron	6 mg	3.0-13.7 mg
Magnesium	n/a	35 mg
Phosphorus	350 mg	63-105 mg
Potassium	520 mg	648 mg
Sodium	n/a	3 mg
Zinc	n/a	0.290 mg
Copper	n/a	0.288 mg
Manganese	n/a	0.298 mg
Beta Carotene (A)	20-259 IU	50 IU
Thiamine (B$_1$)	0.070 mg	0.030-0.090 mg
Riboflavin (B$_2$)	0.080 mg	0.100-0.160 mg
Niacin (B$_3$)	4.4-6.9 mg	1.4-2.2 mg
Pantothenic Acid (B$_5$)	n/a	0.780 mg
Pyridoxine (B$_6$)	n/a	0.192 mg
Folic Acid (B$_9$)	n/a	2.6 mcg
Ascorbic Acid (C)	30 mg	0 mg

Health Benefits

pH 4.14–6.40. In early medicine, dates were one of the four fruits renowned for curing throat and chest ailments (the other three were the fig, the raisin, and the jujube). Because of their tannin content, dates have been used medicinally as an astringent for intestinal troubles. Dates are heat-producing because of their high natural sugar content and give energy to people who engage in physical exercise and hard work. This natural sugar is much better for a person than highly refined white sugar. The fiber or cellulose of the date is very soft and will not irritate a sensitive bowel or stomach but does have a slight constipating tendency.

VARIETIES

Dates are classified as soft, semi-dry, or dry/hard, depending upon the give of the ripe fruit. The soft or semi-dry varieties contain a considerable amount of moisture and are more perishable than dry dates unless dried by either natural or artificial means. Dry dates, also called hard or camel dates, are not dates that have been deliberately dehydrated but that simply contain relatively little moisture when ripe. Dry and fibrous even when fresh, they become extremely hard and sweet when further dried and will keep for years; these are the staple food dates of the Arab world, particularly for nomads.

Barhi dates are a very soft, very sweet fruit when fully ripe. Although they are traditionally eaten in the Middle East and Indian subcontinent at a stage when they are immature, starchy, rather astringent, and low in sugar, westerners prefer them riper and sweeter. They are nearly cylindrical, with thick and richly flavored light amber to dark brown flesh.

Blonde dates are a medium sweet, creamy, soft date. They are a close relative of the honey date but are lighter in color. Blonde dates are available only in a few locations.

Deglet Noor dates are native to Algeria, where the name means "fingers of light." This variety is the leading commercial variety in the United States, constituting 85 percent of all date production. The medium-to-large oblong fruits are a coral red that ripens to amber and cures to a deep rich brown. Very sweet and soft, they have a chewy caramel flavor, with the highest sugar content of any date. Many people prefer Deglet Noor dates because they are chewier than Medjools and not quite

LORE AND LEGEND

The Arabs believe that, when creating the world, Allah formed the date palm not from common clay but out of material left over from the making of Adam. One of the most ancient symbolic forms of the Tree of Life in the subtropical desert regions of the Near East, the date palm is almost worshiped by the local nomadic inhabitants, for whom the tree is a symbol of fertility, and because its fruit is the main food supply for both man and beast. Among the Egyptians it is the symbolic Tree of the Year, because it produces one new set of branches every year. The palm leaf was the sacred emblem of Judea after the Exodus from Egypt, but the Roman legions in 53 B.C. took over the leaf as the emblem of their triumph and victory over Judea, and as a symbol of their plunder and destruction of Jerusalem. The Christians in A.D. 29 believed the palm leaf was symbolic of the triumphant entry of Christ into Jerusalem, when his path was strewn with palm leaves in defiance of the Roman rulers. The leaves of the palm are still used today as religious symbols by Christians on Palm Sunday and by Jews on Passover.

as sweet. Bread dates are Deglet Noors that have been dried to a lower moisture content and are hard, dry, and chewy but not sticky.

Halawi dates are light amber in color and look much like smaller versions of Deglet Noors. This date of Iraqi origin and name (meaning "sweet") is drier and chewier than the Medjool, with a more distinctly sweet, brown sugar taste.

Khadrawi dates are early-ripening, dark-skinned, soft, sticky, chewy dates that can crystallize or become sugary, but this will not affect the eating quality. Important in Saudi Arabia and Iraq (where the name means "green"), the khadrawi is the cultivar most favored by Arabs.

Medjool dates are the most commonly available fresh date. Sweet, soft, and meaty, Medjools are known for their remarkable size, up to an ounce or more in weight, and are often four to five times larger than the Deglet Noor. They are the main Moroccan variety. Medjools were first grown in the California desert in the 1930s from eleven offshoots imported by the U. S. Department of Agriculture from Morocco. The original trees in Morocco were destroyed by Bayoud disease, and all Medjool dates grown in the world today are descended from those offshoots brought to the California desert.

Zahidi dates are the oldest known cultivar of dates. They are not quite as sweet as other dates and are generally smaller in size. Zahidis are cylindrical, light golden-brown, and semi-dry; they are harvested and sold in three stages: soft, medium hard, and hard. Very popular for culinary purposes, they keep well for months.

Duku and Langsat
(Lansium domesticum)

The genus name *Lansium* derives from the Malayan name *lansa* or *lanseh. Domesticum* means "domesticated."

General Information
Native to West Malaysia, these trees take about fifteen years to reach maturity, but the long wait is worthwhile since they then bear clusters of fruit twice a year. Langsats are typically the wild variety, while dukus are slightly more domesticated, although both are widely cultivated. In the Philippines the tree is being utilized in reforestation of hilly areas. Langsat trees produce about twenty fruits per cluster, each oval and just under 1½ inches long, with a thin, pale fawn skin. Dukus have only about ten fruits per cluster. They are round and larger than the langsat, about two inches in diameter, with thicker skins.

Culinary Uses
The flesh of both fruits is usually white (in some cultivated varieties of duku it is pink), juicy, and refreshing, with a taste ranging from sour to sweet. Each fruit is composed of five

Langsat / Nutritional Value Per 100 g Edible Portion			
	Raw		Raw
Protein	0.8 g	Beta Carotene (A)	13 IU
Fiber	2.3 g	Thiamine (B₁)	89 mcg
Calcium	20 mg	Riboflavin (B₂)	124 mcg
Phosphorus	30 mg	Ascorbic Acid (C)	1 mg

LORE AND LEGEND

According to Philippine folklore, dukus and langsats used to be so sour as to be quite inedible, and indeed were even toxic. But it happened one day that a beautiful woman with a child, traveling through the countryside, could find nothing else to eat but *lanzones* (their Philippine name). She accordingly picked one and gave it to the child. From then on the fruit acquired its present desirable characteristics, for the woman was none other than the Virgin Mary. However, the transformation that she wrought was not complete, since some *lanzones* still turn out to be very sour.

segments, some of which may contain bitter, inedible seeds. They can be eaten raw (once the inedible peel is removed) or preserved with sugar, and the seedless ones bottled in syrup.

Health Benefits
The dried peel is burned in Java, the aromatic smoke serving as a mosquito repellent and incense. An arrow poison has been made from the fruit peel and the tree bark, both of which possess a toxic property, lansium acid, which has been shown to arrest heartbeat in frogs.

Durian
(Durio zibethinus)

Durian and Brazil Nut. An odd pair? Yes, but they have this in common, that you have to be careful they don't drop on your head.

—ALAN DAVIDSON

Duri is the Malay word for "spike," and the tree takes both its botanical and its common name from the hard, spiky shell of the fruit. *Zibethinus* means "foul smelling" or, more specifically, "smelling like a civet cat."

General Information
The durian is one of the longest-established inhabitants of the rainforests of Southeast Asia, especially Borneo and other islands of the Malay Archipelago. A full-grown fruit

may be anywhere from grapefruit- to volleyball-sized and weigh five pounds or more. This round or ovoid fruit is covered with stout, sharply pointed spines. When ripe, it ranges in color from brown to a dull yellow. Death by durian is not uncommon, since the tree may grow as high as one hundred feet, and the fruit is not fully ripe until it drops to the ground. It is wise to take care when walking near such trees during the durian season, keeping an eye out not only above but below as well, since the fruit has a strange appeal for tigers. The best of the many varieties is said to be grown in Thailand, and the Thai government has plans to can and export the fruit. Though there is a cultivar that has no smell, almost all durians have a distinctive odor. The subject of striking comparisons, the smell has been compared to the civet cat, sewage, stale vomit, or (more mildly) onions and overripe cheese. Even Indonesians acknowledge that prolonged exposure to the smell may have negative effects, and the carriage of durians on public transport is forbidden. The fruits must be eaten shortly after harvest because they quickly turn rancid and sour.

Buying Tips

Pick a fruit that is intact, comparatively light, and with a large and solid stem. When you shake a mature durian, you should hear the seeds moving, and it should exude a strong—but not sour—aroma. The fruit will start to split along the seam lines when fully ripe. If it passes these tests, insert a knife in the center; if the knife comes out sticky, the fruit is ripe.

Culinary Uses

Most people find that while the smell of durian repels them, they are no longer aware of it once they start eating; it somehow combines with nonsmelly but tasty substances to produce a characteristic rich, aromatic flavor. Alfred

Durian / Nutritional Value Per 100 g Edible Portion			
	Raw		Raw
Calories	144	Beta Carotene (A)	20–30 IU
Protein	2.5–2.8 g	Thiamine (B$_1$)	0.240–0.352 mg
Fat	3.1–3.9 g	Riboflavin (B$_2$)	0.200 mg
Fiber	1.7 g	Niacin (B$_3$)	0.683–0.700 mg
Calcium	7.6–9.0 mg	Ascorbic Acid (C)	23.9–25.0 mg
Iron	0.73–1.0 mg	Tocopherol (E)	"high"
Phosphorus	37.8–44.0 mg		

LORE AND LEGEND

From Southeast Asia to the Philippines everyone knows the durian, and whether it is loved or not, this most controversial of tropical fruits is always talked about. The fruit is widely believed to be an aphrodisiac in Malaya, Thailand, Indonesia, and the Philippines. An old Malay saying has it that "when the durians fall, the sarongs rise." The fruit is so well regarded by Oriental lovers that the ownership of just one tree can make a man as well off as if he owned a small business. It's a rough life, though, for owners often have to sleep under their trees to guard them. In the late 1920s Durian Fruit Products of New York City launched a product named Dur-India as a "health-food accessory." The bottles sold for nine dollars a dozen, about a three-month supply. The tablets reputedly contained durian and a species of *Allium* from India, as well as a considerable amount of vitamin E; the company claimed the supplement provided "more concentrated healthful energy in food form than any other product the world affords," to keep the body vigorous and tireless, the mind alert with faculties undimmed, and the spirit youthful. The product never sold well and soon disappeared.

Russel Wallace, a widely traveled British naturalist, described the smell this way in 1872:

> A rich custard highly flavored with almonds gives the best idea of it, but there are occasional wafts of flavour that call to mind cream cheese, onion-sauce, sherry wine and other incongruous dishes. Then there is a rich glutinous smoothness in the pulp which nothing else possesses, but which adds to its delicacy. It is neither acid, nor sweet, nor juicy; yet it wants none of these qualities, for it is in itself perfect. It produces no nausea or other bad effect, and the more you eat of it the less you feel inclined to stop. (*The Treasury of Botany*, Vol. I, p. 435)

The common procedure for eating the fruit is to split open the shell, which reveals five cells enveloped in a firm, cream-colored, sticky pulp, each containing up to four large, chestnut-sized seeds. Well-chilled durian has a better flavor than it does at room temperature. Durian is sometimes cooked and made into a sausage-shaped cake that retains some of its proper flavor but very little smell. The flesh has been canned in syrup for export, as well as dried for local use and export. Blocks of durian paste are frequently sold in native markets. Javanese prepare the flesh as a sauce to be served with rice; they also combine the minced flesh with minced onion, salt, and diluted vinegar as a kind of relish. The large seeds can be roasted like chestnuts and are said to taste like them.

Health Benefits

Durian flesh is believed to serve as a vermifuge. Eating the fruit is alleged to restore the health of ailing humans and animals, as well as acting as an aphrodisiac.

Elderberry

(Sambucus nigra, S. canadensis, S. mexicana)

The genus *Sambucus* is named after the sambuca, an ancient reedlike musical instrument. *Nigra* means "black"; *canadensis* means "from Canada"; *mexicana* means "Mexican." The English word *elder* is from the Anglo-Saxon *aeld*, meaning "fire," because of the ancient practice of removing the pith from young branches to use as blowing tubes to kindle fires. These tubes were also made into shepherds' pipes, and thus another common name for the elder is the pipe tree.

General Information

Elderberry bushes are found almost everywhere in Europe, western Asia, and North America, wherever there is low damp ground. The trees bear white flower clusters and abundant deep purple or nearly black berries, both of which are edible when cooked. There are also red- and blue-berried elder bushes, but the red variety are generally considered poisonous. Familiar to children of all ages, the straight-growing tough branches, from which the pith may be easily extracted, have been used through the years as simple peashooters, whistles, and blowpipes for kindling fires. An ancient musical instrument, the sambuca, which is trombonelike in tone, was fashioned from many such reedlike sticks. Elder wood once served to make shoemakers' pegs, butchers' skewers, and needles for weaving nets.

Culinary Uses

When raw, elderberries contain small amounts of a poisonous alkaloid and have a sickly smell and taste. Cooking destroys the alkaloid and transforms the taste. In cooking, elderberries are often added to other fruits, especially apples. They yield an excellent wine and, combined with crab apples, produce a pretty jelly. The dried berries are used to make a fruity, flavorful tea much sought after by herbal tea aficionados. Elderflowers are sometimes mixed with batter and baked into cakes; they are also used to flavor cooked fruit and jam by stirring the panful with a spray of flowers until the flavor is judged strong enough. Elderberry cordial, an unfermented and nonalcoholic concentrate, makes a delicious summer drink and can also be used as a topping for ice cream.

Health Benefits

Elderberry tea is an old folk remedy for such conditions as colds, coughs, and influenza. A heavy syrup from the berry juice used as a hot drink was a remedy for coughs, and cold sufferers comforted themselves with hot toddies of mulled elderberry wine. Elderberry juice can relieve spasms of the face (known as tic douloureux or trigeminal neuralgia) and instigate cures of sciatica; adding 20 percent port wine speeds the healing. Elderflower water has been used to keep skin soft, to keep wrinkles and freckles at bay, and to alleviate weariness. In recent years science has discovered that elderberries contain viburnic acid, a substance that induces perspiration and is useful in cases of bronchitis and similar ailments. The flowers contain a glucoside, eldrin, that is identical to rutin. An Israeli researcher, Dr.

Elderberry / Nutritional Value Per 100 g Edible Portion			
	Raw		Raw
Calories	73	Beta Carotene (A)	600 IU
Protein	0.66 g	Thiamine (B₁)	0.070 mg
Fat	0.50 g	Riboflavin (B₂)	0.060 mg
Fiber	7.00 g	Niacin (B₃)	0.500 mg
Calcium	38 mg	Pantothenic Acid (B₅)	0.140 mg
Iron	1.60 mg	Pyridoxine (B₆)	0.230 mg
Phosphorus	39 mg	Ascorbic Acid (C)	36 mg
Potassium	280 mg		

LORE AND LEGEND

Some claim that the elder is surrounded by a healing "aura." Ancient trees were believed to have a mysterious and supernatural history; carrying an elder twig close to the flesh was said to be a priceless charm for good luck and good health. Spirits were believed to reside in the shrub, and thus some people refused to cut it down or burn it. Legend also relates that the cross Christ was crucified upon was made of elder wood, and thus the bush cannot be struck by lightning.

Madeleine Mumcuoglu, has developed a remarkable elderberry extract she calls Sambucol, which has been shown effective at inactivating viruses, no small feat. In laboratory tests, Sambucol stimulates the body's immune system by increasing production of disease-fighting lymphocytes. It also acts as a potent antioxidant.

Emblic

(Phyllanthus emblica)
Also Known As: Malacca Tree

The botanical name *Phyllanthus* means "leaf-flower," referring to the curious manner in which flowers grow along the edges of the leaflike branches.

General Information

Prized for its fruit in tropical Asia, the emblic tree is native to tropical southeastern Asia. It is regarded as sacred by Hindus, whose religion prescribes that the fruits be included in the diet for forty days after a fast, in order to restore vitality. It is a common practice in Indian homes to cook the fruits whole with sugar and saffron and to give one or two to a child every morning. In 1945 the fruits aroused enthusiasm when analyses found that they contained a rich natural source of vitamin C. However, interest quickly switched to the acerola cherry, which was found to be as rich or richer in the vitamin than the emblic. The fruit is slightly ridged, round, hard to the touch, and almost stemless. Light green when underripe, they ripen to a whitish or dull yellowish green, occasionally red.

Culinary Uses

The skin of the emblic is thin and translucent, the flesh crisp and juicy but extremely acidic and astringent. Tightly embedded in the center of the flesh is a stone containing six small seeds. The fruit can be stewed with sugar, made into jams and relishes, baked into tarts, candied, or added to other foods as seasoning during cooking; its juce can be used to flavor vinegar.

Health Benefits

Antiscorbutic, diuretic, laxative. Because of their high vitamin C content, emblic powder, tablets, and candies were issued to Indian troops during World War II as part of daily rations. Of great importance in Asiatic medicine, the emblic is used in the treatment of a great number of ailments, especially those associated with the digestive organs. For most uses, the fruit juice is fermented or prepared in the form of a sherbet.

Feijoa

(Feijoa sellowiana)
Also Known As: Pineapple Guava

The *Feijoa* genus is named after a botanist and former director of the National History Museum in San Sebastian, Spain, Señor Don da Silva Feijo; *sellowiana* was given in honor of Herr F. Sellow, a German explorer who collected plant specimens in the province of Rio Grande do Sul in southern Brazil.

General Information

The small evergreen feijoa tree with its gray-green leaves is native to extreme southern Brazil, northern Argentina, western Paraguay, and Uruguay. It can be grown in many warm temperate zones of the world and was probably

Emblic / Nutritional Value Per 100 g Edible Portion			
	Raw		Raw
Protein	0.07 g	Beta Carotene (A)	0.01 mg
Fat	0.2 g	Thiamine (B$_1$)	0.030 mg
Fiber	1.9 g	Riboflavin (B$_2$)	0.050 mg
Calcium	12.5 mg	Niacin (B$_3$)	0.180 mg
Iron	0.48 mg	Ascorbic Acid (C)	625-1561 mg
Phosphorus	26.0 mg		

Feijoa / Nutritional Value Per 100 g Edible Portion			
	Raw		**Raw**
Calories	49	Copper	0.055 mg
Protein	1.24 g	Manganese	0.085 mg
Fat	0.78 g	Beta Carotene (A)	0 IU
Calcium	4-17mg	Thiamine (B₁)	0.008 mg
Iron	0.05-0.08 mg	Riboflavin (B₂)	0.032 mg
Magnesium	8-9 mg	Niacin (B₃)	0.289 mg
Phosphorus	10-20 mg	Pantothenic Acid (B₅)	0.228 mg
Potassium	155-166 mg	Pyridoxine (B₆)	0.050 mg
Sodium	3-5 mg	Folic Acid (B₉)	38 mcg
Zinc	0.040 mg	Ascorbic Acid (C)	28-35 mg

brought to southern Europe by the Spaniards. This fragrant tropical fruit has a slightly bumpy, thin skin, with the color ranging from lime green to olive. Resembling a fuzzless kiwi fruit, the small egg-shaped green fruit is commercially grown today in New Zealand and California.

Buying Tips

Select a feijoa with a full aroma, as immature feijoas can be quite bitter. If they are not as tender as a firmish plum or soft pear, leave to ripen for a few days until they are. Fully ripened fruit should have a pronounced bouquet of floral fruitiness.

Culinary Uses

The thin green skin of the feijoa encloses a cream to tan, granular, medium-soft flesh surrounding a jellyish central cavity filled with tiny edible seeds. The scent and taste are tart and perfumy, suggestive of pineapple, quince, spruce, and Concord grapes, with a dash of lemon and menthol— all this with a texture gritty like a dense Bosc pear. A slightly underripe fruit is not unpleasant, but it does not have the full, rich flavor that develops with maturity. To prepare the fruit, peel and serve in the desired manner. When served raw, feijoas are usually cut in half like miniature melons, with the flesh spooned out of the shell. Or the fruits can be peeled and sliced as an exotic addition to a fruit salad or compote. Feijoas may be used in any preparation calling for apples, but be aware that their distinctive flavor may dominate more subtly flavored dishes.

Health Benefits

The fruit is rich in water-soluble iodine compounds. The percentage varies with locality and from year to year, but the usual range is 1.65 to 3.90 milligrams per kilogram of fresh fruit.

Fig
(Ficus carica)

Shape is a good part of the fig's delight.

—JANE GRIGSON

Figs are restorative, and the best food that can be taken by those who are brought low by long sickness . . . professed wrestlers and champions were in times past fed with figs.

—PLINY, ROMAN NATURALIST (A.D. 23–79)

The term *Ficus* is the old Roman name for this fruit. Of the many different varieties, the best was considered to be that flourishing in Caria in Asia Minor, hence the modern botanical classification *Ficus carica*. The English name *fig* derives from the Latin *ficus*.

General Information

The fig is a native of western Asia. It can be found over a vast uninterrupted area stretching from eastern Iran through the Mediterranean countries to the Canary Isles, and it is now grown in southwestern areas of the United States. The genus *Ficus* is unique in that no flowers ever form on the trees; instead, it bears its flowers inside nearly closed receptacles that ripen into the fleshy, pear-shaped fruits, of which only the female fruits are edible. There are over 750 species in this genus. Some figs ripen underground, while others grow high in the air on plants dangling from other trees. Some figs are parasites that strangle and kill their hosts; others grow on low trailing shrubs in the desert or on tall trees in tropical forests. There are large figs and small figs, round figs and ovoid figs, spring figs, summer figs, and winter figs, and figs colored black, brown, red, purple, violet, green, yellow-green, yellow, and white.

The cultivation of figs goes back to the very earliest times. Drawings of figs dating back several centuries before Christ were found in the Gizeh pyramid. Fig trees were grown in King Nebuchadnezzar's famous Hanging Gardens of Babylon and are mentioned frequently throughout the Bible and even in Homer's *Odyssey*. While the fruit may not have had the eight hundred uses of the date palm (although its leaves were a more convenient size and shape for the specialized requirements of the Garden of Eden), the fig sometimes fruited well where the date did not, most notably in Greece, where it found a place in the diet of rich and poor alike. The

Greeks are said to have received the fig from Caria in Asia Minor, and they in turn introduced the plant to neighboring countries, although at one point in Greek history figs were in such high demand that their exportation was forbidden by law. In the mid–eighteenth century, the Spanish fathers introduced this fruit to California and planted figs at the first Catholic mission in San Diego, California. This black mission fig is still an important variety in that state, which grows nearly 100 percent of the entire U.S. fig crop.

Buying Tips

Ripe fresh figs vary in color from greenish-yellow to purple, depending on the variety. Fresh fruits should be plump and teardrop-shaped, be evenly colored, and yield under gentle pressure; occasionally they are slightly wrinkled or cracked. Softness, moistness, and oozing nectar all indicate perfect ripeness, but fresh figs are highly perishable at this stage and will not last long, even in the refrigerator. Avoid any that smell sour. Unripe figs, which exude a milky liquid from the stem, should be left at room temperature to mature. Dried figs are best if they still have some "give" to them and are covered with a light dusting of sugar crystals (formed from the fruit itself).

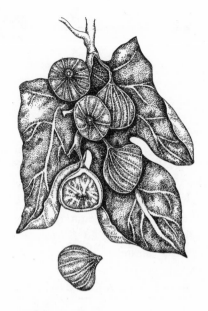

Fig / Nutritional Value Per 100 g Edible Portion		
	Raw	Dried
Calories	80	274
Protein	1.2-1.3 g	4.3 g
Fat	0.14-0.30 g	1.30 g
Fiber	1.2-2.2 g	5.6 g
Calcium	35.0-78.2 mg	126.0 mg
Iron	0.60-4.09 mg	3.00 mg
Magnesium	17 mg	59 mg
Phosphorus	22.0-32.9 mg	77.0 mg
Potassium	194-232 mg	640 mg
Sodium	1-2 mg	11-34 mg
Zinc	0.150 mg	0.510 mg
Copper	0.070 mg	0.313 mg
Manganese	0.128 mg	0.388 mg
Beta Carotene (A)	20-270 IU	80-133 IU
Thiamine (B$_1$)	0.034-0.060 mg	0.071 mg
Riboflavin (B$_2$)	0.053-0.079 mg	0.088 mg
Niacin (B$_3$)	0.320-0.412 mg	0.694 mg
Pantothenic Acid (B$_5$)	0.300 mg	0.435 mg
Pyridoxine (B$_6$)	0.113 mg	0.224 mg
Folic Acid (B$_9$)	n/a	7.5 mcg
Ascorbic Acid (C)	12.2-17.6 mg	0.8 mg

Culinary Uses

Cultivated for centuries as one of the most prized and nutritious of fruits, figs are highly cherished for their rich, sweet, alluring taste, which is nearly addictive (they have one of the highest sugar contents of cultivated fruits). Ripe figs are delicious; peeled or unpeeled, the fruits may be eaten on their own; cooked into pies, puddings, cakes, bread, and other bakery products; or added to ice cream mixes. Hard, unripe figs are best stewed, then used in cakes, jams, or pickles, but they lack the robust flavor of those that are fully ripe. Dried figs can be substituted in recipes that call for apricots, dates, or other dried fruits, and are especially tasty in baked goods; also try adding chopped dried figs to baked sweet potatoes or winter squash for a delicious new sensation. Over 85 percent of the fig crop is dried for market. Fig Newtons, those ubiquitous fig cookies, were first advertised in 1892 and named after the town of Newton, Massachusetts.

Health Benefits

pH 5.05–5.98. Laxative, restorative. The medicinal use of figs is almost as ancient as the plant itself, and the fruit has been used to treat nearly every known disease. Containing more mineral matter and more alkalinity than most fruits,

LORE AND LEGEND

The fig tree is revered nearly everywhere as the Tree of Life and Knowledge, from central Africa—where the natives believe their ancestral spirits live in fig trees—to the Far East—where Siddha Gautama found wisdom and divine illumination under the Bo tree (*Ficus religiosa*) and became the Buddha. The most revered fig tree in the world grows in the ruined city of Anuradhapura (now in Ceylon), said to have come from a cutting of the very Bo tree under which the Buddha sat, meditating his way to perfect knowledge. It was sent to Ceylon in 288 B.C., a present from the Indian emperor Asoka. Even the Muslims held the fig tree sacred, calling it the Tree of Heaven, as it was considered to be the most intelligent of all trees. Early Greek and Roman mythology claimed that the sacred fig was a gift to the people from the Greek god of wine and agriculture, Dionysus, and his Roman counterpart, Bacchus. When Cato the Elder advocated to the Roman Senate the conquest of Carthage, he used as his crowning argument the advantage of acquiring fruits as glorious as North African figs,

specimens of which he pulled from his toga as exhibits. The fig's reputation spread far beyond the lands in which they grew. In the third century B.C., Bindusara, king of the Maurya dominions in India, wrote to Greece asking for some grape syrup, some figs, and a philosopher. Grape syrup and figs, he was told with cool courtesy, would be sent to him with pleasure, but it was "against the law in Greece to trade in philosophers."

In Egypt baskets of figs were included among the tomb furnishings of dynastic times, but they were not always there for gastronomic enjoyment. The Egyptians as a people were preoccupied by their digestion, believing that more illnesses had their source in the alimentary canal than any other bodily place, and they bombarded that system with every remedy in their less-than-prepossessing pharmacopoeia. The fig, with its mild laxative properties, must have qualified as that rare substance, a food that not only tasted good but was also beneficial. It was undoubtedly more palatable than the senna and castor oil that, then as now, were the main alternatives.

figs are great producers of energy and vitality. Either fresh or sun-dried, they work as an excellent natural laxative for sluggish bowels; the high mucin content and tiny seeds help gather toxic wastes and mucus in the colon and drag them out. The gums and pectin found in figs cleanse your cells by bonding to, and removing, the acids that would otherwise accumulate fat globules. Studies show that figs also help kill pernicious bacteria while promoting the buildup of friendly acidophilus bacteria in the bowel. Those who do not drink milk may want to add figs to their regular diet since the fig is one of the highest sources of readily assimilable calcium in the plant world. Although fresh raw figs are best, dried figs also give nourishment and energy to the body, especially during the winter months. Dried figs are typically preserved with potassium sorbate to help keep them moist without spoiling. Milk from the unripe fruit applied twice daily to warts helps remove them. Calimyrna figs have in their skins and kernels a substance that rips the skin of round-

worms. It would be wise to eat some figs once in a while just to make the environment in the intestine sweet and to make it an undesirable environment for unwanted visitors. Intestinal parasites are destroyed by enzymes in fig juice, but all enzymes are destroyed by cooking.

VARIETIES

Adriatic fig trees are prolific bearers, producing light green or yellowish-green fruits with pale pink or dark red flesh, very similar in appearance to Calimyrna but smaller and not as sweet. While good fresh, this variety is also frequently sold dried and is the principal variety used in making fig bars and fig paste.

Black Mission figs are black or dark purple with pink flesh and are of medium to large size. They have a moist, chewy texture and distinctive, sweet flavor. Spanish missionaries established a Franciscan mission in San Diego in 1769 and began to grow a Spanish black common fig that, under the names *Mission*, *Black Mission*, or *Franciscana*, is still one of the leading varieties. The dried version is smaller and drier, with an intense, dark, almost burned flavor.

Calimyrna, or **California Smyrna,** is a large greenish-yellow fig that is less moist and not quite as sweet in its fresh state as the Black Mission fig. Considered to have a more traditional fig flavor and texture, this is the most popular dried variety. Often referred to as a caprifig, the Calimyrna is not self-pollinating and relies on an unusual method of pollination to produce mature edible fruit. Early growers of the Calimyrna (which started from the Turkish Smyrna) were puzzled because the fruit would drop off the tree before maturing. Finally, a researcher discovered that Calimyrna figs would remain on the trees if they received the pollen from an inedible fig called the caprifig. Each caprifig has a colony of small fig wasps, called blastophaga, living inside. When the wasp larvae mature, they go in search of another fig to serve as a nest in order to reproduce. Calimyrna growers intervene just prior to this point and place baskets of caprifigs in their orchards. Female wasps then work their way into the Calimyrna figs, carrying a few grains of caprifig pollen on their wings and bodies. Once inside, the wasps discover that the structure of the Calimyrna fig is not suitable for laying eggs and depart, leaving the pollen behind. Thick-skinned Calimyrna figs are usually peeled when used fresh.

Kadota is a small, thick-skinned fig that is generally canned or sold fresh. Actually greenish yellow in color with a violet-tinted flesh, it has only a few small seeds.

Gandaria
(Bouea gandaria)

General Information
Native to Malaya and Sumatra, the gandaria is the best known of the small mangolike fruits borne by this genus of trees. The fruit is oval or round, with thin, smooth, edible skin, yellow or apricot-colored when ripe. These "miniature mangoes" vary greatly in edibility, but the best are well worth eating.

Culinary Uses
The yellow or orange pulp is juicy, varies from acid to sweet, and adheres to the leathery, whiskered stone. Most fruits are

Gandaria / Nutritional Value Per 100 g Edible Portion			
	Raw		Raw
Protein	0.112 g	Beta Carotene (A)	0.043 mg
Fat	0.04 g	Thiamine (B₁)	0.031 mg
Fiber	0.6 g	Riboflavin (B₂)	0.025 mg
Calcium	6 mg	Niacin (B₃)	0.286 mg
Iron	0.31 mg	Ascorbic Acid (C)	75 mg
Phosphorus	10.8 mg		

eaten in the same manner as mangoes, but they may also be made into jam or chutney. When still immature, they are pickled in brine and used in curries. In Indonesia, the young leaves are marketed and eaten raw with rice.

Goji Berry
(Lycium tibetica, L. barbarum)

Tibetica means "from Tibet," while *barbarum* means "from the countryside."

General Information
The Tibetan Goji berry, *Lycium tibetica*, is a member of the Solanecea family. The Chinese wolfberry, *L. barbarum*, is grown in China. Tibetan Goji berries are grown in protected valleys in wild and cultivated areas of Inner Mongolia in million-year-old soil where pesticides have never been used. These little berries are plumper and sweeter than the Chinese ones, although the Chinese variety claims to be the heirloom strain.

Buying Tips
Goji berries are only sold dried outside of their native countries.

Culinary Uses
The taste of these berries is not quite as sweet as a raisin and not as tart as a dried cranberry. They are pleasing to most people. In Tibet and Mongolia, people love the berries so much that they devote two weeks a year to celebrating them, probably something like the European wine fests of times past.

Health Benefits
The most commonly cited side effect of eating too many berries is increased laughter. It is said that a handful in the

morning will make you happy all day. The Goji berry has been used in traditional Mongolian and Tibetan medicine for centuries. The fruit contains polysaccharides, which have been demonstrated to strongly fortify the immune system. These same polysaccharides have been found to be a secretagogue, that is, a substance that stimulates the secretion in the pituitary gland of human growth hormone, a powerful innate antiaging hormone. The berry is also the richest source of carotenoids, including beta carotene (it has more beta carotene than carrots), of all known foods or plants on earth. The Goji berry is among the most revered of sexual tonic herbs in Asian herbalism and has been recognized as increasing sexual fluids and enhancing fertility. In Mongolia it is commonly used by first-trimester mothers to prevent morning sickness. It is a gentle and soothing fruit that is loaded with available vitality. In several study groups with elderly people, the berry was given once a day for three weeks, with many beneficial results. The berries contain twenty-one trace minerals (the main ones being zinc, iron, and copper) and five hundred times the amount of vitamin C by weight of oranges. It is also loaded with vitamins B_1, B_2, B_6, and E.

Gooseberry
(Ribes uva-crispa, R. hirtellum, R. grossularia)

Ribes probably derived from *ribas*, the Arabic name for *Rheum ribes*, although some believe it to be the latinized form of *riebs*, which is an old German word for "currant." *Uva-crispa* means "curved berry"; *hirtellum* means "somewhat hairy." The English name *gooseberry* is not a corruption of gorse-berry, as is often suggested, but comes from the Flemish *kruys*, meaning "cross," referring to the triple spines at the nodes. The word may also be related to the German *krauselbeere*, meaning "crisp berry," which became *groseille* in French, hence *grossularia*, the specific name.

General Information
Gooseberries are derived mostly from two species: the European gooseberry (*Ribes uva-crispa*), native to the Caucasus Mountains and North Africa; and the American gooseberry (*R. hirtellum*), native to the northeastern and north-central United States and Canada. Popularity of the berry soared in eighteenth-century England, when gardeners began vying to see who could grow the largest fruits. European gooseberries were brought to North

LORE AND LEGEND

In one tale, a wart will vanish if pricked by a gooseberry spine that has passed through a wedding ring.

America by early settlers, but most cultivars quickly succumbed, and only later, when the European and American species were hybridized, did cultivation succeed in North America. The berries themselves vary enormously, running from fuzzy-prickly to downy or satin-smooth, from translucent to opaque, from white through shades of green to deep purple, from the size of a blueberry to that of a cherry tomato, and from mouth-puckering to lightly sweet. The white gooseberry has a veined, smooth, transparent skin, while the red gooseberry has a hairy surface. Most common in American markets are the small to medium-sized, celery-green summer berry and the very large, striated, yellow-green to purplish winter berry.

Buying Tips
Choose hard, dry berries with a rich sheen. Those found in supermarkets, most often from New Zealand, are smooth, like large glass marbles. Avoid mushy berries or those with skins marred by splits or blemishes. The pink or purplish berries tend to be less tart.

Culinary Uses
Gooseberries have a flavor all their own that ranges over a wide spectrum. At one end are fruits with sour pulp and

Gooseberry / Nutritional Value Per 100 g Edible Portion			
	Raw		Raw
Calories	44	Copper	0.070 mg
Protein	0.88 g	Manganese	0.144 mg
Fat	0.58 g	Beta Carotene (A)	290 IU
Fiber	1.90 g	Thiamine (B₁)	0.040 mg
Calcium	25 mg	Riboflavin (B₂)	0.030 mg
Iron	0.31 mg	Niacin (B₃)	0.300 mg
Magnesium	10 mg	Pantothenic Acid (B₅)	0.286 mg
Phosphorus	27 mg	Pyridoxine (B₆)	0.080 mg
Potassium	198 mg	Ascorbic Acid (C)	27.7 mg
Sodium	1 mg	Tocopherol (E)	0.370 mg
Zinc	0.120 mg		

tough skin, while at the other are those whose tender skins envelop an aromatic, sweet pulp. Generally those found in the supermarket are the underripe, tart, sour kinds. Unless they are going to be puréed, top and tail them (taking off the spiny axis from top and bottom with scissors or knife) so as not to spike your guests. Date sugar is best for sweetening the cooked berries, or honey can be added after cooking. In Scandinavia, Hungary, and Russia, a chilled or hot soup of gooseberries and chicken stock, thickened with potato flour or cornstarch and topped with whipped or sour cream, is a favorite first course. England's gooseberry fool is a classic dish. Gooseberries may also be made into conserves, jams, jellies, or pies and pastries when combined, perhaps, with apples.

Health Benefits
pH 2.80–3.10. Gooseberries have a beneficial effect on constipation, liver ailments, poor complexion, arthritis, and dyspepsia. Their oil is rich in gamma-linoleic acid.

Gooseberry, Otaheite
(Phyllanthus acidus)

The botanical name *Phyllanthus* means "leaf-flower," referring to the curious manner in which flowers grow along the edges of the leaflike branches; since the flowers develop into fruits, the fruits also occupy this odd position. *Acidus* means "acidic." The *Otaheite* part of the name seems to indicate a connection with Tahiti, while the fruit's tart flavor recalls that of gooseberries.

General Information
The Otaheite gooseberry tree has been cultivated for centuries in southern India and parts of Southeast Asia. It is an astonishingly abundant bearer, often providing two crops a year. The fruits are ribbed, grape-sized, and green

Gooseberry, Otaheite / Nutritional Value Per 100 g Edible Portion			
	Raw		Raw
Protein	0.155 g	Beta Carotene (A)	0.019 mg
Fat	0.52 g	Thiamine (B₁)	0.025 mg
Fiber	0.8 g	Riboflavin (B₂)	0.013 mg
Calcium	5.4 mg	Niacin (B₃)	0.292 mg
Iron	3.25 mg	Ascorbic Acid (C)	4.6 mg
Phosphorus	17.9 mg		

at first but ripen to a light yellow. Tightly embedded in the center is a hard, ribbed stone containing four to six seeds. The tart flavor is similar to the gooseberry's, but there is no other connection between the two fruits.

Culinary Uses
The flesh must be sliced from the stone, or the fruits cooked and then pressed through a sieve to separate the stones. They can be made into pickles and preserves, added to dishes or drinks as a flavoring, or cooked with sugar to provide a compote or pie filling. If cooked long enough with plenty of sugar, the fruit and juice turn ruby red and yield a tasty jelly.

Health Benefits
In India the fruits are taken as a liver tonic and to enrich the blood, while the syrup is prescribed as a stomachic.

Grape and Raisin
(Vitis vinifera, V. labrusca, V. rotundita)

The sun, with all those planets revolving around it and dependent on it, can still ripen a bunch of grapes as if it had nothing else in the universe to do.

—GALILEO

Vitis is the classical Latin name for the plant and also has the general meaning of "vine" or "branch." The term *vinifera* means "wine-bearing." *Labrusca* signifies the wild vine, while *rotundita* means "small and round." The English word *grape* comes from the Germanic word *krapfo*, meaning "to hook." The English word *raisin* is derived from the Latin *racemus*, meaning "a bunch of grapes or berries."

General Information
Grapes go so far back in time that the vine is thought to have been already established throughout the world even before the coming of humans. Unquestionably, it was humankind's universal interest in the production of stimulating drinks that led to the vast amount of effort put into viticulture (grape cultivation) from late prehistoric times onward. The beginnings of viticulture originate somewhere around the Caspian Sea, an area also considered the place

of origin of *Vitis vinifera*, our most common grape. By the first century B.C., viticulture was a major source of revenue for the Romans (and thus encouraged by the government) and wine was popular throughout their empire. A precious trade item in the ancient Near East and also highly valued in ancient Rome, at one time two jars of raisins could be exchanged for a slave. Europeans encountering raisins on the Crusades recognized their keeping qualities as well as the intensely sweet, tangy richness lacking in their fresh counterpart. Returning home, they incorporated dried fruit and spices into their otherwise bland cooking. Until medieval times, raisins with their high sugar content were used as a sweetener second only to honey. As new colonization and widespread advance of peoples occurred, grapes were carried along; today they are cultivated on all continents and islands that are suitable in climate. There are between six and eight thousand varieties of grapes (though only forty to fifty are important commercially), nearly half of which are native to North America; in fact, when Leif Eriksson and the Vikings landed in the eleventh century,

they named the area Vinland after the wild grapes that were so abundant. The new land remained Vinland until Amerigo Vespucci arrived and named it after himself. Martha's Vineyard, an island off the coast of Massachusetts, was also named for the abundant grapes growing on it (by Gosnold, an Englishman, in 1603).

Harvested in August, grapes are spread on paper trays and sun-dried for two to three weeks in the vineyard; then the stems are removed and the grapes sorted and packaged. Grapes are grown with more chemical fertilizers, pesticides, and growth hormones than any other fruits. Thus most raisins, as concentrated grapes, contain the highest level of pesticide residue of any fruit. Organic raisins, however, are free of toxic residues. Rather than being fumigated with methyl bromide, organic raisins are frozen to −5 degrees Fahrenheit to achieve insect kill.

Buying Tips

When buying fresh grapes, choose plump ones firmly attached to their stems. Any remaining bloom shows minimal handling. Darker varieties should be free from any green tinge, while the greenish-white grapes will show a slight amber color when ripe. The stems should be green; if they are dry, brown, or black, the grapes will lack flavor; any puckering at the stem indicates that the grapes are old. Store raisins in a dark, cool cupboard to prolong their shelf life and to prevent flavor and texture deterioration. If refrigerated for more than six months, they become sugary.

Culinary Uses

Grapes come in many colors and sizes, of which the tiny seedless grapes are said to be the finest. This fruit constitutes the largest fruit industry on the globe; they are sold fresh, dried into raisins, crushed for juice and wine, and preserved or canned for jelly and fruit cocktail. Grapes are used in fruit salads, desserts, and pies. Young, tender grape leaves are eminently edible. Used as a wrapper for rice and other fillings in Greek and Middle Eastern cooking, they are also used to wrap some French cheeses. Bottled or canned grape leaves are sold in Greek and Middle Eastern groceries, but if you have grapes growing on your property, you can use your own leaves as long as they are unsprayed. Fresh leaves should be blanched or steamed to soften them; canned leaves, usually packed in brine, should be rinsed to reduce their sodium content. Grape seed oil is a pale, delicate oil extracted from grape seeds. When refrigerated, it will not cloud, and it has a very high smoke point. Raisins

Grape / Nutritional Value Per 100 g Edible Portion			
	Raw (American) Concord	Raw (European) Muscat/Tokay	Processed Juice
Calories	63	71	61
Protein	0.63 g	0.66 g	0.56 g
Fat	0.35 g	0.58 g	0.08 g
Fiber	0.76 g	0.45 g	n/a
Calcium	14 mg	11 mg	9 mg
Iron	0.29 mg	0.26 mg	0.24 mg
Magnesium	5 mg	6 mg	10 mg
Phosphorus	10 mg	13 mg	11 mg
Potassium	191 mg	185 mg	132 mg
Sodium	2 mg	2 mg	3 mg
Zinc	0.040 mg	0.050 mg	0.050 mg
Copper	0.040 mg	0.090 mg	0.028 mg
Manganese	0.718 mg	0.058 mg	0.360 mg
Beta Carotene (A)	100 IU	73 IU	8 IU
Thiamine (B$_1$)	0.092 mg	0.092 mg	0.026 mg
Riboflavin (B$_2$)	0.057 mg	0.057 mg	0.037 mg
Niacin (B$_3$)	0.300 mg	0.300 mg	0.262 mg
Pantothenic Acid (B$_5$)	0.024 mg	0.024 mg	0.041 mg
Pyridoxine (B$_6$)	0.110 mg	0.110 mg	0.065 mg
Folic Acid (B$_9$)	3.9 mcg	3.9 mcg	2.6 mcg
Ascorbic Acid (C)	4.0 mg	10.8 mg	0.1 mg

are one of the all-time classic snack foods. Soft, sweet, and bite-sized, they can be eaten alone, added to granola and trail mix, or combined with all manner of dishes. They add color and sweetness to garden salads, custard pies, and rice pudding and are frequent additions to candy, hot cereals, cookies, and breads. Raisin paste, made by grinding raisins in a food grinder until crushed and sticky, is a fine substitute or replacement for other sweeteners in baked goods and candies. Try mixing it with sesame tahini, sunflower seeds, and a bit of honey, and rolling into bite-sized balls.

Health Benefits

Grapes: pH 2.80–3.82; raisins: pH 3.80–4.10. Grapes are called "the queen of fruits" because of their excellent cleansing properties, and they rank among the most potent of all medicinal foods. Among their most effective therapeutic applications are as a cure for constipation, gastritis, and chronic acidosis, common complaints for those who live on Western diets. The black variety of grapes are by far the most potent, being excellent detoxifiers of the whole body but especially good for the digestive tract, liver, kidneys, and blood. Those following a diet solely of grapes for several days or weeks (known as the grape cure or ampelotherapy) will feel their powerful detoxifying and alkalinizing properties. Since eating grapes in quantity acts freely on the kidneys, this promotes the expulsion of poisons from the system. Grapes offer a natural combination of fruit acid, natural sugar, and various bitter-astringent properties that will help keep your cellular network cleansed. Grapes are also rich in malic acid, free acids, tannin, volatile acid, and an unusual water—combined with nutrients and fermentable sugar—that provides a superior energy source, improves elimination, and simply makes you feel good. The best grapes are those that have seeds, for the outside of the seed contains tartaric acid (cream of tartar), which helps cut the mucus and catarrh of the body so they can be eliminated. The fruit's high water content adds to the fluids necessary to eliminate hardened deposits that may have settled in the body, their high iron content makes them good blood builders, and their magnesium promotes peristalsis, although the skins and seeds can sometimes be irritating to those with colitis or ulcers.

Recently, scientists have discovered that the ellagic acid found in grapes scavenges carcinogens as it moves through the body; they also have extraordinarily high levels of caffeic acid, which has been shown to be a strong anticancer substance. A study published in *Science* magazine found

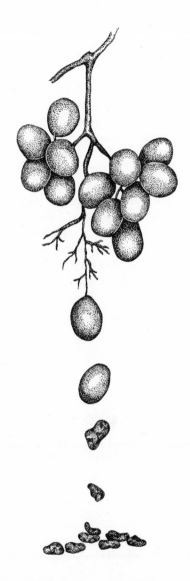

cancer-preventive properties in resveratrol, a phytochemical found in the skins and seeds of red and green grapes. Another reason to eat this delicious fruit is for its high content of boron, a mineral that helps ward off osteoporosis. Grapes fight tooth decay and stop viruses in their tracks.

Raw grape juice is easily assimilated and called the "nectar of the gods" and "vegetarian milk" owing to its ability to sustain nursing infants deprived of mother's milk; it is a far superior option to pasteurized cow's milk. Combining grape juice equally with a nut milk quickly furnishes the system with new blood of the purest kind and is an excellent remedy for anemia. A study conducted at the University of Wisconsin showed that two cups of grape juice a day can reduce platelet aggregation, a risk factor for heart disease.

Grape seed extract is very similar to pine bark extract as it contains a unique type of bioflavonoid called proanthocyanidins, which are synergistic with vitamin C—that is, they greatly enhance the activity of vitamin C. In fact, some researchers believe that grape seed extract helps vitamin C enter cells, thus strengthening the cell membranes and protecting the cells from oxidative damage. In 1970 a biochemist in France isolated from grape seed a material that improves blood circulation—oligomeric proanthocyandin (OPC). It also reduces swelling and may even prevent heart disease. OPC is one of the substances in red grape juice and red wine that has been shown to have some protective properties against heart disease. Because of their OPCs, grapes are now harvested not only for the food and drink products we are familiar with but also as a source

of these therapeutically active ingredients. First and foremost, OPCs are antioxidants, which help the body to handle assaults, such as cigarette smoke and environmental chemicals, that could eventually cause disease. They are different from a broader category of stress protectors called adaptogens, which also protect you from chemical or physical substances. Both antioxidants and adaptogens protect you from physical and mental exhaustion and help you recover after an illness. They may help us avoid at least two of the big killers today: cardiovascular disease and cancer.

Raisins have less acid than grapes since the acid has been dried out of them, but they are very high in sugar so should be used in moderation. They have almost as much iron by weight as cooked dried beans or ground beef. Most raisins have been dried naturally in the sun, but some have been treated with sulfur or other preservatives to retain their color and moistness.

VARIETIES

There are four major classes of grapes grown in the United States: the American grape (*V. labrusca*), the European grape (*V. vinifera*), the muscadine (*V. rotundifolia*), and hybrids of the three. American grapes—sometimes referred to as fox or Concord grapes—are native to the Northeast and grow in bunches, have skins that slip off easily, and are generally eaten fresh or made into jelly, juice, and occasionally wine. These are the grapes that Viking explorer Leif Eriksson found growing so abundantly on the eastern coast of North America, and of which Concord is the most familiar. The European grapes have tight skins and a typically winey flavor. They separate into three main categories: the wine grapes, the dessert grapes, and the raisin grapes. Tokay is the prototype of *vinifera*; these types grow only in California in a rather limited area. Among the "white" *vinifera* are Olivetta, with oval berries, and Thompson seedless. Ribier heads the "black" *vinifera*, which are actually a very deep blue. Muscadine grapes, best characterized by the Scuppernong, are native to the southeastern United States. They grow in loose clusters, have a slightly spicy and musky flavor, and are eaten fresh or made into jelly and occasionally into a fruity wine. From the muscadines come the seedless packaged raisins. Only three varieties of grapes in this country are widely used in the production of raisins: Thompson seedless, muscat, and black Corinth. Nearly all the commercially grown raisins in the United States (and about one-half of the total world

Raisin / Nutritional Value Per 100 g Edible Portion	Raw Brown Seedless	Raw Golden Seedless	Raw Currants
Calories	300	302	283
Protein	3.22 g	3.39 g	4.08 g
Fat	0.46 g	0.46 g	0.27 g
Fiber	1.28 g	1.43 g	1.57 g
Calcium	49 mg	53 mg	86 mg
Iron	2.08 mg	1.79 mg	3.26 mg
Magnesium	33 mg	35 mg	41 mg
Phosphorus	97 mg	115 mg	125 mg
Potassium	751 mg	746 mg	892 mg
Sodium	12 mg	12 mg	8 mg
Zinc	0.270 mg	0.320 mg	0.660 mg
Copper	0.309 mg	0.363 mg	0.468 mg
Manganese	0.308 mg	0.308 mg	0.469 mg
Beta Carotene (A)	8 IU	44 IU	73 IU
Thiamine (B$_1$)	0.156 mg	0.008 mg	0.160 mg
Riboflavin (B$_2$)	0.088 mg	0.191 mg	0.142 mg
Niacin (B$_3$)	0.818 mg	1.142 mg	1.615 mg
Pantothenic Acid (B$_5$)	0.045 mg	0.140 mg	0.045 mg
Pyridoxine (B$_6$)	0.249 mg	0.323 mg	0.296 mg
Folic Acid (B$_9$)	3.3 mcg	3.3 mcg	10.2 mcg
Ascorbic Acid (C)	3.3 mg	3.2 mg	4.7 mg

Grapes figure prominently in the ancient literature and art of both the Western and Eastern Hemispheres. Saturn gave the grape to Crete, Dionysos to Greece, Bacchus to Rome, Osiris to Egypt, and Geryon to Spain. Adam and Eve, as well as Noah, planted grapevines. The grape is certainly the fruit most associated with frivolity, as those who worshiped the gods of grapes and wine were notoriously addicted to wine, wild dances, and hedonistic excesses. The Greek poet Euripides praised the grape in eloquent terms, and the ancients gave clusters to newlyweds in the belief that their many seeds would bless the couple with many children. Clusters of grapes were frequently used on ancient coins (as well as some recent Italian and Israeli ones), and grapes and grapevines often appear as motifs on buildings and in illuminated manuscripts. After the fall of the Roman Empire, during the ensuing Dark Ages when Christianity became a dominant religion, wine became associated with the church. Considered symbolic of the blood of Christ, wine became part of the Communion ritual, and (in moderation) was believed one of the good things in life. Most monasteries soon had their own vineyards, tended by monks who slowly refined the process of wine making, developing regional wines and techniques of fermentation still in use today.

supply) now come from the San Joaquin valley of California, where the raisin industry began booming in the 1870s after a heat wave dried the grape crop on the vine.

Black Beauty also called **Beauty Seedless** is the only seedless black grape. They are spicy and sweet, resembling Concords in flavor. Their season runs from late May to early July.

Calmeria is a pale green oval fruit with a mildly sweet flavor, comparatively thick skin, and a few small seeds. They are sometimes called **Lady Finger** grapes because of their elongated shape. Their season is only January and February.

Cardinal is a cross between the Flame Tokay and the Ribier. These large, dark red grapes have a pearly gray finish, a full fruity flavor, and few seeds. Their season runs mid-May through mid-August.

Champagne or **Black Corinth** is a tiny, purple, seedless fruit with a deliciously winey sweetness. Their season is September and October. Black Corinth grapes that have been dried primarily for the confectionery market are sometimes labeled "Zante currant," referring to the Greek island where this type of grape first grew. About one-quarter the size of regular raisins, these tiny fruits are incorrectly called "currants" because of their resemblance to currant berries and the mispronounced name of the grape (*Corinth* sounds like *currant*). Substitute them in any recipe that calls for raisins; their small size does not interfere with the slicing of bread and cutting of cookies the way large raisins sometimes do. Their delicate flavor lends itself to exotic recipes, such as spiced rice or stuffed mussels and grape leaves.

Concord is a medium-sized, seeded, dark blue-black or purple tough-skinned grape with a powdery bloom. This variety is native to North America and originated in the 1840s near the Massachusetts town whose name it bears. It is very flavorful, with a sweet-tart tang and perfumy fragrance. Savored as table grapes, the Concord is the principal juice grape and also highly favored for jelly and wine. Its season is September and October.

Emperor is a European seeded variety with a mild cherry-like flavor that becomes quite sugary as it softens. The clusters are large, long, and well filled. The fruit is a uniform elongated obovoid, light red or reddish purple to deep purple in color, with a tough skin. Second only to Thompson seedless in quantity grown, Emperors are heavily cultivated in Latin America. California Emperors, a Thanksgiving and Christmas favorite, have a season that starts in October and runs well into March.

Flame Tokay is one of the prettiest of all the grape varieties. It is a long, elegant, bright red grape, with a definite velvety coat, a firm texture, and large seeds. With abundant juice and sweetness, the Tokay has the most grape flavor of all the American grapes, which, although they are sweet, are not sugary. Their season runs from late fall through January. Flame seedless raisins are extra-large and have a generously sweet, rich grape flavor.

Monukka is an especially large grape, nearly twice as large as Thompson seedless, with a rich, robust grape flavor. An old variety used specifically for drying, it makes a large raisin with a pleasing, mellow sweetness. Compared to the more intensely sweet common raisin (made from Thompson grapes), Monukkas are pricier and more subtly flavored. A favorite among raisin connoisseurs, they are produced in limited quantities. Look for them at specialty shops and health food stores.

Muscat is very large, very round, slightly bronzed, dusty green or green-yellow grape. They have a distinct musky wine flavor that conjures up monastic stone wine cellars full of oak kegs brooding in flickering candlelight. At their peak they are an excellent fruity table grape with a unique and enjoyable flavor; they are especially good with cheese and bread and are also pressed for muscatel wine. Sometimes their aroma precedes their flavor, and the combination is heady. It is very difficult to find bad muscat grapes since their season is so short, running only from early October through Thanksgiving. Raisins made from muscat grapes are large, brown, and particularly fruity tasting. Since this variety contains seeds, the raisins are either seeded mechanically or sold with seeds. Muscat raisins are considered a specialty item used mostly for holiday baking, especially fruitcakes, and thus are usually sold just in the autumn and winter months.

Red Flame was created by grafting and hybridizing the Flame Tokay grape, which has seeds, with a round seedless variety like the Perlette. They are a plump, round, deep red, seedless grape that is best when hard as a marble. At their peak these grapes are crisp, sweet, and meaty, with the touch of wine flavor that characterizes their Tokay parent. Their season runs May through October.

Ribier is a very large, very dark purple-black, mildly sweet grape. They may not be seedless, but they are so sweet and juicy that nobody cares. There is another round black variety, called the Exotica, which is just like the Ribier, only bigger, harder, and blacker. Most stores sell Exoticas under the Ribier name. Their season is July through February.

Sultana is a large, pale yellow-green grape originally from Smyrna and grown for the Turkish sultans. The raisins from Sultana grapes are more popular in Europe than in the United States. Particularly flavorful and soft, they can sometimes be purchased in gourmet shops and health food stores.

Thompson Seedless was first grown in California near Yuba City by Mr. William Thompson and is now the most common variety, making up half of the California grape acreage. Fresh Thompson seedless clusters are large, long, and well filled, with grapes that are light green, medium-sized, and ellipsoidal. When fully ripe, the grapes are firm yet tender, with a flavor that is a tasty blend of sweet juicy meat and tart skin. Their season runs from late June into November. Natural seedless raisins are sun-dried Thompson seedless grapes. They account for 95 percent of California raisins. The green grapes naturally develop a dark brown color as they dry in the sun, a process that takes from two to three weeks. Golden raisins are Thompson seedless grapes that have been oven-dried to avoid the darkening effect of sunlight. They may also have been treated with sulfur dioxide, which destroys most of the fruit's nutrients, to preserve their light color. Check the labels well or use another variety of raisin.

Grapefruit
(Citrus x paradisi)

> There's a lot more juice in a grapefruit than meets the eye.
>
> —Anonymous

The term *Citrus* derives from the Greek term for the citron, *kedromelon*. *Paradisi* means "coming from paradise." The English name was coined in 1814 in the West Indies by Jamaican farmers. Several attempts have been made to change the name of the fruit to something "more appropriate," but the name *grapefruit* has prevailed, except in Spanish-speaking areas, where it is called *toronja*.

General Information
The grapefruit is a relative newcomer to the citrus clan, an accidental hybrid between the pummelo and the orange. It was first described in 1750 by Griffith Hughes, who called it the "forbidden fruit" of Barbados. Seeds were brought to Florida by the French Count Odette Phillipe in 1823, but at first the trees were grown only as a novelty and the fruit little utilized. Florida started sending small shipments of the fruit to New York and Philadelphia between 1880 and 1885, thus setting in

LORE AND LEGEND

Following the United States stock market crash in 1929, citrus fruits could be had free for orange-colored food stamps (the color and name of the chief citrus fruit were only coincidental). This brought the grapefruit into families that had previously been so ignorant of it that welfare boards received the same complaint numerous times: that the fruit had been boiled for hours and still remained tough.

motion the colossal Florida citrus industry. For many years the grapefruit was not extremely popular because of its slightly bitter taste, but sweeter varieties were eventually bred. Red grapefruit were first spotted in the Rio Grande valley of Texas during the 1920s and have since been transplanted to other parts of the world; the red grapefruit is now designated the state fruit of Texas. The thin-skinned, shiny, heavy Florida grapefruit is considered by many to be the juiciest, sweetest, most nutritious variety available.

Buying Tips

Grapefruit of good quality should be heavy, well shaped, and even-colored, with a smooth, thin, shiny skin that is firm but springy to the touch. The heavier fruits are usually thinner-skinned and contain more juice than those with coarse, puffy, or spongy skins. Grapefruit will keep for up to eight weeks in the refrigerator.

Culinary Uses

There are several varieties, each good for different uses: white is best for juicing, pink is sweet enough to be eaten like an orange, and red is sweeter still. Generally considered a breakfast fruit, grapefruit is also used to make juice and marmalades, is added to fruit salads, ices, cakes, and other desserts, and can be baked or grilled. It is best to eat grapefruit alone or with other acid fruits, and not in combination with sweet fruits or starches. The habit of sweetening them (with sugar or another sweetener) causes a fermentation of the sweetener in the system, which then produces an acidic reaction in the body. Served before the main meal, grapefruit will stimulate the appetite and aid digestion. Once the grapefruit or its juice has been canned or in any way preserved, the value of the organic elements is lost.

Health Benefits

pH 3.00–3.75. Digestive. Fresh grapefruit, because of its salicylic acid content, has proved to be one of the most valuable fruits as an aid in the removal or dissolving of inorganic calcium that may have formed deposits in the joints (as in arthritis) as a result of excessive consumption of devitalized white flour and pasteurized milk products. Naringin, a flavonoid isolated from grapefruit, has been shown to promote the elimination of old red blood cells from the body and to normalize hematocrit levels (percentage of red blood cells per volume of blood). A compound called galacturonic acid, found only in grapefruit, adds a unique therapeutic benefit: it breaks up and dislodges the fatty plaque buildup in arteries and whisks it away. Used externally, the juice is a natural antiseptic for wounds and is valuable as a drug or poison eliminator.

Grapefruit / Nutritional Value Per 100 g Edible Portion			
	Fresh Fruit	Fresh Juice	Sweetened Canned Juice
Calories	34.4-46.4	37.0-42.0	46.0
Protein	0.50-1.00 g	0.40-0.50 g	0.58 g
Fat	0.06-0.20 g	0.1 g	0.09 g
Fiber	0.14-0.77 g	trace	0 g
Calcium	9.2-32.0 mg	9.0 mg	8.0 mg
Iron	0.24-0.70 mg	0.20 mg	0.36 mg
Magnesium	8 mg	12 mg	10 mg
Phosphorus	15.0-47.9 mg	15.0 mg	11.0 mg
Potassium	135-139 mg	162 mg	162 mg
Sodium	1.0 mg	1.0 mg	2.0 mg
Zinc	0.070 mg	0.050 mg	0.060 mg
Copper	0.047 mg	0.033 mg	0.048 mg
Manganese	0.012 mg	0.020 mg	0.020 mg
Beta Carotene (A)	10-440 IU	10-440 IU	0 IU
Thiamine (B$_1$)	0.040-0.057 mg	0.040 mg	0.040 mg
Riboflavin (B$_2$)	0.010-0.020 mg	0.020 mg	0.023 mg
Niacin (B$_3$)	0.157-0.290 mg	0.200 mg	0.319 mg
Pantothenic Acid (B$_5$)	0.283 mg	n/a	0.130 mg
Pyridoxine (B$_6$)	0.042 mg	n/a	0.020 mg
Folic Acid (B$_9$)	10.2 mcg	n/a	10.4 mcg
Ascorbic Acid (C)	36.0-49.8 mg	36.0-40.0 mg	26.9 mg
Tocopherol (E)	0.250 mg	n/a	n/a

One word of caution, though: avoid the extensive overuse of all citric acid fruits, as they are powerful dissolvers of the catarrhal accumulations in the body, and the elimination of too much toxic material all at once may cause boils, irritated nerves, diarrhea, and other problems. Citrus seed extract, usually derived primarily from grapefruit seeds, is available as a major ingredient in liquid extracts, capsules, and ointments. Grapefruit seed extract is extremely effective at killing dozens of bacteria, fungi, yeast, and other harmful organisms. When diluted, it can help knock out a sore throat, stop a bout of food poisoning, curb acne, clear up traveler's diarrhea, and kill off a candida infection. Used full strength, it even makes warts vanish.

Ground Cherry

(Physalis pruinosa, P. alkekangi, P. pubescens)
Also Known As: Chinese Lantern, Husk Cherry, Husk Tomato, Strawberry Tomato

Physalis is Greek for "bladder," so named because of its thin calyx, which enlarges and encloses the fruit at maturity. *Pruinosa* means "with a hoary bloom," and *alkekangi* comes from the Persian name *kakunaj*, while *pubescens* means "pubescent" or "downy." The fruit does not ripen until it falls to the ground, hence its English name *ground cherry*.

General Information
Native to the Americas, these small fruits of the nightshade family grow in open fields and along roads throughout the United States. In size and shape most ground cherries resemble a small, fanciful cherry tomato enclosed within a red Chinese paper lantern. Inside the paper husk there is a thin, waxy skin that surrounds a very juicy, dense pulp of the same brilliant color, whorled with soft, tiny, edible seeds. The berries drop to the ground before they are ready to eat, but in a week or two the husk dries and the fruit within turns a golden-yellow. The ground cherry most commonly grown as an edible garden vegetable is *P. pruinosa*, which bears a canary-yellow fruit encased in a brownish husk.

Culinary Uses
Its unusual taste is part tomato, part strawberry, part gooseberry, and part grape, yet the total effect is all its own: sweet and pleasantly acid, with a lightly bitter aftertaste. It has traditionally been used as a dessert fruit in pies and preserves or else dried in sugar and eaten like raisins. Prepare it as you would a tomato, either raw or cooked, but remember to remove the husk prior to eating, as it is inedible and slightly toxic. Green or immature wild ground cherries may be toxic. Use only those that are yellow or yellow-orange and have a fresh-looking husk.

Ground Cherry / Nutritional Value Per 100 g Edible Portion			
	Raw		Raw
Calories	53	Phosphorus	40 mg
Protein	1.9 g	Beta Carotene (A)	720 IU
Fat	0.7 g	Thiamine (B₁)	0.11 mg
Fiber	2.8 g	Riboflavin (B₂)	0.04 mg
Calcium	9 mg	Niacin (B₃)	2.8 mg
Iron	1.0 mg	Ascorbic Acid (C)	11 mg

Grumichama
(Eugenia brasiliensis)

The genus *Eugenia* was named in honor of Prince Eugene of Savoy. *Brasiliensis* means "native to Brazil."

General Information
Native to southern Brazil and Peru, this tree bears a long-stalked crimson fruit between one-half and three-quarters of an inch in diameter, with soft flesh and mild flavor. The skin is thin and firm and exudes dark red juice. The grumichama tree is cultivated in and around Rio de Janeiro, as well as in Paraguay. Over the years there have been efforts to encourage interest in the virtues of the grumichama in Florida and Hawaii, mainly because of the beauty and hardiness of the tree and the pleasant flavor of the fruits, but the sepals are a nuisance, and there is too little flesh in proportion to seed for the fruit to be taken seriously.

Culinary Uses
The red or white pulp is juicy and tastes much like a true cherry except for a touch of aromatic resin. It exists in several varieties, distinguished by the color of the flesh (dark red, vermilion, or white), all of equal merit. There are usually two or three hard inedible seeds. Fully ripe grumichamas are pleasant to nibble out of hand. In Hawaii, half-ripe fruits are made into pie, jam, or jelly.

Grumichama / Nutritional Value Per 100 g Edible Portion			
	Raw		Raw
Protein	0.102 g	Beta Carotene (A)	0.039 mg
Fiber	0.6 g	Thiamine (B$_1$)	0.044 mg
Calcium	39.5 mg	Riboflavin (B$_2$)	0.031 mg
Iron	0.45 mg	Niacin (B$_3$)	0.336 mg
Phosphorus	13.6 mg	Ascorbic Acid (C)	18.8 mg

Guava
(Psidium guajava, P. cattleianum, P. littorale var. longipes)

The genus name *Psidium* comes from the Greek *psidion*, meaning "pomegranate," so named because the many small hard seeds recall the pomegranate. *Guajava* is a derivative of the Haitian native name *guayavu*, which our English name also derives from. *Cattleianum* means "similar to the *Cattleyas* of the orchid family," which are named after William Cattley, an early English horticulturist and naturalist.

General Information
The guava is a small, fragrant, tropical tree of the myrrh family, originally from Peru and Brazil. Europeans first encountered and enjoyed the fruit when they arrived in Haiti, where the local name for it was *guayavu*; Spanish and Portuguese mariners soon spread the tree and its name to other regions. It apparently did not arrive in Hawaii until the early 1800s but now occurs throughout the Pacific Islands wild, as a home fruit tree, and in small commercial groves. This "apple of the tropics" is a prolific tree and grows freely, springing up from seeds dropped by birds. There are more than a hundred guava species, ranging in size from a tangerine to an orange. A relative of cinnamon and feijoa, these fruits are most memorable for their floral aroma, which fills tropical and subtropical markets when guavas are at their prime. The fruit has an outer and inner zone, the last with many small gritty seeds, but like citrus fruits there are seedless varieties. The strawberry or Cattley guava (*P. cattleianum*) originated in Brazil; it is round, about 1½ inches in diameter, and dark crimson, with soft, spicy, strawberry-flavored flesh and many hard inedible seeds.

Buying Tips
Guavas range in size from that of an apple to that of a plum; they may be round or pear-shaped, rough- or smooth-skinned, and greenish-white, yellow, or red in color. Large, pear-shaped, white ones are considered the best. The skin will give to gentle pressure when the fruit is ripe, and the whole fruit will have a pleasant floral scent. Since the flavor varies considerably from guava to guava, select one with the aroma most enticing to you. A guava with a rank, foul smell is immature and not worth purchasing. To finish ripening, wrap the fruit in a paper bag with a banana and leave out at room temperature until the guava is soft to the touch. Do not refrigerate until it is fully ripe, and then use within two days.

Culinary Uses
Inside this very aromatic fruit is a white, yellow, pink, or red flesh with a strangely exotic juicy flavor, acid yet sweet, along with a few sharp-edged seeds. Unripe guavas are astringent, but if picked when nearly ripe are soon ready to eat. Available fresh or canned, they are delicious in fruit

Guava / Nutritional Value Per 100 g Edible Portion			
	Raw		Raw
Calories	36-50	Zinc	0.230 mg
Protein	0.9-1.0 g	Copper	0.103 mg
Fat	0.1-0.5 g	Manganese	0.144 mg
Fiber	2.8-5.5 g	Beta Carotene (A)	200-792 IU
Calcium	9.1-17.0 mg	Thiamine (B$_1$)	0.046 mg
Iron	0.30-0.70 mg	Riboflavin (B$_2$)	0.03-0.04 mg
Magnesium	10-25 mg	Niacin (B$_3$)	0.6-1.068 mg
Phosphorus	17.8-30.0 mg	Pantothenic Acid (B$_5$)	0.150 mg
Potassium	284 mg	Pyridoxine (B$_6$)	0.143 mg
Sodium	3 mg	Ascorbic Acid (C)	100-500 mg

salads, ices, cool drinks, desserts, and cakes, and their sharp taste makes them useful for stewing and making custards, tarts, and preserves. To eat fresh guava, cut the fruit into quarters, remove the seeds and peel, and eat the flesh and pips. Canned guavas bear only a faint resemblance in flavor to the fresh fruit. Bars of thick, rich guava paste and guava cheese are staple sweets in some countries, and guava jelly is almost universally marketed.

Health Benefits
pH 3.70–4.00. The guava is beneficial for the skeletal and lymphatic systems. It is known for its astringent and laxative properties.

Huckleberry
(Gaylussacia baccata)
Also Known As: Bilberry, Whortleberry, Hurtleberry

The botanical name *Gaylussacia* was given in honor of Joseph L. Gay-Lussac, a French chemist and physicist; *baccata* means "berry-producing." The English name *huckleberry* is believed a corruption of *hurtleberry*.

General Information
Huckleberries, a member of the heath family, are believed to have been used for human consumption since prehistoric times, even perhaps twenty-five to thirty centuries before Christ; this plant is reputedly one of the oldest living plants on earth. A single plant found in western Pennsylvania covers several square miles and is estimated by botanists to be over thirteen thousand years old (older than the oldest California redwood); it is one of the last

LORE AND LEGEND

Because huckleberries grew wild everywhere in cold-weather climates, they readily became associated by the 1700s with anything rural, tranquil, untouched. From there it was hardly a stretch to transform the meaning in the 1800s to "simple," "small," or "insignificant." Mark Twain used the word *huckleberry* in that sense in *A Connecticut Yankee in King Arthur's Court*, referring to some sharpie as "no huckleberry." His Huckleberry Finn, of course, represented the simple joys of bucolic childhood.

surviving examples of the box huckleberry. Although the huckleberry resembles the blueberry and the two plants grow in the same regions, they are not actually related. The dark blue to black fruit of the true huckleberry is distinguished by the ten bony nutlets (or seeds), while the seeds of blueberries are so small as to be scarcely noticeable. The red "huckleberry" of the Pacific Coast is more likely the red whortleberry (*Vaccinium parvifolium*), related to both cranberries and blueberries. All huckleberries are edible, but some species are not very tasty. The garden huckleberry, which was developed by Luther Burbank, is closely related to the tomato.

Buying Tips
Look for bright, clean berries with good uniform color. Check the bottom of the container to make sure it has not been stained from mushy or moldy fruit.

Culinary Uses
This round, shiny fruit is sweet and pleasantly flavored but more "seedy" than blueberries. Huckleberries are most often used in the preparation of sweets, preserves, and confectionery (they make an excellent pie) and can be used interchangeably with blueberries in many recipes.

Health Benefits
pH 3.38–3.43 (cooked). Eating fresh huckleberries has been observed to regulate bowel action, stimulate appetite, end intestinal putrefaction, and expel ascarids. The fresh berries may require some individual experimentation,

since they tend to produce diarrhea in some people while stopping it in others. Huckleberries are especially helpful in aiding the pancreas in digesting sugars and starches; they have the advantage of passing through the stomach without affecting it, then beginning to work in the small intestine. The dried berries have been found to be valuable in cases of edema. They are low in fat and high in fiber, potassium, iron, phosphorus, sodium, calcium, vitamin B complex, and vitamin C.

Ilama

(Annona diversifolia)

Annona means "year's harvest" and is suggested by the Haitian name *anon*, which is applied to one of the species; *diversifolia* means "having leaves of two or more forms." The name *ilama* is derived, via Spanish, from the native Mexican name *illamatzapotl* (which translates as *zapote de las viejas*, or "old woman's sapote").

General Information

Native to Mexico, the ilama grows wild in foothills from the Southwest coast of Mexico to the Pacific coast of Guatemala and El Salvador. The earliest known record of the fruit was made in 1570 by Francisco Hernandez, who was sent by King Philip II of Spain to note any possible useful products of Mexico. For many years the tree was confused with either the soursop or the custard apple, and only in 1911 was it fully investigated and described by a W. E. Safford of the U.S. Department of Agriculture's Bureau of Plant Industry and given its current botanical name. Like other members of its family, the fruit is conical, heart-shaped, or ovoid, with a rough skin that may be anything from green to magenta-pink with a white bloom. Generally the fruits are studded with protuberances, although some may be quite smooth.

Culinary Uses

In green varieties, the flesh is white and sweet. Pink varieties usually have pink-tinged flesh near the rind and around the seeds and are somewhat tarter in flavor. The flesh of both is somewhat fibrous but smooth and custardy, with a quantity of hard, smooth, inedible seeds. Always consumed raw, the flesh is served either in the half shell or scooped out, chilled, and served with cream and sugar to intensify the flavor.

Jaboticaba

(Myrciaria cauliflora)

The genus name *Myrciaria* is probably related to *Myrtus*, the myrtle family. *Cauliflora* refers to the fact that the tree develops flowers (*flora*) directly on the stem (*caulis*). The word *jaboticaba* is said to have been derived from the Tupi term *jabotim*, for "turtle," and means "like turtle fat," presumably referring to the fruit pulp.

General Information

Native to and widely cultivated in the region of Rio de Janeiro, Brazil, this tree bears its fruits directly on its trunk, main limbs, and branches. The trees were introduced into California at Santa Barbara about 1904; a few were still living in 1912, but by 1939 all had died. Those introduced into Florida have done much better, and some still grow there today. The fruits are round and about one inch in diameter, bright green to maroon or purple in color, and not unlike a grape but with a thicker skin.

Culinary Uses

The white or pinkish pulp is translucent and has an overall subacid to sweet, grapelike flavor that is sometimes quite astringent and spicy. There may be one to five light brown

Ilama / Nutritional Value Per 100 g Edible Portion			
	Raw		Raw
Protein	0.447 g	Beta Carotene (A)	0.011 mg
Fat	0.16 g	Thiamine (B₁)	0.235 mg
Fiber	1.3 g	Riboflavin (B₂)	0.297 mg
Calcium	31.6 mg	Niacin (B₃)	2.177 mg
Iron	0.70 mg	Ascorbic Acid (C)	13.6 mg
Phosphorus	51.7 mg		

Jaboticaba / Nutritional Value Per 100 g Edible Portion			
	Raw		Raw
Calories	45.7	Phosphorus	9.2 mg
Protein	0.11 g	Thiamine (B₁)	0.020 mg
Fat	0.01 g	Riboflavin (B₂)	0.020 mg
Fiber	0.08 g	Niacin (B₃)	0.210 mg
Calcium	6.3 mg	Ascorbic Acid (C)	22.7-30.7 mg
Iron	0.49 mg		

seeds, which cling tenaciously to the pulp. The fruit is generally eaten fresh, without the skin and seeds. By squeezing the fruit between the thumb and forefinger, one can cause the skin to split and the pulp to slip into the mouth. Children in Brazil spend hours searching out and devouring the ripe fruit and eating the seeds with the pulp, but properly the seeds should be discarded. Jaboticabas are often used for making jelly and marmalade, with the addition of pectin (and the removal of the skins from at least half the fruit to avoid a strong tannin flavor). Once harvested, the fruit ferments quickly at ordinary temperatures, but if refrigerated will last for up to two weeks.

Health Benefits

Regular quantities of the skins should not be consumed because of their high tannin content.

Jackfruit

(Artocarpus heterophyllus)

Artocarpus comes from the Greek words *artos*, meaning "bread," and *carpos*, meaning "fruit"; *heterophyllus* means "having leaves of more than one form." The English name *jack* was given to this fruit by the Portuguese in the sixteenth century since it sounded like *tsjaka*, the Malayan name for the plant.

General Information

This tropical evergreen tree is believed to be indigenous to the rainforests of India and the Malayan Peninsula. The fruits grow sporadically on the tree trunk and large branches, a somewhat unusual habit called "cauliflory," which also occurs on the cacao and jaboticaba trees. Under normal conditions, a single tree may bear 150 to 250 huge fruits per year. Among the largest fruits of any tropical plant, the elongated green jackfruits, with their fissured hexagonal patterning and large spikes, frequently measure up to three feet long and eighteen inches wide; they weigh forty to fifty pounds, with some weighing in at over a hundred pounds. Like the pineapple, the jackfruit is a composite fruit, but not nearly so tidy, since the sections are clustered in irregular clumps. The interior is complex, consisting of large bulbs of yellow flesh enclosing a smooth oval seed, massed among narrow ribbons of tougher tissue and surrounding a central pithy core.

Buying Tips

There are two main jackfruit varieties: one with soft flesh and sweet juicy pulp, and a crisp variety that is less juicy and sweet. Purchase a fruit that is without bruises or soft spots. The jackfruit is ripe when its skin is stretched out, the spikes stand clear of each other, and it starts to give off an aroma. Very fragrant jackfruit are overly ripe. Because of its size, jackfruit is often sold precut.

Culinary Uses

The smell of a ripe fruit before it is opened is disagreeable to most (resembling decayed onions), but the thick, sweet, firm interior flesh has a sweet aroma and flavor reminiscent of pineapple and banana. Most often eaten fresh, the golden pulp may also be cooked with coconuts and spices, mixed in curries as a vegetable, included in fruit salads, boiled and dried for storage, or preserved in syrups. Westerners generally find the jackfruit most acceptable in the full-grown but unripe stage, at which time it is simply cut into chunks for cooking, boiled in lightly salted water until tender, and the flesh cut from the rind and served as a vegetable. There may be up to five hundred large, starchy, kidney-shaped, edible seeds of medium size contained with the flesh. The raw seeds or "nuts" are indigestible because of a powerful trypsin inhibitor, but this is removed by boiling or roasting, after which the seeds taste much like European chestnuts. Once cooked, the seeds can be added to soups, stewed with meat, or made into a starchy flour. Store a whole, immature jackfruit at room temperature for three to ten days. Refrigerate when ripe.

Health Benefits

The Chinese consider jackfruit pulp and seeds to be tonic, cooling, nutritious, and useful in overcoming the influence of alcohol on the system. The ripe fruit is somewhat laxative, and if eaten in excess will cause diarrhea.

Jackfruit / Nutritional Value Per 100 g Edible Portion			
	Raw		Raw
Calories	98	Sodium	2 mg
Protein	1.3–1.9 g	Zinc	0.42 mg
Fat	0.1–0.3 g	Copper	0.187 mg
Fiber	1.0–1.1 g	Manganese	0.197 mg
Calcium	22–34 mg	Beta Carotene (A)	297–540 IU
Iron	0.5 mg	Thiamine (B₁)	0.030 mg
Magnesium	37 mg	Niacin (B₃)	0.400 mg
Phosphorus	38 mg	Pyridoxine (B₆)	0.108 mg
Potassium	407 mg	Ascorbic Acid (C)	8–10 mg

Jambolan

(Syzygium cumini)
Also Known As: Java Plum, Black Plum

Syzygium derives from the Greek word meaning "united" and refers to the calyptrate petals. The name *cumini* is of Semitic origin but unknown meaning.

General Information

The jambolan is native to India, Burma, Ceylon, and the Andaman Islands. By 1870 it had become established in Hawaii and occurs in a semi-wild state on all the Hawaiian Islands. In southern Florida the tree was once commonly planted and still fruits heavily, but only a small amount of the crop is utilized. The fruit, which grows in clusters, is round or oblong and a half to two inches long. Starting green, it ripens to light magenta, then dark purple or nearly black.

Culinary Uses

This fruit's juicy flesh is either white or purple, depending on the variety, and encloses at least one seed. The white-fleshed kind is generally sweeter than the purple, but the taste of both is always astringent. Jambolans of good size and quality are eaten raw or may be made into tarts, sauces, and jam. Less desirable fruit can be generously rubbed with salt before eating or used as a good basis for cool drinks. All but decidedly inferior fruits have been utilized for their juice, which is much like grape juice. Jambolan vinegar, made throughout India, is an attractive clear purple, with a pleasant aroma and mild flavor.

Health Benefits

The fruit is stated to be astringent, stomachic, carminative, antiscorbutic, and diuretic. Cooked to a thick jam, it is

LORE AND LEGEND

In southern Asia the tree is venerated by Buddhists, and it is commonly planted near Hindu temples because it is considered sacred to Krishna. The leaves and fruits are employed in worshiping the elephant-headed god, Ganesha or Vinaijaka.

eaten to allay acute diarrhea. Juice from ripe fruits or jambolan vinegar may be administered in India in cases of enlargement of the spleen, chronic diarrhea, and urine retention. Diluted juice is used as a gargle for sore throats and as a lotion for ringworm of the scalp. The seeds contain an alkaloid, jambosine, and a glycoside, jambolin or antimellin, which halts the diastatic conversion of starch into sugar. The leaves, stems, flower buds, opened blossoms, and bark have some antibiotic properties.

Jujube

(Zizyphus jujuba, Z. mauritiana)
Also Known As: Chinese Jujube, Chinese Date

Zizyphus derives from *zizouf*, the Arabian name. *Mauritiana* means "coming from the Mauritius Island" in the Indian Ocean. The English name *jujube* is a convoluted derivation of the Latin name.

General Information

The Chinese jujube (*Z. jujuba*) is the fruit of a small spiny tree that originated in China and grows in mild-temperate, dry, and subtropical regions of both hemispheres. In China, this fruit has been grown and eaten for more than four thousand years, and even now China has more jujube trees than any other type of fruit tree (persimmons are second). The Roman scholar Pliny recorded that jujubes were brought to Rome from Syria sometime near the end of Augustus's reign, and from there they spread throughout southern Europe and northern Africa. The tree reached America in 1837 and aroused some interest among horticulturists as an ornamental, but the fruit itself never caught on. Ranging in size from that of a cherry to that of a plum, the jujube is oblong or spherical in form, with a thin, reddish-brown skin and a whitish flesh of mealy texture and sweet flavor. The Indian jujube (*Z. mauritiana*) is native from

Jambolan / Nutritional Value Per 100 g Edible Portion			
	Raw		**Raw**
Calories	60	Sodium	14.0-26.2 mg
Protein	0.70-1.29 g	Copper	0.230 mg
Fat	0.15-0.30 g	Beta Carotene (A)	10-80 IU
Fiber	0.3-0.9 g	Thiamine (B$_1$)	0.008-0.030 mg
Calcium	8.3-15.0 mg	Riboflavin (B$_2$)	0.009-0.010 mg
Iron	1.20-1.62 mg	Niacin (B$_3$)	0.200-0.290 mg
Magnesium	15-35 mg	Pyridoxine (B$_6$)	0.038 mg
Phosphorus	15.0-16.2 mg	Folic Acid (B$_9$)	3 mcg
Potassium	55-79 mg	Ascorbic Acid (C)	5.7-18.0 mg

the province of Yunnan in southern China to Afghanistan, Malaysia, and Queensland, Australia. It is cultivated to some extent throughout its natural range but mostly in India, where it is grown commercially; its flavor is generally considered less desirable than that of the Chinese jujube.

Culinary Uses

Slightly underripe fruits have flesh that is juicy, acid or subacid to sweet, and somewhat astringent, much like that of a crab apple. When just ripe, the fruit is mahogany-colored and as shiny and smooth as if buffed with a cloth. At this stage, the flesh is crisp and sweet, reminiscent of an apple. If left to ripen a bit longer, the skin begins to wrinkle as the fruit loses water, and the flesh changes from light green to beige and becomes soft, musky, more datelike. In China jujubes are eaten fresh, dried, smoked, pickled, candied, and puréed as a butter. In candied form they are even more reminiscent of dates, with their long pointed (inedible) seeds and caramel-like texture. The fruit can also be boiled with rice or baked with breads, much like raisins.

LORE AND LEGEND

When the Greek hero Ulysses reached the Land of the Lotus Eaters (now identified with the Tunisian island of Djerba), Homer tells us that his companions abandoned themselves to the local diet, forgetting home and families and desiring nothing except to remain in the country of the lotus, in perpetual idleness, forever. The Lotophagoi, according to ancient writers, lived on the lotus exclusively and also made an intoxicating drink from it. The lotus of Homer was most likely not the lotus of Buddha or of the Nile, but the Chinese date or jujube.

Jujube / Nutritional Value Per 100 g Edible Portion	Chinese Raw	Chinese Dried	Indian Raw	Indian Dried
Calories	79-105	287	n/a	473/lb
Protein	1.20 g	3.70 g	0.80 g	1.44 g
Fat	0.20 g	1.10 g	0.07 g	0.21 g
Fiber	1.40 g	3.00 g	0.60 g	1.28 g
Calcium	21.0 mg	79.0 mg	25.6 mg	n/a
Iron	0.48 mg	1.80 mg	0.76-1.80 mg	n/a
Magnesium	10 mg	37 mg	n/a	n/a
Phosphorus	23.0 mg	100.0 mg	26.8 mg	n/a
Potassium	250 mg	531 mg	n/a	n/a
Sodium	3 mg	9 mg	n/a	n/a
Zinc	0.050 mg	0.190 mg	n/a	n/a
Copper	0.073 mg	0.265 mg	n/a	n/a
Manganese	0.084 mg	0.305 mg	n/a	n/a
Beta Carotene (A)	40 IU	n/a	0.021 mg	n/a
Thiamine (B$_1$)	0.020 mg	0.210 mg	0.020-0.024 mg	n/a
Riboflavin (B$_2$)	0.040 mg	0.360 mg	0.020-0.038 mg	n/a
Niacin (B$_3$)	0.900 mg	0.500 mg	0.700-0.873 mg	n/a
Pyridoxine (B$_6$)	0.081 mg	n/a	n/a	n/a
Ascorbic Acid (C)	69.0 mg	13.0 mg	65.8-76.0 mg	n/a

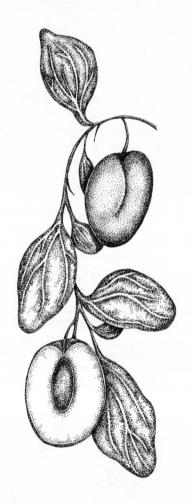

Health Benefits
The jujube has a high concentration of sugar—about 22 percent. Dried ripe fruit is a mild laxative, while fresh fruits are applied to cuts and ulcers or, when mixed with salt and chili peppers, are given for indigestion and biliousness.

Juneberry
(Amelanchier alnifolia, A. canadensis, A. laevis, A. oreophila, A. spicata)
Also Known As: Serviceberry, Shadbush

> *Amelanchier* is from *amelancier*, the French Provençal name of *A. ovalis* and *A. vulgaris*. *Alnifolia* refers to the fact that the leaves are similar to alder (*Alnus*) leaves. *Canadensis* refers to a Canadian origin; *laevis* means "smooth, free from hairs or roughness"; *oreophila* means "mountain-loving"; spicata means "having spikes." The English name *juneberry* refers to the berries' season of ripening. The plant received its alternate name *serviceberry* because of its resemblance to the service tree, an ignored English fruit (*Sorbus domestica*); the name *shadbush* refers to the fact that the bush blossoms just when the shad appear in the rivers.

General Information
There are at least twenty-four different species of juneberry, and the plant grows wild throughout every province of Canada and every state in the continental United States. The American Indians pounded the berries with the meat and fat of game animals to make pemmican, and the berries were a staple of early white settlers on the northern plains. The various species include scrubby plants that hug the ground, trees fifty feet tall, and all sizes of trees and shrubs in between. Not a true berry botanically, the juneberry is a pome fruit akin to the apple and pear. Large quantities of the dark blue or purplish-black berries develop each summer, blueberry-sized or larger.

Culinary Uses
The round fruit has a sweet and pleasant odor and an equally sweet flavor. The berries are delicious any way you want to serve them. Dry them for the winter, cook them into sauces, or make them into jams, jellies, pies, puddings, muffins, even wine. The few small seeds are edible and impart a slight almond taste.

Kiwano
(Cucumis metuliferus)
Also Known As: Horned Melon, Horned Cucumber, Jelly Melon

> *Cucumis* is the old Latin name for the cucumber family. Its alternate name of *horned melon* gives a good description of its appearance.

General Information
This emigrant from Africa definitely wins prizes for its strange appearance. A brilliant golden-orange oval about five inches long, it has small protuberances all over its skin. Its appearance is at once startling and droll, like a comic-book creature from either the deep sea or outer space. It is the size of a fist, with a bland, unremarkable flavor vaguely reminiscent of bananas and cucumbers. Select a bright yellow or orange kiwano with firm spikes and firm, undamaged skin. Do not purchase one with dull-colored skin. Today, kiwanos are grown in New Zealand and California and are available year-round in specialty sections of supermarkets.

Culinary Uses and Health Benefits
The rich green flesh, gelatinous and juicy, holds lots of white seeds like those of other melons. Its flavor is very subtle—many would say bland. The most spectacular use of a kiwano is to halve it, scoop out its flesh, and use its shells to hold individual servings of fruit soup or salad. When sweetened, its juice makes a tasty summer beverage. Its main health benefit is that it is a cooling fruit that helps relieve thirst. The kiwano keeps at room temperature for up to six months.

Kiwi
(Actinidia chinensis)
Also Known As: Chinese Gooseberry

> Someone once threw me a small, brown, hairy kiwi fruit, and I threw a wastebasket over it until it was dead.
>
> —Erma Bombeck

The genus name *Actinidia* comes from the Greek *aktin*, meaning "ray " or "motion" and referring to the lighter colored rays in the crosswise-sliced fruit. The term *chinensis* denotes its Chinese origin. In 1962 New Zealand growers began calling this strange little fruit "kiwi fruit" to give it more market appeal, and this name has become widely accepted. The term was commercially adopted as the trade name in 1974. The name *Chinese gooseberry* results from the fruit's flavor and flesh color, which resembles that of the gooseberry. The translation of the French term for the kiwi (*souris vegetales*) is "vegetable mouse," which is more descriptive than any of its other names but might make some squeamish.

General Information

The kiwi plant, a vigorous climber, is native to the Yangtze valley in northern China and the Zhejiang province in eastern China, but the Chinese have never been overly fond of the fruit, regarding it primarily as a tonic for growing children and for women after childbirth. Kiwi fruits start out with rough green skins, which turn brown and fuzzy when ripe. E. H. ("Chinese") Wilson, the well-known plant explorer, shipped the first seed lots from Asia to England, France, and the United States around 1900. Most introductions emphasized the ornamental qualities of the vines; not so in New Zealand, where the fruits were recognized for their commercial potential. From a single seed lot planted in 1906, the "Chinese gooseberry" quickly flourished. Years later, with increasing foreign demand and anticommunist sentiments running high, enterprising New Zealanders renamed the fruit after their national treasure, the kiwi bird. An appropriate choice, since these brown, fuzzy, egg-shaped fruits are as strange looking as their namesake bird.

Buying Tips

When buying kiwis, look for undamaged fruit that yields evenly to gentle pressure, much like a not-quite-tender nectarine. Those that are still overly firm will soften and sweeten in a week at room temperature. If the fruit is refrigerated (and humidity maintained at 95 percent in a small plastic bag with a few holes), it will keep for nine months.

Culinary Uses

Kiwi fruit has a sparkling emerald-green interior flesh with a distinct bright center starburst and a cluster of very small dark purple or black edible seeds. Reminding some people of a cross between strawberries and bananas, the flesh is tart-sweet and slightly crisp-textured. Their hairy skin is inedible and must be removed before eating. Kiwis can be eaten on their own, sliced and added to salads, desserts, cakes, and jams, or used as an attractive garnish. Like pineapple and papaya, kiwi contains an enzyme that tenderizes meat. It also curdles milk (but not heavy cream) and interferes with the action of gelatin. If you want to add kiwi fruit to gelatin, you should first briefly cook the fruit, which deactivates the actinidin enzyme. Similarly, it must be cooked before it is added to foods containing dairy products such as ice cream or yogurt, to which it would otherwise impart an off-flavor.

Health Benefits

pH 3.2–4.1. Kiwi fruit helps remove excess sodium buildup in the body and contains enzymes similar to those in papaya and pineapple that help in correcting digestive problems.

Kumquat
(Fortunella margarita)

This fruit was named in honor of Robert Fortune, an English traveler and collector of plants for the Royal Horticultural Society in London, who introduced the kumquat into Europe in 1846. *Margarita* means "pearl," probably for the fruit's small size. The English name *kumquat* comes from the Chinese *kam kwat*, which means "golden orange," a fitting description of this brilliant fruit.

General Information

Said to be a native of Southeast China, this diminutive citruslike fruit is not a true citrus but is closely related; its pollen pollinates citrus blossoms and vice versa, creating crosses, such as limequats, lemonquats, and others. It was included in the *Citrus* genus until about 1915, when Dr. Walter Swingle set it apart in the genus *Fortunella*. Kumquat

Kiwi / Nutritional Value Per 100 g Edible Portion			
	Raw		Raw
Calories	66	Potassium	332 mg
Protein	0.79 g	Sodium	5 mg
Fat	0.07-0.44 g	Beta Carotene (A)	175 IU
Fiber	1.10 g	Thiamine (B₁)	0.02 mg
Calcium	16-26 mg	Riboflavin (B₂)	0.05 mg
Iron	0.51 mg	Niacin (B₃)	0.50 mg
Magnesium	30 mg	Ascorbic Acid (C)	75-105 mg
Phosphorus	40-64 mg		

trees were known to exist at least by the seventeenth century, when their name entered the English language in the form of "cam-quit," but the fruit was not introduced into Europe until 1846. In Western countries, kumquat plants used to be placed on the table at fashionable dinners so that guests could pick the small tasty fruit at will. Kumquat fruits are small (one to two inches in length), oblong or roundish, bright orange in color, and with the same kind of peel texture as that of citrus fruits.

Buying Tips

Check to make sure the kumquats are plump, golden, and firm, not soft-wet; if they come with foliage, you can gauge their freshness by the leaves. Because of their thin skins, they keep less well than oranges and other citrus fruits. Left at room temperature they will mold, so refrigerate (do not wrap in plastic) and use within two weeks.

Culinary Uses

Kumquats have an aromatic, sweet, but slightly bitter skin and a tartly sour and spicy interior flecked with little green seeds. The most popular way of treating kumquats in China has been to preserve them in honey. In the West, they are generally eaten whole, rind and all; they should be squeezed first to break and blend the juicy pulp. They can also be simmered in sugar, brandied, pickled, preserved, made into a sauce, or used whole as companions to fowl. They make a beautiful garnish, especially with dark chocolate desserts. Canned kumquats are exported from Taiwan and frequently served as dessert in Chinese restaurants. Limequats, a pale yellow Mexican lime-kumquat hybrid produced by Dr. Swingle in 1909, are a useful lime substitute that are eaten whole like the kumquat, either with or without the pit.

Kumquat / Nutritional Value Per 100 g Edible Portion			
	Raw		Raw
Calories	274	Potassium	995 mg
Protein	3.8 g	Zinc	0.080 mg
Fat	0.4 g	Copper	0.107 mg
Fiber	3.7 g	Manganese	0.086 mg
Sodium	30 mg	Beta Carotene (A)	2,530 IU
Calcium	266 mg	Thiamine (B$_1$)	0.350 mg
Iron	1.7 mg	Riboflavin (B$_2$)	0.400 mg
Magnesium	13 mg	Ascorbic Acid (C)	151 mg
Phosphorus	97 mg		

Lemon
(Citrus limon)

Anytime the perfume of orange and lemon groves wafts in the window, the human body has to feel suffused with a languorous well-being.

—FRANCES MAYES, *Bella Tuscany*

Huge lemons, cut in slices, would sink like setting suns into the dusky sea, softly illuminating it with their radiating membranes, and its clear, smooth surface aquiver from the rising bitter essence.

—RAINER MARIA RILKE (1875–1926)

The term *Citrus* derives from the Greek term for the citron, *kedromelon*. The species name *limon* is derived from the Arabic *laymun*, which also provided the English name.

General Information

The lemon tree is native to the tropical regions of northern India. The fruit is a bright yellow ovoid berry, about three inches long, smooth, and nipple-shaped at the end, with an acid, pale yellow pulp. Lemons were being cultivated in Greece and Rome in the fourth century A.D., but were always rare and expensive. It is the Moors who are credited with establishing the lemon orchards of Andalusia and introducing the fruit into Sicily. Northern Europe most likely did not receive lemons until between A.D. 1000 and 1200, when the Crusaders were returning from the Near East. Columbus introduced the lemon into the Western Hemisphere when he stopped at one of the Canary Islands in October of 1493 and gathered seeds of citrus fruits as well as other plants. Once the lemon reached the New World, it spread rapidly. Lemons were planted in St. Augustine, Florida, in 1565, when the Spanish settled there. Two centuries later, seeds were taken to California by the Franciscan fathers when they moved from Mexico. Since 1950, California has produced more lemons than all of Europe combined. A single tree has been known to produce three thousand lemons a year, because lemon trees will bloom and ripen fruit in every month of the year. Commercial lemons are not permitted to grow until fully ripe, for they lose their desirable acidulous properties when allowed to mature and sometimes grow to enormous sizes. The main varieties of lemon sold in the United States are Eureka and Lisbon. The small, sweet, thin-skinned Meyer is rarely shipped to markets.

Buying Tips

When purchased, lemons should be semi-soft with a bright golden yellow color. Those tinged with green have not been properly "cured" and will be more acidic. Thick-skinned lemons will have less juice than thinner-skinned varieties.

Culinary Uses

Lemons have long been considered the most versatile of the citrus family, except that the tart pulp is too sour for most people to eat raw. An important acidifying and flavoring agent, the lemon has a primary role in the taste of many dishes. It is a common accompaniment to fish and meat, as well as iced and hot tea. Lemon zest and/or juice will add a wonderful tang to soups, desserts, cakes, jams,

and pickles; the juice can substitute perfectly for vinegar and is not irritating to the stomach lining; and slices of lemon make pretty garnishes for a wide range of sweet and savory dishes. One of the most common uses of lemons is for lemonade. The ascorbic acid in lemon juice will also prevent fruits like avocados and apples from oxidizing or turning brown when exposed to air after being cut. Another good use for lemon juice is to bleach linen or muslin: just moisten the cloth in lemon juice and then spread to dry in the sun. As well, the juice removes ink stains, iron rust, and fruit stains from fabrics. Rub the stain well with lemon juice, cover with salt, and put in the sun; repeat if necessary.

Health Benefits

pH 2.00–2.60. Astringent, antiseptic, refrigerant. Lemon juice has long been heralded as a tonic throughout the world; it is used as a gargle for sore throats, a lotion for sunburn, a cure for hiccups, and a popular home remedy for numerous ailments, particularly colds, coughs, and sore throats. Hot lemonade is noted as a diaphoretic, increasing perspiration and the production of fluids in the body, and thus is good to take prior to going to bed with a cold. Lemon is a loosening and cleansing agent. Its potassium strengthens and energizes the heart, its oxygen builds vitality, its hydrogen activates the sensory nervous system, its calcium strengthens and builds the lungs, its phosphorus knits the bones, its sodium encourages tissue building, its magnesium acts as a blood alkalizer, its iron builds the red corpuscles, and its silicon aids the thyroid for deeper breathing. Lemons, along with the rest of the citrus family, work as strong solvents in the body, stimulating the liver and gallbladder, and stirring up any inactive acids and latent toxic settlements that cannot be eliminated any other way. They contain a substance known as limonene, which is used to dissolve gallstones and which shows extreme promise as an anticancer agent. The highest content of limonene is found in the white spongy inner parts of the fruit. Lemons are wonderful for fevers, because a feverish body responds to citric acid fruits better than to any other food. Although acidic to the taste, citrus fruits have a strong alkaline reaction on the body (their alkaline content is five times greater than their acidic content), provided that no sugar is added. They destroy putrefactive bacteria in both the intestines and mouth, and they alleviate flatulence and indigestion in general. Lemons are an outstanding source of vitamin C, but much of this valuable

Lemon / Nutritional Value Per 100 g Edible Portion				
	Raw Fruit w/o Peel	Fresh Juice	Unsweetened Processed Juice	Undiluted Frozen Lemonade
Calories	29	25	23	195
Protein	1.10 g	0.38 g	0.40 g	0.20 g
Fat	0.3 g	0 g	0.1 g	0.1 g
Fiber	0.4 g	trace	trace	0.1 g
Sodium	2.0 mg	1.0 mg	1.0 mg	0.2 mg
Calcium	26 mg	7 mg	7 mg	4 mg
Iron	0.60 mg	0.03 mg	0.20 mg	0.20 mg
Magnesium	n/a	6 mg	n/a	n/a
Phosphorus	16 mg	6 mg	10 mg	6 mg
Potassium	138 mg	124 mg	141 mg	70 mg
Zinc	0.060 mg	0.050 mg	n/a	n/a
Copper	0.037 mg	0.029 mg	n/a	n/a
Manganese	n/a	0.008 mg	n/a	n/a
Beta Carotene (A)	29 IU	20 IU	20 IU	20 IU
Thiamine (B$_1$)	0.040 mg	0.030 mg	0.030 mg	0.020 mg
Riboflavin (B$_2$)	0.020 mg	0.010 mg	0.010 mg	0.030 mg
Niacin (B$_3$)	0.100 mg	0.100 mg	0.100 mg	0.300 mg
Pantothenic Acid (B$_5$)	0.190 mg	0.103 mg	n/a	n/a
Pyridoxine (B$_6$)	0.080 mg	0.051 mg	n/a	n/a
Folic Acid (B$_9$)	10.6 mcg	12.9 mcg	n/a	n/a
Ascorbic Acid (C)	53 mg	46 mg	42 mg	30 mg

LORE AND LEGEND

In the third century A.D. the Romans believed that lemons were an antidote for all poisons, as illustrated by the tale of two criminals thrown to venomous snakes; the one who had eaten a lemon beforehand survived snakebite, while the other died. So great was the lemon's reputation that it became an accompaniment for fish meals in the belief that if a fishbone got stuck in the throat, the lemon juice would dissolve it. In Ceylon there is a story that all the ogres dwelling in Ceylon live in a single lemon and if one can but find that lemon and cut it into pieces, they will all perish. The British navy used lemon and lime juice extensively to combat the scurvy plaguing their seamen (see also **Limes**). During the California Gold Rush, scurvy was so rampant and fresh produce so scarce that miners were willing to pay a dollar apiece for lemons. The world's largest lemon weighed in at a whopping five pounds, thirteen ounces and was grown by Violet Philips of Queensland, Australia, in 1975.

Lime / Nutritional Value Per 100 g Edible Portion		
	Raw Fruit	Fresh Juice
Calories	30	27
Protein	0.070-0.112 g	0.440 g
Fat	0.04-0.17 g	0.10 g
Fiber	0.1-0.5 g	trace
Calcium	4.5-33.3 mg	9.0 mg
Iron	0.19-0.33 mg	0.03 mg
Magnesium	n/a	6 mg
Phosphorus	9.3-21.0 mg	7.0 mg
Potassium	102 mg	109 mg
Sodium	2 mg	1 mg
Zinc	0.110 mg	0.060 mg
Copper	0.065 mg	0.030 mg
Manganese	n/a	0.008 mg
Beta Carotene (A)	10 IU	10 IU
Thiamine (B$_1$)	0.019-0.068 mg	0.020 mg
Riboflavin (B$_2$)	0.011-0.023 mg	0.010 mg
Niacin (B$_3$)	0.140-0.250 mg	0.100 mg
Pantothenic Acid (B$_5$)	0.217 mg	0.138 mg
Pyridoxine (B$_6$)	n/a	0.043 mg
Folic Acid (B$_9$)	8.2 mcg	n/a
Ascorbic Acid (C)	30.0-48.7 mg	29.3 mg

vitamin is lost if the juice is left exposed to air or stored for very long. Externally, lemon juice can be used on sunburn, warts, and corns, and is currently enjoying a revival of interest as a hair rinse and facial astringent. It is a strong natural antiseptic; the juice destroys harmful bacteria found in cuts and other areas of infection. For skin problems, lemon juice can be applied directly to the skin and allowed to dry. Fresh lemon or lemon juice applied to the inflammation of poison ivy will bring immediate relief (an orange also works well).

Lime
(Citrus hystrix, C. aurantifolius, C. latifolia)

The term *Citrus* derives from the Greek term for the citron, *kedromelon*. *Hystrix* means "porcupine-like"; *aurantifolia* means "golden-leaved"; *latifolia* means "broad-leaved." The English name *lime* is derived from the Arabic *lim*.

General Information

Of the two sour varieties of lime, the Mexican lime, also known as the West Indian or Key lime, is the variety longest known and most widely cultivated, often referred to simply as "lime." The Mexican lime is native to the Indo-Malayan region, and the tree has been cultivated for thousands of years both for its fruit and for its decorative foliage. It is assumed to have been carried to North Africa and the Near East by Arabs and taken by Crusaders from Palestine to Mediterranean Europe. It was taken by Columbus to Hispaniola (now Haiti), and Spanish settlers soon established it in Florida. There it acquired its modern name *Key lime* from the southerly chain of islands. They became a commercial crop in the Keys after 1906, when the combination of a severe hurricane and soil depletion forced the locals to abandon pineapple culture. Production peaked in 1923, but the hurricane of 1926 dealt a death blow to the Florida lime groves, and they were never restored. During the 1950s an education campaign was introduced in the Florida Keys to arouse interest in the lime so that its cultivation would not disappear, but today there are no regular commercial sources of Key limes in the Florida Keys. Most

LORE AND LEGEND

Sir James Lind, the Scottish naval surgeon, observed the dramatic effect of eating oranges and lemons on sailors during long voyages. At the end of the eighteenth century it was accepted, by the British navy at least, that the juice of citrus fruits was the only medicine that could conquer the scurvy (caused by lack of vitamin C) that was killing more seamen than enemy action. The Admiralty stood by this decision to the tune of 1.6 million gallons of lemon or lime juice in the period between 1795 and 1815. The mortality rate during this period showed a gratifyingly steep decline. British sailors acquired the nickname *limeys* from their daily ration of lime juice, which they drank along with their ration of rum. Limes could be imported cheaply and without risk from the English colony Jamaica, while lemons had to be bought from Mediterranean countries with whom Britain was often at war.

now come from Mexico. All limes are harvested before they ripen. If left to mature on the tree, they lose their acidity, become sweet, and turn yellowish.

The origin of the Tahiti lime (or Persian lime) is unknown, but it is presumed to be a hybrid of the Mexican lime and the citron or, less likely, the lemon. It is believed that the tree was introduced into the Mediterranean region by way of Iran (formerly Persia); Portuguese traders later carried it to Brazil, and it didn't reach California until between 1850 and 1880. Today Florida produces 90 percent of the national crop for making fresh juice and for canned or frozen juice and concentrate. The Tahiti lime is bigger and lends itself more easily to large-scale agriculture than the Key lime because it keeps better, has no thorns, and grows a thick skin that withstands handling and long shipping. The fruit is very similar in size and coloring to the lemon, being oval or oblong, occasionally ribbed, or with a short neck, and between 1½ and 2½ inches wide and two to three inches long. The peel is vivid green until ripe, at which time it turns a pale yellow.

The Kaffir lime (*Citrus hystrix*) is knobby and bitter but highly aromatic. The plant received its name *hystrix*, which means "porcupine" in Greek, because of its many thorns. The wrinkled, rough, yellow fruit is sometimes used for its acid juice, but the leaves and rind are a more common ingredient and appear frequently in Southeast Asian dishes. When gently rubbed, the richly perfumed leaves release a luscious citrus scent. Kaffir lime leaves are often added to Thai soups, stir-fries, and curries, along with garlic, galangal, ginger, chilies, and fresh Thai basil. Although lime or lemon peel is the nearest approximation, Kaffir lime's strong perfume cannot easily be duplicated. The rind, powdered or grated, is available in Asian markets. Because dried Kaffir lime leaves lose their flavor readily, they are best kept frozen.

Buying Tips

Look for firm fruits with a good weight for their size. Avoid any that look shriveled or soft, as well as those that have decayed spots or skin punctures.

Culinary Uses

The small Mexican limes are nearly spherical and thin-skinned and usually contain several seeds. The green fruits are actually the immature fruits; these are the most desirable commercially because of their extreme acidity. The fully ripe, yellow lime does not have as high an acid content as the immature fruit and may be prepared and used like a lemon, although the lime will be slightly sweeter. Because of its special bouquet and unique flavor, the Mexican lime is ideal for serving as a garnish and flavoring for fish and meats, for adding zest to cold drinks, and for making limeade. The juice is made into syrups, sauces, preserves, and pies similar to lemon pie. Key lime pie is internationally famous but today is largely made from the frozen concentrate of the Tahiti lime. The Tahiti lime usually has a seedless, light greenish-yellow pulp that is tender and acid, but without the distinctive bouquet of the Mexican lime. Its flesh may be used in the same ways as the Mexican lime—as a flavoring, an alternative to vinegar, and for limeade. Other uses for lime juice include cleaning the interiors of coffeepots or dissolving calcium deposits in teakettles.

Health Benefits

pH 2.00–2.80. Astringent, antiseptic, refrigerant. Limes have all the same benefits to the body as do lemons. Lime juice has been applied to relieve the effects of stinging corals with good results. Limes also contain furocoumarins, which make the skin less sensitive to light and help to prevent severe sunburn—but don't use limes as a substitute for sunscreen.

Lingonberry
(Vaccinium vitis idaea)

Vaccinium is the ancient Latin name for plants of the blueberry family, derived from *vacca*, meaning "cow," and given because cows like the plant. *Vitis* means "vine" or "branch"; *idaea* refers to either Mount Ida in Turkey or Mount Ida in Crete. The English name *lingonberry* derives from the Swedish *lingon*, meaning "mountain cranberry."

General Information
This plant bears oval red berries similar to cranberries, with a piquant flavor. The lingonberry is greatly esteemed in the Nordic countries; in Finland it is the most popular berry because of its pleasant flavor and good keeping quality.

Culinary Uses
Crushed with sugar or made into a sauce, it is often served with meat; roast veal with cream sauce and lingonberry jam is one of the classic dishes of Finland.

Loganberry
(Rubus ursinus loganobaccus)

Rubus refers to the redness of the berry, while *ursinus* means "pertaining to bears," and *loganobaccus* melds the name of Judge Logan, in whose garden they originated, with that of the Greek god Bacchus, the god of agriculture and wine.

General Information
Loganberries originated in the Santa Cruz, California, garden of Judge James H. Logan. A natural hybrid of raspberries and dewberries, loganberries are dark red, more acidic, and very long in comparison to either blackberries or raspberries. Grown mostly for wine making, as they are generally considered too acidic to eat raw, they have a sharp flavor and can be eaten in the same ways as blackberries and raspberries. One offspring of the loganberry is the olallieberry, a bright black, firm, sweet berry

Loganberry / Nutritional Value Per 100 g Edible Portion			
	Raw		Raw
Calories	55	Copper	0.117 mg
Protein	1.52 g	Manganese	1.247 mg
Fat	0.31 g	Beta Carotene (A)	35 IU
Fiber	3.0 g	Thiamine (B$_1$)	0.050 mg
Calcium	26 mg	Riboflavin (B$_2$)	0.034 mg
Iron	0.64 mg	Niacin (B$_3$)	0.840 mg
Magnesium	21 mg	Pantothenic Acid (B$_5$)	0.244 mg
Phosphorus	26 mg	Pyridoxine (B$_6$)	0.065 mg
Potassium	145 mg	Folic Acid (B$_9$)	25.7 mcg
Sodium	1 mg	Ascorbic Acid (C)	15.3 mg
Zinc	0.340 mg		

that was the result of a cross between the loganberry and youngberry.

Culinary Uses and Health Benefits
pH 2.70–3.50. Same as blackberries.

Longan
(Dimocarpus longan)
Also Known As: Dragon's Eyes

The genus name *Dimocarpus* is believed to derive from the Greek words *di* (two), *morph* (form), and *carpos* (fruit), thus meaning "a two-formed fruit." The species and English name *longan* is derived from the Chinese *bung yen* or *long yan*, which literally means "dragon's eye."

General Information
Native to southern China and southeast Asia, the longan fruit ripens later than its relative the lychee and withstands lower temperatures, thus making it a more commercially viable prospect. Introduced into Florida from southern China by the U.S. Department of Agriculture in 1903, the tree flourished in a few locations but never became widely popular. The spherical-to-ovoid fruit ranges from the size of an olive to that of a baby plum and is covered with a thin, rough-to-prickly brown shell (pericarp). It is sometimes called "dragon's eye" because once the brown shell is peeled the transparent, jellylike fruit contains a large, dark seed in its center, which looks much like a large eye.

Longan / Nutritional Value Per 100 g Edible Portion

	Raw	Dried
Calories	60	286
Protein	1.31 g	4.90 g
Fat	0.10 g	0.40 g
Fiber	0.40 g	2.00 g
Calcium	1 mg	45 mg
Iron	0.13 mg	5.4 mg
Magnesium	10 mg	46 mg
Phosphorus	21 mg	196 mg
Potassium	266 mg	658 mg
Sodium	0 mg	48 mg
Zinc	0.050 mg	0.220 mg
Copper	0.169 mg	0.807 mg
Manganese	0.052 mg	0.248 mg
Thiamine (B_1)	0.031 mg	0.040 mg
Riboflavin (B_2)	0.140 mg	n/a
Niacin (B_3)	0.300 mg	n/a
Ascorbic Acid (C)	84 mg	28 mg

Buying Tips
Look for heavy, uncracked longans. They will last several weeks if refrigerated.

Culinary Uses
Once the outer shell is removed, which is rather like peeling a hard-boiled egg, the juicy, translucent, gray-white pulp is revealed. This clings to a large, smooth, ebony-colored seed that makes any kind of consumption other than pulling with your teeth rather tricky. The soft meat feels like a peeled grape to the tongue and has a sweet taste with hints of gardenia, spruce, and musk. The stone itself is not edible. Longans are most commonly eaten raw, but they can also be poached in syrup or dried.

Health Benefits
The flesh of the fruit is administered as a stomachic, febrifuge, and vermifuge, and it is regarded as an antidote for poison; in both North and South Vietnam, the "eye" of the longan seed is pressed against a snakebite in the belief that it will absorb the venom. A decoction of the dried flesh is taken as a tonic and treatment for insomnia and neurasthenic neurosis.

Loquat
(*Eriobotrya japonica*)
Also Known As: Japanese or Chinese Medlar

The name *Eriobotrya* is a Greek word meaning "woolly cluster," and *japonica* relates the fruit's Japanese heritage. The English name *loquat* was adapted from the Cantonese *lu-kwyit*, meaning "rush-orange."

General Information
The loquat is native to tropical regions of China and southern Japan, though it may have been introduced into Japan very early. It is closely related to the apple and pear of the temperate zones, and those who find other tropical fruits too sweet and rich will enjoy the loquat. The fruits grow in clusters of four to thirty and are oval, rounded, or pear-shaped and one to two inches long. A little bit larger than the kumquat, and looking slightly like the medlar, the two are often confused, with the loquat sometimes called Japanese medlar in English. The species originally spread and became popular, despite the fact that it is not one of the tastiest of fruits, mostly because its fruits ripen extraordinarily early in the springtime, close to the beginning of the year. Today there is nothing unusual in having fresh fruit available year-round, but in the past it was considered exceptional and somewhat luxurious to have early fruits in the middle of winter.

Buying Tips
Select large fruits that are tender and sweetly scented. Refrigerate only if on the verge of spoiling.

Loquat / Nutritional Value Per 100 g Edible Portion

	Raw		Raw
Calories	47	Sodium	1 mg
Protein	0.43 g	Zinc	0.050 mg
Fat	0.20 g	Copper	0.040 mg
Fiber	0.50 g	Manganese	0.148 mg
Calcium	16 mg	Beta Carotene (A)	1,528 IU
Iron	0.28 mg	Thiamine (B_1)	0.019 mg
Magnesium	13 mg	Riboflavin (B_2)	0.024 mg
Phosphorus	27 mg	Niacin (B_3)	0.180 mg
Potassium	266 mg	Ascorbic Acid (C)	1 mg

Culinary Uses

This golden-skinned fruit resembles a small apricot in size and color, turning from green to yellow or orange when ripe. Its delicate yet firm, sweet-tart flesh can be orange, yellow, or white and tastes randomly like plums, grapes, or cherries. It should be picked when perfectly ripe so that the sugar content and juicy, refreshing pulp are at their best. If you take just one bite, the fruit might have a bitter taste; however, if you put the whole thing in your mouth and start chewing, it will be very sweet. The skins are edible, but the large brown seed is not. If you live in a tropical or semi-tropical climate, just throw the seeds into your garden, as they sprout easily into trees. Although best when eaten straight from the tree, the fruit may also be added to fruit salads, blended with other fruits to make a delicious drink, made into preserves, stewed, or added to confectionery. When cooked, they have a flavor similar to poached plums.

Health Benefits

The fruit is said to act as a sedative and is eaten to halt vomiting and thirst.

Lychee
(Litchi chinensis)

The lychee is to a table grape as a haiku is to pop music.

—NORMAN VAN AKEN

Litchi is the Chinese name for this fruit, while *lychee* is the anglicized version; *chinensis* specifies that it is of Chinese origin.

General Information

The lychee is native to lower elevations of the Kwangtung and Fukien provinces in southern China, where it flourishes along rivers and near the seacoast. Part of the soapberry family, lychee trees prefer a subtropical climate and will flourish only if conditions are exactly right. Once rooted, however, they often live for a thousand years. The trees are beautiful, with branches that curve down like an open umbrella from heights of thirty to forty feet, and are prolific bearers, often producing heavily for two centuries. A comparative latecomer to North America, the first lychee crops ripened in Florida in 1916, and California

now produces a moderate amount. The fruit is the size of a plumply round walnut or small plum and is bright red or brown with a hard, scaly outer covering. The edible portion is the delicate whitish pulp between the outer covering and large brown interior seed.

Buying Tips

Ripe lychees should be plump and semi-firm to the touch, with a tight skin and a sweet, flowery fragrance. Avoid those that are cracked, leaking, or giving off a fermented aroma. The shells may be mottled with brown, which does not affect the fruit's flavor.

Culinary Uses

Once stripped of their shells, the fruits look like and have the consistency of large white grapes, with their juicy, translucent-looking flesh containing a large glossy brown pit in the middle. The taste and aroma are reminiscent of muscat grapes and roses, but sweeter, and have been compared by some to jellied incense. To eat the fresh lychee, break off a piece of the rind at one end and force the pulp and seed into your mouth by pressing with your fingers. Discard the inedible seed. Fresh lychees are best, but the fruits must be picked without delay when ripe because they lose their flavor and color after a few days. They may be kept a year or more in frozen storage if the temperature

Lychee / Nutritional Value Per 100 g Edible Portion	Raw	Dried
Calories	63-64	277
Protein	0.68-1.00 g	2.90-3.80 g
Fat	0.30-0.58 g	0.20-1.2 g
Fiber	0.23-0.40 g	1.40 g
Calcium	8-10 mg	33 mg
Iron	0.4 mg	1.7 mg
Magnesium	10 mg	42 mg
Phosphorus	30-42 mg	181 mg
Potassium	170 mg	1,110 mg
Sodium	1-3 mg	3 mg
Zinc	0.070 mg	0.280 mg
Copper	0.148 mg	0.631 mg
Manganese	0.055 mg	0.234 mg
Thiamine (B$_1$)	0.011 mg	0.010 mg
Riboflavin (B$_2$)	0.065 mg	0.570 mg
Niacin (B$_3$)	0.603 mg	3.100 mg
Ascorbic Acid (C)	24-60 mg	42-183 mg

LORE AND LEGEND

According to legend, lychees once caused a war in ancient China. In the emperor's court there was a beautiful girl who liked fresh and dried lychees better than any other food. Eager to please his lovely subject, the emperor sent soldiers to a distant province where lychees grew; after battling victoriously, the troops harvested the fruit and uprooted the trees to take them back to the emperor's court. Traditionally the favorite fruit of southern China, during the first century A.D. the lychee was considered the finest of southern delicacies and a special courier service with swift horses was set up to bring fresh fruit from Canton north to the Imperial Court. When the Sung dynasty poet Su Tung-po was exiled to Hainan Island in the eleventh century, he declared that he could reconcile himself to banishment anywhere if he could but have three hundred lychees to eat every day.

is continuously held near zero degrees Fahrenheit. In China, the traditional method of preserving the fruits is to hang them in clusters to dry in the sun; sun-dried fruits are considered to have a more delectable flavor than kiln-dried. Lychee "nuts" are made by drying the fruit, which then becomes firm, sweet, and very dark in color. Like a nut with a raisinlike center, the flavor is often compared to a combination of nuts and muscat grapes. Canned lychees, with rind and seed removed, retain some but not all of the hauntingly aromatic flavor of the fresh fruit. Lychees are frequently used as ingredients in sauces and jams, or made into wine.

Health Benefits

Ingested in moderate amounts, the lychee is believed to relieve coughing and to have a beneficial effect on tumors and enlargements of the glands. The Chinese believe that excessive consumption of the raw fruit causes fever and nosebleed.

Mamey
(Mammea americana)
Also Known As: Mammee, Mammee Apple, St. Domingo Apricot, South American Apricot

Mammea derives from *mamey*, an aboriginal West Indian name for the fruit. *Americana* means "native to the Americas."

General Information
Native to the West Indies and northern South America, the mamey fruit is the size of an orange or larger; it's round with slight points at the top and bottom. The tough skin, yellowish russet in color, is bitter, as is the covering of the three seeds.

Culinary Uses
The fragrant golden-yellow or orange pulp between the skin and seeds varies from firm and crisp to tender, melting, and juicy. The fruit is appealingly fragrant and pleasantly subacid in the best varieties, resembling the apricot or red raspberry in flavor. Fruits of poor quality may be either too sour or mawkishly sweet. To facilitate peeling, score the skin from top to bottom and remove in strips. The whitish membrane beneath, which must also be removed, is usually scraped off, and the flesh is then cut off in slices, leaving any part that may adhere to the seed and trimming off any particles of seed covering. Tender varieties are delicious raw, either plain in fruit salads, or served with cream and sugar or wine. Sliced flesh may also be cooked into pies or tarts and is widely made into preserves such as spiced marmalade and pastes. Slightly underripe fruits, rich in pectin, are made into jelly.

Health Benefits
An antibiotic principle was reported by the Agricultural Experiment Station, Rio Piedras, Puerto Rico, in 1951. In

Mamey / Nutritional Value Per 100 g Edible Portion			
	Raw		Raw
Calories	44.5–45.3	Sodium	15 mg
Protein	0.088–0.470 g	Beta Carotene (A)	230 IU
Fat	0.15–0.99 g	Thiamine (B₁)	0.017–0.030 mg
Fiber	0.80–1.07 g	Riboflavin (B₂)	0.025–0.068 mg
Calcium	4.0–19.5 mg	Niacin (B₃)	0.160–0.738 mg
Iron	0.15–2.51 mg	Pantothenic Acid (B₅)	0.103 mg
Phosphorus	7.8–14.5 mg	Ascorbic Acid (C)	10.2–22.0 mg
Potassium	47 mg		

some persons, the fruit produces discomfort in the digestive system, so those trying it for the first time should eat only a small portion.

Mamoncillo
(Melicoccus bijugatus)
Also Known As: Genip, Honeyberry

Melicoccus derives from a Greek term meaning "honey berry," referring to the sweet taste of the fruit. *Bijugatus* means "two yoked together" or "having two pairs joined."

General Information
The mamoncillo fruit is borne on a large tree native to Colombia, Venezuela, and the island of Margarita. With its smooth leathery skin, the cherry-sized green fruit looks like a small lime. The pulp is salmon-colored or yellowish, translucent, and juicy, but scant and somewhat fibrous.

Culinary Uses
When fully ripe, the pulp is pleasantly acid-sweet and reminiscent of grapes, but if unripe, acidity predominates. In most fruits there is a single large hard-shelled seed. For eating out of hand, the rind is merely torn open at the stem end, the pulp-coated seed squeezed into the mouth, and the juice sucked from the pulp until there is nothing left of it but the fiber. More commonly, the peeled fruits are boiled; the resulting juice is prized for cold drinks. The seeds are eaten after roasting.

Health Benefits
In Venezuela the astringent roasted seed kernels are pulverized, mixed with honey, and given to halt diarrhea. A dye that leaves an indelible stain has been made experimentally from the juice of the raw fruit.

Mamoncillo / Nutritional Value Per 100 g Edible Portion			
	Raw		Raw
Calories	58.11-73.00	Phosphorus	9.8-23.9 mg
Protein	0.5-1.0 g	Beta Carotene (A)	70 IU
Fat	0.08-0.20 g	Thiamine (B₁)	0.030-0.210 mg
Fiber	0.07-2.60 g	Riboflavin (B₂)	0.010-0.200 mg
Calcium	3.4-15.0 mg	Niacin (B₃)	0.150-0.900 mg
Iron	0.47-1.19 mg	Ascorbic Acid (C)	0.8-10.0 mg

Mango
(Mangifera indica)

The Latin name for this plant is very descriptive: it means simply "mango-bearing [*mangifera*] plant from India [*indica*]." The English word *mango* is the native name for one species of the plant.

General Information
This favorite fruit of the Orient, one of the finest of the tropics, is a native of Southeast Asia and India. Cultivated for over six thousand years, the enormous mango tree is a member of the sumac family and is related to the cashew. Creating an oasis wherever they stand with their thick, shiny green leaves, mango trees bear their fruit like giant upside-down lollipops hanging from long stems. Of the fifty species that grow naturally in the region from India eastward to the Philippines and Papua New Guinea, the Indian mango is indisputably supreme, being, as one Indian poet so elegantly described, "sealed jars of paradisical honey." Baskets of mangoes there are considered a warm gesture of friendship. The fruit comes in varying shapes, sizes, and colors: pear, peach, heart, or kidney shapes are the most common, but some are long, thin, and S-shaped. Their size ranges from that of a plum to that of a large apple, and although they are usually orange, they may cover the full spectrum from green to yellow or red. Mangoes are one of the leading fruit crops in the world. In fact, more mangoes are consumed on a regular basis by more people in the world than are apples.

Buying Tips
Choose firm, heavy fruits that yield evenly to pressure, are almost as tender as an avocado, and are without blemishes.

Mango / Nutritional Value Per 100 g Edible Portion			
	Raw		Raw
Calories	62.1-63.7	Copper	0.110 mg
Protein	0.36-0.40 g	Manganese	0.027 mg
Fat	0.30-0.53 g	Beta Carotene (A)	3,894 IU
Fiber	0.85-1.06 g	Thiamine (B₁)	0.020-0.073 mg
Calcium	6.1-12.8 mg	Riboflavin (B₂)	0.025-0.068 mg
Iron	0.20-0.63 mg	Niacin (B₃)	0.025-0.707 mg
Magnesium	9 mg	Pantothenic Acid (B₅)	0.160 mg
Phosphorus	5.5-17.9 mg	Pyridoxine (B₆)	0.134 mg
Potassium	156 mg	Ascorbic Acid (C)	7.8-172.0 mg
Sodium	2 mg	Tocopherol (E)	1.12 mg
Zinc	0.040 mg		

LORE AND LEGEND

The sixteenth-century Mogul Emperor Akbar, who ruled northern India from 1556 to 1605, was so taken with the taste and fragrance of mangoes that he ordered an orchard of one hundred thousand trees to be planted at Darbhanga in Bihar. A Hindu legend relates that the beautiful daughter of the sun once escaped from a wicked sorceress by jumping into a lake and transforming herself into a golden lotus. The king of the land fell so in love with the lotus that the evil sorceress burned it to ashes. From the ashes grew a tree, the tree flowered, and the king then fell in love with this second flower. The flower became a fruit, a glorious mango, and the king fell in love with the mango. When the mango was ripe, it fell to the ground and split open; out stepped the daughter of the sun in all her resplendent glory, and the king recognized her as the wife whom he had lost long ago.

In India, there is a story that during one incarnation the Buddha was a merchant and trader. One day he stopped a traveling caravan at the edge of a forest to warn them that poisonous trees grew in the forest and that before tasting any unfamiliar fruit they should consult him. Having thus promised, the traders proceeded into the forest. Within the forest was a village, and within the village a what-fruit tree grew; the what-fruit tree looks exactly like a mango tree and the fruit tastes exactly like a mango, but is poisonous and causes immediate death. Some of the caravan's greedier members immediately hurried up to the tree and ate its luscious-looking fruit, while the others consulted the merchant, who told them not to touch it. As for the foolish members who were by now deathly ill, the merchant treated them kindly. Caravans on many other occasions had stopped by this tree, rashly eaten its fruit, and died, at which time the villagers would fall upon and loot the caravan. On this particular day, they came expecting the usual spoils and found everyone alive and well. Surprised, they questioned the merchant as to how he knew that the tree was poisonous and not a mango. He said, "When near a village grows a tree/ Not hard to climb, 'tis plain to me/ Nor need I further proof to know/ No wholesome fruit thereon can grow!"

They should have a sweet, aromatic fragrance; when over-ripe, they are soft and the aroma is heady and slightly fermented. Green skins indicate the fruit will not fully ripen, while black-spotted skins indicate overripe fruit. Unlike most fruit, mangoes should not be stored in paper bags because they give off a large amount of ethylene gas and can easily overripen. Mangoes can be kept at room temperature or stored in the refrigerator for up to two weeks. As imported mangoes are heat-treated to kill fruit flies and other pests, favor domestic mangoes.

Culinary Uses

Mangoes have a unique-tasting orange flesh that is quite unlike any other fruit. When chilled, they have been described as a delicate blend between sweet and sour, as good as any peach-pineapple-apricot mousse you can concoct, rich and sweet but never cloying. If unchilled, they sometimes have the faintest trace of turpentine flavor. These are some of the most awkward fruits to handle, as the flesh is very soft. The best way is to cut a thick slice lengthwise down either side of the stone, as near to it as possible, then scoop out the flesh. The skin is edible but chewy and is generally peeled off; the large stone is inedible. Overly fibrous fruits are massaged, the stem end cut off, and the juice squeezed directly into the mouth. Mangoes can be eaten on their own or used in fruit salads, cakes, drinks, jams, and chutneys. They go with all tropical fruits and flavorings, taking well to ginger, chilies, and coconut. They can be bought fresh or canned and are also available dried.

Health Benefits

pH 3.40–4.63. Mangoes are beneficial for the kidneys, combat acidity and poor digestion, are wonderful disinfectants in the body, relieve clogged pores of the skin, and reduce cysts. Many people claim the mango is a great blood cleanser and that the juice will help reduce excessive body heat as well as fevers. The mango is among four botanical relatives—the others being poison ivy, poison oak, and poison sumac—that contain urushiol. For people with allergies, this toxic resin can cause contact dermatitis or blistering skin. The peel and juice of a mango—especially of immature fruits—seem to be more of a problem than the flesh. Eating mangoes to excess may cause itching or skin eruptions.

Mangosteen
(Garcinia mangostana)

The genus *Garcinia* was named after Laurence Garcin (1673–1751), who lived and collected plants in eighteenth-century India. *Mangostana* and the English name *mangosteen* derive from the Malay term *mangustan*.

General Information
The mangosteen is the fruit of a small tropical tree that is believed native to Malaysia and Indonesia. Requiring a hot and humid climate, the mangosteen is a slow-growing tree that may not begin to bear fruit until it is between ten and fifteen years old. Many people say that this Malaysian fruit, with its exquisite, milky, sweet juice, is maybe the most delicious tropical fruit there is. The fruit is about the size of a mandarin orange, round and slightly flattened at each end, with a smooth, thick rind and rich red-purple color.

Buying Tips
To select the best fruits, choose those with the highest number of stigma lobes at the apex, for these always have the highest number of fleshy segments and the fewest seeds. Because mangosteen propagation is difficult and because its flavor is best when fresh, availability is sketchy in the United States. Keep them cool and dry if you do manage to find one.

Culinary Uses
The thick inedible interior pulp encloses the nearly translucent white segments lying loose in the cup. The texture of each segment resembles that of a well-ripened plum but is so delicate that it melts in the mouth like ice cream, with a flavor that is sweet, subacid, yet indescribably delicious. The mangosteen has often been described as the "queen of fruits," or at least as one of the world's best-flavored fruits. Jacobus Bontius compared it to nectar and ambrosia, said that it surpassed the mytical golden apples of the Hesperides, and that it was "of all the fruits of the Indies by far the most delicious." The fruit is usually eaten fresh as a dessert. Holding the stem end downward, cut around the middle completely through the rind, and lift off the top half. This leaves the fleshy segments exposed in the colorful cup, or bottom half of the rind, which can be lifted out with a fork. More acidic fruits are best for preserving.

Health Benefits
Dried fruits are shipped to Calcutta and China for medicinal use. The sliced and dried rind is powdered and administered to overcome dysentery and other forms of infectious diarrhea. The plant's astringent qualities are useful in preventing dehydration and the loss of essential nutrients from the GI tract of diarrhea sufferers. The Chinese and Thais also take advantage of the mangosteen's antimicrobial and antiseptic properties to treat infected wounds, tuberculosis, malaria, urinary tract infections, syphilis, and gonorrhea. Made into an ointment, it is applied to eczema and other skin disorders. Among the phytoceuticals in the mangosteen is a newly discovered class of highly active substances called xanthones. In 2001 a single pharmacological study from a European university indicated the following properties of mangosteen's xanthones: antidepressant, antituberculosis activity, antimicrobial (bacteria and fungus), antiviral, anti-leukemic, antitumor activity, antiulcer, and antidiabetic activity. Additionally, polyphenols and catechins, powerful antioxidants and antitumor agents, are present in significant quantities. The fruit's polysaccharides are apparently responsible for its antibacterial and antifungal effects.

Mangosteen / Nutritional Value Per 100 g Edible Portion			
	Raw		Raw
Calories	60–63	Iron	0.20–0.80 mg
Protein	0.50–0.60 g	Phosphorus	0.02–12.00 mg
Fat	0.1–0.6 g	Thiamine (B₁)	0.03 mg
Fiber	5.0–5.1 g	Ascorbic Acid (C)	1–2 mg
Calcium	0.01–8.00 mg		

May Apple
(Podophyllum peltatum)

Podophyllum derives from Tournefort's *anapodophyllum*, "duck's foot leaf," from a fancied resemblance in the foliage. *Peltatum* means "stalked from the surface" rather than the edge (peltate). The English name *May apple* was given because of the plant's habit of blooming in April and fruiting in May.

General Information
The May apple is a beautiful but ill-smelling plant of the barberry family that grows in dense patches along fences, roadsides, and in open woods. Native to eastern and midwestern North America, the edible fruit, which ripens in July or August, is about two inches long, egg-shaped, and yellow when ripe, with a many-seeded pulp within a rather tough skin.

Culinary Uses
The fruits are best for eating when the plants are dying and falling to the ground. Then they are fully ripe, almost a golden-yellow, and have the flavor of a strawberry. Many who know the fruit prefer to eat it raw, scooping the flesh from the skin with a spoon. The raw May apple may also be squeezed for juice or spread on bread as a raw jam. Do not eat the fruit when green, or any other part of the plant, because the roots, leaves, and stems contain a bitter resinous substance that is poisonous.

Health Benefits
The highly toxic roots of the plant were used by Native Americans as an emetic, purgative, and vermifuge. May apple roots also contain a resin called podophyllin, which was used by natives to cure venereal warts; this resin was "rediscovered" by the German physician Dr. Schopf in 1787. May apple was listed in the first edition of the pharmacopoeia of the Massachusetts Medical Society in 1808 and gained entry into the *United States Pharmacopoeia* in 1820, where it remains as the standard treatment for venereal warts today. Studies show that the constituents of the podophyllotoxin obtained from the rhizomes actually suppress lymph cells while boosting the immune system.

Medlar
(Mespilus germanica)

Mespilus is from an old Greek substantive name, *mespilon*. *Germanica* means "native to Germanic regions" (which it is not, but is where the taxonomists first encountered it). The English name *medlar* derives from the Latin name.

General Information
This unusual, applelike fruit, with its five seed vessels visible through the open bottom end, is most likely native to the west coast of the Caspian Sea, although remnants have also been found in East Germany. It may have been cultivated as far back as thirty centuries ago, but because the name *medlar* was also applied to the Cornelian cherry, stone fruits (*Prunus* spp.), and especially the hawthorn and cotoneaster, it is difficult to know for sure whether this is the fruit written about. Reaching their peak of popularity during the Middle Ages, medlars were familiar components of walled monastery gardens and were a common market fruit as late as the nineteenth century. Today the plant is rarely cultivated in Europe or elsewhere. The fruits resemble small green russeted apples, tinged dull yellow or red. They must be fully matured on the tree before harvest, through the entire growing season and including perhaps the first few frosts, or else they will shrivel in storage and never attain a good flavor. Although the fruits do fully ripen in Italy, they rarely do so in cooler climates. The usual process in England, France, and central Europe is to pick the still-hard fruits, spread them out on shelves or straw, and give them two or three weeks to become well softened. This process is called "bletting," and the end result is that the hard, cream-colored interior turns brown and soft. Once bletted, medlars will keep for several weeks.

Culinary Uses

Properly aged medlars have a flesh soft as a baked apple, with a brisk flavor incorporating apples, wine, and cinnamon. Embedded in the pulp are five large inedible seeds. Once popular in Victorian Britain, these "wineskins of morbidity," as D. H. Lawrence so elegantly described them, were served with sugar and cream, or made into jelly and cheese (mixed with eggs and butter like the more familiar lemon curd). The easiest way to eat a medlar is to suck the fruit empty, leaving skin and seeds behind. Or the pulp can be scooped out and folded into cream for a tasty dessert. The fruit is also well suited to baking whole, stewing with butter, and making jams, jellies, tarts, and syrups.

Melon

(Cucumis melo)

Cucumis is simply the old Latin name for this family of plants. The term *melo* is short for *melopepon* and comes from the Greek *melon*, which was a term applied to almost any kind of round fruit, and *pepon*, meaning "an edible gourd."

General Information

Melons, which belong to the same family as the cucumber, originated in the Near East and perhaps the northwest of India, and from there spread throughout Europe. It was during the Roman Empire that melons were introduced into Europe; however, they were not well known in northern Europe until the fifteenth century, when they became hugely popular at the French royal court. Melon seeds were carried to Haiti by Columbus, where they thrived and spread. The despair of gardeners and taxonomists alike, all melons belong to the same species and interbreed and overlap so readily that seed growers must plant different varieties at least a quarter mile apart to prevent cross-pollination from producing results very different than those desired. There are two types of melons—the muskmelon and the watermelon. The latter has its seeds imbedded in its juicy flesh like a cucumber, while in muskmelons the seeds are contained in a hollow central cavity, like a squash or pumpkin.

Buying Tips

Selecting a perfect melon is nearly impossible. For the best

Melon / Nutritional Value Per 100 g Edible Portion			
	Raw Cantaloupe	Raw Honey dew	Raw Casaba
Calories	35	35	26
Protein	0.88 g	0.46 g	0.90 g
Fat	0.28 g	0.10 g	0.10 g
Fiber	0.36 g	0.60 g	0.50 g
Calcium	11 mg	6 mg	5 mg
Iron	0.21 mg	0.07 mg	0.40 mg
Magnesium	11 mg	7 mg	8 mg
Phosphorus	17 mg	10 mg	7 mg
Potassium	309 mg	271 mg	210 mg
Sodium	9 mg	10 mg	12 mg
Zinc	0.160 mg	n/a	n/a
Copper	0.042 mg	0.041 mg	n/a
Manganese	0.047 mg	0.018 mg	n/a
Beta Carotene (A)	3,224 IU	40 IU	30 IU
Thiamine (B$_1$)	0.036 mg	0.077 mg	0.060 mg
Riboflavin (B$_2$)	0.021 mg	0.018 mg	0.020 mg
Niacin (B$_3$)	0.574 mg	0.600 mg	0.400 mg
Pantothenic Acid (B$_5$)	0.128 mg	0.207 mg	n/a
Pyridoxine (B$_6$)	0.115 mg	0.059 mg	n/a
Folic Acid (B$_9$)	17.0 mcg	n/a	n/a
Ascorbic Acid (C)	42.2 mg	24.8 mg	16.0 mg
Tocopherol (E)	0.14 mg	n/a	n/a

results, look for symmetry in shape, even coloring, and a warm, flowery aroma. For cantaloupe there are three major signs of ripeness: (1) no stem, but a smooth, shallow basin where the stem was once attached; (2) thick, coarse, and corky netting or veining over the surface; and (3) a yellowish-buff skin color under the netting. Overripeness is characterized by pronounced yellowing of the skin and a soft, watery, and insipid flesh.

Culinary Uses

Melons are much prized for their sweet, delicate flavor. Usually eaten alone, they are also delicious in salads, preserves, ice creams, sorbets, and desserts. Ginger in any form seems to go uncommonly well with the fruit. Remove the seeds before serving. Given the sweetness of a perfectly ripe melon, it seems surprising that its sugar content accounts for only 5 percent of its weight, only half as much as for an apple or pear; yet since a melon is 94 percent water, this still gives sugar a five-to-one advantage over all the other taste-producing elements.

Health Benefits

pH 5.78–6.67. Melons are excellent cleansers and rehydrators of the body, and this makes them very desirable during the hot summer months. They rejuvenate and alkalinize the body with their highly mineralized distilled water, as well as aiding in elimination. Their silicon content is high, especially when eaten right down to the rind. Cantaloupe has been shown to contain the anticoagulant compound adenosine, which is currently being used in patients with heart disease to keep the blood thin and to relieve angina attacks. All melons are such a perfect food for humans that they require no digestion whatsoever in the stomach; instead, they pass quickly through the stomach and into the small intestines for digestion and assimilation. This can happen, however, only when the stomach is empty and melons are eaten alone. If consumed with or after other foods that require complex digestion, melons cannot pass into the small intestines until the digestion of other foods is complete, and thus they sit and stagnate, quickly fermenting and causing gastric distress. Sliced melons, if left uncovered in the refrigerator, lose 35 percent of their vitamin C content within twenty-four hours.

VARIETIES

There are many different varieties of melon, of which the most common are cantaloupe, honeydew, and watermelon. Most are available year-round, except for watermelon, which is in season only during the summer and early autumn.

Cantaloupes, botanically muskmelons, are native to India and Guinea, and have been cultivated for more than two thousand years. Their name comes from the town of Cantalupo (wolf howl) in Italy, site of a palatial papal vacation home outside Rome, where the melons were reputedly first cultivated during the sixteenth century. For a ripe cantaloupe, pick one that is heavy for its size, with a pleasant aroma, the most pronounced coarse cream or golden netting, and an even, dull color. The stem should be completely gone, with that end being smooth, slightly depressed, and yielding to slight pressure. Available late May through September; most abundant in June and July.

Casabas are a Turkish native, coming from Kasaba, where this melon was apparently first identified. It is a large, pumpkin-shaped fruit with light yellow or light

---

LORE AND LEGEND

One story recounted by Waverley Root tells of a melon half that was pitched by a heckler at Demosthenes during the course of a political debate in Greece. Demosthenes, never at a loss for words, is said to have promptly clapped the melon on his head and thanked the thrower for finding him a helmet to wear while fighting Philip of Macedonia. In one of the stories in the *Arabian Nights*, a child buys a melon to quench his thirst. Upon cutting it open he sees a tiny city, so he enters this microcosm, filled with buildings, people, and animals. On Mount Carmel there is a field of stones supposedly transformed from melons when a man named Elias ate too many, became ill, and cursed the whole lot. When the library of the town of Cavaillon in the south of France asked the great and prolific French author Alexandre Dumas for a complete set of his works, he told them that they were asking for over four hundred books, but that he would do his best to comply if they would send him every year a consignment of Cavaillon melons. They did, and he reciprocated; a highly satisfactory exchange for both parties.

---

green skin and a rind with deep wrinkles that gather at the stem end. When the fruit is fully ripe, the skin becomes slightly sticky, and you can tell it is ready. The fruit will not have any fragrance unless it is a great vine-ripened specimen, which will give off a very light floral scent. The flesh is pale, soft, sweet, and juicy, with a tinge of yellow around the seed bed. The casaba can give you the farthest extremes of the melon taste spectrum. When it is good, it is very, very good; but when it is bad . . . Casabas appear during melon-mania season, July through December.

Crenshaws are a hybrid between the casaba and Persian melons and can weigh up to a hefty ten pounds. Considered the kings of melons, Crenshaws have rough, thick, salmon-orange or dark green skins that will bronze when ripe, and the fruit should feel soft to pressure all over, especially at the enlarged end. Those with a noticeably sweet, thick, rose-pepper aroma are fully ripe. The dense salmon-colored flesh is both sweet and spicy. Their season is July through October, peaking August through September.

Honeydews, both orange-fleshed and green-fleshed, originated in Asia, and it is believed that as early as 2400 B.C. this distinct type of muskmelon was growing in Egypt. The varieties that we eat today were developed around the turn of the twentieth century from a French strain called the White Antibes melon. Green honeydews should have a pale, creamy, yellowish-green skin, not a harsh greenish-white one; orange honeydews should have a golden orange cast to their skin and a musky aroma when ripe. A slight "bloom," faint netting or freckles, a gentle "give," and a slightly sticky feeling all indicate a ripe melon. Both kinds should be heavy for their size, but avoid those that feel like billiard balls, as they were picked too soon. The cool lime-green flesh, bursting with juicy flavor and cradled in its thin porcelain shell, is the height of fruit delight. Available year-round, the melon peaks from June through October.

Persian melons could be the ancestor of all melons; historians place their origin somewhere in the Middle East, most likely Persia. If Crenshaws are the king of melons, then Persians are the sultan. Slightly larger than a honeydew and with a greener rind and finer netting than a cantaloupe, they are ripe when they are soft overall, the netting lightens and stands out, and the gray-green skin color turns to gray-gold. At its best the Persian exudes a perfume that is highly aromatic and unforgettable. Inside, the flesh is a deep orange, thick, firm, juicy, and full-flavored. Persian melons may not be as plentiful as the cantaloupe, but they are equally delicious and widely esteemed as having the thickest and richest-tasting flesh. Eating a Persian melon is an exotic and sensual experience; they make you sit up and take notice. Their season runs June through November, peaking in August and September.

Santa Claus melons are also called Christmas melons because they are widely available at Christmastime. They are oval, light green melons that resemble a small green-and-gold-striped watermelon. About a foot long, they have mild, crisp flesh that is not as sweet as other melons. Their season is September through December.

Spanish melons are large with a dark green corrugated skin. They are difficult to select, as their skin remains green and hard even at maturity, but when ripe they will have a slight aroma and lose their slick surface, producing a subtle glow and stickiness. The yellow, juicy, firm flesh has a taste very similar to the Crenshaw.

Watermelon—see separate reference.

Mombin
(Spondias purpurea, S. mombin)
Also Known As: Spanish Plum, Hog Plum

> *Spondias* derives from a Greek word used by Theophrastus for this family of plants. *Purpurea* means "purple-colored."

General Information
The red (purple) mombin (*S. purpurea*) is a native of tropical America, from southern Mexico through northern Peru and Brazil. Spanish explorers carried the tree to the Philippines, where it has been widely adopted. Varying greatly in size, form, and palatability, the fruits are commonly oval or roundish and from one to two inches long, ranging from deep red to yellow in color. The yellow mombin (*S. mombin*) is native to Brazil and Costa Rica, with golden-yellow fruits that are aromatic and 1 to 1½ inches in diameter.

Culinary Uses
Good fruits have rich, juicy flesh with a fairly acid, spicy flavor, not unlike that of the cashew fruit but less pronounced. They may be eaten fresh, preferably ice-cold,

Mombin / Nutritional Value Per 100 g Edible Portion		
	Raw Purple	Raw Yellow
Calories	n/a	21.8-48.1
Protein	0.096-0.261 g	1.280-1.380 g
Fat	0.03-0.17 g	0.10-0.56 g
Fiber	0.20-0.60 g	1.16-1.18 g
Calcium	6.1-23.9 mg	31.4 mg
Iron	0.09-1.22 mg	2.80 mg
Phosphorus	31.5-55.7 mg	n/a
Beta Carotene (A)	0.004-0.089 mg	71 IU
Thiamine (B$_1$)	0.033-0.103 mg	95 mcg
Riboflavin (B$_2$)	0.014-0.049 mg	50 mcg
Niacin (B$_3$)	0.540-1.770 mg	n/a
Ascorbic Acid (C)	26.4-73.0 mg	46.4 mg

stewed with sugar, or boiled and dried. The large, hard core at the center may be cracked and eaten like a nut. The fruits of the yellow mombin have flesh that is scant, fibrous, mildly acidic, juicy, and generally considered inferior to those of the red mombin. They are appreciated by children, and the juice is used to prepare ice cream, beverages, and preserves.

Health Benefits
Juice from the mombin is drunk as a diuretic and febrifuge.

Monstera
(Monstera deliciosa)
Also Known As: Ceriman, Swiss-Cheese Plant, False Breadfruit

> *Monstera* derives from the Latin *monstrum*, meaning "monster," and refers to the fruit's unnaturally marvelous shape, size, and deviation from normal form. *Deliciosa* means "delicious."

General Information
The monstera is definitely a fruit for those who have a bent for the exotic. More people are familiar with the plant than the fruit. A creeping vine of the arum lily family, the monstera is the familiar split-leaf philodendron, grown as a houseplant for the sake of its unusual leaves. Native to wet forests of southern Mexico and Guatemala, in its natural habitat the plant grows to a great size and bears fruits that somewhat resemble long green corncobs. The cream-colored spadix is at first sheltered by a waxy, white, calla-lily-like spathe but soon develops into a green compound fruit eight to twelve inches or more in length and 2 to 3½ inches thick. Made up of hexagonal plates or "scales," the thick, hard rind covers individual segments of ivory-colored juicy, fragrant pulp. Generally there are no seeds, but occasionally hard seeds resembling large, pale green peas may occur in a few of the segments. Oxalic acid in the unripe fruit, the thin black particles between segments (floral remnants) on the spadix, and

Monstera / Nutritional Value Per Edible Portion			
	Raw		Raw
Calories	335/lb	Fat	0.20%
Protein	1.81%	Fiber	0.57%

even the ripe fruit itself may cause irritation for some people. It is best to eat the fruit sparingly on the first occasion to make sure there are no undesirable reactions.

Culinary Uses
The fruit should be cut from the plant with at least an inch of stem when the tilelike sections of rind separate slightly at the base, making it appear somewhat bulged. If kept at room temperature, the monstera will ripen progressively toward the apex over a period of five or six days. Wrapping the fruit in plastic or aluminum foil will often help it ripen in a more uniform way. As it ripens, the rind loosens along the whole length of the fruit; when it's fully ripe, the hexagonal plates on its surface split apart, exposing a creamy, tart-sweet fruit that looks something like a banana, with a pineapple-banana flavor. The flesh should be eaten only from fully ripened portions. The ripe pulp, once pulled away from the inedible core, can be incorporated into fruit salads or served with ice cream. In the unlikely event of having an excess of fruit, it can be preserved by stewing segments with sugar and lime juice, then storing in jars.

Mulberry
(Morus alba, M. nigra, M. rubra)

> *Morus* and *morarius* were the classical Latin names for the mulberry and come from the Latin verb *morari*, meaning "to delay," after the tree's habit of delaying spring bud formation until the cold weather has passed. The terms *alba* (white), *nigra* (black), and *rubra* (red) distinguish the three varieties. The English name *mulberry* is derived from the Latin.

General Information
The mulberry is a beautiful tree, growing in a weeping willow style, with the thin hanging branches forming an umbrella reaching almost to the ground. The white mulberry originated in the central and eastern mountainous regions of China, where it is thought to have been cultivated for at least five thousand years for feeding silkworms. Since the berries are almost pure sugar and virtually tasteless, and since silkworms seem to prefer the white mulberry leaves, this tree is used exclusively for the production of silk. White mulberry trees were introduced into the United States two hundred years ago in attempts at silk culture, but the experiment proved a failure. The black

mulberry appears to have originated either in the southern part of the Caucasus or in the mountains of Nepal; it now grows almost exclusively in Europe. This variety, having a better fruit, was spread and cultivated for human use while the other species were used almost exclusively for silkworm culture. The comparatively large black berries are sweet and pleasant. The red mulberry tree is native to the eastern United States from New York west to Nebraska and down to the Gulf coast. The red berries are very sweet and flavorful but do not keep well. Although a mulberry fruit superficially resembles a blackberry, it is actually a cluster of small berries, each with an individually lobed surface and each formed from one of a cluster of flowers. The fruit must be allowed to ripen fully before being gathered; then, rather than being picked, it is allowed to fall off the tree. The berries' propensity for staining clothes and fingers is well known in the areas where they grow.

Culinary Uses

Mulberries are unusual berries both in taste and in the quality of their juice. They are delicious when fully ripe and fresh from the tree. Eat them by themselves or with cream, or use them to make pies or jams, a mildly astringent syrup, or mulberry wine. In medieval England, mulberries were made into murrey, a blue-black purée added to spiced meats or used as a pudding. Dried mulberries are a winter staple for some peoples living in the high foothills of the Himalayas.

Health Benefits

Nutritionally, this fruit has the same kind of high mineral content as figs and other berries. If you find them (probably in their natural state, since few if any are commercially cultivated), you will enjoy a refreshing, delightful fruit with rather high amounts of important

LORE AND LEGEND

The mulberry tree was referred to as the "wisest" of trees by Pliny, for it refrained from budding until all danger of frost was over, at which time it burst into full flower overnight, making a great noise as it did so. Because it was wise, the tree was dedicated by the Greeks to Minerva, one of their goddesses of wisdom. In classical legend the red berries of the mulberry tree acquired their color only after two young, ill-fated Babylonian lovers, Pyramus and Thisbe, bled and died under a white mulberry tree. This legend is the source of the much-loved Shakespearean story of Romeo and Juliet.

minerals and better-than-average fruit protein. At one time, mulberries were highly regarded as a general tonic for the whole system. Mulberries are excellent for stomach ulcers, help strengthen the blood, and are soothing to the nervous system because of their high phosphorus content. Mulberry juice is especially good for the digestive system.

Nance

(Byrsonima crassifolia)

The genus name *Byrsonima* refers to the use of some species in the tanning process in Brazil. *Crassifolia* means "thick-leaved."

General Information

The nance is a slow-growing shrub native to southern Mexico through the Pacific side of Central America to

Mulberry / Nutritional Value Per 100 g Edible Portion			
	Raw		Raw
Calories	43	Potassium	194 mg
Protein	1.44 g	Sodium	10 mg
Fat	0.39 g	Beta Carotene (A)	25 IU
Fiber	0.96 g	Thiamine (B₁)	0.029 mg
Calcium	39 mg	Riboflavin (B₂)	0.101 mg
Iron	1.85 mg	Niacin (B₃)	0.620 mg
Magnesium	18 mg	Ascorbic Acid (C)	36.4 mg
Phosphorus	38 mg		

Nance / Nutritional Value Per 100 g Edible Portion			
	Raw		Raw
Protein	0.109-0.124 g	Beta Carotene (A)	0.002-0.060 mg
Fat	0.21-1.83 g	Thiamine (B₁)	0.009-0.014 mg
Fiber	2.5-5.8 g	Riboflavin (B₂)	0.015-0.039 mg
Calcium	23.0-36.8 mg	Niacin (B₃)	0.266-0.327 mg
Iron	0.62-1.01 mg	Ascorbic Acid (C)	90-192 mg
Phosphorus	12.6-15.7 mg		

Peru and Brazil. Throughout its natural range, the fruit is consumed mainly by children, birds, and animals; some trees are under cultivation in Mexico and Central America. The orange-yellow fruit is particularly odorous, round, and from one-half to three-quarters of an inch wide, with a thick skin. They fall to the ground when fully ripe and are very perishable; however, they can be stored for several months merely by being submerged in water.

Culinary Uses

The white, juicy, oily pulp of the nance varies in flavor from insipid to sweet, acidic, or cheeselike. There is a single stone that contains from one to three seeds. Most fruits are eaten raw, but they may also be cooked into desserts and used in soups or stuffings. Carbonated and fermented beverages can also be made from the fruit.

Naranjilla
(Solanum quitoense)

Solanum comes from the Latin *solamen*, meaning "solace" or "quieting." The plant was given its scientific name of *quitoense* in 1793 by Jean-Baptiste Pierre Antoine de Monet de Lamarck, who is better known for his theory of evolution and zoological work than for his many botanical contributions. Lamarck was aware that the naranjilla came from Quito, which at that time referred not only to the city but also to the country that later became Ecuador. When the Spanish came to the New World, they called the fruit *naranjilla*, or "little orange," because at maturity the white hairs rub off the fruits and they resemble small oranges.

General Information

The usually spineless naranjilla is believed to be indigenous to and is most abundant in Peru, Ecuador, and southern

Naranjilla / Nutritional Value Per 100 g Edible Portion			
	Raw		Raw
Calories	23	Phosphorus	12.0–43.7 mg
Protein	0.107–0.600 g	Beta Carotene (A)	600 IU
Fat	0.10–0.24 g	Thiamine (B$_1$)	0.040–0.094 mg
Fiber	0.3–4.6 g	Riboflavin (B$_2$)	0.030–0.047 mg
Calcium	5.9–12.4 mg	Niacin (B$_3$)	1.190–1.760 mg
Iron	0.34–0.64 mg	Ascorbic Acid (C)	31.2–83.7 mg

Colombia. Many introductions of the plant were made into the United States, but the resulting plantings in California, Florida, and northern greenhouses flourished only briefly and eventually all died. The exhibition of fruits and fifteen hundred gallons of freshly made juice of Ecuadorian naranjillas at the New York World's Fair in 1939 aroused a great deal of interest. For a short while, the pulp was shipped to the States, blended with apple or pineapple juice, but the experiment failed due to improper processing and a resultant metallic taste. A most striking plant, it has huge, dark green leaves and orange fruits that are all rather densely pubescent, or fuzzy. Unaffected by season, fruit is produced throughout the year. The fruit can grow up to three inches across, is covered with a brown hairy coat that rubs off easily, and splits into four sections divided by membranes.

Culinary Uses

Its acidulous, yellowish-green pulp encloses many tiny, flat, edible seeds and tastes somewhat like a cross between a pineapple and either a strawberry or a lemon. Ripe naranjillas, freed of hairs, may be casually consumed out of hand by cutting them in half, squeezing the contents of each half into the mouth, and discarding the empty shells. The flesh also is good added to ice cream mixes, made into sauces for native dishes, or used in pies and various other desserts. The shells may be stuffed with a mixture of banana and other ingredients and baked. The most popular use of the naranjilla is to make juice, which is sweetened and served with ice cubes as a cool, foamy drink. Fully ripe naranjillas soften and ferment very quickly.

Nectarine
(Prunus persica var. nucipersica; P. persica var. nectarina)

Talking of Pleasure, this moment I was writing with one hand, and with the other holding to my mouth a Nectarine—how good how fine. It went down all pulpy, slushy, oozy, all its delicious embonpoint melted down my throat like a large, beatified Strawberry.

—JOHN KEATS (1795–1821)

The nectarine is part of the large plum (*Prunus*) genus and was believed to have come from Persia (thus *persica*).

In the sixteenth and seventeenth centuries the nectarine was called *nucipersica* (Persian nut) because it resembled the walnut in smoothness and color of the outer skin, as well as in size and shape. The English word *nectarine* is believed to be derived from the Greek word *nektar*, which was the drink of the gods in Greek and Roman mythology, and to which this fruit was compared because of its superb flavor.

General Information

The origin of the nectarine, first described by a European writer in 1587, is a mystery. Nectarines are a true peach, not a cross between a peach and a plum as some suppose. Experiments show that peach trees can produce nectarines by bud variation, and nectarine trees also produce peaches; peach and nectarine trees may each produce a fruit that is half peach and half nectarine. Generally smaller than peaches, with a smooth fuzzless skin, nectarines have a slightly firmer flesh and tangier flavor. There are more than 150 nectarine varieties (both clingstone and freestone), each differing slightly in size, shape, taste, texture, and skin coloring. Of the two color variations, red and yellow, the red varieties are the larger, but both are usually deeply cleft. The yellow are more oval than round, golden in color, with a pink center near the stone.

Buying Tips

Nectarines should be firm but not hard, slightly soft along their seam, golden with a red blush, and with a sweet, fragrant aroma. Avoid those that are excessively hard, have green areas on them, or are dull in color. Tree-ripened nectarines, locally available in season at farmer's markets, are incomparably superior to commercial nectarines. Soften nectarines at room temperature and eat within a few days.

Culinary Uses

Nectarines may be used in any of the ways peaches or apricots are used: fresh as a table fruit, cut into fruit salads, stewed, baked, or made into preserves, jams, and ice cream. They can also be canned or dried.

Health Benefits

pH 3.92–4.18. Nectarines make an excellent digestive aid and body cleanser when eaten raw.

Orange

(Citrus sinensis, C. aurantium, C. reticulata)

> I recall a little grove of orange trees,
> at the gates of Blidah, it is there that they were
>   beautiful!
> In the dark, shiny, glossy foliage,
> The fruits were brilliant as coloured glass
> And gilded the air about with that halo of
>   splendour
> Which surrounds the radiant flowers.
>
> —Alphonse Daudet

The term *Citrus* derives from the Greek term for the citron, *kedromelon*. *Sinensis* means "of Chinese origin"; *aurantium* is a color designation meaning "orange-red"; *reticulata* means "reticulated" or "netted." According to some authorities, the English word *orange* derives from the Arabic *narandj*, which is derived from the Sanskrit *nagarunga*, meaning "fruit favored by the elephants"; others claim it derives from the Persian *narang*, meaning "golden" or "orange."

General Information

Oranges, native to China and the Far East, are a special kind of berry called a hesperidium. The earliest mention of citrus trees occurs in the *Shu-King*, popularly known as the *Book of History*; this collection of documents is believed to have been edited by Confucius around 500 B.C. Throughout antiquity, the golden color of oranges marked them for the court and the temple and made them generally coveted. Originally very small, bitter, and full of seeds,

Nectarine / Nutritional Value Per 100 g Edible Portion			
	Raw		Raw
Calories	49	Copper	0.073 mg
Protein	0.94 g	Manganese	0.044 mg
Fat	0.46 g	Beta Carotene (A)	736 IU
Fiber	0.40 g	Thiamine (B₁)	0.017 mg
Calcium	5 mg	Riboflavin (B₂)	0.041 mg
Iron	0.15 mg	Niacin (B₃)	0.990 mg
Magnesium	8 mg	Pantothenic Acid (B₅)	0.158 mg
Phosphorus	16 mg	Pyridoxine (B₆)	0.025 mg
Potassium	212 mg	Folic Acid (B₉)	3.7 mcg
Sodium	0 mg	Ascorbic Acid (C)	5.4 mg
Zinc	0.090 mg		

Orange / Nutritional Value Per 100 g Edible Portion

	Raw Fruit	Fresh Juice	Processed Juice	Frozen Concentrate	Raw Tangerine	Tangerine Juice
Calories	47-51	40-48	42	158	46	43
Protein	0.7-1.3 g	0.5-1.0 g	0.6 g	2.3 g	0.8 g	0.5 g
Fat	0.1-0.3 g	0.1-0.3 g	0.1 g	0.2 g	0.2 g	0.2 g
Fiber	0.5 g	0.1 g	0.1 g	0.2 g	0.5 g	0.1 g
Calcium	40-43 mg	10-11 mg	8 mg	33 mg	40 mg	18 mg
Iron	0.2-0.8 mg	0.2-0.3 mg	0.4 mg	0.4 mg	0.4 mg	0.2 mg
Magnesium	10 mg	11 mg	11 mg	n/a	12 mg	8 mg
Phosphorus	17-22 mg	15-19 mg	14 mg	55 mg	18 mg	14 mg
Potassium	190-200 mg	190-208 mg	175 mg	657 mg	126 mg	178 mg
Sodium	1 mg	1 mg	2 mg	2 mg	2 mg	1 mg
Zinc	0.070 mg	0.050 mg	0.070 mg	n/a	n/a	0.030 mg
Copper	0.045 mg	0.044 mg	0.057 mg	n/a	0.028 mg	0.025 mg
Manganese	0.025 mg	0.014 mg	0.014 mg	n/a	0.032 mg	0.037 mg
Beta Carotene (A)	200 IU	200 IU	175 IU	710 IU	420 IU	420 mg
Thiamine (B$_1$)	0.100 mg	0.090 mg	0.060 mg	0.300 mg	0.105 mg	0.060 mg
Riboflavin (B$_2$)	0.040 mg	0.030 mg	0.028 mg	0.050 mg	0.022 mg	0.020 mg
Niacin (B$_3$)	0.400 mg	0.400 mg	0.314 mg	1.200 mg	0.160 mg	0.100 mg
Pantothenic Acid (B$_5$)	0.250 mg	0.190 mg	0.150 mg	n/a	0.200 mg	n/a
Pyridoxine (B$_6$)	0.060 mg	0.040 mg	0.088 mg	n/a	0.067 mg	n/a
Folic Acid (B$_9$)	30.3 mcg	n/a	n/a	n/a	20.4 mcg	n/a
Ascorbic Acid (C)	45-61 mg	37-61 mg	34 mg	158 mg	31 mg	31 mg
Tocopherol (E)	0.24 mg	0.04 mg	n/a	n/a	n/a	n/a

through constant efforts in cross-fertilization and selection, over two hundred varieties of this delicious fruit are now cultivated, with a tremendous improvement in quality. Arab traders brought the bitter orange from the East and propagated it around the Mediterranean. The Moors introduced it to Spain, where it established itself and became known as the Seville orange. This sour orange (*Citrus aurantium*), appreciated for the scent of its flowers and peel and for the sourness of its juice in cooking, was followed in the fifteenth century by the introduction of the sweet orange, also from China, by the Portuguese. The sour orange is now more widely used as a propagation rootstock than for its fruit. The much more popular sweet variety was probably a mutant of the bitter orange, which appeared in China at least by the beginning of our era and probably before. Columbus and other European explorers brought bitter and sweet orange seeds and seedlings with them to the New World in the hope of starting profitable orange plantations. Florida's groves were planted by Spanish missionaries, the most famous perhaps being the groves of St. Augustine, which were laid out in 1565. When Father Junipero Serra and his Franciscan monks began establishing a chain of missions in southern California in 1769, they also brought and planted orange seeds.

Buying Tips

Oranges should be weighty and firm, with smooth, thin, shiny skins, and should give off a sweet, fragrant aroma. Colors range from green-flecked yellow for the smaller juice oranges to deep orange for navels and mandarins. Avoid lightweight or thick-skinned oranges, as they are liable to have less juice. Also avoid those with soft or puffy spots. Buy tree- and sun-ripened fruit whenever possible, as the acids from green or immature fruit may cause adverse reactions in the body. Additionally, most citrus fruits are heavily treated with chemical dips and fumigants, so tree-ripened organic oranges are well worth searching for. Sweeter fruits also have greater food value.

Culinary Uses

Because they oxidize so rapidly, oranges should be used within fifteen minutes of the time they are cut or peeled. Squeezed into juice is the most common way to use oranges, but the segments can also be used in fruit salad or added to smoothies. Thin slices, peel and all, are frequently used as edible garnishes in Asian cooking. Zest is the outer part of the peel from citrus fruits, most commonly lemons or oranges. Zest gives the concentrated flavor of the fruit without adding acid, as would the flesh or juice. The easiest—and least messy—way to take zest is to grate it from an uncut fruit. Be careful to remove only the outermost skin, not the white pith, which is bitter. Use grated orange, lemon, or lime zest, fresh or dried, as a flavoring in savory and sweet dishes. Cut into julienne strips, zest is an attractive garnish. To make a tea, simmer fresh or dried peel, alone or with herbs, for fifteen minutes. Use only organic lemons, oranges, grapefruit, and limes for zest.

Health Benefits

pH 3.00–4.34. Carminative, stimulant, stomachic, tonic. The daily use of an orange will aid in toning up and purifying the entire system, acting as an internal antiseptic, tonic stimulant, and supportive agent. The natural acid and sugar in the orange aid digestion and stimulate the activity of the glands in the stomach. University of Florida scientists have discovered natural antiviral compounds in orange juice that lessen the respiratory symptoms of German measles (rubella) in humans and increase the number of rubella-fighting antibodies in the blood. Freshly squeezed orange juice is predigested food in a delicious and attractive form, ready for immediate absorption and utilization; rich in lime and alkaline salts that counteract the tendency to acidosis, orange juice also has a general stimulating effect on the peristaltic activity of the colon. The amount of food value contained in the juice of a single large orange is about equal to that found in a slice of bread, but orange juice needs no digestion, whereas bread must undergo digestive processing for several hours before it can be used for energizing and strengthening the body.

However, although oranges are an excellent source of water-soluble vitamin C, this vitamin is the least stable of all the vitamins. Orange juice may lose all of its vitamin C within half an hour of being squeezed. Storage of orange juice at low temperatures destroys the vitamin to some extent, while sterilization (pasteurization) may destroy it completely. Additionally, orange juice is one of the ten

LORE AND LEGEND

Oranges are a favorite fruit in mythology, having been identified as the golden apples that grew in the mythological garden of the Hesperides, which in actual fact were probably the Canary Islands. Legend has it that the golden apple presented by Gaea, the ancient Greek goddess of the earth and fertility, as a wedding gift to Hera on the day she married Zeus, was in fact an orange, and the seeds planted in the garden of the Hesperides. When the Moors invaded Spain in the tenth century, they brought oranges with them, but as a sacred fruit, to be used only in religious rites, for medicinal purposes, or as an exquisite flavoring in food and drink. Grown only within walled gardens, the fruits were guarded so jealously that any Christian who ate or even touched an orange did so on pain of death. Five hundred years later, when the Moors were driven out of Spain, these orange groves were perhaps their most valuable legacy. Long a symbol of love, orange blossoms were used by courtesans to sprinkle over their bedsheets and throughout their rooms. Ancient lovers bathed together in orange blossom water, and the fruit itself was given to newlyweds in the belief that its prolific number of seeds would ensure fertility and bless them with many offspring. The custom of using orange blossoms in wedding ceremonies dates back to Saracen brides, who wore orange blossoms on their wedding day; the blossoms were regarded as a symbol of prosperity and fecundity due to the fact that the orange tree bears ripe fruit and blossoms at the same time, and wearing the blossoms represented an appeal to the spirit of the orange tree that the bride should not be barren. The orange, as a traditional Chinese symbol of good luck and prosperity, is still used today in Chinese New Year's celebrations.

most common allergens, and thinking that it's a must is one allergy indicator. Can you start the day *without* OJ? Allergic or otherwise, you might consider choosing the fruit rather than its juice. Too much juice contributes to hypoglycemia or blood sugar imbalance. Unlike juice, a whole orange provides fiber and a powerful antioxidant called glutathione. Eat the whole orange, excluding the very outer skin, to get the full benefits from the fruit.

All varieties of oranges provide purifying energy for both body and mind. In some Wiccan rituals, orange juice is drunk instead of wine, and orange peel tea is said to keep one from getting drunk or muddleheaded. While citrus flesh and juice are cooling, its peel is warming because of its high oil concentration, which make it a useful medicine for cold and deficiency symptoms. The peel contains numerous potent nutraceuticals. Liminoids, for example, are antioxidants that help combat carcinogens in the liver. Citrus peel enhances digestive energy and helps relieve intestinal gas, pain, swelling, and constipation. It also helps decongest the lungs and reduce mucus conditions.

VARIETIES

Bergamot (*Citrus bergamia*) is a variety of bitter orange (see also Seville) used mainly for perfumery and essential oils.

Blood oranges may be uniformly orange, a spotted blend of orange and red, or totally colored a flamboyant red, garnet, or purple. The original mutation that produced the color probably happened in seventeenth-century Sicily and is the result of a pigment (anthocyanin) not usually present in citrus fruits but common in other red fruits and flowers. Used primarily for eating, blood oranges are exceptionally sweet and juicy, literally bursting with rich, zesty, full-bodied citrus flavor, with a deep raspberry aftertaste. The seedless pulp is juicy but firm, less acidic than common oranges, and the membranes separating the segments are downy and soft unless stored too long. Their season begins in December and runs through June.

Clementines (*C. reticulata*), Algerian in origin, are a cross between a mandarin and a bitter orange. They are named for one Brother Clement, a gardener who first cultivated this tree at an orphanage. When the clementine is grown in solid blocks (not near other citrus varieties), it is seedless; otherwise not. The clementine is a medium-sized fruit with a slightly puffy peel and a deep orange, glossy color. It has a unique floral aroma and tastes something like apricot nectar.

Mandarins (*C. reticulata*) are also known as **tangerines.** Although the names are frequently used interchangeably in the United States, a tangerine is technically a subgroup of the mandarin orange. The name *mandarin* was originally no more than a nickname given to this small, loose-skinned, orangelike fruit, brought to England from China by Sir Abraham Hume in 1805. It derives either from the sense of superiority implied by the title or from the color of a mandarin's robes. The name *tangerine* comes from Tangiers, the Moroccan seaport from which they were shipped. Between the years 1840 and 1850, the Italian consul brought the mandarin orange to Louisiana, planting it on the consulate grounds at New Orleans. Always smaller and less acidic than oranges, mandarins have a loose, pebbly, dark orange or reddish-orange skin that separates easily from the flesh. Most are quite seedy and may be slightly tart, but very juicy. Quality mandarins should be heavy for their size, indicating ample juice content. Of the many varieties, probably the best known are the satsumas, developed in Japan during the sixteenth century. They are seedless and bright orange, with loose dullish skin; the smaller ones are usually the sweetest. Mandarins are predominantly eaten out of hand, though the sections are also utilized in fruit salads, gelatins, and puddings or on cakes. Very small types are canned in syrup. Their season runs November through May, peaking in December and January.

Navel oranges are a native of Bahia, Brazil, and are named for the belly-button-like spot at their blossom end. Navels were introduced to the United States in 1870 to fill the need for a good early variety of orange; since they were sponsored by the U.S. Department of Agriculture in Washington, D.C., they came to be called "Washington navels." Their skins are quite bumpy, an indication of their thickness. These seem to be the preferred orange for eating out of hand; their thick rinds are easy to peel, and the flesh is sweet and moist, usually seedless. Juice pressed from navels turns bitter with exposure to air. Their season begins in November, with the peak from March through May.

Ortaniques are a cross between an orange and a tangerine. Flattened in shape, with a medium skin, this hybrid is very juicy and makes a good substitute for either of its parent fruits. Ortaniques can be eaten on their own or in salads, ice creams, desserts, and cakes.

Sevilles (*C. aurantium*), also known as **bitter** or **sour oranges,** are native to southeastern Asia and are reported to have been brought from the East by the Moors, who cultivated plantations of the trees around Seville, from which they derive their name. For five hundred years they were the only orange in Europe, and they were the first orange to reach the New World. Usually imported from Spain, they are considered too sour to be enjoyed out of hand and instead are used for candied peel, marmalade, and liqueur. To approximate the tangy juice, combine three tablespoons each of orange and grapefruit juice with two tablespoons of lemon juice and one teaspoon of grated grapefruit zest to make one-half cup. The leaves and flowers, more aromatic than those of the sweet orange, are used in cosmetics for fragrance.

Tangelos are deliberate or accidental hybrids of the mandarin orange and either the grapefruit or the pummelo. They look rather like large unsymmetrical oranges, with skin a deep orange shaded with bronze. The most popular variety, **Minneola**, has a very distinct knoblike projection on the stem end. Look for hard shiny specimens that feel heavy in your hand. Their colorful orange flesh is juicy but not seedless, with a taste like a blend of orange and tangerine that can be either very tart or very sweet. Peel and prepare like oranges, or squeeze for a wonderfully refreshing juice. Their season runs October through April, peaking November through February.

Tangors are a cross between the tangerine and the sweet orange. Like a tangerine, this fruit is loosely skinned. The most readily available tangors are the **Hamlin**, the **honey tangerine** (also called the Murcott honey orange), the **pineapple orange**, and the **temple orange**.

Valencia oranges are the most widely grown orange, accounting for about half the domestic crop produced each year. They range in size from small to nearly grapefruit-sized, with a smooth, thin skin and slightly oval shape. Their sweet, juicy pulp may have numerous seeds but is well worth eating and makes an outstanding juice as well. Both the California and the Florida varieties produce for about eight or nine months a year. Florida oranges reach their low point in late fall, California ones in late spring. Their season runs March through December.

Papaya
(*Carica papaya*)
Also Known As: Mando (Brazil), Lichasa (Puerto Rico), Paw Paw (Caribbean), Melon Zapote (Mexico)

The genus *Carica* refers to the ancient region called Karia in Asia Minor. The English name *papaya* is a corruption of the Carib name *ababai*.

General Information
The papaya originated in the lowlands of eastern Central America and is second only to the banana in importance to South and Central America. Spanish and Portuguese invaders took to the fruit and quickly spread it to their other settlements in the West and East Indies; it was also taken to the Pacific Islands and by 1800 was being grown in all tropical regions. An extraordinarily generous bearer, the papaya plant is not really a tree but rather a large shrub, similar in appearance to a palm, which puts forth a branchless trunk. This "trunk" grows to about twenty feet but does not harden to bark. Atop this shaft rests a radiating crest of giant leaves under which cluster the ponderous fruits, giving the whole the look of a coconut palm. The large oval or pear-shaped fruit (sometimes called "the melon that grows on trees") can range in size from one to twenty pounds, maturing in eighteen months from the time the seed is planted.

Buying Tips
Choose fruit that feels heavy for its size, is slightly soft to the touch, and is at least half yellow or yellow-orange rather than green. By smelling the stem end, you can tell whether the papaya is sweet or bitter. Avoid overly soft or

Papaya / Nutritional Value Per 100 g Edible Portion			
	Raw		Raw
Calories	23.1-25.8	Zinc	0.07 mg
Protein	0.081-0.340 g	Copper	0.016 mg
Fat	0.05-0.96 g	Manganese	0.011 mg
Fiber	0.5-1.3 g	Beta Carotene (A)	2,014 IU
Calcium	12.9-40.8 mg	Thiamine (B$_1$)	0.021-0.036 mg
Iron	0.25-0.78 mg	Riboflavin (B$_2$)	0.024-0.058 mg
Magnesium	10 mg	Niacin (B$_3$)	0.227-0.555 mg
Phosphorus	5.3-22.0 mg	Pantothenic Acid (B$_5$)	0.218 mg
Potassium	257 mg	Pyridoxine (B$_6$)	0.019 mg
Sodium	3 mg	Ascorbic Acid (C)	35.5-71.3 mg

bruised fruit, or any with soft or hard spots. Papayas will stay fresh for approximately one week when refrigerated.

Culinary Uses

Hawaiian papayas are the size of an average hand and are rich and sweetly flavored. Mexican papayas can be as large as a small watermelon, but they tend to have a thin, gamey flavor that is less attractive. Papayas vary widely in size and color, but the most common varieties are yellow- or orange-skinned and shaped something like an elongated melon or pear. Papaya's lush pink to orange flesh has a fairly sweet flavor similar to apricots and ginger, but sometimes with a peppery bite. In the central cavity lie shiny, gray-to-black peppercorn-sized seeds that are edible, although most people dislike and discard them. To eat a papaya, slice it open and scoop out the seeds. Papaya combines wonderfully with sliced kiwi fruit for breakfast. Peeled chunks can be used raw in salads or baked, sautéed, poached, or otherwise used in desserts and preserves. Cooked papaya does not turn mushy but remains firm and pliant. The black seeds are crunchy and have a peppery taste like mustard and cress. They can be used as a garnish or as a substitute for capers, eaten raw, or crushed for a mildly spicy condiment. The seeds also make a tasty salad dressing ingredient—purée them in a blender and add oil, vinegar, and your choice of seasoning. Dried papaya, if it has any flavor at all, has been sugar-sweetened. *Honey-sweetened papaya* is a dishonest term, the fruit having been soaked in a sugar solution with only a small amount of honey added.

Health Benefits

pH 5.20–5.72. Digestive, stomachic, vermifuge, vulnerary. An extremely nutrient-dense fruit, an average papaya supplies more than a full day's supply of vitamin A, three days' supply of vitamin C, and a high quantity of potassium, calcium, phosphorus, and iron. Externally, papaya juice has been used to remove freckles; internally it cleanses the digestive tract, eliminating gastric indigestion, reducing gas, soothing irritation and inflammation, and cleansing and detoxifying the entire body. Incorporated daily into one's diet, papaya will greatly improve skin, nails, and hair, as well as keep the eyes bright and clear.

Papaya is probably best known for its ability to aid digestion and tenderize meat—two-thirds of all papaya use in the United States is as meat tenderizer (it is also used as a beer-stabilizing agent). Papaya is useful in these capacities because of its content of papain, a proteinase enzyme similar to pepsin (produced by the gastric juices of the stomach). The enzyme is found only in the fresh milky juice of the unripe fruit or the brownish powder to which it dries; very little if any is found in the fully ripe fruit. Papain helps to cleanse the tissues and intestinal walls of all waste matter in the form of excessive mucus and dead tissue. It is harmless to living tissue and is a must for maintenance of health in the intestinal tract. A home remedy to reduce mosquito-bite irritation is to rub the bite with a piece of green papaya, its seeds, or a meat tenderizer made of papain. The papain digests or breaks down the irritating proteins injected by the insect. (However, if you have allergic reactions to insect venom, do *not* use this kitchen remedy.) Part of the protein broken down by papain is converted into arginine, which, in its natural form, has been found to influence the production of Human Growth Hormone (HGH). HGH is produced in the pituitary gland and is directly responsible for DNA and RNA replication as well as synthesis in liver, muscle, cartilage, and adipose tissues. HGH helps to increase muscle tone and decrease body fat.

Papaya seeds are an effective vermicide. In traditional veterinary medicine, papaya seeds also are used as dewormers; in Indonesia and the Philippines, air-dried seeds are ground and mixed with water (three grams of seeds per kilogram of body weight), and this mixture is given to animals once a day for six days. The seeds are also excellent digestive aids. There are more enzymes in one papaya seed than in a whole bottle of store-bought digestive enzyme capsules, plus the seeds have all the nutrients necessary for almost instant assimilation. Eat several before or immediately after a meal and you might be surprised.

Passion Fruit

(Passiflora edulis, P. ligularis, P. quadrangularis, P. molissima)
Also Known As: Granadilla

The flower was named by the Jesuit fathers *flos passionis* (passionflower), or *flor de las cinco llagas* (flower of the five wounds). The term *edulis* means "edible"; *ligularis* means "ligulate" or "strap-shaped"; *quadrangularis* means "quadrangular" or "four-angled"; *molissima* means "softest" or "mildest." The English name *passion fruit* is from an interesting interpretation of the fruit's flowers, which are said

Passion Fruit / Nutritional Value Per 100 g Edible Portion				
	Raw Purple	Raw Sweet	Raw Giant	Raw Banana
Calories	97	n/a	n/a	25
Protein	2.200 g	0.340-0.474 g	0.112-0.299 g	0.600 g
Fat	0.70 g	1.50-3.18 g	0.15-1.29 g	0.10 g
Fiber	10.95 g	3.20-5.60 g	0.70-3.60 g	0.30 g
Calcium	12.0 mg	5.6-13.7 mg	9.2-13.8 mg	4.0 mg
Iron	1.60 mg	0.58-1.56 mg	0.80-2.93 mg	0.40 mg
Magnesium	29 mg	n/a	n/a	n/a
Phosphorus	68 mg	44-78 mg	17-39 mg	20 mg
Potassium	348 mg	n/a	n/a	n/a
Sodium	28 mg	n/a	n/a	n/a
Beta Carotene (A)	700 IU	to 0.035 mg	0.004-0.019 mg	n/a
Thiamine (B$_1$)	n/a	to 0.002 mg	to 0.003 mg	n/a
Riboflavin (B$_2$)	0.130 mg	0.063-0.125 mg	0.033-0.120 mg	0.030 mg
Niacin (B$_3$)	1.500 mg	1.420-1.813 mg	0.378-15.300 mg	2.500 mg
Ascorbic Acid (C)	30.0 mg	10.8-28.1 mg	14.3 mg	70.0 mg

to represent elements of the Passion (crucifixion) of Christ.

General Information

Several types of passion fruit are grown: purple, sweet, giant, and banana. The purple passion fruit (*P. edulis*) is a climbing perennial native from southern Brazil through Paraguay to northern Argentina and widely cultivated in tropical regions. Nearly perfectly round, the three- to six-inch fruit has a tough rind ranging in hue from dark purple to light yellow or pumpkin-colored; within the rind the cavity contains an aromatic mass of membranous sacs filled with orange-colored, pulpy juice and hundreds of small, hard seeds. Sweet passion fruits, or granadillas (*P. ligularis*), are native to Central and South America. The fruits are orange-yellow when ripe and have a sprightly, aromatic flavor. The giant passion fruit (*P. quadrangularis*), often called "giant granadilla," is native to the hotter regions of tropical America and is the largest of the passion fruits. Up to eight inches long, the delicate skin is a pale greenish or yellow color, often blushing with pink and shading to brown when ripe. The fruit gives off a pleasing aroma but is often bland in flavor and is best combined with other, more flavorful fruits. Banana passion fruits (*P. molissima*) are oval and long, more banana-like in shape, with pulp that is not quite as sweet as the purple variety.

LORE AND LEGEND

In the sixteenth century, when the Jesuit missionaries arrived with the conquistadores in South America, they found a blooming vine, which they believed to be the same flower that, according to Christian legend, was seen growing upon the cross in one of the many visions of St. Francis of Assisi (1182–1226). In this vine, whose various parts are said to represent certain aspects of the Passion (crucifixion) of Christ, the Jesuit missionaries fancied that they had not only discovered a marvelous symbol, but also received an assurance of the ultimate triumph of Christianity. The ten white petals represented the ten faithful apostles. Two are absent, representing Peter, who deceived and denied his Lord, and Judas, who betrayed him. The corona symbolized the crown of thorns or halo that surrounded Jesus's head, and the five bright red stamens the five wounds. The ovary signified the hammer, and the three styles, with their rounded heads, the three nails. The tendrils are suggestive of the cords or whips with which he was beaten, while the small seed vessel is the sponge filled with vinegar that was offered to quench Jesus's thirst. When the flower is not entirely opened, it resembles a star, the Star of the East as seen by the three wise men.

South American natives, who had been cultivating these vines since time immemorial, feasted upon its yellow egglike fruits, and the Jesuit fathers interpreted this too as a heavenly sign, that the Indians were hungering for Christianity. Throwing themselves with great religious zeal into converting these yearning heathens to Christianity, the fathers succeeded in a remarkably short time.

Buying Tips

Ripe fruit should be firm and heavy with wrinkled skins. If the skin is not deeply wrinkled but only shriveled and unappealing, keep the fruit at room temperature until the wrinkles become more pronounced.

Culinary Uses

Passion fruit may be eaten straight from the skin like a melon, added to fruit salads, made into juice, puréed and used as a sauce to decorate and flavor desserts, or cooked into jam. The flavor is strong, tangy, almost punchy, combining pineapple, lemon, and guava. The pulp of the banana passion fruit is not quite as juicy and sweet as that of the purple passion fruit, but it is still tasty.

Pawpaw
(Asimina triloba)

Asimina is from *Asiminier,* a French and Indian name of unknown definition. *Triloba* means "three-lobed." The English name *pawpaw* (sometimes spelled *papaw*) is derived from the American Indian name for the fruit.

General Information

This small native North American tree is generally found growing in thickets along riverbanks as far north on the East Coast as New York State and as far west as Nebraska. In 1916 the American Genetic Association offered a prize of one hundred dollars for the most impressive specimens—fifty dollars for the largest tree and fifty dollars for the best fruit. Since then, however, little has been done to spread and improve the tree. The pawpaw tree has the appearance of being an escapee from the tropics and is in fact a member of the tropical and subtropical custard apple family. The fruits when mature resemble stubby bananas with obtuse ends, often four or five inches long and more than 1½ inches thick. When ripe, they are greenish-yellow, turning speckled and streaked with brown a few days after they are pulled from the tree. The smooth skin, without the knobs or reticulations characteristic of its tropical relatives, encloses pulp that is creamy yellow, soft, and smooth, surrounding two rows of large inedible brown seeds. A few pawpaw trees yield fruit with orange pulp, and these are considered the finest.

Pawpaw / Nutritional Value Per 100 g Edible Portion			
	Raw		Raw
Calories	85	Fat	0.9 g
Protein	5.2 g		

Buying Tips

Pawpaws should not be picked until after the first heavy frost. Choose greenish-yellow fruit that is slightly soft.

Culinary Uses

Pawpaws have a rich, sweet, creamy flavor evocative of bananas but with the additional hints of vanilla custard, pineapple, and mango. All this is overlaid with a heavy fragrance that some may find cloying. Fully ripe fruit does not store very well, but the fruit will last several months if picked firm-ripe and refrigerated. The best way to eat fresh pawpaw is to halve the fruit and scoop the flesh out with a spoon; another way is to peel the skin like a banana, though it does not separate quite as easily. Pawpaw is usually eaten raw. It does not take kindly to cooking, as its flavor is easily driven away by heat, but it can be baked with care or made into various desserts.

Peach
(Prunus persica vulgaris)

An apple is an excellent thing—until you have tried a peach.

—George du Maurier

A Georgia peach, a real Georgia peach, a backyard great-grandmother's orchard peach, is as thickly furred as a sweater, and so fluent and sweet that once you bite through the flannel, it brings tears to your eyes.

—Melissa Fay Greene, *Praying for Sheetrock*

This tree is part of the large plum family, thus the *Prunus* genus. *Persica* is simply an epithet meaning "Persian," partly because the fruit flourished so well in Persia that it came to be regarded as a native Persian fruit and partly because one of its many nicknames was the Persian plum. *Vulgaris* refers to the fact that it was a commonly grown plant. The English name *peach* derives ultimately from the Latin *persica.*

General Information

The peach tree is a low, spreading tree cultivated in both China and Persia since ancient times, and probably Chinese in origin, being found in Chinese writings as far back as the tenth century B.C. It began its long westward journey in caravans that carried it to India and on to Persia, where it became naturalized and where invading Roman legions encountered it, calling it *malus Persicus*, or Persian apple. The Roman emperor Claudius is credited with establishing it in Greece, and soon Greek legend and myth were filled with stories of the Persian apple, the golden fruit of the gods. Peaches were among the first trees the Spaniards planted in Mexico, Brazil, the West Indies, and the California missions. Early explorers and settlers planted peaches up and down the eastern seaboard of North America, while the Native Americans carried the fruit westward, planting peach stones about their campsites and along trails from Florida to the Great Lakes. By the mid-1700s, the fruit was so firmly established that some botanists assumed that the peach was native to America. Today the peach is one of the most widely culti-

Peach / Nutritional Value Per 100 g Edible Portion		
	Raw	Dried, Sulfured
Calories	43	262
Protein	0.7 g	3.1 g
Fat	0.09 g	0.70 g
Fiber	0.64 g	3.1 0g
Calcium	5 mg	48 mg
Iron	0.11 mg	6.00 mg
Magnesium	7 mg	n/a
Phosphorus	12 mg	117 mg
Potassium	197 mg	950 mg
Sodium	0 mg	16 mg
Zinc	0.140 mg	n/a
Copper	0.068 mg	n/a
Manganese	0.047 mg	n/a
Beta Carotene (A)	535 IU	3,900 IU
Thiamine (B$_1$)	0.017 mg	0.010 mg
Riboflavin (B$_2$)	0.041 mg	0.190 mg
Niacin (B$_3$)	0.990 mg	5.300 mg
Pantothenic Acid (B$_5$)	0.170 mg	n/a
Pyridoxine (B$_6$)	0.018 mg	n/a
Folic Acid (B$_9$)	3.4 mcg	n/a
Ascorbic Acid (C)	6.6 mg	18.0 mg

vated fruit trees throughout the world, wherever the soil and climate are suitable. They are the third most popular fruit grown in the United States, coming in right behind apples and oranges, and are among the most popular fruits for eating out of hand.

Buying Tips

Ripe peaches should be firm and free from blemishes, yielding to gentle pressure. They should have a warm, fragrant aroma and a fresh, softly colorful appearance of either whitish or yellowish color, combined with a red color or blush, depending on the variety. Those tinged with green

LORE AND LEGEND

The peach tree in China is called the Tree of the Fairy Fruit. It is the symbol of immortality because the Peach Tree of the Gods, which grew in the mythical gardens of Hsi Wang My, the Royal Lady of the West, bloomed only once every three thousand years, to yield the ripened Fruits of Eternal Life. Those who eat of these fruits have health, virility, and the gift of immortality conferred upon them. The sacred food of the Eight Taoist Immortals, and the most important sacred plant in the Chinese Taoist religion, the peach was considered a symbol of immortality and of the Tao, the way of attaining this immortality. Even today the Chinese consider the peach a symbol of longevity, and plates and bowls used for birthday celebrations are often decorated with peaches and their blossoms.

In Japan there is a popular folktale that goes as follows: One day, while washing her clothes at the river, an old woman saw a large, round, pink object splashing and rolling about in the water. Carefully fishing it out, she found it was a peach so large that it would feed her husband and herself for several days. When they broke it open, a tiny child was found inside the stone. Bringing him up with great love and devotion, they gave him everything they could afford. When he was grown, he invaded the Island of the Devils, where he defeated the demons and seized their treasure, laying it at the feet of his beloved foster parents.

Culinary Uses

The flavor of peaches should be warm, syrupy, and sensuous, the very epitome of summer. Peaches do not gain in sugar content after being picked, as there is no reserve of starch to draw from. They are best eaten straight from the tree, edible fuzzy skin and all, but they can be added to fruit salads, baked in desserts, or made into jams and jellies. Peaches go beautifully with other fruit, especially raspberries and other drupes or stone fruits—apricots, cherries, plums, and almonds—that ripen at the same time. Peaches and cream are natural companions. When sugar is added, the reaction in the body becomes acidic; when cooked or canned, their vital elements are lost.

Health Benefits

pH 3.28–4.20. Diuretic, expectorant, laxative, sedative. Peaches are easily digested, have a strong alkaline reaction on the body, stimulate the secretion of the digestive juices, help improve the health of the skin, and add color to the complexion. They have both laxative and diuretic qualities and are an aid in cleansing the system whenever there is kidney and bladder trouble. With fewer calories and a higher water content than apples or pears, peaches are an excellent fruit for hot summer days. For a "peaches and cream" complexion, apply a poultice of blended fresh peach on the face, let dry, then rinse and pat dry. Peach leaf taken as a tea is used for morning sickness, to cleanse the kidneys, and to destroy intestinal worms.

VARIETIES

There are hundreds of varieties of peaches but two basic categories—clingstone and freestone—denoting whether the flesh adheres to or breaks free of the pit. Both categories include both red and yellow peaches. White peaches, with their delicate perfume and exquisite juiciness, are worth seeking out. They are more fragile and expensive, but peach perfectionists prize them.

Clingstone peaches arrive first in the season, appearing in June and lasting until August. Most have skins that are either all yellow or yellow with a large red area, and flesh that is red around a stone that cannot be removed easily. They tend to be juicier, sweeter, and softer-textured than freestones, making excellent dessert peaches by themselves or blended into fruit shakes and ice cream. Less convenient to prepare

were picked immature and will not ripen satisfactorily; they will develop only a pale weak color, little or no flavor, and tough rubbery flesh. Fuzzy peaches are less likely to have been heavily sprayed with pesticides, since fuzz indicates they have escaped the commercial "bathhouse." You can keep peaches at room temperature until they are as soft as you prefer, then store them in the refrigerator and use within a few days. Remember that ripe peaches bruise easily, so handle them with care.

because of the stones, these are the type most commonly used for canning and jam.

Freestone peaches tend to show up later, arriving in July and lasting into September. These are the most popular varieties for eating fresh since they can be split in half by hand and the stones easily removed. Freestones are larger than clingstones, are less juicy, and have a firmer texture, but they are nevertheless very fragrant and sweet tasting and are excellent for canning and baking into pies.

Pear
(Pyrus communis)

> There are only ten minutes in the life of a pear when it is perfect to eat.
>
> —RALPH WALDO EMERSON

Pyrus is the classical Latin name for the pear tree, while *communis* means "common, general, or gregarious." The English word *pear* derives from the Latin term.

General Information
The pear tree seems to have originated in western Asia around the Caspian Sea. Some pears are the distinctive pear shape, while others are elongated, and still others are round. The Romans introduced this fruit into Europe. More than five thousand varieties can now be listed, some spread throughout the world, others found in only one country or even limited to a small locality. In 1850, pears were so popular in France that it was the fashion among the elite to see who could raise the best specimen, and the fruit was celebrated in song and verse. In the United States the pear is almost as much a national favorite as the apple, to which it is related—both are members of the rose family and pome fruits (those with a distinct seeded core). Pear trees were brought to North America by early colonists, who used cuttings from European stock, and the fruit was introduced into California by Franciscan monks, who planted them in mission gardens. Today 95 percent of American-produced commercial pears are grown in Washington, Oregon, and California. Unlike most tree fruits, pears are best ripened off the tree; when tree-ripened, they develop little grit cells, or stones, in the flesh. Separated from the tree, this process cannot take place, and they ripen evenly and smoothly, with a creamy texture.

Buying Tips
Most pears are yellow and have brown or reddish overtones to them, depending on their variety. Select firm, unblemished fruit. They are fully ripe when they give to gentle pressure. Since pears ripen from the core outward, be careful not to let them soften too much, as they will turn to mush. Avoid those that are bruised, have rough scaly areas, or have soft flesh near the stem. Let pears ripen at home either on the counter or in a brown paper bag. Never store a pear sealed in plastic. Without freely circulating oxygen, the core will turn brown and brown spots will develop under the skin. When fully ripe and soft, pears should be stored in the refrigerator and used within a couple of days.

Culinary Uses
Pears are elegantly seductive. Sweet, juicy, wonderfully textured, and highly nutritious, they have the most subtle taste of all orchard fruit and leave the palate delightfully fresh and clean. They are probably the easiest fruit to identify by their shape: the small stem end gradually broadens to a plump blossom end like a bell. Properly ripened, pears are so tender they were once called the "butter fruit." They can be used in all the same ways as apples, including for cider (called "perry"). Fresh pears make wonderful companions for wine, bread, and a mixture of sharp cheeses. Hollowed pear halves make attractive boats for various fillings.

Health Benefits
pH 3.50–4.60. Pears are extremely rich in alkaline elements, have a strong diuretic action, are helpful for constipation and

Pear / Nutritional Value Per 100 g Edible Portion			
	Raw		Raw
Calories	59	Copper	0.113 mg
Protein	0.39 g	Manganese	0.076 mg
Fat	0.40 g	Beta Carotene (A)	20 IU
Fiber	1.40 g	Thiamine (B$_1$)	0.020 mg
Calcium	11 mg	Riboflavin (B$_2$)	0.040 mg
Iron	0.25 mg	Niacin (B$_3$)	0.100 mg
Magnesium	6 mg	Pantothenic Acid (B$_5$)	0.070 mg
Phosphorus	11 mg	Pyridoxine (B$_6$)	0.018 mg
Potassium	125 mg	Folic Acid (B$_9$)	7.3 mcg
Sodium	0 mg	Ascorbic Acid (C)	4 mg
Zinc	0.120 mg	Tocopherol (E)	0.50 mg

poor digestion, and are valuable as general cleansers of the system. Their iodine content helps to keep the thyroid functioning properly and the metabolism balanced. Pears are an excellent source of water-soluble fibers, including pectin. In fact, pears are actually higher in pectin than apples. Pectin reduces serum cholesterol and cleanses the body of environmental and radioactive toxins. The regular consumption of pears is believed to result in a pure complexion and shiny hair. Dried pears are a good energy producer in the wintertime as well as a delicious snack year-round.

VARIETIES

Anjou (Beurre d'Anjou) are the most abundant winter variety of pear. Originating in France or Belgium in the nineteenth century, they are a round, yellowish-green pear that tapers bluntly to the stem end, with a thick, barely noticeable neck and no waistline. Belonging to the bergamot group of pears, their skin remains green but develops a definite glow when ripe; they should be eaten only when they yield to gentle pressure. Although the skin is not tough, it is not as sweet as the meat and has a slightly grainy texture. The flesh is spicy-sweet and juicy with a firm texture. Anjous are a wonderful dessert pear; their firm texture makes them the best pear for cooking and baking, since they never seem to lose their shape. Available from October through May.

Bartletts were first raised in 1770 in Berkshire, England, by a schoolmaster named John Stair. Arriving in London, this variety of pear was called **Williams** after Mr. Williams of Middlesex, who distributed them. In 1798 or 1799, it was brought to the United States and planted in Dorchester, Massachusetts, under the name of **Williams' Bon Chretien**. Enoch Bartlett acquired the estate in 1817 and, not knowing the true name of the pear, distributed it under his own name. In other parts of the world it is still known as Williams or Williams' Bon Chretien. The Bartlett is a true pyriform pear, with a definite waistline and a long stem; it is a large, golden-yellow summer pear, bell-shaped, with smooth, clear skin, often blushed with red. It has white, finely grained flesh that is juicy and delicious. The yellow variety ripens very quickly once picked and bruises easily (even loud noises are said to hurt them); they are best eaten while still flecked with green. The most common variety grown today, Bartletts comprise more than 65 percent of commercial production. They are excellent canners and dessert fruit but are too fragile for lunch bags and picnic baskets. Available July through December.

Bosc (Beurre Bosc) are a member of the conical pear family and are long, tapered, and waistless. They are generally medium-sized, dark yellow, with rough brown skins and long, narrow necks. When properly ripened, they become a dark russet color and respond to gentle pressure. The meat is firm and almost crunchy, cream-colored, very juicy, and smooth-textured. The larger ones usually have the best flavor and sweetness. An excellent pear for eating out of hand, the Bosc holds up well in lunch pails, picnic baskets, and fruit bowls; it is also wonderful baked, broiled, poached, or preserved. Available from October through May.

Clapp pears are hardly ever shipped but are frequently available at roadside stands and farmer's markets. The green Clapp pear has a thinner skin than most, while the red Clapp has a heavier skin and a slightly firmer texture. Of medium size, they have very white flesh, a high sugar content, and plenty of juice.

Comice (Doyenne du Comice)—meaning "best of the show") pears have the reputation of being the sweetest and most flavorful pears. They have a definite pyriform shape, with a short, wide stem end, a waistline, and a very wide blossom end. Somewhat squat and irregularly formed, they are heavily perfumed, with a heady, musky fragrance. Their color during peak ripeness is a soft green that glows with a golden aura and is sometimes slightly bronzed or flecked. Similar in size to the Anjou, they are distinguished from their cousin by a red blush. Their skin is so thin and the flesh so wet that anything more than a gentle stroke leaves a mark; their creamy smooth flesh literally melts in the mouth. Best when eaten fresh, they are also delectable baked into desserts. Available from October through January.

Packhams (Packham's Triumph) are mostly imported, although some are grown in California. Coming in primarily medium and large premium sizes, this pear has a definite pear shape, but the wide bottom is irregular, with a deep blossom end. They also have a perfume that adds to their exotic flavor. Very, very juicy and sweet, a Packham pear at its peak (just turning soft gold all over) begs to be taken home. Available from late June to September.

Red Bartletts are a development of Northwestern pear growers and are fast becoming increasingly available. The red skin is heavier than the yellow variety, the pigment resists disease better, and the ripening process is not quite so quick. Three-quarters red, solid at the cone end, and striped below the waist, they are ripe when the yellow area shows slight green and the striped area is still red, not russet or brown.

Seckels are a true American pear, having been discovered as a mutant sometime around the time of the Revolution. They take their name from the man who acquired the land in Delaware where the original tree was discovered. They have hard green skin that turns slightly golden and develops a light red blush when ripe, a spicy aroma, and crisp but sweet flesh. Always very small and frequently only bite-sized, these are a fun fruit for all but make an especially good children's fruit because of their size. Served fresh, poached, or pickled whole, these eye-catchers are sure to please with their sweet flesh. Available from September through January.

Pear, Asian
(Pyrus ussuriensis, P. pyrifolia)
Also Known As: Sand Pear

Pyrus is the classical Latin name for the pear tree, while *ussuriensis* means "coming from Ussuri" (in east Asia); *pyrifolia* means "having foliage like the common pear." The English name *Asian pear* was given because these members of the pear family are Asian in heritage.

General Information
The sand or Asian pear developed in Asia. The Chinese have been growing and eating Asian pears for the past twenty-five hundred to three thousand years. By the time of the Han dynasty (first century B.C.), there were large orchards planted along the Huai and Yellow rivers. There are currently over three thousand cultivars grown in China, but only twenty-five varieties or so are known in the United States. Asian pears were introduced to North America during the Gold Rush by Chinese miners who grew the trees along streams of the Sierra Nevada. Distinguished from the European "butter fruit" pear, with its soft, melting flesh, sand pears have hard flesh with numerous "sand" or grit cells. Since there are numerous Far Eastern pear varieties marketed under the same name, you will find a wide range of seemingly disparate fruits: they can be petite and chartreuse, mammoth and reddish brown, smooth-skinned and lacquerlike, or sprinkled with a confetti of russeting.

Buying Tips
Choose the most fragrant Asian pears. They are hard when ripe but should be stored in the refrigerator.

Culinary Uses
Asian pears are all crunch and juice, so crisp-firm they can be cut paper-thin, their sweet nectar welling up and pouring off each slice. Ready to eat when you buy them, they can be stored for a long period if refrigerated. Looking like and eaten like apples, their flavor ranges from sweet with just a hint of perfume to sweet with a strong floral aroma. They have a mellower flavor and more juice than either apples or European pears but are granular in texture. Cooked, they resemble the European pears in flavor, but the flesh remains slightly firm and meaty. Allow a much longer cooking time than you would for other pears.

Pear, Asian / Nutritional Value Per 100 g Edible Portion			
	Raw		Raw
Calories	42	Copper	0.050 mg
Protein	0.50 g	Manganese	0.060 mg
Fat	0.23 g	Beta Carotene (A)	0 IU
Fiber	n/a	Thiamine (B₁)	0.009 mg
Calcium	4 mg	Riboflavin (B₂)	0.010 mg
Iron	n/a	Niacin (B₃)	0.219 mg
Magnesium	8 mg	Pantothenic Acid (B₅)	0.070 mg
Phosphorus	11 mg	Pyridoxine (B₆)	0.022 mg
Potassium	121 mg	Folic Acid (B₉)	8 mcg
Sodium	0 mg	Ascorbic Acid (C)	1.2 mg-3.8 g
Zinc	0.02 mg		

Pejibaye
(Bactris gasipaes)
Also Known As: Peach Palm

Bactris derives from the Greek *bactron*, meaning "cane," as the young stems of this plant were used for walking sticks.

General Information
The pejibaye is indigenous to the Amazonian areas of Colombia, Ecuador, Peru, and Brazil and is little known outside of tropical Central America. Yellow to orange or scarlet, turning purple when fully ripe, the one- to three-inch fruit is ovoid, oblate, cylindrical, or conical. The skin

Pejibaye / Nutritional Value Per 100 g Edible Portion			
	Raw		**Raw**
Protein	0.340–0.633 g	Beta Carotene (A)	0.290–2.760 mg
Fat	3.10–8.17 g	Thiamine (B$_1$)	0.037–0.070 mg
Fiber	0.8–1.4 g	Riboflavin (B$_2$)	0.099–0.154 mg
Calcium	8.9–40.4 mg	Niacin (B$_3$)	0.667–1.945 mg
Iron	0.85–2.25 mg	Ascorbic Acid (C)	14.8–41.4 mg
Phosphorus	33.5–55.2 mg		

is thin, the flesh yellow to light orange, sweet yet occasionally with a trace of bitterness, and dry and mealy. Some fruits are seedless, but normally there is a single conical seed. Borne in bunches of up to three hundred fruits, there may be as many as thirteen bunches on a single trunk, and under ideal conditions two crops are harvested per year.

Culinary Uses

Because the fruit is caustic in its natural state, it is commonly prepared by boiling in salted water for three hours, or by roasting. Once boiled or roasted, the flesh and inedible skin separate easily from the seed. The white seed kernel, said to have a flavor like coconut, is sometimes cooked and eaten. However, the seeds are considered to be difficult to digest. Young flowers may be chopped and added to omelets, while palm hearts are served in salads or prepared with eggs and vegetables in a casserole.

Health Benefits

Pejibaye fruit can provide more carbohydrate and protein per hectare (2.47 acres) than corn. This protein contains seven of the eight essential amino acids (excluding only tryptophan), along with ten other nonessential amino acids.

Pepino

(Solanum muricatum)

Also Known As: Melon Pear, Mellowfruit

Solanum comes from the Latin *solamen*, meaning "solace" or "quieting." *Muricatum* means "muricate," or roughed by means of hard points. The English word *pepino* means "cucumber" in Spanish, in reference to the fruit's shape.

General Information

The pepino is a member of the nightshade family, like potatoes, peppers, and tomatoes. This small bush is native to temperate Andean areas of Peru and Chile, and cultivated elsewhere in Central and South America. Efforts to promote the pepino as a commercial crop in California during the 1920s were unsuccessful, but it has since been brought into cultivation in Australia and New Zealand. The shape of the fruit is evocative of a large acorn, a skewed heart, or a giant teardrop, while its skin is yellow-gold and frequently streaked with lavender. The thin skin is very smooth, like that of its relative the eggplant. One variety (Rio Barba) is vinelike and its fruits resemble small cucumbers, thus the name *pepino*. A typical fruit is about three inches in diameter near the stem end and five inches long.

Buying Tips

Choose aromatic fruits (the size does not affect the flavor) that give to gentle pressure like a partly ripe plum, avoiding those with dents or bruises. The fruit should smell lightly sweet, almost honeysuckle-like. The undercolor of the skin should be golden to pinky-apricot when fully ripe, not greenish or mustardy. The flesh is similar to honeydew melon—watery, subtly flavored, and not overly sweet.

Culinary Uses

Pepinos range from plum- to cantaloupe-sized, are slightly heart-shaped, and have fragrant yellow-gold flesh surrounding a central pocket of seeds, like a melon. The mild pulp compares to the finest-textured and juiciest melon, although less sweet, while its aroma suggests a perfumed Bartlett pear blended with vanilla and honey. Serve pepino like melon, or use it in fruit salads. Both seeds and skins are edible, but the skins tend to be tough and unpalatable so are best pulled off once the fruit is sliced.

Health Benefits

Pepinos are low in fat and high in fiber and vitamin C.

Persimmon

(Diospyros virginiana, D. kaki)

> Write me down as one who loved poetry, and
> persimmons.
>
> —SHIKI

Diospyros comes from the Greek words *dios*, meaning "god" (in this case Jupiter or Jove), and *pyros*, meaning "grain"; thus the name means "Jove's grain," alluding to this plant's succulent edible fruits. One of the European species of *Diospyros* is said to have caused oblivion, transporting the eater to heaven, the land of Jove. The term *virginiana* means that this variety was first encountered in that state (Virginia); *kaki* is the Japanese name for the fruit. The English name *persimmon* comes from the Algonquian Indian *putchamin* or *pessemin*, meaning "dried fruit," since well into the colonial era dried persimmons were stored and eaten like figs or mixed with wild nuts and jerked game as pemmican.

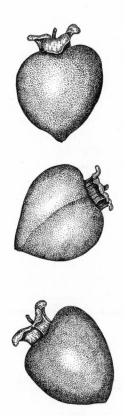

General Information

The persimmon that is native to the United States (*D. virginiana*) grows wild from Connecticut to Florida and from Texas to Kansas. This persimmon is much smaller than the Oriental variety—about the size of a walnut or cherry tomato—but resembles the larger heart-shaped Oriental persimmon in both its bright coloring and the gooey texture of the inner flesh; it also has a stronger fragrance and flavor, sweet and luscious, approaching the richness of dates. Sufficient quantities grow to satisfy local demand, but few outside the region have tasted the fruit, since little or no shipping is done. Native Americans recognized the honeyed sweetness of the ripe fruit hanging like small orange balls from the bare branches of the tree in late autumn. They dried persimmons to eat during the long winters or baked them into breads and puddings. The Oriental persimmon (*D. kaki*) is probably native to China and is widely cultivated in both China and Japan. The Japanese consider it their national fruit, but it is more properly called the Oriental rather than the Japanese persimmon. Commodore Perry's expedition, which opened Japan to world commerce in 1852, is credited with the introduction of this variety to the United States. Contrary to popular folklore, persimmons do not need a frost to fully ripen; those fruits with a dark orange color can be picked while still solid and ripened fully off the tree. You can wait for them to become so ripe that they fall off the tree by themselves, or by shaking the tree you can bring down a shower of fruit. In Israel a form of persimmon known as Sharon fruit is grown without the high tannic acid content.

Buying Tips

Good-quality fruit is well shaped, plump, smooth, and highly colored, with an unbroken skin and an attached stem cap. They are very fragile when fully ripe, so handle with care. Too-firm persimmons will ripen in a few days on their own, or faster if enclosed in a bag with a banana or an apple, whose natural ethylene gas will help them ripen.

Culinary Uses

Persimmons look rather like bright orange plastic tomatoes. Allow them to ripen at room temperature until soft and rather mushy, much like a soft ripe plum. Underripe fruits can be very unpleasantly astringent because of their tannin content, but this tannin disappears as the fruit ripens and sweetens. In general, persimmons that have dark-colored flesh are sweeter and less astringent; these may be eaten before they become too soft. Varieties with light-colored flesh, with the exception of the Fuyu variety, are astringent until they soften. To eat, remove the stem cap, cut in half, and scoop out the soft, brilliantly colored, sensuous flesh. Their texture and flavor are rich, soft, sweet, and spicy, with the texture of a very ripe warm mango, the taste of apricot-papaya custard, and the sweetness of a tree sap like maple syrup. Persimmons are best enjoyed on their own or in fruit salads, but they can be added to puddings and cakes or made into jams and chutneys. They take to many of the same simple flavorings as do mango and papaya, so a touch of citrus or ginger sets them off nicely. In eastern Asia the custom has been to dry them for winter use. In this process the flesh turns blackish, and a fine coating of sugar develops on the surface. These sweet dried fruits are a particular favorite in China for the New Year celebration in February. Surplus persimmons may be converted into molasses, cider, beer, and wine. Roasted seeds have been used as a coffee substitute.

LORE AND LEGEND

In Japan every child knows the origins of the persimmon tree from one of the miraculous tales about the childhood of the great Samurai leader of the twelfth century, Yoshitsune. Yoshitsune and the great giant Benkei met in a confrontation one day, and the giant was knocked over by a blow from Yoshitsune, who was no bigger than a boot, but braver than a tiger. The noise of the fall was so tremendous that the earth shook and split open; out of the crack came a tree covered with beautiful orange-red fruits that were full of juice for the two thirsty fighters. From then on the two warriors were inseparable, and Benkei became Yoshitsune's champion fighter.

Health Benefits

pH 4.42–4.70. Persimmons soothe sore throats and irritated intestinal tracts, are noted for their mild laxative qualities, and contain enzymes that break down damaged cells and foreign microbes. Chinese medicine advises that combining persimmon and crab at the same meal can produce extreme diarrhea.

VARIETIES

Fuyus are the yellow-orange, tomato-shaped variety of persimmon most commonly grown and enjoyed in Israel and Japan. Hard and crisp like an apple, they can be eaten out of hand or peeled and cut in slices across the fruit to reveal the beautiful flower formation in the center.

Hachiya persimmons are the largest and most handsome Oriental variety grown in this country. As a rule, California produces a seedless variety, while the Hachiya grown in Florida has one or more seeds. They are the size of a nectarine or large plum, slightly teardrop-shaped, with a glossy, deep red-orange skin. To be ripe, this large showy fruit with its deep yellow or pink flesh must be very soft, with an almost pudding-like consistency.

Persimmon / Nutritional Value Per 100 g Edible Portion	Raw Japanese	Raw American
Calories	70	127
Protein	0.58 g	0.80 g
Fat	0.19 g	0.40 g
Fiber	1.48 g	1.50 g
Calcium	8 mg	27 mg
Iron	0.15 mg	2.50 mg
Magnesium	9 mg	n/a
Phosphorus	17 mg	26 mg
Potassium	161 mg	310 mg
Sodium	1 mg	1 mg
Zinc	0.11 mg	n/a
Copper	0.113 mg	n/a
Manganese	0.355 mg	n/a
Beta Carotene (A)	2,167 IU	n/a
Thiamine (B$_1$)	0.030 mg	n/a
Riboflavin (B$_2$)	0.020 mg	n/a
Niacin (B$_3$)	0.100 mg	n/a
Folic Acid (B$_9$)	7.5 mcg	n/a
Ascorbic Acid (C)	7.5 mg	66.0 mg

Pineapple
(Ananas comosus)

Ananas was the Carib name for this plant, which despite the sound has nothing to do with bananas but comes from a Guarani word meaning "excellent fruit." *Comosus* means "with long hair." The fruit is neither a pine nor an apple, and its English name, *pineapple*, is only an illustrative term for its form, which resembles a pinecone.

General Information

The unusual-looking pineapple plant is native to southern Brazil and Paraguay; it was carried by Indians throughout South and Central America to Mexico and the West Indies long before the arrival of Europeans. The sailors of the Columbus expedition of 1493 encountered the pineapple on the island of Guadeloupe and were both astonished and delighted by its qualities. The native Indians believed that the pineapple had been brought to Guadeloupe from the Amazon many generations before by the warlike and ferocious Caribs, whose custom it was to bring home seeds, roots, and plants from the places they invaded. The plant consists of a rosette of stiff, sharp-pointed, thorn-edged leaves, with a stem rising from the center that reaches a height of three or four feet. Near the summit of the stem, it swells into a fruit. Resembling a pinecone, the pineapple is not even a fruit in the ordinary sense of the word, but a sorosis, a multiple organ that forms when the fruits of a hundred or more separate flowers on a spike coalesce to form a pulpy mass. There are no records of just when or how the pineapple arrived in Hawaii, although the most generally accepted theory is that they either floated in from a wrecked Spanish or Portuguese ship or were brought ashore by sailors and discarded. The first white settlers found the fruit growing wild beside the sugarcane, and it did not take many years for them to realize its possible commercial value, with the first commercial plantings being set out about 1840. In 1898 the young J. D. Dole arrived in Hawaii, along with hundreds of settlers who had been granted Hawaiian homesteads. He persuaded the homesteaders to plant their land to pineapples, and soon the pineapple industry was born. For many years Hawaii supplied 70 percent of the world's canned pineapple and 85 percent of the canned pineapple juice, but labor costs have shifted a large segment of the industry from Hawaii to the Philippines.

Buying Tips

Pineapples, unlike most other fruits, do not ripen or sweeten after picking. Since they have no reserve of starch to be converted into sugar, they start to deteriorate instead. Look for large, plump, heavy fruit with fresh, deep green plumage. Skin coloring may be green or yellow-gold, depending on the variety. The base should be slightly soft, and there is generally a sweet, but not fermented, aroma. Avoid fruit that is old looking, dry, or starting to decay at the base. To ensure a uniformly sweet fruit, remove the leaves and stand the pineapple upside down at room temperature so the sweet juice concentrated at the base can run throughout. Pineapples can be stored at room temperature if used within a few days. Cut into chunks, the fruit can be kept in a plastic container in the refrigerator for four or five more days.

Culinary Uses

One of the most popular tropical fruits because of its high sugar content and lush flavor, it is not a fruit to make a whole meal out of. Pineapples contain a large amount of bromelin, a protein-digesting enzyme, which is so powerful that plantation and cannery workers have to wear rubber gloves to avoid having their hands literally eaten away. Recognizing this quality, early Hawaiians cooked and baked their meat overlaid with chunks of pineapple; this had a tenderizing effect on the toughest animal meat and was the culinary forerunner of ham decorated with pineapple slices. Bromelin is also responsible for the fact that a gelatin dessert made with fresh pineapple will not set unless an additional jelling agent such as agar-agar is

Pineapple / Nutritional Value Per 100 g Edible Portion			
	Raw		Raw
Calories	49	Copper	0.110 mg
Protein	0.39 g	Manganese	1.649 mg
Fat	0.43 g	Beta Carotene (A)	23 IU
Fiber	0.3-0.6 g	Thiamine (B$_1$)	0.048-0.138 mg
Calcium	6.2-37.2 mg	Riboflavin (B$_2$)	0.011-0.040 mg
Iron	0.27-0.05 mg	Niacin (B$_3$)	0.130-0.267 mg
Magnesium	14 mg	Pantothenic Acid (B$_5$)	0.160 mg
Phosphorus	6.6-11.9 mg	Pyridoxine (B$_6$)	0.090 mg
Potassium	113 mg	Folic Acid (B$_9$)	10.6 mcg
Sodium	1.0-1.4 mg	Ascorbic Acid (C)	27.0-65.2 mg
Zinc	0.080 mg	Tocopherol (E)	0.10 mg

Europeans were completely infatuated with pineapples, even though their climate was unsuited to growing them. Eating them took some getting used to, however. Charles V, king of Spain and Holy Roman Emperor, refused to taste a specimen for fear of being poisoned, while Louis XIV of France rashly bit into the strange fruit before it could be peeled, and thus cut his mouth on the scaly skin. In 1700 a Leyden merchant named La Cour devised a glass house in which a pineapple that was sweet and fragrant was grown to good-sized maturity. The event caused great excitement, and greenhouses soon became an extremely popular hobby and status symbol. The pineapples thus grown became a popular dessert among the privileged, but many of the fruits were considered too valuable to simply eat, and were first rented out for table decorations. Native West Indians hung pineapples or pineapple crowns on village gates and dwelling entrances as signs of abundance and hospitality within (but they planted thick hedges of pineapple plants around their villages to keep strangers out—effective protective barriers, for the sharp, spiky edges of pineapple leaves can inflict nasty cuts). The association of pineapples with hospitality and abundance was copied by the Spanish; pineapples were carved on doorways and gateposts, and cabinetmakers decorated bedposts, desk finials, chests, and chairs with them. A century later the pineapple motif had found its way back to America and was used especially in the Southern colonies.

America's second most popular sherbet flavor, after orange, is pineapple, and pineapple is its third most popular canned fruit, after applesauce and peaches.

Dried pineapple is almost always "honey-dipped" or, more precisely, immersed in a sugar-water solution that may or may not have a small amount of honey added. The end product is up to 80 percent sugar. Unsweetened dried pineapple, which is dipped in pineapple juice concentrate, is dark in color and harder to find.

Health Benefits

pH 3.20–4.10. Detoxicant, diuretic. The pineapple early on became an important medicinal plant. Its fermented juice was made into an alcoholic drink, used for fevers and to relieve body heat in hot weather; externally pineapple juice was used for dissolving painful corns and to cure skin ailments. Pineapples contain a fair amount of acids—notably citric, malic, and tartaric—which in their organic form exert a diuretic action, aid digestion and elimination, and help clear mucous waste from bronchial tissues. They are very rich in bromelin, a proteolytic (protein-digesting) enzyme that literally "digests" dead or diseased cells and foreign microbes in the throat. It helps dissolve mucous formations and speeds up the removal of fats via the kidneys. The greatest value of pineapple juice lies in its digestive power, which closely resembles that of human gastric juices. Pineapple also has important citric and malic acids needed to improve the process of fat flushing, and manganese, an essential part of certain enzymes needed to metabolize protein and carbohydrates.

Plum and Prune
(*Prunus domestica, P. americana, P. salicina*)

Green plum—it draws her eyebrows together.

—BUSON

added. Cooked or canned pineapple and juice no longer contain bromelin, since the enzyme is quickly destroyed by heating. To prepare fresh pineapple, slice off the crown and bottom, then cut downward along the skin with a heavy, sharp knife. Remove the "eyes" with a knife tip. The central core is tough and fibrous, so it is usually cut out. Fresh pineapple is best eaten with other acidic or subacid fruits.

The large plum tree family was given the genus *Prunus*, a name derived from the ancient Greek name *proumne*. The term *domestica* refers to the domesticated variety as opposed to the wild one; *americana* signifies the American variety, while *salicina* means "willowlike." The interchangeable use of the terms *plum* and *prune* dates back several centuries. The English word *plum* is originally Anglo-Saxon, while *prune* is French; at one time they were probably synonymous. It is uncertain just when the word *prune* was first used to designate a dried plum or a plum suitable for drying.

General Information

Plums are the second most cultivated fruit in the world, after apples, and have thousands of varieties, of which only twenty are grown commercially. Technically a drupe—a pitted fruit—related to the nectarine, peach, and apricot, the plum is far more diverse than its relatives, coming in a wider range of shapes, sizes, and colors: it can be red, maroon, black, pink, green, or yellow. Its flavor also may vary from extremely sweet to quite tart. All plums have skins that are shiny when unripe and that change to a dull matte color as they ripen and sweeten; plums left to ripen on the tree until they soften develop dark brown areas that taste bitter. The early colonists found plums growing wild along the entire eastern coast; these native plums today have little commercial value, and the European plum (*P. domestica*) has replaced them. The European variety is believed indigenous to western Asia in the region south of the Caucasus Mountains and to have been introduced to the Mediterranean regions by Alexander the Great. These are smaller, denser, and less juicy than their Japanese counterparts; their skin color is always blue or purple, and their pits are usually freestone. The Japanese variety (*P. salicina*) are the nonprune plums. Originally from China, these plums were introduced into Japan some three hundred years ago, and the Japanese were so diligent about cultivating and improving them that they have made them their own. In the late nineteenth century, dozens of varieties from Europe and Asia were assiduously cultivated in America, primarily in California. One of the most influential plum breeders (alone developing sixty varieties) was the famed horticulturist Luther Burbank, who in 1907 developed a variety called Santa Rosa, which now accounts for about one-third of the total domestic crop. California as a whole supplies about 90 percent of the U.S. commercial crop.

Prunes can be either fresh or dried. Compared to plums, prunes have a firmer, meatier flesh, higher sugar content, and often a higher acid content; they are adaptable to drying. Ripe, fresh prunes are never wrinkled and are always blue or purple; the flesh is greenish but browns up slightly at the stone, which is always freestone and easily removed. The present dried prune industry is based on the French prune, *prune d'Agen*, named after a town in Aquitaine in the southwest of France. This variety was taken to California in 1856 by Louis Pellier, a young apprentice seaman who jumped ship in San Francisco Bay in 1849. He never struck it rich panning for gold, but he and his brothers fared well with their prune orchard. California production is now so great that it dominates the commerce in prunes and provides a high proportion of those sold in France itself. Commercial dried prunes are made by drying prune plums, which are dipped in a mild alkaline solution so that tiny cracks will form in their skins, allowing moisture to escape evenly as they dry. They are not usually treated with sulfur dioxide but may have undergone other processes to tenderize them or soften the skins, and they may be coated with mineral oil.

Buying Tips

Plums of good quality are plump, clean, fresh looking, full-colored for the particular variety, and soft enough to yield to slight pressure. The test for a good plum is temperature. Pass your hand over a bin of fresh plums, and they emit a perceptible coolness. If not, they are old and will taste insipid. Avoid shriveled, split, or hard fruit. Mature but not fully ripened plums will come to full fragrance and softness in a few days at room temperature. Once softened, they keep for a week or more in the refrigerator.

Culinary Uses

Plums fall into two basic categories, dessert and cooking, though there are many varieties of each. Although both

Plum and Prune / Nutritional Value Per 100 g Edible Portion				
	Raw Damson	Raw Japanese	Raw Prune-Type	Raw Dried Prune
Calories	66	48	75	239
Protein	0.5 g	0.5 g	0.8 g	2.6 g
Fat	trace	0.2 g	0.2 g	0.5 g
Fiber	0.4 g	0.6 g	0.4 g	2.0 g
Calcium	18 mg	12 mg	12 mg	51 mg
Iron	0.50 mg	0.50 mg	0.50 mg	2.48 mg
Phosphorus	17 mg	18 mg	18 mg	79 mg
Potassium	299 mg	170 mg	170 mg	745 mg
Sodium	2 mg	1 mg	1 mg	4 mg
Beta Carotene (A)	300 IU	250 IU	300-1,340 IU	1,987 IU
Thiamine (B$_1$)	0.08 mg	0.03 mg	0.03 mg	0.08 mg
Riboflavin (B$_2$)	0.03 mg	0.03 mg	0.03 mg	0.16 mg
Niacin (B$_3$)	0.50 mg	0.50 mg	0.50 mg	1.96 mg
Pyridoxine (B$_6$)	0.05 mg	0.05 mg	0.03 mg	0.26 mg
Ascorbic Acid (C)	n/a	6.0 mg	4.0 mg	3.3 mg

LORE AND LEGEND

The founder of Taoism, the Asian philosophy that urges one to follow nature and not interfere with the natural goodness of the human heart, was Lao-tse, supposedly born white-haired under a plum tree in 604 B.C. Lao-tse's family name (*Li*) also means "plum tree." Although many other trees play significant roles in Chinese mythology, the plum tree is singularly associated with great age and therefore wisdom. Plum blossoms carved on jade symbolize resurrection.

dessert and cooking plums can be cooked, only dessert plums are sweet enough to be eaten raw. Plums can be eaten in pies, puddings, cakes, jams, and desserts. Chopped plums add sweetness to muffins, quick bread, or coffee cake, while sliced plums bring new color and texture to a variety of salads. Prunes, both fresh and dried, are excellent for snacking or baking and make a tasty addition to many dishes.(See note on oxalic acid below.)

Health Benefits

pH 2.80–4.45. Laxative, stimulant. The plum is a dynamic fruit, energy giving and stimulating to the nerves. An acid fruit, plums are not recommended for people with stomach ulcers or inflammations. Some of their acids have a tendency to irritate the kidneys. Both plums and prunes contain oxalic acid, which in its natural state is excellent for both constipation and an inactive liver; however, when cooked, this oxalic acid becomes inorganic and is harmful to the body. It is therefore best to eat this fruit either raw or dried, and not cooked into any sort of sauces or pastries. Because of their high oxalic acid content, even raw plums should be eaten in moderation, otherwise they may deplete calcium from the body. Prunes are known for their strong laxative action. When dried they contain a high phosphorus content, and their content of other salts is valuable as food for the blood, brain, and nerves. Unripe plums (and apples) are rich in citric, malic, and succinic acids, and contain phenolic compounds and hydrolyzable tannins, which help increase hydrochloric acid levels.

Pomegranate
(Punica granatum)

> Eat the pomegranate, for it purges the system of hatred and envy.
>
> —MUHAMMAD

The Romans called the pomegranate *Malus punica* or *Punicum malum*, "the Punic apple," indicating its transmission to Italy via Carthage (Punicus), where the best pomegranates grew. The English name *pomegranate* was derived from the Latin *pomum*, meaning "apple," and *granatum*, meaning "with seeds," bestowed on account of its many seeds.

General Information

A Persian and south Asian native, the unusual pomegranate is one of the oldest fruits known to humans. It has vied for leadership in popularity and importance with the fig and the grape since the earliest times. Long considered a native of China, it was actually brought to that country from Kabul, Afghanistan, under the Han dynasty in 126 B.C. When the Moors conquered Spain in about A.D. 800, they introduced the pomegranate into the Iberian Peninsula, and the fruit became the emblem of Granada, whose name was derived from it. When an explosive shell that strewed metal particles over a wide area was invented, the French military, mindful of the seed-scattering characteristics of the pomegranate, called the explosive "grenade," and the special regiments founded in 1791 who launched these new weapons were called "grenadiers." The Spanish conquistadores brought the pomegranate to America, where it quickly escaped from cultivation, no doubt because of the plenitude of its seeds.

Pomegranate / Nutritional Value Per 100 g Edible Portion			
	Raw		**Raw**
Calories	63-78	Sodium	3 mg
Protein	0.05-1.60 g	Beta Carotene (A)	trace
Fat	0.3-0.9 g	Thiamine (B₁)	0.003-0.030 mg
Fiber	3.4-5.0 g	Riboflavin (B₂)	0.012-0.030 mg
Calcium	3-12 mg	Niacin (B₃)	0.180-0.300 mg
Iron	0.3-1.2 mg	Pantothenic Acid (B₅)	0.596 mg
Phosphorus	8-37 mg	Pyridoxine (B₆)	0.105 mg
Potassium	259 mg	Ascorbic Acid (C)	4.0-4.2 mg

LORE AND LEGEND

The pomegranate, with its mystic origin and early sacred associations, has been a central character in the myths and legends of many peoples. It was long revered by the Persians and Jews, an old tradition having identified it as the forbidden fruit given by Eve to Adam. The ripe and half-open pomegranate, displaying its many seeds, was the symbol of fecundity, abundance, and eternal life in Semitic antiquity; along with wheat and grapes, the pomegranate was regarded as one of the prime attributes of Ibritz, the Hittite god of agriculture. It also became the Chinese symbol for numerous male offspring who rise to fame and glory and behave in a virtuous and filial manner. At weddings the sugared seeds were offered to the guests and, when the newlyweds entered their bedchamber, pomegranates were thrown to the floor so that the bursting fruits strewed their seeds all over the room, signifying that the marriage should be happy and blessed with many children.

However, actually eating the fruit is a different story altogether. When Adam and Eve ate this fruit of the forbidden tree, they exchanged Paradise for nine-to-five, mortgage and car payments, and atomic bombs. Persephone (the Greek goddess of spring and fruit and the daughter of Demeter, goddess of agriculture), while held captive by Hades in the underworld, vowed not to eat until her release but she soon succumbed and ate a pomegranate, spitting out all the seeds except six, which she swallowed. Thus was created the yearly cycle of six months of growth and abundance and six months of winter. (The story varies geographically: Californians say she ate only one or two seeds, while Eskimos say she ate the whole thing.) Muhammad advised his followers to eat pomegranates, for he believed they purged the system of hatred and envy.

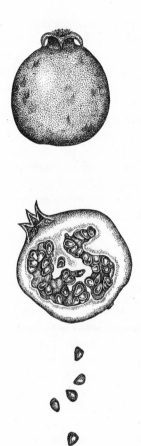

Buying Tips

A pomegranate of good quality should be fresh looking, plump, and heavy for its size, with a hard, reddish-brown rind. Favor larger fruits over smaller ones, and heavier over lighter, as these promise more juice.

Culinary Uses

This "seedy apple" is unique in that its thin, rough rind contains a multitude of seeds, each surrounded by bright red or crimson juicy pulp, and sectioned by a bitter spongy membrane. Cut in half, the fruit is so decorative that a favorite fabric of Renaissance Italy carried the design of the opened fruit. Each section contains a considerable number of long, angular seeds embedded in the pink-to-crimson pulp so inextricably as to oblige the eater either to develop skill in sucking the pulp away from the seeds or to swallow seeds and all. One way to obtain its refreshing juice easily is to bruise the fruit by rolling it on a hard surface until entirely soft, then puncture the end of it, insert a straw, and drink the piquantly sweet juice. Or cut a thin slice off the stem end, cut the fruit into sections, and peel back the skin to free the pips; to release the juice, press the seeds in a sieve over a bowl. The juice can be used as a flavoring in fruit juices, jelled desserts, and sauces. The seeds are edible, and some people readily enjoy their crunch and color, adding them as a garnish to salads, soups, sauces, and desserts. Grenadine is a popular, nonalcoholic sweet liqueur made from pomegranate juice. It adds a sweet tang to sauces, marinades, and dressings, and its red color looks great in sorbets and ice cream. Grenadine is sugar-sweetened, while the pomegranate syrup available in Middle Eastern markets is unsweetened. Pomegranate molasses, made by boiling down and concentrating the juice, is used in Persian cuisine.

Health Benefits

pH 2.93–3.10. Anthelmintic, astringent. Pomegranate juice is cleansing and cooling to the system, is excellent for bladder disorders, and has a slight purgative effect. The rind and partitions of the pomegranate are not generally eaten because of their high tannic acid content. The astringent quality of the rind does, however, make for an excellent skin wash. Galen (A.D. 129–199), the foremost physician in the Roman world, and Dioscorides also recommended the use of pomegranate for birth control. The seeds were typically used as a pessary (vaginal suppository), though one contemporary medical text documents use of pomegranate seed being taken orally as a postcoital contraceptive. The best-known literary reference to the pomegranate's contraceptive power is the Greek myth of Persephone and Hades: Persephone had eaten six pomegranate kernels while in the underworld, and for that many months, during the fall and winter, the land was infertile.

Prickly Pear

(*Opuntia ficus-indica, O. megacantha*)
Also Known As: Barbary Pear, Cactus Pear, Indian Pear, Indian Fig

Here we go round the prickly pear
Prickly pear prickly pear
Here we go round the prickly pear
At five o'clock in the morning.

—T. S. Eliot, "The Hollow Men"

Opuntia was an old Latin name used by Pliny for this plant, probably derived from Opus, a town in Greece. *Ficus-indica* means "Indian fig"; *megacantha* is a term meaning "of great angle." The English name *prickly pear* is an apt description of the fruit's appearance.

General Information

Neither a pear nor a fig, this fruit comes from any of numerous cacti of the genus *Opuntia*, which are native to the drier regions between Central America and the great deserts of the United States. Soon after the discovery of the Americas, the plant was exported to Spain and found a hospitable climate in Sicily and other dry regions of the Mediterranean. Both fruits and "leaves" are enjoyed there as delicacies. Technically a berry, the cactus "pear" is the size of a small pear or large egg. Hostile and thorny, the fruit grows on a cactus with many sharp thorns. Fruit skins range from medium green to dark magenta, while the interior may be a brilliant red-violet or ruby color. All domestic prickly pears are gently processed to remove the glasslike thorns that dot the surface of the fruit, but be careful since there are usually a few hidden ones left. The "leaves" are most commonly used as a vegetable and are discussed in the vegetable section under **Nopal Cactus**.

Buying Tips

Choose prickly pears that are tender but not squishy, full- and deep-colored, not faded. The darker-colored fruits tend to be sweeter and tastier. Beware of moldy spots, which warn of interior mush. If the fruit is very firm, let it soften a few days at room temperature.

Culinary Uses

This prickly fruit does not even remotely look like it wants to be eaten. But the inedible spiny skin encloses a bril-

Prickly Pear / Nutritional Value Per 100 g Edible Portion			
	Raw		Raw
Calories	41	Potassium	220 mg
Protein	0.73 g	Sodium	5 mg
Fat	0.51 g	Beta Carotene (A)	51 IU
Fiber	1.81 g	Thiamine (B₁)	0.014 mg
Calcium	56 mg	Riboflavin (B₂)	0.060 mg
Iron	0.30 mg	Niacin (B₃)	0.460 mg
Magnesium	85 mg	Ascorbic Acid (C)	14 mg
Phosphorus	24 mg		

liantly colored pulp, which may be red, purple, deep orange, or rose-pink. Soft and spongy, juicy, tartly sweet yet refreshing, it has an aroma very similar to watermelon. The easiest way to eat this daunting fruit is to use a knife and fork, cutting lengthwise and slicing the pulp away from the skin. Watch out for the multiple small, hard, bony seeds, which, though some say they are edible, are a nuisance. Some people may desire to add a bit of sweetener to offset the fruit's taste, which can be tart. Prickly pears can be eaten by themselves, used in fruit salads, puréed and added to fruit drinks or iced beverages, or even made into jelly and candy. In the Middle East fruit vendors sell them from trays of shaved ice, and they make a pleasant, cool treat on a hot day.

Pulasan
(Nephelium mutabile)

Nephelium is an ancient name transferred from the burdock, because of some similarity in the rough fruits. *Mutabile* means "changeable, mutable."

General Information
Closely related to the rambutan and sometimes confused with it, the pulasan is native to western Malaysia and Thailand. It is little known elsewhere in the New World except in Costa Rica, where it is occasionally grown and the fruits sometimes appear in the marketplaces. The ovoid fruit is two or three inches long and red or yellow, with a thick, leathery rind.

Culinary Uses
The glistening white or yellowish-white flesh clings to the seed but has a flavor generally much sweeter than the rambutan. The fruits are eaten raw or made into preserves. Boiled or roasted seeds are used to prepare a cocoalike beverage.

Pulasan / Nutritional Value Per 100 g Edible Portion			
	Raw		Raw
Protein	0.82 g	Calcium	0.01-0.05 mg
Fat	0.55 g	Iron	0.002 mg
Fiber	0.14 g		

Pummelo
(Citrus grandis, C. maxima)
Also Known As: Pomelo, Shaddock

The term *Citrus* derives from the Greek term for the citron, *kedromelon*; *maxima* means "largest." The name *pummelo* derives from the Dutch *pompelmous*—*pomp*- from the beginning of the name for "pumpkin" and -*limoes* meaning "citron." In other words, the name means "large pumpkin-sized citron." The alternative name *shaddock* was given this fruit to honor Captain Shaddock, the seventeenth-century English ship commander who introduced the fruit to Europe via the West Indies.

General Information
A strange fruit with an interesting past, the pummelo originated in southeastern Asia and Malaysia and is the world's largest citrus fruit. A beneficial attribute of the pummelo is its relatively high tolerance to saline conditions, such that it can easily be grown around river deltas and brackish marsh areas. Said to be the grandparent of the grapefruit, this sour, pulpy fruit can weigh up to twenty-two pounds and ranges in size from that of a baby cantaloupe to nearly that of a basketball. It is slightly pear-shaped or round and greenish to yellow or pinkish, with an enormously thick, rather soft pith and rind that begs to be conserved. Its spread westward was in the wake of other, more prized citrus fruits. Arabs took it to Spain, where it is still cultivated on a small scale.

Buying Tips
If you have a choice of pummelos, look for what you would in a grapefruit: heaviness, filled-out skin, and a rich aroma. Avoid those with soft or pitted patches.

Culinary Uses
The quality of the pale-yellow-to-pink fruit differs dramatically from one variety to another: from pleasantly juicy to dryish, from slightly acid to very sweet, from enormously seedy to seedless, from insipid to spectacular. It is usually eaten on its own like grapefruit; make sure to remove the entire thick layer of inedible white pith. For the best flavor, each segment must also be skinned. This strange fruit is eaten with salt in southeast Asia, and a delicious, paradisical dessert or salad is made in China with pieces of pummelo combined with oranges, dates, nuts, and mayonnaise.

Pummelo / Nutritional Value Per 100 g Edible Portion			
	Raw		Raw
Calories	25–58	Zinc	0.08 mg
Protein	0.50–0.74 g	Copper	0.048 mg
Fat	0.20–0.56 g	Manganese	0.017 mg
Fiber	0.30–0.82 g	Beta Carotene (A)	20 IU
Calcium	21–30 mg	Thiamine (B$_1$)	0.040–0.070
Iron	0.3–0.5 mg	mg	
Magnesium	6 mg	Riboflavin (B$_2$)	0.027 mg
Phosphorus	20–27 mg	Niacin (B$_3$)	0.300 mg
Potassium	216 mg	Pyridoxine (B$_6$)	0.036 mg
Sodium	1 mg	Ascorbic Acid (C)	30–43 mg

Health Benefits

In the Philippines and southeast Asia, decoctions of the leaves, flowers, and rind are given for their sedative effect in cases of epilepsy and convulsive coughing. The fruit juice is taken as a febrifuge.

Quince

(Cydonia oblonga, C. cydonia)

The Greeks first obtained the quince from Cydonia in Crete (now Canea), from which place the fruit derived its name of *Cydonia*, and of which the English name *quince* is a corruption. *Oblonga* is a descriptive term meaning "oblong."

General Information

Quinces grew wild in Kashmir long before recorded history. In the warm Persian climate, quinces were able to develop sweetness and succulence, so their cultivation spread to other parts of the Mediterranean even before the apple. The Greeks encountered them in Cydonia on the island of Crete; when they were carried back to Athens, they assumed the name of the port from which they came— *malus cydonia*, or "apples of Cydonia." Romans held the fruit in high regard, and quinces were preserved in honey (called *melimelum*, or "honey apple"), used as a flavoring, and made into wine. Quinces were once thought to be a type of pear, and in fact pears are now often grown on quince rootstock, but the two fruits simply cannot be hybridized. In medieval times most Europeans ate them fresh as well as cooking and preserving them. Quince preserves were carried as an antiscorbutic, particularly for trop-ical expeditions, on Portuguese and Spanish ships. In the Middle Ages, the best quinces were held to be those from Portugal; the term *marmalade* comes from *marmelo*, the Portuguese word for the quince, the fruit originally used to make marmalade. There are many varieties of this hard and acid Asiatic fruit of the rose family; however, although it is one of the earliest known fruits and was cultivated for some four millennia, it is not one that has a wide contemporary appeal. When first picked, quinces wear a downy coat of fuzz like a peach, but mechanical rubbing usually eliminates this. They are generally a sour, astringent fruit, resembling a hard-fleshed, sandy-textured yellow apple; in the past they were sometimes referred to as "golden apples."

Buying Tips

Choose large, aromatic, smooth fruits, which are easier to peel and less wasteful than small, knotty ones. They are best when tree-ripened in a warm climate, at which time the natural fruit sugars have matured. Although they never soften, they do bruise easily.

Culinary Uses

Quince have a musky, penetrating aroma reminiscent of pineapple, guava, pear, or apple, depending on the variety you have in hand, but their flavor is rather bland and acidic. This green to golden-colored pome is unusual among fruits in that it is almost always eaten cooked. Its yellow flesh tends to be acidic, hard, and rather unpalatable (although on rare occasions one finds a fully tree-ripened one) but when cooked becomes tender, scented, and tasty, turning a delightful shade of pink. The fruit maintains its shape beautifully even with long cooking, and so it affords grandiose experimentation. Stewing,

Quince / Nutritional Value Per 100 g Edible Portion			
	Raw		Raw
Calories	57	Sodium	4 mg
Protein	0.4 g	Copper	0.130 mg
Fat	0.1 g	Beta Carotene (A)	40 IU
Fiber	1.7 g	Thiamine (B$_1$)	0.020 mg
Calcium	11 mg	Riboflavin (B$_2$)	0.030 mg
Iron	0.7 mg	Niacin (B$_3$)	0.200 mg
Magnesium	8 mg	Pantothenic Acid (B$_5$)	0.081 mg
Phosphorus	17 mg	Pyridoxine (B$_6$)	0.040 mg
Potassium	197 mg	Ascorbic Acid (C)	15 mg

LORE AND LEGEND

The Greeks and Romans held the quince sacred to Venus, who is often depicted with a quince in her right hand as the gift she received from Paris. Being the sacred fruit of the goddess of love, the quince was regarded as the symbol of love, happiness, and fertility. In Athens quinces were tossed into the bridal chariot in which the groom was conducting his bride to their new home, where she would be offered a piece of wedding cake flavored with sesame, honey, and, as a charm for fruitfulness, either a date or a quince. Quinces were also thought to be the forbidden fruit of the Garden of Eden. In Roman times, as described by Plutarch, the quince was picked green, submerged in honey, and left to ripen in time to serve at Roman wedding feasts as a perfect symbolic dessert. The custom of a newly married pair sharing a quince as a token of love was handed down, and throughout the Middle Ages quinces were used at every wedding feast. The "golden apples" of Virgil are believed to be quinces, as they were the only "golden" fruit known in his time, oranges having only been introduced later at the time of the Crusades. Quinces were also reputed to protect against the Evil Eye, and were painted on the walls and eaves of Roman houses for that purpose.

baking, poaching, or braising brings out the unique quince flavor, which complements meat, savory, or sweet dishes. Stewed, they make an excellent dessert, a breakfast dish with cream, or a side dish. Or add a small proportion of cooked fruit to pear and apple dishes (including pies and applesauce) for a surprising amplification of flavor. Most often, though, the fruit is simply made into preserves, either alone or mixed with other fruits such as apples and pears. It has even more pectin (the thickening agent of preserves) than apples and thus is well suited to this purpose. Although the peel cooks to an edible texture, it is best removed, as it tends to add an undesirable bitterness.

Health Benefits

pH 3.12–3.70. The fruit has an acid taste, is slightly astringent, makes a good sedative, and is an effective stomach medicine, allaying gas and vomiting. When used in its fully ripened state without the addition of sugar, quince is beneficial for the liver, counteracts constipation, and helps alkalinize the system. Underripe fruits are extremely acid-forming. The juice makes an excellent gargle.

Rambutan
(Nephelium lappaceum)

Nephelium is an ancient name transferred from the burdock because of some similarity in the rough fruit. *Lappaceum* means "having small burrs." The English name *rambutan* derives from the Malayan word for hair, *rambut*, because of the long "hairs" on the outside of the fruit.

General Information

Native to the western lowlands of Malaysia, the rambutan is closely related to the lychee. The fruits vary in quality and type. There are crimson-, greenish-, yellow-, and orange-skinned varieties, which are ovoid or ellipsoid in shape and one to three inches long or about the size of a plum, with a leathery rind covered with soft spines. The somewhat hairy covering is responsible for the common name of the fruit.

Buying Tips

Rambutans are available from midsummer through early winter in Asian markets and specialty food stores. Select fruits that show no sign of moisture and have a fresh smell. Refrigerate and use within three days.

Culinary Uses

The flesh is highly aromatic, white or rose-tinted, translucent, juicy, and adhering somewhat to the seed within. The inner part of the fruit is smaller than a lychee, but the outside looks larger because of the long "hairs." The flavor is

Rambutan / Nutritional Value Per 100 g Edible Portion			
	Raw		Raw
Protein	0.46 g	Phosphorus	12.9 mg
Fiber	0.24 g	Ascorbic Acid (C)	30 mg
Calcium	10.6 mg		

usually more acid than the lychee. Most often eaten out of hand after tearing the rind open, the peeled fruits are also occasionally stewed as a dessert or preserved in syrup. The seeds, which are reputedly poisonous when raw, are sometimes roasted and eaten, and it is said they have an almondlike flavor.

Health Benefits

The fruit acts as a vermifuge and febrifuge; it is also taken to relieve diarrhea and dysentery.

Raspberry
(Rubus idaeus, R. strigosus)

> Better than any argument is to rise at dawn and pick dew-wet red berries in a cup.
>
> —Wendell Berry

Rubus is from the Latin *ruber*, meaning "red." The term *idaeus* relates the raspberry to Mount Ida in Asia Minor (Turkey), where it grows in abundance; *strigosus* means that the plant is strigose (having bristles or scales that lie flat). The English name *raspberry* comes from the Old English *raspis*, of obscure origin but probably connected with the slightly hairy, "rasping" surface of the fruit.

General Information

Raspberries are members of the rose family and attest to this by their thorny canes. The European raspberry, *R. idaeus*, sometimes called by its French name of *framboise*, grows almost everywhere throughout Europe, as far north as Scandinavia, and extends through northern Asia into the Orient. The American red raspberry is *R. strigosus*, first heard of in 1607 when the French lawyer, traveler, and writer Marc Lescarbot accompanied an expedition to Canada and reported that his fellow explorers "amused themselves by gathering raspberries." A shrub with prickly stems and pale green leaves, the plant is divided by the color of its fruit into two basic types: red and black. The black tends to be smaller and seedier than the red but is distinctly aromatic. Yellow raspberries, often found growing wild in many areas, particularly in Maryland, are considered a variant of red. Purple raspberries are considered a hybrid between the red and black species but are a little more tart than either. The marketed berry is usually

Raspberry / Nutritional Value Per 100 g Edible Portion		
	Raw Fruit	Leaves, Dried
Calories	49	275
Protein	0.91 g	11.30 g
Fat	0.55 g	1.70 g
Fiber	3.00 g	8.20 g
Calcium	22 mg	1,210 mg
Iron	0.57 mg	101.00 mg
Magnesium	18 mg	319 mg
Phosphorus	12 mg	234 mg
Potassium	152 mg	1,340 mg
Sodium	0 mg	7.7 mg
Zinc	0.46 mg	trace
Copper	0.074 mg	n/a
Manganese	1.013 mg	146.000 mg
Beta Carotene (A)	130 IU	18,963 IU
Thiamine (B$_1$)	0.030 mg	0.340 mg
Riboflavin (B$_2$)	0.090 mg	trace
Niacin (B$_3$)	0.900 mg	38.200 mg
Pantothenic Acid (B$_5$)	0.240 mg	n/a
Pyridoxine (B$_6$)	0.057 mg	n/a
Folic Acid (B$_9$)	n/a	n/a
Ascorbic Acid (C)	25 mg	367 mg
Tocopherol (E)	0.30 mg	n/a

the cultivated red variety. The main difference between blackberries and raspberries is that the blackberry stem core stays with the berries, whereas ripe raspberries detach from the core.

Buying Tips

Look for bright, clean berries with uniform coloring. Check the bottom of the container to make sure it has not been stained from crushed or moldy fruit. Handle them as little as possible, since they are highly perishable. Wash only if absolutely necessary, as this rinses off their heady perfume.

Culinary Uses

The raspberry suggests its probable Asian heritage by being rich, exotic, and spice-laden, with just a hint of musk. Extremely fragile, the berry turns to pulp if simply held in the hand too long. This tendency renders fresh raspberries an expensive and rare summer fruit. Most cultivated raspberries are red, but there are also varieties in yellow, apricot, amber, and purple, all similar in flavor and texture. A sprinkling of fresh raspberries makes an artful garnish for desserts and fruit dishes. Their considerable vitamin properties are mostly lost during cooking, so that although raspberry jellies, jams, and preserves may taste good, they have only a fraction of the berry's raw nutritional value. The addition of sugar renders them acidic and detrimental to the body.

Health Benefits

pH 3.18–3.95. Antiemetic, astringent, laxative. Raspberries lead all the berries nutritionally, and all fresh foods in fully digestible elements, being almost totally assimilated by the body during digestion. They are considered a good cleanser for mucus, for catarrhal conditions, and for toxins in the body. Very beneficial for all female organs and problems, they help relieve menstrual cramps and will decrease the menstrual flow if necessary without stopping it altogether. Raspberry leaf tea is queen among pregnancy herbs, frequently taken by pregnant women to prevent miscarriages, allay nausea and vomiting, increase milk flow, and reduce labor pains. For those who are not pregnant, the tea nourishes the reproductive organs and works as an effective antidiarrheal agent. Raspberry leaves possess the classic properties of astringent herbs, especially the tannins and fruit acids (citric and malic). The nutritional profile shows a manganese content (146 milligrams per 100 grams in the dried leaves) twice as high as any other herb, making it one of the richest sources of this mineral.

Rhubarb

(Rheum rhabarbarum, R. rhaponticum, R. hybridum)

The technical name of the genus is said to be derived from *Rha*, the ancient name of the Volga River, on whose banks the plants grow; other authorities derive the name from the Greek *rheo*, meaning "to flow," in allusion to its purgative properties. *Rhaponticum* refers to the region of the Rha that flows into the Pontus (at the southern end of the Black Sea); *hybridum* means "of mixed parentage," a hybrid. The English name *rhubarb* is a derivative of the Latin phrase *rha barbarum*, indicating the region of the Rha River inhabited by the barbarians (any non-Roman).

General Information

Rhubarb is botanically a vegetable, but the U.S. Customs Court at Buffalo, New York, ruled in 1947 that it should be classed as a fruit, since that is how it is normally used. Part of the buckwheat family, the most popular type of rhubarb comes from a species that originated in Siberia or Mongolia. In 1608 an Italian botanist named Prosper Alpinus decided to introduce Siberian rhubarb into Europe as a possible substitute for the exorbitantly costly Chinese rhubarb, the root of which was used only medicinally. Edible rhubarb remained a curiosity until the early 1800s, when people began using the stalks for pies and puddings. Introduced into what is now Alaska by early-seventeenth-century Russian trappers and traders to counteract the problems of scurvy, rhubarb came into its own in 1880 when gold seekers rushed to Juneau. By the mid–nineteenth century it was popular, particularly in the New England states, as a pie and pastry filling, or pressed into homemade wine. Chinese rhubarb, which is entirely different from our garden variety, has been used medicinally since about 2700 B.C.

Buying Tips

Look for moderately thin pink or red stalks. The greener, thicker stalks are stringier, sourer, and coarser. The leaves are poisonous and should be discarded.

Rhubarb / Nutritional Value Per 100 g Edible Portion		
	Raw	Cooked w/ Sugar
Calories	21	116
Protein	0.90 g	0.39 g
Fat	0.20 g	0.05 g
Fiber	0.70 g	0.80 g
Calcium	86 mg	145 mg
Iron	0.22 mg	0.21 mg
Magnesium	12 mg	12 mg
Phosphorus	14 mg	8 mg
Potassium	288 mg	96 mg
Sodium	4 mg	1 mg
Zinc	0.100 mg	0.080 mg
Copper	0.021 mg	0.027 mg
Manganese	0.196 mg	0.073 mg
Beta Carotene (A)	100 IU	69 IU
Thiamine (B$_1$)	0.020 mg	0.018 mg
Riboflavin (B$_2$)	0.030 mg	0.023 mg
Niacin (B$_3$)	0.300 mg	0.200 mg
Pantothenic Acid (B$_5$)	0.085 mg	0.050 mg
Pyridoxine (B$_6$)	0.024 mg	0.020 mg
Folic Acid (B$_9$)	7.1 mcg	5.3 mcg
Ascorbic Acid (C)	8.0 mg	3.3 mg

Culinary Uses

Rhubarb comes in two main varieties: hothouse-grown (pink or light red stalks, with yellow leaves) and field-grown (dark red stalks, with green leaves). The hothouse variety has a somewhat milder flavor and is less stringy. Never eaten raw, the stalks are very tart and need quite a bit of sweetening to be palatable. Their main use is in sauces and pies. To prepare, trim both ends and cut the stalks into one-inch chunks and stew (or bake) with plenty of sugar. Rhubarb cooks very quickly, fiber and sugar dissolving into a puddle of syrup; cook it no longer than necessary. Use the stems only; the leaves and roots are highly poisonous, and eating them has caused deaths, probably because of the leaves' high oxalic acid content. Even the fleshy stalks are high in oxalic acid, so rhubarb should always be eaten in moderation and is not recommended for people who form calcium oxalate kidney stones, or for those with inadequate calcium absorption.

Health Benefits

pH 3.10–3.40. The purgative principle in rhubarb is a group of substances allied to chrysophanic acid and is present mainly in the root. The stalks contain a substantial amount of oxalic acid, which is harmful if eaten to excess. Few if any other plants have such a high concentration of this acid. Cooking converts the oxalic acid into an inorganic crystalline form that is then deposited in vast quantities throughout the body.

Rose Apple

(Syzygium jambos, S. malaccense, S. samarangense, S. aqueum)

> *Syzygium* derives from the Greek word meaning "united" and refers to the calyptrate petals. *Jambos* is a Malaysian name; *aqueum* means "aqueous" or "watery."

General Information

This group of fruits might be better called by the Indian/Malay name *jambu*. Indigenous to southeast Asia or the Indian subcontinent, they bear a superficial resemblance to apples but are quite different to eat. The true rose apple or Malabar plum (*S. jambos*) tree produces fruit that may reach the size of a small apple; it is round or slightly pear-shaped and about two inches long, with smooth, thin, pale yellow or pinkish waxy skin, capped with a prominent green calyx. The yellowish flesh is crisp, mealy, dry to juicy, slightly rose-scented, but rather tasteless. In the center are several brown seeds that rattle when the fruit is shaken. The Malay rose apple (*S. malaccense*) spread throughout the Pacific Islands in very early times; it is featured in Fijian mythology, and the wood was used by ancient Hawaiians to make idols. The flowers are considered sacred to Pele, the fiery volcano goddess. It has been recorded that before the arrival of missionaries in Hawaii there were no fruits except bananas, coconuts, and the Malay apple. The tree bears fruits that are roundish but slightly oblong and narrowed at the stalk end. These fruits have waxy skins, are rosy with faint white markings when ripe, and have flesh that is scented, juicy, and slightly sweet. The Java rose apple or Samarang rose apple (*S. samarangense*) bears fruits that are nearly round or bell-shaped. They are commonly pale green or whitish, but sometimes pink. The pink fruits are juicier and more flavorful. The skin is very thin, the flesh white, spongy, dry to juicy, subacid, and very bland. There may be one or two seeds. The watery rose apple or water apple (*S. aqueum*) has an uneven shape, wider at the apex than at the base. Color varies from white to bright pink, with flesh that is white or pink, crisp and watery, and sweetly scented. There may be several small seeds.

Rose Apple / Nutritional Value Per 100 g Edible Portion			
	Raw True Rose	Raw Malay Rose	Raw Java Rose
Calories	56	n/a	n/a
Protein	0.5-0.7 g	0.5-0.7 g	0.5 g
Fat	0.2-0.3 g	0.1-0.2 g	n/a
Fiber	1.1-1.9 g	0.6-0.8 g	n/a
Calcium	29.00-45.20 mg	5.60-5.90 mg	0.01 g
Iron	0.450-1.200 mg	0.200-0.820 mg	0.001 g
Magnesium	4 mg	n/a	n/a
Phosphorus	11.70-30.00 mg	11.60-17.90 mg	0.03 g
Potassium	50 mg	n/a	n/a
Sodium	34.1 mg	n/a	n/a
Beta Carotene (A)	123-235 IU	3-10 IU	n/a
Thiamine (B$_1$)	0.010-0.190 mg	15-39 mcg	n/a
Riboflavin (B$_2$)	0.028-0.050 mg	20-39 mcg	n/a
Niacin (B$_3$)	0.521-0.800 mg	0.210-0.400 mg	n/a
Ascorbic Acid (C)	3.0-37.0 mg	6.5-17.0 mg	n/a

Culinary Uses

The ripe fruit of all the rose apples is eaten raw, though many people consider it insipid. Most often, the fruit is eaten by children for its thirst-quenching abilities. The fruit is best stewed with cloves or other flavoring and served with cream as a dessert. The slightly unripe fruits are sometimes used for making jelly and pickles, and are often cooked with acid fruits, to the benefit of both, into sauce or preserves. In Puerto Rico both red and white table wines are made from the Malay apple.

Health Benefits

In India the fruit is regarded as a tonic for the brain and liver. An infusion of the fruit acts as a diuretic. The seeds are employed against diarrhea, dysentery, and catarrh. In Nicaragua it has been claimed that an infusion of roasted, powdered seeds is beneficial to diabetics, while in Colombia the seeds are believed to have an anesthetic property.

Roselle

(Hibiscus sabdariffa)

Also Known As: Red Sorrel, Jamaica Sorrel, Florida Cranberry

Hibiscus is an old Greek name for the mallow. *Sabdariffa* comes from a West Indian name. The English name *roselle* is a diminutive term meaning "little rose."

General Information

Though it is frequently called Jamaica sorrel, roselle did not reach Jamaica until the beginning of the eighteenth century, and it is not a close relation of sorrel. Native from India to Malaysia, the plant is unusual in that its main edible part is not the fruit but the calyx of the fruit, what is familiar as the little green star on top of a tomato or strawberry. In this instance it is red, large, and fleshy, enwrapping a small, useless fruit. Roselle jam was popular for some time at the turn of the twentieth century. In 1892 there were two factories producing roselle jam in Queensland, Australia, which exported considerable quantities to Europe. By 1909 there were no more than four acres left of roselle plantings in Queensland. Currently the plant is attracting the attention of food and beverage manufacturers as well as pharmaceutical concerns, which feel it may have possibilities as a natural food product and as a colorant to replace some synthetic dyes.

Culinary Uses

Roselle is best prepared for use by washing, then making an incision around the tough base of the calyx below the bracts to free and remove it with the seed capsule attached. The calyces are then ready for immediate use and may be merely chopped and added to fruit salads, cooked as a side dish, or stewed to make a cranberry-flavored sauce or filling for tarts or pies. They are made into a refreshing, sour "sorrel" drink (or "ade") in the West Indies, and a Jamaican traditional Christmas drink is prepared by putting roselle into an earthenware jug with a little grated ginger and sugar as desired, pouring boiling water over the mixture, and letting it stand overnight. This liquid is then drained off and served with ice (and a dash of rum). The calyces are marketed dried (usually under the name *Flor de Jamaica*) as well as fresh; they are also the source of a red food coloring. Young leaves and tender stems of roselle are eaten raw in salads, cooked as greens, or added to curries as seasoning.

Health Benefits

In India, Africa, and Mexico all aboveground parts of the roselle plant are valued in native medicine. Infusions of the leaves or calyces are regarded as diuretic, cholerectic, febrifugal, and hypotensive, decreasing the viscosity of the blood and stimulating intestinal peristalsis. Pharmacognosists in Senegal recommend roselle extract for lowering blood pressure, while in Guatemala roselle "ade" is a favorite remedy for the aftereffects of alcohol overindulgence. Wild roselle helps prevent joint pain and inflammation by neutralizing toxins. In addition, it appears to have fairly strong antioxidant properties and is a good source of vitamin C.

Roselle / Nutritional Value Per 100 g Edible Portion			
	Raw		**Raw**
Calories	49	Potassium	208 mg
Protein	1.145 g	Sodium	6 mg
Fat	0.64 g	Beta Carotene (A)	287 IU
Fiber	n/a	Thiamine (B$_1$)	0.011 mg
Calcium	216 mg	Riboflavin (B$_2$)	0.028 mg
Iron	1.48 mg	Niacin (B$_3$)	0.310 mg
Magnesium	51 mg	Ascorbic Acid (C)	12 mg
Phosphorus	37 mg		

Rowan and Sorb
(Sorbus aucuparia, S. torminalis)

Sorbus is the ancient Latin name for this family of plants. *Aucuparia* means "bird-catching" and refers to the fact that bird catchers in Germany and elsewhere would trap small birds in hair nooses baited with rowan berries; *torminalis* means "useful against colic." The English name *rowan* is of Scandinavian origin, akin to Old Norse *reynir*, meaning "rowan," and to Old English *read*, meaning "red." *Sorb* derives from the French word *sorbe*, meaning "fruit of the service tree," and ultimately from the Latin *sorbum*.

General Information
The rowan bush grows wild in Europe and parts of Asia, especially in mountainous regions. Related to the large rose family, some sixty-seven species are found in North America alone. The bright scarlet berries are pretty but have limited use. North American Indians ate them fresh, dried some to grind the seeds into a mealy flour, cooked the berries into jams and jellies, and even made wine with them. The sorb tends to grow farther south in Europe and bear larger fruits than the rowan. Its fruits are called sorb apples because they are recognizably like small apples or pears in shape and color. The tree is a magnificent sight, conspicuous across the open fields. The hard, fine-grained wood of the sorb tree was once much in demand for screws and by wood engravers. In October or late September the fruit turns beautifully yellow and red among the long oval leaves, but it should be left until after the first frosts. Only after the fruit has fallen and turned soft and brown (a process called "bletting") will the astringency be gone and the fruit become palatable. It can also be picked off the tree and brought into the house to gradually soften.

Culinary Uses
Much too sour and astringent to be eaten raw, rowan fruits are best suited to being made into jelly, which has a fine, clear red color; its pleasing tartness makes it a good accompaniment for wild game or fowl. Scandinavians make a rowan liqueur of a curious orange color. Sorb fruits are sour and astringent, although less so after exposure to the mellowing effect of frost. Bletting makes them palatable but not exciting. Earlier in the century the French made a kind of cider from the sorb, and they now make a liqueur that is supposed to be quite good.

LORE AND LEGEND
The Scots believed that if you nailed a rowan branch above the doorway of either the house or barn, no ghosts or evil spirits of any kind could enter therein. Young lambs were forced to jump through a rowan-branch hoop to deter witches from stealing them.

Health Benefits
Early western European doctors considered the sorb good for digestion, for fevers accompanied by diarrhea, and for hemorrhages.

Rumberry
(Myrciaria floribunda)

The genus name *Myrciaria* probably is related to Myrtus, the myrtle family. *Floribunda* means "abounding in flowers," or "freely flowering." The English name *rumberry* most likely refers to the fact that the berry was used to flavor rums and other liqueurs.

General Information
Native to much of Central and South America (where it is also known as guavaberry), the rumberry is a tiny fruit that was once in fair demand. It has occasionally been cultivated in Bermuda but rarely elsewhere. Throughout its natural range, when land is cleared for pastures, the tree is left standing for the sake of its fruits, which are round or oblate, a quarter to a half inch in diameter, yellow-orange or so dark red as to be nearly black, and highly aromatic.

Culinary Uses
The flavor is bittersweet and balsamlike, with one globular seed. In Cuba the fruits are relished out of hand and are also made into jam. People on the island of St. John, where the fruits are said to be unusually good, use the preserved fruits in tarts. The local guavaberry liqueur, made by combining the fruits with pure grain alcohol, rum, raw sugar, and spices, is a special treat at Christmastime. Large quantities of fermented juice, strong wine, and heavy liqueur were at one time made and exported, primarily to Denmark.

Health Benefits
The fruits are sold by herbalists in Camagüey for the purpose of making a depurative syrup; the decoction is taken as a treatment for liver complaints.

Santol
(Sandoricum koetjape)

General Information
Native to Malaya and parts of former Indochina, the medium-sized santol tree occurs in two main forms, one with sweet fruit and leaves, which wither yellow, the other with sour fruit and leaves, which turn to red. The fruit is globose or oblate, with wrinkles extending a short distance from the base, 1½ to 3 inches wide, and yellowish to golden, sometimes blushed with pink.

Culinary Uses
The downy rind may be thin or thick and contains a thin, milky juice. It is edible, as is the white, translucent, juicy pulp surrounding the three to five brown, inedible seeds. Sometimes having an aroma of peach, these fruits are eaten fresh, dried, candied, or pickled. Santol marmalade is sometimes imported into the United States from the Philippines.

Health Benefits
Preserved pulp is employed medicinally as an astringent, as is the quince in Europe.

Santol / Nutritional Value Per 100 g Edible Portion	Raw Yellow	Raw Red
Protein	0.118 g	0.89%
Fat	0.10 g	1.43%
Fiber	0.10 g	2.30%
Calcium	4.3 mg	0.01%
Iron	0.42 mg	0.002%
Phosphorus	17.4 mg	0.03%
Beta Carotene (A)	0.003 mg	n/a
Thiamine (B₁)	0.045 mg	0.037 mg
Niacin (B₃)	0.741 mg	0.016 mg
Ascorbic Acid (C)	8.00 mg	0.78 mg

Sapodilla
(Manilkara zapota)

Manilkara is the Malaysian name for the fruit; *zapota* comes from the Latin American *tzapotl*, which apparently means "soft." The English word *sapodilla* is a diminutive form of *sapota*, the anglicized form of *zapota*.

General Information
The sapodilla is the fruit of the sapota tree, a stately evergreen native to Yucatan and possibly other nearby parts of southern Mexico, as well as northern Belize and northeastern Guatemala. The tree bark contains a milky substance known commercially as chicle, which is used in the production of chewing gum, thus the origin of the name *Chicklets gum*. The fruit is a small round or oval berry between two and four inches in diameter, with a brown fuzz over its yellow skin, making it look much like a furry brown kiwi. The flesh is yellow-brown, sometimes pinkish, with a soft, translucent, meltingly juicy pulp containing several inedible flat black seeds in a central cavity. The aspect of the interior resembles that of a pear, except that the seeds are larger.

Buying Tips
Select fruit that is somewhat soft and smooth—a too-hard exterior can indicate an unpleasant, gritty interior. Until fully ripened, the fruit is too astringent to be edible, but left at room temperature, hard fruit will soften to good taste and texture. It is best when soft as a peach; to test for ripening, scratch off some of the fuzz—if the skin shows green, hold at room temperature for another day or two or until the skin is brown. Once ripened, the fruit can be stored in the refrigerator for two to three days.

Sapodilla / Nutritional Value Per 100 g Edible Portion	Raw		Raw
Calories	83	Sodium	12 mg
Protein	0.44 g	Beta Carotene (A)	60 IU
Fat	1.10 g	Thiamine (B₁)	n/a
Fiber	1.40 g	Riboflavin (B₂)	0.020 mg
Calcium	21 mg	Niacin (B₃)	0.200 mg
Iron	0.80 mg	Pantothenic Acid (B₅)	0.252 mg
Phosphorus	12 mg	Pyridoxine (B₆)	0.037 mg
Potassium	193 mg	Ascorbic Acid (C)	14.7 mg

Culinary Uses

Described as having "the sweet perfumes of honey, jasmine, and lily of the valley," sapodilla has a flavor that has been compared to brown sugar or maple syrup. The yellowish pulp may be smooth or granular but when of good quality is always fragrant and melting like bananas or apricots. It is usually chilled, cut in half, and eaten from the inedible half shell, although in the West Indies the fruit may be boiled down to make a sweet syrup. If the pulp is too soft to slice, mash it for use in puddings, custards, quick breads, or ice creams. Care must be taken not to swallow the seeds, as their protruding hook might lodge in the throat; additionally, ingestion of more than six seeds can cause abdominal pain and vomiting.

Health Benefits

Because of their tannin content, young, immature fruits are boiled and the decoction taken to stop diarrhea. An infusion of young fruits and flowers is drunk to relieve pulmonary complaints.

Sapote, Black

(Diospyros digyna)

Also Known As: Black Persimmon, Chocolate Pudding Fruit, Sapote Negro, Zapote Negro

Diospyros comes from the Greek words *dios*, meaning "god" (in this case Jupiter or Jove), and pyros, "grain"—thus the genus name means "Jove's grain," alluding to the plant's succulent, edible fruits. The English word *sapote* derives from the Mexican name *tzapotl*, a general term applied to all soft, sweet fruits.

General Information

The black sapote is the green-skinned fruit of an ornamental evergreen related to the persimmon. Native to Mexico and grown in south Florida, the Caribbean, Hawaii, and California, the fruits have chocolate-brown flesh and a sweet, rich flavor. The fruit is bright green and shiny at first, oblate or nearly round, and two to five inches wide, with a prominent, four-lobed, undulate calyx clasping the base. On ripening, the smooth, thin skin becomes olive green and then rather muddy green. Within is a mass of glossy, brown to very dark brown or almost black, somewhat jellylike pulp that is soft, sweet, and mild in flavor. In the center there may be one to ten flat, smooth, brown seeds, but the fruits are often seedless. They ripen quickly, at which point the flesh becomes very soft.

Buying Tips

Fruits picked when full grown but unripe (bright green) ripen in ten days at room temperature. Firm, olive-green fruits will ripen in two to six days.

Culinary Uses

Generally eaten fresh with lemon juice or a little vanilla, black sapotes are especially useful in ice creams and mousses. They can also be used for preserves and in breads and desserts. In the Philippines the seeded pulp is served as dessert with a little milk or orange juice poured over it. The addition of lemon or lime juice makes the pulp desirable as a filling for pies and other pastry. In Mexico the pulp may be mashed, beaten, or passed through a colander and mixed with orange juice or brandy and then served with or without whipped cream. A foamy, delicious beverage is made by mixing the pulp with canned pineapple juice in a blender.

Health Benefits

The ascorbic acid content (vitamin C) of this fruit is said to be about twice that of the average orange.

Sapote, Mamey

(Pouteria sapota)

Pouteria is a native name for the plant. The English word *sapote* derives from the Mexican name *tzapotl*, a general term applied to all soft, sweet fruits.

General Information

A tropical fruit native to the West Indies, the mamey sapote is just now gaining a market position and is a fruit

Sapote, Black / Nutritional Value Per 100 g Edible Portion (Source: Morton)			
	Raw		Raw
Calories	n/a	Phosphorus	23.0 mg
Protein	0.62-0.69 g	Beta Carotene (A)	0.19 mg
Fat	0.01 g	Thiamine (B$_1$)	n/a
Fiber	n/a	Riboflavin (B$_2$)	0.030 mg
Calcium	22.0 mg	Niacin (B$_3$)	0.200 mg
Iron	0.36 mg	Ascorbic Acid (C)	191.7 mg

to watch for. It is shaped like a large pointed peach with gritty skin and striking flesh that ranges from pink to salmon in color. The mamey's memorable tropical flavor is a blend of honeyed pumpkin and almond essence. Ripen at room temperature until it is soft to the touch and use as you would a mango. Available in the summer, mamey sapote is grown extensively in the Caribbean, Mexico, and South America. The single pit is toxic.

Sapote, White
(Casimiroa edulis)

The genus *Casimiroa* was named in honor of Cardinal Casimiro Gomez de Ortega, a Spanish botanist of the eighteenth century. *Edulis* means "edible." The English word *sapote* derives from the Mexican name *tzapotl*, a general term applied to all soft, sweet fruits.

General Information
The semi-tropical white sapote grows wild in Central America and is cultivated in some Latin American countries. Looking like a green pippin apple, sapotes are orange-sized with a thin, green to yellow skin containing a nearly seedless, coreless white flesh that is mild and creamy-textured. With its ambrosial aroma and soft, juicy texture, it is one of the many new and exotic fruits that is destined to gain in popularity. It has been grown in California since the nineteenth century and also grows in Florida but is still scarce in northern markets. The rarely seen black sapote (see above) is a rather leathery, green-skinned member of the Diospyros clan that has flesh the color and texture of chocolate pudding when fully ripe. The green and yellow varieties of sapote are not commonly exported but are reputed to be of better flavor than the white.

Buying Tips
Choose firm fruits of orange or grapefruit size that are free of bruises and that are green or yellowish green in color. When the fruit has softened so that it has a give like a ripe avocado, it is ripe.

Culinary Uses
This fruit has a very sweet, mild flavor that may hint of peaches, lemons, mango, coconut, caramel, or vanilla, depending upon the variety. The skin is inedible; the seeds, which are embedded at random, may be flat and chiplike or the size and shape of orange seeds; they are toxic if eaten. The fruits are easiest to eat when cut in half so that the delicate, custardy flesh can be scooped out with a spoon, but they can also be used in preserves or fruit sauces. One recommendation is to cut the flesh into sections and serve with cream and sugar.

Health Benefits
Chemists, verifying comments on the fruit made as long ago as the sixteenth century, have found soporific substances in it. Its skin is inedible, and the seed is said to be fatally toxic if eaten by humans or animals.

Soursop
(Annona muricata)
Also Known As: Guanabana, Prickly Custard Apple

Annona means "year's harvest" and is suggested by the Haitian name *anon*, which is applied to one of the species. *Muricata* means "roughened on the surface with sharp, hard points." The English name *soursop* probably comes from the fruit's acidic pulp, which is nearly watery or juicy enough to drink.

General Information
This tropical fruit is native to and common in tropical South America and the West Indies. One of the first fruit trees taken from America to the tropical regions of the Old World, the soursop became widely distributed from southeast China to Australia and the lowlands of East and West Africa. The small tree bears its fruits indiscriminately on twigs, branches, or trunk, flowering and bearing fruit more or less continuously, though there usually is a principal ripening season. The fruits range from four to twelve inches in length and weigh up to nearly eleven pounds.

Sapote, White / Nutritional Value Per 100 g Edible Portion			
	Raw		Raw
Calories	125	Phosphorus	20.4 mg
Protein	0.143 g	Beta Carotene (A)	410 IU
Fat	0.03 g	Thiamine (B₁)	0.042 mg
Fiber	0.9 g	Riboflavin (B₂)	0.043 mg
Calcium	9.9 mg	Niacin (B₃)	0.472 mg
Iron	0.33 mg	Ascorbic Acid (C)	30.3 mg

Culinary Uses

The white flesh consists of numerous segments that are mostly seedless, which is just as well, since the seeds contain toxins and are to be avoided. The quality varies from poor to very good. At its best, it is soft and juicy, with a rich, musky, rather acid, and almost fermented quality and a pleasant aroma reminiscent of pineapple. The soursop is more acid than its relations, but the acidity varies, and some fruits are suitable for eating raw. Others have to be dressed with sugar to make them palatable. Seeded soursop has for years been canned in Mexico and served in Mexican restaurants in New York and other northern cities. Since the fruits are often so juicy that it would be more appropriate to speak of drinking rather than eating them, they are good candidates for use in beverages or sherbets, as well as for jellies and preserves. In the tropics various drinks are made from seeded and sweetened pulp beaten with milk or water.

Health Benefits

The juice of the ripe fruit is said to be diuretic and a remedy for hematuria and urethritis. Taken when fasting, it is believed to relieve liver ailments and leprosy. Pulverized immature fruits, which are very astringent, are decocted as a dysentery remedy.

They are ellipsoid or irregularly ovoid, one side growing faster than the other. The skin has a leathery appearance but is thin and surprisingly tender; dark green to begin with, it later turns yellowish green and yellow when overripe. Because of the soft spines on the skin, the soursop is sometimes called the "prickly custard apple."

Soursop / Nutritional Value Per 100 g Edible Portion			
	Raw		Raw
Calories	53.1–61.3	Sodium	14 mg
Protein	1.0 g	Beta Carotene (A)	2 IU
Fat	0.97 g	Thiamine (B₁)	0.110 mg
Fiber	0.79 g	Riboflavin (B₂)	0.050 mg
Calcium	10.3 mg	Niacin (B₃)	1.280 mg
Iron	0.64 mg	Pantothenic Acid (B₅)	0.253 mg
Magnesium	21 mg	Pyridoxine (B₆)	0.059 mg
Phosphorus	27.7 mg	Ascorbic Acid (C)	29.6 mg
Potassium	278 mg		

Star Apple
(Chrysophyllum cainito)

Chrysophyllum means "golden-leaved." *Cainito* is the West Indian name for the star apple. The English name *star apple* comes from the fact that when the fruit is cut transversely, the seed cells are seen to radiate from the central core like an asterisk or many-pointed star.

General Information

This member of the sapodilla family was long believed to be indigenous to Central America, but the botanists Paul

Star Apple / Nutritional Value Per 100 g Edible Portion			
	Raw		Raw
Calories	67.2	Beta Carotene (A)	0.004–0.039 mg
Protein	0.72–2.33 g	Thiamine (B₁)	0.018–0.080 mg
Fiber	0.55–3.30 g	Riboflavin (B₂)	0.013–0.040 mg
Calcium	7.4–17.3 mg	Niacin (B₃)	0.935–1.340 mg
Iron	0.30–0.68 mg	Ascorbic Acid (C)	3.0–15.2 mg
Phosphorus	15.9–22.0 mg		

Standley and Louis Williams have declared that it is not native to that area, no Nahuatl name has been found, and the tree may properly belong to the West Indies. In Haiti the star apple was the favorite fruit of King Christophe, who held court under the shade of a very large specimen at Milot. The tree is grown occasionally in southern Florida and Hawaii, where it was introduced before 1901. The tree has always been prized for its ornamental value as well as for its fruits. The fruit is the size of a small apple, either white-green or dark purple, with a soft pulp containing a central "star" of six to eleven flat, brown seeds set in translucent jelly. The glossy, leathery skin adheres tightly to the inner rind.

Culinary Uses

Star apple pulp is soft, white, and milky. The flavor is sweet and characteristic of the sapodilla family, but to be good the fruit must be fully ripened on the tree. It is usually chilled and eaten fresh, the flesh spooned out from around the seed cells and core, but it can be made into preserves. A combination of the chopped flesh mixed with mango, citrus, pineapple, and coconut water is frozen and served as "Jamaica fruit salad ice." Fruits must not be bitten into, as the skin and rind are inedible. When opening a star apple, one should not allow any of the bitter latex of the skin to contact the edible flesh.

Health Benefits

The ripe fruit, because of its mucilaginous character, is eaten to soothe inflammation in laryngitis and pneumonia. It is given as a treatment for diabetes mellitus and as a decoction is gargled to relieve angina. In Venezuela the slightly unripe fruits are eaten to overcome intestinal disturbances; however, in excess, they cause constipation.

Strawberry

(Fragaria virginiana, F. vesca, F. moschata)

> Doubtless God could have made a better berry, but doubtless God never did.
>
> —WILLIAM BUTLER

Fraga was the ancient Latin name and refers to the fruit's wonderfully enticing fragrance. The term *virginiana* means "from Virginia"; *vesca* means "weak" or "thin";

moschata means "having a musky scent." The etymology of the English name *strawberry* is often disputed: one group claims that it came about because straw was used between the rows to keep the berries clean and to protect them in wintertime; another explanation is that in Europe ripe berries were threaded on straws to be carried to market; a third contingent claims that the name was originally *strewberry* because the berries appear to be strewn or scattered among the leaves of the plant.

General Information

Strawberries are probably the most popular of all the berries, and indigenous to both the Old and the New World. There are approximately seventy-five varieties of wild strawberries found in the United States alone, all of them edible. The commercial fruits we know today are the result of an 1835 cross between one of the small, wild strawberries native to Europe and North America and a walnut-sized strawberry of Chile. A French spy on a mission to Chile had smuggled the large Chilean strawberry home to France, and in King Louis XV's garden at Versailles the plant was crossed with another strawberry, *F. virginiana*, which Virginian colonists had sent back to England. Although the cross produced a berry of good size and flavor, wild strawberries have a flavor that is unequaled by any commercial berry. The alpine strawberry (*F. vesca*) is a form of wood strawberry, the wild strawberry of antiquity. It was discovered about three hundred years ago east of Grenoble in the low Alps, and since the fruit was larger and the plant bore continuously throughout the growing season, it soon surpassed other wood strawberries in popularity. Some strains of alpine strawberry produce fruits colored creamy white or yellow, slightly larger than the red, and with just a hint of pineapple flavor. The musk strawberry (*F. moschata*) is larger than the alpine strawberry and grows wild to a limited extent in the shaded forests of central Europe, north into Scandinavia, and east into Russia. The strawberry itself is an unusual fruit in that its seeds are embedded in its surface rather than protected within. The sweetest and most nutritious strawberries are those that have been sun-ripened on the plant, because the amount of vitamin C increases the longer the berries remain unpicked in the sun. California provides 80 percent of the nation's fresh and frozen strawberries. Strawberries are one of the foods permitted irradiation.

Buying Tips

All berries should be unblemished, fully and deeply colored without any runny or bleeding spots, slightly soft, and fragrant, with their stems intact. Avoid those with green or white tips as well as overly large varieties, since they have not had enough sun to ripen thoroughly and develop their full sweetness. Both alpine and musk strawberries are flavorless until becoming dead ripe, at which time they become extremely soft and aromatic (plus hard to ship). Strawberries should be refrigerated but taste best at room temperature. Don't take off the cap until just before eating.

Culinary Uses

At their best, strawberries have a musky aroma and are sweet but acid, almost pineapple-like, in flavor. Fruits of the alpine strawberry have an intense, wild strawberry flavor, while the musk strawberry tastes like a combination of strawberry, raspberry, and pineapple. Wash them just before using, if at all, and remove the stems and hulls. An American favorite is strawberry shortcake, but the berries also appear on Belgian waffles, in jams and jellies, and as an adornment for various dishes. A natural complement to strawberries is cream in various forms, whether whipped into clouds, slightly soured, clotted as in Devonshire cream, or enriched with egg into a custard.

Health Benefits

pH 3.00–3.50. Strawberries are highly rated as a skin-cleansing food, even though skin eruptions may increase at first as they rid the blood of harmful toxins. Hives or other allergic reactions to the berries are most likely a

LORE AND LEGEND

The early Greeks had a taboo against eating any red foods, including wild strawberries, and this added mystery to the fruit, leading many to believe that it possessed great powers. Strawberries are often associated with fairy folk, and in Bavaria a basket of the fruit is sometimes tied between a cow's horns to please the elves so that they bless the cow with abundant milk. During the Middle Ages, pregnant women avoided the berries because they believed their children would be born with ugly red birthmarks if they ate them. In art and literature the strawberry is usually a symbol of sensuality and earthly desire.

result of eating them in their unripe state or when they have not been fully vine-ripened. Strawberries are recommended as essential for cardiac health and offer good nutritional energy that is easy to digest and process. All berries, but especially strawberries, are good sources of the anticancer compound ellagic acid. They are among the highest organic sodium fruits and thus are eliminative and good for the intestinal tract; however, the seeds can be irritating where there is colitis or inflammation of the bowel. Their considerable vitamin properties are mostly lost during cooking, so that although strawberry jelly, jams, and preserves may taste good, they have only a fraction of their original natural vitamins. The addition of sugar renders them acidic and detrimental to the body. Strawberry leaf tea has many of the same properties as raspberry leaf tea and may be used to ease diarrhea, increase the flow of milk after birth, and restore strength. A cut strawberry rubbed over the face after washing will whiten the skin and remove a slight sunburn. Research has determined that strawberries have a slight tranquilizing effect; that's why surgical gloves for dentists and masks for children's anesthesia are often perfumed with a strawberry scent. A kitchen remedy to remove tartar and strengthen teeth is to rub a halved strawberry on the teeth and gums and leave on for forty-five minutes, then rinse with warm water.

Strawberry / Nutritional Value Per 100 g Edible Portion

	Raw		Raw
Calories	30	Copper	0.049 mg
Protein	0.61 g	Manganese	0.290 mg
Fat	0.37 g	Beta Carotene (A)	27 IU
Fiber	0.53 g	Thiamine (B$_1$)	0.020 mg
Calcium	14 mg	Riboflavin (B$_2$)	0.066 mg
Iron	0.38 mg	Niacin (B$_3$)	0.230 mg
Magnesium	10 mg	Pantothenic Acid (B$_5$)	0.340 mg
Phosphorus	19 mg	Pyridoxine (B$_6$)	0.059 mg
Potassium	166 mg	Folic Acid (B$_9$)	17.7 mcg
Sodium	1 mg	Ascorbic Acid (C)	56.7 mg
Zinc	0.130 mg	Tocopherol (E)	0.12 mg

Strawberry Pear

(Hylocereus undatus)

Also Known As: Pitaya, Night Blooming Cereus

Hylocereus derives from a Greek term for "wood." *Undatus* means "wavy, not flat, undulate."

General Information

The cacti bearing these fruits are indigenous to Central America. The species reached Hawaii in 1830 among a shipment of plants loaded at a Mexican port en route from Boston to Canton, China. Most of the other plants died and were being discarded during a stopover in Hawaii, but the strawberry pear was still partly alive, so cuttings were planted. The cuttings flourished, and the cactus became a common ornamental throughout the islands, where it blooms spectacularly but rarely sets fruit. The fruit is oval to oblong, up to four inches long, and may be bright red, peach-colored, or yellow.

Culinary Uses

The flesh is sweet, white, and juicy, with numerous tiny black seeds. Most often the fruit is chilled and cut in half so that the flesh can be eaten with a spoon. The juice makes a refreshing beverage. A syrup made of the whole fruit is used in pastries and candy, while the unopened flower bud can be cooked and eaten as a vegetable.

Sugar Apple

(Annona squamosa)

Also Known As: Sweetsop, Scaly Custard Apple

Annona means "year's harvest" and is suggested by the Haitian name *anon*, which is applied to one of the species. *Squamosa* means "having scalelike leaves" or "full of scales." The alternate name *sweetsop* is in contrast to the soursop; the fruit is also sometimes called the "scaly cus-tard apple," in reference to its scales, which cover the greenish-yellow skin under a whitish bloom.

General Information

Sugar apple is the English name used in the West Indies and Americas for the fruit of a small tree commonly cultivated in tropical South America. Its original home is unknown, but the Spaniards probably carried seeds from the New World to the Philippines, and the Portuguese are believed to have introduced the fruit to southern India before 1590. For those living in the interior of Brazil, the sugar apple is one of the most important fruits. The compound fruits, which ripen constantly over a period of six to seven months, are nearly round, ovoid, or conical and $2\frac{1}{3}$ to 4 inches long; their thick rinds, composed of knobby segments, are pale green, gray-green, or bluish green. The fruit is of delicate construction and is liable to come apart when ripe unless carefully handled.

Culinary Uses

The pulp is either yellow or white, tender, delicate, and delicious, uniting an agreeable sweetness with the delightful fragrance of rose water. Many of the segments enclose a single oblong, black or dark-brown inedible seed about a half inch long. There may be as many as thirty-eight seeds per fruit, although some trees bear seedless fruit. The sugar apple is usually eaten as a dessert; the fruit is broken open and the flesh segments spooned out and enjoyed while the inedible seeds are spat out. It may also be used to make sherbets and to flavor ice creams, but it is never cooked.

Health Benefits

The green fruit, which is very astringent, is employed against diarrhea in El Salvador. In India the crushed ripe

Strawberry Pear / Nutritional Value Per 100 g Edible Portion			
	Raw		Raw
Protein	0.159–0.229 g	Beta Carotene (A)	0.005–0.012 mg
Fat	0.21–0.61 g	Thiamine (B₁)	0.028–0.043 mg
Fiber	0.7–0.9 g	Riboflavin (B₂)	0.043–0.045 mg
Calcium	6.3–8.8 mg	Niacin (B₃)	0.297–0.430 mg
Iron	0.55–0.65 mg	Ascorbic Acid (C)	8.0–9.0 mg
Phosphorus	30.2–36.1 mg		

Sugar Apple / Nutritional Value Per 100 g Edible Portion			
	Raw		Raw
Calories	88.9–95.7	Sodium	9 mg
Protein	1.53–2.38 g	Beta Carotene (A)	5–7 IU
Fat	0.26–1.10 g	Thiamine (B₁)	0.100–0.130 mg
Fiber	1.14–2.50 g	Riboflavin (B₂)	0.113–0.167 mg
Calcium	19.4–44.7 mg	Niacin (B₃)	0.654–0.931 mg
Iron	0.28–1.34 mg	Pantothenic Acid (B₅)	0.226 mg
Magnesium	21 mg	Pyridoxine (B₆)	0.200 mg
Phosphorus	23.6–55.3 mg	Ascorbic Acid (C)	34.7–42.2 mg
Potassium	247 mg		

fruit, mixed with salt, is applied to tumors. The seeds are acrid and poisonous.

Tamarillo
(Cyphomandra betacea)
Also Known As: Tree Tomato

Cyphomandra is a Greek term referring to the fruit's hump-shaped anthers. *Betacea* means "beetlike." The New Zealanders, who are the major commercial growers of this fruit, decided to market what was formerly known as the tree tomato as the "tamarillo," and the name stuck.

General Information
Indigenous to Peru, the tamarillo is a tropical fruit related to the tomato. It must have been carried at an early date to East Africa, Asia, and the East Indies, as it is well established in those regions. It was introduced into New Zealand in 1891, where commercial growing on a small scale began about 1920. Flushed by their success in bestowing the name *kiwi* on the Chinese gooseberry, New Zealanders decided that the tree tomato should be called the "tamarillo," and it now widely goes by that name. Shortages of tropical fruits in World War II justified an increased level of production. In nursery catalogs in the United States, the plant is frequently advertised and sold for growing indoors in pots as a curiosity. The size and shape of an egg, the tamarillo fruit looks rather like an elongated plum with its reddish-yellow or crimson skin.

Buying Tips
Look for firm, heavy fruits that yield slightly to pressure. The more predominant the yellow tones, the sweeter and milder the fruit. Hard fruits will ripen at room temperature. Once ripened, they can be refrigerated for up to a week.

Culinary Uses
This stunning and aromatic fruit is reddish yellow or purple when ripe, with the yellower fruit often milder and sweeter than the darker. Inside, the yellow or deep coppery-orange flesh has two purple whorls of black seeds, which are edible, and a plumlike texture that is pleasantly rich, sweet, and slightly astringent. Smelling vaguely of sun-ripened tomatoes, this pleasantly bitter, almost meaty fruit may be eaten raw but is well suited for cooking. Its taste has the sour notes of tomatoes, the subtlety of cooked carrots, and the slight punch of wintergreen. Baked, broiled, or stewed, used in savory dishes, sauces, or preserves, its sweet-spicy flavor will mysteriously deepen and enhance any other fruits when used in moderation. Because of its dense texture and assertive flavor, it holds its own in highly seasoned preparations such as chutneys, salsas, relishes, and other sauces. The fruit should not be cut on a wooden or other permeable surface, as the juice will make an indelible stain. The peel is not edible so must be removed.

Health Benefits
The tamarillo is a good source of vitamins A and C and is low in calories. As a member of the nightshade family, it contains the toxic alkaloid solanine.

Tamarind
(Tamarindus indica)
Also Known As: Indian Date

Tamarindus comes from the Arabic *tamr-hindi*, meaning "Indian date." *Indica* means "native to or introduced from India."

General Information
The tamarind tree is a massive, slow-growing, ornamental leguminous tree native to tropical East Africa. Known as "dates" because of their sticky, fibrous appearance, the fruits are flattish and beanlike. The irregularly curved, cinnamon-colored pods range from three to eight inches long. At first the pods are tender-skinned with green, highly acidic flesh and soft, whitish seeds; as the fruit matures, the pods fill out, the pulp turns brown or reddish brown, and the skin becomes brittle and easily cracked. It is a peculiarity of the fruit that it contains both more acid and more sugar than any other fruit. Although often referred to as "tamarind seed," it is in fact the pulp around the seeds that is used.

Tamarillo / Nutritional Value Per 100 g Edible Portion			
	Raw		Raw
Protein	1.5 g	Beta Carotene (A)	540 IU
Fat	0.06–1.28 g	Thiamine (B₁)	0.038–0.137 mg
Fiber	1.4–4.2 g	Riboflavin (B₂)	0.035–0.048 mg
Calcium	3.9–11.3 mg	Niacin (B₃)	1.100–1.380 mg
Iron	0.66–0.94 mg	Ascorbic Acid (C)	23.3–33.9 mg
Phosphorus	52.5–65.5 mg		

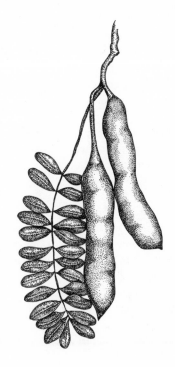

LORE AND LEGEND

There is a superstition that it is harmful to sleep under or to tie a horse to a tamarind tree, probably due to the corrosive effect that fallen leaves have on fabrics in damp weather, and to the fact that few plants survive beneath the tree. Many Burmese believe that the tree represents the dwelling place of the rain god, and that the tree raises the temperature in its immediate vicinity. In Malaya small pieces of tamarind along with coconut milk are placed in the mouth of an infant at birth, and the bark and fruit are given to elephants to make them wise.

Buying Tips

Tamarind is available in the specialty section of supermarkets. In Indian, Asian, and Mexican markets the pulp is available in an easy-to-use paste form. The paste may be stored for a year or more. Tamarind is also available powdered.

Culinary Uses

Tender, immature, very sour pods are cooked as seasoning with rice, fish, and meats in India. The fully grown but still unripe fruits are roasted in coals until the skins burst; the skins are then peeled back and the pulp dipped in wood ashes and eaten. Fully ripe, fresh fruit has a spicy date-apricot flavor and is enjoyed out of hand by children and adults alike. To use the pulp, remove the hard outer shell and strings from the tamarind pods. Cover in water and boil for two minutes. Allow to cool. With your fingers, press the seeds from the pulp. Discard the seeds and pods. Using a fork, purée the pulp with the water to create an extract. The extract can be stored in a closed jar in the refrigerator for up to a week. The pulp is an important ingredient in chutneys, curries, and sauces, including some brands of Worcestershire and barbecue sauce. When purchased dried, the fruit is first soaked in water and the soaking liquid and pulp used (the seeds are discarded). In one sweet preparation, powdered sugar is added to the fresh pulp until it no longer sticks to the fingers, at which time the concoction is shaped into balls and coated with more powdered sugar. Dehydrated tamarinds are also used to prepare confections, and the resulting sweetmeats are commonly found in Jamaica, Cuba, and the Dominican Republic. Combined with guava, papaya, or banana, the pulp makes a delicious preserve. The fruit may also be made into a variety of refreshing beverages and syrups or in sherbet. In India, young leaves and very young seedlings and flowers are cooked and eaten as greens; in Zimbabwe, the leaves are added to soup and the flowers are a common ingredient in salads.

Health Benefits

Anthelmintic, carminative, laxative, refrigerant. The principal use of the ripe, sweet-sour, stringy pulp throughout the Americas and Caribbean is as a mild laxative. The pulp of the fruit contains citric, tartaric, and malic acids, which give it cooling properties; therefore, it is a useful drink for those ill with fever, as well as a popular cooling beverage in

Tamarind / Nutritional Value Per 100 g Edible Portion			
	Raw		**Raw**
Calories	115–230	Sodium	24 mg
Protein	3.10 g	Beta Carotene (A)	15–30 IU
Fat	0.1 g	Thiamine (B$_1$)	0.160–0.428 mg
Fiber	5.6 g	Riboflavin (B$_2$)	0.070–0.152 mg
Calcium	35–170 mg	Niacin (B$_3$)	0.600–1.938 mg
Iron	1.3–10.9 mg	Pantothenic Acid (B$_5$)	0.143 mg
Magnesium	92 mg	Pyridoxine (B$_6$)	0.066 mg
Phosphorus	54–110 mg	Ascorbic Acid (C)	0.7–3.0 mg
Potassium	375–628 mg		

hot countries. Alone, or in combination with lime juice, honey, dates, milk, or spices, the pulp is considered effective as a digestive, as a remedy for biliousness, and as an antiscorbutic. In native practices, the pulp is applied on inflammations, used in a gargle for sore throats, and administered to alleviate sunstroke and alcoholic intoxication. Lotions and extracts made from the leaves and flowers are used in treating conjunctivitis, dysentery, jaundice, hemorrhoids, and many other ailments.

Tomatillo

(Physalis ixocarpa)

Also Known As: Mexican Green Tomato, Mexican Husk Tomato, Tomato Verde, Chinese Lantern Plants

> *Physalis* comes from the Greek *physa,* for "bladder," and was given this plant because the fruit is enclosed within a thin calyx. *Ixocarpa* means "sticky" or "glutinous-fruited." *Tomatillo* is a Spanish word that means "little tomato."

General Information

A prominent staple in Aztec and Mayan economies, the tomatillo plant abounds in Mexico and the highlands of Guatemala. This strange-looking member of the nightshade family has the usual *Physalis* structure, the calyx enlarging with the fruit and becoming straw-colored and papery, often splitting. It resembles a green cherry tomato, ranging in size from an inch in diameter to plum-sized, but is more lustrous and firm. The skin color may be anywhere from yellow-green to purplish, but the fruit is most commonly used in its unripe green state.

Buying Tips

Choose fruits that are firm, hard, and dry, with clean, close-fitting husks that show no blackness or mold. The unhusked fresh fruits can be stored in single layers in a cool, dry atmosphere for several months.

Culinary Uses

The flesh is pale yellow, crisp or soft, and acid to sweet or insipid, with many tiny seeds. In texture and flavor it is reminiscent of a green plum with a sweet-sour taste, though not as sour as a lemon, and with a delightful aroma of freshly mown hay. Like red tomatoes, tomatillo's gelatinous texture makes for great sauce potential. The tangy tomatillo is most frequently featured in southwestern and Mexican cuisine in the form of a sauce known as salsa verde. The fruits are almost always cooked to develop their lemony-herbal flavor and to soften their rather solid hides, but they can be used raw for a sharper flavor. The husk is inedible and must be removed before use.

Health Benefits

It is said in Mexico that a decoction of the calyces will cure diabetes. A member of the nightshade family, this fruit should be used with caution by those with calcium deficiencies.

Ugli Fruit

(Citrus spp.)

> The term *Citrus* derives from the Greek term for the citron, *kedromelon.* The English name *ugli fruit* is copyrighted by the Jamaican exporter G. G. R. Sharp and originated in response to the fruit's appearance.

General Information

A citrus hybrid, the ugli is a cross between the grapefruit and either a tangerine or orange that originated in Jamaica. A chance seedling, it was propagated by F. G. Sharp at Trout Hall, then exported in 1934 to England by his son. Popular in the English markets, where it was generally called the "ugly," it soon made its appearance in other countries. Looking rather like a large, lumpy grapefruit, it has a puffy, thick, knobby, slightly loose-fitting skin that may range from lime green to light orange in color. This skin often forms a furrowed collar or neck on the rounded or slightly pear-shaped fruit. Not altogether an unsightly fruit, it is simply not as sleek and regularly colored as the more common citrus fruits.

Tomatillo / Nutritional Value Per 100 g Edible Portion			
	Raw		**Raw**
Calories	32	Copper	0.079 mg
Protein	0.17–0.70 g	Manganese	0.153 mg
Fat	0.6 g	Beta Carotene (A)	80 IU
Fiber	0.6–1.7 g	Thiamine (B₁)	0.054–0.106 mg
Calcium	6.3–10.9 mg	Riboflavin (B₂)	0.023–0.057 mg
Iron	0.57–1.40 mg	Niacin (B₃)	2.100–2.700 mg
Magnesium	23 mg	Pantothenic Acid (B₅)	0.150 mg
Phosphorus	21.9–40.0 mg	Pyridoxine (B₆)	0.056 mg
Potassium	243 mg	Folic Acid (B₉)	7.0 mcg
Sodium	0.4 mg	Ascorbic Acid (C)	2.0–4.8 mg
Zinc	0.220 mg		

Buying Tips

Look for fruits that are heavy for their size, with a preference for smaller fruits, since they have a sweeter flavor. While there should be no sign of drying at the stem end, any amount of mottling, bronzing, surface scarring, or uneven coloring is perfectly normal. The fruit should have a little bit of give, like a grapefruit.

Culinary Uses

The ugli fruit's loosely adhering coat is a cinch to peel, and the pinkish or yellowy-orange flesh is sweeter than its grapefruit parent and nearly seedless. Once cut, the fruit fairly overflows with sweet juice from its atypically large, tender juice sacs. The acid-sweet flesh is unusually soft and succulent, with a full, zesty flavor. It can be cut and eaten like a grapefruit, peeled and eaten like an orange, or cooked into preserves.

Health Benefits

Low in fat, high in fiber and vitamin C.

Umeboshi

(Prunus salicina)

Also Known As: Salt Plum, Japanese Plum

> This plum is part of the Prunus family—thus the genus name—while *salicina* means "willowlike" or "resembling the willow tree," *Salix* spp.

General Information

The ume or Japanese plum is a sour green fruit resembling an unripe apricot. The tree was introduced to Japan at least thirteen hundred years ago from the Chinese mainland and quickly adapted. The fruit was soon popular among the Japanese, more so than it had been among the Chinese. The hard green plums are picked in the early spring, washed, then packed into vats with crude sea salt for about a month. The salt draws the juice out of the plums by osmosis, so that they are soon covered by a liquid conventionally called "plum vinegar." The plums are then sun-dried while mineral-rich purple shiso leaves (*Iresine herbistii*, also known as "perilla" or "beefsteak") are added to the brine, imparting to it a beautiful deep red color, sweet taste, and fragrant bouquet. The shiso leaves also provide a natural preservative, known to possess over one thousand times the preserving ability of synthetic preservatives. Next, the plums are returned to the brine for additional pickling; they are soaked overnight and dried

daily in the sun for seven days. The plums are then removed and aged for an additional four months to develop subtle qualities of flavor, taste, and appearance.

Culinary Uses

Whole umeboshi plums generally come complete with pit and shiso leaf. The whole plums can be boiled with rice or sliced into stir-fried vegetables. The leaf can also be added while cooking to add flavor and color. Ume extract/concentrate is made by reducing 1 kilogram (2.2 pounds) of fresh plums to 20 grams (less than an ounce) of thick, dark syrup. The concentrate contains no salt, unlike the plums or paste. It is generally made into a drink to relieve acidic conditions but also is an excellent aid for travelers because of its soothing digestive properties. Umeboshi paste is the puréed umeboshi minus pits and shiso. Less expensive than whole umeboshi and more convenient to use, the paste can replace salt in salad dressings, spreads, seasonings, and sauces or be cooked with grains, beans, and vegetables. In paste form or whole, umeboshi keeps for several years at room temperature. Umeboshi vinegar is the pink brine drawn from kegs of mature umeboshi. This liquid has a deep cherry aroma and fruity sour flavor. Technically not a vinegar because it contains salt, it may be substituted for vinegar and salt in any recipe, where it imparts a light, refreshing, citruslike flavor. It especially enhances salad dressings and steamed vegetables.

Health Benefits

Umeboshi has remarkable healing properties, alkalinizing the digestive system, helping to strengthen blood quality, and relieving indigestion due to overeating, overindulgence in alcohol, or morning sickness. Its high citric acid content eliminates from the body lactic acid, a major contributor to fatigue, colds, flu, viruses, diseases, and chronic illnesses. Low in fat, high in iron and vitamin C.

Wampee

(Clausena lansium)

> *Clausena* is from a personal name of unknown origin. The English name *wampee* is derived from the Chinese *huang-p'i-kuo*.

General Information

The wampee is native to southern China and the northern part of former French Indochina. It is cultivated to a limited extent in Queensland, Australia, and Hawaii. Brought to Florida in 1908, a few specimens have been growing for years, but the fruit is generally unknown to most residents. The fruits hang in showy, loose clusters of several strands, being round or conical and up to one inch long with five faint, pale ridges extending a short distance down from the apex. The thin, pliable, but tough rind is a light brownish yellow, minutely hairy, and dotted with tiny raised brown oil glands.

Culinary Uses

The flesh is yellowish white or colorless, grapelike, mucilaginous, juicy, pleasantly sweet, subacid, or sour; it may contain up to five bright green seeds. A fully ripe, peeled wampee is agreeable to eat out of hand; discard the large seed(s). The seeded pulp can also be added to fruit cups, gelatins, and other desserts or made into pie or jam. In Southeast Asia a bottled carbonated beverage resembling champagne is made by fermenting the fruit with sugar and straining off the juice.

Health Benefits

The fruit is said to have stomachic and cooling effects and to act as a vermifuge. The Chinese believe that if one has eaten too many lychees, eating the wampee will counteract the bad effects. Florida-grown fruits have been shown to have 28.8 to 29.2 milligrams of ascorbic acid per 100 grams of flesh.

Watermelon
(Citrullus lanatus, C. vulgaris)

Citrullus is the diminutive form of *Citrus* and is said to be an allusion to the fruit's shape and flesh color, which resembles that of the orange and/or citron. The term *lanatus* means "woolly," while *vulgaris* means that it is an ordinary fruit, commonly grown. The English name *watermelon* is appropriate since the juicy flesh is over 90 percent water.

General Information

Watermelon originated in desert areas of tropical and subtropical Africa and is botanically different from the rest of the melon group. Eaten and cultivated in Egypt and India well before 2500 B.C., the one great advantage of this fruit, which encouraged its spread to lands around the Mediterranean and eastward into Asia, was its over 90 per-

cent water content. This made watermelon a valuable source of drinking water in desert areas and an especially useful source of potable liquid where water supplies were polluted. In 1857 the Scottish missionary and explorer David Livingstone described the abundance of watermelons in the vast dry plateaus of the Kalahari Desert of the Bechuanaland in central South Africa. He noted that the fruits were variable in taste—some bitter and others sweet—and that the natives and all the animals of the region ate them ravenously. There are more than fifty varieties, of various shapes, colors, and sizes, which are generally divided into "picnic" and "icebox" varieties. Picnic types are larger, usually weighing fifteen to fifty pounds; icebox varieties—designed to fit into a refrigerator—weigh between five and fifteen pounds. Watermelons do grow larger under the right conditions, however: the 1991 *Guinness Book of World Records* gives the prize to a 279-pound specimen grown in 1988 by Bill Rogerson of Robertsville, North Carolina. Most watermelons have the familiar red flesh, but there are also orange- and yellow-fleshed varieties, as well as some that are seedless. There is little taste difference among the different varieties. Watermelon consumption in the United States peaked in 1960 at 17.2 pounds per person annually but dropped steadily after that, reaching rock bottom two decades later, when Americans ate only 10.6 pounds per person. Lately, however, these melons are making a comeback.

Buying Tips

Few people can agree on just how to pick a ripe watermelon. Some say that it should have a skin that is dull and slightly waxy, with ends that are not pointy but rounded

Watermelon / Nutritional Value Per 100 g Edible Portion			
	Raw		**Raw**
Calories	32	Copper	0.032 mg
Protein	0.62 g	Manganese	0.037 mg
Fat	0.43 g	Beta Carotene (A)	366 IU
Fiber	0.30 g	Thiamine (B₁)	0.080 mg
Calcium	8 mg	Riboflavin (B₂)	0.020 mg
Iron	0.17 mg	Niacin (B₃)	0.200 mg
Magnesium	11 mg	Pantothenic Acid (B₅)	0.212 mg
Phosphorus	9 mg	Pyridoxine (B₆)	0.144 mg
Potassium	116 mg	Folic Acid (B₉)	2.2 mcg
Sodium	2 mg	Ascorbic Acid (C)	9.6 mg
Zinc	0.07 mg		

and well filled out (evidently the nonpointy ones are female and sweeter), and be heavy for its size, with a bottom that is a pale creamy yellow and not white. Others swear by the thumping method, looking for a deep hollow sound rather than a dull thud. Another method is to look for one with a dry brown stem and then scrape the rind with a fingernail; when the green skin comes off easily, the melon is deemed ready to eat. When the melons are cut, your job is much easier. The best ones have bright red flesh with dark brown or black seeds. Avoid melons with white streaks as well as those that have deeply colored, mealy areas around the seeds. Uncut watermelons can be kept at room temperature for up to two weeks. Wrap any cut leftovers loosely in cellophane and put in the refrigerator, where they will keep for a few days.

Culinary Uses

Almost everyone loves watermelon because it is refreshingly sweet. On a hot summer day nothing beats a freshly cut slice. To serve, either slice or cut into chunks. Italians like to make watermelon puddings, particularly the *gelu u muluni* of Sicily, made with ground almonds, chocolate, and cinnamon. Americans prefer simpler watermelon desserts, such as fruit cups, melon balls, or ices. The rind makes a tasty old-fashioned pickle. Fully ripe seeds are edible and are considered quite tasty by many cultures— see the listing in the **Nuts, Seeds, and Oils** section for more information.

Health Benefits

pH 5.6–6.7. Watermelon is used as a cooling food in hot weather, for treatment of thirst, and to relieve mental depression. As it contains over 90 percent water, it is popular with dieters. Its high-quality water content is an excellent cleanser and detoxifier for the whole body and has the greatest dissolving power of inorganic minerals in the body out of all the fruits and vegetables. Surprisingly, it has only half the sugar (5 percent) of an apple, but it tastes much sweeter because sugar is its main taste-producing element. One of nature's safest and most dependable diuretics, watermelon has a remarkable ability to quickly and completely wash out the bladder. The white rind of the watermelon is one of the highest organic sodium foods in nature, and the outside peel one of the best sources of chlorophyll. The rind can be juiced and drunk, or small amounts can be eaten.

Wood Apple
(Feronia limonia)
Also Known As: Elephant Apple

The genus *Feronia* is named after Feronia, the Roman goddess of forests. *Limonia* perhaps means "lemonlike" or "lemon-scented." Both the tree and its fruit formerly had the botanical name *F. elephantum* because the fruit is a favorite of elephants.

General Information

The small wood apple tree is found in most parts of the Indian subcontinent and eastward to the China Sea. Traditionally a "poor man's food" until processing techniques were developed in the mid-1950s, the tree is now cultivated along roads and occasionally in orchards. Fruit is tested for maturity by dropping samples onto a hard surface from a height of one foot; immature fruits bounce, while mature fruits do not. After harvesting, the fruits are kept in the sun for two weeks to fully ripen, and the hard rinds must be cracked open with a hammer.

Culinary Uses

The round, apple-sized, gray fruits have hard shells and contain an odorous brown, sticky, mealy pulp, which is used to make sherbets, jellies, and chutneys in India. The pulp is also eaten raw with sugar or seasoning but is inconveniently full of small seeds. A bottled nectar is made by diluting the pulp with water, passing it through a pulper to remove seeds and fiber, and then further diluting, straining, and pasteurizing it.

Health Benefits

The fruit is much used in India as a liver and cardiac tonic and, when unripe, as an astringent means of halting diarrhea and dysentery. The pulp is poulticed onto bites and stings of venomous insects, as is the powdered rind.

Wood Apple / Nutritional Value Per 100 g Edible Portion			
Protein	8.00%	Iron	0.07%
Fat	1.45%	Phosphorus	0.08%
Calcium	0.17%		

VEGETABLES

Ho! 'tis the time of salads.
—Laurence Sterne, *Tristram Shandy*

VEGETABLES

VEGETABLES

What is the difference between a vegetable and a fruit? In 1893 this question came before the U.S. Supreme Court, which ruled that a vegetable refers to those edible parts of plants generally eaten as part of the main course, while a fruit refers to a plant part generally eaten as an appetizer, dessert, or out of hand. Typical parts of plants used as vegetables include bulbs (garlic and onion), flowers (broccoli and cauliflower), fruits (pumpkins and tomatoes), leaves (spinach and lettuce), roots (carrots and beets), seeds (legumes, peas, and corn), stalks (celery), stems (asparagus), and tubers (potatoes and yams).

Every vegetable has a history. Some, like taro, are so ancient that no wild variety exists today. Others date from just before cultivation began, while yet others are astonishingly recent—the rutabaga or the orange carrot, for example. All have a tale to tell; all have incidents in their lives that reflect on humankind, on our thoughts and feelings, our vanity and aspirations, our most intimate personal habits and beliefs—as revealing as any archeological remains. Why, for example, have many cultures historically considered the consumption of garlic and onions so vulgar? Why have so many vegetables been considered aphrodisiacs—especially arugula, the seeds of which were strewn around statues consecrated to Priapus. Did the ancient world know something we don't? They certainly valued the medicinal qualities of vegetables and herbs in a way that we have almost lost.

There are hundreds of types and thousands of varieties of vegetables from which to choose. Preference should always be given toward those that are freshest and in season; the tastiest and most nutritious vegetables are those that are consumed immediately after picking or harvesting. Generally speaking, the longer vegetables are exposed to air, heat, and water, the less nutritious they will be. "Fresh" vegetables shipped from long distances and displayed for several days in a store may actually be less nutritious than those that are flash-frozen shortly after harvesting. Canned vegetables (both home-canned and commercially canned) are heated to high temperatures, which destroys some of the vitamin content, including up to 50 percent of the vitamin C. If the canning liquid is not utilized (many people drain the liquid off because of its possible high sodium content), even more nutrients are lost. Canned vegetables, which lack the flavor and texture of produce that is fresh or frozen, should be considered a viable alternative only if no fresh or frozen produce is available. Dehydrated and powdered vegetables are even lower in nutrients than canned, because of their lengthy exposure to air or heat.

The English word *vegetable* derives from the Latin *vegetus*, meaning "active" or "lively," and Roman slave and patrician alike thought all food from the fertile earth was a boon to amatory pursuits. In later cultures vegetables would be spurned by the nobility; our word *garbage*, interestingly enough, comes from the Latin *gerbe*, meaning "green stuff."

A special note on the nightshade family (*Solanaceae*): Nightshade plants are so named because they grow in the shade of the night rather than, like other plants, in the light of the sun. (Corn, a remarkable evolutionary exception, grows during both day and night.) Most nightshades originated in the fertile altiplano region of South America and were introduced to the rest of the world in the fifteenth century. They include three primary crops—potato, tomato, and tobacco. The nightshades contain a toxic alkaloid, solanine, which seems to adversely affect human calcium balance and may be implicated in health complaints ranging from headaches to arthritis. Both macrobiotic and Ayurvedic medicine recommend using the nightshade vegetables, especially tomatoes and potatoes, in moderation if at all. In his book *The Nightshades and Health*, Norman F. Childers, Ph.D., professor of horticulture at Rutgers University, reveals a correlation between rheumatoid arthritis and nightshade consumption. According to his studies, when some people eliminate these foods from their diet, their arthritic symptoms are alleviated or even disappear. Also included in the nightshade family are all the peppers and chilies, eggplant, garden huckleberry, ground cherry, pepino, tamarillo, and tomatillo.

Arracacha

(Arracacia xanthorrhiza)
Also Known As: Peruvian Carrot

The genus name *Arracacia*, as well as the English name, come from the Spanish name for the plant, while *xanthorrhiza* means "yellow-rooted."

General Information

Native to the Andean highlands from Venezuela to Bolivia, arracacha is an herbaceous perennial that produces large, thick, edible, carrot-shaped, starchy roots with a color suggesting parsnip. Secondary tubers (offshoots of the main tuber) are an important carbohydrate foodstuff and are boiled or fried as a table vegetable or used as an ingredient in stews.

Culinary Uses

Arracacha has a delicate flavor, a crisp texture, and either white, creamy-yellow, or purple flesh. The small, young roots may be baked, fried, or used in soups and stews like potatoes. A flour from the roots is used to make breads and pancakes. The older, coarse main rootstocks and mature leaves are used to feed livestock, and the young stems are used for salads or a table vegetable. Harvesting must not be delayed, because roots left in the ground become fibrous and tough and develop a strong, unpleasant flavor.

Health Benefits

The tubers are reported to have a starch content ranging from about 10 to 25 percent and to be similar in many respects to that of cassava; the starch is easily digested and can be used in infant and invalid foods.

Arracacha / Nutritional Value Per 100 g Edible Portion			
Calories	104	Beta Carotene (A)	60 IU
Protein	0.80 g	Thiamine (B$_1$)	0.060 mg
Fat	0.20 g	Riboflavin (B$_2$)	0.040 mg
Calcium	29 mg	Niacin (B$_3$)	3.400 mg
Iron	1.20 mg	Ascorbic Acid (C)	28 mg
Phosphorus	58 mg		

Artichoke, Chinese

(Stachys sieboldii, S. affinis)

Stachys is from an old Greek name meaning "spike," applied by Dioscorides to this and another group of plants; *sieboldii* is in honor of Philipp Franz von Siebold (1796–1866). The English name *Chinese artichoke* refers to this vegetable's resemblance to the Jerusalem artichoke.

General Information

Chinese artichokes are the tubers of an erect, hairy, herbaceous Chinese perennial that resembles the Jerusalem artichoke but are more slender and knotty. These little tubers also go by the name of *crosnes* in Europe; the name comes from the small French town where they were first introduced in 1882 and from where they are still exported. There is no reason why this vegetable should not be sold on a wider scale and relatively cheaply, for it grows easily and abundantly.

Buying Tips

Select tubers that are firm and pearly white, indicating that they are absolutely fresh, or a yellowish beige, which means they are a few days older but still perfectly good to eat.

Culinary Uses

In taste, Chinese artichokes have an exquisite flavor, somewhere between Jerusalem artichokes and salsify, and can be used in the same manners. To cook, trim the ends and rinse thoroughly. Simmer in just enough salted water to cover, or steam them. A dash of lemon juice will heighten their flavor. Cook until tender rather than al dente but not until mushy and collapsing. They are delicious served as they are, with a large pat of butter and a sprinkling of chopped parsley, chervil, chives, or tarragon. They can also be grated into vegetable salads or used as a side vegetable dish. Their peel, which is hard to remove, is edible and can be left on.

Artichoke, Globe

(Cynara cardunculus scolymus, C. scolymus)

These things are just plain annoying. After all the trouble you go to, you get about as much actual "food" out of eating an artichoke as you would from licking thirty or forty postage stamps. Have the shrimp cocktail instead.

—Miss Piggy

The artichoke's botanical name *Cynara*, from the Latin *canina*, meaning "canine," is derived from the similarity of the involucral spines to a dog's tooth; *cardunculus* means "little thistle"; *scolymus* is from the Greek *skolymos*, meaning "thistle." The English name *artichoke* is derived from the Arabic *al-khurshuf*, also meaning "thistle"; the term *globe* results from the vegetable's shape.

General Information

Globe artichokes are an edible variety of thistle in the sunflower family that originated in the Mediterranean. Raised for their fleshy immature flower buds, the plant will produce a beautiful cluster of violet-blue flowers, colorful enough to grace any garden, if not cut down to be used as a vegetable. The edible flower bud is enclosed by green, leaflike scales, or bracts. Both the bracts and the base or "heart" of the flower are edible. Nearly all of the globe artichokes grown in the United States are from Castroville in Monterey County, California, south of San Francisco, the "artichoke capital of the world." Research conducted in the 1930s found that for two-thirds of people, eating artichokes made a drink of water seem sweet. In 1954, it was discovered that the source of this phenomenon was an organic acid called cynarin, unique to artichokes. This substance can stimulate the sweetness receptors, but only in those who are susceptible to it.

Buying Tips

Choose artichokes that are heavy for their size—compact and firm in the winter and spring or somewhat flared and conical in the summer and fall. Overmature artichokes are lighter in color and have tannish leaves that are open or spreading; the tips and scales of the leaves are hard, and the center is fuzzy and dark pink or purple. If you are not sure about the freshness of an artichoke, squeeze it: you will hear a squeaky sound if the leaves are still plump and crisp.

The absolutely best artichokes are those lightly touched by frost, with their outer leaves colored bronze to brown. Artichokes are best eaten within a day of purchase, but they will keep for about five days in a plastic bag in the refrigerator.

Culinary Uses

Globe artichokes have a daunting appearance but are not as difficult to cook as they appear, and their nutlike flavor is worth the attempt. One of the easiest ways to prepare them is by boiling, tops down, in water with the aid of a steamer. They are done when a fork can easily penetrate the base. Once they are cooked, remove the leaves one by one and dip the fleshy ends into melted butter or another favorite sauce, pulling the ends through your teeth to extract the tasty pulp. Inside the bud is the choke, a tuft of slender hay-colored fibers resembling cornsilk. Beneath is the artichoke bottom, sometimes called the "heart," although *artichoke hearts* more correctly refers to younger globes with small or insignificant chokes. Dense and velvety, the entire bottom can be cut into quarters, dipped in sauce, and eaten. The artichoke is the one vegetable that

Artichoke, Globe / Nutritional Value Per 100 g Edible Portion		
	Raw	Cooked
Calories	47	50
Protein	3.27 g	3.48 g
Fat	0.15 g	0.16 g
Fiber	1.17 g	1.25 g
Calcium	44 mg	45 mg
Iron	1.28 mg	1.29 mg
Magnesium	60 mg	60 mg
Phosphorus	90 mg	86 mg
Potassium	370 mg	354 mg
Sodium	94 mg	95 mg
Zinc	0.490 mg	0.490 mg
Copper	0.231 mg	0.233 mg
Manganese	0.256 mg	0.259 mg
Beta Carotene (A)	185 IU	177 IU
Thiamine (B$_1$)	0.072 mg	0.065 mg
Riboflavin (B$_2$)	0.066 mg	0.066 mg
Niacin (B$_3$)	1.046 mg	1.001 mg
Pantothenic Acid (B$_5$)	0.338 mg	0.342 mg
Pyridoxine (B$_6$)	0.116 mg	0.111 mg
Folic Acid (B$_9$)	68 mcg	51 mcg
Ascorbic Acid (C)	11.7 mg	10.0 mg

LORE AND LEGEND

The artichoke, said to have been created when a beautiful woman was turned into a thistle, was popular in Elizabethan England. They became quite fashionable among monarchs and courtiers, and Catherine de Medici—who may have brought them to France from her native Italy—is said to have eaten so many at one sixteenth-century feast that she "nearly burst." Rumored to be a potent aphrodisiac, artichokes were prescribed by doctors for their male patients who sought to increase bedroom performance.

appears to be larger *after* it has been eaten, so compactly are its petals held together on the choke.

Health Benefits

pH 5.60–6.00 (cooked). Diuretic, digestive. Fresh artichokes are low in calories because most of the carbohydrate is in the form of inulin, a polysaccharide or starch that is not utilized by the body for energy metabolism but does provide nutrition to health-promoting bacteria in the intestinal tract. It has also been shown to improve blood sugar control in diabetics. (If the artichoke is stored for any length of time, however, its inulin is broken down into other sugars.) Recent research indicates that the globe artichoke may neutralize the effect of certain toxic substances, as well as benefit heart activity and the gastrointestinal tract. Their active ingredients are caffeylquinic acids (such as cynarin), found in highest concentrations in the leaves but also in the bracts and heart. Artichoke leaf extracts (with their glycosides, flavonoids, and tannins) have demonstrated significant liver-protecting and regenerating effects, promoting the flow of bile and fat to and from the liver. They lower the level of cholesterol in the blood and prevent excessive fatty deposits in liver tissue and the blood, thereby warding off arteriosclerosis.

Artichoke, Jerusalem

(Helianthus tuberosus)
Also Known As: Sunflower Artichoke, Sunchoke

Helianthus is from the Greek words *helios* (sun) and *anthos* (flower); together they signify that the plant is a member of the sunflower genus; *tuberosus* applies to the roots, which are tuberous. The English name *Jerusalem* artichoke does not imply that the plant is native to Palestine, as it might seem. One theory is that *Jerusalem* is a corruption of the Italian *girasola*, meaning "turning to the sun"; another theory is that it is an English alteration of *Ter Neusen*, the Netherlands location from which the plant was introduced into England. *Artichoke* is derived from the Arabic *al-khurshuf*, meaning "thistle."

General Information

Jerusalem artichokes are native to North America, the tubers of a perennial sunflower that produces brilliant yellow flowers. "Discovered" by Sir Walter Raleigh's 1585 expedition to the Virginia region, where the Indians were found growing them, these knobby, gnarled little roots are more accurately represented by their alternate names of *sunflower artichokes* and *sunchokes*. The Jerusalem artichoke plant has numerous creeping roots, which produce tubers like the common potato. These tubers are of a longish, slightly flattened shape and are generally gathered in the spring or fall, although they may be harvested year-round. In Europe, most notably in France, the vegetable has been improved and cultivated, and today there are over two hundred varieties. Twenty years ago Jerusalem artichokes were beige-colored and very knobby and a great deal of bother to clean. Since then varieties have become smoother and tend now to look very much like small, irregular potatoes. Boston Red has an attractive rose-red skin and only a few knobs on it. Stampede is large, white, and earlier maturing than most.

Artichoke, Jerusalem	/ Nutritional Value Per 100 g Edible Portion		
	Raw		Raw
Calories	76	Phosphorus	78 mg
Protein	2.00 g	Manganese	0.060 mg
Fat	0.01 g	Beta Carotene (A)	20 IU
Fiber	0.80 g	Thiamine (B$_1$)	0.200 mg
Calcium	14 mg	Riboflavin (B$_2$)	0.060 mg
Iron	3.40 mg	Niacin (B$_3$)	1.300 mg
Magnesium	17 mg	Ascorbic Acid (C)	4.0 mg

LORE AND LEGEND

A Huron Indian legend explains the origin of the Jerusalem artichoke as follows: A Feast of Dreams was held so that the chief's son could choose his life power force. After feasting on roast dog, the boy became very sick; in his delirium he called upon the thunder god, who was so pleased that he began to roll his thunder drums, alarming the tribe. The tribe chanted and prayed that another image would reveal itself to the child. Finally the boy's eyes opened and he noticed that sunflowers had grown up all around him. These became his symbol. But the thunder god became angry, and sent hailstones down to destroy the flowers. This act brought the sun into battle, pushing the thunder god aside, and causing the hailstones to sink into the earth and become edible tubers. These tubers were Jerusalem artichokes, which would provide food and medicine for the boy's people for many years to come.

Buying Tips
Choose the smoothest, firmest tubers with the fewest protrusions. Avoid any with wrinkled skins or green blotched areas.

Culinary Uses
Knobby and gnarled, resembling a small, nubby potato or a piece of gingerroot, these little roots offer no visual clue to the flavor of their firm white flesh, which is delicate, nutlike, and slightly sweet. Jerusalem artichokes can vary in color from beige to brownish red. Grated or sliced raw chokes add crunch and flavor to either raw or cooked vegetable salads; they can also be snacked on with a creamy dip. The little tubers do not need to be peeled before cooking as the peels are edible (just clean them as well as possible). Cooked and used in the same manner as potatoes, they can be boiled, steamed, or fried and are excellent mashed to a creamy purée and dotted with butter. The vegetable's sweetness invites onion, cream, and dashes of clove, cinnamon, or nutmeg. Be careful not to overcook them (more than twelve minutes) as they can toughen and become rubbery. Combined with a bit of flour and egg, grated sunchokes make hearty pancakes. Flour made from ground dried Jerusalem artichokes makes a nutritious addition to baked goods or pasta.

Health Benefits
pH 5.93–6.00. Jerusalem artichokes contain no starch or oil and little protein. Fifty percent of the choke is indigestible carbohydrate; it makes a good potato substitute for diabetics and others who cannot eat potatoes, since the artichoke stores its carbohydrates in the form of inulin rather than sugar. Inulin is a polysaccharide or starch that is not utilized by the body for energy metabolism but does provide nutrition to health-promoting bacteria in the intestinal tract. It has also been shown to improve blood sugar control in diabetics. The inulin in sunchokes can sometimes cause flatulence; if you have never sampled sunchokes, first try them in small amounts. They are an excellent source of iron, almost on a par with meats, yet with minimal fat content.

Asparagus
(Asparagus officinalis)

The botanical name is derived from *asparag*, the Persian word for all kinds of tender shoots picked and eaten while very young. *Officinalis* means "of the workshop," alluding to apothecaries' shops and signifying that the plant was once part of the official pharmacopoeia of Rome.

General Information
Asparagus originated in the desert regions of eastern North Africa, where the Arabs ate it long before their recorded history. The ancient Phoenicians introduced asparagus to the Greeks and Romans, who cultivated it as early as 200 B.C. Some stalks grown at Ravenna are recorded as weighing three to a pound (meaning, since the Roman pound weighed 0.721 of our pound, that each spear weighed about 3½ ounces), while others in the Getulia plains of Africa were as tall as twelve feet. One intuitively knows that asparagus is a primitive plant when one sees its broad point poking up through the ground, looking alien compared to other garden denizens. It bears no true leaves, but the small scales appearing on the edible stalk perform the function of leaves. There are three types of cultivated asparagus: white, purple, and green, each of which encom-

passes many varieties. White asparagus never sees the light; the furrows in the fields are piled up (as in potato cultivation) in rows, and there is not a plant to be seen. The rarer purple variety is allowed to grow one to two inches above ground before it is cut; it has more flavor than the white. It is, however, green asparagus that we go for in North America. This is allowed to grow six to twelve inches above ground and gets its full complement of chlorophyll. Cultivated asparagus has been a luxury item throughout its history, but it escapes cultivation so easily that it is found wild, free for the gathering, in whatever regions it is cultivated, and many people find the wild varieties tastier than the cultivated. One of spring's first vegetables, asparagus is related to onions, garlic, and other plants in the lily family.

Buying Tips

Only the young green shoots or spears of asparagus are eaten. The spears should be bright green, perfectly straight, firm, and brittle, with tips that are tight, compact, and pointed. Avoid any that are very thin or very thick, as these will tend to be tough and stringy, and any with open, wilted, shriveled, or yellowing tips. Unless you plan to eat

Asparagus / Nutritional Value Per 100 g Edible Portion		
	Raw	Cooked
Calories	23	24
Protein	2.28 g	2.59 g
Fat	0.20 g	0.31 g
Fiber	n/a	0.83 g
Calcium	21 mg	20 mg
Iron	0.87 mg	0.73 mg
Magnesium	18 mg	10 mg
Phosphorus	56 mg	54 mg
Potassium	273 mg	160 mg
Sodium	2 mg	11 mg
Zinc	0.460 mg	0.420 mg
Copper	0.176 mg	0.112 mg
Manganese	0.262 mg	0.152 mg
Beta Carotene (A)	583 IU	539 IU
Thiamine (B$_1$)	0.140 mg	0.123 mg
Riboflavin (B$_2$)	0.128 mg	0.126 mg
Niacin (B$_3$)	1.170 mg	1.082 mg
Pyridoxine (B$_6$)	0.131 mg	0.122 mg
Folic Acid (B$_9$)	128 mcg	146 mcg
Ascorbic Acid (C)	13.2 mg	10.8 mg
Tocopherol (E)	1.98 mg	n/a

it immediately, asparagus is best stored in a cool place—below 41 degrees Fahrenheit or in the coldest part of the refrigerator—with the stems wrapped in a damp paper towel.

Culinary Uses

Fresh asparagus tastes best when cooked only briefly, a fact apparently appreciated by the ancient Roman emperor Augustus, who is said to have described a task quickly done as taking "less time than to cook asparagus." Before steaming, boiling, or grilling asparagus, snap off the tough lower stem ends by holding each spear in both hands and bending it; it will break where the tender and tough parts meet. Asparagus can be served as a hot vegetable, as a cold addition to salads, in soups, or as a sandwich filling. Canned asparagus has lost all of its wholesome qualities and is best avoided.

LORE AND LEGEND

The ancient Egyptians cultivated asparagus and considered it a worthy offering for their gods. Given its blatantly phallic shape, it is inevitable that asparagus has long been considered an aphrodisiac.

Health Benefits

pH 5.00–6.70. Aperient, diaphoretic, diuretic, laxative. Asparagus was used medicinally long before it was eaten as a vegetable. The Greeks and Romans used it for relieving the pain of toothaches and for preventing bee stings. The actual medicinal property is a substance called asparagine, nature's most effective kidney diuretic, which breaks up any oxalic and uric acid crystals stored in the kidneys and muscles and eliminates them through the urine. (Occasionally this will produce a strong odor in the urine, which is only temporary.) According to the National Cancer Institute, asparagus is the food highest in glutathione, an important anticarcinogen. Asparagus also contains substantial amounts of aspartic acid, an amino acid that neutralizes the excess amounts of ammonia that linger in our bodies and make us tired, and rutin, a factor in preventing small blood vessels from rupturing. Its high water content and roughage encourage evacuation of the bowels by increasing fecal bulk with undigested fiber; it is also a good blood builder because of its chlorophyll content, and contains many of the elements that build the liver, kidneys, skin, ligaments, and bones. As a defense against cancer, asparagus is a three-in-one wonder since it's chock-full of two cancer-blocking vitamins—vitamin A and vitamin C—as well as the mineral selenium. These three food-based nutrients have been singled out in several studies as fierce cancer fighters. Folic acid and the B group of vitamins (including vitamins B_1, B_2, and B_3), which asparagus also contains, are said to trigger the production of histamine, a substance in the blood or tissues. In her book *Food and Healing* nutritionist Annemarie Colbin writes that a lack of histamines has been linked to difficulty reaching orgasm in both men and women, which explains why asparagus was used as an aphrodisiac hundreds of years ago.

Avocado
(Persea americana)
Also Known As: Alligator Pear

Persea is an ancient Greek name for an Egyptian tree with sweet fruit; the term *americana* means "coming from the Americas." The English word *avocado* is a corruption of the Nahuatlan Mexican *ahuacatl*, itself an Aztec shortening of *ahuacacuahatl*, which means "testicle tree." The Aztecs explained that their *ahuacatl* was given the name not only because the fruit resembled a testicle and grew in pairs but also because it greatly excited sexual passion. It received its pseudonym *alligator pear* because of its rough leathery skin.

General Information

The avocado is originally from southern Mexico and Central America. The first written account of the avocado is contained in the 1526 report of Gonzalo Hernandez de Oviedo, who saw the tree in Colombia near the Isthmus of Panama. Technically a fruit but generally regarded as a vegetable, avocados are the green, usually pear-shaped fruits of a subtropical tree in the laurel family. They become mature on the tree but will not ripen or soften until picked. Avocado trees must be propagated by budding and grafting from reliable parent trees, a fact that was not recognized until the beginning of this century. Much work in selective breeding has been done since with the three distinct types: the Mexican avocado, with a thick skin, small fruits, anise-scented leaves, and a high oil content; the Guatemalan avocado, with medium-to-large fruits, a thickish skin, and a lower oil content; and the West Indian avocado, which will grow well only in the tropics but whose fruits will reach the size of a melon. These three have spawned nearly five hundred varieties. With great variation in size, shape, and texture, avocados are grown in tropical climates from South America to Australia. Fifty to seventy varieties are grown in the United States. Florida avocados are larger and rounder than their California counterparts and can often be identified by their bright green, smooth-skinned peels; ounce for ounce, these Florida varieties have about half the fat content of the California varieties and thus are not as rich or creamy. Of all the varieties, the most common is the Hass, a dark green to purple-black, rough-skinned avocado that has a higher oil content than most other varieties. About the size and shape of a pear, it is a light greenish yellow inside, with a custardy-smooth texture and rich buttery flavor. Other varieties appearing in stores may include Pinkerton, Fuerte, and Bacon. Pinkerton and Fuerte are pear-shaped and ripen early in the year. Bacon has smooth, rather thin skin and is available from late fall to early spring.

Buying Tips

Avocados are best purchased firm and allowed to sit out and soften until they yield to gentle pressure. Once ripe, they need to be kept refrigerated or they will overripen and turn rancid.

Culinary Uses

Unlike most tree fruits, which are sweet and juicy, avocados are creamy, almost buttery, and have a mild, nutty flavor. Generally used as a vegetable, avocados blend well with almost any flavor and mix well with either vegetables or fruit, making them an excellent addition to salads, sandwiches, guacamole, and other dishes. Avocados must never be cooked because they become bitter and unpleasant; however, they can be served warm, albeit carefully. Avocados produce a bland-flavored oil suitable for everything from salad dressings to sautéing, since it has a very high smoke point of 520 degrees Fahrenheit.

Health Benefits

pH 6.27–6.58. The avocado is one of the world's most perfect foods. At its peak, it contains a high amount of fruit oil, a relatively rare element that gives the avocado its smooth mellow taste, nutlike flavor, and high food energy value. It has a nearly perfectly balanced pH, being neither very acid nor very alkaline, is easily digested, and is rich in mineral elements that regulate body functions and stimulate growth. Especially noteworthy are its iron and copper contents, which aid in red blood cell regeneration and the prevention of nutritional anemia. One of the most valuable sources of organic fat and protein, avocados as a regular part of your diet will improve hair and skin quality as well as soothe the digestive tract; however, those with liver problems will find large quantities of avocados hard to digest because of their fat content. It takes ten avocados to make one teaspoon of pure avocado oil, which can harm the liver, whereas ten avocados in their natural state do no harm to the body.

Avocado / Nutritional Value Per 100 g Edible Portion	California	Florida
Calories	177	112
Protein	2.11 g	1.59 g
Fat	17.33 g	8.87 g
Fiber	2.11 g	2.11 g
Calcium	11 mg	11 mg
Iron	1.18 mg	0.53 mg
Magnesium	41 mg	34 mg
Phosphorus	42 mg	39 mg
Potassium	634 mg	488 mg
Sodium	12 mg	5 mg
Zinc	0.420 mg	0.420 mg
Copper	0.266 mg	0.251 mg
Manganese	0.244 mg	0.170 mg
Beta Carotene (A)	612 IU	612 IU
Thiamine (B$_1$)	0.108 mg	0.108 mg
Riboflavin (B$_2$)	0.122 mg	0.122 mg
Niacin (B$_3$)	1.921 mg	1.921 mg
Pantothenic Acid (B$_5$)	0.971 mg	0.971 mg
Pyridoxine (B$_6$)	0.280 mg	0.280 mg
Folic Acid (B$_9$)	65.5 mcg	53.3 mcg
Ascorbic Acid (C)	7.9 mg	7.9 mg
Tocopherol (E)	1.34 mg	n/a

Bamboo Shoots

(Bambusa, Arundinaria, Dendrocalamus, Phyllostachys spp.)

The genus name *Bambusa* and the English term *bamboo* come from the Malayan word *bambu*. *Arundinaria* is derived from the Latin term *arundo*, meaning "reedlike"; *Dendrocalamus* derives from the Greek terms *dendron*, meaning "tree," and *calamus*, meaning "reed"; *Phyllostachys* means "spike-leaved."

General Information

Bamboo shoots are literally the shoots—the young, sprouting stems—of a bamboo plant, a type of grass rather than a tree. These new shoots can grow up to a foot in twenty-four hours. Usually cut shortly after they first appear, most bamboo shoots are cone-shaped, six to twelve inches tall, and three inches in diameter. The shoots may also be "hilled"; they are piled with soil as they grow, which prevents the development of the green pigment chlorophyll. Once the tough overlapping sheath is stripped off, the white shoot is ready for eating either raw or cooked.

LORE AND LEGEND

The bamboo plant is symbolic of many attributes, including long life, strength, and grace, and serves a multitude of functions for the peoples of Asia.

Buying Tips

Purchase bamboo shoots that are creamy white, with preference being given to smaller-sized shoots.

Culinary Uses

The young shoots taste something like sweet, young corn. Fresh whole bamboo shoots should have the outer layer peeled to expose the white flesh. Cut small-diameter shoots into rings one node at a time; cut large shoots into slices. If the shoots are sweet, they are edible raw in salads or with dips as an appetizer. However, most shoots are bitter until parboiled for fifteen to twenty minutes. Change the water after the first ten minutes, and drain the shoots when done boiling. The raw shoots deteriorate very quickly, so it is best to process or serve them on the day they are purchased. Use as you would any boiled vegetable. Serve with butter, salt, and pepper, use in stir-fries, or add to casseroles. The texture and sweetness of bamboo shoots make them an exotic addition to soups and stews. Be extra careful in preparing fresh shoots, as some varieties are covered with fine sharp hairs that can perforate the intestines if not removed before eating. The canned form are precooked and need only be heated through after rinsing; however, the flavor does not compare in succulence with the fresh variety.

Bamboo Shoots / Nutritional Value Per 100 g Edible Portion		
	Raw	Cooked
Calories	27	12
Protein	2.60 g	1.53 g
Fat	0.30 g	0.22 g
Fiber	0.70 g	0.65 g
Calcium	13 mg	12 mg
Iron	0.50 mg	0.24 mg
Magnesium	3 mg	3 mg
Phosphorus	59 mg	20 mg
Potassium	533 mg	533 mg
Sodium	4 mg	4 mg
Beta Carotene (A)	20 IU	0 IU
Thiamine (B₁)	0.150 mg	0.020 mg
Riboflavin (B₂)	0.070 mg	0.050 mg
Niacin (B₃)	0.600 mg	0.300 mg
Ascorbic Acid (C)	4 mg	0 mg

Basella

(Basella alba, B. rubra)
Also Known As: Ceylon Spinach, Malabar Spinach, Pasali, Pu-tin-choi

Basella is the native Malabar name for the plant. *Alba* means "white"; rubra means "red." The red variety has leaves, stems, and flowers that are slightly tinged with red or purple.

General Information

Native to India and the tropical regions of the Far East, basella does not withstand frosts and grows poorly, if at all, in cold weather. In tropical regions, the plant is cultivated as both an ornamental and vegetable perennial, while in temperate regions it can be grown as an annual, warm-weather substitute for spinach. This little-known plant shares many of the same characteristics of the beet and spinach family. The more common dark green variety has round or oval, very thick leaves on vines that grow up to four feet in length. If given climbing supports, the plants will produce clean, grit-free leaves all summer. To harvest, simply cut the tips of the vines, about three to five inches in length.

Culinary Uses

Basella's thick, succulent leaves have a flavor much milder than that of chard or turnip tops. Being smooth, they are easy to clean and prepare. Flowers, unless very young, are tough; very old leaves are also undesirable. Asian cooks prepare both leaves and stems as a potherb, steaming or stir-frying them. The vegetable can also be added to light soups or mixed with other vegetables. Try it as a substitute in your favorite spinach recipes. Although the odor of the cooking leaves is rather strong, the leaves themselves have a mild, delicate flavor. Take care not to overcook them, or the stems will become somewhat gelatinous.

Health Benefits

The leaves are rich in vitamins A and C, as well as being a good source of calcium and iron.

Bean, Broad/Fava
(Vicia faba)

Vicia is a classical name for the *vetch* (a variety of legume); *faba* comes from the Greek word *phago*, meaning "to eat." As its English name suggests, the broad bean is substantial in size.

General Information

The broad bean is considered native to the Mediterranean basin and is probably the only bean native to the Old World. Seeds have been found in Egypt dating back to between 2400 and 2200 B.C.; a brown Egyptian variety provides the staple *ful*. A large bean resembling a lima in size and shape, the broad bean is about 1¼ inches long and light brown in color, with a dark line running down the ridge where it is split. As a vegetable the broad bean retained its popularity in Europe not only because it could be dried and stored but also because for many centuries it was the only bean readily available. The broad bean was so important that, together with other pulses, from the early Middle Ages onward there was a death sentence for theft from open fields of beans, peas, and lentils. It has remained a favorite throughout the major continents, with the exception of North America, where it is just now becoming more available.

Buying Tips

Look for the smallest, crispest, most evenly green pods, with some discoloration to be expected.

Culinary Uses

Young, fresh broad beans are usually shelled, but the young pods are sometimes tender enough to be eaten. Young beans can be eaten raw, while older ones are best cooked and added to salads or used as a side vegetable. Try gently stewing them in a little butter, lightly touched with savory, thyme, or sage. Cook large, heavy beans longer, then crush to make a purée, adding cream, butter, and a little lemon juice. Unless the beans are very young, they benefit from having their bitter outer layers removed.

Health Benefits

See the reference under **Legumes**.

Bean, Drumstick
(Moringa oleifera, M. stenopetala, M. pterygosperma)

Moringa probably derives from the Malayan name *murinna*. *Oleifera* means "oil-bearing." The English name *drumstick* bean refers to the bean's drumstick shape.

General Information

Native to India, the drumstick bean grows on a small tree in warm, humid climates. Also known as the horseradish tree, the roots actually taste like that popular European seasoning. This is a miracle tree for many areas where hunger and malnutrition are serious problems. Not only is it fast growing, drought-tolerant, and pest-resistant, it is a multipurpose plant. Along the Nile valley it is known as *shagra al rauwaq*, or "tree for purifying," because it is used to purify dirty water. The nine-ribbed pods are often 1½ inches long and contain minute, three-angled, winged seeds; these are ground into a powder, and when a small amount is mixed into a bucket of dirty water from a local stream, an amazing thing happens: the dirt quickly settles to the bottom. Even more amazingly, the bacteria in the water attach themselves to the oily powder in a coagulated

Bean, Broad/Fava / Nutritional Value Per 100 g Edible Portion		
	Fresh Raw	Fresh Cooked
Calories	72	56
Protein	5.60 g	4.80 g
Fat	0.60 g	0.50 g
Fiber	2.20 g	1.90 g
Calcium	22 mg	18 mg
Iron	1.90 mg	1.50 mg
Magnesium	38 mg	31 mg
Phosphorus	95 mg	73 mg
Potassium	250 mg	193 mg
Sodium	50 mg	41 mg
Beta Carotene (A)	350 IU	270 IU
Thiamine (B₁)	0.170 mg	0.128 mg
Riboflavin (B₂)	0.110 mg	0.090 mg
Niacin (B₃)	1.500 mg	1.200 mg
Ascorbic Acid (C)	33.0 mg	19.8 mg

Drumstick Bean / Nutritional Value Per 100 g Edible Portion				
	Leafy Tips Raw	Leafy Tips Cooked	Pods Raw	Pods Cooked
Calories	64	60	37	36
Protein	9.40 g	5.27 g	2.10 g	2.09 g
Fat	1.40 g	0.93 g	0.20 g	0.19 g
Fiber	1.50 g	1.72 g	1.30 g	1.84 g
Calcium	n/a	n/a	30 mg	20 mg
Iron	4.00 mg	2.32 mg	0.36 mg	0.45 mg
Magnesium	147 mg	151 mg	45 mg	42 mg
Phosphorus	112 mg	67 mg	50 mg	49 mg
Potassium	337 mg	344 mg	461 mg	457 mg
Sodium	9 mg	9 mg	42 mg	43 mg
Beta Carotene (A)	7,564 IU	7,013 IU	74 IU	70 IU
Thiamine (B_1)	0.257 mg	0.222 mg	0.053 mg	0.046 mg
Riboflavin (B_2)	0.660 mg	0.509 mg	0.074 mg	0.068 mg
Niacin (B_3)	2.220 mg	1.995 mg	0.620 mg	0.590 mg
Pyridoxine (B_6)	1.200 mg	n/a	0.120 mg	n/a
Ascorbic Acid (C)	51.7 mg	31.0 mg	n/a	n/a

mass. The resulting clear water that can be poured off has been found to have low bacterial levels.

Culinary Uses

The grated root has a peppery flavor similar to horseradish. The young shoots are succulent but when purchased outside of their native country tend to be rather tough. The leaves are delicious, with an almost spicy taste. They are sometimes eaten raw as a salad green but most often used as a potherb or added to soups, stews, and other dishes. They can also be dried and powdered for easy storage. The flowers are eaten raw or cooked—either batter-fried, sautéed, or stir-fried. The immature seedpods, or drumsticks, are cooked and eaten like green beans; when they get a little larger they can be diced and roasted, boiled, or steamed as you would okra.

Bean, Green/Snap

(Phaseolus spp.)

The scientific name *Phaseolus* was bestowed in 39 B.C. by Calumella, who observed that the seeds look like a "small boat."

General Information

Green beans, or snap beans as they are more properly called, are said to be native to Central or South America

and were introduced into Europe in the sixteenth century. Among the most common vegetables grown and eaten in North America, these edible-podded legumes are grown for their pods, which are picked while young and the seeds still small and tender. There are over 150 varieties of green beans in cultivation today, including thick runner beans, the more slender French beans, and the yellow wax bean.

Buying Tips

Green beans should be crisp, firm, long, and slender, feel velvety, and look fresh and bright-colored. At their best, beans break with a crisp snap and the insides are fresh and juicy. Growing plants take in carbon dioxide and give up oxygen, but once picked, fruits and vegetables do the opposite. The technical term is *respiration*, according to Dr. Robert Shewfelt, one of the world's authorities on postharvest care of fruits and vegetables. While a potato gives off a mere eight milliliters of carbon dioxide per kilogram per hour, green beans top the vegetable respiration rate, giving off 250 milliliters. The faster the respiration rate, the faster a vegetable expires. To keep vegetables fresher long, limit their oxygen supply by wrapping them

Bean, Green/Snap / Nutritional Value Per 100 g Edible Portion		
	Raw	Cooked
Calories	31	35
Protein	1.82 g	1.89 g
Fat	0.12 g	0.28 g
Fiber	1.10 g	1.43 g
Calcium	37 mg	46 mg
Iron	1.04 mg	1.28 mg
Magnesium	25 mg	25 mg
Phosphorus	38 mg	39 mg
Potassium	209 mg	299 mg
Sodium	6 mg	3 mg
Zinc	0.240 mg	0.360 mg
Copper	0.069 mg	0.103 mg
Manganese	0.214 mg	0.294 mg
Beta Carotene (A)	668 IU	666 IU
Thiamine (B_1)	0.084 mg	0.074 mg
Riboflavin (B_2)	0.105 mg	0.097 mg
Niacin (B_3)	0.752 mg	0.614 mg
Pantothenic Acid (B_5)	0.094 mg	0.074 mg
Pyridoxine (B_6)	0.074 mg	0.056 mg
Folic Acid (B_9)	36.5 mcg	33.3 mcg
Ascorbic Acid (C)	16.3 mg	9.7 mg
Tocopherol (E)	0.020 mg	n/a

Up until the nineteenth century, snap beans had strings along their pods, just as other members of the bean family do. In the varieties grown specifically for their seeds (great northern and navy beans, for example), this tough line of fiber was useful because it acted as a seam that split and released the plump, edible beans inside. However, in the kinds of beans eaten pod and all, the strings served no useful purpose and detracted from the vegetables' appeal. In the late 1800s, American plant scientists became interested in the "stringiness" problem and set to work to build a better green bean. One pioneer researcher of the period succeeded in producing nine different types, all tasty and "stringless." Over time, other experts followed up with improvements of their own, and today all snap beans are stringless at the harvesting stage.

in plastic. Green beans wrapped in plastic can be stored in the refrigerator for four or five days.

Culinary Uses

Boiled, steamed, stir-fried, or sautéed, green beans can be eaten cold in salads, as a vegetable in their own right, or added to savory dishes and quiches. The heirloom varieties of beans have strings that need to be removed prior to cooking; this is a time-consuming process, but it's worth the effort, since these varieties are generally more flavorful.

Health Benefits

pH 5.60. Green beans, with their abundance of potassium, supply the alkaline needs of the pancreas and salivary glands. The yellow or wax bean is considered inferior to the green bean in nutritional value.

Bean, Winged

(Psophocarpus tetragonolobus)
Also Known As: Asparagus Pea, Goa Bean

Winged beans were given the botanical name *Psophocarpus* from the Greek words for "noise" and "fruit," referring to the fact that the pods, when gathered and laid in the sun, inflate and explode with a loud noise. The term *tetragonolobus* refers to the pod, which is four-angled. The English term *winged* refers to the bean's winged flares.

General Information

Grown almost exclusively in tropical Southeast Asia, New Guinea, the Philippines, and Ghana, the winged bean is a tropical climbing plant that has had a long use as a staple legume in those countries and was virtually unknown in the rest of the world until 1975. A twining vine, it grows to over nine feet when supported and continuously bears pods once mature. The pods have four longitudinal jagged "wings" and contain up to twenty seeds. The smooth, shiny seeds may be white, brown, black, or mottled. The winged bean is cultivated largely for its decorative young, tender pods, which are picked when no more than one or two inches long, and then sliced and cooked like green beans.

Buying Tips

Choose the smallest pods—those in which seeds have not yet developed—for the best flavor, and then cook them immediately, for they wilt and collapse within a few days.

Culinary Uses

The whole plant is edible—seeds, tubers, leaves, and flowers. Young leaves and shoots are said to taste like spinach; the flowers are sweetened by nectar and resemble mushrooms in flavor when lightly sautéed. The immature seeds within the young pods taste like a cross between garden peas and asparagus; when mature, the seeds must be cooked before eating and are usually roasted and eaten like peanuts. Cooked beans have a flavor between that of a string bean and a shell bean: meatier, blander, and starchier tasting than string beans but crunchier and greener-flavored than a shell bean. Winged beans can be used in any manner you would string beans—they do well in soups or stir-fries, boiled as a side dish, or pickled. The seeds can also be ground into flour for bread, pressed to yield an edible oil, or sprouted and turned into bean curd. The protein-rich roots are not wasted either, with the immature tubers eaten like potatoes.

Health Benefits

Winged beans have an exceedingly high nutritional value, very similar to that of soybeans. The seeds are rich in tocopherol, an antioxidant that increases vitamin A use in the human body.

Bean, Winged / Nutritional Value Per 100 g Edible Portion

	Beans Fresh, Raw	Beans Fresh, Cooked	Beans Dried, Raw	Beans Dried, Cooked	Leaves Raw	Tuber Raw
Calories	49	38	409	147	74	159
Protein	6.95 g	5.31 g	29.65 g	10.62 g	5.85 g	11.60 g
Fat	0.87 g	0.66 g	16.32 g	5.84 g	1.10 g	0.90 g
Fiber	2.57 g	1.38 g	6.85 g	2.45 g	2.50 g	7.40 g
Calcium	84 mg	61 mg	440 mg	142 mg	224 mg	30 mg
Iron	1.50 mg	1.09 mg	13.44 mg	4.33 mg	4.00 mg	2.00 mg
Magnesium	34 mg	30 mg	179 mg	54 mg	8 mg	n/a
Phosphorus	37 mg	25 mg	451 mg	153 mg	63 mg	45 mg
Potassium	223 mg	274 mg	977 mg	280 mg	176 mg	n/a
Sodium	4 mg	4 mg	38 mg	13 mg	n/a	n/a
Beta Carotene (A)	128 IU	88 IU	0 IU	0 IU	n/a	n/a
Thiamine (B$_1$)	0.140 mg	0.086 mg	1.030 mg	0.295 mg	n/a	n/a
Riboflavin (B$_2$)	0.100 mg	0.072 mg	0.450 mg	0.129 mg	n/a	n/a
Niacin (B$_3$)	0.900 mg	0.652 mg	3.090 mg	0.830 mg	n/a	n/a
Pyridoxine (B$_6$)	0.113 mg	0.082 mg	0.175 mg	0.047 mg	n/a	n/a
Folic Acid (B$_9$)	n/a	n/a	44.6 mcg	10.4 mcg	n/a	n/a
Ascorbic Acid (C)	n/a	9.8 mg	0 mg	0 mg	n/a	n/a

Bean, Yard-Long

(Vigna unguiculata sesquipedalis)

Also Known As: Asparagus Bean, Chinese Long Bean, Pea Bean, Dow Gok

This genus was named *Vigna* in honor of Dominic Vigni, a Paduan commentator on Theophrastus in the seventeenth century. The term *unguiculata* means "clawed" or "clawlike," while *sesquipedalis* means "a foot and a half in length," the bean's normal length when picked for cooking. The English name *yard-long bean* similarly refers to the pod, which on occasion will reach up to a yard in length.

General Information

A native of Asia and other semi-tropical regions, the climbing herbaceous yard-long bean is a close relative of the black-eyed pea. Of the several varieties, the two most common contain black or red beans. With stalks that reach up to twelve feet in height, the plants produce very long, pliable, string-bean-like pods. The beans are generally sold in their immature stage, when the pods are between eighteen and twenty-four inches in length. Several varieties of long bean are eaten in Asia, as are the leaves and the mature beans.

Bean, Yard-Long / Nutritional Value Per 100 g Edible Portion

	Fresh Raw	Fresh Cooked	Dried Raw	Dried Cooked
Calories	47	47	347	118
Protein	2.80 g	2.53 g	24.33 g	8.29 g
Fat	0.40 g	0.10 g	1.31 g	0.45 g
Fiber	n/a	1.51 g	4.77 g	1.62 g
Calcium	50 mg	44 mg	138 mg	42 mg
Iron	0.47 mg	0.98 mg	8.61 mg	2.64 mg
Magnesium	44 mg	42 mg	338 mg	98 mg
Phosphorus	59 mg	57 mg	559 mg	181 mg
Potassium	240 mg	290 mg	1,157 mg	315 mg
Sodium	4 mg	4 mg	17 mg	5 mg
Zinc	n/a	n/a	3.500 mg	1.080 mg
Copper	n/a	n/a	0.879 mg	0.225 mg
Manganese	n/a	n/a	1.590 mg	0.487 mg
Beta Carotene (A)	865 IU	450 IU	52 IU	16 IU
Thiamine (B$_1$)	0.107 mg	0.085 mg	0.887 mg	0.212 mg
Riboflavin (B$_2$)	0.110 mg	0.099 mg	0.235 mg	0.064 mg
Niacin (B$_3$)	0.410 mg	0.630 mg	2.158 mg	0.551 mg
Pantothenic Acid (B$_5$)	n/a	n/a	1.556 mg	0.398 mg
Pyridoxine (B$_6$)	n/a	n/a	0.371 mg	0.095 mg
Folic Acid (B$_9$)	n/a	n/a	657.9 mcg	145.7 mcg
Ascorbic Acid (C)	18.8 mg	16.2 mg	1.6 mg	0.4 mg

Buying Tips

Purchase pods that are pencil-thin and firm, in which the peas have not matured. They will be comparatively flexible, but should not appear dry or overly limp. Long beans are more fragile than green beans and so are best used within a few days.

Culinary Uses

Yard-long beans are not crisp and sweet like fresh common green beans, but they have a crunch that is solid if not juicy and a flavor that is leguminous, reminiscent of asparagus combined with peas. The paler variety cooks up to become somewhat sweeter and meatier than the deeper-colored, which tends to be more fibrous and less delicate. When treated as a green bean—steamed or boiled—the taste is pleasant, though not spectacular. However, the bean is perfect for sautés and stir-frying, which brings out the best of its texture and flavor, especially when combined with the rich flavors and textures of ginger, nuts, fermented black beans, garlic, assertive herbs, or chili peppers.

Beet
(Beta vulgaris)

The beet is said to get its botanical name *Beta* from the Greek letter *beta*, because the swollen root was thought to more or less resemble it. The term *vulgaris* means "common." The English word *beet* derives either from the French word *bete*, meaning "beast," because the vegetable reminded early cooks of a bleeding animal when it was cut open, or from the Celtic word for "red."

General Information

The beet is descended from a wild, slender-rooted plant that grew abundantly in southern Europe, especially in sandy soil near seacoasts. A member of the ubiquitous goosefoot family, beets are related to chard, spinach, sugar beets, and quinoa. There are actually four types of beets: the garden beet, the "leaf" beet (also called chard), the sugarbeet, which is processed into refined sugar, and the mangold beet, grown mostly in Europe for cattle feed. Beets with rounded roots, like those we eat today, are a comparatively recent variety, propagated in northern Europe in about the sixteenth century. There are many more shapes to the beet than the simple round one, including ovoid, and long and tapering like a carrot. Red beet and white

chard were both known to the ancients, but only the leaves were used for culinary purposes, while the root was employed medicinally. Beet greens, whether ornamental or edible, are among the most intensely hued of plants, and the roots also come in yellow and a dramatic candy-cane red and white.

Buying Tips

Fresh, first-quality beets should have a good globular shape, with smooth, firm flesh and a deep red color. Avoid those with short necks, deep scars, or several circles of leaf scars around the top of the beet, as these have remained in the ground too long and are liable to be tough and woody. Beets store well—up to a few weeks if necessary. After that they will certainly start to soften and after two months will not be worth cooking.

Culinary Uses

Beets, with their distinctive ruby-red coloring and sweet earthy flavor, complement many foods. Most people are all

Beet / Nutritional Value Per 100 g Edible Portion				
	Beet Raw	Beet Cooked	Greens Raw	Greens Cooked
Calories	44	31	19	27
Protein	1.48 g	1.06 g	1.82 g	2.57 g
Fat	0.14 g	0.05 g	0.06 g	0.20 g
Fiber	0.80 g	0.85 g	1.30 g	1.05 g
Calcium	16 mg	11 mg	119 mg	114 mg
Iron	0.91 mg	0.62 mg	3.30 mg	1.90 mg
Magnesium	21 mg	37 mg	72 mg	68 mg
Phosphorus	48 mg	31 mg	40 mg	41 mg
Potassium	324 mg	312 mg	547 mg	909 mg
Sodium	72 mg	49 mg	201 mg	241 mg
Zinc	0.370 mg	0.250 mg	0.380 mg	0.500 mg
Copper	0.083 mg	0.057 mg	0.191 mg	0.251 mg
Manganese	0.352 mg	0.240 mg	n/a	n/a
Beta Carotene (A)	20 IU	13 IU	6,100 IU	5,100 IU
Thiamine (B$_1$)	0.050 mg	0.031 mg	0.100 mg	0.117 mg
Riboflavin (B$_2$)	0.020 mg	0.014 mg	0.220 mg	0.289 mg
Niacin (B$_3$)	0.400 mg	0.273 mg	0.400 mg	0.499 mg
Pantothenic Acid (B$_5$)	0.150 mg	0.097 mg	0.250 mg	0.329 mg
Pyridoxine (B$_6$)	0.046 mg	0.031 mg	0.106 mg	0.132 mg
Folic Acid (B$_9$)	92.6 mcg	53.2 mcg	n/a	n/a
Ascorbic Acid (C)	11.0 mg	5.5 mg	30.0 mg	24.9 mg
Tocopherol (E)	n/a	n/a	1.50 mg	n/a

too familiar with the poor flavor of canned beets; try preparing fresh beets at home and see if perhaps you like them after all. They can be shredded raw into salads, pickled, boiled, baked, or added to soups such as the popular Russian borscht. The young leaves are also edible and make a great side dish either sautéed or steamed; they can also be shredded and added to fresh garden salads.

Health Benefits

pH 4.90–6.60. One of nature's best bodily cleansers, beets will help dissolve and eliminate acid crystals from the kidneys, eliminate blood toxemia, build strong blood by enriching the red corpuscles, detoxify the liver and gallbladder, and eliminate pocket acid material in the bowel. The power is in their unique low-level iron that cleanses blood cells and serves as a strong washing agent for flushing away fatty deposits. Beets also contain natural chlorine, which helps wash away fat that might otherwise accumulate in the cells of the liver, kidneys, and gallbladder. They also tend to stimulate lymph fluid, the straw-colored portion of the blood that dislodges fatty deposits from adipose cells. Since beets lubricate the intestines, they are recommended for constipation. For most people, beets also have the propensity for turning bodily waste products bright pink or red, as the group of pigments known as betacyanins are not easily metabolized. According to nutritionist Jeffrey Bland, Ph.D., pink urine may indicate an iron deficiency while a magenta stool indicates adequate iron. Beet greens are higher in nutritional value than beet roots, but the cooked greens have a high content of oxalic acid and so moderation is advised.

Bitter Melon

(Momordica charantia)

Also Known As: Carilla Fruit, Kareli, Balsam Pear, Bitter Cucumber

Momordica comes from the Latin *momordi* and *mordeo*, meaning "to bite," since the seeds appear to have been bitten; *charantia* is a pre-Linnaean name. The English name *bitter melon* is appropriate, since this fruit is distinctly bitter.

General Information

The warty-skinned bitter melon is not a true melon but rather an immature summer squash shaped like an Anaheim pepper. Native to tropical Asia and Africa, this climbing plant produces fruits up to eight inches in length with lumpy, ridged skin the color of pale jade that turns yellow or orange when the fruit is ripe. Its flesh is the same tone, only lighter, and contains brown seeds. Generally it is eaten in its unripe state. This classic Chinese and East Indian vegetable is rarely seen in grocery stores but can be grown easily in most home gardens and yards.

Buying Tips

Choose small melons that are firm, not shriveled, and free from blemishes or damage. The smaller the melon the less bitter it is; the least bitter are between three and four inches in length. Favor those that are pale green—if dark green, they are immature and extremely bitter. If orange, they are overmature. Select fruits with shiny, even-colored, pale green skin, and store in the refrigerator. Most people consider the fruits inedible once they start to turn yellow.

Culinary Uses

Although the bitter melon is a popular ingredient in Indian and Asian cookery, it is a novelty food for most Americans. As its name indicates, it is indeed bitter; in fact, it is advisable to first soak it in salted water, boil it lightly, and then discard the water before continuing to cook it further. The flesh is soft when cooked, somewhat

Bitter Melon / Nutritional Value Per 100 g Edible Portion				
	Leafy Tips Raw	Leafy Tips Cooked	Pods Raw	Pods Cooked
Calories	30	35	17	19
Protein	5.30 g	3.60 g	1.00 g	0.84 g
Fat	0.69 g	0.20 g	0.17 g	0.18 g
Fiber	2.28 g	1.87 g	1.40 g	1.05 g
Calcium	84 mg	42 mg	19 mg	9 mg
Iron	2.04 mg	1.02 mg	0.43 mg	0.38 mg
Magnesium	85 mg	94 mg	17 mg	16 mg
Phosphorus	99 mg	77 mg	31 mg	36 mg
Potassium	608 mg	602 mg	296 mg	319 mg
Sodium	11 mg	13 mg	5 mg	6 mg
Beta Carotene (A)	1,734 IU	1,733 IU	380 IU	113 IU
Thiamine (B$_1$)	0.181 mg	0.147 mg	0.040 mg	0.051 mg
Riboflavin (B$_2$)	0.362 mg	0.282 mg	0.040 mg	0.053 mg
Niacin (B$_3$)	1.110 mg	0.995 mg	0.400 mg	0.280 mg
Folic Acid (B$_9$)	n/a	87.6 mcg	72.0 mcg	n/a
Ascorbic Acid (C)	88.0 mg	55.6 mg	84.0 mg	33.0 mg

like that of summer squash. The definite bitter taste comes from the presence of quinine; if you like quinine water or strong beer, you will probably like bitter melon. It goes well in stir-fries, soups, or baked vegetable dishes. Pieces of bitter melon are a common ingredient in Indian pickles and are sometimes used in curries. The tender shoots and leaves can be cooked as a kind of spinach.

Health Benefits

Bitter melon was originally an Asian medicine believed to purify the blood, and the leaves were used to treat sore-eyed elephants. The fruit soothes irritated tissues, lowers fever, cleanses toxins from the body, and has diuretic and laxative properties. Bitter melon also contains an insulin-like compound referred to as polypeptide-P or "vegetable insulin." Since polypeptide-P and bitter melon appear to have fewer side effects than insulin, they have been suggested as replacements for insulin in some patients. The ripe fruit has also been shown to exhibit some rather profound anticancer effects, especially in leukemia. The ripe seeds are reputedly a purgative.

Bottle Gourd

(Lagenaria siceraria)
Also Known As: Doodhi, Calabash Gourd

Lagenaria comes from the Latin *lagena*, meaning "large flask." This vegetable is called the "bottle" gourd because when dried it is scooped out and used as a container.

General Information

Native to tropical regions, the bottle gourd now grows both wild and commercially in temperate zones. It is a climbing annual vine reaching up to forty feet in length, clinging to whatever will support it. The gourds are of various shapes and interesting colors, giving rise to the ornamental uses for which many people acquire them. The narrow necks of gourds have made excellent tobacco pipes, while the rounded bodies have been used for dippers, cups, pitchers, or any other kind of cooking utensil. Various American Indian tribes used mature gourds as rattles for dances and ceremonies, since the seeds in mature gourds rattle. The bottle gourd usually resembles a large, pale green cucumber, and has been cultivated for so long that its exact origins are unknown. Because it dries out so well, it can be preserved indefinitely, and remains of it have been

Bottle Gourd / Nutritional Value Per 100 g Edible Portion		
	Raw	Cooked
Calories	14	15
Protein	0.62 g	0.60 g
Fat	0.02 g	0.02 g
Fiber	0.56 g	0.63 g
Calcium	26 mg	24 mg
Iron	0.20 mg	0.25 mg
Magnesium	11 mg	11 mg
Phosphorus	13 mg	13 mg
Potassium	150 mg	170 mg
Sodium	2 mg	2 mg
Zinc	0.70 mg	n/a
Beta Carotene (A)	0 IU	0 IU
Thiamine (B$_1$)	0.029 mg	0.029 mg
Riboflavin (B$_2$)	0.022 mg	0.022 mg
Niacin (B$_3$)	0.320 mg	0.390 mg
Pyridoxine (B$_6$)	0.040 mg	n/a
Folic Acid (B$_9$)	5.9 mcg	n/a
Ascorbic Acid (C)	10.1 mg	8.5 mg

found in Mexico dating from 7000 B.C. and in Egypt dating from 4000 B.C.

Buying Tips

Choose gourds that are free from blemishes and not withered. They are available summer through autumn.

Culinary Uses

Only the young fruits with their comparatively soft shells are eaten. The bottle gourd has a bland flavor and is a useful vegetable for stews and curries. To cook it, peel and remove any large seeds.

Broccoli

(Brassica oleracea italica)

The Latin name *Brassica* derives from the Celtic *bresic*, and although the Romans are usually credited with introducing broccoli into Europe, it is possible that the Celts preceded them. The term *oleracea* refers to a vegetable garden herb that is used in cooking; *italica* means "coming from Italy." The English name *broccoli* derives from the Italian plural diminutive of *brocco*, which means "arm, branch, or shoot" (and which itself derives from the Latin *braccium*).

Broccoli / Nutritional Value Per 100 g Edible Portion

	Raw	Cooked
Calories	28	28
Protein	2.98 g	2.98 g
Fat	0.35 g	0.35 g
Fiber	1.11 g	1.11 g
Calcium	48 mg	46 mg
Iron	0.88 mg	0.84 mg
Magnesium	25 mg	24 mg
Phosphorus	66 mg	59 mg
Potassium	325 mg	292 mg
Sodium	27 mg	26 mg
Zinc	0.400 mg	0.380 mg
Copper	0.045 mg	0.043 mg
Manganese	0.229 mg	0.218 mg
Beta Carotene (A)	3,000 IU	1,388 IU
Thiamine (B$_1$)	0.065 mg	0.055 mg
Riboflavin (B$_2$)	0.119 mg	0.113 mg
Niacin (B$_3$)	0.638 mg	0.574 mg
Pantothenic Acid (B$_5$)	0.535 mg	0.508 mg
Pyridoxine (B$_6$)	0.159 mg	0.143 mg
Folic Acid (B$_9$)	71.0 mcg	50.0 mcg
Ascorbic Acid (C)	93.2 mg	74.6 mg
Tocopherol (E)	0.46 mg	n/a

General Information

Closely related to cauliflower, broccoli has thick stems that branch into clusters of flower buds. Although commercially grown in France and Italy in the sixteenth century, broccoli was not well known in the United States until 1923, when the D'Arrigo Brothers Company made a trial planting of Italian sprouting broccoli in California. A few crates were sent to Boston, and by 1925 the market was well established. Sprouting broccoli is the most familiar variety, but others such as Calabrese, Chinese (see below), and heading are also available.

Buying Tips

Look for fresh green color in the heads, leaves, and stems. Stalks should be tender and firm, with compact buds. Avoid broccoli that feels rubbery. If the lower portion of the stalk is tough and woody, and if the bud clusters are open and yellow, the broccoli is overly mature and will be tough. Store fresh broccoli in a plastic bag in the refrigerator, but it does not keep very long, so use it quickly.

Culinary Uses

Florets, stalks, and leaves are all edible and have an excellent cabbage-related taste that is all their own. Raw broccoli florets are excellent added to salads or used for vegetable dip platters; steamed broccoli goes well with almost any dish; stalks can be peeled and cut or shredded for sautéed vegetable dishes, soups, or casseroles. The leaves may be prepared like other greens such as chard or spinach.

Health Benefits

pH 5.20–6.85. Raw broccoli contains almost as much calcium as whole milk and is linked to lowering the risk of cancer. It is best if undercooked; the more green that is left in broccoli, the more chlorophyll will be left to counteract the sulfur compounds that form gas. All *Brassica* genus vegetables contain dithiolthiones, a group of compounds that have anticancer and antioxidant properties; indoles, substances that protect against breast and colon cancer; sulfur, which has antibiotic and antiviral characteristics; and lutein and zeaxanthin, pigments that protect against the harmful effects of photo-oxidation by filtering out visible blue light. This family of vegetables also mildly stimulates the liver and other tissues out of stagnancy. A recent study found that one ounce of broccoli sprouts contains more isothiocyanate, a potent anticarcinogenic, than two pounds of broccoli. This study from Johns Hopkins University was released in September 1997, and within three months broccoli sprouts were selling fast in U.S. markets. Despite their bitter tang, broccoli sprouts make a tasty addition to salads and sandwiches.

Broccoli, Chinese

(Brassica oleracea alboglabra)
Also Known As: Chinese Kale, Gai Laan, Jie Lan

The Latin name *Brassica* derives from the Celtic *bresic*. The term *oleracea* refers to a vegetable garden herb that is used in cooking. The English name *broccoli* derives from the Italian plural diminutive of *brocco*, which means "arm, branch, or shoot" (and which itself derives from the Latin *braccium*).

General Information

Chinese broccoli was probably introduced to China by the Portuguese after 1517; it is a close relative of the

Portuguese cabbage *couve tronchuda*. The two most delightful things about Chinese broccoli are its delicate edible flowers and its sweet flavor, which is like garden-fresh broccoli. Unlike market-variety broccoli stems (stout) and leaves (puny), Chinese broccoli stems are tender, smooth, and slender (about one-half inch thick), and the plant is abundantly bestowed with broad, blue-green leaves.

Buying Tips

Look for Chinese broccoli with solid stems, unblemished leaves, and flower buds that are just starting to open. A year-round feature in Asian markets, this vegetable is becoming increasingly available in natural food and farmer's markets.

Culinary Uses

Use as you would regular broccoli—sautéed, steamed, braised, boiled, and in soup. Chinese broccoli cooks in less time, however, since it's a less dense vegetable. The stems require longer cooking time than the leaves, and the leaves longer cooking than the blossoms, so cut and cook the vegetable accordingly. The blossoms, usually yellow but sometimes white, red, or pink, perk up any dish. Use them fresh as a garnish on the side of a plate or float them on a steaming bowl of soup. For stir-fried dishes, don't add the blossoms until the last minute so they retain their color.

Health Benefits

Low in fat and high in fiber, potassium, calcium, and vitamins A and C.

Broccoli Raab

(Brassica oleracea rapa, B. rapa parachinensis, B. campestris)

Also Known As: Rape, Rapini, Cima di Rapa, Choy Sum, Turnip Tops

The Latin name *Brassica* derives from the Celtic *bresic*. The term *oleracea* refers to a vegetable garden herb that is used in cooking; *rapa* is from the Latin for "turnip," *parachinensis* means "coming from near China," and *campestris* means "of the fields or plains." The English name *broccoli* derives from the Italian plural diminutive of *brocco*, which means "arm, branch, or shoot" (and which itself derives from the Latin *braccium*).

General Information

Resembling thin, leafy, sparsely budded broccoli stalks, broccoli raab is the tender shoot of the wintered-over turnip. A hardy biennial, the turnip produces a well-developed root and/or luxuriant leaves the first year; then the leaves die back, and the root gradually gets less succulent and more woody. Come spring, the plant sends up a pulpy and juicy stem with a seedpod at its tip. This sprout grows to twelve inches or so before flowering, its tip resembling a miniature head of broccoli. The dark, bluish-green stems with their flat, bright green leaves and small tassel of little yellow flowers taste best when six to eight inches long, since the longer, older shoots will be thick and tough at the base.

Buying Tips

Broccoli raab should be dark forest green and succulent looking, not wilted, and the stalks should not be overly fat or they will be tough. There may be some flowering buds, but most should be closed.

Culinary Uses

With a taste that varies from slightly bitter to ferociously acerbic, broccoli raab would never be called mild. Very pungent, it has hints of spinach, broccoli, collards, and mustard greens, with pleasantly sour or tart notes. Stalk, leaf, and flowers can all be used in the same manner as cabbage and kale, adding zest to bland dishes and holding their own with stronger-flavored ones. The leaves, when properly cooked, are delightfully tender and leave a fresh, brisk taste on the palate. When steamed, broccoli raab should be cooked slowly until just tender and then served with a drizzle of olive oil, a squirt of lemon juice, and fresh-ground pepper.

Health Benefits

Low in fat and high in fiber, potassium, calcium, and vitamins A and C, broccoli raab is beneficial to the heart, lungs, and intestines.

Brussels Sprouts

(*Brassica oleracea*, Gemmifera group)

The Latin name *Brassica* derives from the Celtic *bresic*. The term *oleracea* refers to a vegetable garden herb that is used in cooking; the term *gemmifera*, meaning "diamond maker," comes from this vegetable's reputed ability to enhance mental prowess. These little cabbages carry the name *brussels* because they were first grown in Brussels, Belgium. The Germans call this plant *rosenkohl*, or "rose cabbage," an apt name.

General Information

A relative newcomer to the cabbage family, brussels sprouts are generally believed to have evolved from a variety of savoy cabbage during the seventeenth or eighteenth century. One of the few vegetables to have originated in northern Europe, this vegetable is one of the weirdest-looking plants in a garden: twenty to forty "baby cabbages" grow in spiral fashion on a tall-stemmed stalk, which instead of having a single large head at its end sprouts numerous small heads along its stem. Simply plucked off

Brussels Sprouts / Nutritional Value Per 100 g Edible Portion		
	Raw	Cooked
Calories	43	39
Protein	3.38 g	2.55 g
Fat	0.30 g	0.51 g
Fiber	1.51 g	1.37 g
Calcium	42 mg	36 mg
Iron	1.40 mg	1.20 mg
Magnesium	23 mg	20 mg
Phosphorus	69 mg	56 mg
Potassium	389 mg	317 mg
Sodium	25 mg	21 mg
Zinc	0.420 mg	0.330 mg
Copper	0.070 mg	0.083 mg
Manganese	0.337 mg	0.227 mg
Beta Carotene (A)	883 IU	719 IU
Thiamine (B$_1$)	0.139 mg	0.107 mg
Riboflavin (B$_2$)	0.090 mg	0.080 mg
Niacin (B$_3$)	0.745 mg	0.607 mg
Pantothenic Acid (B$_5$)	0.309 mg	0.252 mg
Pyridoxine (B$_6$)	0.219 mg	0.178 mg
Folic Acid (B$_9$)	61.1 mcg	60.0 mcg
Ascorbic Acid (C)	85.0 mg	62.0 mg
Tocopherol (E)	0.88 mg	0.85 mg

the stem as they mature, these pale green nubbins are prized for their miniature shape and mild cabbage flavor.

Buying Tips

The smaller the sprout, the better the flavor, with the best being no greater than 1½ inches in diameter; old or overly large brussels sprouts have a disagreeable and bitter flavor. Good sprouts are firm, compact, bright green, and fresh looking. Puffy, soft sprouts are usually inferior in quality and flavor, and leaves that are wilted or yellow indicate aging. Brussels sprouts should be stored in a plastic bag in the refrigerator and used within a few days.

Culinary Uses

The hearty, nutlike flavor of brussels sprouts actually improves with a frost, so they are a favored fall and winter food. Young, tender sprouts can be eaten raw; lengthwise slices, which reveal an attractive cross section, are suitable for salads or for dipping. They can also be steamed as a side vegetable, but their flavor will easily overshadow very mild or delicate foods. They are best paired with assertive seasonings and strong-flavored foods, such as sharp cheese.

Health Benefits

pH 6.00–6.30. Brussels sprouts are rich in alkalizing elements, with specific affinity for the pancreas, and help reduce the risk of cancer, especially colon cancer. A Cornell University study found that brussels sprouts are full of glucosinolates, which kill aflatoxin, a fungal mold linked to high rates of liver cancer. Brussels sprouts stimulate sluggish glands and promote the release of hormones that have a cleansing effect on adipose (fatty) cells and tissues. Minerals in brussels sprouts stimulate the kidneys to release more water, making it easier for dislodged fatty wastes to be flushed out of the body.

Burdock Root

(*Arctium lappa*)
Also Known As: Gobo, Great Burdock, Beggar's Button

Arctium is derived from the Greek *arktos*, meaning "bear" (the animal), an allusion to the roughness of the burrs; *lappa* comes either from a word meaning "to seize" or from the Celtic *llap*, meaning "hand," on account of the root's prehensile properties. The English name *burdock* is a combination of *bur*—from the Latin *burra*, meaning "lock of wool," such as is often found entangled with the plant when sheep have passed by—and *dock*, Old English for "plant."

General Information
This Siberian native is cultivated primarily in Japan under the name of *gobo* but thrives throughout many parts of the world as a common weed. The long, thin taproot is unbelievably difficult to dig out, as it penetrates deep into the soil and clings tenaciously. The skin of the root is brown, while its somewhat fibrous flesh is white.

Buying Tips
Choose soil-covered specimens that are firm and relatively crisp, like a fresh carrot, not limp and bendable like an old one. Store for a few days at most, wrapped in a damp cloth or paper towel in the refrigerator.

Culinary Uses
Burdock has the rich, heady aroma of freshly dug earth, while its delicious, earthy flavor is very similar to that of artichoke hearts or salsify. Never used raw, the rather fibrous root is first peeled and then slivered or cut into chips and added to delicate soups, stews, vegetables, and bean or grain dishes, where it imparts a pleasantly chewy texture and subtly sweet taste. It may also be cooked in the same manner as carrots, but allow a longer cooking time. This plant is also used as an herb (see the reference in the **Herbs, Spices, and Other Foods** section).

Burdock Root / Nutritional Value Per 100 g Edible Portion		
	Raw	Cooked
Calories	72	88
Protein	1.53 g	2.09 g
Fat	0.15 g	0.14 g
Fiber	1.94 g	1.83 g
Calcium	41 mg	49 mg
Iron	0.80 mg	0.77 mg
Magnesium	38 mg	39 mg
Phosphorus	51 mg	93 mg
Potassium	308 mg	360 mg
Sodium	5 mg	4 mg
Beta Carotene (A)	0 IU	0 IU
Thiamine (B$_1$)	0.010 mg	0.039 mg
Riboflavin (B$_2$)	0.030 mg	0.058 mg
Niacin (B$_3$)	0.300 mg	0.320 mg
Ascorbic Acid (C)	3.0 mg	n/a

Health Benefits
Burdock is esteemed for its blood-purifying qualities and for its ability to strengthen the kidneys and sexual organs.

Cabbage
(Brassica oleracea capitata)

> Cabbage: a familiar kitchen-garden vegetable about as large and wise as a man's head.
>
> —Ambrose Bierce

> Welcome to the Church of the Holy Cabbage. Lettuce pray.
>
> —Anonymous

The Latin name *Brassica* derives from the Celtic *bresic*. The term *oleracea* refers to a vegetable garden herb that is used in cooking; *capitata* means "capitate," or "headed." The English name *cabbage* comes from the Latin *caput*, meaning "head," because of this vegetable's head-shaped form.

General Information
Cabbage is one of the most ancient vegetables; there is evidence that it has been in cultivation for more than four thousand years and has been domesticated for at least twenty-five hundred years. The modern-day cabbage developed from a wild variety brought to Europe from Asia by roving bands of Celtic people around 600 B.C. Cabbage spread as a food crop throughout northern Europe because it was well adapted to growing in cooler climates, had high yields per acre, and could be stored over the winter in cold cellars. It became immensely popular among the ancient Greeks and Romans, although the cabbage eaten then seems to have been a nonheading variety with loose leaves. During the Middle Ages, farmers in northern Europe developed compact-headed varieties with overlapping leaves that were capable of thriving in cold climates, and people who had little else to eat came to rely upon this sturdy vegetable to survive the harsh winters. Brought to the Americas by the French navigator Jacques Cartier in 1536, cabbage has been cultivated here ever since in many varieties. Centuries of cultivation have produced other forms of the cabbage family, including kale, kohlrabi, cauliflower, broccoli, and brussels sprouts.

Buying Tips

When selecting cabbage, look for heads that are compact and of reasonable size, with leaves that are tender, not withered, puffy, or damaged by shipping or insects. The heads should be heavy for their size. If raw and uncut, cabbage can be kept refrigerated for up to ten days in a plastic bag.

Culinary Uses

Cabbage is not the most glamorous of vegetables. It refuses to draw attention to itself, either in the garden, on the shelf, or on a plate. However, the economical cabbage has a crisp texture and strong flavor. Raw cabbage can be cut into wedges for an appetizer or shredded for salads, with leafy types torn like lettuce rather than shredded. Cabbage can also be steamed, boiled, stir-fried, or made into the infamous German sauerkraut or Russian cabbage soup. Red cabbage reacts like litmus paper when cooked—it turns blue in the presence of an alkali (such as the lime in tap water), so if you want to preserve the color, add some type of acid, like vinegar.

Health Benefits

pH 5.20–6.80. Cabbage, both red and green, is one of the least expensive of the vitamin-protective foods and one of the most healthful. Raw cabbage detoxifies the stomach and upper bowels of putrefactive wastes, thereby improving digestive efficiency and facilitating rapid elimination. It also works to alkalinize the body, stimulate the immune system, kill harmful bacteria and viruses, soothe and heal ulcers, help prevent cancer, and clear up the complexion. Raw, unsalted sauerkraut is excellent for cleansing and rejuvenating the digestive tract; it promotes better nutrient absorption as well as the growth of healthful intestinal flora (acidophilus). For those lacking body heat, cabbage's sulfur and iron content will improve circulation. Cabbage contains iodine and is a rich source of vitamin C; the outer leaves are concentrated in vitamin E and contain at least a third more calcium than the inner leaves. Red cabbage also contains phenolic compounds, which give it its characteristic color as well as additional antioxidant properties. This family of vegetables also mildly stimulates the liver and other tissues out of stagnancy. All *Brassicas* contain isothio-

Cabbage / Nutritional Value Per 100 g Edible Portion

	Green Raw	Green Cooked	Red Raw	Red Cooked	Savoy Raw	Savoy Cooked
Calories	24	21	27	21	27	24
Protein	1.21 g	0.96 g	1.39 g	1.05 g	2.00 g	1.80 g
Fat	0.18 g	0.25 g	0.26 g	0.20 g	0.10 g	0.09 g
Fiber	0.80 g	0.60 g	1.00 g	0.76 g	0.80 g	0.70 g
Calcium	47 mg	33 mg	51 mg	37 mg	35 mg	30 mg
Iron	0.56 mg	0.39 mg	0.49 mg	0.35 mg	0.40 mg	0.38 mg
Magnesium	15 mg	15 mg	15 mg	11 mg	28 mg	24 mg
Phosphorus	23 mg	25 mg	42 mg	29 mg	42 mg	33 mg
Potassium	246 mg	205 mg	206 mg	140 mg	230 mg	184 mg
Sodium	18 mg	19 mg	11 mg	8 mg	28 mg	24 mg
Zinc	0.180 mg	0.160 mg	0.210 mg	0.150 mg	n/a	n/a
Copper	0.023 mg	0.028 mg	0.097 mg	0.069 mg	n/a	n/a
Manganese	0.159 mg	0.129 mg	0.180 mg	0.129 mg	n/a	n/a
Beta Carotene (A)	126 IU	86 IU	40 IU	27 IU	1,000 IU	889 IU
Thiamine (B$_1$)	0.050 mg	0.057 mg	0.050 mg	0.034 mg	0.070 mg	0.051 mg
Riboflavin (B$_2$)	0.030 mg	0.055 mg	0.030 mg	0.020 mg	0.030 mg	0.020 mg
Niacin (B$_3$)	0.300 mg	0.230 mg	0.300 mg	0.200 mg	0.300 mg	0.024 mg
Pantothenic Acid (B$_5$)	0.140 mg	0.063 mg	0.324 mg	0.220 mg	n/a	n/a
Pyridoxine (B$_6$)	0.095 mg	0.064 mg	0.210 mg	0.140 mg	0.190 mg	0.152 mg
Folic Acid (B$_9$)	56.7 mcg	20.3 mcg	20.7 mcg	12.6 mcg	n/a	n/a
Ascorbic Acid (C)	47.3 mg	24.3 mg	57.0 mg	34.4 mg	31.0 mg	17.0 mg
Tocopherol (E)	1.67 mg	n/a	n/a	n/a	n/a	n/a

LORE AND LEGEND

The Romans claimed that their prized cabbages originated either from the sweat of Jupiter, shed while nervously attempting to explain away the rival pronouncements of a pair of opposing oracles, or from the tears of Lycurgus, king of the Edonians, unluckily apprehended by the god Dionysus in the shortsighted act of tearing up the sacred grapevines. While trussed and awaiting his unspeakable punishment, Lycurgus wept profusely, and with good reason. Dionysus, not known as "the raging god" for nothing, first blinded Lycurgus and then tore him limb from limb. Meanwhile, Lycurgus's tears, which had fallen to the ground, sprang up as cabbages. As revered in Greece and Rome as the onion in Egypt, and so sacred that one swore oaths on it, cabbages were considered a panacea for all ills. The Roman consul Cato the Elder, in the second century B.C., attributed such mystical powers to cabbages that he believed men could live solely on them as a diet. He remained convinced even after his wife and son died, his cabbages unable to cure their illnesses. The Emperor Claudius (a glutton and drunkard, but no gourmet) once convoked the Senate to vote on the question of whether any dish surpassed corned beef and cabbage; the Senate dutifully responded that none did. The pharaohs of Egypt considered cabbage an aid to drinking and ate large quantities of cooked cabbage before their drinking bouts on the premise that this would enable them to imbibe more beer and wine without succumbing. The world's largest cabbage was grown by William Collingwood of County Durham, England, in 1865, and weighed in at 123 pounds.

cyanate, or mustard oil, which is partially responsible for their pungency and which has been used in higher concentrations as a toxic chemical weapon. Those with the highest mustard oil content are horseradish, watercress, wasabi, mustard, and canola (rape). Cabbage in excess, however, can aggravate thyroid problems and possibly cause goiter, although this is likely to happen only in areas where the drinking water is also low in iodine.

VARIETIES

Most cabbage is green, but there are also red, white, and purple varieties. Heads can vary in size from round to oval or conical and be firm or loose, with some even having curly, crinkled leaves. The most common are the smooth-leaved green varieties that have a compact round head with many thick, overlapping leaves.

Danish, also called *Hollander,* is a late-season type with round, oval, or slightly flattened heads and smooth, tightly compacted leaves that will keep longer than other types.

Domestic types form slightly looser, round, or flattened heads, with curled leaves that are more brittle than any of the Danish types. Pale green in color and considered an early-season cabbage, the domestic type is often used to make sauerkraut. It does not store well.

Early Jersey Wakefield is an heirloom cabbage variety that has remained popular. The conical heads mature early and weight in at two to three pounds. Young leaves can be used as a salad adjunct.

Lasso is an early-heading Danish red cabbage. It takes its name from an island in Denmark's archipelago. The heads are not large, but they form a firm, trim ball with few outer leaves.

Red or *purple* is similar to domestic cabbage but has reddish-purple and white-streaked leaves. Red cabbage takes longer to mature than green varieties and thus frequently has tougher leaves. Usually cooked with vinegar to preserve its color, red cabbage is frequently pickled.

Savoy is a type of green cabbage, probably of Italian origin. Yellowish green with loose, crinkly leaves that form its head, the savoy is the most tender and sweet of the cabbages. Its wrinkly leaves, which make a decorative alternative to the plain ones of the green cabbage, are used in recipes for stuffed cabbage leaves.

Wrapped heart mustard cabbage looks like a loose-leaved savoy cabbage but has a mustard-sharp taste. A near relative of mizuna, mustard cabbage needs ample moisture when growing or it becomes too hot to eat. Younger leaves are less fiery than older leaves and can be used in salads. Mature plants are best pickled, stir-fried, or cooked until soft in a soup. The blossoms are also edible.

Cardoon
(Cynara cardunculus altilis, Scolymus cardunculus)

The botanical name *Cynara*, from the Latin *canina* or *canine*, results from the similarity of the involucral spines to the dog's tooth. *Cardunculus* means "little thistle," and *altilis* means "rather tall." *Scolymus* is from the Greek *skolymos*, meaning "thistle." The English name *cardoon* is derived from the Latin *carduus*, also meaning "thistle."

General Information
This member of the thistle family, native to the Mediterranean region, is relatively unknown in North America but is quite common in Italian and French cuisine. The Romans relished the cardoon's huge leaf stalks so much that they imported them from Libya and Spain in massive quantities. Growing to heights of four feet, the cardoon looks very much like a globe artichoke plant, but its leaves are spinier, its flower heads are spiny-tipped, and it has a less appetizing appearance. The silver-gray stalks grow in bunches like celery but are flatter, longer, and wider, with slightly notched sides and a brushed suede finish. The tender stalks and root, rather than the fruiting head, are eaten. Cardoons brought a high price in second-century Rome, and in Spain an extract from the dried flowers was used for curdling milk to produce cheese.

Cardoon / Nutritional Value Per 100 g Edible Portion	Raw	Cooked
Calories	20	22
Protein	0.70 g	0.76 g
Fat	0.10 g	0.11 g
Fiber	n/a	n/a
Calcium	70 mg	72 mg
Iron	0.70 mg	0.73 mg
Magnesium	42 mg	43 mg
Phosphorus	23 mg	23 mg
Potassium	400 mg	392 mg
Sodium	170 mg	176 mg
Beta Carotene (A)	120 IU	118 IU
Thiamine (B$_1$)	0.020 mg	0.018 mg
Riboflavin (B$_2$)	0.030 mg	0.031 mg
Niacin (B$_3$)	0.300 mg	0.294 mg
Ascorbic Acid (C)	2.0 mg	1.7 mg

Buying Tips
Choose smallish, comparatively firm stalks with little browning or wilting. A short shank indicates a young, tender plant. Leaves should be very dark green. Cardoons are available in specialty markets in the winter and early spring. Because they are blanched by enclosing the stalks in cardboard, they are an energy intensive crop and therefore expensive. Avoid heads with wilt or rust.

Culinary Uses
The cardoon's flavor is complex, bitter, and sweet, with hints of artichoke heart, celery, and salsify. Some say the juicy stalks possess mushroom and asparagus sweetness laced with escarole bitterness. Very tender, young stalks may be added raw to salads. Larger stalks are blanched and used like celery in casseroles, soups, and vegetable dishes, where their soft meatiness will impart a subtle, mysterious flavor. Try them prepared like french fries for a conversation starter. The roots and leaves are also edible, the roots being used as a cooked vegetable and either being used in soups, salads, and casseroles. The dried flowers are used to curdle milk.

Carrot
(Daucus carota sativa)

Daucus is the old Greek name for the wild ancestor of the carrot, still to be found in the hedgerows of Europe, which has long been of service as food and medicine. *Carota* is the Latin name for the same plant, perhaps deriving from a Greek verb meaning "to burn," in reference to the flaming color of the vegetable; *sativa* indicates that this plant has long been cultivated.

General Information
Most probably native to the region of Afghanistan, where there still exists the greatest diversity, the carrot has not always been orange nor so very sweet. The wild carrot that the ancients knew was, and is, small, pale purple, and tough. During the ninth and tenth centuries, the carrot spread throughout the Islamic world, reaching Holland by the fourteenth century. Horticultural changes are credited to the Hollanders, who introduced it to England during the Elizabethan period. Over decades of breeding, they changed the coloring from purple to pale white and then increasingly to bright orange. Orange won out over purple because the orange color doesn't bleed in cooking. The carrot's orange

pigment (carotene) is the most durable, especially compared to chlorophyll's green, which turns olive drab with cooking. Two particular varieties of carrot, the Long Orange and the Horn, are the source of almost all our finest eating carrots today. Americans were late in embracing the carrot; only after the First World War did true enthusiasm for it develop here. One of the most valuable root crops grown for human consumption, the carrot comes in an amazing variety of colors— including orange, yellow, red, white, and purple—and shapes, including long, short, slender, stubby, pointed, blunt, and even bulbous. However, the only carrots widely grown in North America are the slender, pointed, orange ones.

Buying Tips

Carrots come many shapes and sizes. Regardless, it is easy to buy good carrots. Look for firm, smooth, well-shaped ones of good color and fresh appearance, with fresh green tops. If newly picked carrots with their lacy green fronds are available, these are the freshest and tastiest. Cellophane packages of carrots have frequently been stored for months and have therefore lost some of their flavor and nutrients. Smaller carrots tend to be more flavorful than large ones, since the bigger ones can be fibrous and woody. Avoid dry, rubbery carrots. Strong orange color is directly related to nutrition; the more color a carrot has, the higher its concentration of carotene, which the body turns into vitamin A. Do not store carrots near apples because doing so makes the carrots acquire a bitter taste.

Culinary Uses

Carrots are so versatile as to be considered an important part of appetizers, main dishes, and desserts. They contain more sugar than any other vegetable except beets, which partly accounts for their popularity, and their bright color makes them an appealing addition, cooked or raw, to many dishes. The tastiest and most nutritious way to eat them is pulled fresh from the garden and washed, but if you do not have that luxury, then cut them into sticks or shred them in salads. It is preferable not to peel carrots, as many of the nutrients are in or just under the peels; simply scrub well to remove any dirt and cut off the ends. As the late food writer M. F. K. Fisher observed in *The Art of Eating*, "All of them, whether tender or hard, thick skinned or thin, die when they are peeled . . . even as you and I." There isn't much that has not been done to the carrot: whether served raw, sautéed, boiled, puréed, gratinéed, made into soufflés, cooked in cream, glazed in butter, or

added to stocks and casseroles, they are always delicious. Don't ignore the carrot greens (tops); because of their high phosphorus content these should also be eaten, either raw in salads or cooked in soups.

Peeled baby carrots—now ubiquitous in markets, restaurants, and salad bars—are not really babies. They are adult carrots whittled down to junior size, with the bits and pieces that are removed going into soups or TV dinners. Peeled carrots may develop a "white blush" (to use the industry term) if they are dehydrated. Soak them in water and they will color back up again. Better yet, toss them in the trash and purchase fresh, whole carrots.

Health Benefits

pH 4.55–6.10. Anthelmintic, carminative, diuretic, stimulant. Carrots and their juice are one of the best detoxifiers when consumed in quantity—alkalinizing, cleansing, nourishing, and stimulating to almost every system in the body. Carrots deliver abundant supplies of readily assimilable vitamins, minerals, and enzymes to cells, giving them the fuel they require to slough off morbid wastes and rebuild healthy cells. One of the best foods for the liver and digestive tract, they help kidney function, help prevent and treat cancer, balance the endocrine and adrenal systems, depress blood cholesterol, and increase bulk elimination from the colon. Quality carrots are very rich in the antioxidant beta carotene, the precursor to vitamin A, which makes them beneficial for the eyes and vision (carrots were used during wars to help aviators overcome night blindness). Beta carotene appears to protect against cancer on at least two counts. First, it acts as an antioxidant, countering the destructive action of oxygen free radicals that can lead to cell alterations and cancer. Second, beta carotene helps your immune system produce natural "killer cells" that fight cancer and other diseases. They also contain large amounts of silicon and thereby strengthen the connective tissues and aid calcium metabolism; as well, they contain an essential oil that kills parasites and unhealthy intestinal bacteria. Their potassium salts account for the diuretic action, while at the same time carrot soup makes an effective remedy for diarrhea and is easily digestible for those suffering from stomach and intestinal problems. Carrots contain plentiful amounts of pectin, the soluble fiber that can reduce blood cholesterol levels, and their high fiber also promotes regularity and prevents constipation.

BYPRODUCTS

Carrot juice is a perennial favorite health drink and is excellent for liver rejuvenation and cleansing. The juice is more medicinal in action when taken on an empty stomach. Use in moderation, though, as carrot juice is a refined food. This surprises people, especially those who like to juice their own carrots. But consider how many carrots go into one glass of juice and how much pulp remains. Imagine cramming that many whole carrots into your stomach in the same amount of time it takes to drink their juice. While whole carrots don't raise blood sugar because their fiber slows digestion, carrot juice is a liquid form of simple sugars, and it does raise blood sugar. Therefore, when serving it to children, dilute it first; and the next time you drink it, notice the rush of energy it gives. Carrot juice may also be applied directly to burns to aid in their healing.

Carrot / Nutritional Value Per 100 g Edible Portion		
	Raw	Cooked
Calories	43	45
Protein	1.03 g	1.09 g
Fat	0.19 g	0.18 g
Fiber	1.04 g	1.47 g
Calcium	27 mg	31 mg
Iron	0.50 mg	0.62 mg
Magnesium	15 mg	13 mg
Phosphorus	44 mg	30 mg
Potassium	323 mg	227 mg
Sodium	35 mg	66 mg
Zinc	0.200 mg	0.300 mg
Copper	0.047 mg	0.134 mg
Manganese	0.142 mg	0.752 mg
Beta Carotene (A)	28,129 IU	24,554 IU
Thiamine (B$_1$)	0.097 mg	0.034 mg
Riboflavin (B$_2$)	0.059 mg	0.056 mg
Niacin (B$_3$)	0.928 mg	0.506 mg
Pantothenic Acid (B$_5$)	0.197 mg	0.304 mg
Pyridoxine (B$_6$)	0.147 mg	0.246 mg
Folic Acid (B$_9$)	14.0 mcg	13.9 mcg
Ascorbic Acid (C)	9.3 mg	2.3 mg
Tocopherol (E)	0.44 mg	0.42 mg

LORE AND LEGEND

The ancient Greek word for the carrot, *philon*, comes from their word for "love," as this root was considered a potent aphrodisiac. The Emperor Caligula, who had a fun-loving streak, once fed the entire Roman Senate a feast of carrots in the hope of watching them run sexually amok. Fashionable ladies in the English court once thought carrot foliage and flowers so attractive that they used them to adorn their hair and hats.

Cassava
(Manihot utilissima, M. esculenta)
Also Known As: Manioc, Brazilian Arrowroot, Yuca, Tapioca

Manihot is the plant's native Brazilian name. The term *utilissima* designates a plant that is very useful, while *esculenta* means "esculent," or "edible." The English word *cassava* is from a Taino term, *cac abi*, while *tapioca* comes from the Tupi (Brazilian) word *typyoca*.

General Information
A native of equatorial America and Florida and one of the important plant foods of the tropics, the cassava plant is little known to most people in the temperate zones except in the form of tapioca. Cassava belongs to the Euphorbiaceae, or spurge family, which includes the Para rubber tree, our best source of natural rubber, and the poinsettia, a well-known Christmas ornamental. The edible part of the rather tall and shrubby plant is the long, starchy, tuberous root, which somewhat resembles a sweet potato but is usually much larger, some growing to a yard in length and weighing several pounds. There are two broad groups, the sweet maniocs and the bitter. The tubers of the sweet varieties, which contain negligible traces of toxic compounds, are eaten as cooked vegetables. Bitter varieties contain far higher concentrations of poisonous hydrocyanide compounds and require special preparation to make them safe to eat. The native technique was either to boil the dark brown roots very thoroughly and then mash them, or to peel and grate the roots and then squeeze out the juices under heavy pressure. These juices, boiled hard, were used to make *cassareep* sauce and also threw a starchy sediment

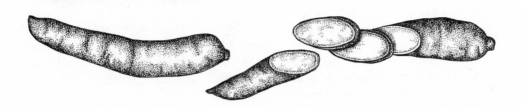

that became granular when dried: tapioca. The pulp was shaped into flat cakes, slowly cooked on a griddle, and eaten as well. The long boiling time would dissipate the toxic compounds, leaving a perfectly safe foodstuff.

Buying Tips

Look for cassava that is as completely bark-covered as possible, although the bark is always patchy. If the bark on the skin is cut or damaged and the cassava is not used immediately, it becomes toxic. There should be no sliminess, mold, or hairline cracks, and the root should smell clean and fresh. Do not buy tubers that show any grayish-blue fibers or even the slightest darkening near the skin. Ask your grocer to cut into one to assure that its flesh is clear and without darkened areas near the skin. Or buy extra and discard any discolored pieces. Do not refrigerate a cassava; rather, store it in a very cool, dry area for a day or two.

Culinary Uses

The swollen roots are shaped like long, narrow sweet potatoes and covered with what looks like bark. Beneath the rough brown coat, through which may be visible rosy or tan patches, is flesh that is as hard, dense, and white as coconut. The softly fibrous, starchy flesh becomes almost translucent when cooked, with a sweetness, butteriness, and glutinous chewiness that is much appreciated by many, but not all. At its simplest, it is boiled or baked, and almost always sauced. In stews, it both thickens and absorbs juices. At one time cassava was in great demand in the United States in the form of tapioca, but this popular pudding has now largely been replaced by gelatins and instant puddings.

Health Benefits

Cooked into pudding, tapioca makes a light, nutritious, and easily digested food for invalids.

Cauliflower
(Brassica oleracea botrytis)

> Cauliflower is nothing but a cabbage with a college education.
>
> —MARK TWAIN

The Latin name *Brassica* derives from the Celtic *bresic*. The term *oleracea* refers to a vegetable garden herb that is used in cooking, while *botrytis* is a Greek word meaning "clusterlike" or "grapelike." The English word *cauliflower* comes from the Latin words *caulis*, meaning "stem" or "cabbage," and flos, "flower."

General Information

Cauliflower, like its cousin broccoli, is a member of the cabbage family, and it took centuries of cultivation to produce

Cassava / Nutritional Value Per 100 g Edible Portion		
	Dry Raw	Pearl Tapioca
Calories	120	341
Protein	3.10 g	0.19 g
Fat	0.39 g	0.02 g
Fiber	2.49 g	n/a
Calcium	91 mg	20 mg
Iron	3.60 mg	1.58 mg
Magnesium	66 mg	1 mg
Phosphorus	70 mg	7 mg
Potassium	764 mg	11 mg
Sodium	8 mg	1 mg
Beta Carotene (A)	10 IU	n/a
Thiamine (B₁)	0.225 mg	0.004 mg
Riboflavin (B₂)	0.101 mg	0 mg
Niacin (B₃)	1.400 mg	0 mg
Ascorbic Acid (C)	48.2 mg	0 mg

a tight head of clustered flower buds in place of the compact leaves of the cabbage head. Thousands of tiny white flower buds are closely packed into even larger buds, forming the florets that make up the single large round head or "flower." Cauliflower was introduced into medieval Europe by the Arabs during their occupation of Spain, and by the twelfth century Spaniards were eating as many as three varieties of the vegetable. In sixteenth-century England, cauliflower was called "Cyprus coleworts," probably because it was first imported from the island of Cyprus. A new green variety has been developed commercially that is a cross between conventional cauliflower and broccoli. The head resembles cauliflower, but the color is chartreuse, rather than the dark green of broccoli.

Buying Tips

Quality cauliflower is creamy or snowy white, clean, heavy, firm, and compact, with outer leaves that are fresh and green. Avoid any that has the appearance of being ricelike

LORE AND LEGEND

In Queen Anne's time the term *cauliflower* was a comical phrase for a clerical wig, later referring to anyone who wore powder on his head.

or granular, speckled, or spotted, or that has yellowing leaves. The size of the vegetable has little to do with its quality. Keep cauliflower in a plastic bag in the refrigerator.

Culinary Uses

Cauliflower can be served either raw in salads and vegetable dip platters or cooked as a vegetable on its own or combined with other vegetables. However, if cauliflower is cooked too long, its sulfur compounds will decompose and form an offensive odor. Green cauliflower has a pleasant taste, cooks more quickly than the white variety, and is less apt to give off the usual cabbagelike odor while cooking. Since cauliflower is a type of cabbage, the leaves, flower stalk, and midveins of the big leaves make excellent eating.

Health Benefits

pH 5.60–6.80. Cauliflower is not as nutrient-dense as many of the other cabbage family vegetables. Its white color is a sign that it contains far less of the beneficial carotenes and chlorophyll, but it is a good source of boron because cauliflower does not grow well in boron-deficient soils. Cauliflower helps purify the blood, aids bleeding gums if eaten raw, and is helpful in cases of asthma, kidney and bladder disorders, high blood pressure, and constipation. Because its high sulfur content may cause indigestion and hinder the assimilation of food, cauliflower should be used in moderation and not combined with other sulfur-rich foods. All *Brassica* genus vegetables contain dithiolthiones, a group of compounds that have anticancer, antioxidant properties; indoles, substances that protect against breast and colon cancer; and sulfur, which has antibiotic and antiviral characteristics. This family of vegetables also mildly stimulates the liver and other tissues out of stagnancy.

Cauliflower / Nutritional Value Per 100 g Edible Portion		
	Raw	Cooked
Calories	24	24
Protein	1.99 g	1.87 g
Fat	0.18 g	0.17 g
Fiber	0.85 g	0.82 g
Calcium	29 mg	27 mg
Iron	0.58 mg	0.42 mg
Magnesium	14 mg	11 mg
Phosphorus	46 mg	35 mg
Potassium	355 mg	323 mg
Sodium	15 mg	6 mg
Zinc	0.180 mg	0.240 mg
Copper	0.032 mg	0.091 mg
Manganese	0.203 mg	0.178 mg
Beta Carotene (A)	16 IU	14 IU
Thiamine (B$_1$)	0.076 mg	0.063 mg
Riboflavin (B$_2$)	0.057 mg	0.052 mg
Niacin (B$_3$)	0.633 mg	0.552 mg
Pantothenic Acid (B$_5$)	0.141 mg	0.122 mg
Pyridoxine (B$_6$)	0.231 mg	0.202 mg
Folic Acid (B$_9$)	66.1 mcg	51.2 mcg
Ascorbic Acid (C)	71.5 mg	55.4 mg
Tocopherol (E)	0.03 mg	n/a

Cee Gwa

(Luffa acutangula)
Also Known As: Chinese Okra, Angled Luffa

Luffa is the Arabic name for this family of plants; *acutangula* means "acutely or sharply angled."

General Information

This close relative of the loofah sponge is presumed native to India. Distinguished by its ten sharp ridges and dull green skin, the long, narrow cee gwa squash rather resembles large okra pods in that it is tapered and grows wider away from the stem. The fruit on the market, which may be three feet long, is actually immature; fully mature fruits reach nine feet in length. They are best when only six inches long. The fruits need to be harvested young, as old ones become fibrous; it is the old ones that are used as scrubbers.

Culinary Uses and Health Benefits

Cee gwa can be eaten raw in salads but most often is used cooked, when it has a pleasant earthy flavor and a texture reminiscent of zucchini. To prepare, slice off the ridges and both ends and scrape the skin lightly. In China this strange vegetable is frequently deep-fried or used in soups. One early-nineteenth-century English botanical writer, William Roxburgh, said that cee gwa was almost as good as green peas when boiled, dressed with butter, and seasoned with salt and pepper. The juice from mature fruits is valued medicinally as a purgative.

Celeriac

(Apium graveolens var. rapaceum)
Also Known As: Celery Root, Knob Celery

There is another kind of celery called Capitatum, which is grown in the gardens of St. Agatha, Theano, and other places in Apulia, granted from nature and unseen and unnamed by the Ancients. Its bulb is spherical, nearly the size of a man's head. It is very sweet and odorous. . . .

—Baptista Porta

Apium derives either from the Latin *apis*, meaning "bee," because bees go dotty over its tiny white flowers, or from a prehistoric Indo-European word for "water," which would be appropriate, since celeriac prefers wet soils and salt marshes. The term *graveolens* means "heavy-scented"; *rapaceum* means "pertaining to turnips" or "turniplike." The English name *celeriac* derives from the Latin *celer*, meaning "quick-acting" or "swift," in reference to its remedial reputation.

General Information

Swiss botanists gave the first description of celeriac in about 1600. Not a true root, celeriac is a special variety of celery that is cultivated for its swollen stem base rather than its upper branches. Technically a corm of a type of celery and looking like an irregular, brown turnip, with many small roots extending from its base, the swollen form would be at home in tales by the brothers Grimm. Between an apple and a cantaloupe in size, the two- to four-inch lopsided sphere is embossed and channeled, decorated with whorls, crevices, and disorderly rootlets, and often scruffy and muddy. It became popular in Europe in the eighteenth century but has never been very popular in England or the United States.

Celeriac / Nutritional Value Per 100 g Edible Portion		
	Raw	Cooked
Calories	39	25
Protein	1.50 g	0.96 g
Fat	0.30 g	0.19 g
Fiber	1.30 g	0.83 g
Calcium	43 mg	26 mg
Iron	0.70 mg	0.43 mg
Magnesium	20 mg	12 mg
Phosphorus	115 mg	66 mg
Potassium	300 mg	173 mg
Sodium	100 mg	61 mg
Beta Carotene (A)	0 IU	0 IU
Thiamine (B$_1$)	0.050 mg	0.027 mg
Riboflavin (B$_2$)	0.060 mg	0.037 mg
Niacin (B$_3$)	0.700 mg	0.427 mg
Pyridoxine (B$_6$)	0.165 mg	0.101 mg
Ascorbic Acid (C)	8.0 mg	3.6 mg

Buying Tips

In choosing celeriac, favor smaller roots over larger, as the latter tend to be pithy, and buy only those that are firm, pressing the tops of the roots to check for internal rot. Cut off any stems and refrigerate. The root will keep up to a week. Peel and discard the skin just prior to use.

Culinary Uses

Celeriac tastes much like a combination of celery and parsley, only stronger and with a smoky flavor. It is one of the few vegetables that must be peeled before using, and the innermost woody section may be too fibrous to use. You can do anything with celeriac that you can with turnips, and more. Once peeled, it can be eaten raw in salads or blanched, steamed, boiled, puréed, or stir-fried. Cut into matchsticks, its chewy crunch and assertive flavor are easy crowd pleasers. Cooked celeriac mixed with an equal quantity of potato makes a delicately flavored purée. The stalks and leaves are not eaten.

Health Benefits

pH 5.71–5.85. As a celery-related plant, celeriac has been known for its diuretic qualities and is useful to those with kidney stones and arthritic conditions. Celeriac is beneficial to the lymphatic, nervous, and urinary systems.

Celery
(Apium graveolens)

> Did woman know what celery
> Bestows upon a man,
> She would go forth to search for it
> From Rome to Turkestan.
>
> Did man but know what celery would do for
>   him,
> Nought else would fill his garden rim to rim.
>
> —AUTHOR UNKNOWN

Apium derives either from the Latin *apis*, meaning "bee," because bees go dotty over its tiny white flowers, or from a prehistoric Indo-European word for "water," which would be appropriate, since celery prefers wet soils and salt marshes. The term *graveolens* means "heavy-scented." The English name *celery* derives from the Latin *celer*,

meaning "quick-acting" or "swift," in reference to its remedial reputation.

General Information

Originally a wild plant that grew along the muddy Mediterranean wetlands where sea and land waters mingled, wild celery has a bitter flavor and pungent odor. Celery as we know it today is a sweeter, less woody variety developed during the seventeenth century by the Italians and French. It belongs to the same plant family (Umbellifer) as carrots, parsley, and fennel, all of which get their characteristic flavor from the volatile oils found in the stems, leaves, and seeds. Celery is typically harvested after its first year of growth, when the stalks are thick and leafy. Some plants, however, are allowed to grow a second year, which results in the formation of seeds. The seeds, as well as the dried leaves, called celery flakes, are popular as seasonings. There are two main varieties: green-ribbed celery (also called Pascal celery), with large green leaves, and golden celery, either blanched with ethylene gas or grown in darkness to change the typical green color to light white

Celery / Nutritional Value Per 100 g Edible Portion		
	Raw	Cooked
Calories	16	18
Protein	0.75 g	0.83 g
Fat	0.14 g	0.16 g
Fiber	0.80 g	0.88 g
Calcium	40 mg	42 mg
Iron	0.40 mg	0.42 mg
Magnesium	11 mg	12 mg
Phosphorus	25 mg	25 mg
Potassium	287 mg	284 mg
Sodium	87 mg	91 mg
Zinc	0.130 mg	0.140 mg
Copper	0.034 mg	0.036 mg
Manganese	0.102 mg	0.106 mg
Beta Carotene (A)	134 IU	132 IU
Thiamine (B₁)	0.046 mg	0.043 mg
Riboflavin (B₂)	0.045 mg	0.047 mg
Niacin (B₃)	0.323 mg	0.319 mg
Pantothenic Acid (B₅)	0.186 mg	0.195 mg
Pyridoxine (B₆)	0.087 mg	0.086 mg
Folic Acid (B₉)	28.0 mcg	22.0 mcg
Ascorbic Acid (C)	7.0 mg	6.1 mg
Tocopherol (E)	0.36 mg	n/a

LORE AND LEGEND

Although at times it has been associated with funerals and thought an omen of ill luck, the ancient Greeks valued celery highly, and awarded it as a prize to winners in many of their sporting contests. Legend has it that medieval magicians tucked celery seeds into their shoes in order to fly.

or golden, with yellow-green leaves. Our domestic crop is grown primarily in California, Florida, and Texas, with Michigan providing it in hot weather.

Buying Tips

Choose crisp stalks of medium length, thickness, and solidity, brittle enough to snap easily. Whole heads should have plenty of small inner stalks and "heart." Look for outer stalks with a uniform length. The leaves should be fresh and green. Avoid celery bunches that have cracked, bruised, or loosened stalks. Celery hearts are the tender inner branches.

Culinary Uses

The flavor of celery is distinctively sharp and tangy, the small, deep green leafy types being sharper than the larger white varieties. Of the most benefit when eaten raw either alone or in sandwiches or with dips, celery is also flavorful when cooked with tomatoes or green peppers. Celery leaves, because they are so tough and strongly flavored, should be chopped, liquefied, and added to other vegetables to lessen their strong taste.

Health Benefits

pH 5.37–6.00. Diuretic. Since Greek times, celery has been valued as a hangover cure and blood cleanser. The 1897 Sears Roebuck & Co. catalog advertised a celery tonic that was good for the nerves, reports Irena Chalmers in *The Great Food Almanac*. Clinical studies show that it significantly reduces blood pressure by relaxing the muscle tissue in artery walls and thus enhancing blood flow. Celery contains compounds known as coumarins, which appear to be useful in cancer prevention and which enhance the activity of certain white blood cells; these compounds also tone the vascular system, lower blood pressure, and may be useful in treating migraines. A favorite reducing food because of its few calories, celery's high water content makes it especially good to eat with foods that are more concentrated, particularly heavy starches. Strongly alkaline, it counteracts acidosis, halts digestive fermentation of foods, purifies the bloodstream, aids digestion, and can help clear up skin problems. Stiffness, creaking, or cracking in the joints may indicate a lack of organic sodium (the "youth" element that helps keep muscles limber and pliable) and a buildup of inorganic calcium deposits. Celery's rich organic sodium content dislodges these calcium deposits from joints and holds them in solution until they can be eliminated through the kidneys. Celery also provides organic calcium and silicon for the repair of damaged ligaments and bones. It is rich in magnesium and iron, two minerals that nourish blood cells, cleanse and wash fatty deposits, and eliminate accumulated wastes. The greener stalks are an especially good source of vitamin A, which fights aging, and are excellent for people suffering from arthritis, neuritis, rheumatism, or high blood pressure. Celery may also promote the onset of menstruation; use it only in moderate amounts during pregnancy.

Chaya
(Cnidoscolus chayamansa)

General Information

This fast-growing ornamental and shade shrub is a source of nutritious green leaves and shoots. The plants vary from smooth to hairy, and the hairy plants sting like nettles, so that harvesters must wear gloves. The stinging hairs disappear with cooking. Cultivated plants are almost free of stinging hairs.

Culinary Uses and Health Benefits

Chaya must be cooked before eating: the fresh leaves contain toxic hydrocyanic glycosides, which cooking deactivates. The young shoots and tender leaves are cooked and eaten like spinach. They are probably suitable for canning or freezing for local and export markets, but this has not yet been attempted. Reportedly they are high in protein, calcium, iron, carotene, thiamine, riboflavin, niacin, and ascorbic acid.

Chinese Cabbage
(Brassica chinensis, B. rapa)

The Latin name *Brassica* derives from the Celtic *bresic*; *chinensis* designates the plant's Chinese origins.

General Information

Long appreciated for its delicate flavor and crisp texture, Chinese cabbage has been cultivated since before the Christian era. It has been described as a cabbage that even cabbage haters love—it is crisper, juicier, sweeter, and more tender than common cabbage. There are several varieties of Chinese cabbage, the two most popular being bok choy and Pe-tsai. All form a head, but the head varies from round like cabbage to elongated like romaine lettuce; also, the crinkly leaves may curl inward or outward.

Buying Tips

In most markets, at least one form or another of Chinese cabbage is available year-round. Select fresh, light-colored greens with plump ribs. Squeeze the heads to find a firm, heavy one. Avoid those that have wilted leaves with any rot spots. Small dark specks, however, are naturally occurring. Chinese cabbage stores exceptionally well (but not so long

as cabbage), and the flavor even improves when it is slightly wilted.

Culinary Uses

Chinese cabbage's sweet flavor is enhanced with long simmering, and the leaves become silky soft but hold their form. Try it in soups and stews, baked, or braised. It's also delicious when lightly cooked (stir-fried, steamed, or blanched) or even raw in a salad, where its thin, crispy-crunchy leaves add great texture and make an excellent salad base on their own. The blanched leaf makes a flexible and excellent wrapper that is, compared to common cabbage, easier to work with yet more delicate. Pickled Chinese cabbage, *kim chee*, the signature dish of Korea, is as easy to make as sauerkraut, the pickled cabbage of equal prominence in German cuisine.

Health Benefits

Chinese cabbage is cooling and beneficial to the lungs, stomach, and liver channels. It also moistens the intestines and treats constipation. It is an anti-inflammatory and useful in cases of yellow mucus discharge and other heat symptoms, including fever. According to Oriental medicine, stalk vegetables raise energy and are expansive and cooling foods. All *Brassica* genus vegetables contain dithiolthiones, a group of compounds that have anticancer, antioxidant properties; indoles, substances that protect against breast and colon cancer; and sulfur, which has antibiotic and antiviral characteristics.

VARIETIES

Bok choy (also called **Chinese chard** and **Chinese mustard**) originates from southeastern China. The cluster of thick, greenish-white stalks are ten to twenty inches long with broad, dark green leaves. Select fresh, crisp, firm heads with leaves that do not look wilted. One advantage that bok choy shares with many members of the leafy green cabbage family is an excellent shelf life. The crunchy stalks have a delicately mild, juicy sweetness that suggests romaine lettuce, while the leaves are soft, somewhat peppery, and cabbagey. Often cut into pieces and stir-fried, bok choy stalks can also be served raw in salads or added to soups. The leaves withstand cooking better than spinach and do not become gooey, but they should always be steamed, never boiled.

Pe-tsai (also called **Chinese cabbage, celery cabbage,** or **napa cabbage**) belongs to the napa cabbage family. It looks very much like romaine lettuce, with its fairly

Chinese Cabbage / Nutritional Value Per 100 g Edible Portion				
	Bok Choy Raw	Bok Choy Cooked	Pe-tsai Raw	Pe-tsai Cooked
Calories	13	12	16	14
Protein	1.50 g	1.56 g	1.20 g	1.50 g
Fat	0.20 g	0.16 g	0.20 g	0.17 g
Fiber	0.60 g	0.60 g	0.60 g	0.50 g
Calcium	105 mg	93 mg	77 mg	32 mg
Iron	0.80 mg	1.04 mg	0.31 mg	0.30 mg
Magnesium	19 mg	11 mg	13 mg	10 mg
Phosphorus	37 mg	29 mg	29 mg	39 mg
Potassium	252 mg	371 mg	238 mg	225 mg
Sodium	65 mg	34 mg	9 mg	9 mg
Zinc	n/a	n/a	0.23 mg	0.18 mg
Beta Carotene (A)	3,000 IU	2,568 IU	1,200 IU	967 IU
Thiamine (B$_1$)	0.040 mg	0.032 mg	0.040 mg	0.044 mg
Riboflavin (B$_2$)	0.070 mg	0.063 mg	0.050 mg	0.044 mg
Niacin (B$_3$)	0.500 mg	0.428 mg	0.400 mg	0.500 mg
Pantothenic Acid (B$_5$)	n/a	n/a	0.105 mg	0.080 mg
Pyridoxine (B$_6$)	n/a	n/a	0.232 mg	0.177 mg
Folic Acid (B$_9$)	n/a	n/a	78.7 mcg	53.4 mcg
Ascorbic Acid (C)	45.0 mg	26.0 mg	27.0 mg	15.8 mg
Tocopherol (E)	n/a	n/a	0.12 mg	n/a

compact, conical head, but the crinkled leaves are pale green. Pe-tsai has a delicate, mild flavor; the tender, crisp, and juicy leaves are favored for stir-fried vegetable dishes, and the white heart of the head is a real delicacy.

Collards
(Brassica oleracea acephala)

The botanical name *Brassica* derives from the Celtic *bresic*; *oleracea* refers to a vegetable garden herb that is used in cooking; *acephala*, meaning "without a head," refers to the plant's loose-leaved, nonheading shape. The English name is a corruption of the Anglo-Saxon *coleworts* or *colewyrts*, meaning "cabbage plants."

General Information
Collards are native to the eastern Mediterranean countries or to Asia Minor and are one of the oldest members of the cabbage family. They made their way to the New World in the seventeenth century with the slave trade. Extremely hardy and adaptable to both hot and cold climates, collards are unfussy growers and abundant producers of "greens," or leaves. The deep bluish-green leaves, each on a fairly long, heavy stalk (too tough to eat), resemble cabbage leaves but are oval, fairly flat, and paddlelike, not round and curved like heading cabbage. Despite their long history and nutritional benefits, collards have never gained wide acceptance except in the southeastern United States.

Buying Tips
Choose relatively small, firm, springy leaves that show no yellowing or insect holes. Store collards in a plastic bag and refrigerate, using them as soon as possible.

Culinary Uses
Collard greens are more tender than kale and less pungent than mustard greens, with an assertively earthy flavor. Young greens can be eaten raw, chopped into a mixed green salad. Older leaves need to be cooked, in the manner of spinach. Substantial enough to replace meat, this traditional southern favorite is commonly cooked with bacon or salt pork.

Health Benefits
All *Brassica* genus vegetables contain dithiolthiones, a group of compounds that have anticancer, antioxidant properties; indoles, substances that protect against breast and colon cancer; and sulfur, which has antibiotic and antiviral characteristics. This family of vegetables also mildly stimulates the liver and other tissues out of stagnancy.

Corn
(Zea mays saccharata)
Also Known As: Sweet Corn, Maize

Sex is good, but not as good as fresh sweet corn.

—GARRISON KEILLOR

The greatest drawback is the way in which it is necessary to eat it. . . . It looks awkward enough: but what is to be done? Surrendering such a vegetable from considerations of grace is not to be thought of.

—HARRIET MARTINEAU, ENGLISHWOMAN, ON CORN ON THE COB (1835)

In 1737 Linnaeus christened the species *Zea mays*, from the Greek *zeia*, for "grain" or "cereal," and the Taino Indian

Collards / Nutritional Value Per 100 g Edible Portion		
	Raw	Cooked
Calories	31	27
Protein	1.57 g	1.35 g
Fat	0.22 g	0.19 g
Fiber	0.57 g	0.49 g
Calcium	29 mg	23 mg
Iron	0.19 mg	0.16 mg
Magnesium	9 mg	7 mg
Phosphorus	10 mg	8 mg
Potassium	169 mg	131 mg
Sodium	20 mg	16 mg
Zinc	0.130 mg	0.110 mg
Copper	0.039 mg	0.032 mg
Manganese	0.276 mg	0.226 mg
Beta Carotene (A)	3,330 IU	2,727 IU
Thiamine (B$_1$)	0.029 mg	0.021 mg
Riboflavin (B$_2$)	0.064 mg	0.052 mg
Niacin (B$_3$)	0.374 mg	0.290 mg
Pantothenic Acid (B$_5$)	0.064 mg	0.052 mg
Pyridoxine (B$_6$)	0.067 mg	0.052 mg
Folic Acid (B$_9$)	12.0 mcg	6.0 mcg
Ascorbic Acid (C)	23.3 mg	12.1 mg

mahiz. The term *saccharata* means "containing sugar" or "sweet." The English word *corn* comes from the Old Norse word *korn*, which means "grain-sized lump" of something. The term has historically meant any sort of kernel or grain, whatever the dominant grain of the country happened to be. In England, for example, *corn* refers to wheat, and in Scotland or Ireland the term refers to oats.

General Information

The only cereal that is native to North America, corn is actually a type of grass; its proper name is *maize*, a word of Indian origin. Sweet corn was being grown by the Indians at least by the beginning of the seventeenth century on the eastern side of the Appalachians, where the Iroquois were raising it along the headwaters of the Susquehanna River in central New York. It was "discovered" there in 1799 and planted along the coast, but it evoked no particular interest among the colonists and began to be widely cultivated only after the Civil War. Today canned sweet corn is America's favorite preserved vegetable and has been outselling all others since World War I. Harvested at an immature stage so that the kernels are tender and juicy, at its peak of flavor

sweet corn contains 5 to 6 percent sugar by weight. For more information about corn, see the reference in the Grains section.

Buying Tips

When buying fresh sweet corn, look for creamy-colored cobs/ears surrounded by green leaves. If possible, pull back the husk and puncture a kernel with your fingernail. If the corn is fresh, the kernel will exude a milky liquid; if not ripe, it will exude water; and if past its prime, the kernels will be tough and the milk doughy. Store corn on the cob with the husks intact in the refrigerator and use as soon as possible.

Culinary Uses

Many varieties of sweet corn are introduced each year, and nowadays fresh and frozen corn on the cob is available year-round. Once picked, sweet corn should be eaten as soon as possible, for the sugar begins to turn to starch immediately after the cob is separated from the stalk. Usually boiled and eaten off the cob, the kernels can be scraped off after cooking and eaten separately or added to baked goods.

Health Benefits

pH 5.92–7.68. Fresh corn on the cob has properties similar to dried corn but contains more enzymes and more of certain vitamins, so it is better eaten fresh in the warmer seasons. Very high in fiber, corn is one of the best-balanced starches (along with brown rice and barley), and its carbohydrate is the easiest of all the grains to digest. Yellow corn is helpful in building bone and muscle, and it is excellent food for the brain and nervous system. Corn is said to help prevent cancer and lower the risk of heart disease and cavities.

Corn / Nutritional Value Per 100 g Edible Portion			
	Raw	Cooked	Frozen & Cooked
Calories	86	108	81
Protein	3.22 g	3.32 g	3.02 g
Fat	1.18 g	1.28 g	0.07 g
Fiber	0.70 g	0.60 g	0.48 g
Calcium	2 mg	2 mg	2 mg
Iron	0.52 mg	0.61 mg	0.30 mg
Magnesium	37 mg	32 mg	18 mg
Phosphorus	89 mg	103 mg	47 mg
Potassium	270 mg	249 mg	139 mg
Sodium	15.2 mg	17 mg	5 mg
Zinc	0.450 mg	0.480 mg	0.350 mg
Copper	0.054 mg	0.053 mg	0.033 mg
Manganese	0.161 mg	0.194 mg	0.180 mg
Beta Carotene (A)	281 IU	217 IU	248 IU
Thiamine (B$_1$)	0.200 mg	0.215 mg	0.069 mg
Riboflavin (B$_2$)	0.060 mg	0.072 mg	0.073 mg
Niacin (B$_3$)	1.700 mg	1.614 mg	1.283 mg
Pantothenic Acid (B$_5$)	0.760 mg	0.878 mg	0.217 mg
Pyridoxine (B$_6$)	0.055 mg	0.060 mg	0.100 mg
Folic Acid (B$_9$)	45.8 mcg	46.4 mcg	22.8 mcg
Ascorbic Acid (C)	6.8 mg	6.2 mg	2.6 mg

Cucumber

(Cucumis sativus, C. melo)

> *Cucumis* is the old Latin name for this plant, derived from the Latin word for gourd. *Sativus* indicates that this plant has long been cultivated; *melo* means "melon."

General Information

The ordinary cucumber, a member of the gourd and squash family and a native of India and Egypt, was cultivated very early in Asia and Europe and was a popular vegetable with the Greeks and Romans. Centuries before

LORE AND LEGEND

In biblical times eating cucumbers was thought to offer protection against deadly insects and snakes. There is some mention of the cucumber as an emblem of fertility; one Buddhist legend tells of Sagara's wife, who had sixty thousand offspring, the first of which was a cucumber that climbed to heaven on its own vine. The Roman emperor Tiberius is reputed to have been so fond of cucumbers that he ate them daily, ten a day. They were even grown in special movable frames so that his supply would never be interrupted when he traveled. It was customary to pick cucumbers at the full of the moon, in the hope of getting the very biggest, which were also considered the very best. One medieval gardener advised draping the plants in comforting "thin coverlets" in the event of violently inclement weather, as they were said to be frightened of thunderstorms.

thermos jugs, travelers in desert caravans carried cucumbers because the green skins effectively protected the cool fresh liquid within, which could assuage thirst, and the flesh provided a refreshing food. The cucumber was introduced into Europe by Alexander the Great. Centuries later, Julius Caesar exalted it in Rome after his eastern campaigns. Cucumbers came to the Western Hemisphere with Columbus, who planted them in his experimental gardens in 1493. There are three basic types of cucumbers: the long, thin, smooth variety known as the Oriental (or European) hothouse or greenhouse cucumber; the shorter, thicker, slicing cucumber; and the small round varieties known as "pickling" cucumbers. Oriental cucumbers are smooth-skinned, about a foot in length, and are generally sweeter and more tender than their field-grown cousins. In contrast to the other varieties, they are always cultivated in greenhouses. The slicing cucumbers most often seen are six to nine inches long and have glossy, dark green skin and tapering ends. Pickling varieties are smaller and squatter, with bumpy, light green skins.

Buying Tips

Cucumbers should be firm, fresh, bright, well shaped, of medium or dark green color, with small immature seeds. Withered or shriveled specimens should be avoided. Store cucumbers in the refrigerator and use within a few days.

Culinary Uses

Cucumbers often come to market waxed to slow the rate of spoilage and so should be peeled. Generally eaten raw as part of a salad, they may also be served thinly sliced for a delightful summer dish. Some might prefer them lightly cooked, as they are served in the East. Over 70 percent of the U.S. cucumber crop is used to make pickles.

Health Benefits

pH 5.12–5.78. Pickled 3.20–4.60. Diuretic, laxative. Cucumbers are an alkaline, nonstarchy, cooling vegetable, rich in minerals that neutralize blood acidosis. It has been said that the lowly cucumber is the best natural diuretic known, facilitating excretion of wastes through the kidneys so that they need not be purged through the skin and helping dissolve uric acid accumulations such as kidney and bladder stones. Among other enzymes, the cucumber contains erepsin, an enzyme that helps to digest proteins, and thus it is beneficial as a digestive aid; this property also enables cucumbers to destroy worms, especially tapeworms. Its potassium content makes the cucumber highly useful for conditions of both high and low blood pressure. It is a superior source of silicon, which is integral for calcium absorption and a nutrient that is generally lacking in the modern diet. Although slightly bitter, cucumber skins are rich in silicon and chlorophyll, and they also contain the predominant share of the cucumber's nutrients, including all of its vitamin A.

Cucumber / Nutritional Value Per 100 g Edible Portion			
	Raw		Raw
Calories	13	Copper	0.040 mg
Protein	0.54 g	Manganese	0.061 mg
Fat	0.13 g	Beta Carotene (A)	45 IU
Fiber	0.60 g	Thiamine (B$_1$)	0.030 mg
Calcium	14 mg	Riboflavin (B$_2$)	0.020 mg
Iron	0.28 mg	Niacin (B$_3$)	0.300 mg
Magnesium	11 mg	Pantothenic Acid (B$_5$)	0.250 mg
Phosphorus	17 mg	Pyridoxine (B$_6$)	0.052 mg
Potassium	149 mg	Folic Acid (B$_9$)	13.9 mcg
Sodium	2 mg	Ascorbic Acid (C)	4.7 mg
Zinc	0.230 mg	Tocopherol (E)	0.15 mg

Eggplant
(Solanum melongena, var. esculentum)
Also Known As: Aubergine, Guinea Squash

> Gleaming skin; a plump elongated shape: the
> eggplant is a vegetable you'd want
> To caress with your eyes and fingers, even if you
> didn't know its luscious flavor.
>
> —ROGER VERGÉ

> How can people say they don't eat eggplant when
> God loves the color and the French love the name?
> I don't understand.
>
> —JEFF SMITH, THE FRUGAL GOURMET

The name *Solanum melongena*, which means "soothing mad apple," is a result of the eggplant's unwarranted reputation for inducing instant insanity in the unwary eater. According to available records, the early types of eggplant had small ovoid white fruits resembling eggs, which accounts for its English name.

General Information

Botanists believe the original eggplant blossomed somewhere in south-central Asia—possibly India—where its peculiar-looking fruits, bitter taste, and nasty thorns did little to recommend it. Nonetheless, some hardy soul eventually domesticated it, and by the third century A.D. the Chinese were gingerly debating its dietary potential. Reaching Europe in the twelfth century by way of Arab merchant caravans, the eggplant was eventually introduced to the United States by Thomas Jefferson, who experimented with the seeds and cuttings of many foreign plants. Until the twentieth century, Americans valued the eggplant more as an ornament or table decoration than as a flavorful, versatile food. This was a result in part of its reputation in Europe, where eating it was suspected to cause madness, not to mention leprosy, cancer, and bad breath. The large berries vary in shape from round to oblong and in color from white to purple, with some even striped. The most common eggplant variety sold in the United States is large and purple with a shiny, patent-leather-like skin, developed because it showed bruise marks less and grew to a larger size. Increasingly, you will find other varieties, including miniature eggplants, that come in a range of shapes and colors. These small eggplants are generally sweeter and more tender than their larger counterparts; they also have thinner skins and contain fewer seeds.

Buying Tips

Look for a well-rounded, symmetrical eggplant with a satin-smooth, uniformly colored skin; tan patches, scars, or bruises on the skin indicate decay, which will appear as discolorations in the flesh beneath. Any with wrinkled or flabby-looking skin will probably be bitter. Those that are light for their size have fewer seeds. A mature eggplant may be as long as twelve inches or as small as two inches; medium-sized specimens, three to six inches in diameter, are likely to be young, sweet, and tender, while oversized specimens may be tough, seedy, and bitter. Store eggplant whole in a cool room or in the refrigerator, where it will keep for about a week.

Culinary Uses

Eggplants have such a pleasing color and shape that they are almost as enjoyable just to look at as they are to eat.

Eggplant / Nutritional Value Per 100 g Edible Portion		
	Raw	Cooked
Calories	26	28
Protein	1.10 g	0.83 g
Fat	0.10 g	0.23 g
Fiber	1.00 g	0.97 g
Calcium	36 mg	6 mg
Iron	0.55 mg	0.35 mg
Magnesium	11 mg	13 mg
Phosphorus	33 mg	22 mg
Potassium	219 mg	248 mg
Sodium	4 mg	3 mg
Zinc	0.150 mg	0.150 mg
Copper	0.112 mg	0.108 mg
Manganese	0.140 mg	0.136 mg
Beta Carotene (A)	70 IU	64 IU
Thiamine (B$_1$)	0.090 mg	0.076 mg
Riboflavin (B$_2$)	0.020 mg	0.020 mg
Niacin (B$_3$)	0.600 mg	0.600 mg
Pantothenic Acid (B$_5$)	0.081 mg	0.075 mg
Pyridoxine (B$_6$)	0.094 mg	0.086 mg
Folic Acid (B$_9$)	17.6 mcg	14.4 mcg
Ascorbic Acid (C)	1.6 mg	1.3 mg
Tocopherol (E)	0.03 mg	n/a

LORE AND LEGEND

At about the same time that Gerard was lamenting the eggplant's aphrodisiac effect in England, the concubine Rada-Hera was concocting the most famous of aphrodisiac eggplant dishes for her husband, the legendary Turkish bey Mustaph Mehere—the same who weighed 400 pounds and took 170 wives and innumerable concubines over his 123-year life span (1488–1611). Rada-Hera (his second wife) made the dish so well that she was the only wife he never discarded, mainly because she kept the recipe secret and Mustaph believed that the purée was the key to his virility and longevity. So while all Mustaph's other wives were discarded when they turned twenty, Rada-Hera had free run of the palace until she died a natural death in 1571.

Astonishingly adaptable, they can be fried, boiled, baked, stuffed, or sautéed; they are excellent served individually as a main dish, as an appetizer, or as part of a larger cast of ingredients. The beautiful skin is edible and does not need to be removed. A traditional substitute for meat in Middle Eastern cooking, they are quite spongy and soak up whatever oils or juices they are cooked in. Eggplant is used for a number of national dishes, including Turkey's *imam biyaldi*, eggplant simmered in olive oil for several hours; France's ratatouille, a stew of onions, garlic, zucchini, spices, and chopped eggplant; and Italy's *caponata*, pickled eggplant.

Health Benefits

pH 4.75–5.50. Since eggplant is more than 90 percent water, it is low in calories. It helps clear stagnant blood by dissolving the congealed blood and accumulations such as tumors, and it has a hemostatic action (reduces bleeding). Eggplant is a rich source of bioflavonoids, which renew arteries and prevent strokes and other hemorrhages. As it has a soothing and stabilizing effect on the nervous system and a protective action on arteries damaged by cholesterol, and it even helps to prevent certain cancers, eggplant has a strong future. However, eggplant is part of the nightshade family (see introduction).

Fennel

(Foeniculum vulgaris)
Also Known As: Finocchio

Foeniculum is the diminutive of the Latin word for "hay," referencing in part to this plant's smell; *vulgare* means "common." The English word *fennel* is derived from its Latin name.

General Information

Fennel is apparently a native of southern Europe, but it has been naturalized in many places around the world. A member of the parsley family prized for its mild licorice flavor, and particularly valued by the Italians and French, fennel is slowly gaining a wider appreciation in the United States. There are three kinds of edible fennel: one is an herb and two are vegetables. Common fennel (*F. vulgaris*) is grown for its seeds and leaves, which are used to flavor soups and fish sauces (see the reference in the **Herbs, Spices, and Other Foods** section); Sicilian fennel (*F. vulgaris azoricum*) is grown in southern Italy for its tender young stems, which are eaten like celery or asparagus; Florence fennel or finocchio (*F. vulgaris dulce*) is cultivated for its very thick basal leaf stalks. The plant resembles a plump celery plant, except that its leaves are finer and more feathery, like dill; its three swollen leaf bases overlap to form a sort of false bulb. If you attempt to grow the bulb fennel in your garden, it quickly turns into the herb fennel. The bulb has to be harvested very early in its growth, with the stalks not more than a foot high. It is the expanding leaf stems that make up the bulb, and once they grow aboveground very far there is no bulb left to speak of.

Fennel / Nutritional Value Per 100 g Edible Portion			
	Raw Bulb		Raw Bulb
Calories	31	Copper	0.066 mg
Protein	1.24 g	Manganese	0.191 mg
Fat	0.20 g	Beta Carotene (A)	n/a
Fiber	n/a	Thiamine (B$_1$)	0.010 mg
Calcium	49 mg	Riboflavin (B$_2$)	0.032 mg
Iron	n/a	Niacin (B$_3$)	0.640 mg
Magnesium	17 mg	Pantothenic Acid (B$_5$)	0.232 mg
Phosphorus	50 mg	Pyridoxine (B$_6$)	0.047 mg
Potassium	414 mg	Folic Acid (B$_9$)	27.0 mcg
Sodium	52 mg	Ascorbic Acid (C)	12.0 mg
Zinc	0.200 mg		

Buying Tips

Choose Florence fennel bulbs that are 2½ to 3 inches in diameter; beyond that they become tough and stringy. Bulbs should be firm and clean, the stalks straight and firm, and the leaves fresh and green; if any flowers are present on the stalks, the bulb is overmature. Avoid any bulbs that show brown spots or signs of splitting.

Culinary Uses

Fennel has a mild, sweet flavor akin to licorice or anise. All parts of it are edible, from the overlapping layers of bulb all the way to the stems and leaves. Once the bulb has been trimmed of its tough outer leaves, it can be sliced whichever way you like—across in rings or downward. The stalks and bulb can be used raw, chopped into salads, or cooked. Sautéing fennel in butter highlights its pleasant taste, and steamed fennel with cream sauce is also excellent. English cooks in centuries past made a cold fennel soup with the sliced stalks, some wine, sugar, ginger, and almonds. The leaves are used as an herb. When juicing fennel, mix it with carrots, apples, pears, or celery to cut down on its licorice-like intensity.

Health Benefits

pH 5.48–6.02. Among herbalists, fennel is viewed in several ways: as an intestinal antispasmodic, for relieving intestinal spasms or cramps; as a carminative, for relieving or expelling gas; as a stomachic, for toning and strengthening the stomach; and as an anodyne, for relieving or soothing pain. Fennel also contains substances known as phytoestrogens, weak plant estrogens, which make it useful in treating many female complaints, especially menopause. It also contains the antioxidant flavonoid quercetin and is therefore anticarcinogenic and of special use for cancer patients following radiation or chemotherapy.

Flower Blossoms and Other Edible Blossoms

General Information

Flower and other edible blossoms invite the eye and delight the heart. Their fragrance and essential oils, which are related to warmth, add a magical warming touch to a meal. Indeed, a blossom's inner temperature is higher than the temperature outside, though sometimes only a microthermometer will show this. Blossoms invite a pause and a deep breath. They uplift the spirit and somehow make the whole meal taste better. The culinary use of flowers dates back thousands of years; the first recorded mention was 140 years before the Christian Era. When choosing flowers, there are several important guidelines that should be followed. First, be sure to use only edible blossoms. Ensure that the flowers selected have been grown without the use of pesticides or other chemical sprays. Flowers from the florist are quite often treated, so those from a reliable source, such as an untreated home garden, are best. If gathering flowers from the garden, pick them early in the day and in dry weather. Rinse quickly under gently running cool water. Do not gather more than one day in advance, as the blossoms wilt quickly. Before using in any preparation, remove the pistils, stamens, and the white part at the base of the petals; this "heel" will impart a bitter flavor to the finished dish.

Culinary Uses

With their delicate flavors and wild colors, flowers add poetry to any meal. Some, like squash or zucchini blossoms, are large enough to be stuffed and cooked, while others simply add their sweet scent and piquant coloring to salads, festive desserts, or platters. Use a salad dressing that is light in vinegar or lemon juice, as a highly acidic dressing will both discolor the petals and overwhelm their subtle flavor. For centuries in Europe, flowers flavored salads, puddings, tarts, custards, liqueurs, and candies. They were eaten raw, pulped, and fried, as well as used in stuffing fowl. The Chinese make tea from many flowers, including jasmine, rose, lotus, peony, narcissus, and marigold. Not all flowers are edible, though, and those that are must be acquired from safe sources so as to avoid pesticides, herbicides, and other toxic chemicals.

Health Benefits

Blossoms, often the brightest and most striking part of the plant, convey the most energy. To sensitive individuals, blossoms may cause allergic reactions. Moreover, some are poisonous. Do not eat Oriental lilies, lily of the valley, sweet pea, or any of the narcissus family (daffodils, narcissus, paper-whites, and jonquils).

VARIETIES

Flower blossoms that are edible include the following: borage, calendula, carnation, chrysanthemum, daisy, daylily, fuchsia, geranium (scented), gladiolus, hibiscus,

LORE AND LEGEND

With their wild beauty and connection with the mysteries of reproduction, flowers were often associated with magic, sorcery, and witchcraft. One popular brew of flowers in the Middle Ages was said to enable one to see fairies.

hollyhock, honeysuckle, lavender, lilac, lobelia, marigold (some varieties are very bitter, so beware), nasturtium, pansy, rose, Scotch broom, sweet pea, and violet. Nasturtium buds or young seedpods are often pickled and used as a substitute for capers, and their tender, young leaves add a peppery flavor to salad. Only the flowers are edible on sweet peas; the pods are poisonous. Avoid flowers from bulbs, as some may be toxic (such as daffodils and tulips).

Fruit blossoms are almost too precious to eat, but if there is an abundance, then indulge in some. All edible fruits have edible blossoms; apple, peach, plum, orange, and lemon are all fragrant and delicately flavored. Cherry and strawberry blossoms are a special delicacy.

Herb blossoms include bee balm, borage, calendula, chamomile, chive, dandelion, dill, garlic, marjoram, mint, mustard flowers, oregano, rosemary, savory, tarragon, and thyme.

Vegetable blossoms for the table include all those from the cabbage, bean, and gourd families, including arugula, bean, chicory, cucumber, pea, and squash. Blossoms can be picked from any squash, winter or summer variety, but zucchini plants produce particularly luxuriant blooms.

Glasswort

(Salicornia europea, S. herbacea)
Also Known As: Marsh Samphire, Saltwort, Sea Asparagus, Sea Bean, Sea Pickle

Salicornia is from the Latin words for *salt* and *horn*, since these are saline plants with hornlike branches. *Europea* means "European," while *herbacea* means "herbaceous" or "not woody." Because this vegetable grows in cliff crevices, the French called it *Saint-Pierre* for Saint Peter, the rock upon which Christ built his church. Along the way the name became *sampyre* and then *samphire* (a name shared by an old-fashioned parsley relative that also grows in rocky places). The name *glasswort* comes from a related plant, *S. stricta*, which was used in glass manufacturing. Glasswort belongs to the branch of the Chenopodiaceae that contains plants that are particularly rich in soda, such as *Salsola kali* and Spanish *sativa*, among others, which were used in the process of making both soap and glass. There was a thriving trade from the Mediterranean, sending the ashes of these plants, called barilla, to northern Europe for the production of glass.

General Information

Jointed like green coral polished smooth and shiny by the sea, glasswort is a mild seashore succulent that grows profusely on mudflats below the high-tide line. The plant grows about sixteen inches high and looks like a leafless, skinny, branching succulent. Its leaves are like scales, which give the branches a bumpy look. Resembling baby aloe, glasswort is sold by fishmongers from spring through early summer and is at its prime in May, when the shoots are large enough to have some substance but before the central core begins to get woody. By fall the plant turns orange-red.

Buying Tips

Select plants that are firm and bright, not flabby or slimy. No soft or discolored spots should be evident. When foraging, harvest the plant tips from late spring until early summer. The mature plant has a fibrous center, which you may eat around, but glasswort is superior when younger.

Culinary Uses

Glasswort is very crunchy and salty, like brined baby string beans. When young, it is crisp, pleasantly deep-sea tasting, an unusual summer pleasure that grows in abundance along the Atlantic and Pacific coasts. Use it raw as a trail nibble or an attractive garnish, or pickle it, a favorite historical use. Toss it into salads, fresh, for a saline crunch. Slightly older plants need to be steamed or boiled briefly for only a few minutes. To prepare, rinse thoroughly and trim off any damaged parts and the woody base. Eat like asparagus with melted butter, or chill to combine with vegetables, seafood, or meat in a composed salad. Glasswort has a natural affinity with fish and does well when prepared jointly. A whole bass surrounded by a bed of glasswort is said to be a sight that inspires rapture.

Good King Henry
(Chenopodium bonus-henricus)
Also Known As: Wild Spinach, Lincolnshire Asparagus, Fat Hen

Chenopodium is a Greek word meaning "goosefoot" and alludes to the shape of the leaves; *bonus-henricus* simply means "good Henry." The English name *Good King Henry* is only vaguely related to King Henry VII of England; in fact, the original German had nothing to do with a monarch at all. The plant got its name from Tudor herbalists who translated the German *Guter Heinrich* (good Henry), which was used to distinguish it from *Boser Heinrich* (bad Henry), a poisonous plant (*Mercurialis perennis*) that it resembles. Delighted with the title "good Henry," these herbalists decided that a little royal flattery might not be a bad thing.

General Information
Once widely cultivated in European and American gardens, this British native is now rarely seen. A member of the goosefoot family, it is a coarse, many-branched plant that grows to a height of about two feet and has leaves that are smooth, arrowhead-shaped, and dark green with purplish centers.

Culinary Uses
Cut the young stalks as they appear in early spring; they need no further preparation other than cleaning before they are cooked in whatever manner is preferred. Older stalks should be peeled to remove the tough outer skin before cooking. The stalks are said to resemble asparagus in flavor and are similarly prepared. Young leaves can be harvested and steamed like spinach or other greens. Older leaves tend to be very bitter.

Health Benefits
The plant's medicinal properties were held in high regard during times past, when it was widely known as "Mercury goosefoot" and "wild Mercury," in honor of the ancient Roman god of medicine. At that time it was esteemed for its blood-purifying and laxative effects, as well as its use for indigestion and to counter anemia.

Heart of Palm
(Euterpe edulis)

The genus *Euterpe* is named after the muse of music and lyric poetry from Greek mythology; *edulis* means "edible."

General Information
A tropical delicacy, palm hearts are the growing tips of palm trees, the cylindrical bundle of leaf bases that may be several inches in diameter and several feet long. Unfortunately, cutting out the heart also completely destroys the tree. Hearts of palm are an important vegetable in Brazil, have spread northward to Florida, and are now becoming popular in the fashionable cuisines of the United States and Europe.

Culinary Uses
Slender, ivory-colored, and delicately flavored, hearts of palm resemble white asparagus, sans tips, and taste something like an artichoke. It is rare to find them fresh outside Brazil, but the canned, marinated varieties are also excellent used as a vegetable or added to salads and appetizers.

Hops
(Humulus lupulus)

Humulus is derived from *humus*—moist earth, the type of soil the plant thrives in; *lupulus* means "small wolf"; apparently, in ancient Rome hops grew wild among willows and, with its aggressive weedlike growth, had an effect on the willows comparable to a wolf among sheep, a propensity Linnaeus alluded to when he gave the plant its scientific name. The common name *hops* is taken from the Anglo-Saxon *hoppen*, meaning "to climb," because the twining perennial plant attaches itself to neighboring objects and grows to a great height.

General Information
Hops will grow anywhere except in desert areas, growing vertically and rampantly. The bracts (modified leaves) and flowers of the female hop plants are used to flavor beer, whether it be commercial or home brew. The edible flowers are small, papery green cones that are harvested in fall. The resemblance of its conelike catkins to a grapevine may have first drawn attention to the hop as a plant suitable for

active principle is lupulin, a glandular powder. The volatile oil is responsible for the peculiar, fragrant odor. Hops has a calming effect on the nervous system. Hops tea is recommended for nervous diarrhea, neuralgia, and restlessness. Hops has been used to help stimulate appetite and to treat flatulence, boils, headaches, toothaches, earaches, pain, intestinal cramps, jaundice, nervous tension and stress, worms, mucous colitis, gonorrhea, ulcers, poor circulation, inflamed rheumatic joints, muscle cramps, neuritis, neuralgia, and shock. It is also used a blood purifier. Combined with valerian (for antispasmodic properties), it is taken for coughs. A cold tea, taken one hour before meals, is particularly good for digestion. Hops also has diuretic properties and can be taken for various problems with water retention and excess uric acid. Externally, a poultice can be used for inflammations, boils, ringworm, tumors, painful swellings, and old ulcers. Hops contains a high amount of estrogen, and as a result too much beer can lead to loss of libido in men.

Horseradish
(Armoracia lapathifolia, A. rusticana)

Armoracia was the Roman name for a wild radish that cannot be identified with certainty as horseradish. The term *rusticana* means "rustic" or "pertaining to the country." The English name *horseradish* was given because of the radish's large size, to distinguish it from the common radish.

General Information
Horseradish is a member of the mustard family and is believed native to Hungary or Russia. Its characteristic hot flavor is produced by mustard oil, which dissipates rapidly after the radish is cut or grated and is thoroughly destroyed by heat. Each root has quite a different shape, but they are generally from six inches to a foot long and from one to three inches in diameter, with several rounded protuberances at one end. Beauty is definitely not this root's strong point; the skin is the color and texture of a scruffy, wrinkled, gnarled parsnip root. It may or may not have a green top.

making beverages. To the ancient Romans the hop was a garden plant: Pliny says the young shoots of hops were eaten as a salad in the spring. Hops gives beer its pleasantly bitter taste, improves its ability to keep well, and imparts certain sedative qualities. Pillows stuffed with hops are a traditional cure for insomnia: King George III and Abraham Lincoln used such pillows in the search for much-needed rest.

Culinary Uses
The conelike flowers are used as a seasoning. Young spring shoots, which look like thin-branched asparagus, are a delicious spring favorite in France. To prepare them for eating, snap off the top six inches of the shoot. The whole tender tip is eaten. Cook and serve as you would asparagus. They are particularly good with a cream sauce.

Health Benefits
Anaphrodisiac, anodyne, anthelmintic, diuretic, febrifuge, hypnotic, nervine, sedative, soporific, stomachic, tonic. The

Buying Tips

Horseradish is available as a whole fresh root, as a dried powder, or in commercial preparations. Look for roots that are exceptionally hard and free of spongy or soft spots; avoid sprouting, greenish-tinged ones, which may have a bitter layer that requires deep paring. The whole root stays fresh in the refrigerator for months; once grated, however, horseradish spoils rapidly.

Culinary Uses

The flavor of horseradish is hot and biting, but with a pungency that is somehow refreshing and cooling. By far the strongest-flavored of cultivated vegetables, horseradish roots are best when raw and freshly grated, as the pungent taste is completely destroyed by cooking. Like good-quality pepper, it should be grated directly onto the food soon before eating, before its volatile flavor dissipates. Add horseradish to vegetables, soups, meats, dressings, anything you want to spice up. This root is most familiar to Westerners in condiment form, which is made by peeling and grinding the roots, then mixing them with vinegar.

Health Benefits

pH 3.56–5.35. Antiscorbutic, antiseptic, diuretic, rubefacient, stimulant. Horseradish has long been famed for its medicinal qualities. It is an excellent solvent of excess mucus in the system and thus is a potent herb for the sinuses and lungs, opening up sinus passages and increasing circulation there. If you're troubled with respiratory disorders such as sinusitis or allergies, a pinch of horseradish may swiftly cleanse the debris and waste from your respiratory system and help you breathe better. Horseradish also stimulates the appetite and aids in the secretion of digestive juices, but if taken in excess it may be irritating to the kidneys and bladder. Applied as a poultice, the mustard oil (allylisothiocyanate) in horseradish irritates the skin and causes the small blood vessels just under the surface to dilate, increasing the flow of blood and making the skin feel warm. An infusion of horseradish in milk makes an excellent cosmetic for the skin and helps restore freshness and color to the cheeks; horseradish juice, mixed with white vinegar and applied externally, is reputed to remove freckles. It is low in fat and high in fiber, sulfur, fluorine, potassium, and vitamin C.

Jicama

(Pachyrhizus erosus, P. tuberosus)
Also Known As: Yam Bean, Sa Kot

Pachyrhizus comes from two Greek words meaning "thick root"; *erosus* means "erose," or jagged, as if gnawed; *tuberosus* means "tuberous." The English name *jicama* is derived from the Nahuatlan Indian *xicama*, meaning "edible storage root."

General Information

Native to Mexico and the headwater region of the Amazon in South America, jicama is the fleshy underground tuber of a leguminous plant. Aboveground this plant is a high-climbing vine with showy flowers and inedible pea pods; below ground the large tuber is top-shaped, with a rough brown skin.

Buying Tips

Always choose jicamas that look firm and unblemished. Smaller roots, up to three pounds in weight, are juicier than the larger ones. Store jicama at room temperature for a few days or refrigerate for up to two weeks. Do not freeze.

Culinary Uses

The jicama's juicy snowy-white interior is crunchy and sweetly bland, tasting like a cross between an apple and pear. Specimens that are heavy-skinned and dryish may be fibrous and starchy instead of sweet—as dull as a raw potato; these are best used in a cooked dish. Jicama could not be easier to prepare, requiring only the peeling of its thinnish, sandy-tan, matte skin. Do not peel jicama until just before it is to be served or eaten, because this vegetable tends to dry out and become hard and fibrous once cut. Its relatively bland taste makes it suitable for almost every type of dish, from salads and fruit medleys to stir-fries. Jicama may be eaten as you would Jerusalem artichokes or potatoes, and although its flavor diminishes with cooking, it doesn't lose its crunch. The Chinese use it as they do water chestnuts, in stir-fries, because of its similar taste and texture. Delicious when served raw in salads or when added to soups or stews for an extra-crispy texture, jicama can even be baked like a potato or grated and used as a pie filling. A popular Latin American preparation is to season raw slices with lime juice, salt, and chili pepper to taste.

Health Benefits

Low in fat and high in fiber, potassium, iron, calcium, and vitamins A, B complex, and C.

Jinengo

(Dioscorea pentaphylla)

Also Known As: Mountain Yam, Wild Yam, Dioscorea, Long Potato, Yamaima

> This family of plants was given the genus name *Dioscorea* in honor of Dioscorides, a Greek naturalist of the first or second century A.D.; *pentaphylla* means "five-leaved."

General Information

This buff-colored tuber is slightly hairy and grows to lengths of three feet. Native Americans and Asians value this wild mountain yam both as a food and for its medicinal properties.

Buying Tips

You will find jinengo root stored in sawdust in Asian markets. Break off as large a section as you wish to purchase. Refrigerate it. Although the cut ends become discolored, the jinengo will keep for a week or more. Purchased jinengo dried for use in medicinal teas.

Culinary Uses

Grated raw jinengo is one of the most gooey substances imaginable; because of this mucilaginous quality, it is often used as a binder to hold other ingredients together, but it loses this quality when cooked. Jinengo may be cooked like potato chips or potato patties.

Health Benefits

Add tamari to grated raw jinengo and you have a digestive aid highly esteemed in Japanese and macrobiotic cuisines, containing even more of the starch-digesting enzyme diastase than does daikon. Jinengo also contains allantoin, which is beneficial for stomach ulcers and asthma. Sweet tasting and warming, jinengo contains hormone precursors that affect the female menstrual cycle and help to reduce pain. In fact, jinengo extract was the original source for diosgenin in birth control pills (today it is synthesized). It yields the anti-inflammatory steroid cortisone, which treats rheumatism. It strengthens the lungs, spleen, pancreas, and kidneys, increases stamina, rejuvenates and supports the liver and gallbladder, and is used for treatment of various digestive disorders.

Kale

(Brassica oleracea var. acephala)

> The Latin name *Brassica* derives from the Celtic *bresic*; *oleracea* refers to a vegetable garden herb that is used in cooking. The distinctive part of kale's scientific name is *acephala*, meaning "headless," which separates it (and collards, a noncurly sibling) from the rest of the cabbage brood. The Latin word *caulis*, meaning "stem" or "cabbage," is the root of the English name *kale*.

General Information

Kale is native either to the eastern Mediterranean region or to Asia Minor. It is believed to have been introduced to North America by Benjamin Franklin when he returned from a visit to Scotland. Two centuries later, most people know kale only as a garnish with as much gustatory appeal as the dusty little trees on model train layouts. A botanically primitive, "headless" member of the cabbage family, kale appears in today's gardens in much the same form as it did several thousand years ago. Perhaps kale has changed so little over time simply because horticultural fiddling

Jinengo / Nutritional Value Per 100 g Edible Portion		
	Raw	Cooked
Calories	67	82
Protein	1.34 g	1.73 g
Fat	0.10 g	0.08 g
Fiber	0.45 g	0.56 g
Calcium	26 mg	8 mg
Iron	0.44 mg	0.43 mg
Magnesium	12 mg	10 mg
Phosphorus	34 mg	40 mg
Potassium	418 mg	495 mg
Sodium	13 mg	12 mg
Beta Carotene (A)	0 IU	0 IU
Thiamine (B$_1$)	0.102 mg	0.086 mg
Riboflavin (B$_2$)	0.019 mg	0.014 mg
Niacin (B$_3$)	0.481 mg	0.130 mg
Ascorbic Acid (C)	2.6 mg	0 mg

seemed unnecessary. In addition to being among the most vigorous, prolific, and easy-to-grow vegetables, this uncomplicated plant is resistant to cold, is simple to harvest, store, and prepare, and is rich in vitamins and minerals. There are two common varieties: Scotch kale has curly, bright green to greenish-yellow leaves; blue kale has deep green to bluish leaves that are plumelike with frilled edges. The flowering variety is also edible but is not generally as tender and serves better in an ornamental role. Kale supplies fresh greens throughout the year; frost only heightens the flavor by releasing its high sugar content.

Buying Tips

Select small, deep-colored bunches with clean, slightly moist leaves. The more crinkled the leaves, the better the taste, with the younger plants being the most tender. Store kale in a plastic bag and refrigerate, using as soon as possible.

Culinary Uses

Kale has a cabbagelike flavor, with a sharpness that some people dislike. During the winter months, the leaves are at their most flavorful and tender. As versatile as cabbage or spinach, baby kale can be part of a green salad (in moderation, as it is strong tasting and chewy). The leaves, whole or cut into strips, can also be cooked: steamed for a few minutes; stir-fried with ginger and garlic; or sautéed with butter and oil, plus garlic, onion, caraway, or fennel to your liking. In the spring the young shoots may be gathered; they have a more delicate flavor than the leaves, with a taste that suggests hazelnuts.

Health Benefits

pH 6.36–6.80 (cooked). Kale is valuable as an internal body cleanser but has a tendency to generate flatulence when the body is overly acidic. It is also beneficial for the digestive and nervous systems, builds up the calcium content of the body, and is one of the cancer-preventive foods. Kale contains the nutraceuticals lutein and zeaxanthin, which protect the eyes from macular degeneration, and indole-3-carbinol, which may protect against colon cancer. All *Brassica* genus vegetables contain dithiolthiones, a group of compounds that have anticancer, antioxidant properties; indoles, substances that protect against breast and colon cancer; and sulfur, which has antibiotic and antiviral characteristics. This family of vegetables also mildly stimulates the liver and other tissues out of stagnancy.

Kale / Nutritional Value Per 100 g Edible Portion				
	Blue Raw	Blue Cooked	Scotch Raw	Scotch Cooked
Calories	50	32	42	28
Protein	3.30 g	1.90 g	2.80 g	1.90 g
Fat	0.70 g	0.40 g	0.60 g	0.41 g
Fiber	1.50 g	0.80 g	1.23 g	0.85 g
Calcium	135 mg	72 mg	205 mg	132 mg
Iron	1.70 mg	0.90 mg	3.00 mg	1.93 mg
Magnesium	34 mg	18 mg	88 mg	57 mg
Phosphorus	56 mg	28 mg	62 mg	38 mg
Potassium	447 mg	228 mg	450 mg	274 mg
Sodium	43 mg	23 mg	70 mg	45 mg
Zinc	0.440 mg	0.240 mg	0.370 mg	0.240 mg
Copper	0.290 mg	0.156 mg	0.243 mg	0.156 mg
Manganese	0.774 mg	0.416 mg	0.648 mg	0.417 mg
Beta Carotene (A)	8,900 IU	7,400 IU	3,100 IU	1,994 IU
Thiamine (B$_1$)	0.110 mg	0.053 mg	0.070 mg	0.040 mg
Riboflavin (B$_2$)	0.130 mg	0.070 mg	0.060 mg	0.039 mg
Niacin (B$_3$)	1.000 mg	0.500 mg	1.300 mg	0.792 mg
Pantothenic Acid (B$_5$)	0.091 mg	0.049 mg	0.076 mg	0.048 mg
Pyridoxine (B$_6$)	0.271 mg	0.138 mg	0.227 mg	0.139 mg
Folic Acid (B$_9$)	29.3 mcg	13.3 mcg	n/a	13.3 mcg
Ascorbic Acid (C)	120.0 mg	41.0 mg	130.0 mg	52.8 mg

VARIETIES

Dinosaur, Italian, or **Tuscan** is an old variety with narrow, almost black-green, savoylike leaves and a sweet, mild flavor.

Lacinato is an heirloom variety. The hue and contours of its leaves set it apart, as does its chewy texture. Lacinato is tolerant of weather extremes.

Ornamental grows like a flat bouquet of ruffled-edged violet and cream leaves; it is more dramatic than many flowers. Not as flavorful as the more modest varieties, however, it is most typically used as a garnish or as a border along a flower bed.

Red Russian did indeed originate in Russia and traveled through Canada to the United States. Along the way it picked up the alternative names **Canadian broccoli** and **Ragged Jack.** The flavor is noticeably sweet even before frosts nip the plants. Red ribs contrast nicely with the cool grayish blue-green of the leaves—Red Russian looks like a photograph that is badly (or wonderfully) in need of color correction. Young leaves add interest to mesclun mixes and other salads.

Scotch or **curly kale** is dark green or even blue-green with very curly leaves.

Verdura, compact and tender, comes from the Netherlands. It is especially sweet and can be harvested through the fall.

White Russian is a variety of Red Russian that offers less color but is especially mild and has less trouble with cold weather.

Kohlrabi

(Brassica oleracea gongylodes caulorapa)

The Latin name *Brassica* derives from the Celtic *bresic*; *oleracea* refers to a vegetable garden herb that is used in cooking. The term *gongylodes* means "roundish" or "swollen" while *caulorapa* means "stem-turnip." The English name *kohlrabi* is derived from the Latin words *caulis*, meaning "stem," and rapa, meaning "turnip."

General Information

The odd-looking kohlrabi is native to northern Europe, another member of the large cabbage family. Instead of a head of closely packed leaves, this cabbage mutant has a globular swelling of the stem just above the ground, either green or purple, some three or four inches in diameter. Our parochialism about edibles and ornamentals keeps us from appreciating the colors, shapes, textures, and sheer scale of kohlrabi. True, when short of leaves it is the uncontested oddball of the produce department. But in the garden, kohlrabi's mantle of waxy leaves gives it a grace all its own. The purple variety is particularly stunning, and at certain times of day it seems to glow with an inner light.

Buying Tips

The condition of the tops is a good indication of quality; tops should be young and green, and the thickened stem firm and crisp, with the smaller ones milder and sweeter. Kohlrabi keeps for a time in the refrigerator but otherwise may quickly lose its crispness after harvest, and crispness is key to enjoying it raw, as a crudité or in salads.

Culinary Uses

Kohlrabi has a crisp texture and tangy, turniplike taste, but it is sweeter, juicier, crisper, and more delicate than any turnip. Some compare it to fresh water chestnuts with a slight touch of radish and celeriac. Kohlrabi is eaten either raw or cooked. It can be sliced, grated, or julienned. In salads it provides a taste reminiscent of radishes. Cooked in any manner—blanched, steamed, boiled, braised, or sautéed—it tastes more like turnips or mild cabbage. Kohlrabi, unlike cabbage, does not become sulfurous with long cooking. The leaves, when young, are similar in flavor to kale or collards.

Health Benefits

pH 5.72–5.82. Kohlrabi is an excellent blood and kidney cleanser, helping to clear poor complexions resulting from toxemia, and is also good for the skeletal, digestive, and lymphatic systems. It helps stabilize blood sugar imbalances and is used for hypoglycemia and diabetes. All *Brassica* genus vegetables contain dithiolthiones, a group of compounds that have anticancer, antioxidant properties; indoles, substances that protect against breast and colon cancer; and sulfur, which has antibiotic and antiviral characteristics. This family of vegetables also mildly stimulates the liver and other tissues out of stagnancy.

Kohlrabi / Nutritional Value Per 100 g Edible Portion		
	Raw	Cooked
Calories	27	29
Protein	1.70 g	1.80 g
Fat	0.10 g	0.11 g
Fiber	1.00 g	1.10 g
Calcium	24 mg	25 mg
Iron	0.40 mg	0.40 mg
Magnesium	19 mg	19 mg
Phosphorus	46 mg	45 mg
Potassium	350 mg	340 mg
Sodium	20 mg	21 mg
Beta Carotene (A)	36 IU	35 IU
Thiamine (B$_1$)	0.050 mg	0.040 mg
Riboflavin (B$_2$)	0.020 mg	0.020 mg
Niacin (B$_3$)	0.400 mg	0.390 mg
Pantothenic Acid (B$_5$)	0.165 mg	n/a
Pyridoxine (B$_6$)	0.150 mg	n/a
Ascorbic Acid (C)	62.0 mg	54.0 mg

Lettuce and Other Salad Greens
(Lactuca sativa)

> Lettuce is like conversation: it must be fresh and crisp, and so sparkling that you scarcely notice the bitter in it.

> —CHARLES DUDLEY WARNER

The botanical name *Lactuca* is derived from the Latin word *lac*, meaning "milk," and refers to the plant's milky, mildly soporific juice. *Sativa* indicates that this plant has long been cultivated. The English name *lettuce* is a derivative of the Latin.

General Information
Wild lettuce originated along the Mediterranean littoral and was known as an edible green throughout antiquity. Belonging to the plant family that includes daisies and thistles, lettuce in its primitive forms had long stems and large leaves. It appeared in Greek and Roman gardens five hundred years before the start of the Christian Era but was considered a luxury and reserved for feast days and the tables of the wealthy. Brought into common favor by Antonius Musa, physician to the Emperor Augustus, lettuce was prescribed as a health-giving food; before that, it was usually eaten as a dessert. Emperor Domitian invented salad dressing, and lettuce quickly became an hors d'oeuvre. Horace later relates that no proper patrician feast began without a salad of lettuce and radishes to stimulate the appetite and "to relax the alimentary canal," preparing the body for a surfeit of food. Columbus brought lettuce to America in 1493; a quick crop, it was favored by greens-hungry early explorers. Sometime during the sixteenth century, close-packed heads of lettuce were developed, with loose-headed ones appearing about a century later. Under the domineering aegis of Louis XIV, who liked his lettuce seasoned with tarragon, pimpernel, basil, and violets, the seventeenth-century French popularized the lettuce salad. There are five general types of common lettuce:

Lettuce & Salad Greens / Nutritional Value Per 100 g Edible Portion

	Arugula	Belgian Endive	Bibb and Boston	Celtuce	Curly Leaf Endive	Escarole	Iceberg
Calories	25	15	13	22	17	20	13
Protein	2.58 g	1.00 g	1.29 g	0.85 g	1.25 g	1.70 g	1.01 g
Fat	0.66 g	0.10 g	0.22 g	0.30 g	0.20 g	0.10 g	0.19 g
Fiber	n/a	n/a	n/a	0.40 g	0.90 g	0.90 g	0.53 g
Calcium	160 mg	n/a	n/a	39 mg	52 mg	81 mg	19 mg
Iron	n/a	0.50 mg	0.30 mg	0.55 mg	0.83 mg	1.70 mg	0.50 mg
Magnesium	47 mg	13 mg	n/a	28 mg	15 mg	n/a	9 mg
Phosphorus	52 mg	21 mg	n/a	39 mg	28 mg	54 mg	20 mg
Potassium	369 mg	182 mg	257 mg	330 mg	314 mg	294 mg	158 mg
Sodium	27 mg	7 mg	5 mg	11 mg	22 mg	14 mg	9 mg
Zinc	0.470 mg	n/a	0.170 mg	n/a	0.790 mg	n/a	0.220 mg
Copper	0.076 mg	n/a	0.023 mg	n/a	0.099 mg	n/a	0.028 mg
Manganese	0.321 mg	n/a	0.133 mg	n/a	0.420 mg	n/a	0.151 mg
Beta Carotene (A)	2,373 IU	0 IU	970 IU	3,500 IU	2,050 IU	3,300 IU	330 IU
Thiamine (B$_1$)	0.044 mg	0.070 mg	0.060 mg	0.055 mg	0.080 mg	0.070 mg	0.046 mg
Riboflavin (B$_2$)	0.086 mg	0.140 mg	0.060 mg	0.070 mg	0.075 mg	0.140 mg	0.030 mg
Niacin (B$_3$)	0.305 mg	0.500 mg	0.300 mg	0.550 mg	0.400 mg	0.500 mg	0.187 mg
Pantothenic Acid (B$_5$)	0.437 mg	n/a	n/a	n/a	0.900 mg	n/a	0.046 mg
Pyridoxine (B$_6$)	0.073 mg	0.045 mg	n/a	n/a	0.020 mg	n/a	0.040 mg
Folic Acid (B$_9$)	97 mcg	n/a	73.3 mcg	n/a	142.0 mcg	n/a	56.0 mcg
Ascorbic Acid (C)	n/a	10.0 mg	8.0 mg	19.5 mg	6.5 mg	10.0 mg	3.9 mg
Tocopherol (E)	n/a	n/a	n/a	n/a	n/a	n/a	0.40 mg

crisphead (iceberg), butterhead (Boston, Bibb), cos (romaine), leaf (bunching), and stem. Mesclun—a mix of tender young lettuces, herbs, and sometimes edible blossoms—commonly includes butterhead lettuce, loose-leaf lettuce, chicory, red romaine, cress, and frisée.

Buying Tips

Make sure all salad greens are fresh and crisp, not wilted; if a headed variety, the head should be fairly firm to hard. Rust-colored spots, though not aesthetically pleasing, are harmless—they are caused by wide fluctuations in temperature during the growing process. Loose outer leaves, called "wrapper leaves," are usually the most nutritious. Unless damaged, they should not be trimmed off. To store lettuce, wash and pat dry before storing in a plastic bag in the refrigerator; use within a few days.

Culinary Uses

The flavor of lettuce ranges from mild and watery to sharply pungent. Its most common use is as a salad ingredient. For extra crispness and crunchiness, place your completed salad in the freezer for a few minutes before serving. Lettuce is compatible with all fruits and vegetables and has only about 70 calories per head, so don't be shy when building your salads.

Health Benefits

pH 5.05–6.15 (mixed greens). Anodyne, antispasmodic, expectorant, sedative. Lettuce of every variety is among humankind's most valuable healing foods because of its large organic water content, ranging from 92 to 95 percent. Nearly all the necessary vitamins are found in lettuce, with the outer leaves being the most valuable. A good rule of thumb is that the greener and darker the leaf, the more nutritious it is. Of all common vegetables lettuce contains the most silicon, a nutrient that helps renew joints, bones, arteries, and all connective tissues. The plant is at its medicinal best when it has bolted to seed; at that point it contains a milky juice whose sedative, narcotic, and anesthetic qualities are well recognized. It contains the sedative lactucarium, which relaxes the nerves, and is a superior source of magnesium, which contributes to its soothing properties. Lettuce helps cure insomnia and nightmares and can allay excessive physical desire. An old name for it is "the herb of eunuchs," yet in one of those paradoxes of nature, lettuce is also the plant of fertility, since it is exceptionally rich in vitamin E, a key element in the reproductive process.

VARIETIES

Arugula (*Eruca vesicaria sativa*), also known as **rucola** and **rocket,** is a Mediterranean-region type of lettuce that grows so plentifully in the wild that it was not cultivated until recently. Its common name is derived from the Latin *eruca*, which denotes a downy stem like a caterpillar. There is no doubt that the ancient world considered arugula to possess aphrodisiac properties; it was sown around the base of statues consecrated to Priapus and believed to restore vigor to the genitalia. The early Christian church knew of its supposed erotic properties and frowned upon its use and cultivation. Numerous writers spoke of its "hotness and lechery," and at one point the church went so far as to ban its cultivation in monastic gardens. The serrated leaves are attractive, between oak-leaf lettuce and dandelion in shape, and have an appealing but sharp flavor and an

Loose-Leaf	Mâche	Radicchio	Romaine
18	21	23	16
1.30 g	2.00 g	1.43 g	1.62 g
0.30 g	0.40 g	0.25 g	0.20 g
0.70 g	0.80 g	n/a	0.70 g
68 mg	n/a	19 mg	36 mg
1.40 mg	n/a	n/a	1.10 mg
11 mg	n/a	13 mg	6 mg
25 mg	n/a	40 mg	45 mg
264 mg	n/a	302 mg	290 mg
9 mg	n/a	22 mg	8 mg
n/a	n/a	0.620 mg	n/a
n/a	n/a	0.341 mg	n/a
n/a	n/a	0.138 mg	n/a
1,900 IU	n/a	27 IU	2,600 IU
0.050 mg	n/a	0.016 mg	0.100 mg
0.080 mg	n/a	0.028 mg	0.100 mg
0.400 mg	n/a	0.255 mg	0.500 mg
0.200 mg	n/a	0.269 mg	n/a
0.055 mg	n/a	0.057 mg	n/a
n/a	n/a	60.0 mcg	135.7 mcg
18.0 mg	n/a	8.0 mg	24.0 mg
n/a	n/a	n/a	n/a

LORE AND LEGEND

Because the "milk" in lettuce was believed to possess aphrodisiac qualities, the Egyptian fertility god Min had lettuce offered to him. Early Greek fertility festivals (seventh century B.C.) were known as Adonis festivals, and quick-growing lettuce was planted in pots and carried to symbolize the transitory quality of life. These potted plants, called the Gardens of Adonis, were possibly the beginnings of the custom of raising plants in pots around the house. In central Europe lettuce was looked upon as the zealously guarded property of the devil, but his demons lurked in the lettuce beds only during the day; at night, when the demons were off on their nefarious business, however, witches were likely to be abroad. Only from dawn to sunrise were the beds left unguarded, and the peasants were very careful to gather the lettuce at that time and no other.

aroma that is earthy, peppery, and mustardlike. Like watercress, it is more than a leafy green but less than a strong herb. Favored as a salad herb in Italy, Greece, and France, it is best used when the leaves are no more than three inches long and then only as a seasoning herb.

Belgian or **French endive** (*Cichorium* spp.), a member of the chicory family, is really witloof (whiteleaf) chicory. The first Belgian endives were grown by accident in the nineteenth century when some chicory roots that had been left in a dark spot began to sprout. A Brussels horticulturist then set to work developing the vegetable in earnest. Later, when a shipment of cultivated endives sent to Paris became a hit, the Belgian endive industry was launched. Looking like small, tightly wrapped, white-husked ears of corn, or perhaps like a fat cigar, these little plants have a distinctive, pleasantly bitter taste. The fresh leaves are smooth and waxlike and add an appealing pungency and crispness to salads. Cooked whole, Belgian endives have a tenderness and succulence all their own. While they have even fewer vitamins and minerals than iceberg lettuce, they do have more flavor. The supply and quality are best between September through April.

Bibb and **Boston** lettuce are two of the more common types of butterhead lettuce. Bibb lettuce was named after Major John Bibb, its developer. It is a small cup-shaped lettuce, with leaves similar to the petals of a rose. The tender leaves are a deep, rich green, blending to a whitish green toward the core. This lettuce has a distinct crispness and flavor—delicate, mild, and sweet. It is considered the choicest member of the lettuce family and is also the most expensive. Boston lettuce is a little larger than a softball, loosely headed, with leaves that have an oily feeling. The outer leaves are a deep dark green, while the inner leaves shade almost to white along the stalk. Not especially crisp, the leaves are sweet and soft and become increasingly so as you reach the heart.

Celtuce (*Lactuca sativa asparagina*), also known as **asparagus lettuce** or **stem lettuce,** is a native of China. In 1938 a missionary from western China, close to the Tibetan border, sent a few seeds of a vegetable eaten there to an American seed company. This plant, given the English name *celtuce* because it looks like a cross between celery and lettuce, is now grown in the United States to some extent. Celtuce produces light green leaves in the shape of a rosette; these are comparable in taste and texture to romaine or cos lettuce rather than to the more delicate kinds of leaf lettuce. Older leaves contain a milky sap that makes the leaves too bitter even for those who fancy bitter foods. As the plant bolts to a seed head, the stalk that bears the leaves elongates and can reach heights of up to five feet. This celery-like stem remains tasty until the flower buds develop. For the tastiest dining, the stem should be harvested when about one inch in diameter at the base. Before eating, peel off the outer skin to get rid of the sap tubes that carry the bitter milky sap. What remains is a soft, cool green core that lies somewhere near cucumber or mild summer squash in flavor. The stalks can be served raw (some prefer them peeled) as a finger food with a dip, or sliced into a salad. Their crispness also makes them a natural choice for stir-frying, or for serving au gratin. The young leaves and heart are eaten like lettuce.

Garden cress (*Lepidium sativum*), also known as **curled cress** and **peppergrass,** is thought to have originated in western Asia and was a popular garden vegetable in ancient Greece. A cool-weather plant, it flourishes in most temperate regions all over the world in clearings, fields, and alongside roads where the soil is somewhat dry. Sometimes crisped like parsley, garden cress has small green leaves and varies greatly from species to species and from habitat to habitat. Growing upright anywhere from eight to twenty-four inches tall, the plant produces white or reddish flowers, followed by tiny, papery pouches containing hot seeds that add a special tang to soups and salad dressings. Garden cress is generally eaten at the seedling stage, when it has a peppery taste and can be used raw in salads and sandwiches. **Winter cress** (*Barbarea verna, B. vulgaris, B. praecox*), also known as **American cress** and **land cress,** is indigenous to America and Europe. This variety was named after Saint Barbara in the belief that eating these greens on that saint's special day (December 4) would bring good luck. Often found growing wild along streams and roadside swamps, the hardy, low-growing winter cress has dark green leaves that form a rosette pattern and look rather like those of watercress, though somewhat thinner and less succulent. It will grow from eight to thirty inches long and sends forth small clusters of edible, bright yellow flowers followed by pointed, 1½- to 2½-inch-long seedpods that supply good birdseed. Winter cress greens taste like watercress when raw but more like mustard greens when cooked.

Curly-leafed endive (*Cichorium endiva crispa*) is often called **chicory** in other countries. Although closely related botanically, these are different plants; the word *endive* is used to designate plants with narrow, finely divided, curly leaves, while chicory is a wild-looking green plant with narrow, raggedy leaves and a bitter taste. Endive has a large, loose head with crisp, narrow white ribs. Slightly bitter in flavor, it can be served raw or lightly cooked like spinach. Endive is especially rich in minerals.

Escarole (*Cichorium endiva latifolium*), a variety of endive, is sometimes confused with curly-leafed endive. Broad, fleshy, ruffled green leaves that shade from deep green on the outside to butter yellow in the center make up the flat head of escarole. Sturdy and crisp, escarole adds a slightly sharp flavor to tossed salads and is particularly good in combination with sweeter leaves such as romaine. It may also be lightly cooked like spinach.

Iceberg, also known as **crisphead lettuce,** is the most commonly used but least nutritious of all the varieties of lettuce. After potatoes, this head lettuce is the second most consumed vegetable in the United States. The name *iceberg* apparently resulted from the commercial practice in years past of shipping lettuce in ice-filled railcars to maintain crispness. Most iceberg lettuce is still grown in California and shipped elsewhere. A headed lettuce with large, crisp, pale green leaves, firm heads, and little flavor, commercial iceberg is one of the most chemically treated crops. Its one nutritional benefit is that it offers bulk to the intestinal tract.

Loose-leaf, bunching, or **leaf lettuce** is the type most often grown in home gardens. A tasty bunch, they are a mixture of nonheading greens whose flat, frilled, or double-ruffled leaves in bright green, dark red, and bronze are ornamental as well as delectable in the salad bowl. Quite delicate, leaf lettuce does not store or ship well. Its semi-crisp texture and mild flavor make for soft, gentle salads with a sweet flavor.

Mâche (*Valerianella olitoria, V. locusta*), also known as **corn salad, Fetticus,** and **lamb's lettuce,** is an attractive blue-green European salad herb. This hardy vegetable thrives in cold, wet regions and even grows through frost and snow. A favorite garden plant, it produces long before and continues after other salad greens. The leaves may be variably broad or narrow, dark or medium green, round or spoon-shaped, and sweetly nutty or simply green-flavored. The largest of its diminutive leaves are five inches long and about 1½ inches wide. The soft, young leaves are best. Slightly chewy and firm in texture, they make beautiful arranged salads and may also be used as an attractive and flavorful garnish for cream soup or delicate vegetable purées.

Mesclun is the French term (*misticanza,* in Italian) for a mix of various greens harvested young. Mesclun may seem to be a faddish restaurant item, but it's really just a twist on a very old practice—snipping spring greens soon after they nose above the ground. The year's first leafy things have been regarded as a tonic by many cultures over the centuries. In Pennsylvania Dutch country, good health would be yours in the year ahead if you ate spring greens on Maundy Thursday, the Thursday before Easter. The Greeks stalk whatever wild spring greens they can find to make *hortopita,* a zippier version of spanokopita. In parts of North America, dandelion foraging is still a rite of spring.

Mizuna (*Brassica rapa*), also known as **Siu Cai,** is yet another leafy green of the cabbage family. Unlike many of its relatives, it can be eaten raw as well as cooked. It has a deeply serrated, almost lacy leaf. Less sulfurous than bok choy, mizuna is an excellent potherb or salad or sandwich green. It makes an exceptionally beautiful garnish. Mizuna is interchangeable with spinach in any recipe. The stalks, more fibrous than the leaves, need to be coarsely chopped before serving.

Radicchio (*Cichorium intybus*), also known as **red chicory,** is another member of the chicory family and hails from the Treviso area in northern Italy. Its brash striated magenta color and firm crisp leaves make it a dramatic addition to mixed salads and an excellent garnish; its arresting flavor, which borders on sweet yet slightly bitter and peppery, also endears it to many palates. Select small-headed radicchio that have a firm white core and that look garden-fresh rather than travel-weary, since old radicchio is decidedly bitter. Mostly commonly thought of as a salad green, the sturdy leaves afford much wider use. It may be freely substituted in any chicory or endive recipe; briefly sautéed for a warm salad with mushrooms, cheese, and olives; or added to soups. Individual leaves may be used as salad cups or wrappers for tasty tidbits.

Romaine or **cos lettuce** (*Lactuca sativa longifolia*) has heads that are loose, long, and cylindrical, with stiff, broad leaves that shade from yellowish-white at the center to dark green at the tips. Individual leaves are elongated ovals, rather loaf-shaped, reminiscent of kitchen tasting spoons; although coarse in texture, the leaves have a semisweet taste, with the lighter inner leaves being particularly tender and flavorful, considered by many salad lovers a necessity in tossed green salads. The common name *romaine* is a corruption of *Roman*; the even older name *cos* is taken from the Greek island of Kos, the birthplace of the famous physician Hippocrates and the place where the Romans originally obtained these mildly tangy leaves. One of the best lettuces nutritionally, romaine contains a substantial amount of iron, potassium, and vitamin E.

Watercress—see separate reference in this section.

Lotus
(Nelumbo nucifera)

Nelumbo comes from the name of the plant in Singhalese (Sri Lanka), and *nuciferum* means "nut-bearing." The English word *lotus* is derived from the Hebraic *lot*, meaning "myrrh."

General Information
The lotus plant grows in tropical paddies with its sausage-shaped roots submerged in the mud and its beautiful leaves and blossoms floating on top of the water. The blossom, widely featured in Indian and other Asian art, is edible as well, as are the leaves, roots, and seeds (see the reference in the **Nuts, Seeds, and Oils** section).

Buying Tips
The sausage-shaped lotus root varies between five and twelve inches in length and from two to three inches in diameter. It may be clean or dirt-caked. The skin is thin but tough and a fawn to pinkish color.

Culinary Uses
The flesh of the root varies from buff to rose or salmon-tinted, and each is pierced with ten air tunnels that, when the root is sliced crosswise, look something like snowflakes; the slices themselves looks like strangely symmetrical rounds of Swiss cheese. The starchy yet crunchy flesh is

Lotus Root / Nutritional Value Per 100 g Edible Portion		
	Raw	Cooked
Calories	56	66
Protein	2.60 g	1.58 g
Fat	0.10 g	0.07 g
Fiber	0.80 g	0.85 g
Calcium	45 mg	26 mg
Iron	1.16 mg	0.90 mg
Magnesium	23 mg	22 mg
Phosphorus	100 mg	78 mg
Potassium	556 mg	363 mg
Sodium	40 mg	45 mg
Beta Carotene (A)	0 IU	0 IU
Thiamine (B$_1$)	0.160 mg	0.127 mg
Riboflavin (B$_2$)	0.220 mg	0.010 mg
Niacin (B$_3$)	0.400 mg	0.300 mg
Ascorbic Acid (C)	44.0 mg	27.4 mg

LORE AND LEGEND

"In the beginning were the waters. Matter readied itself. The sun glowed. And a lotus slowly opened, holding the universe on its golden pericarp." The elegant, sweet-scented lotus has long been regarded with reverence by those in the East. The Egyptian lotus, dedicated to Horus, god of the sun, was the age-old solar symbol of reproductive power and fertility since it grew upon the life-giving Nile; Horus himself was represented in mythology as issuing from the cup of the lotus blossom, thus signifying immortality and eternal youth. The Hindu god Brahma was also born in the sacred bosom of the flower. The five petals of the flower symbolize the five stages in the Hindu wheel of life: birth, initiation, marriage, rest from labor, and death. Chinese Buddhists believe in the Western Heaven with its Sacred Lake of Lotuses, a place where souls of the deceased faithful sleep in lotus buds until the appointed time when they are admitted to Paradise.

slightly sweet and mild, tasting somewhat like water chestnuts. The crunchy texture does not dissipate with cooking. Thin, lacy slices make a nice garnish for salads; the root may also be sliced or grated for use in soups, stews, sautés, or stir-fries. It can be cooked like other starchy vegetables such as turnips, potatoes, jicama, or water chestnuts. Peel before use. Dried lotus root, available in many specialty shops, may be reconstituted and substituted for the fresh root in most dishes. Lotus root flour is made from the dried and powdered root; this gluten-free flour is used in Chinese and Japanese cooking as a thickener for sauces. Tender young lotus leaves are used either raw as part of a green salad or lightly cooked as a hot vegetable. The mature leaves are used as a wrapping and impart their aroma to what is inside. The seeds can be dried, roasted, or pickled (they cannot be eaten raw). Flower petals may be floated on a clear soup.

Health Benefits

In Oriental medicine lotus root is considered a warming food. It is prescribed for lung-related ailments and to increase energy, control blood pressure, neutralize toxins, and help digestion. The linking part between the two roots is considered the most potent.

Martynia

(Proboscidea louisianica, P. annua, P. parviflora)
Also Known As: Unicorn Flower, Proboscis Plant, Devil's Claw, Ram's Horn

The genus name *Proboscidea* means "proboscis-like," which this plant certainly qualifies as; *louisianica* means "coming from Louisiana," *annua* means "annual," and *parviflora* means "small-flowered." The plant was given its English name *martynia* in honor of John Martyn (1699–1768), a professor of botany at Cambridge.

General Information

Native to southwestern North America, martynia is a warm-weather annual with heavy stems, coarse roots, and soft, crinkly foliage. Rather wide spreading, the plant has hairy stems that tend to wander off in all directions. The showy flowers come in a variety of hues, including purple, pink, and yellow. Following the flowers come the edible seedpods, soft and fuzzily green, which resemble curved okra pods. Seedpods left to mature and dry on the vine gradually harden, darken, and split until two dark horns form at the beaked end. The outer skin drops off and the black seeds fall, leaving a "devil's claw" (one of the plant's alternate names).

Culinary Uses

Young seedpods can be pickled or used in soups.

Mushrooms, Truffles, and Other Fungi

The word *mushroom* is derived from the Frankish word *mussiriones*, which referred to the meadow mushroom, and from the French *mousseron*, meaning they grow on moist moss.

General Information

Of all the world's foods, perhaps the strangest are mushrooms. For centuries these primitive plants have been linked with magic and myth. Fungi without roots, leaves, flowers, or seeds, mushrooms lack chlorophyll to photosynthesize nourishment from sunlight, and so must receive their nourishment instead from other organic matter, as do scavengers or parasites. Rather than cringing at this image, use it to understand why mushrooms so effectively detoxify: in nature, mushrooms draw upon that which is decaying; in the human body, mushrooms are said to absorb and then safely eliminate toxins. These toxins include undesirable fat in the blood, pathogens, and excess mucus in the respiratory system.

The mushroom is perhaps the most fertile plant in the world, each one producing not just billions but trillions of spores. Mushroom spores are everywhere; they impregnate the earth, awaiting the opportunity to grow. Though thousands of mushroom species grow in the wild, many of these are poisonous. By the 1600s the French had begun cultivating edible mushrooms to keep up with the local demand. Most of the farming took place in caves that had once been mined for building stone. In 1867 one cave in Mery was said to contain twenty-one miles of beds and to produce three thousand pounds of mushrooms daily.

The part of the mushroom that we recognize is the fruit of the fungus. The majority of the plant remains underground. Colors range across the palette, from the glowing yellow of the chanterelle to the shrouded black horn-of-plenty (called *trompettes-des-mortes*, or "death's trumpets," by the French) and everything in between: violet, purple, pastels, and even bright enamel. These wonders of natural design often have stunning appearances, from the vaulted, arched ribs of the chanterelle to the honeycombed morel and the ostrich-egg-sized giant puffball.

Buying Tips

Choose young, fresh, firm specimens with no bruising or discoloration. As with other life-forms, the quality of a mushroom is greatly determined by the quality of its nourishment. Foraged mushrooms have a flavor superior to commercial varieties grown in a sterile medium of organic waste (straw, corncobs, sawdust, bark, gypsum, and potassium) in windowless, controlled-atmosphere sheds. However, if you gather them yourself, remember that

Mushrooms and Truffles / Nutritional Value Per 100 g Edible Portion

	Common Raw	Common Cooked	Enoki Raw	Shiitake Dried	Shiitake Cooked
Calories	25	27	35	296	55
Protein	2.09 g	2.17 g	1.54 g	9.58 g	1.56 g
Fat	0.42 g	0.47 g	0.39 g	0.99 g	0.22 g
Fiber	0.75 g	0.87 g	n/a	11.50 g	1.96 g
Calcium	5 mg	6 mg	1 mg	11 mg	3 mg
Iron	1.24 mg	1.74 mg	n/a	1.72 mg	0.44 mg
Magnesium	10 mg	12 mg	16 mg	132 mg	14 mg
Phosphorus	104 mg	87 mg	113 mg	294 mg	29 mg
Potassium	370 mg	356 mg	381 mg	1,534 mg	117 mg
Sodium	4 mg	2 mg	3 mg	13 mg	4 mg
Zinc	0.73 mg	0.87 mg	0.57 mg	n/a	n/a
Copper	0.492 mg	0.504 mg	0.067 mg	n/a	n/a
Manganese	0.112 mg	0.115 mg	0.082 mg	n/a	n/a
Beta Carotene (A)	0 IU	0 IU	7 IU	0 IU	0 IU
Thiamine (B$_1$)	0.102 mg	0.073 mg	0.086 mg	0.300 mg	0.037 mg
Riboflavin (B$_2$)	0.449 mg	0.300 mg	0.105 mg	1.270 mg	0.170 mg
Niacin (B$_3$)	4.116 mg	4.460 mg	3.645 mg	14.100 mg	1.500 mg
Pantothenic Acid (B$_5$)	2.200 mg	2.160 mg	0.926 mg	n/a	n/a
Pyridoxine (B$_6$)	0.097 mg	0.095 mg	0.043 mg	n/a	n/a
Folic Acid (B$_9$)	21.1 mcg	18.2 mcg	30.0 mcg	n/a	n/a
Ascorbic Acid (C)	3.5 mg	4.0 mg	11.9 mg	3.5 mg	0.3 mg
Tocopherol (E)	0.08 mg	n/a	n/a	n/a	n/a

many edible species have poisonous look-alikes. Also, avoid busy roadsides or old mining and industrial sites, because mushrooms tend to concentrate any toxic substances such as heavy metals that occur in the vicinity. Don't allow mushrooms to steam and sweat in a plastic bag on the way home, whether they are wild or cultivated; they travel best in a basket, lightly wrapped or covered. Once home, most varieties will keep in the refrigerator for a few days at most. Before using, wipe or dust off dirt particles with a soft brush or a damp paper towel rather than washing; there is no need to peel most types. Cut off any stem bases that are woody. Follow specific instructions for individual mushroom species.

Culinary Uses

Mushrooms are among the most costly, exotic, and delectable of foods. Like a sponge, they soak up the essence of whatever they are cooked in; the more finely they are sliced, the more flavor they absorb. Mushrooms are excellent simply prepared, and they add a rich flavor to sauces, soups, stuffing, and stir-fries. The larger varieties are meatlike sliced and grilled. Roasting concentrates their flavors. Mushrooms are a rich source of glutamic acid (the natural version of the flavor enhancer monosodium glutamate) and so enhance the flavor of any savory food that they are cooked with. If you have a glut, it is best to keep them by drying, pickling, preserving in oil, or cooking and then freezing them. Drying intensifies the flavor of mushrooms and is a convenient way to keep favorite varieties on hand. Reconstitute dried mushrooms by pouring boiling water over them and letting them sit for half an hour. Use the soaking water whenever possible, as it contains a great deal of the flavor. However, do strain the soaking water carefully to eliminate any grit.

Health Benefits

pH 6.00–6.70. Mushrooms have no sugars (and are therefore a good food for diabetics), very little carbohydrate (mostly in the form of indigestible cellulose), many minerals and vitamins (varying with the species), and a good deal of protein (not all of it assimilable). The contemporary practice of eating raw mushrooms lacks historical precedents—and with good reason: carcinogenic compounds found in raw common mushrooms are destroyed in cooking. Asian mushrooms (shiitake, oyster, enoki, and mo-er, or black tree fungus) have been found to thin the blood, which lowers cholesterol and helps prevent strokes

LORE AND LEGEND

Mushrooms, the edible fungi that the ancients called "the plant without leaves," have captured the attention of many peoples. Most ancient cultures believed that the mushroom was magic fare, that it was created by bolts of lightning. Because ordinary citizens did not rate such magic food, in Egypt none but the pharaohs were permitted to partake of this "mysterious night-growing" vegetable. The Greeks and Romans likewise placed mushrooms in a class by themselves, considering them to be food of and for the gods, although that did not stop upper-class Romans from eating them. Julius Caesar even passed stringent laws specifying who could enjoy them and who could not. The Greek city Mycenae possibly takes its name from *mykes* or mushrooms, the legend being that Perseus, hot and thirsty, picked a mushroom and drank the water flowing from it, and then expressed his gratitude by naming the city in its honor. In Asian folklore, mushrooms are esteemed as a longevity tonic. In fact, the symbol for the Chinese god of longevity, Shoulau, is a walking stick capped by a mushroom ornament.

and heart attacks. They also stimulate the immune system, help prevent cancer, and possibly help conditions such as rheumatoid arthritis and multiple sclerosis. Studies at Budapest's Institute of Pathology and Experimental Cancer Research have shown that lentinan, a polysaccharide found in shiitakes, is a promising anticancer agent and immune system stimulant. Mushrooms are among the few rich organic sources of germanium, which increases oxygen efficiency, counteracts the effects of pollutants, and increases resistance to disease. They are also rich in zinc, which is valuable in treating skin injuries, regulating prostate gland function, and helping the metabolism of animal and plant proteins. Mushrooms in general neutralize toxic residues in the body from the consumption of animal protein.

VARIETIES

Chanterelles (*Cantharellus cibarius*), also known as **Girolle** or **egg mushrooms,** range from bright yellow to orange in color and are shaped like a curving trumpet. There is enormous variation in flavor and size among chanterelles from different locations: they can range from pleasantly mild and meaty to flowery, nutty, and softly cinnamony. Most smell faintly of apricots and taste slightly peppery when cooked. The intensity of a raw chanterelle's aroma foretells the strength of its flavor when cooked. Available fresh from mid-June through February, they can also be found dried or canned. However, the dried version tends to be tough as rawhide, while the canned ones are too often insipid. For maximum enjoyment, lightly sauté fresh chanterelles in olive oil and add a dash of salt or tamari. Their firm flesh requires longer cooking than other varieties and will remain chewy.

Cloud ears (*Auricularia polytricha, A. auricula-judae*), also called **black mushrooms, black fungus, wood ears, tree ears, Judas' ear,** and **Jew's ear,** do actually resemble the ear with a small stretch of the imagination. Long a staple of Chinese cooking, they have been available dried but now are occasionally found fresh. Mild tasting and chewy, cloud ears are used to add texture to stir-fries or cold vinaigrette salads. To rehydrate dried cloud ears, cover them with boiling water and allow to soak for thirty minutes; the charcoal-black matter blossoms back into its suspended glutinous texture.

Common or **button mushrooms** (*Agaricus bisporus, A. campestris*), relatives of the wild field mushroom, are bred for their shipping and keeping properties, not their taste. Generally plump and domelike, they have a delicate flavor and can be snow white, tan, or brown in color. All commercial strains have the same subtle, nutty-sweet taste, but they lack the vitality, medicinal properties, and flavor of wild mushrooms. They are also one of the most chemically treated crops. Choose those with caps that are closed or just slightly open. Avoid those with wide-open caps and dark gills, those that are markedly pitted or discolored, and those with a spongy texture.

Cremini (*Agaricus brunnscens*), also known as **Roman** or **browntop mushrooms,** are similar to white button mushrooms in size and shape but have a darker color and deeper flavor. Like their white cousins, the best specimens are firm with tightly closed caps. Substitute cremini for white buttons in any recipe.

Enokis (*Flammulina velutipes*), also known as **snow puffs** or **golden needles,** are long, slender, sproutlike mushrooms with diminutive round heads and creamy white color. They have a crisp texture with a mild, slightly tangy and citrusy taste and are best served raw, as you would sprouts, in salads and sandwiches or floated on top of soups. Cook only lightly, as they will toughen if cooked for very long. Supermarkets usually carry enokis with roots still attached in sealed plastic packages; they will stay fresh for several days in the refrigerator in these packages. Trim off the roots and rinse before serving. Enokis stimulate the immune system, helping to fight off viruses and tumors. Don't eat too many of these raw with any frequency, however, as enokis contain flammutoxin, a protein toxic to the heart (this substance is rendered harmless when cooked).

Maitake (*Grifola frondose*), also known as **hen-of-the-woods** or **sheep's head mushrooms,** grow in clumps at the base of tree stumps in the woods. The stalks of their fan-shaped caps fuse together at the base to form a mass sometimes as large as a football. The Japanese word *maitake* means "dancing mushrooms" because, so tradition tells us, when people found maitake they would dance for joy. What was so joyous about this fungus? For one thing, it was worth its weight in silver. Today, these mushrooms grow wild throughout the northern hemisphere and have been successfully cultivated since 1990. Use them thinly sliced and sautéed in butter with herbs; they may also be baked, grilled, or added to casseroles or soups. Rehydrate dried maitake in water for at least thirty minutes, or until softened. The polysaccharide in maitake—Beta 1, 6-Glucan—is unique to this mushroom and is a potent immuno-stimulant, apparently helping to neutralize tumors and to ameliorate cancer, AIDS, chronic fatigue, and problems of obesity. It lowers blood pressure and benefits diabetes sufferers by lowering blood glucose. Historically, maitake were valued for promoting longevity and maintaining health.

Matsutake or **pine mushrooms** (*Armillaria ponderosa, A. edodes*) are among the most appealing edible mushrooms, with their sweetly scented pine aroma and superb flavor. The stems are thick and meaty, and the slightly pointed, unopened caps are enclosed in a veil, making them look distinctly phallic. As the caps flare open, the market price declines. Matsutake mushrooms thin blood and thus lower cholesterol and help prevent strokes and heart attacks. By stimulating the immune system, they help prevent cancer and other degenerative conditions. Matsutake contain germanium, which increases oxygen efficiency and counters the effects of environmental pollutants. In Asia, matsutake mushrooms are traditionally broken into pieces, rather than sliced, and simmered in broth to best reveal their spicy aroma. While they can flavor many savory dishes, they are usually showcased alone or in a simple preparation. Matsutake mushrooms are foraged near stands of red pine in China, Japan, and the Pacific Northwest. They are recently under limited cultivation; this factor, plus their short foraging season, makes them extremely expensive. Dried matsutake have limited availability, and drying diminishes their flavor. To reconstitute dried matsutake, soak them in water or an unsalted, seasoned broth for twenty minutes, or until softened.

Morel or **sponge mushrooms** (*Morchella esculenta, M. vulgaris*) are easy to recognize, with their brown, spongelike caps pitted with hollows in which the spores are produced. These long-capped mushrooms are black, ivory, or yellow and tiny to fist-sized or larger. A favorite in French cuisine, morels offer an unusually intense, earthy flavor that is hard to describe but may suggest warm autumn leaves, hazelnuts, or even nutmeg. Dried morels are richer, smokier, and even more intense than the fresh; they should have a strong woodsy flavor. Soak the dried variety just a couple of minutes in warm water before use. Morels are excellent with pasta, noodles, or rice dishes. When they are available fresh, during spring and early summer, select those that smell sweet and look fresh. This tasty mushroom tends to harbor grit and sometimes insects in its honeycombed cap, so it needs careful washing.

Oyster mushrooms (*Pleurotus ostreatus*), also known as **tree oysters** or **chilblains,** can be as tiny as peas or as broad as fried eggs, depending on the strain and its provenance. Pearl to gray in color, usually ruffled and fan-shaped, the smooth deep-gilled caps narrow at the base to a short stubby stem, which attaches them to their cluster of kin. Oyster mushrooms have a flavor that is delicate and mellow; they can be eaten raw, but when cooked their dense, chewy texture becomes tender and oyster-flavored. It is best not to overpower them with other strong flavors; break or cut them into bite-sized pieces and add to sautés, stir-fries, or soups near the end of cooking. Fresh oyster mushrooms are most abundant in spring and fall in the wild, but cultivated ones are available year-round.

Porcini (*Boletus edulis*), also known as **cèpes** or **boleti,** received the Italian name *porcini* because of their resemblance to little pigs. With their coolie-style caps and bulging stems, they also resemble the dancing mushrooms in *Fantasia*. The Greeks and Romans used the term *bolites* to describe the best edible mushrooms, but this term has since been applied only to the genus *Boletus*. These wild mushrooms are generally imported dried from Italy. They lose nothing in the transition, though, because they are cut and dried at their peak of ripeness; in fact, the flavor actually intensifies. Fresh porcini range in color from white to reddish brown and have a smooth, meaty texture and a pungent, woodsy, earthy flavor. Caps range from one to ten inches in diameter, and one fresh mushroom can weigh up to a pound. To choose good-quality porcini, look for caps that are fully opened (but not to the gills), fleshy, and whole, with a stout stem. Porcini are traditionally used to flavor sauces, stews, and rice dishes, but are also good sautéed for a pasta topping or grilled with olive oil and herbs. They are not generally used raw. The dried variety can be rehydrated by soaking in warm water for fifteen to thirty minutes; rinse to remove any remaining dirt or grit. In the folk medicine of Bohemia and Bavaria, this mushroom is credited with cancer prevention, and this folk wisdom is supported by studies at Sloan-Kettering Institute for Cancer. It is also an ingredient in the Chinese medicinal "tendon-easing pills," which ease lumbago, leg pain, numbness in limbs, bone and tendon discomfort, and leukorrhea.

Portobello or **brown mushrooms** (*Agaricus bisporus*) are among the giants of the mushroom world, with their thick, flat, deep brown caps sometimes reaching ten or more inches in diameter. Both the caps and the sturdy stems are edible; just trim the gritty stem end and wipe the top with a damp cloth. Available year-round in many markets, their flavor and texture are almost steak-like when grilled, which is a favorite preparation. They are also excellent added to stews and soups. We now have **baby bellos**, small mature portobellos that are even more succulent than the larger type.

Reishi (*Ganoderma lucidum*), also known as **Ling Zhi,** is called the "herb of spiritual potency." The reishi outshines many other mushrooms for its well-documented medicinal properties. Although it grows throughout the world, the reishi is best known and valued in China and Japan, where it has been used in folk medicine for more than four thousand years. Reishi mushrooms are not produced for the commercial market and are not available fresh. Dried, they may be reconstituted and prepared as other fungi. They are primarily found as an ingredient in herbal preparations. An immuno-stimulant, it is helpful for people with AIDS, leaky gut syndrome, Epstein-Barr, chronic bronchitis, and other infectious viruses. It is also used as an aid to sleep, as a diuretic, as a laxative, and to lower cholesterol. They are available dried, in tinctures, in tablets, and in liquid form at natural food stores and from Chinese herb dealers.

Shiitake (*Lentinus edodes*), also known as **golden oak mushrooms** or **Oriental black mushrooms,** are large, umbrella-shaped mushrooms, dark brown to almost black in color. Shiitake mushrooms take their name from the shii tree on which they grow, although they will also grow on oak and hornbeam. Once sold only in dried form, shiitake are now readily available fresh; they are succulent, meltingly tender, and high-priced mushrooms that enhance almost any dish. Try them in soups, stews, sauces, and stir-fries; fresh ones are also delicious baked or grilled. The stems and caps are both edible (although the stems tend to be tough and fibrous), and their rich, meaty flavor goes a long way. When purchasing fresh shiitake, look for firm, fleshy specimens that are flat and dark, with more cap than stem, and still a little closed rather than open. The more aromatic, the more flavorful they will be. Dried shiitake are readily available in most markets. To reconstitute them, submerge them in warm water for at least thirty minutes (one or two hours is preferable, or even overnight); discard the tough stems before use. Shiitakes contain numerous enzymes and vitamins not normally found in plants (including D, B_2, and B_{12}), which may explain the healing qualities traditionally associated with them, now being corroborated in scientific studies.

Straw mushrooms (*Volvariella esculenta*) look like story-book toadstools. These small, conical mushrooms have pointed crowns that are dark brown at the tips and shade to taupe at the base. They have a delicate texture and a distinct flavor.

Truffles (*Tuber melanosporumm, T. magnatum, T. aestivum*) are fungi, but they have taken on a value far beyond any type of mushroom. Reputed as the most delicious food known to humans, the truffle has long been regarded as an aphrodisiac without peer. Truffles might very well act as a general stimulant to the system, for they contain a not inconsiderable dose of invigorating mineral salts—including iron. Additionally, an interesting discovery has recently been made: it appears that truffles contain an aromatic steroid (5 a-androstenol) found in human sperm and underarm sweat. Defying cultivation until the 1970s, now 90 percent of the crop is cultivated in oak or hazelnut orchards in France, New Zealand, and North Carolina. The ancient Greeks believed that truffles were created by thunderbolts striking the earth during pre-autumnal storms—a legend based on the fact that heavy August rains tend to bring a good truffle crop. The plants grow underground, attached to the roots of host trees (usually oaks or hazels), and must be sniffed out by pigs or dogs trained specifically to detect their scent. All truffles have a textured surface and dense flesh; their earthy, sometimes garlicky flavor is imparted to any food with which they are stored, cooked, or served. Their almost meaty flavor comes from their high glutamic acid content, which not only enhances the flavor of other foods but also acts as a tenderizer. Because of their intense flavor and high price, truffles are used sparingly, either sliced or grated raw over hot foods. Two main types of truffles exist: the black Perigord (from France and southern Italy) and the white Piedmontese (from northern Italy). Black truffles are usually peeled before serving and the peelings saved to flavor soups and stocks. They are also available canned and in a paste form, but canned truffles do not have the aroma and flavor of fresh ones. White truffles are never cooked but rather sliced thin and sprinkled over whatever dish they are to adorn; if it is a hot dish, they are added at the last moment, after the cooking is over.

Mustard Greens

(Brassica juncea rugosa)

The Latin name *Brassica* derives from the Celtic *bresic*; *juncea* means "rushlike"; *rugosa* means "rugose" or "wrinkled." The English name *mustard* is derived from the Latin *mustum ardens*, or "burning must," referring to the early French practice of grinding the pungent seeds with grape must (the still-fermenting juice of wine grapes).

General Information

There are three varieties of mustard grown for greens: one has large, smooth, broad, oval leaves with thick, white ribs; another has wider, bright yellow-green leaves that are curly at the tips; the third has large, smooth leaves with narrow ribs. These greens vary in size and texture, but all have the same pleasantly pungent and bitter taste.

Buying Tips

Select smaller leaves, as these will be more tender. They should be of good color, fresh, tender, and crisp. Poor quality is indicated by leaves that are discolored, wilted, or spotted. While some varieties are naturally yellow, avoid overly yellow or brown leaves, as well as those that are very dry with fibrous stems.

Culinary Uses

Mustard greens have a strong, pungent flavor not appreciated by everyone. Young tender leaves can be used in salads, while the stronger-flavored older leaves are cooked like spinach. They are especially delicious lightly sautéed with garlic. Mixing them with other vegetables helps cut down on their biting taste.

Health Benefits

Because of their high water content, mustard greens are a good cleansing food and an excellent tonic, useful in ridding the system of poisonous substances. They are also used as a counterirritant in mustard plasters and stimulating liniments. All *Brassica* genus vegetables contain dithiolthiones, a group of compounds that have anticancer, antioxidant properties; indoles, substances that protect against breast and colon cancer; and sulfur, which has antibiotic and antiviral characteristics. This family of vegetables also mildly stimulates the liver and other tissues out of stagnancy.

Nopal Cactus

(Opuntia ficus-indica, O. megacantha)
Also Known As: Prickly Pear, Barbary Pear, Cactus Pear, Indian Pear, Indian Fig

Opuntia was an old Latin name used by Pliny for this plant, probably derived from Opus, a town in Greece. *Ficus-indica* means "Indian fig"; *megacantha* means "large-fruited." The English name *nopal* comes from the Nahuatl *nopalli*.

General Information

Nopal cactus pads or leaves (nopales) come from any of numerous cacti of the genus *Opuntia*, native to the drier regions between Central America and the great deserts of the United States. The Spanish imported this plant from Mexico to Europe soon after the discovery of America; it found a hospitable climate in Sicily and other Mediterranean regions, where it is cultivated and highly enjoyed. The fleshy spiked leaves take the form of flattish disks or pods stacked one on another, inspiring the American name *beavertail cactus* for the plant. See also **Prickly Pear** in the **Fruits** section.

Mustard Greens / Nutritional Value Per 100 g Edible Portion		
	Raw	Cooked
Calories	26	15
Protein	2.70 g	2.26 g
Fat	0.20 g	0.24 g
Fiber	1.10 g	0.69 g
Calcium	103 mg	74 mg
Iron	1.46 mg	0.70 mg
Magnesium	32 mg	15 mg
Phosphorus	43 mg	41 mg
Potassium	354 mg	202 mg
Sodium	25 mg	16 mg
Beta Carotene (A)	5,300 IU	3,031 IU
Thiamine (B$_1$)	0.080 mg	0.041 mg
Riboflavin (B$_2$)	0.110 mg	0.063 mg
Niacin (B$_3$)	0.800 mg	0.433 mg
Pantothenic Acid (B$_5$)	0.210 mg	0.120 mg
Ascorbic Acid (C)	70.0 mg	25.3 mg
Tocopherol (E)	2.01 mg	n/a

Buying Tips

Nopales should be small, bright green, about eight inches long, and resilient, not limp or dry. They will likely be de-spined, or of a cultivated spineless variety, but you will still need to trim the "eyes" just in case there are any tiny prickers remaining.

Culinary Uses

The flavor of nopales is said to resemble artichoke hearts, string beans, or lima beans, with a texture similar to okra. Peeled and cooked, they exude a mucilaginous substance that does not appeal to some, but their soft, crunchy texture and pleasant mild flavor make them worth experimenting with at least once. While some recommend steaming the pads (and then serving them with lemon juice), others use this strange vegetable in gumbo, vegetable soups, omelets, and casseroles; it can also be chopped into salads or sliced and served like carrot sticks. Nopalitos—sliced or diced nopales—are available canned or bottled with additional spices and herbs and are a tolerable substitute for fresh in cooked dishes, bearing in mind the extra seasoning, which is usually chili-hot.

Health Benefits

Nopal is marvelously rich in all minerals, vitamins, and protein. Low in fat and high in calcium, magnesium, phosphorus, iron, beta carotene, and vitamins A, B complex, and C.

Okra

(Hibiscus esculenta, Abelmoscus esculentus)

Hibiscus is an old Latin name of unknown meaning for this family of plants; *esculenta* means "esculent" or "edible." The English name *okra* derives from *nkruman* or *nkrumun*, from the Twi language spoken on the Gold Coast of Africa. In other parts of the world where the vegetable is popular—the Caribbean, South America, the Middle East, India, and Africa—it is still referred to as *gumbo*, from the *Umbundun ochinggombo* or *ngombo*.

General Information

Okra originated in Africa, probably in the region of Ethiopia, where it still grows wild, and was brought to the European continent by the Moors. It is believed that the French introduced the plant into the United States early in the eighteenth century, because it is a popular ingredient in the famed French cuisine of New Orleans. This tall, warm-weather plant, related to hibiscus and cotton, is raised for its edible pods; okra grows on a showy, flowering bush, and the foliage in some types can reach a height of seven to ten feet. The fingerlike pods, sometimes called "lady fingers," are actually immature seedpods that develop from the plant's pretty red-throated yellow blooms. If allowed to fully ripen, okra becomes fibrous and indigestible. In most varieties, the pods are slender, deep green, and ridged, growing up to seven inches long but picked for commercial use before reaching this length. One miniature type, marketed as "Chinese okra," has plumper, more rounded pods that are two to three inches long.

Buying Tips

Choose small pods that are firm, springy, resilient when pressed, and richly green, with no signs of surface discoloration. Those less than three inches long are preferable; large pods are often hard or tough, but these can be dried and ground into a protein-rich flour.

Okra / Nutritional Value Per 100 g Edible Portion		
	Raw	Cooked
Calories	38	32
Protein	2.00 g	1.87 g
Fat	0.10 g	0.17 g
Fiber	0.94 g	0.90 g
Calcium	81 mg	63 mg
Iron	0.80 mg	0.45 mg
Magnesium	57 mg	57 mg
Phosphorus	63 mg	56 mg
Potassium	303 mg	322 mg
Sodium	8 mg	5 mg
Zinc	0.600 mg	0.550 mg
Copper	0.094 mg	0.086 mg
Manganese	0.990 mg	0.911 mg
Beta Carotene (A)	660 IU	575 IU
Thiamine (B$_1$)	0.200 mg	0.132 mg
Riboflavin (B$_2$)	0.060 mg	0.055 mg
Niacin (B$_3$)	1.000 mg	0.871 mg
Pantothenic Acid (B$_5$)	0.245 mg	0.213 mg
Pyridoxine (B$_6$)	0.215 mg	0.187 mg
Folic Acid (B$_9$)	87.8 mcg	45.7 mcg
Ascorbic Acid (C)	21.1 mg	16.3 mg

Culinary Uses

A favorite vegetable throughout the southeastern United States, okra has a subtly tart yet clean flavor that falls between that of eggplant and that of asparagus (some compare it to green beans and gooseberries). Wash the pods just before preparing and cut off the woody stem ends, but only at the last moment because the pods will quickly start oozing. Inside the tapering, fuzzy green pod is a soft tissue that exudes a sticky juice when cooked. This stickiness is what makes okra useful as a thickener; it is also why many people turn up their noses at the mere mention of okra. The trick to cooking okra is simply not to overcook it; prolonged cooking only promotes gooeyness. Frying is the main way to avoid the mucilaginous quality. Okra fried for no more than a minute or two with just a little olive oil and perhaps a chopped hot chili makes an excellent appetizer. But the mucilage will only seep out if you add liquid and cook longer than a few minutes. Frying also allows for making the okra either fairly soft or crisp on the outside. A main ingredient in gumbos and curries, okra will thicken any dish to which it is added. It can be boiled, baked, sautéed, stuffed, or fried with meat, onions, tomatoes, or other vegetables. When cooked in utensils made of copper, brass, iron, or tin, okra may discolor and turn an extremely unappetizing black. Okra flour is a nutritious addition to broths and soups.

Health Benefits

pH 5.50–6.60. Okra contains a vegetable mucin that is soothing to irritated membranes of the intestinal tract.

Onion

(Allium cepa)

Red onions are especially divine. I hold a slice up to the sunlight pouring in through the kitchen window, and it glows like a fine piece of antique glass. Cool watery-white with layers delicately edged with imperial purple . . . strong, humble, peaceful . . . with that fiery nub of spring green in the center . . .

—MARY HAYES GRIECO

Life is like an onion: You peel it off one layer at a time, and sometimes you weep.

—CARL SANDBURG

Allium is the ancient Latin name for the garlic family, possibly taken from the Celtic *all*, meaning "pungent"; *cepa* is an old Latin term for the onion. Because the onion bulb is a single united entity rather than a conglomeration of separate cloves as found in garlic, it was referred to by the Roman Columella in A.D. 42 as *unio* or *unionem*, meaning "united" and from which the common English name is derived.

General Information

The onion is considered to be of central Asian origin and to have been propagated by the Indo-European tribes in their separate migrations. A member of the lily family along with asparagus, the onion family itself has about 325 members and is one of the oldest vegetables known to humans, its use going back many millennia. The oldest known body of law, the Code of Hammurabi, stipulates that the needy shall receive a monthly ration of bread and onions. Evidently onions were regarded as primarily a food for the poor, who ate them raw on bread, a combination that formed their staple diet. In America, Cortez saw onions on his way to Tenochtitlán, while farther north and a century later Père Marquette told of being saved from starvation by eating wild native American onions. This was in 1624, when Marquette's explorations took him from Green Bay to a point on the southern shore of Lake Michigan that still commemorates its abundance in onions by having taken for its name the Indian word for their odor: *chicago*. This slightly less assertive cousin of garlic offers many varieties, with a wide range of shapes, sizes, colors, and pungencies. An indispensable pantry staple and the most universally eaten vegetable, the onion is truly an all-season food.

Buying Tips

Onions should be firm and well shaped, with dry, paper-like skins. Avoid those that are sprouting or have a wet, soggy feeling at the neck. Size has nothing to do with quality. Scallions and chives should have fresh green tops.

Culinary Uses

The flavor and aroma of the onion are familiar to everyone. Milder than garlic yet still pungent, all types of onions, from the small white ones to the large Spanish variety, are indispensable in the kitchen. The strongest and most pungently flavored are the white onions; yellow onions are milder and sweeter, and red varieties even more so. All varieties can be eaten raw in salads, or baked, boiled, steamed, fried, braised, or stuffed. During the cooking process, some of the pungent volatile oils are lost, and their flavor becomes sweeter and milder. Dehydrated or frozen onions have less flavor, so you will need to add more than when using fresh onions. Holding an onion under cold water while peeling prevents the oil fumes from rising and causing tears. The fumes contain ammonia, an irritant to the eyes and nose.

Health Benefits

pH 5.30–5.85. Anthelmintic, antiseptic, antispasmodic, carminative, detoxicant, diuretic, expectorant, stimulant, stomachic, tonic. Folklore about the curative powers of this versatile vegetable is plentiful, including claims that you can soothe the pain of a toothache with a raw onion or stifle a cough with a sweetened brew of simmered onions. Onions are similar to their cousin garlic in medicinal factors; it is used as an infection fighter and antibiotic, a diuretic, blood pressure regulator, expectorant, heart tonic (reducing the heart rate), contraceptive, and

aphrodisiac. Both onion and garlic contain allyl disulfate, a natural antiseptic oil, and cycloallin, an anticoagulant that helps to dissolve clots that form on the walls of blood vessels. Historically used for asthma, onions relax the bronchial muscle and also inhibit the production of compounds that cause the bronchial muscle to spasm. Onion is excellent for bee stings, as it will suck the pain right out. It also works wonders on sprains and bad bumps. Secure onion slices on an injured site with a bandage and by morning it will be better except where the onion didn't actually touch the skin. The person may smell strongly for the night, but the method works. Onions are rich sources of the potent anticancer bioflavonoid quercetin, which is not destroyed by cooking. The sulfur compounds in onions help to end putrefactive and fermentation processes in the gastrointestinal tract, remove heavy metals and parasites, retard the retention of fluids, and cleanse the system of urea and sodium. Eaten raw, they promote transpiration and cleanse the pores as effectively as a good sauna bath. Half a raw onion a day has been shown in studies to give a 30 percent boost of beneficial

Onion Family / Nutritional Value Per 100 g Edible Portion

	Onion Raw	Onion Cooked	Onion Powder	Powder 1 tsp.	Leek Raw
Calories	38	44	347	7	61
Protein	1.16 g	1.36 g	10.12 g	0.21 g	1.50 g
Fat	0.16 g	0.19 g	1.05 g	0.02 g	0.30 g
Fiber	0.59 g	0.69 g	5.69 g	0.12 g	1.51 g
Calcium	20 mg	22 mg	363 mg	8 mg	59 mg
Iron	0.22 mg	0.24 mg	2.56 mg	0.05 mg	2.10 mg
Magnesium	10 mg	11 mg	122 mg	3 mg	28 mg
Phosphorus	33 mg	35 mg	340 mg	7 mg	35 mg
Potassium	157 mg	166 mg	943 mg	20 mg	180 mg
Sodium	3 mg	3 mg	54 mg	1 mg	20 mg
Zinc	0.190 mg	0.210 mg	2.320 mg	0.050 mg	n/a
Copper	0.060 mg	0.067 mg	0.177 mg	n/a	n/a
Manganese	0.137 mg	0.153 mg	0.374 mg	n/a	n/a
Beta Carotene (A)	0 IU	0 IU	trace	n/a	95 IU
Thiamine (B$_1$)	0.042 mg	0.042 mg	0.418 mg	0.009 mg	0.060 mg
Riboflavin (B$_2$)	0.020 m	0.023 mg	0.056 mg	0.001 mg	0.030 mg
Niacin (B$_3$)	0.148 mg	0.165 mg	0.647 mg	0.014 mg	0.400 mg
Pantothenic Acid (B$_5$)	0.106 mg	0.113 mg	n/a	n/a	n/a
Pyridoxine (B$_6$)	0.116 mg	0.129 mg	n/a	n/a	n/a
Folic Acid (B$_9$)	19.0 mcg	15.0 mcg	n/a	n/a	64.1 mcg
Ascorbic Acid (C)	6.40 mg	5.20 mg	14.69 mg	0.31 mg	12.00 mg
Tocopherol (E)	0.31 mg	n/a	n/a	n/a	0.92 mg

HDL blood cholesterol. Chewing raw onions for five minutes kills all the germs in your mouth, making it sterile; this could be a beneficial practice the next time you get a cold. According to researchers in the United States and India, onions also kill the germs that cause tooth decay. Because their action is stimulating and hot if taken internally, onions are not recommended for those practicing celibacy.

VARIETIES

Bermuda or **Spanish onions** are medium to large, round or oval, moderately mild white onions with dry white shells and dark green or gray stripes running vertically from the root to the stem. It is my understanding that true Bermuda onions are no longer available in the United States; however, Americans call any white onion a Bermuda onion, although they are really "Bermuda-type" onions, a variety of the original. Mostly imported from Mexico, they are available from late summer through December.

Leek Cooked	Shallot Raw	Spring Raw
31	72	32-34
0.81 g	2.50 g	1.83-1.90 g
0.20 g	0.10 g	0.19-0.40 g
0.82 g	0.70 g	0.95-1.00 g
30 mg	37 mg	18-72 mg
1.10 mg	1.20 mg	1.48 mg
14 mg	n/a	20 mg
17 mg	60 mg	37-49 mg
87 mg	334 mg	276 mg
10 mg	12 mg	16 mg
n/a	n/a	0.390 mg
n/a	n/a	0.083 mg
n/a	n/a	0.160 mg
46 IU	n/a	385 IU
0.026 mg	0.060 mg	0.055 mg
0.020 mg	0.020 mg	0.080 mg
0.200 mg	0.200 mg	0.525 mg
n/a	n/a	0.075 mg
n/a	n/a	n/a
24.3 mcg	n/a	64.0 mcg
4.20 mg	8.00 mg	18.80-27.00 mg
n/a	n/a	n/a

LORE AND LEGEND

Praise of the onion has been sung throughout history, except perhaps in India, where onions and garlic were never truly regarded as quite respectable. There the vegetable is not considered fit to be eaten by Brahmins, a tradition that goes back at least to the Ordinances of Manu (about the sixth century B.C.) where it is written "garlic, onions also, leeks and mushrooms, are not to be eaten by the twice-born, as well as things arising from impurity." The Turks have a legend that places the onion and garlic right at the beginning of time; when the Devil was sent out of Paradise and first set foot on earth, on the spot where he placed his right foot there grew the onion and in the place of the left sprang up garlic. Early Egyptians esteemed the onion as a source of strength; the thousands of slaves who built the pyramids were fed a diet consisting largely of onions and garlic, which at the least would have given them remarkably strong breath. Part of the everyday diet of common Egyptians, the onion was not eaten by the priests, but it appeared on the altars of gods and in religious rituals, even as a temple decoration as a representation of eternity. The lowly onion symbolized the universe, since in their cosmogony the various spheres of hell, earth, and heaven were concentric, like its layers. According to a Native American Indian legend, a group of seven young Indian wives were fond of eating onions, but their husbands, disliking the pungent smell, became angry and forbade the practice. The wives, having thought it over and discussed it among themselves, decided that they preferred their onions to their husbands, so they used magical ropes made of eagle down to float up into the sky, where they remain as the Pleiades, presumably eating onions to their hearts' content.

Chives—see the reference in the **Herbs, Spices, and Other Foods** section.

Cipolline onions are small, 1 to 1½ inches in diameter, with flattened ends and a mild, sweet flavor. They are delicious grilled or used on kababs.

Globe onions, also called **yellow** or **white onions,** are the best all-purpose onions and the ones most often seen in supermarket bins. These ubiquitous medium-sized onions encompass many different varieties, with subtle differences in taste or texture, the smaller ones generally being more pungent and the larger sweeter. These are available year-round and are the best keeping variety.

Leeks (*A. ampeloprasum*) are the most subtle and sweet-tasting members of the onion family, with a flavor described as less fine but more robust than asparagus. They look like overgrown green onions with broad, flat leaves eight to fifteen inches long that shade to dark green at the tips and a white cylindrical base up to two inches in diameter. They can be substituted for onions in any dish. Raw leeks taste hot and bitter, but cooked they have a creamy, almost buttery, onion flavor, which makes them good in soups, casseroles, and dressings. To prepare, cut off the roots and tops, leaving eight to ten inches of bulb and lower leaf. Slice down the middle almost to the core, hold under running water or immerse in a basin of water, and gently pull each layer away from the bulb. Rinse well to remove any soil, which the plant is prone to accumulate. The tiny rootlets are also usable and add valuable minerals and nutrients to many cooked dishes. Cut them—as a cluster—from the root base. Soak to loosen any embedded sand and then carefully rinse. Mince the rootlets and use in any soup or sautéed or simmered vegetable dish; they are too fibrous to add to salads or lightly cooked dishes. There is a legend in Wales that when the Saxons invaded in the sixth century A.D., Saint David, patron saint of Wales, directed the Britons to wear leeks on their caps to distinguish them from the enemy. In memory of the heroic resistance by the Britons, the leek became the national emblem of Wales. Even today in Wales and Ireland, house leeks often cover the cottage roofs, and in their midst a few garden leeks are planted, not to have them handy for picking but as a protection against lightning and witches, for lightning greatly dislikes a leek and will go elsewhere, and no witch will supposedly come near this plant, which is sacred to Saint David. Leeks share many of the same healthful qualities as onions and garlic but are considerably less potent. They are, however, an excellent source of the lesser-known carotenoids lutein and zeaxanthin. Leeks are available from September through March.

Maui onions are grown, not surprisingly, in Maui, Hawaii, and are usually pearly pale and flattened but may also be yellowish and globose. The Hawiian soil and weather conditions produce a delicious onion that is low in bite and high in sugar and moisture; the same onion grown elsewhere is more like a common yellow onion. This sweet, moist onion appears in markets from April through June, primarily on the West Coast.

Pearl and **small white onions** are miniature onions that are best peeled and cooked whole. The smallest of all onions, they are mild and tasty. So densely planted that they may be no more than an inch in diameter, they may have layered skins like miniature onions or a single flesh layer like a garlic clove. Available in various colors, they're great creamed, gratinéed, and in kebabs. Pickled pearl onions (used mostly in salads or as a garnish for cocktails) can be purchased in jars at the supermarket. Small white onions look like a slightly larger version of pearls. Both are used whole in soups and stews or simmered with other vegetables, affording great eye appeal in fancy dishes. They are available from September through December.

Red Italian, Creole, or **red-purple onions** are always sweet unless they have been stored too long. They have a stronger flavor than Bermuda and Spanish onions but are still mild enough to be eaten raw. Fresh-picked small ones can be eaten whole like a small apple with a minimum of damage to social conversation. Their purplish color makes them a good addition to salads and sandwiches, and they can also be chopped and used as a garnish. They are best when they are hard, with deep maroon dry shells and shiny first layers. Avoid those that have been peeled to an inner layer, those with double bulbs (generally hotter), or any that are soft at the stem end. Larger ones are generally stronger than smaller ones, and round ones sweeter than flat. Available from early summer through fall.

Scallions or **spring onions** (*A. fistulosum*), often referred to as **green onions,** are a fast-growing type of onion without bulbs. The term *scallion* comes from the biblical Ashkalon, where the plants were called *ascalons*. Technically, scallions are harvested before there is any bulb formation, while green onions have developed small bulbs—about one to two inches in diameter. Both have dark green cylindrical stalks that are white at the root base. These mild-flavored onions are edible from their crisp tops down to their tender white bulbs. Not only do they add color and texture to salads, but their zippy bite affords a counterpoint to heavier soups and entrées. They are available year-round, peaking between April and November.

Shallots (*A. cepa*) were brought to England and France from Syria by knights returning from Crusades during the twelfth century; they acquired the French name *eschalot* from the erroneous belief that they came from Ashkalon in Palestine. A small mild variety of onion, shallots smell and taste like onions, but they look like dark garlic, with clusters of brown- or gray-skinned bulbs. When you want just a hint of onion and garlic flavor, especially in sauces, use shallots. They not only have a mild flavor but are also tender, so they cook quickly. Considered indispensable for such classic sauces as béarnaise, the shallot cooks down to a creamy, thick consistency. Shallots can also be roasted whole or added, finely chopped, to salad dressings. Three to four medium shallot bulbs equals the flavor of one medium yellow onion. When peeled, a shallot bulb divides into two halves; a recipe calling for one shallot refers to both halves. They are usually available from September through December, although they are appearing at other times of the year as well.

Vidalia onions are named after the town in Georgia where they grow. Said by many to be the most delicious variety of onion, they are coppery-colored, elongated, and very hard. These juicy sweet onions (with more sugar than apples) have unlimited uses but are mostly eaten raw and in salads. Availability is limited: only in May and June, although occasionally in July.

Yellow onions—see **Globe Onions**, above.

Walla Walla onions are grown in Washington State in and around the city whose name they bear. For the most part they are light gold-beige, quite round, and creamy, with very thick layers that make for perfect onion rings. They range widely in size, from a mere three ounces to nearly 1½ pounds. At their best raw or only lightly cooked, they quickly become mushy when subjected to heat. Walla Wallas make their appearance from July through October.

Wild leeks, also called **ramps,** are unusual onions. Their scallion-slim stalks, streaked with violet, put out broad, tapering, graceful leaves resembling those of lily of the valley. The leaves emerge in early spring and then die back soon after. Wild leeks have a wild, woodsy aroma and ferocious onion-garlic flavor despite their ladylike appearance. In the southern Appalachians, their appearance is the cause of spring celebrations throughout the area, most notably the Ramp Romp in West Virginia. Choose wild leeks that are firm, springy, and bright green. The roots should always be intact and downright dirty; if trimmed or washed, they develop an unpleasant smell and lose their fresh flavor. To prepare, slip off the first layer of skin from the bulbs, trim the roots, and remove any yellowing or wilted leaves. Generally considered too pungent for raw consumption, they can be cooked in just about any manner that you would cultivated leeks, but with discretion, as they are quite a bit stronger.

Orachee

(Atriplex hortensis)

Also Known As: Salt Bush, Musk Weed, Mountain or French Spinach

> *Atriplex* derives from a Greek name for the plant; *hortensis* means "belonging to the hortus," or garden. The name *orachee* is a corruption of *aurum* (gold), because the seeds mixed with wine were supposed to cure yellow jaundice.

General Information

Native to Europe and Siberia, garden orachee has a long history as one of the oldest cultivated plants. Widely recognized among the ancient Greeks and Romans as a medicinal plant, orachee became very popular in medieval Europe both for culinary and medicinal purposes. Early settlers brought orachee to the New World, where it became a fairly standard vegetable; during the nineteenth century, however, it fell out of favor and has widely been replaced by spinach. There are three main types: white orachee, which has pale green leaves; red orachee, which has dark reddish stems and leaves; and green orachee. The white variety is generally considered the sweetest and most tender.

Culinary Uses

Orachee has a mild flavor and contains much less acid than most other varieties of spinach. The tender leaves that arise from the top of the plant are considered the best to eat. Older leaves are tough and unpleasant tasting. Young stems and stalks can be used in all the same manners that spinach or sorrel are used. Boiled and buttered, creamed, added to quiches, rolled up in crepes, tossed in salads, or added to soups, orachee is delicious in its own right. The French and English use orachee in various soups and stews or serve it steamed as a side dish, while the Italians add it to their pasta.

Health Benefits
Early Greeks and Romans used orachee to soothe sore throats, ease indigestion, and cure jaundice. It stimulates the metabolism and is used internally to dispel sluggishness.

Parsley Root
(Petroselinum crispum tuberosum)
Also Known As: Hamburg Parsley, Turnip-Rooted Parsley

The ancient Greek Dioscorides named this plant *petroselinum* from the Greek words *petros*, meaning "rock," because it grew in rocky places, and *selinon*, meaning "celery." *Crispum* means "curled"; *tuberosum* means "tuberous" or "root." The English word *parsley* is a corruption of the Latin.

General Information
Parsley is believed to be indigenous to Sardinia, Turkey, Algeria, and Lebanon, where it still grows wild. This variety of parsley is grown not for its leaves but for its root. The small, irregularly shaped root looks like a small parsnip (often double-rooted) attached to large, feathery parsley leaves (which are edible but bland).

Buying Tips
Select roots that are firm and preferably have their greens intact.

Culinary Uses
Parsley root tastes somewhere between celeriac and carrot; it is aromatic, slightly aggressive, and herbal-pungent. Most often used to flavor soups and stews, the root adds depth and aroma to hearty main-course dishes and combines well with other roots and tubers. It can also be used on its own—creamed, puréed, steamed, or boiled and buttered.

Health Benefits
Low in fat and high in fiber, sodium, and vitamin C.

Parsnip
(Pastinaca sativum)

The parsnip was once a major Roman foodstuff called *pastinacea*, after the Latin word *pastus*, for "food." *Sativum* indicates that this plant has long been cultivated. The English name *parsnip* is a derivative of the Latin.

General Information
Parsnips grew wild (and still do) in parts of Europe and the Caucasus long before their cultivation. This member of the carrot family looks like a large, rather anemic white carrot, with a starchy root that is among the most nourishing in the whole carrot family. Since the Middle Ages, the potato has gradually replaced the parsnip as a filling, high-starch vegetable, but there was a time when the sweet, nutty, aro-

Parsnip / Nutritional Value Per 100 g Edible Portion		
	Raw	Cooked
Calories	75	81
Protein	1.20 g	1.32 g
Fat	0.30 g	0.30 g
Fiber	2.00 g	2.20 g
Calcium	36 mg	37 mg
Iron	0.59 mg	0.58 mg
Magnesium	29 mg	29 mg
Phosphorus	71 mg	69 mg
Potassium	375 mg	367 mg
Sodium	10 mg	10 mg
Zinc	0.590 mg	0.260 mg
Copper	0.120 mg	0.138 mg
Manganese	0.560 mg	0.294 mg
Beta Carotene (A)	0 IU	0 IU
Thiamine (B$_1$)	0.090 mg	0.083 mg
Riboflavin (B$_2$)	0.050 mg	0.051 mg
Niacin (B$_3$)	0.700 mg	0.724 mg
Pantothenic Acid (B$_5$)	0.600 mg	0.588 mg
Pyridoxine (B$_6$)	0.090 mg	0.093 mg
Folic Acid (B$_9$)	66.8 mcg	58.2 mcg
Ascorbic Acid (C)	17.0 mg	13.0 mg
Tocopherol (E)	1.0 mg	n/a

LORE AND LEGEND

Parsnips have carried some strange superstitions: carrying one was said to ward off snakebite, but if you forgot and got bitten, according to the Greeks you could crush a parsnip and mix it with the pork fat they used to grease their chariot wheels, spread the paste on the wound, and be cured. Many people thought parsnips were dangerous—especially old ones, which were believed to cause insanity.

matic flavor of parsnips was a popular table delight for emperors and peasants alike. In ancient Rome parsnips were reserved for the aristocracy, who liked them drowned in honey or combined with fruit in little cakes. The Roman emperor Tiberius was so fond of their sweet, nut-like flavor that he had them specially imported from Germany when they were out of season in Italy. It is probably because parsnips are dismissed as pale-complexioned carrots that they aren't used more often today. They are treated by both gardening books and gardeners as one of the minor vegetables, but they do inspire something like devotion among those who have figured out how to grow them well.

Buying Tips

Look for straight, smooth-skinned roots that are a tan or creamy-white color, firm and fresh looking, without gray, dark, or soft spots. Softness may indicate decay, and discoloration may indicate freezing. Small to medium-sized are generally the best quality; large roots tend to be woody, but some grow up to twenty inches long and are still tender and sweet. A parsnip that is allowed to remain in the ground at least two weeks past the first frost is unbelievably sweet and satisfying; frost turns the starch in the roots to sugar, and thus parsnips are best in late fall to midwinter.

Culinary Uses

Parsnips have a sweet, nutty flavor that some actually complain is too sweet. They are best after being exposed to cold temperatures so that their starch content is converted into sugar. If tender, parsnips can be eaten raw. Small pieces of raw parsnip add texture and a tingly taste to mixed green salads. If cooked, they should be steamed, not boiled, to obtain their full flavor and then peeled and served, preferably with salt, pepper, and butter. Because of their strong, dominating flavor, use parsnips with discretion in soups and stews.

Health Benefits

pH 5.30–5.70. Diuretic. Parsnips hold a specific affinity toward the kidneys, stomach, and spleen and are helpful in conditions of bladder and kidney stones. Loaded with more food energy than most common vegetables, they help detoxify and cleanse the body and improve bowel action.

Pea
(Pisum sativum)

I eat my peas with honey,
I've done it all my life.
It makes the peas taste funny
But it keeps them on my knife.

—ANONYMOUS

How luscious lies the pea within the pod.

—EMILY DICKINSON

The word *pease*, of Sanskrit origin, became *pisum* in Latin and *pease* in early English. The final *e* was dropped in the mistaken belief that the word was a plural. *Sativum* indicates that this plant has long been cultivated.

General Information

The pea is such an ancient food plant that its center of origin is uncertain, although it is usually attributed to a band of territory sweeping from the Near East into central Asia. Part of the legume family, peas in their dried form have been used as a staple food since ancient times, being found even in Egyptian tombs. Hot pea soup was peddled in the streets of Athens, while fried peas were sold to spectators in lieu of popcorn at the Roman circus and in theaters. Upper-class Romans ate their peas with salted whale meat, while the lower classes had to make do with porridge. A new, sweet-tasting pea was introduced in the sixteenth century, tailor-made for the new custom of eating peas fresh. When Catherine de Medici married King Henry II of France, she introduced his countrymen to small, sweet, fresh *piselli novelli* (new peas), which she had brought from her home in Florence, Italy. These tender gems were adopted enthusiastically by the fashionable French, who dubbed them *petits pois*, the name still in use worldwide for a very tasty type of baby pea. The first peas in America were planted by Christopher Columbus in 1493 on Isabella Island, and the new vegetable was adopted enthusiastically by the Indians. The cultivated pea is comprised of two main varieties—the field pea, now used mostly for forage and for dried peas, and the garden pea, with its high sugar content, considered by some to be the aristocrat of the pea family.

Buying Tips

Choose crisp, young, uniformly green, well-filled pods. Fresh garden peas have a very limited summer season, alas, so make the most of them. Look for pods that are a clear fresh green, not dull, and that have a bouncy shape, never drooping. Prepare them on the day that you buy them. A yellowish pod indicates overmaturity.

Culinary Uses

Fresh garden peas have a delicate, sweet flavor that is well worth the time-consuming effort of shelling them. Use as soon as possible after buying because their sugar quickly turns to starch and they lose flavor. The finest of all are those picked very young and called *petits pois* (tiny, sweet, very young, and tender), but other varieties are also delectable. Peas can be boiled or steamed, puréed, and used in soups, salads, savory dishes, and casseroles; they are delicious served with fresh mint. Canned or frozen peas lack much of the flavor of fresh peas.

Health Benefits

pH 4.90–6.88. Fresh peas are of much greater value medicinally when eaten raw in salads than when cooked, but it takes a strong digestive tract to properly digest raw peas. Slightly diuretic, peas help control blood sugar levels and

Pea / Nutritional Value Per 100 g Edible Portion						
	Raw	Cooked	Edible Pod Raw	Edible Pod Cooked	Sprouted Raw	Sprouted Cooked
Calories	81	84	42	42	128	118
Protein	5.42 g	5.36 g	2.80 g	3.27 g	8.80 g	7.05 g
Fat	0.40 g	0.22 g	0.20 g	0.23 g	0.68 g	0.51 g
Fiber	2.21 g	2.31 g	2.50 g	1.04 g	2.78 g	3.3 g
Calcium	25 mg	27 mg	43 mg	42 mg	36 mg	26 mg
Iron	1.47 mg	1.54 mg	2.08 mg	1.97 mg	2.26 mg	1.67 mg
Magnesium	33 mg	39 mg	24 mg	26 mg	56 mg	41 mg
Phosphorus	108 mg	117 mg	53 mg	55 mg	165 mg	24 mg
Potassium	244 mg	271 mg	200 mg	240 mg	381 mg	268 mg
Sodium	5 mg	3 mg	4 mg	4 mg	20 mg	3 mg
Zinc	1.240 mg	1.190 mg	n/a	0.370 mg	1.050 mg	0.780 mg
Copper	0.176 mg	0.173 mg	n/a	0.077 mg	0.272 mg	0.020 mg
Manganese	0.410 mg	0.525 mg	n/a	0.168 mg	0.438 mg	0.325 mg
Beta Carotene (A)	640 IU	597 IU	145 IU	131 IU	166 IU	107 IU
Thiamine (B$_1$)	0.266 mg	0.259 mg	0.150 mg	0.128 mg	0.225 mg	0.216 mg
Riboflavin (B$_2$)	0.132 mg	0.149 mg	0.080 mg	0.076 mg	0.155 mg	0.285 mg
Niacin (B$_3$)	2.090 mg	2.021 mg	0.600 mg	0.539 mg	3.088 mg	1.072 mg
Pantothenic Acid (B$_5$)	0.104 mg	0.153 mg	0.750 mg	0.673 mg	1.029 mg	0.683 mg
Pyridoxine (B$_6$)	0.169 mg	0.216 mg	0.160 mg	0.144 mg	0.265 mg	0.128 mg
Folic Acid (B$_9$)	65.0 mcg	63.3 mcg	n/a	n/a	144.0 mcg	36.3 mcg
Ascorbic Acid (C)	40.0 mg	14.2 mg	60.0 mg	47.9 mg	10.4 mg	6.6 mg
Tocopherol (E)	0.13 mg	n/a	n/a	n/a	n/a	n/a

Most peas in ancient times were consumed dried, the drying process being considered essential to cure the pea of its "noxious and stomach-destroying" qualities. Uncured peas were occasionally left on the vines by farmers with the intention of poisoning pestiferous rabbits, which may have gotten the better end of the deal. Abundant in folklore, peas were a favorite of Thor, the thunder god of Norse mythology, and are still eaten on Thor's day, or Thursday, in Germany. They were often connected with wooing, possibly as a fertility symbol, and were used for divination: to dream of a dry pea was a portent of a coming marriage. In parts of Europe, peas are still thrown in the lap of a bride on her wedding day to ensure fertility. Then there's the Hans Christian Andersen story that everyone knows, of a princess so sensitive that she could feel a pea under all those mattresses.

contain lectins, which dissolve clumps of red blood cells that are destined to become clots. Peas also contain antifertility agents. In areas of Tibet where there are high consumptions of peas, the fertility rate is considerably suppressed, reduced by more than 50 percent.

VARIETIES

English peas have pods that are not edible. The large, bulging, grass-green pods enclose peas that are typically round and sweet. Most are picked when they are still immature and their sugar content is highest. As they continue to ripen, some of the sugar turns to starch, and the amount of protein increases. Peas intended for drying are left to mature.

Snow peas have firm, crisp, flat, bright green edible pods that taper at both ends and contain very small, underdeveloped peas. The classic snow pea must be picked before the inner peas begin to bulge out and stringiness develops; like other peas, they should be consumed as soon after picking as possible, since their high sugar content quickly turns to starch. For snow peas that are crisp, sweet, and colorful, steam, blanch, or stir-fry for no more than a brief minute or two. Snow peas nourish the liver, stomach, and spleen-pancreas; they are also a good source of calcium and potassium as well as iron and phosphorus.

Sugar snap peas, also known as **mangetouts,** are a hybrid developed by breeder Calvin Lamborn of the Gallatin Valley Seed Company in Twin Falls, Idaho, in the 1970s. Looking just like traditional English peas, the sugar snap pea is the result of a cross between a tough-podded mutant of a processing pea and a conventional snow pea, giving the best of both varieties. These peas have stubby, crunchy, sweet, edible pods enclosing fat, sweet peas. Uncooked, the peas and their pods are crisp and delicious. When ever-so-lightly steamed or blanched, their color turns a dazzling emerald green and their sweetness intensifies. They should be quickly sautéed or stir-fried, for only about two minutes, as overcooking destroys their crisp texture. Older peas may need to be strung on both seams.

Peppers and Chilies
(*Capsicum annuum, C. frutescens*)

The botanical term *Capsicum* arrived on the scene in 1700 under the auspices of Joseph Pitton de Tournefort, early plant taxonomist and plant hunter for the spectacular gardens of Louis XIV. The name is thought to come from either the Latin *capsa,* meaning "box," for the hollow box-like shape of some varieties of the fruit, or from the Greek *kapto,* meaning "to bite," for the pepper's acrid, tongue-searing pungency. The term *annuum* signifies an annual or yearly plant; *frutescens* means "shrubby" or "bushy." Columbus voyaged to the New World in search of India and its black pepper; unsuccessful but undaunted, he named the most pungent New World food "pepper" and the people who cultivated it "Indians." The English word *chili* is from the Nahuatl name *chilli,* the term applied to all members, and also means "red."

General Information
Native to the Americas, peppers and chilies are not related in any manner to black pepper. Along with corn, beans, and squash, the capsicums were among the first plants cultivated in the agriculturally revolutionized Americas. Today there are over one hundred sweet pepper cultivars

LORE AND LEGEND

Tabasco is an Indian word meaning "land where the soil is humid," and the place where the sauce of that name was invented—Louisiana, with its bayous and swamps, its trees hung with Spanish moss—has summers in which the inhabitants steam lightly. The recipe for Tabasco sauce (chilies, salt, and vinegar) was devised by Edmund McIlhenny for his own use in the 1850s. A New Orleans banker, he had been given a handful of dried hot peppers by a friend on his return in 1848 from the war in Mexico. McIlhenny planted the seeds in his father-in-law's plantation, Avery Island, in southern Louisiana. The plants flourished, and there he made his sauce and gave bottles away to a few friends. After the Civil War, with the Southern states defeated and the economy in ruins, McIlhenny saw no future in banking. But the chili had taken over Avery Island, and by 1869 over 350 bottles of Tabasco Pepper Sauce had been dispatched to selected wholesalers. The product never looked back. After the chilies are picked, they are mashed, placed in oak barrels with salt, and left to mature for three years. A wooden top with holes is covered with a layer of salt. This allows any gas to escape when the chilies are fermenting, but the salt insulates the contents from any bacteria. After fermentation, the mashed chilies are tipped into hundred-gallon vats, and white vinegar twice the strength of table vinegar is added. The contents of the vat are kept moving for twenty-eight days, and finally the juice is strained and poured off. Tabasco sauce stings and catches the throat, seeming almost to scrape the lining of the windpipe. Those who love the stuff never seem to have any coughs or colds, however.

Peppers & Chilies / Nutritional Value Per 100 g Edible Portion

	Bell	Hot Chili	Canned Pimiento
Calories	27	40	23
Protein	0.89-1.00 g	2.00 g	1.10 g
Fat	0.19-0.21 g	0.20 g	0.30 g
Fiber	0.44 g	1.80 g	1.05 g
Calcium	9-11 mg	18 mg	6 mg
Iron	0.46 mg	1.20 mg	1.68 mg
Magnesium	10-12 mg	25 mg	6 mg
Phosphorus	19-24 mg	46 mg	17 mg
Potassium	177-212 mg	340 mg	158 mg
Sodium	2 mg	7 mg	14 mg
Zinc	0.120-0.170 mg	0.300 mg	0.190 mg
Copper	0.065-0.107 mg	0.174 mg	0.049 mg
Manganese	0.116-0.117 mg	0.237 mg	0.092 mg
Beta Carotene (A)*	238-5,700 IU	770-10,750 IU	2,655 IU
Thiamine (B$_1$)	0.028-0.066 mg	0.090 mg	0.017 mg
Riboflavin (B$_2$)	0.025-0.030 mg	0.090 mg	0.060 mg
Niacin (B$_3$)	0.509-0.890 mg	0.950 mg	0.615 mg
Pantothenic Acid (B$_5$)	0.080-0.168 mg	0.061 mg	n/a
Pyridoxine (B$_6$)	0.168-0.248 mg	0.278 mg	0.215 mg
Folic Acid (B$_9$)	22.0-26.0 mcg	23.4 mcg	6.0 mcg
Ascorbic Acid (C)	89.3-190.0 mg	242.5 mg	84.9 mg
Tocopherol (E)	0.68 mg	n/a	n/a

*Red varieties highest

on the market and over half as many hot. Chili peppers refuse to be tamed, codified, classified, or otherwise put in their place. Adventurous and spirited, they mix and match, reproduce unpredictably and prolifically, and generally run their own show. Even though pepper varieties are legion, they fall neatly into two categories. The difference between the chilies and the sweet peppers is that chilies contain fiery capsaicin and are used primarily as a spice; sweet peppers lack capsaicin—and therefore heat—and are used primarily as a vegetable. They vary in size and shape, and anyone who judges the spiciness or sweetness of a pepper by its color is bound to be misled. The hotness of a pepper is determined by its capsaicin, a bitter substance located in its skins, seeds, and interior ribs. When the skins and seeds are removed, peppers are less spicy.

In 1912, while working as a chemist for the Parke Davis pharmaceutical company, Wilbur Scoville developed a method to measure the heat level of a chili pepper. Named the Scoville Organoleptic Test, the test is a dilution-taste procedure. In the original test, pure ground chilies were blended with a sugar-water solution and given to a panel of testers, who sipped the concoctions in increasingly diluted concentrations, until they reached the point where the liquid no longer burned the mouth. A number was then assigned to each chili based on how much it needed to be diluted before you could taste no heat. The pungency of chili peppers is measured in multiples of a hundred units, from the bell pepper at zero Scoville units to the incendiary habanero at three hundred thousand Scoville units. One part of chili "heat" per million drops of water rates as only 1.5 Scoville Units, while pure capsaicin rates over fifteen million Scoville Units. The general rule on pepper hotness is that any fresh green pepper is one-third as hot as a red-ripe pepper of the same kind; the dried pepper is generally two to ten times hotter than the fresh red-ripe pepper of the same variety.

Buying Tips

Look for sweet peppers that are firm and well shaped. They should be thick-fleshed and either bright red or green. Avoid those that have punctured skins or look wilted and tired. Peppers and chilies will keep for about a week in the refrigerator. Chilies can be bought fresh, dried, canned, and pickled. Fresh red chili peppers will, if not used within a week or two, dry out and can be kept for many months, as long as they have dried out hanging up within an airflow. Dried red chilies can be bought and stored in a clean jar; they will keep seemingly forever. Dried chilies can also be purchased flaked or ground to a powder, or in the form of Tabasco and a host of other hot sauces.

Culinary Uses

Peppers have many uses, and their popularity as a comestible—condiment, spice, and vegetable—is growing rapidly. Sweet varieties are served raw in salads and as finger foods; they are also stuffed, sautéed, and puréed. They are excellent combined with apples, cheese, nuts, and dried fruits. Hot chili peppers add zest to any number of dishes, and are an important ingredient in Mexican- and Spanish-style foods. In the United States perhaps the best-known use of capsicums is in chili, a dish named after its peppery prime ingredient. For those not accustomed to their fire, they should be used sparingly. Fresh chili peppers should be minced as small as possible, so the eater does not get an overwhelmingly hot bite. Experiment with the different types of chilies to learn their pungency and to develop a taste or tolerance for them. Take care when handling chilies, as capsaicin is a skin irritant, especially painful if any gets into scratches or cuts. Severe burning can result from rubbing your eyes, nose, or lips with your hands after you have handled chilies.

LORE AND LEGEND

Chili peppers were cultivated by the Incas of Peru, and were among the gifts with which the Inca king attempted to bribe Pizarro. One variety among those given to Pizarro is known as Rocoto; although described as "murderous" and by latter-day Peruvians as "hot enough to kill a gringo," it evidently did not do the trick. Pizarro accepted his peppers, macaws, llamas, gold, and silver, and went on to destroy the Inca civilization anyway. Peppers were so highly valued in ancient Peru that the pods were employed as a medium of exchange. In fact, until the middle of the twentieth century, one could purchase items in the plaza of Cuzco with a handful of pepper pods, known as *rantii*. Peru's government has recently decreed that hot chili sauce has decidedly aphrodisiac qualities and ordered it not to be used in prison food, advising that the sauce is not "appropriate for men forced to live a limited life style."

Health Benefits

pH 4.65–5.93. Antibacterial, antiseptic, stimulant. The capsaicin in peppers is one of the best stimulants; when properly stimulated, the body can begin healing and cleansing, allowing itself to function normally. Peppers and chilies normalize blood pressure, improve the entire circulatory system, boost secretion of saliva and stomach acids, increase peristaltic movement, and feed the cell structure of the arteries, veins, and capillaries so they will regain elasticity. Peppers contain vitamin A, which makes bodily tissues more resistant, especially to colds, and promotes growth and the feeling of well-being; vitamin B, which aids in food absorption and normalizes the brain and nervous system by increasing metabolic processes; and vitamin C (up to six times as much as oranges), which is a wonderful health promoter as it wards off acidosis. We get the benefit of this vitamin C if we eat fresh, raw green peppers; they lose about 30 percent of it when fully matured or cooked, and the vitamin essentially vanishes when dried. Our ancestors used hot pepper extract as a painkiller. Modern-day researchers have discovered that capsaicin short-circuits the nerves that make us feel pain.

Folk healers applied capsaicin directly to toothaches. They also applied it to sore eyes because it reduces pain along with the inflammation that accompanies conjunctivitis, or "red eye." Capsaicin gives you a natural "high." When the chemical sends a signal to kill pain, the brain secretes more than its usual output of endorphin, a natural morphine that blocks pain sensation and induces a pleasurable or euphoric feeling. Some people who regularly eat chili peppers, says psychologist Dr. Paul Rozin, may be addicted to them for these very feelings of pleasure. Researchers at the Oxford Polytechnic Institute discovered that adding three grams of hot chili sauce plus three grams of ordinary yellow mustard—commonly called "ballpark mustard"— to a meal can raise a person's metabolic rate by as much as 25 percent. However, fiery hot chili peppers are irritants and, if overeaten, can be overstimulating to the digestive tract, particularly the intestines, kidneys, and bladder. They work wonders for clearing out the sinuses.

HOT VARIETIES

Anaheim, also known as **California long green, New Mexico chile, chile verde, red chile, chile Colorado,** are the longest of the peppers (up to eight inches in length) and are narrow, slightly twisted, and usually a medium to light green, deepening to red at maturity. Legend has it that the original ancestor of the Anaheim was brought to New Mexico from Mexico in 1597 by Don Juan de Oñate, the founder and first governor of Santa Fe. Some three hundred years later a visiting Californian named Emilio Ortega acquired some descendants of Oñate's peppers and with them established a highly successful chili cannery in 1900 at Anaheim, California. The most common chili pepper available in the United States, the mildly hot Anaheims are frequently stuffed for chilies rellenos and are used for the ubiquitous red or green sauce that accompanies the food of New Mexico. One of the least fiery of the chilies, it is the favorite of those with less macho taste buds. This chili can easily be added to any dish in strips or chopped bits to wake up simple vegetable, meat, or egg dishes. Roasted and peeled, it becomes tender and succulent, with a pleasantly bittersweet, fresh taste. In its mature red stage, it is used in the preparation of chili powder and paprika. Dried maroon Anaheims are woven into the festive ropes or *ristras* seen hanging on porches and in shops throughout the Southwest.

Bishop's crown looks like a hat that someone mistook for a seat cushion. Remove the seeds and membrane to moderate its heat.

Bulgarian carrot is a curious heirloom from Bulgaria that produces highly ornamental clusters of what appear to be shiny little carrots. The small plants can be grown in pots wherever mixed flower beds are looking a little thin and weary. The peppers have a fruity heat, and their color recommends them for salsas, chutneys, and marinades.

Cascabels or **cascabellas** are small, round, moderately hot peppers with smooth skins. About 11/2 inches in diameter, cascabels in their fresh state may be either green or barnyard red. Their nutty flavor comes to the forefront with roasting. Dried, their skins turns a brownish translucent red, and the seeds rattle around inside, from whence the pepper received its name, meaning "jingle bell" in Spanish.

Cayenne peppers received their name from Cayenne, French Guiana. These long, thin peppers are exceedingly hot, so fiery that removal of the veins and seeds is highly recommended. Whole fresh or dried cayennes, which vary in size from four to twelve inches, are the favored spice of Creole and Cajun cooks to give their gumbos, shrimp creoles, and crayfish dishes special zest. With a flavor similar to the Tabasco pepper prevalent in bottled hot sauces, cayennes are highly favored for sauces. The prepared condiment "cayenne pepper" may or may not contain true cayenne peppers.

Chilhuacle rojo may not have blistering heat, but the peppers take on notes of cherry and licorice when dried.

Chimayo chile is a New Mexico pepper; its changing color is an indicator of its temperature—mild when green and moderately hot when ripened to red. The peppers are used to make *ristras*.

De Arbor, also known as **tree chili,** looks something like its relative the cayenne, and like that pepper it is often dried and powdered. The flavor is complex and quite hot.

Fresnos are a medium-sized, light green pepper that matures to cherry red; they are pointed and about the same size as the more familiar jalapeño. Named after the city of Fresno, California, this pepper is very hot and best used as a seasoning rather than as a vegetable. Use while green and mince sparingly into dips, salads, or guacamole.

Habaneros (*Capsicum chinense*) are small lantern-shaped peppers, measuring about two inches by two inches. Curvaceous and bright, habaneros come in orange, green, red, and yellow. In their crayon-box colors, these little peppers look something like kids' toys, but behind their cheery appearance is one of the world's hottest gustatory experiences. How hot? Chew on a piece of jalapeño and multiply that heat by thirty, forty, or even fifty, and that's a habanero. However, they aren't just pure burn but offer a fruitiness—mango, papaya—to those who can handle them. Prevalent in the Caribbean, the Yucatan, and South America, they are also grown commercially in California and the Carolinas. They have a burning heat and deep floral flavor; their heat can sneak up on you, so beware of taking a second bite if you think the first one was not hot enough (which is unlikely). Use judiciously in marinades, soups, salads, and sauces.

Hinkelhatz, in the midst of hot peppers with Latino names, is a Pennsylvania Dutch specialty. The name means "chicken heart," for its appearance. It is available at present only through backyard seed savers. Hinkelhatz are traditionally used to flavor pickled foods and vinegar.

Jalapeños originated in Mexico and were named for the town of Xalapa in the state of Veracruz. Blunt-tipped, smooth-skinned, and slightly tapered, they have unusually dense, rich flesh for their petite size. Usually deep green, this pepper occasionally appears in the market in its mature red form, which is prone to show a slight cracking lengthwise. Its powerful bite has assured its place on nachos and other bland, melted-cheese combinations; a small amount in corn breads, soufflés, sauces, and pasta dough makes a snappy difference. Roasting intensifies their flavor but reduces their heat. Smoke-dried jalapeños are known as chipotles (see below). In her book *The Cure for All Diseases*, Dr. Hulda Clark states that taking forty jalapeño seeds (in capsules) three times a day for fourteen days will help remove asbestos from the body.

Jamaican hots are members of a fiery triumvirate that includes habaneros and Scotch bonnets. They are used in all manner of Caribbean dishes.

McMahon's Texas Bird comes from Texas. An army captain stationed there in 1812 sent seeds to Thomas Jefferson at Monticello. Jefferson passed on the seeds to a Philadelphia nurseryman whose name stuck to the pepper. Monticello continues to make the variety available to gardeners.

Poblanos, also known as **anchos** in their dried form, are named after the valley of Puebla, south of Mexico City, where they were first cultivated. This glossy, richly green pepper, shiny as patent leather, resembles a slightly flattened green bell pepper but is pointed at the tip and rather heart-shaped. It is four or five inches long and two to three inches wide. Usually very mild, with an occasional pungent aberration, this variety has a remarkably full, earthy, herbal, and fruity flavor and aroma; cooked and peeled it develops even greater taste and tenderness. With thick flesh that makes it perfect for stuffing, this versatile pepper is a delicious, enlivening addition to corn dishes, soups, vegetables, sauces, and salads. Dried anchos are flat, wrinkled, and heart-shaped, ranging in color from oxblood to almost black. Rehydrated, they become crimson again.

Rocotillos are a distant cousins of the Scotch bonnet and are widely available in Puerto Rico and the Bahamas. They have much less heat than their cousin and give off an intensely fruity, tropical aroma. Small, multicolored, and shaped like a tiny pattypan squash, rocotillos are also known as **ajisitos**. They are great for salads.

Santa Fe grande, also called **Caloro, Caribe,** and **goldspike,** is a tapered, conical pepper that is generally marketed yellow but can also be orange to red. Moderately hot to very hot, with a pleasant sweetness, these peppers are primarily used for pickles, uncooked sauces, and relishes. They may also be roasted and peeled and then cut in tiny strips or minced for garnishing cooked vegetable salads or adding to cornmeal mixes.

Scotch bonnets appear to be cute and cuddly, but these peppers are not recommended for the heat-sensitive. It is interchangeable with the habanero because it is just as hot and colorful, with a rich, smoky flavor that finds its way into Caribbean curries.

Serranos are searing, suitable for those who enjoy

breathing fire. It is believed that the serrano originated on the mountain ridges (*serranias*) north of Puebla and Hidalgo in Mexico. This smooth, sleek, small, narrow, green-to-orange chili pepper, one to two inches long and no more than once inch wide, is deceptively innocuous looking. Packing a tremendous wallop, the burn is intense, immediate, and lasting. More widely used in Mexico and the southwestern United States than any of the other fresh chili peppers, it may be made into an uncooked sauce or mixed raw or roasted with whatever one wishes to spice up.

Thai peppers are thin, pointy, and either green, orange, or red, with needlelike heat penetration and a lingering afterburn. They are popular in Southeast Asian food, including soups, stir-fries, and sauces.

Yellow squash is a squat hot pepper also called **yellow mushroom** for its shape. A red form is available as well.

SWEET VARIETIES

Aconcagua, an Argentine variety, is sweet when still green, unlike familiar bell peppers. Aconcaguas can be used raw in salads, or try them fried or roasted.

Banana peppers, also known as **sweet banana, Hungarian yellow wax,** and **hot Hungarian wax,** are fairly long (five to six inches), tapering, and moderately narrow. They start a pale, translucent, creamy yellow and ripen into orange and scarlet on the vine. Their size, shape, and color have caused them to be compared to bananas. The sweet form is generally called the banana pepper, while the hot variety is the Hungarian wax. Both of them are scarlet when fully mature; however, one seldom sees the red stage because they are consumed before maturity is reached and the Hungarian wax gets so hot it is almost inedible. Traditionally, these peppers are pickled, but they can be slivered fresh into salads or added to bean and grain dishes, where they add flavor and color—but test the pungency first. The hot variety is particularly good in salsas, salads, and pickled vegetables.

Bell, also known as **green** or **sweet peppers,** are usually box- or heart-shaped. The most common is the green bell pepper, which has thick green flesh, a minimum of seeds, and a heavy outer skin. Red bell peppers are actually green peppers that have been allowed to ripen on the plant; ripening makes them softer and sweeter than green peppers. There are also white, deep purple, and bright yellow varieties, which taste much like the red varieties but tend to be a little crisper. Bell peppers can be sautéed and served as a vegetable, chopped and added to casseroles, used in ethnic dishes, and served raw in salads or as a garnish. Because of their unique shape, you can stuff them with any number of mixes—from cheese to rice or nut stuffings.

Corno di Toro is native to Italy; the name means "bull's horn," and the fruits do grow into long, sharply pointed shapes. The flavor is mild but not without character. Use them raw in salads, or grill or sauté them to bring out their character.

Pimientos are small, roughly heart-shaped, richly sweet peppers that were reintroduced to this hemisphere via Spain in 1911. *Pimiento* is a Spanish word meaning "pepper" and is the name adopted by the Associated Pimiento Canners of Georgia for this sweet, thick-fleshed, bright red pepper that is usually canned or stuffed into green olives. Very aromatic, attractive, and tasty, the pimiento is regrettably known to most people solely in its stuffed form. Fresh pimientos are mild yet flavorful, and their thick, meaty flesh makes them delicious in salads and vegetable dishes, as well as excellent candidates for roasting.

DRIED VARIETIES

Chipotles are smoke-dried jalapeños. They can be either a two-toned brown or brick red, ranging in size from two to three inches long and about three-quarters of an inch wide. Chipotles come from Mexico in powder form, *en escabeche* (pickled), and in tomato sauce. Their characteristic very hot to searing flavor comes from the smoke-drying process. They add fire and smoky spiciness to chili con carne and barbecue sauces and are a bold flavoring for mild bean, rice, corn, or cheese dishes.

Pasilla de Oaxaca, from the Mexican state of Oaxaca, gives off tobacco, smoke, and considerable heat. Its principal use is for *rellenos*. The fresh peppers are brownish black when fully ripened. Their heat is concentrated in the veins and seeds; the flesh itself is quite mild.

Plantain
(Musa paradisiaca)

The plant was given the genus designation *Musa* to honor Antonio Musa, physician to Octavius Augustus, the first emperor of Rome (63–14 B.C.). *Paradisiaca* means "of parks or gardens." The English name *plantain* derives from the Latin *platanus* and the Greek *platys*, meaning "broad," referring to the large leaves.

General Information
Plantains are a type of banana that is only eaten cooked. Figuring prominently in Latin American and Asian cookery as a starchy substitute for bread or potatoes, plantains are slowly being introduced to the United States. The most common varieties of plantain look like a large, straight banana and come in various colors, among them green, yellow, red, red-violet, and mottled black.

Buying Tips
Avoid any that are cracked or overly soft, but do not be intimidated by a black or brown peel, for as plantains ripen they also darken. Fully ripe black plantains should give like firm bananas.

Culinary Uses
Plantains have a mild, bland, almost squashlike flavor that begs for spices. When the peel is green or yellow, the flavor of the flesh is bland and its texture simply starchy. As the plantain ripens and the peel changes to brown or black, it plays the role of both fruit and vegetable, having sweetness and a banana aroma but keeping a firm shape when cooked. Never eaten raw, the salmon-colored pulp can be fried, boiled, mashed, sautéed, or baked. Cooked, chopped ripe plantains also make a more than acceptable component of soups, stews, and omelets.

Health Benefits
Plantains have been employed in cases of dyspepsia and ulcers, since they strengthen the surface cells of the stomach lining. Unripe green plantains are the most potent against ulcers.

Plantain / Nutritional Value Per 100 g Edible Portion		
	Raw	Cooked
Calories	122	116
Protein	1.30 g	0.79 g
Fat	0.37 g	0.18 g
Fiber	0.50 g	n/a
Calcium	3 mg	2 mg
Iron	0.60 mg	0.58 mg
Magnesium	37 mg	32 mg
Phosphorus	34 mg	28 mg
Potassium	499 mg	465 mg
Sodium	4 mg	5 mg
Zinc	0.140 mg	0.130 mg
Copper	0.081 mg	0.066 mg
Beta Carotene (A)	10-1,200 IU	909 IU
Thiamine (B$_1$)	0.052 mg	0.046 mg
Riboflavin (B$_2$)	0.054 mg	0.052 mg
Niacin (B$_3$)	0.686 mg	0.756 mg
Pantothenic Acid (B$_5$)	0.260 mg	0.233 mg
Pyridoxine (B$_6$)	0.299 mg	0.240 mg
Folic Acid (B$_9$)	22.0 mcg	26.0 mcg
Ascorbic Acid (C)	18.4 mg	10.9 mg

Potato
(Solanum tuberosum)

Pray for peace and grace and spiritual food,
For wisdom and guidance, for all these are good,
But don't forget the potatoes.

—JOHN TYLER PETTEE

What I say is that, if a man really likes potatoes, he must be a pretty decent sort of fellow.

—A. A. MILNE

Only two things in this world are too serious to be jested on, potatoes and matrimony.

—IRISH SAYING

Solanum comes from the Latin *solamen*, meaning "solace" or "quieting"; *tuberosum* means "tuberous." The English name *potato*, derived from the West Indian name *batata* for the sweet potato, is a mistake that goes back to the time of its introduction into Europe.

General Information

Native to the bleak Andean highlands of South America, the potato is related to the eggplant, pepper, and tomato. One of the world's major food crops, potatoes are tubers, swollen stems that grow underground and are propagated by budding rather than by seeds. Potatoes crossed the Atlantic to Europe before landing in North America in the early 1700s. Except in a few European countries where it became popular soon after its introduction, and a few other places like Ireland where its cultivation precisely met contemporary needs, the beloved potato was only reluctantly accepted as food, and it took well over two hundred years for it to become widely distributed. Although crop failures meant mass starvation, the peasants of Europe remained remarkably obdurate and refused to eat the potato because they believed it caused diarrhea, poisoned the soil, and helped spread the dreaded plague. Today there are over five thousand varieties, and new and improved hybrids are being developed daily; try them all and find your own favorite. In 1900 Americans ate 200 pounds of potatoes per person annually; by 1980, Americans ate only 120 pounds—75 pounds of fresh potatoes and 45 pounds of processed potatoes (frozen, dehydrated, french-fried, or chipped). That works out to about a potato a day, according to USDA figures. One in every three restaurant meals includes potatoes. Over five billion pounds of potatoes a year go to make french fries alone.

Buying Tips

Choose potatoes that are firm, without sprouts, green skins, or spots, indicating exposure to light during storage or growth. Potatoes should be stored in a cool, dark, and well-aired bin or paper bag. It is best to eat them within a week or two of purchasing.

Culinary Uses

Potatoes are a starchy vegetable that everybody has a preferred method of preparing and eating. Both sprouts and green spots contain solanine and are potentially toxic, so they should be mercilessly excised before cooking and eating. Otherwise, the skins should be left on, as significant quantities of vitamins and minerals are either in or just beneath the skin; in peeling, these nutrients and fiber are lost and practically nothing is left except acid-forming starch. Although potatoes may be grated or sliced raw and used in salads, most people prefer to either bake, boil, fry, or mash theirs.

Health Benefits

pH 5.10–5.90. Potatoes are excellent fuel food, despite their reputation of being fattening. Most of the elements are in the skin and eyes, from which roots and shoots grow; the rest of the potato is largely carbohydrate to supply nutrients until roots can take over and extract them from the soil. Raw potatoes contain a sugary carbohydrate that is readily digested and enters the bloodstream slowly to provide the constant energy we need. When potatoes are cooked in any manner except steaming, the value of the mineral elements and most of the vitamins are lost, and the sugars are converted into starchy carbohydrates, which leave an acid end product in the process of digestion. Steamed potatoes retain the most vitamins and minerals and are still strongly alkaline. Fried in fat, potatoes are not only indigestible but also have a tendency to create a disturbance of the liver and gallbladder.

Potato / Nutritional Value Per 100 g Edible Portion					
	Raw Flesh	Raw Skin	Baked w/ Skin	Boiled w/ Skin	Flour
Calories	79	58	109	87	351
Protein	2.07 g	2.57 g	2.30 g	1.87 g	8.00 g
Fat	0.10 g	0.10 g	0.10 g	0.10 g	0.80 g
Fiber	0.44 g	1.79 g	0.66 g	0.32 g	1.60 g
Calcium	7 mg	30 mg	10 mg	5 mg	33 mg
Iron	0.76 mg	3.24 mg	1.36 mg	0.31 mg	17.20 mg
Magnesium	21 mg	23 mg	27 mg	22 mg	n/a
Phosphorus	46 mg	38 mg	57 mg	44 mg	178 mg
Potassium	543 mg	413 mg	418 mg	379 mg	1,588 mg
Sodium	6 mg	10 mg	8 mg	4 mg	34 mg
Zinc	0.390 mg	0.350 mg	0.320 mg	0.300 mg	n/a
Copper	0.259 mg	0.423 mg	0.305 mg	0.188 mg	n/a
Manganese	0.263 mg	0.602 mg	0.229 mg	0.138 mg	n/a
Beta Carotene (A)	n/a	n/a	n/a	n/a	0 IU
Thiamine (B$_1$)	0.088 mg	0.021 mg	0.107 mg	0.106 mg	0.420 mg
Riboflavin (B$_2$)	0.035 mg	0.038 mg	0.033 mg	0.020 mg	0.140 mg
Niacin (B$_3$)	1.484 mg	1.033 mg	1.645 mg	1.439 mg	3.400 mg
Pantothenic Acid (B$_5$)	0.380 mg	n/a	0.555 mg	0.520 mg	n/a
Pyridoxine (B$_6$)	0.260 mg	0.239 mg	0.347 mg	0.299 mg	n/a
Folic Acid (B$_9$)	12.8 mcg	17.3 mcg	11.0 mcg	10.0 mcg	n/a
Ascorbic Acid (C)	19.7 mg	11.4 mg	12.9 mg	13.0 mg	19.0 mg
Tocopherol (E)	0.06 mg	n/a	n/a	0.04 mg	n/a

LORE AND LEGEND

Francisco Pizarro, who stumbled upon the potato somewhere outside of Quito, Ecuador, must have had an imaginative palate, describing his vegetable find as "a tasty, mealy truffle." Under the name *tartuffo*, the potato was introduced to Spain in 1534. Hailed as a revitalizer for impotence, potatoes were sold on the strength of that belief for fantastic prices, in some instances as high as one thousand dollars a pound. From there, the potato meandered into Italy and France, where it was rejected by the general public on the grounds that the knobby, deep-eyed tubers resembled leprous hands and feet and were doubtless carriers of the disease. In 1565 Sir John Hawkins brought the potato plant to Ireland, and in 1585 Sir Francis Drake introduced it to England. A few of Drake's potatoes were given to Sir Walter Raleigh, who planted them on his estate near Cork, Ireland, and later gallantly made a gift of potato plants to Queen Elizabeth I. The local gentry were promptly invited to a royal banquet featuring potatoes at every course. Unfortunately, Queen Elizabeth's cooks, uneducated in the matter of potatoes, tossed out the lumpy-looking tubers and brought to the royal table a dish of boiled stems and leaves (quite poisonous), which promptly made all in attendance deathly ill.

Understandably, potatoes were banned from court, and it was some centuries before they managed to live down their public image.

In the early part of the nineteenth century the potato had become the dominant food in Ireland. The overcrowded Irish could supply their food needs without difficulty when growing potatoes on small plots of land. In fact, it was almost the sole food of the peasantry, with a typical family (man, wife, and four children) said to consume up to 250 pounds of the tubers weekly, eked out with forty pounds of oatmeal, a little milk, and an occasional salted herring. Two things are too serious to joke about, an old Irish saying goes: marriage and potatoes. The potato-dependent Irish referred to their tubers—seriously—as the Apples of Life. When blight struck in 1845 and 1846, wiping out nearly the entire crop, famine followed. An estimated one and a half million people died as a result, and another million emigrated, many of them to the Americas.

Perhaps the most creative use of the potato in history was that of master criminal John Dillinger, who carved a pistol out of a potato, stained it with iodine (iodine turns starch black), and used it to escape from jail.

Fresh potato juice is considered to have antibiotic properties and is a rich source of vitamin C, enzymes, and minerals. It is very high in vitamin C complex, a better vitamin C pattern than is found in citrus fruit, as it contains a lot of tyrosinase fraction, the organic copper blood builder. Potato juice must be used either in a little tomato juice or with a little lemon juice added to prevent its darkening by oxidation; it is so perishable that it will not keep, even if dehydrated.

VARIETIES

Fingerlings are shaped like long, chubby fingers. Colored yellow, pinkish, purple, or white, these potatoes are superlative. An heirloom Peruvian crop now grown in the United States, fingerlings have a silky fine texture and a creamy, pleasing flavor.

New potatoes are not a specific variety but refer to any freshly harvested potato with thin, flaking skins and a sweet flavor. New potatoes require less cooking and retain their shape better than mature potatoes; they are best boiled or steamed within one week of purchase.

Purple potatoes are similar in flavor and shape to the russet, with an indigo skin and a lighter purple flesh. When fried, purple potatoes turn a dingy gray color, so boiling, steaming, or baking is recommended.

Red potatoes are characterized by a thin, reddish skin, ranging from pink to dark red in color. Moister than a russet or long white potato, with a waxy, white, crisp flesh, the red potato is best boiled, but it can also be roasted or fried.

Russet potatoes, also called **Idaho potatoes** or **baking potatoes,** have an elongated cylindrical shape and yellowish brown skin. Their dry, floury, or mealy texture suits them to being baked, fried, or made into potato pancakes or dumplings.

White potatoes are round or long, with a smooth, tan-colored skin and a firm texture. This is an all-purpose potato for baking, steaming, mashing, and frying.

Yellow Finn, also called **Finnish yellow wax,** is a waxy, yellow-fleshed potato, excellent for salads and soups.

BYPRODUCTS

Chuno is a naturally freeze-dried potato or oca from the Andean altiplano. Don't be put off by the chuno's appearance; it looks more like a chunk of pumice than a food, but the earthy flavor and pleasing texture (something like deep-fried tofu) make it worth seeking out in a Latino market. The Quechuas and Aymaras preserve their just-harvested potatoes or ocas in this manner. They're left on the ground for several days, covered with a cloth to keep off the dew; each night they freeze. During the day, they are trampled by foot, to express their water. Once freeze-dried in this manner, they'll keep for years. Chunos are an excellent stew ingredient, taking on other flavors while imparting their own potato goodness.

Papa seca, or **dried potato,** another preserved Peruvian potato, is boiled rather than trampled before being left out to freeze.

Potato flour, also known as **potato starch,** is made of the entire cooked, dried, and ground potato. A useful item around the kitchen, it can serve as a binder for meat and vegetable patties or used in baking to condition the dough (as well as add subtle flavor and nutrients); it is an ideal thickener for sauces, gravies, and soups, as it cooks quickly and smoothly and leaves no raw taste. To use as a thickener, substitute one tablespoon potato flour for two tablespoons all-purpose flour.

Pumpkin
(Cucurbita maxima, C. mixta, C. pepo)

> Go to sleep now, my pumpkin,
> I will cover your toes.
> If you sleep now, my pumpkin,
> You'll turn into a rose.
>
> —LULLABY

Cucurbita is the old Latin name for gourd; *mixta* means "mixed," and *pepo* comes from the Greek word *pepon,* meaning "sun-ripened" or "mellow." The English name *pumpkin* derives from the Greek word, to which was later added the diminutive *-kin* ending.

General Information
The pumpkin, along with other squashes, is native to the Americas. The first Pilgrims barely survived their first winter in 1620 with the help of the lowly pumpkin; they knew sweet and fragrant melons but had never seen these hardy cousins, which the Indians grew as staples between corn and beans. Ranging in size from less than a pound to more than a hundred pounds (*National Geographic World* reported an 816-pound monster grown in Nova Scotia in 1990), the pumpkin also comes in a variety of colors ranging from

Pumpkin / Nutritional Value Per 100 g Edible Portion	Raw	Cooked
Calories	26	20
Protein	1.00 g	0.72 g
Fat	0.10 g	0.07 g
Fiber	1.10 g	0.83 g
Calcium	21 mg	15 mg
Iron	0.80 mg	0.57 mg
Magnesium	12 mg	9 mg
Phosphorus	44 mg	30 mg
Potassium	340 mg	230 mg
Sodium	1 mg	1 mg
Beta Carotene (A)	1,600 IU	1,082 IU
Thiamine (B₁)	0.050 mg	0.031 mg
Riboflavin (B₂)	0.110 mg	0.078 mg
Niacin (B₃)	0.600 mg	0.413 mg
Ascorbic Acid (C)	9.0 mg	4.7 mg
Tocopherol (E)	1.0 mg	n/a

LORE AND LEGEND

The best of the pumpkin tales is one of Aesop's fables, which tells of a man who lay beneath an oak tree, criticizing the Creator for hanging a tiny acorn on so huge a tree, but an enormous pumpkin on such a slender vine. Then, the story goes, an acorn fell and hit him on the nose. Jack-o'-lanterns are an essential part of Halloween, the day before All Saints' Day on November 1. Several Indian tribes carved the shells into ritual masks, a practice that continues, but shorn of its religious implications. Who Jack was is far from certain, but an Irish legend has it that there was a man named Jack who, forbidden to enter heaven because of his stinginess and barred from hell because of his practical jokes, was condemned to walk the earth with his lantern until Judgment Day. The pumpkin was a symbol of fruitfulness, rebirth, and health in early China, where it is still called the Emperor of the Garden. In 1988 Leonard Stellpflug of Rush, New York, trucked a 653½-pound pumpkin to the annual World Pumpkin Confederation weigh-in in Collins, New York. It broke the old squash record by almost 50 pounds. When asked how he grew it, Stellpflug shrugged and said, "Well-rotted manure and twenty-two pounds of fertilizer per plant."

white and peach to even blue and aqua. Deep orange is the color most familiar to Americans. European pumpkins mature sooner than their American counterparts and are generally pale yellow in color, with flesh that is less firm than the American variety; Russian pumpkins have white flesh and pale green skins. First cultivated by American Indians, who dried and made them into a type of flour, pumpkins are now most commonly used either for the traditional Halloween jack-o'-lantern or for pumpkin pie.

Buying Tips

Pumpkins of quality should be heavy for their size and free of blemishes, with a hard rind; the sugar pumpkin, which is quite small, is the variety generally considered best for cooking.

Culinary Uses

Nobody can argue the popularity of pumpkin pie . . . or pumpkin bread, pumpkin butter, pumpkin bars, and even pumpkin ice cream. To prepare a pumpkin, scrape out all the interior seeds and membrane, saving the seeds if you plan to eat them later. Peel off the skin with a vegetable peeler or sharp knife. Generally thought of only as a cooked vegetable, pumpkin can be eaten raw and is delicious when very finely grated and served in combination with grated carrots and beets as a base for salads. It can also be baked or boiled like other winter squash and used in soups, stews, and many baked goods (including corn bread) in addition to pies. In the Caribbean pumpkin is braised into spicy, fragrant stews with chilies, legumes, and sometimes meat. The French cook it into soup and serve it within its own tureen-like shell. The early male blossoms can be picked for salads, sautéing, or stuffing. The seeds are also edible and are discussed in the **Nuts, Seeds, and Oils** section.

Health Benefits

pH 4.90–5.50. Diuretic, laxative. Pumpkin is alkaline in reaction and raises the blood pressure, thus helping the blood to carry nourishment to various parts of the body. Cooked pumpkin destroys intestinal worms but not as effectively as pumpkin seeds. Cooking pumpkins converts them from a readily digested sugar to a starchy carbohydrate.

Radish
(Raphanus sativus)

> A tiny radish of passionate scarlet, tipped modestly in white.
>
> —CLEMENTINE PADDLEFORD

The botanical name *Raphanus* is from the Greek expression *raphanos*, meaning "easily raised." *Sativus* indicates that this plant has long been cultivated. The common English name *radish* comes from the Latin *radix*, meaning "root."

General Information

Radish plants are native to China and are believed to have been under cultivation in Europe as early as Neolithic times. Radishes have been eaten in Egypt since the beginnings of civilization. Herodotus records an Egyptian inscription indicating that the builders of the Great Pyramid ate enormous quantities of a radish called *gurmaia*, together with onion and garlic (History II.cxxv). The first cultivated radishes in Egypt were probably those grown for radish seed oil, which was widely used before Egypt acquired the olive. Radish seed oil was still so important in Pliny's time that he complained about farmers who ceased to grow grain in order to sow radishes because they produced great quantities of profitable, high-priced oil. This member of the mustard family has been widely propagated and now has many different varieties—those we are familiar with in salads, some grown only for cooking, and even some grown solely for their green tops.

Buying Tips

A good-quality radish is brightly colored, well formed, smooth, firm, and crisp. Those that are soft, spongy, or wilted should be avoided. Fresh radishes with the greens attached can be stored for three to five days in the refrigerator, while radishes with the greens removed can be stored in the refrigerator for two to four weeks.

Culinary Uses

The flavor of radishes can vary widely from mild to peppery, and you may see radishes that are white, pink, purple, or black, as well as ruby red; each size and color has its own degree of hotness. Best used when young, radishes become woody and difficult to digest when too old. Most often eaten raw, radishes make beautiful garnishes and are a good brightener for any green salad, with their crisp texture and fresh flavor. They can also be cooked; briefly steaming them transforms their tangy bite into a delicate, sweet flavor much like a sweet turnip. As with many other root vegetables, their green tops are edible and lend a peppery taste to salads and soups; however, the tops do not lend themselves to steaming or boiling.

Health Benefits

pH 5.52–6.05. Antibacterial, antifungal, diuretic, stimulant. Radishes contain a volatile ether that has a particular affinity for dissolving mucus or phlegm, cleansing and expelling gallstones from the bladder, and cleansing the kidneys. They are especially good for hoarseness, sinus

Radish / Nutritional Value Per 100 g Edible Portion						
	Small Red Raw	Daikon Raw	Daikon Cooked	Daikon Dried	Icicle Raw	Seeds Sprouted
Calories	17	18	17	271	14	41
Protein	0.60 g	0.60 g	0.67 g	7.90 g	1.10 g	3.81 g
Fat	0.54 g	0.10 g	0.24 g	0.72 g	0.10 g	2.53 g
Fiber	0.54 g	0.64 g	0.49 g	8.37 g	0.70 g	n/a
Calcium	21 mg	27 mg	17 mg	629 mg	27 mg	51 mg
Iron	0.29 mg	0.40 mg	0.15 mg	6.73 mg	0.80 mg	0.86 mg
Magnesium	9 mg	16 mg	9 mg	170 mg	9 mg	44 mg
Phosphorus	18 mg	23 mg	24 mg	204 mg	28 mg	113 mg
Potassium	232 mg	227 mg	285 mg	3,494 mg	280 mg	86 mg
Sodium	24 mg	21 mg	13 mg	278 mg	16 mg	6 mg
Zinc	0.300 mg	n/a	n/a	n/a	n/a	0.560 mg
Copper	0.040 mg	n/a	n/a	n/a	n/a	0.120 mg
Manganese	0.070 mg	n/a	n/a	n/a	n/a	0.260 mg
Beta Carotene (A)	8 IU	0 IU	0 IU	0 IU	0 IU	391 IU
Thiamine (B$_1$)	0.005 mg	0.020 mg	0 mg	0.270 mg	0.030 mg	0.102 mg
Riboflavin (B$_2$)	0.045 mg	0.020 mg	0.023 mg	0.680 mg	0.020 mg	0.103 mg
Niacin (B$_3$)	0.300 mg	0.200 mg	0.150 mg	3.400 mg	0.300 mg	2.853 mg
Pantothenic Acid (B$_5$)	0.088 mg	n/a	n/a	n/a	0.184 mg	0.733 mg
Pyridoxine (B$_6$)	0.071 mg	n/a	n/a	n/a	0.075 mg	0.285 mg
Folic Acid (B$_9$)	27.0 mcg	n/a	n/a	n/a	14.0 mcg	94.7 mcg
Ascorbic Acid (C)	22.8 mg	22.0 mg	15.1 mg	0 mg	29.0 mg	28.9 mg

LORE AND LEGEND

A talmudic story relates that Judea was once widely renowned for producing enormous garden plants, and in fact one radish was so large that a fox was able to hollow it out and make it his home. After he left, curious onlookers weighed the vegetable and found it to be nearly a hundred pounds! A German botanist in the mid-sixteenth century did report seeing some radishes that weighed a hundred pounds, giving credence to the story. Oaxaca, Mexico, celebrates the Night of the Radishes on December 23 by carving giant radishes into fantastic figures of animals and people.

congestion, and sore throats. They have antibacterial and antifungal action, and regular use will help prevent viral infections such as the common cold and influenza. Radishes have enzymes that aid the secretion of digestive juices, most beneficial when eating heavy starchy foods such as grains, pastas, and potatoes. European folk medicine recommends eating radishes—several a day—on an empty stomach to help melt gallstones and kidney stones.

VARIETIES

Black radishes are sturdy characters that look like sooty black or matte brown-black turnips. Select very firm, comparatively heavy dark globes that show no flabbiness, pitting, sponginess, or cracks. The firm, dry, creamy white flesh may be almost as pungent as horseradish and can be either coarsely shredded (with or without skins) or sliced thin and added raw to salads and cheeses; their peppery bite also works well in stir-fries, soups, and stews. Excellent keeping vegetables, black radishes store well for months in the refrigerator but will mellow during storage. They are available primarily in winter and early spring.

Daikon or **Japanese radish** is known in Japan as the "giant white radish." This sturdy winter radish is six inches to a foot long (weighing up to fifty pounds if the farmer permits), white, cylindrical, and tapered at the tip like a carrot. Look for those that have a satiny sheen and are firm, not spongy. The root should be heavy, solid, and unblemished, with the pungent smell of radish. Sweet and juicy, it has a cleansing, mildly sharp flavor that provides a crisp counterpoint to salty food. Raw daikon can be slivered, grated, diced, or sliced to add its crunch and zip to relishes and salads. It can also be used in soups and stir-fries or pickled whole. Fresh raw daikon is known to contain diuretics, decongestants, the digestive enzymes diastase, amylase, and esterase, and a substance that inhibits the formation of carcinogens in the body. It is available year-round, peaking in July through November.

Horseradish—see separate reference.

Icicle radishes are white both inside and out. They are usually several inches long, with a bite that may be either mild or hot.

Red radishes are the most common variety of radish in North America. Typically they are the size and shape of cherries, though some markets now offer elongated red radishes that are more pungent than the small round ones.

Rutabaga

(Brassica napus napobrassica)
Also Known As: Swedish Turnip

The Latin name *Brassica* derives from the Celtic *bresic*; *napobrassica* means "turnip-cabbage." The English word *rutabaga* comes from the Swedish *rotabagge*, which means "round root."

General Information

The rutabaga was developed by the Swiss botanist Gaspard Bauhin from a series of judicious turnip-cabbage crosses. The result turned out to be tailor-made for the fields of the chilly north; the plants are slow growers that prefer a cool climate and will not thrive where summers are exceedingly hot. At its best during the winter, this member of the cabbage family has a large yellow-orange bulb that is either globular or elongated and is both larger and sweeter than turnips. Before they are shipped to market, their large, blue-green tops are usually trimmed and their bulbs waxed to prevent loss of moisture. There is some confusion over

the root's name: in America it is called "rutabaga," which is the French name for the large yellow variety, while in France the other varieties have the prettier name of *chou-navet*; the English called the vegetable "turnip-rooted cabbage" before it came to be known as "swede" when Sweden began to export their crop to England in the 1780s; but in Scotland what they call a "swede" is in fact a turnip.

Buying Tips

The roots should be firm and fairly smooth, with few leaf scars around the crown or fibrous roots at the base. Avoid those that are light for their size, or soft and shriveled, as they are likely to be tough, woody, or hollow. It is common practice to encase the root in paraffin to extend its shelf life, so it needs to be peeled.

Culinary Uses

Rutabagas have a mild, sweet flavor and readily absorb other flavors. Use them raw in salads or for hors d'oeuvres by peeling and then cutting them into cubes, curls, sticks, or triangles. They can also be steamed, baked, roasted with meat, sliced and fried, boiled and mashed (delicious mixed with potatoes and carrots), or cubed, blanched, and added to stews and soups.

Health Benefits

Rutabagas are sometimes recommended for cases of constipation, but they are apt to cause flatulence because of their mustard oil content and should not be used by anyone who suffers from kidney troubles. All *Brassica* genus vegetables contain dithiolthiones, a group of compounds that have anticancer, antioxidant properties; indoles, substances that protect against breast and colon cancer; and sulfur, which has antibiotic and antiviral characteristics. This family of vegetables also mildly stimulates the liver and other tissues out of stagnancy.

Rutabaga / Nutritional Value Per 100 g Edible Portion		
	Raw	Cooked
Calories	36	34
Protein	1.20 g	1.10 g
Fat	0.20 g	0.19 g
Fiber	1.10 g	1.04 g
Calcium	47 mg	42 mg
Iron	0.52 mg	0.47 mg
Magnesium	23 mg	21 mg
Phosphorus	58 mg	49 mg
Potassium	337 mg	287 mg
Sodium	20 mg	18 mg
Zinc	0.340 mg	0.300 mg
Copper	0.040 mg	0.036 mg
Manganese	0.170 mg	0.153 mg
Beta Carotene (A)	0 IU	0 IU
Thiamine (B$_1$)	0.090 mg	0.072 mg
Riboflavin (B$_2$)	0.040 mg	0.036 mg
Niacin (B$_3$)	0.700 mg	0.630 mg
Pantothenic Acid (B$_5$)	0.160 mg	0.137 mg
Pyridoxine (B$_6$)	0.100 mg	0.090 mg
Folic Acid (B$_9$)	20.5 mcg	15.5 mcg
Ascorbic Acid (C)	25.0 mg	21.9 mg
Tocopherol (E)	0.15 mg	0.15 mg

Salsify

(Tragopogon porrifolius)
Also Known As: Oyster Plant, Vegetable Oyster, Goatsbeard

Tragopogon means "goat's beard" and refers to the milky white seed filaments (like dandelion fluff) that distinguish members of this genus. *Porrifolius* means "leek-leaved" and describes to a degree the grassy, flat greens. The English word *salsify* comes from the Italian *sassefrica*, meaning "plant that accompanies stones," after its predisposition for rocky land. The oyster association most likely comes from the milky fluid that oozes from a cut in the fresh greens rather than from its having an oysterlike flavor.

General Information

Salsify is a member of the chicory family believed to be native to the Mediterranean basin, possibly first on the African side. The English began growing salsify both as a vegetable and as an ornamental sometime after 1500, and it appeared on the American scene during the 1700s. Salsify produces fleshy roots the first year and then sets purple or rose-colored flowers the next. Generally imported to North American markets from Belgium, it is also a popular vegetable in home gardens and readily grows wild. The long, buff-skinned root, which looks like a hairy and undernourished parsnip, has white, mild-tasting flesh. In the United States it is often difficult to find salsify in the markets, while in Europe it is readily available during its season and turns up frequently in fritters, as a basis for cream soups, or even cooked like asparagus.

Buying Tips

The root will be up to eight inches long and have many tiny protruding rootlets. Select those that are firm and crisp rather than soft, and prefer smaller ones over larger ones, which may be pithy.

Salsify / Nutritional Value Per 100 g Edible Portion		
	Raw	Cooked
Calories	82	68
Protein	3.30 g	2.73 g
Fat	0.20 g	0.17 g
Fiber	1.80 g	1.49 g
Calcium	60 mg	47 mg
Iron	0.70 mg	0.55 mg
Magnesium	23 mg	18 mg
Phosphorus	75 mg	56 mg
Potassium	380 mg	283 mg
Sodium	20 mg	16 mg
Beta Carotene (A)	0 IU	0 IU
Thiamine (B$_1$)	0.080 mg	0.056 mg
Riboflavin (B$_2$)	0.220 mg	0.173 mg
Niacin (B$_3$)	0.500 mg	0.392 mg
Ascorbic Acid (C)	8.0 mg	4.6 mg

Culinary Uses

The flavor of salsify combines a slightly sour-sweet taste with a mild, salty flavor. Delicious steamed, boiled, sautéed, baked, deep-fried, or chunked into soups and stews, this vegetable is something to look forward to in the fall, especially after a frost, when their flavor improves. Salsify skin is edible but needs a good scrubbing before cooking. The immature purple bud may be cooked and eaten—it is reminiscent of asparagus in flavor—and the tender young leaves are a good salad ingredient. In the early spring, the young flower stalks can be eaten raw or cooked like asparagus.

Health Benefits

pH 5.72–5.80 (cooked). Salsify contains inulin, a natural insulin that helps the pancreas digest starches. It also nourishes the kidneys and intestines. However, for some people salsify has been known to cause serious gastric grumbling, so test in moderation to find your tolerance.

Salsify, Black

(Scorzonera hispanica)
Also Known As: Scorzonera

Scorzonera comes from either *scorzanera*, Italian for "black bark," or from *escorco*, the Catalan word for "viper," so named because the plant's juices were thought to provide an antidote to snakebite. The plant was introduced to European culture through Spanish seed, hence *hispanica*. The English word *salsify* comes from the Italian *sassefrica*, meaning "plant that accompanies stones," after its predisposition for rocky land.

General Information

Indigenous to central and southern Europe, black salsify was relatively unknown except to wild food gatherers until the sixteenth century. During the Middle Ages it became one of the most important vegetables in Europe, considered a potent tonic and a remedy for smallpox. The Spanish began to cultivate the plant during the eighteenth century, and its use spread to kitchens all over the English-speaking world. The vegetable fell out of flavor in the Victorian era, supposedly because fastidious cooks began peeling the "dirty" black skin from the root before cooking. This practice not only ruined the flavor but also put an end to whatever tonic properties the root possessed.

Not visually appealing, this delectable root resembles a muddy brown, nontapering, petrified carrot. It is usually more regularly shaped, longer, and smoother than white salsify. *Scorzonera* is described by some as inferior to salsify, and by others as superior.

Culinary Uses

Black salsify has a faint coconut or oyster flavor. Generally eaten steamed, baked, boiled, or fried, the roots should always be soaked well before using to remove the bitter taste. The skin is edible and needs only a light scrubbing rather than peeling; it offers interesting color relief and flavor to all manner of dishes. The southwest of France has a specialty of cooking omelets with unopened *Scorzonera* buds, described as more exquisite than asparagus tips.

Health Benefits

Like Jerusalem artichokes and salsify, black salsify roots contain inulin and are thus valuable to diabetics, who can use them as a source of carbohydrate. The inulin is responsible for the sweet quality in the flavor. Some people find that salsify causes serious gastric grumbling, so test in moderation to determine your tolerance. Low in fat and high in fiber, calcium, and iron.

Sea Kale
(Crambe maritima)
Also Known As: Sea Colewort

Maritima means "maritime" or "of the sea."

General Information

Growing wild along the sandy cliffs and beaches of the English, Continental, and Irish coasts, sea kale is quite a large plant, with broad, toothed, bluish-green leaves and white flowers borne on a two-foot-long stalk. This is a beautiful and mysterious plant when still in its wild state. There it sits, like a great silver-green bouquet splayed over the shingle. Sea folk must have eaten the plant since time began, knowing the places along the shore where it grows and waiting to cover the growing shoots with seaweed to blanch them. The young shoots and leaves were recognized as a delicate and choice food by the Romans, who gathered and preserved them in barrels for eating throughout long sea voyages. But not until the late eighteenth century was the plant given a place in the garden. It is recorded as being brought to England from Italy in about 1760, and the seeds sold at a high price as a rarity. Once planted, sea kale will continue to yield for about ten years. Harvested in the spring, the shoots must be blanched to be tender. In mid-summer the plants produce attractive flowers.

Culinary Uses

Choose shoots that are six to nine inches long. These have a delicate, nutty, slightly bitter flavor and are delicious when eaten raw with cheese, in salads, or prepared like asparagus. Traditionally, the leaf stalks are tied in bundles and cooked in salted water for about twenty minutes, then served hot with melted butter. The shoots are boiled for ten minutes.

Sea Vegetables

A Piece of Sea Weed serves for a Barometer;
It gets wet and dry as the weather gets so.

—William Blake

General Information

The culinary and medicinal uses of seaweeds and sea vegetables are not new but were originally confined mostly to Asia. These sea plants have no roots, as land plants do, nor do they have branches and stalks in the same sense but cling by means of holdfasts. Over 435 varieties have been discovered so far, and these are generally grouped into three kinds, based on color—the brown, the red, and the green. The particular color is related to the spectrum of light available to the plants for photosynthesis. Sea vegetables are now becoming more well known and accepted in the western hemisphere.

Culinary Uses

Seaweeds and sea vegetables are highly versatile foods, easily incorporated into numerous styles of cuisine, thereby enhancing and complementing the flavors and textures. Depending on the variety, they can be grilled, broiled, stir-fried, or chopped and added to soups, stews, salads, and many other dishes. An easy way to incorporate seaweeds into the diet is by shaking a little of the dried flakes of any variety onto salads or soups. This will provide flavor plus a whole range of beneficial nutrients. Most dried seaweeds expand considerably when soaked, and since their flavor goes a long way, only a small amount is needed. All of us probably eat a large quantity of seaweed every day without knowing it—it appears as a binder and thickener in foods such as ice creams, candies, jams, soups, and sauces, not to mention its use in toothpaste, cosmetics, and certain medications.

Health Benefits

The medicinal properties of sea vegetables are voluminous. Human blood contains all one hundred or so minerals and trace elements in the ocean; since seaweeds contain these elements in ten to twenty times the quantities as in land plants and in a highly assimilable form, they are an excellent source for food and medicine, particularly for people with degenerative diseases. Sea vegetables are used to reduce blood cholesterol and help disorders of the genito-urinary and reproductive systems. They have antibiotic properties known to be effective against penicillin-resistant bacteria. They are also credited with antiaging properties and have long been acclaimed as beauty aids, believed to help maintain beautiful, healthy skin and lustrous hair.

They hold considerable water when passing through the digestive tract, forming a gel that increases the bulk and speed of the stools. Kelp and other seaweeds are used by the Chinese to soften and reduce hardened masses in the body.

Studies conducted at Canada's McGill University have shown that some seaweeds (including arame, hiziki, and kombu) can help remove radioactive strontium from the body by means of alginic acid, which binds with strontium in the blood and carries it out of the system. Red seaweeds bind plutonium poison; brown binds strontium 90 and cadmium poisons; and green seaweed binds calcium and mercury poison. Seaweeds are one of the few good sources of organic fluorine, a nutrient that boosts the body's defenses and strengthens the teeth and bones. Since fluorine is lost with even minimal cooking, one must eat dried seaweeds raw (after soaking) to gain any fluorine benefit. The iodine content in seaweed prevents goiter and is indispensable to thyroid function; the thyroid influences digestive and metabolic efficiency, and a deficiency of iodine can result in a lack of energy, an inability to metabolize foods, and weight gain.

VARIETIES

Alaria (*Alaria esculenta, A. marginata*) is biologically almost identical to wakame but is harvested primarily in Maine. Shep Erhart, who makes a living foraging different kinds of seaweed in Maine, reports that alaria "is the most beautiful to look at, the most delicate to the taste, and the most dangerous to harvest." Alaria loves rocky, windswept peninsulas, where it curls and crashes with every breaking wave. It has a wilder taste than wakame and requires longer cooking. Dried alaria can be added to soups or cooked with other vegetables or tofu. Baked, it can be crumbled and used as a garnish. Alaria is high in iodine, bromine, and all the B vitamins.

Arame (*Eisenia arborea*) is a kelp closely related to wakame and kombu that is harvested in Japan, Peru, and the Pacific North American coast. The blades, which grow in wide leaves up to a foot in length, are sliced into long, stringlike strands, cooked for seven hours, sun-dried, and packaged. with its mild, sweet taste, this variety is enjoyed by most westerners immediately. Arame is noted for treatment of the spleen and pancreas, female disorders, and high blood pressure. It is highly concentrated in iron and calcium and one of the richest sources of iodine.

Sea Vegetables / Nutritional Value Per 100 g Edible Portion					
	Dulse, Dried	Irish Moss	Kombu	Nori	Wakame
Calories	n/a	49	43	35	45
Protein	13.30 g	1.51 g	1.68 g	5.81 g	3.03 g
Fat	n/a	0.16 g	0.56 g	0.28 g	0.64 g
Fiber	n/a	n/a	1.33 g	0.27 g	0.54 g
Calcium	632 mg	72 mg	168 mg	70 mg	150 mg
Iron	79.20 mg	8.90 mg	2.85 mg	1.80 mg	2.18 mg
Magnesium	593 mg	n/a	121 mg	2 mg	107 mg
Phosphorus	386 mg	157 mg	42 mg	58 mg	80 mg
Potassium	2,270 mg	63 mg	89 mg	356 mg	50 mg
Sodium	9,917 mg	67 mg	233 mg	48 mg	872 mg
Zinc	3.900 mg	1.950 mg	1.230 mg	1.050 mg	0.380 mg
Copper	n/a	0.149 mg	0.130 mg	0.264 mg	0.284 mg
Manganese	3.700 mg	0.370 mg	0.200 mg	0.988 mg	1.400 mg
Beta Carotene (A)	8,010 IU	n/a	116 IU	5,202 IU	360 IU
Thiamine (B_1)	0.160 mg	0.015 mg	0.050 mg	0.098 mg	0.060 mg
Riboflavin (B_2)	0.110 mg	0.466 mg	0.150 mg	0.446 mg	0.230 mg
Niacin (B_3)	3.200 mg	0.593 mg	0.470 mg	1.470 mg	1.600 mg
Pantothenic Acid (B_5)	n/a	0.176 mg	n/a	n/a	n/a
Pyridoxine (B_6)	n/a	n/a	n/a	0.159 mg	n/a
Folic Acid (B_9)	n/a	n/a	180.0 mcg	n/a	n/a
Ascorbic Acid (C)	12.0 mg	n/a	n/a	39.0 mg	3.0 mg
Tocopherol (E)	n/a	n/a	0.87 mg	n/a	n/a

Bladder wrack (*Fucus*), also known as **Rockweed,** is highly regarded as an effective medicine for obesity, hypothyroid function, and edema. It is not, however, a diuretic as its name suggests. *Wraec* is an Old English word for "seaweed," while *bladder* refers to its swollen, bladderlike frond tips. Bladder wrack has a pleasing, sweet flavor, but its slippery gel is a texture most people don't like. It is used primarily in stock or as an ingredient in food supplements.

Dulse (*Rhodymenia palmata, Palmaria palmata*) is a red seaweed with flat, fan-shaped fronds that grows from the temperate to frigid zones of the Atlantic and Pacific. The use of dulse as a food dates back to the eighteenth century in the British Isles, where it was commonly eaten with fish, potatoes, and butter. An unlikely tavern snack food, dulse was nonetheless served in Boston pubs, especially in Irish neighborhoods, through the 1920s. Dried dulse can be eaten raw; chopped or crumbled for salads, soups, and vegetable dishes; or twisted on a tong and roasted. When quickly rinsed under running water, dulse holds its color and is tender and delicious in a green salad, in dressings, or as a garnish. Because of its salty taste, it is frequently used as a salt substitute. One favorite use is as a bacon substitute in a BLT sandwich. Dubbed the "beef jerky of the sea" because of its chewy, stringy texture and salty taste, it is often an immediate favorite of those first tasting seaweed, which may not be true for other sea vegetables. This highly alkaline vegetable is an excellent source of iron and also contains high quantities of iodine and manganese, which activate enzyme systems.

Hijiki (*Hizikia fusiforme*) has been used for hundreds of years in Japan, where it is known as the "bearer of wealth and beauty." It grows over the rocks and sea bottom like a carpet of stem roots or erect like a bush up to six feet high. The harvested plants are cut and sun-dried, boiled until soft, then dried again. The black dried hijiki should be soaked before use; the soaking process will cause it to quadruple in size, and the color to lighten to a deep brown. With a milder taste than dulse, kombu, or nori, hijiki blends well with many foods. Hijiki is very mineral-rich; because of its calcium and iron contents, this sea vegetable is highly recommended during pregnancy. In the Far East, it is esteemed as a food that increases beauty and strengthens and adds luster to the hair.

Irish moss (*Chondrus crispus*), also known as **carrageen,** is found in great abundance off the Atlantic coasts of Europe and America. The name *carrageen* in fact comes from a coastal town in southeastern Ireland. During the potato famine of the mid–nineteenth century, thousands of Irish saved themselves from starvation by eating this flat, red, fernlike seaweed. Inedible when raw, Irish moss can be cut up and added to soups or stews. It is somewhat cartilaginous and flexible but when dried becomes brittle. It bleaches to creamy-white when exposed to sunlight. Most harvested Irish moss is processed for its jellylike extract, carrageenan, used as a thickening agent. Carrageenan is popular in desserts, puddings, yogurt, and other dairy products because it will jell in cool water. Boiled with milk and sugar, it makes a tasty white pudding with a high mucilage content—a soothing food for people with sore throats. Long noted for its medicinal properties, Irish moss is used in cough preparations; for digestive disorders and ulcers, kidney ailments, heart disease, and glandular irregularities; and as a bowel regulator. It contains calcium chloride, which acts as a heart tonic and glandular balancer, and is especially high in iodine and potassium.

Kelp (*Fucus* and *Laminaria* spp.) is the fastest-growing plant on land or in the sea, growing up to two feet a day and reaching lengths of over one thousand feet. The kelp family includes nearly nine hundred known varieties, including kombu, wakame, and arame, which are packaged under their own names. After being harvested and dried, kelp that is to be sold for human consumption is usually powdered for use in capsules or added to supplements and seasonings. Powdered kelp has a "sea" flavor that adds a subtle salty dimension to salads, soups, vegetables, baked goods, and beverages. Dried kelp can be diced and added to soups and stews. Considered the most completely mineralized food, kelp greatly increases the nutritional value of all food prepared with it.

Kombu (*Laminaria longicruris, L. digitata*), also called **tangle, oarweed,** and **sea cabbage,** is one of the better-known and more versatile sea vegetables. A brown seaweed that has been eaten by people in Russia, Wales, and Iceland for several hundred years, its broad blackish-gray ribbons are dried, boiled, compressed, dried again, and finally shredded or powdered. Usually sold in five- to six-inch dried pieces, it is also sold as **natto kombu** (shredded kombu that cooks quickly), **tororo kombu** (vinegared, shaved kombu that needs little or no cooking), **shio-kombu** (boiled, soy-sauce-flavored kombu), **kombu-zuke** (lightly pickled kombu), **kombu-ko** (powdered kombu that can be sprinkled on food or used in drinks), **ne kombu** (the holdfast or root, which is a strengthening food), and **sweet kombu** (a premier kombu harvested from the Pacific only during a one-week period; it has a sweet mineral taste). Kombu can be eaten raw as a vegetable, added to stews or soup stock, used as a food wrapper, or eaten on its own either deep-fried or baked. When crisped (without hydration) for a few minutes in the oven, it becomes a delicious chip; however, if it blisters, it was overtoasted and will taste bitter. Added to a pot of beans, kombu helps them to cook faster and renders them more digestible because it balances the protein and oils as well as softens their tough fibers. Especially delicious with root vegetables, it should first be soaked for fifteen minutes and then cooked beneath the vegetables. More than any other sea vegetable, kombu takes preeminent place in Japan, where it is the foundation for the numerous broths and stocks (dashi) that flavor so many Japanese dishes. Kombu contains significant amounts of glutamic acid, the basis of monosodium glutamate (MSG), but acts as an antidote to excess sodium consumption, reduces blood cholesterol, and lowers hypertension. High in sugar, potassium, iodine, calcium, and vitamins A and C.

Nori (*Porphyra tenera*), also called **laver** when cultivated, is classified as a red seaweed, although it is bright lavender in the water. Dried, it turns a dark purple or black color but then turns green when cooked or toasted. High-quality nori possesses a deep color and brilliant luster, while lesser-quality nori is dull and flat.

Gaelic people of the British Isles have long made flat breads from flour and laver, known as laver bread. In south Wales it is a traditional breakfast food, coated in oatmeal before being fried and served with bacon and eggs. In the Far East nori is sometimes boiled to produce a gel in cooking, but most often it is simply wrapped around rice balls, used for sushi, or lightly toasted and cut into strips for garnishes. It can also be chopped or broken and added to soups and salads. Nori has the highest protein content (48 percent of dry weight) of the seaweeds—higher than soybeans, milk, meat, fish, or poultry—and is the most easily digested. It also contains an enzyme that helps break down cholesterol deposits. Nori contains more vitamin A than carrots. It is also high in B vitamins and vitamins C and D, and it is a good source of calcium, iron, potassium, iodine, and many trace elements.

Sea lettuce (*Ulva* spp.) is a bright green, ribbed plant that resembles leaf lettuce. Gossamer-thin—literally two cells thick—blades of sea lettuce cover rocks on the intertidal zone. This seaweed, which feels like waxed paper, has a mild flavor similar to nori. It is good as a fresh, finely chopped salad green when picked at an early stage. It can also be added to sandwiches in place of regular lettuce. Older fronds may be dried and added to soups.

Sea palm (*Postelsia palmaeformis*) looks like a miniature palm tree. A brown seaweed found on the north Pacific coast of North America, it has a texture, appearance, and flavor that fit right into family fare. Mildly sweet, with a pleasing al dente texture, sea palm comes in long, flat, ribbed strands. Crushed into bits with a pestle, it can be tossed into soups or added to grains, beans, or any pot that's wanting enhanced flavor, mineral enrichment, and eye appeal. Like other brown sea vegetables, it contains algin, which fixes and removes radioactive particles and heavy metals from the body.

Wakame (*Undaria pinnatifida*) is a brown Japanese seaweed that grows in long, thin, ribbonlike strands and sporophylls—fingerlike protrusions—that reportedly taste like peanuts. This versatile and sweet-tasting seaweed can be toasted and crumbled for use as a condiment or an ingredient in soups, salads, and vegetable dishes. The Japanese use it to flavor fish stock (dashi); it can also be soaked and cut into strips for making sushi. The best-quality wakame has a thin rather than a wide center stipe, but since it is impossible to determine the stipe size when the plant is dried, purchasing reputable brand names is the surest way to obtain quality wakame. Once rehydrated, the stipe is generally cut out and reserved for soup stock. As with other sea vegetables, wakame contains alginic acid, a polysaccharide component that is released by gastric acids during digestion. When the alginic acid enters the intestines it can combine with sodium or heavy metals and eliminate them from the system. As a result, eating wakame will alleviate hypertension caused by excessive sodium consumption and reduce the heavy-metal toxicity of the body.

Skirret
(Sium sisarum)

Sium comes from *sion*, the old Greek named used by Dioscorides; *sisarum* means "like sisal." The English name *skirret* is derived from the Dutch *suikerwortel*, meaning "sugar root."

General Information
A member of the carrot and parsley family native to China and Japan, skirret is cultivated for the bunch of wrinkled, grayish roots that form the crown. During the fifteenth century skirret enjoyed a fairly wide acceptance in Europe, and during the seventeenth and eighteenth centuries it ranked as one of the major kitchen vegetables in English and American gardens. The seventeenth-century gardeners Parkinson and Evelyn praised skirret as one of the most acceptable and pleasant root vegetables; they provided recipes for boiled, stewed, and roasted skirret. In the end, however, skirret lost out to the carrot, salsify, and even the parsnip.

Culinary Uses
The roots have a sweet, tender white flesh that, when cooked like salsify or parsnips, is highly esteemed in Asian cuisine. To prepare, simply scrub the roots and cut them into suitable lengths for cooking; they can then be boiled with a bit of salt and served with butter. They can also be stewed, braised, baked, batter-fried, or creamed. They are delicious when mashed with potatoes. Raw skirret can be grated or chopped into mixed salads or dressed on its own in a vinegar marinade.

LORE AND LEGEND
The Emperor Tiberius is said to have been so fond of skirret roots that he sought tributes of them from the warring Germans.

Spinach
(Spinacia oleracea)

Spinacia comes from the term *spina*, meaning "spine," and alludes to the plant's spiny fruit; *oleracea* refers to a vegetable garden herb that is used in cooking.

General Information
Spinach originated in or near Persia, where it was cultivated for the delectation of their exotic long-haired cats. This member of the goosefoot family was entirely unknown to the Greeks and Romans. It reached Spain by way of the invading Moors around A.D. 1100–1200. Spinach was probably brought to the United States early in colonial days, but commercial cultivation did not start until about 1806, and the first curly-leaved variety was introduced in 1828. Popularized in comic strips by the Herculean feats of Popeye the sailor, spinach is not usually a favorite vegetable among children. There are three basic types of spinach. Savoy, with its crinkly, curly, dark green leaves, is the type sold in fresh bunches at most markets. Flat or smooth-leaved spinach has unwrinkled, spade-shaped leaves that are easier to clean than savoy; varieties of this type are generally used for canned and frozen spinach as well as for soups, baby foods, and other processed foods. Increasingly popular are semi-savoy varieties, which have slightly crinkled leaves. These offer some of the texture of savoy but are not as difficult to clean; they are cultivated for both the fresh market and for processing.

Buying Tips
Leaves should be a dark green, and fresh looking. Avoid bunches with yellow leaves or those that are wilted, bruised, or crushed. Spinach will store for a week at most in the refrigerator, so use quickly.

Culinary Uses
Raw spinach is an excellent salad green—light and tasty. Cooked spinach has a slightly acid aftertaste; many cooks

LORE AND LEGEND

Spinach has been regarded in folklore as a plant with remarkable abilities to restore energy, increase vitality, and improve the quality of the blood. The popular cartoon Popeye is a testament to this.

enjoy this flavor, but if you are not one of them, try adding two pats of butter or a splash of milk or cream. The secret of cooking spinach is to cook it quickly in very little water; it reduces in size dramatically, so be sure to buy sufficient quantity. Spinach can also be used as a stuffing for pancakes and in soups, omelets, quiches, and other savory dishes.

Health Benefits

pH 5.50–6.80. Laxative. Raw spinach is one of nature's best antidotes for lower bowel stagnation, detoxifying the digestive tract, restoring the pH balance, soothing intestinal inflammation, promoting peristalsis, and providing the organic mineral salts required for repair and maintenance of the colon. Its rich iron and chlorophyll content helps build healthy blood, while its vitamin A content is valuable for the eyes. The oxalic acid found in spinach is in a natural and beneficial form when raw. Cooking converts this acid into an inorganic form that binds with calcium to form a compound that the body cannot absorb; this compound is then deposited in the kidneys and can contribute to a calcium deficiency within the body.

Spinach, New Zealand
(Tetragonia expansa, T. tetragonioides)

Tetragonia is a Greek word meaning "four-angled" and refers to this plant's four-angled seed; *expansa* means "expanded" and suggests its willingness to spread widely.

General Information

New Zealand spinach is, not surprisingly, native to New Zealand and Australia. The man who was chiefly responsible for the transfer of New Zealand spinach to Europe was Captain James Cook. On his first circumnavigation of the world, he took along Sir Joseph Banks, a botanist who discovered the plant in New Zealand in 1770 and brought back samples of seeds. Planted in Kew Gardens in 1772,

Spinach / Nutritional Value Per 100 g Edible Portion	Raw	Cooked
Calories	22	23
Protein	2.86 g	2.97 g
Fat	0.35 g	0.26 g
Fiber	0.89 g	0.88 g
Calcium	99 mg	136 mg
Iron	2.71 mg	3.57 mg
Magnesium	79 mg	87 mg
Phosphorus	49 mg	56 mg
Potassium	558 mg	466 mg
Sodium	79 mg	70 mg
Zinc	0.530 mg	0.760 mg
Copper	0.130 mg	0.174 mg
Manganese	0.897 mg	0.935 mg
Beta Carotene (A)	6,715 IU	8,190 IU
Thiamine (B$_1$)	0.078 mg	0.095 mg
Riboflavin (B$_2$)	0.189 mg	0.236 mg
Niacin (B$_3$)	0.724 mg	0.490 mg
Pantothenic Acid (B$_5$)	0.065 mg	0.145 mg
Pyridoxine (B$_6$)	0.195 mg	0.242 mg
Folic Acid (B$_9$)	194.4 mcg	145.8 mcg
Ascorbic Acid (C)	28.1 mg	9.8 mg
Tocopherol (E)	1.88 mg	n/a

Spinach, New Zealand / Nutritional Value Per 100 g Edible Portion	Raw	Cooked
Calories	14	12
Protein	1.50 g	1.30 g
Fat	0.20 g	0.17 g
Fiber	0.70 g	0.61 g
Calcium	58 mg	48 mg
Iron	0.80 mg	0.66 mg
Magnesium	39 mg	32 mg
Phosphorus	28 mg	22 mg
Potassium	130 mg	102 mg
Sodium	130 mg	107 mg
Beta Carotene (A)	4,400 IU	3,622 IU
Thiamine (B$_1$)	0.040 mg	0.030 mg
Riboflavin (B$_2$)	0.130 mg	0.107 mg
Niacin (B$_3$)	0.500 mg	0.390 mg
Pantothenic Acid (B$_5$)	0.312 mg	0.256 mg
Ascorbic Acid (C)	30.0 mg	16.0 mg

they were promptly forgotten; apparently, it did not occur to anybody that the plant might be edible. On Cook's second voyage, a botanist named Foster found the plant growing abundantly near Queen Charlotte's Strait and was reminded by its thick, fleshy leaves of the spinach substitute orachee. He took it aboard ship as a possible remedy for scurvy, which had been plaguing the crew, and discovered that it did indeed offer protection against that malady. Europeans were not very excited about the new plant, cultivating it almost exclusively as a curiosity in botanical gardens or, later, as a houseplant for its attractive, fleshy, triangular leaves. Even today one would be hard put to find New Zealand spinach in the markets; usually those who want to eat it have to grow it themselves. Chiefly used for furnishing greens during the hot summer months, when common spinach does not grow well, it endears itself to gardeners for its ability to withstand heat, actually thriving in the hot summer sun.

Culinary Uses

New Zealand spinach tastes very similar to regular spinach but is somewhat tougher. With leaves that are smaller and more porous, it has the same uses. Most experts agree that it has to be cooked in order to be considered palatable. Once cooked, it becomes a pulpy mass, more unctuous than spinach in consistency, which some think makes it more agreeable eating, while others think not. Young tender leaves are much superior to older ones, which tend to develop a taste too assertive to please everyone. One system for picking leaves is to take only the leafy tips of branches where new growth is developing.

Health Benefits

New Zealand spinach contains much the same health-giving elements as true spinach, though with considerably less iron and more oxalic acid.

Sprouts

General Information

Sprouts result when almost any bean, grain, or seed is soaked overnight and allowed to grow, releasing all of its stored nutrients in a burst of vitality as it attempts to become a full-sized plant. When you eat these tiny, easy-to-digest plants, you are literally getting the best of what the plants have to offer, since they are at their nutritional peak. During sprouting, vitamin and enzyme content increase dramatically, while starch is converted into simple sugars, protein is turned into amino acids and peptones, and crude fat is broken down into free fatty acids. Hence, the sprouting process predigests the nutrients, making them easier to assimilate and metabolize. Ancient manuscripts show that by 3000 B.C. the Chinese were eating bean sprouts on a regular basis. The emperor of China at that time also recorded certain therapeutic uses of sprouts in a book about medicinal herbs.

Buying Tips

General guidelines for buying sprouts are that the sprouts should be fresh looking and fresh smelling with no dark soggy spots, and if they are to the leafy stage, the leaves should be green not yellow.

Culinary Uses

Sprouts have now gone mainstream, with alfalfa and mung bean sprouts showing up in almost every grocery store, but many more besides can be sprouted right in your own kitchen. Their crisp, crunchy texture makes them a great addition to salads and sandwiches, and you can use them fresh or cooked in a great many dishes, adding them whole for just the last brief minute. If you are sprouting at home, use only seeds that are whole and preservative-free and eat the sprouts soon after they are "ripened" (exposed to sunlight for chlorophyll) to get the full nutritional benefit. The rinse schedule will depend upon where you live, since the more humidity in the air, the less you should water, as excessive moisture will promote mold; you may have to rinse three or four times a day in Phoenix, Arizona, but only once or twice a day in Miami, Florida. Sprouted wheat berries may be ground and added to bread dough, where they assist in the rising process and give the bread a special flavor. If adding a cup of sprouted wheat berries, subtract half a cup of flour and half a cup of water from the recipe; the berries may be left whole but are better ground, as some hard ones may lurk in the crust.

Health Benefits

Stimulant. In the late sixteenth century Li Shih Chen's *Pen Ts'ao Kang Mu*, an exhaustive work on Chinese pharmaceuticals and herbs, which took over twenty-six years to complete, discussed the medicinal value of sprouts, suggesting their use in reducing inflammation, obtaining a laxative effect, remedying dropsy and rheumatism, and building and toning the body. The life energy and enzymes in fresh sprouts stimulate the body's inherent self-cleansing and self-healing abilities, and if no heavy cooked foods are taken at the same time, the overall metabolism is speeded up because it is not weighed down by hard-to-digest food. Their high water content helps flush toxins from the system, thus slowing the aging clock. Sprouts even enhance the sex life, providing more and better quality vitamin E (known as a fertility vitamin) than wheat germ.

VARIETIES

Aduki sprouts are a fine, grasslike sprout with a sweet, nutty taste and texture. Their mild flavor and crunchy texture make them versatile in salads, Chinese-style marinated vegetables, green drinks, sprout loaves, and sandwiches.

Alfalfa is sprout queen and ubiquitous in every salad bar. These threadlike white sprouts, with tiny green tops and a mild nutty flavor, are a favorite in salads and sandwiches. One of the most nutritious foods you can eat, these require the shortest soaking time (only five hours) and provide large quantities—two tablespoons of seeds will yield one full quart of sprouts. People with autoimmune diseases, particularly rheumatoid arthritis and lupus, have noted aggravations of symptoms when eating alfalfa sprouts, but no problems have been noted using nongrain sprouts such as clover, sunflower, or buckwheat.

Almond sprouts have a crunchy texture and are easy to digest. They are an excellent source of protein, vitamins, and minerals.

Barley sprouts are particularly high in vitamin C and the B complex group, and they contain several key amino acids. Like most other grain sprouts, they should be eaten when less than one inch long, or else they will weave themselves into a thick thatch.

Buckwheat must have its outer hull intact for sprouting. Seven-day-old buckwheat sprouts have rich red stems and round, deep green leaves. More palatable than wheatgrass, buckwheat sprouts can be eaten on their own or used in salads, juices, and soups. They are delicious up to the flowering stage.

Clover sprouts are usually those of red clover. They look very similar to alfalfa sprouts and are sprouted in the same manner. Tangy and crisp, these sprouts have a milder, sweeter taste than alfalfa.

Fenugreek sprouts have an aggressive flavor that is best

Sprouts / Nutritional Value Per 100 g Edible Portion					
	Alfalfa, Raw	Mung, Raw	Radish, Raw	Lentil, Raw	Green Pea, Raw
Calories	29	30	41	106	128
Protein	3.99 g	3.04 g	3.81 g	9.00 g	8.80 g
Fat	0.69 g	0.18 g	2.53 g	0.55 g	0.68 g
Fiber	1.64 g	0.81 g	n/a	22.14 g	28.26 g
Calcium	32 mg	13 mg	51 mg	25 mg	36 mg
Iron	0.96 mg	0.91 mg	0.86 mg	3.10 mg	2.26 mg
Magnesium	27 mg	21 mg	44 mg	37 mg	65 mg
Phosphorus	70 mg	54 mg	113 mg	173 mg	165 mg
Potassium	79 mg	149 mg	86 mg	322 mg	381 mg
Sodium	6 mg	6 mg	6 mg	11 mg	20 mg
Zinc	0.92 mg	0.41 mg	0.56 mg	1.51 mg	1.05 mg
Beta Carotene (A)	155 IU	21 IU	391 IU	45 IU	166 IU
Thiamine (B$_1$)	0.076 mg	0.084 mg	0.102 mg	0.228 mg	0.225 mg
Riboflavin (B$_2$)	0.126 mg	0.124 mg	0.103 mg	0.128 mg	0.155 mg
Niacin (B$_3$)	0.481 mg	0.749 mg	2.853 mg	1.128 mg	3.088 mg
Pantothenic Acid (B$_5$)	0.563 mg	0.380 mg	0.733 mg	0.578 mg	1.029 mg
Pyridoxine (B$_6$)	0.034 mg	0.088 mg	0.285 mg	0.190 mg	0.265 mg
Folic Acid (B$_9$)	36.0 mcg	60.8 mcg	94.7 mcg	9.9 mcg	144.0 mcg
Ascorbic Acid (C)	8.2 mg	13.2 mg	28.9 mg	16.5 mg	10.4 mg

combined with other sprouts. They provide a tangy seasoning in salads and vegetable dishes. One tablespoon will yield about a quart of sprouts, which are ready when one inch long. If you cook them, do not do so for more than three or four minutes, or else they will become bitter. Fenugreek sprouts are a powerful liver and kidney cleanser and an excellent source of phosphorus and iron.

Lentil sprouts are peppery and crisp, tastier if allowed to grow longer than the recommended one-half inch. Three-quarters of a cup of lentils yields one quart of sprouts, requiring only four hours of soaking.

Mung bean sprouts are larger and crunchier than alfalfa sprouts, with a blander flavor. These popular "Chinese bean sprouts" are a staple in Asian dishes and are excellent in stir-fries, soups, and salads. One-half cup of mung beans will yield one quart of sprouts, ready to eat in about four days.

Pumpkin sprouts are a fast-growing sprout since the seeds are always hulled. Best when eaten after about twenty-four hours of sprouting, pumpkin sprouts are very nutritious and contain high-quality proteins.

Radish sprouts have a zesty, tangy flavor that is delicious in salads. Ready to eat when they are an inch long, they are a powerful liver and kidney cleanser and high in potassium.

Sesame sprouts are best grown from unhulled seeds, since they have not been treated with chemical solvents (to remove the hulls). These tiny seeds require only a short time for sprouting—usually one to three days—and are best when small, as they get bitter quickly.

Soybean sprouts have a stronger flavor than mung sprouts and are best used cooked, since in their raw state they are both hard to digest and contain small amounts of toxins that could be harmful if consumed frequently in sizable quantities. Soak overnight, allow to sprout for three to five days, and use when the sprouts are under one inch in length.

Sunflower seed sprouts are mildly flavored, like alfalfa, but much crunchier. These seeds are ready in two to three days, and develop a bitter taste if allowed to sprout over one-quarter of an inch. Two cups of seeds will produce one quart of sprouts.

Wheat sprouts are sweetest if the sprout does not exceed the length of the grain. Considered the most delicious of the sprouting grains by some sprout devotees, they quickly turn into wheatgrass if you grow them longer.

Squash
(Cucurbita spp.)
Also Known As: Marrow, Gourd

Cucurbita is the old classical Latin name for a gourd. The English name *squash* comes from the Narragansett Indian word *askutasquash*, which means "green-raw-unripe," which was the way the Naragansetts ate it. The Iroquois said *isquotersquash*; the Pilgrims simplified it to squash.

General Information

Marrows, squashes, and gourds are all part of a large family (over 805 species) of edible gourds that grow on vines. The Europeans who encountered squashes and pumpkins in America had to compare them to melons or some other European vegetable or fruit, because they had never seen anything quite like them before and had no word for them. It is possible that squash was the very first food to be cultivated by American Indians; it seems at least to have been the first within what has been called the Indian triad—maize, beans, and squash. Archeological finds in Mexican caves, dated variously from 4000 to 9000 B.C., yielded squash seeds of cultivated varieties, while beans found with them were still from wild plants; maize did not appear at all until much later. There are as many different varieties of squash as there are shapes. Summer squash, with their fanciful shapes and bright colors, are a welcome summer vegetable. Their soft, thin skins enclose small, edible seeds, and their tender flesh is mild but charmingly flavorful when they are small and garden-fresh; as their size or time past harvest increases, their flavor rapidly diminishes. These prolific plants produce offspring continuously throughout the growing season, moving from bud to table in just a matter of days. Winter squash are generally larger in size than summer squash, with hard, inedible, shell-like skins and fully developed seeds. They are slower growing, months passing from the time they blossom until the time they are fully mature and ready to be harvested in the fall. Their dense, sweet flesh reflects a whole summer of accumulating energy from sun and soil.

Culinary Uses

Fresh young summer squash has soft, moist flesh that cooks quickly. Served finely sliced in salads or as crudités, they are also popular steamed, baked, and as ingredients in stir-fries, casseroles, and soups. Overly mature summer squash, with their tough skin and dry flesh, are best suited to stuffing and baking. Winter squash is generally prepared by first removing the fibrous matter and seeds from the center and then steaming, broiling, or baking them (on the half shell or with a stuffing mix); those with the deepest-colored flesh are usually the sweetest. Most winter squash varieties can be used interchangeably in recipes, where their sweet, moist flesh adds sensational color and flavor to baked goods, custards, soufflés, soups, spreads, and, of course, pies. Spaghetti squash is often prepared as a substitute for spaghetti by baking or steaming until the rind softens; then it is cut in half lengthwise and the spaghetti-like strands removed and flavored with a favorite seasoning (pasta sauce, etc.). For those with young children, puréed and strained squash makes an excellent baby food. The blossoms of all members of the squash family are edible. Picked just before they open, these yellow flowers are delicious sliced and tossed into salads, stuffed and baked, or batter-coated and deep-fried. All flowers of the gourd family are edible, whether male or female. However, when gathering squash blossoms from your garden, pick only male flowers, leaving a few on each plant for a bee or bug to do its pollinating work. How to tell the male from the female? It's easy: the male blossoms are narrow-stemmed, while the female blossoms attach to the stem with a large bulge, which is, in fact, the nascent squash. The seeds are also edible and, once hulled, can be eaten in the same manner as pumpkin seeds.

Health Benefits

pH 5.18–6.20. Both summer and winter squash are highly alkaline foods and excellent remedies for acidosis of the liver and blood. Summer squashes, with their light, bright flavor, are more suited for the hot summer months. Winter squash are apt fare for cold winter days, since they are a concentrated food and substantially filling. Compared with summer squash, winter squash contains greater amounts of natural sugars, carbohydrates, and vitamin A. Nutritionally packed and one of the mildest and easiest vegetables to digest, squashes are low in calories and particularly high in vitamin A and potassium. According to Chinese medicine, squash helps to reduce inflammation, while consumption of the raw seeds expels roundworms and tapeworms.

Squash, Summer / Nutritional Value Per 100 g Edible Portion										
	Chayote Raw	Chayote Cooked	Crookneck Raw	Crookneck Cooked	Pattypan Raw	Pattypan Cooked	Spaghetti Raw	Spaghetti Cooked	Zucchini Raw	Zucchini Cooked
Calories	24	24	19	20	18	16	33	29	14	16
Protein	0.90 g	0.62 g	0.94 g	0.91 g	1.20 g	1.03 g	0.64 g	0.66 g	1.16 g	0.64 g
Fat	0.30 g	0.48 g	0.24 g	0.31 g	0.20 g	0.17 g	0.57 g	0.26 g	0.14 g	0.05 g
Fiber	0.70 g	0.58 g	0.55 g	0.60 g	0.55 g	0.48 g	1.40 g	1.40 g	0.45 g	0.50 g
Calcium	19 mg	13 mg	21 mg	27 mg	19 mg	15 mg	23 mg	21 mg	15 mg	13 mg
Iron	0.40 mg	0.22 mg	0.48 mg	0.36 mg	0.40 mg	0.33 mg	0.31 mg	0.34 mg	0.42 mg	0.35 mg
Magnesium	14 mg	12 mg	21 mg	24 mg	23 mg	19 mg	12 mg	11 mg	22 mg	22 mg
Phosphorus	26 mg	29 mg	32 mg	39 mg	36 mg	28 mg	12 mg	14 mg	32 mg	40 mg
Potassium	150 mg	173 mg	212 mg	192 mg	182 mg	140 mg	108 mg	117 mg	248 mg	253 mg
Sodium	4 mg	1 mg	2 mg	1 mg	1 mg	1 mg	17 mg	18 mg	3 mg	3 mg
Zinc	n/a	n/a	0.290 mg	0.390 mg	0.290 mg	0.240 mg	0.190 mg	0.200 mg	0.200 mg	0.180 mg
Copper	n/a	n/a	0.102 mg	0.103 mg	0.102 mg	0.083 mg	0.037 mg	0.035 mg	0.057 mg	0.086 mg
Manganese	n/a	n/a	0.157 mg	0.213 mg	0.157 mg	0.128 mg	n/a	n/a	0.127 mg	0.178 mg
Beta Carotene (A)	56 IU	47 IU	338 IU	287 IU	110 IU	85 IU	50 IU	110 IU	340 IU	240 IU
Thiamine (B$_1$)	0.030 mg	0.026 mg	0.052 mg	0.049 mg	0.070 mg	0.051 mg	0.037 mg	0.038 mg	0.070 mg	0.041 mg
Riboflavin (B$_2$)	0.040 mg	0.040 mg	0.043 mg	0.049 mg	0.030 mg	0.025 mg	0.018 mg	0.022 mg	0.030 mg	0.041 mg
Niacin (B$_3$)	0.500 mg	0.420 mg	0.454 mg	0.513 mg	0.600 mg	0.464 mg	0.950 mg	0.810 mg	0.400 mg	0.428 mg
Pantothenic Acid (B$_5$)	0.483 mg	0.408 mg	0.102 mg	0.137 mg	0.102 mg	0.079 mg	0.360 mg	0.355 mg	0.083 mg	0.114 mg
Pyridoxine (B$_6$)	n/a	n/a	0.109 mg	0.094 mg	0.109 mg	0.085 mg	0.101 mg	0.099 mg	0.089 mg	0.078 mg
Folic Acid (B$_9$)	n/a	n/a	22.9 mcg	20.1 mcg	30.1 mcg	20.7 mcg	12.0 mcg	8.0 mcg	22.1 mcg	16.8 mcg
Ascorbic Acid (C)	11.0 mg	8.0 mg	8.4 mg	5.5 mg	18.0 mg	10.8 mg	2.1 mg	3.5 mg	9.0 mg	4.6 mg
Tocopherol (E)	n/a	n/a	n/a	n/a	n/a	n/a	n/a	n/a	n/a	n/a

SUMMER SQUASH VARIETIES

Choose summer squashes that are tender and fresh looking, with skin that is soft enough to puncture with a fingernail. They perish easily, so store them in the refrigerator and use as soon as possible.

Chayote (*Sechium edule*) is a pear-shaped squash native to Mexico and Central America (its name is from the Aztec Nahuatl *chayotl*). Also known as **mango squash, pepinello,** and **vegetable pear,** the chayote has soft, pale skin that varies from creamy white to dark green. Female fruit is smooth-skinned and lumpy, with slight ridges. It is fleshier and preferred over the male fruit, which is covered with warty spines. Although they are furrowed and slightly pitted by nature, they should not look as though these indentations have been made by external forces; nor should they look shriveled, but be completely firm to the touch. Choose smaller chayotes over larger, as they get insipid with size. Use as quickly as possible; if stored in the refrigerator for a week or more, they soon develop an unpleasant, moldy flavor. The pale green flesh is crisp and finely textured, with a taste and consistency that blends cucumber, zucchini, and a bit of kohlrabi. Young chayote need not be peeled, while older ones are best peeled. The fruits, young shoots, leaves, and large fleshy roots are all used as culinary vegetables. Baked or fried, creamed for desserts or soups, chayote may be substituted in any recipe calling for summer squash. However, their bland flavor begs for big, gutsy flavorings—chilies, spices, garlic, tomatoes, or cheese. Their mild, almost non-existent taste also means they can be, and often are, used in sweet dishes, simmered in a scented syrup like pears and served cold or baked in slices with cinnamon, nutmeg, and sugar, or honey, lemon, and butter. The single large seed, which is edible once cooked, has a taste reminiscent of lima bean and almond. The root, large and tuberous and up to twenty pounds in weight, looks and tastes like a yam.

Crookneck and **straightneck squash** (*Cucurbita moschata*) ranges from four to six inches long and has a bulbous blossom end. The crookneck has a long, curved neck reminiscent of a goose and bumpy, bright yellow skin and creamy yellow flesh. The straightneck varieties have a straight neck but same bumpy yellow skin.

Gooseneck squash (*Trichosanthes cucu-meriana*), also known as **snake squash,** is a curled, eye-catching squash native to southeast Asia and Australia, but it can be grown in America and Europe. Eaten in the summer when immature and thin-skinned, it is usually sliced into rounds and steamed or boiled and served with butter, salt, pepper, and herbs such as tarragon, dill, or marjoram.

Pattypan or **scallop squash** looks rather like a thick, round pincushion with scalloped edges. They are their best when they do not exceed four inches in diameter and are pale green rather than their mature white or cream. Their flesh has a somewhat buttery taste, and the skin, flesh, and seeds are all edible.

Spaghetti squash (*Cucurbita pepo*) is a large, oblong summer squash with smooth, lemon-yellow skin. Once cooked, the creamy golden flesh separates into miles of swirly, crisp-tender, spaghetti-like strands. The taste is quite bland, lightly sweet and fresh, its light squash flavor making a perfect saucing medium. Look for very hard, smooth, evenly colored squash without ridges, spots, or bumps. Avoid greenish, honeydew-colored squash, which may be immature or have sprouting seeds. Larger spaghetti squash have better flavor and thicker strands.

Zucchini (*Cucurbita pepo*), called **marrow** by the British, **courgette** by the French, and zucchini by the Italians, is by far the most popular summer squash. This prolific, shiny green squash ranges in size from four inches to baseball bat size but is best when five to eight inches long; longer zucchini tend to have seeds that are large, tough, and preferably removed before using. Unrivaled in versatility, zucchini may be eaten raw in salads, marinated, stir-fried, stuffed and baked, puréed for soups or sauces, or even made into pickles and marmalade. The blossoms are a special delicacy, tossed into a salad or batter-dipped and deep-fried or stuffed with a combination of cheese, meat, herbs, nuts, eggs, bread crumbs, rice, or potatoes. The world's longest zucchini was raised by Nick Balaci of Johnson City, New York, who grew a 69½-inch Romanian zucchini in 1987.

WINTER SQUASH VARIETIES

Choose winter squashes with thick rinds that are heavy for their size and free of soft spots. They are hardy and will keep for several months if stored in a cool, dry place, such as a basement.

Acorn squash (*Cucurbita pepo*), sometimes called **table queen,** is shaped like a giant, ribbed acorn with a definite pointed end. The slightly dry, orange-colored flesh of both green and golden varieties has a distinct nutlike flavor, with the golden variety tending to be a little sweeter and the green moister. Their large seed cavities are perfect for stuffing, and they are best when baked. Unlike most winter squashes, acorns do not contain much beta carotene, but they are still considered medicinal for the stomach and spleen.

Banana squash (*Cucurbita maxima*) is very large, long, and cylindrical and may weigh up to thirty pounds. Its thick, hard skin ranges in color from pale yellow to ivory, and its finely textured flesh is creamy orange or pink, sweet, and dry. Often available cut into manageably sized pieces, this squash is excellent combined with baked potatoes.

Butternut squash (*Caryoka nuciferum*) is reminiscent of a peanut in shape and color, with a large, round, fleshy bottom that encloses the seeds and a cylindrical upper part that is solid flesh. Its smooth hard skin is a deep butterscotch color (avoid those with streaks of green), and its flesh is a deep orange, with a distinctive butterscotch flavor that most people find delicious. Very small butternuts are especially sweet, and because their skins are thinner than those of other winter squash, they may be cooked and puréed with the skin intact. Steamed or baked like other squashes, they make excellent single servings when cut in half, cooked until soft, then served with a topping of butter and maple syrup.

Calabaza (*Cucurbita moschata*) are huge squashes whose mottled skin may be evergreen, sunset, or buff, speckled or striated, though they are always relatively smooth and hard-shelled when mature. Usually sold in chunks or slices, since few could tote the entire large vegetable, this versatile squash may be easily substituted for any other winter squash in dishes where it does not stand alone. The best calabazas are fine-grained, sweet, moist but not watery, and ravishingly orange.

Delicata (*Cucurbita pepo*) is an elongated green and tan-striped squash with tender yellow flesh. Also called **bohemian** or **sweet potato squash,** it first arrived on the scene as early as 1894, introduced by the Peter Henderson Company of New York City. The size and shape of a large cucumber, the delicata has a moist, creamy yellow flesh that tastes and smells like a blend of corn, butternut squash, and sweet potato. Younger squashes may have skins tender enough to eat once cooked. They are best when steamed or baked and are not recommended for soups or baking into desserts.

Golden nugget (*Cucurbita maxima*) is a small round squash that looks like a miniature fairy-tale pumpkin. Salmon-colored, with a finely ridged, very hard shell, this squash was developed at North Dakota State University in 1966 and is a close relative of the acorn squash. The moist, smooth, bright orange flesh has a mild squash flavor, which can range from delightfully sweet and buttery to not-so-sweet and dull-bland. Choose those that have a dull, matte look to the rind; a shiny finish indicates that the squash was picked immature and will be tasteless. Golden nuggets can be opened like pumpkins, scooped clean, brushed inside with butter and seasonings, and baked whole. They can also be split and baked like acorn squash.

Hubbards (*Cucurbita maxima*) are named after Elizabeth Hubbard of Massachusetts and are an old, extensive group of squashes that are usually plump and round in the middle, with tapered necks. Ranging from dark green to blue-gray and orange-red and weighing from five to twenty pounds, these warty, thick-skinned squashes have sweet, dry, orange flesh. Excellent in pumpkin pie, they have a thicker, firmer texture than fresh pumpkin, "set up" easier, and require less sugar.

Kabocha is a generic grouping for many strains of Japanese pumpkin and winter squash of both *Cucurbita maxima* and *Cucurbita moschata* species. Resembling the buttercup or turban squash, with its flattened drum or turban shape, they range from one to seven pounds, with rough, mottled rinds that are thick and deep green (sometimes orange), with paler uneven stripes and markings. The mustard-yellow flesh is sweet and rich-tasting, tender and floury dry, like a balance between sweet potato and pumpkin. Almost fiberless and with the highest sugar content of any squash, it is excellent baked with butter and served as a side dish or stuffed with vegetables for a main course.

Pumpkin—see separate reference.

Turban (*Cucurbita maxima*), also called **buttercup,** was developed in 1932 at North Dakota Agricultural College (now State University) by Dr. A. F. Yeager. Long esteemed by many growers as the ideal winter squash, this turban-shaped squash with its distinctive pale "beanie" is hard, thin-skinned, and dark bluish green with dramatic reddish-orange flecks and stripes; it ranges in size from three to five pounds. The bright orange flesh is tender, sweet, and custardy smooth when steamed; when baked it is denser and drier. It may be used in any manner you would butternut or acorn squash.

Sweet Potato
(Ipomoea batatas)
Also Known As: Batata, Boniato

The scientific name comes from the Greek *ips*, meaning "worm" or "bindweed," and *homoios*, meaning "like" or "similar to," since Carolus Linnaeus—the eighteenth-century Swedish botanist, famed for his system of plant classification—thought the twining vines looked unpleasantly like worms. The plants were called *batatas* in their native West Indies and southern United States.

General Information

Sweet potatoes are not related to potatoes or yams but are a plump, smooth-skinned, tuberous member of the morning glory family native to the West Indies and southern United States. Discovered by Columbus on his second trip to the New World, the sweet potato was sent back to Spain in 1494 along with many other new foods. The Chinese found the sweet potato in the Philippines in

Squash, Winter / Nutritional Value Per 100 g Edible Portion

	Acorn Raw	Acorn Cooked	Butternut Raw	Butternut Cooked	Hubbard Raw	Hubbard Cooked
Calories	40	56	45	40	40	50
Protein	0.80 g	1.12 g	1.00 g	0.90 g	2.00 g	2.48 g
Fat	0.10 g	0.14 g	0.10 g	0.09 g	0.50 g	0.62 g
Fiber	1.40 g	1.96 g	1.40 g	1.26 g	1.40 g	1.74 g
Calcium	33 mg	44 mg	48 mg	41 mg	14 mg	17 mg
Iron	0.70 mg	0.93 mg	0.70 mg	0.60 mg	0.40 mg	0.47 mg
Magnesium	32 mg	43 mg	34 mg	29 mg	19 mg	22 mg
Phosphorus	36 mg	45 mg	33 mg	27 mg	19 mg	22 mg
Potassium	347 mg	437 mg	352 mg	284 mg	320 mg	358 mg
Sodium	3 mg	4 mg	4 mg	4 mg	7 mg	8 mg
Zinc	0.130 mg	0.170 mg	0.150 mg	0.130 mg	0.130 mg	0.150 mg
Copper	0.065 mg	0.086 mg	0.072 mg	0.065 mg	0.064 mg	0.045 mg
Beta Carotene (A)	340 IU	428 IU	7,800 IU	7,001 IU	5,400 IU	6,035 IU
Thiamine (B$_1$)	0.140 mg	0.167 mg	0.100 mg	0.072 mg	0.070 mg	0.074 mg
Riboflavin (B$_2$)	0.010 mg	0.013 mg	0.020 mg	0.017 mg	0.040 mg	0.047 mg
Niacin (B$_3$)	0.700 mg	0.881 mg	1.200 mg	0.969 mg	0.500 mg	0.558 mg
Pantothenic Acid (B$_5$)	0.400 mg	0.504 mg	0.400 mg	0.359 mg	0.400 mg	0.447 mg
Pyridoxine (B$_6$)	0.154 mg	0.194 mg	0.154 mg	0.124 mg	0.154 mg	0.172 mg
Folic Acid (B$_9$)	16.7 mcg	18.7 mcg	26.7 mcg	19.2 mcg	16.4 mcg	16.2 mcg
Ascorbic Acid (C)	11.0 mg	10.8 mg	21.0 mg	15.1 mg	11.0 mg	9.5 mg
Tocopherol (E)	n/a	n/a	n/a	n/a	n/a	n/a

1594, when a famine in the Fujian province prompted the governor to send an expedition there in search of food plants. Now growing in all warm, moist areas of the world, the large, thick, sweet, and mealy root almost entirely replaces the use of potatoes in some regions. The sweet potato has an unusually high yield, four times that of rice. It tolerates poor soils and is resistant to drought, making it an important secondary crop throughout subtropical countries. There are literally hundreds of sweet potato varieties, most having yellow-brown or coppery-colored skins with yellow, bright orange, or yellow-red flesh and ranging in shape from long and slender to round. Varieties with yellowish, fawn-colored skins are relatively dry and mealy; this type is most popular in the North and is sometimes called Jersey because it was once the main type grown in New Jersey. Sweeter, moister varieties with reddish skins and vivid orange flesh are more common in the southern United States. These softer-fleshed varieties are usually fatter or rounder than the firm-fleshed type and are most often mistakenly referred to as yams.

Buying Tips

Choose sweet potatoes that are firm and relatively unblemished, without soft or moldy ends. Buy organic whenever possible, because sweet potatoes tend to pick up a musty taste from soil that has been treated with pesticides. They should be kept in a cool, dry place, where they will keep for a month or longer; at normal room temperatures they should be used within a week. Never store them in the refrigerator, where they are likely to develop a hard core and an off flavor.

Culinary Uses

Sweet potatoes are probably best known for their role as a traditional accompaniment to Thanksgiving dinner, but they should be enjoyed more frequently. Much like a regular potato, sweet potatoes can be roasted, boiled, steamed, or baked in casseroles and sweet dishes. Whenever possible, they should be cooked in their edible skins to conserve the nutrients. Cooked and mashed sweet potatoes can replace up to one-quarter of the wheat flour in breads and are excellent in other baked goods such as cakes, cookies, muffins, or pies, where their flavor is enhanced by a sprinkling of sweet spice such as cinnamon, nutmeg, ground cloves, or allspice.

Health Benefits

pH 5.3–5.6. So nutritious that people can live on them (and have), the sweet potato is easily digestible and good for the eliminative system, ulcers, inflamed colons, and poor blood circulation. Sweet potatoes show strong antioxidant properties; the darker the orange of the flesh, the greater the concentration of beta carotene. When raw, they are very alkaline for the system; cooking affects these tubers in the same way as regular potatoes, making them much more acidic. They are also beneficial for detoxifying the system, since they contain substances called phytochelatins that can bind heavy metals like cadmium, copper, mercury, and lead. If a child accidentally swallows a metallic object such as a coin, feed him plenty of sweet potato; the sweet potato will stick to the object and allow it to pass through easier.

Sweet Potato / Nutritional Value Per 100 g Edible Portion				
	Raw	Baked in Skin	Boiled No Skin	Candied
Calories	105	103	105	137
Protein	1.65 g	1.72 g	1.65 g	0.87 g
Fat	0.30 g	0.11 g	0.30 g	3.25 g
Fiber	0.85 g	0.80 g	0.85 g	0.39 g
Calcium	22 mg	28 mg	21 mg	26 mg
Iron	0.59 mg	0.45 mg	0.56 mg	1.13 mg
Magnesium	10 mg	20 mg	10 mg	11 mg
Phosphorus	28 mg	55 mg	27 mg	26 mg
Potassium	204 mg	348 mg	184 mg	189 mg
Sodium	13 mg	10 mg	13 mg	70 mg
Zinc	0.280 mg	0.290 mg	0.270 mg	0.150 mg
Copper	0.169 mg	0.208 mg	0.161 mg	0.102 mg
Manganese	0.355 mg	0.560 mg	0.337 mg	n/a
Beta Carotene (A)	20,063 IU	21,822 IU	17,054 IU	4,189 IU
Thiamine (B$_1$)	0.066 mg	0.073 mg	0.053 mg	0.018 mg
Riboflavin (B$_2$)	0.147 mg	0.127 mg	0.140 mg	0.042 mg
Niacin (B$_3$)	0.674 mg	0.604 mg	0.640 mg	0.394 mg
Pantothenic Acid (B$_5$)	0.591 mg	0.646 mg	0.532 mg	n/a
Pyridoxine (B$_6$)	0.257 mg	0.241 mg	0.244 mg	0.041 mg
Folic Acid (B$_9$)	13.8 mcg	22.6 mcg	11.1 mcg	11.4 mcg
Cobalamin (B$_{12}$)	n/a	n/a	n/a	0.030 mg
Ascorbic Acid (C)	22.7 mg	24.6 mg	17.1 mg	6.7 mg
Tocopherol (E)	4.56 mg	n/a	n/a	n/a

Swiss Chard

(Beta vulgaris cicla)
Also Known As: Chard, Leaf Beet, Spinach Beet

Beta is believed to have come from the Greek letter *beta*; *vulgaris* means "vulgar" or "common"; and *cicla* is derived from *sicula*, which refers to Sicily, one of the places where chard first grew. The English word *chard* is derived from the Latin word for "thistle," *carduus*. Although chard is not part of the thistle family, the word eventually came to refer to the stalk or ribs of some vegetables, such as chard and cardoon. This vegetable was dubbed *Swiss chard* because of a Swiss botanist who, in the sixteenth century, described yellow chard.

General Information

Wild chard, like other wild beets, probably originated in the Mediterranean region and can still be found there, as well as in Asia Minor and the Near East. This member of the beet family does not develop an enlarged fleshy root like the others but is grown for its large crisp leaves and fleshy leaf stalks. Varying in color from yellowish to dark green or even red, the large glossy leaves have thickened midribs and may be either smooth or crinkled. The stalks resemble thin, flattened celery and range from a pale celadon color to vivid scarlet. Red varieties are known as rhubarb chard.

Buying Tips

Choose crisp bunches with firm, bright leaves. Very rarely will you find anything smaller than ten to twelve inches in the market; for smaller ones, you will have to grow your own.

Culinary Uses

Swiss chard has a mild, delicate flavor, earthy and sweet like a combination of beets and spinach. The green-leaved, cream-stemmed variety tastes closer to spinach. Young leaves and stalks can be chopped and added raw to salads, where they add a pleasant and zesty beetlike flavor and a spinachy texture. Those of medium size can be quickly sautéed, with or without the stalks, for a pleasant side vegetable. Older leaves and stalks are best steamed, boiled, or added to soups. Any treatment that suits spinach will suit chard leaves, but chard must be cooked longer, although not too long, as the vitamin content decreases with cooking. Avoid cooking in aluminum or iron pans, which can discolor chard.

Health Benefits

pH 6.17–6.78 (cooked). Chard has a high oxalic acid content, beneficial in the uncooked state but harmful when cooked because it becomes inorganic and is destructive of calcium. Swiss chard is beneficial to the digestive system.

Swiss Chard / Nutritional Value Per 100 g Edible Portion		
	Raw	Cooked
Calories	19	20
Protein	1.80 g	1.88 g
Fat	0.20 g	0.08 g
Fiber	0.80 g	0.94 g
Calcium	51 mg	58 mg
Iron	1.80 mg	2.26 mg
Magnesium	81 mg	86 mg
Phosphorus	46 mg	33 mg
Potassium	379 mg	549 mg
Sodium	213 mg	179 mg
Beta Carotene (A)	3,300 IU	3,139 IU
Thiamine (B₁)	0.040 mg	0.034 mg
Riboflavin (B₂)	0.090 mg	0.086 mg
Niacin (B₃)	0.400 mg	0.360 mg
Pantothenic Acid (B₅)	0.172 mg	0.163 mg
Ascorbic Acid (C)	30.0 mg	18.0 mg

Taro

(Colocasia esculenta, C. antiquorum)

Also Known As: Eddo, Dasheen, Malanga, Tania,
Elephant Ear

Colocasia is an old Greek name for this plant; *esculenta* means "esculent" or "edible"; and *antiquorum* means "of or relating to the ancients." The common Jamaican name for the root, *dasheen*, derives from *de Chine* (from China), as the root was imported from southeast Asia to feed the slaves in the West Indies. The English word *taro* is the Polynesian name for the plant.

General Information

Of East Indian origin, the taro is a potato-like plant whose globose rhizome, of considerable weight and size, constitutes a staple food for populations living in the tropical areas of Africa and Asia. The plant produces two types of tubers. The most commonly seen are the large, brown, shaggy, turnip-shaped corms (the swollen tip of an underground stem that stores carbohydrates for the plant's growth). These are often cut to expose the smooth, very light flesh inside. The other type is small and elongated, about the size of a plump Brazil nut, and although smoother is still quite hairy and may sprout a pinkish bud at the tip. These little subsidiary tubers, called cormels, grow attached to the main corm by rootlets, six to twenty

per corm. Reportedly, thousands of varieties of taro are known, with the flesh color of the corms ranging from white to yellow and pink. The pink-fleshed variety, which is one of the favorites today, reputedly was reserved for royalty in early times in Hawaii. It is puzzling that taro achieved the status of a staple food, because toxic crystals of calcium oxalate lie just beneath the skin. These produce an allergic reaction, so the vegetable must be peeled under running water (or wear gloves). The toxin is rendered harmless by cooking.

Buying Tips

Choose taro that is very firm and plump, with no sign of withering. Store as you would potatoes—in a cool, well-ventilated place—and use before they start to soften. Do not refrigerate.

Culinary Uses

The flavor of taro combines chestnuts and potatoes. Large corms are dry, nutty, and sweet, while the small cormels are moist and smooth, best for steaming or boiling whole. Although taro's most familiar use is probably for Hawaiian poi, a sticky fermented paste that few visitors find palatable, the rhizomes can be eaten in many of the same ways as potatoes. Small or large corms can be steamed or boiled and take well to soups and stews, absorbing rich and fatty juices without disintegrating. When baked, their delicate, nutty

Taro / Nutritional Value Per 100 g Edible Portion							
	Raw	Cooked	Chips	Leaves Raw	Leaves Cooked	Shoots Raw	Shoots Cooked
Calories	40-107	44-142	477	42	24	11	14
Protein	1.50-2.79 g	0.52-4.16 g	2.04 g	4.98 g	2.72 g	0.92 g	0.73 g
Fat	0.20-0.97 g	0.11-0.68 g	25.47 g	0.74 g	0.41 g	0.09 g	0.08 g
Fiber	0.80-1.75 g	0.86-2.28 g	1.18 g	2.02 g	0.54 g	0.58 g	0.54 g
Calcium	43-129 mg	18-149 mg	45 mg	107 mg	86 mg	12 mg	14 mg
Iron	0.55-1.30 mg	0.72-1.56 mg	1.35 mg	2.25 mg	1.18 mg	0.60 mg	0.41 mg
Magnesium	33-47 mg	30-51 mg	84 mg	45 mg	20 mg	8 mg	8 mg
Phosphorus	45-84 mg	67-76 mg	131 mg	60 mg	27 mg	28 mg	26 mg
Potassium	591-606 mg	484-623 mg	824 mg	648 mg	460 mg	332 mg	344 mg
Sodium	11-50 mg	15-54 mg	369 mg	3 mg	2 mg	1 mg	2 mg
Beta Carotene (A)	0-2,045 IU	0-1,764 IU	0 IU	4,825 IU	4,238 IU	50 IU	n/a
Thiamine (B₁)	0.062-0.095 mg	0.044-0.107 mg	0.053 mg	0.209 mg	0.139 mg	0.040 mg	n/a
Riboflavin (B₂)	0.025-0.244 mg	0.028-0.198 mg	0.029 mg	0.456 mg	0.380 mg	0.050 mg	n/a
Niacin (B₃)	0.600-0.995 mg	0.480-0.510 mg	0.040 mg	0.456 mg	0.380 mg	0.050 mg	n/a
Ascorbic Acid (C)	4.5-96.0 mg	5.0-38.0 mg	n/a	52.0 mg	35.5 mg	21.0 mg	n/a

flavor becomes intensified and meaty, but they dry out considerably and need to be basted with butter or another sauce. Pan-fried or deep-fried taro is excellent, with more texture and flavor than most fried starches, crisping while keeping its identity. Be aware that its light flesh turns a dappled gray or violet when cooked, and that it must be served piping hot or it becomes unpleasantly dense and waxy. Once peeled, keep taro in salted water to prevent discoloring unless you are going to cook them at once. Wear gloves when peeling taro, to avoid skin irritation.

Note: Taro must be eaten cooked, never raw, as it contains a poisonous substance that must be deactivated by heat.

The large green leaves of the taro plant, called callaloo, are also eaten in soups and stir-fries. Callaloo has given its name to a Caribbean soup of salt pork, bacon, crab, shrimp, onions, and okra flavored with garlic, hot chili, lime, and coconut milk. The leaves have a string attached to the stem that must be removed before cooking. In the Pacific Islands they are thoroughly boiled and then often used to wrap vegetables or meat and cooked again in an *umu* (cooking oven). The leaves are poisonous if eaten raw.

Health Benefits

Easily digested, taro has been recommended for use in baby foods and is used medicinally to prepare external plasters for the treatment of cysts, tumors, and boils as it has the ability to dissolve masses. In Chinese medicine, taro is used to strengthen the stomach and spleen-pancreas and for loss of appetite and fatigue owing to weak digestion.

Tomato

(Lycopersicon esculentum)

> It's difficult to think anything but pleasant thoughts while eating a homegrown tomato.
>
> —LEWIS GRIZZARD

Lycopersicon is the latinized nickname "wolfpeach," given the tomato by the French botanist Tournefort during the mid–sixteenth century, when it was often mistaken for the wolf peach written about by Galen thirteen centuries before. *Peach* was for its luscious appearance, *wolf* for its presumptive poisonous qualities, in analogy to pieces of aconite-sprinkled meat thrown out as bait to destroy wolves. The term *esculentum* means "esculent" or "edible." The English word *tomato* is a Spanish rendering of the Nahuatl (Mexican Indian) *tomatl.*

General Information

The tomato is a member of the nightshade family that came originally from western South America, where small-fruited wild forms, described by botanists as weedy and aggressive, still proliferate. The invading Spaniards saw the tomato growing in Montezuma's gardens in 1519 and described it recognizably, though in less than glowing terms: they found the sprawling vines scraggly and ugly. Still, Cortez brought tomato seeds back with him to Europe, along with the more spectacular plunder, and tomato plants were soon growing as curiosities in the sunny gardens of Renaissance Spain. In 1544 the Renaissance botanist Pietro Andrea Mattioli called them *pomi d'oro*—golden apples—so presumably it was a yellow variety he knew. However, he also called them *mala insane* (unhealthy fruit), and for centuries there was much confusion about the tomato's goodness and healthfulness. There are thousands of known tomato varieties, which differ greatly in color and shape, with cultivars adapted to any number of climates. The most common shapes are the large, round varieties such as Jersey and Beefsteak; the small, pear-shaped plum or Italian Roma tomatoes, which make such good sauces; and the small, round cherry tomatoes. Yellow varieties tend to be the least acidic. By cultivation and use the tomato is a vegetable, but botanically it is a fruit and can be classified as a berry, since it is pulpy and contains one or more seeds that are not stones. As the result of a tariff dispute, when an importer contended that the tomato was a fruit and therefore not subject to vegetable import duties, the plant was officially proclaimed a vegetable in 1893 by the U.S. Supreme Court. They ruled it should be classified a vegetable because it was most frequently served in soup or with the main course of a meal, as a vegetable would be. Joseph Campbell brought out his famous canned tomato soup in 1897, shortly after chemist John Dorrance, at a weekly salary of $7.59, worked out the formula for condensing it. After potatoes and iceberg lettuce, tomatoes are the most commonly consumed vegetable in the United States. But tomatoes rank above all produce in the popular fervor they inspire; they are considered a dietary necessity.

Buying Tips

Choose firm, plump tomatoes with an aromatic tomato fragrance. Avoid soft, overripe tomatoes with blemishes, bruises, soft spots, or growth cracks. As they are extremely fragile when ripe, most commercial tomatoes are picked and shipped green and then artificially ripened in ethylene gas chambers. They may need a little help to finish ripening—keep them upside down at room temperature, out of direct sunlight, until they turn richly red. Those tomatoes whose skins are red but whose seeds or internal parts are still green were picked too soon; when a tomato is fully ripe, the seeds inside are brown. Fully vine-ripened tomatoes are sweet and juicy, with a slight tang. Because they are best when picked straight from the vine, even people who are not avid gardeners like to grow them. Hydroponically grown tomatoes may be cosmetically perfect, but they tend to lack flavor. Researchers at the USDA found that vine-ripened tomatoes grown outdoors in sunlight are twice as rich in vitamin C as their greenhouse counterparts. Store tomatoes in a warm location but not in direct sunlight. They will keep for about a week. Do not refrigerate tomatoes as this drains their flavor and gives them a mealy texture.

Culinary Uses

Tomatoes add flavor and color to a wide variety of both raw and cooked dishes. They are used in more spicy sauces, canned in more soups, drunk in more juices, added to more salads, and spread on more pizzas than any other vegetable. No other fruit or vegetable has such mass appeal. Cherry tomatoes, because of their small size, are perfect for tossing whole into salads. Sun-dried tomatoes have an explosively concentrated flavor that provides a tremendous boost to many dishes. One other very important application for the tomato (or tomato juice) is as a neutralizer for butyl mercaptan, the nose-shriveling prime ingredient in the defense spray of skunks.

Health Benefits

pH 3.50–4.90. Tomatoes are over 93 percent water. A natural antiseptic, fresh raw tomatoes contain a great deal of citric acid, which has an alkaline reaction if digested when no starches or sugars are present. Their chlorine content increases the alkalinity of the blood and helps to stimulate the liver in its function as a filter for body and toxic wastes. Raw tomato (both whole and juice form) is especially effective in reducing liver inflammation from hepatitis and cirrhosis. Tomatoes are a good source of vitamin A as carotene—not beta carotene but a different kind, called lycopene. Studies have found that Hawaiians who ate a large number of tomatoes had a lower risk of stomach cancer, Norwegians who ate lots of tomatoes had a lower risk of lung cancer, and Americans who ate much of this fruit had a lower rate of prostate cancer and lower death rates from all cancers. Another large population study in Wales found that tomatoes ranked high in protecting people from acute appendicitis. The highest vitamin content is in the jelly that surrounds the seeds, so de-seeding tomatoes reduces their food value. Never eat raw green tomatoes, as they contain a toxin known as solanine and the acids in the green tomato are very detrimental to the body. Cooked or canned tomatoes have many of their nutrients destroyed.

Tomato / Nutritional Value Per 100 g Edible Portion				
	Raw	Cooked	Sun-Dried Dry	Sun-Dried Oil-Packed
Calories	21	27	258	213
Protein	0.85 g	1.07 g	14.11 g	5.06 g
Fat	0.33 g	0.41 g	2.97 g	14.08 g
Fiber	0.65 g	0.82 g	n/a	n/a
Calcium	5 mg	6 mg	110 mg	47 mg
Iron	0.45 mg	0.56 mg	n/a	n/a
Magnesium	11 mg	14 mg	194 mg	81 mg
Phosphorus	24 mg	31 mg	356 mg	139 mg
Potassium	222 mg	279 mg	3,427 mg	1,565 mg
Sodium	9 mg	11 mg	2,095 mg	266 mg
Zinc	0.090 mg	0.110 mg	1.990 mg	0.780 mg
Copper	0.074 mg	0.093 mg	1.423 mg	0.473 mg
Manganese	0.105 mg	0.132 mg	1.846 mg	0.466 mg
Beta Carotene (A)	623 IU	743 IU	874 IU	1,286 IU
Thiamine (B$_1$)	0.059 mg	0.070 mg	0.528 mg	0.193 mg
Riboflavin (B$_2$)	0.048 mg	0.057 mg	0.489 mg	0.383 mg
Niacin (B$_3$)	0.628 mg	0.749 mg	9.050 mg	3.630 mg
Pantothenic Acid (B$_5$)	0.247 mg	0.295 mg	2.087 mg	0.479 mg
Pyridoxine (B$_6$)	0.080 mg	0.095 mg	0.332 mg	0.319 mg
Folic Acid (B$_9$)	15.0 mcg	13.0 mcg	68.0 mcg	23.0 mcg
Ascorbic Acid (C)	19.1 mg	22.8 mg	39.2 mg	101.8 mg
Tocopherol (E)	0.34 mg	n/a	n/a	n/a

LORE AND LEGEND

Although the early Aztecs of Mexico considered the tomato a "health" food and reverently offered it to their gods of healing, Europeans shunned it because of its association with known poisonous plants, and because its bright shiny colors—red, orange, yellow, and white—were highly suspicious. The turning point for the pro-tomato faction in America, according to time-honored legend, occurred on the steps of the Salem, New Jersey, courthouse on September 26, 1820. That was the day when Colonel Robert Gibbon Johnson ate, in public and without ill effect, an entire basketful of tomatoes. Colonel Johnson, an enthusiastic gardener, had earlier introduced the tomato to the farmers of Salem after a trip abroad in 1808, and each year offered a prize for the largest fruit grown. A forceful individualist and notorious eccentric, the colonel wanted his introduction to be regarded as more than an ornamental bush, so when he announced that he would in public eat not one, but a *whole basket* of "wolf peaches," a large crowd of some two thousand curious people from miles around gathered to watch him commit certain suicide. Dressed in his habitual black suit with impeccable white ruffles, a tricorn hat, black gloves, and gold-topped walking stick, the colonel made an imposing figure as he ascended the courthouse steps at high noon to the accompaniment of a dirgelike tune played by the local firemen's band. Selecting a tomato from his basket, he held it aloft and launched into his spiel:

> The time will come when this luscious, golden apple, rich in nutritive value, a delight to the eye, a joy to the palate, whether fried, baked, broiled, or eaten raw, will form the foundation of a great garden industry, and will be recognized, eaten and enjoyed as an edible food . . . And to help speed that enlightened day, to help dispel the tall tales, the fantastic fables that you have been hearing about the thing, to show you that it is not poisonous, that it will not strike you dead, I am going to eat one right now!

—Hendrickson, *Foods for Love*, pp. 188–189.

Colonel Johnson bit into the tomato, and the juicy bite could be heard through the silence, until he bit again, and again—at least one female spectator screaming and fainting with each succeeding bite. The crowd was amazed to see the courageous colonel still on his feet as he devoured tomato after tomato. He soon converted most onlookers, but not until the entire basket was empty did the band strike up a victory march and the crowd begin to chant a cheer. The colonel's personal physician, Dr. James Van Meeter, had taken a dim view of the proposed tomato eating and had been quoted as saying, "The foolish colonel will foam and froth at the mouth and double over with appendicitis. All that oxalic acid! One dose and you're dead." Barring immediate effects, it was feared that the tomato skins would stick to the lining of the stomach and eventually cause cancer (tomatoes were generally held to induce cancer until nearly the end of the nineteenth century). Dr. Van Meeter stayed, black bag in hand, until the whole basketful of tomatoes had been devoured, and then quietly slunk away. The colonel, undaunted, continued to live in undisputed health to the ripe old age of seventy-nine.

Ketchup started out at *ketsiap*, a sauce developed in the seventeenth century by the Chinese that would never have appealed to westerners. It was a tangy potion of fish entrails, vinegar, and spices, and was used mainly on fish. Exported to Malaya, where it was called *kechap*, the strange purée was sold to English sailors in the early eighteenth century. Back in England it caught on quickly, but English cooks substituted mushrooms for the fish entrails. The first printed recipe, from Richard Brigg's 1792 cookbook *The New Art of Cookery*, called it catsup and included tomatoes as an ingredient (a rarity for the time, because tomatoes were still considered poisonous). Henry Heinz was the first to use the term *ketchup* when he started advertising the product in the early 1900s; he liked the unique spelling. Other competitors slowly followed suit, the last making the change in 1988. Ketchup is now consumed at the rate of seven 14-ounce bottles per person annually.

Turnip
(Brassica rapa)

The Latin name *Brassica* derives from the Celtic *bresic*; *rapa* was the Latin name for the turnip. Our Engish word *turnip* derives from the Middle English name for the plant, *nepe* or *naep*, which when combined with the Anglo-Saxon word *turn*, meaning "to make round," became *turnaep* and then *turnip*.

General Information
The turnip is reported to have come from Russia, Siberia, and the Scandinavian peninsula. Introduced into the New World by Jacques Cartier when he visited Canada in 1540, the vegetable flourished there and quickly spread southward. The Virginia colonists must have brought seeds with them; turnips are said to have grown there in 1609. The Indians took to them at once, for they were superior to the wild roots they had been eating. Indian women baked or roasted them whole in their skins, a method that brought out their full flavor. In 1850 a turnip weighing one hun-

dred pounds was grown in California. This member of the cabbage family has round or top-shaped roots, white skin with purplish or greenish crowns, and thin, green, hairy leaves. Since it flourishes in poor and impoverished soils and keeps well, this rustic vegetable has endeared itself to the poor and given some cause to scorn it. Often confused with its cousin the rutabaga, the turnip is smaller and more perishable; it can also be eaten raw and is most frequently sold with its tops. The two do taste somewhat similar, however, and in many recipes are interchangeable.

Buying Tips
Look for smooth, firm roots with their root end and stem base intact. If these parts are trimmed away and the root is yellowed at the incision, the turnip will be lacking in flavor. Favor small or medium-small turnips, as large ones are often pithy and lack flavor.

Culinary Uses
Raw turnips have a refreshing, tangy flavor similar to mild radish and when cooked are pleasantly sweet. Those grown during the hot summer months are decidedly pungent but mellow somewhat with cooking. When fresh and young, turnips can be used raw in salads. When cooked with other foods, they have the remarkable ability to absorb flavors, making them succulent and rich. Turnip greens can be cooked in the same manner as spinach, slivered and stir-fried, or, as they have been for generations, stewed with pork. They do not make good salad greens, as they are much too bitter and tough. The tops are generally found separate from the familiar roots. Look for relatively small, tender leaves that are moist and well cooled. The stems are not used. Do not cook in aluminum or iron pans, as these will discolor the root or leaves.

Health Benefits
pH 5.29–6.20. Raw grated turnip serves as a digestive aid and cleans the teeth. Because of its sulfur content, it warms and purifies the body, while its alkalizing nature helps detoxify the body. The mildly pungent qualities are easily destroyed through cooking; sliced raw turnip is superior to the cooked, but cooked turnips are also a warming food and said to energize the stomach and intestines. If you have a weak digestive system, turnips may cause flatulence. Turnip juice is especially good for mucous and catarrhal conditions. All *Brassica* genus vegetables contain dithiolthiones, a group of compounds that have anticancer, antioxidant properties; indoles, substances

Turnip / Nutritional Value Per 100 g Edible Portion				
	Root Raw	Root Cooked	Greens Raw	Greens Cooked
Calories	27	18	27	20
Protein	0.90 g	0.71 g	1.50 g	1.14 g
Fat	0.10 g	0.08 g	0.30 g	0.23 g
Fiber	0.90 g	0.71 g	0.80 g	0.61 g
Calcium	30 mg	22 mg	190 mg	137 mg
Iron	0.30 mg	0.22 mg	1.10 mg	0.80 mg
Magnesium	11 mg	8 mg	31 mg	22 mg
Phosphorus	27 mg	19 mg	42 mg	29 mg
Potassium	191 mg	135 mg	296 mg	203 mg
Sodium	67 mg	50 mg	40 mg	29 mg
Zinc	n/a	n/a	0.190 mg	0.140 mg
Copper	n/a	n/a	0.350 mg	0.253 mg
Manganese	n/a	n/a	0.466 mg	0.337 mg
Beta Carotene (A)	0 IU	0 IU	7,600 IU	5,498 IU
Thiamine (B$_1$)	0.040 mg	0.027 mg	0.070 mg	0.045 mg
Riboflavin (B$_2$)	0.030 mg	0.023 mg	0.100 mg	0.072 mg
Niacin (B$_3$)	0.400 mg	0.299 mg	0.600 mg	0.411 mg
Pantothenic Acid (B$_5$)	0.200 mg	0.142 mg	0.380 mg	0.274 mg
Pyridoxine (B$_6$)	0.090 mg	0.067 mg	0.263 mg	0.180 mg
Folic Acid (B$_9$)	14.5 mcg	9.2 mcg	194.4 mcg	118.4 mcg
Ascorbic Acid (C)	21.0 mg	11.6 mg	60.0 mg	27.4 mg
Tocopherol (E)	n/a	n/a	2.24 mg	n/a

LORE AND LEGEND

There is an old story about an ancient king who was exceedingly fond of a certain fish and requested it of his chef for dinner. The chef, being unable to find any of that particular kind of fish, instead bought a large white turnip, carved it into the shape of a fish, baked it, and then served it to the king on a fish platter. The king was delighted and exclaimed that it was the best fish he had ever eaten!

that protect against breast and colon cancer; and sulfur, which has antibiotic and antiviral characteristics. This family of vegetables also mildly stimulates the liver and other tissues out of stagnancy.

Note: Turnips and rutabagas contain especially high amounts of compounds (goitrogens) that interfere with thyroid function. Their use by individuals with low thyroid function should be limited, or else foods high in iodine, such as kelp, should also be consumed.

Wasabi
(Eutrema wasabi, Wasabia japonica)
Also Known As: Japanese Horseradish

Japonica means "coming from Japan."

General Information
Wasabi is the green Japanese radish with the assertive flavor and sinus-clearing effect you may have enjoyed with sushi. Although not related to common horseradish, it is often called Japanese horseradish because its kick is nearly as potent. The more fragrant of the two, wasabi root is gnarled and warty on the outside, with pale, soft green flesh on the inside.

Buying Tips
Look for plump and fresh-looking roots that preferably are not sprouting; avoid those that are withered.

Culinary Uses
Used sparingly, wasabi adds a pungent "cleansing" bite to foods and makes an interesting addition to soy sauce and other dipping sauces. Prior to grating the fresh root, remove the "eyes" and pare away the tough skin. Powdered wasabi, in convenient small tins or foil envelopes, is more frequently available. It should be greenish gray, and not bright green. Mix it into a paste with equal amounts of water just before serving to preserve its flavor and digestive enzymes. Wasabi paste is often used to season sushi or its dipping sauce. In a pinch, it can also substitute for horseradish in recipes. The digestive enzymes in wasabi quickly dissipate; therefore, grate fresh wasabi, or reconstitute powdered wasabi, just prior to use.

Health Benefits
This aromatic root provides more than bite. Wasabi has an abundance of protein-digesting enzymes that make it a perfect condiment with raw fish dishes such as sashimi and sushi. It is used as a kitchen antidote to fish poisoning.

Water Chestnut
(Eleocharis dulcis, Trapa natans, T. bicornis)

Eleocharis is a Greek word that means "delighting in marshes"; the term *dulcis* signifies something that is sweet tasting. *Trapa* is an abbreviation of the Old English *calca-trippe* or *caltrap*, an ancient instrument of war. The insidious iron ball with four sharp-pointed spikes was employed to impede and harass the enemy's cavalry; since the dark brown, hard-shelled, woody fruit of the water chestnut has four woody horns or spikelike projections that resemble that dreaded military weapon, it was named after it. *Natans* means "floating" or "swimming." The English name *water chestnut* was given because it looks like a grubby chestnut in size and shape and because it grows underwater.

General Information
The name *water chestnut* alone usually refers to *Trapa natans*, the European water chestnut, the fruit of an annual herbaceous plant belonging to the evening primrose family. Native to tropical Africa, central Europe, and eastern Asia, these annual floating aquatic plants, with their beautifully mottled foliage, grow luxuriantly in standing water, floating on the surface of ponds, pools, lakes, and irrigation tanks. The edible part is technically a corm—the swollen tip of an underground stem that stores carbohydrates for the plant's growth. The corms are two to

three inches wide from tip to tip of their horns and about one inch in depth. One large, white, starchy kernel is enclosed within each corm.

The Chinese water chestnut (*Eleocharis dulcis*) is the corm or tuber of an Asiatic sedge, a grasslike annual plant common to marshy environments. The corms, about 1½ inches in diameter, are formed on rhizomes down to a depth of some ten inches. At harvesttime the corms have often formed a solid mass of edible material. Once harvested, they look rather like muddy little tulip bulbs, dressed in shabby brown-to-black coats decorated with frayed leaf scales.

Another variety sold in Asian markets is the water caltrops or horned water chestnut (*Trapa bicornis*), related to the European water chestnut. These shiny black, rather nefarious-looking horned nuts grow on a floating water plant like their cousin but have two horns instead of four. This variety must be boiled for an hour before use to destroy possible parasites harmful to the digestive system. The Chinese eat them shelled and cooked in various vegetable and meat combinations or preserved as sweetmeats.

Buying Tips
Select fresh corms that are rock-hard and free of withering or soft spots. Do not worry if they are very dirty, for they clean up well. Always buy more than you think you will need, as there is large waste in peeling, and there will usually be a few bad ones in the lot.

Culinary Uses
Water chestnuts have a delicate and delicious flavor, reminiscent of sugarcane, sweet corn, and coconut. They look like gladiolus bulbs, with fibrous chestnut-brown skins enclosing the sweet firm flesh. The most memorable property of the water chestnut is its crunch. Although jicama and Asian pears come close to the refreshing crisp texture of this water vegetable, they do not match its refreshing delicacy or its juicy sweet flavor. Once the skins are removed, water chestnuts may be added raw to fresh fruit salads, hot or cold vegetables, rice, or noodles. It does not take many, as the texture and flavor are distinct and satisfying. In China the corms are eaten raw out of hand, as a substitute for fresh fruit, or cooked alone as a winter vegetable. Cooking enhances the flavor and does not detract from their texture or crispness. The readily available canned water chestnuts lose some sweetness, though they retain their crispness and color.

Health Benefits
pH 6.20. Originally valued as a medicinal plant, the water chestnut is considered yin, or cooling, and is thought to disperse excess heat, be beneficial for diabetes and jaundice, and sweeten the breath. Water chestnuts also inhibit infectious diseases such as staphylococcus and *E. coli* and are said to aid vision. A paste made from dried ground water chestnuts is fed to children who accidentally swallow coins.

Watercress
(Nasturtium officinale)

Nasturtium is a contraction of the Latin phrase *nasus tortus*, meaning "convulsed nose," on account of the plant's pungency. *Officinale* means "of the workshop," alluding to apothecaries' shops and signifying that the plant was once part of the official pharmacopoeia of Rome. The English name *watercress* comes from the fact that the plant is one of the water-loving members of the cress family.

General Information
Eurasian in origin, watercress is a succulent, leafy, vivid green aquatic plant of the mustard family. No wild edible

Water Chestnut / Nutritional Value Per 100 g Edible Portion	Chinese Raw	Canned w/ Liquid
Calories	106	50
Protein	1.40 g	0.88 g
Fat	0.10 g	0.06 g
Fiber	0.80 g	0.58 g
Calcium	11 mg	4 mg
Iron	0.60 mg	0.87 mg
Magnesium	22 mg	5 mg
Phosphorus	63 mg	19 mg
Potassium	584 mg	118 mg
Sodium	14 mg	8 mg
Zinc	n/a	0.38 mg
Beta Carotene (A)	0 IU	4 IU
Thiamine (B₁)	0.140 mg	0.011 mg
Riboflavin (B₂)	0.200 mg	0.024 mg
Niacin (B₃)	1.000 mg	0.360 mg
Ascorbic Acid (C)	4.0 mg	1.3 mg

LORE AND LEGEND

One hot summer day while out hunting, King Louis IX of France was overcome by thirst and called for a drink. Since no liquid was within reach, he was instead handed a bunch of watercress. Louis crunched its peppery leaves and found himself so surprisingly refreshed that he decided on the spot to honor both the plant and the place that had provided it. The arms of the city of Vernon, now in the French department of Eure, to this day bear three fleurs-de-lis, the royal symbol, on one side, and three bunches of watercress on the other.

plant has enjoyed a longer and more accepted spot in history, from the ancient Middle East to Old England. Cultivated and wild watercress are the same variety, but the domesticated plant is generally larger—up to seven inches—and has a thicker stem. The first attempt to cultivate watercress on any scale was in the sixteenth century at Erfurt in Germany, for the extraction of its blue dye. It was not until 1808 that a William Bradbury created the first watercress beds at Springhead in England. Freshly cut watercress was sold at markets as a breakfast food, with bread, for industrial workers. A Victorian, E. S.

Dallas, comments, "They are the one vegetable eaten by rich and poor in England, for health even more than for food." Watercress of the wild variety was probably introduced to America in the 1600s as a familiar plant that could be grown in the numerous freshwater streams near the first settlements. It provided a salad green much of the year, as well as a boiled vegetable to serve with meat; more importantly, it was a powerful antiscorbutic. Weedlike in its hardiness, it has spread and now thrives in each of the fifty states. With its small, round, pungent leaves, watercress grows alongside gently flowing streams and ponds, but it should be gathered only from those with clean, clear water.

Buying Tips

Choose bunches that look fresh and have no yellowed leaves. Very young cress is light bright green, but the knowledgeable prefer their cress "sunburnt"—that is, slightly older—when the leaves have acquired a delicate bronze. Wilted, bruised, or yellowing leaves are signs of inferior quality and improper handling. Wash with extra care, as the leaves are prone to harbor aquatic insects.

Culinary Uses

Just as delightful as chancing upon a pure stream boasting watercress is munching on this lively, peppery plant. Surprisingly, the bite and aroma are not fiery but leave the palate cool and refreshed. As a salad green, watercress should be used with lettuce or other mild-tasting leaves. Or use it as a garnish, as an ingredient in soups, or in an avocado sandwich. It also tastes delicious in stuffings,

Watercress / Nutritional Value Per 100 g Edible Portion			
	Raw		Raw
Calories	11	Sodium	41 mg
Protein	2.30 g	Beta Carotene (A)	4,700 IU
Fat	0.10 g	Thiamine (B₁)	0.090 mg
Fiber	0.70 g	Riboflavin (B₂)	0.120 mg
Calcium	120 mg	Niacin (B₃)	0.200 mg
Iron	0.20 mg	Pantothenic Acid (B₅)	0.310 mg
Magnesium	21 mg	Pyridoxine (B₆)	0.129 mg
Phosphorus	60 mg	Ascorbic Acid (C)	43.0 mg
Potassium	330 mg	Tocopherol (E)	1.0 mg

omelets, mashed potatoes, or other cheese dishes. When steamed, it loses much of its bite and tastes quite unique. Add it to completed dishes and use daily if possible.

Health Benefits

pH 5.88–6.18. Antiscorbutic, diuretic, expectorant, purgative, stimulant, stomachic. Watercress has an ability to energize the internal organs, aids in breaking up kidney or bladder stones, and is one of the best foods for purifying the blood and taking care of catarrhal conditions. It also has antibiotic properties similar to those of the onion family. Watercress is excellent in vegetable juices or herb teas. Especially kind to the skin, if crushed and applied with a swab of cotton it relieves irritations and helps heal acne, eczema, and other skin irritations and infections. Watercress has an abundant iodine content.

Wax Gourd

(Benincasa hispida)

Also Known As: Chinese Winter Melon, Ash Melon, Chinese Fuzzy Gourd, Doan Gwa

The genus *Benincasa* was named in honor of an Italian nobleman; *hispida* means "hispid" or "bristly."

General Information

Grown throughout the Asian tropics, the wax gourd is little known elsewhere. There are two main varieties: the smaller fuzzy melon and the large winter melon. Fuzzy

Wax Gourd / Nutritional Value Per 100 g Edible Portion		
	Raw	Cooked
Calories	13	13
Protein	0.40 g	0.40 g
Fat	0.20 g	0.20 g
Fiber	0.50 g	0.51 g
Calcium	19 mg	18 mg
Iron	0.40 mg	0.38 mg
Phosphorus	19 mg	17 mg
Potassium	6 mg	5 mg
Sodium	111 mg	107 mg
Beta Carotene (A)	0 IU	0 IU
Thiamine (B$_1$)	0.040 mg	0.034 mg
Riboflavin (B$_2$)	0.110 mg	0.001 mg
Niacin (B$_3$)	0.400 mg	0.384 mg
Ascorbic Acid (C)	13.0 mg	10.5 mg

melons come in two shapes: either narrow and cylindrical, like squash, or like a stubby pill capsule. Harvested young at around one pound, they are easy to spot because they are truly hairy. Winter melon is watermelon green and grows to one hundred pounds. Its melonlike fruit has a thick flesh that is white, crisp, and juicy. An outstanding feature is its resistance to spoilage. Preserved from microorganisms by its waxy coating, the fruit can be stored without refrigeration for as long as a year. An annual creeping vine, the plant resembles a pumpkin vine. It is a rapid and prolific grower, producing three or four crops each year. Most often sold cut, the fruit has pale green skin with a thick and waxy bloom that looks like frost. The wax itself is actually a wax source for candles in Asia.

Buying Tips

Select one that is firm and unblemished. A whole melon, when stored in a cool, dark, dry place, will keep for many months. When buying by the slice, look for a firm-fleshed, evenly colored piece. Slices should be used within several days of purchase.

Culinary Uses

Young leaves, flower buds, and vine tips are boiled and eaten as greens. The fruit's sweetish white flesh can be consumed during various stages of maturity but is not generally eaten raw. The subtle-flavored, easily digested mature flesh may be used as a cucumber substitute, a cooked vegetable, or a food extender, since it takes on the flavors of other foods it is cooked with yet retains its pleasing crispness. Many compare its flavor to the chayote. It is a favorite soup ingredient in Asian cuisine, while in India and Cuba a popular dessert is made by cooking the pulp in syrup. The melon is also found in savory concoctions, candies, and pickles. The pulp has many flat, oval, light-brown seeds, which can be fried and eaten like pumpkin seeds. The seeds also yield a pale oil.

Health Benefits

Like watermelon, Chinese winter melon is 95 percent water, which explains why it is a cooling fruit with diuretic and anti-inflammatory properties and why it is popularly used in China in reducing diets. Nutritionally and medicinally, the wax gourd is closer to summer squash than to winter. The melon contains anticancer terpenes.

Yam

(Dioscorea rotundata, D. cayenensis, D. composita)

The genus name *Dioscorea* was given in honor of Dioscorides, a Greek physician and naturalist of the first or second century A.D. The term *rotundata* means "rotund" or "portly"; *cayenensis* means "coming from Cayenne," the island that is the capital of French Guiana; *composita* means "composite." The English name *yam* is of African origin, coming from the Guinean verb *nyami*, meaning "to eat."

General Information

Yams are large, tuberous roots largely confined to the tropics of West Africa and Asia, although they are found in a few other tropical regions. In the United States, yams can be grown only in the Deep South. Not to be confused with the American "yam," which is just another name for a moist-fleshed variety of sweet potato, true yams may grow to a remarkable size, up to six feet long and more than six hundred pounds. Instead of growing underground like potatoes, yams grow on plants and hang from plant stems. Their weight causes the stems to bend to the soil, and the yams become partially embedded like an exposed underground tuber. Every country and district that grows yams has its

own particular favorite that it cultivates, harvests, and cooks. In some Pacific Islands yams are venerated as nature's pantry, for they can be left in the ground to grow to an enormous size. Their flesh may be white, yellow, red, or even purple. Of the more than six hundred species, those most commonly encountered are brown, black-brown, or rusty tan, and all are shaggy-coated. Common types are elephant's foot or *suram*, taro or dasheen, and the cocoyam, all of which look similar to enormous potatoes. The boniato looks like a sweet potato with its ruddy pink skin but has white flesh; a bit tubbier than the American sweet potato, it has flesh that is drier—more like that of a regular white potato.

In 1936 Japanese chemists formulated by partial synthesis steroidal sapogenins, primarily diosgenin, from the glycoside saponins richly found in the barbasco, a wild yam native to Mexico. By 1940 diosgenin was able to be converted into progesterone, an intermediary in cortisone production. While progesterone can be derived from diosgenin, this can only be done by a chemist in the laboratory; humans cannot produce progesterone in their bodies from yams or their extracts. In 1956 Dr. Gregory Pincus announced that he had formulated a drug that would stop ovulation and hence prevent conception. Up to that time, steroids that prevented conception had to be taken by injection, whereas it now became possible to use oral administration. Although most birth-control pills are wholly synthetic today, dioscorea still figures in their origin. Other steroid drugs derived from diosgenin include anti-inflammatory compounds such as topical hormones and systemic corticosteroids, androgens, estrogens, progestogens, and other sex-hormone combinations.

Buying Tips

Choose yams that are regularly shaped and very hard, with no cracks or soft or shrunken spots. Although they are available in many sizes, those with the best flavor weigh less than two or three pounds. Sometimes the yams will be cut open to show how moist and creamy the interior is; if not, scrape one with your fingernail to see if it is juicy. Store as you would potatoes—never in the refrigerator but rather in the potato bin or any cool, dry, dark place. Yams are most often available in Latino and Asian markets. Frequently you can buy them by the piece, according to the weight you need.

Culinary Uses

Yams have a flavor and texture much like a mealy potato—loose, coarse, dry, and rather bland. The raw flesh is crisp, slippery, and mucilaginous. As versatile as the potato, yams

Yam / Nutritional Value Per 100 g Edible Portion		
	Raw	Cooked
Calories	118	116
Protein	1.53 g	1.49 g
Fat	0.17 g	0.14 g
Fiber	n/a	n/a
Calcium	17 mg	14 mg
Iron	0.54 mg	0.52 mg
Magnesium	21 mg	18 mg
Phosphorus	55 mg	49 mg
Potassium	816 mg	670 mg
Sodium	9 mg	8 mg
Zinc	0.240 mg	0.200 mg
Copper	0.178 mg	0.152 mg
Beta Carotene (A)	0 IU	0 IU
Thiamine (B₁)	0.112 mg	0.095 mg
Riboflavin (B₂)	0.032 mg	0.028 mg
Niacin (B₃)	0.758 mg	0.552 mg
Pantothenic Acid (B₅)	0.314 mg	0.311 mg
Pyridoxine (B₆)	0.293 mg	0.228 mg
Folic Acid (B₉)	23.0 mcg	16.0 mcg
Ascorbic Acid (C)	17.1 mg	12.1 mg

LORE AND LEGEND

It may well be that yams are worshiped because they can become awesomely huge. In the Pacific Island of Ponape, the size of yams is described as two-man, four-man, or six-man, designating the number of men needed to lift the tuber. Tubers up to six feet long and weighing six hundred pounds have been recorded. The Trobriand Islanders build intricately decorated wooden "yam houses" where the splendid tubers are ensconced to be viewed by neighbors. In Cuba, yams are considered festival food, to be saved for special occasions.

can be boiled, roasted, mashed, fried, or made into casseroles; they are a perfect foil for strong, spicy vegetable mixtures. They absorb other flavors well but are enhanced by a sprinkling of sweet spice such as cinnamon, nutmeg, ground cloves, or allspice. Unlike potatoes, the skin is not edible so should be removed. Wash under running water and then peel thickly to remove both the skin and the layer beneath. All yams contain dioscorine, which is poisonous (although cooking completely destroys it); this lies near the peel. Cut the yam into whatever size pieces you want. If not cooking at once, keep in salted water, because yam discolors easily. Added to soups or stews, yam's delicate nutty flavor will sweeten the pot. Frequently it is used in place of sweet potatoes in stews, chilies, and soups. On the islands where the boniato is a common food, people are fond of turning it into chips, much as we do with the common potato.

Health Benefits

pH 5.79–6.81 (cooked). Antiarthritic, antispasmodic, diuretic, emmenagogue. The yam is hailed as a medicinal tonic for many uses, working as an agent to prevent miscarriages and to treat asthma. It also contains simple peptide substances called phytochelatins that can bind heavy metals like cadmium, copper, mercury, and lead and thus help detoxify the body. Those species of yam containing diosgenin are medicinally efficacious for fatigue, inflammation, spasms, stress, colitis, Irritable Bowel Syndrome, PMS, and menopausal complaints. The yam's plant estrogen (phytoestrogen) seems to act as a key to unlock and potentiate existing estrogen in the body, thus eliminating or easing many of the symptoms of low estrogen.

Yautia
(Xanthosoma sagittifolium)
Also Known As: Cocoyam, Dasheen, Malanga, Tannia

Xanthosoma is Greek for "yellow body" and refers to the *stigma; sagittifolium* means "arrow-leaved." This vegetable is called *yautia* by Puerto Ricans and *malanga* by Colombians.

General Information
The funny-looking, potato-like yautia originated in the Americas in both dry and swampy soils. The forty or so species of this vegetable, all native to the American tropics, include some of the oldest root crops in the world. Their close resemblance to a related tuber, *Colocasia esculenta* (most commonly known as taro), has produced a score of common names that overlap the two, blurring the distinguishing characteristics. Like the taro, the yautia is a thin-skinned shaggy cormel that surrounds a larger rootlike corm, but it is larger than the taro and frequently club-shaped. Only the cormels are normally used for human consumption, while the corms are used for animal feed and for replanting. This plant is also grown for its long-stalked, arrow-shaped leaves, which are often sold separately from the tubers and can be boiled and eaten like Swiss chard ribs.

Buying Tips
Select relatively light-colored, very hard specimens with no soft, shriveled, or moldy areas. They should have a fresh smell.

Culinary Uses
The yautia has a unique, creamy texture and a more pronounced flavor than most starchy tropical tubers—vaguely musty and earthy, tending more toward nuts than potatoes. The interior may be cream, yellow, or pinkish, with an extremely crisp, slippery texture. Do not consume raw; once peeled, yautias can be boiled, baked, fried, or ground into flour. The smooth, melting quality that the crisp tuber develops when boiled is most surprising—somewhere between cooked dried pinto beans and waxy new potatoes. It flavors, thickens, and adds creaminess to stews. Yautia makes an excellent bland foil for spicy side dishes or condiments.

Health Benefits
Low in fat and high in thiamine, riboflavin, vitamin C, and iron. As a kitchen remedy, the yautia may be used to regulate energy, support digestion, and disperse congestion.

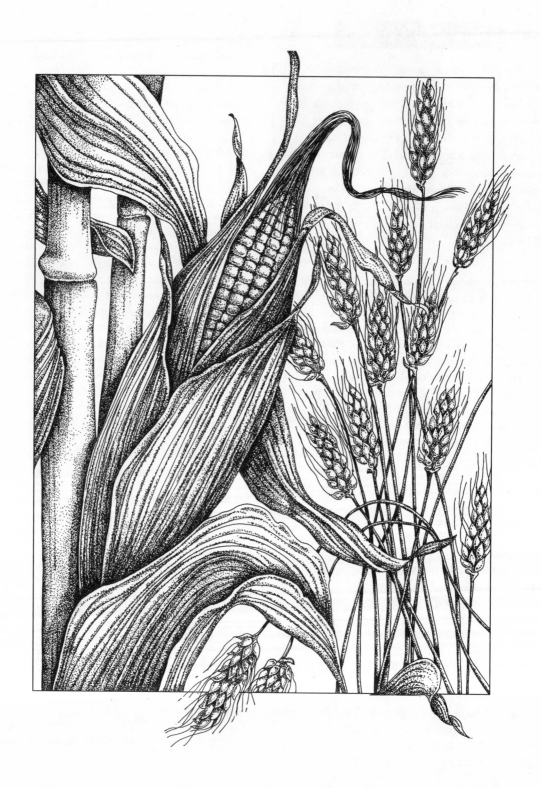

GRAINS

The smallest grain of meal would suit my necessity better than this pearl.

—La Fontaine, Fables

GRAINS

GRAINS

Grains are the seeds and fruits of cereal grasses that grow in a wide variety of climates and conditions; members of this cereal grass family are commonly referred to as cereal grains. The word *cereal* is derived from Ceres, the Roman goddess of agriculture. Archeological evidence shows that wheat and barley were used over ten thousand years ago by people living in the Fertile Crescent, a broad, crescent-shaped area that curved northward and eastward from what is now the eastern border of Egypt to the Taurus Mountains of southern Turkey, across the Zagros Mountains of western Iran, and down to the Persian Gulf. By 4000 B.C., millet farming was well established along the upper Yellow River in China. About the same time, rice was being cultivated in Southeast Asia. Since dried grains store well, it is not surprising that their cultivation spread as people traveled to new lands.

Good-quality grain is whole and contains few specimens that are broken, scratched, or deteriorated. It might seem that cosmetically beautiful grains of the same size and color would indicate quality, but these grains are actually from hybridized seed, which is less vital than unhybridized varieties. Whole grains are perfect examples of complex carbohydrates, containing as they do a complete package, with bran layer, endosperm, and germ intact. Anatomy and structure are basically the same for all grains. The bran is composed of tissues between the outer seed coat and the thin aleurone layer of the endosperm. This bran layer contains fiber, minerals, and protein, adds bulk to the digestive system, and stabilizes blood sugar. Inside the bran layer is the endosperm, the storage compartment of the grain. This starchy interior section is meant to sustain the seedling until it grows leaves for manufacturing its own food. Life springs from the embryo, or germ, which is a rich source of valuable protein, minerals, and vitamins, particularly vitamin E, an antioxidant that prevents the destruction of cells by compounds known as free radicals and is also critical to reproductive function, circulation, and healthy skin. Whole grains are an important source of vegetable lignins, a group of compounds with antitumor and antioxidant properties. The rich fiber in grains produces short-chain fatty acids, including butyrate, acetate, and propionate, which inhibit candida yeast growth. Butyrate in particular has been shown to suppress the growth of colon cancer in humans and cancer in general in animals.

Before a grain has fully turned to starch and is considered ripe, it can be eaten raw. This milky stage is when the grain is highest in grape sugar content (similar to that found in thoroughly ripe fruit); once ripened, the sugars in the grain have turned to starch, and before starch can be used by the body, the outer cellulose wall must be broken by grinding or cooking. All grains in their mature state have a tendency to cause acidosis because they contain mostly protein, carbohydrate, and phosphoric acid. Soaking grains overnight before cooking them starts the sprouting process, which helps to break down the starch and protein into compounds that are easier to digest, thus substantially increasing the protein, vitamin, and enzyme content available. The grain may be cooked in this water, as it is rich in nutrients.

For the fun of it, as well as for the flavor and nutritional variations, experiment with the whole realm of different grain flours. Each flour excels in its own way and can transform what might otherwise be a mundane dish into a culinary masterpiece. Any whole-grain flour has a limited shelf life. It is ideal to grind your own flour eight to twelve hours prior to use. Flour used sooner is "green" and performs erratically; the cells of the dough it is used for are not tough enough to retain gas, and the loaf does not rise as much, nor does it produce an even-textured slice. During the few hours of aging flour, some of the enzymes that might otherwise have interfered with yeast activity have oxidized, taming the flour enough to give consistent results. Further aging, however, does not further improve the flour. To the contrary: each day after grinding, depending on storage conditions, flour loses from 10 to 20 percent of its oxidizable enzymes and vitamins. Traditionally, when bread was made, the dough was allowed to rest for a number of hours to allow time for certain enzymes to work on the phytin (an organic phosphorus compound that interferes with the utilization of nutrients); in the same time, the moistened bran had a chance to become softened and more easily digested.

The type of mill that grinds the grain has a surprising effect on a flour's performance, flavor, and nutrition. Stone-ground flour is a superior-quality flour. Since the layers are simply flaked off the grains, this milling process does not overheat the flour and the nutrients are retained. Making flour with steel roller mills and hammer mills is a fast way of doing it, where the grain is not so much ground as it is splintered and crushed. There are both gross and subtle differences between steel-crushed and stone-ground flour. On the gross level, stone-ground flour comes out both cooler and coarser, resulting in higher food and fiber values. As well, there is a definite consensus among people who have worked with both that stone-ground flour tastes better, with a richer, fuller, nuttier flavor. A number of stone flour mills, both manual and electric, are available for home use, and for those who do a lot of baking these home mills are an excellent investment. Be aware, however, that certain flours cannot be made with stone mills. Oats have a high fat and moisture content and tend to clog stone mills readily unless the grain has been oven-dried in advance. Corn is also a problem, since the kernels are so hard they tend to pit the stones quickly.

FLOUR MILLING HISTORY

For centuries grain was ground in small water- or wind-powered mills scattered throughout the countryside. These old mills pulverized the oily germ of the grain along with the starchy endosperm, with the germ giving the flour its characteristic yellow-brown color and also turning it rancid within a few weeks. According to the adjustment of the stones and the fineness of the sifter, different grades could be produced, but the quality was not consistent, and much of the grain ground in this manner was not very clean.

A new higher-speed method of milling flour was developed in Hungary during the 1840s, where iron rollers processed the grain more consistently than the old stone mills. These new roller mills squeezed the grain in such a way that the endosperm popped out of its coating, leaving the germ behind to be sieved off with the bran. As a result, the new roller-milled flour was whiter than stone-ground and could be stored for months, even years, without deteriorating. This pleased not only the millers, bakers, and grocers, but their customers as well, and with the introduction in the 1870s of porcelain rollers—which didn't rust and were easier to clean—this type of milling became the general practice. The discarded wheat germ and bran, unfortunately, contained most of the grain's nutrients. Unlike the refining of gold, which removes impurities and makes the product much more valuable, the refining of cereal grains makes the grain much less valuable from a nutritional standpoint.

RANCIDITY AND STORAGE

Though they have a long shelf life compared to fruits and vegetables, whole grains are still subject to spoilage. Their natural oils will turn rancid, and they can also fall prey to insect infestation and mold. Grains tightly sealed in closed containers or plastic bags will keep for about three months in a cool, dry place (less in hot or humid weather), and storage in the refrigerator will hold them for at least six months. Frozen grain will keep almost indefinitely; the exceptions are oats and oat bran, which are higher in fat than other grains and so can turn rancid after being frozen in only two or three months; buy only as much as you will need in that period of time. Telltale signs of age and spoilage in grains are not as obvious as in fruits and vegetables. Of primary concern is mold, which indicates either that the grain is old or that it has been improperly stored and allowed to absorb too much moisture. Green or partially green grains in wheat, barley, or rye are not immature but moldy. The exception to this rule is rice, where immature green grains are common and inconsequential.

When grains are cracked, rolled, or milled in any manner, their vitality is compromised. Without its protective sheath, the oil inherent in the grain begins to oxidize and turn rancid. Light and heat speed the process. Rancid foods are toxic to the body and are considered by many to be carcinogenic. Whole-grain flour that is over three months old and has not been kept in the freezer should be discarded.

GLUTEN-RELATED HEALTH HAZARDS

In 1820 French physiologist F. Magendie found that coarse dark bread kept dogs in good health, while feeding them bread made from white flour saw the dogs die within two months. *The Lancet* (March 11, 1826) reported, "A dog fed on fine white bread and water, both at discretion, does not live beyond the fiftieth day. A dog fed on the coarse bread of the military, lives and keeps his health."

Some people cannot tolerate gluten, a composition of two proteins (gliadin and glutenin) that are found in many grains but are highest in wheat, followed at a distance by rye, oats, and barley. Gluten is what gives flour elasticity and strength. It is what allows breads to "rise." (When kneaded, gluten traps the carbon dioxide produced by yeast or a chemical leavening agent, resulting in the expansion or "rising" of the dough.) This combination of proteins has been found to contribute to the cause of several serious diseases, including schizophrenia, celiac disease, and dermatitis herpetiformis. Celiac disease, also known as nontropical sprue, is an intestinal disorder caused by the inability to utilize gluten. It is characterized by diarrhea, malabsorption of nutrients, and an abnormally small intestinal structure that reverts back to normal when dietary gluten is removed and thereafter avoided. The elimination of gluten from the diet causes rapid improvement in the health of most people with celiac disease and dermatitis herpetiformis, and a few of those with schizophrenia. Oats are also often found on a list of foods for gluten-sensitive individuals to avoid. However, when fed to patients with celiac disease, they generally do not cause reactions. A one-pound loaf of bread contains about 40 grams of gluten. This amount of gluten, if eaten in a single day, can cause problems even for people without celiac disease. Gluten causes changes in the intestinal lining that retard the absorption of nutrients.

Amaranth

(Amaranthus hypocondriacus, A. melancholicus, A. caudatus, A. cruentus)
Also Known As: En Choy, Pigweed, Yin Tsoi

Amaranthus, as well as the English *amaranth*, comes from the Greek *amarantos*, meaning "deathless" or "unfading," because this plant's flowers retain their color and appearance even when dried. *Hypocondriacus* means "having a somber appearance"; *melancholicus* means "melancholy," "hanging," or "drooping"; *caudatus* means "caudate" or "tailed"; *cruentus* means "bloody" and refers to the plant's often blood-red coloring.

General Information

Amaranth is the seed of a broadleaf plant rather than a grass, and thus it is not strictly speaking a grain, but the edible seed is classed by use as such. Amaranth plants are members of an elite group of photosynthetic superperformers that botanists call the "C4 group." C4 plants utilize a photosynthetic process or pathway that has above-normal efficiency in converting soil, sunlight, and water into plant tissue. Thus amaranth has enhanced environmental adaptation and is extraordinarily nutritious. There are about five hundred species of amaranth, with types that thrive in environments ranging from wet tropics to semiarid lands and from sea level up to altitudes of ten thousand feet. Indigenous to India and the Americas, amaranth is so hardy that it grows vigorously under the most adverse conditions, tolerating very acid or highly alkaline soils, long equatorial days or short temperate ones, dry spells, heat, and mildly salty conditions. Each seed head resembles a bushy corn tassel and yields hundreds of small round seeds the size of poppy seeds. A single plant, with its multiple seed heads, may produce up to fifty thousand seeds, in colors of cream, gold, or pink. The leaves also vary in color, with stems and flowers of purple, orange, red, or gold. One variety grown for its leaves, frequently known as Chinese spinach (*Amaranthus gangeticus*), has dark green leaves that are tinged with red and slightly fuzzy. Like spinach, the whole plant can be eaten, but the leaves and tender stems are preferred. Plants grown for grain are pale-seeded since their appearance, flavor, and popping capability are considered best. The wild, dark-seeded varieties are generally used as potherbs and ornamentals; they are not as suitable for grain. Amaranth sustained the Aztec culture until 1521, when Cortez arrived and banished the crop. Surviving in remote pockets in the wild, it was "rediscovered" in 1972 by a United States botanical research team.

Culinary Uses

Amaranth is unusual because, like quinoa and unlike other grains, it is edible as both a vegetable and a grain. The greens, with their widely varied colors, add vibrant depth to salads and make a nutritious as well as tasty green vegetable. Although soft, the leaves are rough-textured and grow in clusters on slender stalks from one to six feet tall. Their immature fleshy seed heads are eaten like broccoli. The leaves are described as being similar in taste to spinach but with a more assertive pepperiness, while the stems taste more like artichokes. Older stems may be tough, so the younger the better. Amaranth greens and stems can be used in every way you would use spinach and other greens—in quiches, omelets, casseroles, vegetable medleys, soups, and purées. They are particularly concentrated, with an abundance of nutrients.

The amaranth grain is one that, unless you have an inquisitive palate, may take some adjusting to. It has a

Amaranth / Nutritional Value Per 100 g Edible Portion			
	Raw Whole Grain	Raw Leaves	Cooked Leaves
Calories	374	26	21
Protein	14.45 g	2.46 g	2.11 g
Fat	6.51 g	0.33 g	0.18 g
Fiber	3.77 g	0.98 g	1.31 g
Calcium	153 mg	215 mg	209 mg
Iron	7.59 mg	2.32 mg	2.26 mg
Magnesium	266 mg	55 mg	55 mg
Phosphorus	455 mg	50 mg	72 mg
Potassium	366 mg	611 mg	641 mg
Sodium	21 mg	20 mg	21 mg
Zinc	3.18 mg	0.90 mg	n/a
Copper	0.777 mg	0.162 mg	n/a
Manganese	2.260 mg	n/a	n/a
Beta Carotene (A)	n/a	2,917 IU	2,770 IU
Thiamine (B$_1$)	0.080 mg	0.027 mg	0.020 mg
Riboflavin (B$_2$)	0.208 mg	0.158 mg	0.134 mg
Niacin (B$_3$)	1.286 mg	0.658 mg	0.559 mg
Pantothenic Acid (B$_5$)	1.047 mg	n/a	n/a
Pyridoxine (B$_6$)	0.223 mg	n/a	n/a
Folic Acid (B$_9$)	49.0 mcg	85.3 mcg	n/a
Ascorbic Acid (C)	4.2 mg	43.3 mg	41.1 mg

LORE AND LEGEND

The amaranth, both plant and grain, has frequently been connected with religious ceremonies throughout history. Montezuma collected a tribute of some two hundred thousand bushels of amaranth seed annually—almost the equal of the tribute in maize—from seventeen provinces of the Aztec Empire. The grain had a great religious significance for the Aztecs, who fashioned statues of their war and fire gods from the grain paste, mixing it either with honey or sacrificial blood. These statues were then carried in ceremonial processions, at the end of which they were broken and eaten by the Aztecs or fed to the slaves who were about to be sacrificed. To the Christian Cortez and his followers, this was nothing more than heathen idolatry, a pagan travesty of the Eucharist. Thus the fields of amaranth were burned and it was decreed that anyone in possession of the grain would have both hands cut off. Zuni legends relate that amaranth was one of the plants brought up from the underworld at the Zunis' emergence, and it was a staple grain until the Corn Maiden brought them corn. To the Greeks, the unfading amaranth was a symbol of immortality, and they used the plant to embellish the images of their gods and tombs. The early Christian church also adopted the amaranth as symbolic of immortality. Whether in monastery gardens or on altars during the Middle Ages, their rich purples, royal reds, and golds blended perfectly with the exquisite colors of stained-glass windows, saints' robes, and altar hangings in church and shrine. In 1653 Queen Cristina of Sweden set up the Amaranter Order of Knighthood, obviously bearing in mind the plant's mystical associations.

strong but pleasantly nutty wild flavor and can be used whole, popped like corn, steamed and flattened into a flake, or ground into flour. The whole grain cooks easily and quickly to a cereal-like consistency, but it retains its shape and the hulls stay firm and chewy, never getting soft or mushy. Added in moderation, amaranth lends a distinctive peppery-spicy flavor that enhances the mild taste of grains like rice, buckwheat, millet, or oats. It has marvelous versatility as an ingredient in a range of dishes: breads, salads, soups, candies, pancakes, pilafs, and breakfast cereals. Adding small quantities of the whole cooked grain to batters helps baked goods retain moisture and lightness.

Health Benefits

pH 6.0. Astringent. Nutritionally, amaranth is higher in protein than either corn or beans, higher in fiber than wheat, corn, rice, or soybeans, rich in vitamins, and exceptionally rich in the essential amino acid lysine, absent or very low in most other cereal grains. It is also higher in calcium and the supporting calcium cofactors—magnesium and silicon—than milk and has an iron content up to four times that of brown rice. This makes it an especially helpful food for nursing or pregnant women, infants, children, people who do heavy physical labor, and people wanting to gain weight. The seed is appreciated for its remarkable vitality. As an herb, amaranth works as an astringent, having the effect of contracting tissues and limiting gland secretion; thus it is helpful for excessive menstrual bleeding or diarrhea.

BYPRODUCTS

Amaranth flour, because it has no gluten, is especially appreciated by those who have grain or gluten sensitivities. Added in small amounts to baked goods, the flour boosts both flavor and nutrition. Generally, only a small portion is used in leavened products, while unleavened products such as flatbreads, crackers, and cookies may use a higher percentage. Some cultures commonly use the flour for gruel, pancakes, tortillas, breads, and other baked goods.

Popped amaranth, with its nutty flavor, can be eaten like popcorn or added to a range of recipes to add flavor and lightness. One cup of amaranth will yield three to four cups popped. Small amounts are easiest popped in a Japanese sesame seed toaster (available at most Japanese supply shops); larger amounts can be done in a wok or heavy skillet. Popped amaranth will not keep long and quickly turns rancid.

Barley
(Hordeum vulgare, H. distichon, H. hexastichon)

Hordeum is an ancient Latin name for barley. *Vulgare* means "vulgar" or "common"; *distichon* refers to the two-rowed variety; *hexastichon* is the six-rowed. The English word *barley* is a corruption of the Latin *far*, another name used for this grain.

General Information
Barley is a hardy cereal grain believed to have originated from a wild form somewhere in western Asia or the Ethiopian highlands. It was used as a feedstuff for both man and beast in ancient Egypt between 6000 and 5000 B.C., and in China by 2800 B.C.. It was also one of the grain staples in early Europe until it was replaced by rye and wheat; when leavened bread became common, barley lost much of its importance for bread making because of its low gluten content. The several varieties are usually divided according to the number of grain rows along the ear: the two-rowed coffee or Peruvian barley (*H. distichon*); the four-rowed spring or common barley (*H. vulgare*); and the six-rowed variety (*H. hexastichon*), which was popular in ancient times. Probably the most ancient cultivated grain, barley is considered one of the five most important cereal crops in the world, its grains being used for human food, in malt brewing, and as livestock feed. It was brought to the New World by Dutch and British colonists primarily to make beer, and over one-third of the current crop is still used for that purpose, with less than one-tenth being used for human consumption (the rest is used for animal feed). In fact, beer was even named after this grain, which was once called bere. Barley has two inedible outer hulls that are typically removed by machine. The next inner layer, the aleurone, is rich in protein, B vitamins, and fiber. Most barley, however, is subjected to further processing ("pearling") to remove this layer as well. Pearled barley is thus nutritionally inferior to hulled whole barley.

Culinary Uses
Most barley found in stores is pearled, and it is this form that most people are familiar with. Its mild, sweet flavor and chewy texture has made it a traditional favorite for thickening soups and stews. Cooked on its own it makes a pleasant alternative to potatoes, rice, or pasta, as well as an innovative salad and casserole ingredient.

Health Benefits
pH 5.19–5.32 (cooked). Barley is highly regarded as a nutritious food, excellent for underweight individuals. Soothing to the digestive tract and liver, it is said to help heal stomach ulcers, prevent tooth decay and hair loss, and improve the condition of finger- and toenails. Barley has blood-cholesterol-lowering abilities, and in some areas of the world where barley is a staple, both as a cereal and as a flour, heart disease rates are low. Whole barley, sometimes called "sproutable," is mildly laxative and contains far more nutrition than the commonly used "pearled" variety. Roasting before cooking makes barley, considered the most acid-forming grain, more alkalinizing. Sprouted barley treats indigestion from starchy food stagnation, strengthens weak digestion, and tonifies the stomach. Dried sprouted barley contains sixty-six thousand International Units of beta carotene (vitamin A) per hundred grams. Processing removes many of its nutrients and health benefits, so the less processed, the better. Black barley, a variety of the more prosaic common barley, has an earthy sweetness and is considered medicinal to the kidneys. In Tibet black barley was traditionally favored for beer making and light barley for the daily staple tsampa.

Barley / Nutritional Value Per 100 g Edible Portion	Raw Whole Grain	Raw Pearled	Cooked Pearled	Malt Syrup
Calories	354	352	123	318
Protein	12.48 g	9.91 g	2.26 g	6.20 g
Fat	2.30 g	1.16 g	0.44 g	0 g
Fiber	2.85 g	0.74 g	0.23 g	n/a
Calcium	33 mg	29 mg	11 mg	61 mg
Iron	3.60 mg	2.50 mg	1.33 mg	0.96 mg
Magnesium	133 mg	79 mg	22 mg	72 mg
Phosphorus	264 mg	221 mg	54 mg	236 mg
Potassium	452 mg	280 mg	93 mg	320 mg
Sodium	12 mg	9 mg	3 mg	35 mg
Zinc	2.770 mg	2.130 mg	0.820 mg	0.140 mg
Copper	0.498 mg	0.420 mg	0.105 mg	0.200 mg
Manganese	1.943 mg	1.322 mg	0.259 mg	0.100 mg
Beta Carotene (A)	n/a	22 IU	n/a	0 IU
Thiamine (B₁)	0.646 mg	0.191 mg	0.083 mg	n/a
Riboflavin (B₂)	0.285 mg	0.114 mg	0.062 mg	0.393 mg
Niacin (B₃)	n/a	4.604 mg	2.063 mg	8.120 mg
Pantothenic Acid (B₅)	n/a	0.282 mg	0.135 mg	0.171 mg
Pyridoxine (B₆)	0.318 mg	0.260 mg	0.115 mg	0.500 mg
Folic Acid (B₉)	19.0 mcg	23.0 mcg	16.0 mcg	12.0 mcg
Ascorbic Acid (C)	0 mg	0 mg	0 mg	0 mg
Tocopherol (E)	0.57 mg	0.02 mg	n/a	n/a

LORE AND LEGEND

Barley was used as the basic unit of the Sumerian measuring system from 4000 to 2000 B.C. The Babylonian Code of Hammurabi (1750 B.C.) records that it was frequently used as a means of simple monetary exchange, and even among the Ethiopians, land rent or laborers could be paid in this manner. For the Hebrews, Greeks, and Romans (who represented their agricultural goddess Ceres with barley plaited into her crown) it was the chief bread flour crop and was heralded as a food for potency and vigor. The Greeks trained their athletes on barley mush because it was considered the mildest of all cereals, while Roman gladiators, called *hordearii* (barley eaters), ate the grain to build up strength. Barley in ancient India was dedicated to the god Indra, known as "He who ripens barley"; Hindus still use the grains in their religious celebrations, at weddings, childbirths, funerals, and other rites. In the writings of ancient China, the seed-rich, heavily bearded barley was considered a symbol of male potency, and the grain is mentioned as one of the five most sacred cultivated crops, the others being rice, millet, soybeans, and wheat.

BYPRODUCTS

Barley flakes, or **rolled barley,** are processed in exactly the same manner as oatmeal, which allows them to cook quicker than the whole-grain form. The flakes can be cooked for a chewy breakfast porridge, eaten raw in muesli, or toasted and used as a thickening agent in soups, stews, and baked goods.

Barley flour is starchy and soft, with a sweet, earthy taste. Whole-grain barley flour yields a cakelike crumb (and sometimes a grayish color) and can be substituted for all or part of the wheat flour in recipes. Some suggest that a blend of flours is more desirable for bread baking since barley has a very low gluten content and will not rise much on its own; its maltose content, which enhances the growth of yeast cells in leavened breads, may make up for this. The flour can also be used as a thickening agent.

Barley grass juice, the juice of the chlorophyll-rich grass of young barley plants, is nutritionally comparable to wheatgrass juice. Of the two, barley grass juice is more alkaline and therefore balanced, while wheatgrass juice is stronger and faster acting. As excellent a protein source as meat, both grasses are nearly as high in chlorophyll and vitamin A as micro-algae. In addition, barley grass offers important digestive enzymes, can resolve toxic substances, and contains nutrients that slow deterioration and mutation.

Barley grits are coarsely ground whole hulled barley grains that have been toasted. More similar to bulgur than to corn (hominy) grits, barley grits cook quickly and are excellent served in place of rice, as a breakfast cereal, and in baking.

Hulled barley, also known as **groats, pot barley,** and **Scotch barley,** is the whole grain that has gone through two pearlings to remove the inedible spikelet (two outer husks). "Hull-less" barley is a special variety that has a softer, easily removable hull. Hulled barley is the most nutritious form of the grain because the bran remains, making it rich in dietary fiber, vitamins, and minerals. These light brown grains require strenuous chewing in order to be fully digested but have a pronounced, appealing flavor. They can be used as a whole-grain cereal or added to soups and casseroles; their cooking time is longer than the pearled variety.

Malt powder/malt sugar is a buff-colored, crystalline powder made by evaporating the water out of malt syrup. Primarily used for brewing, malt sugar is becoming increasingly available in stores as a sugar replacement. Since malt powder absorbs moisture very easily (in the process becoming rock-hard), it needs to be stored in a well-sealed glass jar. Stored properly, malt powder has a lengthy shelf life. Malt sugar is easy to substitute for sugar, and unlike natural liquid sweeteners, it gives the same tender crumb that sugar does. Substitute measure for measure. The result is a lighter sweetness with a pleasing malt flavor.

Malt syrup is made from raw, unhulled barley soaked in drums of temperature- and humidity-controlled water to allow it to sprout. Sprouting activates the enzymes in the grain that begin breaking down the starch into simple sugars (maltose). After two or three day, this sprouted grain is kiln-dried, and the grain is then ground, briefly dipped in an acid solution, and heated with water to form the mildly sweet, concentrated liquid we know as malt syrup. If this liquid is subjected to further heating and evaporating, it will become malt extract and maltose (malt sugar), a crystalline, colorless powder. Malt syrup is about 65 percent maltose, which tastes only 20 to 30 percent as sweet as sucrose (white sugar). It should be stored in a cool place, as warmth may cause it to ferment. Malt syrups are also made from wheat, rice, barley and rice, or barley and corn. Malt syrup is less concentrated in flavor than other sweeteners and adds a subtle and mild, rather than bold, sweetness to cooked or baked products. Traditionally used in beer making, hot and cold malted milk drinks, and some breakfast cereals, malt syrup added to bread recipes not only promotes yeast activity but also gives better body and texture while enhancing the flavor of other ingredients; it also adds a warm, rich color. Because malt syrup is high in complex carbohydrates, it enters the bloodstream slowly and can be considered a balanced sweetener that will not upset blood sugar levels.

Pearl barley is the most commonly found form of this grain in the United States. These uniform, ivory-colored granules are produced when the barley grains are scoured six times during milling to completely remove their double outer husk (the spikelet) and the bran layers. The thorough milling, however, removes almost all of their fiber, along with over half their protein, fat, and mineral content; thus pearl barley is an inferior product, nutritionally, compared to the whole hulled variety. However, it is used in times of illness when other foods cannot be tolerated, as it is the mildest and least irritating of the cereals. It has a very mild, nutlike taste, cooks quickly, and readily absorbs the flavors of its companion ingredients in soups, salads, and side dishes. An instant form of pearl barley, called quick barley, cooks even faster because it is precooked by steaming.

Buckwheat
(Fagopyrum esculentum, F. tartaricum)

The scientific name *Fagopyrum* is derived from *fagus*, meaning "beech tree," and *pyrum*, meaning "cereal," because of the resemblance between the buckwheat fruits and those of the beech tree. *Esculentum* means "esculent" or "edible"; *tartaricum* means "coming from Tartary" (an indefinite historical region in Asia and Europe, extending

LORE AND LEGEND

How does a horse get sunburned? A light-colored horse or cow grazing in a buckwheat field on a sunny day may become sunburned and suffer temporary hair loss. Buckwheat inhibits our tanning element, melanin, and judging from farmers' stories about sunburned livestock, apparently it inhibits a horse's melanin as well. Perhaps this is why buckwheat is a staple of the dark-complexioned Siberian peoples but not of the fair-skinned Scandinavians. If you are dark-skinned, a melanin inhibitor keeps your skin a shade lighter and thus enables you to absorb more of the sun's rays—and therefore more vitamin D, a hard-to-obtain vitamin during long, dark winters. In the Deep South, buckwheat is an old kitchen remedy for lightening the skin.

from the Sea of Japan to the Dnieper River in Russia). The English name *buckwheat* is a corruption of the Dutch *bockweit*, meaning "beech wheat," reflecting the grain's physical resemblance to beechnuts and its nutritional similarity to wheat.

General Information
Buckwheat is native to the regions of Manchuria and Siberia, an ancient hardy plant that grows rapidly even in poor, rocky soil and extreme climates. Instead of growing tall and straight, buckwheat is branching and weedlike, with heart-shaped leaves and fragrant white flowers that are attractive to bees. The three-cornered seed has an inedible black outer hull that must be removed, yielding a tan-colored interior kernel. First cultivated in China, it was introduced to Europe in the Middle Ages by the Crusaders, who brought it back to Venice from Asia Minor. During the sixteenth century the plant spread throughout Europe and achieved some importance because of its ability to thrive in poorer soils; at that time it was generally known as Saracen wheat or corn, *Saracen* being a term given to most foreign things but especially those introduced by the Muslims and Turks. Until the turn of the twentieth century, impoverished cultures from eastern Europe to the United States' Deep South depended

on buckwheat for porridge and as an extender for costly wheat flour. Its popularity declined rapidly in the early part of the twentieth century, but it is now making a strong comeback in health food circles. The Japanese especially make wide use of it for many types of noodles (called soba). Buckwheat, due to its extreme hardiness and resistance to disease, is one of the few commercially grown grains that is not routinely doused with insecticides.

Culinary Uses

The buckwheat grown in Europe has a rather mild taste, distinctly different from the buckwheat grown in the United States, which can be quite strong and musky. After harvesting, the black, hard, inedible outer shell has to be removed in order to gain access to the inner kernel. This kernel is then split into pieces, called groats, which are either sold raw or roasted (known by the Russian name *kasha*). The unroasted groats are a greenish color, have a mellow flavor, and are frequently substituted for white or brown rice. Although the raw groats are nutritionally superior, roasting brings out the flavor and increases the availability of iron. The roasted variety usually works best for

LORE AND LEGEND

Japanese goldsmiths have long used buckwheat dough to collect the gold dust in their shops, and the grain is therefore considered a potent charm for collecting riches. When a Japanese family moves to a new house, presents of buckwheat noodles (soba) are given to all the neighbors to express wishes for their good fortune and for long-lasting friendships between them; these noodles are also eaten each New Year's Eve in the hope of acquiring the luck for amassing money during the coming year.

culinary purposes, unless used for cereal. Buckwheat can be eaten as a cereal, or side dish, or incorporated into a main dish, where it blends well with onions, dill, mushrooms, winter squash, and cabbage. It imparts a delicious flavor to stuffings, pilafs, soups, and stews. Most people are familiar with buckwheat only in the form of pancakes or crepes. Of all the grains, buckwheat has the longest transit time in the gut and therefore is the most filling and stabilizing for blood sugar.

Health Benefits

Buckwheat is a power-packed grain, special in that it contains all eight essential amino acids as well as the glucoside rutin, a substance that is helpful in strengthening the capillaries, aiding in circulation, and protecting against the effects of radiation. It is an excellent food for cold-weather months because of its warming and drying effects on the body; however, because of this astringent action, it is not recommended for those with skin eruptions, allergies, or cancer as it may prevent cells from cleansing themselves. Buckwheat also has the reputation of being a good blood builder and neutralizer of toxic acidic wastes in the system. Since it is gluten-free many people with food allergies rely upon buckwheat. Roasted buckwheat (kasha) is a rich source of fiber and silica, which forms butyrate, a short-chain fatty acid, thus detoxifying the intestines and suppressing the growth of cancers. The roasting process converts buckwheat into one of the few alkalinizing grains. Young buckwheat greens (from seeds with the hard, inedible black coverings that drop off after sprouting) are excellent sources of chlorophyll, enzymes, and vitamins.

Buckwheat / Nutritional Value Per 100 g Edible Portion

	Raw Whole Grain	Cooked Kasha	Whole-Grain Dark Flour	Light Flour
Calories	343	92	335	347
Protein	13.25 g	3.38 g	12.62 g	6.40 g
Fat	3.40 g	0.62 g	3.10 g	1.20 g
Fiber	9.90 g	0.52 g	1.60 g	0.50 g
Calcium	18 mg	7 mg	41 mg	11 mg
Iron	2.20 mg	0.80 mg	4.06 mg	1.00 mg
Magnesium	231 mg	51 mg	251 mg	n/a
Phosphorus	347 mg	70 mg	337 mg	88 mg
Potassium	460 mg	88 mg	577 mg	320 mg
Sodium	1 mg	4 mg	n/a	n/a
Zinc	2.400 mg	0.610 mg	3.120 mg	n/a
Copper	1.100 mg	0.146 mg	0.515 mg	n/a
Manganese	1.300 mg	0.403 mg	2.030 mg	n/a
Thiamine (B$_1$)	0.101 mg	0.040 mg	0.417 mg	0.080 mg
Riboflavin (B$_2$)	0.425 mg	0.039 mg	0.190 mg	0.040 mg
Niacin (B$_3$)	7.020 mg	0.940 mg	6.150 mg	0.400 mg
Pantothenic Acid (B$_5$)	n/a	0.359 mg	0.440 mg	n/a
Pyridoxine (B$_6$)	0.210 mg	0.077 mg	0.582 mg	n/a
Folic Acid (B$_9$)	30.0 mcg	14.0 mcg	54.0 mcg	n/a
Ascorbic Acid (C)	0 mg	0 mg	0 mg	0 mg

BYPRODUCTS

Buckwheat flour is a beautiful gray-and-black-speckled flour with an assertive, musky, slightly bitter flavor. Dark buckwheat flour is preferable to light buckwheat flour; it has had only 20 percent of the husk removed, whereas the lighter flour has had 50 percent removed. Since the husk is rich in lysine, favor the darker flour. This beautifully light flour has been traditionally used for making pancakes and crepes; their Russian counterparts, called blinis, are not limited solely to the breakfast table. Buckwheat flour will not rise on its own since it does not contain gluten, but combined with wheat flour it makes delicious bread with the density of a brick but the tender moistness of pudding.

Buckwheat grits are groats that have been coarsely cracked. Sold as buckwheat cereal or cream of buckwheat, these finely ground, unroasted groats cook quickly and develop a soft, creamy texture. Because they have been broken, grits lack the vitality and freshness of the whole groat but are easily digestible. Popular as a filler in many Polish sausages, they are also excellent in soufflés and a rice-pudding-style dessert.

Buckwheat groats are the seeds that have been hulled. Whole buckwheat with the inedible black hull intact is suitable only for sprouting. These hulls, incidentally, are used for stuffing cushions and pillows. The groats are available either unroasted (white or lightly green) or roasted (brown, known as kasha). The tan unroasted groats have a fairly mild flavor and can be substituted in dishes that call for white or brown rice. Roasted buckwheat has a more assertive, almost scorched, flavor, which many people prefer.

Kasha is the brown roasted buckwheat groats, which come in four forms: fine grind, which cooks quickly and is less chewy than the other grinds; medium and coarse grinds, which are good for all-around use; and the whole roasted groat, which is uncracked and good for pilafs. Kasha is also ground to make a flour that can be used for pancakes, crisp thin cakes, and Japanese soba noodles.

Corn/Maize
(Zea mays)

The Indians called this grain *mahiz*. In 1737 Linnaeus christened the species *Zea mays*, from the Greek *zeia*, meaning "grain" or "cereal," and *mays*, a spelling variant of the original Indian *mahiz*. The term *corn* comes from the Old Norse word *korn*, which means "grain-sized lump" of something. The term has historically meant any sort of kernel or grain, whatever the dominant grain of the country happened to be. Be aware that if you ask for corn in Scotland or Ireland, the term refers to oats, while in Europe you may be given wheat; if you request maize, it will be assumed that you mean to feed it to your pigs, for that is the destiny of most corn in Europe.

General Information

Corn, or maize, originated as a spiky little weed in Central and South America, where it is thought to have grown wild about nine thousand years ago. The Indians of that region had been using corn for so long that by the time Europeans arrived they had no record of where it had come from; the wild form had by that time disappeared and been replaced by a multitude of cultivated varieties. Corn was so plentiful that it was planted along the roadsides so that those in want might help themselves; nobody in Mexico could die of hunger at a time when Europeans could and frequently did. Geneticists group the world's corn into races, some three hundred at last count. The Incas of Peru hybridized corn and used vast irrigation systems for their fields; by the time of the Spanish conquest, they were in fact probably the most skilled cultivators of maize in America, and it is reasonable to assume that they had extensive knowledge and experience in selectively breeding only those varieties they considered of special value as food. By the time of Columbus's arrival, the Indians had already developed more than two hundred types of maize—one of the most remarkable plant-breeding achievements in history. Of all the new foodstuffs Columbus encountered, maize was to be the most important in later history; yet because his search was for exotic spices and elusive gold, he hardly took notice when the Indians gave him a gift of the grain. He evidently mistook corn for a plant native to Europe and reported that the Indians ate the fruit of the wild sorghum. While yellow corn predominates today, the Native Americans prized corn with colorful kernels—blue, red, pink, and black—or with bands, spots, or stripes. The rainbow of coloring resulted primarily from concentrations of different pigments (such as carotenes and flavonoids) contained in the aleurone (the outer layer of the endosperm) and from centuries of breeding for traits such as size, flavor, and pest resistance.

Corn has a unique cob structure such that the numerous kernels are firmly attached to a rigid axis, the cob, instead of being covered by floral glumes, and the entire ear is enclosed by modified leaf sheaths. This communal rather than individual protection has the great disadvantage of impeding grain dispersal, and the domestic form we know today is in fact dependent upon human intervention for its continued survival. Corn has remained a grain of the Americas, sustaining the diets and pocketbooks of many, and modern Americans would be hard-pressed to find a way to live without it. In a single typical day one might wear cotton clothes that have had their fibers strengthened by cornstarch; eat cornflakes for breakfast, or eggs laid by corn-fed chickens; drive to work in a car powered in part by ethanol, a fuel derived from corn; read a magazine that has had its paper fibers bound with cornstarch to keep them together as they race through high-speed presses; drink a cola sweetened with corn syrup; and eat possibly several varieties of meat from animals fattened on corn feed. Corn products show up in toothpaste, alcohol, dog food, trash bags, glue, canned goods, shoe polish, fireworks, lotions, crayons, ink, batteries, margarine, marshmallows, mustard, ice cream, aspirin, paint, cosmetics—the list keeps going, ad infinitum.

Culinary Uses

Throughout history, corn—or maize, as it is known in most places—has turned up in a hundred different forms and has provided the base grain for many thousands of dishes in cultures around the world. Available in a myriad of forms, there is one to suit any purpose or taste preference. The most common use is in baking, and all types of cornmeal and corn flour can be used to provide a crumbly, somewhat gritty texture. Because cornmeal is unique in flavor and texture, there is no substitute for it.

Corn / Nutritional Value Per 100 g Edible Portion

	Raw Whole Grain	Whole-Grain Cornmeal	Degermed Enriched Cornmeal	Bran	Germ	Whole-Grain Corn Flour
Calories	365	362	366	224	490	361
Protein	9.42 g	8.12 g	8.48 g	8.36 g	17.00 g	6.93 g
Fat	4.74 g	3.59 g	1.65 g	0.92 g	25.00 g	3.86 g
Fiber	2.90 g	1.84 g	0.62 g	8.46 g	20.80 g	1.34 g
Calcium	7 mg	6 mg	5 mg	42 mg	0 mg	7 mg
Iron	2.71 mg	3.45 mg	4.13 mg	2.79 mg	7.80 mg	2.38 mg
Magnesium	127 mg	127 mg	40 mg	64 mg	672 mg	93 mg
Phosphorus	210 mg	241 mg	84 mg	72 mg	1,587 mg	272 mg
Potassium	287 mg	287 mg	162 mg	44 mg	1,420 mg	315 mg
Sodium	35 mg	35 mg	3 mg	7 mg	31 mg	5 mg
Zinc	2.210 mg	1.820 mg	0.720 mg	1.560 mg	10.600 mg	1.730 mg
Copper	0.314 mg	0.193 mg	0.078 mg	0.248 mg	0.500 mgr	0.230 mg
Manganese	0.485 mg	0.498 mg	0.105 mg	0.140 mg	n/a	0.460 mg
Beta Carotene (A)	n/a	469 IU	413 IU	71 IU	60 IU	n/a
Thiamine (B$_1$)	0.385 mg	0.385 mg	0.715 mg	0.010 mg	1.700 mg	0.246 mg
Riboflavin (B$_2$)	0.201 mg	0.201 mg	0.407 mg	0.100 mg	0.750 mg	0.080 mg
Niacin (B$_3$)	3.627 mg	3.632 mg	5.034 mg	2.735 mg	2.200 mg	1.900 mg
Pantothenic Acid (B$_5$)	0.424 mg	0.425 mg	0.312 mg	0.636 mg	n/a	0.658 mg
Pyridoxine (B$_6$)	0.622 mg	0.304 mg	0.257 mg	0.152 mg	1.410 mg	n/a
Folic Acid (B$_9$)	n/a	n/a	48.0 mcg	4.0 mcg	90.0 mcg	25.0 mcg
Ascorbic Acid (C)	0 mg	0 mg	0 mg	0 mg	4 mg	0 mg
Tocopherol (E)	0.490 mg	n/a	0.150 mg	n/a	n/a	n/a

Health Benefits

pH 5.9–7.6. One of the best-balanced starches, fresh raw (or lightly steamed) corn is easy to digest, but after the grain has been dried, corn and corn cereals are some of the most difficult of all the cereals to digest. Yellow corn is helpful in building bone and muscle and is excellent food for the brain and nervous system. Corn is said to help prevent cancer and lower risk of heart disease and dental cavities. Corn oil is high in linoleic acid and also has fair amounts of oleic, linolenic, and arachidonic acids. The whole-grain oil has been found to correct overalkalinity of the bodily system, and some doctors recommend it (either taken by spoonful or applied directly to the skin) in cases of eczema-type skin disorders.

VARIETIES

There are five basic types of corn: dent corn, flint corn, flour corn, popcorn, and sweet corn. Each of these was once grown in varieties of four different colors: red, white, yellow, and blue, some of which are still available today.

Dent corn (*Z. mays indentata*) is the most widely grown corn in the United States. A hard variety whose seeds literally indent after drying, this is the variety commonly available in stores and is the grain from which most yellow cornmeal is milled. Harder and starchier than sweet corn, 90 percent of dent corn is used for animal feed, and the rest is processed into breakfast foods, cornstarch, corn oils, and corn syrups.

Flint corn (*Z. mays indurata*), also known as Indian corn, is a hard-kerneled corn most often used as animal feed, with some of the colored varieties now gaining in popularity commercially. **Blue corn** is literally blue, and has a sweeter, more delicate flavor than the yellow variety, along with about 20 percent more protein and higher levels of minerals and the amino acid lysine. This open-pollinated flint corn has been grown by the Indians of the Southwest for centuries and is now being used by corn chip and tortilla manufacturers to make uniquely colored products with a rich corn flavor. Open-pollinated corn has a wider genetic base than hybridized varieties and produces a crop that resembles the previous generation; these varieties are available through specialized seed companies selling heirloom seeds. **Multicolored corn** has stunning ears with colors that include yellow, black, blue, violet, red, pink, and white. No two ears are alike in the pattern of their colors. If you have access to a flour mill, buy some to grind into a rich-tasting, sweet cornmeal that can be used as you would other cornmeals.

Flour corn (*Z. mays amylacea*) has a thin outer layer and a soft inner endosperm that is easy to grind and chew. This is the variety that is most often ground into corn flour or cornstarch, used as a thickening agent.

Popcorn (*Z. mays everta*) is a type of maize that looks similar to other types of corn, except that the ears and kernels are smaller. First cultivated by the Incas, it is grown specifically for its use as a snack food. The kernels have a hard outer hull and endosperm, which seal in its relatively high moisture content of 14 percent. When heated, this moisture turns to steam and since there is no place for it to escape, the kernel literally explodes, everting or turning inside out, to relieve the pressure. Two agronomists, Charles Bowman and Orville Redenbacher, started developing the modern varieties of popcorn in the 1940s, while seeking to develop large and fluffy popcorn with a low percentage of duds. They succeeded in 1952, and although the

Cornstarch	Plain Popcorn	Light Corn Syrup	High-Fructose Corn Syrup
381	386	282	281
0.26 g	12.70 g	0 g	0 g
0.05 g	5.00 g	0 g	0 g
0.09 g	2.20 g	0 g	0 g
2 mg	11 mg	3 mg	0 mg
0.47 mg	2.70 mg	0.05 mg	0.03 mg
3 mg	n/a	2 mg	0 mg
13 mg	281 mg	2 mg	n/a
3 mg	n/a	4 mg	0 mg
9 mg	3 mg	121 mg	2 mg
0.060 mg	n/a	0.020 mg	0.020 mg
0.050 mg	n/a	0.010 mg	0.029 mg
0.053 mg	n/a	0.088 mg	n/a
n/a	n/a	0 IU	0 IU
n/a	n/a	0.011 mg	n/a
n/a	0.120 mg	0.009 mg	0.019 mg
n/a	2.200 mg	0.020 mg	0 mg
n/a	n/a	0.023 mg	0.011 mg
n/a	n/a	0.009 mg	0 mg
n/a	n/a	0 mg	0 mg
0 mg	0 mg	0 mg	0 mg
0 mg	n/a	n/a	0 mg

LORE AND LEGEND

The Incas of Peru, the Mayans of Central America, and the Aztecs of Mexico used maize not only as a food, but as currency, fuel, jewelry, and building material. Every maize-growing tribe had its corn gods, corn mothers, or corn maidens—deities of maize, revered by special corn-sowing dances, rain ceremonies, prayer rites for the sprouting seed, and festivals of thanks at harvesttime. The Hopi Indians, who predominantly used blue corn, relate one corn myth: "Yaapa, the Mockingbird, placed many different kinds of corn before the tribes. The Navajo took yellow ears, Sioux picked the white, Havasupai wanted the red, Ute selected the flint, Apache chose the longest ears. My people picked up the last and smallest ear, the blue corn. This meant the Hopi would have a long-lasting but hard life." Another tale, much like that of the Greek Apollo and Daphne, tells of a brave who was so in love with a beautiful maiden that he slept outside her hut to offer her his protection. One night he found her walking in her sleep and followed her. Although she ran fast, he finally caught her, but it was not a young woman whom he embraced. In her fear she had prayed that she might be transformed, and was changed into a tall cornstalk, her hair turning into silk and her hands into cobs. Perhaps the most beautiful symbolic fable is about White Earth, the only survivor in the world after all men were destroyed. She was told by her brother that she would be courted by five suitors, and to accept none until the fifth appeared. First came Usama: when he was rejected, he became tobacco. Next came Wapako, round and pudgy, who turned into a pumpkin. Third was Ashkossim, a melon, and fourth was Kokees, a bean. Then came a sound like music in the wind, and it was the fifth suitor, whom White Earth immediately chose as her husband. The rains came after the wedding and all the previous suitors grew and flourished, but the tallest and best was the corn, her husband, Mondahmin.

companies that sold popcorn were not interested because the new strain cost too much to produce and market, Orville was so convinced the public would buy his new popcorn that he packaged and distributed it himself. Only a few years later his popcorn became the nation's number one seller. Because of this "popcorn pioneer," there are now varieties that can be popped to forty times their original kernel size. Popcorn is harder to digest than other varieties of corn.

Sweet corn is used as a vegetable—see the reference in the **Vegetables** section).

BYPRODUCTS

Corn bran, the outer layer of the corn kernel, can be used in exactly the same way as wheat bran, oat bran, or rice bran, to add soluble fiber to the diet.

Corn flakes are not to be confused with the cornflake of supermarket breakfast cereal notoriety. This is the crushed whole kernel of corn, with all its natural goodness intact. Unlike most whole flaked grains, which need only to be soaked before eating, corn flakes require light cooking.

Corn flour/cornstarch is a fine silken powder milled generally from only the inner endosperm layer of the grain (usually dent corn), although it can also be made from the whole kernel. Because corn has a high oil content, whole-grain corn flour quickly turns rancid, while the degerminated corn flour, which has had the hull, germ, and nutrients refined out, has an indefinite shelf life, though it is limp and bland in comparison. Usually used as a thickening agent for sauces, soups, or pudding, it can also be used to make tortillas and other flatbreads. Corn flour absorbs more water than other flours and will yield a drier, crumblier product with a sweet corn flavor and beautiful golden color. When mixed with water to a creamy consistency and boiled, it will form a clear jelly. Cornstarch mixed into a paste with castor oil provides an excellent poultice to relieve skin irritations. The dry starch is a good baby powder and frequently an ingredient in commercial baby talc products.

Corn germ is the heart of the corn and is nutritionally the richest part. Compared to wheat germ, corn germ has more vitamin E, iron, zinc, and fiber, and it is a complete protein, rich in lysine. It has all the uses of wheat germ—for baking or sprinkling on cereals, soups, and salads—and one more: being a bit bigger and crunchier than wheat germ, it makes a delicious snack eaten right out of the container.

Corn grits are made by coarsely grinding whole dried kernels of yellow or white corn. Almost all the bran and germ are removed during processing. Therefore, grits provide less nutrition than does whole corn (fully one-half to two-thirds of the vitamins are lost). Grits are often artificially enriched with vitamins and minerals to replace those lost during processing. They make a savory, quick-cooking cereal and can be used to make pancakes and soufflés.

Corn oil is one of the most popular oils, and its domestic use dates back to the American Indians. Because of corn's low oil content, extremely high temperatures and toxic solvents are needed to extract what oil there is efficiently. Oil that has been pressed from the whole grain rather than just the germ is dark gold or amber in color and has a rich, buttery corn flavor and a heady, popcornlike aroma. Most commercial oil, however, is extracted from only the germ, a byproduct of such products as breakfast cereals, cornstarch, and corn syrup. This pallid oil is then further filtered, deodorized, and bleached for commercial sale, giving consumers a bland, tasteless product. Half the corn oil produced is usually made into margarine and the rest processed as salad or cooking oil, mayonnaise, salad dressings, or shortening. Corn oil is not suitable for deep-frying since it foams easily.

Corn syrup was originally made by the Peruvians and Mexicans from the stalks of the corn plant rather than the kernels. Juice from the stalks was pressed out and then boiled down to a sweet syrup, similar to the process used for sorghum molasses. Production of commercial corn syrup, which is made from chemically purified cornstarch (from the starchy endosperm), started in the early 1900s. It was initially marketed as "glucose" (corn syrup is almost pure glucose), a name which evidently did not catch on because consumers thought the syrup was made from glue. To overcome this prejudice, the company renamed it "corn syrup," and the product then became popular. To create corn syrup, cornstarch is mixed with water and either hydrochloric or sulfuric acid, then steamed to convert it to "commercial glucose," a highly refined glucose. This dark and odd-smelling substance is deodorized and filtered to produce the odorless, clear, and virtually tasteless liquid called corn syrup. Oftentimes, the syrup is mixed with sugar to increase its sweetness. So-called dark corn syrup is often artificially caramel-colored. Corn sugar—also called solid glucose, dextrose, or starch sugar—is made in the same manner as corn syrup, although more acid is used and the product is steamed for a longer period of time. You may be a big user of corn syrup and not know it, since it makes an appearance in almost all commercial candies and baked goods. The syrup is commonly added not only as a sweetener but also to thicken or add body to foods (such as ketchup), to prevent crystallization in ice cream and other frozen foods, and to retain moisture. **Dried and powdered corn syrup** solids are found in nondairy creamers, imitation fruit drinks, and pudding mixes and are a primary ingredient in imitation maple syrup.

Cornmeal is the coarsely ground grain, which may or may not have been hulled and degerminated. The absolutely best cornmeal is stone-ground whole-grain corn, which retains not only the germ but also a robust flavor and the full complement of vitamins and minerals. The commercial supermarket's degerminated, overmilled, overheated, synthetic, vitamin-enriched cornmeal contains less than half the nutrients of whole-grain cornmeal and even less taste. Cornmeal can be made into a porridge known as cornpone or used in cakes, breads, tamales, desserts, and pancakes. Since it has a low gluten content, it will not leaven bread but can be used for sprinkling over the bread or baking surface before baking, thus adding a distinct flavor and texture. Blue cornmeal, or "Hopi corn," is a favored ingredient in breads of the American Southwest. Slightly grainier and sweeter than yellow corn, it makes a purple-pink, blue-green, or lavender-tinged baked product, depending on the type of ingredients it is combined with. A squeeze of lime juice into blue corn batter will change it to pink. It needs a bit more fat when used to make muffins, biscuits, and tortillas and is available in a variety of grinds.

Dried corn is usually dent corn that has had most of the water removed in the drying process, although any of the varieties can be similarly dried. It can be used in its dry form by grinding it into meal or flour, or it can be reconstituted in water and then added to soups, casseroles, and other dishes.

Hominy is made by taking whole field corn and treating it with slaked (hydrated) lime or a combination of unslaked lime, calcium carbonate, lye, and wood ash. This acts to loosen the hulls and partially "cook" the kernels, while also puffing them up. The corn is then washed to remove the hulls, bleached (depending on use), dried, and used in dishes such as soups and stews. Very little nutritional value remains after processing corn in this manner.

Masa is made from whole-kernel corn that is soaked or boiled in dilute alkalis (lime, calcium hydroxide), wood ashes (potassium hydroxide), or lye (sodium hydroxide) for thirty minutes. The kernels are then drained, washed, and ground into a paste, or masa. This paste can be shaped into balls, flattened, and cooked on a hot griddle like a pancake.

Parched corn, also called corn nuts and corn nuggets, is a snack food made from whole corn kernels. These crunchy morsels are made by soaking the corn in water or brine (salted water) until they swell. They are then deep-fat-fried or baked until golden brown, and heavily salted. Although not very nutritious, they are tasty. Besides eating them as snacks, try them in cookies, casseroles, or breads as you would real nuts.

Polenta is simply cooked cornmeal (either whole or degerminated). Frequently, prepared polenta is made from the coarse meal left after the oil has been squeezed out of the kernels. It has a fine granular texture more similar to semolina than cornmeal. Formerly used primarily by the poor, in recent years it has become popular in sophisticated cuisine; either fried or grilled, it is usually served with vegetables or as an accompaniment to sauces. In Italy the name *polenta* is also given to the dish made from it.

Posole is slaked, parched, and dried white corn; it needs to be parched, or else dried corn is virtually impossible to cook whole. Posole is made when whole dried corn is boiled with wood ash or slaked lime until the hull is soft-

ened and washed off. This traditional Mexican food has a delicately sweet flavor and is delicious on its own, cooked with other grains, or ground into meal. Throughout the Americas, most corn was processed into posole, enhancing the flavor, shortening preparation time, and increasing mineral and vitamin content. Posole is 20 to 300 percent higher in calcium than dried corn, depending upon what it was slaked with. According to one study, half a cup of blue corn contains 1 milligram of calcium; when slaked in juniper wood ash it contains 334 milligrams of calcium. The niacin in posole is also more bioavailable than it is from dried corn.

Job's Tears
(Coix lacryma-jobi)
Also Known As: Hato Mugi

Coix comes from the Greek name *koix*, for the doom palm. *Lacryma* are tears, and *jobi* means "of Job." This grain's name is derived from the fanciful resemblance between its gleaming pearl-white seeds and teardrops (legend had it they were from Job) as they fall sparkling from the eye.

General Information

Job's tears, a relative newcomer to the health food scene, is a true cereal grain of the millet family. Native to India and the Philippines, this large pearled barley look-alike has long been respected in the Far East for its many virtues and light, refreshing taste. When its hard, dark, tear-shaped hull is intact, it is used as a decorative bead for necklaces and rosaries. Its black, impervious hull, which makes it a sturdy bead, is inedible. Once hulled, this grain looks like a giant pearl-gray barley and has a sweet flavor. You can

---

LORE AND LEGEND

Christian legend relates that this plant grew from the tears of Job, whose proverbial sufferings and troubles did not make him lose faith in God. These beadlike seeds, staple food to the hill tribes of India and medicine to the Chinese, were used for rosaries in the Near East and for magic necklaces in ancient Persia.

purchase Job's tears from herb stores, Chinese pharmacies, and full-service whole food suppliers or as a prepared cereal or beverage from Asian markets.

Culinary Uses

Job's tears has a light and refreshing taste that is excellent either on its own or combined with other grains, being less sticky than either rice or barley. It is best to soak it prior to use, as this will reduce the lengthy cooking time. It can also be added to long-cooking soups for body and flavor.

Health Benefits

This grain has soothing properties for the stomach and nervous system, helps purify the blood, and restores general health. In macrobiotic literature Job's tears is acclaimed for its anticancer properties; it is considered too strong to consume during pregnancy and menstruation. In Ayurvedic medicine it is used as a blood purifier. Low in fat and high in calcium and iron.

Kamut
(Triticum durum)

Linnaeus provided the genus name *Triticum*, an old Latin name for "cereal"; *durum* means "hard." *Kamut* is an ancient Egyptian word that is believed to refer to wheat. The organically grown, pure, uncrossed strain has received the registered trademark name *Kamut*; this trademark belongs to the company Montana Flour & Grains (the Quinn family).

General Information

Kamut is an ancient relative of modern durum wheat, a variety believed to have originated some six thousand years ago around Egypt and the Tigris/Euphrates River basin. Although later nearly completely replaced by other strains of wheat, kamut was nonetheless continuously grown until the mid–twentieth century by farmers who prized its rich flavor. Because kamut has not been hybridized and scientifically "improved," its self-pollinating kernels replicate those from ancient history, grown thousands of years ago.

Culinary Uses

Kamut is a truly versatile grain with a rich, almost buttery, delicious flavor. When cracked into a coarse meal and cooked, it makes one of the best-tasting cereals you will ever eat. Kamut pasta is as pleasing in texture and taste as the finest semolina (refined durum) pasta. Ground into a flour, it produces light-textured, delicious whole-grain breads and other baked goods, and since it contains gluten, it can be used for yeasted breads. You can do almost anything with kamut that you can do with ordinary wheat, adding it to salads, pilafs, or stews. Consumer experience indicates that many with wheat allergies tolerate kamut products without negative effects.

Kamut / Nutritional Value Per 100 g Edible Portion			
	Raw Whole Grain		Raw Whole Grain
Calories	359	Sodium	3.8 mg
Protein	17.3 g	Zinc	4.3 mg
Fat	2.6 g	Thiamine (B₁)	0.450 mg
Fiber	1.8 g	Riboflavin (B₂)	0.120 mg
Calcium	31.0 mg	Niacin (B₃)	5.540 mg
Iron	4.2 mg	Pantothenic Acid (B₅)	0.230 mg
Magnesium	153 mg	Pyridoxine (B₆)	0.080 mg
Phosphorus	411 mg	Folic Acid (B₉)	37.5 mcg
Potassium	446 mg	Tocopherol (E)	1.7 mg

In 1949, following World War II, a U.S. airman stationed in Portugal was given thirty-six kernels of a large and unique Egyptian grain; each kernel was two to three times the size of common wheat, and had a distinctive hump in the middle. Told that the oversized kernels had been found in King Tut's tomb (untrue, but it made for an intriguing story), he mailed the seeds to his father, a wheat farmer in Fort Benton, Montana. Thirty-two of the seeds germinated, and for a while the harvest of those few plants attracted some attention at local county fairs as "King Tut's Wheat." Then the novelty wore off and the grain was all but forgotten, the fields eventually going to cattle feed. In the 1970s another wheat farmer from Montana, Bob Quinn, remembered seeing this grain in his childhood and sought out what he could find of the remaining seed. In 1977 he located a pint jar of the Egyptian grain, and the father-and-son team of Mack and Bob Quinn spent the next decade carefully selecting and propagating it on their ranch near Big Sandy, Montana. A sample of kamut was taken to the Natural Products Expo West '86 in Anaheim, California, where serious commercial interest started and has grown steadily ever since. It has since been introduced to the natural food market, where it is gaining rapidly in popularity.

Health Benefits

pH 6.0. Kamut is a high-energy grain of greater nutritional value than regular wheat strains; it is also easier to digest and more compatible with human physiology. It does have less fiber, though, because the huge size of the grain gives a lower ratio of hull to volume. Although it contains gluten, most gluten-sensitive individuals find they are able to tolerate it in moderation.

Millet

(Panicum miliaceum, P. italica, Setaria italica)

Panicum is an old Latin name for Italian millet; *miliaceum* is a term meaning "pertaining to millet," while *italica* means "coming from Italy." The English name derives from the Latin *mille*, meaning "a thousand" and referring to the prolificacy of the seed.

General Information

Native to the East Indies and North Africa, millet been cultivated in India, Africa, and the Middle East since time immemorial. In ancient Egypt it was used to make bread, and it was a staple in China before rice was introduced. In fact, the first written reference to millet is dated at about 2800 B.C. and lists the five sacred crops of China as rice, soybeans, barley, wheat, and millet. Millet seems to have been brought overland by the Mongols into the Middle East and the Mediterranean basin. Frequently noted in the New Testament, millet flourished throughout the Roman Empire and into the Middle Ages, during which time it was a dominant food crop before being supplanted by modern wheat. Botanically, this grass is more ancient than rice, barley, wheat, or rye. Particularly well suited to poor soil and adverse climates, millet manages to lie dormant through long periods of drought, then sprouts with the first rainfalls and is ready to harvest in just forty-five days. A surprisingly large variety of different plants fall under this genus, ranging from sorghum, t'ef, and Job's tears to the small, pearl-like grains that we know and eat as "common" millet. While most corn is fed to cattle, and most barley is brewed for beer, most millet is used as birdseed. (The eastern Colorado town of Otis, population seven hundred, claims to be the Bird Seed Capital of America.) In North America this delicious grain is only beginning to be appreciated; it is widely used in the eastern hemisphere and is renowned as a staple food of the long-living Hunzas of the Himalayas.

Culinary Uses

Available in several forms, this tiny, round, yellowish seed (resembling a mustard seed) has a bland to slightly nutty flavor. The whole grain swells to a fluffy texture in cooking; toasting it in a little oil before cooking enhances the flavor and keeps the tiny grains from clumping together. It can be cooked into a tasty breakfast porridge served with nuts and dried fruit or can be eaten raw when sprinkled over other foods. Millet also makes an excellent substitute for rice and a tasty addition to stuffed vegetables, croquettes, stews, casseroles, pilafs, breads, and gravies. If cooked with a little liquid (1 cup millet to 2¼ cups liquid), it makes a light, dry, fluffy pilaf. Increase the liquid to three cups and the millet takes on a smooth texture like mashed potatoes or polenta. Because millet has a more fragile shelf life than other grains, it should be purchased in small quantities from a natural food market that has a high turnover, and stored in a cool pantry or refrigerated. If it has an acrid, harsh aftertaste, the grain is rancid and should be discarded.

Health Benefits

pH 6.0. Millet is a gluten-free, easily digestible grain that is one of the most outstanding alkaline foods in the world, as well as one of the least allergenic. Exceedingly nutritious, it contains an abundance of minerals and vitamins, and the most complete protein of any of the true cereal grains. Millet is rich in fiber and silica, which detoxify the intestines and form butyrate, a short-chain fatty acid that has been shown to suppress the growth of cancers. It is also antifungal and one of the best grains for those with candida problems. Cooking it with winter squash increases its medicinal value to the stomach and spleen-pancreas.

Millet / Nutritional Value Per 100 g Edible Portion		
	Raw Whole Grain	Cooked Whole Grain
Calories	378	119
Protein	11.02 g	3.51 g
Fat	4.22 g	1.00 g
Fiber	1.03 g	0.36 g
Calcium	8 mg	3 mg
Iron	3.01 mg	0.63 mg
Magnesium	114 mg	44 mg
Phosphorus	285 mg	100 mg
Potassium	195 mg	62 mg
Sodium	5 mg	2 mg
Zinc	1.680 mg	0.910 mg
Copper	0.750 mg	0.161 mg
Manganese	1.632 mg	0.272 mg
Thiamine (B$_1$)	0.420 mg	0.106 mg
Riboflavin (B$_2$)	0.290 mg	0.082 mg
Niacin (B$_3$)	4.720 mg	1.330 mg
Pantothenic Acid (B$_5$)	0.848 mg	0.171 mg
Pyridoxine (B$_6$)	0.384 mg	0.108 mg
Tocopherol (E)	0.050 mg	n/a

BYPRODUCTS

Cracked millet falls between whole millet and millet meal in size and can serve as a substitute for either. Finer in texture and quicker cooking than the whole grain, it will add a slightly crunchy texture to breads or main dishes. Used as a cereal, it is excellent liberally laced with toasted sesame seeds and honey.

Millet flour has a distinctive, sweet flavor and gives a dry, delicate, cakelike crumb and yellow color to baked goods. On its own it can be used interchangeably with t'ef flour and is often used to prepare injera flatbreads. To make a leavened product, though, it needs to be combined with other flours because it is low in gluten. Added to any product, it will add flavor and nutrition; use it as a thickener in soups and stews, for texture in baked goods, or in myriad other ways.

Millet meal is a coarsely ground meal used for baked goods and cereal. It can be purchased preground or it can be ground at home from whole millet, using a home mill or small electric spice (or coffee) grinder. It is best when freshly ground, because the meal acquires a bitter taste fairly quickly. The ancient Romans made their bread of millet meal and wheat flour; try adding one-half cup meal to each five cups of wheat flour in your next batch of bread and enjoy the rich flavor.

Puffed millet is the whole grain that is puffed under pressure. Sold in specialty food stores or natural food outlets, it is an excellent snack food, makes a light and tasty addition to puddings and bread, and is a superior breakfast cereal.

Oats
(Avena sativa)

There is great healing power in the sight of oats,
the faintly blue color of their stems,
the knack of each seed head to hold a single,
radiant drop of moisture after rain.

—Tom Ireland, "Birds of Sorrow"

Avena is the old Latin name for the plant, while *sativa* means "cultivated." The English name *oat* comes from the Old English *ate*.

General Information

Oats seem to be of western European origin, probably developed from two wild grasses, the common wild oat (*A. fatua*) and the wild red oat (*A. sterilis*), around 2500 B.C. Most likely oats traveled to northern Europe along with the raiders, the merchant caravans, the invaders, and the plunderers, who would have carried them as feed for their horses. In cold northern climes such as the British Isles and Scandinavia, where few other grains would grow, oats were of great importance and soon became a staple food. By the thirteenth century oats, then known as pilcorn, were a part of every Scot's daily fare. They were also a popular food among the poor, who could not grow wheat or afford wheat flour. Oats arrived in the New World in 1602 and were planted on the Elizabeth Isles off the coast of Massachusetts, where they soon flourished. An annual grass, oats can grow to heights of two to five feet; only about 5 percent of the entire crop is consumed by humans, with the rest grown primarily as livestock feed. There are both winter and spring varieties, as with wheat. The grains, known as groats, are most often crushed to make oatmeal, oat flour, and oat flakes. Americans consume only about eleven pounds of oats per capita annually, mostly in the form of oatmeal for breakfast.

Culinary Uses

Unlike other grains, oats must be steamed before their two inedible outer hulls can be removed. As with other grains, the more processed oats are, the more their flavor and nutrients are compromised. For all of northern Europe, oats are a part of the culinary heritage, and for the Scots no celebration or cookbook would be complete without their appearance. While the whole groat (minus the inedible outer hull) may be cooked like brown rice, most oats are consumed in the form of oatmeal. Oats contain moderate amounts of gluten and can be used for thickening and enriching soups, for extending meat loaves, for stuffings, pilafs, cakes, breads, muffins, pancakes, granola, and muesli. Oats also contain an antioxidant that delays rancidity; thus the groats can be ground into flour that is longer lasting than whole-wheat flour.

Health Benefits

pH 6.20–6.60. Oats contain a higher proportion of fat and protein than most other grains, and rightly have a reputation for being a warming food appropriate for cold climates. Oats are the one adaptogen grain, meaning that

LORE AND LEGEND

The Romans conquered the English but found the wild Scotsmen invincible. One old account attributed the Highlanders' prowess and guerrilla-like mobility to their staple food. Each Highlander carried a pouch of oatmeal, and dinner was as quick as mixing seawater with it to form a cake that baked in minutes on a hot stone over an open fire. Eighteen centuries later Samuel Johnson in his famous English dictionary defined *oats* as "A grain which in England is generally given to horses, but in Scotland supports the people," to which a Scotsman replied, "England is noted for the excellence of her horses; Scotland for the excellence of her men."

Oats / Nutritional Value Per 100 g Edible Portion

	Raw Whole Grain	Raw (Rolled) Oatmeal	Cooked Oatmeal	Raw Bran	Cooked Bran
Calories	389	384	62	246	40
Protein	16.89 g	16.00 g	2.60 g	17.30 g	3.21 g
Fat	6.90 g	6.30 g	1.00 g	7.03 g	0.86 g
Fiber	n/a	1.10 g	0.20 g	2.17 g	0.37 g
Calcium	54 mg	52 mg	8 mg	58 mg	10 mg
Iron	4.72 mg	4.21 mg	0.68 mg	5.41 mg	0.88 mg
Magnesium	177 mg	148 mg	24 mg	235 mg	40 mg
Phosphorus	523 mg	474 mg	76 mg	734 mg	119 mg
Potassium	429 mg	350 mg	56 mg	566 mg	92 mg
Sodium	2 mg	4 mg	1 mg	4 mg	1 mg
Zinc	3.970 mg	3.070 mg	0.490 mg	3.110 mg	0.530 mg
Copper	0.626 mg	0.343 mg	0.055 mg	0.403 mg	0.066 mg
Manganese	4.916 mg	3.630 mg	0.585 mg	5.630 mg	0.964 mg
Beta Carotene (A)	n/a	101 IU	16 IU	n/a	n/a
Thiamine (B$_1$)	0.763 mg	0.730 mg	0.110 mg	1.170 mg	0.160 mg
Riboflavin (B$_2$)	0.139 mg	0.140 mg	0.020 mg	0.220 mg	0.034 mg
Niacin (B$_3$)	0.961 mg	0.780 mg	0.130 mg	0.934 mg	0.144 mg
Pantothenic Acid (B$_5$)	1.349 mg	1.245 mg	0.200 mg	1.494 mg	0.217 mg
Pyridoxine (B$_6$)	0.119 mg	0.120 mg	0.020 mg	0.165 mg	0.025 mg
Folic Acid (B$_9$)	56.0 mcg	32.0 mcg	4.0 mcg	52.0 mcg	6.0 mcg
Ascorbic Acid (C)	0 mg	0 mg	0 mg	0 mg	0 mg
Tocopherol (E)	1.090 mg	1.510 mg	n/a	n/a	n/a

they improve resistance to stress and thus support the system being in a healthy state of balance. Oats help stabilize blood sugar, regulate the thyroid, soothe the nervous and digestive systems, reduce the craving for cigarettes, and reduce cholesterol. The rolled variety are easily and quickly digested and take less time to cook than steel-cut oats. They are best eaten alone, as milk and sugar will cause them to ferment in the stomach, with all the possible benefits lost. Many people find that oats act as a mild laxative because of their high fiber content. Eating oats can lower cholesterol, as the soluble fiber acts like little sponges, binding cholesterol and carrying it out of the body. Oats are reputedly beneficial for those with an underfunctioning thyroid gland, and their rich silicon content helps renew the bones and all connective tissue. Externally, oats have an anti-inflammatory effect on certain skin problems such as contact eczema, and some physicians recommend oatmeal packs to treat psoriasis. Oat flour is an effective skin cleanser and can replace soap when necessary. Added to bathwater it will soothe the itch of irritations such as eczema, poison ivy, and poison oak, or if made into a thick poultice it can be applied directly to the affected areas.

BYPRODUCTS

Oat bran is the outer covering of the hulled oat groat. Although not the universal panacea for health problems that was originally claimed, studies show that the consumption of oat bran does help lower blood cholesterol levels, as do rice, corn, and wheat bran, because of their fiber content. Oat bran is a delicious and nutritious addition to any baked product. Since it is the oil in the bran that contains the nutrients, all types of bran need to be stored in the refrigerator to prevent rancidity.

Oat flour, also known as **flaked oats,** retains most of the nutrients present in whole oats, as the bran and germ remain intact in processing. It can be used interchangeably with whole-wheat pastry flour in some recipes, giving a moist, delicate sweetness to breads, pancakes, biscuits, scones, and other pastry products. The addition of oat flour to baked goods gives the added benefit of a natural antioxidant, which enables baked products to retain their freshness longer. Oats have only a moderate gluten content, so they need to be combined with wheat flour or other high-gluten-content flour when making leavened bread. Oat flour can also be used as a thickening agent in sauces, soups, and stews. If you can't find oat flour at a health food store, you can make your own by whirring rolled oats in an electric blender and then sifting to remove the coarser elements.

Oat groats are hulled, whole kernels that have been cleaned and dried. They are roasted slightly during the cleaning and hulling process but have virtually the same nutrients as the whole grain; plus, the roasting process adds richness to the flavor. Softer than a wheat berry, oat groats can be pounded with a wooden mallet or rolled on a flat surface with a rolling pin so they will cook quicker than in their original form. They are used in baking, as a cereal, or added to other grains for chewiness.

Rolled oats are made from hulled groats that have been steamed and rolled flat into flakes. "Instant" or "quick oats" are groats that have been precooked in water, dried, and rolled superthin; although quicker to cook, they have less nutritional value because of their exposure to high heat during processing. Both varieties may be ground into a coarse meal suitable for bread making or used whole in cereals, cookies, cakes, and breads or as toppings for fruit crisps. Rolled oats made from the whole grain are subject to rancidity within one to three months after milling; thus it is advisable to store any bulk quantities that will not be used within one month below 40 degrees Fahrenheit.

Steel-cut oats, also known as **Scotch** or **Irish oats,** are natural, unrefined oat groats that have been processed with a minimal amount of heat by steel blades, which cut them into two or three small pieces. These are available in coarse and fine grinds—the finer the slicing, the quicker the grain cooks. They still contain everything that is in the whole oat, retaining most of their B vitamins even through processing. With their fairly long cooking time they are best used for tasty, chewy cereals; however, cooked steel-cut oats can be blended with various flours for baking.

Whole oats are unprocessed and retain the beneficial bran and germ. This whole form stores well without

LORE AND LEGEND

In ancient plant lore an offering of oats showed an appreciation for someone's music; this evidently was an allusion to the shepherd's pipe, the popular "oaten straw" of pastorals. Tea made from oats achieved a curious reputation in the early part of the twentieth century as being able to "cure the opium habit," and reduce the craving for cigarettes.

substantial deterioration. They can be used in baking (after being cooked), as a cereal, added to other grains for chewiness, or sprouted. Sprouting dramatically increases the supply of B vitamins and also releases other minerals for use.

Quinoa

(Chenopodium quinoa)

Chenopodium means "goose-footed," and this plant genus characteristically has leaves shaped like a goose's foot. *Quinoa* means "mother" in Quechua Indian, one of two primary Andean languages of the South American altiplano.

General Information

Quinoa (pronounced *keen-wah*) was a principal grain of the Incas, given sacred status as a "mother grain" and thus targeted by Spanish colonization tactics. For four hundred years it survived only in remote, inaccessible areas of the Andean altiplano (high plains), but it is now enjoying a resurgence in popularity. Botanically, quinoa is not a true grain since it belongs not to the grass family but to the Chenopodium family, which also includes beets, spinach, lamb's quarters, chard, and sugar beets. Best grown at altitudes above ten thousand feet, this grain positively flourishes under extreme conditions, including poor soil, thin cold air, hot sun, frost, short growing days, minimal rainfall, and even drought. There are hundreds of varieties, with Peruvian and Bolivian seed banks alone having over eighteen hundred different ecotype samples. The Aymara Indians on the altiplano of Bolivia still use the entire plant from top to bottom. The seeds are eaten whole in the manner of rice or toasted and ground into flour for tor-

Quinoa / Nutritional Value Per 100 g Edible Portion		
	Raw Whole Grain	Flour
Calories	374	354
Protein	13.10 g	10.40 g
Fat	5.80 g	4.00 g
Fiber	n/a	3.80 g
Calcium	60 mg	94 mg
Iron	9.25 mg	5.60 mg
Magnesium	210 mg	n/a
Phosphorus	410 mg	129 mg
Potassium	740 mg	n/a
Zinc	3.300 mg	n/a
Copper	0.820 mg	n/a
Thiamine (B$_1$)	0.198 mg	0.190 mg
Riboflavin (B$_2$)	0.396 mg	0.240 mg
Niacin (B$_3$)	2.930 mg	0.700 mg
Ascorbic Acid (C)	0 mg	0 mg

LORE AND LEGEND

Inca legend says quinoa was the remains of a heavenly banquet, easy to believe once you have seen its multitude of vivid colors. In 1976 Dr. Stephen L. Gorad and his friend Don McKinley were told about quinoa by Oscar Icharo, the Bolivian religious leader who had mentioned quinoa in his teachings as "a very nutritious food which is good to eat when doing mystical work." When Gorad went to La Paz, Bolivia, in 1978, he searched out the grain, found a sample, tried and liked it, and returned with fifty pounds. Availability problems stopped the two from marketing quinoa in the United States, because gathering grain by going from one remote Indian settlement to another was not economically feasible, and there was at that time no support for developing quinoa on a commercial basis. In 1982, while Dr. Gorad was living in Chile and teaching and writing about holistic health, he received a letter from Don McKinley asking for seed. The first crops were planted in the eight-thousand-foot-high San Luis valley. These first crops were successful, and more fields have been planted in the high altiplano regions of Colorado and western Canada to help supply current demand.

tillas; the leaves are eaten as a vegetable and used to feed farm animals; the stalks are burned as fuel; and even the wash water from rinsing the seeds is frequently used as a shampoo.

Growing three to nine feet in height, with its seeds in large clusters at the end of the stalk, quinoa comes in a dazzling array of colors: red, pink, orange, yellow, lavender, purple, green, black, and white. Store-bought seeds are usually a pale yellow color and look like a cross between sesame seed and millet. These small, disk-shaped seeds are slightly raised in the center, with a thin band running around their periphery; when the seeds are cooked, the band partially separates from the seed, but the curved form of the seed remains. Each seed is thickly covered with saponin, a resinlike substance with an extremely bitter, soapy taste, which protects the grains from birds and insects. Seeds sold commercially have already been washed to remove this substance (although more washing wouldn't hurt), but any seed grown at home needs to be rinsed and drained five or ten times under cold running water; the more rinsing, the milder the flavor of the cooked grain.

Culinary Uses

Quinoa is fast becoming a popular staple in North America because of its mild flavor and fluffy texture. Sometimes called "vegetarian caviar" because of its soft, crunchy consistency, this tiny grain has a delicious nutty flavor reminiscent of couscous and peanuts, and most who try it for the first time immediately like it. Toasting it lightly before cooking will enhance its flavor even further. Ready to eat in less than fifteen minutes, it puffs up to four times its dry volume and becomes fairly translucent, looking rather like cooked couscous sprinkled with little crescent-moon spirals. The few small black or colored seeds are "wild quinoa," and with the exception of looking a bit different and not cooking fully, they are no problem; it is not necessary to spend time removing them. Quinoa makes a quick and tasty substitute for bulgur, rice, or couscous; it can also be added to soups, stews, casseroles, salads, and cookies.

Health Benefits

pH 6.0. Quinoa is valued in fitness circles as a high-energy food, and among the convalescing for its ease of digestion. It also appears to be gluten-free, which makes it valuable for those with wheat allergies. Quinoa offers a great amount of high-quality protein; its protein content is far higher than that of corn, barley, or rice, and only a few types of wheat even approximate the favorable variety and levels of amino acids it provides (including the critical lysine). Quinoa has more calcium than milk and is higher in fat than most other grains. The Peruvian Indians used this grain liberally, not only because it is rich in minerals, but also because of its benefit to nursing mothers, in that it is a powerful stimulant to the flow of milk.

BYPRODUCTS

Quinoa flour happily combines the best features of whole-grain and white flours, imparting a light, delicate crumb full of flavor and nutrients. It is a preferred flour for fine pastries and increases the flavor range and depth of the finished product, but because it lacks gluten, it is best combined with wheat or other gluten-containing flour for leavened products. Add this versatile flour to pancakes, muffins, crackers, cookies, pastries, and breads. Because of its high oil content, quinoa flour should be refrigerated to prevent rancidity and used within three to six months. Quinoa flour is quick and easy to make at home in your blender. To make one cup of flour, place three-fourths of a cup of quinoa in a blender or nut grinder and whiz for several minutes. Much softer than wheat or corn, quinoa pulverizes within a few minutes, yielding a slightly beady flour that is finer than cornmeal.

Rice
(Oryza sativa)

Grain upon grain
Fresh and delightful as frost
A dazzling jewel
To what can I compare this treasure?

—Yang Ji (Ming Dynasty)

Rice is a beautiful food. It is beautiful when it grows, precision rows of sparkling green stalks shooting up to reach the hot summer sun. It is beautiful when harvested, autumn gold sheaves piled on diked, patchwork paddies. It is beautiful when, once threshed, it enters granary bins like a (flood) of tiny seed-pearls. It is beautiful when cooked by a practiced hand, pure white and sweetly fragrant.

—Shizuo Tsuji

The scientific name *Oryza*, depending on the scholar, comes from either the Greek *oriza*, meaning "Orient," the Arabic name *Eruz*, or an ancient Chinese name; *sativa* means "widely cultivated." The common name in all Western tongues (*riso* in Italian, *reis* in German, *riz* in French, *arroz* in Spanish, and *rice* in English) is derived from the Greek *oriza*.

General Information

There are over seven thousand varieties of rice, each with its own distinct flavor, texture, aroma, color, length of grain, and degree of translucency. One of the principal Asian foods and a staple grain for over half the world's population, rice was developed from wild grasses found in Asia and Indochina. It is said that when Buddhism spread from the Indian subcontinent to the Far East, it brought along the custom of eating rice. The Chinese word for rice means "good grain of life"; in many parts of the Far East, the word for rice is the same as that for life, food, or agriculture. Reaching Japan during the second century B.C., rice became so important in feudal times that a man's holdings were ranked not according to their acreage but according to the amount of rice they produced, and samurai were paid in rice. Rice is now widely cultivated throughout the world in areas with warm climates and abundant water. It is difficult for westerners, who eat less than twenty pounds of rice annually, to appreciate all the many subtleties of rice in Asia, where it plays a central rather than a supporting role in cuisine. Among the varieties present in Song dynasty China were pink rice, white rice, yellow rice, mature rice, and winter rice, each with its own unique characteristics, and some with an almost flowerlike fragrance. For many in the Far East, rice provides half the daily caloric intake, and up to four hundred pounds per person may be eaten annually.

Rice came to the United States in 1693, when a ship bound for England from Madagascar was blown off-course by a severe storm, forcing it to dock at Charleston, South Carolina. To pay for repairs and emergency supplies, the captain of the ship gave the colony's governor several bags of seed rice. Henry Woodward, described as one of the founders of the Carolinas, planted it in his own garden in dry soil, where it died. Lord Ashley, a member of the London proprietary board for the Carolinas, later sent a hundred-pound bag of seed rice and perhaps some instructions for planting. By the year 1700 rice was Carolina's leading export. In 1784, seventeen years before he entered the White House, Thomas Jefferson served as American minister to France, where his most urgent task was to establish an export market for American goods. French interest could be aroused in only one product—rice from the plantations of Carolina and Georgia. However, there was a small problem in that during the Revolution, the British occupying Charleston and Savannah had shipped all of America's rice, including seed stocks, to England; now, with no seed available, none could be produced for the French market. While wrestling with his dilemma, Jefferson learned of the existence of a new and improved

LORE AND LEGEND

Since rice is such an important staple, it has always served as an emblem of happiness, nourishment, and fecundity. The Chinese considered it a gift direct from heaven, and in the annual ceremony of sowing five kinds of seeds (rice, wheat, barley, millet, and soybeans), instituted by the Emperor Shen-nung or Chinnong in 2800 B.C., rice plays the principal part; the reigning emperor himself must sow it, whereas the four other species may be sown by the princes of his family. Being a symbol of fertility, it was used to pelt newlywed couples in order to bring them good luck and assure them many children; this custom still exists today in many countries. Upsetting a rice bowl was said to be an omen of great ill fortune, and to deliberately overturn someone else's bowl was the greatest insult to that person and his family. In Malayan tradition, rice has a soul similar to humans and is presided over by the great Rice Mother; flowering rice is therefore treated with the great consideration and respect accorded a pregnant woman, and no sudden or loud noises are allowed in its vicinity for fear that it should take fright and miscarry. In Japan there is a special deity, Inari the rice bearer, whose shrines dot the rural landscape. The most popular folk festival, the Hatsuuma, is held before these shrines on the twelfth of February, to pray for a good crop of rice.

Italian strain of rice; he also learned that to prevent its cultivation by competing nations Italy had prohibited its export, imposing harsh penalties for violators. Undaunted, he went to Italy, somehow obtained two sacks of the grain, and smuggled out his contraband successfully. Jefferson's illicit rice soon revitalized America's languishing rice plantations. The United States grows about 1 percent of the world's rice and exports about 60 percent of this crop. Less than 2 percent of the U.S. production is brown or whole-grain rice.

Rice is covered with an inedible husk that has to be removed before eating, a task presently done commercially with rubber rollers. Beneath the hull lies another layer, similar to the bran in wheat, which contains 10 percent of the protein, 85 percent of the fat, 70 percent of the minerals, and a large amount of the B vitamins. This layer is left on for whole-grain (or brown) rice, while for processed (or white) rice it is removed; its removal helps the rice cook faster but also results in the loss of important fiber, vitamins, and minerals.

Culinary Uses

Rice dishes run the gamut from basic to elaborate. Plain steamed or simmered rice is, of course, a fine accompaniment to almost any meal. Rice is so versatile that it should be experimented with—make risotto, pilaf, or pudding, or eat it as a breakfast cereal. All cooked rice is an excellent addition to bread dough. "A meal without rice," according to one Chinese saying, "is like a beautiful girl with only one eye." In the Philippines you can stuff your guests with food, but if there is no rice it is not considered that you have offered them a meal.

Health Benefits

pH 6.00–6.83 (cooked). Rice is said to calm the nervous system, relieve mental depression, and strengthen the internal organs. Although lower in protein than many other cereal grains, its protein level is still good because it contains relatively high levels of the amino acid lysine.

VARIETIES

Long-grain rice accounts for 75 percent of the U.S. domestic crop. These slender grains are four to five times longer than they are wide. If properly cooked, they will be dry, light, and fluffy, with separate grains. This is the type most often used in Indian cooking. Long-grain rice is richer in the starch amylose, which helps render a dry, fluffy cooked product. *Medium-grain rice* is popular in Asian and Latin American cultures and is the type most commonly processed to make cold cereals. About twice as long as it is wide, it cooks up moister and more tender than long-grain varieties. *Short-grain rice* is a popular feature of Asian cuisine. This variety may be oval or almost round in shape and upon cooking tends to have a stickier, softer texture than its counterparts. Of the three types of rice, short-grain has the highest percentage of amylopectin, the

Rice / Nutritional Value Per 100 g Edible Portion

	Raw Brown Long-Grain	Cooked Brown Long-Grain	Raw Brown Medium-Grain	Cooked Brown Medium-Grain	Raw White Enriched Medium-Grain	Cooked White Enriched Medium-Grain	Cooked White Enriched Short-Grain	Cooked White Glutinous
Calories	370	111	362	112	360	130	130	97
Protein	7.94 g	2.58 g	7.50 g	2.32 g	6.61 g	2.38 g	2.36 g	2.02 g
Fat	2.92 g	0.90 g	2.68 g	0.83 g	0.58 g	0.21 g	0.19 g	0.19 g
Fiber	1.32 g	0.34 g	0.95 g	0.29 g	0.26 g	0.09 g	0.10 g	0.07 g
Calcium	23 mg	10 mg	33 mg	10 mg	9 mg	3 mg	1 mg	2 mg
Iron	1.47 mg	0.42 mg	1.80 mg	0.53 mg	4.36 mg	1.49 mg	1.46 mg	0.14 mg
Magnesium	143 mg	43 mg	143 mg	44 mg	35 mg	13 mg	8 mg	5 mg
Phosphorus	333 mg	83 mg	264 mg	77 mg	108 mg	37 mg	33 mg	8 mg
Potassium	223 mg	43 mg	268 mg	79 mg	86 mg	29 mg	26 mg	10 mg
Sodium	7 mg	5 mg	4 mg	1 mg	1 mg	0 mg	0 mg	5 mg
Zinc	2.020 mg	0.630 mg	2.020 mg	0.620 mg	1.160 mg	0.420 mg	0.400 mg	0.410 mg
Copper	0.277 mg	0.100 mg	0.277 mg	0.081 mg	0.110 mg	0.038 mg	0.072 mg	0.049 mg
Manganese	3.743 mg	0.905 mg	3.743 mg	1.097 mg	1.100 mg	0.377 mg	0.357 mg	0.262 mg
Thiamine (B$_1$)	0.401 mg	0.096 mg	0.413 mg	0.102 mg	0.578 mg	0.167 mg	0.164 mg	0.020 mg
Riboflavin (B$_2$)	0.093 mg	0.025 mg	0.043 mg	0.012 mg	0.048 mg	0.016 mg	0.016 mg	0.013 mg
Niacin (B$_3$)	5.091 mg	1.528 mg	4.308 mg	1.330 mg	5.093 mg	1.835 mg	1.493 mg	0.290 mg
Pantothenic Acid (B$_5$)	1.493 mg	0.285 mg	1.493 mg	0.392 mg	1.342 mg	0.411 mg	0.397 mg	0.215 mg
Pyridoxine (B$_6$)	0.509 mg	0.145 mg	0.509 mg	0.149 mg	0.145 mg	0.050 mg	0.059 mg	0.026 mg
Folic Acid (B$_9$)	20 mcg	4 mcg	20 mcg	4 mcg	9 mcg	2 mcg	2 mcg	1 mcg
Tocopherol (E)	0.680 mg	n/a	0.680 mg	n/a	n/a	n/a	n/a	n/a

starch that makes rice clump together when cooked. This makes it easy to eat with chopsticks and ideal for dishes like sushi.

Arborio rice is a popular short-grain rice imported mainly from the Po valley region of Italy. This favorite of Italian cuisine is a starchy, nearly round, white rice, with a translucent outer portion and opaque center. Arborio absorbs up to five times its weight in liquid as it cooks, yielding a firm, creamy product with an al dente consistency and lots of flavor. Traditionally used for cooking the Italian dish risotto, it also works well for paella and rice pudding.

Basmati is a long-grain rice named after the tropical basmati blossom of Southeast Asia. This aromatic variety is also available in Calmati and Texmati varieties, grown respectively in California and Texas. Generally, basmati rice is aged for at least a year after harvest in order to fully develop its nutty flavor. Unlike other types of rice, the grains elongate more than they plump as they cook, and because it is lower in starch than other long-grain types, basmati turns out flaky and separate. Fluffy,

light, with an aroma of buttered peanuts, and very popular in cooking, basmati comes in both brown and white versions.

Brown rice is the whole rice kernel from which only the outer hull has been removed; it is available in three sizes: short-, medium- and long-grain. It has a richer, chewier texture than white rice and a sweet, nutty flavor. Because it has not been highly processed, brown rice is the only form of the grain that contains vitamin E and retains most of its B vitamins. If the long cooking time is intimidating, there are also quick-cooking and instant forms sold. Brown rice is subject to rancidity within one to three months after milling. Storage is advised at under 40 degrees Fahrenheit for any bulk quantities that will not be used within one month.

Glutinous white rice is a short-grain rice popular in Japan and other Asian countries. Very sticky, chewy, and resilient, this starchy grain turns translucent when cooked and can be formed into balls, without added ingredients, or used in the preparation of sushi. See also **sweet brown rice.**

Raw White Unenriched Long-Grain	Cooked White Enriched Long-Grain	Parboiled Cooked White Enriched Long-Grain	Instant Cooked White Enriched Raw Long-Grain	Raw Rice Bran	Cooked Rice Polish	Brown Rice Cream	White Rice Flour	Rice Flour
365	129	114	98	316	265	50	363	366
7.13 g	2.69 g	2.29 g	2.06 g	13.35 g	12.10 g	0.80 g	7.23 g	5.95 g
0.66 g	0.28 g	0.27 g	0.16 g	20.85 g	12.80 g	trace	2.78 g	1.42 g
0.30 g	0.10 g	0.17 g	0.10 g	11.50 g	2.40 g	trace	1.29 g	0.80 g
28 mg	11 mg	19 mg	8 mg	57 mg	69 mg	2 mg	11 mg	10 mg
0.80 mg	1.10 mg	1.13 mg	0.63 mg	18.54 mg	16.10 mg	0.70 mg	1.98 mg	0.35 mg
25 mg	13 mg	12 mg	5 mg	781 mg	n/a	n/a	112 mg	35 mg
115 mg	47 mg	42 mg	14 mg	1,677 mg	1,106 mg	13 mg	337 mg	98 mg
115 mg	39 mg	37 mg	4 mg	1,485 mg	714 mg	trace	289 mg	76 mg
5 mg	2 mg	3 mg	3 mg	5 mg	trace	176 mg	8 mg	0 mg
1.090 mg	0.460 mg	0.310 mg	0.240 mg	6.040 mg	n/a	n/a	2.450 mg	0.800 mg
0.220 mg	0.063 mg	0.094 mg	0.065 mg	0.728 mg	n/a	n/a	0.230 mg	0.130 mg
1.088 mg	0.467 mg	0.260 mg	0.235 mg	14.210 mg	n/a	n/a	4.013 mg	1.200 mg
0.070 mg	0.163 mg	0.250 mg	0.075 mg	2.753 mg	1.840 mg	0.060 mg	0.443 mg	0.138 mg
0.049 mg	0.013 mg	0.018 mg	0.046 mg	0.284 mg	0.180 mg	0.010 mg	0.080 mg	0.021 mg
1.600 mg	1.476 mg	1.400 mg	0.880 mg	33.995 mg	28.200 mg	0.800 mg	6.340 mg	2.590 mg
1.014 mg	0.390 mg	0.324 mg	0.178 mg	7.390 mg	n/a	n/a	1.591 mg	0.819 mg
0.164 mg	0.093 mg	0.019 mg	0.010 mg	4.070 mg	n/a	n/a	0.736 mg	0.436 mg
8 mcg	3 mcg	4 mcg	4 mcg	63 mcg	n/a	n/a	16 mcg	4 mcg
0.110 mg	n/a	n/a	n/a	n/a	n/a	n/a	n/a	n/a

Golden rose brown rice is a medium-grain brown rice with the nutty flavor of a short-grain and fluffy texture of a long-grain. It is very versatile and can be used interchangeably with other varieties.

Instant white rice is a medium-grain white rice that has been milled and polished, fully cooked, and then dehydrated. Much less nutritious than brown rice and lacking the satisfying texture of regular white rice, it takes about five minutes to prepare.

Japonica, or **Thai black rice,** is a deep purple long-grain rice from Thailand. Though grown in Thailand for centuries, it is among the newest novelty imports to become available. Unlike most varieties of long-grain rice, Japonica rice is quite sticky and shiny, with a grasslike flavor; in Thailand it is usually used for making desserts. Another unusual aspect is that its dark-colored bran dissolves when cooked and imparts the dark color to both the water and the whole grain.

Jasmine rice is a long-grain white rice grown in the southern United States and Thailand. Popular in southeast Asian cuisine, this rice is soft and slightly sticky, very white, delicately flavored, and aromatic. Very similar in flavor to basmati, jasmine rice can easily be substituted for both the domestic and imported varieties.

Parboiled (converted) rice is a medium-grain rice that is steamed (or boiled) and pressurized before milling. The steaming process forces about 70 percent of the nutrients from the hull, bran, and germ back into the starchy part of the grain; when milled into white rice, then, the biggest loss is that most of the fiber is forfeited. The term *parboiled* is slightly misleading; the rice is not precooked and is actually somewhat harder than regular rice. More nutritious than regular white rice, parboiled rice takes longer to cook, and the result is grains that are very fluffy and separate.

Pudding rice is a variety that can be either black or white. Used mainly in China and Japan, it becomes sticky and sweet when boiled and is therefore employed mainly in baking and confectionery.

Red rice, or **Christmas rice,** is a short-grain russet-brown rice similar in color to Wehani with an unusual wild mushroom flavor. This strain is now being grown domestically in California by the Lundberg family.

Sweet brown rice is a short-grain rice that is a favorite among children. Esteemed for its warming and strengthening properties, it has a sweet flavor and sticky texture ideal for making sushi or the Japanese delicacy mochi. Roasted and ground, it makes an unusually tasty and easily digested hot breakfast cereal; ground into flour it is marvelous in baked goods, gravies, and pancakes.

Wehani rice is a plump, reddish-brown long-grain rice. It was developed by the Lundberg brothers, California farmers who pioneered the cultivation of organic rice, and is named after its developers—Wendell, Eldon, Homer, Albert, and Harlan Lundberg. It has a chewy texture and earthy aroma (smelling distinctly like popping corn) and tastes very much like a slightly stronger flavored, sticky, short-grain brown rice. The water it is cooked in will turn mahogany from the color in the bran and stain the whole grain.

White rice is produced by stripping off the outer brown layer of bran, leaving a pure white starchy carbohydrate. Most of the vitamins, minerals, and fiber are lost during this process, and without its natural protective outer layer, the central core of carbohydrate is exposed to molds, bacteria, and insects. To prevent loss from spoilage, some manufacturers coat the rice with an outer layer of talc and glucose (sugar). Talc is the amorphous form of the same substance that asbestos consists of, and talc used for coating rice is often contaminated with large numbers of actual asbestos fibers. When ingested, asbestos fibers are suspected of causing various cancers. Package recommendations to wash the rice before using are futile, because even after nine thorough washings some talc remains. Talc-coated rice is sold mostly in Hawaii, California, and Puerto Rico.

Wild pecan rice is a rather exotic-sounding long-grain variety that was developed by Louisiana State University and that is grown only in the Acadian bayou country of southern Louisiana. A cross between a Louisiana long-grain rice and several species of Indochina aromatic rices, it is a rather sticky, dark brown rice that is gently milled to retain most of the bran and that has a taste slightly evocative of the pecan nut.

BYPRODUCTS

Amasake is made by introducing koji enzymes (*Aspergillus oryzae*) from fermented rice into whole-grain cooked sweet rice and then incubating the whole mixture. The enzymes convert the complex carbohydrates of the rice into simple sugars, mainly maltose and glucose, much like malting barley. Made for hundreds of years by the Japanese, this traditional food is produced in the first fermentation of sake making; the name literally means "sweet sake." In the summer this refreshingly sweet beverage was served cool, while in the winter it was served hot with grated ginger. Amasake is sold as either a plain or a flavored beverage. Imported amasake is thicker and richer than the domestic varieties, more like rice pudding. It can be drunk as is or used as a dessert, a leavener in baking, a natural sweetening agent, a baby food, or a salad dressing; it also makes great kefir and smoothies, and frozen amasake makes excellent ice cream. Because amasake is a fermented food, it is readily digestible and aids in the digestion of other foods.

Brown rice syrup is prepared by adding dried sprouted barley or barley enzymes to cooked whole-grain rice and fermenting the mixture until the malt enzymes convert some of the rice starch into glucose (about 3 percent) and maltose (about 45 percent). This liquid is then cooked until it thickens to a syrupy consistency. Syrup made from organic brown rice has a slight butterscotch flavor. With only about two-thirds the sweetening power of white sugar, one-half that of maple syrup, and one-third that of honey, it adds a subtle and mild, rather than bold, sweetness to cooked or baked products. Because brown rice syrup is high in complex carbohydrates, it enters the bloodstream slowly and can be considered a balanced sweetener that will not upset blood sugar levels. Very easy to digest, it is also hypoallergenic and contains no fructose or sucrose. Made from only slightly polished whole-grain rice, it contains all the nutritional benefits of the rice. Rice syrup has a powdered counterpart, made by pulverizing crystals prepared from the liquid; these crystals will dissolve readily in liquid.

Puffed rice is made by puffing rice under pressure, thus filling the grains with air. Puffed rice makes an excellent cold breakfast cereal and can also be used for making cakes and candy.

Rice bran is made from the outer layer of the rice kernel that contains the bran and a small part of the germ. We owe its existence to the fact that the majority of people in North America eat refined white rice, the processing of which leaves a rich "waste" bran. Nearly twice as high in soluble dietary fiber as oat bran, it can be used the same way: sprinkled on cereal or as an ingredient in baked cookies, breads, and muffins.

Rice cream is a roasted brown rice flour that is generally used for making a cooked breakfast cereal, pudding, or thick broth. You can make your own by toasting brown rice in a heavy frying pan, grinding it to a powder in a blender, and then re-roasting it over medium heat.

Rice flakes are made from brown and/or white rice that is heated and pressed flat under pressure, much as rolled oats are, but a bit thicker. These can be used for a variety of mueslis, cooked breakfast cereals, or breads and other baked goods.

Rice flour is a gluten-free flour made from primarily brown rice; this sweet, slightly gummy flour has a crystalline appearance and contains a wide range of vitamins and minerals. It is most successfully used in low-ratio combinations with other flours. Adding brown rice flour to baked goods usually results in a drier product but imparts a lively, seedlike flavor. Excellent for piecrusts, breads, crackers, noodles, cakes, and biscuits, this flour is also used as a thickening agent, as well as for dusting bread dough because it absorbs moisture slowly, drying the dough's surface without adhering to it.

Rice grits are coarsely ground brown rice grains that are good for quick hot cereals, puddings, and dishes in which the fluffy texture of whole rice is not required.

Rizcous is a precooked cracked rice that may be used interchangeably with bulgur wheat or couscous.

Rice, Wild
(Zizania aquatica)

Zizania is an old Greek name for a weed, probably the darnel that grows among wheat. *Aquatica* simply means "aquatic."

General Information
Though it is cooked and used like a grain, wild rice is neither a rice nor a grain, but the seed of an aquatic grass native to the Great Lakes region. This tall, tubular, reedy aquatic grass grows four to eight feet above the waterline in swamps and along the borders of streams in shallow water. The slender grains are nearly three-quarters of an inch long, round, and almost black, and they fall soon after ripening. About 40 percent of the harvesting is still done by hand in the traditional manner by Native Americans in canoes. The rest is cultivated in man-made paddies and machine-harvested, with California being the largest producer. Hand-harvested rice is immediately parched over open fires, giving it a variety of distinct matte colors, from a ruddy red-brown to a subtle gray-green. Heirloom rice is scarified to remove part of its bran and thus has a mottled brown, gray, and black coloring. Paddy rice is left to cure (and slightly ferment) out in the weather for several weeks after harvesting, where it develops its characteristic shiny, dark kernels and distinctive taste. It is then heated, which gelatinizes the starch and deepens the coloring. Labels usually note if the rice is hand-harvested or cultivated, but the color will tell you immediately how it was grown. Tame wild rice is one of four hybrid varieties selected for responsiveness to petrochemical fertilizers, herbicides, insecticides, and fungicides, as well as for ease of mechanical

Rice, Wild / Nutritional Value Per 100 g Edible Portion	Raw	Cooked
Calories	357	101
Protein	14.73 g	3.99 g
Fat	1.08 g	0.34 g
Fiber	1.44 g	0.33 g
Calcium	21 mg	3 mg
Iron	1.96 mg	0.60 mg
Magnesium	177 mg	32 mg
Phosphorus	433 mg	82 mg
Potassium	427 mg	101 mg
Sodium	7 mg	3 mg
Zinc	5.960 mg	1.340 mg
Copper	0.524 mg	0.121 mg
Manganese	1.329 mg	0.282 mg
Beta Carotene (A)	19 IU	0 IU
Thiamine (B₁)	0.115 mg	0.052 mg
Riboflavin (B₂)	0.262 mg	0.087 mg
Niacin (B₃)	6.733 mg	1.287 mg
Pantothenic Acid (B₅)	1.074 mg	0.154 mg
Pyridoxine (B₆)	0.391 mg	0.135 mg
Folic Acid (B₉)	95 mcg	26 mcg

LORE AND LEGEND

In the Chippewa region of the Great Lakes, wild rice is called *manomin* by the Native Americans, meaning "gift from the Creator."

harvesting and factory production. The Canadian hybrid rice is typically an inch long and is ebony black in color.

Culinary Uses

There are three grades of wild rice: (1) "Select," which contains short broken grains; (2) "Extra-fancy," which has uniform half-inch-long grains and is the most common variety available; and (3) "Giant," the most expensive, with grains that are uniformly one inch in length. All grades can be used interchangeably in recipes. Known as the "gourmet grain," it has actually been a staple in the Chippewa and Sioux Indian diets for centuries. Each brand of wild rice has its own particular taste, so if you have experienced some very strong or bitter types, experiment with other brands. If you find the chewy, nutty, smoky flavor of wild rice too strong on its own, use it in combination with other rices to mellow the intense woodsy flavor, or use the more delicately flavored hand-harvested varieties. Properly cooked wild rice will split and be fluffy. It is frequently used in pilafs, soups, salads, and stuffings. When precooked it makes an excellent addition to yeast breads, muffins, and pancakes; even a small amount imparts its distinctive character to other ingredients. The hulled seeds can be eaten raw as a snack, but few people probably eat wild rice this way.

Health Benefits

Wild grasses, including foraged wild rice, are more robust, nutritious, and flavorful than their tame cousins. Wild rice has almost twice as much protein and iron as brown rice and is an excellent source of soluble fiber.

BYPRODUCTS

Wild rice flour is good in baked goods, pancakes, waffles, and muffins, where it adds its distinctive nutty flavor.

Rye
(Secale cereale)

Secale is an ancient Latin name, said to be derived from *seco*, meaning "to cut"; *cereale* means "pertaining to Ceres" (the Roman goddess of agriculture), or to agriculture itself. The English word *rye* derives from the Lithuanian *rugys*.

General Information

Rye is a large herbaceous annual plant whose stalks can grow to more than three feet in height. A feisty, scrappy survivor that is able to sustain itself in severe climates, it seems to have developed from a wild species of northeastern European grain and was cultivated early on by inhabitants in the colder regions of western Asia and in the mountainous northern regions of Europe. For the rest of Europe and the Mediterranean, rye was a rather late bloomer; the Egyptians and Sumerians did not include it among their range of crops, and the ancient Greeks and Turks considered it only an intrusive and obnoxious weed. Rye was taken to Britain by the Saxons in A.D. 500 and was widely distributed throughout Europe during the Middle Ages. The basic bread of medieval Britain consisted of coarsely ground rye and pea flours, sometimes with a little barley flour mixed in. For poorer folk in much of Europe during the Middle Ages, this cereal grain was a staple, and it is still consumed in much of eastern Europe and Russia, where it gained favor because it was able to tolerate the severe climate better than other grains. It probably came to North America with the Dutch, German, and French settlers, the French first planting it in seventeenth-century Nova Scotia. The popularity of rye spread throughout the West as the frontier was pushed to the Pacific Ocean, not because the pioneers thought so highly of black bread but because rye whiskey has always been one of the largest uses for this grain in America. Of the world's cereal crops, rye makes up only about 1 percent, though its popularity is starting to revive after a long decline.

Rye has from time to time made spectacular appearances on the stage of history because of its greatest weakness—its susceptibility to ergot, which rarely appears in any other cereal. Ergot is a parasitic fungus (*Claviceps purpurea*) that forms hornlike, purplish-black masses that are easily identified in the grain and, when found, are separated out before processing. The fungus is highly toxic to humans and provokes uncontrollable muscular contractions. One of ergot's principal poisons (out of a possible twenty) is ergotamine.

When ergotamine gets into flour and the flour is made into dough and baked, the poison is transformed into lysergic acid diethylamide, or LSD. During the Middle Ages, ergot was responsible for frequent epidemics of what was called Holy Fire or Saint Anthony's Fire—a condition characterized by various effects, from violent manifestations that led to death to milder reactions, which may not have been perceived as having been provoked by any external agent: deafness, dimming eyesight, or psychotic disorders, including hallucination. Frequently there was a loss of blood flow to the extremities, resulting in intense pain and eventually gangrene. Ergot also causes miscarriage, and medieval women used it to provoke abortions (it is still being used for this purpose in some areas today).

Culinary Uses

Slenderer than wheat, rye has blue-gray overtones and a strong, full, robust, and tangy flavor. Because of this hearty flavor, rye has been used mainly in breads such as the well-known Scandinavian crispbread and in drinks such as whiskey in America, gin in Holland, and beer in Russia. Available in whole, cracked, flake, and flour forms, the grain is very versatile and has a wide range of uses: try simmering rye berries with either wheat berries or brown rice, combining cracked rye with cracked wheat, or cooking rye flakes in combination with oatmeal. Or enjoy rye's distinctive flavor on its own, using the berries in wheat-berry recipes, cracked rye in cracked-wheat recipes, and rye flakes in oatmeal dishes. The flour is used to make the dark, heavy "black bread" that, though many people affect to dislike it, stays fresh longer than wheaten bread, has more taste, and is very filling. It is lower in gluten content than wheat and thus is well suited to making pastries, in which the development of gluten would produce toughness. On the other hand, it is more difficult to work into a loaf that will rise nicely.

Health Benefits

pH 6.0. Rye is said to build muscles and promote energy and endurance. It also cleanses and renews arteries; aids fingernail, hair, and bone formation; and benefits the liver. Rye possesses the power to reenergize anemic bodies and rebuild the entire digestive system through its high carbohydrate content and its richness in nitrogenous matter. Eaten in its raw, sprouted state or as soaked flakes, rye provides fluorine, which increases tooth enamel strength. Rye fiber supplies a rich source of noncellulose polysaccharides, with a high water-binding capacity. By binding water in the intestinal tract, rye breads give the sensation of fullness. Rye breads are gently laxative and help prevent arteriosclerosis.

BYPRODUCTS

Cracked rye or **rye cereal** is made of whole rye berries that have been broken or ground into small pieces. It can be cooked for a hot breakfast cereal, combined with cracked wheat or rolled oats for variety, or added to soups.

Rye berries are the whole kernels with just the outer husks removed. Rye berries can be sprouted and used in soups, salads, or breads; unsprouted they can be used for the same dishes or cooked like rice.

Rye flakes are whole grains that have been heated until soft and then pressed and rolled between high-pressure rollers, and lightly toasted. The flakes look very similar to rolled oats but are slightly thicker. Rye flakes can be cooked and eaten as a hearty breakfast cereal and are excellent added to breads and muffins; they are also

Rye / Nutritional Value Per 100 g Edible Portion	Whole Grain	Dark Flour	Medium Flour	Light Flour
Calories	335	324	354	367
Protein	14.76 g	14.03 g	9.39 g	8.39 g
Fat	2.50 g	2.69 g	1.77 g	1.36 g
Fiber	1.50 g	1.46 g	1.40 g	1.30 g
Calcium	33 mg	56 mg	24 mg	21 mg
Iron	2.67 mg	6.45 mg	2.12 mg	1.80 mg
Magnesium	121 mg	248 mg	75 mg	70 mg
Phosphorus	374 mg	632 mg	207 mg	194 mg
Potassium	264 mg	730 mg	340 mg	233 mg
Sodium	6 mg	1 mg	3 mg	2 mg
Zinc	3.730 mg	5.620 mg	1.990 mg	1.750 mg
Copper	0.450 mg	0.750 mg	0.287 mg	0.250 mg
Manganese	2.680 mg	6.730 mg	5.460 mg	1.970 mg
Thiamine (B$_1$)	n/a	0.316 mg	0.287 mg	0.331 mg
Riboflavin (B$_2$)	n/a	0.251 mg	0.114 mg	0.090 mg
Niacin (B$_3$)	n/a	4.270 mg	1.727 mg	0.800 mg
Pantothenic Acid (B$_5$)	n/a	1.456 mg	0.492 mg	0.665 mg
Pyridoxine (B$_6$)	0.294 mg	0.443 mg	0.268 mg	0.234 mg
Folic Acid (B$_9$)	n/a	60 mcg	19 mcg	22 mcg
Tocopherol (E)	1.280 mg	1.410 mg	0.790 mg	0.430 mg

frequently used as a meat extender in meat loaves or as a thickener for soups.

Rye flour is sweet and tangy rather than sour. Whole-grain rye flour is best, followed by dark rye flour and lastly by light rye flour, the difference being how much bran is left. The main ingredient in black bread, pumpernickel bread, and some crispbreads, rye flour also makes excellent pancakes. Since it has little gluten, rye flour has to be mixed with up to two-thirds wheat or other gluten-containing flour when used to make leavened breads. True pumpernickel bread is generally made from rye kernels coarsely ground into a meal and the dough then flavored with caraway or dill seed.

Rye grits are the whole grain that has been cracked into six or eight separate pieces. They are often used as a cereal, as a main-course replacement for rice or potatoes, or mixed with other grains or gluten flour for breads. Rye grits require slightly longer cooking than most other grain grits—about forty-five minutes.

Rye meal is simply coarsely ground whole-rye flour, of the consistency of cornmeal, that can be used in the same manner as regular flour. Rye meal will give the crunchy texture that is characteristic of some types of bread.

Sorghum
(Sorghum bicolor)

The word *sorghum* comes from the Latin *Syricum granum,* meaning "Syrian grain." *Bicolor* means "two-colored."

General Information

Grain sorghum is native to Africa and is believed by some to have been domesticated either in the savanna zone of eastern Africa or in India. In the seventeenth and eighteenth centuries, sorghum, then called "guinea corn," was brought to the West Indies and the British colonies by slave ships traveling from Africa. Somewhat resembling maize in vegetative features and bearing its grain in a terminal cluster, this grain is more drought-tolerant than most cereals and hence is of great importance in semi-arid regions that will not support the growth of the major cereal plants. Widely used by people in Africa and Asia, where it is known by its Arabic name of *dourra,* only recently has grain sorghum became an important crop in the United States; grown in the Southwest, it is used primarily for

Sorghum / Nutritional Value Per 100 g Edible Portion		
	Raw Whole Grain	Syrup
Calories	339	290
Protein	11.30 g	0 g
Fat	3.30 g	0 g
Fiber	2.40 g	0.10 g
Calcium	28 mg	150 mg
Iron	4.40 mg	3.80 mg
Phosphorus	287 mg	56 mg
Potassium	350 mg	1,000 mg
Thiamine (B$_1$)	0.237 mg	0.100 mg
Riboflavin (B$_2$)	0.142 mg	0.155 mg
Niacin (B$_3$)	2.927 mg	0.100 mg

animal feed. The grain sorghums grown in the United States are classified into seven groups, the best of which are kafir, milo, and durra. The kafirs come from southern Africa and have thick, juicy stalks, large leaves, and cylindrical heads that bear white, pink, or red seeds. The milos are from east-central Africa and have wavy leaves, less juicy stalks, and larger salmon, pink, or cream-colored seeds. The durras, from North Africa and the Near East, have bearded, fuzzy heads, large flat seeds, and dry stalks. Other important varieties of sorghum are the great or Turkish millet (*S. durra, S. vulgare*) and sugar sorghum (*S. saccharatum*), which is cultivated chiefly for the sugary syrup contained within the stems.

Culinary Uses

The whole grains can be used much like rice, either boiled or ground into meal for bread or porridge. Sorghum flour is gluten-free and so produces flattish bread on its own.

Spelt
(Triticum aestivum)
Also Known As: Dinkel, Farro

Linnaeus provided the genus name *Triticum,* an old Latin name for "cereal." *Aestivum* means "summer." The English word *spelt* of is Germanic origin, possibly meaning "split."

General Information

Spelt is believed to be among the most ancient of cultivated wheat types. Its recorded use has been most prevalent in Europe, where its history goes back about nine thousand

LORE AND LEGEND

Saint Hildegard of Bingen, a twelfth-century mystic, cured every imaginable ailment with spelt. "When someone is so weakened by illness that he cannot eat," she wrote, "then simply take whole spelt kernels and boil them vigorously in water, add butter and egg. . . . Give this to the patient and it will heal him from within like a good healing salve." Modern science has supported Saint Hildegard's theories by showing that spelt's water solubility is remarkably different from that of common wheat. Hold a few spelt kernels in your mouth and—unlike other types of wheat—they immediately soften. Spelt is also, therefore, readily assimilated into the body.

years. Because the plant tolerates poorly drained, low-fertility soils, it was and still is an excellent alternative to common wheat for many farmers. Throughout history, spelt remained a popular bread wheat until the twentieth century, when it was rejected by both Hitler and the "green revolution" of the 1960s, because of its bulky edible husks and because its yields were lower than modern high-yield varieties. Fortunately, it was still cultivated by enough visionary or stubbornly independent small farmers in out-of-the-way fields in Europe until its popularity began to grow again. Part of its rise in popularity is attributed to new translations of the mystical writings of Saint Hildegard of Bingen, a twelfth-century mystic who praised spelt as the grain best tolerated by the body. Widely recognized among many Europeans, this grain is now becoming familiar to American households.

Culinary Uses

To the eye, spelt looks like a common grain of wheat, but in the mouth it immediately softens. Like kamut, spelt provides both the versatility and the familiarity of common wheat while delivering optimum flavor and nutrients along with a low allergenic profile. As a whole grain, it may be substituted for common wheat, and as a flour it may be substituted for whole-wheat flour in cookies, sauces, and baked goods. It is an excellent bread wheat, producing a satisfying and fine-textured bread.

Health Benefits

pH 6.0. Spelt's high water solubility equates with bioavailability, meaning that the nutrients dissolve rapidly in liquid and become readily available to the body with only a minimum of digestive work. Because it is not a hybridized grain, it is generally higher in protein, vitamins, and minerals than common wheat. Although spelt contains gluten, those with gluten sensitivity can usually tolerate it.

Spelt / Nutritional Value Per 100 g Edible Portion			
	Raw Whole Grain		Raw Whole Grain
Calories	293	Phosphorus	463 mg
Protein	12.7 g	Potassium	420 mg
Fat	1.98 g	Sodium	2 mg
Fiber	13.9 g	Thiamine (B₁)	0.430 mg
Calcium	6 mg	Riboflavin (B₂)	0.110 mg
Iron	2.79 mg	Niacin (B₃)	3.620 mg

T'ef/Teff
(Eragrostis tef, E. abyssinica)

Eragrostis comes either from the Greek *eros*, meaning "love," or from *er*, meaning "spring," combined with *agrostis*, which means "grass"; *abyssinica* means "coming from Abyssinia." The name *t'ef* literally translates from the Ethiopian Amharic word *teffa* as "lost," because much of the tiny seed disappears when handled and cannot be found if dropped.

General Information

T'ef originated at the source of the Blue Nile in the rugged, windswept African alps. As with many other grains, this grain was a foraged wild grass that eventually became cultivated. There are now more than two thousand individual strains of this important, fine-bladed cereal grass, varying from short to tall and from compact to spreading in form. The historically fierce and proud Ethiopians attribute their prowess to this iron-rich and iron-colored grain; other grains, easier to cultivate and harvest, thrive in Abyssinia, but for millennia t'ef has been the premier crop. It is also cultivated for hay in Kenya and Australia, and the straw is still used to make adobe in Ethiopia. Only twice the size of the period at the end of this sentence, with 150 grains equal in weight to one single kernel of wheat, minuscule t'ef is difficult to harvest. Like other heirloom plants, t'ef is not monochromatic—its seeds may be white, red-purple, or brown. It is a superb garden ornamental, with its silvery stalks and brightly colored heads.

Culinary Uses

Because of its excellent nutritional value and pleasing flavor, t'ef is no longer an ethnic secret. It is available in three colors—white, red, or brown—each with its own distinctly pleasant flavor. The mild white t'ef has an almost chestnutlike flavor, while the darker colors are more earthy, with a taste like hazelnuts. For people who like small grains

LORE AND LEGEND

T'ef was introduced to the United States by an Idaho farmer, Wayne Carlson, who was in Ethiopia working on a medical research project. He developed a taste for the native staple, a spongy fermented flatbread called injera, and when he returned to Idaho found himself hungering for this unusual grain. Since none was available, he imported seed, and today t'ef is grown commercially in the high desert volcanic fields of Idaho and distributed through natural food stores.

T'ef / Nutritional Value Per 100 g Edible Portion			
	Raw Whole Grain		Raw Whole Grain
Calories	328	Phosphorus	313 mg
Protein	9.6 g	Beta Carotene (A)	5 mg
Fat	2.6 g	Thiamine (B₁)	0.130 mg
Fiber	2.7 g	Riboflavin (B₂)	0.120 mg
Calcium	172 mg	Niacin (B₃)	1.400 mg
Iron	75.5 mg		

like amaranth, the texture of t'ef is enjoyable. Others, who object to the tiny size of the whole grain, will enjoy the flour. Whole-grain t'ef can be cooked into a tasty breakfast porridge, with the darker grains giving a rich rustic flavor and the white more of a delicate creamy cereal. It can also be added to soups or stews, where it will burst open and provide body and flavor if cooked for at least thirty minutes; it is not well suited to pilafs and salads, as it will give more of a gritty texture than is generally desirable. T'ef flour can be mixed in combination with any other grain to impart its light, pleasing flavor (although it will add some grittiness). It is unique in that it has its own symbiotic yeast, similar to grapes, which remains through harvesting and milling. Because of this intrinsic yeast, t'ef is an ideal starter for naturally leavened bread. Mix one cup of t'ef flour with 1½ cups of water, cover, and allow to stand at room temperature for a day; this fermented mixture can then be substituted for sourdough starter in bread. By itself, t'ef flour is best suited for flatbreads, quick breads, and dessert breads. Do not add t'ef to a yeast bread because the synergy between the two is wild—the dough will run amok and create a fetid stench that takes hours to air out.

Health Benefits

The overall nutrition of this small grain is outstanding. T'ef is packed with nutrients because it is so tiny that it has proportionally more hull (pericarp) than other grains; this outer layer is nutritionally superior to the inner layer. Plus, its tiny size makes it impractical to hull or degerm, so the entire grain is milled, which leaves all the nutrients intact. T'ef is lower in manganese than other cereals, but it more than compensates for that with its higher mineral content, which includes iron, calcium, copper, and zinc. The darker varieties are higher in iron than the white, while the white tends to be higher in protein. Also important is its low allergenic profile; initial reports indicate that most people suffering from wheat and corn allergies may safely eat t'ef.

BYPRODUCTS

T'ef flour is a granular rather than starchy flour that is highly versatile and lends itself to numerous dishes. Because of its symbiotic yeast, it is unsuitable on its own for most leavened breads (combine it with wheat or other gluten-containing flour only up to 20 percent), although this property makes it excellent as a substitute for sourdough starters. T'ef flour may be substituted for wheat flour in many cookie, sauce, pancake, muffin,

and quick bread recipes. The white variety is lighter and more suited to cakes and pastries than the darker varieties. T'ef flour is easily made at home in a grain, coffee, or nut mill.

Triticale
(Triticum secale)

This grain started its life as a hybrid between wheat and rye, as is reflected by its name, *Triticum* being the Latin genus for wheat and *secale* being the genus for rye. The English name *triticale* is a contraction of the two names.

General Information
Triticale is a cereal grain developed in 1875 by Swedish researchers by cross breeding several different species of durum wheat, hard red winter wheat, and rye, to combine the high lysine content and ruggedness of rye with the overall high protein content of wheat. The few seeds produced from the first hybrid plant were sterile, but in 1937 a French researcher succeeded in producing a fertile cross, and triticale became the first human-engineered grain in

Triticale / Nutritional Value Per 100 g Edible Portion	Raw, Whole Grain	Whole-Grain Flour
Calories	336	338
Protein	13.05 g	13.18 g
Fat	2.09 g	1.81 g
Fiber	2.60 g	1.50 g
Calcium	37 mg	35 mg
Iron	2.57 mg	2.59 mg
Magnesium	130 mg	153 mg
Phosphorus	358 mg	321 mg
Potassium	332 mg	466 mg
Sodium	5 mg	2 mg
Zinc	3.450 mg	2.660 mg
Copper	0.457 mg	0.559 mg
Manganese	3.210 mg	4.185 mg
Thiamine (B$_1$)	0.416 mg	0.378 mg
Riboflavin (B$_2$)	0.134 mg	0.132 mg
Niacin (B$_3$)	1.430 mg	2.860 mg
Pantothenic Acid (B$_5$)	1.323 mg	2.167 mg
Pyridoxine (B$_6$)	0.138 mg	0.403 mg
Folic Acid (B$_9$)	73 mcg	74 mcg
Tocopherol (E)	0.900 mg	0.200 mg

history. Subsequent research during the 1950s led to significant improvements; triticale as we now know it is twice as large and heavy as wheat, and in some field tests the plant has yielded nearly twice as much grain. Considered by its developers to be "science's gift to the world," it gained some popularity during the 1970s but then waned and is only now regaining some of its former popular appeal.

Culinary Uses

Triticale's flavor is richer and more nutlike than that of wheat, without the assertiveness of rye. Buy the whole grain, if available, and sprout it, and then enjoy the chewy texture on its own as a snack or add the sprouts (best when no longer than the grain itself) to salads, soups, casseroles, or brown rice dishes. The whole grains can also be cooked like rice, with a resultant flavor resembling whole wheat and pecans. When used in combination with other flours, triticale flour adds a distinctive flavor to breads and other baked goods. The flour contains enough gluten to be used alone as a bread flour; however, it is tricky to turn into a good loaf of bread.

Health Benefits

pH 6.0. Triticale is slightly higher in lysine than wheat, and depending on growing conditions its protein content ranges from 13 to 20 percent.

BYPRODUCTS

Cracked triticale is the coarsely ground whole kernel. Like any processed grain, it has a shorter cooking time than the whole grain. You can make your own cracked triticale by processing whole kernels in a blender until they are coarsely ground. Cracked triticale can be used in the same manner as cracked wheat.

Triticale flakes are the berries that have been steamed and flattened, much like rolled oats. The flakes can be used in the same manner as oat flakes but require a slightly longer cooking time.

Triticale flour is a nutritious, sweet-tasting flour that gives a pleasingly nutty and slightly ryelike flavor to bread. Although it has enough gluten to be used on its own, it is best used in combination with wheat flours for the best texture and leavening capacity. **Leavened triticale bread** will only stand gentle kneading, and one rising is sufficient. The flour can also be used in quick breads, cookies, and pancakes.

Wheat
(Triticum)

Bread is the warmest, kindest of words.
Write it always with a capital letter,
Like your own name.

—Russian café sign

When you have only two pennies left in the world,
Buy a loaf of bread with one, and a lily with the other.

—Chinese proverb

Linnaeus provided the genus name *Triticum*, an old Latin name for "cereal." The English name *wheat* appears to have two derivatives, the Sanskrit *sveta* and the Old English *hwaete*, both meaning "white," and thus distinguishing this grain from the other, darker cereals with which the Germanic races were familiar.

General Information

Wheat dates back thousands of years in Chinese and Egyptian records. There is evidence of wheat cultivation in the Middle East as early as ten thousand years ago. By 4000 B.C. it was growing in the Indus and Euphrates valleys, by 2500 B.C. in China, by 2000 B.C. in Europe west to England. It was of paramount importance to Rome, and it has been suggested that many of her initial overseas conquests were undertaken in order to obtain areas most favorable to the cultivation of wheat, in particular Sicily and Sardinia, Carthaginian Africa, and Egypt. The invasions of northern Germanic peoples into Europe largely displaced wheat and replaced it with their preferred rye. As Europe emerged from the Dark Ages, wheat bread regained its popularity but was largely restricted to the rich; the poor had to make do with various mixtures of grains, leguminous plants, and nuts to make bread flour. Only during the nineteenth century did wheat bread become accessible for all.

There was no wheat in North America when the white man came, nor was there any rye, oats, barley, or millet. In 1493 Columbus planted wheat in the West Indies "to prove the soil." Spanish ships took the grain to Mexico, and by 1687 wheat was widely grown in the vice royalty of

New Spain. Almost all American colonists brought wheat with them from Europe. As the country expanded beyond the Appalachians, wheat went with the pioneers. By the mid–nineteenth century wheat was well established in what would later become America's grain belt. In 1898 the United States Department of Agriculture sent Mark Carleton to Russia to find a spring wheat to complement the sole crop of winter wheat. The result of his visit was the introduction to the United States of durum wheat, the hardest-kerneled of all wheat, rust-resistant, and adapted to dry conditions. Because of our current preference for white bread, wheat is the world's most widely distributed and cultivated cereal grain, grown in nearly every country. For many cultures, wheat has replaced the more traditional (and often more nutritious) grains of corn, buckwheat, rye, barley, quinoa, t'ef, and millet as the staple grain. More wheat is produced in the United States than anywhere else in the world, but the greatest part of that is consumed in highly refined forms. Since the late 1920s wheat has been genetically altered for smut resistance. It is theorized that this manipulation may be a contributing factor in the plethora of wheat allergies.

Culinary Uses

For most of the ten thousand years that wheat has been cultivated, the grain has been used as it is harvested or ground into various grades of flour, mixed with water, and cooked to produce one of the many kinds of bread that are staples the world over.

Health Benefits

pH 6.0. Wheat tends to stimulate the liver to cleanse itself of toxins. This cleansing may be experienced as an "allergy" if there is an abundance of toxins stored there; once the liver has regained its healthful state, wheat consumption does not generally produce any reaction. This relatively recent phenomenon of wheat allergy is partly a result of its being consumed in so highly refined a form. Many people have found that it is the commercial, highly processed wheat they are allergic to, not organically grown wheat in its whole-grain form. Heirloom varieties of wheat, such as kamut and spelt, also seem to cause fewer allergic reactions. As well, those with allergies to wheat or other cereals are almost never allergic to them in their grass or sprouted stage.

Whole wheat is the most nutritious form of this grain, since the nutritious bran and germ are left intact. Whole wheat also contains traces of barium and vanadium, both essential to the health of the heart. Refined wheat has been stripped of both bran and germ, losing as much as 80 percent of its vitamins and minerals and 93 percent of its fiber. So-called enriched white bread, which has had all of its original vitamins and minerals removed, has nothing left but raw starch of such little nutritive value that even most bacteria will not voluntarily eat it. Into this insipid starch synthetic chemicals are added, which form only part of the missing vitamin B complex and which are not properly ingestible by humans because they are not properly balanced. Naturally leavened breads are easier to digest, since they contain lactobacillus, essential to the proper digestion of complex carbohydrates, and contain no phytic acid, which has been tied to anemia, rickets, and nervous disorders. Naturally leavened breads are also believed to be cancer inhibitors, whereas yeasted breads explode the starch cells of the bread, creating cell patterns and bioelectrical energy identical to cancer cells.

In Denmark, when a combination of a severe drought and the Allied blockade threatened to cause massive starvation in 1917, an experiment was conducted on a large scale. Dr. M. Hinhede, superintendent of the State Institute for Food Research in Copenhagen, ordered 80 percent of the pigs and 66 percent of the cattle slaughtered. The cereal grains thus saved were fed to the human population in the form of whole rye bread, to which was added 12 to 15 percent wheat bran. The results were striking. The mortality from all causes fell in the first rationing year by 17 percent to the lowest level ever seen in any country up to that time. When the great worldwide pandemic of influenza struck in 1918, Denmark was the only country in Europe without an increase in mortality. The Danish death rate from all causes actually decreased, while in other European countries it rose by as much as 46 percent.

In India, where wheat has been a major part of the diet for many

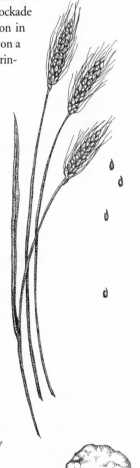

thousands of years, the ancient medical traditions have ascribed it special and unique properties. It is said to be particularly prone to produce growth, thus being especially suitable as a food for growing children. It is also prescribed for convalescents, but traditional Indian physicians are wary of its growth-producing tendency in adults and suspect it of aggravating the tendency to develop cysts and other benign growths and tumors in the body. Wheat is also especially good at helping put on extra pounds, whether they are wanted or not.

This traditional "staff of life" is now consumed in such gluttonous amounts that almost everybody overconsumes it. In many families wheat in some form is served three times a day at meals and then snacked on in between, culminating in a habit of eating bread with almost everything. This habit excludes other important foods, and wheat becomes more of a poison than a benefit to the body. Undigested carbohydrates from the excess bread begin to cause mucus. If bread is consumed more than three days in a row, energy levels begin to drop and thinking becomes cloudy.

VARIETIES

There are literally thousands of varieties of wheat grown around the world—some agronomists count as many as thirty thousand—but many of these varieties have declined in popularity and are restricted to cattle feed. The most common species grown and distributed are common wheat (*T. vulgare*), which is primarily milled into flour to be used in breads and cakes, winter or Lammas wheat (*T. hybernum*), spring or summer wheat (*T. aestivum*), and durum wheat (*T. durum*).

Common wheat is primarily milled into flour to be used in breads and cakes. Of the common wheat varieties, there are subspecies including hard and soft wheats, red and white wheats, and spring and winter wheats.

Durum wheat (from the Latin *durus*, meaning "hard" or tough) is a hard spring wheat that was crossed with a wild cereal called oat grass thousands of years ago. Of desert ancestry, durum wheat is famous for its ability to

Wheat / Nutritional Value Per 100 g Edible Portion									
	Hard Red Spring Wheat	Hard Red Winter Wheat	Soft Red Winter Wheat	Hard White Wheat	Soft White Wheat	Durum Wheat	Raw Bran	Raw Germ	Toasted Germ
Calories	329	327	331	342	340	339	216	360	382
Protein	15.40 g	12.61 g	10.35 g	11.31 g	10.69 g	13.68 g	15.55 g	23.15 g	29.10 g
Fat	1.92 g	1.54 g	1.56 g	1.71 g	1.99 g	2.47 g	4.25 g	9.72 g	10.70 g
Fiber	2.28 g	2.29 g	1.72 g	n/a	n/a	n/a	7.19 g	2.82 g	2.30 g
Calcium	25 mg	29 mg	27 mg	32 mg	34 mg	34 mg	73 mg	39 mg	45 mg
Iron	3.60 mg	3.19 mg	3.21 mg	4.56 mg	5.37 mg	3.52 mg	10.57 mg	6.26 mg	9.09 mg
Magnesium	124 mg	126 mg	126 mg	93 mg	90 mg	144 mg	611 mg	239 mg	320 mg
Phosphorus	332 mg	288 mg	493 mg	355 mg	402 mg	508 mg	1,013 mg	842 mg	1,146 mg
Potassium	340 mg	363 mg	397 mg	432 mg	435 mg	431 mg	1,182 mg	892 mg	947 mg
Sodium	2 mg	2 mg	2 mg	n/a	n/a	2 mg	2 mg	12 mg	4 mg
Zinc	2.780 mg	2.650 mg	2.630 mg	3.330 mg	3.460 mg	4.160 mg	7.270 mg	12.290 mg	16.670 mg
Copper	0.410 mg	0.434 mg	0.450 mg	0.363 mg	0.426 mg	0.553 mg	0.998 mg	0.796 mg	0.620 mg
Manganese	4.055 mg	3.985 mg	4.391 mg	3.821 mg	3.406 mg	3.012 mg	11.500 mg	13.301 mg	19.956 mg
Beta Carotene (A)	n/a	n/a	n/a	n/a	n/a	n/a	n/a	n/a	n/a
Thiamine (B$_1$)	0.504 mg	0.383 mg	0.394 mg	0.387 mg	0.410 mg	0.419 mg	0.523 mg	1.882 mg	1.670 mg
Riboflavin (B$_2$)	0.110 mg	0.115 mg	0.096 mg	0.108 mg	0.107 mg	0.121 mg	0.577 mg	0.499 mg	0.820 mg
Niacin (B$_3$)	5.710 mg	5.464 mg	4.800 mg	4.381 mg	4.766 mg	6.738 mg	13.578 mg	6.813 mg	5.590 mg
Pantothenic Acid (B$_5$)	0.935 mg	0.954 mg	0.850 mg	n/a	n/a	n/a	2.181 mg	2.257 mg	1.387 mg
Pyridoxine (B$_6$)	0.336 mg	0.300 mg	0.272 mg	0.368	0.378	0.419	1.303 mg	1.300 mg	0.978 mg
Folic Acid (B$_9$)	43 mcg	38 mcg	41 mcg	n/a	n/a	n/a	79 mcg	281 mcg	352 mcg
Ascorbic Acid (C)	0 mg	0 mg	0 mg	0 mg	0 mg	0 mg	0 mg	0 mg	6.0 mg
Tocopherol (E)	1.01 mg	1.01 mg	1.01 mg	1.01 mg	1.01 mg	1.01 mg	1.49 mg	14.07 mg	n/a

* Dried grass

thrive despite hardships and has for millennia been the most important food crop produced in most Mediterranean countries. The most esteemed durums have jewel-like, near-transparent kernels that are a lustrous, beautiful, amber-yellow color. Durum wheat makes especially excellent pasta because of its hard starch granules, which stick together.

Hard wheat is a bronze-colored wheat with a high gluten content that is used for bread. It is gluten (from the protein in the starchy center—the endosperm—of the grain) that imparts elastic and tenacious consistency to dough and allows the leavening and rising process. Color and growing season also are indicative of gluten content: red wheat tends to be higher in gluten than white wheat, and spring wheat is generally higher in gluten than winter wheat. Hard spring wheat is a fast-growing wheat cultivated where the winters are severe; sown in the spring and harvested in the fall, it is the wheat of choice for bread making. Hard winter wheat is cultivated where winters are mild; it is sown in the fall, at which time it germinates, but then lies dormant through the winter and starts growing again in the spring. Harvested in the late spring or early summer, winter wheat is normally higher in minerals because it has a longer growing season and thus establishes a more extensive root system.

Soft wheat is a light golden color and is often called white wheat. With more starch and less gluten than hard wheat, it is less suited to bread making; however, the fluffier grains make it a good choice for cakes, pastries, desserts, and sauces. As with hard wheat, soft wheat may be either a winter or a spring variety.

BYPRODUCTS

Bulgur, also known as **wheat pilaf,** is made from wheat berries that have been pearled (the bran removed), steamed, dried, and then cracked into a variety of textures. This process yields a quicker-cooking, lighter-textured, and nuttier-flavored dish than does cracked or whole wheat. The difference between bulgur and cracked wheat is that cracked wheat has simply been cracked but not yet cooked, while bulgur has been cooked; bulgur will be uniform in color, while cracked wheat will have a lighter-colored interior. Bulgur originated in the Middle East, where it is a dietary staple, much like rice in Asia and kasha in Russia. Since conservation of fuel was and still is of great importance, large quantities of wheat berries were processed into bulgur, then cooked quickly in small batches for daily consumption. The original method was to roast it in open braziers, dry it in the sun, then crack it with a mortar and pestle. Today the methods have been mechanized, but the basic process remains similar. Dark bulgur has a slightly stronger taste and is made from hard red wheat, while white bulgur is made from soft white wheat and has a more delicate flavor. When cooked, bulgur swells to a fluffy texture similar in appearance to couscous, and the two can often be used interchangeably. It is the main ingredient in the Lebanese dish tabbouleh and can be used in salads, pilafs, casseroles, stuffings, and bread doughs. As bulgur is a whole-grain product, it does become rancid. Purchase bulgur that smells fresh and nutty, and store it in airtight containers in the refrigerator or freezer.

Couscous is the steamed, dried, and cracked grains of durum wheat, using only the inner starchy endosperm (although a whole-wheat couscous is now available). More refined than bulgur, it has a pale creamy color, a

Sprouted	Dry Whole-Grain Bulgur	Cooked Whole-Grain Bulgur	Dry Couscous	Cooked Couscous
198	342	83	376	112
7.49 g	12.29 g	3.08 g	12.76 g	3.79 g
1.27 g	1.33 g	0.24 g	0.64 g	0.16 g
n/a	1.78 g	0.35 g	0.58 g	0.14 g
28 mg	35 mg	10 mg	24 mg	8 mg
2.14 mg	2.46 mg	0.96 mg	1.08 mg	0.38 mg
82 mg	164 mg	32 mg	44 mg	8 mg
200 mg	300 mg	40 mg	170 mg	22 mg
169 mg	410 mg	68 mg	166 mg	58 mg
16 mg	17 mg	5 mg	10 mg	5 mg
1.650 mg	1.930 mg	0.570 mg	0.830 mg	0.260 mg
0.261 mgr	0.335 mg	0.075 mg	0.247 mg	0.041 mg
1.858 mg	3.048 mg	0.609 mg	0.780 mg	0.084 mg
66,000 IU*	n/a	n/a	n/a	n/a
0.225 mg	0.232 mg	0.057 mg	0.163 mg	0.063 mg
0.155 mg	0.115 mg	0.028 mg	0.078 mg	0.027 mg
3.087 mg	5.114 mg	1.000 mg	3.490 mg	0.983 mg
0.947 mg	1.045 mg	0.344 mg	1.243 mg	0.371 mg
0.265 mg	0.342 mg	0.083 mg	0.110 mg	0.051 mg
n/a	27 mcg	18 mcg	20 mcg	15 mcg
2.6 mg	0 mg	0 mg	0 mg	0 mg
n/a	0.06 mg	n/a	n/a	n/a

Wheat has long been the symbol of prosperity, fertility, abundance, and life. All ancient fertility gods and goddesses of harvest, from the Hittite Ibritz and the Egyptian Nepri and Isis to the Greek Demeter and Roman Ceres, took wheat as one of their symbols. For it was the fertility gods and goddesses who looked after the continuance of the race both from within itself, by begetting children, and from without, in assuring that there would always be sufficient food to eat. Following mother's milk, wheat was—in the fullest sense of the word—the principal food, the veritable staff of life for people of European and Mideastern ancestry. Wheat in a sheaf, as well as being the emblem of agriculture and fertility, stands for autumn, harvest, and death. This is consistent with fertility gods of ancient myth, who died (and were resurrected) yearly for the benefit of humankind. Bearded wheat stands for faithfulness, rejuvenating fire, and the vital (including sexual) urge.

The great religious significance of bread goes back to the proud days of ancient Rome, when bread was so important that a special goddess of the ovens, Fornax, was honored each year by placing flowers over all ovens. Bakers, usually freed slaves, were not permitted to change their vocations, and their sons had to follow in their fathers' floury footsteps. For Christians, bread symbolizes the body of Christ; bread in the form of wafers plays a central role in the fundamental Christian sacrament of Holy Communion, while Christ himself said, "I am the bread of life." In Italy, each and every loaf of bread is an extension of the church wafer. Bakers cross themselves to bless the bread before closing the oven door. Leave a knife in a loaf and you have put a knife into the heart of Jesus; be prepared for bad luck. Placing a loaf upside down on the table or dropping a slice on the floor brings more bad luck. Purgatory is the punishment for wasting bread. For Jews too, bread—in the form of matzoh, an unleavened bread—has major religious significance, for it is eaten during Passover to symbolize their escape from Egyptian bondage more than three thousand years ago.

pleasant light texture, and a pastalike flavor when cooked. It is the main ingredient of the North African dish of the same name, but it is also delicious served with vegetable stew, used in place of rice, mixed with vegetables or salad ingredients, or made into desserts and cakes. The nutritional benefits of couscous are similar to any refined pasta product. The name is derived from an Arabic word meaning "to pulverize or crush."

Cracked wheat consists of whole wheat berries that are machine-cracked into coarse or medium granulation. Not to be confused with bulgur, cracked wheat has a white interior, while bulgur (because it is cooked) has a uniform coloring. Cracked wheat has an agreeably wheaty flavor and can replace rice or other grains in most recipes; baked or boiled, it makes an excellent substitute for rice with its fairly sticky texture and slight crunchiness. It also makes a popular breakfast cereal and is good added to casseroles, soups, and breads or substituted for bulgur in tabbouleh and other main dishes. For better flavor and greater nutritional value,

purchase whole wheat and coarsely grind it yourself at home in a flour mill or blender rather than purchasing the commercial variety.

Diastatic malt is made by sprouting wheat berries until the sprouts are the same length as the grain, which takes about two days. Drain well, spread in thin layers on large baking sheets, and dry in an oven at 150 degrees Fahrenheit, maximum, for about eight hours. The dried sprouts can then be ground into a meal that keeps indefinitely in a tightly closed glass jar stored in the refrigerator or freezer. The malt is good for baking loaves of bread without some sort of sweetener added. The action of the malt enzymes on the yeast and flour improves the flavor and appearance of a loaf of bread; it also gives the bread a finer texture and helps it stay fresh longer. Use only one tablespoon for a batch of dough yielding three or four loaves of bread; too much will make bread overly sweet, dark, and sticky.

Farina, also known as **cream of wheat,** can be made either from the whole grain minus the hull or simply from the inner starchy endosperm. Looking like minuscule white pellets, farina is generally used as a hot breakfast cereal and can also be used for desserts and dumplings. These "middlings," or small hard bits of wheat, were typically the middle product in the process of making wheat into flour. After the germ and bran were removed from the wheat, it was ground and bolted (sifted through a coarsely woven fabric) for the end product of flour; the granular nubbins that were too coarse to go through the cloth were called farina, the Italian word for "meal" or "flour."

Gluten is the protein found principally in wheat. When made into a dough, this protein becomes glutenous (elastic) and traps gas bubbles released from the yeast; in fact, without gluten, yeast cannot perform its leavening function. Most professional bakers and many home bakers add the pale yellow gluten flour to their bread dough. The addition of just 5 to 10 percent gluten flour significantly increases a dough's leavening power, which corresponds to a higher, lighter loaf. Unlike whole-grain flours, gluten has an indefinite shelf life because the germ has been refined away. Some people are allergic to gluten and so use the gluten-free grains, which are amaranth, corn, millet, quinoa, and rice.

Green wheat berries are the kernels of wheat picked while still green and unripe and then dried. They have a grassy flavor and are commonly used for casseroles, soups, stews, and pilafs; they can also be ground into flour.

Seitan is made from whole-wheat flour that is mixed with water, kneaded, and rinsed to remove the starch and some bran until a glutenous dough is obtained. After boiling in water, this dough is called kofu, which can be further processed into many forms, just one of which is seitan; by simmering kofu in a stock of tamari soy sauce, water, and kombu sea vegetable, the dough becomes seitan. Seitan typically comes in margarine-sized tubs. The thick brown paste can be used in sandwiches or as a meat substitute in cooked dishes.

Wheat berries are the whole grain, which can be cooked and eaten like rice, sprouted into wheat grass, or ground into flour. Available in either hard or soft varieties, cooked whole wheat berries provide more jaw exercise than other grains and thus are rarely eaten.

Wheat bran accounts for about 15 percent of the wheat kernel and is composed of six fibrous protective outer layers of the grain. A byproduct of white-flour produc-tion, wheat bran is relatively rich in nutrients but less so than wheat germ. Typically added to provide bulk and fiber for the deficient American diet, it is used in breakfast cereals, casseroles, and baked goods. It is highly recommended as a natural cure for constipation. Better than just adding the bran, however, would be to remove refined products from the diet and substitute whole-grain versions.

Wheat flakes, also known as **rolled wheat,** are wheat berries that have been heated and pressed in the same manner as rolled oats. The flakes are quick cooking and can be used as a hot breakfast cereal, for muesli, or in baked goods.

Wheat germ is the heart of the wheat, the embryo from which the new plant grows. Although it comprises only 2 to 3 percent of the whole wheat berry, it is nutritionally the densest part, being a rich source of protein, vitamin B complex, vitamin E, phosphorus, iron, and magnesium. Wheat germ is one of the very few places in nature in which the entire vitamin B complex is found. Widely available as a waste product from the milling of white flour, it comes either raw or toasted. Raw wheat germ goes rancid within seventy-two hours of milling and even faster if it is not refrigerated. Rancidity occurs because most wheat germ is rolled into flakes, which breaks open the sac containing the wheat germ oil and exposes it to air. Since its vitamin E content acts an antioxidant, there is a brief grace period. But you can be almost certain that if the wheat germ flakes were not vacuum-packed within the day they were rolled, they will be rancid. Most people have not tasted fresh, sweet, raw wheat germ, since most of that sold in stores is not of the highest quality. Unrolled wheat germ, variously known as embryo, chunk, or unflaked wheat germ, is the best form of this product, but it is hard to find. Thus it is better to buy the lightly toasted kind, which, although it may have slightly fewer nutrients, is still beneficial in the diet and has a pleasant nutty flavor. Wheat germ has traditionally been added to cereals, fruit, and breads. The best way to get wheat germ, however, is to eat whole-grain products or the whole grain itself.

Wheat germ oil, an extract of the heart of the wheat berry, is generally consumed not as a cooking or salad oil but as a dietary supplement. However, wheat germ oil goes rancid rapidly once the bottle is opened (within a week). Not only are all the beneficial vitamins, including the all-important vitamin E, destroyed when wheat germ oil turns rancid, but the harmful chemicals created by the process of oxidation can cause many serious health disorders on their own, including cancer. Quality wheat germ oil is rich in inositol, which enhances the metabolism of fats, thereby reducing the excretory burden on skin. It also contains pyridoxine, which enhances peristalsis and improves digestion, assimilation of nutrients, and elimination of wastes; octacosanol, which protects the heart and improves heart function; and high amounts of zinc and vitamin E. Consuming wheat germ oil between meals or when the stomach is empty will allow the nutrients to be better utilized and less affected by any rancid fats that may be present in the digestive tract.

Wheatgrass is wheat that has been sprouted to the point where it resembles grass. Young grass less than four days old may be finely cut and added to salads or blended with other foods. When using it with cooked foods, do not cook it with the food but add just before serving. Older grass can be chewed to extract the juice (the pulp is then spit out) or juiced in a special grinder. Wheatgrass has been known for centuries for its healing qualities and as a blood detoxifier and purifier. It is a very active solvent that works directly on the liver to release old medicines, drugs, nicotine, chemicals from food, and other toxins, and it stimulates the liver's rejuvenation abilities. It is also very alkalinizing to the bowel and soothing to ulcers, cuts, and abrasions of all kinds, both inside and out. Wheatgrass efficiently neutralizes the toxicity of sodium fluoride, which is used in the fluoridation of tap water (and as a rat poison). It may be taken internally, used as a wash for throat and eyes, or as a topical application (scalp tonic, cleanser). Chlorophyll makes up nearly 70 percent of the plant's solid content and is its most important nutrient; nearly identical to human blood, chlorophyll differs only in that it uses magnesium as a bond instead of iron. Wheatgrass contains virtually a full selection of minerals, vitamins, enzymes, and protein. If grown in rich soil, it can pick up more than 90 minerals out of the estimated possible 102. Cereal grasses offer unique digestive enzymes not available in such concentration in other foods—enzymes that help resolve indigestible and toxic substances in food. Also present are the antioxidant enzyme superoxide dismutase (SOD) and the special fraction P4D1, both of which slow cellular

deterioration and mutation and are therefore useful in the treatment of degenerative disease and in the reversal of aging. People with allergies to wheat or other cereals are almost never allergic to them in their grass stage.

Wheatgrass juice is an extract made from cut wheatgrass, juiced in a special wheatgrass press. The flavor has been described as so sweet that it borders on astringency and is therefore one that few people claim to enjoy. The juice can be mixed with other juices and is also available in tablet form. (Also see the **Wheatgrass** section above.)

VARIETIES OF FLOUR

Flour is a soft, dry powder that is usually ground from grain, though it can also be made from vegetables, fruits, legumes, or nuts. Wheat flours are available in many forms, most of which are high in gluten and excellent for bread making and general baking. The refining of flour can drastically change the content and proportion of vitamins, minerals, protein, and even in some cases toxic contaminants. When whole wheat is milled into white flour, 83 percent of the nutrients are removed, leaving a product that is so useless as a food that it must be fortified with synthetic vitamins. As Henry A. Schroeder, M.D., points out in his book *Trace Elements and Man*, "The milling of wheat into refined white flour removes 40 percent of the chromium, 86 percent of the manganese, 76 percent of the iron, 89 percent of the cobalt, 68 percent of the copper, 78 percent of the zinc, and 48 percent of the molybdenum, all trace elements essential for life or health. Only iron, and that in a form poorly absorbed, is later added to flour. The residue, or millfeeds, rich in trace elements, is fed to our domestic animals. And by the same process, most of eight vitamins are removed from wheat, three are added to make the flour enriched; millfeeds are rich in vitamins. Likewise, most of the bulk elements are removed from wheat: 60 percent of the calcium, 71 percent of the phosphorus, 85 percent of the magnesium, 77 percent of the potassium, 78 percent of the sodium, which appear in millfeeds. While some people disdain whole-wheat flour products because they are denser, others prefer them because of their hearty, full-bodied flavor. White flour has little or no flavor of its own; it relies on other ingredients for flavor. A naturally leavened bread made of fresh, stone-ground whole-wheat flour, pure water, and sea salt is incomparable in texture and flavor to any other bread. It has multiple nuances of flavor and is fundamentally satisfying. Stone-ground flour is the highest quality available, since the oil in the germ is distributed evenly throughout the flour, and the flour is not overly heated during milling. High-speed mills heat the flour, which turns the oil rancid, and do not distribute the oil evenly, thus creating masses of rancid oil that flavor the flour and spoil it.

American interest in unrefined flour arose over a century ago and was primarily the result of the efforts of one man, Sylvester Graham (1794–1851), for whom graham crackers and graham flour are named. In his remarkable little book, *Treatise on Bread and Bread-Making*, published in Boston in 1837, Graham very concisely gave the history of bread, the virtues of not discarding any part of the grain, and the chemistry and techniques of bread making, and he vigorously attacked the use of noxious ingredients by the bakers. The facts that he assembled, the force of his logic, and the apparent success of those who followed his advice made converts on a wide scale.

It has been found by experiment that if cattle are fed on grain from which the germ has been removed, they will continue to gain in weight and appear to remain in perfect health. But before many months they begin to drop dead from heart failure. There is no warning in their behavior and no apparent change in their condition of health (Gullickson, T. and Calverley, E. E., "Cardiac Failure in Cattle on Vitamin E-free Rations as Revealed by Electrocardiograms." *Science*, 104: 312–313, 1946).

Proper storage of flour is extremely important. White flour will not deteriorate for several years, even if left out in an open container. Whole-wheat or unbleached flour, however, contains all its vital nutrients and thus will not only go rancid quickly but may also attract unwanted insects. Ideally, fresh-ground flour should be used within five days of milling, but it will last approximately three months refrigerated and six months to a year frozen. If the flour does become infested, you can use it as is with the extra protein, sift out the insects and eggs, and then either use or freeze it for later use, or throw out the whole offending lot.

All-purpose/enriched flour, the flour with which most people are familiar, is the ultimate result of modern milling techniques. It is consistently fine, soft, and pure white, blends well with other ingredients, and keeps indefinitely on the shelf. Milled from the starchy endosperms of a blend of hard and soft wheat, this flour does not contain the germ or bran, which are rich in minerals, vitamins, proteins, and fiber. The freshly milled flour is slightly yellow; to whiten it manufacturers may add up to thirty chemicals (such as benzoyl peroxide or acetone peroxide) to make it whiter and fluffier and also to improve its workability as dough. This processing gives the flour more immediate gluten-producing potential. The manufacturer may also add a number of additives, such as emulsifiers, colorings, flavorings, preservatives, and antioxidants, to prolong shelf life. Enriched flour is so called because of the addition of three synthetic B vitamins and iron to replace several times as many natural factors. This serves to aggravate the effects of deficiency of those factors not added. The most important result of this aggravation is the development of liver disease that arises from the lack of the lipocaic group of the B complex. Other results of this deficiency can be allergies, angina pectoris, arteriosclerosis, diabetes, and gallbladder disease. In the dog-feeding tests on enriched flour, the animals had a tendency to become senile in deportment and drop dead suddenly in their tracks, just as the middle-aged

Wheat Flour / Nutritional Value Per 100 g Edible Portion					
	Whole Wheat	Enriched White Bread	Enriched White Cake	All-Purpose Enriched White	Enriched Semolina
Calories	339	361	362	364	360
Protein	13.70 g	11.98 g	8.20 g	10.33 g	12.68 g
Fat	1.87 g	1.66 g	0.86 g	0.98 g	1.05 g
Fiber	2.10 g	n/a	n/a	0.25 g	n/a
Calcium	34 mg	15 mg	14 mg	15 mg	17 mg
Iron	3.88 mg	4.41 mg	7.32 mg	4.64 mg	4.36 mg
Magnesium	138 mg	25 mg	16 mg	22 mg	47 mg
Phosphorus	346 mg	97 mg	85 mg	108 mg	136 mg
Potassium	405 mg	100 mg	105 mg	107 mg	186 mg
Sodium	5 mg	2 mg	2 mg	2 mg	1 mg
Zinc	2.930 mg	0.850 mg	0.620 mg	0.700 mg	1.050 mg
Copper	0.382 mg	0.182 mg	0.139 mg	0.144 mg	0.189 mg
Manganese	3.799 mg	0.792 mg	0.634 mg	0.682 mg	0.619 mg
Thiamine (B$_1$)	0.447 mg	0.812 mg	0.892 mg	0.785 mg	0.811 mg
Riboflavin (B$_2$)	0.215 mg	0.512 mg	0.430 mg	0.494 mg	0.571 mg
Niacin (B$_3$)	6.365 mg	7.554 mg	6.790 mg	5.904 mg	5.990 mg
Pantothenic Acid (B$_5$)	1.008 mg	n/a	0.458 mg	0.438 mg	0.580 mg
Pyridoxine (B$_6$)	0.341 mg	0.037 mg	0.033 mg	0.044 mg	0.103 mg
Folic Acid (B$_9$)	44 mcg	29 mcg	19 mcg	26 mcg	72 mcg
Tocopherol (E)	n/a	0.030 mg	0.040 mg	n/a	0.260 mg

businessman often dies, as reported daily in the newspapers. All-purpose flour is used for general cooking and baking purposes, but it does not perform as well as other flours.

Bolted wheat flour is produced through a refining technique developed by the Romans. The ground flour was sifted through bolts of finely woven silk fabric to remove hulls and up to 50 percent of the bran and germ. The light delicate loaves that could be prepared from such sifted flour were the prerogative of the privileged classes and were considered an enviable delicacy; in fact, to serve anything but white bread on a ceremonial occasion was considered an insult. Of limited availability today, bolted flour yields a bread with a higher volume than 100 percent whole-wheat flour and more nutritional value than white flour.

Bread flour is a high-gluten blend of 98 percent refined hard wheat flour, with malted barley to improve yeast activity. It may or may not contain potassium bromate to increase the gluten's elasticity.

Durum flour is made of 100 percent durum wheat and is used primarily for whole-wheat pasta.

Gluten flour is a mixture of wheat flour and gluten, the proteins of wheat that remain after the starch, bran, and germ are washed from the flour. Made to contain twice the gluten strength of regular bread flour, gluten flour is used as a strengthening agent with other flours that are low in gluten-producing potential. It is frequently found in commercial wheat bread and other baked goods.

Graham flour is named after its developer, Sylvester Graham, an American physician who in the early nineteenth century was already fighting for dietary reform. He spoke out against the atrocity of worthless white bread, saying thousands of people "eat the most miserable trash that can be imagined, in the form of bread, and never seem to think that they can possibly have anything better, nor even that it is an evil to eat such vile stuff as they do." Brown in color and coarse in texture, graham flour is the whole-wheat flour from winter wheat that has had the endosperm very finely ground and the bran layers and germ returned; it makes delicious if somewhat densely textured bread, which takes longer to rise than the white variety. Commercial graham flours will often have some of the germ removed to allow for a prolonged shelf life.

Granary flour is a blend of whole-wheat and rye flours, malted grains, and caramel. As its constituents suggest,

it has a slightly sweet, malted flavor and makes excellent bread and pastry.

Matzoh meal is made by grinding matzohs, Jewish unleavened crispbreads made of wheat flour and water, into meal consistency. Of medium or fine grind, matzoh meal is used for Jewish Passover cakes, to thicken soups, and in place of flour or bread crumbs.

Panocha is a flour ground from sprouted wheat, the sprouting process having converted carbohydrates into easily digestible simple sugars. Subtle yet satisfyingly sweet, panocha is a popular ingredient in Mexican holiday baked goods and can be found in the Southwest and in Latin American markets.

Self-raising flour is all-purpose white flour (see above) with additional salt, a leavening agent such as baking soda or baking powder, and an acid-releasing substance. The strength of the leavening agent deteriorates within two months, so it needs to be used immediately after purchase, especially in damp climates. Because of delays in merchandising or storing, the leavens may have already lost their potency by the time the flour is purchased. This flour is not recommended, since it is neither nutritious nor suitable for making breads or any leavened product; used in pastry, it gives a spongy rather than a flaky texture.

Semolina is a refined flour produced from the starchy inner endosperm of durum wheat. Semolina flour is not the same as semolina meal, which is a coarse-ground cereal like farina that is used like cornmeal. Semolina flour is most often used to make pasta and couscous because its chemical structure allows it to retain whatever shape it is made into, and it will not dissolve when boiled. It can also be used in gnocchi and desserts or as a tasty addition to Italian-style breads.

Unbleached wheat flour is all-purpose flour that has been spared the bleaching process, and which may or may not have some of the bran and germ added back in. For those who find 100 percent whole-wheat products too heavy, the addition of some unbleached flour will yield a lighter product. A more nutritious alternative is to buy a good multigrain flour, which also yields a lighter product.

Wheat germ flour is made by finely grinding raw wheat germ. It can be added to breads, cakes, and cookies, and lends a finer texture to baked goods than adding the unground wheat germ. This flour is very perishable and must be kept refrigerated or frozen.

White flour is made strictly from the starchy endosperm, with no additional bran or germ. Because the germ is the part that decomposes most readily, omitting it from the flour greatly increases the shelf life of the product. The bran, although it is not subject to spoilage, is also removed from the flour because it makes bread heavy and dark and interferes with the springy texture that is often desired. This flour is then bleached and treated with a multitude of chemicals to form a lighter, fluffier product. One of the substances added during the bleaching process is alloxan, which destroys the beta cells of the insulin-producing pancreas. After bleaching, white flour often has dough conditioners added that reduce the need for kneading. White flour can remain in the grocery store at room temperature almost indefinitely without becoming rancid, a boon for retailers but not for consumers. This fake food, with little or negative nutritional value, is an integral part of more than 90 percent of the baked products sold.

Whole-wheat bread flour is the finely ground grains of hard wheat kernels, where the germ, bran, and endosperm are all used. Since hard wheat contains a higher amount of gluten than soft wheat, this flour is ideal for bread making. Once milled, the oil in the wheat germ starts to oxidize and go rancid; store any whole-wheat flour in a cool dark place (preferably the refrigerator or freezer) and use within a month of milling. Flour with a bitter taste is rancid and should be discarded. The highest-quality flour is stone-ground; the oil released from the germ is distributed evenly throughout and is not rancid because it has not been heated to extremes.

Whole-wheat pastry flour is made from soft rather than hard wheat. Because soft wheat flour is lower in gluten, it is the preferred flour for pastries, cakes, cookies, and other delicate baked goods, although it can be mixed with hard wheat flour to make bread. This flour requires the same care as whole-wheat bread flour.

LEGUMES

Let me put my faith in the bean.
—Maxine Kumin, "Shelling Jacob's Cattle Beans"

LEGUMES

LEGUMES

A staple food throughout the world for thousands of years, beans are so ancient that the word frequently referred to any seed, and the original root word was probably associated with the Sanskrit verb "to eat." It was the Romans who gave the name *legumen* to all edible seeds that form in pods. The great merit of these seeds to past generations was that they could be dried and stored through the winter, to be made into purées and porridges or ground into flour, but they also have great food value when consumed fresh. The dried seeds of pod-bearing plants, which include all types of beans, peas, and lentils, are also known as pulses, a word that is linked to the Latin word *puls*, meaning "porridge," and the Greek *poltos*, meaning "poultice." The French call any vegetable a legume, while nutritionists name any bean, pea, peanut, or lentil a legume and botanists consider a leguminous fruit one that splits into two halves.

In ancient times beans and lentils were associated with men and women of immense strength and were consumed when preparing for strenuous activities. The Greeks and Romans made much use of pulses in their diet; chickpea and lupine seeds were sold hot in the streets, providing a nourishing, cheap meal for the poor, and Pliny, always ready to condemn the extravagant tastes of his time, highly recommended such economical fare. Roman literature contains many references to beans, though one is left with a feeling that they were considered a food more properly fit for the proletariat. Beans have also been the staple food of armies and navies from ancient Rome to the modern juggernauts, since they store easily and are not highly perishable. Legumes were crucial to the survival of the ancient Indians of the Americas, both North and South; their dried beans frequently saw them through the harsh winters. The history of beans in the Massachusetts Colony of Boston dates as far back as the middle of the seventeenth century, when beans were used for elections each year—white beans for "yea" votes, black beans for "nays" or abstentions.

As food plants, the bean family comes a close second to the grasses. It covers the immense range of beans, peas, and lentils, as well as clovers, vetches, and alfalfa. Many of these plants not only furnish food for humans and animals but also provide edible oils, fibers, and raw materials for industry. Soybeans and peanuts yield oils. Tamarind and carob provide intense flavorings. Gum arabic and gum tragacanth are used extensively in food production. Ornamental members of the family include acacia, mimosa, and wisteria.

Legumes add color, variety, texture, taste, and protein to the diet, so do not avoid them because of their notorious flatulent reputation. This reputation stems from the fact that they are one of the most difficult foods of the vegetable realm to digest. Because the human digestive system cannot break down some of the complex trisaccharide sugars (stachyose and raffinose) found in legumes, they end up intact in the large intestine, where bacteria ferment them and produce carbon dioxide and hydrogen, the two main components of gastrointestinal gas. Fortunately, you can make your beans more user-friendly by following these tips: (1) Soak the beans overnight in an appropriate amount of water. This leaches out not only the indigestible sugars but also the phytic acid that is bound with the minerals, thus making the minerals more bioavailable. Ideally, soak beans until they are uniformly soft. This may take from two to twenty-four hours, depending upon the variety. For long soaking, refrigerate to prevent the beans from souring. If the beans are unrefrigerated or in a hot and humid kitchen, change the soaking water after eight hours or when it develops bubbles. Beans that do not need to be soaked are lentils, split peas, and aduki beans. (2) Never cook beans in their soaking water, which contains large amounts of the indigestible natural sugars. Drain the soaked beans and add fresh liquid before thorough cooking. (3) Try adding a pinch of ginger, Mexican epazote (an herb with a flavor similar to cilantro), Indian asafetida (also known as hing), or summer savory to the beans during cooking. These spices cut down on production of gas as well as add flavoring. (4) Sprout the beans first by soaking for eight hours, then draining and rinsing twice daily for two days. Sprouting increases their protein content, decreases their starch content, and shortens their cooking time. It also helps provide more bulk and nutrition without increased cost, and the sprouting process greatly reduces the aftereffects of stomach gas. (5) Keep your meals simple. A staple dinner of rice, beans, and vegetables is less likely to cause flatulence than one that also contains bread, fruit, and dairy products.

Purchase beans from a bulk bin or in a see-through wrapper. Favor those with a vibrant look, for they will be the current crop, and buy only a pound or so at a time. Dull, faded beans are older and tougher and take longer to cook. Select well-formed legumes with few broken, chipped, or split seeds. Uniformity of shape and color is not desirable—it indicates a hybrid, which is less vital than an heirloom variety. A bean's color indicates the organ it most benefits, and so while beans as a category strengthen the kidneys, green-colored beans, like mung beans and split peas, also benefit the liver; red beans, including aduki and kidney beans, influence the heart; yellow beans, like chickpeas and soybeans, support the spleen and pancreas; and navy, lima, and other white beans energize the lungs and colon. Black beans are doubly supportive to the kidneys.

Beans help reduce blood cholesterol, control insulin and blood sugar, lower blood pressure, regulate colon functions, and prevent constipation. Nearly all peas, beans, and lentils are recommended for cleansing arteries, partly because legumes are a good source of choline, a lipotrophic agent that controls fat metabolism; choline is also a primary component of lecithin. They are a superior carbohydrate for people with diabetes or blood sugar imbalances, since they are slowly digested and cause only a gradual rise in blood sugar levels.

Aduki/Adzuki Bean
(*Phaseolus angularis*)
Also Known As: Azuki, Adsuki, Asuki

The scientific name *Phaseolus* was bestowed in 39 B.C. by Calumella, who observed that the seed looks like a "small boat"; *angularis* means "angular" or "angled." The English name *aduki* comes from the Japanese name *azuki*, which means "good health."

General Information
Adukis have been cultivated for millennia in China and Japan, where they are known as the "king of beans." Brought to America from Japan in 1854 by Admiral Perry, this small dark bean, about a quarter inch long and oval in shape, looks almost too good to eat, more like a polished stone to be treasured than a mere dried bean. They are usually dark red with a thin white line down the ridge, although straw-colored, brown, and even black aduki beans can be found. Adukis imported from Japan are lightly polished to a bright sheen and are the most costly. Domestic and Chinese adukis are not polished and as a result have a just-noticeable gritty texture.

Aduki/Adzuki Bean / Nutritional Value Per 100 g Edible Portion	Dried Raw	Dried Cooked
Calories	329	128
Protein	19.87 g	7.52 g
Fat	0.53 g	0.10 g
Fiber	5.26 g	2.02 g
Calcium	66 mg	28 mg
Iron	4.98 mg	2.00 mg
Magnesium	127 mg	52 mg
Phosphorus	381 mg	168 mg
Potassium	1,254 mg	532 mg
Sodium	5 mg	8 mg
Zinc	5.040 mg	1.770 mg
Copper	1.094 mg	0.298 mg
Manganese	1.730 mg	0.573 mg
Beta Carotene (A)	17 IU	6 IU
Thiamine (B₁)	0.455 mg	0.115 mg
Riboflavin (B₂)	0.220 mg	0.064 mg
Niacin (B₃)	2.630 mg	0.717 mg
Ascorbic Acid (C)	0 mg	0 mg

LORE AND LEGEND
Since the Han Dynasty in China (206 B.C.–A.D. 220), red beans have meant good fortune because of their color and are eaten without fail on festive occasions. This tradition was adopted by the Japanese, and a steamed glutinous rice and red bean dish is consumed at birthdays, weddings, and on New Year's—at which time the bean is also scattered about the house to keep bad spirits away.

Culinary Uses
Aduki beans can be eaten pod and all if picked young and tender. Cook them as you would snap beans. Mature shelled beans have a creamy texture and a pleasant nutty flavor. Those who follow a macrobiotic regimen use them in an endless variety of ways—alone as a vegetable, mixed with rice or other grains to give them a festive pink hue, in soups, and even as pie filling. In the Orient aduki beans are eaten fresh, dried, sprouted, mashed into a sweet candied paste, and sometimes ground into flour. Sprouted, they taste very similar to mung beans, but when cooked they are a little chewier; they require from eight to ten minutes of cooking instead of the three or four typical for mung bean sprouts. Aduki beans are also available powdered or in a paste form, which consists of mashed red beans, shortening, and sugar.

Health Benefits
Adukis are one of the most digestible beans and are reputedly healers of the kidneys.

Black-Eyed Bean/Pea
(*Vigna unguiculata, V. sinensis, Dolichos unguiculatus*)
Also Known As: Black-Eyed Suzies, Cow Peas, Southern Peas, Lobia Dal, Lady Peas, Cream Peas, Brown-Eyed Peas, Crowder Peas, China Peas

The genus *Vigna* was named in honor of Dominic Vigni, a seventeenth-century Paduan commentator on Theophrastus. *Dolichos* comes from a Greek word meaning "long" or "racecourse." The term *unguiculatus* means "clawed" or "clawlike"; *sinensis* means "of Chinese origin." The English name comes from the fact that the beans have a black area known as an eye on one side.

LORE AND LEGEND

Black-eyed peas, traditionally eaten on New Year's Day, are supposed to bring luck for the following year.

General Information

Since this bean is related to the mung bean and other Chinese legumes, it is thought to have originated in China. From there it probably traveled by sea to the Arabic countries and into Africa, where it is still found growing wild. It reached the West Indies before the mainland of North America, probably arriving in Jamaica about 1674. When it arrived in the southern United States, the bean became known as the black-eyed pea from the black spot on one end; it is also sometimes called the blackeye bean, or simply the blackeye. Black-eyed beans are similar to small haricot beans, medium in size (about half an inch long), creamy white in color, slightly kidney-shaped, and plump, with an irregular dark purple or black circle along the ridge of the bean.

Black-Eyed Bean/Pea / Nutritional Value Per 100 g Edible Portion

	Fresh Raw	Fresh Cooked	Dried Raw	Dried Cooked	Canned	Young Pods Raw	Young Pods Cooked
Calories	90	97	336	116	77	44	34
Protein	2.95 g	3.17 g	23.52 g	7.73 g	4.74 g	3.30 g	2.60 g
Fat	0.35 g	0.38 g	1.26 g	0.53 g	0.55 g	0.30 g	0.30 g
Fiber	1.80 g	1.94 g	4.58 g	2.31 g	0.68 g	1.70 g	1.70 g
Calcium	126 mg	128 mg	110 mg	24 mg	20 mg	65 mg	55 mg
Iron	1.10 mg	1.12 mg	8.27 mg	2.51 mg	0.97 mg	1.00 mg	0.70 mg
Magnesium	51 mg	52 mg	184 mg	53 mg	28 mg	n/a	n/a
Phosphorus	53 mg	51 mg	424 mg	156 mg	70 mg	65 mg	49 mg
Potassium	431 mg	418 mg	1,112 mg	278 mg	172 mg	215 mg	196 mg
Sodium	4 mg	4 mg	16 mg	4 mg	299 mg	4 mg	3 mg
Zinc	1.010 mg	1.030 mg	3.370 mg	1.290 mg	0.700 mg	n/a	n/a
Copper	0.130 mg	0.133 mg	0.845 mg	0.268 mg	0.117 mg	n/a	n/a
Manganese	0.560 mg	0.572 mg	1.528 mg	0.475 mg	0.283 mg	n/a	n/a
Beta Carotene (A)	817 IU	791 IU	50 IU	15 IU	13 IU	1,600 IU	1,400 IU
Thiamine (B$_1$)	0.110 mg	0.101 mg	0.853 mg	0.202 mg	0.076 mg	0.150 mg	0.090 mg
Riboflavin (B$_2$)	0.145 mg	0.148 mg	0.226 mg	0.055 mg	0.074 mg	0.140 mg	0.090 mg
Niacin (B$_3$)	1.450 mg	1.403 mg	2.075 mg	0.495 mg	0.354 mg	1.200 mg	0.800 mg
Pantothenic Acid (B$_5$)	0.151 mg	0.154 mg	1.496 mg	0.411 mg	0.190 mg	n/a	n/a
Pyridoxine (B$_6$)	0.067 mg	0.065 mg	0.357 mg	0.100 mg	0.045 mg	n/a	n/a
Folic Acid (B$_9$)	168.0 mcg	127.0 mcg	632.6 mcg	207.9 mcg	51.2 mcg	n/a	n/a
Ascorbic Acid (C)	2.5 mg	2.2 mg	1.5 mg	0.4 mg	2.7 mg	33.0 mg	17.0 mg

Culinary Uses

Very young, unripe black-eyed beans in the pod are used the same way as green beans. The adult beans are savory and robust, with a subtle, earthy, yet sweet, nutty flavor and a smooth, buttery texture. Used fresh or dried, they are excellent in salads or combined with steamed greens. They are particularly useful because they cook in about forty minutes without soaking. Black-eyed peas are the basis for the famous dish Hoppin' John, a mixture of black-eyed peas and rice.

Broad/Fava Bean
(*Vicia faba, Faba vulgaris*)
Also Known As: Horse Beans, Daffa Beans, Windsor Beans, Grosse Bohnen

Vicia is a classical name for the vetch family (a type of legume) and is believed to come from the Latin *vincire*, meaning "to bind" or "to twist." *Faba* comes from the Greek *phago*, meaning "to eat," as this plant yields edible seeds. The specific term *vulgaris* means "common." As its English name suggests, the broad bean is substantial in size.

General Information

The broad bean is considered native to the Mediterranean basin, with seeds being found in Egypt dating back to between 2400 and 2200 B.C. A large bean—about 1¼ inches long—resembling a lima in size, it is light brown in color and oval in shape, with a dark line running down the ridge where it is split. As a vegetable the broad bean retained its popularity in Europe not only because it could be dried and saved for eating later but also because for many centuries it was the only readily available bean. So important was it, together with other pulses, that from the early Middle Ages onward there was a death sentence for theft from open fields of beans, peas, and lentils. It has remained a favorite throughout the major continents, with the exception of North America, where it is just now becoming widely available. Ful medames are a small variety of broad bean widely eaten in the Middle East; its white counterpart is called ful nabed. This smaller variety has given its name to one of Egypt's national dishes (ful medames), in which the beans are baked with eggs, cumin, and garlic. The name is thought to derive from *mudammas*, meaning "buried," because a dish was cooked by being buried in hot ashes and left overnight. *Ful* is simply the Arabic word for the fava bean.

Culinary Uses

Fresh fava beans are large, flat, and oval, with a firm creamy texture and dainty, nutty taste. Young beans are quite tender, but as they mature, the skin covering the bean becomes coarser and tougher. Older beans need this coarse outer skin removed or "slipped" before they are eaten. If you are fortunate enough to be in possession of young beans, cook them whole. Simply trim the ends, rinse, and cook in boiling water for four to five minutes. The young pods are unexpectedly filling, and you will find one pound in weight will happily satisfy six to eight people as a side dish. Dried favas look like large lima beans and have a mealy, granular texture and an assertive flavor; they need long, slow cooking and their thick skins peeled before eating. Favas can be eaten on their own, in casseroles, or in salads. Served hot with melted butter, seasoned with salt and freshly ground pepper, and sprinkled with chopped parsley or basil, they are delicious. In most recipes, favas can be substituted for limas.

Broad/Fava Bean / Nutritional Value Per 100 g Edible Portion	Dried Raw	Dried Cooked	Canned
Calories	341	110	71
Protein	26.12 g	7.60 g	5.47 g
Fat	1.53 g	0.40 g	0.22 g
Fiber	2.97 g	0.95 g	0.42 g
Calcium	103 mg	36 mg	26 mg
Iron	6.70 mg	1.50 mg	1.00 mg
Magnesium	192 mg	43 mg	32 mg
Phosphorus	421 mg	125 mg	79 mg
Potassium	1,062 mg	268 mg	242 mg
Sodium	13 mg	5 mg	453 mg
Zinc	3.140 mg	1.010 mg	0.620 mg
Copper	0.824 mg	0.259 mg	0.109 mg
Manganese	1.626 mg	0.421 mg	0.288 mg
Beta Carotene (A)	53 IU	15 IU	10 IU
Thiamine (B$_1$)	0.555 mg	0.097 mg	0.020 mg
Riboflavin (B$_2$)	0.333 mg	0.089 mg	0.050 mg
Niacin (B$_3$)	2.832 mg	0.711 mg	0.960 mg
Pantothenic Acid (B$_5$)	0.976 mg	0.157 mg	0.119 mg
Pyridoxine (B$_6$)	0.366 mg	0.072 mg	0.045 mg
Folic Acid (B$_9$)	422.9 mcg	104.1 mcg	32.7 mcg
Ascorbic Acid (C)	1.4 mg	0.3 mg	1.8 mg

LORE AND LEGEND

In the Greek and Roman world the broad bean was highly regarded, although there have been some very curious beliefs regarding these beans. Herodotus (History, II.xxxvii) recounts that the Egyptian priests regarded broad beans with horror as unclean, and Pythagoras, who imported many Egyptian elements into his religion, similarly despised them. A tenet of his doctrine of metempsychosis is that souls may transmigrate into beans after death. This may have some connection with the fact that bean feasts traditionally ended funerals, and that they figured in rites to rid households of the evil effects occasioned by the nocturnal visits of lemurs, the wandering souls of the wicked (in England, several beans were placed in graves to keep ghosts away, and if you happened to see a ghost, you were to spit a bean at it). Yet broad beans were popular enough with the lay folk, to whom they were distributed by candidates for public office at election times. The politicians were not simply currying favor, since the beans were used as voting tokens during magisterial elections. This custom was later remarked upon by Plutarch, whose proverbial dictum *abstineto a fabis* (abstain from beans) passed into English. No one is sure now whether this was an injunction to refrain from politics and bribery, or from involvement in civil affairs (a continuing of the Pythagorean and priestly prejudice), or a warning against dabbling in the supernatural, since beans have been connected not only with ghosts and death but also with supernatural spirits and witches. Scottish witches, it was once believed, rode not on a broomstick but on a beanstalk. Since the Middle Ages (and earlier in Rome at the Saturnalian festivities, the holiday that became transformed into Twelfth Night), beans were the main ingredient in the Twelfth Night Cake, which also contained honey, flour, ginger, and pepper. This was a sacred cake: one portion was for God, one for the Holy Virgin, and three for the Magi. In Rome even now, a holiday cake is baked with one fava bean hidden inside; the one who gets the piece with the bean is crowned king (or queen) of the festivities.

Health Benefits

Fava beans provide nutritional benefits similar the kidney bean family.

Note: Favism is a painful blood condition brought on by eating fava beans or by inhaling the pollen from the flowering plant. Evidently this is an inborn error of metabolism, a genetic defect that causes the red blood cells to rupture after the individual comes in contact with them. There is no known way to remove or inactivate the responsible substances. Favism is thought to affect up to 35 percent of some Mediterranean populations and 10 percent of African Americans. Symptoms of favism include dizziness, nausea, and vomiting, followed by severe anemia.

Chickpea

(*Cicer arietinum*)

Also Known As: Garbanzo, Ceci, Gram, Kali Chana, Kabuli Chana

Cicer is the ancient Latin name for the vetch plant. *Arietinum* translates as "ramlike," since the ancient Romans thought the bean resembled a ram's head with curling horns. The curious name of *chickpea* that English has fastened to this Asiatic legume is either a phonetic adaptation of the original Latin *cicer* and the French *pois chiche*, or from the fact that the chickpea has a projecting nascent radicle that looks like a chicken's beak.

General Information

Chickpeas are said to have been first cultivated about 5000 B.C. in ancient Mesopotamia; they then migrated to the eastern Mediterranean, India, and other parts of Asia. They were introduced into Europe through Spain, where they are called garbanzos. Chickpeas do not resemble garden peas at all and are unlike other legumes in two ways. First, while beans and lentils are smooth-surfaced, a chickpea is not; it's wrinkled and roundish but compressed and flattened at the sides. Second, while most legumes share a pod with half a dozen or so other seeds, a chickpea has only one or rarely two mature peas per pod. Roughly the size and shape of small hazelnuts, these medium-sized (three-eighths of an inch) dried peas are usually tan-colored, but there are also other varieties—red, white, black, and a small, dark brown variety.

Culinary Uses

Chickpeas have a flavor that is full-bodied, nutty, and rich, reminiscent of chestnuts with a bit of crunch. A popular legume in many parts of the world, chickpeas are very hard and need to be soaked well before long, slow cooking. They are the most important of the pulse crops in India, where they are made into cakes, puddings, and savory dishes. In the Middle East, one of the two most popular puréed chickpea dishes is called humous, or hummus, a

savory spread made with sesame paste, garlic, and lemon; the other is falafel, a ball or patty made of ground chickpeas and spices that is fried as a fritter. Whole cooked chickpeas, which maintain their shape, can be used in salads, casseroles, and other dishes.

Health Benefits

pH 6.48–6.80. Among the legumes, the lowly chickpea is the most hypocholesteremic agent; germinated chickpeas were reported to be effective in controlling cholesterol levels in rat studies.

LORE AND LEGEND

There is a legend that the chickpea plant was cursed by the Virgin Mary because it refused to hide the Holy Family. Since the plant grows to only eighteen inches in height, the Holy Family would have had to be dwarfs to be hidden at all.

BYPRODUCTS

Chickpea flour, also known as **besan, gram,** or **garbanzo flour,** is made from ground chickpeas; in color it resembles corn flour, but it performs more like the flour ground from millet. This high-protein flour cooks dry and powdery, almost chalky, and lends a sweet, rich chickpea flavor. Since it is gluten-free, it is used only in small quantities for leavened breads. A good thickening agent for soups and stews, it needs to be stirred vigorously to eradicate all the lumps. In India, the flour mixed with water forms a batter that is used to coat foods for frying.

Jack Bean
(Canavalia ensiformis, C. gladiata)

Canavalia comes from an aboriginal name for the plant. *Ensiformis* and *gladiata* both mean "swordlike" or "sword-shaped."

General Information

Jack beans are native to the tropics of both hemispheres and were used in Mexico as early as 3000 B.C. Prostrate

Chickpea / Nutritional Value Per 100 g Edible Portion	Dried Raw	Dried Cooked	Canned
Calories	364	164	119
Protein	19.30 g	8.86 g	4.95 g
Fat	6.04 g	2.59 g	1.14 g
Fiber	4.09 g	2.50 g	1.36 g
Calcium	105 mg	49 mg	32 mg
Iron	6.24 mg	2.89 mg	1.35 mg
Magnesium	115 mg	48 mg	29 mg
Phosphorus	366 mg	168 mg	90 mg
Potassium	875 mg	291 mg	172 mg
Sodium	24 mg	7 mg	299 mg
Zinc	3.430 mg	1.530 mg	1.060 mg
Copper	0.847 mg	0.352 mg	0.174 mg
Manganese	2.204 mg	1.030 mg	0.604 mg
Beta Carotene (A)	67 IU	27 IU	24 IU
Thiamine (B$_1$)	0.477 mg	0.116 mg	0.029 mg
Riboflavin (B$_2$)	0.212 mg	0.063 mg	0.033 mg
Niacin (B$_3$)	1.541 mg	0.526 mg	0.138 mg
Pantothenic Acid (B$_5$)	1.588 mg	0.286 mg	0.299 mg
Pyridoxine (B$_6$)	0.535 mg	0.139 mg	0.473 mg
Folic Acid (B$_9$)	556.6 mcg	172.0 mcg	66.8 mcg
Ascorbic Acid (C)	4.0 mg	1.3 mg	3.8 mg

trailing or twining plants, they now grow wild in the tropics of Asia and Africa and are cultivated as vegetables in Australia. Although grown mainly as a green manure or fodder crop, the seedpods are quite edible. The pods reach a length of ten to fourteen inches, with the pod walls becoming very hard and dense when ripe. The large, white, turgid beans bear a prominent seed scar and are packed crosswise into the pod, embedded in a very thin, white, papery lining.

Culinary Uses
Pods of jack beans make passable snap beans when not more than four to six inches long. The beans, when roasted and ground, are also said to make a suitable coffee substitute.

Health Benefits
Low in fat and high in fiber.

Kidney Bean Family
(Phaseolus vulgaris)

The scientific name *Phaseolus* was bestowed in 39 B.C. by Calumella, who observed that the seed looks like a "small boat." The specific term *vulgaris* means "common." The bean takes its English name *kidney* from the anatomically suggestive shape and color of the seeds.

General Information
Kidney beans are an ancient cultivar of some seven thousand years ago from southwestern Mexico, where this common bean developed into hundreds of different varieties. In the sixteenth century Spanish explorers exported it to Europe, where it and its traveling companion, the potato, caused an entire revolution in eating habits.

Culinary Uses
Kidney beans have a robust flavor and a rich, creamy texture. The skins of these beans contain toxins that must be removed after the beans have been soaked by boiling them fast for ten minutes and then replacing this first cooking water with fresh water. Best known for their use in spicy Mexican dishes, kidney beans are also used in soups, casseroles, and salads. In the West Indies they are cooked with coconut milk, hot chilies, and herbs.

VARIETIES

There are now some five hundred varieties and many more subvarieties of kidney beans. Most people are only familiar with the ubiquitous red kidney bean, but there are many more varieties and colors to choose from.

Anasazi beans take their name from a Navajo word meaning "ancient ones." Cultivated in past centuries by the cliff-dwelling Anasazi Indians of the American Southwest, these beans are still grown and treasured by inhabitants of that region. Generally believed to be descendants of the Jacob's cattle bean, which they closely resemble, the beautiful, mottled-purple-and-white anasazi beans are a bit smaller and plumper but lack the distinguishing freckles. Their rich smoky flavor combines the best of both flavor and texture of pinto and kidney beans and may be freely substituted for either. Compared to other beans, anasazi are easier to digest, because they contain only one-fifth the complex sugars that tend to cause flatulence.

Appaloosa beans are an old legume grown in the Palouse area of eastern Washington State and northern Idaho, famed for the speckled horse of the same name. These comparatively large (three-quarters of an inch), thinly shaped beans are a beautiful creamy white with a distinguishing black diagonal splotch. Appaloosa beans have a tender texture with a rich, earthy, mushroom flavor. Wonderful in ethnic soups and stews, they are especially receptive to seasonings like jalapeños, fresh ginger, turmeric, and cilantro.

Black beans are small, oblong, matte black beans with creamy white flesh. Also known as turtle beans and frijoles negros, they are a staple throughout much of Latin America. These pea-sized beans have a strong, slightly sweet, earthy flavor and a soft, creamy texture. Very versatile, they make terrific chilies, bean pancakes, soups, and refried beans, and they also work well as part of a bean salad. They are the basis for feijoada, Brazil's once-weekly traditional national dish, as well as Cuban black bean soup with rum, and Moros y Cristianos (Moors and Christians), a dish of white rice and black beans.

Bolitas take their name from the Spanish term meaning "little ball." Also known as pink beans, bolitas are obviously a relative of the pinto bean but are highly irregular in size, shape, and color, looking as diverse as a

LORE AND LEGEND

The Egyptians made the kidney bean an object of sacred worship due to its close resemblance to the male testicle, and forbade its use as food. In Italy beans are distributed among the poor on the anniversary of a death.

handful of pebbles in a creek. Predominantly pink, but ranging from buff to yellow, bolitas have a sweet, rich, meaty flavor with a slightly mealy texture and may be used interchangeably in any pinto or kidney bean recipe.

Calypsos are named after the island nymph in Greek mythology who detained Odysseus on his journey home from Troy. A plump, nearly round, kidney-shaped bean with a dramatic appearance, calypsos are half white and half black, with the addition of one black polka dot for emphasis; this novel bean looks as though the ancient Chinese yin-and-yang symbol of harmony had been imprinted on its surface. Their smooth, silky texture makes them a terrific addition to soups and stews, and they are especially well suited to cuisine from India and the American Southwest.

Cannellini are white kidney beans originally cultivated in South America but associated with and extremely popular in central Italy, Greece, and France. These large white beans are sold in canned form and often used in Italian dishes. Their smooth, nutty flavor makes them a top choice for minestrone soup and other Mediterranean dishes.

China yellow beans, also known as sulfur beans, are not native to China but are a traditional bean from Maine. This small, oval, sulfur-colored bean possesses a silky soft texture and a mellow flavor. They are delicious simmered into a smooth purée with ginger, turmeric, and corn oil, and they make an excellent gravy for grains, pasta, or vegetables.

Cranberry beans, also known as **October beans, Romans, borlotti,** and **shellouts,** are a dark tan bean with a pink cast and wine-colored dappling. The pods of these beans resemble the bean itself, with wine-colored stripes on a cream background. About the same size as pinto beans, cranberry beans have a mealier texture but a sweeter, more delicate flavor. They become

tender very easily and absorb aromatic spices and herbs well, but in the process of cooking they lose their markings and become a solid pink color. In New England the beans, either freshly shelled or dried, are used in succotash, but they can be used in any recipe calling for kidney or pinto beans, in bean patties, with cooked pasta, or in casseroles, chilies, and soups.

European soldier beans received their name from the splash of color shaped in the silhouette of a soldier standing at attention. Chalk-white, kidney-shaped beans that are grown in Maine and other cool regions of North America, they are easily distinguished by their colored pattern. European soldiers are excellent in vegetable soups such as garbure or minestrone.

Flageolet get its name from a corruption of the Latin genus name *Phaseolus*, strengthened by an imagined likeness to the flutelike musical instrument of that name. A dwarf variety of the haricot, this "Rolls-Royce of beans" originated in the Americas but was commercially developed in France during the 1800s. Instead of being allowed to fully mature, the young beans are removed from their pods while still a soft pale green. Delicate in flavor, color, and texture, flageolets can be eaten fresh or dried but are best fresh, when their soft, creamy texture and delicate taste make them especially good as a vegetable or in salads. Just boil and serve with butter and freshly ground black pepper.

Great northern beans are larger than navy beans, flattish, slightly kidney-shaped, and bright white. They have a mild flavor and creamy texture that makes them ideal in any baked bean recipe or casserole, as well as in soups and stews.

Haricot/navy beans were such an integral part of the French traditional meat-and-vegetable stew known as hericoq that they eventually took over the name as their own. While in India, Alexander the Great encountered great fields of haricot beans. He ordered his cook to prepare them and was so pleased with the result that he brought a large quantity of the beans back to Europe, where they eventually became the fare of the lower classes. The term *haricot* usually refers to the large white haricot or to its smaller counterpart, the pearl haricot. Both have a slightly green undertone produced by pale veining. Haricots are probably best known for their use in commercial baked beans but are also a traditional ingredient of the French cassoulet. Navy beans, a smaller member of the large haricot family, are sometimes referred to as pea

Kidney Beans / Nutritional Value Per 100 g Edible Portion

	All Types Sprouted Raw	All Types Sprouted Cooked	Black Bean Dried Raw	Black Bean Dried Cooked	Bolita Dried Raw	Bolita Dried Cooked	Cranberry Dried Raw	Cranberry Dried Cooked	Great Northern Dried Raw	Great Northern Dried Cooked
Calories	29	33	341	132	343	149	335	136	339	118
Protein	4.20 g	4.83 g	21.60 g	8.86 g	20.96 g	9.06 g	23.03 g	9.34 g	21.86 g	8.33 g
Fat	0.50 g	0.58 g	1.42 g	0.54 g	1.13 g	0.49 g	1.23 g	0.46 g	1.14 g	0.45 g
Fiber	n/a	n/a	5.28 g	2.03 g	2.90 g	1.60 g	2.49 g	1.00 g	6.74 g	2.98 g
Calcium	17 mg	19 mg	123 mg	27 mg	130 mg	52 mg	127 mg	50 mg	175 mg	68 mg
Iron	0.81 mg	0.89 mg	5.02 mg	2.10 mg	6.77 mg	2.30 mg	5.00 mg	2.09 mg	5.47 mg	2.13 mg
Magnesium	21 mg	23 mg	171 mg	70 mg	182 mg	65 mg	156 mg	50 mg	189 mg	50 mg
Phosphorus	37 mg	38 mg	352 mg	140 mg	415 mg	165 mg	372 mg	135 mg	447 mg	165 mg
Potassium	187 mg	194 mg	1,483 mg	355 mg	1,464 mg	508 mg	1,332 mg	387 mg	1,387 mg	391 mg
Sodium	n/a	n/a	5 mg	1 mg	8 mg	2 mg	6 mg	1 mg	14 mg	2 mg
Zinc	n/a	n/a	3.650 mg	1.120 mg	2.550 mg	0.960 mg	3.630 mg	1.140 mg	2.310 mg	0.880 mg
Copper	n/a	n/a	0.841 mg	0.209 mg	0.810 mg	0.271 mg	0.794 mg	0.231 mg	0.837 mg	0.247 mg
Manganese	n/a	n/a	1.060 mg	0.444 mg	1.376 mg	0.548 mg	0.920 mg	0.370 mg	1.423 mg	0.518 mg
Beta Carotene (A)	2 IU	2 IU	17 IU	6 IU	0 IU	0 IU	2 IU	0 IU	3 IU	1 IU
Thiamine (B₁)	0.370 mg	0.362 mg	0.900 mg	0.244 mg	0.772 mg	0.257 mg	0.747 mg	0.210 mg	0.653 mg	0.158 mg
Riboflavin (B₂)	0.250 mg	0.273 mg	0.193 mg	0.059 mg	0.192 mg	0.063 mg	0.213 mg	0.069 mg	0.237 mg	0.059 mg
Niacin (B₃)	2.920 mg	3.024 mg	1.955 mg	0.505 mg	1.892 mg	0.570 mg	1.455 mg	0.515 mg	1.955 mg	0.681 mg
Pantothenic Acid (B₅)	n/a	n/a	0.899 mg	0.242 mg	0.997 mg	0.299 mg	0.748 mg	0.240 mg	1.098 mg	0.266 mg
Pyridoxine (B₆)	n/a	n/a	0.286 mg	0.069 mg	0.527 mg	0.175 mg	0.309 mg	0.081 mg	0.447 mg	0.117 mg
Folic Acid (B₉)	n/a	n/a	444.3 mcg	148.8 mcg	463.2 mcg	168.3 mcg	604.4 mcg	206.8 mcg	482.0 mcg	102.2 mcg
Ascorbic Acid (C)	38.7 mg	35.6 mg	0 mg	0 mg	0 mg	0 mg	0 mg	0 mg	5.3 mg	1.3 mg
Tocopherol (E)	n/a	n/a	n/a	n/a	n/a	n/a	n/a	n/a	n/a	n/a

beans because of their size. They received their name as a result of their universal (if not always acceptable) appearance aboard all ships at sea, including frigates, battleships, and submarines. Some packagers do not differentiate between navy beans, pea beans, and even great northern beans, and thus there may be several varieties in one package. French navy beans have a delicious baconlike flavor and a unique silken texture.

Jacob's cattle beans are also known as **coach dogs, dalmatian beans,** and **trout beans**. A relatively long (five-eighths of an inch), slim, creamy white bean with a large, dark maroon-colored splotch and tiny satellite freckles of the same color, Jacob's cattle beans have been grown in New England since colonial days and are a favorite of that region. They can be used interchangeably with anasazi or pinto beans and are excellent in bean salads. A favorite for baking, their taste strikes some people as similar to potatoes and others as like molasses. Their name is taken from the biblical story of Jacob and the spotted cattle.

Maine yellow eyes are also known as **molasses face,** so called for the brown pattern around the eye. They are small oval beans with a pale gold hue and a creamy texture. These beans are likely the original ingredient in Boston baked beans and are still used today instead of black-eyed peas for the southern dish Hoppin' John. They are delicious substituted for mung beans in the Indian stewed rice and bean dish kitcheree.

Pinto beans are native to India and are the most commonly grown bean in the United States after soybeans. This highly hybridized bean is identified by its squarish, blunt shape and its buff-to-pink coloring, which is splotched like a pinto pony. (The name means "painted" or "spotted" and derives from the Spanish *pinctus.*) Pinto beans have an earthy, full-bodied flavor and a mealy texture. They are the traditional bean used for tacos and frijoles refritos (refried beans) in southwestern and Mexican cooking; they are also used in chilies, soups (especially minestrone), salads, and pâtés. A high-yield pinto bean was hybridized in the 1930s and soon afterward, with encouragement from agricultural colleges and county farm agents, bean growers favored the more-bushel-per-acre pinto over regional

Navy Sprouted Raw	Navy Sprouted Cooked	Navy Dried Raw	Navy Dried Cooked	Pinto Dried Raw	Pinto Dried Cooked	Red Dried Raw	Red Dried Cooked	Great Northern Canned	Kidney Canned	Navy Canned	Pinto Canned
67	78	335	142	340	137	337	127	114	85	113	78
6.15 g	7.07 g	22.33 g	8.70 g	20.88 g	8.21 g	22.53 g	8.67 g	7.37 g	5.25 g	7.53 g	4.56 g
0.70 g	0.81 g	1.28 g	0.57 g	1.13 g	0.52 g	1.06 g	0.50 g	0.39 g	0.34 g	0.43 g	0.32 g
2.50 g	2.88 g	5.52 g	3.14 g	6.01 g	3.02 g	6.19 g	2.81 g	2.27 g	0.93 g	1.86 g	1.26 g
15 mg	16 mg	155 mg	70 mg	121 mg	48 mg	83 mg	28 mg	53 mg	24 mg	47 mg	37 mg
1.93 mg	2.11 mg	6.44 mg	2.48 mg	5.88 mg	2.61 mg	6.69 mg	2.94 mg	1.57 mg	1.26 mg	1.85 mg	1.61 mg
101 mg	111 mg	173 mg	59 mg	159 mg	55 mg	138 mg	45 mg	51 mg	28 mg	47 mg	27 mg
100 mg	103 mg	443 mg	157 mg	418 mg	160 mg	406 mg	142 mg	136 mg	94 mg	134 mg	92 mg
307 mg	317 mg	1,140 mg	368 mg	1,328 mg	468 mg	1,359 mg	403 mg	351 mg	257 mg	288 mg	301 mg
n/a	n/a	14 mg	1 mg	10 mg	2 mg	12 mg	2 mg	4 mg	341 mg	448 mg	416 mg
n/a	n/a	2.540 mg	1.060 mg	2.540 mg	1.080 mg	2.790 mg	1.070 mg	0.650 mg	0.550 mg	0.770 mg	0.690 mg
n/a	n/a	0.879 mg	0.295 mg	0.774 mg	0.257 mg	0.699 mg	0.242 mg	0.160 mg	0.150 mg	0.208 mg	0.140 mg
n/a	n/a	1.309 mg	0.556 mg	1.130 mg	0.556 mg	1.111 mg	0.477 mg	0.408 mg	0.242 mg	0.375 mg	0.229 mg
4 IU	4 IU	4 IU	2 IU	5 IU	2 IU	8 IU	0 IU	1 IU	0 IU	1 IU	1 IU
0.390 mg	0.381 mg	0.645 mg	0.202 mg	0.555 mg	0.186 mg	0.608 mg	0.160 mg	0.143 mg	0.105 mg	0.141 mg	0.101 mg
0.215 mg	0.235 m	0.232 mg	0.061 mg	0.238 mg	0.091 mg	0.215 mg	0.058 mg	0.060 mg	0.088 mg	0.055 mg	0.063 mg
1.220 mg	1.263 mg	2.063 mg	0.531 mg	1.446 mg	0.400 mg	2.110 mg	0.578 mg	0.461 mg	0.456 mg	0.487 mg	0.292 mg
n/a	n/a	0.680 mg	0.255 mg	0.763 mg	0.285 mg	0.780 mg	0.220 mg	0.278 mg	0.150 mg	0.172 mg	0.136 mg
n/a	n/a	0.437 mg	0.164 mg	0.443 mg	0.155 mg	0.397 mg	0.120 mg	0.106 mg	0.022 mg	0.103 mg	0.074 mg
n/a	n/a	369.7 mcg	139.9 mcg	506.3 mcg	172.0 mcg	394.1 mcg	129.6 mcg	81.3 mcg	50.6 mcg	62.3 mcg	60.2 mcg
18.8 mg	17.3 mg	3.0 mg	0.9 mg	7.3 mg	2.1 mg	4.5 mg	1.2 mg	1.3 mg	1.1 mg	0.7 mg	0.7 mg
n/a	n/a	0.34 mg	n/a	n/a	n/a	n/a	n/a	n/a	n/a	n/a	n/a

heirloom varieties. For greater flavor range and vitality, consider a nonhybrid such as pinquito, anasazi, or Jacob's cattle bean.

Lentil
(Lens culinaris esculenta, Vicia lens)

Lens is the ancient name for the lentil family, while *vicia* is the classical Latin name for the vetches, believed to derive from the Latin *vincire*, meaning "to bind" or "to twist." The term *culinaris* refers to the kitchen or food; *esculenta* means "esculent" or "edible." The English word *lentil* derives from a diminutive of the Latin *lens*.

General Information
The lentil is a small, pealike plant of the vetch family that produces small pods containing two lentils apiece. The plant probably originated in the Near East or Mediterranean region and still has an important dietary place there. Because of their Asian origin, many lentils are often referred to by their Indian names, as types of dal. Lentils were known in Egypt and India around 2000 B.C., and they were eaten by the ancient Jews, as indicated in the story of Esau, who renounced his birthright for a dish of lentils (pottage). Considered one of the most delicious and nutritious of the legumes, lentils are eaten throughout the world as an inexpensive source of protein. In Catholic countries lentils were standard Lenten fare for those who could not afford fish. Consistently cheap in comparison with most other available foods, lentils have earned the contempt of the snobbish and pretentious, who call them "poor man's meat," although they have simultaneously received praise from those capable of judging foods by criteria other than price. The country that consumes the greatest number of lentils is India, which grows more than fifty varieties.

Culinary Uses
In recent years lentils have become one of the most popular legumes, and a wide variety are used in Europe, the Middle East, India, and Africa. In the United States red,

Lentil / Nutritional Value Per 100 g Edible Portion

	Dried Raw	Dried Cooked	Sprouted Raw	Sprouted Cooked
Calories	338	116	106	101
Protein	28.06 g	9.02 g	8.96 g	8.80 g
Fat	0.96 g	0.38 g	0.55 g	0.45 g
Fiber	5.20 g	2.76 g	3.05 g	1.10 g
Calcium	51 mg	19 mg	25 mg	14 mg
Iron	9.02 mg	3.33 mg	3.21 mg	3.10 mg
Magnesium	107 mg	36 mg	37 mg	35 mg
Phosphorus	454 mg	180 mg	173 mg	153 mg
Potassium	905 mg	369 mg	322 mg	284 mg
Sodium	10 mg	2 mg	11 mg	n/a
Zinc	3.610 mg	1.270 mg	1.510 mg	1.600 mg
Copper	0.852 mg	0.251 mg	0.352 mg	0.337 mg
Manganese	1.429 mg	0.494 mg	0.506 mg	0.502 mg
Beta Carotene (A)	39 IU	8 IU	45 IU	41 IU
Thiamine (B$_1$)	0.475 mg	0.169 mg	0.228 mg	0.220 mg
Riboflavin (B$_2$)	0.245 mg	0.073 mg	0.128 mg	0.090 mg
Niacin (B$_3$)	2.621 mg	1.060 mg	1.128 mg	1.200 mg
Pantothenic Acid (B$_5$)	1.849 mg	0.638 mg	0.578 mg	0.571 mg
Pyridoxine (B$_6$)	0.535 mg	0.178 mg	0.190 mg	n/a
Folic Acid (B$_9$)	432.8 mcg	180.8 mcg	99.9 mcg	n/a
Ascorbic Acid (C)	6.2 mg	1.5 mg	16.5 mg	12.6 mg

brown, and green lentils are the most common varieties. These small, disk-shaped beans cook quickly, need no presoaking, and have a distinctive, somewhat peppery flavor. The smaller yellow and orange lentils purée very easily, which makes them useful in soups. The others retain their shape well after cooking and can be served as a vegetable, on their own, or in casseroles and salads. Lentils play a particularly important part in Indian curries and other dishes (where they are known as dal).

Health Benefits

pH 6.30–6.83. Lentils are very easily digested, neutralize muscle acids, help build glands and blood, and provide a rich supply of minerals for nearly every organ, gland, and tissue in the body. They are especially good for the heart, and when puréed they are soothing for those suffering from stomach ulcers and colitis.

VARIETIES

Brown lentils are probably the most common variety in the United States. Smaller and plumper than the green

LORE AND LEGEND

The Egyptians held lentils in the highest esteem; they were served liberally to children because it was believed that the beans enlightened their minds, opened their hearts, and made them cheerful. On the other hand, the Romans felt lentils slowed the mind, and one scholar went so far as to trace their name to the Latin word *lentus*, meaning "slow and sluggish." Their famed shape inspired astronomers and physicists to name their disk-shaped double convex optic glass a lens.

variety, they have a more defined earthy taste and remain whole when cooked.

French lentils are a Persian strain prized for their subtle yet distinctive, slightly peppery flavor. These tiny, plump, olive- green- and slate-colored beans are so heavily mottled they are almost black. They cook up firmer than most other varieties.

Green lentils are an unusual Persian variety grown primarily in the Northwest. About half the size of common lentils, they are among the heartiest and most full-flavored of the legumes. They cook to a rich, earthy brown and are tender but retain their shape.

Puy lentils, popular in France, are considered by some to be the best-flavored lentil. They retain their shape when cooked.

Lima/Butter Bean
(Phaseolus limensis, P. lunatus)
Also Known As: Madagascar, Burma, Rangoon, Habas Grandes (large varieties); Baby Limas, Sieva Beans, Butter Beans, Civet Beans, Dixie Speckled Butter Beans, Florida Speckled Pole Limas (small varieties)

The scientific name *Phaseolus* was bestowed in 39 B.C. by Calumella, who observed that the seed looks like a "small boat." The specific term *limensis* means "coming from Lima," while *lunatus* means "crescent- or moon-shaped." Lima beans are named after their city of approximate origin in Peru.

General Information

These beans, christened *lima* after the capital of Peru, are native to the Peruvian altiplano, with origins that can be traced back to about A.D. 1000. Known and used by the pre-Columbian Incas, this "aristocrat of the bean family" was introduced to Mauritius and Madagascar around the eighteenth century, where its cultivation became of great importance. Today this large creamy-white or pale green bean is the main legume crop in tropical Africa. The large, thick-seeded, "potato"-type limas have large pods and are fleshy but are not likely to split at maturity. The baby lima bean is a smaller, milder-tasting variety; the pods are small and numerous and will split open when mature. Christmas limas are an heirloom bean larger than the regular lima, about 1 to 1¼ inches long, and plumper, with a maroon batiklike pattern on a creamy background. Prized for their buttery, chestnutlike flavor as well as their beauty, Christmas limas are smoother than supermarket limas and cook without soaking. They are delicious in bean side dishes and salads.

Culinary Uses

Lima beans have a soft, floury texture and a smooth, creamy, savory, slightly starchy flavor. When selecting lima beans, look for quality pods that are fresh, bright green in color, and well filled. The beans themselves when shelled should be plump, with tender green to greenish-white skins that puncture easily when tested. Hard, tough skins mean the bean is overmature and will probably lack flavor. The beans are also available dried, canned, or frozen; of these, frozen are the most flavorful, but they are salted. Lima beans are delicious in salads and soups or with corn and other vegetables. Served hot with melted butter and chopped chives or dill, or with sautéed onions and mushrooms, they are delicious.

Lima Bean / Nutritional Value Per 100 g Edible Portion							
	Fresh Raw	Fresh Cooked	Dried Raw	Dried Cooked	Large Dried Raw	Large Dried Cooked	Large Canned
Calories	113	123	335	126	338	115	79
Protein	6.84 g	6.81 g	20.62 g	8.04 g	21.46 g	7.80 g	4.93 g
Fat	0.86 g	0.32 g	0.93 g	0.38 g	0.69 g	0.38 g	0.17 g
Fiber	1.89 g	2.09 g	5.71 g	3.59 g	6.34 g	3.09 g	1.23 g
Calcium	34 mg	32 mg	81 mg	29 mg	81 mg	17 mg	21 mg
Iron	3.14 mg	2.45 mg	6.19 mg	2.40 mg	7.51 mg	2.39 mg	1.81 mg
Magnesium	58 mg	74 mg	188 mg	53 mg	224 mg	43 mg	39 mg
Phosphorus	136 mg	130 mg	370 mg	127 mg	385 mg	111 mg	74 mg
Potassium	467 mg	570 mg	1,403 mg	401 mg	1,724 mg	508 mg	220 mg
Sodium	8 mg	17 mg	13 mg	3 mg	18 mg	2 mg	336 mg
Zinc	0.780 mg	0.790 mg	2.600 mg	1.030 mg	2.830 mg	0.950 mg	0.650 mg
Copper	0.318 mg	0.305 mg	0.665 mg	0.215 mg	0.740 mg	0.235 mg	0.180 mg
Manganese	1.215 mg	1.252 mg	1.686 mg	0.585 mg	1.672 mg	0.516 mg	0.363 mg
Beta Carotene (A)	303 IU	370 IU	5 IU	0 IU	0 IU	0 IU	0 IU
Thiamine (B$_1$)	0.217 mg	0.140 mg	0.574 mg	0.161 mg	0.507 mg	0.161 mg	0.055 mg
Riboflavin (B$_2$)	0.103 mg	0.096 mg	0.218 mg	0.055 mg	0.202 mg	0.055 mg	0.034 mg
Niacin (B$_3$)	1.474 mg	1.040 mg	1.712 mg	0.660 mg	1.537 mg	0.421 mg	0.261 mg
Pantothenic Acid (B$_5$)	0.247 mg	0.257 mg	1.265 mg	0.472 mg	1.355 mg	0.422 mg	0.259 mg
Pyridoxine (B$_6$)	0.204 mg	0.193 mg	0.327 mg	0.078 mg	0.512 mg	0.161 mg	0.091 mg
Folic Acid (B$_9$)	n/a	n/a	400.2 mcg	149.9 mcg	395.1 mcg	83.1 mcg	50.4 mcg
Ascorbic Acid (C)	23.4 mg	10.1 mg	0 mg	0 mg	0 mg	0 mg	0 mg

Health Benefits

pH 6.50. Unlike other beans, the lima bean contains enough of the potentially toxic cyanide compounds to require special cooking attention. Boil the beans in an uncovered pot so that the hydrogen cyanide gas will escape with the steam. It is advisable to prepare all lima beans—fresh, dried, or sprouted—in this manner. Fresh lima beans are a high-protein, alkaline food of great value to the muscular system. Dry limas are hard to digest, and the dry skin is irritating to an inflamed digestive system.

Lupine
(Lupinus sativus)

The genus name *Lupinus* comes from the Latin *lupus*, meaning "wolf" or "destroyer," because it was thought that these plants depleted (wolfed) the fertility of the soil by their numbers and strong growth. *Sativus* indicates that this plant has long been cultivated.

General Information

The lupine originated in the Mediterranean basin and can still be found growing wild in Sicily and other regions. Cultivated in Egypt about 2000 B.C., this plant has been a staple food for the poor and used as animal forage. In ancient Rome cooked lupines were distributed free to the people on holy and festival days. In recent years, the lupine has often been grown as green manure to enrich the soil because of the nitrogen-fixing bacteria nodules found on the roots.

Culinary Uses

Although of high nutritive value, the lupine is of very little importance today as food; it is used more as a snack, like peanuts, salted almonds, and roasted pumpkin seeds. The tan beans are available dried or in jars of brine. They look like wide yellowish full moons, and to eat them requires coordination and a little practice. Slipping the bean into your mouth, apply just enough pressure to pierce the tough seed coat and slip out the crunchy, chewy bean. Discard the translucent seed covering. The beans are very mild, requiring salt, pepper, and vinegar to add zip. They are best purchased precooked, for cooking is a laborious process that takes several days.

Mung Bean
(Phaseolus aureus, Vigna radiata)
Also Known As: Green Grams, Black Grams, Split Golden Grams, Sabat Moong (whole), Moong Dal (hulled)

The scientific name *Phaseolus* was bestowed in 39 B.C. by Calumella, who observed that the seed looks like a "small boat." The specific term *aureus* means "golden." The English name *mung* derives from the Sanskrit *mudga*.

General Information

The mung bean is native to India, where it was first cultivated about 1500 B.C. It later spread to China, becoming a favorite there. These humble, olive-green beans are best known to us as the slender, silvery bean sprout of Chinese cuisine.

Culinary Uses

The sweet-flavored pods of the mung bean are eaten as a green vegetable when they are young and tender. The dried beans cook more quickly than most and become soft, rich, starchy, and sweet, similar to split peas. Although they are commonly used in stews, on their own, or in Indian curries, they are perhaps best known in their sprouted form as bean sprouts. Whole beans are available at natural food stores; split and skinless beans are sold as mung (moong) dal at Indian grocery stores. Mung bean flour, ground from the dried beans, is widely used in India.

Lupine / Nutritional Value Per 100 g Edible Portion	Dried Raw	Dried Cooked
Calories	371	119
Protein	36.17 g	15.57 g
Fat	9.74 g	2.92 g
Fiber	13.77 g	0.67 g
Calcium	176 mg	51 mg
Iron	4.36 mg	1.20 mg
Magnesium	198 mg	54 mg
Phosphorus	440 mg	128 mg
Potassium	1,013 mg	245 mg
Sodium	15 mg	4 mg
Zinc	4.750 mg	1.380 mg
Copper	1.022 mg	0.231 mg
Beta Carotene (A)	n/a	n/a
Thiamine (B₁)	0.640 mg	0.134 mg
Riboflavin (B₂)	0.220 mg	0.053 mg
Niacin (B₃)	2.190 mg	0.495 mg

Mung Bean / Nutritional Value Per 100 g Edible Portion				
	Dried Raw	Dried Cooked	Sprouted Raw	Sprouted Cooked
Calories	347	105	30	21
Protein	23.86 g	7.02 g	3.04 g	2.03 g
Fat	1.15 g	0.38 g	0.18 g	0.09 g
Fiber	5.27 g	0.46 g	0.81 g	0.52 g
Calcium	132 mg	27 mg	13 mg	12 mg
Iron	6.74 mg	1.40 mg	0.91 mg	0.65 mg
Magnesium	189 mg	48 mg	21 mg	14 mg
Phosphorus	367 mg	99 mg	54 mg	28 mg
Potassium	1,246 mg	266 mg	149 mg	101 mg
Sodium	15 mg	2 mg	6 mg	10 mg
Zinc	2.680 mg	0.840 mg	0.410 mg	0.470 mg
Copper	0.941 mg	0.156 mg	0.164 mg	0.122 mg
Manganese	1.035 mg	0.298 mg	0.188 mg	0.140 mg
Beta Carotene (A)	114 IU	24 IU	21 IU	14 IU
Thiamine (B$_1$)	0.621 mg	0.164 mg	0.084 mg	0.050 mg
Riboflavin (B$_2$)	0.233 mg	0.061 mg	0.124 mg	0.102 mg
Niacin (B$_3$)	2.251 mg	0.577 mg	0.749 mg	0.817 mg
Pantothenic Acid (B$_5$)	1.910 mg	0.410 mg	0.380 mg	0.243 mg
Pyridoxine (B$_6$)	0.382 mg	0.067 mg	0.088 mg	n/a
Folic Acid (B$_9$)	624.9 mcg	158.8 mcg	60.8 mcg	n/a
Ascorbic Acid (C)	4.8 mg	1.0 mg	13.2 mg	11.4 mg

Pea, Dried / Nutritional Value Per 100 g Edible Portion		
	Dried Raw	Dried Cooked
Calories	341	118
Protein	24.55 g	8.34 g
Fat	1.16 g	0.39 g
Fiber	3.72 g	1.97 g
Calcium	55 mg	14 mg
Iron	4.43 mg	1.29 mg
Magnesium	115 mg	36 mg
Phosphorus	366 mg	99 mg
Potassium	981 mg	362 mg
Sodium	15 mg	2 mg
Zinc	3.010 mg	1.000 mg
Copper	0.866 mg	0.181 mg
Manganese	1.391 mg	0.396 mg
Beta Carotene (A)	149 IU	7 IU
Thiamine (B$_1$)	0.726 mg	0.190 mg
Riboflavin (B$_2$)	0.215 mg	0.056 mg
Niacin (B$_3$)	2.889 mg	0.890 mg
Pantothenic Acid (B$_5$)	1.758 mg	0.595 mg
Pyridoxine (B$_6$)	0.174 mg	0.048 mg
Folic Acid (B$_9$)	273.8 mcg	64.9 mcg
Ascorbic Acid (C)	1.8 mg	0.4 mg
Tocopherol (E)	0.09 mg	n/a

Health Benefits

One of the most important beans therapeutically, mung beans are particularly useful because of their capacity to cleanse the heart and vascular system. Sprouted mung beans are very cooling and are used to detoxify the body. According to Donna Gates, author of *The Body Ecology Diet,* mung beans are the one sprout that ferments, and so they are not advised in an anticandida diet.

Pea, Dried

(Pisum sativum)

The word *pease,* of Sanskrit origin, became *pisum* in Latin and *pease* in early English. The final *e* was dropped in the mistaken belief that the word was a plural. *Sativum* indicates that this plant has long been cultivated.

General Information

The garden pea appears to have derived from the field pea (*Pisum arvense*) through centuries of cultivation and selection for certain desired characteristics. Dried peas hail from the Middle East and date back to about 6000 B.C. Their use spread throughout the Mediterranean, and they were eaten in this form by both the Greeks and Romans. Today, almost 80 percent of the world's crop is utilized as dried peas rather than as fresh peas. In the United States, however, this is reversed, with 90 percent of the peas being eaten as green peas (see the reference in the **Vegetables** section). Dried peas are a useful part of the store cupboard, particularly as fresh ones have such a short season. Once these peas are dried and their skins removed, they split apart naturally. Whole green peas are those that have been shelled from the pod and dried. Green split peas have their outer seed coat removed and are then divided in half.

Culinary Uses

Both split and whole peas are small and possess a soft, grainy texture marked with a certain distinctively sweet flavor. The whole dried peas are the "pease porridge" of our nursery rhymes—cooked to a purée and then mashed. Whole peas can also be used as a side vegetable, while the split varieties make excellent purées and yield a good flour that flavors and thickens beautifully. Green split peas are favored in the United States and Great Britain, while yellow split peas, which have a more pronounced, nutlike flavor, are preferred in Scandinavian and other northern European countries.

Health Benefits
pH 6.43–6.80. Split peas are highly digestible and help tone the stomach and liver.

BYPRODUCTS

Split pea flour, made from dried and ground yellow split peas, cannot be used on its own as a flour in the conventional sense but makes a good thickener for soups or stews.

Pigeon Pea
(Vigna sinensis)
Also Known As: Gunga Peas, Longo Peas, Toor Dal, Congo Peas, No-Eyed Peas, Catjang Beans, Red Grams

This genus was named *Vigna* in honor of Dominic Vigni, a seventeenth-century Paduan commentator on Theophrastus. The specific term *sinensis* means "coming from China."

General Information
Probably native to Africa, the pigeon pea had reached tropical Asia in prehistoric times. Cultivated in Egypt four thousand years ago, this very old bean was brought to the southern parts of the United States and the Caribbean by slaves from Africa. Widely grown in India, these peas in that country are known as red grams and are one of most important pulses after chickpeas. Closely related to the cow pea, the pigeon pea grows in semi-arid tropical conditions, doing well in places like Florida. Its long, twisted, fuzzy pods enclose beans that are grayish yellow in color, about a quarter of an inch long, and plump, in the shape of a pouch or purse with an elongated eye on the flattish cotyledon.

Culinary Uses
This pungently flavored bean is used in combination with rice in many dishes throughout Hispanic communities. In Indian cuisine the split seeds are cooked to provide dal, the familiar pulse dish. With its tough outer skin, the pigeon

Pigeon Pea / Nutritional Value Per 100 g Edible Portion				
	Fresh Raw	Fresh Cooked	Dried Raw	Dried Cooked
Calories	136	111	343	121
Protein	7.20 g	5.96 g	21.70 g	6.76 g
Fat	1.64 g	1.36 g	1.49 g	0.38 g
Fiber	2.67 g	2.90 g	3.12 g	1.10 g
Calcium	42 mg	35 mg	130 mg	43 mg
Iron	1.60 mg	1.32 mg	5.23 mg	1.11 mg
Magnesium	n/a	40 mg	183 mg	46 mg
Phosphorus	127 mg	105 mg	367 mg	119 mg
Potassium	552 mg	456 mg	1,392 mg	384 mg
Sodium	5 mg	4 mg	17 mg	5 mg
Zinc	n/a	n/a	2.76 mg	0.90 mg
Beta Carotene (A)	140 IU	130 IU	28 IU	3 IU
Thiamine (B$_1$)	0.400 mg	0.350 mg	0.643 mg	0.146 mg
Riboflavin (B$_2$)	0.170 mg	0.166 mg	0.187 mg	0.059 mg
Niacin (B$_3$)	2.200 mg	2.153 mg	2.965 mg	0.781 mg
Pantothenic Acid (B$_5$)	0.680 mg	0.630 mg	1.266 mg	0.319 mg
Pyridoxine (B$_6$)	n/a	n/a	0.283 mg	0.050 mg
Folic Acid (B$_9$)	n/a	n/a	456.0 mcg	110.8 mcg
Ascorbic Acid (C)	39.0 mg	28.1 mg	0 mg	0 mg

pea requires longer cooking than other, more common bean varieties.

Scarlet Runner Bean
(Phaseolus multiflorus, P. coccineus)
Also Known As: Multiflora, Painted Lady Bean

The scientific name *Phaseolus* was bestowed in 39 B.C. by Calumella, who observed that the seed looks like a "small boat." The specific term *multiflorus* means "many-flowered"; *coccineus* means "scarlet." The English name comes from the vividly hued flowers that appear on the plant's low-growing runner vines.

General Information
From the mountainous slopes of South or Central America come scarlet runner beans, first cultivated for their large ornamental blossoms. These large, intensely scarlet, showy flowers are edible and taste very similar to the bean itself before they mature. In its native climate this bean is a perennial whose bulbous root lies dormant in the ground during the winter, sending up new shoots the following spring; in North America it must generally be treated as an

annual. The plant was brought to the British Isles in the seventeenth century as an ornamental and decorative plant. Runner beans can be eaten as snap beans when the pods are young, in their immature form as green shell beans, or matured for dried shell beans. The green, eight- to nine-inch pods contain three or four large kidney-shaped seeds, between seven-eighths and one inch long, and are russet red with heavy black mottling near the eye of the bean. There is also a white runner bean grown in the Netherlands and preferred there to its scarlet cousin.

Culinary Uses

The scarlet runner, like many other legumes, can be used either fresh or dried. The pods can be picked young— leaving some on the plant to mature for drying—and eaten whole like string beans. Slightly older pods produce beans with finer-textured flesh and a thinner, more tender skin than the dried variety, which present a floury compact meat and tough skin. The fully mature fresh beans are prepared like fresh lima beans and are quite tasty with herb butter, sautéed shallots, or cheese. These brightly colored, vibrantly flavored beans are excellent in chili and salads.

Health Benefits

Low in fat and high in fiber.

Soybean/Soya Bean

(Glycine max, Soja max)

> *Glycine* comes from the Greek word *glukos*, for "sweet," while *max* means "large." The English word *soy* derives from the Cantonese *shi-yau*.

General Information

The soybean is first mentioned in China about 2800 B.C. but had been cultivated for a considerable time before that. Just as wheat became respectable under the Han Dynasty in China, so did the soybean, formerly regarded as a coarse rustic food; the index of extreme poverty was having nothing but soybeans to chew and water to drink. The primary recommendation of the bean was that it produced a good crop even in bad years, but a few of its many other virtues seem to have been made manifest in the early days of the Han. Not until the sixth century did the soybean find its way to nearby Japan, and Europe did not see it

LORE AND LEGEND

A Japanese myth relates that the god of the sea, Susano, angrily refused his watery realm and was disowned by the Creator. He wandered around, causing trouble, until he became hungry and visited the goddess of food. But he didn't like what she offered him, so he killed her and crushed her body into the ground. On the site sprang five plants: rice, millet, barley, large beans, and soybeans.

until the eighteenth century, when missionaries sent the bean back to Europe. It was introduced into the United States by Dr. Charles Fearn, an Englishman who discovered them on a trip to China; President Woodrow Wilson asked Dr. Fearn to assist the war effort during World War I, and the versatile soybean with its many byproducts was suggested as a nourishing substitute or extender for scarce foods. Its great advantages were cheapness, high protein content, and bland flavor, which was easily enhanced. In 1954 an invention by R. A. Boyer made possible a method of spinning soy protein into fibers, similar to the manufacture of rayon. The fibers were stretched and molded into forms resembling various meats (especially ham and chicken) and then flavored appropriately to suggest the product they imitated. The products were tasty, nourishing, and cheap, but they met with consumer resistance in many areas. Only now are many soy products finding widespread acceptance.

In the period between the two world wars, the soybean became an important crop. The United States is now the world's largest grower of soybeans, but over 90 percent of the crop still goes to feed animals rather than humans. Most of that used for human consumption is made into margarine, shortening, salad oil, and cooking oil. The rows of "vegetable oil" on supermarket shelves are primarily soy oil. The process of extracting oil from soybeans is particularly difficult, as the beans must be roasted and treated with high heat and chemical solvents (usually hexane) before they will yield any quantity of oil. Once extracted, the oil is bleached, "deodorized," and lightly hydrogenated to stabilize the flavor. The end product is a fully refined edible oil without much flavor.

Culinary Uses

The preeminent legume crop in the world, the soybean is a staple in Asian countries, where it has been regarded as the "meat of the earth" for millennia. There are over a thousand varieties, including white, yellow, brown, black, and multicolored. Over the centuries the soybean has become a complete food industry in itself, providing a milk substitute, curd (tofu), sauce, cheese, oil for cooking and making margarine and salad dressings, flour to enrich pasta and breakfast cereals, and bean sprouts. Young soy sprouts are very tasty and make a fine dish by themselves or an excellent addition to a vegetable salad. Cooked on their own, soy beans have a rich deep flavor and are wonderfuly palatable. The whole cooked bean does not soften like other beans and has a gelatinous, slippery texture that most Americans find unpleasant. Young soy sprouts are very tasty and make a fine dish by themselves or an excellent addition to a vegetable salad. Unless well cooked, soy-

beans are difficult to digest. The fermentation process, such as that used in tempeh, tofu, miso, and soy sauce, eliminates this problem, and the resulting products are highly digestible.

In natural food stores you may be able to find a few expeller-pressed, unrefined soy oils. Dark in color, they have a strong "beany" odor and a nutlike flavor. Because of its strong flavor, the oil may not be suitable for some dishes, although it is excellent for use in baking, since its high lecithin content gives preservative qualities to breads, cakes, and cookies. The oil can foam during frying, which may not be desirable in some dishes. Refined soy oil has one of the highest smoke points of all vegetable oils, so it is frequently used as a cooking oil.

Health Benefits

Soybeans are unique among beans in containing the eight essential amino acids and are concentrated in essential fatty

Soybean / Nutritional Value Per 100 g Edible Portion

	Green Raw	Green Cooked	Sprouted Raw	Sprouted Cooked	Kernels Roasted w/ Salt	Mature, Dry Raw	Mature, Dry Cooked	Miso
Calories	147	141	122	81	471	416	173	206
Protein	12.95 g	12.35 g	13.09 g	8.47 g	35.22 g	36.49 g	16.64 g	11.81 g
Fat	6.80 g	6.40 g	6.70 g	4.45 g	25.40 g	19.94 g	8.97 g	6.07 g
Fiber	2.05 g	1.85 g	2.30 g	1.95 g	4.60 g	4.96 g	2.03 g	2.47 g
Calcium	197 mg	145 mg	67 mg	59 mg	138 mg	277 mg	102 mg	66 mg
Iron	3.55 mg	2.50 mg	2.10 mg	1.31 mg	3.90 mg	15.70 mg	5.14 mg	2.74 mg
Magnesium	n/a	n/a	72 mg	60 mg	145 mg	280 mg	86 mg	42 mg
Phosphorus	194 mg	158 mg	164 mg	135 mg	363 mg	704 mg	245 mg	153 mg
Potassium	n/a	n/a	484 mg	355 mg	1,470 mg	1,797 mg	515 mg	164 mg
Sodium	n/a	n/a	14 mg	10 mg	163 mg	2 mg	1 mg	3,647 mg
Zinc	n/a	n/a	1.170 mg	1.040 mg	3.140 mg	4.890 mg	1.150 mg	3.320 mg
Copper	n/a	n/a	0.427 mg	0.330 mg	0.828 mg	1.658 mg	0.407 mg	0.437 mg
Manganese	n/a	n/a	0.702 mg	0.710 mg	2.158 mg	2.517 mg	0.824 mg	0.859 mg
Beta Carotene (A)	180 IU	156 IU	11 IU	11 IU	200 IU	24 IU	9 IU	87 IU
Thiamine (B$_1$)	0.435 mg	0.260 mg	0.340 mg	0.205 mg	0.100 mg	0.874 mg	0.155 mg	0.097 mg
Riboflavin (B$_2$)	0.175 mg	0.155 mg	0.118 mg	0.053 mg	0.145 mg	0.870 mg	0.285 mg	0.250 mg
Niacin (B$_3$)	1.650 mg	1.250 mg	1.148 mg	1.092 mg	1.410 mg	1.623 mg	0.399 mg	0.860 mg
Pantothenic Acid (B$_5$)	n/a	n/a	0.929 mg	0.743 mg	0.453 mg	0.793 mg	0.179 mg	0.258 mg
Pyridoxine (B$_6$)	n/a	n/a	0.176 mg	n/a	0.208 mg	0.377 mg	0.234 mg	0.215 mg
Folic Acid (B$_9$)	n/a	n/a	172.0 mcg	n/a	211.0 mcg	375.1 mcg	53.8 mcg	33.0 mcg
Cobalamin (B$_{12}$)	n/a	n/a	n/a	n/a	n/a	0 mcg	0 mcg	0.21 mcg
Ascorbic Acid (C)	29.0 mg	17.0 mg	15.3 mg	8.3 mg	2.2 mg	6.0 mg	1.7 mg	0 mg
Tocopherol (E)	n/a	n/a	n/a	n/a	0.85 mg	n/a	n/a	n/a

acids (including omega-3); they are also the primary commercial source of lecithin, an essential nutrient that helps control cholesterol. The beans help regulate insulin and blood sugar levels, improve bowel functions, and help prevent certain cancers, most notably of the stomach. Soybeans, like peas and other legumes, are rich in isoflavones, also known as phytoestrogens (plant estrogens). These isoflavones actually bind to estrogen receptors and thus prevent the binding of the body's own estrogen to the receptor. Phytoestrogens are currently under study, and there is controversy over whether they are beneficial or not.

Health Precautions

Soybeans, if consumed in high quantities, can block protein absorption. Soy foods that are not fermented, such as soy milk and protein powders, also contain substances that can block thyroid function, mineral absorption, and glucose uptake in the brain. This means that soy milk is not a good food to feed infants and children on a regular basis. Like all foods, soy should be eaten in moderation, and the focus of consumption should be on fermented products, which include tempeh and miso. Because of the controversial nature of soybeans and soy products, it would be wise to do a little research to see if you wish to include these food products in your diet.

BYPRODUCTS

Edamame or **fresh green soybeans** are the Japanese version of popcorn. Harvested immature in their green seedpods, they are steamed or boiled whole, then drained and set out in bowls for munching. Popped from their shells, the beans have a buttery taste and smooth nonstarchy texture that appeals as much to kids as it does to adults. You may be able to find raw green soybeans in the freezer case of a health food store or

Okara	Shoyu	Flour, Full-Fat Raw	Flour, Full-Fat Roasted	Flour Low-Fat Raw	Flour Defatted Raw	Isolate (prepared with sodium)	Soy Meal Defatted, Raw	Soy Milk	Soy Sauce (imitation)
77	53	433-436	439-441	326-370	327-329	334-338	337-339	33	41
3.22 g	5.17 g	34.54-37.80 g	34.80-38.09 g	46.53-50.93 g	47.01-51.46 g	80.69-88.32 g	44.95-49.20 g	2.75 g	2.43 g
1.73 g	0.08 g	20.65 g	21.86 g	6.70 g	1.22 g	3.39 g	2.39 g	1.91 g	0.08 g
4.12 g	0 g	4.72 g	2.23 g	4.23 g	4.27 g	0.26 g	5.79 g	1.10 g	0 g
80 mg	17 mg	206 mg	188 mg	188 mg	241 mg	178 mg	244 mg	4 mg	5 mg
1.30 mg	2.02 mg	6.37 mg	5.82 mg	5.99 mg	9.24 mg	14.50 mg	13.70 mg	0.58 mg	1.49 mg
26 mg	34 mg	429 mg	369 mg	229 mg	290 mg	39 mg	306 mg	19 mg	6 mg
60 mg	110 mg	494 mg	476 mg	593 mg	674 mg	776 mg	701 mg	49 mg	93 mg
213 mg	180 mg	2,515 mg	2,041 mg	2,570 mg	2,384 mg	81 mg	2,490 mg	141 mg	152 mg
9 mg	5,715 mg	13 mg	12 mg	18 mg	20 mg	1,005 mg	3 mg	12 mg	5,689 mg
n/a	0.370 mg	3.920 mg	3.580 mg	1.180 mg	2.460 mg	4.030 g	5.060 mg	0.230 mg	0.310 mg
n/a	0.115 mg	2.920 mg	2.221 mg	5.080 mg	4.065 mg	1.599 mg	2.000 mg	0.120 mg	0.097 mg
n/a	n/a	2.275 mg	2.077 mg	3.080 mg	3.018 mg	1.493 mg	3.800 mg	0.170 mg	n/a
0 IU	0 IU	120 IU	110 IU	40 IU	40 IU	0 IU	40 IU	32 IU	0 IU
0.020 mg	0.050 mg	0.581 mg	0.412 mg	0.380 mg	0.698 mg	0.176 mg	0.691 mg	0.161 mg	0.042 mg
0.020 mg	0.130 mg	1.160 mg	0.941 mg	0.285 mg	0.253 mg	0.100 mg	0.251 mg	0.070 mg	0.109 mg
0.100 mg	3.360 mg	4.320 mg	3.286 mg	2.160 mg	2.612 mg	1.438 mg	2.587 mg	0.147 mg	2.828 mg
n/a	0.320 mg	1.590 mg	1.209 mg	1.820 mg	1.995 mg	0.060 mg	1.976 mg	0.048 mg	0.269 mg
n/a	0.170 mg	0.461 mg	0.351 mg	0.522 mg	0.574 mg	n/a	0.569 mg	0.041 mg	0.143 mg
n/a	15.5 mcg	345.0 mcg	227.4 mcg	410.0 mcg	305.4 mcg	176.1 mcg	302.6 mcg	1.5 mcg	13.0 mcg
0 mcg	0 mcg	n/a	n/a	n/a	n/a	n/a	n/a	n/a	n/a
0 mg	0 mg	0 mg	0 mg	0 mg	0 mg	0 mg	0 mg	0 mg	0 mg
n/a	n/a	n/a	n/a	n/a	n/a	n/a	n/a	n/a	n/a

Soybean / Nutritional Value Per 100 g Edible Portion

	Sufu	Tamari	Tempeh	Tofu Raw, Firm	Tofu Raw, Regular	Tofu Dried-Frozen
Calories	116	60	199	145	76	480
Protein	8.15 g	10.51 g	18.95 g	15.78 g	8.08 g	47.94 g
Fat	8.00 g	0.10 g	7.68 g	8.72 g	4.78 g	30.34 g
Fiber	0.31 g	0 g	2.99 g	0.15 g	0.08 g	0.16 g
Calcium	46 mg	20 mg	93 mg	205 mg	105 mg	364 mg
Iron	1.98 mg	2.38 mg	2.26 mg	10.47 mg	5.36 mg	9.73 mg
Magnesium	52 mg	40 mg	70 mg	94 mg	103 mg	59 mg
Phosphorus	73 mg	130 mg	206 mg	190 mg	97 mg	483 mg
Potassium	75 mg	212 mg	367 mg	237 mg	121 mg	20 mg
Sodium	2,873 mg	5,586 mg	6 mg	14 mg	7 mg	6 mg
Zinc	n/a	0.430 mg	1.810 mg	1.570 mg	0.800 mg	4.900 mg
Copper	n/a	0.135 mg	0.670 mg	0.378 mg	0.193 mg	1.179 mg
Manganese	n/a	n/a	1.430 mg	1.181 mg	0.605 mg	3.689 mg
Beta Carotene (A)	n/a	0 IU	686 IU	166 IU	85 IU	518 IU
Thiamine (B$_1$)	n/a	0.059 mg	0.131 mg	0.158 mg	0.081 mg	0.494 mg
Riboflavin (B$_2$)	n/a	0.152 mg	0.111 mg	0.102 mg	0.052 mg	0.317 mg
Niacin (B$_3$)	n/a	0.152 mg	4.630 mg	0.381 mg	0.195 mg	1.189 mg
Pantothenic Acid (B$_5$)	n/a	0.376 mg	0.355 mg	0.133 mg	0.068 mg	0.415 mg
Pyridoxine (B$_6$)	n/a	0.200 mg	0.299 mg	0.092 mg	0.047 mg	0.286 mg
Folic Acid (B$_9$)	n/a	18.2 mcg	52.0 mcg	29.3 mcg	15.0 mcg	91.5 mcg
Cobalamin (B$_{12}$)	0.84 mcg	0 mcg	0 mcg	0 mcg	n/a	n/a
Ascorbic Acid (C)	n/a	0 mg	0 mg	0.2 mg	0.1 mg	0.7 mg

Asian market. Steam or boil them (fresh or frozen) for ten to fifteen minutes, drain, and serve.

Miso is a fermented food, made by adding an enzymatic culture (*Aspergillus oryzae*) to a base of cooked soybeans or a combination of soybeans and a variety of grain (usually wheat, barley, or rice). Salt and water are the only other ingredients of natural miso. The mixture is packed into earthenware or wooden vessels, sealed airtight, and fermented, slowly in cool weather or more quickly in warm weather. Through this aging process, the enzymes reduce the proteins, starches, and fats into amino acids, simple sugars, and fatty acids. The flavors marry and mellow, and the paste becomes thick, dark, salty, and pungent. There are several types of miso: mugi (barley), hatcho (soy only), and kome (brown rice) are among the most common. Mugi miso, also called red miso, is dark-colored and of medium flavor strength. It is the preferred miso for everyday use, particularly in temperate weather. Hatcho miso is usually the thickest and strongest in flavor and therefore preferred in cold weather. It is lower in salt and higher in

protein than its grain-containing counterparts. This is the variety favored by famous warlords and the emperor of Japan. Kome miso, also called light miso or white miso, is yellow to amber in color and relatively sweet and mild; it is used particularly in hot weather. In addition to being a soup base, miso is great for flavoring sauces, gravies, grains, dips, spreads, dressings, and marinades. An excellent spread can be made by mixing miso with roasted tahini (sesame butter), chopped scallions, and herbs. Always use unpasteurized miso, since this is a live food, and remember that prolonged cooking and/or high temperatures kill the beneficial microorganisms. Because miso absorbs toxins from plastic containers, it should be transferred into glass, wood, or enamel for prolonged storage. Miso has nutrients that can block our uptake of radioactive substances such as cobalt-60 and strontium-90; it also contains a binding agent called zybiocolin, which is effective in detoxifying and eliminating radioactive elements from the body. Low in calories and fat, miso is a superb source of easily assimilated complete protein; it actually increases the protein quality of other foods with which it is combined. Rich in minerals and vitamins, including the elusive B_{12}, unpasteurized miso contains live microorganisms and enzymes that facilitate digestion and promote an alkaline environment in the body. According to traditional medicine, miso promotes long life and good health.

Natto, steamed fermented soybeans, is an unusual, powerful-tasting food. Fondly called the Limburger of soy, this traditional Japanese condiment looks like innocuous brown soybeans until you dip a spoon in and out, at which point hundreds of hair-fine strands, up to ten inches long, stretch from the bowl to your spoon. These strands contain countless enzymes, bacteria, and fungi. For some people, natto is an acquired taste. Others love it from the first encounter, including many children, who call it "string beans." When serving natto as its own dish, mix it with mustard, soy sauce, and chopped scallions to taste. Allow one tablespoon per serving as a condiment for rice or other grains. Natto is also tasty stirred into soups and noodles. Natto is a potent digestive aid because it is fermented and because its own culture of enzymes assists in the digestion of other foods. It is considered medicinal for the regenerative organs and it helps regulate blood sugar. This condiment contains no salt and is an excellent source of protein. Available frozen in well-stocked natural food stores and Asian markets, it should be keep frozen until it is to be used. Once defrosted, it should be covered tightly and can be refrigerated for up to five days.

Okara is the fibrous pulp that remains after soy milk processing, when the "milk" is strained from the beans. It is highly perishable and must be used quickly or frozen for later use. Okara has a mild, almost neutral flavor and is used in second-generation soy products such as soy sausage or soy burgers. When baked, okara develops a texture and flavor akin to coconut and can be added to granola or cookies. If you want to experiment with okara without making soy milk, you can get some from a local tofu processor, or look for ready-made okara patties in a natural food store's freezer case.

Shoyu is fermented from whole soybeans, wheat koji (a cultured starter), salt, and water. After aging for a year or two, a superior shoyu has a full, round flavor and mellow aftertaste. Thinner and lighter in flavor than tamari, much of its sweet aroma and flavor is lost during long cooking, so it is best used as a seasoning added just before serving. About 95 percent of the soy sauce consumed in Japan is shoyu, and about 95 percent of the "tamari" imported to the West is actually mistakenly identified shoyu. Commercial shoyu is made from defatted soy meal, and the fermentation process is artificially accelerated by temperature control; it may also contain preservatives and other additives.

Soy cheese and **yogurt soy cheese** were designed as substitutes for dairy cheese, but they simply do not taste like, feel like, or melt like real cheese. Moreover, some companies have added casein, a milk protein, so that their product will melt better. Soy yogurt is cultured from rich soy milk, using active bacteria cultures. It is available in many flavors and has the advantages of being lactose- and cholesterol-free.

Soy flour contributes to a tender, moist, and nicely browned finish in baked goods, and it adds a good color and slightly nutty flavor to foods; it also extends the keeping ability of foods, inhibits fat absorption, and provides a nutritional boost. It can successfully replace up to 25 percent of wheat flour in baked goods, although less should be used in breads that require rising since soy flour contains no gluten. Defatted soy flour is from soy meal left after the chemical solvent method of extraction for soy oil and contains less than 1 percent fat and 50 percent protein. Similarly, low-fat soy flour is from soy meal left by the expeller method of extraction for oil and contains 6 percent fat and 45 percent protein. Full-fat soy flour is made from whole soybeans that have been hulled, cracked, and heat-treated to remove the beany flavor, as well as to increase the value of the protein and deactivate certain enzymes that cause deterioration during storage. The beans are then cooled and ground into a flour that contains about 20 percent fat and 35 percent protein.

Soy grits are made from raw or partially cooked soybeans that have been cracked into eight or ten pieces. The bland grits are a good texturizer and make a nutritious addition to cooked grains such as rice without altering the flavor. However, soy grits are not a whole food and have not been processed to eliminate the enzymes that inhibit digestion.

Soy milk is made either by boiling soybeans and pouring off the water or by finely grinding soaked beans, mixing them with water, and straining off the "milk." The resulting thick, heavy liquid is brought to a boil before it can be used; otherwise it tastes "green" and "beany" and contains an enzyme that prevents digestion. Soy milk has a slightly nutty flavor and works as a universal substitute for dairy milk in everything from breakfast cereal to cooked and baked products (but is not very successful in tea or coffee). Rich soy milk, made with proportionally more soybeans per volume of water, can be whipped like cream or made into homemade soy yogurt and ice cream. Fresh soy milk can be kept in the refrigerator for about four days; after that it tends to become sour and separate (clabber), at which time it can be used in place of buttermilk or yogurt in cooking and baking. A longer-lasting soy milk comes in aseptic cartons; in this form it has an indefinite shelf life before opening and lasts for several weeks in the refrigerator after opening. Soy milk is not an advised milk substitute for infants and children.

Soy nuts are a tasty alternative to peanuts. Since they are not widely available commercially, try making them at home. Soak a quantity of soybeans for eight hours, drain, spread them on oiled cookie sheets, and roast at 350 degrees Fahrenheit for about thirty minutes, stirring occasionally. When they are golden brown, remove them from the oven and season to taste with a sprinkle of plain or garlic salt; for a spicier version, add some cayenne pepper or Cajun seasoning mix. Store in an airtight container in a cool place. Coarsely ground soy nuts can be used in place of bacon bits in salads and sandwiches. However, be aware that because soy nuts have not gone through the fermentation process, they are hard to digest.

Soy oil in its unrefined state is dark in color and has a strong, "beany" odor and a nutlike flavor. Because of its strong flavor, the oil may not be suitable for some dishes, although it is excellent for use in baking, since its high lecithin content gives preservative qualities to breads, cakes, and cookies. The oil can foam during frying, which may not be desirable in some dishes. You may be able to find a few expeller-pressed, unrefined soy oils in natural food stores. Refined soy oil has one of the highest smoke points of all vegetable oils, so it is frequently used as a cooking oil.

Soy protein isolate is made from the meal remaining after the beans have been processed for oil. This meal is then bathed in acid, base, and alcohol solutions to remove any carbohydrate remaining. The protein content of the resulting product is between 90 and 95 percent. These isolates are used in various products, including infant formulas, meal-replacement formulas, meat products, dairy-type whipped toppings, frozen desserts, and milk alternatives. It is best to exclude from your diet any products that list soy protein isolate as an ingredient. These products have been heavily refined and bathed in far too many chemicals.

Soy sauce is a generic term applied to three different but related products: tamari, shoyu, and common soy sauce. Each is a dark brown, richly flavored liquid made from a soybean base. Soy sauce is a salty brown sauce made, like miso, by fermenting soybeans with *Aspergillus oryzae* and wheat. It originated in China over twenty-five hundred years ago and was introduced into Japan in the seventh century A.D. Unfortunately, much of the popular soy sauce sold today is made literally overnight. The soybeans are broken down chemically and mixed with caramel coloring, salt, corn syrup, water, and usually a preservative. Look for high-quality brands that brew it traditionally. Superior soy sauce supplies good amounts of free amino acids, but its popularity is primarily a result of the flavor that it imparts to other foods. An essential ingredient in Asian cooking, soy sauce is used to enhance virtually all dishes—among them sauces, rice, and soups. The average annual per capita consumption of soy sauce in Japan is about three gallons. Its pH level is between 4.40 and 5.40.

Sufu is inoculated and fermented tofu, pickled in rice wine and brine, which is eaten as a condiment.

Tamari is a natural byproduct of making miso; it is the liquid that forms on the top of miso as it ferments. The name itself means "liquid pool" in Japanese. Tamari has a rich, full-bodied flavor and is smoother and more complex than ordinary soy sauce. It is not usually available commercially; much of what is labeled "tamari" is actually shoyu or an inferior soy sauce made without wheat.

Tempeh is an ancient Indonesian staple made from cooked, split, fermented soybeans bound together with a white, threadlike mycelium (*Rhizopus oligosporus*), which makes the soy easier to digest and provides many valuable vitamins. Tempeh comes in plain soy form or in various combinations with grains, vegetables, or nuts. With its nutty aroma and dense chewy texture, it is frequently used as a meat substitute in dishes like stir-fries or sloppy joes. Because tempeh is a whole, fermented food, it is more beneficial than tofu. Additionally, the *Rhizopus* mold produces a medicinal antibiotic to increase the body's resistance to infections and free it of chemical toxins. When tempeh was first introduced into America in the 1970s, it was generally produced by cottage industries, and its B_{12} levels often were quite high (4 mcg/100 g). But by the late 1980s most tempeh contained no B_{12} whatsoever, since it was being produced in larger batches and in machines and facilities designed to be more easily cleaned (B_{12}-rich bacteria thrive in less sanitary conditions). Some companies have now taken the B_{12} listing off their containers, while others inoculate the tempeh with bacteria that produce the vitamin.

Textured Vegetable Protein, or ***TVP,*** is made from the soybean meal left after the oil is processed out. This meal is then put through various acid, base, and alcohol solutions to remove virtually all the carbohydrate, leaving soy protein isolate. This is how it is done: The protein is removed from ground soybeans with petroleum solvent, alcohol, and hydrochloric acid; the refined protein is dissolved in alkali and then precipitated into an acid bath as filaments; the isolate can then be "textured" by means of fiber-spinning or extrusion and processed into marketable foodstuffs. The extrusion process creates small chunks of soy protein that are firm and chewy like meat but lacking in flavor and color. With the addition of flavorings, seasonings, and sometimes wheat gluten or other grains, these products can simulate a wide variety of animal foods. Used commercially as a meat extender and appearing in many popular vegetarian convenience foods, these meat analogs were first developed and produced in response to the needs of Seventh-Day Adventists and World War II meat rationing. Although these highly processed products may be convenient, the finished product is comparable chemically to plastic.

Tofu is made by first soaking, blending, and cooking soybeans and then filtering them through cloth to yield soy milk. A coagulant—generally a mineral salt such as calcium sulfate, calcium chloride, or magnesium chloride—is added to the soy milk to make it curdle. After the semi-solid curds separate from the liquid "whey," the curds are pressed and formed into compact blocks of ivory-colored tofu. Tofu comes in several varieties, from soft to extra-firm, depending upon the amount of liquid removed. Soft tofu is often used to make frostings for cakes and dips for chips and vegetables, while

firmer styles, which hold their shape, are used in stir-fries and soups. Freezing and thawing tofu will change it dramatically, creating a chewy, meatlike texture that absorbs marinades and flavorings, great for "American" dishes like chili and tacos. Tofu is also used as a substitute for eggs and other dairy products in baked goods, where it imparts a light, moist texture yet does not alter the flavor. Tofu has a cooling nature and helps relieve inflammation of the stomach and neutralize toxins.

Yuba is a meat substitute made from the skins formed on hot soybean milk, layered and pressed into slabs or cakes. It must be soaked before use and makes an unusual addition to braised vegetables.

Tepary Bean
(Phaseolus acutifolius latifolius)

The scientific name *Phaseolus* was bestowed in 39 B.C. by Calumella, who observed that the seed looks like a "small boat." The specific term *acutifolius* means "acutely leaved" or "sharp-leaved"; *latifolius* means "wide-leaved." The English name *tepary* is of unknown origin.

General Information
Tepary beans were heavily cultivated by Mexican Indians near Tehuacan about five thousand years ago. In all probability the tepary formed one of the principal food crops of that ancient and unknown agricultural race, the ruins of whose cities and irrigating canals are now the only witnesses to their former presence and prosperity. The beans reached Europe as an archeological specimen in 1888, part of an exhibit of materials excavated from the Los Muertos prehistoric site in Arizona. This drought-resistant bean is a rapid grower, ideally suited to the hot, dry climates of western Texas, Arizona, and New Mexico. The pods are about three inches long, two-fifths of an inch wide, and somewhat flattened; the beans themselves are the size of navy beans and may be white, yellow, brown, or dotted. One variety, the blue speckled tepary, is from the southern Mexican highlands. As with others of the species, it is delicately patterned and has its own attractive scent and flavor.

Culinary Uses
Resembling the great northern or navy bean, with coloring ranging from white to brown, the tepary bean has gener-

ally been limited to regional dishes in the areas in which it grows. Well-cooked teparies are light and mealy and have a rich, beany aroma. Serve them simply, with oil, vinegar, and a bit of salt. They're too fine to burden with molasses and smoked ham.

Health Benefits
The tepary bean is less gas-forming than many other beans. Medical studies in Australia have shown that it has a significant effect on controlling blood glucose responses while flattening blood sugar levels, both important factors in controlling adult-onset diabetes. Low in fat and high in fiber.

Urd Bean
(Phaseolus mungo)
Also Known As: Urd Dal, Black Gram

The scientific name *Phaseolus* was bestowed in 39 B.C. by Calumella, who observed that the seed looks like a "small

Urd Bean / Nutritional Value Per 100 g Edible Portion		
	Dried Raw	Dried Cooked
Calories	351	105
Protein	25.06 g	7.54 g
Fat	1.83 g	0.55 g
Fiber	4.43 g	1.33 g
Calcium	196 mg	53 mg
Iron	6.84 mg	1.75 mg
Magnesium	260 mg	63 mg
Phosphorus	575 mg	156 mg
Potassium	1,025 mg	231 mg
Sodium	26 mg	7 mg
Zinc	3.080 mg	0.830 mg
Copper	0.659 mg	0.139 mg
Manganese	1.614 mg	0.412 mg
Beta Carotene (A)	114 IU	31 IU
Thiamine (B$_1$)	0.355 mg	0.150 mg
Riboflavin (B$_2$)	0.280 mg	0.075 mg
Niacin (B$_3$)	1.800 mg	1.500 mg
Pantothenic Acid (B$_5$)	1.920 mg	0.433 mg
Pyridoxine (B$_6$)	0.275 mg	0.058 mg
Folic Acid (B$_9$)	628.2 mcg	94.4 mcg
Ascorbic Acid (C)	4.8 mg	1.0 mg

boat." The specific term *mungo* comes from the Indian name, *moong*, for this type of bean. The English name *urd* is from the Hindi name for the plant.

General Information

The urd bean is thought to be native to India and is widely grown there and in the Far East. The long, hairy pods contain oblong, blackish seeds similar in size and shape to their cousin the mung bean.

Culinary Uses

Urd beans taste very similar to mung beans. Available whole, split, and skinless, they can be cooked whole as a side vegetable or puréed and used in soups.

NUTS, SEEDS, AND OILS

The hardy nut, in solid mail secure,
Impregnable to winter's frosts,
Repays its hoarder's care.
—WILLIAM SOMERVILLE, "HOBBINOL"

Though I do not believe that a plant will spring up where no seed has been,
I have great faith in a seed. Convince me that you have a seed there,
and I am prepared to expect wonders.
—HENRY DAVID THOREAU, "THE DISPERSION OF SEEDS"

God gives the nuts but he does not crack them.
—GERMAN PROVERB

NUTS, SEEDS, AND OILS

NUTS, SEEDS, AND OILS

The term *nut* comes from the Old English *hnutu* and the Latin *nux*, or *nutriens*, meaning "to nourish." Botanically, nuts are oily, single-seeded, dry, hard-shelled fruits that must be cracked open, but the term is also used for any seed or fruit with an edible kernel in a hard or brittle shell. Technically speaking, not everything we call a nut is a nut: almonds and pistachios are fruits; the peanut is a legume; and pine nuts and Brazil nuts are seeds. Nuts and seeds are compact packages of highly concentrated nutrients prepared by nature to supply all the requirements of a living plant, be it a flower, bush, or tree. They are hermetically sealed within their protective shells to guard against bacterial contamination and are doubly protected by the skin covering the kernel. Nuts and seeds are marketed in a variety of forms: shelled or in the shell, raw or roasted, salted or spiced or unseasoned, prepackaged or in bulk. In general, the more processing and packaging they have been subjected to, the higher the price. Although considered by most Americans to be strictly snack food, nuts and seeds are a valuable source of vitamins, minerals, and protein, and they can be used in cooking just like any other vegetable.

When buying nuts and seeds in the shell, look for clean ones with bright, well-shaped shells that are heavy for their size, as this indicates fresher, meatier kernels. The shell is a natural protector against free-radical damage caused by light and air. Make sure that the shells are free from splits, cracks, stains, holes, or other surface imperfections. When purchasing nuts already shelled, avoid limp, rubbery, dark, or shriveled nut meat, and do not eat or use moldy nuts or seeds, since these may not be safe. Whole nuts and seeds in the shell will remain freshest for the longest period of time, while those that have been further processed (chopped, ground, or roasted) are more prone to spoilage or rancidity and should be refrigerated. Most packages of crushed, slivered, and broken nut pieces are already rancid when purchased, so if possible process your own. Almonds are less prone to rancidity, while walnuts and pecans are more prone to it because of their higher oil content. This rich oil content also concentrates pesticides, so seek out organic nuts and seeds. All nuts and seeds should be stored in their shells in glass containers (oil-rich foods combine with plastic to form plasticides) in a cold, dark place such as the refrigerator or freezer.

Add these versatile foods ground to baked goods, mix them chopped or ground slightly into casseroles or salads, brown and serve them with cooked or raw vegetables, purée them into smooth butters, or soak and then grind and strain them to make nut and seed "milks."

Nuts and seeds are endowed with a nearly complete array of vitamins and minerals. They are rich in protein of high biological value; a study of the relative protein content of nuts, milk, and meat showed that pound for pound most nuts contain as much or more protein than meat and milk, and nut protein is easily assimilated and does not form uric acid. Nuts are fairly rich in starches and sugars, are three to four times richer in mineral salts than flesh or milk, and contain far more vitamins. Most nuts are good sources of calcium, phosphorus, magnesium, and potassium. They are also high in essential fatty acids, which facilitate oxygen transport, assist proteins in building body cells, aid glandular activity, convert carotene into vitamin A, and complement vitamin D and calcium. Because they are such a dense and concentrated food, nuts must be properly chewed before swallowing for ease of digestion. Nuts and seeds, along with legumes, contain compounds known as phytosterols. These plant compounds are structurally similar to cholesterol and steroid hormones. Phytosterols function to inhibit the absorption of cholesterol by blocking absorption sites and thus lower total cholesterol count. Phytosterols have also been shown to enhance immune functions, inhibit the Epstein-Barr virus, prevent chemically induced cancers in animals, and exhibit numerous other anticancer effects.

Traditional folk medicines associate the energy affiliated with nuts with sexual energy, a kind of energy not associated with rational behavior—nutty, in a word. In addition, nuts are the most concentrated vegetable source of oils and, if eaten in excess, challenge the liver. An overtaxed liver may lead to another kind of nutty behavior—spring fits and a restless spring fever. That's the excessive side of nuts. In moderate quantities, however, for high-strung and nervous people, nuts are calming. Valued as a restorative and warming food in both Ayurvedic and Chinese medicine, nuts help build body mass and strength. The trick is how to determine the dose, and that will depend upon your ability to digest oil. Nuts are best used sparingly, if at all, by people with a compromised liver or digestive system, an overweight problem, or a sluggish condition (such as candida, yeast, or viral problems, edema, tumors, or cysts). Such people would do best to favor the less fatty nuts.

Here is a list of the fat content of various nuts (in grams of fat per 100 grams of edible portion), from most fatty to least fatty:

Macadamia	72	Black Walnut	59	Cashew	46
Pecan	71	Almond	54	Coconut	35
Brazil Nut	67	Pistachio	54	Acorn	5
English Walnut	65	Peanut	48	Chestnut	2
Hazelnut	62	Pine Nut	47		

OILS

Fat is sexy. The most critical part of any plant is its seed's fatty acids, which store sunlight energy to start anew. No wonder these delicate oils found in the plant's reproductive parts contain more flavor and aroma than the rest of the plant. Consider, for example, an eight-foot-tall corn plant, including its root system. Only the kernels of this huge plant contain oil, and each kernel contains only 5 percent fat. One huge plant yields only a few precious grams of oil. We all need fat. Dietary fats produce body fat needed to provide energy as well as insulate and regulate bodily temperature. The fat-soluble vitamins—vitamins A, D, E, and K—need fat to be bioavailable. Fats help us feel grounded, soothed, and comforted. Refined fats, however, are carcinogenic; they suppress the immune system; they cause gastric distress and irritated lungs and mucous membranes; and they speed aging. Overconsumption of fats of any type can cause a person to be mentally, physically, or emotionally heavy, overly materialistic, or grasping. Excessive fats and/or poor-quality fats challenge the liver and exacerbate cancer, candida, tumors, cysts, edema, obesity, and some forms of high blood pressure.

Nuts and seeds have long been used as a source of oil for culinary, medicinal, and cosmetic purposes. Certain oils offer advantages over others for specific applications. For example, olive, sesame, and coconut oil are more stable than other vegetable oils, so they are preferred for use when exposing foods to heat. Highly polyunsaturated oils such as flax, safflower, and sunflower should not be heated because heat changes the chemical structures of the fatty acids and forms free radicals; these oils are best suited for salad dressings. Oils such as cottonseed and palm should be avoided. These consist primarily of saturated fat (which is usually solid at room temperatures). Cottonseed oil may contain toxic residues because the plants are so heavily sprayed during cultivation and because the oil contains gossypol, a substance known to inhibit sperm function. In fact, gossypol is being investigated for its potential as a "male birth-control pill."

In a modern oil-pressing facility, the starting material (whether seed, nut, grain, or legume) is first mechanically cleaned to prepare it for either chemical or mechanical extraction. With chemical extraction, the material is typically rolled into meal (for example, seed meal or cornmeal) and then mixed with a chemical solvent such as hexane. Once the solvent has separated the oil from the meal, the mixture is exposed to high heat to distill the solvent. Although most of the solvent is removed by this means, traces can still be found. The oil to be produced is then usually further processed (degummed, bleached, deodorized, and so on) to produce a "refined" oil. A refined oil is one that has had some or all of its impurities removed. Many of these "impurities"—vitamin E, lecithin, chlorophyll, carotenes, aromatic oils, and free fatty acids—have important health-promoting properties. In the process of refining, the oil is exposed not only to extremely high heat but also to caustic substances such as phosphoric acid and sodium hydroxide. Because the refined oil has been stripped of most of its natural protection against damage, synthetic antioxidants like BHT are then added as stabilizers and preservatives.

The mechanical method usually differs only in how the oil is initially extracted. The starting material may or may not be cooked at high temperatures for up to two hours to liquefy the oil content and then mechanically pressed through an expeller.

The pressure can be as high as several tons per square inch, which results in the generation of heat, usually around 200 degrees Fahrenheit. The higher the heat, the better the oil yield. Oil pressed in this manner can be filtered and sold either as "cold-pressed," since no external heat was added during the extraction, or as natural, crude, or unrefined oil; it can also be processed further to produce a refined oil. Even oil that has undergone refinement can still be labeled "cold-pressed" as long as no external heat was applied during the extraction. Although far from ideal, the best oils commonly available in the United States are the cold-pressed unrefined oils. Do not expect these oils to taste as "clean" as the highly processed commercial varieties you may have grown accustomed to. Cold-pressed unrefined oils still retain much of their original flavor.

The rancidity process in oil starts immediately. Both heat and air will speed up its deterioration. Therefore, all oil is best kept in a closed container at a temperature of no more than 65 degrees Fahrenheit, preferably lower (the refrigerator is best). The highly monounsaturated oils tend to solidify at very cool refrigerator temperatures, which does not present a problem. The effect of light on oil is far worse than air because it rapidly alters the unsaturated fatty acids into free-radical chains. To counteract this tendency, store all oil in dark or opaque containers. Also, oil readily combines with most types of plastic to form toxic plasticides. If you purchase oil packaged in plastic, remove the oil from its container as soon as possible and store it in a glass container. Better yet, refuse to buy any oil that is sold in plastic.

Although margarine is frequently believed to be more healthful than butter, the truth is that they have the same caloric value and contain equal amounts of fat; what's more, margarine will contribute to the very problems the commercials imply it will prevent, particularly heart disease. The hydrogenated fats in margarine cause extremely elevated cholesterol levels, and deaths from heart disease and cancer are highest among consumers of this type of fat. Most margarines made from soy and safflower oils and sold as "natural" are also hydrogenated and just as harmful as any other margarine. High-quality butter in moderate amounts can be handled by the body much more easily than margarine, which is a chemical compound.

Butter is excellent fuel for the body's basic metabolic functions and contains many nourishing substances. Among the foremost of these is butyric acid, an easily digested short-chain fatty acid that has powerful antiviral, antifungal, and anticancer properties; it also raises the level of the antiviral chemical interferon in the body. Butyric acid also has characteristics found to be helpful in the prevention and treatment of Alzheimer's disease. Butter does contain cholesterol, but cholesterol is required for the proper functioning of bodily cells. While the average North American diet is severely deficient in the vitamins, minerals, and fiber needed to metabolize cholesterol and fats, good-quality butter in a diet rich in nutrients and fiber poses no health risk. The best-quality butter comes from organic farms, where no pesticides or antibiotics are used. Try to find raw organic butter whenever possible, as that is the highest quality.

Ghee is clarified butter, or butter from which the water and milk solids have been removed; it an excellent appetizer, helps digestion by stimulating the secretion of digestive juices, and enhances the flavor of foods. Like butter, ghee contains butyric acid. When used with various herbs, ghee carries their medicinal properties to the tissues. It does not increase cholesterol as many other oils do but promotes the healing of wounds; relieves chronic fever, anemia, and blood disorders; aids in detoxification; alleviates peptic ulcer and colitis; and is good generally for the eyes, nose, and skin. Indian lore also purports that ghee helps to enhance intelligence, understanding, and memory.

It doesn't take a Ph.D. in chemistry to discern good oils from bad. It's as simple as using your taste and smell senses. Compare a superior extra-virgin olive oil with a pure olive oil. If the oil smells and tastes like the food from which it was pressed, that's one indication of quality. If it leaves a fresh, rather than an acrid, burning, or metallic taste in your mouth, it passes a second test. There is also a third indicator: how the oil feels in your mouth. Within seconds of swallowing a teaspoon of vital oil, your mouth feels fresh and clean. It's as if your body, knowing that good oil is indispensable, invites it right in. Conversely, an oil denatured by oxygen or high heat (from shoddy production or storage) has a greasy taste, coats the mouth, and isn't readily soluble. The body doesn't want to absorb it. If denatured oil tastes greasy in your mouth, imagine how it gums up arteries and challenges the liver, the organ primarily responsible for fat metabolism.

Acorn
(Quercus alba, Q. virens, Q. rubra)

Quercus is derived from the Celtic *quer*, meaning "fine," and *cuez*, meaning "tree." Ultimately, the word is believed to have been derived from the Sanskrit word for "door"; many cultures believed trees in general to be doorways to other worlds and dimensions. *Alba* means "white"; *virens* means "green." The English word *acorn* is derived from the Old English *aecern*, meaning "oak fruit" or "fruit of the tree."

General Information

The oak is indigenous to temperate regions of the northern hemisphere and to high altitudes in the tropics. A member of the beech family, oak trees are prolific producers, annually producing more nuts in North America than all of the region's other nut trees taken together, both wild and cultivated. Acorns are round to oblong in shape and fit into cups of rough bark; when the nuts are ripe, the cups separate and the nuts drop to the ground. Many Greek and Latin writers referred to acorns as wholesome fare. Early Athenians evidently ate them, and several classical writers say the same of the idyllic Arcadians in the "Golden Age" of innocence. With the rising abundance of cereal grains, the acorn lost its importance as a staple food and was relegated to the role of poor man's fare and swine fodder. The

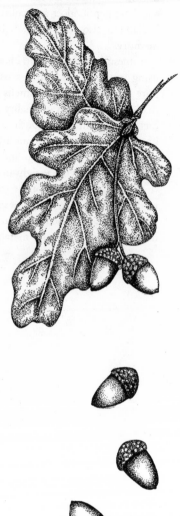

Acorn / Nutritional Value Per 100 g Edible Portion		
	Raw	Dried
Calories	369	509
Protein	6.15 g	8.10 g
Fat	23.86 g	31.41 g
Fiber	2.57 g	3.38 g
Calcium	41 mg	54 mg
Iron	0.79 mg	1.04 mg
Magnesium	62 mg	82 mg
Phosphorus	79 mg	103 mg
Potassium	539 mg	709 mg
Sodium	0 mg	0 mg
Zinc	0.510 mg	0.670 mg
Copper	0.621 mg	0.818 mg
Thiamine (B$_1$)	0.112 mg	0.149 mg
Riboflavin (B$_2$)	0.118 mg	0.154 mg
Niacin (B$_3$)	1.827 mg	2.406 mg
Ascorbic Acid (C)	0 mg	0 mg

drawback to most acorns is their bitter taste, which comes from tannic acid. Of the almost three hundred species of oaks, only a very few (particularly the white oak and evergreen oak) produce nuts that are sweet, naturally delicious, and edible when they drop ripe from the tree. Acorns represented an important source of food for American Indians, who removed the bitter substance by boiling the nuts until the kernels were palatable or by grinding them and placing the resultant meal in water for a day to soak out the bitter substances.

LORE AND LEGEND

Of all the trees in prehistoric times, the oak was the most widely venerated because in many ancient mythologies it was the primordial first tree and the tree from which humanity sprang. Abraham received the angel of Jehovah under its branches; the Greeks dedicated it to Zeus because his oracle in Dodona was located in a grove of oaks; and the Romans held it sacred to Jupiter. It has long been associated with thunder gods in European culture; this may be due to the fact that oaks seem to attract more lightning than any other tree. Because the oak provided the life-giving acorn, the main food for many Nordic tribes, the tree became a symbol of fecundity and immortality, and was under the immediate protection of the Norse god Thor. It was considered an act of sacrilege to mutilate these trees to even a small degree. The oak tree was also the sacred tree of the pagan Dagda, the Good God and Creator of the ancient Irish Gaels. It was the celestial tree of the Celtic Druids, and no Druidic ceremony or rite took place without the aid of the oak tree and its satellite, the mistletoe; even their diet consisted mainly of acorns and berries. In fact, the name *Druid* derived from the Greek word for "tree" (particularly oak), *drus;* a wood nymph was a *druas.* Aesop recounts the fable of the man who lay beneath an oak tree criticizing the Creator for placing so tiny an acorn on so huge a tree, while the mammoth pumpkin grows on so delicate a vine. But when an acorn fell and hit him on the nose, he decided that perhaps the Creator was right after all, for what if that acorn had been in proportion to the tree?

To Romans during Pliny's day the oak symbolized bravery, and a crown of oak leaves was a glorious reward for outstanding military valor, particularly for saving a citizen's life in battle. The northern European peoples also believed in the heroic and victorious symbolism of the oak leaf cluster, and this symbolism survives today in American military decorations, with the Oak Leaf Cluster bestowed as an additional honor on those already decorated for exceptional service.

Culinary Uses

The flavor of acorns seems to be a matter of opinion. Some consider it to be rough and disagreeable, while others claim that fresh sweet acorns, roasted and salted, provide a good snack food, tasting like a cross between sunflower seeds and popcorn. They are considered "one of the most palatable wild foods" by H. D. Harrington, who ate his way through uncounted edibles while researching his classic reference book, *Edible Native Plants of the Rocky Mountains.* Chestnutlike in texture, the thin-shelled, starchy seed is nestled in a tiny basal cup. To remove the bitter tannins, the nuts must be soaked in several changes of water until sweet tasting. This leaching process may take from a few hours to a few days, depending upon the variety. Ground into meal, acorns can be used in the same manner as cornmeal.

Health Benefits

Acorns help to stabilize blood sugar and thus are used for both hypoglycemia and hyperglycemia. They are a nurturing food, helping build mass and supporting the stomach and spleen-pancreas meridians.

Alfalfa

(Medicago sativa)

Also Known As: Chilean Clover, Buffalo Grass, Lucerne, Purple Medic

The name *Medicago* is derived from the Media region in Persia, where this important plant was thought to have originated. The Greeks called it *medicai,* the Romans *medica* or *herba medica,* all meaning "coming from Media." *Sativa* means "cultivated." The Arabs named this herb *al-fac-facah,* meaning "father of all foods," which the Spanish changed to *alfalfa.*

General Information

Alfalfa is a deep-rooting, bushy perennial resembling leggy clover that grows to three feet in height and produces the smallest, but most popular, seeds of the legume family. The plant was introduced into the Mediterranean Greek and Roman world about 470 B.C., during the time of the Persian Wars. The ancient Arabs fed it to their horses in the belief that it made them swift and strong, and the Romans (believing or at least hoping the same) started cultivating it as a forage crop starting in the first or second century A.D. Not until the seventeenth century did alfalfa arrive in western Europe, at which time it was given the name *lucerna*, meaning "lamp," after the bright, shiny appearance of the seeds. Ultimately, alfalfa reached North America with the Spanish conquistadores, who planted it in Mexico and Chile. Gold prospectors carried it from South America into California. Although still highly prized by farmers as animal forage, the sprouted seeds have become so popular for human consumption in the last thirty years that they are now found in stores and restaurants everywhere.

Culinary Uses

The leaves, flowering tops, seeds, and sprouts of alfalfa are all edible, but it is the sprouts that are most often seen and eaten. Easily grown, alfalfa sprouts find their way into salads and sandwiches of every kind, where their delicate taste endears them to many hearts and palates. The light brown unsprouted seeds may also be sprinkled over salads, casseroles, breads, and pastries for a delicious, nutty flavor.

Health Benefits

Nutritive, stomachic, tonic. Alfalfa is one of the most complete and nutritionally rich of all foods tested. It is noteworthy for its exceptional amount of trace minerals, for having all eight essential amino acids, and for being high in vitamins A and D, calcium, phosphorus, iron, and potassium. Medicinally, it has anti-inflammatory properties; is very effective in cleansing toxins from the large intestine and bloodstream; is a natural pain reliever; contains natural fluorine, which prevents tooth decay and helps rebuild decayed teeth; and provides a boost to the immune system. Its high beta carotene (the precursor to vitamin A) content acts to strengthen the epithelial cells of the mucous membranes of the stomach, while its high chlorophyll content works as a natural deodorizer, infection fighter, and blood purifier. Alfalfa-and-mint tea is regarded as a soothing beverage and an aid to digestion, probably because alfalfa contains the digestive enzyme betaine. Alfalfa tea provides a nutrient boost, prevents exhaustion, and relieves bloating, arthritis, rheumatism, colitis, ulcers, and anemia.

Note: Alfalfa sprouts and seeds should be avoided by those with rheumatoid arthritis and systemic lupus, because of their rich content of the amino acid canavanine, which can ignite inflammations in these conditions. Alfalfa leaf, however, is not a source of this amino acid and may be used by those with rheumatoid diseases.

Almond
(Prunus dulcis, P. amygdalus)

The almond tree is part of the plum family—thus the genus *Prunus*. *Dulcis* means "sweet," while *amygdalus* is the old Latin name for the almond. The English word *almond* came from the French *amande*, a derivative of *amygdalus*.

General Information

The graceful almond tree is native to North Africa, west Asia, and the Mediterranean. Botanically, almonds are a fruit—the ancient ancestor of later fruits that have large stones for seeds, like nectarines, peaches, plums, and apricots. The almond itself has a tough, greenish-gray hull that looks very much like a small, elongated peach. This hull splits open at maturity, revealing the familiar almond shell, which encases the edible nut. Two types of almonds are

Alfalfa / Nutritional Value Per 100 g Edible Portion	Sprouted Raw	Dried
Calories	29	269
Protein	3.99 g	19.9 g
Fat	0.69 g	4.30 g
Fiber	1.64 g	21.00 g
Calcium	32 mg	899 mg
Iron	0.96 mg	26.00 mg
Magnesium	27 mg	230 mg
Phosphorus	70 mg	150 mg
Potassium	79 mg	1,200 mg
Sodium	6 mg	17 mg
Zinc	0.920 mg	trace
Copper	0.157 mg	n/a
Manganese	0.188 mg	2.530 mg
Beta Carotene (A)	155 IU	24,800 IU
Thiamine (B₁)	0.076 mg	0.190 mg
Riboflavin (B₂)	0.126 mg	1.420 mg
Niacin (B₃)	0.481 mg	9.700 mg
Pantothenic Acid (B₅)	0.563 mg	n/a
Pyridoxine (B₆)	0.034 mg	n/a
Folic Acid (B₉)	36.0 mcg	n/a
Ascorbic Acid (C)	8.2 mg	147.0 mg

grown: sweet and bitter. The sweet is the only one used as a nut, mostly for desserts and confectionery items. Bitter almonds are cheaper and easier to grow but contain prussic acid and are suitable for use only after the removal of this poison by heat. The bitter almond provides the main source of bitter almond oil, which is used both as a flavoring and as an ingredient in cosmetic skin preparations. Early on, almonds became popular throughout Europe. An inventory of the household goods of the queen of France in 1372 listed five hundred pounds of almonds, versus only twenty pounds of sugar. Almonds were brought to California in 1843 by Spanish missionaries, and today this state produces the world's largest share of almonds. They remain a dominant nut in world trade and the most widely grown and eaten tree nut.

Culinary Uses

For freshness, purchase whole almonds and then slice or chop them just prior to use. The thin brown skin of a shelled almond should be intact and unscratched, as it provides some protection from rancidity. Slice an almond kernel in half and examine its texture. A solid white nutmeat denotes freshness, while a honeycomb-textured kernel or yellow color indicates rancidity. Although the skin is edible, some authorities claim that it should be removed because of its astringent tendencies. Almonds are widely used in confectionery, are made into drinks and liqueurs, combine successfully with cheese and vegetables to make a good stuffing, and may be added raw to salads. Use almonds in tandem with almond oil for reinforced flavor in baking or to give body to a salad dressing. Raw, whole almonds will sprout. Indeed, sprouted almonds are

LORE AND LEGEND

Greek mythology relates that a beautiful Thracian princess named Phyllis was deserted on her wedding day by her lover, Demophon. After waiting many years for him to return, she eventually died of a broken heart. In sympathy and for eternal compensation, the gods transformed her into an almond tree (called *phylla* by the Greeks), a symbol of hope. When Demophon finally returned it was too late, and when the leafless, flowerless, and forlorn tree was shown him as the memorial of Phyllis, he clasped it in his arms, whereupon it burst forth into bloom—an emblem of true love inextinguishable by death. In Greece almonds in uneven numbers of three, five, or seven are offered to guests for good fortune and happiness at christenings, weddings, and the ordination of priests. Shelled almonds and raisins, combined, were early symbols of good luck for Jews. The nuts and fruits, packaged together, are still popular in eastern Europe.

Another beautiful legend comes from Portugal. A Moorish prince from the deep south of Portugal (Algarve) married a Scandinavian princess, who pined away in that snowless land for lack of winter and the sight of snow. Her prince relieved her homesickness by planting almond trees so thickly along the entire coast that when they bloomed, their white blossoms covered the land each spring with a snowy-white blanket.

Almond / Nutritional Value Per 100 g Edible Portion			
	Dried, Unblanched		Dried, Unblanched
Calories	589	Copper	0.942 mg
Protein	19.95 g	Manganese	2.273 mg
Fat	52.21 g	Beta Carotene (A)	0 mg
Fiber	2.71 g	Thiamine (B₁)	0.211 mg
Calcium	266 mg	Riboflavin (B₂)	0.779 mg
Iron	3.66 mg	Niacin (B₃)	3.361 mg
Magnesium	296 mg	Pantothenic Acid (B₅)	0.471 mg
Phosphorus	520 mg	Pyridoxine (B₆)	0.113 mg
Potassium	732 mg	Folic Acid (B₉)	58.7 mcg
Sodium	11 mg	Ascorbic Acid (C)	0.600 mg
Zinc	2.920 mg	Tocopherol (E)	24.01 mg

very delicious; many people consider them to have a much better flavor than dry, unsprouted almonds. Don't sprout them for longer than twenty-four to thirty-six hours or else the sprouts may turn rancid.

Health Benefits

pH > 6.0. Demulcent, emollient. Almonds are traditionally regarded as having special healing and protecting properties; some doctors even "prescribe" almonds daily for their patients. The most alkaline of all nuts (but still slightly acidic), almonds are particularly valuable as an essential "building food" for those who are underweight. Their high fat, carbohydrate, and protein content make them an ideal food for strengthening the body when there is no need to worry about the increase in the supply of fat. Almonds contain a small amount of amygdalin, better known as laetrile, which has resulted in their gaining a reputation as an anticancer food. According to Ayurvedic medicine, almonds build and strengthen the bones, nerves, and reproductive system. Best eaten raw, they are easy to digest when well masticated or ground fine.

Note: Since almonds have a high ratio of arginine to lysine, they should be avoided by individuals susceptible to cold sores or herpes infections; arginine promotes (and lysine prevents) the activation of the virus.

BYPRODUCTS

Almond butter is made from either raw or roasted almonds ground to a creamy consistency. It can be used on toast or in baked goods, wherever you would use peanut butter.

Almond extract is made from the oil of the bitter almond, a cousin to the sweet almond. The oil is diluted with water and alcohol to make this common flavoring.

Almond milk is made from almonds that have been soaked, crushed, and strained. This delicately sweet and satisfying beverage is a wonderful dairy-free and soy-free milk that can be directly substituted for cow's milk. Although it is available commercially, almond milk can be produced easily at home, and the result is fresher and sweeter.

Almond oil is made by crushing whole raw almonds to extract the oil. Food-grade almonds are expensive, making a quality almond oil expensive and very difficult to find in a truly cold-pressed form. Unrefined almond oil is sweet, pleasant tasting, and known for its high content of vitamins A and E. Therapeutically, the oil has been used for treating gastric ulcers, as a laxative, and as an antiseptic for the intestines, as well as to help stabilize the nervous system. It is also a time-honored balm for dry or sunburned skin, a skin beautifier, and a massage oil.

Almond, Tropical
(Terminalia catappa)

The scientific binomial is descriptive, for *Terminalia* refers to the manner in which the leaves are borne in bunches on the branch ends, while *catappa* comes from a Malayan name for the tree.

General Information
Native to the sandy coasts of Malaysia and other regions of southeast Asia, the tropical almond tree was taken by Captain Bligh to Saint Vincent in the West Indies in 1793, along with the breadfruit. The fruits are about the size of a plum and are slightly compressed on two sides. They have a tender skin and a thin layer of edible, juicy pulp surrounding a thick, spongy shell, which is very difficult to crack.

Culinary Uses
The crisp, white nutmeat of the small, slender kernel has a delicious flavor reminiscent of the true almond, to which the tropical almond is not related. The nuts are edible raw or roasted. Having been described by one writer as "beyond comparison the most delicious nut of any kind India affords," they are popular and highly regarded in the Far East. The kernels yield a sweet, colorless, nondrying, edible oil—Indian almond oil—which resembles true almond oil in flavor and odor. Highly esteemed as a table oil in India and Malaysia, it does not readily become rancid.

Almondette
(Buchanania lanzan)
Also Known As: Calumpang, Chironji

The English name *almondette* means "little almond."

General Information
The almondette tree is native to southeast Asia and grows best in the deciduous forests of hot, dry regions. The tree bears black, single-seeded fruits measuring about half an inch in diameter, with pear-shaped kernels enclosed within; often mottled, these kernels are no more than a quarter inch in length. Virtually unknown in the United States, the almondette is an important article of commerce in central India, where it is known as chironji.

Culinary Uses

The delicious flavor of almondettes may be compared to a combination of almond and pistachio. In India the nuts are eaten raw or roasted, as substitutes for almonds, and since early times they have been prized as a sweetmeat when cooked. One of the native Indian breads consists of pounding the dried fruits (with the kernel intact) and then drying and baking the resulting nut loaf. These nuts also yield a light yellow, wholesome oil, which has a pleasant aroma and makes a satisfactory substitute for either almond or olive oil.

Health Benefits

Almondette nuts are composed of over 50 percent oil and 12 percent protein.

Beechnut
(Fagus grandifolia, F. sylvatica)

Fagus is from the Greek word *phagein*, meaning "to eat," referring to the edible character of the nuts. The term *grandifolia* means "large-leaved," while *sylvatica* means "forest-loving." The common name *beech tree*, found in varying forms throughout the Teutonic dialects, means, with difference of gender, either "a book" or "a beech."

General Information

The stately beech tree, with its smooth, silvery-gray bark, blue-green leaves, and symmetrical round canopy, is one of the most beautiful trees found in North America and Europe. The nuts are larger and more numerous in more northerly climes. Like their relative the acorn, beechnuts are now used primarily as animal fodder, although some regions in Scandinavia still use them to make meal for bread.

Culinary Uses

The beechnut is similar to the chestnut in flavor but has a much higher fat content. One of the sweetest nuts from

Beechnut / Nutritional Value Per 100 g Edible Portion			
	Dried		**Dried**
Calories	576	Fiber	3.70 g
Protein	6.20 g	Calcium	1 mg
Fat	50.00 g		

LORE AND LEGEND

The beech has been intimately associated with books and writing since antiquity, and thus has become the symbolic tree of the graphic arts. Early runic tablets were made from thin slabs of smooth beech bark, and as a monumental tree the beech has no rival: for many centuries its bark has served as a convenient place to register challenges to the enemy, post epitaphs, and carve the initials of loved ones.

the northern forests, those gathered from the wild may be eaten fresh, dried, or roasted. Unless properly dried, fresh nuts will deteriorate within a few weeks. Flour or meal is prepared by mashing the nutmeats, allowing the resultant paste to dry out, and then grinding it. This meal can then be used to make bread and biscuits or combined with other flours in baked products.

Health Benefits

Beechnuts, according to some authorities, contain small amounts of toxins and thus should either not be consumed in quantity or be avoided entirely.

Brazil Nut
(Bertholletia excelsa)
Also Known As: Para Nut, Cream Nut

This tree was given its Latin name *Bertholletia* in honor of Louis Claude Berthollet, a French chemist; the term *excelsa* means "tall." The nut's English name indicates its place of origin, Brazil.

General Information

From the Amazon River forests come Brazil nuts, fruits of huge broad leaf evergreen trees whose trunks may grow up to six feet in diameter and reach straight up to immense heights of 150 feet. These trees are not cultivated but grow wild, and all attempts thus far at cultivation have met with resounding failure. Each tree bears between two and four hundred large fruits, which when ripe are dark brown, pear-shaped, and about the size of a man's head, weighing between two and four pounds; in total these fruits contain approximately five hundred pounds of unshelled Brazil nuts. Most are harvested by waiting for the fruit to ripen and fall to the ground—a potentially lethal event, since they fall from great heights. When the fruits are broken open, there is a coconut-like pod containing between twelve and twenty-four nuts all packed neatly together like orange segments. Each dark brown nut is up to two inches in length and triangular in shape. Harvesting of the nuts is done by laborers called caboclo, who gather the pods in baskets and carry them to trading posts. In-shell nuts are dried in automatic dryers to produce a moisture content of 11 percent before shipment. Shelled nuts are dried to 6 percent moisture content. A quarter of the crop is shelled before export, chiefly from the city of Para. The shelling operation is largely a manual one. Nuts are soaked for twenty-four hours and then put in boiling water for three to five minutes to soften the shell. Cracking machines are hand-operated and resemble a home bottle capper. In some small plants, a piece of iron or a wooden club suffices. Although these trees are important to the Brazilian economy, the nuts are not a regular part of the native diet since the climate is too hot for so oily a food. For the most part, Brazil nuts are enjoyed as a delicacy in foreign lands thousands of miles away from where they grow.

Culinary Uses

Brazil nuts are sweet and flavorful, with a rich, creamy texture and a delicate flavor. They are best purchased in the shell, since their high oil content predisposes them to turn rancid quickly; after purchasing, they should always be refrigerated and used within two or three months. Brazil nuts are excellent for eating raw in muesli and salads, as a stuffing for dates, or just as a snack on their own. They also can be added to vegetarian loaves and burgers, casseroles, stuffings, and soups. Try them as the "core" of baked apples.

Health Benefits

The Brazil nut is among the most acid of nuts because of its high protein content and has an oil content of nearly 70 percent. Brazil nuts are good sources of the amino acids methionine and cysteine, making them a complementary protein source for vegetarians. For those doing hard physical work, both the nuts and the butter made from them are very nourishing.

Breadnut
(Artocarpus altilis, Brosimum alicastrum)

Artocarpus comes from the Greek words *artos*, meaning "bread," and *carpos*, meaning "fruit." The term *altilis* refers to the tallness of the tree. *Brosimum* derives from a Greek term meaning "edible." The English name *breadfruit* comes from the fact that when the fruit is roasted whole between hot stones, the pulp achieves the consistency and taste of freshly baked bread. The English name *breadnut* is probably a contraction of *breadfruit tree nut*.

General Information

Two related trees produce nuts or seeds that are designated as breadnuts: the breadnut tree and the seeded variety of the breadfruit tree. The evergreen breadnut (*Brosimum alicas-*

Brazil Nut / Nutritional Value Per 100 g Edible Portion			
	Dried, Unblanched		Dried, Unblanched
Calories	656	Copper	1.770 mg
Protein	14.34 g	Manganese	0.774 mg
Fat	66.22 g	Thiamine (B₁)	1.000 mg
Fiber	2.29 g	Riboflavin (B₂)	0.122 mg
Calcium	176 mg	Niacin (B₃)	1.622 mg
Iron	3.40 mg	Pantothenic Acid (B₅)	0.236 mg
Magnesium	225 mg	Pyridoxine (B₆)	0.251 mg
Phosphorus	600 mg	Folic Acid (B₉)	4 mcg
Potassium	600 mg	Ascorbic Acid (C)	0.70 mg
Sodium	2 mg	Tocopherol (E)	7.60 mg
Zinc	4.590 mg		

Breadnut / Nutritional Value Per 100 g Edible Portion				
	Breadfruit Seeds, Raw	Breadfruit Seeds, Boiled	Breadnut Seeds, Raw	Breadnut Seeds, Dried
Calories	191	168	217	367
Protein	7.40 g	5.30 g	5.97 g	8.62 g
Fat	5.59 g	2.30 g	0.99 g	1.68 g
Fiber	1.69 g	1.80 g	2.53 g	5.60 g
Calcium	36 mg	61 mg	98 mg	94 mg
Iron	3.67 mg	0.60 mg	2.09 mg	4.60 mg
Phosphorus	175 mg	124 mg	67 mg	178 mg
Beta Carotene (A)	256 IU	n/a	248 IU	216 IU
Thiamine (B₁)	0.482 mg	0.290 mg	0.055 mg	0.030 mg
Riboflavin (B₂)	0.301 mg	0.170 mg	0.055 mg	0.140 mg
Niacin (B₃)	0.438 mg	5.300 mg	0.880 mg	2.100 mg
Pantothenic Acid (B₅)	0.877 mg	n/a	n/a	n/a
Ascorbic Acid (C)	6.6 mg	n/a	27.4 mg	46.6 mg

LORE AND LEGEND

The seeded breadfruit, native of the hot, moist Pacific Islands, was regarded for years as a romantic symbol of abundance and easy living.

trum) is native to southern Mexico, Central America, and the Caribbean. Ripe breadnut fruits are yellow and about one inch in diameter, with a single seed or breadnut about the size of a small chestnut. The scanty pulp is edible. The breadfruit tree (*Artocarpus altilis*) is a handsome tree believed native to a vast area extending from New Guinea through the Indo-Malayan Archipelago to western Micronesia. A member of the mulberry family, the bread-fruit is a valuable crop from southern Florida to Brazil and during its eight-month season provides the natives around the Gulf of Mexico and the Caribbean Sea with an important fruit, often the mainstay of their diet. Both seedless and seeded forms of breadfruit are known. The seeded type is grown primarily for its seeds, called breadnuts, which when cooked and eaten are said to taste like chestnuts.

Culinary Uses
When breadnut seeds are boiled, their flavor is somewhat like potatoes. Ground breadnut seeds may be added to cold milk and sugar to make a nutritious and tasty milk shake. Roasted seeds develop a nutty cocoa flavor, and a beverage somewhat similar to coffee can be prepared by grinding the roasted seeds and steeping them in boiling water. The seeds from seeded breadfruit are usually boiled, roasted, or fried before being eaten, when they are said to be so close to chestnuts in flavor and texture that they may be freely substituted in any chestnut recipe. See also the **Breadfruit** reference in the **Fruits** section.

Butternut
(Juglans cinerea)
Also Known As: Oilnut, White Walnut

The generic term *Juglans* is a contraction of the Latin *Jovis glans*, meaning "nut of Jupiter" or "nut of the gods," after the ancient belief that the gods dined on walnuts. The term *cinerea* means "ash-colored" and refers to the color of the foliage. The English term *butternut* comes from the nut's high oil content.

General Information
The butternut is native to North America and grows over most of the eastern half of the United States. It differs from the black walnut in that the tree is usually smaller and has lighter-colored bark. The oblong or cylindrical fruits that enclose the nuts are about 2½ inches in length and sharp-pointed at the apex, with a rough, jagged surface. A thin husk with numerous sticky hairs and a pungent but not unpleasant odor covers the outside. The shell is hard, rough, and walnutlike. Since the shell is so hard and thick, it is generally difficult to crack the nuts without shattering the kernels.

Culinary Uses
Butternuts have a deliciously sweet yet distinctive, slightly spicy flavor. Young tender butternuts, gathered in the

Butternut / Nutritional Value Per 100 g Edible Portion			
	Dried		Dried
Calories	612	Phosphorus	446 mg
Protein	24.90 g	Potassium	421 mg
Fat	56.98 g	Sodium	1 mg
Fiber	1.87 g	Zinc	3.130 mg
Calcium	53 mg	Copper	0.450 mg
Iron	4.02 mg	Manganese	6.560 mg
Magnesium	237 mg		

summer while still green, can be pickled in the same manner as walnuts. Fully mature nuts are good eaten alone or in baked goods. The trees can also be tapped for their sweet sap, like sugar maples.

Candlenut
(Aleurites moluccana)

Aleurites is from a Greek term meaning "farinose" or "floury"; *moluccana* means "coming from the Moluccas." The nut derives its English name from the fact that natives of Hawaii string the kernels on a stick and light them as we do candles. Because the nuts are very oily, they serve this purpose well.

General Information
This small evergreen tree is native to most warm countries of the East: India, southern Japan, Malaysia, and nearly all the islands of the Pacific Ocean.

Culinary Uses
The nuts are round and one to two inches across, each containing either one or two waxy white kernels possessing a flavor similar to walnuts. They are widely consumed as a flavoring ingredient after suitable preparation. The usual practice is to roast the nuts until they can be cracked open and then to sauté the kernels crushed with other ingredients such as shallots, garlic, and chili peppers; the result is an aromatic mixture that can be used in savory dishes.

Canola Oil
(Brassica rapa oleifera, B. campestris, B. napus)

Brassica is the old Latin name for this family of plants; *rapa* is from the Latin for the turnip, *oleifera* means "oil-bearing," *campestris* means "from the fields," *napus* means "turnips."

General Information
Canola oil is made from the seeds of rape, a plant in the cabbage and turnip family that dates back to antiquity in eastern Europe and Asia. The small, round, usually black seeds grow in long slender pods similar to mustard and have a nutty flavor like sesame seeds but with a surprising sweetness and tang. With a name like *rape seed*, neither the seeds nor the oil caught on in the United States, so currently they are under production using their Canadian name, *canola* (shorthand for "Canadian oil/low-acid"), both as a snack seed and for oil production.

Culinary Uses
Unrefined canola oil has a fresh golden color and rich, savory flavor, but most canola oil found in stores is highly processed and rather mild. This highly processed oil is best suited for dishes where you do not want a pronounced flavor, or it can be used directly on salads, raw vegetables, potatoes, and grains. Because of its omega-3 fatty acid content, canola oil should not be used for cooking at over 320 degrees Fahrenheit.

Health Benefits
Canola oil contains one of the lowest amounts of saturated fat and is among the highest for monounsaturated fat content of any edible oil. Therapeutically, it has been used to protect artery walls and as protection against blood clots. Unfortunately, rape seeds contain erucic acid, which causes fatty degeneration of the heart, kidneys, adrenals, and thyroid.

Cashew
(Anacardium occidentale)

The generic name *Anacardium* means "heart-shaped"; *occidentale* means "western." The English word *cashew* is derived from the Brazilian Tupi-Indian word *acaju*.

General Information
The tropical evergreen cashew tree, whose relatives include the delicious mango and pistachio along with the not-so-pleasant poison ivy and poison oak, is native to the West Indies and Brazil. In the sixteenth century Portuguese

explorers carried the cashew from Brazil to India, where it proved to be well adapted to the south Indian and East African climate. The cashew is a medium-sized spreading tree, attaining a height of thirty to fifty feet. It requires a minimum of attention and can exist in many different types of soil and climates, growing at sea level on beaches and at altitudes of up to three thousand feet on mountainsides and thriving in areas with rainfall anywhere from 20 to 150 inches a year. The nut is actually the seed of the fleshy, orange-colored, pear-shaped cashew apple (see the reference in **Fruits**); instead of being on the inside of the fruit, however, it hangs like an appendage from the base. Since the cashew apple spoils within twenty-four hours of harvest, it is almost never exported; the fortunate few who have tried this fruit, either ripe or in preserves, say it is even tastier than the cashew nut. The kidney-shaped nuts have hard shells with two layers; between the layers is a black resinous liquid called cardol, which is caustic and can burn the skin, like its relative poison ivy. During processing (roasting at 350 degrees), this liquid is removed and used to make paints, varnishes, and insecticides. After peanuts, cashews are the most popular snack nut in the United States. In 1998 the United States imported about a hundred million pounds of cashew nuts; nearly all came from Brazil and India, with smaller quantities from Indonesia and Vietnam.

Culinary Uses

Cashew nuts are bean-shaped, eggshell white, and plump, with a slightly sweet, bland flavor. They are never sold in the shell and cannot be considered a raw nut since they are heated during processing. The cashew nut is very versatile; it can be eaten plain or used in making nut milks and butters, cream soups, ice cream, breads, and stuffings. For a special main dish, try mushroom and cashew Stroganoff. "Raw" cashews are hard to digest, but roasting enhances both their flavor and their digestibility. Because they are not shelled domestically, cashews are frequently stale. Fresh cashews are crisp, solid, and white. Even though whole cashews are more expensive, they are definitely fresher and a better buy than cashew pieces.

Health Benefits

Cashews are helpful for emaciation, problems with teeth and gums, and lack of vitality. They are a nutritive and warming food because of their 47 percent fat content. They contain a high content of oleic acid (versus polyunsaturated oils).

BYPRODUCTS

Cashew butter is made by grinding cashews in a blender or food grinder until the consistency of peanut butter. This spread can then be used on crackers and bread or in sauces and soups as a thickener. Another type of cashew butter is made by melting regular butter, adding seasonings, and mixing in cashew pieces; use this as a sauce with vegetables.

Cashew milk made from soaked and ground cashews may be used to replace whole dairy milk in the same proportions for almost all recipes. Because the cashew nut is soft, it can be blended to a smooth white liquid with no residue.

Castor Oil
(Ricinus communis)

Ricinus is the name in classical languages applied to the castor bean seed; *communis* means "common" or "widely known." The English name *castor* comes from the Greek term for "beaver," *kastor*, and is related to the earlier Sanskrit term *kasturi*, meaning "musk." Beaver musk (*castoreum*) was a valuable commodity, used not only as a perfume base but also as a cathartic in ancient medicine. Since the oil of the castor bean was similarly used as a cathartic, it was named after the beaver.

General Information

The castor oil plant, native to western Asia and Africa, often grows thirty or forty feet high. The mature seed

Cashew / Nutritional Value Per 100 g Edible Portion			
	Dry-Roasted		Dry-Roasted
Calories	574	Copper	2.220 mg
Protein	15.31 g	Beta Carotene (A)	0 mg
Fat	46.35 g	Thiamine (B₁)	0.200 mg
Fiber	0.70 g	Riboflavin (B₂)	0.200 mg
Calcium	45 mg	Niacin (B₃)	1.400 mg
Iron	6.00 mg	Pantothenic Acid (B₅)	1.217 mg
Magnesium	260 mg	Pyridoxine (B₆)	0.256 mg
Phosphorus	490 mg	Folic Acid (B₉)	69.2 mcg
Potassium	565 mg	Ascorbic Acid (C)	0 mg
Sodium	16 mg	Tocopherol (E)	0.57 mg
Zinc	5.600 mg		

capsules, each containing three beanlike seeds, explode and scatter their seeds as they dry. From the seeds a pale, viscous oil has been pressed since antiquity. This oil, with its unpleasant, acrid taste, is one of the oldest medicinal prescriptions and has been used throughout the ages as a purgative for many ills of the stomach, spleen, bowels, and uterus and as a cure for intestinal worms. The Egyptians used castor oil as lamp oil and as an unguent; they also purged their systems three times a month by drinking the oil mixed with beer. The Greeks and Romans—taking note, no doubt, that the beans are poisonous—used the oil only externally, and it was not until the late eighteenth century that it regained its ancient role as a laxative. All parts of the plant, but especially the seeds, are toxic to humans and animals and should never be eaten. Eating a single castor bean can kill a child. The toxic action is because of ricin, a severe irritant that produces nausea, vomiting, gastric pain, diarrhea, thirst, and dimness of vision. Hulled and crushed at temperatures below 100 degrees Fahrenheit, the beans yield a clear or yellowish, poison-free oil rich in ricinolein, which irritates the intestines, causing them to expel their contents.

Health Benefits

Laxative. Castor oil is a mild enough laxative to use even for small babies. For chronic constipation, one tablespoon of castor oil should be taken with a cup of ginger tea; this tonic will neutralize toxins and relieve gas and constipation. The oil may also be applied externally for itches and other cutaneous complaints, or rubbed on the nipples of a nursing mother after each feeding in order to prevent soreness. Used as an external poultice, it dissolves and draws out cysts, tumors, warts, growths, and other toxic accumulations. It also has an emollient effect, helping to soften and remove scars. For these purposes, soak a wool flannel cloth with castor oil and apply one or more times daily to the affected area for one or two hours. For increased effectiveness, put a protective layer on the poultice and apply heat directly on top of it with a hot-water bottle or heating pad. Castor oil also makes an excellent hair tonic and massage oil. The tea of the castor root is used as an anti-inflammatory to treat many disorders such as arthritis, sciatica, chronic backache, and muscle spasms.

Chestnut
(Castanea sativa, C. dentata)

> [Chestnuts are] delicacies for princes and a lusty and masculine food for rusticks, and able to make women well-complexioned.
>
> —JOHN EVELYN (1620–1706)

Castanea is said to have been derived either from the city Kastanea in Pontus, Asia Minor, or from a town of the same name in Thessaly, Greece, from where chestnuts were first introduced into Europe. *Sativa* indicates that this nut has long been cultivated; *dentata* means "toothed," usually with sharp, outward-pointing teeth. The English word *chestnut* is derived from the Latin.

General Information

Most of the chestnut trees now found in the United States are a variety native to southern Europe. The native American chestnut grew abundantly in the United States

Chestnut / Nutritional Value Per 100 g Edible Portion				
	Raw Unpeeled	Boiled Steamed	Roasted	Flour
Calories	213	131	245	362
Protein	2.42 g	2.00 g	3.17 g	6.10 g
Fat	2.26 g	1.38 g	2.20 g	3.70 g
Fiber	1.71 g	0.70 g	1.90 g	2.00 g
Calcium	27 mg	46 mg	29 mg	50 mg
Iron	1.01 mg	1.73 mg	0.91 mg	3.20 mg
Magnesium	32 mg	54 mg	33 mg	n/a
Phosphorus	93 mg	99 mg	107 mg	164 mg
Potassium	518 mg	715 mg	592 mg	847 mg
Sodium	3 mg	27 mg	2 mg	11 mg
Zinc	0.520 mg	0.250 mg	0.570 mg	n/a
Copper	0.447 mg	0.472 mg	0.507 mg	n/a
Manganese	0.952 mg	0.854 mg	1.180 mg	n/a
Beta Carotene (A)	28 IU	n/a	24 IU	n/a
Thiamine (B₁)	0.238 mg	n/a	0.243 mg	0.230 mg
Riboflavin (B₂)	0.168 mg	n/a	0.175 mg	0.370 mg
Niacin (B₃)	1.179 mg	n/a	1.342 mg	1.000 mg
Pantothenic Acid (B₅)	0.509 mg	n/a	0.554 mg	n/a
Pyridoxine (B₆)	0.376 mg	n/a	0.497 mg	n/a
Folic Acid (B₉)	62 mcg	n/a	70 mcg	n/a
Ascorbic Acid (C)	43 mg	n/a	26 mg	n/a

LORE AND LEGEND

The Greek Xenophon's army supposedly lived on chestnuts during its retreat from Asia Minor in 401–399 B.C. In Tuscany the nuts have a sacred connotation: they are eaten on Saint Simon's Day, and on the Feast of Saint Martin are distributed to the poor.

until the early twentieth century, when some diseased trees imported from Asia and planted on Long Island in 1904 spread a fungus that nearly obliterated all the native trees. Only a few groves in California and the Pacific Northwest escaped the general destruction. New stocks have been planted, but most of the chestnuts sold for eating today are imported from Italy and Japan. Once considered a staple food, the mound-shaped, smooth, brown, thin-skinned nuts grow two or three inside of a hard prickly burr. After the burrs fall to the ground, they are gathered and the chestnuts removed. Although the chestnut is called a "nut," looks and feels like a nut, and has a shell like a nut, it is shown by analysis to be more closely related to the starchy grains. Furthermore, chestnuts are sweet and soft, without the characteristic crunchiness of nuts.

Processing varies somewhat by variety. Chinese chestnuts are cured by being spread on a floor and stirred frequently for a period of five to ten days. European chestnuts receive similar treatment, but they are cured or allowed to "sweat" for only two days. American chestnuts are prone to weevil infestation, for which they are dipped in hot water (110 to 120 degrees Fahrenheit) for thirty to forty-five minutes. They are then cured for one to two days in a manner similar to Chinese chestnuts. Most chestnuts are sold in-shell.

Culinary Uses
Chestnuts have graced tables on several continents for centuries in the widest variety of forms, from the exalted marrons glacés to common porridge. Fresh chestnuts are quite starchy and not very sweet when first picked, but after a few days of curing, some of the starch turns to sugar and the large, soft nuts develop a gentle sweetness. Available during the fall and winter in many supermarkets, select fresh chestnuts in the shell with clear, silky smooth, brown shells rather than dry or brittle shells. To roast or bake them, first deeply score the shells with a paring knife; otherwise, they

may explode. They may also be boiled and then shelled. The only nut treated as a vegetable, they are never eaten raw because of their tannic acid content. The cooked nuts can be used chopped in stuffings, sprinkled over vegetables, or puréed in soups. Because of their high starch content, Europeans often use them as a substitute for potatoes or noodles, and the combination of chestnuts and sweet potatoes is a favorite of many. Dried chestnuts are a useful time-saving standby; they are considered sweeter than fresh chestnuts, although their texture is less floury, and they need to be soaked for about an hour and then cooked like legumes before use. In replacing fresh chestnuts with the dried variety, allow one part dried to three parts fresh. Dried chestnuts are always more expensive than the fresh, but they are a great convenience and are available year-round. Canned whole chestnuts and chestnut purée (available either plain or sweetened) are used in soups, desserts, crepes, and cakes. Whole chestnuts preserved in sugar or syrup as marrons glacés make a sweet treat or garnish.

Health Benefits
The chestnut has the lowest fat content of all major nuts (4 to 6 percent) and contains substantial amounts of carbohydrates.

BYPRODUCTS

Chestnut flour is a fragrant, sweet-tasting flour that forms a firm and unyielding paste. Rather heavy on its own, it is best combined with other grain flours to sweeten, lighten, and add creaminess to pastries, cookies, and tarts. Chestnut flour is generally available in specialty shops.

Chia
(Salvia columbariae, S. hispanica)

Salvia is derived from the Latin *salvere*, which means "to save" or "to be well or healthy"; *columbariae* and *hispanica* mean "Columbian" and "Hispanic or Mexican," referring to their places of origin. The English name *chia* comes from the Mayan *chiabaan*, meaning "strong" or "strengthening."

General Information
The chia plant is native to the warm and temperate regions of the southwestern North American deserts and Central

America. This small member of the sage family appears on the plains, hills, and valleys over much of California and northern Mexico, growing from an annual root with a slender branching stem terminated by several curious whorls containing the seeds. The seeds are flat and round, with a slippery feeling to the touch. *Columbariae*'s seeds are a golden tan, while *hispanica*'s are a grey-black (a few are white) and look rather like flattened, washed-out poppy seeds. Used as a staple long before corn was developed, chia seeds were used by indigenous people as a highly nutritious and energy-generating food and medicine.

Culinary Uses

Chia seeds by themselves taste much like wheat germ. Both varieties of chia seeds are hard and smooth as long as they are dry, but when placed in warm water, or any liquid for that matter, they rapidly begin to soften and swell, increasing their original size by four or five times. If plain water surrounds the seeds, it turns to a clear gelatin and the entire tapioca-like substance is pleasant to eat, especially if a little sweetener is added. Others prefer to grind the seeds in a blender and then sprinkle the meal directly on cereal. This meal can also be added to salads, soups, and baked products. The sprouted seeds taste much like watercress. As the seeds cannot be sprouted in the conventional manner because of their highly mucilaginous nature, there are earthenware containers (usually animal-shaped) made especially for this purpose.

Health Benefits

The energizing value of chia seeds was well known to the American Indians, who made use of the potent seeds to sustain them on long desert marches and runs. It is said that a handful of seeds, roasted and ground, will maintain a person throughout a day of hard exertion, such as continuous running. Next to flax, chia seeds are the highest

source of omega-3 fatty acids. Chia seeds of the small southwestern variety (*S. columbariae*) are more nutritious than the Mexican variety.

Chilean Wild Nut
(Gevuina avellana)

This plant was named after Avella Vecchia, near Naples in southern Italy. *Gevuina* derives from the Chilean name.

General Information

Also known as the Chilean hazel, this evergreen tree is a member of the macadamia family. The natural habitat of the tree is the cold region of southern Chile, extending from the snowline on the Pacific slopes of the Andes down to the seacoast. The fruits are fleshy drupes about the size of cherries that become coral-red when ripe and contain a single seed, somewhat smaller than the macadamia nut, which is enclosed within a hard, woody shell.

Culinary Uses

These nuts are pleasant tasting, similar in flavor to the European hazelnut—thus their common name in Chile, *avellano*. The kernels may be eaten fresh, but they are usually roasted and sold in small paper bags like peanuts.

Coconut
(Cocos nucifera)

The generic name *Cocos* and the English name *coconut* are derived from the Spanish/Portuguese word *coco*, meaning "monkey face." Sixteenth-century Spanish and Portuguese explorers gave the coconut this name because the three scars or markings on the base of the shell resemble a monkey's face: two of the germinating holes represent the eyes, the third the nose. The term *nucifera* means "nut-bearing."

General Information

The coconut palm is believed to be native to Polynesia, Malaysia, and southern Asia. Considered the "king of plants" by the local inhabitants of tropical and subtropical regions, it is often the only cash crop and may be the primary source of food as well. In Sanskrit the coconut palm is called *kalpa vriksha*, meaning "tree that gives all that is

Chia / Nutritional Value Per 100 g Edible Portion			
	Dried		Dried
Calories	472	Zinc	5.320 mg
Protein	16.62 g	Copper	1.660 mg
Fat	26.25 g	Beta Carotene (A)	36 IU
Fiber	25.30 g	Thiamine (B₁)	0.869 mg
Calcium	529 mg	Riboflavin (B₂)	0.166 mg
Iron	10.00 mg	Niacin (B₃)	5.817 mg
Phosphorus	604 mg		

necessary for living." Practically all parts of the plant can be used in one manner or another: the trunk provides excellent wood, the leaves are used for basket weaving and roofing material, the husks for rope making, the shells for drinking vessels, and the young terminal buds for food, under the name of "palm cabbages." Like citrus trees, coconut palms bloom and fruit year-round. Ten to thirteen times a year a new flower spike emerges from the crown of the tree, developing into a cluster of six to twelve nuts. The individual coconuts require a year to reach full maturity from the time they first begin to take shape, but since new nuts are constantly being produced, there is a continuous yield. In some years an individual palm may bear two hundred coconuts, but a good annual harvest averages sixty coconuts. Cultivated trees start bearing in seven to ten years, produce mature crops from fifteen to fifty, and continue to bear up to seventy years of age.

It is the fruit, botanically classed as a drupe and not a nut, that gives the plant its greatest economic importance. The largest seed known, each nut is encased in a smooth outer layer, a fibrous middle layer, or coir, and a strong inner portion or shell, which encloses the single seed. Very buoyant and easily waterborne, coconuts have been carried on the Gulf Stream to places as unlikely as Norway. Those appearing in markets have generally had the outer layers removed so that only the inner fibrous husk shows.

A young coconut between six and nine months contains between 1½ and 2 cups of "water." The coconut is a natural water filter that takes almost nine months to filter each 2 cups of water. This prehistoric plant can survive many months floating at sea with fresh water stored sterile in the nut itself. Coconuts in their young stage of growth are the most health enhancing. As the coconut matures, its juice eventually becomes hard flesh and it loses some of its nutritional benefits. Besides being highly nutritious, young coconuts have also been exceedingly revered as having medicinal qualities for heart, liver, and kidney disorders.

Buying Tips

Coconuts may be found on the market all year, but October through December are the peak months. Young coconuts are the "white" ones sold in Asian markets and a few health food stores. They look white because the green outside is cut away before they are shipped from Thailand or Philippines. Ripe, mature coconuts are the brown ones commonly found. A quality nut is one that is heavy for its size and that sloshes with liquid when shaken. Do not choose one without liquid, as this indicates spoilage; also avoid those with moldy or wet "eyes," as these are unsound.

Culinary Uses

The coconut's first dividends are reserved for those who live in its habitat. At six months, while the pulp is still gelatinous and no harder than that of a melon, it has a fresh, fruity flavor, more nutlike than sugary. Unripe coconuts, preferred by natives over ripe ones, are eaten with a spoon, fed to babies, and used as a healing food. Ripe coconuts have a meat that is solid, pure white, and very sweet. Opening a young coconut requires a hefty knife and a few good whacks to pop the top off. To crack the mature coconut, pierce the soft spots or "eyes" at the top of the shell with an ice pick or other sharp object and then drain the liquid. Tap all around the hard shell with a hammer until it cracks and falls away, or heat the coconut in the oven at 350 degrees Fahrenheit for thirty minutes, at which point the shell will easily break away. Coconut flesh can be eaten fresh out of hand, grated with a grater, or chopped in the blender. The thin brown seed coat adhering to the white meat is edible and contains nutrients in addition to fiber. Fresh coconut is more flavorful and less expensive than packaged coconut and is free of preservatives. Coconut can also be purchased dried, desiccated, flaked, shredded, or as coconut cream. Keep all of these in the refrigerator or freezer, or store them in airtight jars and use quickly, as the high oil content makes them prone to rapid rancidity. Shredded or flaked coconut is a wonderful garnish for cakes and candies and makes a tasty addition to baked goods, granolas, and vegetable and rice dishes. Coconut is especially useful in Indonesian and West Indian dishes, where it is an important ingredient in curries, chutneys, and stews. Avoid coconut that is sweetened and has glycerine (a coal-tar product) added.

Health Benefits

pH 5.52–6.18 (fresh). Coconut contains the organic iodine necessary to prevent thyroid gland problems, and soothes internal membranes with their laxative properties. It digests best when combined with salads and cooked vegetables; with starches or sugars, including honey, it digests with difficulty. Coconut milk is warming, sweet, and thirst quenching. Coconut water is one of the highest sources of electrolytes known. It's a natural isotonic beverage, with the same level of electrolytic balance that we have in our blood, but with less sodium, more potassium, more magnesium, and added medicinal benefits. Plasma makes up 55 percent of human blood, and coconut water is identical to human blood plasma, which makes it the universal donor. By drinking coconuts we give ourselves an instant blood transfusion. In fact, during the Pacific War of 1941 to 1945, both sides in the conflict regularly used coconut water—siphoned directly from the nut—to give emergency plasma transfusions to wounded soldiers.

BYPRODUCTS

Coconut milk is the liquid that is extracted from grating the fresh kernel, mixing it with water, and then straining the mixture. It is an important food commodity for millions of people throughout the tropical world, used in place of oil, fat, and butter. Coconut milk can be used in cooking and baking or as a liquid refreshment. In chemical balance it compares to mother's milk and is a complete protein food when taken in its natural form. Coconut milk is widely available canned, where the cream separates from the milk

Coconut / Nutritional Value Per 100 g Edible Portion				
	Raw	Dried Unsweetened	Raw Cream	Raw Milk	Raw Water
Calories	354	660	330	230	19
Protein	3.33 g	6.88 g	3.63 g	2.29 g	0.72 g
Fat	33.49 g	64.52 g	34.68 g	23.84 g	0.20 g
Fiber	4.27 g	5.31 g	n/a	n/a	0.02 g
Calcium	14 mg	26 mg	11 mg	16 mg	24 mg
Iron	2.43 mg	3.32 mg	2.28 mg	1.64 mg	0.29 mg
Magnesium	32 mg	90 mg	n/a	37 mg	25 mg
Phosphorus	113 mg	206 mg	122 mg	100 mg	20 mg
Potassium	356 mg	543 mg	325 mg	263 mg	250 mg
Sodium	20 mg	37 mg	4 mg	15 mg	105 mg
Zinc	1.100 mg	2.010 mg	0.960 mg	0.670 mg	0.100 mg
Copper	0.435 mg	0.796 mg	0.378 mg	0.266 mg	0.040 mg
Manganese	1.500 mg	2.745 mg	1.304 mg	0.916 mg	n/a
Beta Carotene (A)	0 mg	0 mg	0 mg	0 mg	0 mg
Thiamine (B₁)	0.066 mg	0.060 mg	0.030 mg	0.026 mg	0.030 mg
Riboflavin (B₂)	0.020 mg	0.100 mg	0 mg	0 mg	0.057 mg
Niacin (B₃)	0.540 mg	0.603 mg	0.890 mg	0.760 mg	0.080 mg
Pantothenic Acid (B₅)	0.300 mg	0.800 mg	n/a	n/a	0.043 mg
Pyridoxine (B₆)	0.054 mg	0.300 mg	n/a	n/a	0.032 mg
Folic Acid (B₉)	26.4 mcg	9 mcg	n/a	n/a	n/a
Ascorbic Acid (C)	3.3 mg	1.5 mg	2.8 mg	2.8 mg	2.4 mg
Tocopherol (E)	0.73 mg	n/a	n/a	n/a	n/a

LORE AND LEGEND

In New Guinea a native belief holds that the coconut palm originated by sprouting from the head of the first man to die. Thousands of miles away in northern India, the coconut is considered the sacred fruit of the "Tree of Life." A symbol of prosperity and fertility, coconuts are often given by priests to women who wish to conceive. In Bali, however, women are forbidden to touch coconut palms lest the fertility of the tree be drained off into the fertility of the woman. Do not pick up what looks to be an abandoned coconut lying by the road in Samoa unless you are looking for trouble; somebody knows it is there and has proprietary rights to it. On the Nicobar Islands in the Indian Ocean, whole coconuts comprised the local currency until the early twentieth century, with the value of goods reckoned in number of coconuts. Disks carved from coconut shells formed part of the shell-money strings that served as currency on some islands in the Carolines and in the Bismarck Archipelago in the South Pacific. According to an old South Sea proverb: "He who plants a coconut tree plants food and drink, vessels and clothing, a habitation for himself, and a heritage for his children."

and rises to the top. To blend the two, shake the can before you open it. Or after opening a can, lift off the cream and use it separately as a garnish or extra-rich ingredient. Cans labeled "light coconut milk" have had the cream removed. Bypass sugar-sweetened coconut milk intended for beverage use.

Coconut oil — see the reference below.

Coconut water is the liquid found inside the coconut upon opening. Ripe coconuts have a liquid that is cloudy, aromatic, and pleasing to the taste and body. The liquid of young coconuts is clear and light, with a taste that is both delicious and cleansing. Both the ripe and young liquids are either drunk straight from the shell or used in tropical drinks, fruit shakes, cocktails, or spiced vegetables dishes.

Shredded or *desiccated coconut* is made from the meat of the coconut, the white inner lining of the kernel. Following shelling, the reddish-brown skin is pared off the outside surface of the white meat; the meat is then washed, pasteurized, blanched, shredded, dried, and graded into extra-fine, fine, medium, and coarse qualities. The finished product has a moisture content of less than 3 percent and an oil content of about 68 percent. Although coconut meat has its own natural sweetness, some commercial shredded coconut makers add extra sugar and propylene glycol (a preservative) to retain moisture. If you cannot get whole fresh coconut, try to find unsweetened shredded or flaked coconut without additives.

Thai or *young water coconuts* are immature coconuts. Today cultivars are specifically bred to be sold at this stage. The thin, exceptionally delicious flesh ranges from jellylike in very young coconuts to a softer "meat" in slightly older ones. Large water coconuts are available in specialty or Asian markets cut down to form eight-inch white cubes. Cut through the cube to get to the delicately flavored flesh within.

Coconut Oil/Butter
(Cocos nucifera)

General Information

Coconut oil is the most versatile of all vegetable oils. It is obtained from mature coconuts that have fallen to the ground. These are split in half, and the interior white flesh is shredded. The resultant flakes (copra) are then pressed at 90 degrees Fahrenheit, and the oil is extracted and filtered. Fluid in warm tropical climates, the oil changes to a solid fat with the consistency of butter at temperatures below 78 degrees Fahrenheit. In its liquid state the oil has for thousands of years been used for cooking; in a semi-solid state, it is a substitute for lard, but unlike lard coconut fats are easily digested and metabolized and do not tend to cause weight gain. Most coconut oil is not sold in its unrefined state but has been refined by bleaching, deodorizing, and hydrogenating it into a clear liquid that has neither the taste nor the odor of the coconut. This refined oil has an astonishingly high percentage of saturated fat—over 90 percent, even higher than the animal fats butter and lard. Since it is quite resistant to oxidation, coconut oil is frequently used in ice cream, salad dressings, and confections, as a spray oil on crackers, and especially for nondairy coffee creamers and whipped toppings (where it is better at raising blood cholesterol than cream).

Culinary Uses

Coconut oil is the premier oil for cooking, as it enhances the flavor of all types of cuisine. It is also the most stable of any known oil or butter at high temperatures and is therefore the best to use for heating or cooking any food. Coconut butter should be stored in a cool, dark area. It can be refrigerated after opening, but this is not necessary to ensure freshness. Because all butters and oils are light-sensitive, they should be sealed in dark containers. Look for raw, organic coconut oil.

Health Benefits

Coconut oil has been used in India as a key ingredient in Ayurvedic medicine for over four thousand years, and it is still a primary form of medical treatment for millions of people. It is used in hospitals around the world to treat digestive and malabsorption problems and is commonly given to infants and children who have problems digesting other fats. For this same reason, coconut oil is a primary

Coconut Oil/Butter / Nutritional Value Per 100 g Edible Portion		
	100 g	1 Tbsp
Calories	862	117
Protein	0 g	0 g
Fat	100 g	13.6 g
Fiber	0 g	0 g
Calcium	0 mg	0 mg
Iron	0.04 mg	0.01 mg
Magnesium	0 mg	0 mg
Phosphorus	0 mg	0 mg
Potassium	0 mg	0 mg
Sodium	0 mg	0 mg
Zinc	0 mg	0 mg
Copper	0 mg	0 mg
Manganese	0 mg	0 mg
Beta Carotene (A)	0 IU	0 IU
Thiamine (B1)	0 mg	0 mg
Riboflavin (B2)	0 mg	0 mg
Niacin (B3)	0 mg	0 mg
Pantothenic Acid (B5)	0 mg	0 mg
Pyridoxine (B6)	0 mg	0 mg
Folic Acid (B9)	0 mg	0 mg
Ascorbic Acid (C)	0.00 mg	0.42 mg
Tocopherol (E)	0.09 mg	0.01 mg

ingredient in infant milk formulas. One of coconut oil's most remarkable properties is that it is one of the few significant plant sources of lauric acid. This medium-chain fatty acid (MCFA), which is also found in human breast milk, enhances brain function and the immune system. MCFAs confuse lipid-coated viruses and bacteria because they disrupt their lipid membranes. Thus coconut oil helps protect against disease-causing bacteria and viruses as well as yeast, fungi, and parasites. As Bruce Fife, ND, writes in his book *The Healing Miracles of Coconut Oil*, "Coconut oil is in essence a natural antibacterial, antiviral, antifungal, and antiprotozoal food."

Coconut oil also provides quick energy, improves insulin secretion and utilization of blood glucose, relieves stress on the pancreas and enzyme systems of the body, improves calcium and magnesium absorption for the development of strong bones and teeth, aids in the absorption of minerals and fat-soluble vitamins, and supports thyroid function. High-quality unrefined oil is said to be useful in mitigating muscular aches when massaged into the affected area, in preventing stretch marks during pregnancy, for healing cuts and scratches as well as burns (including sunburns), and as a facial massage and wrinkle remover.

Cola
(Cola nitida, C. acuminata)

Cola is the native name for these nuts, while *nitida* means "shiny" or "glossy," and *acuminata* means "acuminate" or "long-pointed."

General Information
A popular stimulant in West Africa, cola "nuts" are not really nuts but the interior part of the fleshy seeds of tropical trees. Following the harvest, the nuts are removed from the pods, fermented for a few days, then washed, cleaned, sun-dried, and stored in baskets lined with rot-resistant green leaves. From time to time the leaves must be changed; with proper care, the nuts can be stored for several months. The seeds may be pink, white, or purple, the preferred being white.

Culinary Uses
The taste at first is slightly bitter, but after moderate chewing, a sense of well-being is said to spread through the

> ## LORE AND LEGEND
>
> Among a number of tribal groups in West Africa, the cola nut is a symbol of hospitality, given to the guest either upon arrival or departure. In addition, sharing and partaking of cola is an integral part of many social ceremonies. It plays a significant role in early-morning worship, childbirth, child naming, marriage, installation of chiefs, and at funerals. Prayers are generally said over the cola nut before it is shared; it is looked upon not as a luxury, but as a vital necessity of life. If the host does not present his guest with a cola nut, it is considered to be a serious breach of etiquette in many Nigerian communities.

body, leaving a more pleasant taste in the mouth, which causes any food or drink consumed immediately thereafter to seem sweet. Pulverized and boiled in water, cola nuts formed part of a stimulating traditional West African beverage. Their use in beverages accounted for the origin of the word *cola* in several of today's popular soft drinks. Coca-Cola started out during the 1880s as a powerful, caffeine-rich patent medicine, containing carbonated water mixed with a powder of ground cola nuts and an extract of coca (*Erythroxylon coca*) leaves from Peru. The coca leaves contain several alkaloids, including cocaine. While cocaine is not an ingredient in any of today's cola beverages in the United States, extracts of the cola nut are still utilized for natural flavor in many cola-type soft drinks.

Health Benefits
Small pieces of the nut, when masticated, are supposed to benefit the chewer by increasing mental activity, reducing fatigue, dulling appetite, and counteracting intoxication. As a medicine it is reputed to be an effective stimulant—a tonic that will allay thirst, promote digestion, give strength, and "stave off a porter's exhaustion during a forced march in the heat of the tropics while bearing an eighty-pound head load." It will prevent sleep but will not induce a drug habit. The nuts have a similar effect to tea or coffee, since they contain the same alkaloid, caffeine. They also contain smaller amounts of theobromine—as does the related cacao "bean"—and kolanin, a heart stimulant.

Cottonseed Oil
(Gossypium hirsutum)

Gossypium is from the Latin *gossypion*, referring to Pliny's cotton tree; *hirsutum* means "rough" or "shaggy."

General Information
Cottonseed oil is derived from the small, pea-sized seeds of the cotton plant, fifty of which are found in each cotton boll (the fluffy white puff that becomes fiber for clothing). The seeds are freed from the hulls and the kernels crushed, heated, and subjected to high pressure or solvent extraction to produce a reddish raw oil that must be further refined. The final product, the cottonseed oil found on the market, is yellow and has a light flavor and color. A hundred pounds of cotton seed will yield about sixteen pounds of oil; the remaining eighty-four pounds becomes lint and cottonseed meal, the latter used as livestock feed.

Culinary Uses
A high percentage of the cottonseed oil produced is blended with safflower oil, soy oil, or other vegetable oils to produce a generic salad oil, margarine, or shortening. It is popular oil because of its comparatively low cost.

Health Benefits
Because cotton is not considered a food crop, residues from pesticides—which are heavily used in cotton cultivation—may be present in the oil, thus rendering it potentially unsafe for consumption. The oil also contains between 0.6 and 1.2 percent of a fatty acid known as cyclopropen, which has toxic effects on the liver and gallbladder, slows down sexual maturity, and multiplies the power of the cancer-causing aflatoxin fungi. Additionally, cottonseed oil contains gossypol, a substance that irritates the digestive tract and causes water retention in the lungs, shortness of breath, and paralysis. Gossypol is also known to inhibit sperm function and is being investigated as a "male birth-control pill." Its use as an antifertility agent began after studies demonstrated that men who had used substantial quantities of crude cottonseed oil as their cooking oil over a number of years had low sperm counts, followed by total testicular failure.

Flaxseed/Linseed
(Linum usitatissimum)

Linum is the plant's classical name, used by Theophrastus, from the Greek *linon*, meaning "cord" or "flax." The term *usitatissimum* means "most useful." In the southern regions this plant was known as *linum*; in the northern regions it was known as *flahs*, from the Old German, referring to the process of flailing or flaying the fibers.

General Information
Flax is a graceful little plant that grows up to four feet in height, with turquoise-blue blossoms. This highly valuable plant is said by some to be native to Egypt, while others believe it to have come from the elevated plains of central Asia. Flax was already being cultivated in Babylon around 5000 B.C., and flaxseeds and pods, along with wall paintings depicting its cultivation and cloth made of flax fiber (linen), were found in the oldest known burial chambers of the Egyptians (around 3000 B.C.). The French leader Charlemagne pronounced flax more sanitary than wool (because linen is so much easier to launder than woolen fabrics) and ordered his subjects to cultivate it. Until the eighteenth century, when cotton came to the forefront, flax was the most important vegetable fiber in the Western world, being used to produce linen as well as ropes and high-grade paper. About A.D. 750, a paper superior to papyrus or parchment was created of flax fibers in Samarkand, still part of the Muslim Empire. During the next five centuries the Moors built paper mills and introduced flax from Cairo to Morocco and Sicily. The Crusaders during the Middle Ages brought the art of papermaking from flax fibers to Europe. The introduction of mechanical printing about the middle of the fifteenth

century increased the demand for paper far beyond possible flax production, and the French naturalist Rene de Reaumur suggested that paper be manufactured from wood pulp as an alternative. By 1800 mills were producing wood-based paper in France, and the demand for flax in paper production decreased.

The plant was introduced into North America by European colonists, who processed it for cloth. Its economic importance grew as flaxseed was used in a variety of products—from flaxseed cakes, which were used for fattening cattle, to linseed oil, which was employed in making oilcloth and linoleum. Today this multipurpose herb offers something for the weaver, the painter, the physician, and the cook: fibers from the stalk are spun into linen; oil from the seeds is used in paint and linoleum; both the seeds and the oil are used medicinally; and the seeds are combined with other ingredients to bake into a wholesome bread.

Culinary Uses

Flaxseeds are the tiny, shiny, oval-shaped brown seeds of the flax plant. Their smooth, nutty flavor makes them a tasty and crunchy addition to freshly baked bread and an excellent addition to casseroles, sauces, and salads. When placed in water the seeds readily soften, swell, and dissolve, producing a gel. This gelatinous effect accounts for the ability of soaked and cooked flaxseed to be whipped up like egg white. Flaxseed meal keeps fresh only a few days because of its high oil content, after which it becomes rancid to the point of being harmful. Flakes are now available that have been stabilized to prevent spoilage. The oil pressed from the seeds, called linseed or flaxseed oil, is used as a kitchen oil but tends to go rancid quickly. Buy high-quality refrigerated oils and use within two weeks. If you use the oil as a topping for baked potatoes, pasta, or vegetables, do not heat it.

Health Benefits

pH > 6.0. Decongestant, demulcent, emollient, expectorant, laxative, purgative. Flaxseed has been used in medicine since antiquity for liniments, cough syrups, and salves

Flaxseed / Nutritional Value Per 100 g Edible Portion			
	Dried		Dried
Calories	450	Fat	31.9–44.7 g
Protein	17.3–31.6 g	Fiber	24.0–31.6 g

LORE AND LEGEND

In Teuton mythology flax is said to be under the protection of the goddess Hulda, the watchful Guardian of Flax Fields, no doubt because it was she who taught mortals the arts of spinning and weaving. In Bohemia the spindly leaves of flax have the beneficent property of making homely girls beautiful, provided the girls dance among the leaves when precisely seventeen. But not on Saturday, for the plant belongs to the Devil on that day. Even spinning is not done on Saturday. One Saturday, it is told, two old sisters defied the Devil and went right on with their spinning. That night one of them died. The next Saturday the other sister sat again at her spindle. Toward evening she looked up, and there beside her stood the dead woman, enveloped in flames. She had returned from hell to show the punishment that awaited those who dared spin on Saturday. Young women getting married in Thuringia place flax in their shoes as a charm against poverty, and tie a flaxen string around their left leg so the marriage will thrive. To the ancient Egyptians, white linen (woven flax) was a symbol of divine light and purity associated with the great mother-goddess Isis. Linen was worn as a symbol of purity by Greek, Hebrew, and Egyptian priests, and in Egyptian tombs the mummies of pharaohs lay wrapped in fine linen bindings for thousands of years. Detailed wall paintings in the tombs represent the history of flax in the Nile valley, and show that its basic cultivation, processing, and weaving into fabric has changed little through the ages. The Cherokee Indians regarded flax as one of their most nourishing and healing herbs, and the plant was as sacred to them as the eagle feather. They believed that flaxseed oil captured energies from the sun that could then be released and utilized in the body's metabolic processes.

to treat boils and similar infections. This simple domestic herb helps to alleviate the problems of constipation, distension, and discomfort in the abdominal region. The seeds have a thick outer coating of cells that abound in a viscous matter, which in hot water forms a thick mucilaginous fluid. Eating the seeds intact is useful for constipation, as the seeds swell to three times their dry volume in the intestines and encourage elimination by increasing the volume of fecal matter. Flaxseeds are also energizing, help to relieve asthma and chronic cough, enrich the blood, and strengthen the nerves; they are also reputedly good for dry, brittle hair. Flaxseeds contain prussic acid, which in small amounts stimulates the respiration and improves digestion but in excess causes respiratory failure and death (however, it would take a phenomenal amount of flaxseed to do so). They are one of the best vegetarian sources of omega-3, the fatty acid typically found in fish oil that has been shown to reduce serum triglyceride levels in heart patients. The omega-3 and omega-6 fatty acids are highly soothing and anti-inflammatory to the intestinal wall and are a natural laxative. Along with all eight essential amino acids and lecithin, flax also contains up to 60 percent linolenic acid (LNA), which has been shown to inhibit the production of tumor-promoting acid in the body and helps maintain the integrity of cell walls. Ancient Indian scriptures state that in order to reach the highest state of contentment and joy, flaxseeds must be eaten daily.

Flaxseed flour and defatted flaxseed meal, because of their high lignan content, are being used for investigations into the association between high lignan consumption and lowered risk for sex-hormone-dependent cancers. Intestinal bacteria convert plant lignans into enterolactone and enterodiol. These hormonelike substances produce a number of protective effects against breast cancer. Lignans are also found in many other seeds, grains, and legumes. Studies show that omnivorous women with breast cancer typically excrete much lower levels of lignans in their urine than do vegetarian women.

BYPRODUCTS

Fresh flaxseed oil is known for its rich golden color, delicate nutty taste, and ease of digestion. However, it has the dubious distinction of turning rancid faster than any other vegetable oil when exposed to light, oxygen, and heat, and thus special care must be taken in pressing, filling, and storing operations. Avoid any oil that tastes bitter, acrid, or scratchy, since those tastes indicate rancidity. The spoilable "impurities" are the two nutritionally essential fatty acids linoleic acid (LA) and linolenic acid (LNA), found in such high quantities (over 70 percent) that if they were removed, very little oil would be left. LNA helps disperse hardened deposits of saturated fatty acids and cholesterol from cellular membranes; it plays an essential role in keeping veins and arteries soft and pliable.

The oil also contains a substance resembling prostaglandins, which regulate blood pressure and arterial function and are important for calcium and energy metabolism. Flaxseed oil has been found to lower high cholesterol and triglyceride levels and to be effective at treating mood disorders, low vitality, liver disorders, and cancer. Flax is a superior source of lignan, a mildly estrogenic compound that helps normalize a woman's menstrual cycle and that has anticancer, antibacterial, antifungal, and antiviral properties. Many women find that the use of flaxseed oil with a good balanced diet and other nutritional support has cleared up PMS symptoms as well as prevented stretch marks from developing after childbirth. Because it provides essential fatty acids as well as vitamin A, minerals, lecithin, and other vital nutrients, flaxseed oil helps to initiate cell renewal after a radiation burn.

Ginkgo Nut
(Ginkgo biloba)

Because of its unusual leaf shape, the ancient Chinese called the ginkgo tree *Ya-chio*, meaning "duck's foot," a name that got anglicized to *ginkgo*. The term *biloba* means "bi-lobed."

General Information
The celebrated ginkgo tree is a "living fossil" of the distant past, the only surviving member of the Ginkgoaceae, a tree family dominant in the vegetation of the northern hemisphere 125 million years ago, when dinosaurs were still roaming the earth. Probably native to northern China, the ginkgo tree is no longer found in the wild, but for over a thousand years it has been cultivated as a sacred tree in Buddhist temple courtyards around China. Each year it bears drupelike fruit: round, plum-sized, and brown. The fleshy, foul-smelling pulp encloses the seed or nut, which

is cream-colored, oval, and one-half to three-quarters of an inch long, within a smooth, thin, white shell.

Culinary Uses

The ginkgo nut is only edible cooked, when it has a pleasant flavor similar to mild Swiss cheese. The color also changes, from a soft pale yellow to a pale yellowish green. Not yet popular among westerners, ginkgo nuts are consumed for the most part by the Chinese and the Japanese. Most are eaten as appetizers, but they also appear in any "eight-jeweled" Chinese dish. Skewered and grilled, or fried and added to other dishes, they contribute color and a mild, sweet, crisp flavor. While fresh ginkgo nuts appear in the autumn markets, boiled and canned nuts are also available year-round.

Health Benefits

Ginkgo nuts have a high starch content of over 60 percent. They are said to promote digestion and diminish the effects of too much drinking. An extract of the leaves increases peripheral blood circulation, especially to the brain, thus enhancing memory. It is also a powerful antioxidant.

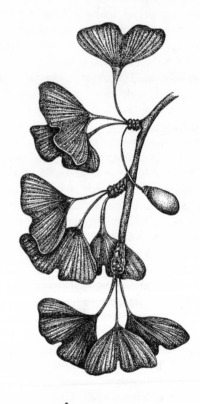

LORE AND LEGEND

Ginkgo nuts have a ritual significance in China and Japan, where they are consumed at feasts and weddings as an Oriental delicacy called "silverfruits." The leaf is a widely used motif in traditional Japanese art, frequently turning up on jewelry, kimonos, and family crests, and is the official emblem of Tokyo University.

Ginkgo / Nutritional Value Per 100 g Edible Portion	Raw	Dried
Calories	182	348
Protein	4.32 g	10.35 g
Fat	1.68 g	2.00 g
Fiber	0.50 g	0.98 g
Calcium	2 mg	20 mg
Iron	1.00 mg	1.60 mg
Magnesium	27 mg	53 mg
Phosphorus	124 mg	269 mg
Potassium	510 mg	998 mg
Sodium	7 mg	13 mg
Zinc	0.340 mg	0.670 mg
Copper	0.274 mg	0.536 mg
Manganese	0.113 mg	0.220 mg
Beta Carotene (A)	558 IU	1,091 IU
Thiamine (B$_1$)	0.220 mg	0.430 mg
Riboflavin (B$_2$)	0.090 mg	0.176 mg
Niacin (B$_3$)	6.000 mg	11.732 mg
Pantothenic Acid (B$_5$)	0.160 mg	1.345 mg
Ascorbic Acid (C)	15.0 mg	29.3 mg

Hazelnut and Filbert
(Corylus avellana, C. maxima)

The genus name *Corylus* comes from the Greek *korys*, meaning "helmet" or "hood," and refers to the shape of the husk enclosing the nut. The specific *epithet avellana* is said to be derived either from the name of an Asian valley or from the town of Abella, Italy; *maxima* means "largest." The English word *hazel* is derived from the Anglo-Saxon word *haesel*, meaning "headdress" or "bonnet," which is a good description of the way the covering fits on the short nut. The word *filbert* is thought by some to have originated from the German *vollbart*, meaning "full beard"; others claim the name is taken from the Frankish abbot Saint Philibert, whose feast day in England on August 20 coincides with the time the nut matures.

General Information

Filbert and hazel trees are small shrubby trees of the birch family. Their clustered, green-skinned nuts once rivaled the popularity of the acorn in Europe. Many species grow wild in temperate areas, but only three are cultivated as a cash crop: the Turkish hazel, the Mediterranean filbert, and the Old World cobnut. Traditionally, the smaller, round nuts not entirely covered by the husk were known as hazels or cobs—*cob* because they were thought to look like a short, stout English horse called a cob. The larger and longer nuts were known as filberts, and they had a tubular husk, often fringed, that completely covered and often extended beyond the end of the oblong nut. Once the nuts were shelled, though, it was difficult to distinguish them. Filbert trees grow wild all across the northern temperate zones of the United States and are grown commercially in Oregon and Washington. The hazelnut is Oregon's official state nut, with good reason—99 percent of the entire U.S. commercial crop is Oregon grown. The mild Willamette valley, stretching from Eugene to Portland, provides the perfect eco-niche for the hazelnut. The first sizable planting was made in 1876 by a Frenchman named David Gernot, who planted seed for fifty trees along a fencerow. Turkey is the world's largest producing country of hazelnuts, and West Germany is the largest user, followed by England. Americans eat an average of only a couple of ounces of hazelnuts a year, while West Germans average about 2½ pounds a year, and no traditional English Christmas feast is complete without hazelnuts and figs.

Culinary Uses

Filberts and hazelnuts have smooth, reddish-brown shells, which are thin and brittle. The tasty kernels are among the most popular nuts (for humans and squirrels both) with their pleasantly sweet, somewhat toasty flavor. The flavor has been likened to browned butter, and in fact the French word for "browned butter," *noisette*, also means "hazelnut." Used mainly in baking and confectionery, they can also be added to stuffings, ice creams, butters, and nut loaves. The nuts when pressed yield a fair amount of oil, which is often used in the preparation of cosmetics and perfumes.

Health Benefits

pH > 6.0. Filberts are a rich food and therefore hard to digest, even for those with good digestion. They are good for the teeth and gums, and aid in normalizing the metabolism. Like most other nuts, filberts and hazelnuts have an acidic reaction on the system and so should be eaten in moderation.

BYPRODUCTS

Hazelnut oil, with its delicate flavor and bouquet, is considered the finest gourmet cooking oil, preferred by many gold-medal chefs for creating fine dishes and desserts. Produced mainly in France, it is expensive and should be used sparingly. Its delicate flavor is lost when heated, but the oil can be whisked into a sauce at the last minute or used for baked goods in combination with hazelnuts. Exceptional on salads and pasta as well as in pancakes, waffles, and muffins, hazelnut oil is rich in monounsaturated fatty acids. Traditionally the oil has

Hazelnut, Filbert / Nutritional Value Per 100 g Edible Portion			
	Dried, Unblanched		Dried, Unblanched
Calories	632	Copper	1.509 mg
Protein	13.04 g	Manganese	2.016 mg
Fat	62.64 g	Beta Carotene (A)	67 IU
Fiber	3.80 g	Thiamine (B$_1$)	0.500 mg
Calcium	188 mg	Riboflavin (B$_2$)	0.110 mg
Iron	3.27 mg	Niacin (B$_3$)	1.135 mg
Magnesium	285 mg	Pantothenic Acid (B$_5$)	1.148 mg
Phosphorus	312 mg	Pyridoxine (B$_6$)	0.612 mg
Potassium	445 mg	Folic Acid (B$_9$)	71.8 mcg
Sodium	3 mg	Ascorbic Acid (C)	1.0 mg
Zinc	2.400 mg	Tocopherol (E)	23.92 g

LORE AND LEGEND

The nut-bearing hazel has long been associated with mystic rites and the occult, and the trees are emblematic of justice, reconciliation, and love. Virgil praised the filbert, stating that it was accorded more honors than the vine, the myrtle, and even the bay tree. In Greek mythology the two sons of Jupiter—Apollo, the god of harmony, and Mercury, the god of eloquence—exchanged gifts with which they would be empowered to provide a better life for humanity. Apollo received a lyre made of tortoiseshell, whose tone would free the artistic spirit of humankind, while Mercury received a winged wand made of hazel, whose touch would enable men to express their thoughts through words. The winged hazel rod, entwined with two serpents, is even today the symbol of communication, reconciliation, and commerce. Among ancient Romans the hazel was intimately connected with marriage, and it was their custom to burn hazel torches during the wedding night to ensure a peaceful and happy union of the newlywed couple.

In Nordic and Teutonic mythology the hazel was dedicated to Thor and Donar, gods of thunder, war, and strength. In Celtic and Old Irish legend it was the Tree of Wisdom, and linked with the magic number nine: the nine hazels of wisdom signify all knowledge of the arts and sciences, the hazel was the ninth tree in the Old Irish tree alphabet, and it was a symbol of the ninth month (August 6 to September 2). So honored was it that anyone caught cutting down a hazel tree could be put to death. In Sweden hazelnuts were reputed to have the power of making a person invisible, and their magical properties placed them in great demand for divination. In France and Germany young girls danced under the hazelnut tree to attract suitors; courting under the tree was the best opportunity to have one's love returned, even by those who had shown no love elsewhere. The cracking of the nuts on All Hallow's Eve, accompanied by fortune-telling, was a traditional amusement linked with British folklore—October 31 was called "Nut Crack Night." Chinese lore relates the hazelnut as being one of the five sacred nourishments bestowed on humans, and the nuts have been cultivated continuously in China for over forty-five hundred years.

---

also been used for massage and in the treatment of tuberculosis, urinary disease, and colitis. Because it is easily digested, it is recommended for people recovering from disease, the elderly, pregnant women, and diabetics.

Heart Nut
(Juglans ailanthifolia, J. sieboldiana cordiformis)

The generic term *Juglans* is a contraction of the Latin *Jovis glans*, meaning "nut of Jupiter" or "nut of the gods." *Ailanthifolia* means "having leaves like the ailanthus tree" (tree of heaven); *sieboldiana* is in honor of Philipp Franz von Siebold (1796–1866); *cordiformis* means "heart-shaped."

General Information
One of the "other walnuts" of the walnut family, the heart nut gets its common English name from the shape of the nut, both before and after hulling. Native to Japan, it is known also as the Japanese walnut and the Siebold walnut. Introduced into the United States from Japan in the 1860s, the heart nut did well for a time, but in the early twentieth century was nearly decimated by the walnut bunch disease; it has since been replaced for the most part by the Persian or English walnut.

Culinary Uses
The nuts, about one inch in diameter, are smaller than butternuts and are easily cracked to remove the kernel. The flavor is mild and pleasant, resembling that of the butternut.

Hemp Seeds and Hemp Seed Oil
(Cannabis sativa)

Linnaeus gave the plant its botanical name in 1753, the term *Cannabis* deriving probably from the Arabic *Qannob* or Greek *Kahnabas. Sativa* means "long cultivated."

General Information

Thought to be of Asian origin, the hemp plant has reached around the globe. The earliest texts describing hemp and its health benefits are the Egyptian Ebers papyrus, dating back thousands of years. Ancient Indian and Chinese medicinal texts describe hemp's broad applications. It is said to slow aging, stimulate and enhance the circulation, and restore the arteries and veins. It helps treat paralysis and neurological impairment due to stroke, increases milk flow in nursing mothers, and promotes hair growth.

The hemp plant is native to central Asia. There is evidence that it was cultivated in China by 4000 B.C.; it has since been distributed throughout the world in every climatic region. As early as 1545, the plant was brought to North America by British, French, and Spanish colonists. Although used throughout history for paper, textiles, food, and medicine, most people associate this plant with narcotic use. All hemp seed products sold in the U.S. today are required to be of minimal drug quality and sterilized, so there is no chance of psychoactive chemicals being present.

Culinary Uses

The most basic hemp seed product is the shelled seed, sometimes referred to as the hemp seed nut. The other major hemp food products are hemp seed nut butter, which resembles peanut and other nut butters, and cold-pressed hemp seed oil and hemp seed flour. These basic products can be consumed alone or used along with or instead of other grains, seeds, nuts, and oils in any appropriate recipe. Hemp seed oil is a green, nutty-flavored oil that is best used unheated. It tastes a little like sunflower oil and is perfect for making such things as pesto or salad dressing. Its greenish hue is the result of chlorophyll, which is rich in magnesium.

Health Benefits

Cannabis has been used in medicine since about 2300 B.C., when the legendary Chinese emperor Shen-Nung prescribed chu-ma (female hemp) for the treatment of constipation, gout, beriberi, malaria, rheumatism, and menstrual problems. He classified chu-ma as one of the Superior Elixirs of Immortality. In the second century A.D., the renowned physician Hua Tuo formulated ma-yo (hemp wine) and ma-fei-san (hemp boiling powder) as anesthetics for the many surgeries he performed. The fourteenth-century text *Ri-Yong-Ben-Cao* (Household Materia Medica), by Wu Rui, described the use of hemp seed as a medicine.

Both the ancient Ayurvedic system of Indian medicine and the Arabic Unani Tibbi system make extensive use of hemp for healing. Usually, it is mixed with other vegetable, mineral, and animal substances that neutralize its narcotic effects and enhance its therapeutic virtues. The ninth-century medical text *Susruta Samhita* describes bhang as an antiphlegmatic against catarrh. The Sanskrit book *Rajbulubha* recommends hemp for the treatment of gonorrhea. The supreme nutritional benefits of hemp-seed oil are mainly because of its perfect ratio of omega-6 and omega-3 fatty acids. These long-chain unsaturated fats provide various benefits including cell membrane fluidity, normal cell growth and maturation, brain development, prostaglandin production, cardiovascular health, nerve cell (myelin sheath) maintenance, and healthy immune response. Research suggests that for humans the ideal ratio of omega-6 to omega-3 is in the region of 3–5:1, since the ration in most cells is at this level. Hemp seed oil, which contains a three-to-one omega-6 to omega-3 ratio, is the only oil to fulfill this profile. Hemp is also the only edible seed to contain substantial amounts of GLA, making it particularly beneficial as an alternative to other GLA-rich sources such as borage or evening primrose oil.

Hemp protein provides a well-balanced array of the essential amino acids for humans. An important aspect of hemp seed protein is a high content of arginine (123 mg/g protein) and histidine (27 mg/g protein), both of which are important for growth during childhood, and of the sulfur-containing amino acids methionine (23 mg/g protein) and cysteine (16 mg/g protein), which are needed for proper enzyme formation. Hemp protein also contains relatively high levels of the branched-chain amino acids that are important for the metabolism of exercising muscle. Animals, especially birds, instinctively prefer hemp seeds. Not only are the feathers of birds that eat help seed more luxurious, but their offspring are stronger and healthier.

Hickory Nut
(*Carya* spp.)

Carya comes from the Greek name *karya*, for the hickory tree. The Algonquin Indians in Virginia in the mid–seventeenth century called the nuts *pokahickery*, which the colonial settlers shortened to *hickory*.

General Information
Hickory trees are a native North American tree of the walnut family. Although all species of hickory trees bear nuts, the only commercially important one is the pecan, which is covered separately. Second in importance is the shagbark hickory (*Carya ovata*), so named for its loose, shaggy bark, which hangs in long strips. Though few of these trees are cultivated, the nut with its thin, flattened, light tan shell is the northern equivalent of the pecan. Another closely related hickory is the shellbark, which produces similar nuts. A natural hybrid nut, called hican, is produced by crossing an edible hickory variety with a pecan tree. The result is a nut larger than the pecan but still as tasty as a hickory.

Culinary Uses
Hickory nuts can be eaten raw but are especially good when baked in cookies.

Hickory Nut / Nutritional Value Per 100 g Edible Portion			
	Dried		Dried
Calories	657	Magnesium	173 mg
Protein	12.72 g	Phosphorus	336 mg
Fat	64.37 g	Potassium	436 mg
Fiber	3.24 g	Sodium	1 mg
Calcium	61 mg	Zinc	4.310 mg
Iron	2.12 mg	Copper	0.738 mg

Jack Nut
(*Artocarpus heterophyllus*)

Artocarpus comes from the Greek words *artos*, meaning "bread," and *carpos*, meaning "fruit"; *heterophyllus* means "having leaves of more than one form." The name *jack* was given to this fruit by the Portuguese in the sixteenth century since it sounded like the Malayan name for the plant, *tsjaka*.

Jack Nut / Nutritional Value Per 100 g Edible Portion		
	Fresh	Dried
Protein	6.6 g	n/a
Fat	0.4 g	n/a
Fiber	1.5 g	n/a
Calcium	0.05-0.55 mg	0.13%
Iron	0.002-1.200 mg	0.005%
Phosphorus	0.13-0.23 mg	0.54%

General Information
This tropical evergreen tree is believed indigenous to the rainforests of India and the Malayan Peninsula. The fruits grow sporadically on the trunk and large branches, a somewhat unusual habit called "cauliflory," which also occurs in the cacao tree. Under normal conditions, a single tree may bear 150 to 250 huge fruits per year. The fruit's interior is complex, consisting of large bulbs of yellow flesh, each enclosing a smooth oval seed, massed among narrow ribbons of tougher tissue and surrounding a central pithy core. There may be up to five hundred large, starchy, kidney-shaped, edible seeds of medium size contained within a single fruit's edible flesh. See also **Jackfruit** in the **Fruits** section.

Culinary Uses
The raw seeds or "nuts" are indigestible because they contain a powerful trypsin inhibitor and have a slightly unpleasant flavor, both of which are removed by boiling or roasting, after which they taste much like European chestnuts. Once cooked, the seeds can be added to soups, stewed with meat, or made into a starchy flour.

Health Benefits
Jack nuts have an unusually low fat content of less than 1 percent, even lower than chestnuts. The Chinese consider jackfruit pulp and seeds to be tonic, cooling, nutritious, and useful in overcoming the influence of alcohol on the system.

Jojoba Nut
(*Simmondsia chinensis*)

When the British naturalist H. F. Link landed in Baja California in 1822 and gathered botanical specimens of jojoba, he named the plant *Simmondsia* in honor of another British botanist, T. W. Simmonds, who had died several years earlier in Trinidad. Subsequently, Link visited China to carry out further plant exploration. When he shipped a box of Chinese botanical specimens back to England, his Mexican jojoba was accidentally mixed in with his Chinese botanical collection; thus the plant was erroneously given the specific name *chinensis*. The English name *jojoba* is of Mexican-Spanish origin.

General Information

A hardy desert shrub native to the Sonora Desert, the jojoba is usually found at elevations of between two and four thousand feet. "Female" plants bear fruit capsules that contain one to three oily, chocolate-brown seeds or nuts, about the size of small hazelnut kernels. Mature plants yield between three and twelve pounds of seed per year. The plant is now the object of a major crop development program, because jojoba seed oil is the only natural substitute for sperm whale oil in the production of liquid wax.

Culinary Uses

Indians of the Southwest desert gathered the nuts and ate them, raw or roasted; their flavor is reminiscent of the hazelnut but more bitter. Jojoba nuts contain about 50 percent oil and 30 percent protein.

Lotus Seed

(Nelumbo nucifera)

Nelumbo comes from the name of the plant in Singhalese (Sri Lanka), and *nucifera* means "nut-bearing." The English word *lotus* is derived from the Hebraic *lot*, meaning "myrrh."

General Information

The spinning-top-shaped, seed-bearing receptacle of the lotus plant contains ten to thirty marble-sized white fruits that look rather like cooked chickpeas, each of which encloses a single seed. When the receptacle dries out and shrinks away from the hardening fruits, the seeds become loose and rattle in their cavities. During harvesting, the edible seeds are removed from the receptacles. The seeds are preferably picked unripe for the best flavor.

Culinary Uses

Immature lotus seeds are eaten raw like nuts, at which stage they have a pleasant nutty flavor. Mature seeds are

Lotus Seed / Nutritional Value Per 100 g Edible Portion		
	Raw	Dried
Calories	89	332
Protein	4.13 g	15.41 g
Fat	0.53 g	1.97 g
Fiber	0.65 g	2.42 g
Calcium	44 mg	163 mg
Iron	0.95 mg	3.53 mg
Magnesium	56 mg	210 mg
Phosphorus	168 mg	626 mg
Potassium	367 mg	1,368 mg
Sodium	1 mg	5 mg
Beta Carotene (A)	13 IU	50 IU
Thiamine (B$_1$)	0.171 mg	0.640 mg
Riboflavin (B$_2$)	0.040 mg	0.150 mg
Niacin (B$_3$)	0.429 mg	1.600 mg

generally roasted or boiled; soak them for several hours, then boil them alone for an hour. Once cooked, many people prefer to push out the bitter center portion of the seeds with a wooden pick before eating them. The starchy lotus seeds are popular ingredients in many Asian meat and vegetable dishes, as well as in puddings, pastes, and candies. They also may be ground into flour or dried for storage.

Health Benefits

Lotus seed increases energy, promotes vitality, and aids digestion.

Macadamia Nut

(Macadamia integrifolia, M. tetraphylla)
Also Known As: Queensland Nut

The tree was named *Macadamia* in 1857 by Baron Ferdinand von Mueller, director of the Royal Botanical Gardens in Melbourne and the foremost botanist of Australia, after his friend John Macadam, M.D. (1827–1865), secretary of the Philosophical Institute of Victoria (Australia). Dr. Macadam died of pleurisy aboard the ship taking him to New Zealand, where he intended to sample the nut that bore his name. The term *integrifolia* means "entire-leaved," while *tetraphylla* means "four-leaved."

General Information

The macadamia is an evergreen tree indigenous to the coastal subtropical rainforests of southeast Queensland and northern New South Wales in eastern Australia. The trees are not truly ever-bearing, although they put forth a few blossoms and nuts throughout the year. Cone-shaped clusters of about twenty nuts form on the tree, each nut having a brown, leathery husk that splits when ripe, causing the nut to fall. The macadamia nut is a rarity—a "new" crop that was domesticated for the first time in 1858 in Australia and the only indigenous Australian plant ever developed as a commercial food crop. They are cultivated on a large scale, however, only in the Hawaiian Islands, where the trees have thrived in the rich volcanic soil since being introduced there in 1882 by William Herbert Purvis. Macadamias are Hawaii's third largest crop; pineapples and sugarcane are the leaders. The island of Hawaii, known as the Big Island, provides 99 percent of Hawaiian macadamias and 95 percent of the world supply.

Culinary Uses

The large (one inch in diameter), spherical, light beige macadamia kernel has a crunchy, sweet, delicate taste and a creamy, rich texture. Given their hard shells, tendency to mildew in the shell, and high oil content, they are almost always sold shelled in vacuum-packed jars. Once the container is opened, the nuts should be consumed quickly, which is usually not a problem. Raw macadamias should be refrigerated or frozen in airtight containers and used within two months. Most macadamias are processed by stripping the husks and dehydrating the nuts to remove almost every bit of moisture, followed by a roasting in coconut oil and a dunk in salt powder. They are mainly eaten as cocktail nibbles straight from the can but are also occasionally used in salads, casseroles, confectionery, sweet dishes, and baked goods.

LORE AND LEGEND

Since the Aborigines had informed Walter Hill, a Scottish botanist and director of the Botanic Gardens at Brisbane (as well as a friend of von Mueller's), that macadamia nuts were poisonous, he was horrified to find his assistant (who had been instructed to crack the shells and plant them) eating the kernels and proclaiming them delicious! A few days later, when the boy did not sicken or die, Hill himself tasted the kernels and was so favorably impressed by their flavor that he immediately became an enthusiastic promoter of macadamia nuts. In 1858 Hill planted what is believed to be the first cultivated macadamia tree on the banks of the Brisbane River in Queensland, which as of 1984 was still alive and producing.

Health Benefits

Macadamia nuts help rejuvenate the liver and discourage the craving for alcohol. They are among the highest in fat (about 70 percent) and calories of the nuts so should be eaten in moderation.

Olive and Olive Oil
(*Olea europaea*)

And the dove came in to him in the evening; and, lo, in her mouth was an olive leaf plucked off: so Noah knew that the waters were abated from off the earth.

—GENESIS 8:11

The whole Mediterranean, the sculpture, the palms, the gold beads, the bearded heroes,
The wine, the ideas, the ships, the moonlight, the winged gorgons, the bronze men,
The philosophers—all of it seems to rise in the sour, pungent taste of these black olives
Between the teeth. A taste older than meat, older than wine. A taste as old as cold water.

—LAWRENCE DURRELL

Macadamia Nut / Nutritional Value Per 100 g Edible Portion

	Dried		Dried
Calories	702	Potassium	368 mg
Protein	8.3 g	Sodium	5 mg
Fat	73.72 g	Zinc	1.710 mg
Fiber	5.28 g	Copper	0.296 mg
Calcium	70 mg	Beta Carotene (A)	0 IU
Iron	2.41 mg	Thiamine (B₁)	0.350 mg
Magnesium	116 mg	Riboflavin (B₂)	0.110 mg
Phosphorus	136 mg	Niacin (B₃)	2.140 mg

The Romans knew this tree as *Olea*, from the root word *oleum*, meaning "oil," since the fruits provide large quantities of this important commodity. The term *europaea* means "European." The English word *olive* derives from the Greek *elaia*.

General Information

Asia Minor is credited as the original home of one of the oldest fruit trees known to humanity, the olive tree. Records show that this slow-growing, picturesque evergreen tree with its leathery leaves and fragrant blossoms was being cultivated by the ancient Egyptians in the seventeenth century B.C., and olives were one of the chief staples of husbandry and trade in the early days of Minoan Crete (3000 B.C.). The Spanish brought the olive tree to America to provide oil for the colonists; it was among the first trees planted in the West Indies. The first recorded planting in North America was at the mission of San Diego de Alcola in about 1769 by Jesuit priests. Hand-picking is still the most reliable method for gathering olives, since the fruits do not ripen simultaneously and picking by hand is least likely to damage them. Spain produces mostly green olives, while Italy produces mainly black olives.

Olive oil comes from the same black or green olives you may eat as an appetizer. Tree-ripened olives are picked when their color changes from green to purplish black and the skins look oily but not too soft. The first pressing is done with gentle pressure, and temperatures produced are not much above room temperature. Oil thus extracted is sold as "extra-virgin"; it contains 1 percent or less oleic acid and has an enticing fragrance and superb flavor. Also look for the appellation "cold-pressed," which indicates that the oil was mechanically pressed without heat or chemical treatments. Oil from the second pressing is sold as "virgin." Fine virgin olive oil contains no more than 1.5 percent acidity and is also delicious; semi-fine virgin may have up to 3 percent acidity but still maintains a pleasant aroma and taste. Oil from subsequent pressings of pulp and pits is processed with chemical solvents at high heat, up to 450 degrees Fahrenheit, and sold as "pure" or "refined" olive oil. Another category of olive oil to enter the market recently is "light" olive oil, which does not refer to fewer calories or fat but rather to a lighter color and minimal taste. A greenish cast to the oil indicates a less refined oil and one of higher quality.

LORE AND LEGEND

"After the ox Aleph, the house Beta, and the camel Gamma, the olive or Zai was the symbol denoting the fourth letter of the most ancient alphabets. Flocks and herds, housing, transport, and agriculture were the four poles of a thriving civilization. And out of all cultivated plants, the olive tree was chosen as a symbol rather than any of the cereals, which may well seem surprising. However, dealing in olive oil was the backbone of the import-export trade in the ancient world."
—Maguelonne Toussaint-Samat,
History of Food

Culinary Uses

Unlike most raw fruits, tree-ripened olives are too bitter to eat and require such manner of preparation that one wonders how they were ever discovered to be edible. Fresh, unprocessed olives are used for the production of olive oil, while the only ones sold for eating are pickled. Of the two types—green and black—the green are the less oily. Plant variety, growing conditions, and region all affect the olive's flavor and quality. Those grown in a particular geographic area generally share a similar character but are by no means identical because of the profound influence of each microclimate, as well as other variables. Olives tend to retain chemical tastes and smells, so organically grown olives in any region are preferred over non-organic. The best olives are sun-dried; revive them in water and then place them back in olive oil. Eaten mainly as finger foods, olives can also be used in pizzas, salads, and cooked savory dishes.

Used for centuries in Greek, French, and Italian cuisines, olive oil is a favorite for giving even ordinary dishes a Mediterranean flavor. It is excellent for sautéing, and it is delicious when used in salad dressings, sauces, and spreads. Like wine, it is distinguished by words such as *smooth, full-bodied, round, fruity, sweet, light,* and *extra bouquet.* Try the many different varieties: brilliant green Italian Tuscan oils usually taste rich and fruity, with peppery accents; southern Italian oils are generally more delicate and mellow; and Greek oils are typically robust and assertive. Unlike most fine wines, olive oil peaks in its first year and does not benefit from aging. Pure olive oil is more stable

Olive and Olive Oil / Nutritional Value Per 100 g Edible Portion

	Black, Canned	Oil
Calories	81-115	884
Protein	0.84-0.97 g	0 g
Fat	6.87-10.68 g	100.00 g
Fiber	n/a	0 g
Calcium	88.00-94.00 mg	0.18 mg
Iron	3.30-3.32 mg	0.38 mg
Magnesium	4.00 mg	0.01 mg
Phosphorus	3.00 mg	1.22 mg
Potassium	8-9 mg	n/a
Sodium	872.00-898.00 mg	0.04 mg
Zinc	0.220 mg	0.060 mg
Copper	0.251 mg	0.226 mg
Manganese	0.020 mg	n/a
Beta Carotene (A)	346-403 IU	n/a
Thiamine (B$_1$)	0.003 mg	n/a
Riboflavin (B$_2$)	0 mg	n/a
Niacin (B$_3$)	0.022-0.037 mg	n/a
Pyridoxine (B$_6$)	0.009-0.012 mg	n/a
Folic Acid (B$_9$)	0 mcg	n/a
Ascorbic Acid (C)	0.9-1.5 mg	n/a
Tocopherol (E)	n/a	11.9 mg

and can sometimes be stored without refrigeration for over a year, but virgin and extra-virgin oils degrade more quickly. Though their vitamin E content helps to preserve them, they should be stored away from heat or bright light, preferably in a dark glass container, as plastic may impart an off-taste. The oil will keep longer in the refrigerator but will congeal, an annoyance because it then has to be brought back to room temperature to be poured; plus frequent changes in temperature instigate rancidity.

Health Benefits

pH 3.60–7.30 (green to black). As with any fatty food, olives tend to slow down body functions and processes. They are considered obstructive and therefore medicinal for a person with high-strung, nervous energy or for someone with diarrhea. A slow-moving person with blocked or stuck energy patterns or one who has a tendency for cysts and tumors might use olives less frequently. High-quality olive oil is easily digested and imparts a generally soothing and healing influence to the digestive tract. Taken internally, olive oil is beneficial for the gallbladder and liver, strengthens and develops body tissue, and is a general tonic for the nerves; it increases the secretion of bile and acts as a

LORE AND LEGEND

The olive tree in ancient times was so important that Moses exempted from military service all men who would work at its cultivation. In scriptural and classical writings, olive oil is symbolic of goodness and purity, and the tree of peace, happiness, and prosperity. The oil, in addition to its wide use in diet and healing, was burned in the sacred temple lamps. The Greeks prayed for prosperity and peace with green olive boughs held in their hands, garlands draped around their necks, and plaited crowns of olive leaves set upon their heads. When the Romans extended their power into Tunis they taxed the Tunisians three-hundred thousand gallons of oil yearly, and special conduits were built for it down to the sea and the waiting ships. Among the Chinese, disputes or quarrels were settled by sending the offended person an olive wrapped in red paper.

In Greek legend the as-yet-nameless newly founded city of Athens was being fought over by Athena and Poseidon, who both desired to become the city's patron. The rest of the gods decreed that the one who gave the best gift to humanity should have this honor. Poseidon struck the seashore with his trident and there sprang forth the horse; Athena smote the ground with her spear and the olive tree arose. Athena's gift, being a symbol of peace and agriculture, was deemed infinitely better for humanity than Poseidon's horse, an emblem of war, and thus Athena became the patron goddess of Athens.

laxative by encouraging muscular contraction in the bowels. Mild in its action, olive oil can be given to children where more potent laxatives or cathartics might be harmful. It is also soothing to mucous membranes and is said to help dissolve cholesterol deposits.

Because it is about 73 percent oleic acid, one of the two fatty acids that make up the phospholipids that form cerebral and nervous tissue, olive oil positively affects cerebral growth in babies. It has the same linolenic acid concentration as breast milk, and it favors the mineralization and development of bones, thus helping to fight osteoporosis. It is also valuable for its content of squalene, found in small amounts in many vegetable oils but especially olive oil. Squalene is a normal component of the human body, a precursor to all steroidal hormonal production (adrenal hormones). Highly concentrated in the skin, where it provides protection from germs and free-radical damage, squalene also has a unique ability to carry oxygen throughout the body, independent of hemoglobin. An amazing immune enhancer, it helps the body protect against all three types of common offenders: bacterial, viral, and fungal infections.

Applied externally, olive oil is good for sunburn or other burns as well as dry skin, minor skin eruptions, and inflammations. Rich in vitamins that nourish the skin's epidermic layer, it may attract the sun's rays and therefore tend to produce sunburns (unless one cup of olive oil is mixed with ten drops of iodine and the juice of a lemon). A lotion made of warm olive oil and a squeeze of lemon juice will quickly undo the damage done to skin by heavy labor or too much scrubbing. The oil mixed with lime water is recommended for burns.

VARIETIES

Black and *green olives* are the two broad types. Most olives are picked green from the tree in October and then held in brine for several months. Those to be sold green must be soaked in a lye solution before brining, while black olives can be brined immediately. Those that wind up black are bombarded continuously with jets of air, a technique that oxidizes the skin and meat to its dark color. Those that are to be marketed as ripe green olives are not aerated but kept immersed in the lye and/or brine solution to prevent oxidation. In either case the final steps are the same: the olives are washed thoroughly to remove all traces of lye and then packed in a dilute salt solution and canned. Green olives are often pitted and stuffed with various ingredients, including almonds, pimientos, anchovies, capers, or onions. The green varieties of olive are much more acidic and may contain residual chemicals; black olives are mellower and richer in flavor.

Greek/Italian olives are not picked until they are fully tree-ripened, at which time they are dark purple, soft, and juicy. They are then put down in rock salt and left for several months before being packed in olive oil and marketed. Kalamatas are the most popular of the Greek olives. These purple-black olives are marinated in a wine vinegar solution. They are medium-sized and have a pleasing aftertaste.

Manzanillas are the most traditional green cocktail olives. A mainstay of the Spanish and California olive industries, they have crisp flesh and a smoky flavor. (Black Mission olives can be substituted in recipes.)

Niçoise olives are small, dark brown or purple olives with a sharp and slightly sour flavor. Because the pits are disproportionately large for the size of the olive, there isn't much fruit left after they're pitted.

Oil-cured olives are jet black and very wrinkled. They're the most bitter of all.

Spanish green olives, after being harvested, are placed in brine solution to which a little sugar has been added. A particular strain of bacteria may then be manually introduced, or the vats may be allowed to receive wild or natural bacteria from the air; the medium is selective, and only acid-forming bacteria will grow in it. The olives are then fermented for several days or weeks at a temperature of 100 degrees Fahrenheit or more, until the correct amount of lactic acid is formed. They are then removed and packed in jars.

Oyster Nut
(Telfairia pedata)

The oyster nut tree was named in honor of Charles Telfair (1778–1833), an Irish botanist and plant collector who lived in Mauritius. *Pedata* means "footed." The name *oyster nut* comes from the nut's resemblance in shape to oysters.

General Information
Native to tropical East Africa, this fast-growing, woody-stemmed, prodigious climbing vine of the gourd family reaches a height of sixty to seventy feet as it climbs and scrambles over tall trees. Individual branches may attain

one hundred feet in length, while a single plant may overrun an area the size of a tennis court. The fruits are deeply ridged and shaped like large footballs, reach one to two feet in length, and eight to twelve inches in diameter, and can weigh up to thirty pounds apiece. Often the trees that originally supported the vines with their heavy gourds become smothered and crushed under the enormous weight. The fruits burst open when ripe, releasing over one hundred pale yellow seeds embedded in a golden-yellow pulp. Large, flat, and circular, about 1½ inches in diameter by half an inch thick, the seeds are washed and dried in the sun for several days, after which they are opened in a manner much like shucking an oyster: they are cut around the edge and the bitter fibrous shells are pried open with a knife to extract the edible kernels.

Culinary Uses

Raw or roasted, the oyster nut has a pleasant flavor somewhat similar to the Brazil nut. In East Africa the kernels are used to make sweets, cakes, and soups, and they are also prepared with a variety of other foods.

Health Benefits

Oyster nuts have a fat content of over 60 percent.

Palm Oil and Palm Kernel Oil
(Elaeis guineensis)

> Its family name derives from the Greek *elaia*, meaning "olive," on account of its fruits rich in oil. *Guineensis* means "native to Guinea."

General Information

The African oil palm tree, which looks like a coconut tree, is unique in that its fruit contains two types of oil—palm oil and palm kernel oil. Palm oil is pressed from fibrous pulp (mesocarp) of the fruit, while palm kernel oil comes from the seed. The oil from the fruit is a vivid red color and constitutes 90 percent of the plant's oil; the oil from the seed is colorless and yields the remaining 10 percent. Both oils are liquid when warm and solid at room temperature. The oil palm produces more oil per acre than any other vegetable crop. In volume of worldwide production, palm oil is second only to soy oil. Although this palm originated in West Africa, it is now grown throughout the tropics, with Malaysia and Indonesia producing the most for export.

Culinary Uses

The Bahins of northeastern Brazil call palm oil *dende*. It's color, unmistakable aroma, and flavor are as integral to their cuisine as olive oil is for the Italians. Available in Indian, Latino, and Asian markets, unrefined palm oil and palm kernel oils are excellent for baking, deep-frying, and sautéing at high temperatures. Look for it in cans, which are light-protective, rather than bottles. Unfortunately, these oils are most commonly available in highly refined forms. Palm oil is frequently used as the frying fat for potato chips and is an ingredient in margarine, gravies, and soups. Palm kernel oil is a familiar ingredient in nondairy coffee creamers, dressings, dips, whipped toppings, candies (especially carob), and cookies and waffles. In a cheap chocolate substitute, palm kernel oil is chemically fractionated to be 100 percent saturated, thus preventing candy coatings from melting at room temperature or on your fingers.

Health Benefits

Unrefined palm oil is among the richest sources of beta carotene (three hundred times that of tomatoes and fifteen times that of carrots). It also has a high content of vitamin E (both tocopherol and tocotrienol), which helps retard oxidation, making it a naturally stable oil. However, since all palm oil used in the Western world is highly refined (crude palm oil has a reddish-brown color, which most consumers would probably reject), most of these vital nutrients are destroyed. Palm oil contains more palmitic acid (39 percent)—the common fatty acid that tends to raise blood cholesterol—than is found in any other food. Palm kernel oil is a highly saturated (82 percent) tropical plant oil. When the oil is unrefined, this high saturation gives it stability, making it a superior culinary oil for cooking at high temperatures. Today palm kernel oil is still denigrated because of its high saturation—rightly so when it is refined palm kernel oil. The saturation in both palm and palm kernel oils enables them to be used for manufacturing purposes without hydrogenation.

Peanut

(Arachis hypogaea)

Also Known As: Monkey Nuts, Groundnuts, Goobers, Pindars

No man in the world has more courage than the man who can stop after eating one peanut.

—CHANNING POLLOCK,
AMERICAN PLAYWRIGHT AND CRITIC

Arachis is a Greek term referring to the plant's hairy stem, which suggests the web of Arachne, the Lydian girl who challenged Athena to a weaving contest and was turned into a spider. The specific name *hypogaea* means "growing beneath the ground." The English word *peanut* comes from the plant's being a member of the pea (legume) family and the seeds looking like nuts.

General Information

The peanut, technically a legume rather than a nut, is the seed of a plant native to Peru and Brazil. Cultivated extensively by the Mayans in Yucatan, by the Incas in Peru, and by various tribes in Brazil, it was spread by Portuguese explorers to East Africa and by Spanish explorers to the Philippines. Later it came to North America via Africa and the slave trade. Rather low and bushy, the plant bears pods that have the peculiar habit of bending groundward and being pushed into the ground by the elongating branches. After the plant withers and dies back, the mature pods, carrying between one and three peanuts each, are ready to be dug out. An additional curious feature is that while other legumes store starch, peanuts store fat and so are more like a nut than a bean. Only toward the end of the nineteenth century was the peanut extensively cultivated as an oil-producing plant. Before that they were grown almost solely for hog feed. A St. Louis physician named Ambrose Straub is credited with creating in 1880 what many consider to be the most exalted state of grace any

Peanut / Nutritional Value Per 100 g Edible Portion								
	Unroasted, Raw	Boiled	Dry-Roasted w/ Salt	Oil-Roasted	Defatted Flour	Commercial Low Fat Flour	Commercial Peanut Butter Chunky	Peanut Butter Smooth
Calories	567	318	585	581	327	428	589	588
Protein	25.80 g	13.50 g	23.68 g	26.35 g	52.20 g	33.80 g	24.05 g	24.59 g
Fat	49.24 g	22.01 g	49.66 g	49.30 g	0.55 g	21.90 g	49.94 g	49.98 g
Fiber	4.85 g	1.96 g	5.10 g	5.33 g	4.05 g	n/a	2.50 g	2.41 g
Calcium	92 mg	55 mg	54 mg	88 mg	140 mg	130 mg	41 mg	34 mg
Iron	4.58 mg	1.01 mg	2.26 mg	1.83 mg	2.10 mg	4.74 mg	1.90 mg	1.67 mg
Magnesium	168 mg	102 mg	176 mg	185 mg	370 mg	48 mg	159 mg	157 mg
Phosphorus	376 mg	198 mg	358 mg	517 mg	760 mg	n/a	317 mg	323 mg
Potassium	705 mg	180 mg	658 mg	682 mg	1,290 mg	1,358 mg	747 mg	721 mg
Sodium	18 mg	751 mg	813 mg	433 mg	180 mg	1 mg	486 mg	478 mg
Zinc	3.270 mg	1.830 mg	3.310 mg	6.630 mg	5.100 mg	5.990 mg	2.780 mg	2.510 mg
Copper	1.144 mg	0.499 mg	0.671 mg	1.300 mg	1.800 mg	2.039 mg	0.515 mg	0.556 mg
Manganese	1.934 mg	1.023 mg	2.083 mg	2.062 mg	4.900 mg	4.231 mg	1.865 mg	1.536 mg
Beta Carotene (A)	0 mg	0 mg	0 mg	0 mg	0 mg	n/a	0 mg	0 mg
Thiamine (B$_1$)	0.640 mg	0.259 mg	0.438 mg	0.253 mg	0.700 mg	n/a	0.125 mg	0.136 mg
Riboflavin (B$_2$)	0.135 mg	0.063 mg	0.098 mg	0.108 mg	0.480 mg	n/a	0.112 mg	0.099 mg
Niacin (B$_3$)	12.066 mg	5.259 mg	13.525 mg	14.277 mg	27.000 mg	n/a	13.689 mg	13.090 mg
Pantothenic Acid (B$_5$)	1.767 mg	0.825 mg	1.395 mg	1.390 mg	2.744 mg	n/a	0.964 mg	0.920 mg
Pyridoxine (B$_6$)	0.348 mg	0.152 mg	0.256 mg	0.255 mg	0.504 mg	n/a	0.450 mg	0.378 mg
Folic Acid (B$_9$)	239.8 mcg	74.6 mcg	145.3 mcg	125.7 mcg	248.2 mcg	n/a	92.0 mcg	78.2 mcg
Ascorbic Acid (C)	0 mg	0 mg	0 mg	0 mg	0 mg	0 mg	0 mg	0 mg
Tocopherol (E)	8.33 mg	n/a	7.80 mg	6.94 mg	n/a	n/a	n/a	n/a

ambitious nut can aspire to: peanut butter. Promoting his peanut butter as a readily digestible, healthy, yet tasty high-protein food, the physician gained a loyal circle of consumers in the St. Louis area. It gained exposure and popularity when he introduced it at the Chicago World's Columbian Exposition of 1893. On February 14, 1903, patent no. 721,651 was granted to Dr. Straub for a "mill for grinding peanuts for butter." The machine was launched at the 1904 St. Louis World's Fair. Soon grocers across the country were stocking peanut butter in bulk in large wooden tubs to satisfy customer demand. During the same period Dr. John H. Kellogg, famous for breakfast cereals, prescribed peanut butter as nourishment for his convalescing patients. How seriously Americans regard peanut butter becomes quite clear when one notes the presence in Chicago of the American Museum of Peanut Butter History. Nearly half the peanuts grown in the United States are turned into peanut butter to satisfy the voracious American appetite; the remainder are used primarily for oil and industrial uses. Three types of peanuts are grown: Spanish, a small, roundish nut; Valencia, a medium-sized, oval-shaped nut most often used for salted-in-the-shell peanuts; and Virginia (or jumbo), the large nuts typically added to cocktail mixed nuts. All three varieties are used for peanut butter, candies, snacks, and home cooking.

Culinary Uses

Peanuts should not be eaten raw because they contain a substance, readily destroyed by heat, that is believed to inhibit the body's ability to absorb nutrients. Avoid peanuts that have been salted in the shell, as this is done by adding salt to a detergent-like compound that transports the salt through the shell. Although their main use is for peanut butter and peanut oil, peanuts make an excellent sauce for serving with salads or lightly cooked vegetables; this sauce is made by reducing lightly roasted peanuts to a purée in a blender or food processor with chili pepper, garlic, and fresh coriander to taste and enough milk, coconut milk, or stock to make a thick sauce. In Indonesia and many African countries, peanuts are often used as the basis of sauces, curries, and stews. Peanut butter and jelly sandwiches are almost synonymous with childhood. Because of its fat content, peanut butter becomes rancid when exposed to light and heat or with long storage. Refrigeration retards rancidity but firms the butter.

LORE AND LEGEND

In ancient Peru pots of peanuts were buried with the dead for sustenance on their long journey into the next world. In Africa gold peanuts hammered from crude ore were trophies of the sixteenth century, being presented by tribal chieftains to warriors, athletes, and hunters.

Health Benefits

pH 6.28. Unfortunately, peanuts are one of the most chemically adulterated crops, since the fields are rotated with cotton that, because it is a nonfood crop, is treated with chemicals too toxic to be allowed on food crops. These chemical residues remain and affect the following peanut crop. Furthermore, peanuts are highly susceptible to the aflatoxin mold (*Aspergillis flavus*), one of the most powerful liver carcinogens known. Aflatoxin is twenty times more toxic than DDT and has been linked to mental retardation and lowered intelligence. This mold is present in both raw and processed peanuts; roasting does not kill it. Peanut oils will not contain it because the strong alkalis used in processing neutralize the toxin. Organic peanuts not only contain fewer chemical residues but are less subject to aflatoxin. In moderate amounts, peanuts can benefit the person with a fast metabolism; they tend to slow metabolic rate so are not recommended for those with slow digestion. Peanuts also have a high content of phosphoric acid, which in combination with their starch and protein makes them a highly acid-forming food. For those trying to lose weight, the peanut should be avoided altogether because of its high fat content.

BYPRODUCTS

Peanut butter of the commercial variety often contains as little as 75 percent peanuts. The rest is made up of hydrogenized fats (to prevent oil separation), sugar (for added sweetness and to mask the taste of inferior peanuts), emulsifiers (against oil separation), texturizers (to aid spreadability and counteract the butter's natural tendency to stick to the roof of the mouth), and degermed peanuts (for infinite shelf life). Buy high-quality peanut butter from natural food stores (often made right in the store) or make your own. Americans consume over eight hundred million pounds of peanut butter annually, or three-plus pounds per person—most of this by children, 92 percent of whom eat peanut butter at least twice a week. According to a 1988 Peanut Advisory Board survey, women prefer chunky peanut butter by a margin of 43 to 39, and most men have no preference.

Peanut flour is made solely of finely ground peanuts or from peanuts that are processed to remove a high proportion of the oil and calories, leaving a flour product that contains about 60 percent protein and less than 1 percent fat. Peanut flour is becoming more popular as a protein extender in bakery and confectionery products, especially for diet-conscious consumers.

Peanut meal is the meal remaining after the peanuts have been processed for oil. It can be used as a substitute for chopped peanuts or to boost the nutritional level of baked goods and lend a delicious taste. This meal is available both roasted and unroasted, with the roasted kind having a more distinctive, nutty flavor.

Peanut oil was one of the first native North American vegetable oils. Peanuts can produce large quantities of oil, since the nut is about 50 percent oil. Peanut oil is frequently used in combination with other vegetable oils to make an all-purpose cooking oil because it is light-colored and bland. With its high smoke point, peanut oil lends itself particularly well to frying and is often used for popping popcorn. However, commercial peanut oil is highly refined and of dubious quality. Buy freshly pressed peanut oil, filtered rather than refined, without antioxidants, preservatives, and solvents. According to tests at the University of Vienna, high-quality unrefined peanut oil is an aid to the transportation of adrenaline and has laxative properties. It also contains traces of calcium, iron, magnesium, potassium, sodium, zinc, and vitamin E.

Pecan
(Carya illinoinensis)

> Nothing rekindles my spirits, gives comfort to my heart and mind, more than a visit to Mississippi. . . . And to be regaled as I often have been, with a platter of fried chicken, field peas, collard greens, fresh corn on the cob, sliced tomatoes with French dressing . . . and to top it all off with a wedge of freshly baked pecan pie.
>
> —CRAIG CLAIBORNE

The pecan was formerly known botanically as *Hicoria pecan*—the Latinate name *Hicoria* having been derived from the American Indian *powcohicoria*, for a milky beverage made from pulverized hickory nuts and water. *Carya* comes from the Greek word *karyon*, which was their name for the tree. Toward the end of the French and Indian Wars, about 1760, fur traders introduced the pecan from the territory of the Illinois Indian to the Atlantic seaboard; thus it became known as the "Illinois" nut (*illinoinensis* means "coming from Illinois"). The English common name *pecan* comes from the Algonquian Indian *paccan*, a word that also included walnuts and hickories—referring to nuts so hard they had to be cracked with a stone.

General Information

A native North American tree belonging to the hickory family and a near relative of walnuts, the pecan tree is a large, stately deciduous tree that under favorable conditions may grow to over one hundred feet in height, with a trunk diameter of six feet and a limb spread of some one hundred feet. These trees are indigenous to the Mississippi River basin, growing as far north as Indiana and Illinois and west into Texas and Kansas. They are very long-lived, with some native trees in the Southeast known to be over a thousand years old. The fruit, like that of the walnut, is enveloped in a hard woody husk, which opens when ripe, releasing four rounded oblong nuts with edible, oily kernels of excellent flavor. Each tree may yield up to five hundred pounds annually. Nuts from these trees, called "seedlings," are very tasty but are usually quite small and have a hard shell. It is difficult to get the kernels out whole without commercial machinery. Once shelled, seedlings find a ready market in candy, baked goods, and ice cream. "Cultivated" or "improved" varieties are pecans selected from seedling trees whose nuts displayed some superior characteristic: thinner shell, larger size, better flavor, brighter color, or higher kernel content. These improved varieties do not grow wild but are planted in orchards and are carefully cultivated. Georgia produces far more improved pecans than any other state. Before the sixteenth century, no European had ever seen a pecan nut, and there was little commercial development of the trees until the 1850s, when a black slave known as Antoine developed the Centennial variety at a Louisiana plantation. It is claimed that the oval-shaped pecan is the second most popular nut in the United States, after the peanut.

Size classifications of pecan halves are established by the

U.S. Department of Agriculture. Classifications are determined by the number of halves it takes to make a pound.

Mammoth	250 or fewer halves per pound
Jr. Mammoth	251-300 halves per pound
Jumbo (Junior)	301-350 halves per pound
Extra-Large	351-450 halves per pound
Large	451-550 halves per pound
Medium	551-650 halves per pound
Topper	651-800 halves per pound

Culinary Uses

Pecan nutmeats have a sweet, pulpy texture. They are great in fruit salads and, if toasted slightly, are a delicious topping for cooked grains or steamed green vegetables. The nuts are particularly enjoyed in the infamous pecan pie, butter pecan ice cream, and the praline—a brown sugar candy of French origin. In most recipes pecans can be substituted directly for walnuts. Try mixing chopped pecans into your favorite nut loaf or bean burgers, or hide a few

Pecan / Nutritional Value Per 100 g Edible Portion		
	Dried	**Flour/ Meal**
Calories	667	329
Protein	7.75 g	31.87 g
Fat	67.64 g	1.43 g
Fiber	1.60 g	1.50 g
Calcium	36 mg	32 mg
Iron	2.13 mg	1.97 mg
Magnesium	128 mg	120 mg
Phosphorus	291 mg	274 mg
Potassium	392 mg	334 mg
Sodium	1 mg	1 mg
Zinc	5.470 mg	5.130 mg
Copper	1.182 mg	1.116 mg
Manganese	4.506 mg	4.249 mg
Beta Carotene (A)	128 IU	n/a
Thiamine (B$_1$)	0.848 mg	n/a
Riboflavin (B$_2$)	0.128 mg	n/a
Niacin (B$_3$)	0.887 mg	n/a
Pantothenic Acid (B$_5$)	1.707 mg	n/a
Pyridoxine (B$_6$)	0.188 mg	n/a
Folic Acid (B$_9$)	39.2 mcg	n/a
Ascorbic Acid (C)	2.0 mg	n/a
Tocopherol (E)	3.10 mg	n/a

LORE AND LEGEND

Some North American Indians believed the pecan tree to be the manifestation of the Great Spirit and valued it so much that the early Spaniards in Florida were able to trade nuts for hides and mats. One tribe that lived in Texas, the Mariames, ate them as their only food for two months of every year.

in sandwiches for a crunchy surprise. Pecans are best purchased in the shell, for their high oil content predisposes them to turn rancid quickly after shelling.

Health Benefits

pH > 6.0. Best characterized as rich, one fully developed pecan kernel has a fat content of almost 70 percent, and in every pound of shelled nuts there are a whopping 3,633 calories. However, the oil in pecans is about 90 percent unsaturated fat, the type associated with boosting levels of "good" cholesterol in the blood. Raw pecans are one of nature's richest source of readily assimilable organic pyridoxine (vitamin B$_6$), which plays an essential role in converting the amino acids from consumed proteins into usable form for the body as well as being important to the nervous system; thus, raw pecans assist in the regeneration of damaged cells in diseased hearts.

BYPRODUCTS

Pecan meal is easily made by grinding these tender nuts in a blender; it can be added to bread and cookie recipes for a nutty flavor and nutritional boost.

Pili Nut
(*Canarium ovatum, C. luzonicum*)

Canarium perhaps refers to the Canary Islands, while *ovatum* means "ovate" or "egg-shaped."

General Information

Native to the Old World tropics of Southeast Asia, the pili nut, also known as the Java almond, gets its common name from the Philippines and is indigenous to that island group.

Pili Nut / Nutritional Value Per 100 g Edible Portion			
	Dried		Dried
Calories	719	Phosphorus	575 mg
Protein	10.80 g	Potassium	507 mg
Fat	79.55 g	Sodium	3 mg
Fiber	2.80 g	Beta Carotene (A)	41 IU
Calcium	145 mg	Thiamine (B$_1$)	0.913 mg
Iron	3.53 mg	Riboflavin (B$_2$)	0.093 mg
Magnesium	n/a	Niacin (B$_3$)	0.519 mg

Female trees begin to produce in their sixtieth year, yielding oblong, black, smooth fruits, which are about 2½ inches in length and grow in clusters. Each fruit contains within a fleshy husk a single, slender, triangular, sweet-tasting, cream-colored nut that is pointed at both ends.

Culinary Uses

The pili has a delicious flavor suggestive of the almond, and it used in the same manner. The thick, bony shell of the nut is hard to crack—so hard that it may be an obstacle to pili orchard development, even though the kernels are very popular locally. Whether the nuts are consumed raw or roasted and salted, the seed coat is always removed before eating. A good-quality edible oil, suitable for culinary purposes, is expressed from the kernels; this oil also serves as a lamp oil in the Philippines.

Pine Nut

(Pinus pinea, P. edulis, P. cembroides, P. koraiensis)
Also Known As: Pignolia, Piñon

> *Pinus* is the ancient Latin name for the tree; *pinea* means "of or from the pine"; *edulis* means "edible"; *koraiensis* means "coming from Korea." *Pignolia* is the diminutive form of *pine*.

General Information

Pine nuts are the seeds from the cones of certain pine tree species. Most of those that are marketed under the name of pine nuts come from the Italian stone pine (*P. pinea*), the Colorado piñon (*P. edulis*), the Mexican piñon (*P. cembroides*), or the Chinese nut pine (*P. koraiensis*). Many classical authors have written about pine nuts, which were valued as an article of food and as a dessert; all speak of the pine woods of Ravenna, which, although much

LORE AND LEGEND

The ancient Greeks held the stone pine sacred to the god Neptune, and both Greeks and Romans appreciated the taste of the nuts (most often preserved in honey). The piñon pine was an integral part of the mythology of many Indians of the Southwest. The Navajo smeared piñon pitch on corpses before burial; the Hopi dabbed pitch on their foreheads as a protection against sorcerers before going out of doors in December; burning piñon gum provided incense for Navajo nocturnal ceremonies, and specially selected piñon branches served as ritual wands. In China and Japan the pine is symbolic of longevity, and the Chinese god of immortality is often pictured sitting beneath a pine tree.

Pine Nut / Nutritional Value Per 100 g Edible Portion			
	Dried		**Dried**
Calories	515-568	Sodium	4-72 mg
Protein	11.57-24.00 g	Zinc	4.250-4.280 mg
Fat	50.70-60.98 g	Copper	1.026-1.035 mg
Fiber	0.80-4.71 g	Beta Carotene (A)	29 IU
Calcium	8-26 mg	Thiamine (B$_1$)	0.810-1.243 mg
Iron	3.06-9.20 mg	Riboflavin (B$_2$)	0.190-0.223 mg
Magnesium	234 mg	Niacin (B$_3$)	3.570-4.370 mg
Phosphorus	35-508 mg	Ascorbic Acid (C)	2.0 mg
Potassium	599-628 mg		

diminished, still remain today one of the greater areas of pine concentration. The seeds do not appear on the Italian stone pine until their fifteenth year of growth, and the greatest production comes only after half a century of life. The Colorado piñon, inhabiting the drier mountainous regions from Colorado south and west into Mexico, does not begin bearing until it is twenty-five years of age, not reaching full production until it is seventy-five, and then it only bears large crops every third or fourth year. Most pine nuts sold have been dried and milled to remove their outer brown skin. Unmilled pine nuts—with their brown jackets—are available in some areas.

Culinary Uses

Pine nuts are a small, thin, white, pellet-shaped nutmeat or seed. Their delicate, buttery taste and soft texture make them suitable, either raw or lightly roasted, for use in a variety of dishes and desserts. Probably best known for their appearance in pesto, they are also delicious in rice and eggplant dishes, in East Indian curries, or as a garnish for fruit and vegetable dishes. The nuts should be either purchased in the shell or kept refrigerated in an airtight glass container, as they spoil very quickly.

Health Benefits

The pine nut is one of the best sources of protein in the nut family and can easily take the place of the finest meats; a very small portion supplies all that the body needs of protein and fats. In general European species of pine nuts are richer in protein and lower in fat than the American varieties, but American pine nuts offer more vitamins and minerals.

Pistachio
(Pistacia vera)
Also Known As: Green Almond

The Latin *Pistacia* and the English name *pistachio* are derived from *pisteh*, the Persian name for this nut. The term *vera* means "true," "genuine," or "standard."

General Information

The diminutive pistachio tree probably originated in the Levant, most notably Persia, from where it spread throughout Palestine and the Mediterranean region and into certain areas of India and Russian central Asia. Tradition says that the pistachio was brought to ancient Rome by the Emperor Vitellius, circa A.D. 50. Related to the sumac and the cashew, this twenty-foot tall deciduous species of turpentine tree flourishes under adverse conditions, literally thriving in poor stony terrain where for most of the year there may be no rainfall, and tolerating long, hot summers with temperatures over 100 degrees Fahrenheit; while resistant to both cold and wind, pistachios cannot tolerate excessive dampness or high humidity. Under favorable conditions, pistachio trees live and produce for centuries: in the Kerman region of Iran a seven-hundred-year-old tree is still standing. Hard, off-white shells surround the uniquely colored pale green nutmeat. The green color comes from the presence of chlorophyll, and varieties of pistachio differ markedly in this respect, with the dark green kernels being the most highly valued and decorative.

A Syrian immigrant introduced pistachios into the United States in the late 1890s. Before migrating to America, he was a nut salesman in Syria and Turkey, traveling his territory by camel. He first imported pistachios

Pistachio / Nutritional Value Per 100 g Edible Portion			
	Dried		**Dried**
Calories	577	Zinc	1.340 mg
Protein	20.58 g	Copper	1.189 mg
Fat	48.39 g	Manganese	0.327 mg
Fiber	1.88 g	Beta Carotene (A)	233 IU
Calcium	135 mg	Thiamine (B$_1$)	0.820 mg
Iron	6.78 mg	Riboflavin (B$_2$)	0.174 mg
Magnesium	158 mg	Niacin (B$_3$)	1.080 mg
Phosphorus	503 mg	Folic Acid (B$_9$)	58.0 mcg
Potassium	1,093 mg	Tocopherol (E)	5.21 mg
Sodium	6 mg		

LORE AND LEGEND

If bad weather or disease prevents the nuts from ripening so that the shells fail to split open, pistachio growers repeat an old Turkish expression, "Too bad, our pistachios are not smiling." The Queen of Sheba was especially fond of pistachio nuts and is said to have monopolized the limited pistachio output of Assyria for herself and her court favorites. By decree of the queen, no subject outside the royal household was allowed to keep any part of the pistachio harvest. Following a social call in Syria, the departing guest is frequently given a small bag of pistachio nuts as a gesture of goodwill; the nuts are also an important ingredient at wedding feasts. One gluttonous emperor of Rome around A.D. 69, Vitellius, would finish off his meal by stuffing his mouth full of pistachios.

for his family and friends in New York, and then in 1906 he became a dealer, and other East Coast competitors soon followed his lead. Ninety-eight percent of the world supply of pistachios is now consumed in the United States. Iran, Turkey, and Afghanistan are the largest producers of pistachios. Commercial crops were planted in California in 1968 and have been steadily gaining on other producers. California pistachios are generally larger than those from the Middle East. Imported pistachios are fumigated with methyl bromide or phostoxin.

Culinary Uses

The pistachio nut is so prized for its pleasant, mild flavor and fetching green color that consumers are willing to pay exorbitant prices for it. The pistachio's shell is naturally tan; those that are red have been dyed to conceal mottled markings caused by the natural drying process, while those overly light may have been whitened with heavy coats of salt and cornstarch—both should be avoided. The greenish kernel (the more pronounced the color, the better the nut) is shaped somewhat like a small almond and is used to flavor and color ice cream, Turkish delight, and halvah. Coarsely chopped or in paste form (or both), the nuts are also delicious in salads and stuffings. Early Persians used to grind pistachios and other nuts and use the paste as a

thickener. Almost all pistachios are sold roasted and salted, but look for the delicious fresh, raw, organic ones. Because the shell splits during the drying process, the pistachio does not have as lengthy a shelf life as do other whole nuts. Do not bother to crack unsplit nuts, as the kernels are immature.

Health Benefits

Pistachio nuts are rich in oil, with an average oil content of about 55 percent, all in a form very easily digested and assimilated. They contain no indigestible cellulose or fiber and are inclined to be alkaline-forming. Raw pistachios are beneficial for constipation and help purify the blood and tone the liver and kidneys. Compared to other nuts, the pistachio is a superior source of protein, calcium, and vitamin A and the best source of iron and potassium.

Poppy Seed
(Papaver somniferum hortense, P. rhoeas)

Papaver, a classical Latin name for the poppy plant, comes from the word *pap*, "teat." *Somniferum* means "sleep-bearing" and is derived from *Somnus*, the Roman god of sleep. The term *hortense* means "belonging to a *hortus*" or garden; *rhoeas* comes from the Greek name *rhoias*, for the corn poppy.

General Information

Poppies are native to Eurasia and have been grown in the Near East since ancient times. The tiny, slate-blue seeds are so small that it takes nearly one million of them to make a single pound. The most notorious of poppies is the garden or opium poppy (*P. somniferum*), with white or bluish-purple blooms. The drug opium is contained in the juicy

Poppy Seed / Nutritional Value Per 100 g Edible Portion			
	Dried		**Dried**
Calories	533	Sodium	21 mg
Protein	18.04 g	Zinc	10.230 mg
Fat	44.70 g	Copper	1.633 mg
Fiber	6.26 g	Manganese	6.833 mg
Calcium	1,448 mg	Beta Carotene (A)	trace
Iron	9.40 mg	Thiamine (B$_1$)	0.849 mg
Magnesium	331 mg	Riboflavin (B$_2$)	0.173 mg
Phosphorus	848 mg	Niacin (B$_3$)	0.976 mg
Potassium	700 mg	Pyridoxine (B$_6$)	0.444 mg

LORE AND LEGEND

The sedative properties of opium were used by the ancient Egyptians, and by the women of Crete, who worshiped a poppy goddess in 1400 B.C. The Greeks, who regarded sleep as the greatest of all physicians and the most powerful consoler of humanity, crowned all their nocturnal gods with a wreath of poppy blossoms. The plant was dedicated to Nix, goddess of night; to Thanatos, god of death; to his twin brother Hypnos, god of sleep; and to the son of Hypnos, Morpheus, god of dreams. The poppy was also an attribute of the love goddess, Aphrodite. When Pluto, god of the underworld, stole Persephone from her mother Ceres, the wheat was neglected and her mother's ceaseless wanderings brought her to Sicily where, nearly exhausted, she climbed Mount Etna to light her torch so she might continue her journey at night. The gods, noting her desperate drive to continue despite extreme fatigue, caused poppies to grow around her feet. Ceres inhaled their fragrance, nibbled on the seeds, and fell into a much-needed, long, peaceful sleep. Once Ceres was properly rested, the wheat began to flourish once again. Thereafter, the seeds were offered to the dead to ensure their peaceful sleep. The poppy is a Christian symbol of fertility, ignorance, and indifference, although when carved on the end of church benches and pews it is supposed to designate heavenly sleep (though preferably not during the services). The red corn poppy, considered the emblem of eternal sleep and oblivion, was believed to spring up on every battleground where men fought and died, deriving its red color from the blood of slain warriors. The battle-torn fields and desolate farms of Flanders were robed in red after one season of calm following the Battle of Waterloo and again after the First World War. The flower was thus chosen as the emblem of remembrance of fallen war heroes, and the Poppies of Flanders were adopted as the emblem of the U.S. Armistice Day, in memory of America's armed forces.

cell walls of the ripening capsule up to twenty days after flowering. The seeds, however, contain no drug, as the opium-yielding power of the plant is lost before the seeds ripen. In addition to slate-blue poppy seeds, there are also yellow and brown varieties with limited availability.

Culinary Uses

Poppy seeds have a pleasantly nutty flavor and aroma. The seeds are frequently sprinkled on breads and rolls and included in recipes for cakes and pastries, salad dressings, and vegetable dishes. Poppy seed butter adds extra flavor and aroma to noodles, rice, vegetables, and fish.

Health Benefits

Poppy seeds are soporific, which means that they sedate and calm the nervous system. They also relieve coughs and are considered medicinal for the colon.

Psyllium Seed
(Plantago psyllium)

Plantago is derived from *planta*, meaning "sole of the foot," and refers to the plant's broad-shaped leaves. The specific name *psyllium* is derived from the Greek word for flea, *psylla*, an allusion to the seed's small size.

General Information

Psyllium is an annual herb related to the plantain; it is native to the Mediterranean regions of southern Europe, the Canary Islands, northern Africa, and as far east as western Pakistan. Widely cultivated in Pakistan, India, and parts of Europe, it is now being grown in North America as well. The plant grows low to the ground and produces small white flowers. The seeds, the only part of the plant that is used, are smooth, dull, pinkish-brown or pinkish-white ovals, varying from one-sixteenth to one-eighth of an inch long. Each seed is enveloped in a thin, white, translucent husk. The seeds have neither taste nor odor but

Psyllium Seed / Nutritional Value Per 100 g Edible Portion			
	Dried		Dried
Calories	235	Sodium	54 mg
Protein	1.5 g	Zinc	2.100 mg
Fat	3.7 g	Manganese	1.600 mg
Fiber	0.3 g	Beta Carotene (A)	4023 IU
Calcium	334 mg	Thiamine (B₁)	0 mg
Iron	20.0 mg	Riboflavin (B₂)	0 mg
Magnesium	51 mg	Niacin (B₃)	0 mg
Phosphorus	63 mg	Ascorbic Acid (C)	0 mg
Potassium	811 mg		

when soaked in water will swell to from eight to fourteen times their original volume because of mucilage complex carbohydrates that attract and hold water.

Culinary Uses
Two forms of psyllium seed are sold—the husks and the meat. The husks are coarse like bran, while the meat made from the husked seed is gentler and easier to digest. The Greeks simply chewed the seeds; other options include blending them in a vegetable juice cocktail or sprinkling them, whole or ground, on cereal or yogurt.

Health Benefits
Laxative. Both psyllium husks and psyllium meat are non-irritating, but the meat surrounds any food that may be consumed with the seed and renders it impermeable by the digestive fluids. As the seeds swell, they create a mucilaginous bulk that expands and sweeps through the entire intestinal tract, pushing out food from blocked areas, pockets, and crevices on its way. They are said to relieve an ailment known as autointoxication, in which the body poisons itself by reabsorbing from impacted areas of the colon an excess of intestinal waste products. The husks are most often used for laxative purposes, since they contain a very soothing indigestible substance with little crude fiber and either take up water from a loose stool or add moisture when it is too dry and hard. In India psyllium is used as a diuretic, while in China related species are used to treat bloody urine, coughing, and high blood pressure.

Pumpkin Seed
(Cucurbita pepo, C. maxima)
Also Known As: Pepito

Cucurbita is the old classical Latin name for a gourd. *Pepo* comes from the Greek word *pepon*, meaning "sun-ripened" or "mellow"; the term *maxima* means "largest." The English name *pumpkin* is a derivative of the Greek *pepon*, with the diminutive *-kin* ending.

General Information
Pumpkins are members of the cucumber family, which includes melons, gourds, and squashes. All pumpkin or squash seeds are edible. Most varieties produce seeds that are enclosed in teardrop-shaped shells thin enough to crack open with your teeth. Some pumpkin varieties have hull-less seeds and are grown specifically for this purpose, but their flesh reportedly is stringier and tastes inferior to other pumpkins. In the early 1970s the U.S. Department of Agriculture released a new, high-yielding pumpkin cultivar called Lady Godiva, which got its name because its rounded, dark green, "naked" seeds have no seed coat. These attractive shell-less seeds are suitable for consumption as a snack food.

Culinary Uses
Although mainly used as a source of oil, hulled or hull-less pumpkin seeds can be used just like any other nut or seed. Either raw or toasted, pumpkin seeds are excellent as a snack on their own, in salads of all kinds, or added to casseroles, breads, and nut loaves. Try them ground into a meal and added to pancakes and other baked goods or mixed with peanut butter for a protein-rich spread.

Health Benefits
pH > 6.0. Anthelmintic. Pumpkin seeds are nature's most nourishing food for the male prostate gland because of their high magnesium and zinc content; they also are valuable sources of omega-3 fatty acids. These seeds have been used worldwide as an aid to remove intestinal worms. The effectiveness of pumpkin seeds as a vermifuge has been attributed to mechanical effects and to a rare amino acid (3-amino-3 carboxypyrrolidine, or cucurbitin) found only in certain *Cucurbita* species. Another constituent of pumpkin is myosin, the chief protein constituent of nearly all muscles in the body, which plays an important role in the chemistry of muscular contraction. The seed oil is helpful for healing burns and wounds.

Pumpkin Seed / Nutritional Value Per 100 g Edible Portion			
	Dried		Dried
Calories	541	Sodium	18 mg
Protein	24.54 g	Zinc	7.460 mg
Fat	45.85 g	Copper	1.387 mg
Fiber	2.22 g	Beta Carotene (A)	380 IU
Calcium	43 mg	Thiamine (B₁)	0.210 mg
Iron	14.97 mg	Riboflavin (B₂)	0.320 mg
Magnesium	535 mg	Niacin (B₃)	1.745 mg
Phosphorus	1,174 mg	Ascorbic Acid (C)	173 mg
Potassium	807 mg		

BYPRODUCTS

Pumpkin seed oil has been used throughout history in India, Europe, and the Americas. This dark green oil is quite tasty and should be used raw, poured directly onto vegetables, pasta, and other dishes. One of the most nutritious of oils, with a good proportion of both omega-3 and omega-6 essential fatty acids, it is commonly recommended for pregnant and lactating women. It has similar properties to the seeds and has been used to nourish and heal the digestive tract, fight parasites, improve circulation, help heal prostate disorders, and help prevent dental caries.

Quandong Nut
(Eucarya acuminata)

Acuminata means "acuminate" or "long-pointed."

General Information
Also known as the Australian native peach, *quandong* is the Aboriginal name for the small trees or shrubs native to and abundant in the Southwest and central desert regions of Australia, where there is little rainfall. The tree produces fruits that are globular, about one-half to three-quarters of an inch in diameter, and usually bright red in color. The edible pulp, rich in vitamin C and with a flavor similar to that of the guava, may be eaten raw, used as a pie filling, or made into preserves and jellies. Within the pitted stone is an edible oily kernel or nut, with a hard shell that is difficult to crack. The kernels, harshly aromatic in flavor, have been prized by the Aborigines for many centuries but are virtually unknown outside of Australia.

Culinary Uses
Although unusually delectable, the flavor of the quandong kernel tends to be too pungent and overpowering for some palates.

Safflower Oil
(Carthamus tinctorius)

Tinctorius means that plant was used as a color dye.

General Information
Safflower oil is extracted from the seeds of the safflower, a plant native to the semi-arid Mediterranean region as well as the mountainous regions of southwest Asia and Ethiopia. Botanically related to lettuce, sunflowers, and daisies, this annual plant was apparently originally domesticated for its flowers, which were used for a dye, and only later for its oil-rich seeds.

Culinary Uses
Safflower oil is probably the most versatile vegetable oil; in its unrefined form, it has a deep amber-yellow color and slightly nutty, earthy flavor. Because of its high fat content, it has a tendency to go rancid much quicker than other oils and should be stored in the refrigerator. Refined safflower oil is typically a very pale yellow with a bland taste. Often used for deep-fat-frying, sautéing, and baking, it is also an ingredient in salad dressings and mayonnaise.

Health Benefits
Safflower oil probably has the highest percentage of unsaturated fats of all the oils and is highest in linoleic acid (78 percent). Although widely touted because of its high content of polyunsaturated fatty acids, safflower oil is considered by many to be excessively irritating and capable of provoking or aggravating a wide variety of disorders.

Sapucaya Nut
(Lecythis usitata)
Also Known As: Paradise Nut

The generic name *Lecythis* is from the Greek term for "oil jar," a rather accurate description of the appearance of the fruit, which looks like a jar complete with a neatly fitting lid; *usitata* means "useful." *Sapucaya* is an Amazonian

Indian word meaning "chicken," since the nut was frequently fed to chickens. The alternate name *paradise nut* owes its origin to the high quality of the nut, said to be even more delicious than the Brazil nut.

General Information

Native to the Amazonian rainforests of northeastern Brazil and the neighboring Guiana region, the *Lecythis* genus includes some fifty species in northern South America, of which the Brazil nut and the paradise nut are the most widely known. The sapucaya tree produces large woody fruits, about eight inches long and ten inches wide, that are suspended upside down from the ends of the branches. When the fruits are mature, their lids drop off and the nuts then gradually become detached and fall to the ground. A single fruit contains thirty to forty irregularly oblong, wrinkled seeds (nuts), each about two inches long, resembling Brazil nuts, although paradise nuts are more rounded and have a lighter brown color and thinner, softer shells.

Culinary Uses

The nut kernels are ivory white with a creamy texture and an unusual, delicate, sweet flavor considered by some connoisseurs to be the finest among nuts. They may be eaten raw or roasted and are utilized to a limited extent in making candies and cakes. An excellent pale yellow, edible oil is expressed from the kernels and used by natives of the Amazon to produce soap and illuminants.

Health Benefits

Containing about 62 percent fat and 20 percent protein, the nuts are highly nutritious. Precautions should be taken in gathering and eating paradise nuts: there are harrowing reports about the fruits of certain poisonous species of *Lecythis* in tropical America that, when eaten, can cause severe nausea, diarrhea, dramatic (if temporary) loss of scalp and body hair, and the shedding of fingernails.

Sesame Seed

(Sesamum indicum)

The English name *sesame* can be traced back through the Arabic *simsim* and the Coptic *semsem* to the early Egyptian *semsemt*, a name mentioned in the Ebers Papyrus (c. 1800 B.C.), which indicates how long humanity has known and used the herb. The term *indicum* means "from India."

LORE AND LEGEND

Sesame seeds are sacred to the Hindu elephant deity Ganesha and are eaten to increase one's basic life force, which the Hindus believe is the hidden creative energy that accumulates at the base of the spine. At one time sesame plants were thought to grow near secret treasures or concealed doorways.

General Information

Sesame seeds come from a tall annual herb native to the East Indies whose single hairy stalk can grow as high as seven feet, although a two- to four-foot stalk is much more common. The heavy glistening stems support variable leaves and rose-colored flowers. The flowers become four-celled capsules containing many tiny black and white seeds; when ripe, the seeds burst suddenly with a pop from

Sesame Seed / Nutritional Value Per 100 g Edible Portion			
	Whole Dried	Kernels Dried	Flour
Calories	573	588	526
Protein	17.73 g	26.38 g	30.78 g
Fat	49.67 g	54.78 g	37.10 g
Fiber	4.60 g	2.96 g	6.39 g
Calcium	975 mg	131 mg	159 mg
Iron	14.55 mg	7.80 mg	15.17 mg
Magnesium	351 mg	347 mg	361 mg
Phosphorus	629 mg	776 mg	807 mg
Potassium	468 mg	407 mg	423 mg
Sodium	11 mg	40 mg	41 mg
Zinc	7.750 mg	10.250 mg	10.670 mg
Copper	4.082 mg	1.460 mg	n/a
Manganese	2.460 mg	1.430 mg	n/a
Beta Carotene (A)	9 IU	66 IU	69 IU
Thiamine (B$_1$)	0.791 mg	0.722 mg	2.684 mg
Riboflavin (B$_2$)	0.247 mg	0.085 mg	0.286 mg
Niacin (B$_3$)	4.515 mg	4.682 mg	13.369 mg
Pantothenic Acid (B$_5$)	0.050 mg	0.681 mg	2.928 mg
Pyridoxine (B$_6$)	0.790 mg	0.146 mg	0.152 mg
Folic Acid (B$_9$)	96.7 mcg	n/a	30.8 mcg
Ascorbic Acid (C)	0 mg	n/a	n/a
Tocopherol (E)	2.27 mg	n/a	n/a

LORE AND LEGEND

In *The Thousand and One Nights*, the story of Ali Baba and the forty thieves, a password was needed to open the door of the robbers' den. The magical command "Open Sesame" may have been chosen because ripe sesame seeds bursting from their pods sound much like the sharp sudden pop of a lock springing open.

the capsule and scatter. Sesame was one of the very earliest plants to be used by human both for the seed and for the oil contained in the seeds. The oil today is still the main source of fat used in cooking in the Near and Far East.

Culinary Uses

Sesame seeds have a pleasant, nutlike aroma and flavor that is heightened by toasting. Whole, unhulled sesame seeds are dark, the hulled seeds are white; tan seeds have been hulled and roasted. The darker variety of sesame have a stronger taste and smell and are worth seeking out (but beware the dyed variety). You can judge the freshness of the seeds by their color: fresh sesame seeds should be white or light yellow, while old and rancid seeds acquire a muddy gray look. The best season to buy them is between September and April, when the new crops have been harvested. Sesame seeds can be sprinkled over breads and cereals, used in salads and biscuits, or processed into tahini, gomasio (see below), and other products.

Health Benefits

pH > 6.0. Emollient, laxative. Sesame seeds will often help relieve local swelling or tumors, and their high vitamin E content strengthens the nerves and heart. Since the sesame seed hull has a bitter flavor and contains 2 to 3 percent oxalic acid—a compound that can interfere with calcium utilization—it is often removed. However, hulled sesame seeds lose their fiber and much of their potassium, iron, vitamins A and B$_6$, folacin, and thiamine. The stronger flavor of black sesame seeds indicates that they are higher in minerals and trace nutrients than lighter-colored sesame seeds. Black sesame is a general building tonic: it nourishes the blood, strengthens the kidneys and liver, and treats constipation, blurry vision, ringing in the ears, low backache, weak knees, stiff joints, headache, and dizziness. Like most nuts and seeds, sesame contains lignans; sesamin, a lignan that exists exclusively and abundantly in sesame, has demonstrated remarkable antioxidant effects and has been put to good use in stabilizing sesame products. In studies with rats, sesamin has been shown to inhibit the absorption of cholesterol from the diet and to inhibit the manufacture of cholesterol in the liver.

BYPRODUCTS

Black sesame butter is sesame butter made from black sesame seeds, which have a richly intense sesame flavor. It has recently become available in some specialty food stores and is worth experimenting with at least once. This black, gooey spread has no comparable match in our culinary tradition and likely poses no threat to the peanut butter industry.

Gomasio is made by finely grinding roasted sesame seeds and adding sea salt (five to eight parts sesame to one part salt). Also known as **sesame salt,** gomasio is widely used in Japan and macrobiotic diets, and its nutty flavor makes it a delicious addition to any dish.

Sesame butter is made of whole (unhulled) roasted sesame seeds and may or may not have salt added. It may be used interchangeably with peanut butter. Differing from tahini, a better-known product, in that it is made from roasted seeds rather than raw, sesame butter is a heavier product with fewer culinary uses. Because of its high vitamin E content, sesame butter has a longer shelf life than other nut butters. Once opened, it should be refrigerated. If it causes a harsh or slight burning sensation in the back of the throat, it is rancid and should be discarded.

Sesame milk is made by blending sesame seeds and water and then straining to remove the hulls. For flavoring, add any of the following singly or in combination: one tablespoon carob powder, six dates, a banana, stewed raisins, and apple or cherry concentrate. Highly nutritious, sesame milk is wonderful for gaining weight and for lubricating the intestinal tract.

Sesame oil is one of the oldest vegetable oils used. Oil-rich sesame seeds are one of the few seeds capable of yielding a commercially acceptable oil without being exposed to high heat or being put through a high-pressure expeller process. Unrefined sesame oil is dark yellow to amber in color and has a pleasant, mild, nutty flavor. A richer, darker, more flavorful oil is made by roasting the seeds before the process of oil extraction. Since the seeds contain sesamol, a natural preservative, the oil pressed from them is very stable and highly resistant to oxidation (rancidity). Highly refined sesame oil is pale yellow and has a bland taste. Sesame oil is utilized in the production of margarine, salad oils, and good-quality cooking oils. The traditional oil for Asian and macrobiotic cooking, it is good for sautéing vegetables, on grains and noodles, and in salad dressings, spreads, pasta toppings, and mayonnaise. Sesame oil is rich in monounsaturated and polyunsaturated fatty acids and in lecithin, which helps build the nervous system and brain cells. It has been used to treat depression and stress as well as to improve circulation. Externally, the oil may be used as for massage and for soothing and healing sunburn or other burns, as well as for minor eruptions of the skin.

Sesame salt—see **Gomasio**, above.

Tahini is a light, creamy spread made from hulled and ground sesame seeds. The roasted variety tastes nuttier; the unroasted is sweeter. Both kinds may contain salt. Commercial tahini is made from seeds that are hulled in caustic chemical baths, neutralized, and bleached; these tahinis tend to be bitter and have a faintly soapy taste. Quality tahini is made from mechanically hulled seeds. This high-protein spread is a staple in Middle Eastern and Asian cookery, where it is added to dressings, sauces, and desserts. It can also serve as an oil, egg, or milk replacement in recipes or be added to nut or soy milk, cream soups, and baby foods. Mixed with peanut butter or honey it makes a delicious spread. Containing approximately 45 percent protein and 55 percent oil, it is easy to digest and very nutritious, especially for bones and teeth.

Souari Nut
(Caryocar nuciferum)

Caryocar is from the Greek word for nut, while *nuciferum* means "nut-bearing." The unusual vernacular name, applied to several species, comes from the Cariban Indian word *sawarie*; it is spelled in a number of different ways. To add to the confusion, the British often refer to the tree as "butternut" since the nuts have a high oil content of about 60 percent.

General Information
The souari is native to northern Brazil and the adjoining Guiana region. The trees produce fruits that are round, soft-wooded capsules, about six inches in diameter. When ripe, these capsules crash to the ground and burst on impact, loosening their two to five nuts, which are brown, kidney-shaped, and about the size of a hen's egg. Surrounding the nuts is an oily, yellow pulp that may be cooked and eaten as a vegetable. The souari nut is found mainly in European and South American seaports; few people in the United States have had the opportunity to sample them.

Culinary Uses
The nuts have a hard, woody, warty shell, about a quarter of an inch thick, which is difficult to crack. The kernels are somewhat larger than Brazil nuts, pure white and soft, and rich and oily, with a sweet, almondlike flavor. Souari nuts are eaten raw or roasted and also serve as a source of cooking oil.

Sunflower Seed
(Helianthus annuus)

The sunflower's botanical name is truly descriptive of the plant: *Helianthus* comes from the Greek words *helios*, meaning "sun," and *anthos*, meaning "flower"; the species name, *annuus*, is derived from the Latin word for "annual." The English name *sunflower* is simply the translation of the Latin name.

General Information
The sunflower originated somewhere in the southwestern part of the United States and has been raised for centuries for its nutritious seeds. More than any other flower, the sunflower proclaims summer. Wild, it bedecks roadways and gilds whole fields with sun-colored mandalas. Cultivated in home gardens it towers to impressive heights of fifteen feet or more and boasts a flower up to two feet in diameter. A single plant may yield several hundred plump, nutlike kernels, which are actually the fruit of the flower. These teardrop-shaped seeds may be white, brown, black, or black with white stripes. Though the seeds have long been used as a dietary staple by American Indians, they were only introduced to Europeans in the sixteenth century. The stalks, when treated like hemp, produce a fine,

silky fiber. The U.S. commercial supply comes primarily from the Red River valley of Minnesota.

Culinary Uses

Whole sunflower seeds are available raw or roasted, with or without hulls. Raw sunflower seeds have an oily taste that is pleasantly nutty, and have virtually no aroma; roasting brings out the nutty flavor further. The best-quality seeds are bought in the hull and then either eaten by cracking the hulls open with the teeth or sprouted; pre-hulled raw or roasted sunflower seeds are almost always rancid. Whole or chopped sunflower seed kernels can be substituted for other nuts in any recipe. Sprinkle a few on top of a casserole before baking, mix them into vegetable or fruit salads, or sauté them with chopped onion and toss with a cooked vegetable just before serving. They are also a good addition to quick breads and muffins, but if used in a recipe that calls for baking soda, they will frequently turn the finished product green.

Health Benefits

pH > 6.0. Diuretic, expectorant. The sunflower seed nourishes the entire body, supplying it with many vital elements needed for growth and repair. It is a rich source of protein of high biological value—richer than most meats, eggs, and cheese (with no putrefying bacteria). As a source of vitamin D, sunflower seeds are superior to cod liver oil, which has many objectionable features. In addition to vitamin D, these seeds are richer in the B complex vitamins than an equivalent amount of wheat germ and also offer vitamins E and K. Fresh sunflower seeds contain pectin, which binds radioactive residues and removes them from the body. The seeds have been found to relieve farsightedness, eyestrain, and extreme sensitivity to light. They also strengthen fingernails that are brittle or peeling. Their trace of fluorine explains the Russians' claim that they are good for the teeth.

BYPRODUCTS

Sunflower seed meal is made from ground sunflower seeds and is easily prepared at home. Because of its high oil content, the meal needs to be kept refrigerated and used within a couple of days. Sunflower-seed meal can be used as a substitute for some of the flour in baked goods; it also makes a delicious addition to soups, cereals, and casseroles. If you prefer, toast the seeds before grinding for a nuttier flavor.

Sunflower seed oil, in its unrefined form, is light amber in color and has a distinctive flavor; refined oil is pale and bland tasting. Be sure to buy pressed sunflower seed oil rather than additive-filled, chemically extracted commercial oil. Although 40 to 65 percent of the U.S. sunflower crop consists of oil varieties, only 20 to 25 percent of this is used in domestic consumption—10 percent as vegetable oil and 15 percent as livestock feed. Often used as an extender for more expensive oils, sunflower oil is used for baking and sautéing; it adds a wonderfully delicate, nutty flavor to salads, baked goods, and other dishes. Rich in polyunsaturated fatty acids, lecithin, linoleic acid, and vitamin E, sunflower oil has a long history of being used to help the endocrine and nervous systems and to reduce cholesterol levels. Many naturopathic physicians believe that sunflower oil helps the formation of healthy tissue and generally aids resistance to disease. The consumption of sunflower oil (one teaspoonful three times a day) has cured paralysis stemming from polyneuritis and greatly reduced symptoms from multiple sclerosis.

Sunflower Seed / Nutritional Value Per 100 g Edible Portion	Kernels Dried	Flour
Calories	570	326
Protein	22.78 g	48.06 g
Fat	49.57 g	1.61 g
Fiber	4.16 g	5.19 g
Calcium	116 mg	114 mg
Iron	6.77 mg	6.62 mg
Magnesium	354 mg	346 mg
Phosphorus	705 mg	689 mg
Potassium	689 mg	67 mg
Sodium	3 mg	3 mg
Zinc	5.060 mg	4.950 mg
Copper	1.752 mg	1.713 mg
Manganese	2.020 mg	1.975 mg
Beta Carotene (A)	50 IU	n/a
Thiamine (B$_1$)	2.290 mg	3.187 mg
Riboflavin (B$_2$)	0.250 mg	n/a
Niacin (B$_3$)	4.500 mg	7.313 mg
Pantothenic Acid (B$_5$)	n/a	6.595 mg

LORE AND LEGEND

As though magnetized by the sun's rays, the great floral disk of the sunflower follows the solar orb in its course through the heavens. Significantly in the Indian hunting calendar, the buffalo were said to be fat with plenty of good meat when sunflowers were tall and in full bloom. The Plains Indians of the prairie regions of North America placed ceremonial bowls filled with sunflower seeds on the graves of their dead for food to sustain them on their long and dangerous journey to their Happy Hunting Grounds. When Francisco Pizarro fought his way into Peru in 1532, he found there the giant sunflower, venerated by the Indians of the Inca empire as the sacred image of their sun god. In the early eighteenth century Peter the Great took the sunflower to Russia, where a historical quirk caused it to become an important food plant. The Holy Orthodox Church of Russia decreed very strict dietary regulations during Lent and the forty days preceding Christmas: nearly all foods rich in oil were proscribed by name and forbidden. Since the sunflower had only recently been introduced to the country and was virtually unknown, it was not on the prohibited list and the sharp-eyed laity eagerly adopted it as a food item and source of oil, thus making the plant very popular yet all the while complying with church regulations.

Tallow Nut

(*Ximenia americana*)
Also Known As: False Sandalwood

This tree is named after Francisco Ximenes, a Spanish friar who translated into Spanish a Latin manuscript describing the Mexican flora and fauna in 1615; *americana* indicates that the plant was found on the American continent.

General Information

The juicy, fleshy pulp of the yellow or reddish-colored, egg-shaped fruit is plumlike in character. Although the fruits have an acid taste like sour apples, they are eaten either raw or cooked and can be made into an excellent jelly. Each contain a large, oily seed, the kernel of which is white.

Culinary Uses and Health Benefits

Reports on the palatability of the tallow nut vary: some extol its flavor, comparing it to the filbert; others warn that the nuts are strongly purgative and should be eaten only a few at a time. The kernels are rich in protein and have a high fat content of about 66 percent; they may be eaten raw or roasted.

Tiger Nut

(*Cyperus esculentus*)
Also Known As: Chufa, Earth Almond, Earth Nut, Rush Nut, Zulu Nut

Cyperus is an ancient Greek name that perhaps refers to the island of Cyprus, while *esculentus* means "esculent" or "edible."

General Information

Tiger "nuts" are not really nuts but edible, underground tubers of the creeping rootstock of a grasslike sedge indigenous to the Mediterranean region and western Asia. When dried, these tough-skinned corms, about one inch long by one-half inch in diameter, look like large, wrinkled peas.

Culinary Uses

Tiger nuts possess an agreeable, slightly sweet, nutlike flavor. The fibrous nuts may be eaten raw out of hand, but they are usually roasted or cooked and added to soups. In confectionery the roasted nuts may be substituted for almonds.

Tiger Nut / Nutritional Value Per 100 g Edible Portion			
Calories	403	Potassium	14 mg
Protein	4.3 g	Sodium	1 mg
Fat	23.8 g	Thiamine (B$_1$)	0.230 mg
Fiber	n/a	Riboflavin (B$_2$)	0.100 mg
Calcium	48 mg	Niacin (B$_3$)	1.100 mg
Iron	3.20 mg	Ascorbic Acid (C)	6 mg
Phosphorus	210 mg		

Health Benefits

In Sierra Leone there is a native belief that the tiger nut has an aphrodisiac effect, and when a Zulu maiden wants to hasten the inception of menstruation, she eats a porridge in which tiger nuts have been mashed. Chufa oil, considered to be a superior table oil that compares favorably to olive oil, is also employed in soap making.

Walnut

(Juglans regia, J. nigra)

The generic term *Juglans* is a contraction of the Latin *Jovis glans*, meaning "nut of Jupiter" or "nut of the gods," after the ancient belief that the gods dined on walnuts. The specific epithet *regia* means "royal," both because of the tree's attractive appearance and because of its historical importance as a source of timber and food. *Nigra* means "blackish." The English name *walnut* is probably of Teutonic origin, the Germans having named the nut *wall-nuss*, or *welsche nuss*, *welsche* signifying "foreign"; another possibility is that the *wal* of *walnut* is derived from the Anglo-Saxon word *wealh*, meaning "foreign" or "alien." The suffix *nut* comes from the Anglo-Saxon *hnutu*, meaning "nut."

General Information

The Romans considered the walnut tree to be of Persian origin, but the tree is now so widespread that it is impossible to discern whether this is true. The majority opinion today seems to be that while Persia does fall within the area where the walnut was cultivated earliest, it covered a great deal more ground, ranging from southeastern Europe and/or Asia Minor to the Himalayas. Ancient Greeks pressed the nuts for their oil; they seem to have been using them nearly a century before the Romans, about the beginning of the fourth century B.C. The first walnuts planted in California were probably brought from Chile around 1770 by Franciscan fathers. Walnut trees are large, often growing one hundred feet high with trunks that may be up to twelve feet in diameter. The nuts are harvested when the green outer husk begins to crack, the thin divider separating the halves of the kernel is no longer leathery but brittle, and the kernel itself still quite moist. The nuts are then mechanically hulled, washed, and dried to 8 percent moisture.

There are about fifteen species of *Juglans*, the walnut genus; all are edible, but *J. regia*, known as the Persian or English walnut, is probably the most delicious and certainly the most important. It has a thin shell that can be easily crushed, with curly nutmeat halves. A good part of its flavor comes from the golden to dark brown papery skin, which is both bitter and astringent. This variety became known as "English" when England became a powerful trading nation in the mid–fourteenth century and English trading ships transported walnuts from the Mediterranean countries to markets all over the world. Attempts to grow walnuts in England didn't pan out. Walnuts, like pecans, are a long-season crop. In England late spring freezes often kill the buds before they can develop into nuts. Today the British countryside is forested in many places with walnut trees, which make lovely shade trees and beautiful furniture lumber, but few nuts. Most of England's walnuts, so essential for a British yule feast, come from southern Europe. Spanish missionaries introduced English walnuts to North America via California, much as they did almonds, and a commercial orchard of

Walnut / Nutritional Value Per 100 g Edible Portion		
	English Dried	Black Dried
Calories	642	607
Protein	14.29 g	24.35 g
Fat	61.87 g	56.58 g
Fiber	4.60 g	6.46 g
Calcium	94 mg	58 mg
Iron	2.44 mg	3.07 mg
Magnesium	169 mg	202 mg
Phosphorus	317 mg	464 mg
Potassium	502 mg	524 mg
Sodium	10 mg	1 mg
Zinc	2.730 mg	3.420 mg
Copper	1.387 mg	1.020 mg
Manganese	2.898 mg	4.271 mg
Beta Carotene (A)	124 IU	296 IU
Thiamine (B$_1$)	0.382 mg	0.217 mg
Riboflavin (B$_2$)	0.148 mg	0.109 mg
Niacin (B$_3$)	1.042 mg	0.690 mg
Pantothenic Acid (B$_5$)	0.631 mg	n/a
Pyridoxine (B$_6$)	0.558 mg	n/a
Folic Acid (B$_9$)	66 mcg	n/a
Ascorbic Acid (C)	3.2 mg	n/a
Tocopherol (E)	2.62 mg	n/a

two hundred trees was planted in 1869. Most of the U.S. domestic supply—and a significant percentage of the world's supply—of English walnuts comes from California.

The eastern black walnut (*J. nigra*) is a native American walnut. The trees grow to enormous size, some reaching a height of 150 feet and a thickness of as much as six feet. Black walnut trees produce beautiful lumber used for furniture and paneling. Because the lumber is so highly prized, production of walnuts may be endangered. Tree "rustling" has become a problem in many areas. There have been reports of people returning home after a vacation trip to find all their black walnut trees cut down and spirited away. Related to the English variety, the nuts have a dark skin covering the white nutmeat and hard, protective, sticky hulls that are difficult to remove. The shells require a cement floor and heavy hammer to crack (some people run over them with their cars). Once split, each morsel of nutmeat needs to be coaxed from the still-unyielding shell. During this process the oil leaves an indelible brown stain on fingers, fabric, and even cement. The amount of meat per nut is small, but its flavor is satisfyingly full, rich, and nutty. The black walnut is less popular for nibbling on its own because the kernel's flavor is considered too strong by most people, but it is prized when combined with other ingredients for baking, in batter and icing, and for the manufacture of both candies and ice cream. Other less commercially cultivated varieties are the Chinese walnut, the Japanese walnut, and the white walnut, more commonly called the butternut.

Culinary Uses

Walnuts are extremely versatile and may be used at different stages of their growth. Freshly shelled walnuts should be brittle and will snap if broken, showing a clean white interior; shriveled or rubbery nuts are already stale or rancid and should be avoided. Some shelled walnuts are darker than others; the darker color develops in those that grow on the sunnier side of the tree, and these are richer and more flavorful. Because of their high oil content, walnuts are prone to rancidity and are best bought in the shell and stored in either the refrigerator or the freezer. Whole walnuts kept in a cool, dry environment can be stored for up to one year.

Shelled commercial walnuts are frequently treated with ethylene gas, fumigated with methyl bromide, dipped in hot lye or a solution of glycerin and sodium carbonate to loosen their skins, and then rinsed in citric acid. The result is a uniform, pale nut that is obviously less healthful than an organic nut but has a longer shelf life. Besides the familiar multitude of dessert uses, walnuts are increasingly used in salads, where they provide a flavorful balance to fruits and strong greens like watercress. The nuts combine especially well with dill, garlic, and parsley. Walnuts are reduced to a paste to bind and thicken certain sauces, usually garlic sauces such as pesto. In the United States the walnut is returning to the role of a full-fledged food in vegetarian dishes because of its high protein content.

Health Benefits

pH 5.42–5.5. Walnuts are a warming and laxative food used to strengthen the kidneys and lungs, to lubricate the large intestine, and to improve metabolism. They may harbor liver flukes, however, so be sure to toast them or, preferably, use them only in cooked dishes. The black walnut is lower in fat and higher in protein and iron than the English walnut and has more vitamin A than most nuts. Black walnuts also contain the essential arachidonic fatty acid associated with alleviating symptoms of bursitis and are a rich source of iodine and the trace mineral chromium. The black walnut has long been considered one of America's most valuable native cathartics. Because it is rich in tannin, a toning substance, it is also called an astringent. An excellent vermicide, sudorific, antiseptic, and febrifuge, the black walnut aids in regulating blood sugar levels and has been used for herpes, impetigo, athlete's foot, ringworm, and hemorrhoidal bleeding in the colon. Black walnut contains natural fluoride (without the side effects of the chemical fluoride used in our water supplies) and will remove plaque and restore tooth enamel if applied directly to the teeth. It has neither a strong taste nor a strong odor and is considered a mild enough herb to try for many disorders by those who are afraid of stronger herbs. For this reason it is very well tolerated by children. Pet owners love to use black walnut as a natural worming option, and it is also used in heartworm programs for a safer approach to killing them than the drugs.

LORE AND LEGEND

Roman lore claimed that in the "Golden Age" when people lived on acorns, the gods feasted upon walnuts, which were considered far superior to other such vulgar nuts as acorns, beechnuts, and chestnuts. Credited with bringing good health, warding off disease, and increasing fertility, handfuls of walnuts were customarily tossed at Roman weddings by the bridegroom—much as we now throw rice—to be scrambled for by young boys. By flinging the nuts away, the bridegroom showed he had laid aside childish amusements and was fully mature. In Romania, however, a bride who does not wish to bear children immediately places one roasted walnut in her bodice for every year she wishes to remain childless. During the Middle Ages, Europeans believed that evil spirits lurked in walnut branches; thus the walnuts themselves were thought useful in warding off lightning, fevers, witchcraft, the evil eye, and epileptic fits. In China, where the cricket has traditionally been considered a creature of good omen, musically trained singing crickets were carried about in intricately carved walnut shells.

BYPRODUCTS

Dried walnuts are the type most often eaten; they are simply an older version of wet walnuts from which the moisture has been allowed to evaporate. A dried walnut is more than half oil, with the pressed oil frequently used for salads. Dried walnuts can be added to salads, savory dishes, cakes, and breads.

Green walnuts, which have not yet developed a hard shell, are still a quarter or more water. They must be peeled before eating because the bitter skin produces a somewhat painful reaction in the mouth. Picked in June or July, green walnuts are used to make pickles (a British delicacy), ketchups, and chutneys. Green walnuts can also be made into walnut marmalade or nut brandy, added to jams, or preserved whole in syrup.

Walnut milk is made from blanched, pulverized walnuts soaked in water and then strained. This makes a tasty milk alternative that was drunk in many early European households that lacked access to or could not afford regular milk.

Walnut oil, cold-pressed from ripe walnuts, is an aromatic, subtly delicious oil. In southern Europe, especially in France, walnut oil has long been a popular cooking oil, one frequently substituted for olive oil, and is also used on salads and vegetables. It is said that at one time half the oil used in France was walnut oil. Walnuts from the Perigord and Dordogne regions in France are said to produce the best oil; in those regions, walnuts are strictly graded for quality and production is small. Heavy, sweet, and characteristically aromatic, the oil loses its fluidity and thickens gradually over several months into a sort of jelly. The unsaturated fats in walnuts are prone to rancidity, and so the oil must be used quickly. Since most of the walnut oils currently available in stores are heavily processed and refined, they cannot be recommended.

Wet walnuts are those that are newly picked in early autumn. These have moist kernels with a hard outer shell; their delicious and fragrant flavor is marvelous in savory dishes.

Watermelon Seed
(Citrullus lanatus)

Citrullus is the diminutive form of citrus, said to be in allusion to the shape of the fruits and color of their flesh. The term *lanatus* means "woolly."

General Information

The edible watermelon seeds vary considerably: they may be black, white, yellow, or reddish but are generally smooth, flat, and up to five-eighths of an inch long by a

Watermelon Seed / Nutritional Value Per 100 g Edible Portion			
Kernels, Dried			
Calories	557	Potassium	648 mg
Protein	28.33 g	Sodium	99 mg
Fat	47.37 g	Beta Carotene (A)	0 mg
Fiber	3.04 g	Thiamine (B$_1$)	0.190 mg
Calcium	54 mg	Riboflavin (B$_2$)	0.145 mg
Iron	7.28 mg	Niacin (B$_3$)	3.550 mg
Magnesium	515 mg	Folic Acid (B$_9$)	57.9 mcg
Phosphorus	755 mg	Ascorbic Acid (C)	0 mg

quarter of an inch wide. A thin shell encloses the oily, nutritious kernel. In some districts of western tropical Africa, watermelons with bitter flesh are grown solely for their edible seeds, and the yellow oil extracted from the seeds is employed for table use instead of peanut oil. These nutritious but neglected seeds might find a modest place in the growing snack nut trade.

Culinary Uses

Although watermelon seeds are not generally considered a delicacy in this country, in other parts of the world they are eaten just like peanuts, either raw or roasted, following removal of the seed coat. The Chinese have for centuries enjoyed watermelon seeds preserved in salt, and in the Near East roasted watermelon seeds are sold in bags like popcorn. To make a seed milk drink, combine the seeds and water in a blender, grind, and strain.

Health Benefits

Watermelon seeds are great for the kidneys. They are tranquilizers for the body and wonderful for the nervous system. The seeds contain cucurbocitrin, a compound that dilates capillaries and lowers high blood pressure, as well as improving kidney function. Watermelon seeds are also a remedy for constipation and are nearly as efficacious as pumpkin seeds in their ability to expel worms.

HERBS, SPICES, AND OTHER FOODS

Awake, O north wind;
And come, thou south;
That the spices may flow out.
—Song of Solomon

If you wish to have a lily white skin
Steep yourself in green without and within.
—Author unknown

HERBS, SPICES, AND OTHER FOODS

From the dawn of civilization thousands of years ago, herbs and spices have been used to bring flavor and color to foods, as well as for medicinal purposes. They played an important role in religious life, being used as ingredients in holy anointing oils and incense and as strewing plants. Taxes were often collected in the form of spices, which during some periods of history were valued as highly as gold. The name *herb* comes from the Latin word *herba*, meaning "grass" or "herbage," and technically refers only to those plants that do not have a woody stem or to a plant or plant part that is used for medicinal purposes. The name *spice* derives from the Latin *species*, meaning "something of a kind" or "to sort things out" into recognizable types. (During the Middle Ages, the four most common spices sold by grocers were saffron, cloves, cinnamon, and nutmeg.) However, the terms *herb* and *spice* intermingle so much that for the purposes of this book, the two groups will be discussed together.

During the Dark Ages, the accumulated knowledge of the Persian, Greek, and Roman herbalists was nearly lost to humanity. In the sixth century the community of Benedictine monks at Monte Cassino in Italy was one of the very few in all of Europe that owned a library of herbal manuscripts or that cultivated an herb and vegetable garden. These monks copied the gardening and agricultural books in their possession time and again for other monasteries, thus keeping the ancient science of the medicinal and nutritional values of plants alive. In later years it became a rule in every monastery that at least one of the monks acquire a thorough knowledge of the use and cultivation of plants. It took the invention of the printing press in the fifteenth century to popularize this knowledge throughout western Europe and England.

One word of warning: conventionally grown and produced herbs, seasonings, and spices may contain some or all of the following: fillers, anticaking agents, artificial colorings, preservatives, monosodium glutamate (MSG), and pesticide residues. Reactions to these various extraneous substances may occur. Look for organically grown, non-irradiated herbs and spices in your local natural food and herb stores; the possible price difference is well worth it.

Agar-Agar

(Gelidium amansii, G. corneum, G. cartilagineum)
Also Known As: Kanten, Chinese Grass, Ceylon Moss,
  "Vegetable Jell-O"

Gelidium is influenced in meaning by the Latin *gelare*, meaning "to freeze" or "to congeal." The term *corneum* means "horn-bearing"; *cartilagineum* means "like cartilage" in texture. The English word *agar* comes from a Malayan term for "alga."

General Information

Agar-agar, or simply agar, is the product of mucilage from several species of Far Eastern seaweeds collectively classed as agarophytes (agar-yielding plants). Three or more agarophytes are usually combined into one agar formula. This group of seaweeds, growing at varying depths between fifteen and two hundred feet, includes some of the world's most beautiful. Most grow in brown, red, or purple fern-like fronds up to three feet long. The colors of the red seaweeds, ranging from a soft rosy pink to a striking purplish red, are a result of pigments that camouflage their green chlorophyll. These pigments serve to soak up light, which is scarce, since the seaweeds inhabit deep, dark waters. Within their plant cells lies an odorless, tasteless, colorless, and transparent substance that is processed out to become agar. Commercially harvested in Japan since 1769, the flat, fernlike seaweed is washed, sun-bleached, and dried. The strips are then boiled in water, the mucilaginous solution strained through a cloth, and the liquid allowed to harden and dry in the sun; this becomes a papery, whitish-clear product and is sold as bars, flakes, or granules. One of agar's most interesting properties is its indigestibility by practically all bacteria; hence, it is an excellent base on which to control the growth of laboratory bacterial cultures. The bacteria consume the medium in which they are grown, but not the agar itself.

Culinary Uses

Having virtually no taste or smell, agar can be used as a thickening and jelling agent for salads and desserts, substituting for gelatin derived from animal sources or pectin. Agar is available in powder form and as flakes, bars, and sticks; the powder dissolves the easiest and is the most concentrated. Bars and sticks are generally harder to find. One teaspoon of agar powder or two teaspoons of flakes firmly gel one cup of liquid. Use less for a softer gel, or for a less rubbery result use one part agar to three parts arrowroot powder. Add agar to a cool liquid, bring the mixture to a boil, lower the heat, and then simmer for about two minutes to fully activate. As it cools, the mixture will gel; at room temperature this takes from twenty to thirty minutes, while in the refrigerator the process takes only half as long. Jellies and jams made with agar rather than commercial pectin need less sweetener, since most of the sugar called for in jelly and jam recipes is required to compensate for the sourness of the pectin product, not the fruit. Commercially, agar is used in the manufacture of silk, textiles, and foods such as ice cream, jelly beans, and preserves. Because it is indigestible by humans, it is a common ingredient of diet foods, filling the stomach without adding calories.

Health Benefits

Demulcent, emollient, hydrophilic, laxative. At 75 percent carbohydrate, agar is high in a form of fiber that passes through the body undigested. Useful in cases of constipation, its high concentration of polysaccharide mucilage swells to many times its bulk upon reaching the intestines, absorbing moisture rapidly and supplying soft fibrous bulk and lubrication, thereby increasing peristaltic action and relieving constipation without painful griping. As well, it is believed to bond with toxins (including heavy metals and radioactive substances) and carry them out of the system.

Agar-Agar / Nutritional Value Per 100 g Edible Portion		
	Raw	Dried
Calories	26	306
Protein	0.54 g	6.21 g
Fat	0.03 g	0.30 g
Fiber	0.45 g	0.70 g
Calcium	54 mg	625 mg
Iron	1.86 mg	21.40 mg
Magnesium	67 mg	770 mg
Phosphorus	5 mg	52 mg
Potassium	226 mg	1,125 mg
Sodium	9 mg	102 mg
Manganese	0.373 mg	4.300 mg
Beta Carotene (A)	0 IU	0 IU
Thiamine (B$_1$)	0.005 mg	0.010 mg
Riboflavin (B$_2$)	0.022 mg	0.222 mg
Niacin (B$_3$)	0.055 mg	0.202 mg
Ascorbic Acid (C)	0 mg	0 mg

Ajowan

(Carum ajowan, C. copticum, Trachyspermum ammi)
Also Known As: Ajwain, Bishop's Weed

Carum is probably derived from the Caria region in Asia Minor. *Trachyspermum* means "shaggy-seeded," and *ammi* means "of sandy places."

General Information

Native to southern India, ajowan is a pretty plant resembling wild parsley. It is closely related to caraway and cumin, although it tastes strongly of thyme. It has seeds that range from light brown to red in color.

Ajowan / Nutritional Value Per 100 g Edible Portion			
	Seeds		Seeds
Protein	15.0-18.5 g	Zinc	4.3 mg
Fat	21.8-33.5 g	Copper	0.910 mg
Fiber	21.2-22.9 g	Manganese	3.31 mg
Calcium	1,525-1,647 mg	Beta Carotene (A)	0.070-0.080 mg
Iron	17.8-29.9 mg	Thiamine (B₁)	0.210-0.230 mg
Phosphorus	443-478 mg	Riboflavin (B₂)	0.280-0.300 mg
Sodium	56-61 mg		

Culinary Uses

The seeds look similar to large celery seeds; the taste, in addition to the thyme-like flavor, is hot and bitter. Indian breads such as naan, pakora, and paratha are made with ajowan, which imparts a distinctive flavor to the dough.

Health Benefits

Digestive. Besides adding flavor to foods, ajowan helps control flatulence. Ajowan's essential oil, thymol, is used as a germicide and an antiseptic.

Allspice

(Pimenta officinalis, P. dioica)
Also Known As: Clove Pepper, Jamaican Pepper, Pimento

The Spanish called the tree bearing the allspice berries *pimienta*, meaning "pepper," because the berries resembled peppercorns. The term *Pimenta* comes from the medieval term *pigmentum*, meaning "spicy." *Officinalis* means "of the workshop," alluding to apothecaries' shops and signifying that the plant was once part of the official pharmacopoeia of Rome. *Dioica* means "dioecious," having male and female flowers borne on different plants. The English name *allspice* was coined by a gentleman named Ray in 1693 because of the berry's taste, which has been described as a combination of cloves, juniper berries, cinnamon, and pepper.

General Information

Considered among the most aromatic of spices, allspice is made from the dried berries of the West Indian pimento or allspice tree, native to the West Indian island of Jamaica especially but also to Central and South America. This evergreen member of the myrtle family often grows to great heights of forty feet or more, depending on the climate. In July and August the tree produces clusters of half-inch, fleshy, sweet, round berries that are purplish black and rough-surfaced when ripe and contain two kidney-shaped seeds. Since the berries lose their aroma and volatile oil upon ripening, they are collected as soon as they have attained their full size. The unripe green berries are then dried in the hot tropical sun until they turn a dark reddish brown. The Jamaican variety is held to be the best, as the berries are smaller and more aromatic than those of other varieties. Allspice, or pimento, should not be confused with pimientos, the fruits of certain capsicum garden peppers.

Allspice / Nutritional Value Per 100 g Edible Portion		
	Dried, Ground	1 tsp.
Calories	263	5
Protein	6.09 g	0.12 g
Fat	8.69 g	0.17 g
Fiber	21.64 g	0.41 g
Calcium	661 mg	13 mg
Iron	7.06 mg	0.13 mg
Magnesium	135 mg	3 mg
Phosphorus	113 mg	2 mg
Potassium	1,044 mg	20 mg
Sodium	77 mg	1 mg
Zinc	1.010 mg	0.020 mg
Copper	0.553 mg	n/a
Manganese	2.943 mg	n/a
Beta Carotene (A)	540 IU	10 IU
Thiamine (B₁)	0.101 mg	0.002 mg
Riboflavin (B₂)	0.063 mg	0.001 mg
Niacin (B₃)	2.860 mg	0.054 mg
Ascorbic Acid (C)	39.20 mg	0.75 mg

LORE AND LEGEND

In their quest for black pepper, the Spanish discovered the island of Jamaica, which was covered with trees bearing aromatic berries that somewhat resembled peppercorns. Although it is hard to believe that the explorers actually thought the berries were peppercorns, the trees and their small berries were nonetheless called *pimienta* (Spanish for "pepper"). They were long regarded and feared as an aphrodisiac, and Peter the Venerable in 1132 forbade the monks under his charge at Cluny to eat pimento (allspice) because it was "provokative to lust." The leaves of the allspice tree are used in the production of bay rum, and at one time the white bark was sold as clove cinnamon.

Culinary Uses

With its hint of many flavors, allspice can add a warm, rich taste to many meals. Ground allspice is found in many of the blended spice mixtures and can be used on its own in pickles, fruitcakes, plum pudding, and spicy cakes and cookies. Just a pinch will add zip to carrots or other sweet vegetables. Two or three whole berries add a warm, spicy flavor to green pea or other soups.

Health Benefits

Aromatic, carminative, stimulant, stomachic. Allspice promotes digestion and removes gases from the upper intestinal tract. Applying the crushed berries to painful muscles and joints works as an effective pain reliever, and the oil may be applied directly to painful teeth and gums as an anesthetic and/or first aid until professional care can be obtained. Considered a lucky spice, allspice is said to promote health in an individual and prosperity in a family. Allspice is burned as incense to attract money.

Aloe Vera
(Aloe vera, A. barbadensis, A. ferox)

Aloe is derived from the Arabic *alloeh*, meaning "bitter and shiny substance"; *vera* means "true"; *barbadensis* means "coming from Barbados"; *ferox* means "ferocious" or "thorny."

General Information

Aloe vera is a desert plant belonging to the lily family, a succulent native to East and South Africa. In the sixth century A.D., Arab traders carried aloe from Spain to Asia and introduced it to India's traditional Ayurvedic physicians, who heralded its healing properties. References to the healing benefits of aloe are found in Egyptian, Roman, Chinese, Greek, Italian, Algerian, Moroccan, Arabian, Indian, and Christian history. The plant grows extremely well in dry soils and requires little or no care, propagating itself by means of suckers, with small plants growing out from the roots of the parent plant. The basal leaves are long and narrow, fleshy with a spiny margin about two inches in thickness. Decorative as well as medicinal, aloe is particularly effective as a center of floral designs. Some varieties make excellent houseplants, especially for those without green thumbs.

Culinary Uses

The leaves of aloe vera are pressed into juice and administered for liver ailments. Fresh or prepared aloe is sold in various forms, including juice, gel caps, and powders. Fresh juice is readily obtained by breaking off a leaf and squeezing the juice out.

Aloe Vera / Nutritional Value Per 100 g Edible Portion			
	Dried		Dried
Calories	280	Sodium	51 mg
Protein	5.7 g	Zinc	1.100 mg
Fat	0.80 g	Manganese	0.600 mg
Fiber	17.7 g	Beta Carotene (A)	5,080 IU
Calcium	460 mg	Thiamine (B$_1$)	0.080 mg
Iron	4.1 mg	Riboflavin (B$_2$)	trace
Magnesium	93 mg	Niacin (B$_3$)	6.400 mg
Phosphorus	94 mg	Ascorbic Acid (C)	626 mg
Potassium	85 mg		

LORE AND LEGEND

Aloe is one of the few non-narcotic plants to cause a war. When Alexander the Great conquered Egypt in 332 B.C., he heard stories of a plant growing on an island off Somalia with amazing wound-healing powers. Intent on healing his soldiers' wounds—and denying this healer to his enemies—Alexander sent an army to seize the island of Socotra to gain access to the plant, which turned out to be aloe.

Health Benefits

Antibiotic, demulcent, emollient, healing, purgative, vulnerary. Aloe vera is one of the oldest healing remedies known to humans. Most of its tissue does not contain any medicinally active substance, but inside the outer layer of the leaf is a crystal-clear mucilaginous gel. When applied externally, the gel is quickly absorbed, soothing and relieving pain, burning, and itching; it provides a natural protection for the skin, seems to reduce scar tissue formation, does not stain, and has no unpleasant odor. As well, there seems to be some unknown substance that acts as a "wound hormone" to accelerate the healing process of injured surfaces. Documented cases of radiation burn victims show more rapid healing when using aloe than with any other method of burn treatment. If turmeric is added to the gel, the healing process is even faster. In Java aloe juice is massaged into the hair and scalp to improve their condition and stimulate growth. The fresh gel is frequently used in cosmetic skin care products as an emollient and might well be worth a try, as the beautiful Cleopatra is known to have massaged it into her skin. Taken internally, aloe vera aids in assimilation, circulation, and elimination. It purifies the blood and liver, as well as soothing ulcers and hemorrhoids. Aloe contains a colon-stimulating phytochemical called anthraquinone, which increases peristaltic waves, thereby regulating and cleansing the colon. It has been reported to increase endurance and energy, to provide speedy recovery from fatigue, and to aid in muscle function and utilization of vitamins and minerals.

Note: Pregnant women and diabetics are cautioned not to take aloe vera internally.

Angelica

(Angelica archangelica, A. sinensis, A. atropurpurea, A. sylvestris)

Also Known As: Wild Celery, Masterwort, Archangel, Dong Quai

There are several versions of how this plant got its genus name *Angelica*. One group claims the name comes from the old Roman name *herba angelica*, meaning "angelic herb," because it was thought to possess powers against poison and plague. Another possibility is that because *angelica* often blooms around the feast day of St. Michael the Archangel (May 8), the plant was named in his honor. My personal favorite is a legend that holds that during the bubonic plague of 1665, a monk dreamed he met an angel who showed him an herb (*angelica*) that could cure the scourge; the monk then duly named the plant in honor of the angel in his dream. *Archangelica* means "archangel"; *sinensis* means "originating in China"; *atropurpurea* means "dark purple"; and *sylvestris* means "pertaining to the wood," or "growing wild."

General Information

Angelica is a member of the carrot family resembling celery; its roots and fruit furnish a flavorful oil. The European variety (*A. archangelica*), with its preference for cold, moist climates, is native to the north of Europe, while the American variety (*A. atropurpurea*) grows in meadows and marshy woods from Canada to the Carolinas. During the late 1700s, American colonists would eat two-year-old angelica shoots as a vegetable. They also boiled the stalks and rolled them in sugar for a sweet treat. Of the several different species of angelica, the one most sought after comes from China (*A. sinensis*); commonly known as "dong quai," this species is used as a flavorful cooking spice and as a potent herbal medicine. Other species of angelica that come from Europe are used for flavoring wines, perfumes, and liqueurs, as well as in folk medicine.

Culinary Uses

Angelica has a flavor that most people enjoy; reminiscent of licorice and juniper berries, this sweet, hardy flavor permeates the fresh or dried leaves, stem, root, and seeds of the plant. The most celebrated part of angelica is its stem. Fresh stems can be cooked and eaten as a fresh herb, used for seasoning fish, or made into syrup for pudding and ice cream toppings. Candied or crystallized stems are used as a confection once widely known and enjoyed (especially in fruitcake). Savor the stems alone, or use them to decorate cakes, tarts, and other sweet pastries. Fresh leaves provide a slightly sweet, zesty accent to fruit or vegetable soups and green salads. Dried ground leaves reduce the need for sweetener in making pies or sauces and add zip to desserts and pastries. The dried ground root has a taste similar to the leaves but is bolder and earthier; this flavor works well in yeasted and quick breads, cakes, muffins, and cookies.

Health Benefits

Aromatic, carminative, expectorant, stimulant, stomachic, tonic. Angelica has been highly regarded in Europe and Asia for centuries because of its medicinal properties. Angelica stimulates many functions of the body: it strengthens the heart and lungs, opens passageways in the liver and spleen to allow them to function better, reduces gas in the intestines, relieves heartburn and sour stomach, and promotes perspiration and the production of urine. The root is widely used in treating stomach and bowel disorders. In small doses angelica root decreases the production of gastric juices, which is good for ulcer sufferers; in larger doses it increases the production of gastric juices, thus stimulating the appetite. With the regular use of angelica, there seems to arise a distaste for alcoholic drinks. When fasting, make a powder of the roots and take thirty grains at a time (about three-eighths of a teaspoon) to guard against infection. The odor is aromatic and the taste sweetish.

In China the ten different angelica species collectively known as dong quai have been used for several thousand years and are considered second only to ginseng in importance. The brown, fleshy root looks much like gentian

LORE AND LEGEND

European peasants made angelica leaf necklaces to protect their children from illness and witchcraft. The presence of angelica in a woman's garden or cupboard was once used as a defense against spurious charges of witchcraft, as it was reputedly the only herb never used by witches.

root, while its odor is strong, resembling celery, but the taste is warm, sweetish, and aromatic. Ranking next to licorice in frequency of use, it is much prescribed for female complaints, colds, flu, and many other health problems. Dong quai was introduced into Western medicine in 1899 by the Merck company in the form of a liquid extract, sold under the name of Eumenol, recommended for menstrual disorders. The active constituents of dong quai appear to be aromatic volatile oils that affect the uterus, liver, heart, blood pressure, and nervous system.

Note: Fresh angelica roots contain poisonous elements eliminated only by thorough drying. Unless you are a confident field botanist, do not collect angelica in the wild, as it is too easy to confuse the plant with the extremely poisonous water hemlock (*Cicuta maculata*). Do not take this herb for prolonged periods of time as it can cause a slight skin rash and make some folks more sensitive to the sun's rays.

Anise/Aniseed
(Pimpinella anisum)

Pimpinella possibly derives from the Latin *bipinnula*, meaning "bipinnate" (having similar parts arranged on opposite sides). The early Arabic name for the plant was *anysum*, from which was derived the Greek *anison* or *anneson*, the Latin *anisum*, and the English *anise*.

General Information

Native to western Asia and Egypt, anise is an annual oil-bearing seed plant of the carrot family. This dainty annual reaches two feet in height and has feathery leaves divided into many leaflets and umbrella-like clusters of tiny white or yellow flowers, which bloom in midsummer and produce small, downy, ribbed fruits (seeds) in late summer.

Angelica / Nutritional Value Per 100 g Edible Portion			
	Chinese, Dried (Dong Quai)		Chinese, Dried (Dong Quai)
Calories	320	Sodium	trace
Protein	13.0 g	Zinc	trace
Fat	1.8 g	Manganese	2.600 mg
Fiber	17.2 g	Beta Carotene (A)	2,010 IU
Calcium	282 mg	Thiamine (B₁)	trace
Iron	88 mg	Riboflavin (B₂)	0.340 mg
Magnesium	265 mg	Niacin (B₃)	6.800 mg
Phosphorus	334 mg	Ascorbic Acid (C)	30.4 mg
Potassium	1,070 mg		

The whole plant has a fragrant odor, and the pungent seeds taste warm, sweet, and reminiscent of licorice when chewed.

Culinary Uses

Anise is used both as a seed and a leafy herb. Before the seed heads are produced, the leaves and stalks can be used as a salad herb; they have a sweet licorice-like taste and are delicious served freshly chopped into salads and cream sauces; they can also be steamed or sautéed with a bit of olive oil, garlic, and lemon juice. Aniseeds are classed as one of the four great hot seeds. Available either whole or powdered, aniseed has a sweet yet spicy aroma and licorice flavor; it is used to flavor cakes and cookies, pickles, salad dressings, and soups. Using the whole seed is preferable, since many of the volatile oils quickly become lost after grinding. Try adding just a dash to applesauce for a delightful change.

Health Benefits

Antispasmodic, aphrodisiac, aromatic, carminative, diuretic, expectorant, stimulant, stomachic, tonic. Medicinally, anise has warming and moistening properties; it has traditionally been used in European herbal medicine as a mild diuretic, a slight stimulant for vital bodily organs, a treatment for flatulence and indigestion, a breath sweetener, a toothache reliever, and a stimulator of mother's milk. Anise is also an expectorant with antispasmodic action that is helpful in countering menstrual pain, asthma, whooping cough, and bronchitis; it appears frequently as a

Anise/Aniseed / Nutritional Value Per 100 g Edible Portion		
	Whole Seed	1 tsp.
Calories	337	7
Protein	17.60 g	0.37 g
Fat	15.90 g	0.33 g
Fiber	14.60 g	0.31 g
Calcium	646 mg	14 mg
Iron	36.96 mg	0.78 mg
Magnesium	170 mg	4 mg
Phosphorus	440 mg	9 mg
Potassium	1,441 mg	30 mg
Sodium	16 mg	trace
Zinc	5.300 mg	0.110 mg
Copper	0.910 mg	n/a
Manganese	2.300 mg	n/a

LORE AND LEGEND

Anise was so important as a spice and cash crop for ancient cultures that it was frequently used as a medium of exchange and for the payment of taxes. Clay tablets found in Assyria contain praise for the medicinal properties of anise, while ancient Greeks valued its purported effectiveness as an aphrodisiac. The Romans cultivated the herb extensively and anise was one of several spices used to flavor a cake called *mustaceum*, often served as a dessert and digestive aid at feasts. In medieval England the spice was so popular as a flavoring, medicine, and perfume that in 1305 King Edward I placed a special import tax on it to raise money to repair the London Bridge. For some reason, mice seem to find anise quite irresistible, and if a better mouse trap is ever developed, it just may use anise as the bait.

flavoring and active ingredient in cough syrups and lozenges. Chewing aniseed will help induce sleep and alleviate cramps and nausea. To make a pleasant digestive remedy, bruise two teaspoonfuls of aniseeds well in a mortar, then put them in a jug and pour in half a pint of boiling water. Cover and leave to get cold, then bottle. Adults should take two teaspoonfuls, while half a teaspoonful will be sufficient for a very young child. Anise calms and soothes the body and mind. Aniseeds contain a form of plant estrogen, and the aromatic tea made from them deepens meditation. The mild hormonal action of aniseed may explain its ability to increase breast milk production and its reputation for easing childbirth and treating impotence and frigidity.

Annatto

(Bixa orellana)
Also Known As: Achiote, Bija, Bijoul, Roucou, Lipstick Tree

Bixa is derived from a South American name for the plant.

General Information

The annatto tree is an attractive, small flowering tree that grows throughout the Caribbean, Mexico, and Central and South America. It bears large pink flowers that resemble wild roses. However, it is the orange dye from the fifty or so seeds inside the heart-shaped, prickly scarlet fruits that makes the tree commercially important. These rust-colored seeds provide a potent, almost neon orange-red colorant. The intensity of color is comparable to turmeric, only it is predominantly salmon red rather than mustard yellow. The plant's alternate name, lipstick tree, denotes its cosmetic use; but long before the term *lipstick* was coined, Amazonians used annatto as a body dye and insect repellent. The warlike Carib Indians used it to paint their bodies, and it was also used by the ancient Mayans in Guatemala. Annatto was introduced to the Philippines by the Spaniards, and it has since become an important ingredient in many dishes.

Culinary Uses

Annatto is exploited to its fullest in the cooking of the Caribbean and Latin American cultures, where it is used primarily as a coloring although also as a gentle flavoring. It is an ingredient in the spicy sauce that is served over the Jamaican national dish of ackee and salt cod. In Mexico annatto seeds are ground with other herbs and spices for a seasoning mixture that has a fragrant and flowery taste. In Europe and North America annatto is used to color butter and cheese. The seeds, if brick red, will keep indefinitely in a cool, dark place.

Health Benefits

Annatto is mildly bitter and astringent. It contains a high rate of carotenoids and carotenoid factors, which explains its effectiveness as a dye and as a medicinal herb. Annatto's vast ethno-botanical uses include treatment for headaches, cancer, diabetes, inflammation, jaundice, epilepsy, and tumors. It is also used as an aphrodisiac and a douche.

Arrowroot

(Maranta arundinacea)

The botanical name *Maranta* was given by Plumier in 1559 to honor a famous Venetian physician and botanist, Bartommeo Maranto. The term *arundinacea* means "reed-like." The English name *arrowroot* either originates from an American Indian name for all flour-giving roots,

Annatto / Nutritional Value Per 100 g Edible Portion			
	Fresh		Fresh
Calories	54-346	Phosphorus	10-64 mg
Fat	0.3-1.9 g	Beta Carotene (A)	0.090-0.600 mg
Fiber	0.5-3.2 g	Riboflavin (B$_2$)	0.050-0.300 mg
Calcium	7.0-45.0 mg	Niacin (B$_3$)	0.30-1.90 mg
Iron	0.8-5.0 mg	Ascorbic Acid (C)	2.0-13.0 mg

Arrowroot / Nutritional Value Per 100 g Edible Portion			
	Powder		Powder
Calories	357	Copper	0.040 mg
Protein	0.30 g	Manganese	0.470 mg
Fat	0.10 g	Beta Carotene (A)	n/a
Fiber	n/a	Thiamine (B$_1$)	0.001 mg
Calcium	40 mg	Riboflavin (B$_2$)	0 mg
Iron	0.33 mg	Niacin (B$_3$)	0 mg
Magnesium	3 mg	Pantothenic Acid (B$_5$)	0.130 mg
Phosphorus	5 mg	Pyridoxine (B$_6$)	0.005 mg
Potassium	11 mg	Folic Acid (B$_9$)	7.0 mcg
Sodium	2 mg	Ascorbic Acid (C)	0 mg
Zinc	0.070 mg		

araruta, or from the belief that these roots could cure wounds from poisoned arrows.

General Information

Arrowroot powder is a fine, starchy flour extracted from the beaten pulp of tuberous rootstocks of a tropical plant native to South America and the West Indies. There are red and white varieties, the former being the most esteemed. Most of our arrowroot comes from the West Indian island of Saint Vincent. The roots are ground, sun-dried, and powdered.

Culinary Uses

A fine, silky powder without the chalkiness of cornstarch or the graininess of flour, arrowroot can be used to thicken fruit puddings, soups, and gravy. Although it will keep almost indefinitely when stored in a cool, dry cupboard, the general recommendation is that it be used within a year of purchase. One tablespoon of arrowroot powder will thicken a cup of liquid; for a thicker mixture, use two tablespoons per cup. Dissolve the powder by stirring it into an equal amount of cool liquid before adding it to the dish being prepared; stir the mixture in during the last minutes of cooking time. It does not have to reach the boiling point to thicken. Use 1½ teaspoons of arrowroot to replace 1 tablespoon of either cornstarch or flour in recipes. One precaution: arrowroot-thickened sauces tend to break down if overcooked or allowed to stand too long before serving. For this reason it works especially well for fruit desserts and other preparations that require little or no cooking.

Health Benefits

Anticeptic, demulcent. Arrowroot is easily digested and more nutritious than cornstarch. The powder of choice for diaper rash, this absorbent, soothing, natural, and non-toxic powder reduces friction, prevents irritation, and keeps skin dry by absorbing water. People in the Caribbean use the root as a poultice for smallpox sores and as an antiseptic tea for urinary infections. Arrowroot is used in herbal medicine in much the same manner as slippery elm, as a soothing demulcent and a nutrient of benefit in convalescence, and for easing digestion. It helps to relieve acidity, indigestion, and colic, and is a mild laxative. It may be applied as an ointment or poultice mixed with other antiseptic herbs, such as comfrey.

Asafoetida

(Ferula assafoetida, F. foetida regel)

Also Known As: Hing, Stinking Gum, Devil's Dung, Food of the Gods

Ferula is an old Latin name for the plant, likely derived from the verb *ferire*, "to strike," because its stems were used as *ferules* (instruments, such as a flat piece of wood, used to punish children). *Assafoetida* derives from the Persian *aza*, meaning "mastic" (resin), and the Latin *foetida*, meaning "fetid" or "bad-smelling." The *regel* part of the name perhaps refers to Eduard von Regel (1815–1892), the director of the Botanic Gardens in St. Petersburg, Russia.

General Information

Asafoetida comes from a brown resinous substance, known as "gum asafoetida," contained in two varieties of the giant fennels native to Persia and Afghanistan. These are unrelated to the garden and wild fennels, though somewhat similar in appearance, and have a dreadful stink (said by some to resemble rotting garlic) because of their sulfur compounds. In ancient Persia this plant was highly regarded and known as "food of the gods." The leaves and stems were used as a vegetable, the odor disappearing once the plant is boiled. The Romans, who knew asafoetida as Persian Sylphium, valued it for medicinal purposes and as a flavoring for sauces and wines. An expensive imported spice, it became more so when a money-hungry government found it worth taxing, as happened in second century A.D. Alexandria. For a natural pesticide to ward off deer and rabbits, mix one ounce of powdered asafoetida with 1½ quarts water and shake hard, and then apply the mixture around plants.

Culinary Uses

Asafoetida is available in solid waxlike pieces or in powder form. Used sparingly, it will give a flavor redolent of garlic and shallots to vegetables, stews, gravies, and sauces; it goes especially well with fresh or salted fish. The repellent smell quickly disappears with cooking. A frequent ingredient in Indian cooking, it is popular in bean dishes and sauces, where it helps lower their gas-producing tendencies. It is also worth noting that among the ingredients of that long-lived modern favorite, Worcestershire sauce, there are very small quantities of asafoetida. In Afghanistan and Iran the leaves and stems are eaten as a vegetable.

LORE AND LEGEND

As its name suggests, asafoetida in any quantity has a strong repulsive smell and a nauseating taste—characteristics that also burdened it with the name *devil's dung*. In the Middle Ages, a small piece of the gum was worn around the neck to ward off disease; whatever effectiveness it had was probably due more to the antisocial properties of the amulet rather than any medicinal virtue.

Baking Powder / Nutritional Value Per Tablespoon

	Calumet Brand	Brand with Cream of Tartar
Calories	3	7
Protein	0 g	0 g
Fat	0 g	0 g
Fiber	n/a	n/a
Calcium	241 mg	0 mg
Iron	0 mg	0 mg
Magnesium	0 mg	0 mg
Phosphorus	83 mg	0 mg
Potassium	0 mg	361 mg
Sodium	426 mg	694 mg
Zinc	0 mg	0 mg

Health Benefits

Anthelmintic, aphrodisiac, carminative, diaphoretic, diuretic, emmenagogue, expectorant, laxative, stimulant, tonic. Asafoetida will produce a sensation of warmth without any rise in body temperature; it stimulates digestion and the mucous membranes, particularly the alimentary canal, acting like a natural laxative and detoxicant. Occasionally, those who are not accustomed to asafoetida may develop a puzzling diarrhea after ingestion. In ancient Greek and Roman times, extracts of asafoetida were used as a contraceptive and early-term abortifacient.

Baking Powder

General Information

Baking powder is a mixture of the "slow-acting" leavening agent baking soda and a "fast-acting" leavening agent such as calcium acid phosphate (monocalcium phosphate monohydrate), calcium sulfate, or cream of tartar. Those containing sodium aluminum sulfate are viewed with concern, since excessive amounts of aluminum in the body are not desirable. "Double-acting" indicates that the baked product will rise both when the batter is prepared and during baking. Rumford baking powder was invented by two scientists in 1854 (one of them Eben Horsford, a professor who held the Rumford Chair of Applied Science at Harvard University) and named after Count Rumford, formerly known as Benjamin Thompson of Massachusetts (1753–1814). Count Rumford was a politician and inventor; the Leonardo da Vinci of the kitchen, he was the founder of home economics and invented the first kitchen range and other useful kitchen items. He was also a pioneer in studies of light and heat, guns and explosives, ship design, and many other areas. It was Rumford who conceived the idea of an American military academy, but he was denied a role in establishing West Point because of his British sympathies during the Revolution.

Culinary Uses

Baking powders have been in use for more than a hundred years as a yeast substitute. When baking powder is mixed into a batter, carbon dioxide gas is released from the sodium or potassium bicarbonate by the action of an acid or an acid salt. It is this gas that gives volume (rise) and a lighter texture to the finished product. Easily made at home, baking powder can be put together from two parts cream of tartar, one part baking soda, and two parts arrowroot powder.

Health Benefits

Most commercially available baking powders contain aluminum compounds that are deleterious to health as well as flavor, imparting a bitter aftertaste. Look for aluminum-free baking powders instead. Because of its baking soda content, baking powder depletes baked goods of the B vitamins thiamine and folic acid and creates a type of alkalinity in the body that eradicates vitamin C.

Baking Soda
(Sodium bicarbonate)

General Information

Baking soda was developed by John Dwight and his brother-in-law Dr. Austin Church in 1846. Called Dwight's

Saleratus, the powder was made from carbon-dioxide-treated soda ash, and it completely revolutionized the baking industry. Baking soda today is produced by the Solvay method, in which a brine solution is run into saturation tanks, where it mixes with ammonia gas; this ammonia brine is then injected with carbon dioxide to produce bicarbonate of soda. The newly formed soda is insoluble, so it is precipitated out, drawn off, filtered, washed in cold water, dried, and milled into the refined white powder we are all familiar with. Baking soda is used as a leavening agent in quick breads, which do not require kneading and rising before baking, and also in cookies, cakes, pies, pancakes, and any other baked goods using pastry wheat flours or flours other than hard wheat.

Culinary Uses

Baking soda must be used in conjunction with an acid; when mixed in the proper proportions with a liquid, they almost completely neutralize each other, forming water and carbon dioxide gas, which lifts the batter and creates a light, smooth-textured product. A few blandly flavored salts remain of the original baking soda. The most familiar use for baking soda is as an ingredient in baking powder. When cooked with garbanzo or black beans, baking soda makes them lighter and facilitates the cooking process. It is also frequently used as a nontoxic household cleanser and deodorizer.

Health Benefits

Baking soda depletes baked goods of the B vitamins thiamine and folic acid, and creates a type of alkalinity in the body that eradicates vitamin C. An excellent use of baking soda is as a dentifrice, as its highly alkaline properties neutralize plaque acids and eliminate the bacteria that cause tooth decay. It also helps stop the major cause of tooth loss—gum infection and inflammation such as gingivitis and pyorrhea—better than most commercial toothpastes. Baking soda is an effective treatment for athlete's foot: dust

feet liberally in the morning and then put on cotton or wool socks. Baking soda relieves skin infections, hives, and rash, and maintains the health and hygiene of the skin. A paste of baking soda and water can soothe the itch of a mosquito bite; one-quarter to one-half cup added to a warm bath can soothe itchiness resulting from hives, eczema, or minor sunburn, as well as promote circulation and make the skin soft. A pinch mixed with a cup of warm water and the juice of half a lemon relieves stomach acidity, gas, and indigestion. An excellent external treatment in every form of radiation exposure is a bath of sea salt and baking soda. Add one pound each of sea salt and baking soda to a warm bath and soak for twenty minutes; rinse with cool water. Repeat three times a week for one month in cases of serious exposure.

Balm
(Melissa officinalis)
Also Known As: Sweet Balm, Lemon Balm, Melissa

> Sometimes she embraces the lovely narcissus,
> and sometimes
> The rosy hyacinth, and following no particular
> path
> Wanders from meadow to meadow, from
> garden to garden,
> Collecting up a sweet load of melissa or thyme.
>
> —Pierre de Ronsard

Until the fifteenth century, this plant was considered important only as a bee-attracting plant and was known as either *melissophyllon*, Greek for "bee leaf," or *apiastrum*, Latin for "bee plant." Its modern botanical name, *Melissa*, meaning "bee," reflects this early association. *Officinalis* means "of the workshop," alluding to apothecaries' shops and signifying that the plant was once part of the official pharmacopoeia of Rome. The English name *balm* comes from the Greek *balsamon*, meaning "balsam," an oily, fragrant resin; since this plant does not actually exude a balsam, the name probably refers to its fragrant aroma and its ability to soothe and calm the nerves.

General Information

Balm originated in the Middle East but soon found its way to the Mediterranean countries, where it was cultivated for

Baking Soda / Nutritional Value Per 100 g Edible Portion		
	100 g	1 tsp.
Calories	0	0
Protein	0 g	0 g
Fat	0 g	0 g
Fiber	0 g	0 g
Sodium	27,360 mg	1,259 mg

Culinary Uses

Balm has a lemony scent and imparts a lemon-mint, honey-sweet flavor to salads, salad dressings, iced tea, and fruit drinks. The leaves can also be used for flavoring or garnish in soups, stews, custards, puddings, or cookies.

Health Benefits

Antibacterial, antispasmodic, astringent, calmative, carminative, diaphoretic, emmenagogue, relaxant, stomachic, tonic. Because of their antibacterial properties, leaves of balm have been used to dress and heal wounds since ancient times. Recommended for troubles involving the liver, spleen, kidneys, or bladder, balm will help the digestion and relieve nausea and vomiting. It is often helpful in treating attention deficit disorder (ADD). Tea made from the fresh or dried leaves is said to soothe menstrual cramps and headaches, relieve insomnia, act as a sedative, quiet vomiting, relieve colic, and reduce fever. The leaves contain a volatile oil that is used in the manufacture of perfumes and cosmetics.

Basil

(Ocimum basilicum, O. sanctum)
Also Known As: Sweet Basil, St. Josephwort

> A man taking basil from a woman will love her always.
>
> —Sir Thomas Moore

Ocimum is from an old Greek name for the plant, while *basilicum* means "royal" or "magnificent" and *sanctum* means "holy." The common name *basil* is an abbreviation of *basilikon phuton*, Greek for "kingly herb."

General Information

Basil is another member of the mint family, a bushy annual with broad, light green, oval leaves that release a spicy scent when bruised. Native to India, there are many different varieties, including sweet basil, lemon basil, licorice basil, cinnamon basil, and purple basil. Basil makes a safe and natural insect repellent for the garden and house, repelling houseflies, mosquitoes, and cockroaches.

its fragrant lemony-scented leaves. A rather coarse low herb, it is always popular because of this pleasant fragrance and is the special joy of honeybees, which are forever delving into its small white or yellowish flowers. An important herb in the monastic apothecary gardens, balm has a venerable history of use as both a healing herb and as part of a drink to ensure longevity.

Balm / Nutritional Value Per 100 g Edible Portion			
	Seed		Seed
Protein	29.3 g	Fat	11.5 g

Culinary Uses

The flavor of fresh basil is rich and spicy, almost peppery and rather like cloves, with a strong, pungent, sweet smell. The dried leaves taste more like curry. Its pungency, unlike most other herbs, actually increases with cooking, so handle with care. The sweet, clovelike flavor and aroma give basil infinite uses, but it is probably best known for its use with tomato dishes, especially pizza. It combines especially well with rosemary, sage, and summer savory and is used in pasta salads, Mediterranean-style dishes, and herb breads. When purchasing basil, look for crisp, vibrant green leaves with no sign of decay. A successful way to store the fresh leaves is to place them in a jar with a pinch of salt and cover them with olive oil. Dried basil can be used if fresh basil is not available.

Health Benefits

Antiseptic, antispasmodic, appetizer, carminative, emmenagogue, stomachic. Traditionally classified as a warming and moistening herb, basil is regarded as slightly antiseptic and a mild nervine and emmenagogue. It has a good

Basil / Nutritional Value Per 100 g Edible Portion			
	Fresh	Dried	1 tsp.
Calories	27	251	4
Protein	2.54 g	14.37 g	0.20 g
Fat	0.61 g	3.98 g	0.06 g
Fiber	n/a	17.76 g	0.25 g
Calcium	154 mg	2,113 mg	30 mg
Iron	n/a	42.00 mg	0.59 mg
Magnesium	81 mg	422 mg	6 mg
Phosphorus	69 mg	490 mg	7 mg
Potassium	462 mg	3,433 mg	48 mg
Sodium	4 mg	34 mg	trace
Zinc	0.850 mg	5.820 mg	0.080 mg
Copper	0.290 mg	1.367 mg	n/a
Manganese	1.446 mg	3.167 mg	n/a
Beta Carotene (A)	n/a	9,375 IU	131 IU
Thiamine (B$_1$)	0.026 mg	0.148 mg	0.002 mg
Riboflavin (B$_2$)	0.073 mg	0.316 mg	0.004 mg
Niacin (B$_3$)	0.925 mg	6.948 mg	0.097 mg
Pantothenic Acid (B$_5$)	0.238 mg	n/a	n/a
Pyridoxine (B$_6$)	0.129 mg	n/a	n/a
Folic Acid (B$_9$)	64.0 mcg	n/a	n/a
Ascorbic Acid (C)	n/a	61.22 mg	0.86 mg

LORE AND LEGEND

Ancient lore seems to have accorded basil somewhat mixed attributes. In India the herb flourishes freely and from time immemorial has been sacred to the Hindus, consecrated to their god Vishnu, and to his popular incarnation, Krishna (especially *Ocimum sanctum*, "holy basil"). They call it *tulasi*, after the goddess Tulasi, the wife of Vishnu, who when she came to earth took the form of this lowly herb. Thus the plant is revered, and no sprig of it may be broken off except for a worthy reason, and only then gathered with a prayer to Tulasi and Vishnu for forgiveness, for the heart of Vishnu is sorely agitated and tormented when so much as a leaf is broken from the stalk of his wife Tulasi. Yet these leaves are necessary, for no Hindu could rest in his grave unless his head had been bathed with tulasi water just before burial, and a tulasi leaf laid on his breast. According to Greek mythology, basil was named for the baneful basilisk—a fabulous creature, half lizard and half dragon, born of serpents, that was believed to inhabit the deserts of Africa, and whose very look was fatal. Because the plant was regarded as magical protection against this monster, no one carrying a sprig could be injured by his look, by his breath, or even by his bite if a leaf were quickly applied to the wound. In more enlightened days, when the lizard-dragon basilisk had passed into fable, basil leaves became very naturally an antidote for the bite of any venomous creature, even a mad dog. Later Greeks and Romans had a curious belief that, because the herb was a symbol of hostility and insanity, to grow truly fragrant basil one had to shout and swear angrily and outlandishly while sowing its seeds. Even today in French, "sowing basil" (*semer le basilic*) means "ranting."

affinity with the stomach, where it will stimulate the appetite, digestion, and nerves; it also counteracts flatulence, stomach cramps, nausea, vomiting, and constipation. Because of its antibacterial and fungicidal action, basil leaves are used on itching skin, insect bites, and skin eruptions. It is effective against bacterial infections and intestinal parasites. Tea made from the leaves is recommended for nausea, gas pains, and dysentery. For warts, crush up a few basil leaves, place them right on the wart, and cover the area with a bandage. Change this dressing daily, and the wart should disappear within a week or so.

Bay
(Laurus nobilis)

The Bay leaves are of as necessary use as any other in the garden or orchard, for they serve both for pleasure and profit, both for ornament and for use, both for honest civil uses and for physic, yea, both for the sick and the sound, both for the living and the dead; . . . so that from the cradle to the grave we still have use of it, we still have need of it.

—JOHN PARKINSON, *Garden of Flowers* (1629)

Its botanical name emphasizes the respect with which the ancient held this plant: the Latin *Laurus* means "to praise" and *nobilis* means "renowned" or "famous." The English word *bay* derives from the Latin *baca*, meaning "berry."

General Information
The stately, fragrant bay tree is indigenous to the Mediterranean basin, growing especially near the coasts of the three continents surrounding the Mediterranean Sea but also extending its range inland and northeast to the Black Sea coast of Turkey. It was so highly valued in all the Mediterranean regions that a Roman gold coin of 342 B.C. has a laurel wreath modeled upon its surface. Usually a shrub or small tree, the leaves are dark green and somewhat glossy, as leathery and as thin as when they are dried. The leaves are gathered by hand in mid- to late summer by mountain peasants—picked in the morning and dried in the shade lest they turn brown. Leaves from the American bay (*Umbellularia californica*) have a camphor-and-paint smell and an awful taste. These are sometimes sold for culi-

Bay / Nutritional Value Per 100 g Edible Portion		
	Dried Crumbled	1 tsp.
Calories	313	2
Protein	7.61 g	0.05 g
Fat	8.36 g	0.05 g
Fiber	26.32 g	0.16 g
Calcium	834 mg	5 mg
Iron	43.00 mg	0.26 mg
Magnesium	120 mg	1 mg
Phosphorus	113 mg	1 mg
Potassium	529 mg	3 mg
Sodium	23 mg	trace
Zinc	3.700 mg	0.020 mg
Copper	0.416 mg	n/a
Manganese	8.167 mg	n/a
Beta Carotene (A)	6,185 IU	37 IU
Thiamine (B$_1$)	0.009 mg	trace
Riboflavin (B$_2$)	0.421 mg	0.003 mg
Niacin (B$_3$)	2.005 mg	0.012 mg
Ascorbic Acid (C)	46.53 mg	0.28 mg

nary uses but should be avoided. Instead, seek out the best European bay you can find.

Culinary Uses
Bay leaves have an aromatic perfume and a strong, spicy flavor reminiscent of pine, nutmeg, and pepper. When the leaves are shredded or crushed, the aroma and flavor are even more apparent. Fresh leaves are strongly scented, bitter, and not to everyone's taste. They are best left to dry and mellow for a few days, although not for too long, as old dried leaves will be quite flavorless. Newly dried leaves are sweet in the sense that cinnamon and clove are sweet, with a grassy freshness. Popular in Mediterranean cooking, bay leaves are usually used when preparing meats but can also be added to stews, casseroles, and soup stocks. By their very nature, bay leaves provide support to other seasonings. They should be used sparingly because of their strong flavor, with one-half to one leaf all that is needed for a medium-sized pot of soup or stew. The whole leaves do not cook down and should be removed before the dish is served. Bay leaves appear to repel roaches, moths, and fleas. Put a whole leaf in a canister of flour to keep insects out, or put whole leaves on the floor of your closet, in drawers where woolen clothes are stored, or around the drain under the sink in your kitchen.

LORE AND LEGEND

Legend has it that we owe the bay laurel to Apollo, Greek god of prophecy, poetry, and medicine. It seems that one day Apollo scolded Cupid for some unseemly conduct and called him a mere child. The usually charming but mischievous Cupid decided to avenge the insult, and succeeded in shooting Apollo with a golden arrow to induce passionate longing for the first woman he saw; Cupid then loosed a second arrow of lead to cause that woman to be equally repelled. While traversing the verdant forest, Apollo came upon the lithe and lovely wood nymph Daphne, and the effect of the golden shaft was immediate. He saw before him not merely a wood nymph but a goddess of superb beauty with attributes of wisdom and charm beyond all description. However, Daphne felt such repugnance that she fled in panic. Apollo eagerly pursued and entreated her, but she refused to stop; when the capture seemed inevitable, Daphne prayed urgently to the gods to take from her the physical form that had so enchanted Apollo, and under his grasping hands her feet were rooted into the ground, her body and upraised arms thickened into a tree trunk and limbs covered not with silky skin but rough bark, and her blowing hair turned into rustling leaves. The amazed Apollo was inconsolable but determined that his unrequited love would take another form, and thus decreed that the tree would remain green during both summer and winter, and that its leaves would be the badge of honor and glory for those who excelled in courage or accomplishment. Laurel wreaths were given the victors in the Pythian Games and at the first Olympics in 776 B.C. in honor of Apollo.

It was believed that laurel endowed prophets with vision, and the Pythian priestesses at Delphi, the oracle dedicated to Apollo, chewed laurel leaves to induce oracular powers. Since the leaves are mildly narcotic in large doses, they may have induced the required trance states. When the ancient Greek civilization flourished, bay branches from the sacred groves near the healing temples were gathered and woven into wreaths to honor great artistic figures, victors, heroes, and athletes. Physicians, upon completing their studies, were crowned with wreaths of berried laurel branches, the "baca lauris," and students even today receive their baccalaureate degrees.

Health Benefits

Antiseptic, relaxant. Bay has an ancient reputation of being beneficial to the health and happiness of humans. A pleasant tonic that gives tone and strength to the digestive organs, bay is especially good for soothing the stomach, relieving abdominal cramps, and relieving flatulence. Bay oil is said to benefit sprains, bruises, and skin rashes; studies show that it has bactericidal and fungicidal properties, as well as having narcotic and sedative effects on mice. In the past a decoction of the leaves was used to bring on menses and to ease childbirth, bring about a speedy delivery, and expel the afterbirth. Too much, it is said, can cause abortion. American Indians have used bay leaves in hot baths for rheumatism and place them on their heads to cure headaches. They also place a piece of the fresh leaf inside the nostril to clear the breathing passages and refresh the brain. To help prevent tooth decay, buy a toothpaste with bay in it.

Bee Balm
(Monarda didyma)
Also Known As: Bergamot, Oswego Tea

The name *Monarda* honors the Spanish physician and medical botanist Dr. Nicolas Monardes of Seville, who wrote his herbal on the flora of America in 1569, *Joyful Newes Out of the New Founde World.* Dr. Monardes called this herb bergamot because its leaf scent resembles that of the Italian bergamot orange. *Didyma* refers to the leaves, which grow in pairs. The plant received its English name *bee balm* because bees seem especially attracted to its fragrant flowers,

General Information

Bee balm is a member of the mint family native to swampy, moderately acid woodland soils of eastern North

America. In Europe bee balm is an introduced plant, first raised in 1745 by Peter Collinson from seed collected from the shores of Lake Ontario. The flowers are a startling red, borne in heads with red bracts between each floret so that the whole plant resembles a sparkling firework. Used by Native Americans, the plant has a citruslike fragrance.

Culinary Uses

Bee balm's flavor has a bright tang, reminiscent of citrus and mint, with a soft mingling of orange and lemon. Wherever you need a little zip or a little color, throw in some bee balm flowers: into a salad, or float them in a bowl of punch as a bright, colorful garnish. Use the fresh leaves in cooking and the dried leaves in tea blends. Bee balm's citrusy flavor naturally complements many fruits—strawberries, apples, oranges, and melons—as well as working well in combination with other mints.

Health Benefits

Carminative, diaphoretic, diuretic, stimulant. Herbalists recommend an infusion of bee balm for coughs, sore throats, nausea, flatulence, and menstrual cramps. A tea made from the leaves is used as a gentle febrifuge. Scientists have found that the oil contains thymol, which is antiseptic and effective against fungi, bacteria, and some parasites. In lotions and baths, infusions of bee balm stimulate the skin. The Winnebago Indians use a decoction of the leaves as a cure for pimples; Omaha braves made a pomade of the leaves for the hair. Vinegar of bergamot is useful as a scalp wash for dandruff.

Bee Pollen

General Information

A revival of interest in pollen has been slowly developing since the early 1940s, when U.S. biochemists began analyzing the contents of pollen to discover the causative agent of pollen allergies in people. To their surprise, they learned that bee pollen was extremely nutritious and contained amazingly high percentages of protein, vitamins, and minerals when compared to all other plant and animal sources. Also around this time (1945) a report from Russian biologist Nicholas Tsitin was published stating that of the 150 Russian centenarians who replied to a questionnaire inquiring about their age, occupation, and principal foods,

all replied that honey was their principal food. Further investigation by the Longevity Institute of the USSR revealed that it wasn't only honey that was eaten. In fact, it was the waste matter found in the bottom of beehives. This waste matter was largely bee pollen mixed with a small bit of honey. In 1952 a Swedish railway clerk, Gosta Carlsson, produced the first pollen collection machine and started collecting pollen on a large scale.

Bee pollen should not be confused with the pollen that is blown by the wind and is a common cause of allergies. Allergy-causing pollens are called anemophiles; they are light and easily blown by the wind. Bee pollen is heavier and stickier and is collected off bees' legs by special devices placed at the entrance to hives. This type of pollen is called entomophile, or "friend of the insects," and will rarely cause allergy symptoms. Bee pollen is the male seed of a flower blossom that has been gathered by the bees and to which special elements from the bees have been added. The bees' hairy legs are perfectly adapted for the job of pollination and for carrying back to the hive the little pellets of pollen they use for food. As a bee travels from flower to flower, she gathers from each some pollen that is mixed with nectar and certain stomach juices to hold the grains together. Eventually a small pellet is formed weighing about ten milligrams and containing around two million grains of pollen collected from perhaps two to five hundred flowers in a half-hour period. It takes twelve hundred of these pellets to fill a tablespoon, an amount that weighs approximately twelve grams and contains 2.5 billion grains of pollen.

One of the most interesting facts about bee pollen is that it cannot be synthesized in a laboratory. When researchers take away a bee's pollen-filled comb and feed her manmade pollen, the bee dies even though all the known nutrients are present in the lab-produced synthesized food. Many thousands of chemical analyses of bee pollen have been made with the very latest diagnostic equipment, but there are still some elements present in bee pollen that science cannot identify. The bees add some mysterious "extra" of their own. These unidentifiable elements may very well be the reason bee pollen works so spectacularly against so many diverse conditions of ill health.

Culinary Uses

Add bee pollen to your smoothies, fruit puddings, or bowls of mixed fruit. It gives any dish a rich, satisfying flavor.

Buy bee pollen in glass jars and refrigerate or freeze after opening. Do not heat bee pollen as that will eliminate any health benefits. The pollen at first is firm but softens quickly when mixed with juice or moist fruit.

Health Benefits

Adaptogenic, alterative, anabolic, antibiotic, anticatarrhal, antifatigue, anti-infective, antioxidant, antiseptic, antispasmodic, bacteriostatic (antibacterial), biocatalyst, calmative, detoxicant, disinfectant, diuretic, expectorant, febrifuge, immuno-stimulant, nervine, nutritive, rejuvenative, restorative, spasmolytic, stimulant (circulatory and secretolytic), tonic, and virucidal (antiviral). More than forty research studies document the therapeutic efficacy and safety of bee pollen. Clinical tests show that orally ingested bee pollen particles are rapidly and easily absorbed and that they pass directly from the stomach into the bloodstream. Within two hours after ingestion, bee pollen is found in the blood, in cerebral spinal fluids, and in the urine. Bee pollen rejuvenates your body, stimulates organs and glands, enhances vitality, and potentially brings about a longer life span. Bee pollen's ability to consistently and noticeably increase energy levels makes it a favorite substance among many world-class athletes and those interested in sustaining and enhancing quality performance.

Bee pollen contains a wide spectrum of vitamins, hormones, and carbohydrates; it has twenty-two amino acids, twenty-seven mineral salts, thousands of enzymes and coenzymes, fourteen beneficial fatty acids, and more. It is also one of the few vegetable sources rich in vitamin B_{12}. Bee pollen also contains the bioflavonoid rutin, which increases capillary strength. The sugars in bee pollen are predigested, and they convert easily to glycogen in the bloodstream, providing the necessary sugar to feed the muscles quickly. Bee pollen contains a gonadatropic hormone, similar to the pituitary hormone, gonadotropin, which functions as a sex-gland stimulant. Research was conducted at the University of Sarajevo, Yugoslavia, with a group of impotent men treated with bee pollen. After one month of ingesting honeybee pollen, over half showed an improvement in sperm production, in self-confidence, and in sexual performance. Women may use it to alleviate menstrual pain and restore regularity. Experiments show that those who take bee pollen decrease their daily intake of food by 15 to 20 percent.

Bitterroot
(*Lewisia rediviva*)
Also Known As: White Mountain Rose, Spatlum

The genus *Lewisia* commemorates Captain Meriwether Lewis (1774–1809) of the Lewis and Clark expedition; *rediviva* means "restored," or brought back to life. The English name *bitterroot* was given because the root is intensely bitter when raw.

General Information

Bitterroot is a member of the purslane family native to the western United States, from Montana, Wyoming, and Utah west to the Pacific. Probably because of its importance to the American Indians and early settlers, it was made the state flower of Montana, and the high range of mountains between Montana and Idaho received their name from this plant. This stemless perennial is amazingly tenacious. After being uprooted and dried for weeks or even months, it has the power of reviving when placed in water or in the ground, putting forth leaves and flowers. Its dark-colored roots are white and floury inside and resemble arrowroot when boiled; they have great vitality and are capable of a large yield when cultivated.

Culinary Uses

Although the fleshy roots are intensely bitter when raw, this property is chiefly removed by cooking, when they become quite succulent. From the roots the California Indians make a flour known as spatlum (or spatulum), which is surprisingly nourishing, with one ounce said to provide sufficient nourishment for a meal.

Borage
(*Borago officinalis*)

> Borage could say, and it would be true,
> I comfort the heart, I banish all rue.
>
> —Medical school of Salerno

Borage likely gets its name from the Latin root *borra* or *burra*, meaning "rough hair" or "short wool." It may also come from the Arabic *abu araq*, which means "father of sweat." *Officinalis* means "of the workshop," alluding to apothecaries' shops and signifying that the plant was once part of the official pharmacopoeia of Rome.

General Information

A member of the forget-me-not family now widely spread over Europe and North America, borage is originally a wild plant from Syria. It was spread by the Arabs in the Middle Ages and became popular as a culinary herb and as food for bees. A decorative plant, it has coarse, woolly hairs that cover its stems and leaves. In centuries past, borage was most widely known as a bee-plant and for its handsome blue or purplish racemose flowers. There is an old saying that "a garden without borage is like a heart without courage." If you want to impress your friends, try tossing a few borage leaves on the hot coals at your next barbecue. The nitrate in the leaves triggers sparks and pops, creating a mini-display of fireworks.

Culinary Uses

Borage has a fresh, slightly salty, cucumber flavor. The leaves are best when picked young and finely chopped to minimize their hairy texture. They can then be used in salads or cooked and served like spinach. Do not cook borage in an aluminum or iron pot, because the tannins can react with the metal to discolor both pot and borage. If the hairy leaves are not appealing, the stalk can be peeled and cut into chunks. The leaves and stalk are excellent added to lettuce, cucumber, or potato salads; they can also

Borage / Nutritional Value Per 100 g Edible Portion		
	Raw	Cooked
Calories	21	25
Protein	1.80 g	2.09 g
Fat	0.70 g	0.81 g
Fiber	0.92 g	1.07 g
Calcium	93 mg	102 mg
Iron	3.30 mg	3.64 mg
Magnesium	52 mg	57 mg
Phosphorus	53 mg	55 mg
Potassium	470 mg	491 mg
Sodium	80 mg	88 mg
Beta Carotene (A)	4,200 IU	4,385 IU
Thiamine (B$_1$)	0.060 mg	0.059 mg
Riboflavin (B$_2$)	0.150 mg	0.165 mg
Niacin (B$_3$)	0.900 mg	0.940 mg
Ascorbic Acid (C)	35.0 mg	32.5 mg

LORE AND LEGEND

Borage has an ancient reputation for having a wonderfully positive effect on the mind and body, and is believed to drive away sorrow, increase joyfulness, and strengthen the heart. According to old folktales, borage was sometimes smuggled into the drink of prospective husbands to give them the courage to propose marriage.

be used to enhance the flavor of iced tea and fruit drinks. The dried leaves have much less flavor than the fresh ones. The vivid blue flowers are also edible and make a tasty salad ingredient or garnish, are decorative in beverages, and can be candied and eaten as a sweet. Borage wilts rapidly, so unless it's plucked fresh from the garden, dried borage is a better option.

Health Benefits

Diaphoretic, diuretic, emollient, tonic. As its Arabic name suggests, borage stimulates sweat as well as lactation. This bland, cooling herb is a valuable remedy for reducing high fever, soothing irritation of skin and mucous membranes, restoring vitality, and treating chronic catarrh. It also strengthens the heart and is a mild laxative, sedative, and antidepressant. The leaves can be used as a poultice on inflammatory swellings because of their mucilaginous qualities and the healing powers of their natural salts (especially potassium nitrate and calcium oxalate). Borage also seems to have some calming effect on the central nervous system that make it useful for nervous conditions. Borage seeds are an excellent source of the important gamma-linoleic acid (GLA), which regulates hormones and lowers blood pressure.

Note: Internal consumption of large amounts of borage has recently been questioned for safety because of its alkaloid pyrrolizidine.

BYPRODUCTS

Borage seed oil was first used during the Middle Ages, when it was recommended to ensure good blood quality. High in gamma-linolenic acid, borage seed oil has been used to help those struggling with illnesses. This oil should only be used in small amounts, from one-quarter to one-half teaspoon daily, taken plain by mouth or poured directly onto food. It should never be used for cooking and must be kept refrigerated.

Burdock
(Arctium lappa)
Also Known As: Beggar's Button, Cockleburr, Great Burdock, Burr, Lappa

The genus name *Arctium* is derived from the Greek *arktos*, meaning "bear" (the animal), in allusion to the roughness of the burrs; *lappa* is derived either from a word meaning "to seize" or from the Celtic word *llap*, meaning "hand," on account of the plant's prehensile properties. The English name *burdock* is a combination of *bur*, from the Latin *burra*, meaning "lock of wool," such as is often found entangled with the plant when sheep have passed by, and *dock*, an Old English word for "plant."

General Information

A native of Europe, burdock is a coarse composite herb growing to four feet in height. The sticky seed balls of burdock hitchhike everywhere and have even begged a lift across the Atlantic at some stage in the past. The plant has since become naturalized in all regions of North America, where it grows alongside roads, among rubbish, and in cultivated fields. A distinctive and unmistakable plant, burdock ranks among the tallest and most space-consuming herbs, sporting extraordinarily big leaves as well as its notorious burrs. Yet considering its many values, not the least of which is that it gave the inspiration to the invention of

Velcro, it appears to be chronically undervalued. Burdock is rarely welcome in any yard, much less in carefully groomed gardens, though at least the bees and butterflies appreciate it for its generous supply of nectar. Well known for its propensity for attaching burrs to any and all who brush by, the plant seems to grow well under almost any conditions.

Culinary Uses

Tender young burdock leaves have a slightly bitter flavor but are delicious in salads, and the stems of older plants can be peeled, steamed, and served like asparagus. The long grayish-brown roots can be grated into salads, steamed as a vegetable, or sliced into soups, stews, and stir-fried dishes. They can also be boiled and then buttered and served like turnips or potatoes. Do not cook burdock in an aluminum or iron pot, because it can react with the metal to discolor both pot and plant.

Burdock / Nutritional Value Per 100 g Edible Portion			
	Dried		Dried
Calories	205	Sodium	152 mg
Protein	10.6 g	Zinc	2.20 mg
Fat	0.70 g	Manganese	6.00 mg
Fiber	7.2 g	Beta Carotene (A)	7,500 IU
Calcium	733 mg	Thiamine (B$_1$)	1.100 mg
Iron	147 mg	Riboflavin (B$_2$)	0.340 mg
Magnesium	537 mg	Niacin (B$_3$)	1.300 mg
Phosphorus	437 mg	Ascorbic Acid (C)	8.5 mg
Potassium	1,680 mg		

Health Benefits

Cholagogue, demulcent, diaphoretic, diuretic, stimulant, tonic. Burdock contains high concentrations of vitamins and minerals, especially iron, and is actually higher in minerals than beets, carrots, potatoes, or turnips. It contains between 27 percent and 45 percent inulin, a form of starch that is easily digested and the source of most of its curative powers. Volatile oils in the fresh roots account for the diaphoretic and urinary tonic effects. Burdock's overall mode of action can be described as purifying. Used both as folk medicine and in homeopathic remedies, burdock is said to neutralize and eliminate poisons from the body, promote the flow of secretions from the glands to cleanse and normalize their inner membranes, stimulate the action of the stomach, increase perspiration and the flow of urine, and cleanse and eliminate impurities from the blood. Perhaps the most widely used of all blood purifiers, it is the most important herb for treating chronic skin problems. Dried burdock root is sometimes sold in health food stores as "lappa," which is used to make burdock tea, and the tea when taken freely will help heal all kinds of skin diseases, boils, and carbuncles. It has a stimulating effect on the metabolism and gently but persistently activates and tones all the organs of elimination, thus inducing a process of inner cleansing. The leaves, roots, and tea are all used to draw impurities from the body and aid the healing process.

Burdock has a strong hypoglycemic action and is an effective painkiller that alleviates symptoms of arthritis and other inflammatory diseases. Traditionally, burdock is also considered a powerful antitumor herb, and various salves and decoctions have been prepared with it as a home treatment for this purpose. One of the better-known preparations that fall into this category is a tea known as Essiac, of which burdock is a key ingredient. German researchers confirmed antitumor activity in all parts of burdock as long ago as 1964. The Chinese also consider burdock to be a strengthening aphrodisiac.

Burnet
(Sanguisorba minor, S. officinalis)

The Latin name *Sanguisorba* means "blood absorber," from *sanguis* (blood) and *sorbeo* (to stanch), indicating its use on battlefields to stanch bleeding wounds. *Minor* is the lesser or smaller burnet, while *officinalis* means "of the

LORE AND LEGEND

In Hungary burnet is considered a mystic plant and called "Chaba's salve." Tradition says that long ago, King Chaba fought a sanguinary battle with his brother, who was attempting to usurp the throne. Fifteen thousand of Chaba's soldiers were wounded, and the good king cured every one of them with the leaves of burnet. Soldiers fighting in the American Revolution dosed themselves with a tea made from burnet on the night before a battle, on the theory that if they suffered a wound in battle the next day, the burnet in their system would keep them from bleeding to death.

workshop," alluding to apothecaries' shops and signifying that the plant was once part of the official pharmacopoeia of Rome. The English name *burnet* comes from the French diminutive for brown, *brunette*, in reference to its chestnut-brown color.

General Information

The burnets are pleasantly aromatic members of the rose family that are native to Eurasia but were introduced into North America and now are widely naturalized. A hardy perennial, they are of an ornamental character with their odd-pinnate leaves and little heads of flowers with drooping stamens. You can tell the two varieties apart by their flowers: garden or salad burnet (*S. minor*) has light green to yellow-green flowers, while greater burnet (*S. officinalis*) has red ones.

Culinary Uses

Burnet leaves are pleasantly aromatic, with a slightly nutty, cucumber-like flavor. Since the flavor fades when the leaves dry out, pick the most tender leaves and use them as soon as possible in salads, soups, casseroles, and herb butters or as a garnish for fancy dishes and cool summer drinks.

Burnet / Nutritional Value Per 100 g Edible Portion			
	Fresh		Fresh
Protein	11.1 g	Fiber	7.6–24.4 g
Fat	9.4 g		

Burnet blends especially well with rosemary, tarragon, basil, and thyme.

Health Benefits

Astringent, carminative, stomachic, tonic. Burnet has antiseptic and astringent qualities, making it useful for wounds and abrasions. Added to unfamiliar foods along with other herbs, burnet will help prevent digestive upsets. Tea made from its dried leaves is one of the best remedies for a sour stomach and is very useful for cleansing the chest, lungs, and stomach. The roots, rich in tannin, are used as an astringent and are valuable in the treatment of dysentery and enteritis. In weaker doses, a tisane of the leaves or dried roots serves as a stomachic.

Calamus Root

(Acorus calamus)
Also Known As: Sweet Flag

Acorus comes from a Greek word meaning "pertaining to the eye," and *calamus* is a Greek word for "reed canes."

General Information

Calamus is native to southern Asia. It was apparently brought to Europe via the Balkans by Turks, Tartars, and perhaps even the Crusaders. As early as the seventeenth century, it was a popular medicine as well as a culinary herb. A relative of skunk cabbage and jack-in-the-pulpit, this highly aromatic, reedlike plant resembles the cattail in appearance and frequently grows in the same locations: swamps, marshy grounds, and along sluggish streams. Grown for thousands of years for its rhizomes, which were traded as articles of commerce in the Near East, the calamus has fleshy rootstalks that grow in closely matted masses often many feet in extent. The sword-shaped leaves, which smell of tangerine when bruised, resemble those of the iris but are glossy and yellow-green, while those of the iris are dull and bluish green. The interior of the stalk is sweet—hence the name *sweet flag*.

Calamus Root / Nutritional Value Per 100 g Edible Portion			
	Fresh		Fresh
Calcium	704 mg	Sodium	45.9 mg
Iron	35.0 mg	Zinc	trace
Magnesium	110 mg	Copper	0.4 mg
Potassium	1,600 mg	Manganese	30.9 mg

Culinary Uses

The entire calamus plant has a spicy citrus fragrance. Used to flavor milk (left to soak like a vanilla pod), the leaves impart a delicious taste to creams and custards. The fleshy rootstock has a warm, pungent, rather bitter taste; it is sometimes used as a substitute for ginger, cinnamon, or nutmeg because of its spicy nature. It is also candied as a sweetmeat by confectioners. The root should not be peeled, for the vital principles lie just under the surface.

Health Benefits

Carminative, expectorant, stimulant, tonic. The rhizome contains an aromatic essential oil, tannins, and bitter principles, constituents that have a medicinal effect. Calamus was recommended to the French and British armies during the Crimean War in 1854 as a remedy against marsh pestilence, since quinine was in short supply. The pungent powder may be taken into the nose like snuff to relieve sinus congestion, common colds, or sinus headache. It acts on the higher cerebral functions and brain tissue to help expand and bring clarity to the consciousness. In Ayurvedic medicine, calamus is used to help restore mental acuity after damage done by drugs or other causes. An alcohol extract is used externally as a rub to alleviate tired and sore muscles and as a stimulating agent in baths.

Calendula

(Calendula officinalis)
Also Known As: Pot Marigold

It was the Romans who recorded that calendulas were usually in bloom on the first day, or *calends*, of every month; from this observation came the Latin generic name *Calendula*. *Officinalis* means "of the workshop," alluding to apothecaries' shops and signifying that the plant was once part of the official pharmacopoeia of Rome. The plant received its alternative English name *pot marigold* in the fourteenth century because it was called "Mary's gold" by early Christians, after Mary, mother of Jesus, and the color of its flowers, which are bright gold.

General Information

The genus *Calendula* is native to the Mediterranean region from the Canary Islands to Iran. Grown for ornament, as food for bees, and for its medicinal properties, calendula in its cultivated form was first recorded in twelfth century by

Calendula / Nutritional Value Per 100 g Edible Portion

	Fresh		Fresh
Protein	0.64 g	Calcium	3,040 mg
Fat	26.0-45.0 g	Ascorbic Acid (C)	133-310 mg

the Abbess Hildegard of Bingen. The flower heads, either whole along with the green outer bracts or the outer ray florets alone without the stalk, are used in medicines.

Culinary Uses

The brightly colored flowers of calendula used to be frequent additions to cookery. Sown with spinach, they were often cooked along with it. In the eighteenth century no serious soup in the Netherlands was served without calendula petals, which were also used to flavor oatmeal. Cooks made calendula puddings, dumplings, even wine. Used either fresh or dried, the petals impart a delicate aromatic bitterness and strong coloring to dishes. Petals and young leaves can be eaten in salads, added to decorate or color various dishes, or used in cakes, cheeses, or butter.

Health Benefits

Antiseptic, stimulant, tonic, vulnerary. Powdered calendula petals mixed with arrowroot powder, cornstarch, or pure talc make a pleasant way to soothe skin rashes for both adults and children. The crushed petals can also be soaked in olive oil or ointment to speed the healing of cuts, burns, old wounds, or scars and as a general tonic for the complexion. Bathing with calendula petals or an infusion made from them promotes the granulation of damaged tissue and has been successfully used in the treatment of minor burns, frostbite, and varicose ulcers. The plant is a good source of organic iodine, which accounts for its beneficial antiseptic qualities. For women, calendula can be especially appealing, as it helps prevent painful menstrual periods and also helps balance female hormones to ensure regular menstrual cycles.

Cane Sugar, Palm Sugar, and Rapadura Sugar

General Information

Granulated cane sugar from sugarcane juice is a mechanically processed, chemical-free product that physically resembles light brown sugar. This unrefined product has existed

LORE AND LEGEND

The history of calendula is filled with poetry and symbolism, most of which has been in reaction to an unusual characteristic that has fascinated poets and prose writers alike since early times. The golden-orange blossoms rise and open at dawn with the sun, creating the poetic image of a "weeping" flower; the flowers then brighten the day until evening, when they close down again for the night. According to German folklore, if the flowers remain closed after seven o'clock in the morning, there is a strong indication of rain.

in certain tropical areas for five thousand years; it is made simply by evaporating the water from whole sugarcane juice. With between 80 and 85 percent sucrose, it still contains the vitamins, minerals, and other nutrients present in the original cane. Although cane sugar was previously difficult to export because of fermentation resulting from its moisture content, in recent years drier, nonfermenting products are being produced in the West for the first time. One popular brand is Sucanat, a trade name that stands for "sugar cane natural." Containing up to 2.5 percent mineral salts, vitamins, and trace minerals, these fine brown granules have a faint molasses flavor and are more complete (although still processed) than regular brown or turbinado sugar. It is used just like regular refined sugar but should be stored away from excess humidity, as the granules can clump and possibly ferment. Occasionally whole sugarcane can be purchased; take it home and chew on the core for a while—it is quite delicious yet not overly sweet.

Rapadura is unrefined, evaporated cane juice. It is a natural sweetener that has all of sugarcane's minerals, vitamins, and micronutrients intact. Rapadura is made by a simple technology: juice is pressed from sugarcane and cooked to reduce its water content. Today's organic rapadura is then granulated at low temperatures. When traditionally made, this hot, concentrated cane juice is poured into cones or blocks that harden when cool and require grating before use (*rapa* in Portuguese means "to grate"; *dura* means "hard"). Rapadura is 82 percent sucrose; it is high in chromium, the nutrient that diabetics are deficient in. Like sugar, unrefined cane juice can ease

Cane Sugar / Nutritional Value Per 100 g Edible Portion

Protein	1.10 g	Beta Carotene (A)	1,600 IU
Calcium	165 mg	Thiamine (B₁)	20 mcg
Chromium	40 mcg	Riboflavin (B₂)	20 mcg
Phosphorus	50 mg	Niacin (B)	20 mcg

spasms, relieve pain, give a sense of ease and nurture, and, in the short term, boost energy. Because its vitamins, minerals, and micronutrients are intact, rapadura does not pass as quickly into the bloodstream as white sugar does; if used in excess, however, it contributes to the same health problems.

Palm sugar was used long before cane sugar; it is made from the sweet sap of the sugar palm (*Arenga pinnata* or *Borassus flabellifer*) or by tapping the tender, unopened inflorescence of the coconut, date, or toddy palm. This sweet liquid can be drunk fresh or boiled down (like maple sap) to make palm sugar. Not highly refined, palm sugar retains most of its mineral content and is available from Indian and Middle Eastern grocery stores. It is frequently sold compressed into round or rectangular shapes (which may need to be grated or melted before use), in round, slightly domed cakes, or as a thick paste. With a maple-sugar-like flavor and color that varies by brand, palm sugar is sold in Asian markets under a variety of names. Mexican piloncillo and Indian jaggery are sometimes available in ethnic or natural food markets.

Culinary Uses

Cane, palm, and rapadura sugars are easily substituted for refined white sugar. One popular use for the molded sugar is to melt it in a saucepan, strain, and then pour over pancakes or waffles.

Health Benefits

Because these types of sweetener are unrefined, they contain many more vitamins and minerals than refined white sugar. If used in excess, they still contribute to health problems.

Caper
(Capparis spinosa)

Capparis and the English *caper* come from the Greek word *kapparis*, said by some to have been derived from the Arabic name for the plant. *Spinosa* means "full of spines."

General Information

Capers are the unopened flower buds of a low, straggling, spiny shrub that grows wild on mountain slopes, principally those that border the Mediterranean Sea. They frequently inhabit old walls and cliffs, on which they provide a graceful ornament. Native to northern Africa, where the plant is known as the Sahara caper tree, it is clearly designed for desert existence, remaining green, with its stems and leaves juicy with sap, even when the soil around its roots is completely dried up. The greenish flower buds or young berries are most often pickled to bring out their strong, aromatic flavor (the result of their capric acid content).

Culinary Uses

The strongly aromatic caper is most often available pickled, although raw capers may sometimes be found. Like green olives, capers develop their unique flavor in the brine marinade. The little buds are small but explode with a burst of lemony tang. Capers form the basis of the piquant caper sauce as well as many other sauces and dressings, are useful additions to salads and hors d'oeuvres, and make an attractive garnish.

Health Benefits

Because pickled capers are high in sodium, they may increase the body's retention of fluids and raise blood pressure. For salt-free capers, grow your own bushes, which thrive in mild-winter climates.

Caper / Nutritional Value Per 100 g Edible Portion

	Fresh		Fresh
Protein	19.0-22.0 g	Fat	31.6-36.0 g

Caraway
(Carum carvi)

Carum is probably derived from the Caria region in Asia Minor and *carvi* from the Latin *carui*, meaning "dear" or "costly." The English name *caraway* comes from the ancient Arabic name *karawya*, by which it is still known.

General Information

Of unknown origin, the oldest caraway seeds found to date were discovered in Neolithic lake settlements in Switzerland. A biennial, caraway usually produces only leaves during its first year of life and then flowers during its second—and final—year. The ancient Romans may first have received caraway from Gaul, where it was used to season sausages. These flavorful seeds were introduced to Britain during the Victorian age by Prince Albert, who was extremely fond of them. A member of the carrot family, caraway is also sometimes called "Roman cumin" because the ground seed has a flavor similar to, but lighter than, ground cumin. Although found in many meadow plant communities in Eurasia, the caraway used for culinary and medicinal purposes is not obtained from wild plants but only from those especially cultivated for this purpose. The plant's thin, crescent-shaped seeds have a strong flavor that gives rye bread and kummel (a popular liqueur) their characteristic tastes, which not everyone enjoys.

Culinary Uses

The flavor of caraway is pleasantly warm and spicy but rather sharp, seeming to combine both anise and dill but with a tang and surprising nuttiness. A popular feature of German and Austrian cooking, caraway is used in sauerkraut, baked goods, cheese spreads and dips, vegetable dishes, and sweet pickles. Add caraway seeds after the dish is cooked, since long cooking may turn their flavor bitter. The seeds can also be ground and used as a substitute for cumin in homemade curry or chili powders. Young caraway leaves, which have a stronger dill flavor than the seeds, can

Caraway / Nutritional Value Per 100 g Edible Portion		
	Whole Seed	1 tsp.
Calories	333	7
Protein	19.77 g	0.42 g
Fat	14.59 g	0.31 g
Fiber	12.65 g	0.27 g
Calcium	689 mg	14 mg
Iron	16.23 mg	0.34 mg
Magnesium	258 mg	5 mg
Phosphorus	568 mg	12 mg
Potassium	1,351 mg	28 mg
Sodium	17 mg	trace
Zinc	5.500 mg	0.120 mg
Copper	0.910 mg	n/a
Manganese	1.300 mg	n/a
Beta Carotene (A)	363 IU	8 IU
Thiamine (B$_1$)	0.383 mg	0.008 mg
Riboflavin (B$_2$)	0.379 mg	0.008 mg
Niacin (B$_3$)	3.606 mg	0.076 mg

LORE AND LEGEND

Centuries ago caraway was believed to have retentive properties. Love potions were laced with caraway to attract and magnetize a person's love; people also mingled caraway seeds with their prized possessions, in the hope that the seeds would protect their goods from theft, or magically hold any would-be thief in place until the owner returned.

be used to add flavor to many kinds of salads, soups, and cheeses. The root is also edible; having a slightly carrotlike taste, it is generally boiled and served like parsnips.

Health Benefits

Antispasmodic, carminative, emmenagogue, expectorant, stomachic. Caraway is said to strengthen and tone the stomach, prevent fermentation in the stomach, aid the digestion of heavy starches, promote the onset of menstruation, and relieve uterine and intestinal cramping. To treat flatulent infant colic or as a general stomach settler (for child and adult alike), caraway is especially recommended. The main medicinal constituent of the seeds is an essential oil that contains carvone, limonene, and other substances.

Cardamom
(Elettaria cardamomum)

Elettari was the name of the plant in Malabar, a region in India where the best-quality cardamom is still grown. *Cardamomum* comes from the Greek *kardamon* (peppergrass) and *anomon* (fragrant spice plant).

General Information

The cardamom plant is a tropical shrub of the ginger family native to India and Ceylon. It is the world's third most expensive spice, behind saffron and vanilla, because each seedpod must be hand-picked. Sold whole or ground, the pods may be either green (dried indoors in large kilns, resulting in a mild flavor) or a creamy white (bleached; these have the least flavor). Brown cardamom pods are not true cardamom but a related variety, with a flavor and texture not as delicate or pleasant as the green variety. The

LORE AND LEGEND

Because of its superb aroma, cardamom was burned as an offering to the gods and became an ingredient in many perfumes. The alluring power of cardamom is said to increase the strength of marriages and all types of unions, and the ground-up seeds are used to make love potions.

Vikings brought this exotic spice back to their homeland from their long voyages to the spice centers of the East, and it is a popular feature in Scandinavian and other northern European cuisines. Since cardamom contains the same chemical, eucalyptol, that is found in bay leaves, it may help repel household pests. Try a few seedpods in your flour canister; even if it doesn't work, it will at least make the flour smell wonderful.

Culinary Uses

Cardamom has a delightfully pleasant aroma, faintly reminiscent of pine and eucalyptus. The flavor is rich and deep yet airy, gingerlike with a touch of lemon. Because it rapidly loses flavor when ground, this spice is best purchased whole, in its pods. The dark brown or black seeds can then be removed from within the pods and ground as needed. The seed may also be roasted to heighten its warming sweetness. Cardamom's most frequent use is in baked goods and desserts, especially Danish pastries, but it is also a frequent addition to curries, rice dishes, and spiced wine.

Health Benefits

Carminative, stimulant. The seeds contain essential oils that make cardamom a stimulant like cinnamon or ginger. Chewing on the seeds is said to relieve flatulence and indigestion, reduce pain, sharpen the mind, open the bronchial tubes, warm the body, and sweeten the breath.

Carob
(Ceratonia siliqua)

> And John himself was clothed in camel's hair,
> with a leather belt around his waist; and his food
> was locusts [carob pods] and wild honey.
>
> —MATTHEW 3:4

Ceratonia comes from the Greek word *keras*, meaning "horn," in reference to the large pod; *siliqua* is Latin for "pod" or "husk." The Arabic word for "sweetness," *kharru bah*, is generally believed to be the origin for the English word *carob*.

General Information

The carob tree is native to southwestern Europe and western Asia but is also widely cultivated in the Mediterranean region. Peasants have virtually lived on the pods during times of famine, but the tree is valued mostly for providing great amounts of pods for livestock feed. Spanish missionaries introduced the carob into Mexico and southern California, and groves of carob still grow in these regions. This dome-shaped evergreen tree, with its dark green, glossy leaves and small, clustered red flowers, can grow to heights of fifty feet. A ten- or twelve-year-old tree can bear up to one hundred pounds of pods annually. Each long brown seedpod holds five to fifteen seeds within sweet pulp; those grown in Sicily have particularly sweet, fleshy pulp. The pods are harvested in September by shaking the branches of the tree with long sticks; after the pods are sun-dried, the seeds are removed and the pulp ground into carob powder. The seeds are the source of

Cardamom / Nutritional Value Per 100 g Edible Portion		
	Ground	1 tsp.
Calories	311	6
Protein	10.76 g	0.21 g
Fat	6.70 g	0.13 g
Fiber	11.29 g	0.23 g
Calcium	383 mg	8 mg
Iron	13.97 mg	0.28 mg
Magnesium	229 mg	5 mg
Phosphorus	178 mg	4 mg
Potassium	1,119 mg	22 mg
Sodium	18 mg	trace
Zinc	7.470 mg	0.150 mg
Copper	0.383 mg	n/a
Manganese	28.000 mg	n/a
Beta Carotene (A)	trace	n/a
Thiamine (B₁)	0.198 mg	0.004 mg
Riboflavin (B₂)	0.182 mg	0.004 mg
Niacin (B₃)	1.102 mg	0.022 mg

locust bean gum (carob gum), an additive used in ice creams, cheeses, and confections to improve the texture by thickening and stabilizing the food. Carob syrup is made by dissolving the powder in water and boiling the mixture until it has the consistency of honey.

Culinary Uses

The big, handsome, brown carob pods can be eaten fresh and unprocessed out of hand. They are sweet and chewy, something like hard dates. Broken pods smell faintly like Limburger cheese but taste much better. Generally the pods are roasted and ground into a powder (flour) that is used in place of chocolate, owing to the similarity of color, texture, and cooking properties. Both raw and roasted forms of carob powder may be available; the raw is preferred for baking, since it is more flavorful when cooked for the first time. Roasted carob powder is generally used for mixing in liquids to produce carob-flavored drinks, hot or cold. It is a good substitute for hot cocoa or for chocolate flavoring in milk shakes and smoothies. Substitute equal amounts of carob powder for cocoa in recipes. When substituting for chocolate, use three tablespoons of carob

Carob / Nutritional Value Per 100 g Edible Portion		
	Flour	1 Tbsp.
Calories	180	14
Protein	4.62 g	0.37 g
Fat	0.65 g	0.05 g
Fiber	7.19 g	0.58 g
Calcium	348 mg	28 mg
Iron	2.94 mg	0.24 mg
Magnesium	54 mg	4 mg
Phosphorus	79 mg	6 mg
Potassium	827 mg	66 mg
Sodium	35 mg	3 mg
Zinc	0.920 mg	0.070 mg
Copper	0.571 mg	0.046 mg
Manganese	0.508 mg	0.041 mg
Beta Carotene (A)	14 IU	1 IU
Thiamine (B$_1$)	0.053 mg	0.004 mg
Riboflavin (B$_2$)	0.461 mg	0.037 mg
Niacin (B$_3$)	1.897 mg	0.152 mg
Pantothenic Acid (B$_5$)	0.047 mg	0.004 mg
Pyridoxine (B$_6$)	0.366 mg	0.029 mg
Folic Acid (B$_9$)	29.0 mcg	2.3 mcg
Ascorbic Acid (C)	0.20 mg	0 mg

LORE AND LEGEND

Legend has it that Saint John the Baptist once survived in the wilderness by eating locust beans (carob pods) and wild honey, hence carob's nickname of "Saint John's Bread." The word *locust* was originally applied only to the carob tree; later it was also applied to migratory and other grasshoppers, along with a number of other leguminous trees with pinnate leaves and oblong pods. The seeds at one time served as the original "carat" weight measurement for goldsmiths.

powder plus one tablespoon of water for each one-ounce square of chocolate. Since carob powder is 46 percent natural sugar, less sweetener should be used than when using cocoa or unsweetened chocolate. Carob chips are made from barley malt, corn malt, carob powder, and lecithin; since they contain no refined sugar or dairy solids, they are preferred by many for baking over chocolate chips. The roasted seeds have served as a substitute for or adulterant of coffee in Europe.

Health Benefits

Carob powder contains pectin, which is good for regulating digestion. Unlike chocolate, it contains a negligible amount of fat, is naturally sweet (with 46 percent sugar, including sucrose), contains no caffeine, and encourages the absorption of calcium. Sweet, light, and dry, carob is alkaline in nature and nourishes the lungs. It does, however, contain a notable level of tannin—as do cocoa, coffee, and tea—which inhibits the absorption of protein. This may depress the growth rate of young animals, and therefore it is recommended that carob be used in moderation, especially for young children.

Cassia
(Cinnamomum cassia)

The scientific name *Cinnamomum* derives from the Hebraic and Arabic term *amomon*, meaning "fragrant spice plant," and with the prefix -*kin* means "fragrant spice plant of China." The English name *cassia* is of Semitic origin.

General Information

Cassia is the bark of an evergreen tree related to true cinnamon (*Cinnamomum zeylanicum*). It grows wild, especially in the Chinese province of Kwangsi and in Tonkin and Annam in Indochina. Cassia has a stronger scent than cinnamon and instead of tan is a reddish-brown color. Sticks of true cinnamon look like quills, forming a single tube, while those of cassia are rolled from both sides toward the center so that they look like scrolls. Cassia buds, the dried fruit of the cassia tree, are highly aromatic spices that look like cloves; in China they are used for adding a cinnamon flavor to candy and sweet pickles. However, the "cassia blossoms" sold in Asian markets are not truly the blossoms of the cassia tree but are from a member of the jasmine family (*Osmanthus fragrans*); These yellow flowers are sold preserved in a sweetened brine and are used to perfume sweets such as lotus seed soup, various pastries, steamed pears, and Chinese teas and wines. They are also sold embalmed in a sugary paste called "cassia blossom jam."

Culinary Uses

The taste of cassia has been described as warm and very spicy, yet coarser than true cinnamon, with an odor recalling that of the bedbug. If you were to taste plain cassia and plain cinnamon, you would find cassia bitter and cinnamon warm and sweet. Never sold under its own name, cassia bark may be ground and mixed with cinnamon to be marketed as "ground cinnamon" or rolled and sold as "cinnamon sticks." The leaves also have a cassia flavor and can be used as a flavoring like bay leaves. The buds, which look a little like cloves, are useful where a slight cinnamon flavor is needed. While we tend to associate cinnamon (and thus cassia) with sweets, it was first valued as a meat preservative. According to ancient texts,

> ## LORE AND LEGEND
>
> One Chinese legend tells of the celestial World Tree, a cassia or cinnamon tree, that has been growing since time immemorial to an incredible height in Paradise, a garden located far up in the Tibetan Mountains at the source of the Hwang-Ho, or Yellow River. Whoever enters Paradise and eats of the fruit of this tree will gain bliss and immortality.

its culinary value lay with its ability to "eliminate the stench of raw flesh"; it does contain phenols that inhibit the bacteria responsible for putrefaction.

Health Benefits

Cassia has properties similar to cinnamon, but weaker. It contains 1 to 2 percent volatile oil (cassia oil), which is mainly responsible for its spicy aroma and taste. The volatile oil contains many chemicals used in the manufacture of fragrances or flavorings; cinnamaldehyde, the one present in the highest amount (75 to 90 percent), has been demonstrated in scientific experiments to have sedative and pain-relieving effects on mice. Like other bark materials, cassia also contains tannins, sugars, resins, and mucilage, among other constituents. Both cassia and cinnamon have been used for thousands of years in Eastern and Western cultures in treating chronic diarrhea, rheumatism, colds, high blood pressure, kidney conditions, and abdominal pains. Cassia's first recorded use dates back to the Han Dynasty (200 B.C.–A.D. 200), when it was described in the Shennong herbal under the nontoxic category of herbs. It is now considered slightly toxic and to have warming effects. When ingested in relatively large amounts (1.3 ounces and over), it creates toxic symptoms, including dizziness, blurred vision, cough, dry thirst, and decreased urine flow.

Catnip

(Nepeta cataria)
Also Known As: Catmint, Catswort, Field Balm

The name *Nepeta* may derive from the city of Nepi (called Nepete by the Etruscans) in Tuscany, where catnip once grew in great profusion and where it was highly valued.

Cassia / Nutritional Value Per 100 g Edible Portion			
	Dried		**Dried**
Protein	4.3 g	Sodium	4.2-28.7 mg
Fat	3.5 g	Zinc	0.4-1.0 mg
Fiber	27.0 g	Copper	0.2-1.0 mg
Calcium	490-1,357 mg	Manganese	16.7-60.0 mg
Iron	2.5-42.1 mg	Thiamine (B$_1$)	0.100 mg
Magnesium	77-168 mg	Riboflavin (B$_2$)	0.100-0.200 mg
Phosphorus	100 mg	Ascorbic Acid (C)	30.9 mg
Potassium	302-1,550 mg		

Cataria derives from the Latin *catus*, meaning "cat." The English name *catnip* came from the habit cats have of nipping off the leaves to chew with relish.

General Information

Catnip is a temperate herb of the mint family that originated in the milder climes of Europe, Asia, and Africa. The herb was brought to North America about 1620 by a certain Captain John Mason, who considered it one of eleven essential herbs for the fisherman's garden in Newfoundland, and it became a popular everyday tea. Upon its introduction, it quickly escaped from cultivated gardens and spread rapidly across the continent. The plant secretes an oil to ward off insects, but it attracts cats that, in their ecstatic rolling and rubbing, may completely demolish the plants. Although many people think of this herb only in connection with cats, it has a long history of human use. It was a popular garden herb earlier in European history and was used for many centuries in cooking and for medicinal use. Catnip tea was a popular beverage before the importation of Indian and Chinese tea to Europe. Catnip is also helpful around the house, ridding it of pesky ants if you sprinkle their trails with some crushed leaves; they evidently dislike the smell and will leave your house alone.

Culinary Uses

Catnip leaves can be used to add a minty flavor to salads. The young leaves can also be used in the manner of basil to make a flavorful pesto. To get the most flavor from the leaves, chop or rub them against the side of a colander or sieve to release the flavorful oils.

Health Benefits

Aromatic, antispasmodic, carminative, diaphoretic, emmenagogue, tonic. Catnip benefits the body by quieting the nervous system. Tea made from the steeped (not boiled) leaves relieves stomach gas or cramps, aids digestion, helps

LORE AND LEGEND

Early Americans settlers believed eating dried catnip roots made even the kindest person mean. Thus, executioners and hangmen would eat it to ensure the courage and proper mood necessary to carry out their duties.

clean out excess mucus in the body, and is efficacious in the treatment of iron-deficiency anemia, menstrual and uterine disorders, and dyspepsia. Well into the twentieth century, a simmering pot of catnip tea was a fixture on the back burner of many American homes, awaiting colds, fevers, stomach upset, or sleeplessness. Chewing a leaf reportedly relieves headaches. Some find that hot catnip tea taken at bedtime works as a mild sedative and thus helps them sleep better. Researchers at Iowa State University report that nepetalactone, the essential oil in catnip that gives the plant its characteristic odor, is about ten times more effective at repelling mosquitoes than DEET—the compound used in most commercial insect repellents. The same research group discovered that catnip also repels cockroaches.

Note: Herbalists and doctors say it is best to stay clear of catnip if you are pregnant or plan on being pregnant in the near future.

Cayenne
(Capsicum annuum, C. minimum)

The word *capsicum* arrived on the scene in 1700 under the auspices of Joseph Pitton de Tournefort, early plant taxonomist and plant hunter for the spectacular gardens of Louis XIV. It most likely derives either from the Latin *capsa*, meaning "box," for the hollow, boxlike shape of the fruit, or from the Greek *kapto*, meaning "to bite," for the pepper's acrid, tongue-searing pungency. The term *annuum* signifies an annual plant, while *minimum* means "very small," pertaining to some of the fruit's diminutive size. The English name *cayenne* came from the ground dried chili peppers called *kian* native to Cayenne Island, capital of French Guiana.

Catnip / Nutritional Value Per 100 g Edible Portion			
	Dried		Dried
Calories	n/a	Magnesium	207 mg
Protein	9.8 g	Phosphorus	241 mg
Fat	n/a	Potassium	2,350 mg
Fiber	n/a	Sodium	trace
Calcium	616 mg	Zinc	trace
Iron	138 mg	Manganese	37.400 mg

Cayenne / Nutritional Value Per 100 g Edible Portion		
	Dried Ground	1 tsp.
Calories	318	6
Protein	12.01 g	0.22 g
Fat	17.27 g	0.31 g
Fiber	24.88 g	0.45 g
Calcium	148 mg	3 mg
Iron	7.80 mg	0.14 mg
Magnesium	152 mg	3 mg
Phosphorus	293 mg	5 mg
Potassium	2,014 mg	36 mg
Sodium	30 mg	1 mg
Zinc	2.480 mg	0.050 mg
Copper	0.373 mg	n/a
Manganese	2.000 mg	n/a
Beta Carotene (A)	41,610 IU	749 IU
Thiamine (B$_1$)	0.328 mg	0.006 mg
Riboflavin (B$_2$)	0.919 mg	0.017 mg
Niacin (B$_3$)	8.701 mg	0.157 mg
Ascorbic Acid (C)	76.44 mg	1.38 mg

General Information

Cayenne peppers are native to the warmer regions of Asia and America and are cultivated in almost all parts of the world. With its oddly shaped fruit and its colorful presence, the shrubby cayenne plant is as unusual looking as it is biting to the tongue. The hot, pungent spice is made from the dried pods, although other spices are often added to the powder in its commercial form. Varying in color from orange-red to deep red, cayenne is sometimes labeled simply "red pepper." Cayenne from Sierre Leone in Africa is said to be the most pungent and medicinal. Used as a fumigant, cayenne is safe and effective in ridding buildings of vermin. Put a heaping tablespoon of the dried and powdered pepper in a shallow pan over a low flame and allow the fumes to pervade the air. Mice, rats, and even cockroaches abhor the fumes, which are quite harmless to humans and domestic pets. Another good use is to sprinkle a little in your shoes to warm up cold toes.

Culinary Uses

Cayenne is very hot and should therefore be used delicately and respectfully. It can be added to impart a spark to almost any dish, but its most common uses are in white sauces, soups, and stews. Common paprika is the mildest form of cayenne and is also the form with the highest vitamin C content. Cayenne peppers are available in various forms: whole fresh, whole dried, crushed dried, or ground. Select according to recipe specifications.

Health Benefits

Appetizer, digestive, stimulant, tonic. Cayenne is said to be the purest and most certain stimulant, producing a natural warmth and improving circulation. It helps the digestion when taken with meals, arouses all the secreting organs, helps heal stomach and intestinal ulcers, has a cleansing action upon the large intestine and sweat glands, and helps to evacuate the bowel and destroy worms and parasites. Cayenne is good for colds, coughs, and congestion; it produces a natural warmth when used as a poultice for pneumonia and other acute congestions. Don't forget that cayenne is also good for depression. A little cayenne on the tip of tongue will lessen and sometimes completely remove depression. For travelers, a container of red cayenne pepper or a small bottle of pepper sauce (cayenne in vinegar) is a sensible protection in countries where the preparation and serving of food is not always sanitary; cayenne also protects against amebic dysentery.

Celery Seed
(Apium graveolens)

Apium derives either from the Latin *apis*, meaning "bee," because bees go dotty over its tiny white flowers, or from a prehistoric Indo-European word for "water," which would also be appropriate since celery prefers wet soils and salt marshes. *Graveolens* means "heavy-scented." The common name *celery* derives from its remedial reputation—from the Latin *celer*, meaning "quick-acting" or "swift."

General Information
Celery seeds are the dried fruit of a variety of wild celery popularly known as smallage. They are one of the smallest of all the seeds used as flavorings; about 760,000 seeds are required to make just one pound. The seeds are much more intensely aromatic than the leaves or stalks of the plant because they contain proportionally more of the flavorful oil. The wild plant itself is tough and inedible, with an acrid, unpleasant taste. During the seventeenth century, Italian gardeners developed both the familiar stalk celery and celeriac from the wild plant.

Culinary Uses
Celery seed can be used in almost any dish calling for fresh celery. It adds zest to salads, roasts, sauces, and stews. The seeds are also ground and mixed with salt to make "celery salt."

Celery Seed / Nutritional Value Per 100 g Edible Portion		
	Whole Seeds	1 tsp.
Calories	392	8
Protein	18.07 g	0.36 g
Fat	25.27 g	0.50 g
Fiber	11.85 g	0.24 g
Calcium	1,767 mg	35 mg
Iron	44.90 mg	0.90 mg
Magnesium	440 mg	9 mg
Phosphorus	547 mg	11 mg
Potassium	1,400 mg	28 mg
Sodium	160 mg	3 mg
Zinc	6.930 mg	0.140 mg
Copper	1.370 mg	n/a
Manganese	7.567 mg	n/a
Beta Carotene (A)	52 IU	1 IU
Ascorbic Acid (C)	17.14 mg	0.34 mg

LORE AND LEGEND

The ancient Greeks prized celery and gave awards of celery or celery wine to winning athletes. Celery elixirs have been used in healing throughout history, and legend has it that celery was an ingredient of the love potion that had such dire effects on Tristan and Isolde. Medieval magicians, it was believed, tucked celery seeds into their shoes in order to fly.

Health Benefits
Carminative, diuretic, stimulant, tonic. Pharmacologists confirm that celery seed is a carminative, and effective for the relief of gas pains. This herb has been highly recommended for rheumatism and flatulence and as an appetite stimulant.

Chamomile
(Chamaemelum nobile, Anthemis nobilis, Matricaria recutita)
Also Known As: Camomile, Matricaria, Anthemis, Ground Apple

Because the Greeks noted that the plant had apple-scented characteristics, they named it *chamomile*, from *chamai* (on the ground) and *melon* (apple). *Anthemis* comes from the Greek word *anthemon*, meaning "flower," in reference to the great number of flowers the plant produces. *Nobile* and *nobilis* mean "noble" or "famous." The name *Matricaria* is either from the Latin root words *mater* and *cara*, meaning "beloved mother," or from *matrix*, meaning "womb," after the plant's use in treating female disorders. *Recutita* means "skinless," or apparently bare of epidermis. The Spanish call this plant *manzanilla*, which means "little apple." Referring to its medicinal properties, the Germans call it *alles zutraut*, which means "capable of anything."

General Information
Chamomile is actually not one herb but two botanically unrelated plants of the daisy family that produce the same light blue oil used in healing since ancient times. Both have downy stems, pale green feathery leaves, daisylike flowers with yellow centers and white rays, and a distinct apple-like

fragrance and flavor. The flowers are the only edible parts of the plants. Roman chamomile (*Chamaemelum nobile* or *Anthemis nobilis*) is native to western Europe. A perennial plant that rarely exceeds nine inches, it is often used as a ground cover for garden paths. It forms a carpet of fine, ferny foliage that will stay lush if mowed a few times during the summer. The plant does best when occasionally stepped on, since walking on it releases the herb's lovely apple fragrance and does not hurt the plant. German chamomile (*Matricaria recutita*, also known as sweet false chamomile), believed native to southern Europe, is an annual that reaches three feet in height. The German variety is used most frequently medicinally because it is less expensive than the Roman and more concentrated in valuable chemical constituents. Most Roman chamomile is somewhat bitter, and its primary use is in potpourri rather than tea.

Culinary Uses

Only the flowers of chamomile are used. As a flavoring agent, chamomile appears in alcoholic beverages such as vermouth and some bitter tonics, as well as in a variety of teas, desserts, and candies. The flowers can be added fresh or dried to salads or steeped to make an apple-scented tea. Use fresh flowers or a well-sealed tea bag since the volatile oils dissipate rapidly.

Health Benefits

Antispasmodic, aromatic, carminative, tonic. Chamomile soothes, deodorizes, and cleanses wherever there is chaos in the form of flatulence, disturbed metabolism, congestion, cramps, diarrhea, insomnia, or anxiety. The major effects of chamomile are a result of its volatile oils; these actions are strongest on the liver and kidneys, where the oils stimulate the organs to purge themselves of toxins. These oils (including azulene) are bactericidal and fungicidal, espe-

LORE AND LEGEND

Chamomile was cherished by the ancient Egyptians, who claimed that its aromatic tea was a mild elixir of youth. They dedicated it to the sun and worshiped it above all other herbs for its healing properties. In Beatrix Potter's classic Tale of Peter Rabbit, after Peter was chased from Mr. MacGregor's garden, he went scurrying home in great fright. When he arrived, his mother sent him to bed with a cup of soothing chamomile tea to calm his fear.

cially against certain staph bacteria and *Candida albicans*. A cup of chamomile tea, probably the most popular herbal tea, made from three or four fresh flowers to a cupful of boiling water, will soothe and calm fevers and colds, headaches, upset stomachs, flatulence and colic, menstrual cramps, pain and swelling caused by arthritis or injury, and diarrhea. It is an excellent children's remedy, gently calming colicky infants and teething babies. When kids are cranky and irritable, give them a warm chamomile bath by brewing a large pot of tea and pouring the strained tea into the bathtub. As a topical remedy, chamomile soothes the skin and promotes healing, helps soothe burns, sunburn, diaper rash, and even radiation burns. Chamomile is also a frequent ingredient in rinses for blond hair.

Hungarian or German chamomile is derived from wild plants, and its oil is used externally in dental caries and in the ear canal for pain. Roman chamomile was cultivated for medicinal use in Saxony. Its oil is used externally as a rub for hard swellings and pains in the joints. A simple way to make chamomile oil, according to the Egyptians, is to take fresh (preferably) or dry flowers of chamomile (one ounce) and beat them up with pure olive oil. Steep the flowers in the oil for twenty-four hours or more, until their virtues have been extracted, then strain. This oil can then be used as a rub for rheumatism and for massaging overstrained or cramped muscles.

Note: This herb is not recommended during pregnancy, as some herbalists consider it too relaxing to the uterus. Also, some people with hay fever who are sensitive to ragweed, asters, or related plants may be sensitive to chamomile.

Chamomile / Nutritional Value Per 100 g Edible Portion			
	German, Dried		German, Dried
Calories	299	Sodium	258 mg
Protein	11.5 g	Zinc	trace
Fat	3.9 g	Manganese	5.200 mg
Fiber	7.2 g	Beta Carotene (A)	365 IU
Calcium	672 mg	Thiamine (B₁)	0.080 mg
Iron	17 mg	Riboflavin (B₂)	0.430 mg
Magnesium	292 mg	Niacin (B₃)	14.900 mg
Phosphorus	322 mg	Ascorbic Acid (C)	26.7 mg
Potassium	1,320 mg		

Chervil
(Anthriscus cerefolium)
Also Known As: Skirret

Anthriscus derives from the Greek *anthriskos*, probably referring to an anther or beard of grain. *Cerefolium* means "wax-leaved." The English name *chervil* comes from a Greek word meaning "cheer leaf" or "leaf of rejoicing."

General Information
Chervil is of eastern European and Russian origin and was introduced into the Mediterranean region around 400 B.C. The Greeks used it, as we do today, to flavor other foods, but the Romans also cooked it as a vegetable in its own right. The Romans later introduced it to France and Britain, where it found enthusiastic favor in the kitchen. A fernlike annual plant related to carrots, chervil may have either curly or flat leaves; both have the same pleasant flavor, but the curled leaf makes a more decorative garnish. It has been called "gourmet's parsley" since it has a more delicate flavor than parsley and is sweeter and more aromatic, with a scent some say resembles tarragon.

Culinary Uses
Chervil is a subtly aromatic herb that provides a mild, slightly sweet, tender flavor that is part anise and part parsley. Its taste and fragrance fill the senses the way warmth does, slowly, softly, subtly. Although it is available dried, for the very best results it should be used fresh—

LORE AND LEGEND

Because chervil's flavor and fragrance resemble the myrrh brought by the wise men to the baby Jesus, and because chervil symbolized new life, it became traditional in Europe to serve chervil soup on Holy Thursday.

either finely chopped or in tiny sprigs. Its delicate flavor is destroyed by cooking, so it is best used raw or added when the dish is nearly ready. Chervil is an essential ingredient in French cooking, lending its sweet fragrance and flavor to salads and salad dressings, herbal soups, sauces, and vegetables. It is one of the four essential ingredients in the classic French blend fines herbes (the others being chives, parsley, and tarragon). Use it generously in the kitchen; it never overpowers but rather enhances and improves the combination of other herbal flavors.

Health Benefits
Digestive, diuretic, expectorant, stimulant. Chervil has long been used as a spring tonic; it is said to have blood-cleansing and diuretic qualities, as well as having a mild stimulant effect on all functions of the metabolism.

Chickweed
(Stellaria media)

This little plant got its Latin name *Stellaria* because of the starlike (*stella*) shape of its delicate white flowers. *Media* means "medium" or "intermediate," serving to distinguish this plant from both larger and smaller relatives. The plant in English is called chickweed (and was formerly called chickenweed) because chickens and other birds relish the seeds and young foliage. Its ancient Latin name was *Morsus gallinae*, meaning "a bite or morsel for hens."

General Information
The ubiquitous chickweed has changed little since Neolithic times. Before written history it was gathered on the plains of India, as it was gathered later in Greece and Rome, because it was an edible green that provided food through the colder months. In Elizabethan days the plant was gathered to feed falcons, as it had been observed that

Chervil / Nutritional Value Per 100 g Edible Portion		
	Dried	1 tsp.
Calories	237	1
Protein	23.20 g	0.14 g
Fat	3.90 g	0.02 g
Fiber	11.30 g	0.07 g
Calcium	1,346 mg	8 mg
Iron	31.95 mg	0.19 mg
Magnesium	130 mg	1 mg
Phosphorus	450 mg	3 mg
Potassium	4,740 mg	28 mg
Sodium	83 mg	trace
Zinc	8.800 mg	0.050 mg
Copper	0.440 mg	n/a
Manganese	2.100 mg	n/a
Pyridoxine (B$_6$)	1.225 mg	0.007 mg

Chickweed / Nutritional Value Per 100 g Edible Portion			
	Dried		Dried
Calories	213	Sodium	147 mg
Protein	21.7 g	Zinc	5.200 mg
Fat	4.8 g	Manganese	15.300 mg
Fiber	10.8 g	Beta Carotene (A)	7,229 IU
Calcium	1,210 mg	Thiamine (B₁)	0.210 mg
Iron	253 mg	Riboflavin (B₂)	0.130 mg
Magnesium	529 mg	Niacin (B₃)	4.700 mg
Phosphorus	448 mg	Ascorbic Acid (C)	6.9 mg
Potassium	1,840 mg		

flocks of wild birds sought out patches of it as winter feed. Although its arrival in America is not recorded, Puritan housewives most likely brought it with them to grow in their dooryard gardens. The New England climate proved extremely hospitable, and now the prolific weed is easily found in gardens, fields, waste places, cultivated grounds, and woods over most of the country. Chickweed is so common because it blooms as early as March and continues blooming throughout the summer months, with its seeds easily scattered by the wind.

Culinary Uses

Chickweed has no scent, a pleasantly salty taste, and a flavor of mild cabbage. Some eat it cooked like spinach as a vegetable, while others prefer it raw as a salad green. The young leaves are the best tasting, and the plant should be used only when fresh.

Health Benefits

Carminative, demulcent, emollient, laxative, refrigerant. Chickweed is a mild-acting herb that is probably best known as one of the traditional country herbs taken to cleanse the kidneys and liver after a winter of heavy eating. Healing and soothing anything it comes in contact with, chickweed dissolves plaque in blood vessels and carries out toxins. Its most popular use is as a poultice on external abscesses and rashes, where it removes the heat of infection and draws out poisons. It is a mild diuretic, but the effect is only temporary, as the body produces cholesterin to neutralize this effect after about a week.

Chicory

(Cichorium intybus)

Also Known As: Coffeeweed, Blue Sailors, Wild Endive, Blue Dandelion, Succory

Cichorium (from the Greek *kichoreia*) and *intybus* both come from old names of unknown meaning for the plant. The English name *chicory* derives from the Greek through the French *chicoree*.

General Information

Chicory, a member of the sunflower family and closely related to lettuce and dandelion, is native to temperate and northern subtropical regions of Europe, western Asia, and North Africa. It was cultivated by the Egyptians and exported to Rome during Cleopatra's reign. The plant came early to North America with the colonists as a medicinal herb, but Thomas Jefferson and others grew it as a forage crop, as had been done in Europe. Because it does not dry well for hay, it was usually cut and fed green to horses, cattle, sheep, poultry, and rabbits. Chicory quickly escaped from cultivation and became a naturalized weed in pastures and fields, and now grows along much of the country's roadsides. Its leaves resemble those of the dandelion sufficiently to have earned it the occasional nickname *blue dandelion*, and its delicate blue flowers open and close again with clocklike regularity in the morning hours. Chicory

Chicory / Nutritional Value Per 100 g Edible Portion		
	Raw Leaves	Raw Roots
Calories	23	73
Protein	1.70 g	1.40 g
Fat	0.30 g	0.20 g
Fiber	0.80 g	1.95 g
Calcium	100 mg	41 mg
Iron	0.90 mg	0.80 mg
Magnesium	30 mg	22 mg
Phosphorus	47 mg	61 mg
Potassium	420 mg	290 mg
Sodium	45 mg	50 mg
Beta Carotene (A)	4,000 IU	6 IU
Thiamine (B₁)	0.060 mg	0.040 mg
Riboflavin (B₂)	0.100 mg	0.030 mg
Niacin (B₃)	0.500 mg	0.400 mg
Ascorbic Acid (C)	24.0 mg	5.0 mg

LORE AND LEGEND

According to folktale, the flowers of chicory are a beautiful clear blue because they are the transformed eyes of a young maiden weeping for her lover's ship, which was lost at sea, never to return. Because the plant's sky-blue flowers can be counted on to open and close at precisely the same time every day, the Swedish botanist Carolus Linnaeus included it in the floral clock he planted at Uppsala, Sweden.

They may also be chopped and added to salads. Dried chicory root is frequently roasted and used as a coffee substitute; in fact, chicory is the secret ingredient that made Creole New Orleans coffee "black as sin and sweet as love."

Health Benefits

pH 5.90–6.05. Diuretic, laxative, tonic. Chicory shares many of the medicinal and culinary uses of its relative the dandelion. Its tasty, bitter leaves act as a stimulant to the appetite and internal organs, toning up the system in general. A primary component (up to 20 percent) of the root is inulin, the easily digestible carbohydrate that gives Jerusalem artichokes their characteristic flavor. When the roots are roasted, this inulin is converted to oxymethylfurfurol, which smells like coffee but has none of the harmful caffeine. Root extracts have been used as a diuretic and laxative and to treat fevers and jaundice. Laboratory research has shown these root extracts to be antibacterial, anti-inflammatory, and slightly sedative. Leaf extracts have similar effects but are weaker. Chicory is also recommended in herbal tea mixtures that help purify the blood. These are taken mainly in spring to help cleanse the body of residues from heavy food eaten over the cold winter months.

came prominently before the public in the late 1890s and early 1900s, when it was widely cultivated as an adulterant and substitute for coffee. However, the principal consumers of chicory coffee insisted that the European root was superior to the American, and thus American-grown chicory faded back into obscurity. Growers have developed dozens of improved cultivars that scarcely resemble the scrawny roadside weed, including heading chicories such as radicchio; loose-leaf chicory; root chicory, grown either for cooking like parsnips or for roasting to make a coffee substitute; and witloof, or Belgian endive, the roots of which are forced to produce elongated shoots called "chicons."

Culinary Uses

Young chicory leaves have a slightly bitter tang and are best used in salads. The white underground parts of the earliest leaves are good in salad or cooked as a potherb. Later leaves are apt to be bitter, but cooking and serving them like spinach makes them quite tasty. The roots when cooked taste like parsnips but are almost too skinny to bother with.

Chili Powder

General Information

Chili powder is a blend of spices created in New Braunfels, Texas, by Willie Gebhardt, a German, in 1892. This blend is the basis of the fabled chili con carne. A representative chili powder is mostly red (cayenne) pepper, plus cumin, oregano,

Chili Powder / Nutritional Value Per 100 g Edible Portion		
	Dried Ground	1 tsp.
Calories	314	8
Protein	12.26 g	0.32 g
Fat	16.76 g	0.44 g
Fiber	22.23 g	0.58 g
Calcium	278 mg	7 mg
Iron	14.25 mg	0.37 mg
Magnesium	170 mg	4 mg
Phosphorus	303 mg	8 mg
Potassium	1,916 mg	50 mg
Sodium	1010 mg	26 mg
Zinc	2.700 mg	0.070 mg
Copper	0.429 mg	n/a
Manganese	2.165 mg	n/a
Beta Carotene (A)	34,927 IU	908 IU
Thiamine (B$_1$)	0.349 mg	0.009 mg
Riboflavin (B$_2$)	0.794 mg	0.021 mg
Niacin (B$_3$)	7.893 mg	0.205 mg
Ascorbic Acid (C)	64.14 mg	1.67 mg

paprika, salt, and garlic powder. It gets its bite chiefly from capsaicin, the most pungent chemical in cayenne peppers.

Culinary Uses
Since the fire of capsaicin does not dissolve in cold water, ice water just will not do to quench the burning of a hotly spiced, chili-flavored stew. What works best is a glass of cold milk or a chilled beer, since both milk fat and alcohol are capable of dissolving capsaicin to relieve the stinging in your mouth. You can enrich the flavor of any chili powder and make it more interesting by adding a pinch of one of the "sweet" spices: allspice, cinnamon, cloves, or onion.

Health Benefits
Diaphoretic, irritant. Virtually all the effects of chili powder on the body are from the capsaicin in the red pepper. This irritates the mucous membranes lining the nose and throat, causing them to weep a watery secretion. It also irritates the stomach lining, stimulating the flow of gastric juices and triggering the contractions we call hunger pains. The small amount of garlic in chili powder adds antimicrobial powers, while cumin enhances the digestive powers. Eating food spiced with moderate amounts of chili powder may be helpful when you have hay fever or a cold, because it makes it easier to clear the accumulated mucus.

Chive
(Allium schoenoprasum, A. tuberosum)

Allium is the ancient Latin name for the garlic family; *schoenoprasum* is derived from two Greek words—*schoinos* (reedlike) and *prason* (leek); *tuberosum* means "tuberous." The English name *chive* derives from the Latin *cepa*, meaning "onion," which became *cive* in French.

General Information
Native to Asia and Europe, chives have been known for almost five thousand years. The cultivated variety is very closely related to a wild Alpine variety; other wild varieties grow widely over the northern hemisphere. A well-known member of the onion family, chives grow six to eight inches in height and make dense mats of narrow hollow leaves similar to slender scallions but without the swollen bulbs. Their purple cloverlike blossoms come in the early spring, often blooming off and on again all summer. Garlic chives (*A. tuberosum*) are a garlic-flavored chive also called Chinese chives; they have grayish, straplike leaves with white flowers in flat clusters and can be used in the same way as ordinary chives.

Culinary Uses
Unlike most of its onion relatives, chive tops are the only usable part of the plant. These hollow, flat, narrow green leaves are snipped and used as a culinary herb, either fresh or dried. If cut regularly, more will grow and the stalks will remain tender; those left too long have a tendency to become tough and go to seed. Once flowers appear, the leaves become much less flavorful, but the young pink, lavender, purple, or white flower clusters are edible if used before seeds form. Chives have a soft springtime flavor, only mildly oniony and more delicate than that of scallions. They do not benefit from long cooking but should be chopped finely and added at the last moment to soups, vegetables, omelets, sauces, and salads. Garlic chives are frequently used in Asian dishes to give them their characteristic flavor.

Health Benefits
pH 5.20–6.31. Antiseptic, appetizer, digestive. Like the rest of the onion family, chives are an antiseptic because of their sulfur-containing oil but have none of their relative's digestion-disturbing tendencies. Chives have a stimulating effect on the appetite, fight intestinal fermentation, and

Chive / Nutritional Value Per 100 g Edible Portion			
	Fresh, Raw		Fresh, Raw
Calories	30	Copper	0.157 mg
Protein	3.27 g	Manganese	0.373 mg
Fat	0.73 g	Beta Carotene (A)	4,353 IU
Fiber	n/a	Thiamine (B₁)	0.078 mg
Calcium	92 mg	Riboflavin (B₂)	0.115 mg
Iron	1.60 mg	Niacin (B₃)	0.647 mg
Magnesium	42 mg	Pantothenic Acid (B₅)	0.324 mg
Phosphorus	58 mg	Pyridoxine (B₆)	0.138 mg
Potassium	296 mg	Folic Acid (B₉)	105.0 mcg
Sodium	3 mg	Ascorbic Acid (C)	58.1 mg
Zinc	0.560 mg		

are energizing to the stomach and liver. They are also good for the kidneys and help lower blood pressure. Garlic chives are a traditional remedy for urinary incontinence, male impotence from kidney weakness, and low back pain. They are not recommended for people with fever, ulcers, or eye disorders.

Chocolate and Cocoa
(Theobroma cacao)

The high regard in which chocolate had come to be held is readily apparent in the scientific name assigned to cacao in 1720 by the Swedish botanist Carolus Linnaeus during his monumental classification of the world's plant life: *Theobroma cacao*, from the Greek *theos* (god) and *broma* (food)—hence the free translation "cacao, food of the gods." The English name *chocolate* comes from the Mexican *chocolatl*, while *cacao* is from *cacauatl*. Both the tree and its beans are called *cacao*; the powder manufactured from roasted cacao beans after a portion of their butterfat has been removed is called cocoa.

General Information
The cacao tree, native to tropical America, grows up to thirty feet tall and starts bearing fruit in its fourth year. The tree has the unusual habit of bearing its flowers, and subsequently its pods, on the trunk as well as on its branches. Ripe pods are seven to twelve inches in length and dark reddish brown or purple in color; the tough, thick rind encloses a mass of slippery, whitish pulp that surrounds the almond-sized cacao beans. After hand-picked harvesting,

the pods are cut open to remove the pulp and beans (twenty to fifty per pod, four hundred to a pound), and the beans are placed in fermentation tanks to cure. Freshly picked raw beans are very bitter and have no chocolate taste; fermentation causes them to become more reddish and less bitter. Later the beans are cleaned, sorted, roasted (a process called "tonefication"), and cracked to remove their hard shells. Now called "cocoa nibs," they are then ground into a thick, oily paste called "chocolate liquor" and blended according to the desired specifications of chocolate and cocoa manufacturers. The cocoa fat—more than 50 percent of the bean—is rendered into yellowish cocoa butter. Unlike most fats, it is not greasy. It also has a pleasant odor and does not easily become rancid and thus is prized for use in soaps, other toiletry products, and soothing ointments. The fat-free powdered residue is cocoa; mixed with sugar and either hot milk or water, it makes the energizing drink that most people love.

It is chiefly to the Aztecs that we owe our knowledge of

Chocolate and Cocoa / Nutritional Value Per 100 g Edible Portion		
	Unsweetened Cocoa Powder	Cocoa Butter
Calories	229	884
Protein	19.6 g	n/a
Fat	13.7 g	100.0 g
Fiber	5.2 g	n/a
Calcium	128 mg	n/a
Iron	13.86 mg	n/a
Magnesium	499 mg	n/a
Phosphorus	734 mg	n/a
Potassium	1,524 mg	n/a
Sodium	21 mg	n/a
Zinc	6.810 mg	n/a
Copper	3.788 mg	n/a
Manganese	3.837 mg	n/a
Beta Carotene (A)	20 IU	n/a
Thiamine (B₁)	0.078 mg	n/a
Riboflavin (B₂)	0.241 mg	n/a
Niacin (B₃)	2.185 mg	n/a
Pantothenic Acid (B₅)	0.254 mg	n/a
Pyridoxine (B₆)	0.118 mg	n/a
Folic Acid (B₉)	32.0 mcg	n/a
Ascorbic Acid (C)	0 mg	n/a
Tocopherol (E)	n/a	1.80 mg

cocoa. They roasted the beans in pots, then crushed them between stones and formed the paste into cakes. This paste could then be diluted with water and spiced with annatto and anise seeds, crushed long red peppers, and cinnamon. The mixture was beaten and stirred slowly over a low fire until it became a foamy, bubbling liquid: a sort of hot, spicy, deluxe chocolate shake. It was on his fourth voyage, in 1502, that Columbus discovered cacao beans in what is today Nicaragua and sent some back to Spain, to general indifference; probably no one knew how to rid them of their forbidding bitterness. But in 1519 Hernando Cortez tasted chocolate as the Aztecs prepared it—both in drink form and in some form of paste. He brought back not only more beans but also the knowledge of how the Aztecs prepared them. They were given to a monastery, where the roasted ground beans, dampened into a paste, were mixed with cane sugar (another novelty in Europe at that time). The resulting product was so appreciated that Spain attempted to keep its origin and preparation secret. France acquired chocolate when Jews expelled from Spain settled in the region of Bayonne and began to process chocolate there. France regarded chocolate as at best a barbarous product and at worst a noxious drug, and Bayonne forbade making chocolate within the city limits. However, by 1550, only thirty years after the first white men tasted cocoa in Montezuma's palace, chocolate factories of considerable size were operating in Lisbon, Marseilles, Bayonne, Turin, Genoa, and many other cities throughout southern Europe.

The first chocolate factory in the United States was opened in 1765 in Dorchester, Massachusetts, and funded by Dr. James Baker. Baker's chocolate became part of American folklore, and the factory is still in existence today. Switzerland was a late bloomer in chocolate, only starting commercial production toward the middle of the nineteenth century. The Swiss were short on chocolate and sugar but had plenty of milk, so in 1876 milk chocolate was introduced to the rest of the world, a concoction developed by M. Daniel Peter. Milton Snaveley Hershey invented the candy bar in 1894 after seeing a German chocolate-making machine at the 1893 Chicago World's Columbian Exposition. He ordered one of the German machines and began experimenting, loosing on the market a couple of candy bars that are still popular today: the Hershey's Milk Chocolate Bar and the Hershey's Milk Chocolate with Almonds Bar.

Buying Tips

Purchase only organic raw cacao or products made from the organic raw cacao beans. Non-organic products may be fumigated and contain more extraneous material than you desire. There are very few suppliers of this type of product in the United States at this time. Most products sold are from roasted beans.

Culinary Uses

The enticing taste of chocolate has been cherished for centuries in Mexico and the West Indies. Today it is one of the most popular ingredients worldwide. The annual consumption in the United States is an estimated one million tons of cocoa products. While found mostly in candies and baked goods, chocolate and cacoa also make their appearance in delicious drinks, in trail mixes, and in mole sauces. Be aware that because chocolate is naturally bitter, most products with chocolate in them usually contain a lot of sweetener.

Health Benefits

Unroasted (raw) cacao beans are remarkably rich in sulfur and magnesium, and cacao, in fact, seems to be one of the highest sources of magnesium. This is likely the primary reason why women crave chocolate during their menstrual period (when they are low in magnesium). Magnesium balances brain chemistry, builds strong bones, and is associated with more happiness. Magnesium is one of the most deficient major minerals for those who eat the Standard American Diet (SAD); over 80 percent of Americans are chronically deficient in magnesium. Cacao beans are also high in the mineral sulfur, which builds strong nails, hair, and beautiful skin, detoxifies the liver, and supports healthy pancreas functioning.

Although cacao contains subtle amounts of caffeine and theobromine, experiments have shown that these stimulants are far different when consumed raw than cooked. One experiment conducted with a decoction of roasted ground cacao beans in boiling water produced an excitement of the nervous system similar to that caused by black coffee: an increased state of circulation, and an accelerated pulse. Interestingly, when the same decoction was made with raw, unroasted beans neither effect was noticeable, leading the experimenters to conclude that the physiological changes were caused by aromatic substances released during roasting.

LORE AND LEGEND

The cacao beans are so important to the Ecuadorian economy that they are still called *pepe de oro*, seeds of gold. The Aztecs used the cacao bean as currency, the unit eight thousand indicated by a sack holding eight thousand cacao beans, and the Mayans did likewise. In fact, the Mayans even had trouble with "counterfeiters" of cacao beans, the con men filling hollowed beans with dirt and passing them off as the real thing. Emperor Montezuma convinced Europeans that chocolate was ambrosia for the gods; however, this royal drink was forbidden to the women of the court, much to the dismay of the ladies, who had to go to unladylike lengths to get it. Chocolate became more popular than ever with lovers after a Swiss named M. Daniel Peter invented milk chocolate in 1876. Since then it has become the foremost of Valentine gifts, and on Saint Nicholas Eve (December 5) Dutch lovers exchange chocolate initials, or use them as place cards at the dinner table.

Other chemicals found in cacao include phenylethylamine (PEA) and anandamide. PEA is an adrenal-related chemical that is also created and released within the brain when we are in love. This is one of the reasons why love and chocolate have such a deep correlation. PEA also plays a role in increasing focus and alertness. Anandamide is known as "the bliss chemical" because it is released while we are feeling great. Cacao contains enzyme inhibitors that decrease our bodies' ability to break down anandamide. This means that natural anandamide and/or cacao anandamide may stick around longer, making us feel good longer, when we eat cacao.

A recent study showed that only one out of five hundred people thought they were allergic to chocolate actually tested positive. Allergies to chocolate are quite rare. It is typically the case that the person is in fact allergic to milk and dairy products.

There is very little to recommend in terms of roasted chocolate products for the health-conscious. Roasting increases the amount of caffeine along with the tannic and oxalic acids. These can trigger various nervous symptoms including anxiety, insomnia, gastrointestinal complaints, and mood swings.

VARIETIES

Bitter (unsweetened) chocolate consists of 95 percent chocolate liquor with 5 percent added cocoa butter. It is used as a baking ingredient.

Bittersweet (semisweet) chocolate contains sugar and from 35 to 50 percent chocolate liquor, with 15 percent added cocoa butter.

Cocoa powder contains only 18 percent total cocoa butter. The dry cake that remains after pressing cocoa butter is pulverized for use as an ingredient in baking, confectionery, and beverages.

Couverture is a rich chocolate, very high in cocoa butter and characterized by an exceptionally shiny finish.

Dutch-process cocoa powder is an alkali-processed cocoa powder. The alkali, usually potassium carbonate, is used to neutralize the cocoa's acids and make it easier to dissolve. This type of cocoa powder is also labeled "European style."

Milk chocolate contains sugar, added cocoa butter, milk solids, and chocolate liquor.

White chocolate contains only cocoa butter and sugar, or, historically, chestnuts. It has a short shelf life and easily becomes rancid. In cheap, imitation white chocolate, vegetable oil is substituted for cocoa butter.

Cinnamon
(Cinnamomum zeylanicum)

> I have perfumed my bed
> with myrrh, aloes and cinnamon.
> Come, let us take our fill of love till morning . . .
>
> —PROVERBS 7:17

The botanical name *Cinnamomum* derives from the Hebraic and Arabic term *amomon*, meaning "fragrant spice plant," and with the prefix *-kin* means "fragrant spice plant of China." *Zeylanicum* means "of Ceylonese origin." This spice is known as "true cinnamon," to distinguish it from the similar-looking and -tasting cassia (*Cinnamomum cassia*). In many European languages, the name for cinnamon comes from the Latin *canella*, which means "small tube or pipe," referring to how thin strips of the inner bark of the cinnamon tree are sun-dried to form tightly curled quills.

General Information

Cinnamon is the dried, strongly aromatic, and sweet-tasting inner bark of a tropical evergreen laurel species native to India and Sri Lanka (Ceylon). Only small groves of cinnamon trees grew in Arabia, where the spice was so prized that only priests were permitted to gather it, offering the first bundle gathered to the sun god. The tree must grow for eight years before its thick bark is mature enough to be harvested. After the bark is peeled from the tree's shoots during the rainy season, when it is juicy with sap, it is left to dry and ferment for twenty-four hours. Then the outer layer of the bark is scraped off, leaving the inner light-colored layer, which curls into quills as it dries. Removing the outer bark makes the cinnamon less biting and mellows its aroma. Ancient travelers introduced the aromatic herb to the Egyptians, who added it enthusiastically to their embalming mixtures; it was partly the Egyptian demand for cinnamon, as well as for pepper, that provided the chief impetus for the spice trade and world exploration. The strategically situated Arabs monopolized most of the spice traffic with the East until the first century A.D. Much of the cinnamon bark came by the long and hazardous route from Malaya and Indonesia to Madagascar (forty-five hundred miles of open sea in double outrigger canoes) and then on up the coast of East Africa to the Red Sea. The Arabs knew very well where cinnamon came from, and how, but since there was nothing wrong with their commercial instincts, they took care to protect their middleman's profit by giving currency to a number of magical myths about its origins.

Culinary Uses

Cinnamon has a fragrant, spicy, slightly sweet flavor that becomes stronger when the bark is ground. Available in either quills or powder, cinnamon is best purchased whole and ground as needed or purchased ground in small quantities and constantly replaced, as it quickly becomes stale. The thinnest bark is the best quality and has the finest aroma. Frequently used in baked goods, cinnamon also adds a warm flavor to mulled wine, puddings, fruit pies, curries, pilafs, and creams. Much of the cinnamon sold is actually partly cassia, a related plant of lesser quality (see the separate reference).

LORE AND LEGEND

Cinnamon was highly prized in ancient times as a perfume, medicine, preservative, and flavoring spice; small quantities of the precious quills were considered gifts fit for kings. The Arabs, who first brought cinnamon to the West, shrouded its origins in grotesque mysteries to frighten off rival traders. Herodotus, in a credulous mood, reproduced one Arabian account of the cinnamon harvest:

> Where it comes from and what country produces it, they do not know. What they say is that the dry sticks, which we have learned from the Phoenicians to call cinnamon, are brought by large birds (Phoenixes) which carry them to their nests, made of mud, on mountain precipices which no man can climb, and that the method the Arabians have invented for getting hold of them is to cut up the bodies of dead oxen, or donkeys, or other animals, into very large joints which they carry to the spot in question and leave on the ground near the nests. They then retire to a safe distance and the birds fly down and carry off the joints of meat to their nests which, not being strong enough to bear the weight, break and fall to the ground. Then the men come along and pick up the cinnamon, which is subsequently exported to other countries.
>
> —Herodotus, III, iii.

There were equally disarming action-packed tales about frankincense and cassia featuring flying snakes and belligerent bats.

Health Benefits

Antiseptic, aromatic, astringent, carminative. Cinnamon is a good detoxifying herb, as it creates freshness and strengthens and energizes the tissues; it also acts as a pain reliever, promotes digestion, and has a natural cleansing action. Cinnamon can increase digestive fluid secretion and therefore ameliorate intestinal gas. It raises vitality and stimulates all the vital functions of the body, counteracting congestion and aiding the peripheral circulation of the blood. It is useful for treating diarrhea, nausea and vomiting, influenza, arthritis, menstrual cramps, rheumatism, and candidiasis. Cinnamon, ginger, cardamom, and clove are used together as a tea to relieve cough and congestion and to promote digestion. Cinnamon contains a substance that kills various fungi, bacteria and other microorganisms, including *Staphylococcus aureas* (staph infections), *Clostridium botulinum* (botulism), *Aspergillus parasiticus* (many molds), and *A. flavus* (which produces the poison aflatoxin). Cinnamon bark oil, produced in Sri Lanka for over two thousand years, is one of the most antimicrobial essential oils. In modern times it has been demonstrated that viruses cannot live in the presence of cinnamon oil.

Cinnamon may significantly help people with type 2 diabetes improve their ability to regulate blood sugar; one study found that it increased glucose metabolism twentyfold. Dr. Richard A. Anderson, lead scientist at the Maryland-based Human Nutrition Research Center, a branch of the U.S. Department of Agriculture, explained that his mostly unpublished research shows that a compound in cinnamon called methylhydroxy chalcone polymer (MHCP) makes fat cells more responsive to insulin by activating an enzyme that causes insulin to bind to cells and inhibiting the enzyme that blocks this process. While it is too soon to recommend the spice as a regular treatment for type 2 diabetes, Dr. Anderson said patients could try adding a quarter to one teaspoon of cinnamon to their food. "The worst that will happen is it won't do any good and the best is that it will help dramatically," he stated. The aroma of cinnamon has also proven to be an aphrodisiac in a recent study (by Alan Hirsch, M.D., at the Smell and Taste Treatment and Research Foundation in Chicago) in which male subjects sniffed a variety of odors; freshly baked cinnamon rolls scored the highest response of the ten odors tested.

Clove

(Eugenia aromatica, Syzygium aromaticum, E. caryophyllata)

This tree was given the genus *Eugenia* in honor of Prince Eugene of Savoy. Eugenia also means "good birth," from the prefix *eu* (well or good) and *genia* (genesis). *Aromatica* means simply "aromatic"; *caryophyllata* was a name given this plant by Pliny and refers to its nut-shaped leaves. The English name *clove* comes from the Latin *clavus*, meaning "nail," which the buds resemble.

LORE AND LEGEND

Esoterically, clove buds are used to attract love and money and for psychic protection. The Chinese called them "birds' tongues," and Europeans referred to them as "grains of paradise." Cloves are said to help one penetrate illusion, and the Romans burned them as incense to keep others from making up lies or gossiping about them. Clove's aromatic influences have been known to improve memory and create a feeling of protection and courage.

General Information

Cloves are the dried aromatic flower buds of a tropical evergreen tree of the myrtle family. Believed to have originated in China, clove trees are now most commonly found in Southeast Asia. The whole tree is highly aromatic, although the only commercially useful part is the flower buds; since these are small and lightweight, it takes five to seven thousand dried cloves to make a pound of spice. Picked just before opening into pinkish-green blossoms, the buds are dried for forty-eight hours in the sun, during which time they change color from rose to brown. The buds are then separated from their husks and dried for several more days. First cultivated by the Dutch in the Moluccas (Spice Islands), cloves were smuggled out to Mauritius and the West Indies with intricate subterfuge by spice-hungry colonialist nations. In line with the centuries-old battle for a monopoly on cloves, Zanzibar made it a capital offense in 1972 to smuggle cloves out of the country. Fifteen persons were actually sentenced to death for this crime that year. A major portion of the world's clove production goes to Indonesia for use in kretak cigarettes, which contain a mixture of two parts tobacco to one part cloves.

Buying Tips

Freshly dried whole cloves are mahogany red and oily, with a pungent and sweet aroma. If they are black and shriveled, they are old. If ground cloves taste bitter and harsh, they are old and should be discarded.

Culinary Uses

Step into any spice shop and breathe deeply. Chances are that the dominant fragrance comes from rich, warm-smelling cloves. Good-quality cloves should be plump, oily, and not easily broken, with a pungent, spicy taste. Ideally, they should be bought as whole buds and ground as needed, but preground cloves (which are less pungent) are also available. Cloves are excellent added to baked goods and spiced drinks. A few cloves brewed with Oriental tea add an enticing flavor, as well as giving a carminative effect, while clove-spiced mulled wine offers a more exciting way to aid digestion than most commercial concoctions. Whole fresh cloves can be pushed into a thin-skinned orange until the entire orange is covered. The orange can then be rolled in ground cinnamon, wrapped in tissue paper, and set to dry for several weeks to make a beautifully scented pomander ball for the home.

Health Benefits

Anesthetic, antiseptic, carminative, rubefacient. Cloves aid the digestion and utilization of food, promoting the flow of saliva and gastric juices. The clove has antiseptic properties and when taken internally is excreted by the kidneys, skin, liver, and bronchi, thereby stimulating and disinfecting each. Clove oil contains eugenol, a strong anesthetic and antiseptic substance used today to numb gums in dentistry. A natural pain reliever, clove oil can be used to relieve toothaches, as a decongestant, and to benefit cir-

LORE AND LEGEND

Chinese officials during the Han Dynasty of 207 B.C.–A.D. 220 were allowed to approach their monarch only when holding cloves in their mouths to mask their unpleasant breath.

culation. Tinctures of clove oil are effective against many fungi, among them the one that causes athlete's foot. Eating cloves is said by some to work as an aphrodisiac. Tea, made by steeping the buds in boiling water, is said to cure nausea and to rid the stomach and intestines of gas.

Clover, Red
(Trifolium pratense)

Trifolium comes from the Latin *tres* (three) and *folium* (leaf), referring to the plant's trifoliolate leaves. *Pratense* means "growing in meadows," its frequent habitat. The English word *clover* comes from the ancient German word *kleo*.

General Information

Clover is a member of the legume family and native to the Mediterranean and Red Sea areas. From there, it wandered north and westward throughout Europe with the Roman legions, who called it "clava" because its three-petaled leaf reminded them of Hercules's club. By the late twelfth century red clover was well established as a dependable forage crop in the Rhine valley. Albertus Magnus, a Dominican priest and scholar with a deep interest in natural science, cultivated red

Clove / Nutritional Value Per 100 g Edible Portion

	Dried, Ground	1 tsp.
Calories	323	7
Protein	5.98 g	0.13 g
Fat	20.06 g	0.42 g
Fiber	9.62 g	0.20 g
Calcium	646 mg	14 mg
Iron	8.68 mg	0.18 mg
Magnesium	264 mg	6 mg
Phosphorus	105 mg	2 mg
Potassium	1,102 mg	23 mg
Sodium	243 mg	5 mg
Zinc	1.090 mg	0.020 mg
Copper	0.347 mg	n/a
Manganese	30.033 mg	n/a
Beta Carotene (A)	530 IU	11 IU
Thiamine (B₁)	0.115 mg	0.002 mg
Riboflavin (B₂)	0.267 mg	0.006 mg
Niacin (B₃)	1.458 mg	0.031 mg
Ascorbic Acid (C)	80.81 mg	1.70 mg

Clover, Red / Nutritional Value Per 100 g Edible Portion

	Dried		Dried
Calories	326	Sodium	16 mg
Protein	11.5 g	Zinc	trace
Fat	3.6 g	Manganese	5.900 mg
Fiber	9.9 g	Beta Carotene (A)	2,008 IU
Calcium	1,310 mg	Thiamine (B₁)	0.420 mg
Iron	0.035 mg	Riboflavin (B₂)	0.330 mg
Magnesium	349 mg	Niacin (B₃)	12.500 mg
Phosphorus	322 mg	Ascorbic Acid (C)	296.6 mg
Potassium	2,000 mg		

clover in Cologne during the middle of the thirteenth century. In 1240 he built the first greenhouse in the history of horticulture and gave a large dinner party to demonstrate his invention, which made it possible to grow plants throughout the winter. Unfortunately, this miniature plot of spring in the midst of a snowy winter landscape made him suspect of sorcery, but his reputation suffered no permanent damage: in 1931 he was canonized, and is now sometimes referred to as Saint Albert the Great. By the sixteenth century red clover was cultivated throughout much of Italy. Europe's first botanical garden opened in Italy at the University of Padua, and Prosper Alpinus, who had been appointed to the chair of botany, took a particular interest in red clover. By 1750 red clover had been introduced into the English colonies on the Atlantic coast and was growing on scattered farms as forage. It grows in fields, along roadsides, and in waste places in all temperate climates. Children of all ages love looking for four-leaved clovers and picking the pretty blossoms.

LORE AND LEGEND

Because of its importance in early agriculture, red clover has a long history as a religious symbol. The ancient Greeks, Romans, and Celts of pre-Christian Ireland all revered it. In pre-Christian times the three-leaved clover was associated with the triad goddesses of Greek and Roman mythology and with the sacred sun wheel of the Celts. The rare four-leaved clover, also a Christian symbol with its four leaves representing the form of the cross, was said to enable its wearer to ward off evil (including witches), to see fairies and various spirits, to heal illnesses, to have good fortune, and to escape military service. According to an old medieval folk rhyme, each leaf of a four-leaved clover represents a different aspect of happiness. The first leaf stood for fame; the second, wealth; the third for a faithful lover; and the fourth for excellent health. Together these qualities could be said to represent the epitome of good fortune, a completely happy life. The extremely rare five-leaved clover was believed to be unlucky.

Culinary Uses
The leaves of red clover are used in salads, tacos, sandwiches, and coleslaw. Blossoms should be picked when near or in full bloom and immediately eaten in one of these ways or dried for tea making.

Health Benefits
Antispasmodic, depurative. Red clover benefits the entire body, purifying the blood, promoting healing, soothing the nerves, and offering relief for those with coughs or bronchial conditions. It is used as a thick poultice to rid one of athlete's foot and in a tea as a sedative and an antispasmodic. Red clover tea may be imbibed as freely as water; it is pleasant steeped alone or with another aromatic herb. Clover heads, dried quickly, retain their fragrance and color and make a pleasing and effective curative powder.

Note: Because red clover is a blood thinner, it should not be used before surgery or during pregnancy. Its blood-thinning ability comes from its content of coumarin, which inhibits the liver/vitamin K factor to reduce blood clots.

Comfrey
(Symphytum officinale, S. peregrinum)
Also Known As: Knitbone, Bruisewort, Boneset

The genus name *Symphytum* is derived from the Greek word *sympho*, meaning "to unite" or "to grow together," referring to comfrey's healing and mending properties. *Officinale* means "of the workshop," alluding to apothecaries' shops and signifying that the plant was once part of the official pharmacopoeia of Rome; *peregrinum* means "foreign" or "wandering." The English name *comfrey* derives from the Latin *conferva*, meaning "knitting or growing together."

General Information
Comfrey is a very popular herb of the borage family suited to almost every climate. Native to Europe, it was introduced into North America by early settlers and now grows wild throughout much of the continent. The plant sends its taproots over ten feet deep into the subsoil to raise moisture and valuable minerals to the upper levels. A perennial crop lasting up to twenty years, comfrey grows well in drought-prone regions and brings the subsoil into

Comfrey / Nutritional Value Per 100 g Edible Portion		
	Leaves	Root, Dried
Calories	n/a	217
Protein	22 g	9.4 g
Fat	n/a	1.7 g
Fiber	n/a	7.2 g
Calcium	n/a	1,130 mg
Ironn	/a	81 mg
Magnesium	n/a	170 mg
Phosphorus	n/a	211 mg
Potassium	n/a	1,590 mg
Sodium	n/a	351 mg
Zinc	n/a	0.28 mg
Manganese	n/a	6.70 mg
Beta Carotene (A)	n/a	11,000 IU
Thiamine (B₁)	0.500 mg	0.120 mg
Riboflavin (B₂)	1.000 mg	0.720 mg
Niacin (B₃)	5.000 mg	6.700 mg
Cobalamin (B₁₂)	0.700 mg	n/a
Ascorbic Acid (C)	100.0 mg	13.2 mg
Tocopherol (E)	30.0 mg	n/a

the fertility cycle much faster than alfalfa, as well as growing where alfalfa will not. It is easily grown, with a simple root cutting producing an enormous plant up to four feet high and just as wide, with leaves up to thirty-nine inches long and eight inches wide. The rampant tubers run wild and produce offshoot plants at random. The most commonly used comfrey comes from the plant *S. officinale*; a less well-known variety is *S. peregrinum*, or Russian comfrey.

Culinary Uses

Comfrey leaves are somewhat bitter but quite edible. They wilt rapidly after picking, so they should be used immediately in salads, steamed lightly as cooked greens, or juiced with other vegetables for a green drink. The leaves can also be dried, ground, and added to baked goods. The stalks, if blanched, make a good substitute for spinach, while the mild-flavored, spindle-shaped root can be used finely chopped in a salad or ground for use as the base of seed-nutmeat loaves or fruit-carob candies. Comfrey root, along with dandelion and chicory roots, can be made into a coffee substitute without the harmful effects of coffee.

Health Benefits

Astringent, demulcent, emollient, expectorant, nutritive, vulnerary. Comfrey is among the most nutritionally healthful plants and probably used for more purposes than any other herb. With more protein in its leaf structure than any other known member of the vegetable kingdom, it is also the only land plant discovered so far that contains traces of vitamin B₁₂. Comfrey is an excellent detoxicant, especially effective on liver and lung tissues, creating richer, cleaner blood cells that are capable of carrying greater amounts of oxygen and nourishment. All parts of the comfrey plant contain allantoin, a nitrogenous crystalline substance that promotes the healthy proliferation of red blood cells, increases blood circulation, and encourages rapid healing of injured bone and muscle tissue; the plant also contains pepsin and other enzymes to aid digestion. Comfrey, combined with alfalfa, feeds the pituitary gland. Rich in a watery but slightly viscous fluid that forms a paste easily and sets quickly, poultices made of the leaves and root are applied to swellings, bruises, broken bones, and sore breasts. As a tea, comfrey has been found helpful in healing and soothing the inner body as well as loosening mucus. About one-quarter to one-half cup of strong comfrey tea with a teaspoon of honey can end an asthmatic or allergic night cough and bring restful sleep. A daily drink of comfrey, alfalfa, and parsley mixed with fruit juice is a marvelous tonic, very efficacious for general health.

Coriander and Cilantro

(*Coriandrum sativum*)
Also Known As: Chinese Parsley, Mexican Parsley

> The name *Coriandrum*, used by Pliny, comes from the Greek *koris*, a name for an ill-smelling bug or bedbug; it was given to this plant because of the peculiar odor produced when it is struck or broken. *Sativum* indicates that this plant has long been cultivated. *Cilantro* is the Spanish name for the plant.

General Information

Coriander is most probably indigenous to the Mediterranean regions of Africa and Asia and is one of the most ancient of herbs still in use today. Coriander seeds have been found in Bronze Age ruins on the Aegean islands and in the tombs of the pharaohs. Cultivated in Egyptian gardens thousands of years before the birth of Christ, coriander was steeped in

LORE AND LEGEND

Coriander seeds were frequently among the funeral offerings found in Egyptian tombs. The Chinese cultivated coriander as a valuable culinary and medicinal plant as early as the fourth century B.C., and the plant acquired a reputation for bestowing immortality on those who ate the seeds during a state of spiritual purity. Other herbalists developed aphrodisiac concoctions from coriander with lust in mind, for they believed that it aroused passion, a rumor that may have been started by the Arabian fantasy, *The Thousand and One Nights*, in which coriander was referred to as an aphrodisiac.

wine to increase its intoxicating power. Coriander was introduced into Latin America by the Spaniards shortly after they encountered the New World, and it won instant favor with the indigenous people there. Later, it was passed on by them to the American Indians of what is today the southwestern United States. *Cilantro* is the name used for the young, flat, feathery leaves of the coriander plant, a member of the carrot family. The plant grows one to three feet in height, with glabrous, strong-smelling leaves with almost threadlike divisions. Sometimes confused with parsley, this plant has a distinctly different taste. The whole plant has a disagreeable smell until the active principles in the volatile oil reach their apogee and the seeds are fully ripened; then the disagreeable element becomes pleasant and aromatic. The seeds are gathered from the small white or purple-tinged flowers of the plant and dried to bring out their characteristic sweet aroma. The small seeds are pale green to cream or brown in color, round, and ridged. The dried seeds of the plant are sold as the spice coriander.

Buying Tips

Fresh cilantro is available in greengrocers year-round. In Asian markets, it is sold with the root attached, increasing its longevity. Select bunches that look fresh and bright. Cilantro quickly loses its flavor and develops a harsh, unpleasant taste; the leaves rapidly deteriorate, so use it soon after purchase.

Culinary Uses

Coriander seeds have a distinctive, sweetly aromatic flavor and spicy scent when crushed. They are more intensely flavored than the leaves, with a rich, earthy blend of lemon and sage that is brought out even further by toasting and grinding. Unripe coriander seeds have an unpleasant odor that becomes warm and spicy when the seed matures; this is one spice that actually improves with age. A basic spice in Indian curries, along with cayenne pepper, turmeric, and ginger, coriander is also used for pickles and sweet dishes, including certain types of cakes and baked goods. It has a well-established place in the food industry as a seasoning that not only improves the flavor and aroma of food but also makes heavier meats and pickled vegetables more digestible; it has the same effect when used in making breads and as an ingredient of curry powder.

Often confused with some types of parsley, cilantro (coriander leaves) has a fresh, zesty, orange and parsley flavor and is an important ingredient in Mexican, Indian, and Asian dishes because of its cooling effect. It goes especially well with green chili peppers and forms the basis of many Mexican salsas as well as Indian curries and chutneys. Best used fresh, it makes an excellent addition to salads or sauces and can be used as a garnish for soups. Coriander roots taste

Coriander / Nutritional Value Per 100 g Edible Portion		
	Whole Seed	1 tsp.
Calories	298	5
Protein	12.37 g	0.22 g
Fat	17.77 g	0.32 g
Fiber	29.12 g	0.52 g
Calcium	709 mg	13 mg
Iron	16.32 mg	0.29 mg
Magnesium	330 mg	6 mg
Phosphorus	409 mg	7 mg
Potassium	1,267 mg	23 mg
Sodium	35 mg	1 mg
Zinc	4.700 mg	0.080 mg
Copper	0.975 mg	n/a
Manganese	1.900 mg	n/a
Beta Carotene (A)	trace	trace
Thiamine (B₁)	0.239 mg	0.004 mg
Riboflavin (B₂)	0.290 mg	0.005 mg
Niacin (B₃)	2.130 mg	0.038 mg

Cilantro / Nutritional Value Per 100 g Edible Portion			
	Fresh, Raw	Dried	1 tsp.
Calories	20	279	2
Protein	2.36 g	21.83g	0.13 g
Fat	0.59 g	4.76 g	0.03 g
Fiber	0.80 g	10.39 g	0.06 g
Calcium	98 mg	1,246 mg	7 mg
Iron	1.95 mg	42.46 mg	0.25 mg
Magnesium	26 mg	694 mg	4 mg
Phosphorus	36 mg	481 mg	3 mg
Potassium	542 mg	4,466 mg	27 mg
Sodium	28 mg	211 mg	1 mg
Copper	n/a	1.786 mg	n/a
Manganese	n/a	6.355 mg	n/a
Beta Carotene (A)	2,767 IU	n/a	n/a
Thiamine (B₁)	0.074 mg	1.252 mg	0.008 mg
Riboflavin (B₂)	0.120 mg	1.500 mg	0.009 mg
Niacin (B₃)	0.730 mg	10.707 mg	0.064 mg
Ascorbic Acid (C)	10.5 mg	566.71 mg	3.40 mg

more like the leaves than the seeds but with an added nutty flavor; they are most often minced and used fresh.

Health Benefits

Antispasmodic, aromatic, carminative, diuretic, stomachic, refrigerant. Warm, spicy coriander has been used as an herbal digestive aid for thousands of years. It is a natural diuretic, has cooling properties, helps purify the blood and strengthen the heart, and is also useful for gas, indigestion, nausea, and vomiting. A soothing drink is made by infusing half a teaspoon of the crushed seeds in one cup of hot water; if sipped half an hour before meals, this drink will greatly improve digestion. Coriander oil, pressed from the seeds, lowers glucose levels by normalizing insulin levels and supporting pancreatic function; it may be added to food or water as a dietary supplement or flavoring. Both coriander seeds and cilantro help regulate energy, are diuretic, and specifically treat urinary tract infections. They are diaphoretic (support perspiration) and therefore treat fever. They aid digestion, treat nausea, relieve intestinal gas, pain, and distention, and support peristalsis. They also quench thirst and soothe inflammation, rheumatic pain, headaches, coughs, and mental stress.

Cilantro supports the spleen-pancreas, stomach, bladder, and lung meridians. A cooling herb, the leaves may be pulped and applied to the skin to relieve burning sensations. Cilantro is a remarkable heavy-metal detoxifier, in that it pushes mercury out of its storage containers (adipose or fat tissues) within the body. By some still-unknown mechanism, cilantro mobilizes mercury rapidly from the brain and central nervous system; combined with algae, which binds the excreted toxin and drags it out of the body, this is a powerful combination.

Cream of Tartar
(Potassium bitartrate)

General Information

Cream of tartar is a byproduct of the wine-making industry. The sediment (called "crystals of argolis") that forms on the sides and bottoms (lees) of wine barrels during the fermentation process contain tartaric acid. These crystals are ground, purified, dried, and reground to produce cream of tartar. It is frequently used as the acid counterpart to baking soda in formulas for baking powder.

Culinary Uses

The best-known use for cream of tartar is in baking powder, where it combines with baking soda to release carbon dioxide. The cream of tartar is a "fast-acting" leavening agent that encourages the release of carbon dioxide at room temperature, while baking soda is a "slow-acting" leavening agent that releases its carbon dioxide later, when

Cream of Tartar / Nutritional Value Per 100 g Edible Portion		
		1 tsp.
Calories	258	8
Protein	0 g	0 g
Fat	0 g	0 g
Calcium	8.0 mg	0.2 mg
Iron	3.72 mg	0.11 mg
Magnesium	2 mg	0 mg
Phosphorus	5 mg	0 mg
Potassium	16,500 mg	495 mg
Sodium	52 mg	2 mg
Zinc	0.420 mg	0.013 mg
Copper	0.195 mg	0.006 mg
Manganese	0.205 mg	0.006 mg

the batter is heated in the oven. Baking powders that contain baking soda and cream of tartar are called "double-acting" baking powders.

Cubeb

(Piper cubeba)

Also Known As: Tailed Pepper

Piper is an ancient Latin name for the plant. *Cubeba* derives from an Indonesian word, *cabe*, meaning "pepper." The Sanskrit word *pippali* meant "berry" and also "long pepper," and because long pepper (*P. longum*) was at first the most highly regarded pepper, *pippali* became the root of the word *pepper* in European languages.

General Information

The cubeb berry is a drupe from a climbing shrub native to the Indonesian Islands, mainly Java, and now grown in other parts of southeastern Asia and India. The dried black berry is the size of the largest allspice berries and comes with its stem attached (giving rise to one of its other names, of *tailed pepper*). In England in 1307, a pound of cubebs for the "King's Wardrobe" cost nine shillings; cubebs were used then to season meats and other dishes in a highly spiced, even sugared, Muslim-influenced style that would probably unsettle modern palates. This relative of black pepper has long since fallen out of use and is extremely difficult to find in the West.

Culinary Uses

The flavor of cubeb, with its mild muskiness and spice, is reminiscent of tea. Ground in a mortar, the berries release an aroma of nutmeg and cumin. Cooking alters the scent to something more currylike, persistent and still slightly floral, with scarcely a trace of the heat of black pepper. This spice is a feature of Indonesian cuisine, where it lends a distinctive taste, closer to allspice than to pepper.

Health Benefits

Antiseptic, carminative, diuretic. The original use of cubeb was medicinal, mainly as a treatment for respiratory problems and for male reproductive difficulties. Cubeb berries were used in medicinals and aphrodisiacs by Arab physicians in the ninth and tenth centuries. They contain substances that have been used as antiseptics, carminatives, and diuretics. Oil of cubeb is a constituent of some throat lozenges.

Cumin

(Cuminum cyminum, Nigeria sativa, Nigella sativa)

The name *cumin* is of Semitic origin but unknown meaning. *Nigeria* means "of or from Nigeria"; *sativa* means "cultivated."

General Information

Cumin is native to the eastern Mediterranean, especially the upper reaches of the Nile. The seeds resemble caraway in appearance but are slightly longer and lighter in color, with quite a different flavor, being hot and pungent. The white variety is the most common, but if you shop in Indian grocery stores, you may run across black cumin (*Nigeria sativa*), an unrelated plant also known as nutmeg flower or Roman coriander. The black cumin is easier to grow than regular cumin and produces pods with small, dark seeds that smell like fennel and taste something like peppery nutmeg. They can be ground and used like pepper, but the flavor is quite distinctive, so try a little before you season a whole dish.

Culinary Uses

Cumin has a strongly aromatic, spicy taste; it is even a little bitter, but pleasantly so. When darkened several shades by toasting in a hot, dry skillet, the seed releases its gentle perfume, and the taste becomes richer and mellower. In bib-

Cumin was so highly valued in the time of Christ that it had become negotiable for the payment of taxes. It is also supposed to induce a pallid complexion, and Pliny tells of the students of Porcius Patro, the celebrated master of oratory, who consumed cumin to achieve that pallid "studious" look. In early Roman times cumin was the symbol of cupidity and avarice; because he was judged to possess these characteristics, Marcus Aurelius was nicknamed "Cumin." Later, cumin was associated with being a tightwad, and in an era when profligacy was the rule, the exceptional thrift of Emperor Antonius Pius was ridiculed by dubbing him "the cumin splitter."

lical times, cumin seeds were valued for their digestive properties and used for flavoring bread and other dishes during periods of ceremonial fasting to make up for the lack of meat. Available in both seed and powdered form, cumin is most frequently used in commercial curry powder but also makes appearances in Mexican-style rice or bean dishes and in relishes, soups, salads, curries, and baked goods. A true Texan would not consider cooking his pinto beans without cumin (or comino), which also serves as the major ingredient in his chili powder; the Indian or Pakistani also regards cumin as an essential ingredient in dal, the staple dish made from dried beans or peas that is taken with nearly every meal.

Health Benefits

Aromatic, carminative. Cumin is one of the best aromatic spices to strengthen digestion and improve the taste of food while aiding the secretion of digestive juices. It also stimulates circulation, relieves pain and cramping in the abdomen, and helps prevent and relieve flatulence. Roasted cumin powder is effectively used in intestinal disorders such as diarrhea or dysentery.

Curry Powder

Eat your curry, and be brilliant! Why should I make the effort to try something new when I already like the food I eat? Part of the answer lies in the Indian belief that eating more complex and subtly flavored foods exercises the brain, making it better at understanding and appreciating and surviving the subtle complexities of life.

—SPICE HOUSE CATALOG

The word *curry* is derived from the original south Indian *kari*, meaning "sauce."

General Information

Curry is a combination of spices that may consist of a mixture of as few as five or as many as fifty ingredients. At Indian meals several curries—each of them with different flavors—may be served during the course of one meal. The color of most curry powders is derived from the goldenrod yellow of turmeric. True Indian curry bears very little resemblance to the parodies of it served in the West. For Indians, curry is a sauce intended to add relish—no more—to bland basic fare like rice or the wheaten pancakes known as chapatis. A little of it goes, and is meant to go, a long way.

Cumin / Nutritional Value Per 100 g Edible Portion		
	Whole Seed	**1 tsp.**
Calories	375	8
Protein	17.81 g	0.37 g
Fat	22.27 g	0.47 g
Fiber	10.50 g	0.22 g
Calcium	931 mg	20 mg
Iron	66.35 mg	1.39 mg
Magnesium	366 mg	8 mg
Phosphorus	499 mg	10 mg
Potassium	1,788 mg	38 mg
Sodium	168 mg	4 mg
Zinc	4.800 mg	0.100 mg
Copper	0.867 mg	n/a
Manganese	3.333 mg	n/a
Beta Carotene (A)	1,270 IU	27 IU
Thiamine (B₁)	0.628 mg	0.013 mg
Riboflavin (B₂)	0.327 mg	0.007 mg
Niacin (B₃)	4.579 mg	0.096 mg
Ascorbic Acid (C)	7.71 mg	0.16 mg

Curry Powder / Nutritional Value Per 100 g Edible Portion

	Powder	1 tsp.
Calories	325	6
Protein	12.66 g	0.25 g
Fat	13.81 g	0.28 g
Fiber	16.32 g	0.33 g
Calcium	478 mg	10 mg
Iron	29.59 mg	0.59 mg
Magnesium	254 mg	5 mg
Phosphorus	349 mg	7 mg
Potassium	1,543 mg	31 mg
Sodium	52 mg	1 mg
Zinc	4.050 mg	0.080 mg
Copper	0.815 mg	n/a
Manganese	4.289 mg	n/a
Beta Carotene (A)	986 IU	20 IU
Thiamine (B₁)	0.253 mg	0.005 mg
Riboflavin (B₂)	0.281 mg	0.006 mg
Niacin (B₃)	3.467 mg	0.069 mg
Ascorbic Acid (C)	11.41 mg	0.23 mg

Culinary Uses

Commercially prepared curry powder usually contains fifteen or twenty spices, herbs, and seeds. It is prepared by grinding a small quantity of slightly roasted, dried chili peppers to a powder, mixing it with ground turmeric and coriander along with other spices, which may include one or more of the following: allspice, anise, bay leaves, caraway, cardamom, celery seed, cinnamon, cloves, cubeb berries, cumin, dill, fennel, fenugreek (seeds and leaves), garlic, ginger, juniper berries, mace, mint, mustard, nutmeg, pepper (white and/or black), poppy seeds, saffron, sumac seeds, and salt. The pungency is dependent on the amount of chili pepper used. If you wish to make your own curry powder, combine six parts turmeric, four parts cumin, and one part each of cardamom, coriander, cinnamon, black pepper, ground fenugreek, and ginger. This combination will provide maximum flavor but minimal heat. For heat, add as much cayenne pepper as you desire.

Health Benefits

pH 4.60–4.80. Because curry powder promotes perspiration, which acts as a natural air conditioner, cooling the body as the moisture evaporates on the skin, curry powder is a popular seasoning in warm climates. Its pungency may also be helpful to clear the head and nose during a head cold. Most curries contain herbs that not only stop the progress of free radicals but also prevent them from occurring in the first place. Curry also detoxifies and defends against cancer-causing molds that collect on stored food. Curry powder has been shown to increase metabolism, help breathing, and reduce cholesterol.

Dandelion
(Taraxacum officinale)

The derivation of the name *Taraxacum* is clouded by several points of view. Some botanists claim that it derives from the Persian *tark hashgun*, for the wild endive. Others believe that it was taken from an Arabian alteration of a Greek word meaning "edible." The more common theory is that the name is taken from the Greek *taraxos*, meaning "disorder," and *akos*, meaning "remedy," because of the plant's ability to correct a multitude of disorders. *Officinale* means "of the workshop," alluding to apothecaries' shops and signifying that the plant was once part of the official pharmacopoeia of Rome. The English name *dandelion* comes from the French term *dent de lion*, quite literally "lion's tooth," which describes the look of the plant's jagged leaves.

General Information

Dandelions probably originated in Asia Minor but spread throughout the known world long before written history. They were first mentioned in the writings of Arabian physicians in the tenth and eleventh centuries. European settlers deliberately introduced the plant to North America. Perhaps the world's most famous weed, this ubiquitous plant makes its appearance in nearly every country around the world and is the winner of a rogue's reputation, for it grows indiscriminately in lawns, pastures, fields, and gardens. The lowly dandelion is an extremely hardy plant, one that some believe will be among the few to survive all the herbicides we have dumped on this planet. Although lawn owners so feverishly dig it up, the dandelion actually heals the earth by transporting minerals (especially calcium) upward from deep layers, even from underneath hardpan. The dandelion's beautiful golden flower head is made up of tiny blossoms that soon turn to fluffy parachutes tipped by dark seeds—thirty-five thousand of them to the ounce. All parts of this jagged-leaved plant are quite edible, and there is now even a cultivated variety, which produces greens with a milder flavor than the wild. Early spring and fall (after the first frosts of autumn) are the best times to "harvest" dandelions; the plants in summer have matured to the point of being tough and bitter. The dandelion is an important plant for bees and the production of honey, because the flowers open early in the year, even in a cool spring, and furnish considerable quantities of nectar and pollen, while successive blooms continue throughout the year until the late autumn. The plant is highly sensitive: in fine weather the flowers follow the sun, turning toward the warmth, but long before dusk the flowers close up against the dew of the night; they will also close up at the threat of rain during the day.

Culinary Uses

Wild dandelions have more flavor than cultivated ones because they are richer in vitamins and mineral salts. All parts of the dandelion are edible, but be sure to pick early, as the plant gets quite bitter as it matures. Tender young leaves can be chopped and added raw to salads or steamed and seasoned with onion, vinegar, lemon, or herbs, to be served like spinach. Unopened buds are excellent nutlike morsels, delicious in salads and as a tea for tonic and indigestion. Fried in butter, they taste much like mushrooms. Dandelion root has a stronger flavor than the highly cultivated vegetables most of us are accustomed to, with a

LORE AND LEGEND

The feathery seed balls of dandelions were used in olden times as oracles by lovers. Young maidens would blow three times on the fluff to determine if their sweethearts were thinking of them; the maiden was not forgotten if a lone feather remained. Dandelion greens were so highly prized by the Apache Indians that they would spend days or weeks searching the surrounding countryside for them.

marked taste that is both slightly sweet and bitter. Young roots are good chopped and added to salads, peeled and sautéed to be served as a tasty vegetable, or dried, roasted, and ground to be used as a caffeine-free coffee substitute. A kind of beer can be made from the leaves, and from the crushed flower heads a light golden dandelion wine is made that has a taste suggestive of sherry and a reputation as an excellent tonic for the blood.

Health Benefits

Cholagogue, diuretic, laxative, stomachic, tonic. One of the oldest and most versatile of the healing herbs, dandelion is regarded as a blood cleanser, tonic, and digestive aid because of its content of mucilages, which soothe the digestive tract, absorb toxins from ingested food, and regulate intestinal bacteria. Considered one of the finest liver remedies, both as a food and as a medicine, the root has bitter principles that enhance the flow of bile, improving such conditions as liver congestion, bile duct inflammation, hepatitis, gallstones, and jaundice. Its action in increasing bile flow is twofold: it has a direct effect on the liver, causing an increase in bile production and flow to the gallbladder (choleretic effect), and it has a direct effect on the gallbladder, causing contraction and release of stored bile (cholagogue effect). In the spring the root contains levulose, a sugar easily assimilated by diabetics; by autumn this sugar has changed to inulin, an easily assimilated starch. Dandelion leaves are many times richer in vitamin C, potassium (which makes them bitter), and calcium than leaf lettuce or even spinach. The young greens are also an excellent liver cleanser, stimulate the activity of the pancreas and spleen, and detoxify any poisons throughout the body. Because of its cleansing abilities, dandelion has a

Dandelion / Nutritional Value Per 100 g Edible Portion			
	Greens, Raw	Cooked	Dried
Calories	45	33	265
Protein	2.70 g	2.00 g	16.50 g
Fat	0.70 g	0.60 g	1.60 g
Fiber	1.60 g	1.30 g	8.90 g
Calcium	187 mg	140 mg	614 mg
Iron	3.10 mg	1.80 mg	96 mg
Magnesium	36 mg	n/a	157 mg
Phosphorus	66 mg	42 mg	362 mg
Potassium	397 mg	232 mg	1,200 mg
Sodium	76 mg	44 mg	113 mg
Beta Carotene (A)	14,000 IU	11,700 IU	14,000 IU
Thiamine (B$_1$)	0.190 mg	0.130 mg	trace
Riboflavin (B$_2$)	0.260 mg	0.175 mg	0.210 mg
Niacin (B$_3$)	n/a	n/a	3.310 mg
Ascorbic Acid (C)	35.0 mg	18.0 mg	37.6 mg
Tocopherol (E)	2.50 mg	n/a	n/a

beneficial effect on any skin disorders, jaundice, menstrual troubles, and blood pressure irregularities.

Dandelion juice is an excellent tonic used to counteract hyperacidity and normalize the alkalinity of the system; it is beneficial for the teeth and gums. Juice from the broken stems of spring or summer dandelions is reputed to cure warts (autumn and winter juice will not work). Touch the wart with the milky juice and leave on to dry; repeat frequently. In a few days the wart will turn black and fall off. The tea is used as a remedy for fatigue, as a diuretic and a tonic, to promote bowel regularity, and to nourish the liver.

Dill
(Anethum graveolens)

See how unpretentious and ordinary they are, the plants through which miracles are performed. It's only a little Dill mixed with Bay leaves in spring water, but it serves to prepare a bath and a potion.

—APULEIUS

Dill / Nutritional Value Per 100 g Edible Portion					
	Leaves Fresh	Leaves Dried	Leaves 1 tsp.	Whole Seed	Seed 1 tsp.
Calories	43	253	3	305	6
Protein	3.46 g	19.96 g	0.20 g	15.98 g	0.34 g
Fat	1.12 g	4.36 g	trace	14.53 g	0.31 g
Fiber	n/a	11.93 g	0.12 g	21.09 g	0.44 g
Calcium	208 mg	1,784 mg	18 mg	1,516 mg	32 mg
Iron	n/a	48.77 mg	0.49 mg	16.32 mg	0.34 mg
Magnesium	55 mg	451 mg	5 mg	256 mg	5 mg
Phosphorus	66 mg	543 mg	5 mg	277 mg	6 mg
Potassium	738 mg	3,308 mg	33 mg	1,186 mg	25 mg
Sodium	61 mg	208 mg	2 mg	20 mg	trace
Zinc	0.910 mg	3.300 mg	0.030 mg	5.200 mg	0.110 mg
Copper	0.146 mg	0.490 mg	n/a	0.780 mg	n/a
Manganese	1.264 mg	3.950 mg	n/a	1.833 mg	n/a
Beta Carotene (A)	n/a	n/a	n/a	53 IU	1 IU
Thiamine (B₁)	0.058 mg	0.418 mg	0.004 mg	0.418 mg	0.009 mg
Riboflavin (B₂)	0.296 mg	0.284 mg	0.003 mg	0.284 mg	0.006 mg
Niacin (B₃)	1.570 mg	2.807 mg	0.029 mg	2.807 mg	0.059 mg
Pantothenic Acid (B₅)	0.397 mg	n/a	n/a	n/a	n/a
Pyridoxine (B₆)	0.185 mg	1.461 mg	0.015 mg	n/a	n/a
Folic Acid (B₉)	150 mcg	n/a	n/a	n/a	n/a

LORE AND LEGEND

Hanging a bunch of dill over the doorway was said to protect the house from witches. In the American colonies dill (and fennel) seeds were called "meetin' seeds" because they were carried to church by mothers for restless and hungry children to chew on during the interminable sermons.

Anethum is from *anethom*, an ancient Greek name for the dill plant; *graveolens* means "heavy-scented." The English name *dill* is a derivative of the old Norse word *dilla*, which means "to lull."

General Information
Dill is a member of the parsley family native to the Mediterranean region and southern Russia. Used since time immemorial, it makes its first written appearance in an Egyptian medical work of about 3000 B.C. Among the Greeks it was used as a food, a perfume, and an incense. The Romans chewed dill seeds to promote digestion, and they hung dill garlands in their dining halls, believing the herb would prevent stomach upset. The plant yields two different herbs: dill seed (the fruit of the plant) and dill weed, the top eight inches of the graceful, feathery leaves. Dill is highly prized in Scandinavian, Russian, and Polish cooking but is used in the United States primarily in pickles, potato salad, and sauerkraut.

Culinary Uses
Dill is a fragrant, decorative plant whose delicate flavor cannot be matched by any other herb. The feathery green leaves have a subtle, piquant flavor, similar to mild caraway, good for enhancing the natural flavors of cucumbers, green salads, vegetables, soups, and stews. Dill seeds have a slightly sharper taste than the leaves and are quite plainly bitter. They are used in pickles, cheese dishes, salad dressings, potato salads, and occasionally in cakes and pastries. Fresh dill leaves and seeds are preferable to the dried forms.

Health Benefits
Antispasmodic, aromatic, carminative, diuretic, stimulant, stomachic. Dill is an ancient Egyptian remedy that is mentioned as a painkiller in the Ebers papyrus (c. 1500 B.C.). It contains an essential oil that includes carvone and other

components that give it its inimitable fragrance. Dill seed usually contains 2.5 to 4 percent volatile oil, composed mainly of carvone with lesser amounts of numerous other aromatic chemicals. Dill oil has been proven to help lower glucose levels by normalizing insulin levels. Both leaves and seed have a mild soporific effect, and in England a soothing dill water was once given to babies. Herbalists regularly use dill leaves and seeds to dispel flatulence, stimulate the appetite and settle indigestion, induce sleep, and increase mother's milk. Try chewing a few seeds to help clear up halitosis. Seasoning food with dill makes it more appetizing and digestible, with the added bonus of a high vitamin content.

Epazote

(Chenopodium ambrosioides)
Also Known As: Mexican Tea, Wormseed, Jerusalem Oak

Chenopodium is a Greek word meaning "goosefoot," alluding to the shape of the plant's leaves; *ambrosioides* means "ambrosial." The English name is taken from the Aztec words for "skunk," *eptal*, and "sweat," *tzotl*, which aptly describes the plant's intense, musky-sour aroma.

General Information

Epazote is native to the Yucatan Peninsula of tropical America and grows wild in the Americas and parts of Europe. A close relative of lamb's-quarter, it is a nondescript weed that grows several feet high and has irregularly toothed green leaves, sometimes splotched with red or purple.

Culinary Uses

This herb has an aroma similar to that of turpentine or menthol. It is used as a green herb in Mexican cooking and as a

tisane in Europe. When combined with beans, epazote helps to reduce intestinal gas. Because pests are deterred by the leaves, they are stuffed in mattresses and sachets in Brazil.

Health Benefits

An acrid and astringent herb, epazote increases perspiration and relaxes spasms. It is not used during pregnancy because it stimulates downward motion in the pelvis. All parts of the plant are effective externally for fungal infections, barber's itch, athlete's foot, and ringworm, as well as being somewhat antibacterial. Oil from the seeds is used to expel worms, but overdoses have caused death in infants because of its toxic alkaloid. The tea is used by herbalists to treat dysentery. Use this herb only in small quantities.

Fennel

(Foeniculum vulgare dulce, F. piperitum, F. azoricum)
Also Known As: Finocchio, Carosella, Florence Fennel

> There's fennel for you, and columbines; there's rue for you; and here's some for me; we may call it herb of grace o' Sundays.
>
> —WILLIAM SHAKESPEARE, *Hamlet*

The Romans named the plant *foeniculum*, which means "little hay." The name eventually evolved into the more familiar *fennel*. *Vulgare dulce* means "commonly found sweet plant"; *piperitum* means "resembling peppermint" or "being sharply fragrant/flavored"; *azoricum* means "from the Azores." The plant's Greek name, *marathon*, comes from a verb meaning "to grow thin."

General Information

Fennel was originally a maritime plant from southern Europe. The Romans employed all parts of this aromatic plant—roots, stems, leaves, and seeds—both raw and cooked. It was introduced into western North America by Spanish priests and still grows wild around their old missions. Early English settlers brought the plant to the eastern coast. A rather unusual looking vegetable, with a celery-like base and feathery dill-like leaves, it has small yellow flowers, each of which produces two green or yellow-brown seeds about an eighth to five-sixteenths of an inch long, oval in shape, ribbed, and greenish gray. These diminutive seeds are said by some to resemble miniature

Epazote / Nutritional Value Per 100 g Edible Portion			
	Fresh		Fresh
Calories	42-295	Sodium	1.0-6.9 mg
Protein	3.8-30.9 g	Beta Carotene (A)	3.5-43.6 mg
Fat	0.7-5.4 g	Thiamine (B$_1$)	0.060-0.540 mg
Fiber	1.3-12.1 g	Riboflavin (B$_2$)	0.300-2.500 mg
Calcium	304-2,456 mg	Niacin (B$_3$)	0.600-18.500 mg
Iron	5.2-55.7 mg	Ascorbic Acid (C)	11-610 mg
Phosphorus	52-403 mg		

watermelons. There are several varieties of fennel, including Florence fennel and finocchio (*F. piperitum, F. azoricom*), which produce thick stalks that can be eaten like celery, and sweet fennel (*F. vulgare dulce*), whose seeds are used as an herb.

Culinary Uses

Fennel is one of the newer arrivals in North American supermarkets. This strange-looking plant has a flavor slightly reminiscent of anise and licorice, but softer and nuttier. The leaves, tender stems, and seeds are used from the milder sweet fennel variety, while the stalks and bulbs are used from Florence fennel and finocchio. The bulb and stems are eaten like celery; the stalk, stripped of its skin and dressed in vinegar and pepper, makes a tasty celery-like salad called cartucci that is popular in the plant's native Mediterranean area. Feathery leaves of dark green are a tasty addition to mayonnaise, vinaigrette sauces, salads, and soups. Finocchio is used as a vegetable, most often in salads. Fennel seeds can be used in a wide range of dishes, from apple pies to curries and vinegars. Toss a few fennel seeds in your next pot of baked beans, as they will help cut down on the flatulent aftereffects.

Health Benefits

Aromatic, antispasmodic, carminative, diuretic, expectorant, stimulant, stomachic. Fennel has been used to soothe

LORE AND LEGEND

Early Greeks believed that fennel had slimming powers and was able to give a man strength, courage, and long life. The plant's name in Greek was *marathon*; the place where the famous battle with the Persians in 490 B.C. was fought was so called because the soil there was overgrown with fennel. Romans believed that fennel was an aid in sharpening vision and was a symbol of success. The giant variety grown by the Romans was used to flog reluctant students, with the hope that, perhaps by osmosis, new insights and abilities would result. As far back as Pliny there was a belief that serpents ate the leaves of fennel to renew their youth and thus enable them to shed their skins. It was also believed that serpents constantly haunted fennel patches because its strong licorice odor improved their vision, which at best is never very keen. During the Middle Ages people ate fennel seeds to stave off hunger during church fasts. In sixteenth-century Europe, the expression "to give fennel" meant to flatter or give false compliments; just as fennel allayed hunger for a while, bringing no lasting nourishment, a false compliment flatters temporarily but brings no real satisfaction to its recipient.

the stomach and intestines, relieve flatulence, expel pinworms, sweeten the breath, regularize menstrual periods, and increase milk in nursing mothers. It can also be used as a gargle and an eyewash. Fennel seed generally contains 2 to 6 percent volatile oil (fennel oil) and other active constituents. These volatile oils, many which are antimicrobial, are responsible for most of fennel's medicinal properties. Fennel is also reported to have hormonal-like action that helps support the body in reducing PMS and menopausal symptoms. It may also help break up fluids and toxins and cleanse the tissues of the body. Tea made from the crushed seeds, proven scientifically to contain antispasmodic properties, is used to treat indigestion and cramps. Chew the leaves, bulb, or seeds for a pleasant, refreshing taste and breath sweetener. To bathe the eyes,

Fennel / Nutritional Value Per 100 g Edible Portion		
	Whole Seed	1 tsp.
Calories	345	7
Protein	15.80 g	0.32 g
Fat	14.87 g	0.30 g
Fiber	15.66 g	0.31 g
Calcium	1,196 mg	24 mg
Iron	18.54 mg	0.37 mg
Magnesium	385 mg	8 mg
Phosphorus	487 mg	10 mg
Potassium	1,694 mg	34 mg
Sodium	88 mg	2 mg
Zinc	3.700 mg	0.070 mg
Copper	1.067 mg	n/a
Manganese	6.533 mg	n/a
Beta Carotene (A)	135 IU	3 IU
Thiamine (B$_1$)	0.408 mg	0.008 mg
Riboflavin (B$_2$)	0.353 mg	0.007 mg
Niacin (B$_3$)	6.050 mg	0.121 mg

put a teaspoonful of the leaves in a cup, pour in boiling water, allow to cool, and then gently drop the strained liquid into the eyes. Fennel has a specific affinity for the bloodstream and builds strong blood plasma. Other benefits of fennel include its being an excellent obesity fighter, since it acts as an appetite suppressant and accelerates the digestion of fatty foods.

Fenugreek
(Trigonella foenum-graecum)
Also Known As: Greek Hay, Foenugreek

The name *Trigonella* is derived from the old Greek name denoting "three-angled," because of the form of the plant's corolla. The English name *fenugreek* comes from *foenum-graecum*, a Latin phrase meaning "Greek hay," the plant being used to scent inferior hay. Early Greeks mixed the plant into moldy or insect-damaged forage to make it more palatable to their animals and in the process discovered that sick horses and cattle would eat fenugreek when they would not eat anything else.

General Information
Fenugreek, a member of the leguminous bean family, is cultivated primarily for its seeds and is one of the oldest culinary and medicinal plants. Indigenous to Mediterranean shores and western Asia, fenugreek plants resemble white clover but produce pods, each of which contains between ten and twenty aromatic seeds. Each seed is about one-quarter inch long, brownish yellow, and marked with an oblique furrow along half its length. The plant was introduced into central Europe by Benedictine monks, and Charlemagne himself promoted its use during the ninth century. Fenugreek was introduced to the Chinese during the Sung Dynasty (c. 1057 A.D.), and they have since made much use of the plant. The seeds in their natural state have little or no odor; they acquire some when dried, a little more when ground, and a final increment when heated.

Culinary Uses
Young shoots of fenugreek are chopped and added to salads, while the leaves are used as a vegetable. The yellow seeds have a slightly bitter yet pleasant taste, reminiscent of celery and maple, with a similar odor. For cooking, the seeds are best dry-roasted before use to remove their bitter flavor, although over-roasting will leave them just as

unpleasant. If you inadvertently overtoast fenugreek, one taste will let you know and from then on you will have a sense of how much is enough. Sprouted like mustard and cress, the seeds make a tasty, crunchy addition to salads. Ground fenugreek seed is an important ingredient in Indian curry powder, chutneys, and the Jewish sweet dish halvah. The seeds are so hard, however, that they cannot be ground in a mortar but only with a special poppy seed grinding mill. The oil of fenugreek has a maple flavor and can be used for a maple flavoring in cooking and syrups.

Health Benefits
Emollient, expectorant, mucilaginous, tonic. Fenugreek is one of the oldest medicinal plants, dating back to the ancient Egyptians and the Greek Hippocrates. Early Egyptians prepared a thick paste by soaking the seeds in water; this was used to prevent fevers, to soothe stomach disorders, and to treat diabetics. The seeds are high (40 percent) in mucilage, as well as an emollient soothing to the skin, and are used as an emulsifier in drugs and food. They are also rich in fixed oils that are often compared to cod liver oil preparations, as they contain choline and vitamin A (and upon oxidizing produce a distinct "fishy" odor). Nourishing and body building, fenugreek helps treat indigestion, intestinal inflammation, mucous membranes,

Fenugreek / Nutritional Value Per 100 g Edible Portion		
	Whole Seed	1 tsp.
Calories	323	12
Protein	23.00 g	0.85 g
Fat	6.41 g	0.24 g
Fiber	10.07 g	0.37 g
Calcium	176 mg	6 mg
Iron	33.53 mg	1.24 mg
Magnesium	191 mg	7 mg
Phosphorus	296 mg	11 mg
Potassium	770 mg	28 mg
Sodium	67 mg	2 mg
Zinc	2.500 mg	0.090 mg
Copper	1.110 mg	n/a
Manganese	1.228 mg	n/a
Beta Carotene (A)	n/a	n/a
Thiamine (B$_1$)	0.322 mg	0.012 mg
Riboflavin (B$_2$)	0.366 mg	0.014 mg
Niacin (B$_3$)	1.640 mg	0.061 mg
Folic Acid (B$_9$)	57.0 mcg	2.1 mcg
Ascorbic Acid (C)	3.00 mg	0.11 mg

LORE AND LEGEND

Arab women from Libya to Syria ate roasted fenugreek seeds to gain weight and attain the shapely Rubenesque proportions synonymous with beauty from ancient times through the nineteenth century. The lord of the harem, meanwhile, ate them as an aphrodisiac. In many places fenugreek is still considered a potent aphrodisiac. Nursing mothers in Ethiopia increase their intake of fenugreek, for it is believed to promote the production of milk (it does provide a generous 180 mg of calcium per hundred grams of seed). Fenugreek was a major ingredient in Lydia E. Pinkham's famous Vegetable Compound, introduced to the American public in 1875 as a remedy for "female complaints"; the compound also contained a comforting syrup that was about 18 percent alcohol.

ulcers, lung problems, and allergies. Fenugreek tea helps lubricate the intestines, cleaning out poisonous toxins that build up in the body's system; it also helps relieve lower back pain and that general feeling of tiredness often associated with stomach and intestinal troubles. The seeds also contain saponins and spogenins consisting of diosgenin and yamogenin, which are starting materials for the synthesis of steroid hormones and related drugs. Diosgenin is important in the synthesis of oral contraceptives and sex-hormone treatments, as it can be converted to pregnenolone (a steroid formed during the synthesis of hormones) and progesterone, the anti-estrogen hormone secreted by pregnant women.

Galangal

(Alpinia galanga, A. officinarum)
Also known as Greater Galangal, Thai Ginger, Kencur, Laos

The genus *Alpinia* was named after Prosper Alpinus, an Italian botanist. *Officinarum* means "sold as an herb."

General Information

Greater galangal resembles ginger, to which it is related, but its rhizomes are larger and pale yellow with zebralike markings and pink shoots. Called galingale in England, it was popular throughout Europe in the Middle Ages but disappeared from Western cooking when the heavy use of spices went out of favor in the eighteenth century. Dried, ground galangal (often called laos, its Indonesian name) can frequently be found in Asian groceries.

Culinary Uses

With its fiery medicinal taste and wood-chip texture, the fresh root of greater galangal is not to be eaten on its own. Pounded fresh in a mortar with seasonings such as lemongrass, chili peppers, shallots, and garlic, galangal has a much more appealing flavor and is an important ingredient in Thai curry pastes. Dried, ground galangal is added to soups, stews, and curries. Its small black fruits are used as a cardamom substitute. Lesser galangal, yet another ginger family member, is used primarily as a vegetable and medicinal ingredient.

Health Benefits

Like ginger, galangal is reputed to curb nausea and settle the stomach, and grated galangal with lime juice is an all-purpose tonic in Southeast Asia.

Garam Masala

The name of this Indian spice literally translates as "hot mixture."

General Information

Garam masala is an aromatic mixture of toasted, ground spices used as a basic seasoning for many Indian dishes. Although freshly blended and ground in India and the East, here in the West it is bought ready-prepared and may contain such "warm" spices as allspice, cinnamon, coriander, peppercorns, cloves, cumin, and chili pepper.

Culinary Uses and Health Benefits

The primary use of garam masala is in bean dishes, where it adds a great deal of energy and flavor. Garam masala has all the beneficial properties of its constituent spices.

Garlic
(Allium sativum, A. scorodoprasum)

Shallots are for babies; onions are for men; garlic is for heroes.

—AUTHOR UNKNOWN

Tomatoes and oregano make it Italian; wine and tarragon make it French. Sour cream makes it Russian; lemon and cinnamon make it Greek. Soy sauce makes it Chinese; garlic makes it good.

—ALICE MAY BROCK (OF ALICE'S RESTAURANT)

Allium is the ancient Latin name for the garlic family and may derive from the Celtic *all*, meaning "pungent." *Sativum* indicates that this plant has long been cultivated. The English name *garlic* is derived from the Middle English *gar*, meaning "spear," and *leac*, meaning "potherb." During the Middle Ages bald men were called *pilgarlics*, a term meaning "peeled garlics."

General Information
The origin of garlic is unknown, though it is believed to have originated somewhere near Siberia and to have spread from there into the Middle East and Europe. This member of the lily family has a compact bulb divided into a varied number of white or purplish-colored, almond-shaped segments called cloves, each one wrapped in its own papery

LORE AND LEGEND

There has never been a time when humanity ignored garlic, nor has there ever been an herb called upon to play such disparate roles. The entire ancient world from Spain to China revered garlic; in fact, the cultivation of garlic in China is of such ancient origin that it has an ideogram to itself. During the time of the pharaohs, when Egypt was at the peak of its power, garlic was given to the laborers and slaves who were building the pyramids in order to increase their stamina and strength as well as to protect them from disease. In the fifth century A.D. the Greek historian Herodotus wrote that on one of the pyramids there is an inscription describing the amount of garlic, onions, and radishes consumed by those building the great pyramid of King Khufu (Cheops). The use of garlic was evidently not limited solely to slaves, as Herodotus called all Egyptians "the stinking ones" because of their redolent garlic aroma. The Greeks greatly admired garlic and made much of it, and Greek criminals were given garlic to eat in order to purify them of their crimes. However, common folk who smelled of garlic were not allowed to enter the temple of Cybele, the mother goddess of the earth and goddess of untellable name, worshiped throughout the Near East.

Among the Romans garlic was fed to laborers to make them strong and to the army to give it courage, since the plant was dedicated to the war god Mars. They even attributed their success in conquering the world to garlic because "no invader would come into the country that smelled so strong." The lowly bulb was not considered with much favor by the richer classes, however, who viewed garlic breath as a sign of low birth, a belief that lasted well into the twentieth century. In India the priestly brahmins were forbidden to eat garlic, while in the first days of Islam the prophet Muhammad—fearful of offending his hosts by rejecting a dish liberally laced with garlic—explained disarmingly, "I am a man who has close contact with others." Sir John Harrington, in *The Englishman's Doctor*, written in 1609, summarized garlic's virtues and faults thus: "Garlic then have power to save from death; Bear with it though it maketh unsavory breath; And scorn not garlic like some that think; It only maketh men wink and drink and stink." Garlic has an age-old reputation as a stimulant to the sexual appetites and rambunctious thoughts. In many Eastern religious traditions, yogis, monks, and nuns eliminate garlic from their diets for these reasons.

skin. Mentioned in the literature of all the great ancient world kingdoms—Babylon, Persia, Greece, and Rome—garlic has a long history that has always been tied to the working class. A ruffian with a heart of gold and a wealth of talents—serving in the kitchen, the medicine chest, and the vegetable garden—garlic is totally undistinguished of appearance, and its smell (to some) is coarse and offensive. California produces 90 percent of the United States crop (more than 250 million pounds); some of the best is reported to be cultivated around Gilroy. In years when frost strikes the garlic crop, the cloves turn out firmer and smoother. **Elephant garlic** (*A. scorodoprasum*) cloves are roughly the size of quail eggs. Each slips nicely out of its papery skin, and in theory one clove of the big stuff is equal to about eighteen to twenty cloves of the normal-sized garlic. Elephant garlic provides essence and mild taste but not the pungency of regular garlic, and none of the aftereffects.

Culinary Uses

Sold fresh or dried into flakes and powder, garlic is probably the most popular flavoring. It is important in most of the world's cuisines and adds dimension to all foods except desserts; preparing such foods as eggplant, tomatoes, Caesar salads, and pesto is absolutely unthinkable without garlic. Raw garlic has a vibrantly sharp, biting flavor, which some find too strong for their palate. Cooking eliminates the bite and softens the flavor, while roasting garlic gives it a smooth, mild, nutty flavor. Unpeeled cloves are roasted for about fifteen minutes at 350 degrees Fahrenheit and then peeled, mashed, and used in purées, sauces, and soups.

Health Benefits

pH 5.3–6.3. Antibacterial, antifungal, antiseptic, antispasmodic, anthelmintic, antiviral, aromatic, carminative, diaphoretic, digestive, expectorant. Along with its less potent botanical relatives onions, scallions, leeks, chives, and shallots, garlic ranks among the world's oldest medicines. An Egyptian medical papyrus from the sixteenth century B.C. lists twenty-two remedies employing garlic for everything from heart disease and worms to tumors, headaches, and bites. In hundreds of studies biochemists have confirmed the ancient use of garlic as a fungicide and a powerful antibiotic: seventy-two separate infectious agents can be deterred by garlic, including those that cause the common cold, whooping cough, tuberculosis, botulism, vaginal and bladder infections, gangrene, diarrhea, staph, dysentery, and typhoid. One raw crushed clove contains the antibiotic equivalent of one hundred thousand units of penicillin and has proven more effective than either penicillin or tetracycline in suppressing certain types of disease-carrying agents. Dr. Albert Schweitzer, deep in the jungle, with his mainstream pharmaceuticals depleted, gave his patients garlic for amebic dysentery; in Japan a cold-processed, odorless raw garlic substance called Kyolic serves as an antibiotic; and in the former Soviet Union, where garlic is known as "Russian penicillin," officials on one occasion imported some five hundred tons to combat an outbreak of influenza.

Garlic is one of the most beneficial foods for the digestive system and has a strong effect on the lymphatic fluid and tissue, aiding in the elimination of noxious waste matter. In fact, European studies show garlic helps eliminate lead and other toxic heavy metals from the body. Garlic is also effective at ridding the alimentary canal of worms and other parasites, boosting immunological functions, purifying the bloodstream by removing sticky inorganic deposits in the blood vessels, and regularizing the action of the liver and the gallbladder. For protection against dysentery when traveling in foreign countries, chew a clove of garlic before consuming suspect food or water. To ward off mosquitoes, eat garlic at least once daily. As a remedy for athlete's foot, spread freshly crushed garlic over the affected area (which will feel warm for about five minutes) and leave on for half an hour before washing with plain water. Do this once a day for a week. If the skin burns, wash immediately with plain water and try later with less garlic. Another method is to sprinkle powdered garlic daily on wet feet and let dry before wearing socks.

Despite its many beneficial qualities, garlic can also induce blisters, irritation, and dermatitis (especially eczema)

Garlic / Nutritional Value Per 100 g Edible Portion			
	Raw	Powder	1 tsp.
Calories	149	332	9
Protein	6.36 g	16.80 g	0.47 g
Fat	0.50 g	0.76 g	0.02 g
Fiber	1.50 g	1.87 g	0.05 g
Calcium	181 mg	80 mg	2 mg
Iron	1.70 mg	2.75 mg	0.08 mg
Magnesium	25 mg	58 mg	2 mg
Phosphorus	153 mg	417 mg	12 mg
Potassium	401 mg	1,101 mg	31 mg
Sodium	17 mg	26 mg	1 mg
Zinc	n/a	2.630 mg	0.070 mg
Copper	n/a	0.147 mg	n/a
Manganese	n/a	0.545 mg	n/a
Beta Carotene (A)	0 IU	trace	n/a
Thiamine (B$_1$)	0.200 mg	0.466 mg	0.013 mg
Riboflavin (B$_2$)	0.110 mg	0.152 mg	0.004 mg
Niacin (B$_3$)	0.700 mg	0.692 mg	0.019 mg
Folic Acid (B$_9$)	3.1 mcg	n/a	n/a
Ascorbic Acid (C)	31.2 mg	n/a	n/a
Tocopherol (E)	0.01 mg	n/a	n/a

in some individuals. These toxic effects of garlic are a result of, to a large part, the sulfur-containing compounds present in garlic oil. Raw garlic, when eaten to very great excess, may cause various digestive problems. It may also result in burns in the mouth, throat, esophagus, and stomach. Garlic is high in sulfur and iodine.

Geranium, Scented
(Pelargonium graveolens)

The genus name *Pelargonium* is Greek for stork, because the peculiarly shaped fruit is long and slender like a stork's bill; *graveolens* means "heavy-scented." The English name *geranium* derives from the Greek diminutive word for crane, *geranos.*

General Information
The rose geranium, an annual plant grown for its small lavender flowers and wonderful rose aroma, originated in South Africa and was introduced to Europe in 1690. There are also geraniums that smell like apples, cinnamon, coconut, lemon, and mint; these plants are collectively known as scented geraniums. The unusual foliage, pretty blossoms,

easy cultivation, and delightful aromatic properties of these herbs have endeared them to gardeners the world over. The French perfume industry first demanded large-scale cultivation of rose geraniums for their essential oil in 1847.

Culinary Uses
Leaves from all the scented geraniums can be used to add an enticing aroma and delicate, sweet flavor to fresh salads, desserts, baked goods, jellies, and jams. The larger the leaves, the more fragrant they will be. The leaves may also be added whole to cool fruit drinks, crushed in warm water to make a tea, or added to other herb brews, such as peppermint tea. Jars of homemade jam are sealed with a large leaf, or one or two leaves can be placed in jars of apple or blackberry jelly before storing. Rose geranium leaves have the delicate taste and aroma of roses, with just a hint of spice.

Ginger
(Zingiber officinale)

Ginger gets its Latin and English names from the Latin translation of the Sanskrit word *sringavera*, which means "horn-root," from the fancied resemblance of its misshapen flattened rhizome to the horns of an animal. *Officinale* means "of the workshop," alluding to apothecaries' shops and signifying that the plant was once part of the official pharmacopoeia of Rome.

General Information
Ginger, a distant relative of the banana, is an exotic tropical plant that originated in India. First mentioned in China about 400 B.C., the plant has since been naturalized and cultivated in Jamaica, Africa, and the West Indies. It was a popular import item in Europe from the eleventh to the thirteenth centuries. Cultivated for its edible root, the ginger plant thrives in warm, humid climates, growing up to three feet high with wide, erect, stalkless leaves and highly aromatic flowers shooting up from the tuberous underground rhizomes. The best ginger reputedly comes from the island of Jamaica, while the most highly prized of the several varieties of ginger rhizomes has a light brown skin and creamy yellow to light green fibrous flesh.

Culinary Uses
Fresh ginger root is juicy, hot, and fibrous, with a pungent, almost peppery flavor and a refreshing sharpness.

Ginger / Nutritional Value Per 100 g Edible Portion

	Fresh Raw	Dried Powdered	1 tsp.
Calories	69	347	6
Protein	1.74 g	9.12 g	0.16 g
Fat	0.73 g	5.95 g	0.11 g
Fiber	1.03 g	5.91 g	0.11 g
Calcium	18 mg	116 mg	2 mg
Iron	0.50 mg	11.52 mg	0.21 mg
Magnesium	43 mg	184 mg	3 mg
Phosphorus	27 mg	148 mg	3 mg
Potassium	415 mg	1,342 mg	24 mg
Sodium	13 mg	32 mg	1 mg
Zinc	n/a	4.720 mg	0.080 mg
Copper	n/a	0.480 mg	n/a
Manganese	n/a	26.500 mg	n/a
Beta Carotene (A)	0 IU	147 IU	3 IU
Thiamine (B_1)	0.023 mg	0.046 mg	0.001 mg
Riboflavin (B_2)	0.029 mg	0.185 mg	0.003 mg
Niacin (B_3)	0.700 mg	5.155 mg	0.093 mg
Pantothenic Acid (B_5)	0.203 mg	n/a	n/a
Pyridoxine (B_6)	0.160 mg	n/a	n/a
Ascorbic Acid (C)	5.0 mg	n/a	n/a

The flavor and texture of gingerroot varies according to the season in which it is gathered and the length of time it is stored. The older roots tend to be tough, fibrous, and strong tasting, whereas the younger roots are mild and tender. If ginger is young and fresh, the skin will be thin and unnecessary to peel; if the skin is tough or shriveled, the skin needs to be peeled with a paring knife before using. Choose tubers that are fresh looking and firm. The little sprouts that appear on the sides of the root are more delicate in flavor than the main section. Store fresh ginger in the refrigerator. Peeled and ground to a pulp, ginger is a popular ingredient in many curries, grains, and vegetable dishes. Try adding a few bits of ginger to a pot of chamomile tea, to melted butter before pouring it over vegetables, or to rice as it cooks for a delicate, mysterious flavor. Ginger is also available dried and ground to a powder, canned, crystallized in sugar, or preserved in syrup. Candied gingerroot, a favorite treat of children, has recently regained some of its popularity, largely because it is very nearly as healthful as it is pleasurable to eat. Powdered or dried ginger, used primarily in baking, gives a completely different flavor to foods and cannot be substituted for fresh ginger; it adds a delicious flavor to stewed fruit and puddings, baked goods, and other desserts.

Health Benefits

Antispasmodic, appetizer, astringent, carminative, diaphoretic, diuretic, expectorant, stimulant, stomachic. Ginger rhizomes produce the volatile oil that contains such aromatic substances as camphene, phellandrene, zingiberene, and zingerone. These, along with several other chemicals, have made ginger one of the world's oldest and most popular medicinal spices, used in folk medicine almost everywhere. Ginger is regarded as promoting overall circulation of energy in the body and acting as a stimulant for those who are debilitated, lethargic, or convalescing from an illness. It promotes heat, neutralizes

LORE AND LEGEND

Ancient Indians used their native ginger as a physical and spiritual cleanser. They shunned strong-smelling garlic and onion before religious celebrations for fear of offending their deities, but ate lots of ginger because it left them smelling sweet, and therefore presentable to the gods. Ancient Chinese sailors chewed gingerroot to prevent seasickness, and when the root arrived in ancient Greece it was used as a stomach soother. Physicians prescribed it wrapped with bread, eventually leading to the world's first cookie, gingerbread, and later to a folk remedy for upset stomach that is still popular today: ginger ale. Beginning with the twelfth century, gingerbread was a favorite confection in England, but the cost was sufficient to largely confine its pleasure to royalty and the wealthy. The gingerbread man, beloved of children and adults alike, is the impersonalized descendant of the aristocratic gingerbread portraits of the Elizabethan court, when Elizabeth I employed a chef-artist to fashion portraits of honored guests in gingerbread. Being the subject of such attention must have been very flattering, if it didn't presage a more realistic beheading.

toxins, and aids the digestion and assimilation of food, as well as affecting a systematic cleansing through the skin, bowels, and kidneys. Recent research has shown that ginger is helpful in preventing motion sickness and vertigo. Ginger tea, made by boiling pieces of fresh gingerroot in water, promotes cleansing of the system through perspiration and is also said to be useful for menstrual cramps, bloating, or suppressed menstruation. Try some warm ginger tea at the onset of a cold or flu to ease the effects of the usual symptoms. The tea is also gentle enough to use during pregnancy to help ease morning sickness or alleviate colds (however, see the note below regarding use of ginger during pregnancy). Finally, chew the peeled root to stimulate the flow of saliva and to soothe a sore throat.

Note: Germany's Commission E recommends that dried, powdered ginger not be taken for morning sickness during pregnancy; traditional Chinese medicine also recommends against using ginger during pregnancy.

Ginseng
(Panax ginseng, P. quinquefolius, Eleutherococcus senticosus)

The genus name *Panax*, like the word *panacea*, is derived from the Greek words *pan* (all) and *akos* (remedy); thus *panakeia* means "all-healing," in reference to the miraculous virtue ascribed to it by the Chinese, who consider it a sovereign remedy in almost all diseases. The ancient Chinese called the plant *jen shen*, or "essence of the earth in the form of a man," which became the English *ginseng*. The term *quinquefolius* means "five-leaved." *Eleutherococcus* comes from the Greek words *eleutheros*, meaning "free," and *coccus*, which can refer to a berry, seed, or grain.

General Information
Ginseng is the aromatic root of an unassuming ivylike ground cover that commonly grows to a length of two feet or more. Asiatic or Chinese ginseng (*Panax ginseng*) grows in the damp woodlands of Manchuria and is cultivated primarily in Korea. American ginseng (*P. quinquefolius*) is a perennial plant that at one time was found wild in the rich, cool woodlands of eastern North America, from Quebec west to Manitoba and south to northern Florida and Alabama. It is most abundantly found in the Cumberland Gap region of southern Appalachia. Siberian ginseng (*Eleutherococcus senti-*

cosus) has a habitat of primarily Siberia—thus its vernacular name; it is not a true ginseng but is part of the same family as the other two ginsengs and contains similar active chemicals. All three varieties of ginseng are used interchangeably, and as its high reputation in Asia ensures constant demand, world trade consists almost exclusively of cultivated plants. Esteemed by the Chinese above all other botanicals as a cure-all, it has been primarily their centuries-old demand that provoked incredible market fluctuations, astronomical prices, overharvesting, and a lingering curiosity. This curious root, with its distinctive trunk and extremities, which approximate human arms and legs, remains as important in Chinese folk medicine as ever. A Jesuit missionary named Joseph Lafitau in Montreal, Canada, during the early 1700s realized that American ginseng was nearly identical to a medicinal plant much in demand in China, and almost overnight a brisk export trade developed. The first American ship to reach China in 1784, Major Samuel Shaw's *Emperor of China*, carried a cargo of American ginseng and made quite a tidy profit. Popular demand for the roots nearly wiped out the wild supply, and ginseng is now protected by law in many states because of previous overharvesting.

Culinary Uses
Ginseng lovers claim that the fabled herb has a mild licorice flavor, which adds a delightful accent to tea, coffee, and other beverages and dishes. The Chinese have traditionally chewed the root and brewed it into a tea and spring tonic, but today ginseng is also available in powder, capsule, honey, and liquid form.

Health Benefits
Ginseng has been said to be a general panacea, with the ability to promote healing in all ailments—everything from

Ginseng / Nutritional Value Per 100 g Edible Portion			
	Asian, Dried		**Asian, Dried**
Calories	274	Sodium	2.4 mg
Protein	10.9 g	Zinc	trace
Fat	1.77 g	Manganese	1.90 mg
Fiber	7.2 g	Beta Carotene (A)	trace
Calcium	288 mg	Thiamine (B$_1$)	0.170 mg
Iron	trace	Riboflavin (B$_2$)	0.180 mg
Magnesium	48.1 mg	Niacin (B$_3$)	8.000 mg
Phosphorus	52.8 mg	Ascorbic Acid (C)	0 mg
Potassium	243 mg		

LORE AND LEGEND

Ginseng is one of the most fabled ancient healing plants, a plant cloaked in mystery and superstition. According to ancient beliefs, ginseng represented the crystallization of the unseen spirit of nature in the form of a man who dwells in its root. Thus, ginseng roots that were clearly man-shaped held the spirit and power of God and were effective in curing disease and strengthening the weak. In one legend ginseng began as a divine gift to a deserving but miserable young wife who, after several years of marriage, had no children and was frantic with disappointment. Custom made her situation particularly bitter, because after three childless years her husband would be permitted to take a concubine. One night she dreamed about an old man in the mountains who could assist her; searching him out, she took the herbal remedy he offered and soon bore a child. Later, when she made the journey back to see and thank him, she thanked him so prettily that he (who was actually a deity in disguise) filled the woods with this miraculous plant. The plant was ginseng, and has become a Chinese symbol of strength, vigor, long life, and clear judgment. Surpassing even the truffle throughout history as a precious aphrodisiac, one

Chinese emperor reputedly paid ten thousand dollars for a perfect man-figure ginseng root. Like mandrake, the most potent ginseng roots are said to be shaped like a man's body, and the Chinese believe that even better results are obtained when the root is dug up at midnight during a full moon.

Chinese records verify the fact that the renowned Chinese herbalist Li Chung Yun reached 256 years of age. He was born in 1677, and in 1933 the *New York Times* announced the death of this remarkable man. Professor Li gave a course of twenty-eight lectures on longevity at a Chinese university when he was over the age of two hundred. Those who saw him declared that he did not appear older than a man of fifty-two; that he stood straight and strong, and had his own natural hair and teeth. It is claimed that Li Chung Yun's longevity was due to his strictly vegetarian diet, his calm and serene attitude toward life, and the fact that he regularly used powerful rejuvenating herbs prepared as teas. These herbs were Fo-ti (*Polygonum multiflorum*), gotu kola (*Centella asiatica*), and ginseng. With the exception of the ginseng root, Li would eat only food that was produced above the ground.

conquering cancer to rejuvenating male sexuality. It is the only plant used routinely by so great a number of more or less healthy individuals for stimulation, added energy, and a sense of well-being. The main active constituents of ginseng are a group of fifteen ginsenosides, each of which acts differently, stimulating or sedating depending on the particular metabolic needs of the individual. Hence the term *adaptogen* is used to describe ginseng, for it helps to restore and maintain internal homeostasis. Tests have shown that ginseng stimulates the central nervous system and various secretory glands and promotes increased motor coordination, stamina and endurance, mental alertness, adaptability and agility, sensual perception, and learning ability. It has also been found to afford protective medicinal action against radiation exposure.

Chinese medical practitioners classify Asian/Chinese ginseng as yang (warming/male) and use it for increasing

chi (energy), strength, and blood volume; promoting life and appetite; and quieting the spirit and giving wisdom. It is great for individuals who are weak, run cool or cold, have trouble containing heat and/or are on the mend from a long illness, including lung or heart ailments; it is also a good sexual/libido/performance tonic and increases sperm count and quality. This variety of ginseng is best avoided by those who are well muscled and quick to anger. Chinese ginseng has been used for over five thousand years in China and is the most botanically similar to American ginseng; they are capable of cross-pollinating.

Korean ginseng, also *Panax ginseng*, is grown in Korea and is always steamed, thus causing it to become energetically concentrated. Because of this concentration, Korean ginseng is warm to hot—more yang, if you will. This type is more appropriate for those who are looking to really "amp up" their system. Korean ginseng increases sexual vitality a bit more than the other ginsengs do and is perfect for those who are cold or work in the cold, such as in refrigerated environments or outdoors. Korean ginseng can raise the blood pressure and if taken in excess can cause headaches or sleeplessness. It is recommended that moistening herbs, such as licorice, marshmallow, or honey, be added to Korean ginseng to balance its slightly drying nature.

American ginseng is considered a yin (cooling/female) tonic whose action is to reduce heat of the respiratory or digestive systems, relieve fatigue, and enhance reproductive performance and immunity; it is well suited to those with an aggressive constitution. American ginseng is ideal for individuals who have a tendency to run warm or hot and should not be further heated, yet need a chi tonic. It is also recommended for individuals with lung weakness or a history of lung ailments. This ginseng is also good for diabetics and postchemo cancer patients as well as those with neuralgia, rheumatism, gout, poor digestion, and impotency. American ginseng is a gentle and slow-acting herb compared to its relatives. Because it is so well balanced, it may be taken as a simple (single herb), not requiring other herbs to balance it. It is also fine to use in the summer, when the weather is warmer, because it is neutral in temperature and not overstimulating. In North America, American ginseng was an important medicine among many Indian tribes. It was used to induce easy childbirth, to treat nosebleeds, to increase female fertility, and as a general mental tonic.

Siberian ginseng is used for increasing chi, treating energy deficiencies that result in lower back pain and kidney problems, and normalizing body functions. It is especially noted for its adaptogenic action, protecting against the mental and physical effects of stress, aiding in the recovery from stress, and reducing the overall collateral damage caused by stress. It is also a hypotensive (blood pressure regulator) and may even bring blood pressure up if it is too low (however, see the note below regarding this use of Siberian ginseng). It increases immune function as well as being antirheumatic and antispasmodic. It also aids in recovery and reduction of side effects from chemotherapy, as well as overwork, exhaustion, chronic fatigue syndrome, insomnia, mild depression, trauma, surgery, adrenal/endocrine exhaustion, and more. Siberian ginseng is well known for its ability to increase athletic performance, as was witnessed by the world in the Olympic Games of the 1970s and 1980s, where the Russian athletes excelled. Russian cosmonauts also used Siberian ginseng in their space program in the 1970s and found it to be significantly helpful.

Note: Germany's Commission E, a division of the German Federal Health Agency, recommends that Siberian ginseng not be used in cases of high blood pressure.

Gum Karaya
(Sterculia urens)

Sterculia comes either from Sterculius, of Roman mythology, or from *stercus*, meaning "manure," because the leaves and fruits of some species have a particular odor; *urens* means "burning" or "stinging." The English term *gum karaya* comes from the plant's exuding a gummy substance and from a Hindi term, *karayal*, meaning "resin."

General Information

Every spring, harvesters enter the forests of the subtropical Himalayas in search of the soft-wooded trees called karaya. Avoiding the large leaves, which resemble the leaves of grapevines except that their stalks are armed with stinging hairs, they selectively wound some of the larger trees, cutting away two sheets of the smooth bark. A gummy, brownish, vinegary-smelling sap begins to flow, solidifying into ropy strips or huge tears, some of which may weigh as much as ten pounds. The hardened sap is a polysaccharide—a complex form of carbohydrate—whose individual molecules have been reported to outweigh those of water by more than five hundred thousand times. When it comes in contact with water, the absorbent granules of the dried gum swell up like sponges to as much as one hundred times their original size. The paper industry uses karaya as a fiber binder in tissue paper; in construction, it is used to bind the particles of some composition boards.

Culinary Uses

Gum karaya is used as a stabilizer for salad dressings, a binder for meat products, a gummy base for candies, and a thickener of meringue, Popsicles, sherbets, whipped cream, and cheese spreads.

Health Benefits

Laxative. In the intestines, gum karaya swells and triggers peristalsis, pushing food through the digestive system.

Dentists use the powdered gum as a denture adhesive that is resistant both to bacteria and to the enzymes of the mouth.

Honey, Raw

If God had not made brown honey, men would think figs much sweeter than they do.

—Xenophanes

Honey comes out of the air . . . . At early dawn the leaves of trees are found bedewed with honey . . . . Whether this is the perspiration of the sky or a sort of saliva of the stars, or the moisture of the air purging itself, nevertheless it brings with it the great pleasure of its heavenly nature. It is always of the best quality when it is stored in the best flowers.

—Pliny (A.D. 23–79), *Natural History*, Book 20

General Information

Honey is one of the oldest sweeteners known to humans. People collected and ate this sweet, golden substance before they knew how to raise cereal grains or keep dairy animals. Originally, honey was collected by smoking bees from their nests, a method illustrated in Egyptian tomb reliefs of the third millennium B.C., but dating back much earlier. Made throughout the world by only five varieties (*Apis mellifica*) of the ten thousand bee species recorded, honey is the product of the blossom nectar gathered by bees and converted into a sweet, sticky liquid. It takes 160,000 bees numerous trips to two million flowers to gather the four pounds of nectar required to produce just one pound of honey; a single honeybee will produce only one teaspoonful in its entire lifetime. Until the end of the Middle Ages honey was the sweetener par excellence in much of the world, although by no means the only one; some countries used date syrup or fig syrup, others malted grains, still others grape juice, and a few had sugarcane. Having discovered the pleasant flavor and energy-giving properties of honey, people soon found that it had other virtues. Since the golden substance is almost pure sugar and ferments very readily, even the debris of a honeycomb left to soak in water is enough to produce a delicious and mildly intoxicating liquid. Honey ale, generally known as mead, was popular for thousands of years, especially in countries where grapes did not grow and ale-making grains were scarce. In England honey did not lose its hold until the sixteenth century and the dissolution of the monasteries (monks were the primary beekeepers—they used the wax for votive candles and the honey as a commercially valuable byproduct).

Buying Tips and Culinary Uses

Honey is the only food that will not spoil; it has been found perfectly preserved in caves dating from ancient times. It will crystallize but is easily brought back to a fluid state by heating. The lighter-colored honeys are mildest in flavor, while darker honeys are stronger-flavored and have a greater nutritional value. The three most commercially prevalent types are alfalfa, clover, and buckwheat. Alfalfa and clover honey are usually light-colored and mild-flavored; pure buckwheat honey is dark brown and strong-flavored, similar to sorghum. Honey has a sweetening power 140 percent greater than white sugar, so less is needed.

In addition to color, there are several factors to consider when selecting honey. Buy from quality sources only, and avoid those producers who feed their bees antibiotics, sugar syrup, or sulfur drugs, as well as those whose honey contains pesticides or other toxic residues. Good honey is unfiltered (or strained only through cheesecloth to remove any extraneous material) and uncooked. Filtering removes the pollen that gives good honey its cloudiness and valuable nutrients. The U.S. Department of Agriculture grades honey according to its clarity, which is a reflection of how much it is filtered, and in typical government fashion the honeys with the greatest clarity receive the highest grades: Grade A or "Fancy" honey has been screened and filtered

Honey / Nutritional Value Per 100 g Edible Portion			
	Strained		**Strained**
Calories	304	Copper	0.036 mg
Protein	0.3 g	Manganese	0.080 mg
Fat	0 g	Beta Carotene (A)	0 IU
Fiber	n/a	Thiamine (B$_1$)	0 mg
Calcium	6 mg	Riboflavin (B$_2$)	0.038 mg
Iron	0.42 mg	Niacin (B$_3$)	0.121 mg
Magnesium	2 mg	Pantothenic Acid (B$_5$)	0.068 mg
Phosphorus	4 mg	Pyridoxine (B$_6$)	0.024 mg
Potassium	52 mg	Folic Acid (B$_9$)	2 mcg
Sodium	4 mg	Ascorbic Acid (C)	0.5 mg
Zinc	0.220 mg		

LORE AND LEGEND

Milk and honey are frequently mentioned as offerings to gods, or as food of the gods, which indicates how important they were to the ancients. In Greek mythology the young Zeus was rescued from his father Cronus and brought up secretly by the nymphs Amalthea and Melissa, who fed him milk and honey. Aristotle thought honeydew was the nectar of the gods fallen to earth, and had something to do with rainbows; Pliny the Elder thought it a sweet liquid of the heavens, saliva from the stars or juice produced when air purified itself. The Koran teaches that the disappearance of honey would be Allah's punishment of men: "The first good that God will take from man will be honey." As told in an ancient Egyptian legend, one day long ago the god Ra wept, and the tears that dropped from his eyes turned into bees that promptly set about making honeycomb and gathering nectar from the flowers. An old custom is the practice of placing a few drops of honey on the first book presented to a child. The child would lick the honey off the book, thus forever associating books with sweetness.

Health Benefits

pH 3.70–4.20. Antiallergenic, antianemic, antibiotic, anticarcinogenic, antifungal, anti-inflammatory, antiseptic, antiviral, expectorant, laxative. As if we needed a reason to eat honey other than its wonderful flavor, it has been found to possess immune-stimulating, nutritive, and tonic properties. Because of its content of potassium and formic acid, honey has the characteristic of being antiseptic. It is hygroscopic, meaning that honey draws every bit of moisture out of germs, thus killing them. Universally applied to dress external wounds and sores to keep them sterile, honey also hastens the healing process. Honey creates heat in the body, is good for healing internal and external ulcers, carries the medicinal properties of herbs to the bodily tissues, is an excellent blood purifier, and is good for the eyes and teeth. Mixed with lemon juice or vinegar, it makes a soothing cough syrup; taken with water, it energizes the body and helps to flush the kidneys. Honey is probably the best natural source of energy available to humans due to its pure sugar content, which is very easily assimilated by the body. Since honey has the complexity of a whole food, the blood sugar race it triggers will be conducted at a slower speed than the one triggered by processed sugar. Darker honeys are generally richer in minerals than light honey.

Raw honey is teeming with active enzymes, which are deactivated at 117 degrees Fahrenheit. These enzymes may be a key to long life: one study showed that many centenarians in the republic of Georgia were beekeepers who regularly consumed raw honey, complete with pollen. Bee pollen is packed with amino acids (twenty-two, including all the essential ones), vitamins, minerals, hormones, fatty acids, and thousands of enzymes. Bee pollen has been found to be effective in treating allergies, bacterial infections, asthma, capillary weakness, chronic fatigue, immune depression, menopausal symptoms, nutritional disorders, prostate problems, chronic cystitis, and urinary tract infections. It has also been proven to bind environmental poison ¼ teaspoon two times daily). See also the separate listing for bee pollen.

Note: Do not give honey to children under one year of age, as it has been known to cause botulism in infants.

to death. Lower grades are B (Choice), C (Standard), and D (Substandard). These grades imply nothing about the quality of the honey or its source but indicate only the degree of fineness of the screen through which the honey has been filtered. Temperatures up to 145 degrees Fahrenheit can be used with "uncooked" still permitted as a description, but to be meaningful the label should imply not heated over 104 to 117 degrees Fahrenheit, just enough to encourage free flowing but not high enough to destroy vitamins and enzymes. When honey is heated to high temperatures or cooked, its attributes are altered and the resultant product can clog the digestive tract and create toxins within the body by its acidic nature. Truly uncooked honey begins to crystallize at room temperature within several weeks after bottling and if necessary can be reliquefied by setting the jar or can into a pan of warm water.

Hyssop
(Hyssopus officinalis, Agastache foeniculum)

Hyssopus comes from the Greek *hyssopos* and the Hebrew *ezobh*, meaning "holy herb," because it was traditionally used for cleaning sacred places. *Officinalis* means "of the workshop," alluding to apothecaries' shops and signifying that the plant was once part of the official pharmacopoeia of Rome. *Agastache* is derived from the Greek words *agan*, meaning "very much," and *stachys*, meaning "ear of grain." *Foeniculum* means "aniselike" or "anise-scented."

General Information

Hyssop is a perennial shrub of the mint family that is native to southern Europe and temperate Asia. Easily grown, it produces small purple flowers and narrow, pungent leaves. In Elizabethan and Tudor gardens the plant is frequently clipped into miniature hedges for knot gardens. In seventeenth-century Europe hyssop was a popular strewing herb; crushed leaves and flower tops were scattered around homes to mask odors at a time when people rarely bathed and when farm animals often shared human living quarters. When bathing became popular and strewing ceased, hyssop was placed in scent baskets in sickrooms. Hyssop has also been used for centuries as a potherb and for salads. Anise hyssop (*A. foeniculum*) is neither anise nor hyssop, but another completely separate member of the mint family.

Culinary Uses

Hyssop has provided a culinary seasoning for many centuries, with its evocative, spicy and slightly bitter, minty flavor. Although hyssop is too pungent for most modern palates, the Romans liked its taste and made an herbal wine from it; medieval monks also favored the herb, and spiced soups and sauces with it. Hyssop's strong flavor is best used in small quantities, adding a few leaves to salads, breads, and soups, or it can be used as a decorative garnish. Anise hyssop has fragrant licorice and anise-scented leaves that can be used for teas and seasonings. The violet-blue flowers are used fresh or dried to garnish fruit dishes or desserts.

Health Benefits

Antiseptic, aromatic, astringent, carminative, depurative, emmenagogue, expectorant, stimulant, tonic, vermifuge. Hyssop aids the digestion of fat, and is recommended for use with greasy meats and fish. It acts as a general cleansing

LORE AND LEGEND

So powerful is hyssop's fragrance that elderly women in Switzerland and Bavaria are said to press its flowers in their psalm books in the hope that its strong odor will prevent them from falling asleep during boring sermons.

tonic, improves blood quality and circulation, and benefits the bronchial and stomach linings. A tea prepared from the flower tops is used for respiratory problems, easing coughs, hoarseness, sore throats, and loosening phlegm. When the leaves are ground and applied to cuts or wounds, they exert an antiseptic quality and speed healing. The oil from hyssop is said to kill internal worms; applied to the head, it kills lice and cures head itch. The leaves are laid on wounds to cure infection and to promote healing. In fact, penicillin mold grows and thrives on hyssop leaves. Hyssop is used in essentially the same way as sage, with which it is sometimes combined.

Note: If you are taking medication for high blood pressure or you are pregnant, check with your doctor before taking hyssop, just to be safe.

Juniper Berry
(Juniperus communis)

Juniperus is the classical name for this plant. *Communis* means "common."

General Information

Juniper is an evergreen shrub that, unlike most conifers, produces spicy blue-black or purplish berries. The common juniper is a native of Europe but has been introduced into some parts of the United States, where it has become naturalized. The bushes carry berries at all different stages of development since the berries take three years to fully ripen. All parts of the plant contain a volatile oil that imparts an aromatic scent. The berries were at one time popular as a strewing herb to sweeten stale air in overcrowded rooms or hospital wards. Potency of the berries varies by region, with juniper from southern Europe being the most flavorful. Juniper trees are among our most

LORE AND LEGEND

Juniper often figures in stories and legends as a magical plant. During the Middle Ages, Europeans believed planting a juniper beside the front door kept witches out; however, the tree did not provide complete protection, as a witch could still enter if she correctly guessed the number of its needles. Parents burned juniper branches during childbirth in the belief that its smoke prevented the fairies from substituting a changeling for their newborn baby.

common landscape greenery. When foraging, do not harvest berries from red or savin cedars, as their oils are too toxic for internal use. Juniper berries are also available in the spice section of well-stocked health food stores.

Culinary Uses

Juniper berries, used either fresh or dried, are aromatic and spicy and taste slightly of pine. Most people consider them too pungent to be eaten fresh. Frequently used to reduce the strong taste of wild game and to add flavor to sauerkraut, pickles, and chutneys, just a few berries added to stews, casseroles, and vegetable dishes impart an intriguing flavor. To use, remove any seeds, crush the berry, and add as a seasoning ingredient. Ten berries season one pound of meat. When dried, they may be ground in a pepper mill like peppercorns. Oils and extracts of juniper are used in many foods (including gin) and as a fragrance in soaps and perfumes.

Health Benefits

Antiseptic, carminative, diuretic, stimulant, stomachic, tonic. Ripe juniper berries contain a component-rich, aromatic essential oil similar to turpentine oil. They will gently stimulate the appetite, increase the production of hydrochloric acid, counteract flatulence, and help remedy gastrointestinal infections, inflammations, and cramps. An infusion of berries in wine is an appetite stimulant. The berries are used by herbalists for treating some kidney infections, but in conjunction with more cooling herbs. American Indians drank a tea of the berries for fever and steamed on juniper's green boughs to ease the pains of arthritis. They also used a tea of the root to control venereal disease and tea of the berry as a method of birth control. The berries can be dried and strung like beads and are used to dye hair and fabric.

Note: Taken in large quantities, juniper berries occasionally produce irritation of the urinary passages. They are not recommended for pregnant women.

Juniper Berry / Nutritional Value Per 100 g Edible Portion			
	Dried		**Dried**
Calories	341	Sodium	trace
Protein	18.2 g	Zinc	trace
Fat	5.6 g	Manganese	6.30 mg
Fiber	12.0 g	Beta Carotene (A)	2,026 IU
Calcium	849 mg	Thiamine (B₁)	0.120 mg
Iron	15.0 mg	Riboflavin (B₂)	0.060 mg
Magnesium	93 mg	Niacin (B₃)	1.200 mg
Phosphorus	90 mg	Ascorbic Acid (C)	0 mg
Potassium	957 mg		

Kudzu

(Pueraria lobata, P. thunbergiana)
Also Known As: Kuzu

This plant received its genus name in honor of M. N. Puerari, a botanist from Geneva. *Lobata* means "divided into lobes"; *thunbergiana* is given in honor of Carl Peter Thunberg (1743–1822), a Swedish botanist. The English name *kudzu* is derived from *kuzu*, the plant's name in Japan.

General Information

Kudzu is a prostrate Asian leguminous vine whose root has been known for its medicinal and culinary properties in Japan and China for over a thousand years. This "giant of roots" weighs an average of two hundred pounds and grows up to seven feet in length. The traditional way of preparing the starch is a labor-intensive process taking up to 120 days. The root is dug out of the ground during the winter, when the sap is concentrated there; this root is then cleaned, chopped, and pounded into a mash. Eventually a crude fibrous paste forms, which is washed, filtered through cloth, and allowed to settle out in broad, shallow settling ponds. This process is repeated up to fifty times until ultimately a pure white starch is obtained; after the last settling the water is drained off and the damp layer of starch is cut into small blocks and allowed to air-dry naturally for up to two months. There is no way to speed up this drying process since direct sunlight and ovens are too hot and alter the starch's ability to dissolve in water during use. After drying, the cubes are crumbled and packaged for use.

Kudzu was introduced to the United States from Indochina and Japan in 1876. Exhibited at the Philadelphia Centennial Exposition, it was admired by Americans as an attractive ornamental and planted as a shade vine. Between 1910 and 1935 kudzu was widely used in the South as livestock fodder and pasturage and was renamed King Kudzu. However, by 1955 the plant was considered a noxious weed because the fast-growing vine had spread far beyond desired boundaries, covering crops, pastures, and forest. A single vine can grow one hundred feet or more in a single season, pulling down and/or killing everything in its path.

Culinary Uses

Kudzu is used as a thickener in much the same way as cornstarch or arrowroot, or as a gelling agent like agar and gelatin. It adds a subtle sweetness and smoothness to sauces, desserts, and confections. The odorless white starch is unequaled in producing transparent, smooth, and tasty sauces, without the elastic texture or raw, starchy flavor often noticeable in cornstarch-thickened mixtures. Usually sold in chunks, the pieces work best when first crushed to a fine consistency so that they will dissolve more readily. Like cornstarch, kudzu must be dissolved in cold liquid before using. Once dissolved, it can be added to the liquid being prepared and brought to a boil. As it cools, a kudzu sauce thickens; a sauce thickened with arrowroot, on the other hand, thins as it cools.

Health Benefits

As a kitchen remedy, kudzu helps develop an alkaline condition within the body and provides relief from intestinal and digestive disorders, headaches, fever, colds, and hangovers. Recent research confirms its traditional use for suppressing the desire for alcohol. In 1993 Harvard biochemists discovered that a dose of kudzu made alcoholic hamsters cut their imbibing by 50 percent. Apparently the compound daidzin, found in the root, leaves, and flowers of kudzu, reduced the rodents' craving and significantly lowered their blood levels of alcohol. Similar studies found that kudzu works on mice in Japan, and human alcoholics in China. It also helps prevent the eruption of rashes and clears the skin.

Lamb's-Quarter

(Chenopodium album)
Also Known As: Wild Spinach, Goosefoot, Pigweed, Redroot

Chenopodium is a Greek word meaning "goosefoot," alluding to the shape of the leaves; *album* means "white."

General Information

Lamb's-quarter is a relative of garden spinach and beets and grows in gardens and cultivated fields in most temperate climates. The plant seems to have a special affinity for potato fields, coming up after cultivation has ceased. Native to Europe and Asia and introduced early into North America, it is now found everywhere in the United States except the extreme northern section of the country. Four thousand years ago in North America, the cultivated seeds and greens of lamb's-quarter were staple food, until corn became the dominant crop, around A.D. 1200. Of necessity, the greens regained popularity during the 1930s Depression. A "mess of greens" often meant a meal of lamb's-quarter fried in lard and served with a splash of vinegar. Not necessarily an attractive plant, it has histori-

Lamb's-Quarter / Nutritional Value Per 100 g Edible Portion		
	Raw	Cooked
Calories	43	32
Protein	4.20 g	3.20 g
Fat	0.80 g	0.70 g
Fiber	2.10 g	1.80 g
Calcium	309 mg	258 mg
Iron	1.20 mg	0.70 mg
Phosphorus	72 mg	45 mg
Beta Carotene (A)	11,600 IU	9,700 IU
Thiamine (B₁)	0.160 mg	0.100 mg
Riboflavin (B₂)	0.440 mg	0.260 mg
Niacin (B₃)	1.200 mg	0.900 mg
Ascorbic Acid (C)	80.0 mg	37.0 mg

cally been used for "spring greens," since it was found in abundance and easily collected. When small, six to ten inches high, the plants are succulent and tender. The leaves are trilobed, like a goose's foot, and have a silvery cast that almost looks fuzzy. At maturity the stems reach five feet. Increasingly found at farmer's markets, the plant may also be easily foraged.

Culinary Uses

Both the foliage and the seeds of lamb's-quarter are edible. Young, tender leaves or shoots may be used raw in salads; the older leaves and immature seeds can be steamed and served as spinach. Very young leaves are mild tasting with a hint of lemon; once the plant sets seed, however, the leaves are bitter. Fully ripened seeds may be eaten raw or dried and ground into a meal to make bread. Both leaves and seeds can be dried for winter use.

Health Benefits

Antiscorbutic, laxative, vermifuge. Like other wild foods, lamb's-quarter is more energizing than cultivated food, which is evident from eating it as well as from its nutrient profile. Lamb's-quarter contains more vitamin A by weight than carrots and three times the calcium of broccoli. With its slightly slippery texture, it is useful in treating constipation, especially in the elderly. The leaves help cleanse the blood and have a positive action on the liver and lungs. The seeds are effective in treating dysentery, diarrhea, and eczema and also act as a vermifuge.

Lavender
(Lavandula officinalis, L. vera, L. angustifolia)

> When my eyes were closed, at night in my little room, my favourite hill used to come to me, and I would sleep under an olive tree, enveloped in the scent of hidden lavender.
>
> —MARCEL PAGNOL

Lavandula is derived from the Latin *lavandus*, meaning "to be washed," because the plant was used in ancient times to perfume bathwater. *Officinalis* means "of the workshop," alluding to apothecaries' shops and signifying that the plant was once part of the official pharmacopoeia of Rome. *Vera* means "true," perhaps in reference to the existence of false or inferior lavenders. *Augustifolia* means "narrow-leaved."

General Information

Lavender originated in the mountainous regions of the Mediterranean and covers vast tracts of dry, barren land in Spain and Italy. A perennial plant with narrow, gray-green leaves and long, purple-flowered spikes, lavender became popular in ancient Rome as a sensual fragrance for the bath. It was used for a variety of healing purposes in medieval Europe, and in many parts of Europe stalks of lavender leaves and flowers were set in linen closets to impart their fragrance to sheets, pillowcases, blankets, and comforters. Though used in a more limited manner today, lavender still scents sachets, perfumes, and soaps. The dried flowers or sprigs will keep moths away from stored linens and clothes, while the fresh flowers can be rubbed over the skin to deter obnoxious insects.

Culinary Uses

Lavender flowers have a strong, fragrant odor, and an aromatic, warm, bitterish taste. The fragrant leaves and flowers can be used fresh in salads and fruit dishes or added to beverages, cooked sauces, candies, and baked goods. When dried, the leaves are most often used in jellies.

Health Benefits

Aromatic, carminative, diuretic, sedative, stimulant, tonic. Lavender is a wonderfully refreshing and delightfully scented plant with a long history of medicinal use. Its strong scent, like that of mint, is a remedy for dizziness and fainting. The plant has been attributed calmative and

LORE AND LEGEND

Lavender has long had a reputation as an anti-aphrodisiac (counterstimulant), with one old belief advocating sprinkling lavender on your head as an aid in maintaining chastity. In sixteenth-century England women and men had the spicy-smelling flowers of lavender quilted into their hats to "comfort the braines."

sedative properties and used to soothe the nerves, relieve nervous headaches and depression, stimulate the appetite, relieve intestinal flatulence, and soothe colic. A few sprigs in the evening bath will calm jaded nerves and inhibit germs. Crushed leaves can be used as an antiseptic wash for wounds and are quite effective on snakebites. If you are looking for a relaxing herb, make sure the package has one of the botanical names listed above and not *Lavandula stoechas*. The latter is a Spanish variety that actually makes a person feel invigorated, and thus it is definitely not something you want to add to a warm bath before heading off to bed. French chemist Rene-Maurice Gattefosse discovered lavender's healing powers by accident. While working in his perfume lab in the 1920s, he burned his hand. In a panic, he plunged it into the nearest liquid vat, which happened to be filled with lavender oil. He pulled out his hand and voilà: the pain quickly disappeared, and the burn healed without a trace of a scar. Strange but true.

Lecithin

The name *lecithin* is derived from the Greek word for "egg yolk" because that is the source from which it was first isolated.

General Information
A phosphorized fat molecule (phospholipid) that moves well through both fat and water, lecithin is a necessary structural component of all cell membranes in living organisms. Found in many natural foods, including whole grains, nuts and seeds, and unrefined vegetable oils, lecithin is also produced routinely in the body. Soybeans are the primary commercial source of lecithin (phosphatidylcholine). Unrefined soy oil contains approximately 3 percent lecithin. During refining, the lecithin is removed as an "impurity" and then sold for use in baked goods, prepared foods, and pharmaceutical preparations. Lecithin is available in both liquid and granulated forms.

Culinary Uses
Granulated lecithin resembles waxy or oily millet seeds, although it is more golden. These slightly nutty-flavored granules can be sprinkled on cereals, added to beverages, or used in baked goods, where they result in a better texture and a more tender crust and also act as a preservative. Commercially, lecithin is usually referred to as an emulsifier, stabilizer, or thickener, and it holds together everything from margarine and mayonnaise to baked goods, salad dressings, and cosmetics.

Health Benefits
Lecithin is an important constituent of all the bodily organs and aids in the breakdown, absorption, and utilization of fats as well as vitamins A, D, E, and K. Lecithin has demonstrated positive effects in lowering cholesterol levels by preventing cholesterol from collecting and attaching to the walls of blood vessels, and it is actually said to reduce harmful cholesterol levels in the body. It also improves liver and gallbladder function, helps eliminate liver spots, repairs various neurological disorders, and is beneficial in cases of dry skin and psoriasis. Lecithin also provides choline, which is necessary for both liver and brain function, along with phosphorus and inositol.

Lecithin / Nutritional Value Per 100 g Edible Portion	
Calories	763
Fat: Saturated	15.01%
Monounsaturated	11.00%
Polyunsaturated	45.32%

Lemongrass
(Cymbopogon citratus, C. flexuesus)

Cymbopogon comes from the Greek *kumbo* (cup) and *pogon* (beard). *Citratus* means "citruslike" and refers to the plant's pleasant, citrusy aroma; *flexuesus* means "flexuous" or "tortuous, zigzagged." The English name *lemongrass* comes from the plant's scent and appearance.

General Information

The term *lemongrass* refers to several species of grass native to Southeast Asia, all possessing the flavor of lemon because of the presence of citric oils. These are perennial plants with tall, gray-green, grasslike leaves that grow best in cooler tropical climates. A relative of citronella, these plants have long been cultivated for their aromatic oil, which is used in cosmetics and fragrances.

Buying Tips

Fresh lemongrass is sold by the stalk, which is two feet in length and looks something like a scallion, though it is fibrous to the point of being woody. Only the bulblike six- to eight-inch base of the stalk is used, after the top is trimmed and a layer of tough outer leaves peeled off. Store any portion that you will use within a week in plastic in the refrigerator, and tightly wrap and freeze the remainder. Slice off a piece as needed and return the unused portion to the refrigerator or freezer.

Culinary Uses

Lemongrass has a light, airy, floral aroma combining lemon and lime peel with fresh-cut hay. Available dried, powdered (known as sereh powder), and fresh, this plant is frequently used in Southeast Asian cooking to impart a lemony flavor and aroma. The strawlike fresh stalks can lend their flavor to soups and stews or be used for steaming but need to be removed before the dish is served, as they are too harsh-textured to be eaten. It is the inner part of the stalk, a pale, tubular core resembling a firm scallion bulb, that is tender enough to be eaten. This is finely slivered into dishes, adding its inimitable lemony pungency. Since fresh lemongrass is powerful and intensifies with cooking, use it sparingly until its potency is understood. The dried herb possesses only a wisp of its former seasoning power and must be soaked before use. One teaspoon of ground powder is roughly equivalent to one stalk.

Lemongrass / Nutritional Value Per 100 g Edible Portion			
	Dried		Dried
Calories	389	Magnesium	331 mg
Protein	8.2 g	Phosphorus	214 mg
Fat	7.1 g	Potassium	2,300 mg
Fiber	n/a	Sodium	64 mg
Calcium	368 mg	Zinc	trace
Iron	54.3 mg	Manganese	10.40 mg

LORE AND LEGEND

In Indonesia young girls are sent to cut lemongrass, because of an old belief that the grass is at its most fragrant when harvested by someone with a virgin's pure thoughts.

Health Benefits

Analgesic, antispasmodic, digestive. This tropical grass is rich in citral, the active ingredient found in lemon peel. Lemongrass cools, aids digestion (especially in children), and increases perspiration. It relieves spasms, muscle cramps, rheumatism, and headaches and is also effective against infections. Lemongrass is used cosmetically for overactive sebaceous glands, to make the hair lustrous, and as a water or vinegar wash for the face, hair, or body.

Licorice
(Glycyrrhiza glabra)

The botanical name *Glycyrrhiza* derives from the Greek words *glukos*, meaning "sweet," and *riza*, meaning "root," an appropriate description. The term *glabra* means "glabrous" or "smooth." The Romans changed *glycyrrhiza* to *liquiritia*, which evolved into the English word *licorice*.

General Information

Licorice is true to its Greek name, as it is fifty times sweeter than sugar. A member of the pea (and thus legume) family that grows wild in southern Europe and Asia, licorice is a graceful plant with light, spreading pinnate foliage presenting an almost feathery appearance from a distance. Taproots may sink three or four feet and should be harvested in the fall. The use of licorice has been known since ancient times. It was introduced to the Greeks by the Scythians and was also used by the Chinese and Indians. Great quantities of licorice were found with the fabulous treasures of King Tut and other Egyptian rulers; the Egyptians believed that the licorice could be used to prepare a sweet drink, maisus, in the next world. Licorice is cultivated for its sweet-tasting rhizomes (underground stems) and roots, which are used as flavorings. Ninety percent of all natural licorice imported is employed as a conditioning and flavoring agent in tobacco.

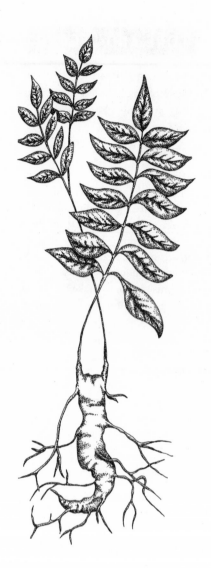

Licorice / Nutritional Value Per 100 g Edible Portion			
	Dried		**Dried**
Calories	268	Sodium	818 mg
Protein	11.0 g	Zinc	0.30 mg
Fat	1.0 g	Manganese	4.70 mg
Fiber	8.4 g	Beta Carotene (A)	trace
Calcium	878 mg	Thiamine (B₁)	0.210 mg
Iron	88 mg	Riboflavin (B₂)	0.160 mg
Magnesium	965 mg	Niacin (B₃)	7.000 mg
Phosphorus	79 mg	Ascorbic Acid (C)	62.6 mg
Potassium	1,140 mg		

flavoring agents to mask bitter, nauseating, or other undesirable tastes in medicine.

Health Benefits

Demulcent, diuretic, expectorant, laxative. The main active component in licorice root is a saponin-like glycoside called glycyrrhizin, which is fifty times sweeter than sugar. Its use as a noncaloric sweetener is limited, however, because of the strong taste it imparts to food. Still, it is one of the most common ingredients in Chinese herbal formulas, for it moderates the strong effects of other ingredients and makes them more effective. Licorice root cleanses the mouth and teeth, arrests tooth decay because of its germicidal action, promotes salivation, and increases secretions in the gastrointestinal tract. Known to improve circulation and cleanse the blood, it is also good for hypoglycemia and the removal of age spots and drugs from the body. Research indicates that licorice may counteract various viruses, including herpes simplex I and HIV. Licorice tea is a mild laxative and a natural expectorant and decongestant; it aids digestion, helps the liver discharge toxins, and strengthens both the heart and the circulatory system. Septic or nonhealing wounds will be healed by the application of licorice tea or licorice ghee.

Note: Glycyrrhizin increases fluid and sodium retention and promotes potassium depletion if licorice is used for long periods. Persons with cardiac problems and hypertension should avoid consumption of significant quantities. Also, licorice is not given to pregnant women or to people with high blood pressure or kidney disease, because in excess it may cause water retention and raise blood pressure.

Culinary Uses

Sweet and slightly astringent, licorice can be purchased as the whole dried root, sliced, or powdered. The root resembles a brown pencil and is usually available in three- to five-inch lengths or cut into chips. Some people use the powder in fruit smoothies or on their food as a seasoning. Licorice flavoring is used in soft drinks, ice cream, candy, desserts, cakes, and confectionery. Licorice candy, which rarely contains more than 2 percent natural licorice extract, is more likely to be flavored with anise (which is unrelated to licorice) or with a synthetic licorice flavoring. Licorice extracts are used extensively as ingredients in cough drops and syrups, tonics, laxatives, antismoking lozenges, and as

Lovage
(Levisticum officinale, Ligusticum scoticum)

The botanical name *Levisticum* is a corruption of the earlier name *Ligusticum*, after Liguria, Italy (a region that includes the Italian Riviera), where lovage once grew in abundance. *Officinale* means "of the workshop," alluding to apothecaries' shops and signifying that the plant was once part of the official pharmacopoeia of Rome. *Scoticum* denotes a variety that comes from Scotland. The English name *lovage* is a corruption of the Latin name.

General Information
Lovage is a tall plant with large, dark green leaves, native to the Balkans and Mediterranean area. The Romans, who used lovage as a medicinal herb, introduced it to much of Europe and Great Britain. In the Middle Ages it was used as a cure-all for most illnesses. This relative of dill, angelica, and parsley sometimes looks, smells, and tastes more like celery than celery itself.

Culinary Uses
The flavor of lovage is similar to strong celery with a bit of anise; some compare it to that of brewer's yeast. Used as a celery substitute, the leaves, stems, and stalks add a slightly spicy taste to any dish. Tender, young leaves are best for salads, while older leaves can be used in soups, stews, and casseroles. Lovage is excellent in potato salads and other salads; in soups and stews its strong flavor persists even after long cooking. The stems, like angelica, may be candied, but the flavor is inferior. If lovage goes to seed, use the seeds for making breads, herb butters, chicken salads, and candy.

Health Benefits
Carminative, diuretic, emmenagogue, expectorant, stimulant, stomachic. Lovage contains a volatile oil called angelic acid, which has antiseptic qualities, plus strong resins and oils that act on the kidneys and bladder and relieve menstrual disorders. This herb is used mostly for its diuretic properties in cases of water retention and urinary difficulties, but it also has a beneficial cleansing effect on the system, remedies digestive difficulties, eases flatulence, and can be applied externally to wounds because of its antiseptic qualities. The leaves bruised and toasted in oil are used in a compress for boils. A powder of the root drunk in wine is said to help the body resist most poisons and infections and to ease all pains. As a cosmetic, the decoction of the root is used as a face wash to remove spots and freckles.

Note: Because it promotes the onset of menstruation, lovage should not be used during pregnancy.

Mallow
(Malva rotundifolia, M. sylvestris)
Also Known As: Malva, Cheese Plant, Low Mallow

This plant got its botanical name *Malva* from the Greek *malake*, meaning "soft," because of its soft emollient leaves. *Rotundifolia* means "round-leaved"; *sylvestris* means "from the woods and forests." The English word *mallow* is a corruption of the Latin name.

General Information
Common or high mallow (*M. sylvestris*) and dwarf mallow (*M. rotundifolia*) are ancient herbs native to Europe and Asia that have been cultivated since the era of the Romans and that now grow wild in North America. Centuries ago Pliny wrote of the wonders of low mallow, to the effect that whoever ate a spoonful of it every day would be free of disease. Other related species having many uses for hundreds of years are hollyhock, okra, and marshmallow.

Culinary Uses
Mallow produces small, round leaves that can be added to salads, boiled and eaten as a vegetable, or brewed into a delicately flavored tea. Its shoots, green seed capsules (known as cheeses), and pink flowers can be chopped and added to salads.

Health Benefits
Astringent, demulcent, emollient, expectorant. Mallow contains the healing substances of asparagin, pectin, and mucilage, all beneficial for the respiratory, alimentary, and urinary organs. It is also an emollient, so it softens and soothes sensitive tissues. American Indians and modern herbalists have recommended poultices made from the plant's leaves to relieve the pain of sores, insect stings and bites, and swellings. Mallow taken in the form of either soup or tea can overcome stubborn constipation.

Lovage / Nutritional Value Per 100 g Edible Portion			
	Fresh		**Fresh**
Protein	20.0 g	Fat	14.7 g

Maple Syrup and Maple Sugar
(Acer saccharum)

Saccharum means "sugar" or "sweet." *Acer* is the ancient Latin name for the maple tree.

General Information

Maple syrup and maple sugar are made only in the United States and parts of Canada, from the sap of sugar maples. American Indians on the Northeast Coast made maple syrup for centuries before the coming of Europeans. The Algonquins called it *sinzibuckwud*, "drawn-from-the-wood." Trees grown elsewhere do not produce enough sap to make syrup, since they require a climate with a long winter that goes from below freezing during the night to above freezing the next day, a condition common in New England and eastern Canada. The sap starts flowing from the trees' roots to the branches in late winter and early spring, bringing nourishment for budding leaves. Collectors drill holes into the tree trunks and insert a spout to divert the clear, tasteless, watery sap into buckets. Each tree averages twelve gallons of sap per season. The sap is boiled in large vats to evaporate the water; between thirty and forty gallons of sap are needed to make one gallon of syrup, which is why pure maple syrup is so expensive. Some syrup producers place a formaldehyde pellet in the tree's tap hole to prolong sap flow, which contaminates the sap. The Canadian government, the state of Vermont, and organic certification codes prohibit use of these pellets. Maple syrup may also be contaminated with high levels of lead, either from the lead seams in the metal cans it is packaged in or from the evaporating pans used by most producers. Since the FDA limits the lead content of imported maple syrup, Canadian brands can be considered safe, as can certified organic brands. Buy organic maple syrup to avoid formaldehyde, chemical antifoaming agents, and mold inhibitors.

Culinary Uses

Buy only high-quality, preferably certified organic maple syrup, avoiding those "maple-flavored" syrups that contain mostly additives and as little as 3 percent real syrup. The syrup should be refrigerated after the container has been opened. Highest-grade (AA or "fancy") maple syrup has the sweetest, most delicate flavor and is best used as a topping. Darker, stronger-flavored grades are ideal for cooking and baking. Maple sugar is maple syrup taken a few steps further, boiled down until it crystallizes and sets solid in sugar cakes. This is then usually pulverized into sugar crystals, with a light tan color and a concentrated maple flavor. Maple sugar can be reconstituted back into maple syrup with the addition of water. Both maple syrup and granules make a good white sugar substitute for cooking and baking, adding a warm, rich flavor to the finished product.

Health Benefits

pH 5.15. Valued for its flavor rather than its nutritive qualities, maple syrup is composed primarily of simple carbohydrates and some trace minerals. Compared to white sugar with its 99 percent sucrose content, maple syrup at 65 percent sucrose is obviously a more healthful choice. Like white sugar, however, it may still cause insulin and adrenaline reactions. Maple syrup is damp-producing and so is best used in moderation if at all by people with candida, malignancies, tumors, cysts, or a compromised immune system.

Maple Syrup and Maple Sugar / Nutritional Value Per 100 g Edible Portion	Syrup	Sugar
Calories	262	354
Protein	0 g	0.1 g
Fat	0.2 g	0.2 g
Fiber	0 g	0 g
Calcium	67 mg	90 mg
Iron	1.20 mg	1.61 mg
Magnesium	14 mg	19 mg
Phosphorus	2 mg	3 mg
Potassium	204 mg	274 mg
Sodium	9 mg	11 mg
Zinc	4.160 mg	6.060 mg
Copper	0.074 mg	0.099 mg
Manganese	3.298 mg	4.422 mg
Beta Carotene (A)	n/a	n/a
Thiamine (B$_1$)	0.006 mg	0.009 mg
Riboflavin (B$_2$)	0.010 mg	0.013 mg
Niacin (B$_3$)	0.030 mg	0.040 mg
Pantothenic Acid (B$_5$)	0.036 mg	0.048 mg
Pyridoxine (B$_6$)	0.002 mg	0.003 mg
Folic Acid (B$_9$)	0 mcg	0 mcg
Ascorbic Acid (C)	0 mg	0 mg

Marjoram
(Origanum majorana, Majorana hortensis)

The botanical name *Origanum* is from the Greek words *oros* and *ganos*, meaning "mountain glamour" or "joy of the mountain," after the attractive appearance and aroma of the bushy flowering plant, which adorns the hilly Mediterranean landscape. *Majorana*, or *maiorana*, is a very old name of unknown derivation by which the plant was known when first introduced to Europe in the Middle Ages. *Hortensis* means "belonging to a hortus," or garden.

General Information

Native to North Africa and southwest Asia, this member of the mint family is now naturalized in the Mediterranean region and cultivated in North America. Marjoram is so closely related to oregano that botanists sometimes use the same botanical name to describe both plants; most distinguish between them by using the name *Majorana hortensis* for the sweet-scented marjoram and *Origanum majorana* or *O. vulgare* for the sharper-flavored oregano.

Culinary Uses

A product of the strong summer sunshine, marjoram brings real heat—not that which burns and assaults but

Marjoram / Nutritional Value Per 100 g Edible Portion		
	Dried	1 tsp.
Calories	271	2
Protein	12.66 g	0.08 g
Fat	7.04 g	0.04 g
Fiber	18.11 g	0.11 g
Calcium	1,990 mg	12 mg
Iron	82.71 mg	0.50 mg
Magnesium	346 mg	2 mg
Phosphorus	306 mg	2 mg
Potassium	1,522 mg	9 mg
Sodium	77 mg	trace
Zinc	3.600 mg	0.020 mg
Copper	1.133 mg	n/a
Manganese	5.433 mg	n/a
Beta Carotene (A)	8,068 IU	48 IU
Thiamine (B$_1$)	0.289 mg	0.002 mg
Riboflavin (B$_2$)	0.316 mg	0.002 mg
Niacin (B$_3$)	4.120 mg	0.025 mg
Ascorbic Acid (C)	51.43 mg	0.31 mg

LORE AND LEGEND

There are many stories regarding the origin of marjoram, but all of them hold the plant as a symbol of youth, beauty, and happiness. Greek legend holds that the plant owes its beginnings to Aphrodite, who was inadvertently wounded by one of Cupid's arrows one day in her garden. Quickly she looked about for a cure to counteract the love dart, but found none at hand. Causing sweet marjoram to spring up, she gave it the wrong magic in her haste, making it enhance the damage rather than cure it. From that day forward sweet marjoram was endowed with great potency as a love plant. Greek couples wore marjoram wreaths at their weddings because of its association with Aphrodite, and young girls placed marjoram in their beds so that Aphrodite would visit their dreams and reveal the identity of their future spouses.

Another legend of its origin comes from the island of Cyprus. The king of the island lived in a beautiful marbled palace looking out to the sea. As ruler, he expected instant obedience and efficient service from his many servants; any laxity or carelessness was met with stern punishment. One day a new page named Amarakos was given a large urn of costly perfume to carry to the king's quarters. As he attempted to shift the heavy burden from one shoulder to the other the urn slipped, falling and shattering on the floor. The boy, seeing the puddling perfume and remembering the demanding reputation of his king, was so paralyzed with fright that he fell dead to the wet floor. As custom demanded, the boy was duly buried, but upon his grave grew a beautiful plant that exuded the same fragrance as the rich perfume he had spilled, which was then named sweet marjoram.

rather the warmth that arouses and fills the individual with elation for life. The flavor of sweet marjoram is delicate, sweet, and spicy, rather similar to thyme but sweeter and more scented. The leaves and flowers are used fresh or dried in salads, soups, stuffings, quiches and pies, omelets, and potato dishes. Marjoram's delicate flavor is destroyed by heat, so it is best added just before the dish is ready or used in lightly cooked dishes. It complements especially well the herbs bay, garlic, onion, thyme, and basil.

Health Benefits

Antispasmodic, calmative, carminative, diaphoretic, expectorant, stimulant, stomachic, tonic. Marjoram will benefit a sour stomach or loss of appetite, increase white blood corpuscles, improve circulation, relieve abdominal cramps, and ease respiratory ailments. Marjoram tea is an age-old remedy to aid digestion, increase sweating, and encourage menstruation. As a steam inhalant, marjoram clears the sinuses and helps relieve laryngitis. Strongly antiseptic, it may be taken to treat respiratory conditions such as coughs, tonsillitis, bronchitis, and asthma. The diluted oil can be applied to a toothache or painful joints. Marjoram oil is also used for soothing the muscles, the respiratory system, and the nerves. Adding dried leaves to a bath can promote a calming effect and relieve insomnia.

Matrimony Vine
(Lycium chinense)

Lycium is derived from the Greek *lykion*, a name later transferred by Linnaeus to this genus. *Chinense* means "belonging to China." The English name of *matrimony vine* was given because the plant is related to a Western species that is so named.

General Information

Shoots of this spiny shrub are increasingly available at Asian produce stands. The thorny stalk is discarded and the leaves used. Traditionally, the leaves are eaten in the spring, the flowers in the summer, the berries (called wolfberries) in the fall, and the root in the winter. The berries look like small, pointed, reddish-orange raisins and have a sweet, slightly licorice flavor. There are abundant matrimony-vine extracts, tinctures, and pills, and even the dried parts of the plant itself, for sale in Chinese herbal shops.

Culinary Uses

The peppermint-flavored leaves are stirred into rich soups just before they are served, or they are traditionally cooked with pork. In China and Japan the leaves are also used to make tea.

Health Benefits

The berries have a reputation for improving eyesight and kidney function. Children in Chinese apothecary shops are often given a handful as a quick, tonic snack.

Mint
(Mentha viridis, M. spicata, M. piperita)

The genus *Mentha* is named after the Greek nymph *Minthe*. *Viridis* means "green"; *spicata* means "spicate" or "having spikes"; *piperita* means "sharply fragrant or flavored." The English name *spearmint* is a corruption of *spire mint*, so called because the tall flower spikes resemble the spires of weathered churches; the name *peppermint* results from this variety's peppery flavor.

General Information

Originally natives of the Near East, the many varieties of mint spread across the globe in part because of their aggressive growth characteristics but also because of the great esteem in which they were held by everyone who came in contact with them. The refreshingly cool, stimulating scent and taste of mint has been valued since antiquity for both culinary and medicinal purposes. All mints are relatively pungent because of their volatile oil containing menthol, carried in resinous dots on the stems and leaves. Best known to most people of the more than two thousand varieties are spearmint (*M. viridis, M. spicata*) and peppermint (*M. piperita*). Spearmint is the oldest variety of mint, and while the leaves closely resemble those of peppermint, the flavor does not; peppermint has more oils and a very strong taste of menthol that is not found in spearmint. The high menthol content accounts for its characteristic sensation of coolness, which invades the mouth after the original pungency has died away. Because it is strongly aromatic, a bouquet of mint hung indoors will pleasantly scent the whole house and give an impression of coolness. The commercial demand for the extracted volatile oil of mint is so great that in a town named Mentha, Michigan, growing this herb is the principal industry.

LORE AND LEGEND

In early Palestine mint was one of the accepted forms for tax payment. Greeks, and Athenians in particular, believed mint to have the aroma of strength, and they would rub leaves over their arms to bolster their endurance. Peppermint oil was mentioned by Aristotle as an aphrodisiac, and the use of wild mint by soldiers of Alexander the Great was forbidden because he felt it so aroused them erotically that it took away all desire to fight. The Romans spread mint on the floors during feasts, as the fragrant aroma was believed to cause humans to rejoice and incline them toward eating (plus, it had the added benefit of frightening away mice). The Arabs have also used mint for centuries, partaking of mint tea as a social drink as well as a virility stimulant. The familiar after-dinner mints evolved from the ancient custom of concluding feasts with a sprig of mint to soothe the stomach.

Pluto, the god of the Greek underworld, fell in love with the beautiful nymph Minthe. His wife soon discovered the romantic affair and went into a fury, which culminated when she threw Minthe to the ground and stamped her to death. Although Pluto could not bring Minthe back to life, he changed her form into that of the fragrant plant. Another tale relates the story of two strangers who were walking through Phrygia. Snubbed by the villagers, who offered them neither food nor drink, the two knocked at the humble house of Philemon and Baucis, and asked for food. The old couple quickly made them welcome and looked around for ways to enhance their plain environment. Gathering some mint that was growing by the door, they used it to scrub the table and impart a sweet fragrance to the room. Upon serving their guests the food intended for their own meal, a radiance soon revealed the true identities of their guests—Zeus and Hermes. The gods richly rewarded Philemon and Baucis for their hospitality, changing their home into a beautiful temple where priests were assigned to serve the humble pair for the rest of their lives.

Buying Tips

Many mints are now widely available fresh in grocery stores. This is the preferred form. If fresh mints are not available, the dried leaves or extracts also provide good flavor.

Culinary Uses

All mints have a distinctive flavor and a refreshing aroma. Mint leaves can be used fresh or dried (although fresh is better) as a tasty addition to potato salads, bean dishes, vegetable and fruit salads, fruit drinks, jellies, and sauces. Peppermint's volatile oil, which contains menthol, is employed in the manufacture of medicines, candies, liqueurs, cigarettes, and other products. Spearmint's pleasant but less potent flavor comes from its leaves and oil; it is an ingredient in mint sauces and jellies, as well as flavoring chewing gum and candy, iced teas, liqueurs and other drinks, and baked goods.

Health Benefits

Antiseptic, antispasmodic, aromatic, carminative, stimulant, stomachic, tonic. Peppermint is considered a general stimulant, cleansing and strengthening the entire body. A strong cup of peppermint tea will act more powerfully on the system than any liquor stimulant, quickly diffusing itself throughout the entire system and bringing back to the body its natural warmth and glow. Because it can allay nausea, peppermint is suggested for use against seasickness. Spearmint is neither as versatile nor popular as peppermint and is used primarily for flavoring foods.

Mint / Nutritional Value Per 100 g Edible Portion			
	Peppermint, Dried		**Peppermint, Dried**
Calories	302	Sodium	195 mg
Protein	24.8 g	Zinc	trace
Fat	5.4 g	Manganese	6.10 mg
Fiber	11.4 g	Beta Carotene (A)	39,579 IU
Calcium	1,620 mg	Thiamine (B$_1$)	1.210 mg
Iron	60 mg	Riboflavin (B$_2$)	3.890 mg
Magnesium	661 mg	Niacin (B$_3$)	11.400 mg
Phosphorus	772 mg	Ascorbic Acid (C)	20.1 mg
Potassium	2,260 mg		

Mint of any kind is a balm for the entire digestive tract, regulating the stomach, liver, gallbladder, and intestines; it also regulates the sexual functions of both men and women. However, mint can as easily stop periods as increase the blood flow, so it is best to be careful during the menstrual cycle. It is effective against stomach gas or spasms, vomiting, intestinal parasites, excessive acidity, and colic. The deodorant properties of mint have been capitalized on as well, as they make frequent appearances in mouthwashes and toothpastes to sweeten the breath.

All mints contain a volatile oil, ranging from about 0.3 to 0.4 percent in peppermint, 0.7 percent in spearmint, and 1 to 2 percent for corn mint. Among dozens of aroma chemicals present in the volatile oil, menthol, menthone, and carvone (which is also present in caraway) are found in the largest amounts. Peppermint oil contains 30 to 50 percent menthol and 20 to 30 percent menthone but only minor amounts of carvone, while spearmint oil contains 50 to 70 percent carvone, with only minor amounts of menthol and menthone. The menthol in peppermint is a time-honored and clinically proven aid to digestion and also a mild antispasmodic that is useful for relieving menstrual cramps and nausea. The utilization of menthol in upper respiratory ailments and as a soothing rub for sore muscles is easily verified by a trip to the local pharmacy, where the labels of many respiratory preparations and rubs indicate its presence. Menthol has also been shown to have antimicrobial properties. Peppermint oil may elevate and open the sensory system, and its aromatic influences are purifying and stimulating to the conscious mind. In addition to volatile oil, mints also contain numerous biologically active constituents, including flavonoids (such as rutin), resins, tannin, and azulene, among others.

Note: Do not give mint tea to children younger than two, as the menthol in it can make them choke.

Molasses

The English name *molasses* comes from the Latin term *mellaceus,* meaning "like honey."

General Information
Molasses is the thick, dark syrup that remains after sugar crystals are removed during the process of sugar refining. The color and flavor differ depending on whether the syrup results from early or later extractions. In Britain and western Europe molasses is often called "black treacle."

Health Benefits
pH 4.90–5.40. Two teaspoonfuls of molasses taken in a glass of milk twice daily for three months helped cure one individual of eczema (after seven years and numerous visits to doctors). Blackstrap molasses is potentially a good mineral supplement; a tablespoon of it contains up to one-third of the minimum daily requirement of some of the minerals and trace elements. British natural healer Cyril Scott used blackstrap molasses to cure a wide variety of mineral deficiencies early in the twentieth century. His classic work, *Crude Black Molasses,* was reprinted by Benedict Lust Publications in 1980.

VARIETIES

Barbados molasses is made from the first press of sugarcane. Lighter in color and more delicate in flavor than blackstrap molasses, one tablespoon of Barbados molasses is about 70 percent sugar and has 2 percent of the RDA of iron.

Blackstrap molasses (sulfured) is the waste residue left after the third extraction of sugar from the sugarcane or beet. It contains all the nutrients that were stripped away from the sugar during the refining process; it also contains all the residues from the chemicals used in growing and refining the sugar—pesticides, lead, and sulfur, to name just a few. Very aromatic, blackstrap molasses has a strong, deep, slightly bitter licorice flavor and is not the kind of syrup you would want to eat straight from the container. It imparts its unique dark flavor to fruit cakes, toffees, gingerbreads, and cookies. Blackstrap molasses is 55 percent sucrose.

Light molasses is the residue left after the first extraction of sugar crystals and is quite sweet (65 percent sucrose).

Medium or dark molasses is obtained from the second extraction and is moderately sweet.

Sorghum molasses, also called **unsulfured** or **West Indies molasses,** is made from the sweet sorghum plant (*Horcus sorghum saccara*), grown specifically for making molasses. This plant grows to a height of fifteen feet and forms a stalk (cane) that is topped by clusters of seeds, much like its relative millet. The

Molasses / Nutritional Value Per 100 g Edible Portion	Regular	Blackstrap	Sorghum
Calories	266	235	290
Protein	0 g	0 g	0 g
Fat	0.1 g	0 g	0 g
Fiber	n/a	n/a	0.1 g
Calcium	205 mg	860 mg	150 mg
Iron	4.72 mg	17.50 mg	3.80 mg
Magnesium	242 mg	215 mg	100 mg
Phosphorus	31 mg	40 mg	56 mg
Potassium	1,464 mg	2,492 mg	1,000 mg
Sodium	37 mg	55 mg	8 mg
Zinc	0.290 mg	1.000 mg	0.410 mg
Copper	0.487 mg	2.040 mg	0.130 mg
Manganese	1.530 mg	2.610 mg	n/a
Beta Carotene (A)	0 IU	0 IU	n/a
Thiamine (B$_1$)	0.041 mg	0.033 mg	0.100 mg
Riboflavin (B$_2$)	0.002 mg	0.052 mg	0.155 mg
Niacin (B$_3$)	0.930 mg	1.080 mg	0.100 mg
Pantothenic Acid (B$_5$)	0.804 mg	0.880 mg	n/a
Pyridoxine (B$_6$)	0.670 mg	0.700 mg	n/a
Folic Acid (B$_9$)	0 mcg	1 mcg	n/a
Ascorbic Acid (C)	n/a	n/a	n/a

stalks of the plant are cut and pressed through rollers, and the sweet, dark, thick liquid released is cooked and clarified into a dark syrup. It takes eight to twelve gallons of sorghum sap to make one gallon of "finished" syrup. Good-quality sorghum is a clear amber color, with little sediment and no gritty or grainy feel in the mouth. From 65 to 70 percent sucrose, it will have a rich, hearty, smoky taste. Because sorghum molasses is not a byproduct of sugar refining, it contains none of the sulfur dioxide, a fairly dangerous chemical used in the manufacturing of white sugar. However, it is usually difficult to find a pure cane syrup since its shelf life is fairly short, and for this reason many additives are often used to help preserve it. Traditionally, sorghum molasses is used on pancakes, corn muffins, and other breads, but it is also a suitable substitute for other sweeteners (using one-half to three-quarters the amount of sweetener called for) in most recipes, where it adds a unique taste. Sorghum can ferment, so refrigerate it if you do not use it often.

Mustard
(Brassica nigra, B. juncea, Sinapis alba)

Brassica is the old classical Latin name for this family of plants. The term *nigra* means "black"; *juncea* means "rush-like"; *alba* means "white." The English name *mustard* is derived from the Latin *mustum ardens*, meaning "burning must" and referring to the early French practice of grinding the pungent mustard seeds with grape must (the still-fermenting juice of wine grapes).

General Information

There are many varieties of mustard, but the three species used for the condiment are the black (*Brassica nigra*), the brown (*B. juncea*), and the white (*Sinapis alba*). The husk of the black seed is a dark purplish red-brown; the husk of the brown may vary from brown to black, yet also yellow; the husk covering the white seed is actually a pale tan yellow. Black mustard originated in Asia Minor and Iran and has scarcely been grown for the past twenty-five years because it is difficult to harvest. The brown seed, which originated in the Himalayan area, has replaced the black in both England and America; it is the mustard of North American Chinese restaurants, and certain varieties are grown for salad greens. White mustard is an eastern Mediterranean native. This is the kind used in the ubiquitous American ballpark mustard, dyed bright yellow. All three kinds have become so thoroughly naturalized in North America that they now grow over much of southern Canada and nearly all of the United States. Mustard seeds contain two chemical compounds, myrosin and sinigrin, which when mixed with water produce a volatile oil that may cause skin blisters or burns upon contact. No mustard has either flavor or fire until the cells are broken and water added, and then it takes a few moments for the potency to show and achieve full force. White mustard heats only the tongue; black and brown can also be felt on the tongue, but they also rise memorably to the nose, eyes, and even the forehead, with a pungency that is more intense and longer lasting than that of the white variety.

Early Romans pounded mustard seeds and mixed them with wine to make an early version of our table mustard. Dijon mustard, made in Dijon, France, was heavily regulated. Mustard seed had to be soaked in and mixed with only good vinegar and aged for twelve days before it could be ground and sold. After grinding, the husks were filtered out of the wet mustard to create a smooth yellow paste. If the husks are left in and ground fine, mustard is brown, as are coarse mustards from dark seed. Jeremiah Colman, who gave his name to the famous English mustard business, early mastered the skill of grinding mustard fine without heating it and bringing out the oil. His company thrived, and in 1866 Colman's was appointed mustard maker to Queen Victoria. In India mustard is also grown for the extraction of mustard oil, an important ingredient in Indian cooking.

Buying Tips

Mustard can be purchased as greens or as seeds. The seeds are available whole, as ground, powdered seeds, and as a prepared condiment.

Culinary Uses

Mustard is a thoroughly economical plant, as its leaves, flowers, and seedpods are all edible. The most common mustard greens are from brown mustard, with soft, slightly fuzzy, thin oval leaves of brilliant parrot or emerald green, frilled or scalloped around the edge and attached to fairly long stems. They have a taste very similar to that of prepared mustard, with just a hint of radish and a pleasant perfumy edge. Slivered mustard greens (the stems are not

<table>
<tr><td colspan="3">Mustard / Nutritional Value Per 100 g Edible Portion</td></tr>
<tr><td></td><td>Whole Seed</td><td>1 tsp.</td></tr>
<tr><td>Calories</td><td>469</td><td>15</td></tr>
<tr><td>Protein</td><td>24.94 g</td><td>0.82 g</td></tr>
<tr><td>Fat</td><td>28.76 g</td><td>0.95 g</td></tr>
<tr><td>Fiber</td><td>6.55 g</td><td>0.22 g</td></tr>
<tr><td>Calcium</td><td>521 mg</td><td>17 mg</td></tr>
<tr><td>Iron</td><td>9.98 mg</td><td>0.33 mg</td></tr>
<tr><td>Magnesium</td><td>298 mg</td><td>10 mg</td></tr>
<tr><td>Phosphorus</td><td>841 mg</td><td>28 mg</td></tr>
<tr><td>Potassium</td><td>682 mg</td><td>23 mg</td></tr>
<tr><td>Sodium</td><td>5 mg</td><td>trace</td></tr>
<tr><td>Zinc</td><td>5.700 mg</td><td>0.190 mg</td></tr>
<tr><td>Copper</td><td>0.410 mg</td><td>n/a</td></tr>
<tr><td>Manganese</td><td>1.767 mg</td><td>n/a</td></tr>
<tr><td>Beta Carotene (A)</td><td>62 IU</td><td>2 IU</td></tr>
<tr><td>Thiamine (B$_1$)</td><td>0.543 mg</td><td>0.018 mg</td></tr>
<tr><td>Riboflavin (B$_2$)</td><td>0.381 mg</td><td>0.013 mg</td></tr>
<tr><td>Niacin (B$_3$)</td><td>7.890 mg</td><td>0.260 mg</td></tr>
</table>

LORE AND LEGEND

In India, where mustard is symbolic of rebirth or reincarnation, there was a beautiful little temple inhabited by the lovely nymph Bakawali. For twelve years she occupied the temple, but the structure fell into disrepair, was dismantled, and the earth over the site plowed and planted with mustard. One day a young couple, who remained childless despite much prayer and the advice of many wise men, walked by the mustard field and picked some of the leaves to take home. After cooking and eating the leaves, the wife discovered she was pregnant. When the tiny, nymphlike infant was born, she was named Bakawali in honor of the original nymph, who may have changed form once more.

used) lend depth and brilliance to soups, or they can be cooked on their own like spinach and served with butter. Cooked mustard leaves lose at least half of their fiery flavor. Mixed in with blander leaves, such as lettuce, they give great zest and interest to the salad. Flowers and seedpods can also be used in salads to add a bright taste.

The tiny mustard seed provides a disproportionate amount of spicy flavor for its size because of its hot-tasting volatile oils. White mustard seeds are milder than the black variety and have a pleasant, mild, nutty flavor. Used primarily for mustard powder, they should not be substituted in recipes calling for dark mustard seeds, because their flavor is quite different. Mustard seed is used for a wide range of dishes, including curries, cocktail dips, sandwich spreads, relishes, cheese dishes, and dressings. So popular is prepared mustard in the United States that it ranks second only to black pepper. Because of its acidity and salt, a store-bought jar of mustard does not spoil, but it does slowly lose flavor as well as fire, even in a vacuum-sealed jar. Heat and pungency begin to decline as soon as they reach their peak twenty minutes after mixing. Buy small jars and use them quickly, or your mustard will taste more acidic than flavorful.

Health Benefits

pH 3.55. Appetizer, counterirritant, digestive, emetic, laxative, rubefacient, stimulant. Mustard is pungent, sharp, penetrating, and oily. It stimulates the appetite, increasing salivation by as much as eight times. Used as a domestic spice, it promotes digestion and neutralizes toxins, as well as preventing indigestion and distension of the abdomen. Mustard contains sulfur, one of the best-known treatments for skin diseases, as it rids the blood of excess impurities and slows the activities of the sebaceous glands, which throw off cellular debris. Oil of mustard is a rubefacient, irritating the skin and dilating the small blood vessels underneath; this increases the flow of blood to the skin, turning it red and making it feel warm, and the increased blood flow carries away any toxic products. The pungent taste and tear-producing properties of mustard seeds are a result of nitrogen- and sulfur-containing compounds called isothiocyanates. These compounds are formed from glucosides called sinigrin (in brown mustard) and sinalbin (in white mustard), which are normally present in ground mustard seeds when the seeds are dry; once water is added, special enzymes (myrosin, for example), also present in the seeds, break down these glucosides to form isothiocyanates. That is why dry mustard powder lacks pungent odor but develops it only shortly after water or vinegar is added.

BYPRODUCTS

Mustard powder is a mixture of ground brown and white seeds combined with turmeric or saffron, which add flavor and color. Dry mustard powder can be added to innumerable dishes and when used sparingly gives an excellent flavor.

Prepared mustard is a ready-to-use blend of mustard seeds, salt, other spices, and vinegar (an acid that acts as a fixative so the mustard retains its strength and flavor). You can easily make your own by boiling together one cup of apple cider vinegar, two tablespoons of honey, an eighth of a teaspoon of turmeric, and half a teaspoon of salt. While the mixture is still hot, pour it into a blender, add half a cup of yellow mustard seeds, and grind. When it has achieved a smooth consistency, add one tablespoon of olive oil.

Nasturtium
(Tropaeolum majus, T. minus)

Tropaeolum comes from a Greek word meaning "to twine." The terms *majus* and *minus* differentiate the larger and smaller varieties. The English name *nasturtium* is derived from the Latin words *nasus tortus* (convulsed nose) on account of the plant's pungency.

General Information

Nasturtium is an annual twining vine originally from Peru with decorative, round, light green leaves and colorful flowers that bloom almost continuously. Both nasturtium and its botanical cousin watercress get their spicy, peppery flavor from mustard oils.

Nasturtium / Nutritional Value Per 100 g Edible Portion

	Fresh Leaf/Stalk		Fresh Leaf/Stalk
Calories	48–350	Phosphorus	85–620 mg
Protein	1.8–13.2 g	Beta Carotene (A)	9.0–66.5 mg
Fat	1.2–8.8 g	Thiamine (B₁)	0.090–0.650 mg
Fiber	0.5–3.6 g	Riboflavin (B₂)	0.350–2.550 mg
Calcium	211–1,540 mg	Niacin (B₃)	1.000–7.500 mg
Iron	1.3–9.5 mg	Ascorbic Acid (C)	200–465 mg

Culinary Uses

The leaves, petals, and seeds of nasturtium have a crisp, pungent, peppery taste. Stems, leaves, and flowers can be chopped and added to salads; the leaves can also be cooked and served as a vegetable. The brilliantly hued blossoms make stunning additions to special sandwiches and green salads, or they can be floated in bowls of punch for a garnish. The still-green seeds may be pickled in vinegar and served as a substitute for capers.

Health Benefits

Antiscorbutic, antiseptic, expectorant, stimulant, tonic. Medicinally, nasturtium builds stronger blood by promoting the formation of blood cells, breaks up congestion in the respiratory passages and chest during colds, is good for nervous depression and constipation, and helps clear the skin and eyes. With its high sulfur content, it is especially good for older people, greatly increasing their energy. Nasturtium also has a reputation for arousing sexual appetites.

Nettle, Stinging

(Urtica dioica)

Urtica is from the Latin *uro*, meaning "to burn." *Dioica* refers to the plant's dioecious character (having separate male and female plants). The English name *nettle* is said to derive from the Latin *nassa*, meaning "fishnet," because the stems were woven into strong nets.

General Information

The stinging nettle is a native of Eurasia. Introduced into America with imported cattle by the first English settlers, it is commonly found in wet waste places. The nettle was mentioned in the 1672 *New England Rarities Discovered*, the first book about the flora and fauna of America. A perennial plant with persistent, spreading roots, it can grow up to seven feet in height. With bristly hairs on its square stems, sawtoothed leaves, and small clusters of dull greenish flowers sprouting near the joints of the leaves and stems, the common nettle is not the prettiest plant. Easily recognized by anyone who has come into contact with it, each tiny flower and hair contains sharp, hypodermic-like points that can easily penetrate the skin and insert their virulent venom, derived from formic acid. Generally regarded as an ugly weed, nettles do have some redeeming characteristics. They are frequently the preferred food of goats, and chickens become ecstatic when offered fresh nettles; when made into hay it also makes excellent feed for cattle and horses. In Scotland and in parts of Europe, the nettle was treated much like flax, the fibers making a cloth similar to linen. In World War I, with cotton imports cut off, the Germans utilized nettle for weaving. This should come as no surprise, since nettles are closely related to hemp, which makes a top-quality fiber.

Culinary Uses

If you want to enjoy nettles as a vegetable, head for a sunlight-dappled streambank or a wooded rural area. Collect young shoots (with gloves on) before they flower, or harvest the tender stem tops; older leaves contain gritty deposits of calcium oxalate and are bitter in taste. Young shoots and leaves provide a good spring green, cooked in the manner of spinach and served with salt, pepper, and a little vinegar or lemon juice. The leaves are tender, with a rather salty, earthy flavor. A famous pudding made of nettles combined with leeks, broccoli, or cabbage and rice, and then boiled in a muslin bag, comes

Nettle, Stinging / Nutritional Value Per 100 g Edible Portion

	Dried		Dried
Calories	n/a	Sodium	4.9 mg
Protein	10.2 g	Zinc	4.70 mg
Fat	2.3 g	Manganese	7.80 mg
Fiber	n/a	Beta Carotene (A)	15,700 IU
Calcium	2,900 mg	Thiamine (B₁)	0.540 mg
Iron	41.8 mg	Riboflavin (B₂)	0.430 mg
Magnesium	860 mg	Niacin (B₃)	5.200 mg
Phosphorus	447 mg	Ascorbic Acid (C)	83 mg
Potassium	1,750 mg		

LORE AND LEGEND

In Scandinavian mythology nettles are sacred to the thunder god Thor. Thus they were thrown on the fire during thunderstorms to protect the home from being destroyed by lightning. When carried about the person, they were believed to give courage to the bearer and drive away fear in times of danger.

from Scotland; nettle cream soup is a specialty in Ireland; and nettle beer is made in regions of Britain. The leaves, with the addition of a little salt, can curdle milk and so can be put to use as a substitute for rennet. The poisonous property of the hair disappears with either cooking or drying.

Health Benefits

Diuretic. A number of references to nettle refer to an infusion of the leaves as a treatment for rheumatism. The seeds also have been given as an infusion for coughs and shortness of breath. The high content of iron, silicic acid, and vitamins A and C in young spring nettle shoots explains the effectiveness of nettle tea, which is said to be good for kidney disorders and to improve the function of the liver, gallbladder, and intestines. Tea made from the seeds is used in modern herbal medicine as a hair tonic and growth stimulant as well as an antidandruff shampoo. An old practice to abate gout and rheumatism was to thrash afflicted joints with nettle shoots; the possible improvement was a result of the increased blood flow to that region. Pressing the boiled leaves against a wound will stop the bleeding and at the same time purify the blood.

Nigella
(Nigella sativa)
Also Known As: Kalonji

Nigella is the diminutive form of the Latin term *niger*, meaning "black," and refers to the plant's seeds; *sativa* indicates that the plant has long been cultivated.

Nigella / Nutritional Value Per 100 g Edible Portion			
	Seed		Seed
Protein	21.2–27.2 g	Iron	14.0 mg
Fat	35.5–41.6 g	Potassium	582 mg
Fiber	5.5 g	Sodium	98 mg
Calcium	1,060 mg	Ascorbic Acid (C)	257.7 mg

General Information

Nigella is native to western Asia, the Middle East, and southern Europe, though today it is grown primarily in India. The pretty plant known as "love-in-a-mist," with its feathery foliage and attractive blue flowers, is a very close relative, and the two are frequently called by the same name. This hardy annual grows to about two feet in height. The very small, black seeds look rather like onion seeds. They must be gathered before they are fully ripe; otherwise, the pods will burst and the seeds will be lost.

Culinary Uses

The small, black seeds are lightly aromatic, with a peppery flavor. They are a familiar ingredient in many spice mixtures of the Indian area and are frequently found sprinkled on breads, including those of Turkey and other Middle Eastern countries. They can usually be purchased in specialty grocery stores under their Indian name, kalonji. In Western dishes, use nigella as a pepper substitute; the taste will be slightly more spicy and bitter. To bring out the most flavor, dry-roast the seeds in a skillet before use. Added to buttered vegetables such as zucchini or cabbage, nigella gives an exotic flavor and a pleasant crunchy texture.

Health Benefits

Pungent-tasting nigella aids digestion, reduces inflammation, eases bronchial complaints, stimulates lactation, and eases painful menstruation and postpartum contractions. It also has laxative properties.

Nutmeg and Mace
(Myristica fragrans)

Myristica is from the Greek word *myrrha*, which refers to the aromatic qualities of the plant; *fragrans* means "fragrant." The English word *nutmeg* derives from the Latin *nux*, meaning "nut," and *muscat*, meaning musky; "mace" derives from the Greek *makir*.

General Information

Nutmeg is native to Indonesia, the dried seed of a fruit resembling a peach or an apricot from a slow-growing evergreen tree of the myrtle family. When the nutmeg fruit is harvested, its outer husk is broken open and the red fibrous covering (aril) is separated by hand from the seed shell inside, while the seed kernel (nutmeg) is left to dry inside the shell. The broken pieces of the aril are dried to develop their strong aroma and then ground to make the powder we call mace. Mace from Indonesia is generally orange in color, while that from the West Indies is yellowish brown. Arab traders brought nutmeg to the Eastern spice markets and introduced it to European palates, but it took several hundred years for westerners to develop both taste and pocketbook for this spice. So expensive was this fragrant, nutlike seed that, in the fourteenth century, a pound of it could be

LORE AND LEGEND

Because nutmeg was so costly, it became fashionable in Europe for ladies and gentlemen alike to carry their own nutmeg, along with tiny graters. At fashionable eating establishments, the diners would bring out their nutmeg and graters to flavor wine or food. Predictably, since the graters were carried about and displayed when used, special designs and shapes were created. Some were made of silver and embossed, some folded inside a case to be worn as a pendant, some pierced in intricate patterns, but all imparted to their users a status of fashion-conscious elegance.

exchanged for two calves, three sheep, or half a cow. Where nutmeg is grown, people eat the fruit fresh or preserve it in syrup, but the seed is dried for export. Nutmeg and nutmeg oil are used extensively in flavoring all types of processed food products. Nutmeg oil is also used in cosmetics and in flavoring pharmaceuticals.

Buying Tips

Nutmeg can be purchased as the whole or ground seed, while mace is available as a ground powder. Whole nutmeg is best, because once ground it rapidly loses its volatile oils, thus altering its flavor.

Culinary Uses

Both nutmeg and mace have a warm, sweet, spicy fragrance and a warm, slightly sharp, pervasive flavor. Grated nutmeg is used in cakes, custards, pies (especially pumpkin), milk puddings, cream soups, and hot drinks. The more pungent mace is used in pickles and preserves, cheese dishes, stewed fruit, and mulled wine; it especially complements dishes with either cherries or chocolate.

Health Benefits

Aromatic, carminative, stimulant. Nutmeg is used for general weakness, for diarrhea, for gas and dull, aching pain in the abdomen, for liver and spleen disorders, and for improving appetite and digestion. Taken with milk, it serves as a tonic for the heart, brain, and reproductive

Nutmeg and Mace / Nutritional Value Per 100 g Edible Portion	Nutmeg Ground	Nutmeg 1 tsp.	Mace Ground	Mace 1 tsp.
Calories	525	12	475	8
Protein	5.84 g	0.13 g	6.71 g	0.11 g
Fat	36.31 g	0.80 g	32.38 g	0.55 g
Fiber	4.02 g	0.09 g	4.77 g	0.08 g
Calcium	184 mg	4 mg	252 mg	4 mg
Iron	3.04 mg	0.07 mg	13.90 mg	0.24 mg
Magnesium	183 mg	4 mg	163 mg	3 mg
Phosphorus	213 mg	5 mg	110 mg	2 mg
Potassium	350 mg	8 mg	463 mg	8 mg
Sodium	16 mg	trace	80 mg	1 mg
Zinc	2.150 mg	0.050 mg	2.300 mg	0.040 mg
Copper	1.027 mg	n/a	2.467 mg	n/a
Manganese	2.900 mg	n/a	1.500 mg	n/a
Beta Carotene (A)	102 IU	2 IU	800 IU	14 IU
Thiamine (B$_1$)	0.346 mg	0.008 mg	0.312 mg	0.005 mg
Riboflavin (B$_2$)	0.057 mg	0.001 mg	0.448 mg	0.008 mg
Niacin (B$_3$)	1.299 mg	0.029 mg	1.350 mg	0.023 mg

organs. Nutmeg contains up to 10 percent volatile oil (nutmeg oil) and many other minor constituents. Nutmeg oil itself contains dozens of chemical constituents, including 4 to 8 percent myristicin and small amounts of safrole. Nutmeg oil supports the adrenal glands for increased energy. It has historically benefited circulation, muscles, joints, arthritis, gout, aches and pains, rheumatism, flatulence, indigestion, sluggish digestion, nausea, and bacterial infection. It also helps to support the nervous system to overcome frigidity, impotence, neuralgia, and nervous fatigue.

Note: Both nutmeg and mace can produce severe toxicity at doses exceeding one teaspoon. Nausea, vomiting, and dizziness accompanied by hallucinations, feelings of unreality, and delusions are some of the symptoms that may develop. Deaths resulting from the ingestion of very large doses of nutmeg have been reported. The hallucinogenic and other psychotropic qualities of nutmeg are believed to be a result of myristicin.

Oregano
(Origanum vulgare)

The botanical name *Origanum* means "joy of the mountain," derived from the Greek words *oros* (mountain) and *ganos* (joy). Those who have visited Greece, where oregano covers the hillsides and scents the warm summer air, would emphatically agree. *Vulgare* means "vulgar" or "common."

General Information
Oregano is a member of the mint family, a relative of basil and marjoram. Native to Europe, oregano is a branching perennial growing about two feet tall and bearing pink or purple flowers. This "pizza herb" has highly aromatic small leaves and young shoots that can be used fresh like those of sweet marjoram or dried for later use.

Culinary Uses
Oreganos vary in flavor, from the mild common oregano to the more strongly flavored Greek and Spanish oregano, all the way to Mexican oregano (also known as Mexican marjoram or Mexican wild sage), which is the strongest of all, strong enough to be used in chili powders and dishes flavored with chili peppers. Oregano is often available fresh, which is the preferred form. If the fresh herb is not available, the whole dried leaves are the best remaining

LORE AND LEGEND

According to Greek folklore, the goddess Aphrodite was so touched by oregano that she bestowed upon it its inviting sweet scent. Through the ages, oregano was known as a symbol of happiness and eternal bliss, and it was woven into garlands for brides and bridegrooms. If this herb grew on a tomb, folks believed that meant the dearly departed was happy in the afterlife. It was also used as a magic charm to ward off the perceived evils of witchcraft during the Middle Ages; oregano's aromatic influences do increase one's feeling of security.

alternative. One of the most frequently used dried herbs, oregano has a hot, peppery flavor. Both oregano and its cousin marjoram are popular in Mediterranean cooking and are best known for their appearance in tomato sauce; oregano also enhances mushroom, eggplant, and zucchini dishes, various salads, pasta sauces, cabbage, broccoli, and onions. Its flavor combines well with those of garlic, thyme, parsley, and olive oil.

Oregano / Nutritional Value Per 100 g Edible Portion		
	Dried	1 tsp.
Calories	306	5
Protein	11.00 g	0.17 g
Fat	0.25 g	0.15 g
Fiber	14.96 g	0.22 g
Calcium	1,576 mg	24 mg
Iron	44.00 mg	0.66 mg
Magnesium	270 mg	4 mg
Phosphorus	200 mg	3 mg
Potassium	1,669 mg	25 mg
Sodium	15 mg	trace
Zinc	4.430 mg	0.070 mg
Copper	0.943 mg	n/a
Manganese	4.667 mg	n/a
Beta Carotene (A)	6,903 IU	104 IU
Thiamine (B₁)	0.341 mg	0.005 mg
Riboflavin (B₂)	n/a	n/a
Niacin (B₃)	6.220 mg	0.093 mg

Health Benefits

Carminative, choleretic, emmenagogue, stimulant, tonic. Oregano will help rid the body of poisons, strengthen the stomach, and expel gas from the gastrointestinal tract. Herbalists have noted that its warming qualities have made it useful as a liniment and rubefacient, and the oil is a frequently mentioned toothache remedy. Oregano also makes a refreshing and invigorating bath additive to treat rheumatic pains and skin infections, in a dilution of two tablespoons dried leaves per two liters of water. Oregano oil is one of the most powerful antimicrobial essential oils. Highly damaging to many kinds of viruses, oregano was recently shown in laboratory research conducted at Weber State University to have a 99 percent kill rate against *Streptococcus pneumoniate*, which is responsible for many kinds of lung and throat infections. Oregano oil may help balance metabolism and strengthen the vital centers of the body.

Note: Go easy on oregano as a medicine until you are sure there are no side effects. Although regarded as a safe herb, oregano does trigger an allergic reaction in a small percentage of the population.

Pandanus Leaf

(Pandanus odorus)
Also Known As: Screw Pine Leaf

Pandanus is the latinized form of a Malayan name for the plant; *odorus* means "fragrant." The alternate name *screw pine*, given the plant by European sailors traveling in the South Pacific, leads one to think the plant looks like a pine tree when in fact it is more akin to palm trees.

General Information

The bush-sized plant produces thin, pointed leaves that are used as a seasoning in Thailand, Malaysia, Indonesia, and elsewhere in Southeast Asia. Leaves up to twenty inches in length are increasingly available at Asian produce stands. Look for leaves that are shiny green on one side; they lose luster as they dry and age.

Culinary Uses

The flavor is best described as new-mown hay with a floral dimension. Typically one or two leaves are cooked in a sugar syrup that is then strained as a first step in turning out various puddings, cakes, and custards made with rice, tapioca, and even mung bean flours. The leaves color the syrup and resultant product green.

Paprika, Sweet Hungarian

(Capsicum tetragonum)

Our word *capsicum* arrived on the scene in 1700 under the auspices of Joseph Pitton de Tournefort, early plant taxonomist and plant hunter for the spectacular gardens of Louis XIV. The name is thought to come from either the Latin *capsa*, meaning "box," for the hollow, boxlike shape of the fruit (at least in some cases), or the Greek *kapto*, meaning "to bite," for the pepper's acrid, tongue-searing pungency. *Tetragonum* means "four-angled," referring to the shape of the pods used for this powder. By the 1560s capsicum peppers had reached the Balkans, where they were called *peperke* or *paparka*—and the Hungarians, by a short linguistic jump, had acquired their famed *paprika* by 1569.

General Information

Paprika always refers to a ground product prepared of highly colored, mild red pods of one or more varieties of capsicums used to flavor and color foods. Sweet paprika is

Paprika / Nutritional Value Per 100 g Edible Portion		
	Dried	1 tsp.
Calories	289	6
Protein	14.76 g	0.31 g
Fat	12.95 g	0.27 g
Fiber	20.89 g	0.44 g
Calcium	177 mg	4 mg
Iron	23.59 mg	0.50 mg
Magnesium	185 mg	4 mg
Phosphorus	345 mg	7 mg
Potassium	2,344 mg	49 mg
Sodium	34 mg	1 mg
Zinc	4.060 mg	0.080 mg
Copper	0.607 mg	n/a
Manganese	0.843 mg	n/a
Beta Carotene (A)	60,604 IU	1,273 IU
Thiamine (B$_1$)	0.645 mg	0.014 mg
Riboflavin (B$_2$)	1.743 mg	0.037 mg
Niacin (B$_3$)	15.320 mg	0.322 mg
Ascorbic Acid (C)	71.12 mg	1.49 mg

mostly pericarp with more than half of the seeds removed, while hot paprika contains some seeds, placenta, calyces, and stalks, depending on the grade. The Hungarian powder is ground from dried, long-podded peppers and is more pungent than the Spanish paprika, which uses a tomato-shaped pepper.

Culinary Uses
Paprika is traditionally used in Hungarian goulash but also appears in cheese dishes, cocktail dips, dressings, sauces, and soups; it makes an attractive and tasty garnish.

Health Benefits
Antibacterial, stimulant. The capsicum in paprika is one of the best stimulants; when the body is properly stimulated, the healing and cleansing process starts, allowing the body to function normally. Paprika normalizes blood pressure, improves the entire circulatory system, boosts secretion of saliva and stomach acids, increases peristaltic movement, and feeds the cell structure of the arteries, veins, and capillaries so they regain elasticity.

Parsley
(Petroselinum crispum)

> Parsley—the jewel of herbs, both in the pot and on the plate.
>
> —ALBERT STOCKLI

The ancient Greek Dioscorides named this plant *Petroselinum* from the Greek words *petros* (rock) and *selinon* (celery). *Crispum* means "curled"; the English word *parsley* is a corruption of the original Latin.

General Information
Parsley is believed to be indigenous to Sardinia, Turkey, Algeria, and Lebanon, where it still grows wild. Sardinian coins, until recent times, were minted with a parsley imprint. A member of the carrot family, there are more than thirty-seven different varieties, including broadleaved, curly-leaved, Hamburg, and Neapolitan (Italian) parsley. The mild curly-leaved is prettier as a garnish, but the flat-leaved (Italian) is more tender and has a stronger, more intense flavor. Considered a protective and purifying herb for over two thousand years, parsley was introduced

into Britain in 1548. German mystic Hildegard of Bingen created a popular tonic made of parsley sprigs, wine, and vinegar that was credited with many miraculous cures during the Middle Ages.

Culinary Uses
There are two main types of parsley available in stores: the strongly flavored flat-leaved parsley (also known as Italian parsley), which stands up well to heat; and the mildly flavored curly parsley, which is a better keeper. Flat-leaved parsley is a deep blue-green; the curly, a lighter green. Select parsley with no sign of wilting. Plunge the stems into a glass of water, keep it in a shady part of the kitchen, and use within three days. Parsley sold in airtight plastic bags seems to keep fairly well in the salad drawer of the refrigerator but not for more than two days. If you have too much fresh parsley, you can chop and freeze it with excellent results. Parsley has a tangy, sweet flavor that helps bring out the flavor of other herbs and seasonings, particularly in soups and stews. The stems have a stronger flavor

Parsley / Nutritional Value Per 100 g Edible Portion					
	Fresh Raw	Dried	1 tsp.	Freeze-Dried	1 Tbsp.
Calories	36	276	1	271	1
Protein	2.97 g	22.42 g	0.07 g	31.30 g	0.13 g
Fat	0.79 g	4.43 g	0.01 g	5.20 g	0.02 g
Fiber	n/a	10.32 g	0.03 g	10.06 g	0.04 g
Calcium	138 mg	1,468 mg	4 mg	176 mg	1 mg
Iron	6.20 mg	97.86 mg	0.29 mg	53.90 mg	0.22 mg
Magnesium	50 mg	249 mg	1 mg	372 mg	1 mg
Phosphorus	58 mg	351 mg	1 mg	548 mg	2 mg
Potassium	554 mg	3,805 mg	11 mg	6,300 mg	25 mg
Sodium	56 mg	452 mg	1 mg	391 mg	2 mg
Zinc	1.070 mg	4.750 mg	0.010 mg	6.110 mg	0.020 mg
Copper	0.149 mg	0.640 mg	n/a	0.459 mg	0.002 mg
Manganese	0.160 mg	10.500 mg	n/a	1.338 mg	0.005 mg
Beta Carotene (A)	5,200 IU	23,340 IU	70 IU	63,240 IU	253 IU
Thiamine (B$_1$)	0.086 mg	0.172 mg	0.001 mg	1.040 mg	0.004 mg
Riboflavin (B$_2$)	0.098 mg	1.230 mg	0.004 mg	2.260 mg	0.009 mg
Niacin (B$_3$)	1.313 mg	7.929 mg	0.024 mg	10.400 mg	0.042 mg
Pantothenic Acid (B$_5$)	0.400 mg	n/a	n/a	2.516 mg	0.010 mg
Pyridoxine (B$_6$)	0.090 mg	1.002 mg	0.003 mg	1.375 mg	0.006 mg
Folic Acid (B$_9$)	152.0 mcg	n/a	n/a	1,535.4 mcg	6.1 mcg
Ascorbic Acid (C)	133.0 mg	122.04 mg	0.37 mg	149.00 mg	0.60 mg
Tocopherol (E)	1.74 mg	n/a	n/a	n/a	n/a

LORE AND LEGEND

Parsley is one of the first herbs to appear in spring, and has been used for centuries in the seder, the ritual Jewish Passover meal, as a symbol of new beginnings. In Greek mythology parsley sprang from the blood of Opheltes, infant son of King Lycurgus of Nemea, who was killed by a serpent while his nanny directed some thirsty soldiers to a nearby spring. One of the soldiers, the seer Amphiarus, seeing the child's death as a bad omen predicting his own death in an upcoming battle, gave Opheltes the surname *Archemorus*, meaning "first to die." For centuries Greek soldiers believed any contact with parsley before battle signaled impending death. Because of this association, parsley was planted on Greek graves, a custom that ironically led to its rehabilitation. To honor the memory of important figures, the Greeks held the Nemean Games, crowning the winners of the athletic contests with wreaths of parsley. Over a few centuries, the herb lost its association with death and came to symbolize strength. The Romans fed it to

their horses on the theory that it made them swift, and wore curly-leaved parsley garlands in their hair, not only because they were attractive but because they believed that nibbling on parsley sprigs enabled one to drink more wine without becoming drunk.

In medieval times parsley was thought to belong to the Devil, with Good Friday being the only day of the year on which it could be sown successfully, and then only if the moon was rising. Before the plant would grow, the seed was thought to go to the Devil and back seven times, and would only grow successfully if the woman was master of the household. In Devonshire parsley is considered a most unlucky plant. One may break off a few leaves, for that is of benefit to the plant, but if one should pull up a stalk, even to transplant it, the sprites who guard the parsley beds would be seriously offended, and would have their revenge by sending death to some member of the family.

than the leaves; both are used to flavor sauces, soups, salads, omelets, and stuffings and as a decorative garnish for virtually any dish. Because of the high vitamin C and iron content of this herb, it should be added to foods whenever possible. Parsley's high chlorophyll content works to absorb odors and thus makes an effective after-dinner breath "mint." Parsley is also available in the form of dried flakes, although these are lacking in both flavor and color compared to the fresh.

Health Benefits

pH 5.70–6.03. Antispasmodic, carminative, diuretic, emmenagogue, expectorant, tonic. Raw parsley facilitates oxygen metabolism, cleanses the blood, dissolves sticky deposits in veins, maintains elasticity of blood vessels, facilitates removal of moderately sized kidney stones and gallstones, stimulates the bowel, treats deafness and ear infections, benefits the sexual system, and stimulates adrenal sections. Chewed after eating a meal heavy in garlic, it will eliminate halitosis (bad breath) because of its chlorophyll content. Parsley tea strengthens the teeth and

makes a face lotion to increase circulation and bring color to the skin. Stir one teaspoonful of parsley leaves in a cup of hot water; cool, stir, and strain before drinking or using as a wash.

Note: Furocoumarins (toxic crystalline acids) present in parsley's volatile oil are phototoxic and may cause skin inflammations and contact dermatitis in sensitive individuals.

Pepper, Black
(Piper nigrum)

Piper is an ancient Latin name for the plant; *nigrum* means "black." The Sanskrit word *pippali* meant "berry" and also "long pepper," and is the root of the word *pepper* in European languages.

General Information

Pepper is the small berry of a tropical vining shrub from the Malabar coast of India that for over three thousand years has been the world's most important spice. Possibly the earliest spice known to humans, it was first cultivated probably around 1000 B.C.; a thousand years later it was carried by Hindu immigrants to Malaysia and Indonesia, where it was established in such places as Malacca, Sarawak, Java, Sumatra, and the Moluccas (Spice Islands). Pepper was the spice par excellence of the classical world and was well known in Greece by the fifth century B.C., although less for cooking than as an item in the official pharmacopoeia. In medieval Europe it was so precious that it was classed with gold, silver, and gems.

Pepper berries are borne on two- to six-inch spikes, with fifty to sixty berries per spike. Black peppercorns are berries that are picked when full-sized but unripe and allowed to dry in the sun to develop their color and flavor. The outer flesh, which contains most of the aromatic power of the spice, shrinks to become the wrinkled black skin; the blackening is caused by enzymes within the berries. On average, it takes eight to ten thousand black peppercorns make a pound. White peppercorns are berries that are allowed to mature to their fully ripe, red stage before being picked; after harvesting they are soaked in water, washed of the soft outer layer to reveal the smooth whitish core, and allowed to dry and bleach in the sun. Sun-drying intensifies white pepper's pungency. Because much of pepper's pungency is in its skin, all forms of white pepper are milder tasting than black pepper; aroma, however, is a different matter, with the fragrance of white pepper excelling that of black pepper. Green peppercorns are harvested in their unripe, green stage and then packed in vinegar or brine or else freeze-dried or dehydrated. The dehydrated green peppercorns are more flavorful than the freeze-dried and are preferred for pepper mills. The spiciness and moderate heat of green peppercorns suggest a less concentrated version of black pepper (which is picked at the same stage).

Red or pink peppercorns come from *Schinus terebinthifolius*, a plant called variously the Brazilian pepper tree, Christmas berry, and Florida holly. This plant is native to Brazil and has become a pest in Florida. The dried spice is usually slightly larger than a peppercorn, with the red-to-pink skin dried to a thin brittle shell loosely surrounding a single seed. The flavor is at first sweet, almost citrusy, and then somewhat menthol and resinous; there is slight bitterness and little if any heat. These novelty peppercorns have caused adverse reactions in some people and for a time were banned from sale by the FDA.

Culinary Uses

Although not as ubiquitous as water or salt, pepper is probably the third most common addition to food. Pepper can be purchased as whole peppercorns or ground into a powder. Whole peppercorns hold their flavor and volatile oils better than ground pepper; since the aromatic qualities of pepper are fleeting and it turns bitter if ground too far in advance, freshly ground pepper is a must. Furthermore, most preground pepper is toasted, and once toasted, pepper acts as an irritant. Black pepper has a very characteristic fragrant aroma with a hot, biting, pungent flavor; white pepper is somewhat milder and more warmly aromatic than the black. Green peppercorns have a fresh and pungent flavor and are usually sold pickled in brine. Pepper flavors nearly all dishes other than desserts, and though it needs to be used sparingly, it can make an enormous difference to the flavor of foods. Lacking the strictly defined personalities of most other spices, pepper enhances and at the same time is submissive. It blends easily with meat, fish, and vegetables; its heat teases gently and burns only when used in ludicrous quantities. As a general aesthetic rule, white pepper is added to pale-colored foods and sauces where little specks of black pepper would spoil the appearance. Whole peppercorns are added to pickles, marinades, and

Pepper / Nutritional Value Per 100 g Edible Portion				
	Black Whole	1 tsp.	White Whole	1 tsp.
Calories	255	5	296	7
Protein	10.95 g	0.23 g	10.40 g	0.25 g
Fat	3.26 g	0.07 g	2.12 g	0.05 g
Fiber	13.13 g	0.28 g	4.34 g	0.10 g
Calcium	437 mg	9 mg	265 mg	6 mg
Iron	28.86 mg	0.61 mg	14.31 mg	0.34 mg
Magnesium	194 mg	4 mg	90 mg	2 mg
Phosphorus	173 mg	4 mg	176 mg	4 mg
Potassium	1,259 mg	26 mg	73 mg	2 mg
Sodium	44 mg	1 mg	5 mg	trace
Zinc	1.420 mg	0.030 mg	1.130 mg	0.030 mg
Copper	1.127 mg	n/a	0.910 mg	n/a
Manganese	5.625 mg	n/a	4.300 mg	n/a
Beta Carotene (A)	190 IU	4 IU	trace	n/a
Thiamine (B$_1$)	0.109 mg	0.002 mg	0.022 mg	0.001 mg
Riboflavin (B$_2$)	0.240 mg	0.005 mg	0.126 mg	0.003 mg
Niacin (B$_3$)	1.142 mg	0.024 mg	0.212 mg	0.005 mg

LORE AND LEGEND

Indian pepper was so important that it was numbered among the five "essential luxuries" on which the whole foreign trade of the Roman Empire was said to have been based (the others were Chinese silk, African ivory, German amber, and Arabian incense). Of the five, only pepper came nearest to being a true essential, not because spices were vital to Roman cuisine but because they transformed the food (often quite bland and boring) of everyday life. Many spices influenced the ebb and flow of history, but it was pepper that launched one of the grandest series of dramas in recorded history. Desire for a readier access to pepper and other spices instigated European attempts to find alternative routes to India, and Columbus's search for a western route ended in the discovery of America. Like other spices, peppercorns were valuable because they were small, were easily transported, and lasted indefinitely at normal temperatures. So high a price did the spice command in medieval times that it was used in payment of levies and taxes instead of coins. Pepper represented a more stable medium of exchange than gold or silver in days when every petty sovereign (and a number of important cities as well) struck his own coins and only an Archimedes could assess their content of precious metal, even without taking into account the common habit of scraping or clipping some of it off as money passed from hand to hand. Today the phrase "peppercorn rent" is sometimes used to denote a nominal sum, but in late medieval times there was nothing nominal about it: a pound of pepper was the barter equivalent of two or three weeks' labor on the land, and worth a pound of gold. The habit even arose in medieval times of expressing a man's wealth in terms not of the amount of land in his estate, but of the amount of pepper in his pantry. One way of saying a man was poor was to say that he lacked pepper. The wealthy kept large stores of pepper in their houses, and let it be known that it was there: it was a guarantee of solvency. In A.D. 408 Alaric, king of the Visigoths, demanded three thousand pounds of pepper as part of the ransom for the city of Rome.

bouillon. Pepper connoisseurs select their pepper by region. Tellicherry, Lampong, and Sarawak produce some of the finest-quality pepper; Malabor and Brazilian pepper are usually considered overly hot and sharp.

Another beneficial use of pepper is as a pest deterrent. Pepper contains piperine, a natural insecticide considered more toxic to houseflies than pyrethrins, the natural insecticide derived from chrysanthemums. Black pepper has been proven toxic against a number of agricultural and household pests, including ants, potato bugs, silverfish, and some roaches and moths. To protect your plants, spray them with a solution of one-half teaspoon freshly ground pepper in one quart of warm water. Or sprinkle ground pepper in areas insects frequent.

Health Benefits

Antiseptic, stimulant. Historically in Eurasia, pepper was valued as an aid to digestion, to cause sneezing, and to relieve gas. It stimulates the flow of energy and blood to the body and, because it opens the pores for sweating, is good at the onset of the common cold. Clinical evidence shows that a major pepper compound, piperine, acts as an anti-inflammatory, protects the liver against solvents like tetrachloride, and acts as a parasite inhibitor; however, it was also found to have antifertility effects and to depress the central nervous system. Most commercial ground pepper is roasted and is an irritant rather than a stimulant. Make your own fresh-ground pepper with a pepper mill and whole peppercorns. Because pepper is hot and pungent, it acts as a digestive stimulant, increasing the secretion of digestive juices, improving the taste of food, and alleviating that uncomfortable heavy feeling after a large meal. Meanwhile, it also irritates the mucous membranes inside the nose and throat, causing them to weep a watery secretion that makes it easier to cough up mucus or blow the nose. Pepper also makes you perspire, and because perspiration acts as a natural air conditioner, cooling the body as the moisture evaporates from the skin, peppery foods are popular in warm climes. Pepper has demonstrated impressive antioxidant and antibacterial properties. The overuse of pepper, however, can provoke chronic hypersecretion followed by a burning sensation in the stomach. A pinch of pepper mixed with ghee and applied externally relieves disorders such as dermatitis and hives.

Pepper, Indian Long
(Piper longum)

Piper is an ancient Latin name for the plant; *longum* means "long." The Sanskrit word *pippali* meant "berry" and also "long pepper," and because long pepper was at first the most highly regarded pepper, *pippali* is the root of the word *pepper* in European languages.

General Information
Indian long pepper is, not surprisingly, native to India. The philosopher Theophrastus, pupil of Aristotle along with Alexander the Great, wrote, "Pepper is a fruit, and there are two kinds. One is round . . . and it is reddish; the other is elongated and black and has seeds like those of a poppy. And this kind is much stronger than the other." A relative of black pepper, long pepper is actually a cluster of tiny berries that merge to a single rodlike fruit of mahogany brown. The entire pod of long pepper is used as the spice; it is about an inch and a half long, less than a quarter inch wide, and slightly tapered. Like black pepper, it is harvested unripe and dried in the sun. Long pepper was much more common in ancient and medieval times than it is today, probably because white and black pepper were scarce in those times. It is possible to find long pepper in southeast Asian markets and in Indian markets that specialize in food from the Bombay region.

Culinary Uses and Health Benefits
The sweet smell of ground long pepper gives no warning of its hot pungency. The taste suggests something of black pepper, wintergreen, cinnamon, and clove. Someone once compared it to the candies called Red Hots. The unripe, dried berry is used mainly in parts of India and Indonesia, where it is added whole to curries and pickles. Crush the rods before use, or use the clusters whole as a pickling spice. Trikatu, the most important stimulant and digestive tonic in Ayurvedic medicine, is made of equal parts black pepper, long pepper, and ground ginger. Combine ½ teaspoon of this blend with one cup of hot water and a tea-spoon of honey. It's a great morning wake-up drink that doesn't have the side effects of caffeinated beverages. Hot and warm with sweet overtones, long pepper has a higher content of piperine (the primary micronutrient in black pepper) than does black pepper. It aids digestion and has decongestant, antibiotic, and analgesic effects. Long pepper improves absorption in the intestines and helps protect the liver from free-radical damage. The Chinese use it externally for toothache.

Peppergrass
(Lepidium virginicum)
Also Known As: Cress, Land Cress, Bird's Pepper

The botanical name *Lepidium* is a Greek term meaning "little scales," alluding to the plant's small, flat pods; *virginicum* means "from Virginia." The English name *peppergrass* comes from its taste.

General Information
Peppergrass is an annual herb of the mustard family that grows in temperate to hot climates. The foliage and pods have an aromatic, peppery flavor; the herbage of some species is used as a salad herb, and the pods are sometimes fed to tame birds (hence the name *bird's pepper*).

Peppergrass / Nutritional Value Per 100 g Edible Portion		
	Raw	Cooked
Calories	32	23
Protein	2.60 g	1.90 g
Fat	0.70 g	0.60 g
Fiber	1.10 g	0.90 g
Calcium	81 mg	61 mg
Iron	1.30 mg	0.80 mg
Magnesium	n/a	n/a
Phosphorus	76 mg	48 mg
Potassium	606 mg	353 mg
Sodium	14 mg	8 mg
Beta Carotene (A)	9,300 IU	7,700 IU
Thiamine (B₁)	0.080 mg	0.060 mg
Riboflavin (B₂)	0.260 mg	0.160 mg
Niacin (B₃)	1.000 mg	0.800 mg
Pyridoxine (B₆)	0.247 mg	n/a
Ascorbic Acid (C)	69.0 mg	23.0 mg
Tocopherol (E)	0.70 mg	n/a

Culinary Uses

The spicy, pungent flavor of peppergrass leaves and seeds greatly enhances soups, coleslaws and salads, green drinks, seed or nutmeat loaves, and pizzas. It should be added when the dish is ready to serve, since it should not be cooked.

Health Benefits

Herbalists use peppergrass to clear lung congestion.

Plantain
(Plantago major, P. media)

The botanical name *Plantago* has as a root element the Latin word *planta*, meaning "sole of the foot" and referring to the broad shape of the leaves. *Major* means "large" or "great," referring to the leaf size; *media* means "medium" or "intermediate." The English name *plantain* is a corruption of the Latin *plantago*.

General Information

Plantain is a humble perennial Eurasian weed with an ancient reputation in Oriental, European, and Native American medicine. There are many varieties of plantain, but the most familiar is common plantain (*P. major*), characterized by its rosette of ribbed, ovate leaves and its spiked stalk. This variety is commonly found in waste places, lawns, dooryards, and roadsides all over North America and Europe. Another variety (*P. psyllium*), known as psyllium seed, is becoming more well known, as the seeds are used for medicinal purposes and are frequent ingredients in laxatives and intestinal cleansing products. See psyllium's separate reference in the **Nuts, Seeds, and Oils** section.

Culinary Uses

Plantain's young, tender leaves have a sour-sharp taste and are used in salads or lightly steamed like spinach.

Health Benefits

Antiseptic, astringent, demulcent, expectorant, hemostatic, vulnerary. The medicinal part of plantain is contained in the

Plantain / Nutritional Value Per 100 g Edible Portion			
	Fresh		Fresh
Protein	18.8 g	Potassium	460 mg
Fat	10.0–22.0 g	Ascorbic Acid (C)	trace
Fiber	19.0 g		

LORE AND LEGEND

According to legend, plantain was once a maiden who spent so much time by the roadside watching and waiting for her absent lover that she eventually was transformed into this common roadside plant. The ancient Saxon book *Lacuna* considered plantain one of the nine sacred herbs, while for early Christians the plant symbolized the well-trodden path of the multitude who sought Christ. American Indians called it White Man's Foot because the plant, resembling miniature cattails to some extent, seemed to follow the white settlers wherever they went.

broad, ribbed leaves; these contain such an effective soothing, mucilaginous fluid that a poultice made of the freshly bruised or ground leaves applied to wounds and sores will often check bleeding. Not only excellent for cuts, skin infections, and chronic skin problems, the freshly crushed leaves are also used on stings and bites and give relief when rubbed on poison ivy. Plantain also contains tannin and is thus an astringent, able to draw tissues together. It is an excellent blood purifier and works to improve kidney function. It also helps prevent gas and diarrhea.

Purslane
(Portulaca oleracea)
Also Known As: Pussley, Indian Cress, Portulaca, Verdolaga

Lord, I confess too when I dine
The pulse is thine,
And all those other bits that be
There placed by thee,
The worts, the purselain, and the mess
Of Water Cress.

—Author unknown

Portulaca is most likely derived from the Latin *porto*, "to carry," and *lac*, "milk," ultimately meaning "milk carrier," because of the plant's milky sap. *Oleracea* means "oleraceous," or a vegetable garden herb used in cooking. The English name *purslane* is derived from the Latin *portulaca*.

General Information

A native of India and Africa, purslane was introduced into Europe as a salad plant by the Arabs during the fifteenth century. During colonial times, purslane was naturalized in America and has spread over this country and into Mexico and South America, acting like a native in the southwestern United States. There are two varieties: the wild form is a sprawling plant that grows no more than two inches high and has reddish-green or purple-tinted stems with greenish purple leaves; cultivated purslane has larger leaves of a golden-yellowish color. Both varieties have thick, fleshy branches and succulent stems that ooze milky fluid when squeezed. The purslane most favored by the North American Indians is the white mountain rose, or bitterroot (*Lewisia rediviva*), discussed separately.

Culinary Uses

Purslane has a sharp yet not unpleasant taste similar to watercress that blends well with other herbs. The leafy new growth is the tastiest part to eat. In salads, purslane leaves are delicious, and the yellow-leaved variety adds a spark of color. The whole plant can be used if cooked as a green; boil or steam for only five minutes and serve garnished with butter and a touch of lemon. It also goes well in stir-fries and is delicious pickled. Purslane's mucilaginous texture gives it thickening power and makes a welcome addition to many soups; use it instead of okra in gumbos and creole dishes.

Health Benefits

Antiscorbutic. Purslane leaves contain tannin, phosphates, urea, and various minerals. They have been used to counteract inflammation and destroy bacteria in bacillary dysentery, diarrhea, and hemorrhoids.

Rose and Rose Hip

(*Rosa pomifera, R. rugosa, R. canina*)
Also Known As: Brier Rose, Dog Rose

> One day Venus, wishing to pick the white rose, wounded herself, tinging it with an immortal purple hue. The flower then appeared to Cupid so beauteous, that he placed upon it a kiss . . . from this comes its perfume!
>
> —EUGENE RIMMEL

> I'd rather have roses on my table than diamonds on my neck.
>
> —EMMA GOLDMAN

The genus name *Rosa* is derived from the Greek word *rodon*, meaning "red." *Pomifera* means "bearing pomelike fruits"; *rugosa* means "rugose," or wrinkled; *canina* means "pertaining to a dog."

General Information

Prized since the dawn of history, the rose is queen of the flowers. But in herbal healing, this plant becomes noteworthy only after the velvety petals have fallen away, revealing the rusty-colored, cherry-shaped rose hips, or

Purslane / Nutritional Value Per 100 g Edible Portion	Raw	Cooked
Calories	16	18
Protein	1.30 g	1.49 g
Fat	0.10 g	0.19 g
Fiber	0.80 g	0.81 g
Calcium	65 mg	78 mg
Iron	1.99 mg	0.77 mg
Magnesium	68 mg	67 mg
Phosphorus	44 mg	37 mg
Potassium	494 mg	488 mg
Sodium	45 mg	44 mg
Beta Carotene (A)	1,320 IU	1,852 IU
Thiamine (B₁)	0.047 mg	0.031 mg
Riboflavin (B₂)	0.112 mg	0.090 mg
Niacin (B₃)	0.480 mg	0.460 mg
Ascorbic Acid (C)	21.0 mg	10.5 mg

Rose Hip / Nutritional Value Per 100 g Edible Portion	Hips, Dried		Hips, Dried
Calories	341	Sodium	4,600 mg
Protein	13.3 g	Zinc	trace
Fat	1.9 g	Manganese	4.000 mg
Fiber	30.0 g	Beta Carotene (A)	7,015 IU
Calcium	810 mg	Thiamine (B₁)	0.380 mg
Iron	trace	Riboflavin (B₂)	0.720 mg
Magnesium	139 mg	Niacin (B₃)	6.800 mg
Phosphorus	256 mg	Ascorbic Acid (C)	740 mg
Potassium	827 mg		

LORE AND LEGEND

According to Greek myth, one cloudy morning Chloris, the deity of flowers, walked through the woods and found the body of a beautiful nymph. Saddened to see such a lovely creature deprived of life, she decided to transform the nymph into a beautiful flower surpassing all others in charm and beauty. She called on the other deities to help with her task: Aphrodite, to give beauty; the three Graces, to bestow brilliance, joy, and charm; her husband Zephyrus, the West Wind, to blow away the clouds so that Apollo, the Sun, could send his blessing through his rays; and Dionysius, the deity of wine, to give nectar and fragrance. When the new flower was finished, the gods rejoiced over its charming beauty and delicate scent. Chloris collected a diadem of dewdrops and crowned the new flower queen of all flowers. Aphrodite then presented the rose to her son Eros, the deity of love. The white rose became the symbol of charm and innocence, and the red rose of love and desire. When Eros in turn gave the rose to Harpocrates, the deity of silence, to induce him to conceal the weaknesses of the gods (especially the amorous affairs of his mother), the rose became the emblem of silence and secrecy. A rose hung in a room or over a table meant that all information spoken was to be kept secret or *sub rosa*—under the rose.

There is another pretty legend about the rose, this one Romanian, of a princess going to bathe in her garden pool. The Sun, passing overhead, fell so in love with her beauty that he stopped still in the heavens to watch her. Hours passed, and there he remained. This fretted the Moon, for she wanted her own chance to parade across the sky; complaining, she approached the god of Night and Day, who promptly changed the princess into a rosebush, so the Sun would go on about his business. The roses were originally white, but when the Sun appeared the next day those nearest him began to blush; and at midday, under his ardent rays, the topmost ones blushed deeply—thus the Romanians have white, pink, and red roses. The Greeks relate that it was Cupid, dancing among them one day, who dashed a goblet of wine over some of them and stained them red. Another legend says that roses were stained red from the blood of Aphrodite, who pricked her foot on a thorn while trying to aid her beloved dying Adonis. The Turks, on the other hand, claim the red rose is stained from the blood of Mohammad; Christian legend says the red rose is colored from the blood of martyrs. The thorns are also attributed to Cupid who, flying over the garden, saw one very lovely rose and alighted to kiss it. However, there was a bee within that angrily stung him on the lip. Crying with indignity, he flew to his mother for comfort; she gave him a quiver of arrows tipped with captive bees, and he shot them at the bush, their stings remaining to this day as thorns on the roses.

Roses were a favorite of the ancient Egyptians, who used the fragrant petals as air fresheners and rose water as perfume. When Cleopatra invited Mark Anthony to her palace, she had the floors covered knee-deep in rose petals so that their scent would rise above him as he walked toward her—such

"false fruit," left after the bloom has died—"false fruit" because in fact the fruits are inside the rose hips. Almost all varieties of roses produce valuable hips, but only some of those produced are pleasant tasting. The others are inclined to be astringent. The best rose hips come from the rugosa rose. Pick fruits when they are fully colored. Do not allow them to become overripe (soft and wrinkled). The plant became important during World War II, when Britain was short of fruit providing vitamin C and schoolchildren were sent to gather rose hips that could then be boiled down to make a syrup issued as a dietary supplement.

Culinary Uses

The small, applelike rose hips have a pleasant flavor that is both fruity and spicy, almost cranberry-like, and many people enjoy eating them fresh, straight off the bush. They are best when left on the bush until the first frost has was her belief in the romantic powers of their perfume. In Greece and Rome the rose was the favorite flower of the goddess of the flowers, the Greek Chloris, and her Roman counterpart Flora. In festivals for these goddesses, people bedecked themselves and their animals with flowers, using mostly roses. At Roman banquets roses were used lavishly for decoration; the Emperor Nero once used millions of the blooms to decorate a hall for a single banquet, with rosewater-saturated pigeons fluttering overhead to sprinkle the guests with scent. For Teutonic peoples, the rose was the flower of the northern goddess of love, Freyja, who was known for her ability to keep secrets. In Scandinavia the rosebush is under the special protection of elves and dwarfs, and it is only by gently asking their permission for each flower taken that one may gather the roses; but one must never pluck a leaf, for it is the leaves that hide the elves from mortal eyes.

A rose by any name signifies joy, beauty, and love; its perfect blossom is associated with love, beauty, youth, perfection, and even immortality; its thorns with the pain of love and guilt; its withering blossom with the ephemeral nature of beauty and youth. The specific meaning of roses depends on the color of the flower: red is for passion and desire; pink for simplicity and happy love; white for innocence and purity; yellow for jealousy and perfect achievement.

touched them, and then picked when bright red and slightly soft to the touch. The seeds inside the vaselike receptacle of the fruit are covered with small, irritating hairs (used by mischievous schoolchildren to make an itching powder) and should be removed. Rose hips are used to make syrups, jellies and jams, teas, wines, soups (especially in Scandinavian cultures), purées, pies, tarts, quick breads, and muffins. Fresh rose petals and leaves tossed either in or on top of a fruit or vegetable salad pro-

vide elegance as well as extra nutrition. Petals can also be used in omelets, fried in batter, crystallized, or made into jam. The Arab countries have many sweets made with roses, and in the eighteenth century there was a rage for dousing everything with rosewater, from meats to sauces. Make sure any rose petals or hips you use come from unsprayed roses.

Health Benefits

Antiscorbutic. Rose hips are an important source of vitamin C. Do not bring them into contact with any metal except stainless steel, for they will quickly lose their color, and the precious store of vitamin C will be depleted. They also contain high amounts of carotene (the vitamin A precursor), vitamin P (bioflavonoids), B complex vitamins, and rutin. Rose hips are excellent for the skin; help stop infection, dizziness, cramps, colds, and stress; and are known to be a blood purifier. Rose hip tea is made by boiling or steeping one teaspoonful of the crushed hips per one cup of water and then pouring the mixture through a sieve to remove the irritating hairs on the fruits. Four to six cups of this tea may be drunk daily. A handful of rose petals thrown into the bath will do wonders for rheumatic pains. Symptoms of sore and irritated eyes are relieved by steeping a few rose petals in a cup of hot water; after careful filtering, the liquid is applied to each eye four or five times a day. Rose vinegar can be prepared (a handful of fresh rose petals steeped in vinegar) and used as a rub, cleansing the skin and acting as a disinfectant for pimples and sores. The essential oil, called attar of rose, is used in aromatherapy as a mildly sedative, antidepressant, and anti-inflammatory remedy. Rose oil has the highest frequency (320 megahertz) of any oil and is very difficult to distill and therefore one of the most expensive oils. Its beautiful fragrance is intoxicating and aphrodisiac. It helps brings balance and harmony and is stimulating and elevating to the mind, creating a sense of well-being.

Rosemary
(Rosmarinus officinalis)
Also Known As: Sea Rose, Incensier, Herb of Crowns, Compass Plant, and Mary's Tree

> There's Rosemary for you, that's for remembrance! Pray you, love, remember.
>
> —WILLIAM SHAKESPEARE (OPHELIA IN *Hamlet*)

> The air was calm, and the strong scents of the hill, like invisible smoke, filled the bottom of the ravine. Thyme, aspic and rosemary turned green the golden fragrance of the resin, whose long, motionless tears shone in the clear shade on the black bark.
>
> —MARCEL PAGNOL

The botanical name *Rosmarinus* comes from the Latin words *ros* (dew) and *marinus* (of the sea). Like the fabled *rosmarine*, a walruslike creature that scaled ocean cliffs to feed on the dew, rosemary thrives best on "dew of the sea." Sometime during the Middle Ages the word *rosmarinus* was changed to *rosemary* in honor of Mary, the mother of Jesus, whose name was then linked to the flower. *Officinalis* means "of the workshop," alluding to apothecaries' shops and signifying that the plant was once part of the official pharmacopoeia of Rome.

General Information

Rosemary is an evergreen shrub of the mint family native to the Mediterranean region, where it often grows by the ocean, a fact reflected in its botanical name. It likes arid growing conditions and seems to prefer watering only by the evanescent humidity that drifts in from the sea; it is true that rosemary is never so richly flavored as when it grows by the ocean. This shrub with its warm, stimulating aroma is a relative of basil and oregano and often grows to heights of six feet, with dark green, silver-tipped, aromatic leaves that look like tiny pine needles. It has the particular characteristic of flowering practically all year, its floral buds blooming continuously or sporadically, depending on the region and the climate. An undemanding plant, rosemary grows all over the areas around the Mediterranean. It is particularly fond of very sunny places with a pronounced summer drought and soil that is chalky or quite clayey but not water-saturated. It forms vast masses in Provence on the uncultivated hills and is also very common in Spain, Morocco, Tunisia, former Yugoslavia, Italy, Greece, and Corsica. A natural insecticide, rosemary protects other plants in the garden by its presence, and sachets of rosemary, either alone or in combination with lavender and ground lemon peel, will repel moths if placed throughout the wardrobe.

Rosemary / Nutritional Value Per 100 g Edible Portion		
	Dried	**1 tsp.**
Calories	331	4
Protein	4.88 g	0.06 g
Fat	15.22 g	0.18 g
Fiber	17.65 g	0.21 g
Calcium	1,280 mg	15 mg
Iron	29.25 mg	0.35 mg
Magnesium	220 mg	3 mg
Phosphorus	70 mg	1 mg
Potassium	955 mg	11 mg
Sodium	50 mg	1 mg
Zinc	3.230 mg	0.040 mg
Copper	0.550 mg	n/a
Manganese	1.867 mg	n/a
Beta Carotene (A)	3,128 IU	38 IU
Thiamine (B₁)	0.514 mg	0.006 mg
Riboflavin (B₂)	n/a	n/a
Niacin (B₃)	1.000 mg	0.012 mg
Ascorbic Acid (C)	61.22 mg	0.74 mg

LORE AND LEGEND

Rosemary's legendary origin is in the steep, barren cliffs of Sicily, where the evil Woman of Etna cast a jealous spell over the island, destroying love and peace and causing only the poisonous mandrake, henbane, and belladonna to grow. The people despaired, and the surrounding sea grew turbulent in anger, but so great was the Woman of Etna's power that she quelled the ocean's rage. But as the last wave crashed upon the cliffs, a maiden was drawn back into the swirling waters crying "Remember, remember"; with these words, where her fingers grappled helplessly with the wet rocks, a beautiful plant burst forth—the rosemary.

Rosemary's ability to preserve meats led to the belief that it helped preserve memory, and Greek students frequently wore garlands of rosemary when going into examinations. It was believed that rosemary would only grow in the gardens of righteous people, and because it was associated with memory, it became the symbol of fidelity, friendship, and affectionate remembrance. Rosemary was also deemed popular with the fairy and elfin folk: should a mortal be so fortunate as to find a four-leaved clover that some fairy has touched and thus given magic sight in passing, he might see whole rows of young fairies perched on rosemary branches while their elders dance amid the thyme.

Steeped in Christian tradition, rosemary has a place as a symbol of fidelity and remembrance in two of the holiest of Christian ceremonies: weddings and funerals. Sprigs were dipped in scented water, and then woven into bridal bouquets or exchanged by the newlyweds as a token of their troth; sprigs were also richly gilded and bound in multicolored ribbons, then presented to the wedding guests as reminders of love and virtuous fidelity. At funerals rosemary sprigs were tossed into the grave as a pledge that the life and good deeds of the departed would not soon be forgotten. Regarded as a powerful defense against evil, sprigs were frequently placed in churches and even used as incense.

The flowers of this pleasant herb were once a dull white, according to Spanish legend. When the Virgin Mary and the Christ child were fleeing from the soldiers of Herod, a thick stand of rosemary bushes parted to enable them to take shelter and rest. Mary remained in that sheltered spot for some time, the sweet pungence of rosemary's fragrance so reviving her that as she left she bestowed upon the flowers the glorious color of her light blue mantle. The flowers were then called the roses of Mary or rosemary. For centuries people thought that a rosemary plant would grow no higher than six feet in thirty-three years, so as not to stand taller than Christ.

Culinary Uses

Rosemary contains oil of camphor, which gives it a wonderful scent and a pleasantly pungent flavor, sometimes described as a cross between sage and lavender with a touch of ginger. These small, needle-shaped leaves are used fresh; they should be crushed or minced to bring out their full flavor before sprinkling over or rubbing into foods. Whole sprigs can be placed in olive oil for an excellent alternative to butter, and the pale blue flowers make a wonderful addition to salads. An extremely versatile herb, rosemary appears in everything from breads and meats to jams and desserts, and it especially complements the herbs bay, chervil, chives, parsley, and thyme. Store-bought dried rosemary has lost most of its oil and fragrance.

Health Benefits

Antiseptic, aromatic, astringent, carminative, diaphoretic, emmenagogue, nervine, stimulant, tonic. Rosemary has a reputation for miracles that is not totally unjustified, for the herb has a wide spectrum of powers. Because of its high essential oil content, rosemary has many effects similar to those of other members of the mint family. It helps alleviate nervous conditions, headaches, and respiratory troubles, corrects and improves the function of the liver and gallbladder, strengthens and tones the muscles of the stomach, acts to raise blood pressure and improve circulation, and even helps with potency disturbances. Its diuretic action is effective in alleviating rheumatism and gout, as well as kidney stones. Rosemary has a long-standing reputation as an invigorating herb, imparting a zest for life that is to some degree reflected in its distinctive aromatic taste. Its aromatic influences stimulate memory, open the conscious mind, and help overcome mental fatigue. The scent alone is said to preserve youth. World-famous biological researcher James Duke makes a drink that he says is his own herbal secret for staying mentally sharp. He calls it his Anti-Alzheimer's Cocktail, made by steeping several sprigs of rosemary in lemonade. Dr. Duke says the antioxidant chemicals in rosemary have a similar effect to those in the latest drugs being used to treat Alzheimer's.

Rosemary oil has been researched for its antiseptic and antimicrobial properties and may be beneficial for skin conditions and dandruff, candida, and impaired immune system. Like thyme, rosemary makes a healthful tea that can be drunk throughout the day with tangible benefits. The tea, because of the oils, is also wonderful for the hair if applied externally as a rinse; it combats dandruff and makes hair more manageable and easier to comb, as well as stimulating new growth. Rosemary has cleansing and antiseptic properties when burned, similar to juniper and cedar. During World War II, French hospitals used rosemary and juniper as incense to kill germs in the air. A sprig of rosemary in the bath water is highly stimulating (some even find it works as an aphrodisiac) and is invaluable in the treatment of slow-healing wounds and rheumatic pains. Rosemary is high in easily assimilable calcium and benefits the entire nervous system. It alleviates depression, eases headaches, preserves good humor, and eliminates negativity of all kinds.

Note: Rosemary should not be used by pregnant women or anyone being treated for epilepsy or high blood pressure.

Rue
(Ruta graveolens)

The name *Ruta* derives from the Greek word *reuo*, meaning "to set free," because of its efficaciousness in treating various diseases; *graveolens* means "heavy-

Rue / Nutritional Value Per 100 g Edible Portion			
	Fresh		Fresh
Fat	37.0 g	Ascorbic Acid (C)	479 mg
Beta Carotene (A)	94.4 mg		

LORE AND LEGEND

The Greeks regarded rue as an antimagical herb, because it served to remedy the nervous indigestion, attributed to witchcraft, that they suffered when eating before strangers. They also wore rue as protection against spells and the Evil Eye. According to mythology, it was the herb given to Ulysses by Mercury to overcome the charms of Circe, as an antidote for her potion and a preserver of chastity. During the Middle Ages, rue was grown in monastery gardens because of its ability to counteract amatory tendencies, and its use prescribed for monks who wished to preserve their purity. Shakespeare called it the Herb of Grace, because at one time holy water was sprinkled from brushes bound from rue at the ceremony "Asperges," usually preceding Sunday celebration of High Mass. It was also used for many centuries as an antidote to poisons, insect bites, and infections, with judges carrying it into court as one of a bouquet of herbs to guard them against infection from prisoners. In the first century B.C., King Mithradates VI of Asia Minor apparently ate rue to immunize himself against being poisoned by enemies, taking the herb in gradually increasing doses. However, this scheme worked so well that it backfired when he attempted suicide by poisoning himself and failed—in the end, he had to persuade a slave to stab him. Both Leonardo da Vinci and Michelangelo claimed that, owing to rue's metaphysical powers, their eyesight and creative inner vision had been improved.

scented." The English name *rue* comes from a mistaken association with the verb "to rue," or "to have regret."

General Information

Rue is native to southern Europe and northern Africa; it was introduced into Britain by the Romans, who needed it to flavor their wine. A hardy evergreen, rue tends to be shrubby in growth but reaches about three feet in height.

Glands distributed over the entire plant contain a volatile oil that accounts for both its unusual smell and its bitter taste. This distinctive fragrance is found pleasant and attractive by some, while others find it objectionable. The oil has the odd power of photosensitizing the skin of some people, causing small water blisters to break out.

Culinary Uses

Rue has a strong aromatic scent and a pungent, acrid taste. Young chopped leaves can be added to salads in small quantities as a strong seasoning. The most common use for rue is to grind up the leaves and apply as a bug deterrent.

Health Benefits

Antispasmodic, aromatic, emmenagogue, irritant, stimulant, stomachic, tonic. Aromatic rue is a valuable stimulant and tonic when taken in small doses only, relieving flatulence and congestion of the uterus and beneficial in menstrual difficulties. An infusion of rue is used for hysteria and as a nervine. Boiled in wine with pepper, it was applied to warts to remove them, and the fresh herb bruised with myrtle was used to remove pimples and marks on the body. The infusion taken internally will kill and expel worms. The ointment is used for sciatica, sore joints, and gout. The seed boiled in wine is said to be an antidote against all poisons. The medicinally important flavonol rutin was isolated for the first time from rue, thus its name.

Note: This plant should not be boiled. It should not be used by pregnant women or in large doses by anyone, as it can cause violent gastrointestinal pains and vomiting, possible abortion, and toxic poisoning. The oil is a dangerous abortifacient, and large doses may produce nerve derangements; however, it rarely causes death. Contact with the sap from the cut stems may cause a skin rash or edema in sensitive people.

Saffron
(Crocus sativus)

The Latin genus *Crocus* is from *krokos*, the Greek name for the plant. *Sativus* indicates that this plant has long been cultivated. The Arabs, who introduced the cultivation of the saffron crocus into Spain as an article of commerce, bequeathed to us its modern title of *zafara*, or *saffron*.

General Information

Saffron is a small perennial plant native to Asia Minor. Cilicia was its most abundant area of cultivation; Sicily also produced a good deal of it, but Mount Tobus in Phrygia was, in the general opinion, the site that produced the best saffron of the ancient world. Saffron is supposed to have entered China when that country was invaded in the thirteenth century by the Mongols, who made considerable use of it in their cooking. The cultivation of saffron was well established in Rome before the birth of Christ, and Pliny the Elder notes that it was an important product of Sicily by the year A.D. 1. A valuable (and extremely costly) dye plant in early Europe and the Orient, saffron produced golden-yellow cloth for the exclusive use of the rich and noble. The plant is now cultivated in many places but particularly in France, Spain, Sicily, and Iran. The spice saffron, made from the dried stigmas, is said to be the most expensive in the world. Each saffron flower has only three stigmas, which must be hand-picked as soon as the flowers open. It takes nearly 150,000 flowers to yield enough flat, tubular, thread-like stigmas to make two pounds of dried saffron; over forty-three hundred flowers are necessary for just one ounce. Paradoxically, this expensive spice is prevalent in the diets of the Pennsylvania Dutch. Since they grow their own saffron and eat it themselves, however, its price on the world market is a negligible factor. Schwenkfelder cake, a recipe found in almost all Pennsylvania Dutch cookbooks, comes from the Schwenkfelder family, who emigrated to the United States in the eighteenth century, bringing with them the materials of the business they had been pursuing in Germany—growing saffron. Saffron flourished in their new home, and the Schwenkfelders and their neighbors acquired such a taste

Saffron / Nutritional Value Per 100 g Edible Portion		
	Dried	1 tsp.
Calories	310	2
Protein	11.43 g	0.08 g
Fat	5.85 g	0.04 g
Fiber	3.87 g	0.03 g
Calcium	111 mg	1 mg
Iron	11.10 mg	0.08 mg
Phosphorus	252 mg	2 mg
Potassium	1,724 mg	12 mg
Sodium	148 mg	1 mg
Copper	0.328 mg	n/a
Manganese	28.408 mg	n/a

LORE AND LEGEND

According to Greek legend, the crocus flower was born of the unfulfilled love of a beautiful youth called Crocus. Consumed by his ardor for a beautiful shepherdess of the hills named Smilax, Crocus pined away and died. Upon his death, the gods changed him into the flower that bears his name. The orange-yellow tones of its dyestuff have held sacred positions in widespread areas of the world. The gods, goddesses, heroes, and nymphs of Greek myths and poetry wore robes dyed golden-yellow with saffron. Then there are the saffron robes of the Buddhist monks; the saffron cloaks once worn by Irish kings; and the saffron shirts alloted to noblemen of the Hebrides through the seventeenth century. The ancients often used this flower to adorn their marriage beds because according to the Greek poet Homer, the crocus plant was one of the flowers of which the couch of Zeus and Hera was composed. In ancient Rome during the time of Nero, the crocus was considered to be a great cordial, a tonic for the heart, and a potent love potion. The luxury-loving Romans of that time were so fond of the blossom that they would strew them throughout their banquet halls, fountains, and the small streams that flowed through their gardens and courtyards, filling the air with a beautiful fragrance.

Returning Crusaders introduced the saffron crocus to the table of King Henry I of England (1068–1135), who quickly became very fond of it. When the court ladies started to use up the entire saffron supply to dye their hair, the king forbade this use of his favorite spice by severe punishment. In the fifteenth century Henry VIII made two demands at his royal table: enormous quantities of food, and dishes flavored with saffron. To eliminate much of the competitive demand for this scarce spice, he issued an edict banning the practice of using saffron to dye beards and hair orange (they soon found a suitable substitute—marigold). He also forbade the Irish to use saffron as a linen dye, because the populace believed that saffron had some manner of sanitary virtue and cloth dyed with it was therefore not as frequently washed. The temptation to adulterate saffron has always been strong, and in the fifteenth century regular saffron inspections were held in Nuremberg. Those unfortunates who had extended their saffron for profit were burned at the stake or buried alive—along with their impure saffron.

In Kashmir saffron cultivation flourished under the monopoly of the rajah. Ownership by others, much less exportation of even a single bulb, carried a penalty of death. Nevertheless, during the reign of Edward III, a traveler disguised as a monk managed to conceal a bulb in his hollow pilgrim's staff and brought it to England. The bulb was planted in the soil of Walden, near London, and thrived. So much saffron was produced in this area from the single original bulb that the place was named Saffron Walden, and the arms of Saffron Walden bear three crocus flowers yet today.

for it that today it is one of the most common spices in Pennsylvania Dutch country.

Culinary Uses

Saffron is available as either whole or ground threads, with the whole thread having the best flavor and least chance of being adulterated. The threads are a brick-red color, about one inch long, and wiry. True saffron has a characteristic penetrating scent with a spicy, aromatic, pungent, and slightly bitter taste. Very little is required to give color and flavor to food; too much saffron overpowers and borders on an unpleasant, medicinal flavor. Commercial powdered saffron is frequently adulterated because of its cost; turmeric can be used as an inexpensive substitute. Saffron is a traditional ingredient in the classic Spanish dish paella and is also used in soups, rice dishes, cakes, and biscuits.

Health Benefits

Anodyne, antispasmodic, aphrodisiac, appetizer, choleretic, emmenagogue, expectorant, sedative. Saffron is considered the most perfect of all spices. Eating saffron dispels depression and eliminates psychological inertia, and it was once

ancing and calming effect on the entire system. It will also promote perspiration and help relive gout and arthritis.

Note: In substantial doses saffron produces a pleasant mania, with sudden changes from hilarity to melancholia. In excessive quantity it can create headaches, cough, and even hemorrhaging, with detrimental effects on the central nervous system and kidneys. Use no more than several threads once per day, since larger amounts can be toxic or even lethal. It should also not be used by pregnant women since it has stimulating effects on the uterus and may cause abortion.

Sage
(Salvia officinalis)

If one consults enough herbals . . . every sickness known to humanity will be listed as being cured by sage.

—VARRO TAYLOR, PH.D. (HERB EXPERT)

The botanical name *Salvia* is derived either from the Latin *salvus*, meaning "health" or "salvation," or from the Latin *salvere*, meaning "to save," both terms alluding to the

thought that you could die of "excessive joy" by eating too much of it. Drinking the tea is said to bestow the gift of clairvoyance and greatly enhance the body's healing powers. The alchemists considered saffron the gold of the plant kingdom and believed it carried the "signature" of the great transmuting agent for which they spent their lives searching. Saffron contains the only water-soluble carotene, crocetin, a dark orange carotene responsible for much of the spice's color and potent antioxidant and anticancer activities. Saffron in small quantities is a pure and natural digestive aid, soothing the entire digestive tract. It has a bal-

Sage / Nutritional Value Per 100 g Edible Portion		
	Dried, Ground	1 tsp.
Calories	315	2
Protein	10.62 g	0.07 g
Fat	12.74 g	0.09 g
Fiber	18.05 g	0.13 g
Calcium	1,652 mg	12 mg
Iron	28.12 mg	0.20 mg
Magnesium	428 mg	3 mg
Phosphorus	91 mg	1 mg
Potassium	1,070 mg	7 mg
Sodium	11 mg	trace
Zinc	4.700 mg	0.030 mg
Copper	0.757 mg	n/a
Manganese	3.133 mg	n/a
Beta Carotene (A)	5,900 IU	41 IU
Thiamine (B₁)	0.754 mg	0.005 mg
Riboflavin (B₂)	0.336 mg	0.002 mg
Niacin (B₃)	5.720 mg	0.040 mg
Ascorbic Acid (C)	32.38 mg	0.23 mg

plant's powerful healing properties. *Officinalis* means "of the workshop," alluding to apothecaries' shops and signifying that the plant was once part of the official pharmacopoeia of Rome. The English word *sage* derives from the French *sauge*.

General Information

Sage is indigenous to northern Mediterranean regions, where it prefers the arid soil of hillsides, especially if it is chalky. Sage finds its most representative natural habitat in Dalmatia—on the chalky, practically bare, and very stony lands overhanging the Adriatic. It probably crossed the Alps along with the monks on their travels. Another member of the enormous mint family, this aromatic woody evergreen shrub has violet-blue flowers and woolly, gray-green leaves. Like many other foods, sage got into the pantry via the medicine chest. Its health-protecting advantages have been forgotten by many, but along the way most people have learned to like its flavor. The French produced so much sage at one time that they exported it in the form of tea; the Chinese became so fond of sage tea that they traded four pounds of their tea for one pound of sage.

Culinary Uses

Sage is available as fresh or dried leaves, the dried being generally preferred over the fresh leaves. Dried sage is either "rubbed" or ground; "rubbed" sage has gone through a minimum grinding into a fluffy, velvety powder, while ground sage is more finely ground. The flavor of sage may be described as warm, pungent, slightly bitter yet lemony, with just a hint of camphor. Chopped fresh or dried leaves are added to salads, kebabs, stuffings, squash dishes, beans, pickles, and cheese. The most popular use of sage is as an ingredient in stuffing at Thanksgiving, but it should be used throughout the year.

Health Benefits

Antiseptic, astringent, expectorant, tonic, vermifuge. Sage is one of those herbs that has been used to cure a multitude of ills. One of its properties is to aid in the digestion of heavy, greasy meats, preventing their oxidation, and thus sage is a common ingredient in pork, sausage, and duck recipes. Sage's action focuses on the mouth, the throat, and the female reproductive system. It increases estrogen and helps treat menopausal sweats. It has long been regarded as a tonic that keeps the stomach, intestines, kidneys, liver, spleen, and sexual organs healthy (although it may temper

LORE AND LEGEND

In the tenth century the medical school at Salerno, Italy, coined the aphorism "Cur moriatur homo cui Salvia crescit in horto?" or "Why should a man die when sage grows in his garden?" To those of the ancient world, sage was associated with immortality, or at least longevity, and was credited with increasing mental capacity, as well as relied upon to cure all manner of ills—from colds to worms, from excessive sexual desire to sexual debility, from nerves to dandruff and even graying hair. The ancient Druids believed that it possessed curative powers so magical that it could even resuscitate the dead. One belief held that sage, like rosemary, flourished in the garden only when the woman dominated the house; another belief was that the plants reflected the fortunes of the man of the house, flourishing when he prospered and withering when he did not. One fanciful legend has it that if young maidens at twilight on Midsummer's Eve go to a pond in a lonely wood, pick a twig of sage, and wave it around their heads seven times while repeating an incantation, their bridegrooms will appear to them at midnight.

sexual desire). Sage is stimulating and cleansing to the skin and scalp, soothing to sore muscles, and restorative to aging skin and hair, encouraging hair growth if the roots have not been destroyed. Its stimulating qualities increase circulation and relieve headaches, break fevers, and help reduce respiratory congestion and other cold symptoms. For sparkling teeth, rub them with fresh sage leaves; this will not only whiten and clean the teeth, but also strengthen the gums and make the breath pleasant. Because sage contains sclereol, which stimulates the body to produce its own estrogen, it may nutritionally support the body during the childbearing years and menopause. It may also help us in coping with despair and mental fatigue.

Sage extracts have powerful antioxidant activity because of the presence of phenolic acids, especially labiatic and carnosic acids. Its volatile oil contains thujone, camphor, cineole (eucalyptus fragrance), and borneol, all of which are antimicrobial and antispasmodic. The carminative property of the oil results from its ability to stimulate the production of digestive fluids and relax smooth muscles. Sage oil supports the cells and hormones. Its aromatic influence calms and enhances the dream state and brings about a feeling of euphoria. Sage tea is very soothing and quieting to the nerves. It has been used as an antidote for sore throats, cold sores, fevers, and congestion and as a tonic for the hair and scalp. It helps regulate hormones, bringing on a late or suppressed menses and lessening an excessively heavy menstrual flow. It also works to expel worms and when taken cold will help dry up milk in nursing mothers (when desired). To make sage tea, steep two or three leaves in one cup of hot water; strain and add one teaspoon of powdered ginger.

Note: If pregnant or epileptic, do not use sage.

Salt
(Sodium chloride)

The name *sodium* derives from the English term *soda*; *chloride* comes from the Greek *chlorid*, meaning "greenish-yellow chemical." The English word *salt* comes from the Roman god of health, Salus, who gave to the English language such words as *salutary, salute,* and *salvation.*

General Information

One of the most traditional of food flavorings, sea salt contains about eighty necessary mineral elements, and in the proper proportions, since they occur in seawater and our blood. Refining this salt produces a table salt that is composed of 40 percent sodium and 60 percent chloride. The process of refining is typically accomplished with the use of chemicals and extremely high heat, reducing salt from a whole food to an ultrarefined compound. According to the standards of the U.S. Food Chemicals Codex, commercial salt must be 97.5 percent pure sodium chloride to qualify for food use. Most commercial brands are iodized, which

Salt / Nutritional Value			
	1 tsp.		1 tsp.
Calories	0	Phosphorus	3 mg
Calcium	14 mg	Potassium	trace
Iron	trace	Sodium	2,100-2,300 mg

means that potassium iodide, an essential nutrient removed during the refining process, has been re-added. There may also be other ingredients added: sodium silico-aluminate, dextrose, sodium bicarbonate, and magnesium carbonate, plus other chemicals to absorb moisture and make the salt flow freely.

Throughout history, there have been groups of people who have not used salt. The fact is that these people who astonished observers by not eating salt did eat salt; what they did not eat was added salt. They were either great drinkers of milk (the Bedouins) or great consumers of animal proteins (the Eskimos) or both. Cow's milk contains 1.6 grams of salt per liter (three times as much as human milk), while meat averages between 0.1 and 0.15 gram of salt per 100 grams of weight. Thus these people's diet provided the necessary salt for their survival; only upon changing to a more cereal- and vegetable-based diet was there a need for supplemental dietary salt.

For every one hundred pounds of salt produced each year, only five go into your saltshaker or prepared food products. The rest is used for packing meat, feeding livestock (both large and small), building roads and keeping them free of winter's ice and snow, tanning leather, and industrial uses such as the manufacture of glass and soap. Of the many salt works in existence during the eighteenth and nineteenth centuries, very few are still in existence today; the suffix *-wich* in an English place name (Norwich, Middlewich, Greenwich) bears testimony to the sites of salt works or brine springs.

Culinary Uses

Salt's potency for heightening and enhancing the taste of food is unmatched. It deepens and unites flavors, balancing acidity and sweetness. Without salt, breads, potatoes, and grains would taste flat and metallic. In the majority of bread recipes, salt is almost a necessity, as it strengthens the gluten (the building fiber of wheat) and helps to form a crisp crust. It also conveniently lowers the freezing point of water in the salt-and-ice mixture of old-fashioned ice cream freezers. Salt is extremely useful to the food industry, since it acts as a natural preservative, masks the flavor of odorous foods, helps inhibit the growth of molds and bacteria, and bleaches and "improves" food color. It also is a processing aid in peeling, sorting, and floating; is useful in drying and freezing foods; and whets the appetite to consume even more processed foods and beverages. Brining, pickling, curing, and salting are processes that produce especially high salt content in foods. Cured ham is twenty times saltier than fresh pork, and potato chips contain 340 times the sodium found naturally in raw potatoes of the same weight. Additional sodium may be ingested from unsuspected sources such as soft drinks, sparkling water, and desserts. Most current guidelines for daily salt consumption recommend about three thousand milligrams, while the average American takes in approximately seventeen thousand milligrams, or about 3½ teaspoonfuls of highly refined salt each day. An estimated 70 percent of the sodium in the American diet comes from processed foods, and Americans now use over one million tons of salt annually for food preparation or processing; this averages out to a horrendous ten pounds per person. Sea salt contains approximately eighty mineral elements, some of which are needed in trace amounts. Thus unrefined sea salt is a better choice of salt than other types on the market. Ordinary table salt bought in the supermarkets has been stripped of its companion elements and contains additive elements such as aluminum silicate to keep it powdery and porous.

Health Benefits

Carminative, stimulant. Many people use salt simply to improve the taste of food; however, it also has medicinal properties. Salt is necessary for converting carbohydrates into fat, for ridding the body of carbon dioxide, and for heart and muscle contractions. It is effective in stabilizing irregular heartbeats and is essential for the regulation of blood pressure (in conjunction with pure water). The chloride in salt is needed by the body to produce hydrochloric acid—the main digestive juice in the stomach—as well as to balance the body's acid-alkaline level and to stimulate the liver. Salt relieves gas and distension of the abdomen, cleanses the mouth, stimulates secretions in the digestive canal, and aids digestion. Salt is vital for balancing the sugar levels in the blood, which is critical for those with diabetes. Insufficient sodium can result in symptoms similar to heatstroke: faintness, nausea, vomiting, weakness, and muscle cramps. If you get leg cramps frequently, you can safely assume that your body needs more salt. In hot climates, when too much sweating causes salt deficiency, one of the symptoms often seen is a lack of energy to undertake any form of activity. If salt is withheld from children, the common reaction is for them to begin eating soap; they have an irresistible desire for sodium compounds, and soap is sodium oleate.

LORE AND LEGEND

Salt has often been associated with magic due to its puzzling properties. A rock rather than a plant, salt can alter the taste of food more powerfully than any organic herb or spice; it will also preserve delicate food, yet destroy solid metal. Because salt is pure (and therefore good), spilling it brought bad luck; and since the Devil hated salt, all you had to do was throw some into his face (he could generally be found lurking over your left shoulder), and all would be well again. In some cultures salt is sprinkled on the threshold and in the corners of new homes to rid the premises of evil influences. Roman Catholics once used salt as part of the baptism rite, placing it on the baby's tongue for protection. Salt was so important in imperial Rome that soldiers were paid with it or given the money to buy it: salt money, *salarium*, was the predecessor of our *salary*. Those lacking in mercenary skill were thought to not be worth their salt. In ancient China a favored way of committing suicide was to eat a pound of salt. For all Semitic peoples, an offer of salt was an offer of hospitality, with all its attendant duties; this obligation could be avoided by strewing salt across the sill of a house or the entrance of a tent to warn strangers that they were not welcome.

Salt is essential to keep the airways of the body clear, including the nasal passageways when you have a cold. Being a strong natural antihistamine, salt also unplugs mucus in the nose and sinuses and stops runny nose in allergic reactions. A little on the tongue will stop persistent dry coughs. Salt is also critical for preserving the serotonin and melatonin levels in the brain. When water and salt perform their natural antioxidant duties and clear the toxic waste from the body, essential amino acids, such as tryptophan and tyrosine, will not be sacrificed as chemical antioxidants. In a well-hydrated body, tryptophan is spared and gets into the brain tissue, where it is used to manufacture serotonin, melatonin, and tryptamine—essential antidepressant neurotransmitters. A natural hypnotic, salt is vital for sleep regulation and prevents excess salivation to the point that it flows out of the mouth during sleep.

Salt helps to reduce a double chin: When the body is short of salt, it really is short of water. The salivary glands sense the salt shortage and are obliged to produce more saliva to lubricate the act of chewing and swallowing and also to supply the stomach with water that it needs for breaking down foods. Circulation to the salivary glands increases, and the blood vessels become "leaky" in order to supply the glands with water to manufacture saliva. The "leakiness" spills beyond the area of the glands themselves, causing increased bulk under the skin of the chin, the cheeks, and into the neck. Salt is absolutely crucial for bone structure, osteoporosis being largely a result of salt and water shortage in the body. A bath of sea salt and baking soda is an excellent external treatment in every form of radiation exposure. Add one pound of both sea salt and baking soda to a warm bath and soak for twenty minutes; rinse with cool water. This can be repeated up to three times a week for one month in cases of serious exposure. A tablespoon of salt dissolved in a cup of warm water is a quick emetic to administer in case of poisoning.

Too much salt (especially of the highly refined type), however, may result in water weight gain, because salt can cause water retention and make you thirsty. It can also contribute to hypertension, high blood pressure, the risk of heart disease, and all the calcium deficiency problems. Although we would die without the 3½ ounces of salt our bodies contain, few people are in danger of dying from insufficient sodium but rather risk death daily by overconsumption. Less than a half teaspoon would satisfy our current daily salt requirements, and most Americans typically consume seven times that amount. Seventy percent of this excess comes from processed foods.

VARIETIES

Flavored salts, such as garlic, onion, and celery salts, are available. This is just salt that has been combined with a proportion of flavoring agent.

Iodized salt contains not more than 0.01 percent potassium iodine, a mineral needed for proper thyroid functioning. Iodine was added to salt in the early 1900s to prevent goiters, caused from deficiency in this mineral, but iodine is now generally plentiful in the diets of North Americans.

Rock salt is obtained from underground land deposits where millions of years ago there were probably living seawaters. Although rock salt is less refined than table salt, the passage of time has removed all trace minerals and left the pure chemical sodium chloride. This is the kind most often sold in the United States.

Sea salt comes either in crystalline or granular form and is obtained by vacuum-drying seawater. This salt, with all its mingled salts of the sea and correspondingly less plain sodium chloride than refined salt, has the stimulating flavor of the ocean. Unrefined, it contains an abundance of trace minerals (iodine in particular) that make it superior to the pure chemical sodium chloride of land-mined salt. The sea salt most rich in minerals is gray in color. Most sea salt sold in the United States is every bit as refined as rock salt, however, unless you can find imported unprocessed salt. Look for high-quality Celtic sea salt, which is solar-dried and contains the most minerals. Europeans generally prefer sea salt to rock salt, saying that it produces a better flavor in foods. That said, in order to benefit from the trace minerals in unprocessed sea salt, you would have to eat far more than is desired. You would get more benefit nutritionally by simply eating fresh fruit and vegetables. Sodium is found in good quantities in many foods, including all seaweeds, beets, turnips, and greens such as chard, spinach, and parsley.

Table salt has been commercially processed to be at least 97.5 percent sodium chloride, with a number of additives to make it more "manageable" and keep it from hardening. One such chemical is YPS (sodium ferrocyanide), which causes small tentacles to form on each grain, preventing them from sticking together.

Savory
(Satureja hortensis, S. montana)

In ancient days savory plants were believed to be under the protection of the satyrs, hence the name *Satureja*. The term *hortensis* means "belonging to a hortus," or garden; *montana* means "pertaining to mountains," and thus to snow and winter. The plant got its English name from the Saxons, who named it *savory* for its pleasantly spicy, pungent taste.

General Information

Summer savory (*S. hortensis*) is a small, compact plant with pink or white flowers that grows only during the summer months. This aromatic plant was brought to England by the Romans, died out during the Dark Ages, and then was reintroduced during the sixteenth century. The ground savory sold in stores is summer savory. Winter savory (*S. montana*) is a small, hardy evergreen perennial from the mountains of southern Europe and North Africa. It looks similar to summer savory with its white or blue flowers but has stiff, dark green, pointed leaves. Also known as Spanish savory, this variety is not generally available in stores.

Culinary Uses

Summer savory's small, green leaves have a pungent, spicy aroma and a peppery flavor reminiscent of thyme. In Europe savory is called "the bean herb" because it not only complements the flavor of beans but also greatly diminishes their flatulent tendencies. Egg dishes profit as well by the addition of summer savory, as do nearly all kinds of meat (especially sausage), stuffings, salads, soups, and stews. In many dishes it makes a flavorful substitute for salt. Winter savory has a stronger, sharper, more piney taste than summer savory and is best used with strong game meats and pâtés.

Savory / Nutritional Value Per 100 g Edible Portion		
	Dried, Ground	1 tsp.
Calories	272	4
Protein	6.73 g	0.09 g
Fat	5.91 g	0.08 g
Fiber	15.27 g	0.21 g
Calcium	2,132 mg	30 mg
Iron	37.88 mg	0.53 mg
Magnesium	377 mg	5 mg
Phosphorus	140 mg	2 mg
Potassium	1,051 mg	15 mg
Sodium	24 mg	trace
Zinc	4.300 mg	0.060 mg
Copper	0.847 mg	n/a
Manganese	6.100 mg	n/a
Beta Carotene (A)	5,130 IU	72 IU
Thiamine (B$_1$)	0.366 mg	0.005 mg
Riboflavin (B$_2$)	n/a	n/a
Niacin (B$_3$)	4.080 mg	0.057 mg

LORE AND LEGEND

For reasons lost to history, the ancient Romans linked summer savory to the mythological licentious satyrs—the lustful, half-man, half-goat creatures who roamed the ancient forests playing their pipes, and who disported endlessly with the nymphs in debauched orgies in honor of Dionysus, god of wine. As a result of this association, savory was forbidden in monastic gardens for many centuries.

Health Benefits

Antiseptic, astringent, carminative, expectorant, stimulant, stomachic. Although not as strong as others in the mint family, the savories make a pleasant digestive aid. Both varieties contain a strong volatile oil that aids digestion and are therefore recommended in dishes that are known to be difficult to digest, such as game, dried beans, and peas. Savory tea is a safe remedy for most stomach and intestinal disorders, including cramps, nausea, indigestion, and lack of appetite. The leaves can be chewed to sweeten the breath or crushed and applied to a bee sting to reduce swelling and pain. Savory also has a long reputation as an "herb of love," and men who nibble on savory swear that their amorous abilities increase tenfold. The Roman naturalist Pliny called summer savory an aphrodisiac and the winter variety a sexual depressant (not surprisingly, summer savory was more popular). The famous French herbalist Maurice Messegue often used summer savory instead of ginseng to help couples retrieve their marital bliss.

Shepherd's Purse

(*Capsella bursa-pastoris*)

Also Known As: Lady's Purse, Pepper and Salt, Rattleweed, Pastor's Purse, Purselet

Capsella is the diminutive form of *capsa*, Latin for "box," and *bursa-pastoris* means "bag or purse belonging to a shepherd." This plant takes both its Latin and English names from the shape of its flat and rather triangular seedpods, which were commonly compared to the leather pouches in which shepherds carried their food.

General Information

Shepherd's purse is a native of the Old World that now thrives around the globe. It is well suited for survival: a single plant can produce up to forty thousand seeds. This small common evergreen plant with arrow-shaped leaves and clusters of small white flowers easily adapts to mild and extreme climates alike. It flowers most of the year and its fruits are shaped like inverted, compressed triangles, each holding twenty to twenty-five small seeds. When broken, the foliage has a peculiar and unpleasant odor and a somewhat biting taste. In mild temperate climates, this member of the mustard family grows year-round and is commonly found in waste areas with sandy, gravelly soil.

Culinary Uses

The leaves of shepherd's purse have a peppery taste and serve as both a cooked vegetable and a salad. The mature seeds can be used in bread making, soups, and salads.

Health Benefits

Antiscorbutic, diuretic, stimulant, styptic, tonic, vasoconstrictor. Shepherd's purse regularizes blood pressure, whether high or low, and heart action. It is effective for various menstrual problems, including difficult menstruation, and will temper the sometimes excessive menstrual flow of pubescent girls or menopausal women. Shepherd's purse is sometimes used to promote uterine contractions during childbirth and can promote bowel movements, having a similar effect on the intestines. An extract applied to internal or external bleeding works as an effective blood coagulant.

Shepherd's Purse / Nutritional Value Per 100 g Edible Portion			
	Fresh		Fresh
Calories	280–330	Potassium	394–3,339 mg
Protein	4.2–35.6 g	Beta Carotene (A)	0.260–2.200 mg
Fat	0.3–36.0 g	Thiamine (B₁)	0.250–2.120 mg
Fiber	1.1–10.2 g	Riboflavin (B₂)	0.170–1.440 mg
Calcium	208–1,763 mg	Niacin (B₃)	0.400–3.400 mg
Iron	4.8–40.7 mg	Ascorbic Acid (C)	36.0–550.0 mg
Phosphorus	60–729 mg		

Shiso

(Perilla frutescens)
Also Known As: Perilla, Beefsteak Plant

Perilla is said to be a native name in India, while others believe it to be a Greek or Latin proper name. *Frutescens* means "shrubby" or "bushy."

General Information

This cousin of basil and mint was eaten by the Chinese as a vegetable over fifteen hundred years ago, and they valued the oil from its seeds for cooking. For some reason, however, the Chinese gave up on shiso as a food staple centuries ago, but the Japanese—to whom they introduced the plant—still eat two varieties: green (ao-jiso) and red (aka-jiso). Found packed in brine in Japanese groceries, the large red leaves' main culinary use is for pickling plums into umeboshi (see separate listing in the **Fruits** section). The smaller green leaves are sometimes sold fresh in small plastic packages.

Culinary Uses

The smaller green leaves are used as a garnish and sometimes fried whole in tempura batter. Most often they are used as an aromatic addition to sushi rolls. The larger red leaves seem to be strictly for umeboshi.

Health Benefits

The Chinese *materia medica* cites shiso as an antidote to fish poisoning.

Sorrel

(Rumex acetosa, R. acetosella, R. scutatus)
Also Known As: Sheep Sorrel, Sour Grass, Little Vinegar

Rumex is an old Latin name for the plant. Both *acetosa* and *acetosella* come from the Latin word for "vinegar" and imply the plant's acid and/or sour character, coming mainly from oxalic acid; *scutatus* means "carrying a shield." The English name *sorrel* derives from the Germanic *sur* and the Old French *surele*, both meaning "sour."

General Information

Sorrel is a perennial plant native to Europe and Asia. From the Middle Ages up until the 1700s, sorrel's jade-green leaves were a regular feature of European vegetable gardens.

This relative of rhubarb is commonly found in damp meadows and along roads and shorelines in both Europe and Asia; it is found only sparingly in North America. There are several varieties, but the main ones are garden sorrel (*R. acetosa*), sheep sorrel (*R. acetosella*), and French sorrel (*R. scutatus*). The leaves of garden sorrel are arrowhead-shaped, with the detached points at the base parallel to the stem. Leaves up to about six inches long are young enough to use for salads; older leaves are coarse and more sour. Sheep sorrel has leaves that are no more than two inches long, in the same arrowhead shape as garden sorrel but with base lobes that splay outward from the stem. The plant is said to have come to America as a weed mixed in with other seed or with hay brought over from Europe to feed shipboard animals. French sorrel grows up to eighteen inches tall with spinachlike leaves that are favored for sorrel soup. Sorrel has a high content of the chemical salt binoxalate of potash, which imparts the highly acidic taste. Oxalic acid was formerly known as "salts of sorrel" and used as a stain remover.

Culinary Uses

Sorrel has a refreshing, slightly bitter, spinachlike taste; the French variety has just a hint of citrus flavor. Use fresh leaves if you can, as the dried leaves have lost most of their distinctive flavor. Fresh young leaves can be combined with other herbs in salads or cooked and served like spinach, usually in combination with either Swiss chard or spinach. Sorrel may also be used to enliven soups, as a garnish and flavoring in small amounts to season eggs and meat, as an ingredient in sauces, or as one of a variety of herbs on which fish is steamed. For most preparations, the leaves are washed and the stems pulled off to remove any coarse veins. Then about two dozen leaves are laid parallel in a neat pile, rolled into a fat cigar, and shredded crosswise with a knife. Place the shreds in a pan with a generous teaspoon of butter or a little water, olive oil, or cream. Over low heat with occasional stirring the leaves will melt into an olive-green purée in about fifteen minutes. If the dish

they are to be used in is elegant or if the leaves are coarse, the purée is put through a fine strainer. Sorrel should not be cooked in an iron pan, as it will draw out a potentially harmful and very unpleasant metallic taste. The juice of the leaves can have the same action upon milk as rennet, forming a junket.

Health Benefits

pH 2.98-3.27. Antiscorbutic, astringent, diuretic, nutritive, tonic. Sorrel is used as a preventive tonic against scurvy, and the tea is given to reduce fevers and quench thirst. Tea made from the leaves also works as a wound cleanser, for treating chronic skin diseases, and as a blood purifier.

Note: The herb's sharp taste comes from its oxalic acid and vitamin C content. Because even small amounts of oxalic acid are toxic to some extent, sorrel should not be served indiscriminately. In large quantities, oxalic acid is extremely poisonous. Persons with gout, rheumatism, or kidney ailments should avoid eating this plant, as it will tend to aggravate those conditions.

Spirulina
(Spirulina platensis, S. maxima, S. pacifica)

The term *Spirulina* is derived from the word *helix* and was given because of the algae's growth pattern of tiny spiraling wires. *Maxima* means "largest"; *pacifica* means "from the Pacific."

General Information

Spirulina is one of a variety of blue-green algae often found in saline—usually highly alkaline—natural lakes like Lake Texcoco near Mexico City and Lake Chad in Africa. It has been used for centuries by the Africans and was a major protein source for the Aztec culture. Natives of the Sahara dry it with grains, vegetables, and seasonings to form *dihe*, practically a meal in itself. Spirulina produces all its nutrients by harvesting sunlight, which it gathers and transforms into green and blue pigments (making it a blue-green algae). The blue is an amino acid group called phycocyanin, found only in spirulina, which accounts for its high concentration of vegetarian protein. The green in spirulina is chlorophyll, one of the best natural detoxifiers known. The alga grows in single cells that resemble filaments—tiny spiral wires—to about one millimeter in length. Its size is

Sorrel / Nutritional Value Per 100 g Edible Portion			
	Fresh		Fresh
Protein	5.6-9.6 g	Phosphorus	1,126 mg
Fat	1.7-3.6 g	Potassium	2,293 mg
Calcium	1,620 mg	Ascorbic Acid (C)	50-1,200 mg
Magnesium	1,085 mg		

measured in microns (millionths of a meter). Another micro-alga is wild blue-green (*Aphanizomenon flos-aquae*), which grows wild in Oregon's Klamath Lake.

In the United States, Korea, and Japan, spirulina is also cultivated in man-made tanks, allowing for its mineralization to be altered toward the maximum values for human nutrition. *Spirulina pacifica* is a superior strain of spirulina compared to other strains, such as *S. platensis*. It contains three times the beta carotene, ten times the calcium, and four times the iron as other spirulina strains. It is cultivated using advanced techniques of strain selection, further refining the algae with each generation.

Culinary Uses

This bland, extremely fine green powder is used most frequently as a food supplement and often combined with nutritional yeast, comfrey, ginseng powder, or bee pollen. It can be added (up to 10 percent by volume) to cereals and other food products to boost their nutritional profile without changing the flavor or creating objectionable tastes.

Health Benefits

Micro-alga exists on the edge between the plant and animal kingdoms and offers some unique nutritional advantages. In its dried state—the usual commercial form—spirulina contains the highest amounts of complete protein, beta carotene, and nucleic acids of any animal or

plant food. It contains the complete B complex vitamins and the essential trace minerals and fatty acids, all in a form easy to digest and absorb. One of the most outstanding of spirulina's nutritional features is its exceptionally high level of the fatty acid GLA. It also contains substantial omega-3 alpha-linolenic acid. GLA, important for growth and development, is found most abundantly in mother's milk; spirulina is the next highest whole food source. Thus it is often recommended for people who were never breast-fed, in order to foster the hormonal and mental development that may not have occurred because of lack of proper nutrition. Its very large store of nucleic acids (RNA and DNA) is known to benefit cellular regeneration and to reverse aging. (Too much nucleic acid, however, can raise the uric acid level in the body, causing calcium depletion, kidney stones, and gout.)

Spirulina works to balance blood sugar and satisfies hunger. It helps the brain function and improves mental clarity. Energy is noticed in a few short days, as well as a keen alertness. It's chlorophyll helps the body to detoxify in a natural way and eventually will rid the body of toxic poisons. It helps the body with mineral absorption and helps reduce cholesterol. Spirulina protects the kidneys against injury that could occur from taking strong prescription medication and helps the liver regenerate after severe damage from malnutrition, alcoholism, or the consumption of nutrient-destroying food or drugs.

Spirulina is richly supplied with the blue pigment phycocyanin, a biliprotein that has been shown to inhibit cancer-colony formation. In recent years researchers have increasingly studied micro-algae such as spirulina because they contain antifungal and antibacterial biochemicals not found in other plant or animal species. Medical scientists find spirulina not only stimulates the immune system but also actually enhances the body's ability to generate new blood cells. With spirulina supplementation, important parts of the immune system—the bone marrow stem cells, macrophages, T-cells, and natural killer cells—exhibit enhanced activity, and the spleen and thymus glands also show enhanced function. Scientists observe spirulina causing macrophages to increase in number, becoming "activated" and more effective at killing germs. EPO (erythropoetin) is produced by healthy kidneys and regulates bone marrow stem cell production of red blood cells. Chinese scientists claim phycocyanin also regulates production of white blood cells, even when bone marrow stem cells are damaged by toxic chemicals or radiation. Based on

Spirulina / Nutritional Value Per 100 g Edible Portion		
	Raw	Dried
Calories	26	290
Protein	5.92 g	57.47 g
Fat	0.39 g	7.72 g
Fiber	0.34 g	3.64 g
Iron	n/a	28.50 mg
Magnesium	n/a	195 mg
Phosphorus	11 mg	118 mg
Potassium	127 mg	1,363 mg
Sodium	98 mg	1,048 mg
Beta Carotene (A)	n/a	250,000 IU
Thiamine (B$_1$)	0.222 mg	2.380 mg
Riboflavin (B$_2$)	0.342 mg	3.670 mg
Niacin (B$_3$)	1.196 mg	12.820 mg
Pantothenic Acid (B$_5$)	0.325 mg	3.480 mg
Pyridoxine (B$_6$)	0.034 mg	0.364 mg
Ascorbic Acid (C)	0.9 mg	10.1 mg

this effect, spirulina is approved in Russia as a "medicine food" for treating radiation sickness. The children of Chernobyl suffer radiation poisoning from eating food grown on radioactive soil. Their bone marrow is damaged, rendering them immuno-deficient, unable to produce normal red or white blood cells. They are anemic and suffer from terrible allergic reactions. When these children are fed just five grams of spirulina tablets each day, they make dramatic recoveries within six weeks, while children not given spirulina remain ill.

Wild blue-green alga has the most extreme properties of the commonly available micro-algae, and one needs to take precautions when using it. Under certain conditions, wild blue-green can transform into an exceptionally toxic plant. Experts claim this toxic state has never been found in Oregon's Klamath Lake, and the companies that harvest there monitor the product closely. Wild blue-green is bitter, cooling, drying, and mildly diuretic, a neurostimulant, antidepressant, and a relaxant. Because bitter substances can focus the mind, certain foods, including wild blue-green algae and peyote, have been used to improve concentration during meditation and prayer.

Star Anise

(Illicium verum, I. anisatum)

The Latin name *Illicium* means "allurement" or "that which entices," given because of the very pleasant scent of the tree and fruit. The term *verum* means "true," "genuine," or "standard"; *anisatum* means "anise-scented." The shape of the fruits as they open account for the *star* in star anise's name. The *anise* comes from the fact that the plant tastes and smells like anise, although the two plants are not botanically related.

General Information

Star anise is a small evergreen tree indigenous to southern Chile. The tree grows to a height of about twenty-six feet and does not bear fruit until approximately six years of age, but once it does it can continue to bear for the next century. Its yellow flowers are followed by brown fruit that opens, when ripe, into star shapes. Each point of the star contains a shiny brown seed that is less aromatic than the pod. These star-shaped fruits with their six to eight points are collected while still green and then sun-dried until they become woody and reddish brown. Both the pod and the shiny, golden-brown, oval seeds contain the same essential oils as anise. Long used as a spice in the East, star anise was not seen in Europe until 1588, when a sample was brought from the Philippines to London. For many years star anise made the journey from the East via the China-Russia tea route (and was called "Siberian cardamom" because of it) but is now quite popular in Western countries.

Culinary Uses

The spicy, sweet flavor of star anise is stronger and more pungent than ordinary anise. The pod is used whole as a garnish and can be broken or crushed to intensify the flavor. A frequent addition to Asian cooking, spicy dishes, casseroles, baked goods, and drinks, star anise adds a delicate aniseed flavor; it is one of the main ingredients of Chinese five-spice powder. Despite the fact that they come from different plants, anise and star anise contain the same essential oil (anethole), have the same composition and flavor, and are considered to be widely interchangeable.

Health Benefits

Carminative, diuretic, expectorant, stimulant. Star anise is used particularly in China, where it is believed to have a beneficial effect on the digestive system and where it is common to chew a piece after meals to sweeten the breath and relieve flatulence. It has a reputation of being mildly sleep inducing.

Stevia

(Stevia rebaudiana)
Also Known As: Sweet Leaf, Sweet Herb

Stevia was named in honor of P. J. Esteve, a Spanish botanist.

General Information

The stevia plant, first cultivated in Paraguay, has been used as an herbal sweetener for centuries in South America. The Guarani Indians of Paraguay have long used it to make a sweet tea, and the dried leaves and twigs of the plant are commonly sold in local markets and pharmacies. An extract is made of the leaves and flowers. Also called "sweet leaf" or "sweet herb," stevia contains a very sweet component called stevioside, with a sweetening effect similar to cane sugar. In Japan, where the government approved the herb in 1970, stevia and its extracts make up 40 percent of the sweetener market, and it is used by companies such as

Coca-Cola and Beatrice to sweeten various products, including Diet Coke. In 1991 the U.S. FDA placed an import ban on stevia, declaring that there was "not adequate evidence to establish that such use in food is safe." This ban was reversed late in 1995, although stevia still is required to be sold as a nutritional supplement rather than as a sweetener.

Culinary Uses

Powdered stevia looks similar to parsley flakes. The powdered leaf can be made into a simple extract by mixing one teaspoon in a cup of water and allowing it to soak overnight. The liquid extract is much better tasting and easier to use than the powdered form. Only a few drops will sweeten a cup of tea; this liquid is also delicious in yogurt, cereal, and baked goods. Stevia's sweet flavor is not affected by heat, and thus it can be used in teas and other beverages, for canned fruits, and for all kinds of baked desserts.

Health Benefits

Tests have shown the sweetening agent glycoside stevioside is thirty times sweeter than granulated table sugar. Because it is a whole herbal food, stevia contains other properties that nicely complement its sweetness. A report from the Hiroshima University School of Dentistry indicates that stevia actually suppresses dental bacteria growth rather than feeding it as other sugars do. Japanese and Latin American scientists have discovered other attributes as well, including its use as a tonic and a diuretic, as well as its ability to combat mental and physical fatigue, harmonize digestion, regulate blood pressure, and assist in weight loss. Stevia is the one sweetener people suffering from candida and other yeast-type conditions can tolerate. As

sweetened foods exacerbate an overly hot and moist internal environment, which fosters yeast overgrowth, people on anticandida diets must forego all sweets—stevia is the sweet exception.

Sweet Cicely
(Myrrhis odorata)

The generic name *Myrrhis* is derived from the Greek word *myrrha*, meaning "fragrant" or "perfume," because of the plant's fragrant, myrrhlike smell; *odorata* means "odorous" or "fragrant." Until the sixteenth century this plant was known as seseli, a name first used by Dioscorides. It is usually prefaced by *sweet* because of the leaf's sweet taste.

General Information

Sweet cicely is a graceful, decorative plant, probably native to central and southern Europe, with lacy, fernlike leaves and small white flowers. The soft green leaves have a myrrhlike scent with overtones of moss, woodland, and a hint of anise. Sweet cicely was very popular in England during the sixteenth and seventeenth centuries and held a highly regarded place in the old kitchen gardens; its leaves, flowering tops, seeds, and fragrant roots were all used in salads, broths, and baked goods. In the north of England the plant was rubbed on beehives to attract bees and the seeds used for polishing furniture. Nowadays sweet cicely is not in demand, and few supermarkets carry it.

Culinary Uses

Sweet cicely smells slightly like anise and has a sugary sweet flavor with licorice overtones. The leaves, flowers, and stem tips can be used fresh in salads, added to soups and stews, or boiled to make a licorice-flavored liquid used in fruit pies and compotes. If the liquid is added to cream, the cream will lose its fatty taste and become sweeter. Sweet cicely's nutty, licorice-flavored small green or black seeds

Stevia / Nutritional Value Per 100 g Edible Portion			
	Dried		Dried
Calories	254	Sodium	89.2 mg
Protein	11.2 g	Zinc	trace
Fat	1.9 g	Manganese	14.700 mg
Fiber	15.2 g	Beta Carotene (A)	12,440 IU
Calcium	544 mg	Thiamine (B₁)	trace
Iron	3.9 mg	Riboflavin (B₂)	trace
Magnesium	349 mg	Niacin (B₃)	trace
Phosphorus	318 mg	Ascorbic Acid (C)	11 mg
Potassium	1,780 mg		

LORE AND LEGEND

Sweet cicely is believed to quicken a dull mind, make the heart merry, aid the memory, and give the aged a new lease on youth.

can be used raw in salads and fruit dishes. The roots are also edible steamed, simmered, or cooked and puréed like parsnips.

Health Benefits

Aromatic, carminative, expectorant, stomachic. Sweet cicely is used in much the same manner as anise—for coughs, indigestion, flatulence, mucous congestion, and lack of appetite. The fresh roots are antiseptic, while the distilled liquid is diuretic. It acts as a gentle stimulant for weak or debilitated stomachs and makes a natural sweetener for diabetics and others who have to avoid sugar.

Szechuan Pepper

(Zanthoxylum piperitum)
Also Known As: Fagara, Anise Pepper, Chinese Pepper

Zanthoxylum comes from two Greek words: *xanthos*, meaning "yellow," and *xylon*, meaning "wood." *Piperitum* means "pepper-scented." *Szechuan pepper* got its English name because it is native to that province.

General Information

Szechuan pepper is made from the dried, rusty-brown seed pods of a woody, prickly, ornamental ash tree native to Japan, Korea, and northern China. Completely unrelated to black pepper, this plant is a member of the citrus family and grows in any temperate climate. Most parts of the plant, but especially the fruits, emit a strong aromatic odor when bruised. The three- to four-millimeter berry has a rough, reddish-brown shell that splits open to reveal a black seed inside. This seed is bitter and can be discarded; the red shell is the part used culinarily. Szechuan pepper was once a standard table condiment in China, to the point that even wines were flavored with it. During the Tang period (A.D. 618–907) it was the vogue to take Szechuan pepper with tea and clotted cream. When black pepper was introduced from the tropics, Szechuan pepper fell out of favor and has never fully regained its popularity.

Culinary Uses

Szechuan pepper has a hot, aromatic flavor that provides a sharp accent to foods. The rusty-brown peppercorns are not piping hot but spicy, mildly piquant, and fragrant. The dried pods make useful additions to soups, stews, and sauces, are delicious on roasted fish, and are a frequent ingredient in five-spice powder. The Chinese often mix this peppery spice with salt, sometimes roasting it first to release its full woodsy flavor. It is available precrushed or in pods; the pods are crushed to a coarse powder or ground in a pepper mill over foods. Seeds and inner bark are cooked or pickled, and fresh leaves are added to soup.

Tamarind

(Tamarindus indica)

Tamarindus comes from the Arabic *tamr-hindi*, meaning "Indian date." *Indica* means "coming from India."

General Information

Tamarind is the dried fruit of the leguminous tamarind tree, native to East Africa. Known as Indian "dates" because of their sticky, fibrous appearance, the fruit is a cinnamon-colored, oblong pod from three to eight inches long, with a thin, brittle shell enclosing a soft, brownish, acidulous pulp. When ripe, the fruit possesses a sweet yet sour taste. It is peculiar of the fruit that it contains more acid and, at the same time, more sugar than any other fruit. Although it is often referred to as "tamarind seed," in fact it is the pulp around the seeds that is used.

Culinary Uses

When fresh and tender, tamarind's spicy date-apricot pulp can be eaten raw or cooked with rice and fish. When purchased dried, the fruit is first soaked in water and the soaking liquid used (the seeds are discarded). Tamarind's spicy pulp is used to add a sour, fruity taste to seasonings, curries, chutneys, and various drinks.

Health Benefits

Anthelmintic, laxative, refrigerant. The principal use of the

Tamarind / Nutritional Value Per 100 g Edible Portion			
	Pulp		Pulp
Calories	115	Potassium	375 mg
Protein	3.10 g	Sodium	24 mg
Fat	0.10 g	Beta Carotene (A)	15 IU
Fiber	5.6 g	Thiamine (B₁)	0.160 mg
Calcium	35-170 mg	Riboflavin (B₂)	0.070 mg
Iron	1.3-10.9 mg	Niacin (B₃)	0.600-0.700 mg
Phosphorus	54-110 mg	Ascorbic Acid (C)	0.7-3.0 mg

ripe, sweet-sour, stringy pulp throughout the Americas and the Caribbean is as a mild laxative. The pulp of the fruit has cooling properties; therefore, it is a useful drink for those ill with fever, as well as a popular cooling beverage in hot countries. Tamarind contains large amounts (16 to 18 percent) of plant acids composed mainly of tartaric acid (the acid of grapes) and malic acid, which give it its tart taste.

Tansy
(Tanacetum vulgare)

The generic name *Tanacetum* means quite literally "a bed of tansy"; *vulgare* means "vulgar" or "common." The English word *tansy* is derived from the Greek *athanatos*, meaning "immortal," tansy having been the plant the gods employed when they granted eternal life to human beings.

General Information
Tansy is an attractive plant with delicate, fernlike leaves native to temperate regions of Europe and Asia. The Benedictine monks at St. Gall in Switzerland were cultivating tansy in their medicinal gardens as early as 1265. By the fifteenth century it was commonly used as a medicine in both France and England, but old herbals caution about its careless use. Used as an embalming agent from ancient days until the time of the American Revolution, tansy was also used to preserve meat from the ravages of storage in pre-refrigeration times. The plant is a natural insecticide, repelling flies, mosquitoes, ants, and other insects; plant it by doorways or sprinkle the dried leaves in cellars and attics to deter pests.

Culinary Uses
The flavor of tansy is hot and peppery, bitter, and largely disliked. Once used as a substitute for pepper, tansy now plays a minor role in flavoring baked goods, salad dressings, and omelets. Among its better known uses is in the manufacture of the liqueur Chartreuse. Because of its strong flavor, it is best used sparingly.

Health Benefits
Anthelmintic, emmenagogue, stimulant, tonic. Tansy is an old remedy used to tone up the system, soothe the bowels, expel parasites, and strengthen a weak heart. An infusion of the leaves and flowers is used as a cosmetic wash to remove

LORE AND LEGEND

Ancient Greeks and Romans regarded tansy as a symbol of immortality, and it was a critical ingredient in a potion that conferred immortality upon a handsome Greek boy named Ganymede, who became the eternal cupbearer for the god Zeus. It developed into a symbolic and pragmatic component in Easter rites, being embraced as one of the bitter herbs of Passover. In the belief that tansy could rejuvenate the human body after a long winter's subsistence on salted meat and fish, and purify the humors of the body after the sparsities of Lent, tansy cakes and other tansy-flavored foods were made as traditional fare after the Lenten fasts were over.

freckles, ease sunburn, and help heal pimply skin, as well as for bruises, sprains, and rheumatism. Boiled with vinegar and honey and with some alum added, it makes an effective gargle to ease toothache, fasten loose teeth, and relieve sore gums. American Indians made a tea from the entire plant to promote suppressed menstruation and induce abortion. Tansy oil is antimicrobial and has been used to help numerous skin conditions and tone the entire system.

Note: In the small quantity used by the cook, the juice of the crushed leaves does little or no harm; in any quantity, however, the volatile oils are toxic. The strength of the poison greatly increases at flowering and seed time. Tansy leaves can no longer be sold for tea-making purposes in the United States because they are considered to be poisonous.

Tarragon
(Artemisia dracunculus)

The genus name *Artemisia* is in honor of the Greek goddess Artemis, daughter of Zeus and sister to Apollo; she is the virgin huntress, goddess of wildlife and childbirth, and protectress of all young things. *Dracunculus* means "little dragon." Ibnal Baithar, an Arabian botanist and pharmacist living in Spain in the thirteenth century, mentioned tarragon by the name of *tarkhun*, meaning "little dragon"; the Spanish called it *tara-goncia* (also meaning "little dragon"), and from this name the English word *tarragon* was derived.

General Information

Tarragon is a tall, weedy plant, one of the very few that was relatively unknown in ancient times. Perhaps the fact that it is native to Siberia and Mongolia accounts for its anonymity, since those places were not on the trade routes and their inaccessibility left them isolated. It is believed to have reached the West with the invading Mongols. Tarragon was unknown in Europe until the latter part of the fifteenth century but was later brought to America by the colonists. Affectionately known in most Western languages as "little dragon," in reference to its dragonlike roots, the plant may actually strangle itself if not divided frequently. In the United States the plant most often sold as tarragon is actually false tarragon, or Russian tarragon (*A. dracunculoides*), which is nearly tasteless. To make sure you are getting true tarragon, grow your own, checking the botanical name when purchasing the plant.

Tarragon flowers are always barren. Several hundred years ago the plant produced fertile seed, but because cultivars propagated by division or root cuttings were favored, the fertile plants were irretrievably lost. There is, incidentally, an ever-increasing number of foods that are incapable of reproducing themselves at all or of reproducing them-

LORE AND LEGEND

Tarragon was once believed to cure the bites of mad dogs and venomous creatures, because in medicinal lore and legend any plant with a serpentine root system is given credit for treating snakebite. By many it was also considered an aphrodisiac.

selves true to form because of hybridization or infertility. If we are what we eat, possibly our rapidly increasing consumption of sterile foods—from eggs and beef to bananas and seedless grapes—may be implicated in the increasing rate of human infertility.

Culinary Uses

Tarragon's long, delicate, polished gray-green, aromatic leaves have a sweet yet slightly bitter flavor. Although some say that tarragon has a slight flavor of licorice, others find no hint of this. The young shoots and tips of the plants were cooked and eaten as a vegetable in earlier times, and they are still served as an appetizer in the Near East. Because tarragon's flavorful oil evaporates when the leaves are dried, fresh tarragon is much more flavorful than dried; the dried leaves also take on a musty, haylike quality. Add the leaves to salads, dressings, sauces, and vegetable, poultry, and fish dishes. Those who make their own tartar sauce will find this herb indispensable. Tarragon can easily take the place of salt, pepper, and vinegar, if necessary, and can also replace garlic. Because it is strongly flavored, tarragon should be used with discretion. Fresh or dried, heat intensifies the flavor.

Health Benefits

Diuretic, emmenagogue, hypnotic, stomachic. A simple infusion of tarragon leaves will stimulate the appetite, relieve flatulence and colic, regulate menstruation, balance the body's acidity, alleviate the pains of arthritis, rheumatism, and gout, and expel worms from the body. Tarragon is also regarded as a mild, nonirritating diuretic that helps the system flush out toxins produced by the digestion of heavy proteins. Drinking tarragon tea before going to bed helps to overcome insomnia. The fresh leaf or root when applied to aching teeth, cuts, or sores is said to act as a local anesthetic.

Tarragon / Nutritional Value Per 100 g Edible Portion		
	Dried, Ground	1 tsp.
Calories	295	5
Protein	22.76 g	0.36 g
Fat	7.24 g	0.12 g
Fiber	7.41 g	0.12 g
Calcium	1,139 mg	18 mg
Iron	32.30 mg	0.52 mg
Magnesium	347 mg	6 mg
Phosphorus	313 mg	5 mg
Potassium	3,020 mg	48 mg
Sodium	62 mg	1 mg
Zinc	3.900 mg	0.060 mg
Copper	0.677 mg	n/a
Manganese	7.967 mg	n/a
Beta Carotene (A)	4,200 IU	67 IU
Thiamine (B$_1$)	0.251 mg	0.004 mg
Riboflavin (B$_2$)	1.339 mg	0.021 mg
Niacin (B$_3$)	8.950 mg	0.143 mg

Thyme
(Thymus vulgaris)

Wind-bit thyme . . . smells like the perfume of the dawn in paradise.

—RUDYARD KIPLING

Those herbs which perfume the air most delightfully, not passed by as the rest, but, being trodden upon and crushed, are three; that is, burnet, wild thyme and watermints. Therefore, you are to set whole alleys of them, to have the pleasure when you walk or tread.

—FRANCIS BACON

It is said that the botanical name *Thymus* is connected with the Greek word *thymon*, meaning "to fumigate," as thyme was used for incense in temples; another derivation is from the Greek *thymos*, which signifies courage and strength, the plant being held in ancient and medieval days to be a great source of invigoration, its cordial qualities inspiring courage. *Vulgaris* means "vulgar" or "common."

General Information

Thyme is a member of the mint family that was originally grown as a decorative rather than a culinary herb in the Mediterranean. Used by the Sumerians, its history goes back to at least 3500 B.C. Thyme has woody stems, clusters of small lavender flowers, and short, oval, gray-green leaves. There are more than one hundred varieties of thyme, all developed from wild thyme (*T. serphyllum*), the so-called mother of thyme; each looks slightly different and has its own flavor and aroma. Thyme from England has broad leaves; French thyme has narrow leaves; and winter thyme, from Germany, stays green all winter. There are also thymes that taste and smell like lemon, mint, pine, licorice, caraway, or nutmeg. Thyme has long been associated with bees and honey, as the plant attracts the insects in great profusion and is thus excellent for orchards. This low, creeping plant was invariably planted along walkways, so that it might creep over the sun-warmed stones and impart its delicious aroma when stepped upon. Thyme, especially the lemon-scented variety, is a mild pest repellent.

Culinary Uses

The gray-green leaves of fresh thyme smell resinous and sweet and have a bright, sharp taste. The strong, aromatic flavor of thyme can easily overpower other, more delicate flavors, so it should be used with discretion. Dried, it loses some of its fragrance and gains pungency. Lemon thyme is milder, with a lemony tang, and blends better in dishes for which garden thyme is too sharp. Thyme especially complements vegetables of the cabbage family but also goes well with potatoes, tomatoes, zucchini, and eggplant. This herb improves the digestion of foods it is prepared with, so it is often found with fatty meats such as lamb or pork and with bean dishes.

Health Benefits

Antiseptic, aromatic, carminative, diaphoretic, expectorant, tonic, vulnerary. Thyme's carminative properties are attributed to its volatile oils, which irritate the gastrointestinal lining, thus stimulating the production of gastric fluids. Oil of thyme (thymol) is antimicrobial and a powerful antiseptic; during World War I it was used as an antiseptic, a local anesthetic, and a deodorant. Thyme oil may be beneficial in supporting immunological functions and overcoming fatigue and physical weakness after illness.

Thyme / Nutritional Value Per 100 g Edible Portion		
	Dried, Ground	1 tsp.
Calories	276	4
Protein	9.10 g	0.13 g
Fat	7.43 g	0.10 g
Fiber	18.63 g	0.26 g
Calcium	1,890 mg	26 mg
Iron	123.60 mg	1.73 mg
Magnesium	220 mg	3 mg
Phosphorus	201 mg	3 mg
Potassium	814 mg	11 mg
Sodium	55 mg	1 mg
Zinc	6.180 mg	0.090 mg
Copper	0.860 mg	n/a
Manganese	7.867 mg	n/a
Beta Carotene (A)	3,800 IU	53 IU
Thiamine (B$_1$)	0.513 mg	0.007 mg
Riboflavin (B$_2$)	0.399 mg	0.006 mg
Niacin (B$_3$)	4.940 mg	0.069 mg

LORE AND LEGEND

Thyme has not always been a seasoning herb, or even primarily so. History records its cultivation for decorative, ceremonial, aphrodisiac, and medicinal purposes. Long valued as an herb of courage, elegance, and grace in Greece, the highest compliment that could be paid a man was to tell him that he smelled of thyme. Indeed, it was very popular as a bath scent and was used in other ways as a male cosmetic. Thyme was held sacred to both Mars and Venus (respectively, Roman god of war and goddess of love); in the Middle Ages thyme sprigs or thyme-embroidered kerchiefs and scarves were given by ladies to their favorite knights in order to protect them in battle. If a young girl wore a corsage of wild thyme flowers, it meant that she was looking for a sweetheart; if a bashful boy drank enough wild thyme tea it would give him the courage to take her up on it. Due to its antiseptic qualities it was included in the embalming fluids used by the Egyptians and the posies carried by European judges and nobility to protect them from the odors and diseases of the common people. Early anatomists named the lymph gland in the chest the thymus because it reminded them of a thyme flower. A bed of thyme was thought to be a favorite for fairies, who would creep out late in the evening and frolic in the garden. Gardeners once set aside a patch of the herb especially for them, much as we provide birdhouses. According to legend, at midnight on Midsummer's Eve the king of the fairies and his followers dance in beds of wild thyme.

used to relieve mental instability, melancholy, and nightmares and to prevent memory loss and inefficiency. The tea sweetened with honey is an excellent, soothing cough mixture that also helps to relieve fevers and headaches, acts as a mood elevator, expels gas, and increases perspiration. Thyme destroys some intestinal hookworms and roundworms. Garden thyme usually contains about 1 percent of a volatile oil (thyme oil) that is composed mainly of thymol and carvacrol, along with minor amounts of many other aroma chemical compounds.

Note: Small amounts of thyme in cooking are okay, but do not ingest large amounts of thyme if you have thyroid problems or high blood pressure or if you are pregnant.

Turmeric
(Curcuma longa)

> *Curcuma* comes from an Arabic name for the plant, *kurkum*, meaning "saffron" or "crocus"; *longa* means "long." The English name *turmeric* comes from the medieval Latin phrase *terra merita*, meaning "deserving earth."

General Information

Turmeric is an East Indian tropical herb of the ginger family. It flourishes in the rich, moist soils of Java, China, India, and Bangladesh and is a valuable cash crop in many other tropical areas of the Far East. It is the underground rhizome of the plant that is used, like ginger, but it is both sweeter and more fragrant than ginger. This aromatic, vivid yellow spice is prepared by washing, peeling, drying, and grinding the thick root. Best known for its bright yellow color and spicy taste to lovers of Indian food, tumeric has medicinal value that is not as well known.

Culinary Uses

Turmeric is sometimes available fresh, when it looks similar to fresh ginger, but is normally bought dried, either whole or ground. Eaten raw in southern India, the bright yellow, aromatic root has a delicate, buttery, slightly peppery and mustardlike taste (some compare it to horseradish) that is clean and refreshing. One of the basic curry spices, turmeric gives a pleasantly warm and rich undertone to food, as well as adding its unmistakable coloring. It can be added to any curried dish or used alone to lend color and subtle spice to grains, beans, chutneys, cream

Thyme is an excellent natural tranquilizer because it contains carvacrol, which has a tonic effect on the nerve centers and also helps retard hair loss by improving the superficial blood vessels of the scalp, whose job it is to feed the roots of the hair. Strengthening to the nervous system, it has aromatic influences that help supply energy in times of physical weakness and stress. In aromatherapy thyme is sauces, and mayonnaise. Turmeric may be used as a cheap substitute for saffron, but its flavor is stronger than the more expensive spice. If you wish to make your own curry powder, combine six parts turmeric, four parts cumin, and one part each of cardamom, coriander, cinnamon, black pepper, ground fenugreek, and ginger. This combination will provide maximum flavor but minimal heat. Add dried, ground chili powder or cayenne pepper to taste for heat.

Health Benefits

Antifungal, cholagogue, choleretic, stimulant. Turmeric is noted as a blood purifier, has a soothing action on respiratory ailments, improves liver function, benefits the circulation, helps regulate the menstrual cycle, and works as a restorative after loss of blood at childbirth. It also helps the body to digest proteins, and when combined with coriander and cumin it aids in the digestion of complex carbohydrates. Turmeric may be used to regulate blood sugar for diabetics. It has antifungal and antibacterial properties and helps heal wounds both internally and externally. For an abrasion, bruise, or traumatic swelling, apply a paste of half a teaspoon of turmeric, a pinch of salt, and water or ghee to the affected area. Turmeric is considered to have beneficial effects on the skin, and it is said that Indian women owe their velvety complexions to the daily

LORE AND LEGEND

The Persian sun worshipers held the golden crocus sacred as the representation on earth of the sun, and used saffron to dye their holy garments and color their skins. The availability of saffron, however, was not sufficient to supply all their needs, so a substitute of equally vibrant color was deemed acceptable for use: turmeric. Even today, turmeric is used as a dye and cosmetic. The faces of Hindu brides are made more glowing by being painted with turmeric, and many ladies use it in place of rouge to add radiance to the skin.

intake of turmeric in their foods. Turmeric contains highly variable amounts (0.3 to 5.4 percent) of a yellow pigment called curcumin, the most active component in turmeric; curcumin has been found effective as an anti-inflammatory and antimicrobial agent and as a cardiovascular and gastrointestinal aid; it also appears to inhibit the development of colon cancer.

Turmeric / Nutritional Value Per 100 g Edible Portion		
	Dried, Ground	1 tsp.
Calories	354	8
Protein	7.83 g	0.17 g
Fat	9.88 g	0.22 g
Fiber	6.71 g	0.15 g
Calcium	182 mg	4 mg
Iron	41.42 mg	0.91 mg
Magnesium	193 mg	4 mg
Phosphorus	268 mg	6 mg
Potassium	2,525 mg	56 mg
Sodium	38 mg	1 mg
Zinc	4.350 mg	0.100 mg
Copper	0.603 mg	n/a
Manganese	7.833 mg	n/a
Beta Carotene (A)	trace	n/a
Thiamine (B₁)	0.152 mg	0.003 mg
Riboflavin (B₂)	0.233 mg	0.005 mg
Niacin (B₃)	5.140 mg	0.113 mg
Ascorbic Acid (C)	25.85 mg	0.57 mg

Vanilla

(Vanilla planifolia, V. tahitensis, V. fragrans)

Vanilla derives both its Latin and English name from the Spanish *vaina*, meaning "sheath" or "pod"; *vainilla* is a diminutive meaning "small sheath," with reference to the thinness of the black capsuled fruit. The Spanish word goes farther back etymologically to the Latin *vagina*, which was what the shape of the bean suggested to a number of people, giving it an aphrodisiac reputation. *Planifolia* means "flat-leaved"; *tahitensis* means "coming from Tahiti"; *fragrans* means "fragrant."

General Information

Vanilla beans are the dried unripe fruits of the only member of the orchid family used as a foodstuff. One of the most expensive spices after saffron, vanilla is grown throughout most tropical areas within twenty degrees of the equator. The plant will grow elsewhere but not produce pods. In the wild of Mexico, vanilla vines climb trees in the shade of the jungle canopy and reach 250 feet or more. Under cultivation the vines are looped over specially planted trees or training stakes seven or eight feet tall to keep them within reach. Flowering lasts two months, with each blossom producing a single bean. The long, thin pods hang in banana-like bunches, growing for eight to nine months before they are harvested. They are filled with a pulpy substance in which are embedded a multitude of all-but-invisible black seeds—the tiny black specks you may see, for instance, in vanilla ice cream. In the plant's natural environment, a tiny hummingbird and a bee called the melipone pollinated the vanilla orchid, but these species are now extinct because of pesticide usage. All vanilla is now hand-pollinated, and pollination must occur within a few hours of the flower's opening. The mature pods must be picked just before the moment when, thoroughly ripened, they would split open by themselves.

Without curing, the vanilla pod would have no great culinary interest. The aroma and flavor develop as a result of a complicated curing process that lasts five to six months or more after harvest. Bourbon beans are first "killed" by dipping baskets of them briefly into near-boiling water; in Mexico the beans are first dried in sheds for several weeks. Next, the beans are laid out on wool blankets in the sun to bake until they are too hot to touch. At night they are wrapped in their blankets and sealed up indoors to "sweat"; this routine may continue for several weeks. The beans shrivel, become flexible, and darken, eventually turning chocolate brown to black. They are then dried for two to three months more in the shade before being tied in bundles and packed away for conditioning. Vanillin, a white crystalline substance, occurs during this fermentation time, and the flavor of vanilla as we know it has developed. During this process, what began as five pounds of green pods are reduced to one pound of dried beans ready for the market. Vanilla beans are sorted and graded before being tied into bundles and packed in tin. The beans that command the highest prices are about eight inches long, pliable, aromatic, and plump. Farmers and plantation owners guard their pods closely throughout the long

LORE AND LEGEND

While some drank vanilla in their pursuit of love, many others found that its delicate, persuasive aroma was just as powerful. The Totonaca wore vanilla beans in their hats and used it to perfume their homes, a practice they continue today. They used the oil from the drying vanilla beans to rub on their skin until their bodies glistened. The Europeans—especially the French—created perfumes from vanilla pods, to fragrance not only their bodies but also their tobacco and snuff. When vanilla extracts came onto the market at the end of the nineteenth century, more than a few savvy women dabbed a little behind their ears and onto their wrists, thereby creating the ultimate in perfumes—a sensual aroma that also conjured up the homey pleasures of food fresh from the kitchen. Smart modern women have found that fragrances with strong vanilla notes draw an attentive audience with minimal effort. In 1991 Sloan-Kettering Cancer Center in New York announced in a news release that the fragrance of heliotropin—a sweet, vanilla-like scent—was the most relaxing and pleasant of five fragrances tested for the reduction of anxiety and distress during a difficult medical procedure.

growing and curing process because they are so valuable. Some growers will tattoo their pods with a series of pinpricks before harvest to prevent theft, while others use guard dogs or human sentries to keep watch.

There is not enough natural vanilla in the world to supply even the American demand alone, which has intensified during the last decades because of the growing popularity of vanilla ice cream. Vanilla accounts for over 50 percent of all ice cream sales, and vanilla is also a constituent of many other flavors of ice cream. In 1980 the United States imported a hundred thousand pounds of vanilla from Mexico and enough from several other small tropical countries to exercise an appreciable effect on their economies. That part of the demand that genuine vanilla cannot meet is furnished by substitutes.

Vanilla / Nutritional Value Per 100 g Edible Portion			
	Cured		Cured
Protein	2.6–10.0 g	Calcium	1,900 mg
Fat	4.7–21.2 g	Phosphorus	70 mg
Fiber	15.3–26.3 g		

Bourbon vanilla is named after the French island of Reunion in the Indian Ocean, formerly known as Ile de Bourbon, after the royal family. Most of Bourbon vanilla is actually grown on the northeastern coast of Madagascar, with smaller amounts coming from relatively nearby Reunion and the Comoro Islands. Madagascan vanilla is particularly smooth and rich, while Reunion has more sweetness and spice. Mexican vanilla is the traditional vanilla. It produces a fine flavor, with just a hint of sharpness or pungency. The best Mexican vanilla comes from the state of Veracruz, and where it grows the air is richly scented. Tahitian vanilla vines produce fatter, thicker-skinned, and more strongly flowery-scented beans compared with the more traditional Mexican vanilla. The plant was taken to Tahiti from Manila in 1848, and botanists still argue whether the specific strain was produced intentionally or by a chance mutation of nature. All the vanilla produced in Tahiti used to be exported to France, but the United States now imports half the crop.

Thomas Jefferson is credited with vanilla's arrival in the United States. When he returned from his ambassadorship in France in 1789, he was dismayed to discover that no one in the States knew about vanilla, so he wrote his French attaché requesting that he send him fifty vanilla pods. Jefferson's personal passion soon became a national one; vanilla was used as a flavoring, a medicine, and—yes—an aphrodisiac. In the 1800s Dr. John King, advised in the *American Dispensatory* that one should use vanilla to "stimulate the sexual propensities." He went on to give a very carefully detailed recipe for a decoction promising amorous evenings. If the good doctor was right, a hefty swig of vanilla extract before bedtime could work like a charm.

Culinary Uses

Vanilla pods should be chocolate brown or coal black in color, flexible, and covered with a frosting of aromatic crystals (*givre*, the French word for "frost"). If washed and dried each time, the pods can be reused after making vanilla extract. They should be stored in a tightly sealed glass jar so that they lose no further moisture or volatile essence. Once they have reached the dry, brittle stage, they have lost their flavor and incomparable character. Vanilla has a wide range of uses in confectionery, being used as a flavoring in sauces, creams, baked goods, cakes, ice creams, and custards. The primary quality that vanilla adds is sweetness, although its sweetness is usually overwhelmed by the sweetness of sugar.

Vanilla beans and vanilla extract can often be substituted for one another, but you will get a more true and interesting flavor from the bean. To use one, carefully cut it in half lengthwise. Run the blade of a sharp knife down the inside, scraping out the fleshy pulp. Add this and the scraped bean to the liquid in your recipe. Ideally, you would allow this to steep for about fifteen to twenty minutes. Remove the bean before serving the dish. To get a bit more mileage from a bean after cooking with it, rinse and dry the halves and then sink them into your sugar bowl. After a couple of weeks you will have a pleasant vanilla sugar for baking or sweetening coffee and tea.

Vanilla extract is made by circulating a mixture of alcohol and water heated to 70 degrees Fahrenheit through chopped beans in a sealed vat and then aging the resultant product for three to six months. The extract manufactured and sold in Mexico is frequently fortified with coumarin, a toxic natural flavoring obtained from the tonka bean. Coumarin contains no vanillin but adds a sweet, smooth flavor close enough to true vanilla to fool most people. Unless you are certain of the purity, it is advisable to avoid buying extract in Mexico. Until 1954, when coumarin was banned in the United States for health reasons, its very sweet flavor was widely employed in artificial and blended vanilla extracts. Pure vanilla extract contains 35 percent alcohol by volume. Vanilla flavoring contains less alcohol and has the same taste components but is less concentrated than vanilla extract.

Imitation vanilla is, at best, made from a sulfite waste byproduct of softwood pulp used in the paper industry; at worst, it is a totally synthetic product (hydroxy-4 methoxy-3 benzaldehyde). Although imitation vanilla simulates the flavor of pure vanilla to some degree, it is by comparison harsh and abrasive, lacking true vanilla's sweet, well-rounded flavor and aroma. There is nothing to recommend the use of imitation vanilla—real vanilla is worth any extra price.

Health Benefits

Aphrodisiac, choleretic, stimulant. There are thirty-six aromatic compounds in vanilla, and the most active component, vanillin, is mildly toxic in both its natural and its synthetic form. The FDA considers it safe, however, because such small amounts are used. Workers who daily handle large quantities may be afflicted with vanillism, which causes headaches and allergic skin reactions.

The medicinal reputation of vanilla has declined over

the years, but it was at one time considered to be a stimulant, an aid to digestion, and an aphrodisiac. Because vanilla was recommended as a stomach calmative in American medical journals, some doctors today provide vanilla extract for those with stomach upset. One woman who was going through a very toxic treatment for uterine cancer said that the extract in water was the only thing that calmed her stomach for two days after each chemotherapy treatment. In aromatherapy, vanilla's consoling aroma is used to support self-confidence, to dissolve pent-up anger and frustration, and to access sensuality.

Verbena
(Verbena officinalis, Aloysia triphylla)

The botanical and English name *verbena* means "green bough" and refers to the sacred branches of laurel, myrtle, or olive carried by heralds and certain priests. *Officinalis* means "of the workshop," alluding to apothecaries' shops and signifying that the plant was once part of the official pharmacopoeia of Rome. *Aloysia* comes from the name *Louisa*, the plant being named after Maria Louisa, wife of King Charles IV of Spain; *triphylla* means "three-leaved."

General Information
Verbena (*Verbena officinalis*) is native to the Mediterranean region but early on spread throughout Eurasia. Even though it is rather undistinguished in appearance and not rare, verbena was long regarded with awe throughout its natural range. The plant was brought to North America by the Puritans and now is widely naturalized throughout temperate North America. Lemon verbena (*Aloysia triphylla*) is an unassuming woody shrub with narrow, shiny, pale green leaves that taste like lemon and smell like a combination of lemons and limes. This plant with its delicate lemony aroma charmed the Spanish explorers who happened upon it in Argentina and Chile. Verbenas wound their way into the hearts of colonial gardeners because they provided both color for the eye and satisfaction for the nose, as well as a savory herb tea that relieved colds and fevers in a pleasant manner. Although people seem to find the fragrance intimate, this and other lemon-scented plants appear to act as natural insect repellents.

LORE AND LEGEND

The European verbena or vervain plant was sacred to Mars, the ancient Roman god of war, and it was believed that the plant had the properties of repelling the enemy. Heralds bore crowns of verbena when dispatched to other nations carrying messages of peace, or to give defiance and challenge to an enemy. Verbena was also considered a great purifying plant, and its green leaves were used to cleanse tables and altars in festivities to honor Zeus and lesser gods. In ancient Gaul and Britain the plant was held in great veneration. It was both an ingredient of medieval witches' love potions and a charm against their evil spells; it even made its way into Christian lore as the plant used to stanch Christ's wounds on Calvary. The Druids regarded the vervain as a plant of spells and enchantment, and used it as a sacred food in rituals, holding it in great reverence because they saw in its leaves a resemblance to the oak. In the north vervain was sacred to Thor, the god of lightning.

Culinary Uses
Lemon verbena leaves are particularly useful because they will not lose their lemony flavor or aroma when dried or cooked. The leaves brighten the taste of vegetable marinades, salad dressings, jams, puddings, beverages, or anything else that needs just a touch of lemon.

Health Benefits
Antispasmodic, aphrodisiac, astringent, diaphoretic, diuretic, sedative, tonic. Scientists have recently substantiated verbena's folk use as a diuretic, gout remedy, and appetite suppressant. In southern Europe verbena is recommended as a remedy for exhaustion and depression. Verbena corrects minor menstrual irregularities, has diuretic properties that eliminate edemas caused by cardiovascular disorders, and helps to treat inflammation of the spleen and liver. The dried leaves are used in sachets and potpourris, as well as in teas as a sedative or antipyretic. The oil is extensively used in perfumery.

Vinegar

The English name *vinegar* comes from the French *vin aigre*, or sour wine, the first major source of vinegar.

General Information

Vinegar is a sour liquid obtained by acetic fermentation, a natural process that occurs when a liquid containing less than 18 percent alcohol is exposed to the air. Bacteria present in the air react with the alcohol to produce a thick skin over the surface of the liquid, called the "mother." This layer of yeast cells and bacteria converts the alcohol into a natural acetic acid, giving vinegar its characteristic sharpness. The most common sources of fermentable sugar are wine, apples, and grains. Like salt, vinegar is one of the oldest condiments used to season, preserve, and tenderize food. Vinegars owe their specific characteristics largely to their source and sometimes to fermentation techniques. In addition to having different degrees of sourness or tartness, acidity, and other traits, vinegars can be tinged with the sweetness of fruits, the tang of an herb, the fragrance of a spice, or a blend of all three.

Buying Tips

Vinegar is a solvent; therefore, vinegar stored in plastic or metal becomes enriched with polycarbons or metallic ions. Purchase traditionally made vinegars, aged in wood and bottled in glass. When cooking with vinegar, use nonreactive cookware, such as an enameled pot, as opposed to a metal one.

Health Benefits

pH 2.40–3.40. Traditional, unpasteurized, unfiltered vinegar contains as many as fifty different nutrients, amino acids, and trace elements, which contribute to vinegar's distinctive taste and also to its medicinal properties. The amino acids counter the effect of lactic acid buildup in the blood and help prevent the formation of toxic fat peroxides, which contribute to aging, fatigue, irritability, and cholesterol formation on blood vessel walls. Apple cider vinegar is rich in potassium, an anti-aging nutrient. One of the most obvious signs of premature aging is the stiffness that invades the joints and often makes even the simple act of walking painful and difficult. But the problem is more often potassium deficiency than old age. Without the proper level of potassium, acid crystals accumulate in the body's joints and tissues, gradually hardening. That accumulation of crystals in the bursa between tendons and bones or in the joints may result in bursitis, arthritis, or rheumatism—diseases most often associated with old age. Nutritionists have found that a recipe of two tablespoons of apple cider vinegar and two tablespoons of raw honey in a glass of warm water, taken daily, flushes those acid crystals out of the body, relieving pain and stiffness and halting the premature aging process. Apple cider vinegar also works in weight control. When the body lacks potassium, sodium makes it retain fluids, which translates into extra inches and pounds. Apple cider vinegar, with its high potassium content, helps the body rid itself of excess sodium.

Apple cider vinegar also contains malic acid, a natural component of apples, which helps create an exhilarating stimulation to your body's digestive processes. Apple cider vinegar can mean the difference between a bad or a mild case of food poisoning. A teaspoon added to a glass of water miraculously soothes the digestive tract even after symptoms appear; take a quarter teaspoonful every fifteen minutes until relieved. Soaking feet daily in vinegar will help clear up athlete's foot. Apply vinegar directly to insect bites or stings to relieve pain. Apple cider vinegar brings fast relief from burns and will retard scarring if applied immediately. Added to bathwater, vinegar stimulates circulation and keeps the pores open. Used as a rinse, it gives hair a glossy appearance and soft texture.

Distilled vinegar should not be used internally, as it is highly demineralizing, leaching out phosphorous, overstimulating the thyroid gland, and rapidly destroying red blood corpuscles.

VARIETIES

Apple cider vinegar, when raw and unpasteurized, has a bright, crisp flavor and is generally used for marinades, salad dressings, and sauces. It has about 5 to 6 percent acetic acid and a pronounced apple-acid flavor.

Balsamic vinegar is made from grapes, pressed and

Vinegar / Nutritional Value Per 1 Tablespoon		
	Apple Cider	Distilled
Calories	2	2
Protein	trace	trace
Calcium	1 mg	n/a
Iron	0.1 mg	n/a
Phosphorus	1 mg	n/a
Potassium	15 mg	2 mg
Sodium	trace	0 mg

cooked into a dark, sweet liquid. This "must" is mixed with wine vinegar and aged in wooden barrels. Because of its smooth, mellow character, balsamic vinegar takes its name from the Italian word for "balm." This dark vinegar makes a delicious salad dressing with olive oil. Balsamic vinegar has a 6 percent acidity and is sweet and woodsy, one of the most flavorful vinegars.

Malt vinegar is usually made from malted barley. Most often used for pickling onions and other vegetables, its strong flavor is overly harsh for use in salad dressings, but it combines well with fish-and-chips.

Rice vinegar, distilled from rice, has less sharpness than cider vinegar and just a hint of sweetness. The Japanese use it to make sushi, dipping sauces, and many pickled dishes, but it is also good for marinating tofu (with soy sauce and ginger) and in grain and bean salads.

White distilled vinegar is the product of fermenting ethyl alcoholic fluids. Strong, acidic, and too sharp for dressings and regular cooking, it is good for washing windows and little else. Substitute lemon, tomato, or grapefruit juice in recipes where white vinegar is called for.

Wine vinegars have a 5 percent acidity and may derive from red, white, or rosé wines. They are robust and perceptibly fruity and combine well with salads, sauces, and dressings.

Violet, Sweet
(*Viola odorata*)

Viola is the Latin form of the Greek name *Ione*; *odorata* means "odorous" or "fragrant." *Violet* is the diminutive of the Latin *viola*.

General Information
Violets come originally from Europe and since the days of Hippocrates have been used in medicines, perfumes, love

LORE AND LEGEND

Greek legend attributes the violet to Jupiter, who changed his beloved Io into a white heifer for fear of Juno's jealousy. When Io shed tears over the coarseness of the common grass she was forced to feed upon, Zeus decided to create a new and more suitable plant for the delicate creature. From her fallen tears he caused to spring forth a sweet-smelling dainty flower, and gave it her name. Ancient Athenians held the plant in high regard for its power both to moderate anger and to cure insomnia. In Greek burials it was the custom to cover the dead with violets as a symbol of both the beauty and the transitory quality of life. The Greeks chose the violet as a symbol for Athens, dedicated this seductively scented flower to Aphrodite, and from it made vast quantities of violet wine, as well as conserves and cosmetics. The flower became so popular that it was cultivated on a large scale to supply the needs of all the Mediterranean countries. In Toulouse, France, violets were given as a poetry prize during the age of troubadours, and in southern Germany during the Middle Ages, the appearance of the first spring violet was celebrated with dancing. The violet (posy) was a love token between Napoleon Bonaparte and Josephine, and later became his political emblem. He sometimes was known as Corporal Violet because of his fondness for the flower, and wearing a violet became a symbol of support among his followers while he was exiled on Elba. Upon his return to power in Paris, violets were strewn along the parade route.

potions, and sweets. Sweet violet, which has heart-shaped leaves, deep purple flowers, and root stalks that creep along the ground, is one of the most fragrant of the more than six hundred species of violet. Suggestive of soft kisses, violets are one of the tenderest of flowers, with an elusive fragrance.

Culinary Uses

Violet flowers are highly fragrant and have a sweet, aromatic flavor. The purple flowers can be candied or used fresh as a garnish in salads. Crystallized flowers are a familiar sight on violet-flavored sweets and chocolates. Violet water, made by weighting and steeping leaves and petals in water until fragrant, is used in tea breads, cupcakes, puddings, ices, fruit compotes, and chilled soups.

Health Benefits

Antiseptic, diuretic, expectorant. Violet flowers contain an abundance of vitamins A and C. The leaves are mildly laxative and contain glucosides that are antiseptic; the roots and seeds are purgatives and emetics, causing severe gastric upset, including nausea and vomiting. The flowers are now principally used as a coloring agent, as a fragrance in perfumes, and in cough syrups.

Wintergreen

(*Gaultheria procumbens*)
Also Known As: Deerberry, Teaberry Shrub, Mountain Tea

> This plant received its botanical name in honor of Dr. Gaultier, a prominent physician in Quebec. *Procumbens* means "procumbent," laying facedown or having stems that trail along the ground without rooting. The English name *wintergreen* was given because this plant stays green and does not lose its leaves throughout the winter.

General Information

Wintergreen is a low-growing evergreen plant native to southern Canada and the United States. A member of the heath family, it has white flowers and spicy red berries. The leaves are sharply astringent and aromatic on account of the volatile oil, known as oil of wintergreen. Anyone who has ever sought relief from a muscle ache by reaching for the Ben-Gay has experienced the soothing qualities of wintergreen's active constituent. Even more familiar is the refreshing, minty taste of oil of wintergreen, a popular flavoring for gum, candy, and toothpaste.

Culinary Uses

Wintergreen's shiny leaves may be nibbled on for a natural chewing gum—but only for half a minute or so because the sweet, aromatic taste soon turns bitter. The bright red berries are prized for their sweet and refreshing flavor and can be eaten as a special treat on their own, with other fruit, or blended with honey to make a wintergreen spread.

Health Benefits

Aromatic, astringent, carminative, diuretic, rubefacient, stimulant. The medicinal virtues of wintergreen leaves reside essentially in the oil of wintergreen, which can be obtained by steam distillation. The oil consists primarily of methyl salicylate, one of the ingredients of aspirin. Not surprisingly, then, the leaves have long been used for headaches and other aches and pains, inflammations, and rheumatism. Until 1874 the only commercial source of aspirin was by hydrolysis of the oils from sweet birch bark or wintergreen leaves. A tea of the leaves can be drunk whenever aspirin might be used, such as for colds, coughs, aches, and flu. Wintergreen tea will also stimulate the stomach and respiration, and it is beneficial as a gargle. The leaves can be used as a compress to help cure skin problems or headache. In addition to being used as a flavoring agent in candies, gum, and mouthwashes, the oil is employed as a counterirritant in ointments and lotions for swollen joints (arthritis and rheumatism).

Yeast Extracts

(*Saccharomyces cerevisiae*)

> *Saccharomyces* derives from the Latin *saccharus*, meaning "sweet," and the Greek *myces*, meaning "fungus" or "mushroom."

General Information

Yeasts are living organisms, microscopic, nonidentical, single-celled fungi with as many as one hundred billion cells per ounce. These tiny plants, which occur naturally in honey, in soil, and on rinds or peelings of fruits such as grapes, metabolize (digest) sugars and produce alcohols and carbon dioxide as byproducts. They differ from other plant cells because they are not surrounded by cellulose, which must be destroyed by proper mastication (chewing), cooking, or fermentation before the cell can be useful as food. Yeast probably came into human use by a happy accident, but it is now widely utilized. The two main functions of commercial yeast are for fermentation and for growing nutrients. Fermenting yeasts include those used in baking and in brewing wine or beer. Nutrient-growing yeasts produce vitamins, enzymes, amino acids, and other microbial nutrients for scientific research as well as for human or animal consumption. At the end of the growth period, the culture is pasteurized to kill the yeast.

The "natural" B vitamins proclaimed in yeast are in fact from synthetic vitamins fed the culture during its growth stage; the end product is then further fortified. This process allows a yeast of any B vitamin potency desired to be produced and used to formulate vitamin pills with "B vitamins derived from yeast." Ammonia also is generally added to the growth medium of the yeast, just as it is used in chemical farming—as a nitrogen fertilizer to increase protein content in the finished product.

Culinary Uses

Nutritional yeast extracts have an agreeable taste, somewhat like cheese, but with a more refreshing aftertaste. For many it is an acquired taste; those who are nauseated by yeast or who find its taste disagreeable should avoid it. Fresh yeast should not be ingested except when the stomach is empty. It should be eaten by itself, allowed to dissolve slowly in the mouth or mixed with warm water or milk—never with anything else. The best times to take fresh yeast are early in the morning, one hour before the evening meal, or at bedtime. Yeasts are used mostly in sandwich spreads or hot drinks but are also used to flavor soups and stews.

Health Benefits

pH 5.65. Yeast is one of the most valuable antidotes against acid or toxic bile; it neutralizes irritation in the bowels, soothes inflamed surfaces, and restores normal bowel movements. Since it contains certain vitamins that help the deranged liver to oxidize fats properly, yeast has a beneficial effect on the skin (incompletely oxidized fats in the diet clog the oil and sebaceous glands and thus cause acne) and has long been used as a remedy for pimples and acne. In their raw state, yeasts are a rich source of the B vitamins and alkaline elements, especially sodium and potassium; cooking partially destroys these nutrients. What B_{12} there is in yeast is included as an additive at the end of its manufacture, or else the yeast is grown in a B_{12}-enriched medium; not all yeasts contain the vitamin. Yeasts do have their disadvantages: they are high in nucleic acids, which when metabolized are converted to uric acid crystals that tend to settle throughout the body and cause gout or kidney stones. While they are exceptionally rich in certain nutrients, they are lacking in others that are needed for bal-

ance; thus, if not properly balanced with other foods, yeasts can cause deficiencies. Another problem with yeast is that microorganisms of this sort tend to induce unhealthy amounts of candida-type yeasts in the body, especially in more susceptible individuals.

VARIETIES

Baker's yeast is used to give lift and lightness to baked products. When given a moist, warm environment, the yeast cells start to grow and outgas carbon dioxide, causing bread to rise. If temperatures are too cold or too hot, the yeast will not function properly, and the baked product will be dense and heavy. Baker's yeast works best with hard wheat flours, not with the softer pastry wheat flours or flours from other grains, because hard wheat is the only grain with sufficient gluten to trap the gases produced by yeast and induce rising. Other grains like rye, barley, and corn have to be mixed with hard wheat flour or gluten flour if you expect them to rise well with yeast. Baker's yeast is available in two forms: compressed or dry. Compressed yeast is a fresh, soft yeast obtainable in one-pound blocks from most bakeries. Extremely perishable, it should be stored in the refrigerator and used within a week, although it can be frozen successfully for longer periods. This yeast is also available in small cakes wrapped in foil, but this size

Yeast Extracts / Nutritional Value			
	Baker's Dry Active 1 pkg.	Brewer's Dry 1 Tbsp.	Torula 1 oz.
Calories	20	25	79
Protein	3 g	3 g	10.9 g
Fat	trace	trace	0.3 g
Fiber	n/a	n/a	n/a
Calcium	3 mg	6-60 mg	120 mg
Iron	1.1 mg	1.4 mg	5.5 mg
Phosphorus	90 mg	140 mg	486 mg
Potassium	140 mg	152 mg	580 mg
Sodium	4 mg	10 mg	4 mg
Beta Carotene (A)	trace	trace	trace
Thiamine (B₁)	0.160 mg	1.250 mg	3.970 mg
Riboflavin (B₂)	0.380 mg	0.340 mg	1.430 mg
Niacin (B₃)	2.600 mg	3.000 mg	12.600 mg
Ascorbic Acid (C)	trace	trace	trace

also must be kept refrigerated and used within a week. When its light gray color turns to brown, it is too old to use. Dry yeast generally comes in small foil packets and will keep for about six months. Many commercial baking yeasts contain BHT (butylated hydroxytoluene), a petroleum-based antioxidant that is best avoided. Baker's yeast, since it is active, should not be used as a nutritional supplement. Live yeast feeds on the foods in the intestinal tract and may cause health problems.

Brewer's yeast, now called **nutritional yeast,** was originally the byproduct of beer production, hence its name. The original yeast was grown on barley malt, rice, corn or corn syrup, and hops. Now most nutritional yeast is grown on a molasses or sugar beet solution for use solely as a nutritional supplement. Once grown, the yeast is removed from the vats, de-bittered, and reduced to a powder by being sprayed through drying chambers kept at a temperature of 250 degrees Fahrenheit—which kills and sterilizes, as well as giving this yeast its characteristic "chicken soup" flavor. The resulting product keeps well but is classed as a "dead" yeast because it will not leaven dough. Nutritionally, brewer's yeast has some strong points and some weak points. It contains a full complement of amino acids, iron, and B vitamins, as well as a few hard-to-get trace elements like selenium and chromium. However, the heating not only reduces the vitamin content but also changes its organic salts into inorganic salts, rendering it acidic to the body. Also, yeast is a high-phosphorus food and as such needs to be balanced out by some sort of calcium supplementation; it is also high in purines, which produce uric acid, a prime factor in gout, a painful disease of the joints. Unlike fresh yeast, nutritional yeast is compatible with any kind of food and causes less flatulence. To most people, it has a pleasant-tasting, cheesy flavor, and it can be used as a condiment on vegetables, baked potatoes, popcorn, and other foods.

Torula yeast is frequently (but not always) grown on food-grade ethyl alcohol, a byproduct of petroleum refining and papermaking. It is frequently added to processed foods such as dessert toppings and pastries. This type of yeast has been found to irritate some people. Torula yeast is not considered by many nutritionists to be a true food.

Yellow Dock
(Rumex crispus)

Rumex is an old Latin term for "lance," in reference to the shape of this plant's leaves; *crispus* means "curled." The English name *dock* most likely comes from the Scottish Gaelic *dogha*, meaning "burdock."

General Information
Yellow dock is a perennial plant of the *Rumex* genus, a group of plants that includes sorrel, rhubarb, and buckwheat. It is native to Europe and Asia but was early introduced into America and is now found nearly everywhere throughout the United States, most often as a troublesome weed in fields and waste places. It quickly inhabits cultivated ground and grows along roadsides, producing copious quantities of seed each fall. Its slender, curly leaves can be used as a vegetable or a potherb; they are best gathered in the spring, when they are young and tender. The most medicinal part of the plant is its root.

Culinary Uses
Young leaves of yellow dock have a sharp, bitter flavor similar to that of spinach but with a slight tinge of lemon. Like dandelion greens, the leaves are tasty only when young and tender, and again after autumn frost has

Yellow Dock / Nutritional Value Per 100 g Edible Portion			
	Raw	Cooked	Dried
Calories	22	20	284
Protein	2.00 g	1.83 g	20.30 g
Fat	0.70 g	0.64 g	4.10 g
Fiber	0.80 g	0.73 g	12.20 g
Calcium	44 mg	38 mg	1,000 mg
Iron	2.40 mg	2.08 mg	76 mg
Magnesium	103 mg	89 mg	320 mg
Phosphorus	63 mg	52 mg	757 mg
Potassium	390 mg	321 mg	1,220 mg
Sodium	4 mg	3 mg	7.7 mg
Manganese	n/a	n/a	14.5 mg
Beta Carotene (A)	4,000 IU	3,474 IU	37,432 IU
Thiamine (B$_1$)	0.040 mg	0.034 mg	0.810 mg
Riboflavin (B$_2$)	0.100 mg	0.086 mg	1.080 mg
Niacin (B$_3$)	0.500 mg	0.411 mg	5.400 mg
Ascorbic Acid (C)	48.0 mg	26.3 mg	405.4 mg

removed their bitterness. Because of their high oxalic content, the leaves should be cooked; they are relatively safe when boiled in water that has been changed twice, since this removes much of the acid. The new leaves make a pleasant steamed green on their own or mixed with spinach, especially when seasoned with a little garlic and olive oil.

Health Benefits

Antiscorbutic, astringent, laxative, tonic. Known as a medicinal plant since ancient times, yellow dock (both leaves and root) has been used as a laxative and a mild, astringent tonic, strengthening the circulatory system, purifying the blood, and cleansing the lymphatic system. A good liver and spleen herb, yellow dock also stimulates the elimination channels (especially the skin) and promotes the elimination of excess lymph fluid. During the nineteenth century, it gained popularity as a remedy for jaundice and as a tonic for the liver and gallbladder and has since been included in nearly all herbal liver remedies. The active principles in yellow dock are the astringent tannins and the purgative anthraquinone glycosides, based on emodin and chrysophenic acid, which have antimicrobial properties. Decoctions of the plant are useful in scrofulous diseases of the skin, including psoriasis and eczema. Yellow dock's astringent and antimicrobial properties also explain the use of the powdered root as an abrasive dentrifice, especially in cases of spongy gums. Ointments and herbal baths with yellow dock make effective treatments for skin conditions such as eczema, itches, sores, hives, and ringworm.

Acrid Unpleasantly pungent or caustic.

Adaptogen An herb that maintains health by increasing the body's ability to adapt to environmental and internal stress, generally by strengthening the immune system, nervous system, and/or glandular system.

Alkaloid A plant-based, nitrogen-containing compound that has a potent effect on body function.

Allergen Any substance that produces an allergic reaction.

Allicin (and other sulfur compounds) Crushed garlic releases pungent sulfur compounds, including allicin, that can lower blood cholesterol and fight the formation of cancerous tumors. These compounds can also help prevent infectious diseases, including colds and flu.

Allyl sulfides Phytochemicals that stimulate levels of glutathione S-transferase, one of the primary detoxification enzymes. They're found in garlic, onions, leeks, and chives.

Amino acids The chief components of proteins, synthesized by living cells or obtained as essential components of the diet. They are made up of nitrogen-containing compounds attached to acids. Eight (some say nine) of the amino acids must be provided by the diet, since the body is not able to manufacture them; hence they are termed "essential." These are tryptophan, valine, threonine, isoleucine, leucine, lysine, phenylalanine, methionine, histidine.

Analgesic An herb that relieves pain without causing loss of consciousness. Some analgesics are also antispasmodics, relieving pain by reducing cramping in muscles; others affect the nerves directly, reducing the pain signals to the brain.

Anaphrodisiac An agent that lessens sexual function and desire.

Anemia A condition in which there is a shortage of red blood cells or hemoglobin or both. Nutritional deficiencies can cause anemia, or it can be caused by other factors, such as prolonged blood loss.

Anesthetic An agent that induces loss of feeling or reduces pain in an area by desensitizing the nerves.

Anodyne A substance that soothes, calms, or comforts.

Anthelmintic An agent that tends to kill and/or expel intestinal parasitic worms. Plants containing substances that are obnoxious to the worms or which act as cathartics have been used for this purpose. Chamomile and tansy are two such examples.

Anthocyanidins Along with pro-anthocyanidins, these are the flavonoids responsible for the red to blue colors of blueberries, blackberries, cherries, grapes, hawthorn berries, and many flowers. These flavonoids are found in the flesh of the fruit as well as the skin. They are able to increase vitamin C levels within the cells, decrease the leakiness and breakage of small blood vessels, protect against free-radical damage, and support our joint structures.

Antibacterial Any substance that has the ability, even in dilute solutions, to destroy or inhibit the growth or reproduction of bacteria and other microorganisms; used especially in the treatment of infectious diseases.

Antibiotic An organic substance that is capable of killing viruses, bacteria, or other microorganisms and is used to combat infections or disease. While many herbal antibiotics have direct germ-killing effects, their primary action is the stimulation of the body's own immune response.

Antibody A protein produced by the body in response to foreign invaders (antigens). Antibodies destroy and deactivate antigens by attaching to them and rendering them harmless.

Anticoagulant A substance that prevents or slows clotting of the blood.

Antidote A remedy to counteract or neutralize poisons and toxins.

Antifungal A substance that destroys or inhibits the growth of fungi.

Antigen Foreign substances (including proteins in food) that provoke an immune response.

Antioxidants Substances that oppose oxidation or inhibit reactions promoted by oxygen or peroxides. These compounds react with oxygen in an effort to protect other substances from oxidation. Antioxidants added to processed foods keep oils and fats from spoiling. Antioxidants (such as vitamin C, vitamin E, and beta carotene) already in foods may protect against cancer, cataracts, and heart disease.

Antiscorbutic A substance that prevents the disease scurvy, caused by a deficiency of vitamin C.

Antiseptic A substance that prevents sepsis, or putrefaction and decay, by arresting the growth or action of noxious microorganisms, either by inhibiting their activity or by destroying them. The term *antiseptic* generally refers to agents applied to living tissue, the term *disinfectant* to those used on inanimate objects such as floors, walls, or clothing.

Antispasmodic A relaxant or nervine that relieves or prevents involuntary muscle contractions or spasms, such as those occurring in epilepsy, painful menstruation, intestinal cramping, or muscle "shock." Antispasmodics are included in most herb formulas to relax the body and allow it to use its full energy for healing.

Aphrodisiac A substance believed to arouse sexual desire and improve sexual potency and power.

Arachidonic acid A liquid, unsaturated fatty acid essential in nutrition, found in peanut oil and soybean extract.

Arginine An amino acid at one time listed as essential. Although it is now agreed that arginine is manufactured by the body, it is also noted that this amino acid is not manufactured quickly enough for quick growth and emergency healing. Arginine is found in peanuts, sesame seeds, and peas. About 80 percent of the spermatozoon (male reproductive cell) is composed of arginine.

Aromatic An herb with a strong, volatile, and fragrant aroma. Medicinally, aromatics are used to relieve flatulence, open nasal passages, or eliminate phlegm, although many people regard them merely as pleasant fragrances; they are often added to medicines to improve their palatability.

Ascorbic acid Vitamin C as made in the laboratory. Natural vitamin C is composed of many factors.

Aspartic acid An amino acid manufactured by the body.

Astringent An agent that causes a constricting, drawing together, or binding effect, such as dehydration, thus checking the discharge of mucus or blood, or that closes skin pores, tightens muscles, and the like.

Atherosclerosis The gradual buildup of plaque on artery and blood vessel walls that can interfere with blood flow. As blood vessels narrow because of plaque buildup, blood flow can eventually be shut off, leading to heart attack or stroke.

Avicenna A Persian physician and philosopher (A.D. 980–1037) whose most famous medical work was a systematic encyclopedia based on the achievements of Greek physicians and his own experience.

Balsamic (1) The resinous, aromatic exudations of certain plants or trees; (2) a substance that has the odor of an aromatic substance called balsam, which is derived from various plants and used in medicinal preparations to heal or soothe.

Basal metabolic rate The rate at which the body burns or uses energy to support life-sustaining activities such as digestion and respiration.

Benzoic acid An acid that occurs naturally in all true resins and in cranberries and prunes. This organic chemical is a very important preservative (look at some food labels)—it prevents the growth of yeasts and molds, retards rancidity, and is odorless, tasteless, and non-toxic. It is also a very strong antiseptic, has diuretic and antipyretic properties, and is the starting point in the manufacture of a large group of chemicals used in medicine, dyes, plastics, and insect repellent. It is used in cosmetics and soaps to retard darkening.

Beta carotene The orange pigment found in many fruits and vegetables. Not a completely formed nutrient, it can be easily converted by the body into vitamin A.

Bile A thick, bitter fluid stored in the gallbladder and secreted by the liver; it aids fat digestion.

Bioflavonoids Formerly called vitamin P or citrin, these substances (plant glycosides) strengthen the walls of the blood capillaries and have a very broad protective influence on the entire inner environment of the body. Naturally occurring flavone or coumarin derivatives show vitamin P activity, notably rutin, hesperidin, and esculin.

Biotin (or vitamin H) A member of the vitamin B complex family. A bacterial growth factor found in liver, egg yolk, and yeast.

Bromelain A mixture of proteolytic (protein-digesting) enzymes obtained principally from the pineapple plant. It improves the activity of antibiotics, has anti-inflammatory action, and enhances circulation and the immune system. In clinical tests bromelain reduces angina pectoris, or chest pain.

Bruise (1) An injury, especially produced by a blow or collision, that does not break the surface of the skin but by rupturing small blood vessels near the surface causes blood to flow into the tissues, resulting in discoloration; (2) to crush or mangle the tissues of a plant to release its properties.

Butyric acid This short-chain fatty acid (SCFA) provides an important energy source for cells that line the colon. In fact, butyrate is the preferred source for energy metabolism in the colon, and its production may be responsible for the anticancer properties of dietary fiber.

Calmative An agent having a mild sedative action.

Calorie A unit of heat. A calorie is the amount of heat required to raise the temperature of one gram of water one degree Centigrade. It is used as a unit for measuring the energy produced by food when oxidized by the body.

Carbohydrate Carbohydrates are short- and long-chain molecules much richer in oxygen than are proteins and fats. The long-chain fibrous polymers make up cellulose, pectins, and, in animals, glycogen. The basic units are simpler sugars that may have from two to six carbon chains. Glucose, fructose, and galactose are simple six-carbon chains. Two hexoses combined form disaccharides such as lactose and sucrose. Long chains make up the complicated carbohydrates such as starch and glycogen. All carbohydrates must be broken down in the digestive tract into the simple sugars, which are then absorbed into the blood. Pure carbohydrates, especially sugars, are not found free in nature. When plants lay down starch in the wheat kernel, it is associated with smaller quantities of protein and fat but also with minerals and vitamins. The enzymes required to convert the sugars into starch are not removed when the process is completed. Germination reverses the chemical reaction and converts starch into the simple sugars, using the same enzymes that were used to synthesize the starch. When this starch in its original form is consumed, the same vitamins and minerals are available to be used by the body. When man refines carbohydrates and sugars, he produces starches and sugars free of the other nutrients with which they are normally associated. This is one of the reasons why excessive consumption of sugar generally depletes the body's stores of vitamins.

Caries Tooth decay.

Carminative An agent that checks the formation of gas in the gastrointestinal tract and aids in dispelling whatever gas has already formed. The after-dinner mint is the most familiar carminative. Among other herbs and spices used as carminatives are anise, caraway, cloves, dill, and ginger.

Carnitine A vitamin-like compound that stimulates the breakdown of long-chain fatty acids by mitochondria (energy-producing units in cells). Carnitine is essential in the transport of fatty acids into the mitochondria; it is synthesized from the amino acid lysine in the liver, kidney, and brain. Carnitine increases HDL ("good") cholesterol levels, while decreasing triglyceride and LDL ("bad") cholesterol levels.

Carotene Carotenes or carotenoids represent the most widespread group of naturally occurring pigments in nature. They are a highly colored (red to yellow) group of fat-soluble compounds that function in plants to protect against damage caused during photosynthesis. Carotenes are best known for their capacity for conversion into vitamin A, for their antioxidant activity, and for their correlation with the maximum life-span potential of humans, other primates, and mammals. The leading sources of carotenes are dark green leafy vegetables and yellow-orange fruits and vegetables.

Catarrh An inflammation of any mucous membrane (usually the nasal and air passages) characterized by congestion and the secretion of mucus.

Cathartic An agent (laxative or purgative) that causes the evacuation of the bowels. A laxative provides a gentle stimulation and quickening of peristaltic action, while a purgative, used only in stubborn conditions, stimulates the secretions of the intestines and is much more forceful.

Chelate A chelate is a compound formed between a metallic ion and an organic molecule having two neighboring groups capable of simultaneously combining with the metal to form a ring structure. The term *chelate* is derived from the Greek *chela*, meaning "claw," because the chelate resembles a claw, with the metal ion clutched between the pincers of the organic molecule. Chelates have very high stability, and as a result the metal in them is no longer available for many of its usual reactions and many of its biological, chemical, and physical properties are changed. EDTA (ethylenediaminetetracetic acid) is probably the most potent chelating agent known, and the chelates that it forms with heavy metals are very stable. In mammals it is very effective for detoxicating poisonous metals such as lead, which are then excreted as nontoxic chelates. The toxicity of this compound is so low that lead EDTA is used clinically as an X-ray contrast material.

Chlorophyll The green pigment of plants found in the chloroplast compartment of plant cells. In the chloroplast, electromagnetic energy (light) is converted into chemical energy through the process known as photosynthesis. The natural chlorophyll found in green plants is fat-soluble and is used as a vulnerary. Chlorophyll seems to thicken and strengthen the walls of the body cells of animals, increase cellular resistance to disease organisms, and inhibit the growth of disease bacteria. It needs to be in contact with living tissues to work.

Cholagogue An agent that stimulates the gallbladder and biliary duct to discharge bile into the small intestine and increase the body's excretion of cholesterol.

Choleretic An agent that stimulates the liver to increase its production of bile, which helps emulsify fats in the duodenum and increase peristalsis.

Cholesterol A crystalline fatty alcohol, insoluble in water, occurring in animal fats, oils, bile, blood, nerve tissue, gallstones, and elsewhere. Large amounts are found in egg yolks, butter, animal fats, and all shellfish. The generally accepted rule for cholesterol is that your count should be kept under 220 (milligrams of cholesterol per hundred milliliters, or about six cubic inches, of blood). Most of what we use does not come from food, however, but is manufactured in our liver and intestinal lining. Cholesterol is a complicated four-ring alcohol that, despite its structural complexity, our body easily makes out of simple acetic acid, the main constituent of ordinary vinegar. Although cholesterol is one of the most important constituents of cells, its function is still mysterious, being somehow involved in their structure and permeability. It is also a major ingredient in bile and of gallstones. From it are made the bile acids, the vitamin D synthesized in the skin by sunlight, and the sex and adrenal hormones. These last include the cortisone group that strongly affects, among other things, the metabolism of proteins, fats, and carbohydrates, immune and inflammatory responses, wound healing, permeability of blood vessels, and muscle integrity.

Choline A vitamin of the B complex. Choline performs the vital function of making the main components of the cell membranes, such as phosphatidylcholine (lecithin) and sphingomyelin. Choline is also required for the proper metabolism of fats; without choline, fats become trapped in the liver and block metabolism. The richest sources of choline are brewer's yeast, soybeans, turnips, mustard and spinach greens, peas, cabbage, and wheat germ.

Citrin Vitamin P, now called bioflavonoids. Citrin reduces the permeability and fragility of capillaries. It is found in lemon juice and paprika, among other sources.

Colic Paroxysmal pain in the abdomen or bowel due to overdistension, toxemia, inflammation, or obstruction.

Contraindication A certain condition for which a particular herb (or other plant) is not recommended.

Corm A solid, swollen part of a stem, usually underground, protected by a thin layer of scale leaves. It differs from a true bulb in that it is solid and sends down a root when a new growing season begins. Usually starchy and edible.

Counterirritant An agent used to produce superficial inflammation of the skin in order to relieve deeper inflammation.

Cruciferous vegetables A group of plants that are members of the mustard family and have cross-shaped blossoms: cauliflower, cabbage, broccoli, collard greens, mustard greens, bok choy, brussels sprouts, radishes, rutabagas, and turnips are all part of this family. Studies conducted on animals found these vegetables may help protect against cancer.

Daidzein Along with genistein, a plant estrogen and isoflavone uniquely abundant in soy foods. An anticarcinogen (especially of breast cancer), daidzein also relieves menopausal symptoms and reduces cholesterol levels.

Decoction A preparation made by simmering roots, bark, seeds, or stems of herbs in water.

Demulcent An agent that is soothing to the intestinal tract, usually of an oily or mucilaginous nature, and that provides a protective coating and allays irritation. It also soothes and softens the part to which it is applied, acting to relieve irritation. Glycerin and olive oil are well-known examples.

Depurative Having cleansing properties, but especially a blood purifier.

Diaphoretic An herb or substance taken internally to increase perspiration, usually through expansion of capillaries near the skin. Such medicines are also called sudorifics and have been used along with sweat baths throughout history to promote general and specific health.

Diastase A starch-changing enzyme.

Dietary fiber Originally the definition of *dietary fiber* was restricted to the sum of plant compounds that are not digestible by the secretions of the human digestive tract. For everyday purposes, however, the term refers to the components of plant cell walls as well as to the indigestible residues. The composition of the plant cell wall varies according to the species of plant. Dietary fiber provides a deterrent to colon and breast cancer and is also responsible for maintaining a healthy gastrointestinal tract and preventing constipation and other problems in the gut. **Soluble fiber** dissolves in water, is important in the digestion and absorption of food, and may help lower blood cholesterol levels. Some studies suggest soluble fiber may also help to regulate blood sugar levels in people with diabetes. Foods rich in soluble fiber include whole-grain oats and barley, oat bran, citrus fruits, and dried beans and other legumes. **Insoluble fiber** does not dissolve in water but provides bulk that helps to satisfy the appetite, as well as hastening transit of wastes through the colon. By diluting carcinogens in the large intestine and stool, fiber may also help protect against their harmful effects. Foods rich in insoluble fiber include vegetables; wheat, corn, and rice bran; whole-grain wheat, corn, and rice; and dried beans and peas.

Dioscorides A Greek medical man of the first century A.D. His *De Materia Medica* was the leading text on pharmacology for sixteen centuries. The treatise details the properties of about six hundred medicinally valuable plants and animal products.

Dithiolthiones Phytochemicals that boost levels of enzymes that stop carcinogens from damaging cells. They're found in abundance in broccoli.

Diuretic An agent that increases the secretion and discharge of urine. Notable herbs are dandelion, juniper berries, and lemon juice.

Dysentery An inflammation of the colon marked by intense diarrhea with the passage of small amounts of mucus and blood, usually caused by pathogenic bacteria or protozoans.

Dyspepsia A condition of disturbed digestion characterized by nausea, heartburn, pain, and gas.

Ecbolic A drug that accelerates uterine contractions, primarily used to facilitate delivery (childbirth).

Edema Abnormal accumulation of serum fluid in an organ or body cavity.

Electrolytes Chemical substances that carry electrical charges when dissolved in water. They are either positive—like sodium, potassium, calcium, and others—or negative, like chloride and phosphate. Potassium, sodium, and chloride are the most prominent of the electrolytes, and they interact to regulate a number of key physiological functions. Electrolytes control osmosis, the movement of water from outside of the cell through the membrane and into the cell; they help maintain the acid-base balance required for normal cellular activity; and they carry electrical currents that travel down nerves—allowing muscles to contract—and release some hormones and neurotransmitters along the way.

Elixir A sweetened aromatic preparation, about 25 percent alcohol, used as a vehicle for medicinal substances for its flavoring or medicinal qualities.

Ellagic acid A phytochemical phenol found in grapes, cherries, and strawberries. One of ellagic acid's primary actions is to protect against damage to our chromosomes and to block the cancer-causing actions of many pollutants. Ellagic acid is a potent antioxidant and has shown an ability to increase many of the body's antioxidant compounds.

Emetic An agent that causes or promotes vomiting.

Emmenagogue A substance that promotes the onset of menstruation. Some emmenagogues are so strong that they have been used to induce abortion.

Emollient An agent that will soften and soothe the surface of the body when applied locally to the skin or other exposed tissue. Similar to demulcents, emollients are used externally.

Emulsion A preparation composed of totally unhomogeneous (non-similar) substances that are intimately mixed, causing one to be suspended in the other—oil and egg in mayonnaise, for example.

Enema A rectal injection of liquid, often used to encourage the evacuation of the bowels.

Enzymes Any of various organic proteins secreted by the body that act as catalysts in inducing chemical changes in other substances, particularly in digestion. Or, in simpler terms, enzymes are the communication particles of the body. They carry and sometimes are the nutrients traveling from one gland or organ to another. They are catalysts and not only allow intercommunication but also facilitate absorption.

Errhine An agent that induces sneezing; also known as a sternutator.

Essence (1) The volatile matter constituting perfume; (2) an alcohol or water-alcohol solution of medicinal substances, usually 10 to 20 percent alcohol.

Expectorant A medicinal substance that helps in the expulsion of mucus or phlegm from the throat or lungs (by coughing, sneezing, or spitting).

Extract A solution representing four to six times the strength of the crude drug.

Exudate The liquid that oozes from an inflamed area; the products, such as gums, resins, and mucilages, formed in the metabolic processes of a number of plants.

Fats The fatty portion of foods, free of nitrogen but containing carbon and hydrogen. Fats range from short-chain fatty acids to long-chain fatty acids and are combined with other constituents. Fats are not soluble in water. They have three main functions: (1) to provide supportive structures; (2) to participate in chemical reactions in the body; and (3) to store extra calories. Each gram provides nine calories. If the same quantity of energy were stored as protein or carbohydrate, twice as much volume would be required. Extra sugar is converted into fat and stored in the fat depots of the body. When required, the fats are released and metabolized. Fats are therefore the reserve depots in the body and buffer the body against variations in food intake. Quality of fats is judged by the degree of unsaturation—saturated fat has no double bonds, while an unsaturated fat does contain double bonds. Unsaturated fats are liquid at room temperature. The liquidity of the fat, therefore, is a measure of the degree of unsaturation. Too much fat in the diet will lead to obesity and perhaps to elevated fat levels in the blood. But this seems to be infrequent, perhaps because it is more difficult to overconsume fat as compared to sugar. When too much fat is present in the diet, one quickly becomes satiated; furthermore, fat tends to decrease the emptying time of the stomach and gives one a sense of fullness that lasts for many hours. This effectively deters the subject from continuing to overconsume fats.

Saturated fats are found in animal products and are hard at room temperature. More than any other type of fat, they infiltrate and fill your fat cells. Sources are butter, cheese, egg yolk, lard, meat, and dairy products. Other saturated fats include coconut and coconut oil along with palm oil, and these appear to be beneficial for your body. Polyunsaturated fats are most commonly found in liquid vegetable oils. Sources are various oils, fish, and margarine. Monounsaturated fats are sometimes called "neutral fats" and may be helpful in washing other fats from your cells. Sources are cashews, olives, and olive oil.

Fatty acids Any of numerous acids that occur naturally, usually in the form of esters in fats, waxes, and essential oils. Omega-3 fatty acids are polyunsaturated fats that may help reduce the risk of heart disease. Saturated fatty acids contain all the hydrogen they are able to carry and tend to be stable; they are ordinarily somewhat solid at room temperature. Unsaturated fatty acids have room for many more hydrogen atoms, which they do not carry. Quality is determined by the length of the chain. Essential fatty acids (EFAs) are long-chain molecules containing eighteen, twenty, and twenty-two carbon atoms per molecule (arachidonic acid, for example). They are related to the prostaglandins. EFAs are essential because the body needs them and cannot manufacture them itself. You must get them through your diet. There are two EFAs—linoleic acid (LA), more commonly called omega-6 fatty acids, and alpha-linolenic acid (LNA), or omega-3 fatty acids. EFAs are precursors to prostaglandins, hormonelike substances with powerful and pervasive effects in the body. Prostaglandins are involved in keeping platelets from clumping together, in the relaxing and contracting of blood vessels, and in controlling inflammation, fever, and pain. Omega-3 fatty acids have been demonstrated to suppress tumor growth. They protect against most of the degenerative diseases, including arthritis, diabetes, and heart disease. They improve immune function and alleviate skin disorders. The richest sources are cold-water fish oils and flaxseed oil. Omega-6 fatty acids are fairly widespread in our diet, as they are found in nuts, seeds, grains, and most vegetable oils. However, because EFAs are so biochemically active, they are extremely unstable. EFA deficiency is associated with cardiovascular disease, atherosclerosis, inflammatory bowel disease, cystic fibrosis, brain and behavioral dysfunction, strokes, hypertension, celiac disease, kidney failure, pressure in the eyes and joints, water retention, allergic response, multiple sclerosis, and cancer. When EFAs are added back to the diet, many of these maladies are ameliorated.

Febrifuge An agent that reduces fever.

Fiber Indigestible substances found in food. Most fibers are carbohydrates such as cellulose, hemicellulose, pectin, and gum. But lignin, a noncarbohydrate woody material that makes up the stems and bark of many plants, is sometimes classified as fiber. While the body lacks enzymes necessary to digest fiber, the substance is critical to health. Fiber can help lower blood cholesterol levels, prevent constipation, and possibly protect against certain types of cancer.

Flavonoids A group of plant pigments largely responsible for the colors of fruits and flowers. In plants flavonoids protect against environmental stress, while in humans they seem to function as "biological response modifiers." Flavonoid molecules are unique in being active against a wide variety of oxidants and free radicals; they also make platelets of blood cells less likely to clot. Bioflavonoids are flavonoids with recognized biological activity.

Fomentation An application of heat and moisture to the body to ease pain or reduce inflammation.

Free radicals Unpaired oxygen molecules that cause cellular damage by stealing molecules from healthy cells.

Galactogogue A substance that increase the secretion of milk.

Genistein A compound found in high concentrations in soybeans and alfalfa sprouts, as well as in cruciferous vegetables, such as broccoli and cabbage. Genistein aids menopausal symptoms, inhibits angiogenesis, and may block some cancers.

Glucose A simple sugar used by the body for quick energy.

Glutathione Called the "supreme antioxidant," glutathione is touted to be able to reverse DNA damage caused by X-rays, excessive sunlight, tobacco smoke, estrogen, drugs, toxins, and other dangerous environmental substances. A deficiency of this enzyme is associated with hemolytic anemia.

Glycoside A complex organic substance that when hydrolyzed (split by the action of water, acids, or enzymes) separates into two parts: a sugar (glycone) component and a nonsugar (aglycone) component. Glycosides also include saponins, a characteristic of which is producing a soapy foam.

Goitrogenic A substance that can induce goiter if the level of iodine in the diet is not fairly high. The thiocyanates in the brassicas (cabbage family), excess calcium, and sulfonamides all act as goitrogenic factors in the diet, while high levels of the halogens, chlorine, bromine, or fluorine may induce goiter by stimulating the excretion of iodine from the body.

Gram (g) A metric unit of mass, equal to a thousandth of a kilogram. There are about 453.6 grams in a pound. Thirty grams are roughly equivalent to one ounce.

Griping A substance that causes a clutching, painful, or grasping feeling in the bowels.

Groat A term referring to any hulled grain, it most often refers to oats and buckwheat.

Hemostatic Any substance that prevents bleeding, arrests hemorrhaging, or promotes clotting of blood.

Hesperiden A crystallizable bioflavonoid also known as vitamin P occurring in most citrus fruits, especially in the white of the rind of oranges and lemons.

High-density lipoprotein (HDL) One of several transport compounds made of protein and various amounts and types of fat. HDL packages carry cholesterol away from the arteries and blood vessels to the liver, where it can be processed. High levels of HDL are associated with a decreased risk for heart disease.

Homeopathy A system of healing and therapeutics developed by Samuel Hahnemann, advocating the administration of small doses of a drug that would, in healthy persons, produce symptoms of the disease being treated.

Hormone One of a group of powerful substances secreted by different body glands and tissues to help regulate different body functions. Insulin regulates blood sugar; thyroid hormones regulate metabolism. Glands that produce hormones include the adrenals, gonads (ovaries and testes), pancreas, thyroid, parathyroid, and pituitary. Other tissues such as the kidneys, intestines, and brain can also secrete hormones.

Hybrid seed A cross between different varieties designed to achieve desired cosmetic, nutritional, or harvesting properties. Not capable of reproducing like heirloom seeds, hybrids have lost the natural integrity and viability of the original seed.

Hydrating Having the capacity to maintain or restore the normal proportion of fluid in the body or skin. Hydrating agents are used in cosmetics to keep the skin moist, firm, and young looking.

Hydrogenation The process of adding hydrogen to unsaturated oils to turn them into semi-solid fats, destroying the double bonds in the fatty acids and saturating the carbon atoms with hydrogen; the resulting fats contain more saturated fat than the liquids from which they were made.

Immunity The ability to resist infection; largely the result of substances in the immune system (antibodies) that recognize and fight off foreign invaders that cause disease.

Infusion A preparation made by pouring boiling water on dried or fresh flowers or leaves and then steeping. All herbal infusions and decoctions should be freshly prepared and used within twelve hours.

Inositol A member of the B complex group. Inositol functions quite closely with choline. It is a primary component of cell membranes, where it is bound as phosphatidylinositol. Like choline, inositol promotes the flow of fat to and from the liver and has shown some promise as a treatment in diabetic neuropathy. Good sources include citrus fruits, whole grains, nuts and seeds, and legumes.

Insulin A hormone secreted by the pancreas in response to an elevation in blood sugar. Insulin is the key that unlocks body cells so that glucose can enter. Without insulin or sufficient amounts of insulin, glucose would concentrate in the blood.

Inulin A polysaccharide found in the roots of various sunflower family members that is medicinal for diabetics.

Ipriflavone An isoflavone or compound that naturally occurs in foods and plants. The chemical name for ipriflavone is 7-isopropoxy isoflavone. Alfalfa is the richest source of ipriflavone, but it is also found in propolis (from bees) and some other plants. The subject of more than sixty different clinical studies in Italy, Japan, and Hungary, ipriflavone has been shown to stimulate the synthesis and secretion of calcitonin, a hormone that promotes calcium metabolism; to promote bone formation and increase bone mineral density; and to decrease fracture rate and complement prescription estrogen.

Isoflavones Found in soybeans, isoflavones block the absorption of estrogen by cells, thus reducing the risk of certain estrogen-dependent malignancies such as breast cancer. Other flavonoids, in fruits and vegetables from berries to carrots, block receptor sites for hormones that may promote cancer.

I.U. (or IU) Abbreviation for International Unit. One milligram of ascorbic acid (vitamin C) is equal to twenty International Units of vitamin C as defined and adopted by the Permanent Commission on Biological Standardization of the League of Nations in June 1934. Other vitamins have different definitions.

Kilogram (kg) A unit of weight and mass equal to one thousand grams.

Lactose A disaccharide (double sugar) composed of galactose and glucose found in milk products. Also called milk sugar. Many people are lactose-intolerant because they lack the enzyme needed to digest milk sugar. Without this enzyme, drinking milk can bring on abdominal pain, nausea, and diarrhea.

Laetrile A substance prepared from apricot pits and used as a cancer treatment in some areas other than the United States.

Laxative An herb, food, or medicine that causes elimination of the feces. Laxatives work by stimulating peristaltic action of the intestinal wall, by moistening the colon, by increasing the secretion of bile, or by relaxing intestinal cramps.

Legume Part of a large plant family of herbs, shrubs, and trees, legumes have pods or seeds that are higher in protein than most other plant foods: kidney beans, soybeans, peanuts, black-eyed peas, and lentils are all part of this family.

Leucine An essential amino acid.

Lignans Compounds found in high-fiber foods that show important properties, such as anticancer, antibacterial, antifungal, and antiviral activity. Flaxseeds are the most abundant source of lignans, but other seeds, grains, and legumes are also good sources.

Liminoid Found in the essential oils of orange and other citrus fruit peels (and the white pulp between segments) as well as in dill, caraway, and lemongrass, liminoid inhibits the formation and reduces the size of tumors in animals.

Limonene Found in citrus fruits, limonene boosts production of enzymes that help neutralize potential carcinogens.

Linolenic acid An unsaturated fatty acid essential in nutrition. Also called an omega-3 fatty acid.

Lipids Fatty compounds present in most tissues and especially in the blood.

Lipoic acid An antioxidant naturally produced in the body instrumental in maintaining the energy system of the body. It differs from other antioxidants in several important ways: first, unlike other antioxidants that have a specific job in the body, lipoic acid is so versatile that it can serve as a "free agent" and pinch-hit for other antioxidants when they are in short supply; second, lipoic acid greatly enhances the potency of vitamins C and E, antioxidants that are more powerful and their beneficial effects more long lasting when combined than when they stand alone; third, lipoic acid raises metabolism, helping those who need extra energy to maintain their strength and stamina by increasing energy production in muscle cells and reducing the soreness and stiffness that frequently accompanies a rigorous workout; lastly, one of its most important functions is to normalize blood sugar levels, particularly helpful for the many middle-aged and older men and women who develop insulin resistance, a condition that affects some sixteen million Americans.

Low-density lipoproteins (LDL) One of several transport compounds made of protein and various amounts and types of fat. LDL carry cholesterol from the liver to body tissues for storage. High levels of LDL are associated with an increased risk for heart disease.

Lutein Along with zeaxanthin, an antioxidant and yellow carotenoid found in the eye. Lutein filters out harmful blue light and protects against macular degeneration, the leading cause of blindness in people over sixty-five years of age. A member of the carotenoid family, lutein is found in deep green leafy vegetables such as spinach, kale, and turnip greens.

Lycopene The pigment that gives tomatoes, watermelon, pink grapefruit, and guavas their red color. It is a fat-soluble antioxidant related to beta carotene. A carotenoid (as is beta carotene), lycopene serves as an antioxidant, blocks UVA and UVB rays, and is strongly suspected of arresting the growth of cancer cells, especially of the prostate. Lycopene is especially plentiful in tomatoes and tomato-based products and works better when combined with a small amount of fat. Lycopene has roughly twice the power of beta carotene and ten times the strength of vitamin E when it comes to neutralizing free radicals. In the human body, you will find lycopene in the blood and the skin.

Lysine An essential amino acid. The best sources are fish, cheese, meat, eggs, and yeast.

Megadose A dose that is ten times the level recommended as safe and adequate. The term is typically used when referring to vitamin supplements that offer a nutrient in excessive amounts, making the nutrient more like a drug and thus bringing on druglike side effects.

Menopause The cessation of menstruation and the fluctuating hormone levels and biological changes that accompany it. Women enter menopause at around the age of forty-five to fifty.

Methionine An essential amino acid. The richest sources of methionine are eggs, cheese, sardines, rice, and sunflower seeds.

Milligram (mg) One thousandth of a gram ($^1/_{1,000}$ g).

Minerals Inorganic elements, some of which are known to be vital to health in small or trace quantities.

Monoterpenes Antioxidants that also boost immuno-protective enzymes. Monoterpenes are found in parsley, carrots, yams, tomatoes, eggplants, basil, citrus fruits, broccoli, and other vegetables.

Mucilage A gel-forming fiber generally found within the inner layer (endosperm) of grains, legumes, nuts, and seeds. Guar gum, found in most legumes, is the most widely studied plant mucilage. Guar gum and other mucilages, including psyllium seed husk and glucomannan, are perhaps the most potent cholesterol-lowering agents of gel-forming fibers. In addition, mucilage fibers have been shown to reduce fasting and after-meal glucose and insulin levels in both healthy and diabetic subjects.

Mucilaginous An herb that is full of or secretes a sticky or slimy, gelatin-like substance that is soothing to inflammations. Mucilages and gums form gels when mixed with water and are used externally to soothe inflamed skin, while internally their bulking effect is laxative and cleansing.

Narcotic A drug that in moderate doses allays sensibility, relieves pain, and produces sleep but if misused, or taken in large doses, is poisonous to the system.

Nervine An herb that relaxes the whole body or a part of the body by affecting the nervous system, giving a feeling of healthy well-being.

Neuralgia A severe recurrent pain along one or more nerves, usually not associated with changes in the nerve structure.

Neurotransmitter A chemical in the body that transmits a nerve impulse from one cell to the next. Serotonin, a compound that may help improve mood, is an example of one of these chemical messengers.

Neutrceutical A term coined in the 1990s by Dr. Stephen Felice and defined as a substance that is a food or is isolated/purified from food, and which has shown medical or health benefits.

Nutrient density The amount of nutrients in a serving of food in relation to that food's total energy contribution. If a food delivers a large amount of nutrients and has very few calories it is considered nutrient-dense.

Nutrients Substances obtained from food that promote growth, maintenance, or repair of worn or injured body tissues. There are six classes of nutrients: carbohydrate, protein, fat, vitamins, minerals, and water.

Nutritive A substance that is thought to gradually increase some function of the body, generally by supplying nutrients rather than by stimulation of the nervous or circulatory system.

Omega-3 fatty acids These include alpha-linolenic acid, eicosapentaenoic acid (EPA), and docosahexaenoic acid (DHA). Alpha-linolenic acid is the original omega-3 fatty acid and is used in the formation of cell membranes. Best food sources include flaxseeds, hemp seeds, pumpkin seeds, walnuts, and dark green leafy vegetables. EPA is a derivative of alpha-linolenic acid needed to make anti-inflammatory, hormone-like prostaglandins. DHA is also a derivative of alpha-linolenic acid and is necessary for proper brain and nervous system development and visual function. Both EPA and DHA are found in cold-water fish (wild not farmed salmon, trout, tuna, herring, mackerel, and sardines) and fish liver oil supplements and are also available in vegetarian supplements made from micro-algae.

Omega-6 fatty acids These include linoleic acid, gamma-linolenic acid, and arachidonic acid. Linoleic acid is the original omega-6 fatty acid and is used in cell membrane formation. Best food sources include sesame seeds, pumpkin seeds, many nuts, and most vegetable oils. Safflower and sunflower oils are the richest sources. Gamma-linolenic acid is a derivative of linoleic acid used to make prostaglandins. Best food sources include evening primrose oil, borage oil, and black currant oil. Arachidonic acid is also a derivative of linoleic acid and is a precursor of inflammatory prostaglandins. Best food sources are meats and other animal products.

Pantothenic acid A member of the B complex family essential for cell growth. The richest sources of pantothenic acid are liver, yeast, rice polish extract, molasses, egg yolks, soybeans, peanuts, wheat germ, and dried peas and beans.

Pectin A substance found in all plant cell walls, as well as in the outer skin and rind of fruits and vegetables. For example, the rind of an orange contains 30 percent pectin, an apple peel 15 percent, and onion skins 12 percent. The gel-forming properties of pectin are well known to anyone who has made jelly or jam. Pectins also lower cholesterol levels by binding it along with bile acids in the intestines and promoting their excretion. Pectin is a type of fiber found in all green land plants. It provides the structural framework for fruits and vegetables and is considered harmless since it is not broken down by the body's digestive enzymes. When it reaches the colon, though, bacterial enzymes split the compound into fragments that raise the weight and frequency of the stool.

Peristalsis Involuntary, wavelike muscle contractions of the digestive tract that move its contents.

Pharmacognosy The science encompassing those phases of knowledge relating to natural products that are generally of medicinal value and primarily of plant origin.

Phenylalanine An essential amino acid. Foods richest in phenylalanine are sesame seeds, cottonseed, oats, cheese, eggs, and liver.

Phlegm Thick mucus, secreted by the respiratory tract lining.

Phosphatidylserine (PS) Phosphatidylserine belongs to a special category of fat-soluble substances called phospholipids. Phospholipids in general are essential components of cell membranes, and phosphatidylserine in particular is found in high concentrations in the brain. Found in only trace amounts in a typical diet, PS is found in very small amounts in lecithin. The body manufactures it from phospholipid building blocks. Along with other phospholipids, PS safely and effectively supports memory, learning, concentration, word recall, and a wide range of other cognitive brain functions.

Phytic acid A heat- and acid-stable astringent acid found in cereals, nuts, and seeds (especially in sesame seeds and soybeans) that protects against some cancers and may help control blood sugar, cholesterol, and triglycerides.

Phytochelatins Large plant molecules that lock around minerals and hold them, thus removing toxic minerals (such as cadmium, copper, mercury, and lead) from the body.

Phytochemical A biologically active substance in plants (*phyto*) responsible for giving them characteristics such as color, flavor, and natural disease resistance. Our common foods contain millions of phytochemicals. They are classified under five groups: indoles, thioallyl derivatives, antioxidants, phenolic compounds, and flavonoids. The indoles group includes broccoli, cabbage, and cauliflower and is necessary for healthy cells. Thioallyl derivates include garlic, leeks, and onions. This group boosts the immune system and helps rid the body of carcinogens. Antioxidants, which include beta carotene and vitamins C and E, are readily available in produce. Critical to the immune system and cellular health, they also promote healing and slow aging. Phenolic compounds, found in fruits, vegetables, and black or green tea, have antitumor and anticancer values. Flavonoids, found in soy products and apples, also contain antioxidants and are key to healthy growth and development of cells.

Phytoestrogens Plant estrogens that seem to act as a key to unlock and potentiate existing estrogen within the body, eliminating or easing many of the symptoms of low estrogen.

Placebo A pill or compound that is similar in appearance to an agent being tested in a clinical trial but has no effect. Often referred to as a sugar pill, it can contain other harmless and inactive substances.

Pliny the Elder (A.D. 23–79) Author of the *Natural History*, a work comprised of thirty-seven volumes; books XX to XXXII deal with medicines derived from plants and from the bodies of humans and other animals.

Polyphenols A phytochemical that may help detoxify carcinogens. Research has shown that polyphenols protect against several kinds of cancer, including that of esophageal, rectal, gallbladder, and endometrial. These chemicals are found abundantly in green tea.

Polysaccharide A carbohydrate that can be decomposed by hydrolysis into two or more molecules of monosaccharides (simple sugars).

Polyunsaturated A chemical term used to describe a fatty acid particle with four, six, or more hydrogen atoms missing. There are three polyunsaturated fatty acids considered essential for nutrition: linoleic, linolenic, and arachidonic.

Potassium-magnesium aspartate A combination of minerals that produces a dramatic increase in physical endurance in over 90 percent of the people who took them, including those with chronic fatigue syndrome. The results were so impressive the compound was sold as a prescription drug in the early 1960s, though shortly thereafter the product was taken off the market. The most common forms of these minerals are oxides, chlorides, and gluconates, but beware: they do not work like the aspartic acid form.

Potpourri A mixture of dried flowers and spices used for scent or perfume.

Poultice A soft mass, usually heated then spread on cloth and applied to sores or inflamed areas to supply warmth, relieve pain, or act as a counterirritant or an antiseptic.

Pregnenolone (Preg) A natural steroid hormone that cannot be patented, Preg is derivative of cholesterol and is made in many organs and tissues that produce steroid hormones. The most common of these organs are the adrenal glands, liver, skin, and gonads (testicles and ovaries). Even the brain and retinas make Preg. It can be easily converted into DHEA, which in turn is converted into androgens, estrogens, and other steroids.

Prophylactic An agent that protects or defends against disease.

Protein A nitrogen-containing foodstuff. Proteins are made up of smaller molecules or units called amino acids. Of the two dozen or so amino acids, eight are considered to be essential since they cannot be made in the body. The others can be synthesized from other substances. However, a deficiency of any amino acid, either because there is too little in the food or because too little can be made in the body, will produce some interference in metabolism. Proteins provide the amino acids that are used by the body to synthesize tissue, enzymes, and so on. They are not primarily calorie sources. Each gram provides four calories (120 calories per ounce of pure protein). Protein requirements vary with state of health, physical activity, and other factors. The optimum quantity of protein has the right amount of essential amino acids to provide for growth and repair. Too little is dangerous. Too much is wasteful. All people should determine from their own sense of well-being what the optimum requirement is for themselves. A protein deficiency or an imbalance of amino acids can cause mental depression, apathy, peevishness, irritability, and a desire to be left alone.

Purgative A cleansing agent that will purge the bowels, such as a strong laxative.

Quercetin A powerful antioxidant that can prevent the oxidation of the LDL form of cholesterol. Quercetin helps block this oxidation, as does vitamin E. Higher intakes of flavonoid-rich foods like black tea, onions, grapefruit, and apples have been shown to reduce the risk of dying by heart attack by 50 percent. Red and yellow onions are a rich source of quercetin, a remarkable phytochemical that is a natural anti-inflammatory and also protects against heart disease and some forms of cancer. Studies have shown that the more onions we eat, the lower our risk of stomach cancer and heart attack.

Recommended Dietary Allowances (RDA) The base amount of a nutrient needed by normal, healthy people, as determined by the Food and Nutrition Board of the National Academy of Sciences.

Refrigerant An old medical term referring to plant drugs that cool the blood and reduce fever.

Restorative A substance that serves to bring a person to consciousness or back to normal vigor.

Resveratol A polyphenol phytochemical found in grapes that may help protect against heart disease.

Rhizome An elongated, thickened, usually horizontal underground plant stem that sends out roots below and shoots above. It is differentiated from ordinary rootstock by the presence of nodes, buds, and occasionally scalelike leaves. One example of a rhizome is ginger.

Rubefacient A substance that increases blood circulation to the area where it is applied (turning it red), usually on the skin but sometimes internally. Its function is to draw inflammation and congestion from deeper areas.

Rutin A bright yellow bioflavonoid obtained chiefly from buckwheat and having an action similar to vitamin P. It is used with vitamin C in the treatment of capillary fragility.

Salve A healing or soothing ointment.

Saponins Compounds that form stable froths or foams when shaken in water. Their healing effect resides in their capacity to break up red blood cells.

Sedative An herb that greatly quiet the nervous system.

Serotonin A neurotransmitter made within the brain from the amino acid tryptophan. It is believed to promote sleepiness and to have a calming effect on mood.

Soporific A substance that induces drowsiness or sleep.

Stimulant An agent that produces a temporary increase in the various functional actions of the body, such as quickening digestion or raising body temperature. It does this quickly, unlike a tonic, which stimulates general health over a period of time. Unlike a narcotic, it does not necessarily produce a feeling of general well-being, which a narcotic produces by depressing nerve centers. Among the best-known plant stimulants are cinnamon, cloves, ginger, horseradish, pepper, peppermint, and sage.

Stomachic An agent that gives strength and tone to the stomach or stimulates the appetite by promoting digestive secretions. Stomachics can also stimulate the secretion of hydrochloric acid.

Styptic An agent that contracts tissues or that checks bleeding by contracting the blood vessels.

Sudorific An agent that induces perspiration: diaphoretic.

Sulforaphane A phytochemical that stimulates the production of enzymes that disarm free radicals before they can harm healthy cells. Sulforaphane is found in broccoli, brussels sprouts, cabbage, and kale.

Tannins Organic substances of diverse composition with pronounced astringent properties that react with protein. One of the best known uses of tannins is in preserving animal hides by turning them into leather; tannins also soothe inflamed mucous membranes and promote wound healing and the formation of new skin.

Tincture An alcohol or water-alcohol fluid extraction of medicinal herbs that concentrates herbal properties and can be kept at full potency for years. Tinctures were particularly popular with herbalists during the late nineteenth and early twentieth centuries. Usually a specified number of drops of tincture are mixed with a small amount of water or juice and taken according to directions.

Tisane An infusion of flowers.

Tocopherol Any of a group of alcohols having the properties of vitamin E. There are four tocopherols, and all possess vitamin E activity: alpha, beta, gamma, and delta. The main source is wheat germ oil.

Tonic An herb usually used by itself to strengthen or tone the body or some part of the body gradually by stimulating the nutrition of tissues within the body. Bitter tonics stimulate the flow of gastric juices, increasing the appetite and promoting the intake of food. Tonics are usually slightly stimulating, as opposed to being only nutritive. Whether an herb is regarded as a tonic, a nutritive builder, or a stimulant often has to do more with the dose or quantity used than with its actual properties. When tonics are used in formulas they are often referred to as "neutrals" (balancers).

Trans-fatty acids The altered fat compounds produced when polyunsaturated vegetable oils are hydrogenated into solid fats like margarine. Studies suggest that trans-fats can raise blood cholesterol levels.

Trypsin A protein-digesting enzyme.

Tryptophan An essential amino acid. The richest sources of tryptophan are leafy greens, mother's milk, and sesame seeds.

Unguent A fatty medicinal preparation for external use that liquefies when rubbed into the skin.

Unsaturated A chemical term used to describe a fatty acid particle with missing hydrogen atoms.

Vermifuge Any substance that destroys and expels intestinal worms and similar intestinal parasites upon ingestion or repeated ingestion. Also called an anthelmintic.

Vitamins Complex organic substances, small quantities of which are vital to health.

Vulnerary Any plant or substance used to treat wounds, usually an antibiotic or antiseptic that promotes healing through cell regeneration and repair. These were extremely important herbs in the days of hand-to-hand combat.

Xanthophyll This carotenoid, found in spinach and collard greens, appears to protect against age-related macular degeneration.

Zeaxanthin Found in green leafy vegetables, this antioxidant is also found in the macula of the eye and is believed to help preserve good vision.

ANNOTATED BIBLIOGRAPHY

Airola, Paavo. *Are You Confused?* Phoenix, Ariz.: Health Plus Publishers, 1971. Broad health overview, somewhat dated and dogmatic.

Andrews, Jean. *Peppers: The Domesticated Capsicums.* Austin, Tex.: University of Texas Press, 1984. Scientific and historical overview of the *Capsicum* genus, with lots of pictures.

Appleton, Nancy, Ph.D. *Lick the Sugar Habit.* New York: Avery Publishing Group, 1988. Exposé on sugar addiction and allergic responses; interesting information and very pertinent to our Western culture.

Baggett, Nancy, Ruth Glick, and Gloria Kaufer Greene. *Eat Your Vegetables!* New York: Times Books, 1985. A brief history of and recipes for the more common vegetables.

Bailey, Adrian (editor). *Cook's Ingredients.* Pleasantville, N.Y.: Reader's Digest Association, 1990. Very brief overview, with lots of pictures of kitchen ingredients, including meats.

Bailey, Liberty H. *How Plants Get Their Names.* New York: Dover Publications, 1963. I used the list of specific Latin names from the appendix. The rest of the book is slanted toward the horticulturist or botanist.

—. *Standard Cyclopedia of Horticulture.* New York: Macmillan, 1922. A discussion of all plants known to cultivation at the time. Encompassing six large volumes, it has a lot more information than most people would ever want or need to know. I used it for the history of plant names.

Baker, Elton, and Elizabeth Baker. *Bandwagon to Health.* Colorado: Drelwood Publications, 1984. Deals with transitional diet from processed to raw foods and leads reader through steps.

—. *The UnCook Book.* Washington: Drelwood Publications, 1980. Excellent book on raw foods and food combining, with delicious recipes.

Baker, Jerry. *Jerry Baker's Herbal Pharmacy.* Michigan: American Master Products, 2000.

Balch, James F., M.D., and Phyllis A. Balch, C.N.C. *Prescription for Nutritional Healing.* New York: Avery Publishing Group, 1990. Fairly comprehensive self-help guide organized by ailment.

Ballentine, Rudolph, M.D. *Diet & Nutrition: A Holistic Approach.* Honesdale, Pa.: Himalayan International Institute, 1982. A comprehensive study of nutrition and diet, and an overview of Ayurvedic principles.

Ballister, Barry. *Barry Ballister's Fruit and Vegetable Stand.* Woodstock, N.Y.: Overlook Press, 1987. Overview of fruits and vegetables written from the greengrocer's view. Some nutritional information and recipes.

Batmanghelidj, F., M.D. *Water for Health, for Healing, for Life: You're Not Sick, You're Thirsty!* New York: Warner Books, 2003.

Shows how water and sea salt can relieve a wide range of medical conditions.

Behr, Edward. *The Artful Eater: A Gourmet Investigates the Ingredients of Great Food.* New York: Atlantic Monthly Press, 1992. Origins and uses of some familiar ingredients.

Bergner, Paul. *The Healing Power of Minerals, Special Nutrients, and Trace Elements.* Rocklin, Calif.: Prima Publishing, 1997. Just what it says. A lot of Price-Potternger Nutrition Foundation information.

Bianchini, Francesco, Francesco Corbetta, and Marilena Pistoia. Translated by Italia and Alberto Mancinelli. *The Complete Book of Fruits and Vegetables.* New York: Crown Publishers, 1975. Beautiful illustrations; the text leans heavily toward botany.

Bicknell, Franklin, and Frederick Prescott. *The Vitamins in Medicine.* London: William Heinemann Medical Books Ltd., 1948.

Bieler, Henry G., M.D. *Food Is Your Best Medicine.* New York: Ballantine Books, 1982. Discusses the body and its operations, the genesis of diseases, and how foods can rebuild the body. Tends to ramble.

Bragg, Paul C. *The Shocking Truth About Water.* Desert Hot Springs, Calif.: Health Science, 1975. Explains why water is a prime requisite for health, what actions it performs within the body, the best types of water, and how to find them. Fascinating little book, well worth reading.

Brandt, Johanna. *The Grape Cure.* St. Catherines, Ontario, Canada: Provoker Press, 1967. Story of the author's miraculous recovery from cancer and her attempts to help others in the United States.

Brothwell, Don, and Patricia Brothwell. *Food in Antiquity: A Survey of the Diet of Early Peoples.* New York: Frederick A. Praeger, 1969. Interesting historical and botanical information on various foods, written from an anthropological viewpoint.

Bruder, Roy. *Discovering Natural Foods.* Santa Barbara, Calif.: Woodbridge Press, 1982. Nice, well-written, and informative introduction to natural foods, written by a former store owner.

Bumgarner, Marlene Anne. *Book of Whole Grains.* New York: St. Martin's Press, 1976. A beginner's book on grains, with a wide selection of recipes (not vegan).

Carroll, Anstice, and Embree de Persiis Vona. *The Health Food Dictionary with Recipes.* New York: Weathervane Books, 1973. Primarily slanted toward a person new to nutrition and healthful eating.

Carper, Jean. *The Food Pharmacy.* New York: Bantam Books, 1988. Discoveries about diet's impact on disease. Goes through fifty-five foods that have had medicinal properties investigated and gives research reports and conclusions. From a traditional scientific/medical background and perspective.

Castleman, Michael. *The Healing Herbs*. Emmaus, Pa.: Rodale Press, 1991. Reputable herbalist; list of possible side effects and contraindications.

Cituk, Kathy, and John Finnegan. *Natural Foods and Good Cooking*. Mill Valley, Calif.: Elysian Arts, 1989. A conservative approach to healthier living. Very basic.

Clute, Willard N. *The Common Names of Plants and Their Meanings*. Indianapolis, Ind.: Willard N. Clute & Co., 1942. A small, rambling book about how plants get their names and some of their meanings.

Coon, Nelson. *Using Plants for Healing*. Emmaus, Pa.: Rodale Press, 1979. History of medicinal plants, preparation, and glossary.

Cost, Bruce. *Bruce Cost's Asian Ingredients*. New York: William Morrow and Co., 1988. A guide to the fresh, preserved, and bottled ingredients arriving in our markets from Asia. Recipes for most ingredients.

Creasy, Rosalind. *The Complete Book of Edible Landscaping*. San Francisco: Sierra Club Books, 1982. Deals mostly with fruit and nut trees.

Cusumano, Camille. *The New Foods*. New York: Henry Holt and Company, 1989. A guide to some of the newer foods (some of which are now very familiar).

Davidson, Alan. *Fruit: A Connoisseur's Guide and Cookbook*. New York: Simon & Schuster, 1991. An informative account of the edible fruits and nuts of the world. The organization is a little unusual, but the illustrations are stunning, and there is a complete index if you get lost.

Davis, Ben. *Rapid Healing Foods*. West Nyack, N.Y.: Parker Publishing Co., 1980. Foods that cleanse the body of poisons and help relieve multiple ailments. Many personal stories, very little scientific research cited.

Dawson, Adele G. *Health, Happiness and the Pursuit of Herbs*. Brattleboro, Vt.: Stephen Greene Press, 1980. Arranged more for gardeners, but still an interesting book.

Diamond, Harvey, and Marilyn Diamond. *Fit for Life*. New York: Warner Books, 1985. Basics on health and nutrition, diet plan for transition to healthier eating, good recipes. Would highly recommend for any and all to read.

——. *Living Health*. New York: Warner Books, 1987. Continuation of *Fit for Life* program, with additional information and recipes.

Diamond, Marilyn. *American Vegetarian Cookbook*. New York: Warner Books, 1990. Completely vegan, good basic book with simple recipes. Lots of information regarding foods and nutrients, with substitute chart for old-style cooking.

Doyle, Harrison. *Golden Chia: Ancient Indian Energy Food*. Vista, Calif.: Hillside Press, 1975. A rambling story about the author's experience with both eating and growing chia seeds.

Dyer, T. F. Thiselton. *The Folk-Lore of Plants*. New York: D. Appleton and Co., 1889. Contains some good information, but difficult to read and not well organized.

Editors of the *East West Journal*. *Shopper's Guide to Natural Foods*. Garden City Park, N.Y.: Avery Publishing Group, 1987. A beginner's introduction to natural foods and food stores.

Elkort, Martin. *The Secret Life of Food: A Feast of Food and Drink History, Folklore, and Fact*. Los Angeles: Jeremy P. Tarcher Inc., 1991. A fun book full of historical information, anecdotes, and definitions.

Elliot, Rose. *The Complete Vegetarian Cuisine*. New York: Pantheon Books, 1988. Beautifully illustrated book, half reference and half cookbook. European-style cookery.

Esser, William L. *Dictionary of Foods*. Bridgeport, Conn.: Natural Hygiene Press, 1953, 1983. Have both old and new versions; makes for a nice encyclopedic listing of natural foods. Ideologies are in line with Herbert Shelton's writings.

Fielder, Mildred. *Wild Fruits: An Illustrated Field Guide & Cookbook*. Chicago, Ill.: Contemporary Books, 1983. Identifies and provides recipes for seventy-eight North American wild fruits.

Finnegan, John. *The Facts About Fats*. Mill Valley, Calif.: Elysian Arts, 1992. Role of fats and oils in diet, how they are processed, uses and abuses.

Friedlander, Barbara. *The Vegetable, Fruit & Nut Book: Secrets of the Seed*. New York: Grosset & Dunlap, 1974. An eclectic gathering of facts, history and myths, and other items of interest about these plants.

Gledhill, D. *The Names of Plants*. New York: Cambridge University Press, 1989. An excellent dictionary of botanical terms and their meanings.

Grieve, Maude. *A Modern Herbal*, Vols. 1 and 2. New York: Dover Publications, 1971. An old-style listing of primarily English botanical herbs with some spices. Wouldn't recommend for the novice reader.

Griggs, Barbara. *The Food Factor*. Middlesex, England: Viking Books, 1986. The fascinating history of nutrition, vitamins, government policy, and the health pioneers.

Grigson, Sophie. *Gourmet Ingredients*. New York: Van Nostrand Reinhold, 1991. Foods from a British point of view, some foods still unseen in North America.

Halpin, Anne Moyer (editor). *Unusual Vegetables*. Emmaus, Pa.: Rodale Press, 1978. Interesting book on some lesser-known and obscure vegetables, as well as some more familiar ones.

Haughton, Claire Shaver. *Green Immigrants: The Plants That Transformed America*. New York: Harcourt Brace Jovanovich, 1978. A fascinating book about many botanical immigrants to America. Well worth reading for those interested in plant history.

Healey, B. J. *A Gardener's Guide to Plant Names*. New York: Charles Scribner's Sons, 1972. Deals primarily with flower names, but there are a smattering of other ones thrown in.

Heifetz, Jeanne. *Green Groceries: A Mail-Order Guide to Organic Foods*. New York: HarperCollins, 1992. An excellent sourcebook for mail-ordering any sort of organic food items; in fact, this is the only book I have seen that puts all these sources together in one place.

Heinerman, John. *Encyclopedia of Fruits, Vegetables and Herbs*. West Nyack, N.Y.: Parker Publishing Company, 1988. From a medical anthropologist, an alphabetical listing of common fruits, vegetables, and herbs, including some of their health-promoting uses. Very useful home-remedy book.

Heiser, Charles B., Jr. *Seed to Civilization: The Story of Food*. San Francisco, Calif.: W. H. Freeman and Company, 1981. A quick history of agriculture and food crops.

Hendrickson, Robert. *Foods for Love*. New York: Stein and Day, 1974. A guide to aphrodisiac edibles, their history, and curious anecdotes. Strange and unusual, but interesting.

Hurd, Frank J., and Rosalie Hurd. *A Good Cook . . . Ten Talents*. Chisholm, Minn.: Frank J. Hurd, 1985. Excellent food-combining cookbook (no dairy, eggs, sugars) and health manual. Some religious dogma.

Jensen, Bernard, and Mark Anderson. *Empty Harvest*. Garden City Park, N.Y.: Avery Publishing Group, 1990. A somber picture of how interconnected humans are to this earth and how this connection is being destroyed. Offers range of practical solutions still available to mend nature's broken links.

Jensen, Bernard. *Foods That Heal*. Garden City Park, N.Y.: Avery Publishing Group, 1993. A guide to understanding and using the healing power of some of the common foods, including their history of use, buyer's tips, therapeutic benefits, nutrient information, and recipes.

———. *The Joy of Living and How to Attain It*. Los Angeles: Bernard Jensen Press, 1946. Mental, physical, and spiritual aspects of living life fully, including diet and exercise.

———. *Tissue Cleansing Through Bowel Management*. Escondido, Calif.: Bernard Jensen Press, 1981. Very graphically shows the power of fasting and colonics.

Kadans, Joseph M., Ph.D. *Encyclopedia of Fruits, Vegetables, Nuts and Seeds*. West Nyack, N.Y.: Parker Publishing, 1973. Alphabetical listing, some interesting information.

Kilham, Christopher S. *The Bread & Circus Whole Food Bible*. Reading, Mass.: Addison-Wesley Publishing Co., 1991. How to select and prepare whole foods. Good for beginners.

Kloss, Jethro. *Back to Eden*. Loma Linda, Calif.: Back to Eden Books Publishing Co., 1992. Originally printed in 1939 and updated for a fiftieth-anniversary edition. Fairly comprehensive, lots of stories, some dogma but quite readable.

Koppel, Dale. *Healing Foods & Juices*. Boca Raton, Fla.: Globe Communications Corp., 1999. Small basic pamphlet on mostly fat-fighting foods.

Kraft, Ken, and Pat Kraft. *Exotic Vegetables*. New York: Walker and Company, 1977. Older book with brief discussion of vegetables, some gardening tips, and a few recipes for each.

Kulvinskas, Viktoras. *Sprouts for the Love of Every Body*. Wethersfield, Conn.: Omango D'Press, 1978. Nutritional values and benefits of sprouts and wheatgrass.

Larkcom, Joy. *The Salad Garden*. New York: Viking Press, 1984. Various information on salad plants and gardening.

Lehner, Ernst, and Johanna Lehner. *Folklore & Odysseys of Food & Medicinal Plants*. New York: Farrar, Straus & Giroux, 1973. Brief history of many plants and resultant products. Lots of old, interesting illustrations.

———. *Folklore and Symbolism of Flowers, Plants and Trees*. New York: Tudor Publishing Co., 1960. A brief overview of many of the sacred plants, the lore and legends surrounding them, and the language of flowers. A small, older book, but still interesting.

Lesser, Michael. *Nutrition and Vitamin Therapy*. New York: Grove Press Inc., 1980. Nutrition and the vitamins and minerals it comes from.

Levy-Bacon, Josephine. *Exotic Vegetables A–Z*. Topsfield, Mass.: Salem House Publishers, 1988. Information on some of the lesser-known vegetables.

Lieberman, Shari, and Nancy Bruning. *The Real Vitamin and Mineral Book*, 2nd edition. New York: Avery Publishing Group, 1997. Guide to vitamins and minerals, optimum supplementation.

Liebman, Malvina W. *From Caravan to Casserole: Herbs and Spices in Legend, History, and Recipe*. Miami, Fla.: E. A. Seemann Publishing, 1977. A brief history of better-known herbs and spices, along with recipes.

London, Sheryl, and Mel London. *The Versatile Grain and the Elegant Bean*. New York: Simon & Schuster, 1992. Covers most of the available grains and beans, giving a brief history and description, as well as cooking instructions, with lots of recipes for each one (nonvegetarian). List of mail-order sources for most products.

Loewenfeld, Claire, and Phillippa Back. *The Complete Book of Herbs and Spices*. New York: G. P. Putnam's Sons, 1974. Older British book, but with very good, concise information. Well laid out and easy to read. Nice sections on description, habitat, and cultivation, as well as flavor and culinary and medicinal uses. Would be a welcome addition to any culinary or herbal library.

Lovelock, Yann. *The Vegetable Book: An Unnatural History*. New York: St. Martin's Press, 1973. Fascinating information about not only the more common vegetables, herbs, and spices but also the unusual ones, which were once popular but now forgotten. From a British perspective; some information gets rather technical and tedious. For the person interested in botany and the historical significance of names, this is an excellent book.

Lucas, Richard. *Common and Uncommon Uses of Herbs for Healthful Living*. West Nyack, N.Y.: Parker Publishing, 1969. Presents herbal folk remedies, with history and uses of herbs.

Lust, John. *The Herb Book*. New York: Bantam Books, 1974. Catalog of plants and various uses. Some history and folklore.

Mailhebiau, Philippe. *Portraits in Oils: The Personality of Aromatherapy Oils and Their Link with Human Temperaments.* England: C. W. Daniel Company Ltd., 1995. Has monographs of twenty-four major essential oils, presenting each oil as an individual entity with detailed and precise characteristics.

Margen, Sheldon (editor). *The Wellness Encyclopedia of Food and Nutrition.* New York: Random House, 1992. Covers the basics on how to buy, store, and prepare almost every common variety (plus a few newer ones) of fresh food. Nicely categorized by section. Promotes no particular lifestyle; has sections on meat, fish, and dairy.

Medsger, Oliver Perry. *Edible Wild Plants.* New York: Macmillan Company, 1966. Guide to identification and preparation of North American edible wild plants. A perusal of these pages makes clear just how little most of us know about the plants around us.

Messegue, Maurice. Translated by Clara Winston. *Maurice Messegue's Way to Natural Health and Beauty.* New York: Macmillan Publishing Co., 1974. Foods and nutrition from a French point of view. Entertaining to read; some of the information is a little old, but a fun book.

Meyerowitz, Steve. *Juice Fasting and Detoxification.* Great Barrington, Mass.: The Sprout House, 1992. Detoxification through juice fasting; programs and remedies. Fun and easy to read.

Morton, Julia F. *Fruits of Warm Climates.* Miami, Fla., 1987. An exceptionally complete book for identifying and growing any of the warm-weather fruits.

Murray, Michael T. *The Healing Power of Foods: Nutrition Secrets for Vibrant Health and Long Life.* Rocklin, Calif.: Prima Publishing, 1993. Explains the components of a healthful diet and the health-promoting properties that specific foods possess. Section on specific food prescriptions for common health problems.

National Academy of Sciences. *Underexploited Tropical Plants with Promising Economic Value.* Washington, D.C., 1975. From the U.S. government, so technical, but still interesting reading.

Neal, Bill. *Gardener's Latin.* Chapel Hill, N.C.: Algonquin Books, 1992. A lexicon giving the origins, lore, and meanings of botanical names.

Null, Gary. *The Vegetarian Handbook: Eating Right for Total Health.* New York: St. Martin's Press, 1987. Reminiscent of John Robbins's books.

Ortiz, Elizabeth Lambert. *The Encyclopedia of Herbs, Spices, and Flavorings.* London: Dorling Kindersley, 1992. A beautifully illustrated book on herbs, spices, and flavorings for the kitchen.

Pedersen, Mark. *Nutritional Herbology.* Bountiful, Utah: Pedersen Publishing, 1991. Nutritional profiles of 106 commonly used herbs and foods.

Pennington, Jean A. T. *Food Values of Portions Commonly Used.* New York: Harper & Row, 1989. Food composition tables.

Pitchford, Paul. *Healing with Whole Foods.* Berkeley, Calif.: North Atlantic Books, 1993. Oriental traditions and modern nutrition.

Pizer, Vernon. *Eat the Grapes Downward: An Uninhibited Romp Through the Surprising World of Food.* New York: Dodd, Mead & Company, 1983. Fascinating facts and insights into the colorful world of food. Examines the role of food in history, religion, politics, the arts, and sex, and probes its influence on nations and cultures.

Poole, Gray Johnson. *Nuts from Forest, Orchard, and Field.* New York: Dodd, Mead & Company, 1974. A quick look at each of the common nuts and their place in history as well as the kitchen.

Price, Weston A. *Nutrition and Physical Degeneration.* New Canaan, Conn.: Keats Publishing, 1989. This nutrition classic is a must-read for anybody seriously interested in good health. Price's research was primarily for dentistry but applies equally for all medical and nutritional fields. Shows how a modern poor diet changes body shape and form, dental structure and quality of teeth, and overall health, including mental health.

Quigley, D. T. *The National Malnutrition.* Milwaukee, Wis.: Lee Foundation, 1943. Reviews diet and shows how to promote vitamin and mineral intake.

Quinn, Vernon. *Leaves: Their Place in Life and Legend.* New York: Frederick A. Stokes Co., 1937. An interesting little book about leaves and their many uses and legends.

Reader's Digest. *Herbs (Home Handbook).* Pleasantville, N.Y.: Reader's Digest Assoc. Inc., 1990. A basic book on herbs and their various uses.

—. *Magic and Medicine of Plants.* Pleasantville, N.Y.: Reader's Digest Assoc. Inc., 1986. A fun book on herbs and other plants.

Reich, Lee. *Uncommon Fruits Worthy of Attention: A Gardener's Guide.* Reading, Mass.: Addison-Wesley Publishing Co., 1991. Guide to the history, cultivation, and use of uncommon but easy-to-grow fruits.

Reid, Daniel P. *Tao of Health, Sex & Longevity.* New York: Simon & Schuster, 1989. Excellent in-depth book on food and its effects on health and longevity. This is the book that started my quest for information regarding food and health.

Riely, Elizabeth. *A Feast of Fruits.* New York: Macmillan, 1993. Descriptions and over 340 recipes for thirty-six different kinds of fruits.

Rinzler, Carol Ann. *The Complete Book of Herbs, Spices and Condiments.* New York: Facts on File, 1990. Orthodox medical viewpoint on herbs, showing nutritional value, medical benefits, adverse effects, and nontraditional uses.

Robbins, John. *Diet for a New America.* Walpole, N.H.: Stillpoint Publishing, 1987. How our food choices affect our health and the health of the planet. A very convincing argument to reduce or eliminate the consumption of meat.

—. *May All Be Fed.* New York: William Morrow, 1992. A continuation of *Diet for a New America*, with much of the same information.

Robertson, Laurel, Carol Flinders, and Bronwen Godfrey. *Laurel's Kitchen*. Petaluma, Calif.: Nilgiri Press, 1976. Basics on vegetarianism, plus plenty of nutritional facts, tables, and recipes.

Robertson, Laurel, Carol Flinders, and Brian Ruppenthal. *The New Laurel's Kitchen: A Handbook for Vegetarian Cookery and Nutrition*. Berkeley, Calif.: Ten Speed Press, 1986. Full of nutritional information; recipes include a lot of dairy and eggs.

Rodale Press. *The Rodale Herb Book*. Emmaus, Pa.: Rodale Press, 1974. Lots of good herbal information for cooking, aromatics, medicinals, history, and more.

—. *Rodale's Illustrated Encyclopedia of Herbs*. Emmaus, Pa.: Rodale Press, 1987. Features entries on more than 140 herbs, including history and lore, cultivation, and storage; accompanied by kitchen tips, charts, and other information. A good reference book.

Roehl, Evelyn. *Whole Food Facts*. Rochester, Vt.: Healing Arts Press, 1988. Excellent book on foods; no medicinal uses, but fairly complete otherwise; foods in sections by classes (grains, fruit, etc.). Recommend for general information.

Rogers, Ford. *Nuts: A Cookbook*. New York: Fireside, 1993. A beautifully photographed cookbook with a wide assortment of dishes to try. Has a short but nice introduction to the major nuts.

Rohe, Fred. *The Complete Book of Natural Foods*. Boulder, Col.: Shambhala Press, 1983. Very basic primer on whole foods and how to make the transition to a more wholesome diet.

Rombauer, Irma S., and Marion Rombauer Becker. *The Joy of Cooking*. New York: Bobbs-Merrill Company, 1975. An American household classic covering everything. Not even remotely vegetarian; I use it as a reference base.

Root, Waverley. *Food*. New York: Simon & Schuster, 1980. An enormous but fascinating tome on food history and a dictionary of world foods.

Rose, Jeanne. *Herbs & Things: Jeanne Rose's Herbal*. New York: Grosset & Dunlap, 1972. A compendium of practical and exotic herbal lore.

Rosengarten, Frederic, Jr. *The Book of Edible Nuts*. New York: Walker Publishing Co., 1984. Discusses botany, ecology, history, and processing. Recipes for many of the nuts. An excellent book for anyone seriously interested in learning more about nut trees, nuts, and their uses.

—. *The Book of Spices*. New York: Livingston Publication Co., 1969. Beautiful, albeit older, book on common spices.

Rosenthal, Sylvia. *Fresh Food*. New York: E. P. Dutton, 1978. How to select, buy, and store the freshest food.

Rupp, Rebecca. *Blue Corn and Square Tomatoes*. Pownal, Vt.: Storey Communications, Inc., 1987. Unusual facts about common garden vegetables. Fun and informative narratives tracing the origin of scientific and common names, investigating the poor reputations of many of our now most popular vegetables, plus some nutritional values and a list of seed suppliers.

Sanecki, Kay N. *The Complete Book of Herbs*. New York: Macmillan, 1974. More herbal information for the beginner.

Schauss, Alexander. *Diet, Crime and Delinquency*. Berkeley, Calif.: Parker House, 1981. Explains connection between poor nutrition and antisocial behavior, and how proper nutrition can dramatically change behavior.

Schlosser, Eric. *Fast Food Nation: The Dark Side of the All-American Meal*. New York: Houghton Mifflin, 2001. The story of the fast-food industry and its effect upon cultural history.

Schmid, Dr. Ronald F. *Traditional Foods Are Your Best Medicine*. Stratford, Conn.: Ocean View Publications, 1987. Reviews traditional diet of longest-lived cultures. Proposes we put more emphasis on fish, meat, and fowl of good quality. Strongly emphasizes benefits of fish and fish oils upon health. Downplays role of fruits and vegetables.

Schneider, Elizabeth. *Uncommon Fruits and Vegetables: A Commonsense Guide*. New York: Harper & Row, 1986. Some of these are not so uncommon anymore. A light, easy-to-read, and interesting review of the more unusual fruits and vegetables. Comes with descriptions and several recipes for each. For anybody seriously interested in experimenting with these foods, it is well worth buying.

Schroeder, Henry A., M.D. *The Trace Elements and Man*. Old Greenwich, Conn.: Devin-Adair Company, 1973. Cover both positive and negative aspects of trace elements and minerals.

Schutte, Karl. *The Biology of the Trace Elements: Their Role in Nutrition*. Philadelphia: J. B. Lippincott Company, 1964. How trace elements affect biology in plants, animals, and humans.

Shannon, Sara. *Diet for the Atomic Age*. Wayne, N.J.: Avery, 1987. How to protect yourself from the radiation that is all around us.

Shelton, Herbert M., M.D. *Superior Nutrition*. San Antonio, Tex.: Willow Publishing, 1982. Hard-to-read tome, heavy with dogma.

Sokolov, Raymond. *Fading Feast: A Compendium of Disappearing American Regional Foods*. New York: Farrar, Straus & Giroux, 1981. Twenty-four pieces on regional foods.

Spencer, Colin. *The New Vegetarian*. New York: Viking Penguin Inc., 1986. European-style (with some very strange foods) cookbook, including a nice illustrated section on herbs, spices, vegetables, and more.

—. *The Vegetable Book*. New York: Rizzoli International Publications, 1996. A picturesque wander through the wild and variegated world of vegetables.

Stanchich, Lino. *Power Eating Program*. Miami, Fla.: Healthy Products Inc., 1989. Details the importance of chewing your food properly (mastication) and the resultant beneficial effects on your health. Promotes macrobiotic lifestyle, stress reduction.

Staten, Vince. *Can You Trust a Tomato in January?* New York: Simon & Schuster, 1993. An entertaining and revealing trip through the supermarket, revealing things you always wanted to know (and a few you didn't) about food in the grocery store.

Stearn, William T. *Botanical Latin.* North Pomfret, Vt.: David & Charles, 1983. Very helpful for finding Latin terminology.

——. *Stearn's Dictionary of Plant Names for Gardeners.* London: Cassell Publishers Ltd., 1992. Used to help find botanical names.

Steinman, David. *Diet for a Poisoned Planet.* New York: Harmony Books, 1990. Guide to common foods, with lists of pesticides and chemical residues found in them. Short detoxification section. Large appendices with sources on organic products, activist groups, certification groups, and testing laboratories.

Stuart, Malcolm (editor). *The Encyclopedia of Herbs and Herbalism.* New York: Crescent Books, 1979. History of herbalism, biology and chemistry of plants, and medicinal, culinary, and other uses. Encyclopedic section organized by Latin botanical name.

Tannahill, Reay. *Food in History.* New York: Crown Publishers, 1988. A world history of food from prehistoric times to today; traces the way in which food (or lack thereof) has influenced the entire course of human development. Fascinating reading; follows culture's perception of diet and nutrition from ancient days to the present.

U.S. Department of Agriculture, Human Nutrition Information Services. *Composition of Foods: Fruits and Fruit Juices; Raw, Processed, Prepared.* Agriculture Handbook No. 8-09, 1982.

——. *Composition of Foods: Nut and Seed Products; Raw, Processed, Prepared.* Agriculture Handbook No. 8-12, 1984.

——. *Composition of Foods: Vegetables and Vegetable Products; Raw, Processed, Prepared.* Agriculture Handbook No. 8-11, 1984.

——. *Composition of Foods: Legumes and Legume Products; Raw, Processed, Prepared.* Agriculture Handbook No. 8-16, 1986.

——. *Composition of Foods: Fats and Oils; Raw, Processed, Prepared.* Agriculture Handbook No. 8-04, 1979.

——. *Composition of Foods: Cereal Grains and Pasta; Raw, Processed, Prepared.* Agriculture Handbook No. 8-20, 1989.

——. *Composition of Foods: Snacks and Sweets; Raw, Processed, Prepared.* Agriculture Handbook No. 8-19, 1991.

——. *Composition of Foods: Spices and Herbs.* Agriculture Handbook No. 8-2, 1977.

——. *Composition of Foods: 1989 Supplement.*

——. *Composition of Foods: 1990 Supplement.*

Waldstein, Steve. *How to Choose the Diet That's Right for You.* New York: Crossing Press, 1984. Vegetarianism, diets, foods, and nutrition. Good section on vitamins and minerals.

Walker, N. W. *Colon Health: The Key to a Vibrant Life.* Phoenix, Ariz.: O'Sullivan Woodwide & Co, 1979. Explains how the health of the colon affects the rest of the body.

——. *Natural Way to Vibrant Health.* Phoenix, Ariz.: O'Sullivan Woodside & Co, 1983. Basics of digestion and nutrition, written in typical rambling Walker style.

Watt, B. K., and A. L. Merrill. *Composition of Foods . . . Raw, Processed, Prepared.* U.S. Department of Agriculture, Agriculture Handbook No. 8, 1963. This is the older version of the Agriculture Handbooks.

Weiner, Michael. *Weiner's Herbal.* New York: Stein and Day, 1980. An okay book, heavy on the botanical descriptions.

Wigmore, Ann. *The Sprouting Book.* Wayne, N.Y.: Avery Publishing Group, 1986. Lots of good information on sprouts, setting up home sprouting, recipes for using sprouts.

Wood, Rebecca. *The Whole Foods Encyclopedia.* New York: Prentice Hall Press, 1988. Encyclopedic style; some good information but not very in-depth.

Yepsen, Roger. *A Celebration of Heirloom Vegetables.* New York: Workman Publishing Company, 1998. Beautifully illustrated guide to some of the older varieties of vegetables.

the politics and practice of sustainable living

CHELSEA GREEN PUBLISHING

CHELSEA GREEN publishes information that helps us lead pleasurable lives on a planet where human activities are in harmony and balance with Nature. Our celebration of the sustainable arts has led us to publish trendsetting books about organic gardening, solar electricity and renewable energy, innovative building techniques, regenerative forestry, local and bioregional democracy, and whole foods. Our works, while intensely practical, are also entertaining and inspirational, demonstrating that an ecological approach to life is consistent with producing beautiful, eloquent, and useful books, and multimedia.

For more information about Chelsea Green, or to request a free catalog, call toll-free (800) 639-4099, or write to us at P.O. Box 428, White River Junction, Vermont 05001. Visit our Web site at www.chelseagreen.com.

CHELSEA GREEN PUBLISHING

the politics and practice of sustainable living

Shelter

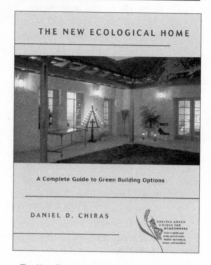

The New Ecological Home: A Complete Guide to Green Building Options
Daniel D. Chiras
ISBN 1-931498-16-4 • $35.00

Food

The Slow Food Guide to New York City
Martins and Watson • ISBN 1-931498-27-X
The Slow Food Guide to Chicago
Gibson and Lowndes • ISBN 1-931498-61-X
$20.00 each

Planet

Limits to Growth: The 30-Year Update
Donella Meadows, Jorgen Randers, and Dennis Meadows
ISBN 1-931498-58-X • $22.50

People

This Organic Life: Confessions of a Suburban Homesteader
Joan Dye Gussow
ISBN 1-931498-24-5 • $16.95